# BUTTERWORTHS
# EMPLOYMENT LAW
# HANDBOOK

Twenty-first edition

Editor
## PETER WALLINGTON QC
Barrister, 11KBW
Sometime Professor of Law at the University of Lancaster
and Brunel University
A Part-time Employment Judge

**Members of the LexisNexis Group worldwide**

| | |
|---|---|
| United Kingdom | LexisNexis, a Division of Reed Elsevier (UK) Ltd, Halsbury House, 35 Chancery Lane, London, WC2A 1EL, and London House, 20–22 East London Street, Edinburgh EH7 4BQ |
| Australia | LexisNexis Butterworths, Chatswood, New South Wales |
| Austria | LexisNexis Verlag ARD Orac GmbH & Co KG, Vienna |
| Benelux | LexisNexis Benelux, Amsterdam |
| Canada | LexisNexis Canada, Markham, Ontario |
| China | LexisNexis China, Beijing and Shanghai |
| France | LexisNexis SA, Paris |
| Germany | LexisNexis GmbH, Dusseldorf |
| Hong Kong | LexisNexis Hong Kong, Hong Kong |
| India | LexisNexis India, New Delhi |
| Italy | Giuffrè Editore, Milan |
| Japan | LexisNexis Japan, Tokyo |
| Malaysia | Malayan Law Journal Sdn Bhd, Kuala Lumpur |
| New Zealand | LexisNexis NZ Ltd, Wellington |
| Poland | Wydawnictwo Prawnicze LexisNexis Sp, Warsaw |
| Singapore | LexisNexis Singapore, Singapore |
| South Africa | LexisNexis Butterworths, Durban |
| USA | LexisNexis, Dayton, Ohio |

© Reed Elsevier (UK) Ltd 2013
Published by LexisNexis
This is a Butterworths title

A CIP Catalogue record for this book is available from the British Library.

ISBN for this volume: 978 1 4057 7879 4

Printed in the UK by CPI William Clowes, Beccles NR34 7TL.

Visit LexisNexis at www.lexisnexis.co.uk

The year 2013 will see a much larger number of employment law and related measures introduced than in many recent years. It had been anticipated that most of the major changes announced for 2013 would at least be on the Statute Book in time for inclusion in this edition of the Handbook, for which the official cut-off date is 6 April, but that has not proved to be so. In particular, problems with the supporting IT led to a last minute deferment of the new Employment Tribunal Rules of Procedure, based on the draft produced by Lord Justice Underhill's working party. The new Rules were finally laid before Parliament on 31 May, just in time for them to be included in the text of this edition (but not the Index); the old Rules, which remain in force until 29 July, have been retained for this edition. Also included are the relevant parts of the Enterprise and Regulatory Reform Act 2013, the Public Service Pensions Act 2013 and Growth and Infrastructure Act 2013, all of which received Royal Assent on 25 April, and the Draft Orders which will introduce fees for employment tribunal claims and appeals to the Employment Appeal Tribunal, which were laid before Parliament at the end of April and are due to come into force at the end of July 2013, subject to Parliamentary approval. The new Acts will in due course be supported by further regulations, but too late for this edition.

The significant new measures mentioned above are far from the end of a long list of measures proposed by the Government for implementation over the next 12 months, (or, for flexible working and reforms to parental leave, in 2015). The underlying agenda may be the reduction of burdens on business and the relaxation of employment regulation, but the means do not yet appear to extend to any real reduction in the *quantity* of law. This edition has thus sadly reverted to type in being longer than its predecessor. As noted in the Preface to the last edition, the trend over more than 30 years of the Handbook has been an inexorable increase in the volume and detail of legislation, from 558 pages in 1979 to some 5 times that now, despite smaller print, and less emphasis on health and safety legislation.

One thing on which almost all shades of opinion about what is the right level of regulation of employment would agree is that there is ample room, and an urgent need, for the drastic simplification of the law. The successful codification of discrimination law in the Equality Act 2010 points the way – there is an urgent need for re-consolidation of the Employment Rights and Employment Tribunals Acts of 1996, and for a Family Rights Act bringing together in a clear and simple format all the burgeoning regulations on maternity, paternity, adoption and parental rights, and rights to flexible working and time off.

The text of the materials included in the Handbook has been fully updated to 6 April 2013, with later changes and new material incorporated so far as possible up to the end of May. The format of the Handbook is as in previous editions. Amendments are indicated as follows: repeals and revocations are indicated by three dots; insertions and substitutions are in square brackets; and prospective repeals and substitutions are in italics, with the text to be substituted set out in the notes. Details of the provenance of changes are given in the notes, together with the effective date (unless this was before April 2008) and details of any savings and transitional provisions in the implementing legislation. Paragraphs are numbered consecutively within each Part: so paragraphs in Part 1 begin [1.1] and in Part 2 [2.1].

Part 1 contains statutes, in chronological order and printed as amended and in force at the time of going to press. Part 2 contains statutory instruments, in similar format and with similar annotations. Part 3 is European material, covering relevant Treaty provisions and EU Regulations, Directives and Recommendations, with subsequent amendments annotated. Part 4 contains statutory Codes of Practice and Guidance on the meaning of disability. Part 5 (Miscellaneous Materials) includes international materials, Practice Directions, Employment Tribunal Claim and Response Forms, and an updated list of useful addresses.

All the materials in this Handbook apply equally to England and Wales and Scotland unless otherwise stated in the annotations. However, no attempt is made to cover Northern

Ireland, and this book is not suitable for researching Northern Ireland domestic legislation; nor does it indicate whether particular materials extend to Northern Ireland.

I am grateful to those, sadly too numerous to name individually, who have contributed, wittingly or otherwise, to the development of the Handbook over the past 34 years, and to this edition in particular. I include those who have drawn my attention to materials or supplied copies and those who have helpfully commented on coverage and format (even those whose suggestions to expand the content have not proved practicable). I am particularly grateful to LexisNexis for its organisational support and commitment and especially to its editorial staff for their efficiency and forbearance in the face of the demanding schedule for publication. Responsibility for the selection of contents is mine.

To end on a lighter note, particularly for the benefit of those who hanker for a golden age when there was no excessive bureaucratic regulation of such matters as working time, my researchers have found the Statute of Artificers, passed by the English Parliament exactly 450 years ago in 1563. Section XII in particular merits quoting:

"And be it further enacted by the Authority aforesaid, That all Artificers and Labourers, being hired for their Wages by the Day or Week, shall betwixt the Midst of the Months of March and September be and continue at their Work at or before five of the Clock in the Morning, and continue at work and not depart until betwixt seven and eight of the Clock at Night (except it be in the Time of Breakfast, Dinner or Drinking, the which Times at the most shall not exceed above two Hours and a Half in a Day, that is to say, at every Drinking one half Hour, for his Dinner one Hour, and for his Sleep when he is allowed to sleep, which is from the midst of May to the midst of August, Half an hour at the most, and at every Breakfast one Half Hour) . . . upon Pain to lose and forfeit one Penny for every Hour's Absence, to be deducted and defaulted out of his Wages that shall so offend."

The idea of drinking and sleeping time may appeal.

Peter Wallington QC

North Berwick, East Lothian

Peter.wallington@11kbw.com

*7 June 2013*

# CONTENTS

# PART 2   STATUTORY INSTRUMENTS

**Chronological list**

## PART 4   STATUTORY CODES OF PRACTICE

### A.  ACAS

### B.  BORDER & IMMIGRATION AGENCY

### C.  EQUALITY AND HUMAN RIGHTS COMMISSION

### D.  FINANCIAL CONDUCT AUTHORITY AND PRUDENTIAL REGULATION AUTHORITY

### E.  HEALTH AND SAFETY EXECUTIVE

## F. INFORMATION COMMISSIONER

## G. SECRETARY OF STATE

## H. CODES MADE BY BODIES REPLACED BY THE EHRC

## PART 5   MISCELLANEOUS MATERIALS

## A. INTERNATIONAL LAW MATERIALS

## B. EMPLOYMENT APPEAL TRIBUNAL PRACTICE DIRECTION & PRACTICE STATEMENT, ETC

## C. CLAIM AND RESPONSE FORMS FOR TRIBUNAL CLAIMS

## D. CABINET OFFICE MATERIALS

## E. USEFUL ADDRESSES

# PART 1
## STATUTES

# APPORTIONMENT ACT 1870

### (1870 c 35)

*An Act for the better Apportionment of Rents and other periodical Payments*

[1 August 1870]

**NOTES**
See *Harvey* BI(1)(B).

**[1.1]**
## 1　Short title
This Act may be cited for all purposes as "The Apportionment Act 1870".

**[1.2]**
## 2　Rents, etc to be apportionable in respect of time
. . . All rents, annuities, dividends, and other periodical payments in the nature of income (whether reserved or made payable under an instrument in writing or otherwise) shall, like interest on money lent, be considered as accruing from day to day, and shall be apportionable in respect of time accordingly.

**NOTES**
Words omitted repealed by the Statute Law Revision (No 2) Act 1893.

**3, 4**　*(Outside the scope of this work.)*

**[1.3]**
## 5　Interpretation
In the construction of this Act—
The word "rents" includes rent service, rentcharge, and rent seck, and also tithes and all periodical payments or renderings in lieu of or in the nature of rent or tithe.
The word "annuities" includes salaries and pensions.
The word "dividends" includes (besides dividends strictly so called) all payments made by the name of dividend, bonus or otherwise out of the revenue of trading or other public companies, divisible between all or any of the members of such respective companies, whether such payments shall be usually made or declared, at any fixed times or otherwise; and all such divisible revenue shall, for the purposes of this Act, be deemed to have accrued by equal daily increment during or within the period for or in respect of which the payment of the same revenue shall be declared or expressed to be made, but the said word "dividend" does not include payments in the nature of a return or reimbursement of capital.

**6**　*(Outside the scope of this work.)*

**[1.4]**
## 7　Nor where stipulation made to the contrary
The provisions of this Act shall not extend to any case in which it is or shall be expressly stipulated that no apportionment shall take place.

# EQUAL PAY ACT 1970 (NOTE)

### (1970 c 41)

**[1.5]**

**NOTES**
The whole of this Act was repealed by the Equality Act 2010, s 211(2), Sch 27, Pt 1, as from 1 October 2010. The Equality Act 2010 (Commencement No 4, Savings, Consequential, Transitional, Transitory and Incidental Provisions and Revocation) Order 2010, SI 2010/2317 (at **[2.1558]** et seq) provides for various transitional provisions and savings in connection with the commencement of the 2010 Act and the repeal of this Act. See, in particular, art 15 (saving where the act complained of occurs wholly before 1 October 2010), and Schs 3, 4 (savings in relation to work on ships, hovercraft and in relation to seafarers).

# SUPERANNUATION ACT 1972

## (1972 c 11)

### ARRANGEMENT OF SECTIONS

*An Act to amend the law relating to pensions and other similar benefits payable to or in respect of persons in certain employment; to provide for distribution without proof of title of certain sums due to or in respect of certain deceased persons; to abolish the Civil Service Committee for Northern Ireland; to repeal section 6 of the Appropriation Act 1957; and for purposes connected with the matters aforesaid*

[1 March 1972]

**NOTES**

Only sections of this Act relevant to employment law are reproduced here. For reasons of space, the subject matter of sections not printed is not annotated.
See *Harvey* BI(9).

*Persons employed in the civil service, etc*

**[1.6]**
**1 Superannuation schemes as respects civil servants, etc**
(1) The Minister for the Civil Service (in this Act referred to as "the Minister")—
  (a) may make, maintain, and administer schemes (whether contributory or not) whereby provision is made with respect to the pensions, allowances or gratuities which, subject to the fulfilment of such requirements and conditions as may be prescribed by the scheme, are to be paid, or may be paid, by the Minister to or in respect of such of the persons to whom this section applies as he may determine;
  (b) may, in relation to such persons as any such scheme may provide, pay or receive transfer values;
  (c) may make, in such circumstances as any such scheme may provide, payments by way of a return of contributions, with or without interest; and
  (d) may make such payments as he thinks fit towards the provision, otherwise than by virtue of such a scheme, of superannuation benefits for or in respect of the persons to whom this section applies as he may determine.
[(1A) Subsection (1) is subject to sections 18 and 19 of the Public Service Pensions Act 2013 (restrictions on benefits provided under existing schemes).]
(2) The Minister may, to such extent and subject to such conditions as he thinks fit, delegate to any other Minister or officer of the Crown any functions exercisable by him by virtue of this section or any scheme made thereunder.
[(2A) Where a money purchase scheme under this section includes provision enabling a member to elect for the benefits which are to be provided to or in respect of him to be purchased from any authorised provider whom he may specify, then—
  (a) notwithstanding subsection (1)(a) above, the scheme may make provision for the making of such an election to have the effect, in such cases as the scheme may specify, of discharging any liability of the Treasury to pay those benefits to or in respect of that member; but
  (b) the scheme shall not be so framed as to have the effect that benefits under it may only be provided in a manner which discharges that liability of the Treasury.]

[(2B) The Minister may, to such extent and subject to such conditions as he thinks fit, delegate to the Scottish Parliamentary Corporate Body any function exercisable by him by virtue of this section or any scheme made thereunder so far as that function or scheme relates to any employees of that Body.]

(3) Before making any scheme under this section the Minister, or, if the Minister so directs in relation to a particular scheme [(other than a scheme mentioned in subsection (3A) below)], another Minister of the Crown specified in the direction, shall consult with persons appearing to the Minister or that other Minister, as the case may be, to represent persons likely to be affected by the proposed scheme or with the last-mentioned persons.

[(3A) Before making any scheme under this section relating to any employees of the Scottish Parliamentary Corporate Body (referred to as "the Parliamentary corporation") the Minister, or, if the Minister so directs, the Parliamentary corporation, shall consult with—

(a) persons appearing to the Minister or the Parliamentary corporation, as the case may be, to represent persons likely to be affected by the proposed scheme, or

(b) the last-mentioned persons.]

(4) This section applies to persons serving—

(a) in employment in the civil service of the State; or

(b) in employment of any of the kinds listed in Schedule 1 to this Act; or

(c) in an office so listed.

[(4A) This section also applies to persons serving in employment or in an office, not being service in employment or in an office of a kind mentioned in subsection (4), where the employment or office is specified in a list produced for the purposes of this subsection (see section 1A).]

(5) Subject to subsection (6) below, the Minister may by order—

(a) add any employment to those listed in the said Schedule 1, being employment by a body or in an institution specified in the order,

(b) add any office so specified to the offices so listed, or

(c) remove any employment or office from the employments or offices so listed.

(6) No employment or office shall be added to those listed in the said Schedule 1 unless [at the date from which the addition has effect] the remuneration of persons serving in that employment or office is paid out of moneys provided by Parliament [the Consolidated Fund or the Scottish Consolidated Fund].

(7) Notwithstanding subsection (6) above, the Minister may by order provide that this section shall apply to persons serving in employment which is remunerated out of a fund specified in the order, being a fund established by or under an Act of Parliament.

(8) An order under subsection (5) or (7) above—

(a) may be made so as to have effect as from a date before the making of the order;

(b) may include transitional and other supplemental provisions;

(c) may vary or revoke a previous order made under that subsection; and

(d) shall be made by statutory instrument, which shall be subject to annulment in pursuance of a resolution of either House of Parliament.

[(9) In this section—

["authorised provider", in relation to the investment of any sums paid by way of voluntary contributions or the provision of any benefit, means—

(a) a person who has permission under [Part 4A] of the Financial Services and Markets Act 2000 to invest such sums or, as the case may be, to provide that benefit;

(b) an EEA firm of a kind mentioned in paragraph 5(a), (b) or (c) of Schedule 3 to that Act, which has permission under paragraph 15 of that Schedule (as a result of qualifying for authorisation under paragraph 12 of that Schedule) to invest such sums or, as the case may be, to provide that benefit and which satisfies the conditions applicable to it which are specified in subsection (9B), (9C) or (9D); or

(c) an EEA firm of a kind mentioned in paragraph 5(d) of Schedule 3 to that Act, which has permission under paragraph 15 of that Schedule (as a result of qualifying for authorisation under paragraph 12 of that Schedule) to invest such sums or, as the case may be, to provide that benefit;]

"money purchase scheme" [has the meaning given by section 181(1) of the Pension Schemes Act 1993].]

[(9A) In subsection (9), the definition of "authorised provider" must be read with—

(a) section 22 of the Financial Services and Markets Act 2000;

(b) any relevant order under that section; and

(c) Schedule 2 to that Act.

(9B) If the EEA firm concerned is of the kind mentioned in paragraph 5(a) of Schedule 3 to the Financial Services and Markets Act 2000, the conditions are—

(a) that, in investing of the sums in question, or in providing the benefit in question, the firm is carrying on a service falling within section A or [B of Annex I to the markets in financial instruments directive]; and

(b) that the firm is authorised by its home state authorisation to carry on that service.

(9C) If the EEA firm concerned is of the kind mentioned in paragraph 5(b) of that Schedule, the conditions are—

  (a)  that, in investing of the sums in question, or in providing the benefit in question, the firm is carrying on an activity falling within Annex 1 to the Banking Consolidation Directive; and

  (b)  that the activity in question is one in relation to which an authority in the firm's home State has regulatory functions.

(9D) If the EEA firm concerned is of the kind mentioned in paragraph 5(c) of that Schedule, the conditions are—

  (a)  that, in investing of the sums in question, or in providing the benefit in question, the firm is carrying on an activity falling within Annex 1 to the Banking Consolidation Directive;

  (b)  that the activity in question is one in relation to which an authority in the firm's home State has regulatory functions; and

  (c)  that the firm also carries on the activity in question in its home State.

(9E) Expressions used in subsections (9B) to (9D) which are also used in Schedule 3 to the Financial Services and Markets Act 2000 have the same meaning in those subsections as they have in that Schedule.]

---

**NOTES**

Sub-s (1A): inserted by the Public Service Pensions Act 2013, s 27, Sch 8, paras 6, 7, as from a day to be appointed.

Sub-s (2A): inserted by the Pensions (Miscellaneous Provisions) Act 1990, s 8(1).

Sub-s (2B), (3A): inserted by the Scotland Act 1998 (Consequential Modifications) Order 2000, SI 2000/2040, art 2(1), Schedule, Pt I, para 5(1), (2), (4).

Sub-s (3): words in square brackets inserted by SI 2000/2040, art 2(1), Schedule, Pt I, para 5(1), (3).

Sub-s (4A): inserted by the Public Service Pensions Act 2013, s 29, Sch 9, paras 1, 2, as from 25 April 2013.

Sub-s (6): words in first pair of square brackets inserted by the Public Bodies Act 2011, s 34, as from 14 February 2012; words in second pair of square brackets substituted by the Scotland Act 1998, s 125, Sch 8, para 14.

Sub-s (9): inserted by the Pensions (Miscellaneous Provisions) Act 1990, s 8(2); definition "authorised provider" substituted by the Financial Services and Markets Act 2000 (Consequential Amendments and Repeals) Order 2001, SI 2001/3649, art 106(1), (2); in definition "authorised provider", words in square brackets in para (a) substituted by the Financial Services Act 2012, s 114(1), Sch 18, Pt 2, para 35, as from 1 April 2013; words in square brackets in the definition "money purchase scheme" substituted by the Pension Schemes Act 1993, s 190, Sch 8, para 6.

Sub-ss (9A)–(9E): inserted by SI 2001/3649, art 106(1), (3); words in square brackets in sub-s (9B)(a) substituted by the Financial Services and Markets Act 2000 (Markets in Financial Instruments) Regulations 2007, SI 2007/126, reg 3(6), Sch 6, Pt 1, para 4.

Modifications: various enactments modify this section so that (i) references to a Minister of the Crown include the Scottish Ministers and the Welsh Ministers, and (ii) references to an officer of the Crown other than a Minister include (for example) the Electoral Commission's chief executive and the chief executive of the Local Government Boundary Commission. These enactments are considered outside the scope of this work.

Orders: a large number of Orders have been made under this section in relation to the admission of various categories of persons and office-holders to Sch 1 to this Act. The list of Orders has been omitted for reasons of space.

---

**[1.7]**

**[1A   List of employments and offices for purposes of section 1(4A)**

(1)  The Minister may specify an employment or office in a list produced for the purposes of section 1(4A) if subsection (2), (3) or (4) applies in relation to the employment or office.

(2)  This subsection applies to an employment or office if—

  (a)  at any time on or after the commencement of this section, the employment or office ceases to be of a kind mentioned in section 1(4), and

  (b)  immediately before that time, persons serving in the employment or office are, or are eligible to be, members of a scheme under section 1 by virtue of section 1(4).

(3)  This subsection applies to an employment or office if—

  (a)  at any time before the commencement of this section, the employment or office ceased to be of a kind mentioned in section 1(4), and

  (b)  at that time, persons serving in the employment or office ceased to be members of a scheme under section 1 or to be eligible for membership of such a scheme.

(4)  This subsection applies to an employment or office if—

  (a)  it is of a description prescribed by regulations, and

  (b)  the Minister determines that it is appropriate for it to be specified for the purposes of section 1(4A).

(5)  The power to specify an employment or office in reliance on subsection (4) may be exercised so as to have retrospective effect.

(6)  The Minister—

  (a)  may at any time amend a list produced under this section, and

  (b)  must publish the list (and any amendments to it).

(7)  The published list must comply with such requirements, and contain such information, as may be prescribed by regulations.

(8)  Regulations made under this section must be made by the Minister by statutory instrument; and an instrument containing such regulations is subject to annulment in pursuance of a resolution of either House of Parliament.]

**NOTES**
Commencement: 25 April 2013.
Inserted by the Public Service Pensions Act 2013, s 29, Sch 9, paras 1, 3, as from 25 April 2013.

**[1.8]**
**2 Further provisions relating to schemes under s 1**
(1) A scheme under section 1 of this Act which makes provision with respect to the pensions, allowances or gratuities which are to be, or may be, paid to or in respect of a person to whom that section applies and who is incapacitated or dies as a result of an injury sustained, or disease contracted, in circumstances prescribed by the scheme may make the like provision in relation to any other person, being a person who is employed in a civil capacity for the purposes of Her Majesty's Government in the United Kingdom, whether temporarily or permanently and whether for reward or not, or is a person holding office in that Government and who is incapacitated or dies as a result of an injury or disease so sustained or contracted.
(2) Any scheme under the said section 1 may make provision for the payment by the Minister of pensions, allowances or gratuities by way of compensation to or in respect of persons—
    (a) to whom that section applies; and
    (b) who suffer loss of office or employment, or loss or diminution of emoluments, in such circumstances, or by reason of the happening of such an event, as may be prescribed by the scheme.
[(3) [Subject to subsection (3A) below,] no scheme under the said section 1 shall make any provision which would have the effect of reducing the amount of any pension, allowance or gratuity, in so far as that amount is directly or indirectly referable to rights which have accrued (whether by virtue of service rendered, contributions paid or any other thing done) before the coming into operation of the scheme, unless the persons consulted in accordance with section 1(3) of this Act have agreed to the inclusion of that provision.]
[(3A) Subsection (3) above does not apply to a provision which would have the effect of reducing the amount of a compensation benefit except in so far as the compensation benefit is one provided in respect of a loss of office or employment which is the consequence of—
    (a) a notice of dismissal given before the coming into operation of the scheme which would have that effect, or
    (b) an agreement made before the coming into operation of that scheme.
(3B) In this section—
"compensation benefit" means so much of any pension, allowance or gratuity as is provided under the civil service compensation scheme by way of compensation to or in respect of a person by reason only of the person's having suffered loss of office or employment;
"the civil service compensation scheme" means so much of any scheme under the said section 1 (whenever made) as provides by virtue of subsection (2) above for benefits to be provided by way of compensation to or in respect of persons who suffer loss of office or employment.
(3C) In subsection (3B) above a reference to suffering loss of office or employment includes a reference to suffering loss or diminution of emoluments as a consequence of suffering loss of office or employment.]
[(3D) So far as it relates to a provision of a scheme under the said section 1 which would have the effect of reducing the amount of a compensation benefit, the duty to consult in section 1(3) of this Act is a duty to consult with a view to reaching agreement with the persons consulted.]
(4) Subject to subsection (3) above, any scheme under the said section 1, or any provision thereof, may be framed—
    (a) so as to have effect as from a date earlier than the date on which the scheme is made; or
    (b) so as to apply in relation to the pensions, allowances or gratuities paid or payable to or in respect of persons who, having been persons to whom the said section 1 applies, have died or ceased to be persons to whom that section applies before the scheme comes into operation; or
    (c) so as to require or authorise the payment of pensions, allowances or gratuities to or in respect of such persons.
(5) Where an order has been made under section 1 (7) of this Act, any scheme under that section may provide for the payment to the Minister out of the fund specified in the order of benefits or other sums paid by him in accordance with the scheme to or in respect of persons to whom that section applies by virtue of the order, together with any administrative expenses incurred in connection with the payment of those sums, and for the payment into that fund of contributions paid in accordance with the scheme by or in respect of those persons and of any transfer values received in respect of them.
(6) Any scheme under the said section 1 may provide for the determination by the Minister of questions arising under the scheme and may provide that the decision of the Minister on any such question shall be final.

(7)   Where under any such scheme any question falls to be determined by the Minister, then, at any time before the question is determined, the Minister may (and if so directed by any of the Courts hereinafter mentioned shall) state in the form of a special case for determination by the High Court, the Court of Session or the Court of Appeal in Northern Ireland any question of law arising out of the question which falls to be determined by him.

(8)   Where such a case is stated for determination by the High Court, an appeal to the Court of Appeal from the determination by the High Court shall lie only with the leave of the High Court or of the Court of Appeal; and where such a case is stated for determination by the Court of Session then, subject to any rules of court, the Minister shall be entitled to appear and be heard when the case is being considered by that Court.

(9)   Any scheme under the said section 1 may amend or revoke any previous scheme made thereunder.

(10)   Different schemes may be made under the said section 1 in relation to different classes of persons to whom that section applies, and in this section "the principal civil service pension scheme" means the principal scheme so made relating to persons serving in employment in the [civil service of the State].

(11)   Before a scheme made under the said section 1, being the principal civil service scheme or a scheme amending or revoking that scheme, comes into operation the Minister shall lay a copy of the scheme before Parliament.

[(11A)   Subsection (11B) below applies if a scheme made under the said section 1 makes any provision which would have the effect of reducing the amount of a compensation benefit.

(11B)   Before the scheme comes into operation, the Minister must have laid before Parliament a report providing information about—

   (a)   the consultation that took place for the purposes of section 1(3) of this Act, so far as relating to the provision,
   (b)   the steps taken in connection with that consultation with a view to reaching agreement in relation to the provision with the persons consulted, and
   (c)   whether such agreement has been reached.]

(12)   Notwithstanding any repeal made by this Act, the existing civil service superannuation provisions, that is to say, the enactments and instruments listed in Schedule 2 to this Act, shall, with the necessary adaptations and modifications, have effect as from the commencement of this Act as if they constituted a scheme made under the said section 1 in relation to the persons to whom that section applies, being the principal civil service pension scheme, and coming into operation on the said commencement and may be revoked or amended accordingly.

**NOTES**

Sub-s (3): substituted by the Pensions (Miscellaneous Provisions) Act 1990, s 9; words in square brackets inserted by the Superannuation Act 2010, s 1(1), (2), as from 16 December 2010 (for effect see s 1(4)–(6) of the 2010 Act at **[1.1812]**).

Sub-ss (3A)–(3C): inserted by the Superannuation Act 2010, s 1(1), (3), as from 16 December 2010 (for effect see s 1(4)–(6) of the 2010 Act at **[1.1812]**).

Sub-ss (3D), (11A), (11B): inserted by the Superannuation Act 2010, s 2(1)–(3), as from 16 February 2011 (for effect see s 2(4) of the 2010 Act at **[1.1813]**).

Sub-s (10): words in square brackets substituted by the Constitutional Reform and Governance Act 2010, s 19, Sch 2, Pt 1, para 2, as from 11 November 2010.

Rules, etc: various Rules and Regulations relating to the Principal Civil Service Pension Scheme which were made under the Superannuation Act 1965 (repealed by this Act) now have effect under this section. They are omitted as outside the scope of this work.

**[1.9]**
## 5   Benefits under civil service superannuation on schemes not assignable

(1)   Any assignment (or, in Scotland, assignation) of or charge on, and any agreement to assign or charge, any benefit payable under a scheme made under section 1 of this Act shall be void.

(2)   Nothing in subsection (1) above shall affect the powers of any court under [section 310 of the Insolvency Act 1986] or section [32(2) and (4)] of the Bankruptcy (Scotland) Act [1985] (bankrupt's salary, pension, etc may be ordered to be paid to the trustee in bankruptcy) or under any enactment applying to Northern Ireland (including an enactment of the Parliament of Northern Ireland) and corresponding to [section 51(2) of the Bankruptcy Act 1914 or [the said section 310]].

**NOTES**

Sub-s (2): words in first and fifth pairs of square brackets substituted by the Insolvency Act 1986, s 439(2), Sch 14; words in second and third pairs of square brackets substituted by the Bankruptcy (Scotland) Act 1985, s 75, Sch 7, para 9; words in fourth pair of square brackets substituted by the Insolvency Act 1985, s 235(1), Sch 8, para 19.

*Persons employed in local government service, etc*

**[1.10]**
**7  Superannuation of persons employed in local government service, etc**
(1)  The Secretary of State may by regulations make provision with respect to the pensions, allowances or gratuities which, subject to the fulfilment of such requirements and conditions as may be prescribed by the regulations, are to be, or may be, paid to or in respect of such persons, or classes of persons, as may be so prescribed, being—
   (a)   persons, or classes of persons, employed in local government service; and
   (b)   other persons, or classes of persons, for whom it is appropriate, in the opinion of the Secretary of State, to provide pensions, allowances or gratuities under the regulations.
[(1A)   Subsection (1) is subject to sections 18 and 19 of the Public Service Pensions Act 2013 (restrictions on benefits provided under existing schemes).]
(2)  Without prejudice to the generality of subsection (1) above, regulations under this section—
   (a)   may include all or any of the provisions referred to in Schedule 3 to this Act; and
   (b)   may make different provision as respects different classes of persons and different circumstances.
(3)  Notwithstanding anything in the Pensions (Increase) Act 1971, regulations under this section may provide—
   (a)   that increases under that Act of such of the pensions, allowances or gratuities payable under the regulations as may be prescribed by the regulations, or such part of those increases as may be so prescribed, shall be paid out of such of the superannuation funds established under the regulations as the regulations may provide; and
   (b)   that the cost of those increases or that part thereof, as the case may be, shall be defrayed by contributions from the persons to whom any services in respect of which the pensions, allowances or gratuities are or may become payable were or are being rendered or by such of those persons as may be so prescribed;
and any provisions of the said Act of 1971, or of regulations made under section 5 thereof, relating to liability for the cost of increases under that Act of pensions, allowances or gratuities payable under the regulations shall have effect subject to the provisions of any regulations made by virtue of this subsection and for the time being in force.
(4)  Without prejudice to subsection (2) above, regulations made by virtue of subsection (3) above may make different provision as respects different classes of pensions, allowances or gratuities.
(5)  Before making any regulations under this section the Secretary of State shall consult with—
   (a)   such associations of local authorities as appear to him to be concerned;
   (b)   any local authority with whom consultation appears to him to be desirable; and
   (c)   such representatives of other persons likely to be affected by the proposed regulations as appear to him to be appropriate.

**NOTES**
  Sub-s (1A): inserted by the Public Service Pensions Act 2013, s 27, Sch 8, paras 6, 8, as from a day to be appointed.
  Transfer of Functions: functions under this section are transferred, in so far as they are exercisable in or as regards Scotland, to the Scottish Ministers, by the Scotland Act 1998 (Transfer of Functions to the Scottish Ministers etc) Order 1999, SI 1999/1750, art 2, Sch 1.
  Regulations: a large number of Regulations have been made under this section constituting and amending what is now the Local Government Pension Scheme. The principal Regulations currently (April 2013) in force for England and Wales are the Local Government Pension Scheme (Benefits, Membership and Contributions) Regulations 2007, SI 2007/1166, the Local Government Pension Scheme (Transitional Provisions) Regulations 2008, SI 2008/238, and the Local Government Pension Scheme (Administration) Regulations 2008, SI 2008/239, all as amended. The equivalent Regulations applying to Scotland are the Local Government Pension Scheme (Administration) (Scotland) Regulations 2008, SSI 2008/228, the Local Government Pension Scheme (Transitional Provisions) (Scotland) Regulations 2008, SSI 2008/229, and the Local Government Pension Scheme (Benefits, Membership and Contributions) (Scotland) Regulations 2008, SSI 2008/230, also as amended.

*Teachers*

**[1.11]**
**9  Superannuation of teachers**
(1)  The Secretary of State may, by regulations made with the consent of the Minister, make provision with respect to the pensions, allowances or gratuities which, subject to the fulfilment of such requirements and conditions as may be prescribed by the regulations, are to be, or may be, paid [to or in respect of teachers by the Secretary of State or, in the case of injury benefit, by the Secretary of State, an employer of teachers or such other person as the Secretary of State may consider appropriate and may specify in the regulations].
[(1A)   Subsection (1) is subject to sections 18 and 19 of the Public Service Pensions Act 2013 (restrictions on benefits provided under existing schemes).]
(2)  Without prejudice to the generality of subsection (1) above, regulations under this section—
   (a)   may include all or any of the provisions referred to in Schedule 3 to this Act; and
   (b)   may make different provision as respects different classes of persons and different circumstances.

[(2A) Where regulations under this section make provision with respect to money purchase benefits, they may also—

    (a) include provision enabling a person to elect for such money purchase benefits as are to be provided to or in respect of him under the regulations to be purchased from any authorised provider whom he may specify; and

    (b) notwithstanding subsection (1) above, provide that the making of such an election shall have the effect, in such cases as may be specified in the regulations, of discharging any liability of the Secretary of State to pay those benefits to or in respect of that person;

but no regulations under this section shall be so framed as to have the effect that any money purchase benefits to be provided under them may only be provided in a manner which discharges that liability of the Secretary of State.]

(3) Where the regulations provide for the making of any such payment as is referred to in paragraph 3, 5 or 6 of the said Schedule 3, they may also provide for the payment to be made by the Secretary of State.

[(3A) Notwithstanding anything in the Pensions (Increase) Act 1971, regulations under this section may provide that the cost of increases under that Act of such of the pensions, allowances or gratuities payable under the regulations as may be prescribed by the regulations, or such part of those increases as may be so prescribed, shall be defrayed—

    (a) by contributions from employers of teachers or from such other persons or classes of person (apart from teachers) as the Secretary of State may consider appropriate and may specify in the regulations; or

    (b) by contributions from such of those employers or other persons as may be so specified;

and any provisions of the said Act of 1971, or of regulations made under section 5 thereof, relating to liability for the cost of increases under that Act of pensions, allowances or gratuities payable under the regulations shall have effect subject to the provisions of any regulations made by virtue of this subsection and for the time being in force.]

(4) Where regulations under this section provide for the establishment of a superannuation fund, the regulations may also provide for the payment by the Secretary of State—

    (a) of the administrative expenses of the persons by whom, in accordance with the regulations, the fund is to be administered; and

    (b) of such travelling, subsistence and other allowances to those persons as the Secretary of State may, with the consent of the Minister, determine.

(5) Before making any such regulations the Secretary of State shall consult with representatives of [local authorities, or, in Scotland, education authorities] and of teachers and with such representatives of other persons likely to be affected by the proposed regulations as appear to him to be appropriate.

[(5A) The powers exercisable by a [local authority] or, in Scotland, an education authority, by virtue of—

    (a) section 111 of the Local Government Act 1972 (subsidiary powers of local authorities), or

    (b) section 69 of the Local Government (Scotland) Act 1973 (similar provision for Scotland),

shall be taken to include, and to have at all times included, power to pay, or arrange for the payment of, injury benefit to or in respect of teachers; but that section shall cease to confer any such power on an authority in either part of Great Britain as from the coming into force of the first regulations under this section which make provision for the payment of injury benefit by such an authority to or in respect of teachers in that part.]

(6) In this section

["authorised provider" has the meaning given in section 1;]

["injury benefit" means a pension, allowance or gratuity payable under the regulations to or in respect of a teacher in consequence of any injury sustained, or disease contracted, by him in the course of his employment in that capacity;]

["local authority" has the meaning given by section 579(1) of the Education Act 1996;]

"money purchase benefits" has the meaning given by [section 181(1) of the Pension Schemes Act 1993];]

"teachers" includes such persons as may be prescribed by regulations made under this section, being persons employed otherwise than as teachers—

    (a) in a capacity connected with education which to a substantial extent involves the control or supervision of teachers; or

    (b) in employment which involves the performance of duties in connection with the provision of education or services ancillary to education.

(7) . . .

---

**NOTES**

Sub-s (1): words in square brackets substituted by the Pensions (Miscellaneous Provisions) Act 1990, s11(1).

Sub-s (1A): inserted by the Public Service Pensions Act 2013, s 27, Sch 8, paras 6, 9, as from a day to be appointed.

Sub-ss (2A), (3A), (5A): inserted by the Pensions (Miscellaneous Provisions) Act 1990, ss 4(1), 8(3), 11(2).

Sub-ss (2A), (3A), (5A): inserted by the Pensions (Miscellaneous Provisions) Act 1990, ss 4(1), 8(3), 11(2).

Sub-s (6) is amended as follows:

Definition "authorised provider" inserted by the Pensions (Miscellaneous Provisions) Act 1990, s 8(4), and substituted by the Financial Services and Markets Act 2000 (Consequential Amendments and Repeals) Order 2001, SI 2001/3649, art 107.

Definition "injury benefit" inserted by the Pensions (Miscellaneous Provisions) Act 1990, s 11(3).

Definition "local authority" inserted by SI 2010/1158, art 5(1), Sch 2, Pt 2, para 27(1), (4), as from 5 May 2010.

Definition "money purchase benefits" inserted by the Pensions (Miscellaneous Provisions) Act 1990, s 8(4).

Words in square brackets in the definition "money purchase benefits" substituted by the Pension Schemes Act 1993, s 190, Sch 8, para 7.

Sub-s (7): repealed by SI 2010/1158, art 5(1), (2), Sch 2, Pt 2, para 27(1), (5), Sch 3, Pt 2, as from 5 May 2010.

Transfer of Functions: functions under this section are transferred, in so far as they are exercisable in or as regards Scotland, to the Scottish Ministers, by the Scotland Act 1998 (Transfer of Functions to the Scottish Ministers etc) Order 1999, SI 1999/1750, art 2, Sch 1.

Regulations: the principal Regulations currently (April 2013) in force under this section are the Teachers' Pensions Regulations 2010, SI 2010/990 (for England and Wales), and the Teachers' Superannuation (Scotland) Regulations 2005, SSI 2005/393 (for Scotland) (in both cases, as amended). Other Regulations are omitted for reasons of space.

*Persons engaged in health services, etc*

**[1.12]**

**10   Superannuation of persons engaged in health services, etc**

(1)   The Secretary of State may, by regulations made with the consent of the Minister, make provision with respect to the pensions, allowances or gratuities which, subject to the fulfilment of such requirements and conditions as may be prescribed by the regulations, are to be, or may be, paid by the Secretary of State to or in respect of such persons, or classes of persons, as may be so prescribed [(in this section referred to as "health staff")], being—

(a)   persons, or classes of persons, engaged in health services other than services provided by a . . . local authority; and

(b)   other persons, or classes of persons, for whom it is appropriate, in the opinion of the Secretary of State, to provide pensions, allowances or gratuities under the regulations.

[(1A)   Subsection (1) is subject to sections 18 and 19 of the Public Service Pensions Act 2013 (restrictions on benefits provided under existing schemes).]

(2)   Without prejudice to the generality of subsection (1) above, regulations under this section—

(a)   may include all or any of the provisions referred to in Schedule 3 to this Act; and

(b)   may make different provision as respects different classes of persons and different circumstances.

[(2A)   Where regulations under this section make provision with respect to money purchase benefits, they may also—

(a)   include provision enabling a person to elect for such money purchase benefits as are to be provided to or in respect of him under the regulations to be purchased from any authorised provider whom he may specify; and

(b)   notwithstanding subsection (1) above, provide that the making of such an election shall have the effect, in such cases as may be specified in the regulations, of discharging any liability of the Secretary of State to pay those benefits to or in respect of that person;

but no regulations under this section shall be so framed as to have the effect that any money purchase benefits to be provided under them may only be provided in a manner which discharges that liability of the Secretary of State.]

(3)   Where the regulations provide for the making of any such payment as is referred to in paragraph 3, 5 or 6 of the said Schedule 3, they may also provide for the payment to be made by the Secretary of State.

[(3A)   Notwithstanding anything in the Pensions (Increase) Act 1971, regulations under this section may provide that the cost of increases under that Act of such of the pensions, allowances or gratuities payable under the regulations as may be prescribed by the regulations, or such part of those increases as may be so prescribed, shall be defrayed—

(a)   by contributions from employers of health staff or from such other persons or classes of person (apart from health staff) as the Secretary of State may consider appropriate and may specify in the regulations; or

(b)   by contributions from such of those employers or other persons as may be so specified;

and any provisions of the said Act of 1971, or of regulations made under section 5 thereof, relating to liability for the cost of increases under that Act of pensions, allowances or gratuities payable under the regulations shall have effect subject to the provisions of any regulations made by virtue of this subsection and for the time being in force.]

(4)   Before making any such regulations the Secretary of State shall consult with such representatives of persons likely to be affected by the proposed regulations as appear to him to be appropriate.

(5)   *(Amends the Superannuation (Miscellaneous Provisions) Act 1967, s 7).*

[(6)   In this section—

["authorised provider" has the meaning given in section 1;]

"money purchase benefits" has the meaning given by [section 181(1) of the Pension Schemes Act 1993].]

**NOTES**

Sub-s (1): words in square brackets inserted by the Pensions (Miscellaneous Provisions) Act 1990, s 4(2); words omitted repealed by the National Health Service Reorganisation Act 1973, ss 57, 58, Sch 5.

Sub-s (1A): inserted by the Public Service Pensions Act 2013, s 27, Sch 8, paras 6, 10, as from a day to be appointed.

Sub-ss (2A), (3A): inserted by the Pensions (Miscellaneous Provisions) Act 1990, ss 4(2), 8(5).

Sub-s (5): amends the Superannuation (Miscellaneous Provisions) Act 1967, s 7.

Sub-s (6): added by the Pensions (Miscellaneous Provisions) Act 1990, s 8(6); definition "authorised provider" substituted by the Financial Services and Markets Act 2000 (Consequential Amendments and Repeals) Order 2001, SI 2001/3649, art 108; words in square brackets in the definition "money purchase benefits" substituted by the Pension Schemes Act 1993, s 190, Sch 8, para 7.

Transfer of Functions: functions under this section are transferred, in so far as they are exercisable in or as regards Scotland, to the Scottish Ministers, by the Scotland Act 1998 (Transfer of Functions to the Scottish Ministers etc) Order 1999, SI 1999/1750, art 2, Sch 1.

Regulations: the principal Regulations currently (April 2013) in force under this section are (for England and Wales) the National Health Service Pension Scheme Regulations 2008, SI 2008/653, and (for Scotland) the National Health Service Pension Scheme (Scotland) Regulations 2008, SSI 2008/224 (in both cases, as amended). Other Regulations are omitted for reasons of space.

## Miscellaneous and Supplemental

**[1.13]**
## 24 Compensation for loss of office, etc

(1)   Subject to subsection (2) below, the Secretary of State may, with the consent of the Minister, by regulations provide for the payment by such person as may be prescribed by or determined under regulations of pensions, allowances or gratuities by way of compensation to or in respect of the following persons, that is to say, persons—

(a)   in relation to whom regulations may be made under section 7, section 9 or section 10 of this Act or section 1 of the [Police Pensions Act 1976] or [in respect of whose service payments may be made under a scheme brought into operation under section 34 of the Fire and Rescue Services Act 2004]; and

(b)   who suffer loss of office or employment, or loss or diminution of emoluments, in such circumstances, or by reason of the happening of such an event, as may be prescribed by the regulations.

[(1A)   Subsection (1) is subject to section 19 of the Public Service Pensions Act 2013 (restrictions on benefits provided under existing schemes).]

(2)   Regulations under this section relating to persons in relation to whom regulations may be made under section 7 of this Act may be made without the consent of the Minister.

(3)   Regulations under this section may—

(a)   include provision as to the manner in which and the person to whom any claim for compensation is to be made, and for the determination of all questions arising under the regulations;

(b)   make different provision as respects different classes of persons and different circumstances and make or authorise the Secretary of State to make exceptions and conditions; and

(c)   be framed so as to have effect from a date earlier than the making of the regulations, but so that regulations having effect from a date earlier than the date of their making shall not place any individual who is qualified to participate in the benefits for which the regulations provide in a worse position than he would have been in if the regulations had been so framed as to have effect only from the date of their making.

(4)   Regulations under this section may include all or any of the provisions referred to in paragraphs 8, 9 and 13 of Schedule 3 to this Act.

(5)   Regulations under this section shall be made by statutory instrument, which shall be subject to annulment in pursuance of a resolution of either House of Parliament.

**NOTES**

Sub-s (1): words in first pair of square brackets substituted by the Police Pensions Act 1976, s 13(1), Sch 2, para 10; words in second pair of square brackets substituted by the Fire and Rescue Services Act 2004, s 53(1), Sch 1, para 37 (for transitional provisions in relation to the Firefighters' Pension Scheme, see the Fire and Rescue Services Act 2004 (Firefighters' Pension Scheme) (Wales) Order 2004, SI 2004/2918 and the Firefighters' Pension Scheme (England and Scotland) Order 2004, SI 2004/2306).

Sub-s (1A): inserted by the Public Service Pensions Act 2013, s 27, Sch 8, paras 6, 11, as from a day to be appointed.

Transfer of Functions: functions under this section are transferred, in so far as they are exercisable in or as regards Scotland, to the Scottish Ministers, by the Scotland Act 1998 (Transfer of Functions to the Scottish Ministers etc) Order 1999, SI 1999/1750, art 2, Sch 1.

Regulations: Regulations made under this section include the National Health Service (Compensation for Premature Retirement) Regulations 2002, SI 2002/1311, the Local Government (Early Termination of Employment) (Discretionary Compensation) (England and Wales) Regulations 2006, SI 2006/2914 at **[2.1048]**, the Teachers' Pensions Regulations 2010, SI 2010/990, and the Local Government (Discretionary Payments) (Injury Allowances) Regulations 2011, SI 2011/2954. Other Regulations are omitted for reasons of space.

# EUROPEAN COMMUNITIES ACT 1972

(1972 c 68)

### ARRANGEMENT OF SECTIONS

#### PART I
#### GENERAL PROVISIONS

*An Act to make provision in connection with the enlargement of the European Communities to include the United Kingdom, together with (for certain purposes) the Channel Islands, the Isle of Man and Gibraltar*

[17 October 1972]

---

**NOTES**

The Parts of this Act which have been reproduced here are those which govern the status in UK law of the European Union Treaties and legislation, and empower the incorporation of EU legislation into UK law.

See *Harvey* PII.

---

### PART I
### GENERAL PROVISIONS

**[1.14]**
## 1   Short title and interpretation
(1)   This Act may be cited as the European Communities Act 1972.
(2)   In this Act . . . —
    ["the EU" means the European Union, being the Union established by the Treaty on European Union signed at Maastricht on 7th February 1992 (as amended by any later Treaty),]
    "the Communities" means the European Economic Community, the European Coal and Steel Community and the European Atomic Energy Community;
    "the Treaties" or "[the EU Treaties]" means, subject to subsection (3) below, the pre-accession treaties, that is to say, those described in Part I of Schedule 1 to this Act, taken with—
    (a)   the treaty relating to the accession of the United Kingdom to the European Economic Community and to the European Atomic Energy Community, signed at Brussels on the 22nd January 1972; and
    (b)   the decision, of the same date, of the Council of the European Communities relating to the accession of the United Kingdom to the European Coal and Steel Community; [and
    (c)   the treaty relating to the accession of the Hellenic Republic to the European Economic Community and to the European Atomic Energy Community, signed at Athens on 28th May 1979; and
    (d)   the decision, of 24th May 1979, of the Council relating to the accession of the Hellenic Republic to the European Coal and Steel Community;] [and
    [(e)   the decisions of the Council of 7th May 1985, 24th June 1988, 31st October 1994, 29th September 2000 and 7th June 2007 on the Communities' system of own resources;]]
    [(g)   the treaty relating to the accession of the Kingdom of Spain and the Portuguese Republic to the European Economic Community and to the European Atomic Energy Community, signed at Lisbon and Madrid on 12th June 1985; and
    (h)   the decision, of 11th June 1985, of the Council relating to the accession of the Kingdom of Spain and the Portuguese Republic to the European Coal and Steel Community;] [and
    (j)   the following provisions of the Single European Act signed at Luxembourg and The Hague on 17th and 28th February 1986, namely Title II (amendment of the treaties establishing the Communities) and, so far as they relate to any of the Communities

or any Community institution, the preamble and Titles I (common provisions) and IV (general and final provisions);] [and

(k)    Titles II, III and IV of the Treaty on European Union signed at Maastricht on 7th February 1992, together with the other provisions of the Treaty so far as they relate to those Titles, and the Protocols adopted at Maastricht on that date and annexed to the Treaty establishing the European Community with the exception of the Protocol on Social Policy on page 117 of Cm 1934] [and

(l)    the decision, of 1st February 1993, of the Council amending the Act concerning the election of the representatives of the European Parliament by direct universal suffrage annexed to Council Decision 76/787/ECSC, EEC, Euratom of 20th September 1976] [and

(m)    the Agreement on the European Economic Area signed at Oporto on 2nd May 1992 together with the Protocol adjusting that Agreement signed at Brussels on 17th March 1993] [and

(n)    the treaty concerning the accession of the Kingdom of Norway, the Republic of Austria, the Republic of Finland and the United Kingdom of Sweden to the European Union, signed at Corfu on 24th June 1994;] [and

(o)    the following provisions of the Treaty signed at Amsterdam on 2nd October 1997 amending the Treaty on European Union, the Treaties establishing the European Communities and certain related Acts—

(i)    Articles 2 to 9,

(ii)    Article 12, and

(iii)    the other provisions of the Treaty so far as they relate to those Articles,

and the Protocols adopted on that occasion other than the Protocol on Article J.7 of the Treaty on European Union;] [and

(p)    the following provisions of the Treaty signed at Nice on 26th February 2001 amending the Treaty on European Union, the Treaties establishing the European Communities and certain related Acts—

(i)    Articles 2 to 10, and

(ii)    the other provisions of the Treaty so far as they relate to those Articles,

and the Protocols adopted on that occasion;] [and

(q)    the treaty concerning the accession of the Czech Republic, the Republic of Estonia, the Republic of Cyprus, the Republic of Latvia, the Republic of Lithuania, the Republic of Hungary, the Republic of Malta, the Republic of Poland, the Republic of Slovenia and the Slovak Republic to the European Union, signed at Athens on 16th April 2003;] [and

(r)    the treaty concerning the accession of the Republic of Bulgaria and Romania to the European Union, signed at Luxembourg on 25th April 2005;] [and

(s)    the Treaty of Lisbon Amending the Treaty on European Union and the Treaty Establishing the European Community signed at Lisbon on 13th December 2007 (together with its Annex and protocols), excluding any provision that relates to, or in so far as it relates to or could be applied in relation to, the Common Foreign and Security Policy;] [and

(t)    the Protocol amending the Protocol (No 36) on transitional provisions annexed to the Treaty on European Union, to the Treaty on the Functioning of the European Union and to the Treaty establishing the European Atomic Energy Community, signed at Brussels on 23 June 2010;] [and

(u)    the treaty concerning the accession of the Republic of Croatia to the European Union, signed at Brussels on 9 December 2011; and

(v)    the Protocol on the concerns of the Irish people on the Treaty of Lisbon, adopted at Brussels on 16 May 2012;]

and [any other treaty entered into by the EU (except in so far as it relates to, or could be applied in relation to, the Common Foreign and Security Policy)], with or without any of the member States, or entered into, as a treaty ancillary to any of the Treaties, by the United Kingdom;

and any expression defined in Schedule 1 to this Act has the meaning there given to it.

(3)   If Her Majesty by Order in Council declares that a treaty specified in the Order is to be regarded as one of [the EU Treaties] as herein defined, the Order shall be conclusive that it is to be so regarded; but a treaty entered into by the United Kingdom after the 22nd January 1972, other than a pre-accession treaty to which the United Kingdom accedes on terms settled on or before that date, shall not be so regarded unless it is so specified, nor be so specified unless a draft of the Order in Council has been approved by resolution of each House of Parliament.

(4)   For purposes of subsections (2) and (3) above, "treaty" includes any international agreement, and any protocol or annex to a treaty or international agreement.

**NOTES**
Sub-s (2) is amended as follows:
Words omitted repealed by the Interpretation Act 1978, s 25(1), Sch 3.
Definition "the EU" inserted by the European Union (Amendment) Act 2008, s 3(1), as from 1 December 2009.
In the definitions "the Treaties" or "the EU Treaties" (originally the "the Treaties" or "the Community Treaties") words "the EU Treaties" substituted by the European Union (Amendment) Act 2008, s 3(3), Schedule, Pt 1, as from 1 December 2009; paras (c), (d) and the word immediately preceding para (c), inserted by the European Communities (Greek Accession) Act 1979, s 1; para (e) and the word immediately preceding it originally inserted (together with para (f)) by the European Communities (Finance) Act 1985, s 1, and substituted, together with the word immediately preceding it, (for paras (e), (f)) by the European Communities (Finance) Act 2001, s 1; para (e) further substituted by the European Communities (Finance) Act 2008, s 1, as from 19 February 2008; para (g) and the word immediately preceding it and para (h) inserted by the European Communities (Spanish and Portuguese Accession) Act 1985, s 1; para (j) and the word immediately preceding it inserted by the European Communities (Amendment) Act 1986, s 1; para (k) and the word immediately preceding it inserted by the European Communities (Amendment) Act 1993, s 1(1); para (l) and the word immediately preceding it inserted by the European Parliamentary Elections Act 1993, s 3(2); para (m) and the word immediately preceding it inserted by the European Economic Area Act 1993, s 1; para (n) and the word immediately preceding it added by the European Union (Accessions) Act 1994, s 1; para (o) and the word immediately preceding it added by the European Communities (Amendment) Act 1998, s 1; para (p) and the word immediately preceding it added by the European Communities (Amendment) Act 2002, s 1(1); words "any other treaty entered into by the EU (except in so far as it relates to, or could be applied in relation to, the Common Foreign and Security Policy)" in square brackets substituted by the European Union (Amendment) Act 2008, s 3(3), Schedule, Pt 1, as from 1 December 2009; para (q) and the word immediately preceding it added by the European Union (Accessions) Act 2003, s 1(1); para (r) and the word immediately preceding it added by the European Union (Accessions) Act 2006, s 1(1); para (s) and the word immediately preceding it added by the European Union (Amendment) Act 2008, s 2, as from 19 June 2008; para (t) and the word immediately preceding it added by the European Union Act 2011, s 15(2), as from 19 July 2011; paras (u), (v) and the word immediately preceding para (u) inserted by the European Union (Croatian Accession and Irish Protocol) Act 2013, s 3, as from 31 January 2013.
Sub-s (3): words in square brackets substituted by the European Union (Amendment) Act 2008, s 3(3), Schedule, Pt 1, as from 1 December 2009.
The reference in sub-s (2)(n) to Norway was superseded by the subsequent decision of Norway not to accede to the Union.
Orders in Council made under this section: omitted as outside the scope of this work.

**[1.15]**
**2   General implementation of Treaties**
(1)   All such rights, powers, liabilities, obligations and restrictions from time to time created or arising by or under the Treaties, and all such remedies and procedures from time to time provided for by or under the Treaties, as in accordance with the Treaties are without further enactment to be given legal effect or used in the United Kingdom shall be recognised and available in law, and be enforced, allowed and followed accordingly; and the expression ["enforceable EU right"] and similar expressions shall be read as referring to one to which this subsection applies.
(2)   Subject to Schedule 2 to this Act, at any time after its passing Her Majesty may by Order in Council, and any designated Minister or department may [by order, rules, regulations or scheme], make provision—
   (a)   for the purpose of implementing any [EU obligation] of the United Kingdom, or enabling any such obligation to be implemented, or of enabling any rights enjoyed or to be enjoyed by the United Kingdom under or by virtue of the Treaties to be exercised; or
   (b)   for the purpose of dealing with matters arising out of or related to any such obligation or rights or the coming into force, or the operation from time to time, of subsection (1) above;
and in the exercise of any statutory power or duty, including any power to give directions or to legislate by means of orders, rules, regulations or other subordinate instrument, the person entrusted with the power or duty may have regard to the [objects of the EU] and to any such obligation or rights as aforesaid.
In this subsection "designated Minister or department" means such Minister of the Crown or government department as may from time to time be designated by Order in Council in relation to any matter or for any purpose, but subject to such restrictions or conditions (if any) as may be specified by the Order in Council.
(3)   There shall be charged on and issued out of the Consolidated Fund or, if so determined by the Treasury, the National Loans Fund the amounts required to meet any [EU obligation] to make payments to [the EU or a member State], or any [EU obligation] in respect of contributions to the capital or reserves of the European Investment Bank or in respect of loans to the Bank, or to redeem any notes or obligations issued or created in respect of any such [EU obligation]; and, except as otherwise provided by or under any enactment,—
   (a)   any other expenses incurred under or by virtue of the Treaties or this Act by any Minister of the Crown or government department may be paid out of moneys provided by Parliament; and
   (b)   any sums received under or by virtue of the Treaties or this Act by any Minister of the Crown or government department, save for such sums as may be required for disbursements permitted by any other enactment, shall be paid into the Consolidated Fund or, if so determined by the Treasury, the National Loans Fund.

(4)   The provision that may be made under subsection (2) above includes, subject to Schedule 2 to this Act, any such provision (of any such extent) as might be made by Act of Parliament, and any enactment passed or to be passed, other than one contained in this Part of this Act, shall be construed and have effect subject to the foregoing provisions of this section; but, except as may be provided by any Act passed after this Act, Schedule 2 shall have effect in connection with the powers conferred by this and the following sections of this Act to make Orders in Council [or orders, rules, regulations or schemes].

(5), (6)   *(Relate to Northern Ireland, the Channel Islands and the Isle of Man.)*

**NOTES**

The words in the first pair of square brackets in sub-s (2), and the words in square brackets in sub-s (4), were substituted by the Legislative and Regulatory Reform Act 2006, s 27(1).

All the other words in square brackets were substituted by the European Union (Amendment) Act 2008, s 3(3), Schedule, Pt 1, as from 1 December 2009.

Transfer of functions and modification in relation to Scotland: various functions under this section are, in so far as exercisable in or as regards Scotland, transferred to the Scottish Ministers by the Scotland Act 1998 (Transfer of Functions to the Scottish Ministers etc) Order 1999, SI 1999/1750, the Scotland Act 1998 (Transfer of Functions to the Scottish Ministers etc) Order 2005, SI 2005/849, and the Scotland Act 1998 (Transfer of Functions to the Scottish Ministers etc) Order 2006, SI 2006/304. References in this section to a statutory power or duty include a power or duty conferred by an Act of the Scottish Parliament or an instrument made under such an Act, and references to an enactment include an enactment within the meaning of the Scotland Act 1998: see the Scotland Act 1998, s 125, Sch 8, para 15(1), (2). In relation to any order, rules, regulations or scheme made by the Scottish Ministers, or an Order in Council made on the recommendation of the First Minister, the word "designated" in the first sentence of sub-s (2), and the second sentence of that subsection, are to be disregarded, and references to an Act of Parliament are to be read as references to an Act of the Scottish Parliament: see the Scotland Act 1998, s 125, Sch 8, para 15(1), (3) (as amended by the Legislative and Regulatory Reform Act 2006, s 27(4)).

See also the Government of Wales Act 2006, s 59(1) which provides that the power to designate a Minister of the Crown or government department under this section may be exercised to so designate the Welsh Ministers.

The number of Orders and Regulations made under this section is so numerous that references are omitted for reasons of space.

**[1.16]**
**3   Decisions on, and proof of, Treaties and [EU instruments], etc**
(1)   For the purposes of all legal proceedings any question as to the meaning or effect of any of the Treaties, or as to the validity, meaning or effect of any [EU instrument], shall be treated as a question of law (and, if not referred to the European Court, be for determination as such in accordance with the principles laid down by and any relevant [decision of the [the European Court])].

(2)   Judicial notice shall be taken of the Treaties, of the [Official Journal of the European Union] and of any decision of, or expression of opinion by, [the European Court] on any such question as aforesaid; and the Official Journal shall be admissible as evidence of any instrument or other act thereby communicated of [the EU] or of any [EU institution].

(3)   Evidence of any instrument issued by an [EU institution], including any judgment or order of [the European Court], or of any document in the custody of an [EU institution], or any entry in or extract from such a document, may be given in any legal proceedings by production of a copy certified as a true copy by an official of that institution; and any document purporting to be such a copy shall be received in evidence without proof of the official position or handwriting of the person signing the certificate.

(4)   Evidence of any [EU instrument] may also be given in any legal proceedings—
   (a)   by production of a copy purporting to be printed by the Queen's Printer;
   (b)   where the instrument is in the custody of a government department (including a department of the Government of Northern Ireland), by production of a copy certified on behalf of the department to be a true copy by an officer of the department generally or specially authorised so to do;
and any document purporting to be such a copy as is mentioned in paragraph (b) above of an instrument in the custody of a department shall be received in evidence without proof of the official position or handwriting of the person signing the certificate, or of his authority to do so, or of the document being in the custody of the department.

(5)   In any legal proceedings in Scotland evidence of any matter given in a manner authorised by this section shall be sufficient evidence of it.

**NOTES**

The words in the second (outer) pair of square brackets in sub-s (1) were substituted by the European Communities (Amendment) Act 1986, s 2.

All the other words in square brackets (including those in the section heading) were substituted by the European Union (Amendment) Act 2008, s 3(3), Schedule, Pt 1, as from 1 December 2009.

Modification in relation to Scotland: references in sub-s (4) to a government department include any part of the Scottish Administration: see the Scotland Act 1998, s 125, Sch 8, para 15(1), (4).

**4–12**   *(In so far as these sections have not been repealed, they are outside the scope of this work.)*

# SCHEDULES
## SCHEDULE 1
## DEFINITIONS RELATING TO [EU]

**NOTES**

The abbreviation "EU" was substituted by the European Union (Amendment) Act 2008, s 3(3), Schedule, Pt 1, as from 1 December 2009.

Section 1

## PART I
## THE PRE-ACCESSION TREATIES

**[1.17]**

**1.** The "ECSC Treaty", that is to say, the Treaty establishing the European Coal and Steel Community, signed at Paris on the 18th April 1951.

**2.** The "EEC Treaty", that is to say, the Treaty establishing the European Economic Community, signed at Rome on the 25th March 1957.

**3.** The "Euratom Treaty", that is to say, the Treaty establishing the European Atomic Energy Community, signed at Rome on the 25th March 1957.

**4.** The Convention on certain Institutions common to the European Communities, signed at Rome on the 25th March 1957.

**5.** The Treaty establishing a single Council and a single Commission of the European Communities, signed at Brussels on the 8th April 1965.

**6.** The Treaty amending certain Budgetary Provisions of the Treaties establishing the European Communities and of the Treaty establishing a single Council and a single Commission of the European Communities, signed at Luxembourg on the 22nd April 1970.

**7.** Any treaty entered into before the 22nd January 1972 by any of the Communities (with or without any of the member States) or, as a treaty ancillary to any treaty included in this Part of this Schedule, by the member States (with or without any other country).

## PART II
## OTHER DEFINITIONS

**[1.18]**

"Economic Community", "Coal and Steel Community" and "Euratom" mean respectively the European Economic Community, the European Coal and Steel Community and the European Atomic Energy Community.

["EU customs duty"] means, in relation to any goods, such duty of customs as may from time to time be fixed for those goods by directly applicable [EU provision] as the duty chargeable on importation into member States.

["EU institution" means any institution of the EU.]

["EU instrument"] means any instrument [issued by an EU institution].

["EU obligation"] means any obligation created or arising by or under the Treaties, whether an [enforceable EU obligation] or not.

["Enforceable EU right"] and similar expressions shall be construed in accordance with section 2(1) of this Act.

"Entry date" means the date on which the United Kingdom becomes a member of the Communities.

["European Court" means the Court of Justice of the European Union.]

"Member", in the expression "member State", refers to [membership of the EU].

**NOTES**

All words in square brackets were substituted by the European Union (Amendment) Act 2008, s 3(3), Schedule, Pt 1, as from 1 December 2009.

Part 1   Statutes

## SCHEDULE 2
## PROVISIONS AS TO SUBORDINATE LEGISLATION

Section 2

**[1.19]**

**1.** (1)   The powers conferred by section 2(2) of this Act to make provision for the purposes mentioned in section 2(2)(a) and (b) shall not include power—

(a)   to make any provision imposing or increasing taxation; or

(b)   to make any provision taking effect from a date earlier than that of the making of the instrument containing the provision; or

(c)   to confer any power to legislate by means of orders, rules, regulations or other subordinate instrument, other than rules of procedure for any court or tribunal; or

(d)   to create any new criminal offence punishable with imprisonment for more than two years or punishable on summary conviction with imprisonment for more than *three months* or with a fine of more than [level 5 on the standard scale] (if not calculated on a daily basis) or with a fine of more than [£100 a day].

(2)   Sub-paragraph (1)(c) above shall not be taken to preclude the modification of a power to legislate conferred otherwise than under section 2(2), or the extension of any such power to purposes of the like nature as those for which it was conferred; and a power to give directions as to matters of administration is not to be regarded as a power to legislate within the meaning of sub-paragraph (1)(c).

[(3)   In sub-paragraph (1)(d), "the prescribed term" means—

(a)   in relation to England and Wales, where the offence is a summary offence, 51 weeks;

(b)   in relation to England and Wales, where the offence is triable either way, twelve months;

(c)   in relation to Scotland and Northern Ireland, three months.]

**[1A.**   (1)   Where—

(a)   subordinate legislation makes provision for a purpose mentioned in section 2(2) of this Act,

(b)   the legislation contains a reference to an [EU instrument] or any provision of an [EU instrument], and

(c)   it appears to the person making the legislation that it is necessary or expedient for the reference to be construed as a reference to that instrument or that provision as amended from time to time,

the subordinate legislation may make express provision to that effect.

(2)   In this paragraph "subordinate legislation" means any Order in Council, order, rules, regulations, scheme, warrant, byelaws or other instrument made after the coming into force of this paragraph under any Act, Act of the Scottish Parliament[, Measure or Act of the National Assembly for Wales] or Northern Ireland legislation passed or made before or after the coming into force of this paragraph.]

**2.**   (1)   Subject to paragraph 3 below, where a provision contained in any section of this Act confers power to make [any order, rules, regulations or scheme] (otherwise than by modification or extension of an existing power), the power shall be exercisable by statutory instrument.

(2)   Any statutory instrument containing an Order in Council or [any order, rules, regulations or scheme] made in the exercise of a power so conferred, if made without a draft having been approved by resolution of each House of Parliament, shall be subject to annulment in pursuance of a resolution of either House.

**[2A.**   (1)   This paragraph applies where, pursuant to paragraph 2(2) above, a draft of a statutory instrument containing provision made in exercise of the power conferred by section 2(2) of this Act is laid before Parliament for approval by resolution of each House of Parliament and—

(a)   the instrument also contains provision made in exercise of a power conferred by any other enactment; and

(b)   apart from this paragraph, any of the conditions in sub-paragraph (2) below applies in relation to the instrument so far as containing that provision.

(2)   The conditions referred to in sub-paragraph (1)(b) above are that—

(a)   the instrument, so far as containing the provision referred to in sub-paragraph (1)(a) above, is by virtue of any enactment subject to annulment in pursuance of a resolution of either House of Parliament;

(b)   the instrument so far as containing that provision is by virtue of any enactment required to be laid before Parliament after being made and to be approved by resolution of each House of Parliament in order to come into or remain in force;

(c)   in a case not falling within paragraph (a) or (b) above, the instrument so far as containing that provision is by virtue of any enactment required to be laid before Parliament after being made;

(d)   the instrument or a draft of the instrument so far as containing that provision is not by virtue of any enactment required at any time to be laid before Parliament.

(3)   Where this paragraph applies in relation to the draft of a statutory instrument—

(a)   the instrument, so far as containing the provision referred to in sub-paragraph (1)(a) above, may not be made unless the draft is approved by a resolution of each House of Parliament;

(b)   in a case where the condition in sub-paragraph (2)(a) above is satisfied, the instrument so far as containing that provision is not subject to annulment in pursuance of a resolution of either House of Parliament;

(c)   in a case where the condition in sub-paragraph (2)(b) above is satisfied, the instrument is not required to be laid before Parliament after being made (and accordingly any requirement that the instrument be approved by each House of Parliament in order for it to come into or remain in force does not apply); and

(d)   in a case where the condition in sub-paragraph (2)(c) above is satisfied, the instrument so far as containing that provision is not required to be laid before Parliament after being made.

(4)   In this paragraph, references to an enactment are to an enactment passed or made before or after the coming into force of this paragraph.

**2B.** (1)   This paragraph applies where, pursuant to paragraph 2(2) above, a statutory instrument containing provision made in exercise of the power conferred by section 2(2) of this Act is laid before Parliament under section 5 of the Statutory Instruments Act 1946 (instruments subject to annulment) and—

(a)   the instrument also contains provision made in exercise of a power conferred by any other enactment; and

(b)   apart from this paragraph, either of the conditions in sub-paragraph (2) below applies in relation to the instrument so far as containing that provision.

(2)   The conditions referred to in sub-paragraph (1)(b) above are that—

(a)   the instrument so far as containing the provision referred to in sub-paragraph (1)(a) above is by virtue of any enactment required to be laid before Parliament after being made but—

(i)    is not subject to annulment in pursuance of a resolution of either House of Parliament; and

(ii)   is not by virtue of any enactment required to be approved by resolution of each House of Parliament in order to come into or remain in force;

(b)   the instrument or a draft of the instrument so far as containing that provision is not by virtue of any enactment required at any time to be laid before Parliament.

(3)   Where this paragraph applies in relation to a statutory instrument, the instrument, so far as containing the provision referred to in sub-paragraph (1)(a) above, is subject to annulment in pursuance of a resolution of either House of Parliament.

(4)   In this paragraph, references to an enactment are to an enactment passed or made before or after the coming into force of this paragraph.

**2C.** Paragraphs 2A and 2B above apply to a Scottish statutory instrument containing provision made in the exercise of the power conferred by section 2(2) of this Act (and a draft of any such instrument) as they apply to any other statutory instrument containing such provision (or, as the case may be, any draft of such an instrument), but subject to the following modifications—

(a)   references to Parliament and to each or either House of Parliament are to be read as references to the Scottish Parliament;

(b)   references to an enactment include an enactment comprised in, or in an instrument made under, an Act of the Scottish Parliament; and

(c)   the reference in paragraph 2B(1) to section 5 of the Statutory Instruments Act 1946 is to be read as a reference to [section 28 of the Interpretation and Legislative Reform (Scotland) Act 2010 (asp 10)].]

**3.** Nothing in paragraph 2 above shall apply to any Order in Council made by the Governor of Northern Ireland or to any [any order, rules, regulations or scheme] made by a Minister or department of the Government of Northern Ireland; but where a provision contained in any section of this Act confers power to make such an Order in Council or [any order, rules, regulations or scheme], then any Order in Council or [any order, rules, regulations or scheme] made in the exercise of that power, if made without a draft having been approved by resolution of each House of the Parliament of Northern Ireland, shall be subject to negative resolution within the meaning of section 41(6) of the Interpretation Act (Northern Ireland) 1954 as if the Order or [any order, rules, regulations or scheme] were a statutory instrument within the meaning of that Act.

**4, 5.**   (*Outside the scope of this work.*)

**NOTES**
    Para 1: for the words in italics in sub-para (1)(d) there are substituted the words "the prescribed term", and sub-para (3) is added, by the Criminal Justice Act 2003, s 283, Sch 27, para 3, as from a day to be appointed; first-mentioned maximum fine in sub-para (1)(d) increased and converted to a level on the standard scale by the Criminal Justice Act 1982, ss 37, 40, 46; words in second pair of square brackets in sub-para (1)(d) substituted by the Criminal Law Act 1977, s 32(3).

Paras 1A, 2A–2C: inserted by the Legislative and Regulatory Reform Act 2006, ss 28, 29, as from 8 January 2007; words in square brackets in para 1A(1)(b) substituted by the European Union (Amendment) Act 2008, s 3(3), Schedule, Pt 1, as from 1 December 2009; words in square brackets in para 1A(2) inserted by the Government of Wales Act 2006 (Consequential Modifications and Transitional Provisions) Order 2007, SI 2007/1388, art 3, Sch 1, para 1; words in square brackets in para 2C(c) substituted by the Interpretation and Legislative Reform (Scotland) Act 2010 (Consequential, Savings and Transitional Provisions) Order 2011, SSI 2011/396, art 11, as from 11 November 2011.

Paras 2, 3: words in square brackets substituted by the Legislative and Regulatory Reform Act 2006, s 27(2), as from 8 January 2007.

Modification in relation to Scotland: para 2(2) has effect in relation to regulations made by Scottish Ministers, or an Order in Council made on the recommendation of the First Minister, under s 2 of this Act, as if the references to each, or either, House of Parliament were to the Scottish Parliament: see the Scotland Act 1998, s 125, Sch 8, para 15(3)(c).

Welsh Ministers: see the note to s 2 at **[1.15]** with regard to the Government of Wales Act 2006, s 59(1). Note also s 59(4) of the 2006 Act which disapplies para 2(2) above in relation to any statutory instrument made by the Welsh Ministers in certain circumstances.

# EMPLOYMENT AGENCIES ACT 1973

## (1973 c 35)

### ARRANGEMENT OF SECTIONS

*An Act to regulate employment agencies and businesses; and for connected purposes*

[18 July 1973]

**NOTES**

Disapplication of Act: this Act does not apply to an employment agency or an employment business in so far as its activities consist of activities for which a licence is required under the Gangmasters (Licensing) Act 2004; see s 27 of that Act at **[1.1332]**.

Regulatory functions: the regulatory functions conferred by, or under, this Act are subject to the Legislative and Regulatory Reform Act 2006, ss 21, 22 at **[1.1495]**, **[1.1496]**; see the Legislative and Regulatory Reform (Regulatory Functions) Order 2007, SI 2007/3544 (made under s 24(2) of the 2006 Act) for details.

See *Harvey* AI(4).

**1–3** *(Repealed by the Deregulation and Contracting Out Act 1994, ss 35, 81(1), Sch 10, para 1(1), (2), Sch 17.)*

*[Prohibition orders*

**[1.20]**
**3A Power to make orders**
(1) On application by the Secretary of State, an [employment tribunal] may by order prohibit a person from carrying on, or being concerned with the carrying on of—
   (a) any employment agency or employment business; or
   (b) any specified description of employment agency or employment business.
(2) An order under subsection (1) of this section (in this Act referred to as "a prohibition order") may either prohibit a person from engaging in an activity altogether or prohibit him from doing so otherwise than in accordance with specified conditions.
(3) A prohibition order shall be made for a period beginning with the date of the order and ending—
   (a) on a specified date, or
   (b) on the happening of a specified event,
in either case, not more than ten years later.

(4)  Subject to subsections (5) and (6) of this section, an [employment tribunal] shall not make a prohibition order in relation to any person unless it is satisfied that he is, on account of his misconduct or for any other sufficient reason, unsuitable to do what the order prohibits.

(5)  An [employment tribunal] may make a prohibition order in relation to a body corporate if it is satisfied that—

(a)    any director, secretary, manager or similar officer of the body corporate,

(b)    any person who performs on behalf of the body corporate the functions of a director, secretary, manager or similar officer, or

(c)    any person in accordance with whose directions or instructions the directors of the body corporate are accustomed to act,

is unsuitable, on account of his misconduct or for any other sufficient reason, to do what the order prohibits.

(6)  An [employment tribunal] may make a prohibition order in relation to a partnership if it is satisfied that any member of the partnership, or any manager employed by the partnership, is unsuitable, on account of his misconduct or for any other sufficient reason, to do what the order prohibits.

(7)  For the purposes of subsection (4) of this section, where an employment agency or employment business has been improperly conducted, each person who was carrying on, or concerned with the carrying on of, the agency or business at the time, shall be deemed to have been responsible for what happened unless he can show that it happened without his connivance or consent and was not attributable to any neglect on his part.

(8)  A person shall not be deemed to fall within subsection (5)(c) of this section by reason only that the directors act on advice given by him in a professional capacity.

(9)  In this section—

"director", in relation to a body corporate whose affairs are controlled by its members, means a member of the body corporate; and

"specified", in relation to a prohibition order, means specified in the order.]

**NOTES**

Inserted, together with ss 3B–3D, by the Deregulation and Contracting Out Act 1994, s 35, Sch 10, para 1(1), (3).

Sub-ss (1), (4)–(6): words in square brackets substituted by the Employment Rights (Dispute Resolution) Act 1998, s 1(2)(a).

**[1.21]**
**[3B  Enforcement**
Any person who, without reasonable excuse, fails to comply with a prohibition order shall be guilty of an offence and liable—

[(a)    on conviction on indictment, to a fine;

(b)    on summary conviction, to a fine not exceeding the statutory maximum].]

**NOTES**

Inserted as noted to s 3A at **[1.20]**.

Words in square brackets substituted by the Employment Act 2008, s 15, as from 6 April 2009.

**[1.22]**
**[3C  Variation and revocation of orders**
(1)  On application by the person to whom a prohibition order applies, an [employment tribunal] may vary or revoke the order if the tribunal is satisfied that there has been a material change of circumstances since the order was last considered.

(2)  An [employment tribunal] may not, on an application under this section, so vary a prohibition order as to make it more restrictive.

(3)  The Secretary of State shall be a party to any proceedings before an [employment tribunal] with respect to an application under this section, and be entitled to appear and be heard accordingly.

(4)  When making a prohibition order or disposing of an application under this section, an [employment tribunal] may, with a view to preventing the making of vexatious or frivolous applications, by order prohibit the making of an application, or further application, under this section in relation to the prohibition order before such date as the tribunal may specify in the order under this subsection.]

**NOTES**

Inserted as noted to s 3A at **[1.20]**.

Words in square brackets substituted by the Employment Rights (Dispute Resolution) Act 1998, s 1(2)(a).

**[1.23]**
**[3D  Appeals**
(1)  An appeal shall lie to the Employment Appeal Tribunal on a question of law arising from any decision of, or arising in proceedings before, an [employment tribunal] under section 3A or 3C of this Act.

(2) No other appeal shall lie from a decision of an [employment tribunal] under section 3A or 3C of this Act; and section 11 of the Tribunals and Inquiries Act 1992 (appeals from certain tribunals to High Court or Court of Session) shall not apply to proceedings before an [employment tribunal] under section 3A or 3C of this Act.]

**NOTES**

Inserted as noted to s 3A at **[1.20]**.
Words in square brackets substituted by the Employment Rights (Dispute Resolution) Act 1998, s 1(2)(a).

**4** *(S 4 was substituted (together with s 3) by a new s 3 only by the Employment Protection Act 1975, s 114, Sch 13, para 4 (s 3 was subsequently repealed as noted ante).)*

### Conduct of employment agencies and employment businesses

**[1.24]**
**5 General regulations**
(1) The Secretary of State may make regulations to secure the proper conduct of employment agencies and employment businesses and to protect the interests of persons availing themselves of the services of such agencies and businesses, and such regulations may in particular make provision—
(a) requiring persons carrying on such agencies and businesses to keep records;
(b) prescribing the form of such records and the entries to be made in them;
(c) prescribing qualifications appropriate for persons carrying on such agencies and businesses;
(d) regulating advertising by persons carrying on such agencies and businesses;
(e) safeguarding client's money deposited with or otherwise received by persons carrying on such agencies and businesses;
[(ea) restricting the services which may be provided by persons carrying on such agencies and businesses;
(eb) regulating the way in which and the terms on which services may be provided by persons carrying on such agencies and businesses;
(ec) restricting or regulating the charging of fees by persons carrying on such agencies and businesses].
[(1A) A reference in subsection (1)(ea) to (ec) of this section to services includes a reference to services in respect of—
(a) persons seeking employment outside the United Kingdom;
(b) persons normally resident outside the United Kingdom seeking employment in the United Kingdom.]
(2) Any person who contravenes or fails to comply with any regulation made under this section shall be guilty of an offence and liable—
[(a) on conviction on indictment, to a fine;
(b) on summary conviction, to a fine not exceeding the statutory maximum].

**NOTES**

Sub-s (1): paras (ea)–(ec) substituted, for the original paras (f), (g) and the subsequent proviso, by the Employment Relations Act 1999, s 31, Sch 7, paras 1, 2(1), (2).
Sub-s (1A): inserted by the Employment Relations Act 1999, s 31, Sch 7, paras 1, 2(1), (3).
Sub-s (2): words in square brackets substituted by the Employment Act 2008, s 15, as from 6 April 2009.
Regulations: the Conduct of Employment Agencies and Employment Businesses Regulations 2003, SI 2003/3319 at **[2.751]**; the Conduct of Employment Agencies and Employment Businesses (Amendment) Regulations 2007, SI 2007/3575; the Conduct of Employment Agencies and Employment Businesses (Amendment) Regulations 2010, SI 2010/1782.

**[1.25]**
**6 Restriction on charging persons seeking employment, etc**
[(1) Except in such cases or classes of case as the Secretary of State may prescribe—
(a) a person carrying on an employment agency shall not request or directly or indirectly receive any fee from any person for providing services (whether by the provision of information or otherwise) for the purpose of finding him employment or seeking to find him employment;
(b) a person carrying on an employment business shall not request or directly or indirectly receive any fee from an employee for providing services (whether by the provision of information or otherwise) for the purpose of finding or seeking to find another person, with a view to the employee acting for and under the control of that other person;
(c) a person carrying on an employment business shall not request or directly or indirectly receive any fee from a second person for providing services (whether by the provision of information or otherwise) for the purpose of finding or seeking to find a third person, with a view to the second person becoming employed by the first person and acting for and under the control of the third person.]
(2) Any person who contravenes this section shall be guilty of an offence and liable—
[(a) on conviction on indictment, to a fine;

(b)    on summary conviction, to a fine not exceeding the statutory maximum].

**NOTES**
Sub-s (1): substituted by the Employment Relations Act 1999, s 31, Sch 7, paras 1, 3.
Sub-s (2): words in square brackets substituted by the Employment Act 2008, s 15, as from 6 April 2009.
Regulations: the Conduct of Employment Agencies and Employment Businesses Regulations 2003, SI 2003/3319 at **[2.751]**; the Conduct of Employment Agencies and Employment Businesses (Amendment) Regulations 2007, SI 2007/3575; the Conduct of Employment Agencies and Employment Businesses (Amendment) Regulations 2010, SI 2010/1782.

**7**    *(Repealed by the Deregulation and Contracting Out Act 1994, s 81(1), Sch 17.)*

*Supplementary provisions*

**8–11, 11A, 11B**    *(S 8 repealed by the Employment Protection Act 1975, ss 114, 125(3), Sch 13, para 5, Sch 18; ss 9–11, 11A, 11B outside the scope of this work.)*

**[1.26]**
**12    Regulations and orders**
(1)    Subject to the next following subsection, the Secretary of State shall have power to make regulations for prescribing anything which under this Act is to be prescribed.
(2)    The Secretary of State shall not make any regulations under this Act except after consultation with such bodies as appear to him to be representative of the interests concerned.
(3)    Regulations under this Act may make different provision in relation to different cases or classes of case.
(4)    The power of the Secretary of State to make regulations and orders under this Act shall be exercisable by statutory instrument.
[(5)    Regulations under section 5(1) or 6(1) of this Act shall not be made unless a draft has been laid before, and approved by resolution of, each House of Parliament.
(6)    Regulations under section 13(7)(i) of this Act or an order under section 14(3) shall be subject to annulment in pursuance of a resolution of either House of Parliament.]

**NOTES**
Sub-ss (5), (6): substituted, for the original sub-s (5), by the Employment Relations Act 1999, s 31, Sch 7, paras 1, 6.

**[1.27]**
**13    Interpretation**
(1)    In this Act—

 . . .

    "employment" includes—
        (a)    employment by way of a professional engagement or otherwise under a contract for services;
        (b)    the reception in a private household of a person under an arrangement whereby that person is to assist in the domestic work of the household in consideration of receiving hospitality and pocket money or hospitality only;
        and "worker" and "employer" shall be construed accordingly;
    "employment agency" has the meaning assigned by subsection (2) of this section but does not include any arrangements, services, functions or business to which this Act does not apply by virtue of subsection (7) of this section;
    "employment business" has the meaning assigned by subsection (3) of this section but does not include any arrangements, services, functions or business to which this Act does not apply by virtue of subsection (7) of this section;
    "fee" includes any charge however described;
 . . .

    "local authority", in relation to England    . . . , means a county council,    . . . , the Common Council of the City of London, a district council or a London borough council [and in relation to Wales, means a county council or a county borough council,] and, in relation to Scotland means a [council constituted under section 2 of the Local Government etc (Scotland) Act 1994];
    "organisation" includes an association of organisations;
    "organisation of employers" means an organisation which consists wholly or mainly of employers and whose principal objects include the regulation of relations between employers and workers or organisations of workers
    "organisation of workers" means an organisation which consists wholly or mainly of workers and whose principal objects include the regulation of relations between workers and employers or organisations of employers;
    "prescribed" means prescribed by regulations made under this Act by the Secretary of State;
    ["prohibition order" has the meaning given by section 3A(2) of this Act;]
 . . .

(2)   For the purposes of this Act "employment agency" means the business (whether or not carried on with a view to profit and whether or not carried on in conjunction with any other business) of providing services (whether by the provision of information or otherwise) for the purpose of finding [persons] employment with employers or of supplying employers with [persons] for employment by them.

(3)   For the purposes of this Act "employment business" means the business (whether or not carried on with a view to profit and whether or not carried on in conjunction with any other business) of supplying persons in the employment of the person carrying on the business, to act for, and under the control of, other persons in any capacity.

(4)   The reference in subsection (2) of this section to providing services does not include a reference—

   (a)   to publishing a newspaper or other publication unless it is published wholly or mainly for the purpose mentioned in that subsection;

   (b)   to the display by any person of advertisements on premises occupied by him otherwise than for the said purpose; [or

   (c)   to providing a programme service (within the meaning of the Broadcasting Act 1990)].

(5)   For the purposes of section 269 of the Local Government Act 1972, this Act shall be deemed to have been passed after 1st April 1974.

(6)   In this Act, except where the context otherwise requires, references to any enactment shall be construed as references to that enactment as amended, extended or applied by or under any other enactment.

(7)   This Act does not apply to—

   (a)   any business which is carried on exclusively for the purpose of obtaining employment for—

      (i)   persons formerly members of Her Majesty's naval, military or air forces; or

      (ii)   persons released from a [custodial sentence passed by a criminal court in the United Kingdom, the Channel Islands or the Isle of Man;]

      and which is certified annually by or on behalf of the Admiralty Board of the Defence Council, the Army Board of the Defence Council or the Air Force Board of the Defence Council or by the Secretary of State (as the case may be) to be properly conducted;

   (b)   *any agency for the supply of nurses as defined in section 8 of the Nurses Agencies Act 1957 or section 32 of the Nurses (Scotland) Act 1951;*

   (c)   *the business carried on by any county or district nursing association or other similar organisation, being an association or organisation established and existing wholly or mainly for the purpose of providing patients with the services of a nurse to visit them in their own homes without herself taking up residence there;*

   (d)   services which are ancillary to the letting upon hire of any aircraft, vessel, vehicle, plant or equipment;

   (e)   . . .

   (f)   the exercise by a local authority   . . .   [or a joint authority established by Part IV of the Local Government Act 1985] of any of their functions;

   [(fza)   the exercise by an authority established for an area in England under section 207 of the Local Government and Public Involvement in Health Act 2007 (joint waste authorities) of any of its functions;]

   [(fzb)   the exercise by an economic prosperity board established under section 88 of the Local Democracy, Economic Development and Construction Act 2009 of any of its functions;

   (fzc)   the exercise by a combined authority established under section 103 of that Act of any of its functions;]

   [(fa)   the exercise by a police and crime commissioner of any of the commissioner's functions;

   (fb)   the exercise by the Mayor's Office for Policing and Crime of any of that Office's functions;

   (fc)   the exercise by a chief constable established under section 2 of the Police Reform and Social Responsibility Act 2011 of any of the chief constable's functions;

   (fd)   the exercise by the Commissioner of Police of the Metropolis of any of the Commissioner's functions;]

   [(ff)   the exercise by the Broads Authority of any of its functions;]

   [(fg)   the exercise by a National Park authority of any of its functions;]

   [(fh)   the exercise by the London Fire and Emergency Planning Authority of any of its functions;]

   (g)   services provided by any organisation of employers or organisation of workers for its members;

   [(ga)   services provided in pursuance of arrangements made, or a direction given, under section 10 of the Employment and Training Act 1973;]

   (h)   services provided by an appointments board or service controlled by—

      (i)   one or more universities;

      (ii)   a central institution as defined in section 145 of the Education (Scotland) Act 1962 or a college of education as defined in the said section 145;

[(i)    any prescribed business or service, or prescribed class of business or service or business or service carried on or provided by prescribed persons or classes of person]:

*Provided that paragraph (b) of this subsection shall not be taken as exempting from the provisions of this Act any other business carried on in conjunction with an agency for the supply of nurses.*

(8)    Subsection (7)(c) of this section shall have effect in its application to Scotland as if at the end there were added the words *"or mainly or substantially supported by voluntary subscriptions and providing patients with the services of a nurse whether or not the nurse takes up residence in the patient's house".*

### NOTES

Sub-s (1) is amended as follows:

First, second and final definitions omitted repealed, and definition "prohibition order" inserted, by the Deregulation and Contracting Out Act 1994, ss 35, 81, Sch 10, para 1(5), Sch 17.

Third definition omitted repealed by the Employment Protection Act 1975, ss 114, 125(3), Sch 13, para 7, Sch 18.

In definition "local authority" first words omitted repealed, and words in first pair of square brackets inserted, by the Local Government (Wales) Act 1994, s 66(6), (8), Sch 16, para 41, Sch 18; second words omitted repealed by the Local Government Act 1985, s 102, Sch 17; words in second pair of square brackets substituted by the Local Government etc (Scotland) Act 1994, s 180(1), Sch 13, para 90.

Sub-s (2): words in square brackets substituted by the Employment Relations Act 1999, s 31, Sch 7, paras 1, 7.

Sub-s (4): words in square brackets substituted by the Broadcasting Act 1990, s 203(1), Sch 20, para 18.

Sub-s (7) is amended as follows:

Words in square brackets in para (a)(ii) substituted by the Criminal Justice Act 1988, s 123(6), Sch 8, para 7.

Paras (b), (c) and the proviso repealed by the Care Standards Act 2000, ss 111(2), 117(2), Sch 6, in relation to England and Wales (the italicised paragraphs remain in force for Scotland).

Para (e) repealed by the Deregulation and Contracting Out Act 1994, ss 35, 81, Sch 10, para 4, Sch 17.

In para (f), words omitted repealed by a combination of the Police Reform and Social Responsibility Act 2011, s 99, Sch 16, Pt 3, para 118(a), as from 16 January 2012, the Serious Organised Crime and Police Act 2005, ss 59, 174(2), Sch 4, para 19, Sch 17, Pt 2, and the Education Reform Act 1988, s 237, Sch 13, Pt I; words in square brackets inserted by the Local Government Act 1985, s 84, Sch 14, para 50. Note that the words repealed by the Police Reform and Social Responsibility Act 2011 were "a police authority established under section 3 of the Police Act 1996"; for general transitional provisions relating to police reform and the abolition of existing police authorities, see Sch 15 to the 2011 Act, and the Police Reform and Social Responsibility Act 2011 (Commencement No 3 and Transitional Provisions) Order 2011, SI 2011/3019.

Para (fza) inserted by the Local Government and Public Involvement in Health Act 2007, s 209(2), Sch 13, Pt 2, para 30.

Paras (fzb), (fzc) inserted by the Local Democracy, Economic Development and Construction Act 2009, s 119, Sch 6, para 40, as from 17 December 2009.

Paras (fa)–(fd) substituted for the original para (fa) (as inserted by the Greater London Authority Act 1999, s 325, Sch 27, para 37) by the Police Reform and Social Responsibility Act 2011, s 99, Sch 16, Pt 3, para 188(b), as from 16 January 2012 (for general transitional provisions relating to police reform and the abolition of existing police authorities, see Sch 15 to the 2011 Act, and the Police Reform and Social Responsibility Act 2011 (Commencement No 3 and Transitional Provisions) Order 2011, SI 2011/3019).

Para (ff) inserted by the Norfolk and Suffolk Broads Act 1988, s 21, Sch 6.

Para (fg) inserted by the Environment Act 1995, s 78, Sch 10, para 11.

Para (fh) inserted by the Greater London Authority Act 1999, ss 325, 328, Sch 27, para 37, Sch 29, Pt I, para 22.

Para (ga) inserted by the Trade Union Reform and Employment Rights Act 1993, s 49(2), Sch 8, para 4.

Para (i) substituted by the Employment Relations Act 1999, s 31, Sch 7, paras 1, 8.

Sub-s (8): substituted by the Care Standards Act 2000, s 111(2), as from a day to be appointed, as follows (note that the substituted subsection was amended by the Regulation of Care (Scotland) Act 2001, s 79, Sch 3, para 6)—

"(8)    This Act, in its application to Scotland, does not apply to—
    (a)    [a nurse agency as defined in section 2(6) of the Regulation of Care (Scotland) Act 2001 (asp 8)] (but excluding any other business carried on in conjunction with such an agency);
    (b)    the business carried on by any county or district nursing association or other similar organisation, being an association or organisation within paragraph (a) or (b) of that definition.".

Regulations: the Employment Agencies Act 1973 (Exemption) Regulations 1976, SI 1976/710; the Employment Agencies Act 1973 (Exemption) (No 2) Regulations 1979, SI 1979/1741; the Employment Agencies Act 1973 (Exemption) (No 2) Regulations 1984, SI 1984/978 (all made under sub-s (7)(i)).

**[1.28]**
### 14   Short title, repeals, commencement and extent

(1)    This Act may be cited as the Employment Agencies Act 1973.

(2)    The enactments specified in the Schedule to this Act are hereby repealed to the extent specified in the third column of that Schedule.

(3)    The Secretary of State may, after consultation with such bodies as appear to him to be concerned, by order repeal any provision of any local Act, being a provision which is not specified in Part II of the said Schedule and which appears to him to be unnecessary having regard to the provisions of this Act, or to be inconsistent with the provisions of this Act, and may by that order make such amendments of that or any other local Act as appear to him to be necessary in consequence of the repeal and such transitional provision as appears to him to be necessary or expedient in connection with the matter.

(4)    This Act shall come into force on such date as the Secretary of State may by order appoint, and different dates may be appointed for different provisions and for different purposes.

(5)  This Act does not extend to Northern Ireland.

**NOTES**

Orders: the Employment Agencies Act 1973 (Commencement) Order 1976, SI 1976/709.

# SCHEDULE

*(Schedule (repeals) outside the scope of this work.)*

# HEALTH AND SAFETY AT WORK ETC ACT 1974

## (1974 c 37)

### ARRANGEMENT OF SECTIONS

### PART I
#### HEALTH, SAFETY AND WELFARE IN CONNECTION WITH WORK, AND CONTROL OF DANGEROUS SUBSTANCES AND CERTAIN EMISSIONS INTO THE ATMOSPHERE

*An Act to make further provision for securing the health, safety and welfare of persons at work, for protecting others against risks to health or safety in connection with the activities of persons at work, for controlling the keeping and use and preventing the unlawful acquisition, possession and use of dangerous substances, and for controlling certain emissions into the atmosphere; to make further provision with respect to the employment medical advisory service; to amend the law relating to building regulations, and the Building (Scotland) Act 1959; and for connected purposes*

[31 July 1974]

**NOTES**

The Act confers extensive powers to make subordinate legislation. Considerations of space preclude reference to all Orders made under the Act, for details of which specialist works on Health and Safety should be consulted.

As to the transfer of railway safety functions to the Office of Rail Regulation and for transitional provisions in connection with the transfer, see the Railways Act 2005, s 2, Schs 1, 3. See also the Health and Safety (Enforcing Authority for Railways and Other Guided Transport Systems) Regulations 2006, SI 2006/557, which provide that the ORR shall be responsible for the enforcement of the relevant statutory provisions (within the meaning of s 53) to the extent that they relate to the operation of a railway, the operation of a tramway, and the operation of any other system of guided transport.

Disapplication: as to the disapplication of this Act in relation to premises to which the Regulatory Reform (Fire Safety) Order 2005, SI 2005/1541 applies, see art 47 of the 2005 Order. See also the Fire (Scotland) Act 2005, s 70 (Consequential restriction of application of Part I of the Health and Safety at Work etc Act 1974).

As to the transfer of the functions of the Minister for the Civil Service to the Treasury, see the Transfer of Functions (Minister for the Civil Service and Treasury) Order 1981, SI 1981/1670.

Regulatory functions: the regulatory functions conferred by, or under, this Act are subject to the Legislative and Regulatory Reform Act 2006, ss 21, 22 at **[1.1495]**, **[1.1496]**; see the Legislative and Regulatory Reform (Regulatory Functions) Order 2007, SI 2007/3544 (made under s 24(2) of the 2006 Act) for details.

See *Harvey* NIII.

# PART I
# HEALTH, SAFETY AND WELFARE IN CONNECTION WITH WORK, AND CONTROL OF DANGEROUS SUBSTANCES AND CERTAIN EMISSIONS INTO THE ATMOSPHERE

**NOTES**

The general purposes of this Part of this Act are extended by the Offshore Safety Act 1992, ss 1(1), 2(1), the Consumer Protection Act 1987, s 36, the Railways Act 1993, s 117(2), (6), (7), and the Energy Act 2008, s 99.

*Preliminary*

**[1.29]**
**1   Preliminary**
(1)   The provisions of this Part shall have effect with a view to—
  (a)   securing the health, safety and welfare of persons at work;
  (b)   protecting persons other than persons at work against risks to health or safety arising out of or in connection with the activities of persons at work;
  (c)   controlling the keeping and use of explosive or highly flammable or otherwise dangerous substances, and generally preventing the unlawful acquisition, possession and use of such substances; . . .
  (d)   . . .
(2)   The provisions of this Part relating to the making of health and safety regulations . . . and the preparation and approval of codes of practice shall in particular have effect with a view to enabling the enactments specified in the third column of Schedule 1 and the regulations, orders and other instruments in force under those enactments to be progressively replaced by a system of regulations and approved codes of practice operating in combination with the other provisions of this Part and designed to maintain or improve the standards of health, safety and welfare established by or under those enactments.
(3)   For the purposes of this Part risks arising out of or in connection with the activities of persons at work shall be treated as including risks attributable to the manner of conducting an undertaking, the plant or substances used for the purposes of an undertaking and the condition of premises so used or any part of them.
(4)   References in this Part to the general purposes of this Part are references to the purposes mentioned in subsection (1) above.

**NOTES**

Sub-s (1): words omitted repealed by the Environmental Protection Act 1990, s 162(2), Sch 16, Pt I.

Sub-s (2): words omitted repealed by the Employment Protection Act 1975, ss 116, 125(3), Sch 15, para 1, Sch 18.

Dangerous substances: for certain purposes, the reference to dangerous substances in sub-s (1)(c) above is extended to include environmentally hazardous substances; see the Health and Safety at Work etc Act 1974 (Application to Environmentally Hazardous Substances) Regulations 2002, SI 2002/282.

Regulations: the Control of Asbestos in the Air Regulations 1990, SI 1990/556.

*General duties*

**[1.30]**
**2   General duties of employers to their employees**
(1)   It shall be the duty of every employer to ensure, so far as is reasonably practicable, the health, safety and welfare at work of all his employees.
(2)   Without prejudice to the generality of an employer's duty under the preceding subsection, the matters to which that duty extends include in particular—
  (a)   the provision and maintenance of plant and systems of work that are, so far as is reasonably practicable, safe and without risks to health;
  (b)   arrangements for ensuring, so far as is reasonably practicable, safety and absence of risks to health in connection with the use, handling, storage and transport of articles and substances;
  (c)   the provision of such information, instruction, training and supervision as is necessary to ensure, so far as is reasonably practicable, the health and safety at work of his employees;
  (d)   so far as is reasonably practicable as regards any place of work under the employer's control, the maintenance of it in a condition that is safe and without risks to health and the provision and maintenance of means of access to and egress from it that are safe and without such risks;
  (e)   the provision and maintenance of a working environment for his employees that is, so far as is reasonably practicable, safe, without risks to health, and adequate as regards facilities and arrangements for their welfare at work.
(3)   Except in such cases as may be prescribed, it shall be the duty of every employer to prepare and as often as may be appropriate revise a written statement of his general policy with respect to the health and safety at work of his employees and the organisation and arrangements for the time being in force for carrying out that policy, and to bring the statement and any revision of it to the notice of all his employees.

(4)  Regulations made by the Secretary of State may provide for the appointment in prescribed cases by recognised trade unions (within the meaning of the regulations) of safety representatives from amongst the employees, and those representatives shall represent the employees in consultations with the employers under subsection (6) below and shall have such other functions as may be prescribed.

(5)  . . .

(6)  It shall be the duty of every employer to consult any such representatives with a view to the making and maintenance of arrangements which will enable him and his employees to co-operate effectively in promoting and developing measures to ensure the health and safety at work of the employees, and in checking the effectiveness of such measures.

(7)  In such cases as may be prescribed it shall be the duty of every employer, if requested to do so by the safety representatives mentioned in [subsection (4)] above, to establish, in accordance with regulations made by the Secretary of State, a safety committee having the function of keeping under review the measures taken to ensure the health and safety at work of his employees and such other functions as may be prescribed.

**NOTES**

Sub-s (5): repealed by the Employment Protection Act 1975, ss 116, 125(3), Sch 15, para 2, Sch 18.

Sub-s (7): words in square brackets substituted by the Employment Protection Act 1975, ss 116, 125(3), Sch 15, para 2, Sch 18.

Exclusion or modification: see s 15(3)(b) and (6)(c) at **[1.42]**.

Regulations: the Employers' Health and Safety Policy Statements (Exceptions) Regulations 1975, SI 1975/1584 (which exempt employers with fewer than 5 employees from the requirements of sub-s (3)); the Safety Representatives and Safety Committees Regulations 1977, SI 1977/500 at **[2.27]**; the Police (Health and Safety) Regulations 1999, SI 1999/860 at **[2.441]**.

**[1.31]**
## 3   General duties of employers and self-employed to persons other than their employees

(1)  It shall be the duty of every employer to conduct his undertaking in such a way as to ensure, so far as is reasonably practicable, that persons not in his employment who may be affected thereby are not thereby exposed to risks to their health or safety.

(2)  It shall be the duty of every self-employed person to conduct his undertaking in such a way as to ensure, so far as is reasonably practicable, that he and other persons (not being his employees) who may be affected thereby are not thereby exposed to risks to their health or safety.

(3)  In such cases as may be prescribed, it shall be the duty of every employer and every self-employed person, in the prescribed circumstances and in the prescribed manner, to give to persons (not being his employees) who may be affected by the way in which he conducts his undertaking the prescribed information about such aspects of the way in which he conducts his undertaking as might affect their health or safety.

**NOTES**

Exclusion or modification: see s 15(3)(b) and (6)(c) at **[1.42]**.

**[1.32]**
## 4   General duties of persons concerned with premises to persons other than their employees

(1)  This section has effect for imposing on persons duties in relation to those who—
  (a)  are not their employees; but
  (b)  use non-domestic premises made available to them as a place of work or as a place where they may use plant or substances provided for their use there,

and applies to premises so made available and other non-domestic premises used in connection with them.

(2)  It shall be the duty of each person who has, to any extent, control of premises to which this section applies or of the means of access thereto or egress therefrom or of any plant or substance in such premises to take such measures as it is reasonable for a person in his position to take to ensure, so far as is reasonably practicable, that the premises, all means of access thereto or egress therefrom available for use by persons using the premises, and any plant or substance in the premises or, as the case may be, provided for use there, is or are safe and without risks to health.

(3)  Where a person has, by virtue of any contract or tenancy, an obligation of any extent in relation to—
  (a)  the maintenance or repair of any premises to which this section applies or any means of access thereto or egress therefrom; or
  (b)  the safety of or the absence of risks to health arising from plant or substances in any such premises;

that person shall be treated, for the purposes of subsection (2) above, as being a person who has control of the matters to which his obligation extends.

(4)  Any reference in this section to a person having control of any premises or matter is a reference to a person having control of the premises or matter in connection with the carrying on by him of a trade, business or other undertaking (whether for profit or not).

**NOTES**
Exclusion or modification: see s 15(3)(b) and (6)(c) at **[1.42]**.

**5** *(Repealed by the Environmental Protection Act 1990, ss 162(2), 164(3), Sch 16, Pt I.)*

**[1.33]**
**6 General duties of manufacturers etc as regards articles and substances for use at work**
[(1) It shall be the duty of any person who designs, manufactures, imports or supplies any article for use at work or any article of fairground equipment—

(a) to ensure, so far as is reasonably practicable, that the article is so designed and constructed that it will be safe and without risks to health at all times when it is being set, used, cleaned or maintained by a person at work;

(b) to carry out or arrange for the carrying out of such testing and examination as may be necessary for the performance of the duty imposed on him by the preceding paragraph;

(c) to take such steps as are necessary to secure that persons supplied by that person with the article are provided with adequate information about the use for which the article is designed or has been tested and about any conditions necessary to ensure that it will be safe and without risks to health at all such times as are mentioned in paragraph (a) above and when it is being dismantled or disposed of; and

(d) to take such steps as are necessary to secure, so far as is reasonably practicable, that persons so supplied are provided with all such revisions of information provided to them by virtue of the preceding paragraph as are necessary by reason of its becoming known that anything gives rise to a serious risk to health or safety.

(1A) It shall be the duty of any person who designs, manufactures, imports or supplies any article of fairground equipment—

(a) to ensure, so far as is reasonably practicable, that the article is so designed and constructed that it will be safe and without risks to health at all times when it is being used for or in connection with the entertainment of members of the public;

(b) to carry out or arrange for the carrying out of such testing and examination as may be necessary for the performance of the duty imposed on him by the preceding paragraph;

(c) to take such steps as are necessary to secure that persons supplied by that person with the article are provided with adequate information about the use for which the article is designed or has been tested and about any conditions necessary to ensure that it will be safe and without risks to health at all times when it is being used for or in connection with the entertainment of members of the public; and

(d) to take such steps as are necessary to secure, so far as is reasonably practicable, that persons so supplied are provided with all such revisions of information provided to them by virtue of the preceding paragraph as are necessary by reason of its becoming known that anything gives rise to a serious risk to health or safety.]

(2) It shall be the duty of any person who undertakes the design or manufacture of any article for use at work [or of any article of fairground equipment] to carry out or arrange for the carrying out of any necessary research with a view to the discovery and, so far as is reasonably practicable, the elimination or minimisation of any risks to health or safety to which the design or article may give rise.

(3) It shall be the duty of any person who erects or installs any article for use at work in any premises where that article is to be used by persons at work [or who erects or installs any article of fairground equipment] to ensure, so far as is reasonably practicable, that nothing about the way in which [the article is erected or installed makes it unsafe or a risk to health at any such time as is mentioned in paragraph (a) of subsection (1) or, as the case may be, in paragraph (a) of subsection (1) or (1A) above].

[(4) It shall be the duty of any person who manufactures, imports or supplies any substance—

(a) to ensure, so far as is reasonably practicable, that the substance will be safe and without risks to health at all times when it is being used, handled, processed, stored or transported by a person at work or in premises to which section 4 above applies;

(b) to carry out or arrange for the carrying out of such testing and examination as may be necessary for the performance of the duty imposed on him by the preceding paragraph;

(c) to take such steps as are necessary to secure that persons supplied by that person with the substance are provided with adequate information about any risks to health or safety to which the inherent properties of the substance may give rise, about the results of any relevant tests which have been carried out on or in connection with the substance and about any conditions necessary to ensure that the substance will be safe and without risks to health at all such times as are mentioned in paragraph (a) above and when the substance is being disposed of; and

(d)   to take such steps as are necessary to secure, so far as is reasonably practicable, that persons so supplied are provided with all such revisions of information provided to them by virtue of the preceding paragraph as are necessary by reason of its becoming known that anything gives rise to a serious risk to health or safety.]

(5)   It shall be the duty of any person who undertakes the manufacture of any [substance] to carry out or arrange for the carrying out of any necessary research with a view to the discovery and, so far as is reasonably practicable, the elimination or minimisation of any risks to health or safety to which the substance may give rise [at all such times as are mentioned in paragraph (a) of subsection (4) above].

(6)   Nothing in the preceding provisions of this section shall be taken to require a person to repeat any testing, examination or research which has been carried out otherwise than by him or at his instance, in so far as it is reasonable for him to rely on the results thereof for the purposes of those provisions.

(7)   Any duty imposed on any person by any of the preceding provisions of this section shall extend only to things done in the course of a trade, business or other undertaking carried on by him (whether for profit or not) and to matters within his control.

(8)   Where a person designs, manufactures, imports or supplies an article [for use at work or an article of fairground equipment and does so for or to another] on the basis of a written undertaking by that other to take specified steps sufficient to ensure, so far as is reasonably practicable, that the article will be safe and without risks to health [at all such times as are mentioned in paragraph (a) of subsection (1) or, as the case may be, in paragraph (a) of subsection (1) or (1A) above], the undertaking shall have the effect of relieving the first-mentioned person from the duty imposed [by virtue of that paragraph] above to such extent as is reasonable having regard to the terms of the undertaking.

[(8A)   Nothing in subsection (7) or (8) above shall relieve any person who imports any article or substance from any duty in respect of anything which—

(a)   in the case of an article designed outside the United Kingdom, was done by and in the course of any trade, profession or other undertaking carried on by, or was within the control of, the person who designed the article; or

(b)   in the case of an article or substance manufactured outside the United Kingdom, was done by and in the course of any trade, profession or other undertaking carried on by, or was within the control of, the person who manufactured the article or substance.]

(9)   Where a person ("the ostensible supplier") supplies any [article or substance] to another ("the customer") under a hire-purchase agreement, conditional sale agreement or credit-sale agreement, and the ostensible supplier—

(a)   carries on the business of financing the acquisition of goods by others by means of such agreements; and

(b)   in the course of that business acquired his interest in the article or substance supplied to the customer as a means of financing its acquisition by the customer from a third person ("the effective supplier"),

the effective supplier and not the ostensible supplier shall be treated for the purposes of this section as supplying the article or substance to the customer, and any duty imposed by the preceding provisions of this section on suppliers shall accordingly fall on the effective supplier and not on the ostensible supplier.

[(10)   For the purposes of this section an absence of safety or a risk to health shall be disregarded in so far as the case in or in relation to which it would arise is shown to be one the occurrence of which could not reasonably be foreseen; and in determining whether any duty imposed by virtue of paragraph (a) of subsection (1), (1A) or (4) above has been performed regard shall be had to any relevant information or advice which has been provided to any person by the person by whom the article has been designed, manufactured, imported or supplied or, as the case may be, by the person by whom the substance has been manufactured, imported or supplied.]

**NOTES**

Sub-ss (1), (1A): substituted, for the original sub-s (1), by the Consumer Protection Act 1987, s 36, Sch 3, para 1(1), (2).

Sub-ss (2), (3), (5), (8), (9): words in square brackets inserted or substituted by the Consumer Protection Act 1987, s 36, Sch 3, para 1(1), (3), (4), (6), (7), (9).

Sub-ss (4), (10): substituted by the Consumer Protection Act 1987, s 36, Sch 3, para 1(1), (5), (10).

Sub-s (8A): inserted by the Consumer Protection Act 1987, s 36, Sch 3, para 1(1), (8).

Exclusion or modification: see s 15(3)(b) and (6)(c) at **[1.42]**.

Enforcing authority: the Office for Rail Regulation is the enforcing authority for the purposes of this section in so far as it relates to articles designed, manufactured, imported or supplied (or substances manufactured, imported or supplied), to be used exclusively or primarily in the operation of railways, tramways and certain other systems of guided transport (or, in the case of sub-s (3)), in so far as it relates to the erection or installation of articles for use at work in the operation of such systems of transport; see the Health and Safety (Enforcing Authority for Railways and Other Guided Transport Systems) Regulations 2006, SI 2006/557.

**[1.34]**
## 7   General duties of employees at work
It shall be the duty of every employee while at work—

(a) to take reasonable care for the health and safety of himself and of other persons who may be affected by his acts or omissions at work; and

(b) as regards any duty or requirement imposed on his employer or any other person by or under any of the relevant statutory provisions, to co-operate with him so far as is necessary to enable that duty or requirement to be performed or complied with.

**NOTES**
Exclusion or modification: see s 15(3)(b) and (6)(c) at **[1.42]**.

**[1.35]**
**8 Duty not to interfere with or misuse things provided pursuant to certain provisions**
No person shall intentionally or recklessly interfere with or misuse anything provided in the interests of health, safety or welfare in pursuance of any of the relevant statutory provisions.

**NOTES**
Exclusion or modification: see s 15(3)(b) and (6)(c) at **[1.42]**.

**[1.36]**
**9 Duty not to charge employees for things done or provided pursuant to certain specific requirements**
No employer shall levy or permit to be levied on any employee of his any charge in respect of anything done or provided in pursuance of any specific requirement of the relevant statutory provisions.

**NOTES**
Exclusion or modification: see s 15(3)(b) and (6)(c) at **[1.42]**.

*[The Health and Safety Executive]*

**[1.37]**
**[10 Establishment of the Executive**
(1) There shall be a body corporate to be known as the Health and Safety Executive (in this Act referred to as "the Executive").
(2) The provisions of Schedule 2 shall have effect with respect to the Executive.
(3) The functions of the Executive and of its officers and servants shall be performed on behalf of the Crown.
(4) For the purpose of any civil proceedings arising out of those functions—
    (a) in England and Wales and Northern Ireland, the Crown Proceedings Act 1947 shall apply to the Executive as if it were a government department within the meaning of that Act, and
    (b) in Scotland, the Crown Suits (Scotland) Act 1857 shall apply to the Executive as if it were a public department within the meaning of that Act.]

**NOTES**
Substituted by the Legislative Reform (Health and Safety Executive) Order 2008, SI 2008/960, arts 3, 4.
Section heading: the Legislative Reform (Health and Safety Executive) Order 2008, SI 2008/960 does not amend the heading immediately before this section. However, in light of the other amendments made by that Order, and in light of the abolition of the HSC by art 2 of that Order, the heading has been changed from "The Health and Safety Commission and the Health and Safety Executive" to "The Health and Safety Executive".

**[1.38]**
**[11 Functions of the Executive**
(1) It shall be the general duty of the Executive to do such things and make such arrangements as it considers appropriate for the general purposes of this Part.
(2) In connection with the general purposes of this Part, the Executive shall—
    (a) assist and encourage persons concerned with matters relevant to those purposes to further those purposes;
    (b) make such arrangements as it considers appropriate for the carrying out of research and the publication of the results of research and the provision of training and information, and encourage research and the provision of training and information by others;
    (c) make such arrangements as it considers appropriate to secure that the following persons are provided with an information and advisory service on matters relevant to those purposes and are kept informed of and are adequately advised on such matters—
        (i) government departments,
        (ii) local authorities,
        (iii) employers,
        (iv) employees,
        (v) organisations representing employers or employees, and
        (vi) other persons concerned with matters relevant to the general purposes of this Part.

(3)   The Executive shall submit from time to time to the Secretary of State such proposals as the Executive considers appropriate for the making of regulations under any of the relevant statutory provisions.

(4)   In subsections (1) to (3)—

(a)   references to the general purposes of this Part do not include references to the railway safety purposes; and

(b)   the reference to the making of regulations under the relevant statutory provisions does not include a reference so far as the regulations are made for the railway safety purposes.

(5)   It shall be the duty of the Executive—

(a)   to submit to the Secretary of State from time to time particulars of what it proposes to do for the purpose of performing of its functions;

(b)   to ensure that its activities are in accordance with proposals approved by the Secretary of State; and

(c)   to give effect to any directions given to it by the Secretary of State.

(6)   The Executive shall provide a Minister of the Crown on request—

(a)   with information about its activities in connection with any matter with which the Minister is concerned; and

(b)   with advice on any matter with which he is concerned, where relevant expert advice is obtainable from any of the officers or servants of the Executive, but which is not relevant to the general purposes of this Part.]

**NOTES**

Ss 11–13 substituted by the Legislative Reform (Health and Safety Executive) Order 2008, SI 2008/960, arts 3, 5.

**[1.39]**
**[12   Control of the Executive by the Secretary of State**

(1)   The Secretary of State may approve any proposals submitted to him under section 11(5)(a) with or without modifications.

(2)   The Secretary of State may at any time give to the Executive—

(a)   such directions as he thinks fit with respect to its functions, or

(b)   such directions as appear to him requisite or expedient to give in the interests of the safety of the State.

(3)   The Secretary of State may not under subsection (2) give any directions with regard to the enforcement of the relevant statutory provisions in any particular case.

(4)   The reference to directions in subsection (2)(a)—

(a)   includes directions modifying the Executive's functions, but

(b)   does not include directions conferring functions on the Executive other than any functions of which it was deprived by previous directions given under subsection (2)(a).]

**NOTES**

Substituted as noted to s 11 at **[1.38]**.

**[1.40]**
**[13   Powers of the Executive**

(1)   Subject to subsection (2), the Executive shall have power to do anything which is calculated to facilitate, or is conducive or incidental to, the performance of its functions, including a function conferred on it under this subsection.

(2)   The power in subsection (1) shall not include the power to borrow money.

(3)   The Executive may make agreements with a government department or other person for that department or person to perform any of its functions, with or without payment.

(4)   Subject to subsections (5) and (6), the Executive may make agreements with a Minister of the Crown, with a government department or with a public authority to perform functions exercisable by that Minister, department or authority, with or without payment.

(5)   The functions referred to in subsection (4)—

(a)   in the case of a Minister of the Crown, include functions not conferred by an enactment;

(b)   shall be functions which the Secretary of State considers can be appropriately performed by the Executive; and

(c)   do not include any power to make regulations or other instruments of a legislative character.

(6)   The Executive may provide services or facilities, with or without payment, otherwise than for the general purposes of this Part, to a government department or public authority in connection with the exercise of that department's or authority's functions.

(7)   The Executive may appoint persons or committees of persons to provide it with advice in connection with any of its functions and, without prejudice to subsection (8), it may remunerate these persons.

(8)   The Executive may, in connection with the performance of its functions, pay to any person—

(a)   travelling and subsistence allowances, and

(b)   compensation for loss of remunerative time.

(9)   Any amounts paid under subsections (7) and (8) shall be such as may be determined by the Secretary of State, with the approval of the Minister for the Civil Service.

(10)   The Executive may—

   (a)   carry out, arrange for, or make payments for the carrying out of, research into any matter connected with its functions, and

   (b)   disseminate or arrange for or make payments for the dissemination of information derived from this research.

(11)   The Executive may include, in any arrangements made for the provision of services or facilities under subsection (6), provision for the making of payments to the Executive, or any person acting on its behalf, by other parties to the arrangements and by persons using those services or facilities.]

**NOTES**

Substituted as noted to s 11 at **[1.38]**.

**[1.41]**
**14   Power of [the Executive] to direct investigations and inquiries**

(1)   This section applies to the following matters, that is to say any accident, occurrence, situation or other matter whatsoever which [the Executive] thinks it necessary or expedient to investigate for any of the general purposes of this Part or with a view to the making of regulations for those purposes; and for the purposes of this subsection—

   [(a)   those general purposes shall be treated as not including the railway safety purposes; but

   (b)   it is otherwise]
immaterial whether the Executive is or is not responsible for securing the enforcement of such (if any) of the relevant statutory provisions as relate to the matter in question.

   [(2)   The Executive may at any time—

   (a)   investigate and make a special report on any matter to which this section applies; or

   (b)   authorise another person to investigate and make a special report into any such matter.

(2A)   The Executive may at any time, with the consent of the Secretary of State, direct an inquiry to be held into any matter to which this section applies.]

(3)   Any inquiry held by virtue of [subsection (2A)] above shall be held in accordance with regulations made for the purposes of this subsection by the Secretary of State, and shall be held in public except where or to the extent that the regulations provide otherwise.

(4)   Regulations made for the purposes of subsection (3) above may in particular include provision—

   (a)   conferring on the person holding any such inquiry, and any person assisting him in the inquiry, powers of entry and inspection;

   (b)   conferring on any such person powers of summoning witnesses to give evidence or produce documents and power to take evidence on oath and administer oaths or require the making of declarations;

   (c)   requiring any such inquiry to be held otherwise than in public where or to the extent that a Minister of the Crown so directs.

[(5)   In the case of a special report made by virtue of subsection (2), or a report made by the person holding an inquiry by virtue of subsection (2A), the Executive may cause the report, or so much of it as the Executive thinks fit, to be made public at such time and in such manner as it thinks fit.]

(6)   [The Executive]—

   (a)   in the case of an investigation and special report made by virtue of [subsection (2)] above (otherwise than by an officer or servant of the Executive), may pay to the person making it such remuneration and expenses as the Secretary of State may, with the approval of the Minister for the Civil Service, determine;

   (b)   in the case of an inquiry held by virtue of [subsection (2A)] above, may pay to the person holding it and to any assessor appointed to assist him such remuneration and expenses, and to persons attending the inquiry as witnesses such expenses, as the Secretary of State may, with the like approval, determine; and

   (c)   may, to such extent as the Secretary of State may determine, defray the other costs, if any, of any such investigation and special report or inquiry.

(7)   Where an inquiry is directed to be held by virtue of [subsection (2A)] above into any matter to which this section applies arising in Scotland, being a matter which causes the death of any person, no inquiry with regard to that death shall, unless the Lord Advocate otherwise directs, be held in pursuance of the Fatal Accidents [and Sudden Deaths Inquiry (Scotland) Act 1976].

**NOTES**

Sub-s (1): words in first pair of square brackets substituted by the Legislative Reform (Health and Safety Executive) Order 2008, SI 2008/960, arts 3, 6(1), (2); words in second pair of square brackets substituted by the Railways Act 2005, s 2, Sch 3, para 4(5).

Sub-ss (2), (2A): substituted, for the original sub-s (2), by SI 2008/960, arts 3, 6(1), (3).

Sub-ss (3), (6): words in square brackets substituted by SI 2008/960, arts 3, 6(1), (4), (6).

Part 1  Statutes

Sub-s (5): substituted by SI 2008/960, arts 3, 6(1), (5).

Sub-s (7): words in first pair of square brackets substituted by SI 2008/960, arts 3, 6(1), (7); words in second pair of square brackets substituted by the Fatal Accidents and Sudden Deaths Inquiry (Scotland) Act 1976, s 8(1), Sch 1, para 4.

Note: the Legislative Reform (Health and Safety Executive) Order 2008, SI 2008/960 does not amend the title of this section. However, in light of the other amendments made by that Order, and in light of the abolition of the HSC by art 2 of that Order, the title of this section has been changed from "Power of the Commission to direct investigations and inquiries" to "Power of the Executive to direct investigations and inquiries".

Regulations: the Health and Safety Inquiries (Procedure) Regulations 1975, SI 1975/335; the Health and Safety Inquiries (Procedure) (Amendment) Regulations 1976, SI 1976/1246.

*Health and safety regulations and approved codes of practice*

**[1.42]**
## 15  Health and safety regulations

[(1)  Subject to the provisions of section 50, the Secretary of State  . . .  shall have power to make regulations under this section for any of the general purposes of this Part (and regulations so made are in this Part referred to as "health and safety regulations").]

(2)  Without prejudice to the generality of the preceding subsection, health and safety regulations may for any of the general purposes of this Part make provision for any of the purposes mentioned in Schedule 3.

(3)  Health and safety regulations—
  (a)  may repeal or modify any of the existing statutory provisions;
  (b)  may exclude or modify in relation to any specified class of case any of the provisions of sections 2 to 9 or any of the existing statutory provisions;
  (c)  may make a specified authority or class of authorities responsible, to such extent as may be specified, for the enforcement of any of the relevant statutory provisions.

(4)  Health and safety regulations—
  (a)  may impose requirements by reference to the approval of [the Executive] or any other specified body or person;
  (b)  may provide for references in the regulations to any specified document to operate as references to that document as revised or re-issued from time to time.

(5)  Health and safety regulations—
  (a)  may provide (either unconditionally or subject to conditions, and with or without limit of time) for exemptions from any requirement or prohibition imposed by or under any of the relevant statutory provisions;
  (b)  may enable exemptions from any requirement or prohibition imposed by or under any of the relevant statutory provisions to be granted (either unconditionally or subject to conditions, and with or without limit of time) by any specified person or by any person authorised in that behalf by a specified authority.

(6)  Health and safety regulations—
  (a)  may specify the persons or classes of persons who, in the event of a contravention of a requirement or prohibition imposed by or under the regulations, are to be guilty of an offence, whether in addition to or or to the exclusion of other persons or classes of persons;
  (b)  may provide for any specified defence to be available in proceedings for any offence under the relevant statutory provisions either generally or in specified circumstances;
  (c)  may exclude proceedings on indictment in relation to offences consisting of a contravention of a requirement or prohibition imposed by or under any of the existing statutory provisions, sections 2 to 9 or health and safety regulations;
  (d)  may restrict the punishments [(other than the maximum fine on conviction on indictment)] which can be imposed in respect of any such offence as is mentioned in paragraph (c) above.
  [(e)  . . . ]

(7)  Without prejudice to section 35, health and safety regulations may make provision for enabling offences under any of the relevant statutory provisions to be treated as having been committed at any specified place for the purpose of bringing any such offence within the field of responsibility of any enforcing authority or conferring jurisdiction on any court to entertain proceedings for any such offence.

(8)  Health and safety regulations may take the form of regulations applying to particular circumstances only or to a particular case only (for example, regulations applying to particular premises only).

(9)  If an Order in Council is made under section 84(3) providing that this section shall apply to or in relation to persons, premises or work outside Great Britain then, notwithstanding the Order, health and safety regulations shall not apply to or in relation to aircraft in flight, vessels, hovercraft or offshore installations outside Great Britain or persons at work outside Great Britain in connection with submarine cables or submarine pipelines except in so far as the regulations expressly so provide.

(10)  In this section "specified" means specified in health and safety regulations.

**NOTES**

Sub-s (1): substituted by the Employment Protection Act 1975, s 116, Sch 15, para 6; words omitted repealed by the Ministry of Agriculture, Fisheries and Food (Dissolution) Order 2002, SI 2002/794, art 5(2), Sch 2.

Sub-s (4): words in square brackets substituted by the Legislative Reform (Health and Safety Executive) Order 2008, SI 2008/960, arts 3, 7.

Sub-s (6): words in square brackets in para (d) inserted by the Criminal Law Act 1977, s 65(4), Sch 12; para (e) added by the Offshore Safety Act 1992, s 4(1), (6), and repealed by the Health and Safety (Offences) Act 2008, ss 2(1), 3(3), Sch 3, para 2(1), Sch 4, as from 16 January 2009, except in relation to offences committed before that date.

"May repeal or modify any of the existing statutory provisions" (sub-s (3)): the power to repeal or modify any of the existing statutory provisions by regulations under this section is extended to the provisions which are deemed by the Offshore Safety Act 1992, ss 1(1), (3), 2(1), (3), and the Railways Act 1993, s 117(1), (4), to be existing statutory provisions within the meaning of this Part of this Act, and these extensions are without prejudice to the generality of sub-s (1) above; see the Offshore Safety Act 1992, ss 1(2), 2(2), the Railways Act 1993, s 117(3); see also the Coal Industry Act 1994, s 55. As to the Secretary of State's power to repeal or revoke any provision of regulations, see the Deregulation and Contracting Out Act 1994, s 37(1)(b).

Regulations: a very large number of regulations has been made under this section, and specialist Health and Safety publications should be consulted for a full list. Among the most important currently in force (many as subsequently amended) are: the Safety Representatives and Safety Committees Regulations 1977, SI 1977/500 at **[2.27]**; the Health and Safety (First-Aid) Regulations 1981, SI 1981/917; the Electricity at Work Regulations 1989, SI 1989/635; the Health and Safety Information for Employees Regulations 1989, SI 1989/682 at **[2.110]**; the Health and Safety (Display Screen Equipment) Regulations 1992, SI 1992/2792; the Manual Handling Operations Regulations 1992, SI 1992/2793; the Personal Protective Equipment at Work Regulations 1992, SI 1992/2966; the Workplace (Health, Safety and Welfare) Regulations 1992, SI 1992/3004; the Reporting of Injuries, Diseases and Dangerous Occurrences Regulations 1995, SI 1995/3163; the Health and Safety (Enforcing Authority) Regulations 1998, SI 1998/494; the Provision and Use of Work Equipment Regulations 1998, SI 1998/2306; the Lifting Operations and Lifting Equipment Regulations 1998, SI 1998/2307; the Control of Major Accident Hazards Regulations 1999, SI 1999/743; the Police (Health and Safety) Regulations 1999, SI 1999/860 at **[2.441]**; the Railway Safety Regulations 1999, SI 1999/2244; the Ionising Radiations Regulations 1999, SI 1999/3232; the Management of Health and Safety at Work Regulations 1999, SI 1999/3242 at **[2.454]**; the Control of Lead at Work Regulations 2002, SI 2002/2676; the Control of Substances Hazardous to Health Regulations 2002, SI 2002/2677; the Work at Height Regulations 2005, SI 2005/735; the Manufacture and Storage of Explosives Regulations 2005, SI 2005/1082; the Control of Vibration at Work Regulations 2005, SI 2005/1093; the Control of Noise at Work Regulations 2005, SI 2005/1643; the Health and Safety (Enforcing Authority for Railways and Other Guided Transport Systems) Regulations 2006, SI 2006/557; the Construction (Design and Management) Regulations 2007, SI 2007/320; the Coal Mines (Control of Inhalable Dust) Regulations 2007, SI 2007/1894; the Carriage of Dangerous Goods and Use of Transportable Pressure Equipment Regulations 2009, SI 2009/1348; the Agency Workers Regulations 2010, SI 2010/93 at **[2.1277]**; the Control of Artificial Optical Radiation at Work Regulations 2010, SI 2010/1140; the Control of Asbestos Regulations 2012, SI 2012/632.

**[1.43]**
**16  Approval of codes of practice by [the Executive]**
(1)  For the purpose of providing practical guidance with respect to the requirements of any provision of [any of the enactments or instruments mentioned in subsection (1A) below], [the Executive] may, subject to the following subsection  . . .  —
  (a)  approve and issue such codes of practice (whether prepared by it or not) as in its opinion are suitable for that purpose;
  (b)  approve such codes of practice issued or proposed to be issued otherwise than by [the Executive] as in its opinion are suitable for that purpose.
[(1A)  Those enactments and instruments are—
  (a)  sections 2 to 7 above;
  (b)  health and safety regulations, except so far as they make provision exclusively in relation to transport systems falling within paragraph 1(3) of Schedule 3 to the Railways Act 2005; and
  (c)  the existing statutory provisions that are not such provisions by virtue of section 117(4) of the Railways Act 1993.]
(2)  [The Executive] shall not approve a code of practice under subsection (1) above without the consent of the Secretary of State, and shall, before seeking his consent, consult—
  (a)  any government department or other body that appears to [the Executive] to be appropriate  . . . . ; and
  (b)  such government departments and other bodies, if any, as in relation to any matter dealt with in the code, [the Executive] is required to consult under this section by virtue of directions given to it by the Secretary of State.
(3)  Where a code of practice is approved by [the Executive] under subsection (1) above, [the Executive] shall issue a notice in writing—
  (a)  identifying the code in question and stating the date on which its approval by [the Executive] is to take effect; and
  (b)  specifying for which of the provisions mentioned in subsection (1) above the code is approved.
(4)  [The Executive] may—
  (a)  from time to time revise the whole or any part of any code of practice prepared by it in pursuance of this section;

(b)   approve any revision or proposed revision of the whole or any part of any code of practice for the time being approved under this section;

and the provisions of subsections (2) and (3) above shall, with the necessary modifications, apply in relation to the approval of any revision under this subsection as they apply in relation to the approval of a code of practice under subsection (1) above.

(5)   [The Executive] may at any time with the consent of the Secretary of State withdraw its approval from any code of practice approved under this section, but before seeking his consent shall consult the same government departments and other bodies as it would be required to consult under subsection (2) above if it were proposing to approve the code.

(6)   Where under the preceding subsection [the Executive] withdraws its approval from a code of practice approved under this section, [the Executive] shall issue a notice in writing identifying the code in question and stating the date on which its approval of it is to cease to have effect.

(7)   References in this part to an approved code of practice are references to that code as it has effect for the time being by virtue of any revision of the whole or any part of it approved under this section.

(8)   The power of [the Executive] under subsection (1)(b) above to approve a code of practice issued or proposed to be issued otherwise than by [the Executive] shall include power to approve a part of such a code of practice; and accordingly in this Part "code of practice" may be read as including a part of such a code of practice.

**NOTES**

Words "the Executive" in square brackets in each place they occur substituted by the Legislative Reform (Health and Safety Executive) Order 2008, SI 2008/960, arts 3, 8.

Other amendments to this section are as follows:

Sub-s (1): words in first pair of square brackets substituted by the Railways Act 2005, s 2, Sch 3, para 9(1); words omitted repealed by the Employment Protection Act 1975, ss 116, 125(3), Sch 15, para 7, Sch 18.

Sub-s (1A): inserted by the Railways Act 2005, s 2, Sch 3, para 9(2).

Sub-s (2): words omitted repealed by the Health and Social Care Act 2012, s 56(4), Sch 7, paras 4, 5, as from 1 April 2013.

For reasons of space the only Codes of Practice made under this section which are reproduced in this work are Safety Representatives and Safety Committees (1978) at **[4.167]** and Time off for the Training of Safety Representatives (1978) at **[4.169]**.

**[1.44]**
**17   Use of approved codes of practice in criminal proceedings**

(1)   A failure on the part of any person to observe any provision of an approved code of practice shall not of itself render him liable to any civil or criminal proceedings; but where in any criminal proceedings a party is alleged to have committed an offence by reason of a contravention of any requirement or prohibition imposed by or under any such provision as is mentioned in section 16(1) being a provision for which there was an approved code of practice at the time of the alleged contravention, the following subsection shall have effect with respect to that code in relation to those proceedings.

(2)   Any provision of the code of practice which appears to the court to be relevant to the requirement or prohibition alleged to have been contravened shall be admissible in evidence in the proceedings; and if it is proved that there was at any material time a failure to observe any provision of the code which appears to the court to be relevant to any matter which it is necessary for the prosecution to prove in order to establish a contravention of that requirement or prohibition, that matter shall be taken as proved unless the court is satisfied that the requirement or prohibition was in respect of that matter complied with otherwise than by way of observance of that provision of the code.

(3)   In any criminal proceedings—
   (a)   a document purporting to be a notice issued by [the Executive] under section 16 shall be taken to be such a notice unless the contrary is proved; and
   (b)   a code of practice which appears to the court to be the subject of such a notice shall be taken to be the subject of that notice unless the contrary is proved.

**NOTES**

Sub-s (3): words in square brackets substituted by the Legislative Reform (Health and Safety Executive) Order 2008, SI 2008/960, arts 3, 9.

*Enforcement*

**[1.45]**
**18   Authorities responsible for enforcement of the relevant statutory provisions**

(1)   It shall be the duty of the Executive to make adequate arrangements for the enforcement of the relevant statutory provisions except to the extent that some other authority or class of authorities is by any of those provisions or by regulations under subsection (2) below made responsible for their enforcement.

(2)   The Secretary of State may by regulations—
   (a)   make local authorities responsible for the enforcement of the relevant statutory provisions to such extent as may be prescribed;

(b)  make provision for enabling responsibility for enforcing any of the relevant statutory provisions to be, to such extent as may be determined under the regulations—

(i)   transferred from the Executive to local authorities or from local authorities to the Executive; or

(ii)  assigned to the Executive or to local authorities for the purpose of removing any uncertainty as to what are by virtue of this subsection their respective responsibilities for the enforcement of those provisions;

and any regulations made in pursuance of paragraph (b) above shall include provision for securing that any transfer or assignment effected under the regulations is brought to the notice of persons affected by it.

(3)  Any provision made by regulations under the preceding subsection shall have effect subject to any provision made by health and safety regulations  . . .  in pursuance of section 15(3)(c).

(4)  It shall be the duty of every local authority—

(a)   to make adequate arrangements for the enforcement within their area of the relevant statutory provisions to the extent that they are by any of those provisions or by regulations under subsection (2) above made responsible for their enforcement; and

(b)   to perform the duty imposed on them by the preceding paragraph and any other functions conferred on them by any of the relevant statutory provisions in accordance with such guidance as [the Executive] may give them.

[(4A)  Before the Executive gives guidance under subsection (4)(b) it shall consult the local authorities.

(4B)  It shall be the duty of the Executive and the local authorities—

(a)   to work together to establish best practice and consistency in the enforcement of the relevant statutory provisions;

(b)   to enter into arrangements with each other for securing cooperation and the exchange of information in connection with the carrying out of their functions with regard to the relevant statutory provisions; and

(c)   from time to time to review those arrangements and to revise them when they consider it appropriate to do so.]

(5)  Where any authority other than  . . .  the Executive or a local authority is by any of the relevant statutory provisions  . . .  made responsible for the enforcement of any of those provisions to any extent, it shall be the duty of that authority—

(a)   to make adequate arrangements for the enforcement of those provisions to that extent; and

(b)   [except where that authority is the Office of Rail Regulation,] to perform the duty imposed on the authority by the preceding paragraph and any other functions conferred on the authority by any of the relevant statutory provisions in accordance with such guidance as [the Executive] may give to the authority.

(6)  Nothing in the provisions of this Act or of any regulations made thereunder charging any person in Scotland with the enforcement of any of the relevant statutory provisions shall be construed as authorising that person to institute proceedings for any offence.

(7)  In this Part—

(a)   "enforcing authority" means the Executive or any other authority which is by any of the relevant statutory provisions or by regulations under subsection (2) above made responsible for the enforcement of any of those provisions to any extent; and

(b)   any reference to an enforcing authority's field of responsibility is a reference to the field over which that authority's responsibility for the enforcement of those provisions extends for the time being;

but where by virtue of [subsection (3) of section 13] the performance of any function of  . . .  the Executive is delegated to a government department or person, references to  . . . .  the Executive (or to an enforcing authority where that authority is the Executive) in any provision of this Part which relates to that function shall, so far as may be necessary to give effect to any agreement under [that subsection], be construed as references to that department or person; and accordingly any reference to the field of responsibility of an enforcing authority shall be construed as a reference to the field over which that department or person for the time being performs such a function.

---

**NOTES**

Sub-s (3): words omitted repealed by the Employment Protection Act 1975, ss 116, 125(3), Sch 15, para 8, Sch 18.

Sub-s (4): words in square brackets substituted by the Legislative Reform (Health and Safety Executive) Order 2008, SI 2008/960, arts 3, 10(1), (2).

Sub-ss (4A), (4B): inserted by SI 2008/960, arts 3, 10(1), (3).

Sub-s (5): first words omitted repealed by the Employment Protection Act 1975, ss 116, 125(3), Sch 15, para 8, Sch 18; second words omitted repealed by the Railways Act 2005, s 59(6), Sch 13, Pt 1; words in first pair of square brackets in para (b) inserted by the Railways Act 2005, s 2, Sch 3, para 10(3); words in second pair of square brackets in para (b) substituted by SI 2008/960, arts 3, 10(1), (4).

Sub-s (7): words omitted repealed, and words in square brackets substituted, by SI 2008/960, arts 3, 10(1), (5).

See also the Health and Safety (Enforcing Authority for Railways and Other Guided Transport Systems) Regulations 2006, SI 2006/557, which provides that the ORR shall be responsible for the enforcement of the relevant statutory provisions to the extent that they relate to the operation of a railway, the operation of a tramway, and the operation of any other system of guided transport.

Regulations: the Petroleum (Consolidation) Act 1928 (Enforcement) Regulations 1979, SI 1979/427; the Railway Safety (Miscellaneous Provisions) Regulations 1997, SI 1997/553; the Health and Safety (Enforcing Authority) Regulations 1998, SI 1998/494; the Ammonium Nitrate Materials (High Nitrogen Content) Safety Regulations 2003, SI 2003/1082; the Adventure Activities (Enforcing Authority) Regulations 2004, SI 2004/1359; the Railways and Other Guided Transport Systems (Safety) Regulations 2006, SI 2006/599; the Manufacture and Storage of Explosives and the Health and Safety (Enforcing Authority) (Amendment and Supplementary Provisions) Regulations 2007, SI 2007/2598; the Health and Safety (Miscellaneous Amendments and Revocations) Regulations 2009, SI 2009/693; the Major Accident Off-Site Emergency Plan (Management of Waste from Extractive Industries) (England and Wales) Regulations 2009, SI 2009/1927; the Control of Asbestos Regulations 2012, SI 2012/632.

**[1.46]**
## 19   Appointment of inspectors
(1)   Every enforcing authority may appoint as inspectors (under whatever title it may from time to time determine) such persons having suitable qualifications as it thinks necessary for carrying into effect the relevant statutory provisions within its field of responsibility, and may terminate any appointment made under this section.
(2)   Every appointment of a person as an inspector under this section shall be made by an instrument in writing specifying which of the powers conferred on inspectors by the relevant statutory provisions are to be exercisable by the person appointed; and an inspector shall in right of his appointment under this section—
  (a)   be entitled to exercise only such of those powers as are so specified; and
  (b)   be entitled to exercise the powers so specified only within the field of responsibility of the authority which appointed him.
(3)   So much of an inspector's instrument of appointment as specifies the powers which he is entitled to exercise may be varied by the enforcing authority which appointed him.
(4)   An inspector shall, if so required when exercising or seeking to exercise any power conferred on him by any of the relevant statutory provisions, produce his instrument of appointment or a duly authenticated copy thereof.

**[1.47]**
## 20   Powers of inspectors
(1)   Subject to the provisions of section 19 and this section, an inspector may, for the purpose of carrying into effect any of the relevant statutory provisions within the field of responsibility of the enforcing authority which appointed him, exercise the powers set out in subsection (2) below.
(2)   The powers of an inspector referred to in the preceding subsection are the following, namely—
  (a)   at any reasonable time (or, in a situation which in his opinion is or may be dangerous, at any time) to enter any premises which he has reason to believe it is necessary for him to enter for the purpose mentioned in subsection (1) above;
  (b)   to take with him a constable if he has reasonable cause to apprehend any serious obstruction in the execution of his duty;
  (c)   without prejudice to the preceding paragraph, on entering any premises by virtue of paragraph (a) above to take with him—
       (i)    any other person duly authorised by his (the inspector's) enforcing authority; and
       (ii)   any equipment or materials required for any purpose for which the power of entry is being exercised;
  (d)   to make such examination and investigation as may in any circumstances be necessary for the purpose mentioned in subsection (1) above;
  (e)   as regards any premises which he has power to enter, to direct that those premises or any part of them, or anything therein, shall be left undisturbed (whether generally or in particular respects) for so long as is reasonably necessary for the purpose of any examination or investigation under paragraph (d) above;
  (f)   to take such measurements and photographs and make such recordings as he considers necessary for the purpose of any examination or investigation under paragraph (d) above;
  (g)   to take samples of any articles or substances found in any premises which he has power to enter, and of the atmosphere in or in the vicinity of any such premises;
  (h)   in the case of any article or substance found in any premises which he has power to enter, being an article or substance which appears to him to have caused or to be likely to cause danger to health or safety, to cause it to be dismantled or subjected to any process or test (but not so as to damage or destroy it unless this is in the circumstances necessary for the purpose mentioned in subsection (1) above);
  (i)   in the case of any such article or substance as is mentioned in the preceding paragraph, to take possession of it and detain it for so long as is necessary for all or any of the following purposes, namely—
       (i)    to examine it and do to it anything which he has power to do under that paragraph;
       (ii)   to ensure that it is not tampered with before his examination of it is completed;

(iii) to ensure that it is available for use as evidence in any proceedings for an offence under any of the relevant statutory provisions or any proceedings relating to a notice under section 21 or 22;

(j) to require any person whom he has reasonable cause to believe to be able to give any information relevant to any examination or investigation under paragraph (d) above to answer (in the absence of persons other than a person nominated by him to be present and any persons whom the inspector may allow to be present) such questions as the inspector thinks fit to ask and to sign a declaration of the truth of his answers;

(k) to require the production of, inspect, and take copies of or of any entry in—
   (i) any books or documents which by virtue of any of the relevant statutory provisions are required to be kept; and
   (ii) any other books or documents which it is necessary for him to see for the purposes of any examination or investigation under paragraph (d) above;

(l) to require any person to afford him such facilities and assistance with respect to any matters or things within that person's control or in relation to which that person has responsibilities as are necessary to enable the inspector to exercise any of the powers conferred on him by this section;

(m) any other power which is necessary for the purpose mentioned in subsection (1) above.

(3) The Secretary of State may by regulations make provision as to the procedure to be followed in connection with the taking of samples under subsection (2)(g) above (including provision as to the way in which samples that have been so taken are to be dealt with).

(4) Where an inspector proposes to exercise the power conferred by subsection (2)(h) above in the case of an article or substance found in any premises, he shall, if so requested by a person who at the time is present in and has responsibilities in relation to those premises, cause anything which is to be done by virtue of that power to be done in the presence of that person unless the inspector considers that its being done in that person's presence would be prejudicial to the safety of the State.

(5) Before exercising the power conferred by subsection (2)(h) above in the case of any article or substance, an inspector shall consult such persons as appear to him appropriate for the purpose of ascertaining what dangers, if any, there may be in doing anything which he proposes to do under that power.

(6) Where under the power conferred by subsection (2)(i) above an inspector takes possession of any article or substance found in any premises, he shall leave there, either with a responsible person or, if that is impracticable, fixed in a conspicuous position, a notice giving particulars of that article or substance sufficient to identify it and stating that he has taken possession of it under that power; and before taking possession of any such substance under that power an inspector shall, if it is practicable for him to do so, take a sample thereof and give to a responsible person at the premises a portion of the sample marked in a manner sufficient to identify it.

(7) No answer given by a person in pursuance of a requirement imposed under subsection (2)(j) above shall be admissible in evidence against that person or the [spouse or civil partner] of that person in any proceedings.

(8) Nothing in this section shall be taken to compel the production by any person of a document of which he would on grounds of legal professional privilege be entitled to withhold production on an order for discovery in an action in the High Court or, as the case may be, on an order for the production of documents in an action in the Court of Session.

**NOTES**

Sub-s (7): words in square brackets substituted by the Civil Partnership Act 2004, s 261(1), Sch 27, para 49.

Regulations: the Ammonium Nitrate Materials (High Nitrogen Content) Safety Regulations 2003, SI 2003/1082.

Fees: see the Health and Safety (Fees) Regulations 2012, SI 2012/1652, regs 23–26 at **[2.1630]–[2.1633]** which introduce fees for breaches of the statutory provisions leading to enforcement action under this Act.

**[1.48]**
## 21 Improvement notices

If an inspector is of the opinion that a person—

(a) is contravening one or more of the relevant statutory provisions; or

(b) has contravened one or more of those provisions in circumstances that make it likely that the contravention will continue or be repeated,

he may serve on him a notice (in this Part referred to as "an improvement notice") stating that he is of that opinion, specifying the provision or provisions as to which he is of that opinion, giving particulars of the reasons why he is of that opinion, and requiring that person to remedy the contravention or, as the case may be, the matters occasioning it within such period (ending not earlier than the period within which an appeal against the notice can be brought under section 24) as may be specified in the notice.

**NOTES**

Fees: see the note to s 20 at **[1.47]**.

**[1.49]**
**22   Prohibition notices**
(1)   This section applies to any activities which are being or are [likely] to be carried on by or under the control of any person, being activities to or in relation to which any of the relevant statutory provisions apply or will, if the activities are so carried on, apply.
(2)   If as regards any activities to which this section applies an inspector is of the opinion that, as carried on or [likely] to be carried on by or under the control of the person in question, the activities involve or, as the case may be, will involve a risk of serious personal injury, the inspector may serve on that person a notice (in this Part referred to as "a prohibition notice").
(3)   A prohibition notice shall—
   (a)   state that the inspector is of the said opinion;
   (b)   specify the matters which in his opinion give or, as the case may be, will give rise to the said risk;
   (c)   where in his opinion any of those matters involves or, as the case may be, will involve a contravention of any of the relevant statutory provisions, state that he is of that opinion, specify the provision or provisions as to which he is of that opinion, and give particulars of the reasons why he is of that opinion; and
   (d)   direct that the activities to which the notice relates shall not be carried on by or under the control of the person on whom the notice is served unless the matters specified in the notice in pursuance of paragraph (b) above and any associated contraventions of provisions so specified in pursuance of paragraph (c) above have been remedied.
[(4)   A direction contained in a prohibition notice in pursuance of subsection (3)(d) above shall take effect—
   (a)   at the end of the period specified in the notice; or
   (b)   if the notice so declares, immediately.]

**NOTES**
   Sub-ss (1), (2): words in square brackets substituted by the Consumer Protection Act 1987, s 36, Sch 3, para 2(a).
   Sub-s (4): substituted by the Consumer Protection Act 1987, s 36, Sch 3, para 2(b).
   Fees: see the note to s 20 at **[1.47]**.

**[1.50]**
**23   Provisions supplementary to ss 21 and 22**
(1)   In this section "a notice" means an improvement notice or a prohibition notice.
(2)   A notice may (but need not) include directions as to the measures to be taken to remedy any contravention or matter to which the notice relates; and any such directions—
   (a)   may be framed to any extent by reference to any approved code of practice; and
   (b)   may be framed so as to afford the person on whom the notice is served a choice between different ways of remedying the contravention or matter.
(3)   Where any of the relevant statutory provisions applies to a building or any matter connected with a building and an inspector proposes to serve an improvement notice relating to a contravention of that provision in connection with that building or matter, the notice shall not direct any measures to be taken to remedy the contravention of that provision which are more onerous than those necessary to secure conformity with the requirements of any building regulations for the time being in force to which that building or matter would be required to conform if the relevant building were being newly erected unless the provision in question imposes specific requirements more onerous than the requirements of any such building regulations to which the building or matter would be required to conform as aforesaid.
   In this subsection "the relevant building", in the case of a building, means that building, and, in the case of a matter connected with a building, means the building with which the matter is connected.
(4)   Before an inspector serves in connection with any premises used or about to be used as a place of work a notice requiring or likely to lead to the taking of measures affecting the means of escape in case of fire with which the premises are or ought to be provided, he shall consult the [fire and rescue authority].
   In this subsection "[fire and rescue authority]"[, in relation to premises, means—
   (a)   where the Regulatory Reform (Fire Safety) Order 2005 applies to the premises, the enforcing authority within the meaning given by article 25 of that Order;
   (b)   in any other case, the fire and rescue authority under the Fire and Rescue Services Act 2004 for the area where the premises are (or are to be) situated].
(5)   Where an improvement notice or a prohibition notice which is not to take immediate effect has been served—
   (a)   the notice may be withdrawn by an inspector at any time before the end of the period specified therein in pursuance of section 21 or section 22(4) as the case may be; and
   (b)   the period so specified may be extended or further extended by an inspector at any time when an appeal against the notice is not pending.
(6)   In the application of this section to Scotland—

(a)   in subsection (3) for the words from "with the requirements" to "aforesaid" there shall be substituted the words—

> "(a)   to any provisions of the building standards regulations to which that building or matter would be required to conform if the relevant building were being newly erected; or
>
> (b)   where the sheriff, on an appeal to him under section 16 of the Building (Scotland) Act 1959—
>
>> (i)   against an order under section 10 of that Act requiring the execution of operations necessary to make the building or matter conform to the building standards regulations, or
>>
>> (ii)   against an order under section 11 of that Act requiring the building or matter to conform to a provision of such regulations,
>
> has varied the order, to any provisions of the building standards regulations referred to in paragraph (a) above as affected by the order as so varied,

unless the relevant statutory provision imposes specific requirements more onerous than the requirements of any provisions of building standards regulations as aforesaid or, as the case may be, than the requirements of the order as varied by the sheriff.";

(b)   after subsection (5) there shall be inserted the following subsection—

> "(5A)   In subsection (3) above "building standards regulations" has the same meaning as in section 3 of the Building (Scotland) Act 1959.".

**NOTES**

Sub-s (4): words in first and second pairs of square brackets substituted, in relation to England and Wales only, by the Fire and Rescue Services Act 2004, s 53(1), Sch 1, para 44; words in third pair of square brackets substituted, in relation to England and Wales only, by the Regulatory Reform (Fire Safety) Order 2005, SI 2005/1541, art 53(1), Sch 2, para 9. Note that this subsection has also been amended, in relation to Scotland only, by the Fire (Scotland) Act 2005 (Consequential Modifications and Amendments) Order 2005, SSI 2005/383, art 2(1), Sch 1, para 4, and by the Fire (Scotland) Act 2005 (Consequential Modifications and Savings) Order 2006, SSI 2006/475, art 2(1), Sch 1, para 6. In relation to Scotland, this subsection (as amended by the Police and Fire Reform (Scotland) Act 2012, s 128(1), Sch 7, Pt 2, para 49, as from 1 April 2013) now reads as follows—

> "(4)   Before an inspector serves in connection with any premises used or about to be used as a place of work a notice requiring or likely to lead to the taking of measures affecting the means of escape in case of fire with which the premises are or ought to be provided, he shall consult—
>
>> (a)   where Part 3 of the Fire (Scotland) Act 2005 (asp 5) applies in relation to the premises, the enforcing authority (as defined in section 61(9) of that Act);
>>
>> (b)   in any other case, the [Scottish Fire and Rescue Service].".

Fees: see the note to s 20 at **[1.47]**.

**[1.51]**
**24   Appeal against improvement or prohibition notice**
(1)   In this section "a notice" means an improvement notice or a prohibition notice.
(2)   A person on whom a notice is served may within such period from the date of its service as may be prescribed appeal to an [employment tribunal]; and on such an appeal the tribunal may either cancel or affirm the notice and, if it affirms it, may do so either in its original form or with such modifications as the tribunal may in the circumstances think fit.
(3)   Where an appeal under this section is brought against a notice within the period allowed under the preceding subsection, then—
(a)   in the case of an improvement notice, the bringing of the appeal shall have the effect of suspending the operation of the notice until the appeal is finally disposed of or, if the appeal is withdrawn, until the withdrawal of the appeal;
(b)   in the case of a prohibition notice, the bringing of the appeal shall have the like effect if, but only if, on the application of the appellant the tribunal so directs (and then only from the giving of the direction).
(4)   One or more assessors may be appointed for the purposes of any proceedings brought before an [employment tribunal] under this section.

**NOTES**

Sub-ss (2), (4): words in square brackets substituted by the Employment Rights (Dispute Resolution) Act 1998, s 1(2)(a).
Regulations: the Employment Tribunals (Constitution and Rules of Procedure) Regulations 2004, SI 2004/1861 at **[2.809]**. For the procedure on appeal, including the time limit prescribed for the purpose of sub-s (2), see reg 16(3)(b) of, and Sch 4 to, those Regulations at **[2.824]** and **[2.892]**.
Fees: see the note to s 20 at **[1.47]**.
**Stop Press:** see the Employment Tribunals (Constitution and Rules of Procedure) Regulations 2013, SI 2013/1237 at **[2.1689]**.

**[1.52]**
**25  Power to deal with cause of imminent danger**
(1)  Where, in the case of any article or substance found by him in any premises which he has power to enter, an inspector has reasonable cause to believe that, in the circumstances in which he finds it, the article or substance is a cause of imminent danger of serious personal injury, he may seize it and cause it to be rendered harmless (whether by destruction or otherwise).
(2)  Before there is rendered harmless under this section—
   (a)  any article that forms part of a batch of similar articles; or
   (b)  any substance,
the inspector shall, if it is practicable for him to do so, take a sample thereof and give to a responsible person at the premises where the article or substance was found by him a portion of the sample marked in a manner sufficient to identify it.
(3)  As soon as may be after any article or substance has been seized and rendered harmless under this section, the inspector shall prepare and sign a written report giving particulars of the circumstances in which the article or substance was seized and so dealt with by him, and shall—
   (a)  give a signed copy of the report to a responsible person at the premises where the article or substance was found by him; and
   (b)  unless that person is the owner of the article or substance, also serve a signed copy of the report on the owner;
and if, where paragraph (b) above applies, the inspector cannot after reasonable enquiry ascertain the name or address of the owner, the copy may be served on him by giving it to the person to whom a copy was given under the preceding paragraph.

**NOTES**
   Fees: see the note to s 20 at **[1.47]**.

**[1.53]**
**[25A  Power of customs officer to detain articles and substances**
(1)  A customs officer may, for the purpose of facilitating the exercise or performance by any enforcing authority or inspector of any of the powers or duties of the authority or inspector under any of the relevant statutory provisions, seize any imported article or imported substance and detain it for not more than two working days.
(2)  Anything seized and detained under this section shall be dealt with during the period of its detention in such manner as the Commissioners of Customs and Excise may direct.
(3)  In subsection (1) above the reference to two working days is a reference to a period of forty-eight hours calculated from the time when the goods in question are seized but disregarding so much of any period as falls on a Saturday or Sunday or on Christmas Day, Good Friday or a day which is a bank holiday under the Banking and Financial Dealings Act 1971 in the part of Great Britain where the goods are seized.]

**NOTES**
   Inserted by the Consumer Protection Act 1987, s 36, Sch 3, para 3.
   Commissioners of Customs and Excise: a reference to the Commissioners of Customs and Excise is now to be taken as a reference to the Commissioners for Her Majesty's Revenue and Customs; see the Commissioners for Revenue and Customs Act 2005, s 50(1), (7).

**[1.54]**
**26  Power of enforcing authorities to indemnify their inspectors**
Where an action has been brought against an inspector in respect of an act done in the execution or purported execution of any of the relevant statutory provisions and the circumstances are such that he is not legally entitled to require the enforcing authority which appointed him to indemnify him, that authority may, nevertheless, indemnify him against the whole or part of any damages and costs or expenses which he may have been ordered to pay or may have incurred, if the authority is satisfied that he honestly believed that the act complained of was within his powers and that his duty as an inspector required or entitled him to do it.

*Obtaining and disclosure of information*

**[1.55]**
**27  Obtaining of information by  . . .  the Executive, enforcing authorities etc**
(1)  For the purpose of obtaining—
   (a)  any information which [the Executive] needs for the discharge of its functions; or
   (b)  any information which an enforcing authority needs for the discharge of the authority's functions,
[the Executive] may, with the consent of the Secretary of State, serve on any person a notice requiring that person to furnish to [the Executive] or, as the case may be, to the enforcing authority in question such information about such matters as may be specified in the notice, and to do so in such form and manner and within such time as may be so specified.

In this subsection "consent" includes a general consent extending to cases of any stated description.

(2) Nothing in section 9 of the Statistics of Trade Act 1947 (which restricts the disclosure of information obtained under that Act) shall prevent or penalise—

(a) the disclosure by a Minister of the Crown to . . . the Executive of information obtained under that Act about any undertaking within the meaning of that Act, being information consisting of the names and addresses of the persons carrying on the undertaking, the nature of the undertaking's activities, the numbers of persons of different descriptions who work in the undertaking, the addresses or places where activities of the undertaking are or were carried on, the nature of the activities carried on there, or the numbers of persons of different descriptions who work or worked in the undertaking there; . . .

(b) . . .

[(3) In the preceding subsection, any reference to a Minister of the Crown or the Executive includes respectively a reference to an officer of that person or of that body and also, in the case of a reference to the Executive, includes a reference to—

(a) a person performing any functions of the Executive on its behalf by virtue of section 13(3);

(b) an officer of a body which is so performing any such functions; and

(c) an adviser appointed under section 13(7).]

(4) A person to whom information is disclosed in pursuance of subsection (2) above shall not use the information for a purpose other than a purpose . . . of the Executive.

**NOTES**

Sub-s (1): words in square brackets substituted by the Legislative Reform (Health and Safety Executive) Order 2008, SI 2008/960, arts 3, 11(1), (2).

Sub-s (2): first words omitted repealed by SI 2008/960, arts 3, 11(1), (3); other words omitted repealed by the Employment Act 1989, s 29(3), (4), Sch 6, para 10, Sch 7, Pt I.

Sub-s (3): substituted by SI 2008/960, arts 3, 11(1), (4).

Sub-s (4): words omitted repealed by SI 2008/960, arts 3, 11(1), (5).

Note: the Legislative Reform (Health and Safety Executive) Order 2008, SI 2008/960 does not amend the title of this section. However, in light of the other amendments made by that Order, and in light of the abolition of the HSC by art 2 of that Order, the title of this section has been changed from "Obtaining of information by the Commission, the Executive, enforcing authorities etc" to "Obtaining of information by the Executive, enforcing authorities etc".

**[1.56]**
**[[27A  Information communicated by Commissioners for Revenue and Customs]**

(1) If they think it appropriate to do so for the purpose of facilitating the exercise or performance by any person to whom subsection (2) below applies of any of that person's powers or duties under any of the relevant statutory provisions, [the Commissioners for Her Majesty's Revenue and Custom] may authorise the disclosure to that person of any information obtained [or held] for the purposes of the exercise [by Her Majesty's Revenue and Customs] of their functions in relation to imports.

(2) This subsection applies to an enforcing authority and to an inspector.

(3) A disclosure of information made to any person under subsection (1) above shall be made in such manner as may be directed by [the Commissioners for Her Majesty's Revenue and Customs] and may be made through such persons acting on behalf of that person as may be so directed.

(4) Information may be disclosed to a person under subsection (1) above whether or not the disclosure of the information has been requested by or on behalf of that person.]

**NOTES**

Inserted by the Consumer Protection Act 1987, s 36, Sch 3, para 4.

Section heading: substituted by the Commissioners for Revenue and Customs Act 2005, s 50(6), Sch 4, para 18(1), (4).

Sub-s (1): words in first and third pairs of square brackets substituted, and words in second pair of square brackets inserted, by the Commissioners for Revenue and Customs Act 2005, s 50(6), Sch 4, para 18(1), (2).

Sub-s (3): words in square brackets substituted by the Commissioners for Revenue and Customs Act 2005, s 50(6), Sch 4, para 18(1), (3).

**[1.57]**
**28  Restrictions on disclosure of information**

(1) In this and the two following subsections—

(a) "relevant information" means information obtained by a person under section 27(1) or furnished to any person [under section 27A above[, by virtue of section 43A(6) below] or] in pursuance of a requirement imposed by any of the relevant statutory provisions; and

(b) "the recipient", in relation to any relevant information, means the person by whom that information was so obtained or to whom that information was so furnished, as the case may be.

(2) Subject to the following subsection, no relevant information shall be disclosed without the consent of the person by whom it was furnished.

(3) The preceding subsection shall not apply to—

(a)    disclosure of information to . . . the Executive, [the Environment Agency, [the Natural Resources Body for Wales,] the Scottish Environment Protection Agency,] a government department or any enforcing authority;

(b)    without prejudice to paragraph (a) above, disclosure by the recipient of information to any person for the purpose of any function conferred on the recipient by or under any of the relevant statutory provisions;

(c)    without prejudice to paragraph (a) above, disclosure by the recipient of information to—
      (i)    an officer of a local authority who is authorised by that authority to receive it,
      [(ii)    an officer . . . of a water undertaker, sewerage undertaker, water authority or water development board who is authorised by that . . . undertaker, authority or board to receive it,]
      (iii)    . . .
      (iv)    a constable authorised by a chief officer of police to receive it;

(d)    disclosure by the recipient of information in a form calculated to prevent it from being identified as relating to a particular person or case;

(e)    disclosure of information for the purposes of any legal proceedings or any investigation or inquiry held by virtue of [section 14(2) or (2A)], or for the purposes of a report of any such proceedings or inquiry or of a special report made by virtue of [section 14(2) or (2A)];

[(f)    any other disclosure of information by the recipient, if—
      (i)    the recipient is, or is acting on behalf of a person who is, a public authority for the purposes of the Freedom of Information Act 2000 [or a Scottish public authority for the purposes of the Freedom of Information (Scotland) Act 2002], and
      (ii)    the information is not held by the authority on behalf of another person].

[(4)   In the preceding subsection, any reference to the Executive, the Environment Agency, [the Natural Resources Body for Wales,] the Scottish Environment Protection Agency, a government department or an enforcing authority includes respectively a reference to an officer of that body or authority (including, in the case of an enforcing authority, any inspector appointed by it), and also, in the case of a reference to the Executive, includes a reference to—

(a)    a person performing any functions of the Executive on its behalf by virtue of section 13(3);

(b)    an officer of a body which is so performing any such functions; and

(c)    an adviser appointed under section 13(7).]

(5)   A person to whom information is disclosed in pursuance of [any of paragraphs (a) to (e) of] subsection (3) above shall not use the information for a purpose other than—

(a)    in a case falling within paragraph (a) of that subsection, a purpose . . . of the Executive or [of the Environment Agency [or of the Natural Resources Body for Wales] or of the Scottish Environment Protection Agency or] of the government department in question, or the purposes of the enforcing authority in question in connection with the relevant statutory provisions, as the case may be;

(b)    in the case of information given to an officer of a [body which is a local authority, . . . a water undertaker, a sewerage undertaker, a water authority, a river purification board or a water development board, the purposes of the body] in connection with the relevant statutory provisions or any enactment whatsoever relating to public health, public safety or the protection of the environment;

(c)    in the case of information given to a constable, the purposes of the police in connection with the relevant statutory provisions or any enactment whatsoever relating to public health, public safety or the safety of the State.

[(6)   References in subsections (3) and (5) above to a local authority include . . . a joint authority established by Part IV of the Local Government Act 1985[, [an economic prosperity board established under section 88 of the Local Democracy, Economic Development and Construction Act 2009, a combined authority established under section 103 of that Act,] an authority established for an area in England by an order under section 207 of the Local Government and Public Involvement in Health Act 2007 (joint waste authorities)] [and the London Fire and Emergency Planning Authority].]

(7)   A person shall not disclose any information obtained by him as a result of the exercise of any power conferred by section 14(4)(a) or 20 (including, in particular, any information with respect to any trade secret obtained by him in any premises entered by him by virtue of any such power) except—

(a)    for the purposes of his functions; or

(b)    for the purposes of any legal proceedings or any investigation or inquiry held by virtue of [section 14(2) or (2A)] or for the purposes of a report of any such proceedings or inquiry or of a special report made by virtue of [section 14(2) or (2A)]; or

(c)    with the relevant consent.

In this subsection "the relevant consent" means, in the case of information furnished in pursuance of a requirement imposed under section 20, the consent of the person who furnished it, and, in any other case, the consent of a person having responsibilities in relation to the premises where the information was obtained.

(8) Notwithstanding anything in the preceding subsection an inspector shall, in circumstances in which it is necessary to do so for the purpose of assisting in keeping persons (or the representatives of persons) employed at any premises adequately informed about matters affecting their health, safety and welfare, give to such persons or their representatives the following descriptions of information, that is to say—

    (a)    factual information obtained by him as mentioned in that subsection which relates to those premises or anything which was or is therein or was or is being done therein; and

    (b)    information with respect to any action which he has taken or proposes to take in or in connection with those premises in the performance of his functions;

and, where an inspector does as aforesaid, he shall give the like information to the employer of the first-mentioned persons.

[(9) Notwithstanding anything in subsection (7) above, a person who has obtained such information as is referred to in that subsection may furnish to a person who appears to him to be likely to be a party to any civil proceedings arising out of any accident, occurrence, situation or other matter, a written statement of relevant facts observed by him in the course of exercising any of the powers referred to in that subsection.]

[(9A)    Subsection (7) above does not apply if—

    (a)    the person who has obtained any such information as is referred to in that subsection is, or is acting on behalf of a person who is, a public authority for the purposes of the Freedom of Information Act 2000 [or a Scottish public authority for the purposes of the Freedom of Information (Scotland) Act 2002], and

    (b)    the information is not held by the authority on behalf of another person.]

[(10)    The Broads Authority and every National Park authority shall be deemed to be local authorities for the purposes of this section.]

---

NOTES

Sub-s (1): words in first (outer) pair of square brackets inserted by the Consumer Protection Act 1987, s 36, Sch 3, para 5; words in second (inner) pair of square brackets inserted by the Railways and Transport Safety Act 2003, s 105(2).

Sub-s (3) is amended as follows:

Words omitted from para (a) repealed by the Legislative Reform (Health and Safety Executive) Order 2008, SI 2008/960, arts 3, 12(1), (2)(a).

Words in first (outer) pair of square brackets in para (a) inserted by the Environment Act 1995, s 120(1), (3), Sch 22, para 30(1), (6)(a).

Words in second (inner) pair of square brackets in para (a) inserted by the Natural Resources Body for Wales (Functions) Order 2013, SI 2013/755, art 4(1), Sch 2, paras 111, 112(1), (2), as from 1 April 2013.

Para (c)(ii) substituted by the Water Act 1989, s 190, Sch 25, para 46, in relation to England and Wales only; words omitted from that paragraph repealed by the Environment Act 1995, s 120(1), (3), Sch 22, para 30(1), (6)(b).

Para (c)(ii), as it applies to Scotland, was substituted by the Environment Act 1995, s 120(1), (3), Sch 22, para 30(1), (6)(c), and further amended by the Water Industry (Scotland) Act 2002 (Consequential Modifications) Order 2004, SI 2004/1822, art 2, Schedule, Pt 1, para 8(a), and now reads as follows—

    "(ii)    an officer of a water undertaker, sewerage undertaker [or Scottish Water] who is authorised by [that undertaker or, as the case may be, Scottish Water] to receive it,".

Para (c)(iii) repealed by the Environment Act 1995, s 120(1), (3), Sch 22, para 30(1), (6)(d).

Words in square brackets in para (e) substituted by SI 2008/960, arts 3, 12(1), (2)(b).

Para (f) added by the Freedom of Information (Removal and Relaxation of Statutory Prohibitions on Disclosure of Information) Order 2004, SI 2004/3363, art 5(1), (2); words in square brackets inserted by the Freedom of Information (Relaxation of Statutory Prohibitions on Disclosure of Information) (Scotland) Order 2008, SSI 2008/339, art 5(1), (2), as from 13 October 2008.

Sub-s (4): substituted by SI 2008/960, arts 3, 12(1), (3); words in square brackets inserted by SI 2013/755, art 4(1), Sch 2, paras 111, 112(1), (3), as from 1 April 2013.

Sub-s (5) is amended as follows:

Words in first (outer) pair of square brackets inserted by SI 2004/3363, art 5(1), (3).

Words in second (inner) pair of square brackets inserted by SI 2013/755, art 4(1), Sch 2, paras 111, 112(1), (4), as from 1 April 2013.

Words omitted from para (a) repealed by SI 2008/960, arts 3, 12(1), (4).

Words in square brackets in para (a) inserted by the Environment Act 1995, s 120(1), (3), Sch 22, para 30(1), (6)(f).

Words in square brackets in para (b) substituted by the Water Act 1989, s 190, Sch 25, para 46; words omitted from that paragraph repealed by the Environment Act 1995, s 120(1), (3), Sch 22, para 30(6)(f).

The words from the beginning of para (b) to "in connection" were substituted by the Environment Act 1995, s 120(1), (3), Sch 22, para 30(1), (6)(f), in relation to Scotland only, and that paragraph was further amended (in relation to Scotland only) by SI 2004/1822, art 2, Schedule, Pt 1, para 8(b). Para (b), as it applies to Scotland, now reads as follows—

    "(b)    [in the case of information given to an officer of a body which is a local authority, a water undertaker [or a sewerage undertaker or to an officer of Scottish Water,] the purposes of the [authority, undertaker or, as the case may be, Scottish Water] in connection] with the relevant statutory provisions or any enactment whatsoever relating to public health, public safety or the protection of the environment;".

Sub-s (6): substituted by the Local Government Act 1985, s 84, Sch 14, para 52; words omitted repealed by the Education Reform Act 1988, s 237, Sch 13, Pt I; words in first (outer) pair of square brackets inserted by the Local Government and Public Involvement in Health Act 2007, s 209(2), Sch 13, Pt 2, para 32; words in second (inner) pair of square brackets inserted by the Local Democracy, Economic Development and Construction Act 2009, s 119, Sch 6, para 42, as from 17 December 2009; words in final pair of square brackets added by the Greater London Authority Act 1999, s 328(8), Sch 29, Pt I, para 23.

Sub-s (7): words in square brackets substituted by SI 2008/960, arts 3, 12(1), (5).

Sub-s (9): inserted by the Employment Protection Act 1975, s 116, Sch 15, para 9.

Sub-s (9A): inserted by SI 2004/3363, art 5(1), (4); words in square brackets inserted by SSI 2008/339, art 5(1), (3), as from 13 October 2008.

Sub-s (10): inserted by the Norfolk and Suffolk Broads Act 1988, s 21, Sch 6, para 13; substituted by the Environment Act 1995, s 78, Sch 10, para 12.

Disclosure: sub-s (7) has effect in relation to the disclosure of information by or on behalf of a public authority as if the purposes for which disclosure is authorised included the purposes mentioned in the Anti-terrorism, Crime and Security Act 2001, s 17; see Sch 4, Pt 1 to that Act.

**29–32**   *(Repealed by the Employment Protection Act 1975, ss 116, 125(3), Sch 15, para 10, Sch 18.)*

*Provisions as to offences*

**[1.58]**
## 33   Offences
(1)   It is an offence for a person—
   (a)   to fail to discharge a duty to which he is subject by virtue of sections 2 to 7;
   (b)   to contravene section 8 or 9;
   (c)   to contravene any health and safety regulations  . . .  or any requirement or prohibition imposed under any such regulations (including any requirement or prohibition to which he is subject by virtue of the terms of or any condition or restriction attached to any licence, approval, exemption or other authority issued, given or granted under the regulations);
   (d)   to contravene any requirement imposed by or under regulations under section 14 or intentionally to obstruct any person in the exercise of his powers under that section;
   (e)   to contravene any requirement imposed by an inspector under section 20 or 25;
   (f)   to prevent or attempt to prevent any other person from appearing before an inspector or from answering any question to which an inspector may by virtue of section 20(2) require an answer;
   (g)   to contravene any requirement or prohibition imposed by an improvement notice or a prohibition notice (including any such notice as modified on appeal);
   (h)   intentionally to obstruct an inspector in the exercise or performance of his powers or duties [or to obstruct a customs officer in the exercise of his powers under section 25A];
   (i)   to contravene any requirement imposed by a notice under section 27(1);
   (j)   to use or disclose any information in contravention of section 27(4) or 28;
   (k)   to make a statement which he knows to be false or recklessly to make a statement which is false where the statement is made—
       (i)   in purported compliance with a requirement to furnish any information imposed by or under any of the relevant statutory provisions; or
       (ii)   for the purpose of obtaining the issue of a document under any of the relevant statutory provisions to himself or another person;
   (l)   intentionally to make a false entry in any register, book, notice or other document required by or under any of the relevant statutory provisions to be kept, served or given or, with intent to deceive, to made use of any such entry which he knows to be false;
   (m)   with intent to deceive, to  . . .  use a document issued or authorised to be issued under any of the relevant statutory provisions or required for any purpose thereunder or to make or have in his possession a document so closely resembling any such document as to be calculated to deceive;
   (n)   falsely to pretend to be an inspector;
   (o)   to fail to comply with an order made by a court under section 42.
[(2)   Schedule 3A (which specifies the mode of trial and maximum penalty applicable to offences under this section and the existing statutory provisions) has effect.
(3)   Schedule 3A is subject to any provision made by virtue of section 15(6)(c) or (d).]
(5), (6)   . . .

**NOTES**

Sub-s (1): words omitted from para (c) repealed by the Employment Protection Act 1975, ss 116, 125(3), Sch 15, para 11, Sch 18; words in square brackets in para (h) added by the Consumer Protection Act 1987, s 36, Sch 3, para 6; words omitted from para (m) repealed by the Forgery and Counterfeiting Act 1981, s 30, Schedule, Pt I.

Sub-ss (2), (3): substituted, for sub-ss (1A), (2), (2A)–(4), by the Health and Safety (Offences) Act 2008, s 1(1), as from 16 January 2009, except in relation to offences committed before that date. Note that sub-ss (1A) and (2A) were originally inserted by the Offshore Safety Act 1992, s 4(2), (3), (6).

Sub-s (5): repealed by the Offshore Safety Act 1992, ss 4(5), (6), 7(2), Sch 2.

Sub-s (6): repealed by the Forgery and Counterfeiting Act 1981, s 30, Schedule, Pt I.

**[1.59]**
## 34   Extension of time for bringing summary proceedings
(1)   Where—
   (a)   a special report on any matter to which section 14 of this Act applies is made by virtue of subsection [(2)] of that section; or

(b)   a report is made by the person holding an inquiry into any such matter by virtue of subsection [(2A)]) of that section; or

(c)   *a coroner's inquest is held touching* the death of any person whose death may have been caused by an accident which happened while he was at work or by a disease which he contracted or probably contracted at work or by any accident, act or omission which occurred in connection with the work of any person whatsoever; or

(d)   a public inquiry into any death that may have been so caused is held under the Fatal Accidents Inquiry (Scotland) Act 1895 or the Fatal Accidents and Sudden Deaths Inquiry (Scotland) Act 1906,

and it appears *from the report or, in a case falling within paragraph (c) or (d) above, from the proceedings at the inquest or* inquiry, that any of the relevant statutory provisions was contravened at a time which is material in relation to the subject-matter of the *report, inquest or inquiry*, summary proceedings against any person liable to be proceeded against in respect of the contravention may be commenced at any time within three months of the making of the report or, in a case falling within paragraph (c) or (d) above, within three months of the *conclusion of the inquest* or inquiry.

(2)   Where an offence under any of the relevant statutory provisions is committed by reason of a failure to do something at or within a time fixed by or under any of those provisions, the offence shall be deemed to continue until that thing is done.

(3)   Summary proceedings for an offence to which this subsection applies may be commenced at any time within six months from the date on which there comes to the knowledge of a responsible enforcing authority evidence sufficient in the opinion of that authority to justify a prosecution for that offence; and for the purposes of this subsection—

(a)   a certificate of an enforcing authority stating that such evidence came to its knowledge on a specified date shall be conclusive evidence of that fact; and

(b)   a document purporting to be such a certificate and to be signed by or on behalf of the enforcing authority in question shall be presumed to be such a certificate unless the contrary is proved.

(4)   The preceding subsection applies to any offence under any of the relevant statutory provisions which a person commits by virtue of any provision or requirement to which he is subject as the designer, manufacturer, importer or supplier of any thing; and in that subsection "responsible enforcing authority" means an enforcing authority within whose field of responsibility the offence in question lies, whether by virtue of section 35 or otherwise.

(5)   In the application of subsection (3) above to Scotland—

(a)   for the words from "there comes" to "that offence" there shall be substituted the words "evidence, sufficient in the opinion of the enforcing authority to justify a report to the Lord Advocate with a view to consideration of the question of prosecution, comes to the knowledge of the authority";

(b)   at the end of paragraph (b) there shall be added the words

"and

(c)   [section 331(3) of the Criminal Procedure (Scotland) Act 1975] (date of commencement of proceedings) shall have effect as it has effect for the purposes of that section".

[(6)   In the application of subsection (4) above to Scotland, after the words "applies to" there shall be inserted the words "any offence under section 33(1)(c) above where the health and safety regulations concerned were made for the general purpose mentioned in section 18(1) of the Gas Act 1986 and".]

---

**NOTES**

Sub-s (1) is amended as follows:

Figures in square brackets substituted by the Legislative Reform (Health and Safety Executive) Order 2008, SI 2008/960, arts 3, 13.

For the first words in italics there are substituted the words "an investigation under Part 1 of the Coroners and Justice Act 2009 is conducted into", for the second words in italics there are substituted the words "from the report or investigation or, in a case falling within paragraph (d) above, from the proceedings at the", for the third words in italics there are substituted the words "report, investigation or inquiry", and for the final words in italics there are substituted the words "conclusion of the investigation", by the Coroners and Justice Act 2009, s 177(1), Sch 21, Pt 1, para 25, all as from a day to be appointed.

Sub-s (5): words in square brackets in para (b) substituted by the Criminal Procedure (Scotland) Act 1975, s 461(1), Sch 9, para 51.

Sub-s (6): added by the Gas Act 1986, s 67(1), Sch 7, para 18.

Criminal Procedure (Scotland) Act 1975: repealed by Criminal Procedure (Consequential Provisions) (Scotland) Act 1995, s 6, Sch 5. Section 331 of the 1975 Act was replaced by s 136 of the Criminal Procedure (Scotland) Act 1995.

Fatal Accidents and Sudden Deaths Inquiry (Scotland) Act 1906; Fatal Accidents Inquiry (Scotland) Act 1895: repealed by the Fatal Accidents and Sudden Deaths Inquiry (Scotland) Act 1976, s 8(2), Sch 2.

Gas Act 1986, s 18(1): repealed by the Offshore Safety Act 1992, ss 3(3)(a), 7(2), Sch 2.

**[1.60]**
## 35  Venue
An offence under any of the relevant statutory provisions committed in connection with any plant or substance may, if necessary for the purpose of bringing the offence within the field of responsibility of any enforcing authority or conferring jurisdiction on any court to entertain proceedings for the offence, be treated as having been committed at the place where that plant or substance is for the time being.

**[1.61]**
## 36  Offences due to fault of other person
(1)  Where the commission by any person of an offence under any of the relevant statutory provisions is due to the act or default of some other person, that other person shall be guilty of the offence, and a person may be charged with and convicted of the offence by virtue of this subsection whether or not proceedings are taken against the first-mentioned person.

(2)  Where there would be or have been the commission of an offence under section 33 by the Crown but for the circumstance that that section does not bind the Crown, and that fact is due to the act or default of a person other than the Crown, that person shall be guilty of the offence which, but for that circumstance, the Crown would be committing or would have committed, and may be charged with and convicted of that offence accordingly.

(3)  The preceding provisions of this section are subject to any provision made by virtue of section 15(6).

**NOTES**
    The Crown: references to the Crown in this section shall be treated as including the Assembly Commission; see the National Assembly for Wales Commission (Crown Status) (No 2) Order 2007, SI 2007/1353, art 2.

**[1.62]**
## 37  Offences by bodies corporate
(1)  Where an offence under any of the relevant statutory provisions committed by a body corporate is proved to have been committed with the consent or connivance of, or to have been attributable to any neglect on the part of, any director, manager, secretary or other similar officer of the body corporate or a person who was purporting to act in any such capacity, he as well as the body corporate shall be guilty of that offence and shall be liable to be proceeded against and punished accordingly.

(2)  Where the affairs of a body corporate are managed by its members, the preceding subsection shall apply in relation to the acts and defaults of a member in connection with his functions of management as if he were a director of the body corporate.

**[1.63]**
## 38  Restriction on institution of proceedings in England and Wales
Proceedings for an offence under any of the relevant statutory provisions shall not, in England and Wales, be instituted except by an inspector[, the Environment Agency or the Natural Resources Body for Wales] [or] by or with the consent of the Director of Public Prosecutions.

**NOTES**
    Words in first pair of square brackets substituted by the Natural Resources Body for Wales (Functions) Order 2013, SI 2013/755, art 4(1), Sch 2, paras 111, 113, as from 1 April 2013; word in second pair of square brackets inserted by the Environment Act 1995, s 120(1), Sch 22, para 30(1), (7).

**[1.64]**
## 39  Prosecutions by inspectors
(1)  An inspector, if authorised in that behalf by the enforcing authority which appointed him, may, although not of counsel or a solicitor, prosecute before a magistrates' court proceedings for an offence under any of the relevant statutory provisions.

(2)  This section shall not apply to Scotland.

**[1.65]**
## 40  Onus of proving limits of what is practicable etc
In any proceedings for an offence under any of the relevant statutory provisions consisting of a failure to comply with a duty or requirement to do something so far as is practicable or so far as is reasonably practicable, or to use the best practicable means to do something, it shall be for the accused to prove (as the case may be) that it was not practicable or not reasonably practicable to do more than was in fact done to satisfy the duty or requirement, or that there was no better practicable means than was in fact used to satisfy the duty or requirement.

**[1.66]**
**41 Evidence**
(1) Where an entry is required by any of the relevant statutory provisions to be made in any register or other record, the entry, if made, shall, as against the person by or on whose behalf it was made, be admissible as evidence or in Scotland sufficient evidence of the facts stated therein.
(2) Where an entry which is so required to be so made with respect to the observance of any of the relevant statutory provisions has not been made, that fact shall be admissible as evidence or in Scotland sufficient evidence that that provision has not been observed.

**[1.67]**
**42 Power of court to order cause of offence to be remedied or, in certain cases, forfeiture**
(1) Where a person is convicted of an offence under any of the relevant statutory provisions in respect of any matters which appear to the court to be matters which it is in his power to remedy, the court may, in addition to or instead of imposing any punishment, order him, within such time as may be fixed by the order, to take such steps as may be specified in the order for remedying the said matters.
(2) The time fixed by an order under subsection (1) above may be extended or further extended by order of the court on an application made before the end of that time as originally fixed or as extended under this subsection, as the case may be.
(3) Where a person is ordered under subsection (1) above to remedy any matters, that person shall not be liable under any of the relevant statutory provisions in respect of those matters in so far as they continue during the time fixed by the order or any further time allowed under subsection (2) above.
[(3A) Subsection (4) applies where a person is convicted of an offence consisting of acquiring or attempting to acquire, possessing or using an explosive article or substance (within the meaning of any of the relevant statutory provisions) in contravention of any of the relevant statutory provisions.]
(4) Subject to the following subsection, the court by or before which [the person is convicted of the offence] may order the article or substance in question to be forfeited and either destroyed or dealt with in such other manner as the court may order.
(5) The court shall not order anything to be forfeited under the preceding subsection where a person claiming to be the owner of or otherwise interested in it applies to be heard by the court, unless an opportunity has been given to him to show cause why the order should not be made.

**NOTES**
Sub-s (3A): inserted by the Health and Safety (Offences) Act 2008, s 2(1), Sch 3, para 2(2), as from 16 January 2009, except in relation to offences committed before that date.
Sub-s (4): words in square brackets substituted by the Health and Safety (Offences) Act 2008, s 2(1), Sch 3, para 2(3), as from 16 January 2009, except in relation to offences committed before that date.

*Financial provisions*
**[1.68]**
**43 Financial provisions**
(1) It shall be the duty of the Secretary of State to pay to [the Executive] such sums as are approved by the Treasury and as he considers appropriate for the purpose of enabling [the Executive] to perform its functions; . . .
(2) Regulations may provide for such fees as may be fixed by or determined under the regulations to be payable for or in connection with the performance by or on behalf of any authority to which this subsection applies of any function conferred on that authority by or under any of the relevant statutory provisions.
(3) Subsection (2) above applies to the following authorities, namely . . . the Executive, the Secretary of State, . . . every enforcing authority, and any other person on whom any function is conferred by or under any of the relevant statutory provisions.
(4) Regulations under this section may specify the person by whom any fee payable under the regulations is to be paid; but no such fee shall be made payable by a person in any of the following capacities, namely an employee, a person seeking employment, a person training for employment, and a person seeking training for employment.
(5) Without prejudice to section 82(3), regulations under this section may fix or provide for the determination of different fees in relation to different functions, or in relation to the same function in different circumstances.
[(6) The power to make regulations under this section shall be exercisable by the Secretary of State . . . ]
(7) . . .
(8) In subsection (4) above the references to a person training for employment and a person seeking training for employment shall include respectively a person attending an industrial rehabilitation course provided by virtue of the Employment and Training Act 1973 and a person seeking to attend such a course.

(9)   For the purposes of this section the performance by an inspector of his functions shall be treated as the performance by the enforcing authority which appointed him of functions conferred on that authority by or under any of the relevant statutory provisions.

**NOTES**

Sub-s (1): words in square brackets substituted, and words omitted repealed, by the Legislative Reform (Health and Safety Executive) Order 2008, SI 2008/960, arts 3, 14(a).

Sub-s (3): first words omitted repealed by SI 2008/960, arts 3, 14(b); second words omitted repealed by the Employment Protection Act 1975, ss 116, 125(3), Sch 15, para 12, Sch 18.

Sub-s (6): substituted, for the original sub-ss (6), (7), by the Employment Protection Act 1975, s 116, Sch 15, para 12; words omitted repealed by the Ministry of Agriculture, Fisheries and Food (Dissolution) Order 2002, SI 2002/794, art 5(2), Sch 2.

Fees: the current Regulations prescribing fees are the Health and Safety (Fees) Regulations 2012, SI 2012/1652 at **[2.1629]**.

Regulations: other Regulations made under this section are considered to be outside the scope of this work (see further the introductory notes to this Act *ante*).

**43A**   *(S 43A (Railway safety levy) outside the scope of this work.)*

*Miscellaneous and supplementary*

**44, 45**   *(S 44 (Appeals in connection with licensing provisions in the relevant statutory provisions), s 45 (Default powers) outside the scope of this work.)*

**[1.69]**
**46   Service of notices**
(1)   Any notice required or authorised by any of the relevant statutory provisions to be served on or given to an inspector may be served or given by delivering it to him or by leaving it at, or sending it by post to, his office.
(2)   Any such notice required or authorised to be served on or given to a person other than an inspector may be served or given by delivering it to him, or by leaving it at his proper address, or by sending it by post to him at that address.
(3)   Any such notice may—
  (a)   in the case of a body corporate, be served on or given to the secretary or clerk of that body;
  (b)   in the case of a partnership, be served on or given to a partner or a person having the control or management of the partnership business or, in Scotland, the firm.
(4)   For the purposes of this section and of section 26 of the Interpretation Act 1889 (service of documents by post) in its application to this section, the proper address of any person on or to whom any such notice is to be served or given shall be his last known address, except that—
  (a)   in the case of a body corporate or their secretary or clerk, it shall be the address of the registered or principal office of that body;
  (b)   in the case of a partnership or a person having the control or the management of the partnership business, it shall be the principal office of the partnership;
and for the purposes of this subsection the principal office of a company registered outside the United Kingdom or of a partnership carrying on business outside the United Kingdom shall be their principal office within the United Kingdom.
(5)   If the person to be served with or given any such notice has specified an address within the United Kingdom other than his proper address within the meaning of subsection (4) above as the one at which he or someone on his behalf will accept notices of the same description as that notice, that address shall also be treated for the purposes of this section and section 26 of the Interpretation Act 1889 as his proper address.
(6)   Without prejudice to any other provision of this section, any such notice required or authorised to be served on or given to the owner or occupier of any premises (whether a body corporate or not) may be served or given by sending it by post to him at those premises, or by addressing it by name to the person on or to whom it is to be served or given and delivering it to some responsible person who is or appears to be resident or employed in the premises.
(7)   If the name or the address of any owner or occupier of premises on or to whom any such notice as aforesaid is to be served or given cannot after reasonable inquiry be ascertained, the notice may be served or given by addressing it to the person on or to whom it is to be served or given by the description of "owner" or "occupier" of the premises (describing them) to which the notice relates, and by delivering it to some responsible person who is or appears to be resident or employed in the premises, or, if there is no such person to whom it can be delivered, by affixing it or a copy of it to some conspicuous part of the premises.
(8)   The preceding provisions of this section shall apply to the sending or giving of a document as they apply to the giving of a notice.

**NOTES**

Interpretation Act 1889, s 26: see now the Interpretation Act 1978, s 7, Sch 2, para 3.

**[1.70]**

**47 Civil Liability**

(1) Nothing in this Part shall be construed—

    (a) as conferring a right of action in any civil proceedings in respect of any failure to comply with any duty imposed by sections 2 to 7 or any contravention of section 8; or

    (b) *as affecting the extent (if any) to which breach of a duty imposed by any of the existing statutory provisions is actionable; or*

    (c) as affecting the operation of section 12 of the Nuclear Installations Act 1965 (right to compensation by virtue of certain provisions of that Act).

*(2) Breach of a duty imposed by health and safety regulations . . . shall, so far as it causes damage, be actionable except in so far as the regulations provide otherwise.*

(3) No provision made by virtue of section 15(6)(b) shall afford a defence in any civil proceedings, *whether brought by virtue of subsection (2) above or not; but as regards any duty imposed as mentioned in subsection (2) above health and safety regulations . . . may provide for any defence specified in the regulations to be available in any action for breach of that duty.*

(4) Subsections (1)(a) *and (2)* above are without prejudice to any right of action which exists apart from the provisions of this Act, and subsection *(3)* above is without prejudice to any defence which may be available apart from the provisions of the regulations there mentioned.

*(5) Any term of an agreement which purports to exclude or restrict the operation of subsection (2) above, or any liability arising by virtue of that subsection shall be void, except in so far as health and safety regulations . . . provide otherwise.*

*(6) In this section "damage" includes the death of, or injury to, any person (including any disease and any impairment of a person's physical or mental condition).*

[(7) The power to make regulations under this section shall be exercisable by the Secretary of State.]

**NOTES**

Sub-s (1): para (b) repealed by the Enterprise and Regulatory Reform Act 2013, s 69(1), (2), as from a day to be appointed, subject to savings in s 69(8)–(10) thereof at **[1.1857]**.

Sub-s (2): words omitted repealed by the Employment Protection Act 1975, ss 116, 125(3), Sch 15, para 14, Sch 18; substituted by new sub-ss (2), (2A), (2B), by the Enterprise and Regulatory Reform Act 2013, s 69(1), (3), subject to savings in s 69(8)–(10) thereof at **[1.1857]**, as from 25 April 2013 (so far as is necessary for enabling the exercise of any power to make regulations) and as from a day to be appointed (otherwise), as follows:

    "(2) Breach of a duty imposed by a statutory instrument containing (whether alone or with other provision) health and safety regulations shall not be actionable except to the extent that regulations under this section so provide.

    (2A) Breach of a duty imposed by an existing statutory provision shall not be actionable except to the extent that regulations under this section so provide (including by modifying any of the existing statutory provisions).

    (2B) Regulations under this section may include provision for—

        (a) a defence to be available in any action for breach of the duty mentioned in subsection (2) or (2A);

        (b) any term of an agreement which purports to exclude or restrict any liability for such a breach to be void.".

Sub-s (3): words omitted repealed by the Employment Protection Act 1975, ss 116, 125(3), Sch 15, para 14, Sch 18; words in italics repealed by the Enterprise and Regulatory Reform Act 2013, s 69(1), (4), as from a day to be appointed, subject to savings in s 69(8)–(10) thereof at **[1.1857]**.

Sub-s (4): for the words "and (2)" and "(3)" in italics there are substituted the words ", (2) and (2A)" and "(2B)(a)" respectively, by the Enterprise and Regulatory Reform Act 2013, s 69(1), (5), as from a day to be appointed, subject to savings in s 69(8)–(10) thereof at **[1.1857]**.

Sub-s (5): words omitted repealed by the Employment Protection Act 1975, ss 116, 125(3), Sch 15, para 14, Sch 18; repealed by the Enterprise and Regulatory Reform Act 2013, s 69(1), (6), as from a day to be appointed, subject to savings in s 69(8)–(10) thereof at **[1.1857]**.

Sub-s (6): repealed by the Enterprise and Regulatory Reform Act 2013, s 69(1), (6), as from a day to be appointed, subject to savings in s 69(8)–(10) thereof at **[1.1857]**.

Sub-s (7): added by the Enterprise and Regulatory Reform Act 2013, s 69(1), (7), subject to savings in s 69(8)–(10) thereof at **[1.1857]**, as from 25 April 2013 (so far as is necessary for enabling the exercise of any power to make regulations) and as from a day to be appointed (otherwise).

**[1.71]**

**48 Application to Crown**

(1) Subject to the provisions of this section, the provisions of this Part, except sections 21 to 25 and 33 to 42, and of regulations made under this Part shall bind the Crown.

(2) Although they do not bind the Crown, sections 33 to 42 shall apply to persons in the public service of the Crown as they apply to other persons.

(3) For the purposes of this Part and regulations made thereunder persons in the service of the Crown shall be treated as employees of the Crown whether or not they would be so treated apart from this subsection.

(4) Without prejudice to section 15(5), the Secretary of State may, to the extent that it appears to him requisite or expedient to do so in the interests of the safety of the State or the safe custody of persons lawfully detained, by order exempt the Crown either generally or in particular respects from all or any of the provisions of this Part which would, by virtue of subsection (1) above, bind the Crown.

(5)   The power to make orders under this section shall be exercisable by statutory instrument, and any such order may be varied or revoked by a subsequent order.

(6)   Nothing in this section shall authorise proceedings to be brought against Her Majesty in her private capacity, and this subsection shall be construed as if section 38(3) of the Crown Proceedings Act 1947 (interpretation of references in that Act to Her Majesty in her private capacity) were contained in this Act.

**NOTES**

The Crown: references to the Crown in sub-ss (1)–(4) shall be treated as including the Assembly Commission; see the National Assembly for Wales Commission (Crown Status) (No 2) Order 2007, SI 2007/1353, art 2.

Secretary of State: the power of the Secretary of State under sub-s (4) above includes power to provide for exemptions in relation to designated premises within the meaning of the Atomic Weapons Establishment Act 1991, or activities carried on by a contractor at such premises; see s 3(1) of, and the Schedule, paras 1, 7(1) to, that Act.

Orders: as of 6 April 2013 no Orders had been made under this section.

**49**   (*S 49 (Adaptation of enactments to metric units or appropriate metric units) outside the scope of this work.*)

**[1.72]**
**50   Regulations under the relevant statutory provisions**
[(1)   Where any power to make regulations under any of the relevant statutory provisions is exercisable by the Secretary of State, that power may be exercised either—
  (a)   so as to give effect (with or without modifications) to proposals submitted by the Executive under section 11(3); or
  (b)   subject to subsection (1AA), independently of such proposals.
(1AA)   The Secretary of State shall not exercise the power referred to in subsection (1) independently of proposals from the Executive unless he has consulted the Executive and such other bodies as appear to him to be appropriate.]
[(1A)   Subsection (1) does not apply to the exercise of a power to make regulations so far as it is exercised—
  (a)   for giving effect (with or without modifications) to proposals submitted by the Office of Rail Regulation under paragraph 2(5) of Schedule 3 to the Railways Act 2005; or
  (b)   otherwise for or in connection with the railway safety purposes.]
(2)   Where the [authority who is to exercise any such power as is mentioned in subsection (1) above proposes to exercise that power] so as to give effect to any such proposals as are there mentioned with modifications, he shall, before making the regulations, consult [the Executive].
(3)   Where [the Executive] proposes to submit [under section [11(3)]] any such proposals as are mentioned in subsection (1) above except proposals for the making of regulations under section 43(2), it shall, before so submitting them, consult—
  (a)   any government department or other body that appears to [the Executive] to be appropriate (and, in particular, in the case of proposals for the making of regulations under section 18(2), any body representing local authorities that so appears . . . );
  (b)   such government departments and other bodies, if any, as, in relation to any matter dealt with in the proposals, [the Executive] is required to consult under this subsection by virtue of directions given to it by the Secretary of State.
(4), (5)   . . .

**NOTES**

Sub-ss (1), (1AA): substituted, for the original sub-s (1), by the Legislative Reform (Health and Safety Executive) Order 2008, SI 2008/960, arts 3, 16(1), (2).

Sub-s (1A): inserted by the Railways Act 2005, s 2, Sch 3, para 13.

Sub-s (2): words in first pair of square brackets substituted by the Employment Protection Act 1975, s 116, Sch 15, para 16(2); words in second pair of square brackets substituted by SI 2008/960, arts 3, 16(1), (3).

Sub-s (3): words in first, second (inner), third and fourth pairs of square brackets substituted by SI 2008/960, arts 3, 16(1), (4); words in second (outer) pair of square brackets substituted by the Employment Protection Act 1975, s 116, Sch 15, para 16(3); words omitted repealed by the Health and Social Care Act 2012, s 56(4), Sch 7, paras 4, 6, as from 1 April 2013.

Sub-ss (4), (5): repealed by the Employment Protection Act 1975, ss 116, 125(3), Sch 15, para 16(4), Sch 18.

**[1.73]**
**51   Exclusion of application to domestic employment**
Nothing in this Part shall apply in relation to a person by reason only that he employs another, or is himself employed, as a domestic servant in a private household.

**[1.74]**
**[51A   Application of Part to police**
(1)   For the purposes of this Part, a person who, otherwise than under a contract of employment, holds the office of constable or an appointment as police cadet shall be treated as an employee of the relevant officer.
(2)   In this section "the relevant officer"—

(a)  in relation to a member of a police force or a special constable or police cadet appointed for a police area, [means—

    (i)  the chief officer of police of that force, or

    (ii)  in the case of a member of the force or a special constable who is, by virtue of a collaboration agreement under section 22A of the Police Act 1996, under the direction and control of a chief officer (within the meaning given by section 23I of that Act), that chief officer,]

[(b)  in relation to a member of a police force seconded to the *Serious Organised Crime Agency to serve as a member of its staff*, means that Agency, and]

(c)  in relation to any other person holding the office of constable or an appointment as police cadet, [means—

    (i)  the person who has the direction and control of the body of constables or cadets in question, or

    (ii)  in the case of a constable who is, by virtue of a collaboration agreement under section 22A of the Police Act 1996, under the direction and control of a chief officer (within the meaning given by section 23I of that Act), that chief officer.]

[(2A)  For the purposes of this Part the relevant officer, as defined by subsection (2)(a) or (c) above, shall[, if not a corporation sole,] be treated as a corporation sole.

(2B)  Where, in a case in which the relevant officer, as so defined, is guilty of an offence by virtue of this section, it is proved—

(a)  that the officer-holder personally consented to the commission of the offence,

(b)  that he personally connived in its commission, or

(c)  that the commission of the offence was attributable to personal neglect on his part,

the office-holder (as well as the corporation sole) shall be guilty of the offence and shall be liable to be proceeded against and punished accordingly.

(2C)  In subsection (2B) above "the office-holder", in relation to the relevant officer, means an individual who, at the time of the consent, connivance or neglect—

(a)  held the office or other position mentioned in subsection (2) above as the office or position of that officer; or

(b)  was for the time being responsible for exercising and performing the powers and duties of that office or position.

(2D)  The provisions mentioned in subsection (2E) below (which impose the same liability for unlawful conduct of constables on persons having their direction or control as would arise if the constables were employees of those persons) do not apply to any liability by virtue of this Part.

(2E)  Those provisions are—

[(a)  section 24 of the Police and Fire Reform (Scotland) Act 2012 (asp 8);]

(b)  section 88(1) of the Police Act 1996;

(c), (d) . . .

(e)  paragraph 14(1) of Schedule 3 to the Criminal Justice and Police Act 2001;

(f)  *section 28 of the Serious Organised Crime and Police Act 2005;*

[(g)  paragraph 20 of Schedule 1 to the Police and Justice Act 2006].

(2F)  In the application of this section to Scotland—

(a)  subsection (2A) shall have effect as if for the words "corporation sole" there were substituted "distinct juristic person (that is to say, as a juristic person distinct from the individual who for the time being is the office-holder)";

(b)  subsection (2B) shall have effect as if for the words "corporation sole" there were substituted "juristic person"; and

(c)  subsection (2C) shall have effect as if for the words "subsection (2B)" there were substituted "subsections (2A) and (2B)".]

(3)  For the purposes of regulations under section 2(4) above—

(a)  the Police Federation for England and Wales shall be treated as a recognised trade union recognised by each chief officer of police in England and Wales,

(b)  the Police Federation for Scotland shall be treated as a recognised trade union recognised by [the chief constable of the Police Service of Scotland], and

(c)  any body recognised by the Secretary of State for the purposes of section 64 of the Police Act 1996 shall be treated as a recognised trade union recognised by each chief officer of police in England, Wales and Scotland.

(4)  Regulations under section 2(4) above may provide, in relation to persons falling within subsection (2)(b) or (c) above, that a body specified in the regulations is to be treated as a recognised trade union recognised by such person as may be specified.]

---

**NOTES**

Inserted by the Police (Health and Safety) Act 1997, s 1.

Sub-s (2): words in square brackets in paras (a), (c) substituted by the Police Reform and Social Responsibility Act 2011, s 99, Sch 16, Pt 3, para 119(1), (2), as from 16 January 2012 (for general transitional provisions relating to police reform and the abolition of existing police authorities, see Sch 15 to the 2011 Act, and the Police Reform and Social Responsibility Act 2011 (Commencement No 3 and Transitional Provisions) Order 2011, SI 2011/3019); para (b) substituted by the Serious

Organised Crime and Police Act 2005, s 59, Sch 4, para 20; for the words in italics in para (b) there are substituted the words "National Crime Agency to serve as a National Crime Agency officer" by the Crime and Courts Act 2013, s 15(3), Sch 8, Pt 2, para 21(1), (2), as from a day to be appointed.

Sub-ss (2A)–(2F): inserted by the Serious Organised Crime and Police Act 2005, s 158(1), (5), with effect for the purposes of any proceedings in or before a court or tribunal that are commenced on or after 7 April 2005 as if this insertion had come into force on 1 July 1998; words in square brackets in sub-s (2A) substituted by the Police Reform and Social Responsibility Act 2011, s 99, Sch 16, Pt 3, para 119(1), (3), as from 16 January 2012 (for general transitional provisions relating to police reform and the abolition of existing police authorities, see Sch 15 to the 2011 Act, and the Police Reform and Social Responsibility Act 2011 (Commencement No 3 and Transitional Provisions) Order 2011, SI 2011/3019); in sub-s (2E), para (a) substituted by the Police and Fire Reform (Scotland) Act 2012, s 128(1), Sch 7, Pt 1, para 2(a), as from 1 April 2013; in sub-s (2E), paras (c), (d) repealed, and para (g) added, by the Police and Justice Act 2006, ss 1(3), 52, Sch 1, Pt 7, para 54, Sch 15, Pt 1; in sub-s (2E) para (f) is substituted by the Crime and Courts Act 2013, s 15(3), Sch 8, Pt 2, para 21(1), (3), as from a day to be appointed, as follows:

"(f)　paragraph 2 of Schedule 4 to the Crime and Courts Act 2013;".

Sub-s (3): words in square brackets in para (b) substituted by the Police and Fire Reform (Scotland) Act 2012, s 128(1), Sch 7, Pt 1, para 2(b), as from 1 April 2013.

Criminal Justice and Police Act 2001, Sch 3: repealed by the Police and Justice Act 2006, s 52, Sch 15.

Regulations under section 2(4): see the Police (Health and Safety) Regulations 1999, SI 1999/860 at **[2.441]**.

**[1.75]**
## 52　Meaning of work and at work
(1)　For the purposes of this Part—
(a)　"work" means work as an employee or as a self-employed person;
(b)　an employee is at work throughout the time when he is in the course of his employment, but not otherwise;
[(bb)　a person holding the office of constable is at work throughout the time when he is on duty, but not otherwise; and]
(c)　a self-employed person is at work throughout such time as he devotes to work as a self-employed person;
and, subject to the following subsection, the expressions "work" and "at work", in whatever context, shall be construed accordingly.
(2)　Regulations made under this subsection may—
(a)　extend the meaning of "work" and "at work" for the purposes of this Part; and
(b)　in that connection provide for any of the relevant statutory provisions to have effect subject to such adaptations as may be specified in the regulations.
[(3)　The power to make regulations under subsection (2) above shall be exercisable by the Secretary of State　.　.　.　]

**NOTES**
Sub-s (1): para (bb) substituted for the original word "and" following para (b) by the Police (Health and Safety) Act 1997, s 2.

Sub-s (3): substituted, for the original sub-ss (3), (4), by the Employment Protection Act 1975, s 116, Sch 15, para 17; words omitted repealed by the Ministry of Agriculture, Fisheries and Food (Dissolution) Order 2002, SI 2002/794, art 5(2), Sch 2.

Modifications: in accordance with sub-s (2) above, the definitions "work" and "at work" are modified, inter alia, by the Health and Safety (Training for Employment) Regulations 1990, SI 1990/1380, which extend the definitions of "work" and "at work" to cover persons engaged in specified training.

Regulations: other Regulations made under this section are considered to be outside the scope of this work (see further the introductory notes to this Act *ante*).

**[1.76]**
## 53　General interpretation of Part I
(1)　In this Part, unless the context otherwise requires—
.　.　.
"article for use at work" means—
(a)　any plant designed for use or operation (whether exclusively or not) by persons at work, and
(b)　any article designed for use as a component in any such plant;
["article of fairground equipment" means any fairground equipment or any article designed for use as a component in any such equipment;]
"code of practice" (without prejudice to section 16(8)) includes a standard, a specification and any other documentary form of practical guidance;
.　.　.
"conditional sale agreement" means an agreement for the sale of goods under which the purchase price or part of it is payable by instalments, and the property in the goods is to remain in the seller (notwithstanding that the buyer is to be in possession of the goods) until such conditions as to the payment of instalments or otherwise as may be specified in the agreement are fulfilled;
"contract of employment" means a contract of employment or apprenticeship (whether express or implied and, if express, whether oral or in writing);

"credit-sale agreement" means an agreement for the sale of goods, under which the purchase price or part of it is payable by instalments, but which is not a conditional sale agreement;

["customs officer" means an officer within the meaning of the Customs and Excise Management Act 1979;]

"domestic premises" means premises occupied as a private dwelling (including any garden, yard, garage, outhouse or other appurtenance of such premises which is not used in common by the occupants of more than one such dwelling), and "non-domestic premises" shall be construed accordingly;

"employee" means an individual who works under a contract of employment [or is treated by section 51A as being an employee], and related expressions shall be construed accordingly;

"enforcing authority" has the meaning assigned by section 18(7);

"the Executive" has the meaning assigned by section [10(1)];

"the existing statutory provisions" means the following provisions while and to the extent that they remain in force, namely the provisions of the Acts mentioned in Schedule 1 which are specified in the third column of that Schedule and of the regulations, orders or other instruments of a legislative character made or having effect under any provision so specified;

. . .

["fairground equipment" means any fairground ride, any similar plant which is designed to be in motion for entertainment purposes with members of the public on or inside it or any plant which is designed to be used by members of the public for entertainment purposes either as a slide or for bouncing upon, and in this definition the reference to plant which is designed to be in motion with members of the public on or inside it includes a reference to swings, dodgems and other plant which is designed to be in motion wholly or partly under the control of, or to be put in motion by, a member of the public;]

"the general purposes of this Part" has the meaning assigned by section 1;

"health and safety regulations" has the meaning assigned by section 15(1);

"hire-purchase agreement" means an agreement other than a conditional sale agreement, under which—

    (a)    goods are bailed or (in Scotland) hired in return for periodical payments by the person to whom they are bailed or hired; and

    (b)    the property in the goods will pass to that person if the terms of the agreement are complied with and one or more of the following occurs—

        (i)    the exercise of an option to purchase by that person;

        (ii)    the doing of any other specified act by any party to the agreement;

        (iii)    the happening of any other event;

and "hire-purchase" shall be construed accordingly;

"improvement notice" means a notice under section 21;

"inspector" means an inspector appointed under section 19;

. . .

"local authority" means—

    (a)    in relation to England  . . . , a county council,  . . . , a district council, a London borough council, the Common Council of the City of London, the Sub-Treasurer of the Inner Temple or the Under-Treasurer of the Middle Temple,

    [(aa)  in relation to Wales, a county council or a county borough council,]

    (b)    in relation to Scotland, a [council constituted under section 2 of the Local Government etc (Scotland) Act 1994] except that before 16th May 1975 it means a town council or county council;

["micro-organism" includes any microscopic biological entity which is capable of replication;]

"offshore installation" means any installation which is intended for underwater exploitation of mineral resources or exploration with a view to such exploitation;

"personal injury" includes any disease and any impairment of a person's physical or mental condition;

"plant" includes any machinery, equipment or appliance;

"premises" includes any place and, in particular, includes—

    (a)    any vehicle, vessel, aircraft or hovercraft,

    (b)    any installation on land (including the foreshore and other land intermittently covered by water), any offshore installation, and any other installation (whether floating, or resting on the seabed or the subsoil thereof, or resting on other land covered with water or the subsoil thereof), and

    (c)    any tent or movable structure;

"prescribed" means prescribed by regulations made by the Secretary of State;

"prohibition notice" means a notice under section 22;

["railway safety purposes" has the same meaning as in Schedule 3 to the Railways Act 2005;]

. . .

"the relevant statutory provisions" means—

    (a)    the provisions of this Part and of any health and safety regulations  . . . ; and

(b)    the existing statutory provisions;

"self-employed person" means an individual who works for gain or reward otherwise than under a contract of employment, whether or not he himself employs others;

"substance" means any natural or artificial substance [(including micro-organisms)], whether in solid or liquid form or in the form of a gas or vapour;

. . .

"supply", where the reference is to supplying articles or substances, means supplying them by way of sale, lease, hire or hire-purchase, whether as principal or agent for another.

(2)–(6)   . . .

**NOTES**

Sub-s (1): definitions "article of fairground equipment", "customs officer", "fairground equipment" and "micro-organism" inserted by the Consumer Protection Act 1987, s 36, Sch 3, para 7; definition "the Commission" (omitted) repealed, and figure in square brackets in definition "the Executive" substituted, by the Legislative Reform (Health and Safety Executive) Order 2008, SI 2008/960, arts 3, 17; in definition "employee" words in square brackets inserted by the Police (Health and Safety) Act 1997, s 6(1); definition "railway safety purposes" inserted by the Railways Act 2005, s 2, Sch 3, para 15(3); in definition "substance", words in square brackets inserted by the Consumer Protection Act 1987, s 36, Sch 3, para 7; definition "substance for use at work" (omitted) repealed by the Consumer Protection Act 1987, s 48, Sch 5; in definition "local authority", second words omitted repealed by the Local Government Act 1985, s 102, Sch 17, first words omitted from that definition repealed, and para (aa) inserted, by the Local Government (Wales) Act 1994, ss 22(3), 66(8), Sch 9, para 9, Sch 18, and words in square brackets in para (b) of that definition substituted by the Local Government etc (Scotland) Act 1994, s 180(1), Sch 13, para 93(3); other words and definitions omitted repealed by the Employment Protection Act 1975, ss 116, 125(3), Sch 15, para 18, Sch 18.

Sub-ss (2)–(6): repealed by the Employment Protection Act 1975, ss 116, 125(3), Sch 15, para 18, Sch 18.

**[1.77]**
**54   Application of Part I to Isles of Scilly**
This Part, in its application to the Isles of Scilly, shall apply as if those Isles were a local government area and the Council of those Isles were a local authority.

**55–76**   *(Ss 55–60 (Pt II: Employment Medical Advisory Service) outside the scope of this work; Pt III (ss 61–76) repealed as follows: ss 61–74, 76 repealed by the Building Act 1984, s 133(2), Sch 7; s 75 repealed by the Building (Scotland) Act 2003, s 58, Sch 6, para 9.)*

## PART IV
## MISCELLANEOUS AND GENERAL

**77–79**   *(S 77 repealed by the Health Protection Agency Act 2004, s 11(2), Sch 4; s 78 repealed by the Regulatory Reform (Fire Safety) Order 2005, SI 2005/1541 and the Fire (Scotland) Act 2005 (Consequential Modifications and Savings) Order 2006, SSI 2006/475; s 79 repealed by the Companies Consolidation (Consequential Provisions) Act 1985, s 29, Sch 1.)*

**[1.78]**
**80   General power to repeal or modify Acts and instruments**
(1)   Regulations made under this subsection may repeal or modify any provision to which this subsection applies if it appears to the authority making the regulations that the repeal or, as the case may be, the modification of that provision is expedient in consequence of or in connection with any provision made by or under Part I.
(2)   Subsection (1) above applies to any provision, not being among the relevant statutory provisions, which—
(a)   is contained in this Act or in any other Act passed before or in the same Session as this Act; or
(b)   is contained in any regulations, order or other instrument of a legislative character which was made under an Act before the passing of this Act; or
(c)   applies, excludes or for any other purpose refers to any of the relevant statutory provisions and is contained in any Act not falling within paragraph (a) above or in any regulations, order or other instrument of a legislative character which is made under an Act but does not fall within paragraph (b) above.
[(2A)   Subsection (1) above shall apply to provisions in [the Employment Rights Act 1996 or the Trade Union and Labour Relations (Consolidation) Act 1992 which derive from provisions of the Employment Protection (Consolidation) Act 1978 which re-enacted] provisions previously contained in the Redundancy Payments Act 1965, the Contracts of Employment Act 1972 and the Trade Union and Labour Relations Act 1974 as it applies to provisions contained in Acts passed before or in the same session as this Act.]
(3)   Without prejudice to the generality of subsection (1) above, the modifications which may be made by regulations thereunder include modifications relating to the enforcement of provisions to which this section applies (including the appointment of persons for the purpose of such enforcement, and the powers of persons so appointed).

[(4) The power to make regulations under subsection (1) above shall be exercisable by the Secretary of State . . . ; but the authority who is to exercise the power shall, before exercising it, consult such bodies as appear to him to be appropriate.

(5) In this section "the relevant statutory provisions" has the same meaning as in Part I.]

**NOTES**

Sub-s (2A): inserted by the Employment Protection (Consolidation) Act 1978, s 159(2), Sch 16, para 17; words in square brackets substituted by the Employment Rights Act 1996, s 240, Sch 1, para 5.

Sub-ss (4), (5): substituted, for the original sub-ss (4)–(6), by the Employment Protection Act 1975, s 116, Sch 15, para 19; words omitted from sub-s (4) repealed by the Ministry of Agriculture, Fisheries and Food (Dissolution) Order 2002, SI 2002/794, art 5(2), Sch 2.

Employment Protection (Consolidation) Act 1978: repealed by the Trade Union and Labour Relations (Consolidation) Act 1992, s 300(1), Sch 1, and the Employment Rights Act 1996, s 242, Sch 3, Pt I.

Redundancy Payments Act 1965; Contracts of Employment Act 1972; Trade Union and Labour Relations Act 1974: the relevant provisions previously contained in those Acts were repealed by the Employment Protection (Consolidation) Act 1978, s 159(3), Sch 17.

Regulations: Regulations made under this section are considered to be outside the scope of this work (see further the introductory notes to this Act *ante*).

**[1.79]**
**81 Expenses and receipts**
There shall be paid out of money provided by Parliament—
(a) any expenses incurred by a Minister of the Crown or government department for the purposes of this Act; and
(b) any increase attributable to the provisions of this Act in the sums payable under any other Act out of money so provided;
and any sums received by a Minister of the Crown or government department by virtue of this Act shall be paid into the Consolidated Fund.

**[1.80]**
**82 General provisions as to interpretation and regulations**
(1) In this Act—
(a) "Act" includes a provisional order confirmed by an Act;
(b) "contravention" includes failure to comply, and "contravene" has a corresponding meaning;
(c) "modifications" includes additions, omissions and amendments, and related expressions shall be construed accordingly;
(d) any reference to a Part, section or Schedule not otherwise identified is a reference to that Part or section of, or Schedule to, this Act.
(2) Except in so far as the context otherwise requires, any reference in this Act to an enactment is a reference to it as amended, and includes a reference to it as applied, by or under any other enactment, including this Act.
(3) Any power conferred by Part I or II or this Part to make regulations—
(a) includes power to make different provision by the regulations for different circumstances or cases and to include in the regulations such incidental, supplemental and transitional provisions as the authority making the regulations considers appropriate in connection with the regulations; and
(b) shall be exercisable by statutory instrument, which [(unless subsection (4) applies)] shall be subject to annulment in pursuance of a resolution of either House of Parliament.
[(4) The first regulations under section 43A(1) shall not be made unless a draft has been laid before and approved by resolution of each House of Parliament.]

**NOTES**

Sub-s (3): words in square brackets in para (b) inserted by the Railways and Transport Safety Act 2003, s 105(3)(a).
Sub-s (4): added by the Railways and Transport Safety Act 2003, s 105(3)(b).
Regulations: the Health and Safety (Fees) Regulations 2012, SI 2012/1652 at **[2.1629]**.

**83** *(Repealed by the Statute Law (Repeals) Act 1993.)*

**[1.81]**
**84 Extent, and application of Act**
(1) This Act, except—
(a) Part I and this Part so far as may be necessary to enable regulations under section 15 . . . to be made and operate for the purpose mentioned in paragraph 2 of Schedule 3; and
(b) paragraph . . . 3 of Schedule 9,
does not extend to Northern Ireland.
(2) Part III, except section 75 and Schedule 7, does not extend to Scotland.

(3)   Her Majesty may by order in Council provide that the provisions of Parts I and II and this Part shall, to such extent and for such purposes as may be specified in the Order, apply (with or without modification) to or in relation to persons, premises, work, articles, substances and other matters (of whatever kind) outside Great Britain as those provisions apply within Great Britain or within a part of Great Britain so specified.

For the purposes of this subsection "premises", "work" and "substance" have the same meanings as they have for the purposes of Part I.

(4)   An Order in Council under subsection (3) above—

   (a)   may make different provision for different circumstances or cases;
   (b)   may (notwithstanding that this may affect individuals or bodies corporate outside the United Kingdom) provide for any of the provisions mentioned in that subsection, as applied by such an Order, to apply to individuals whether or not they are British subjects and to bodies corporate whether or not they are incorporated under the law of any part of the United Kingdom;
   (c)   may make provision for conferring jurisdiction on any court or class of courts specified in the Order with respect to offences under Part I committed outside Great Britain or with respect to causes of action arising by virtue of section 47(2) in respect of acts or omissions taking place outside Great Britain, and for the determination, in accordance with the law in force in such part of Great Britain as may be specified in the Order, of questions arising out of such acts or omissions;
   (d)   may exclude from the operation of section 3 of the Territorial Waters Jurisdiction Act 1878 (consents required for prosecutions) proceedings for offences under any provision of Part I committed outside Great Britain;
   (e)   may be varied or revoked by a subsequent Order in Council under this section;

and any such Order shall be subject to annulment in pursuance of a resolution of either House of Parliament.

(5)   . . .

(6)   Any jurisdiction conferred on any court under this section shall be without prejudice to any jurisdiction exercisable apart from this section by that or any other court.

**NOTES**

Sub-s (1): words omitted from para (a) repealed by the Employment Protection Act 1975, ss 116, 125(3), Sch 15, para 20; words omitted from para (b) repealed by the House of Commons Disqualification Act 1975, s 10(2), Sch 3.

Sub-s (5): repealed by the Offshore Safety Act 1992, ss 3(1)(b), 7(2), Sch 2.

Orders: the Health and Safety at Work etc Act 1974 (Application outside Great Britain) Order 2013, SI 2013/240, which applies provisions of the Act, with appropriate modifications, to various offshore activities.

**[1.82]**
**85   Short title and commencement**

(1)   This Act may be cited as the Health and Safety at Work etc Act 1974.

(2)   This Act shall come into operation on such day as the Secretary of State may by order made by statutory instrument appoint, and different days may be appointed under this subsection for different purposes.

(3)   An order under this section may contain such transitional provisions and savings as appear to the Secretary of State to be necessary or expedient in connection with the provisions thereby brought into force, including such adaptations of those provisions or any provision of this Act then in force as appear to him to be necessary or expedient in consequence of the partial operation of this Act (whether before or after the day appointed by the order).

**NOTES**

Orders: six commencement orders have been made under this section; these are not listed for reasons of space.

## SCHEDULES

### SCHEDULE 1
### EXISTING ENACTMENTS WHICH ARE RELEVANT STATUTORY PROVISIONS
Sections 1, 53

**[1.83]**

| Chapter | Short title | Provisions which are relevant statutory provisions |
| --- | --- | --- |
| 1875 c 17 | The Explosives Act 1875 | The whole Act except sections *30 to 32, 80 and* 116 to 121. |
| 1882 c 22 | The Boiler Explosions Act 1882 | The whole Act. |
| 1890 c 35 | The Boiler Explosions Act 1890 | The whole Act. |
| 1906 c 14 | The Alkali, &c Works Regulation Act 1906 | The whole Act. |

| Chapter | Short title | Provisions which are relevant statutory provisions |
|---|---|---|
| 1909 c 43 | The Revenue Act 1909 | Section 11. |
| . . . | . . . | . . . |
| 1920 c 65 | The Employment of Women, Young Persons and Children Act 1920 | The whole Act. |
| 1922 c 35 | The Celluloid and Cinematograph Film Act 1922 | The whole Act. |
| . . . | . . . | . . . |
| 1926 c 43 | The Public Health (Smoke Abatement) Act 1926 | The whole Act. |
| 1928 c 32 | The Petroleum (Consolidation) Act 1928 | The whole Act. |
| 1936 c 22 | The Hours of Employment (Conventions) Act 1936 | The whole Act except section 5. |
| 1936 c 27 | The Petroleum (Transfer of Licences) Act 1936 | The whole Act. |
| 1937 c 45 | The Hydrogen Cyanide (Fumigation) Act 1937 | The whole Act. |
| 1945 c 19 | The Ministry of Fuel and Power Act 1945 | Section 1(1) so far as it relates to maintaining and improving the safety, health and welfare of persons employed in or about mines and quarries in Great Britain. |
| 1946 c 59 | The Coal Industry Nationalisation Act 1946 | Section 42(1) and (2). |
| 1948 c 37 | The Radioactive Substances Act 1948 | Section 5(1)(a). |
| 1951 c 21 | The Alkali, &c Works Regulations (Scotland) Act 1951 | The whole Act. |
| . . . | . . . | . . . |
| 1952 c 60 | The Agriculture (Poisonous Substances) Act 1952 | The whole Act. |
| . . . | . . . | . . . |
| [ . . . | . . . | . . . ] |
| 1954 c 70 | The Mines and Quarries Act 1954 | The whole Act except section 151. |
| 1956 c 49 | The Agriculture (Safety, Health and Welfare Provisions) Act 1956 | The whole Act. |
| 1961 c 34 | The Factories Act 1961 | The whole Act except section 135. |
| 1961 c 64 | The Public Health Act 1961 | Section 73. |
| 1962 c 58 | The Pipe-lines Act 1962 | Sections 20 to 26, 33, 34 and 42, Schedule 5. |
| 1963 c 41 | The Offices, Shops and Railway Premises Act 1963 | The whole Act. |
| 1965 c 57 | The Nuclear Installations Act 1965 | Sections 1, 3 to 6, 22 and [24A], Schedule 2. |
| 1969 c 10 | The Mines and Quarries (Tips) Act 1969 | Sections 1 to 10. |
| 1971 c 20 | The Mines Management Act 1971 | The whole Act. |
| 1972 c 28 | The Employment Medical Advisory Service Act 1972 | The whole Act except sections 1 and 6 and Schedule 1. |

**NOTES**

In entry relating to the Explosives Act 1875 words in italics repealed by the Fireworks Act 2003, s 15, Schedule, as from a day to be appointed; entry relating to "The Anthrax Prevention Act 1919" (omitted) repealed by the Anthrax Prevention Order 1971 etc (Revocation) Regulations 2005, SI 2005/228, reg 2(2); entries relating to "The Explosives Act 1923", "The Fireworks Act 1951" and "The Emergency Laws (Miscellaneous Provisions) Act 1953" (omitted) repealed by the Manufacture and Storage of Explosives Regulations 2005, SI 2005/1082, reg 28(1), (2), Sch 5, Pt 1, para 14, Sch 6, Pt 1; entry relating to the "Baking Industry (Hours of Work) Act 1954" (omitted) originally inserted by the Sex Discrimination Act 1975, s 23(3), Sch 5, para 3, and repealed by the Sex Discrimination Act 1986, s 9, Schedule, Pt III; in the entry relating to the Nuclear Installations Act 1965, figure in square brackets substituted by the Atomic Energy Act 1989, s 6(3).

Existing enactments that are relevant statutory provisions: (i) as to the power of the Secretary of State to repeal or revoke any provision which is an existing statutory provision for the purposes of Pt I of this Act, see the Deregulation and Contracting Out Act 1994, s 37(1)(a); (ii) Pt I of the Act has effect subject to modifications by the Offshore Safety Act 1992, ss 1(1), 2(1), the Railways Act 1993, s 117(1), (4), and the Gas Act 1995, s 16(1), Sch 4, para 10. These Acts specify that a variety of sector related enactments are relevant statutory provisions within the meaning of this Part.

Boiler Explosions Act 1882; Boiler Explosions Act 1890; Alkali, &c Works Regulation Act 1906; Revenue Act 1909, s 11; Public Health (Smoke Abatement) Act 1926; Hours of Employment (Conventions) Act 1936; Hydrogen Cyanide (Fumigation) Act 1937; Coal Industry Nationalisation Act 1946, s 42; Radioactive Substances Act 1948, s 5(1)(a); Alkali, &c Works Regulations (Scotland) Act 1951; Agriculture (Poisonous Substances) Act 1952; Pipe-lines Act 1962, ss 20–26, 33, 34, 42, Sch 5; Nuclear Installations Act 1965, Sch 2; Mines and Quarries (Tips) Act 1969, ss 8, 9; Mines Management Act 1971: all repealed.

Ministry of Fuel and Power Act 1945, s 1(1): repealed, in so far as it is a relevant statutory provision.

---

## [SCHEDULE 2
## ADDITIONAL PROVISIONS RELATING TO THE CONSTITUTION ETC OF THE
## HEALTH AND SAFETY EXECUTIVE

Section 10

### *The Health and Safety Executive*

**[1.84]**

**1.** The Executive shall consist of—
    (a)    the Chair of the Executive, and
    (b)    at least seven and no more than eleven other members (referred to in this Schedule as "members").

**2.** (1)   The Secretary of State shall appoint the Chair of the Executive.

(2)   The Secretary of State shall appoint the other members of the Executive according to sub-paragraph (3).

(3)   The Secretary of State—
    (a)    shall appoint three members after consulting such organisations representing employers as he considers appropriate;
    (b)    shall appoint three members after consulting such organisations representing employees as he considers appropriate;
    (c)    shall appoint one member after consulting such organisations representing local authorities as he considers appropriate; and
    (d)    may appoint up to four other members after consulting, as he considers appropriate—
       (i)    the Scottish Ministers,
       (ii)    the Welsh Ministers, or
       (iii)    such organisations as he considers appropriate, including professional bodies, whose activities are concerned with matters relating to the general purposes of this Part.

(4)   Service as the Chair or as another member of the Executive is not service in the civil service of the State.

(5)   The Secretary of State, with the approval of the Chair, may appoint one of the other members appointed under sub-paragraph (2) to be the deputy chair of the Executive.

### *Terms of Appointment of the Executive*

**3.** Subject to paragraphs 4 and 5, a person shall hold and vacate office as the Chair or as another member according to the terms of the instrument appointing him to that office.

**4.** The Chair or any other member of the Executive may at any time resign his office by giving notice in writing to the Secretary of State.

**5.** The Secretary of State may remove a Chair or other member who—
    (a)    has been absent from meetings of the Executive for a period longer than six months without the permission of the Executive;
    (b)    has become bankrupt or [has had a debt relief order (under Part 7A of the Insolvency Act 1986) made in respect of him or] has made an arrangement with his creditors;
    (c)    in Scotland, has had his estate sequestrated or has made a trust deed for creditors or a composition contract;
    (d)    has become incapacitated by physical or mental illness; or
    (e)    is otherwise, in the opinion of the Secretary of State, unable or unfit to carry out his functions.

### *Remuneration of Members*

**6.** (1)   The Executive shall pay to each member such remuneration and such travelling and other allowances as may be determined by the Secretary of State.

(2)   The Executive shall pay to, or in respect of, any member, such sums by way of pension, superannuation allowances and gratuities as the Secretary of State may determine.

(3)   Where a person ceases to be a member otherwise than on the expiry of his term of office, and the Secretary of State determines that there are special circumstances which make it right that he should receive compensation, the Executive shall pay to him such amount by way of compensation as the Secretary of State may determine.

### Proceedings of the Executive

**7.** (1)   The Executive may regulate its own procedure.

(2)   The validity of any proceedings of the Executive shall not be affected by any vacancy among the members or by any defect in the appointment of a member.

(3)   The Executive shall consult with the Secretary of State before making or revising its rules and procedures for dealing with conflicts of interest.

(4)   The Executive shall from time to time publish a summary of its rules and procedures.

### Staff

**8.** (1)   The Executive shall, with the consent of the Secretary of State, appoint a person to act as Chief Executive on such terms and conditions as the Secretary of State may determine.

(2)   The Executive shall appoint such other staff to the service of the Executive as it may determine, with the consent of the Secretary of State as to numbers of persons appointed and as to the terms and conditions of their service.

(3)   The Executive shall pay to the Minister for the Civil Service at such times as that Minister may direct, such sums as the Minister may determine in respect of any increase attributable to this paragraph in the sums payable out of monies provided by Parliament under the Superannuation Act 1972.

(4)   A person appointed to the staff of the Executive may not at the same time be a member of the Executive.

(5)   Service as a member of staff of the Executive is service in the civil service of the State.

### Performance of functions

**9.** (1)   Subject to sub-paragraphs (2) to (4), anything authorised or required to be done by the Executive (including exercising the powers under this paragraph) may be done by—
   (a)   such members of the Executive or members of staff of the Executive as the Executive considers fit to authorise for that purpose, whether generally or specifically; or
   (b)   any committee of the Executive which has been so authorised.

(2)   Sub-paragraph (1)(b) does not apply to a committee whose members include a person who is neither a member of the Executive nor a member of staff of the Executive.

(3)   The Executive—
   (a)   shall authorise such of its members of staff as it considers fit to authorise for that purpose, to perform on its behalf those of its functions which consist of the enforcement of the relevant statutory provisions in any particular case; but
   (b)   shall not authorise any member or committee of the Executive to make decisions concerning the enforcement of the relevant statutory provisions in any particular case.

(4)   The Executive shall not authorise any person to legislate by subordinate instrument.

(5)   The Executive shall publish any authorisations which it makes under this paragraph.

### Accounts and Reports

**10.** (1)   It shall be the duty of the Chief Executive—
   (a)   to keep proper accounts and proper records in relation to the accounts;
   (b)   to prepare in respect of each accounting year a statement of accounts in such form as the Secretary of State may direct with the approval of the Treasury; and
   (c)   to send copies of the statement to the Secretary of State and the Comptroller and Auditor General before the end of November next following the accounting year to which the statement relates.

(2)   The Comptroller and the Auditor General shall examine, certify and report on each statement referred to in sub-paragraph (1)(c) and shall lay copies of each statement and his report before each House of Parliament.

(3)   As soon as possible after the end of the accounting year, the Executive shall make to the Secretary of State a report on the performance of the Executive's functions during the year.

(4)   The Secretary of State shall lay the report referred to in sub-paragraph (3) before each House of Parliament.

(5)   In this paragraph, "accounting year" means the period of 12 months ending with 31st March in any year; but the first accounting year of the Executive shall, if the Secretary of State so directs, be of such other period not exceeding 2 years as may be specified in the direction.

*Supplemental*

**11.**   The Secretary of State shall not make any determination or give his consent under paragraph 6 or 8 of this Schedule except with the approval of the Minister for the Civil Service.

**12.**   (1)   The fixing of the common seal of the Executive shall be authenticated by the signature of the Chair or some other person authorised by the Executive to act for that purpose.

(2)   A document purporting to be duly executed under the seal of the Executive shall be received in evidence and shall be deemed to be so executed unless the contrary is proved.

(3)   This paragraph does not apply to Scotland.]

**NOTES**
   Substituted by the Legislative Reform (Health and Safety Executive) Order 2008, SI 2008/960, arts 3, 16(1), (2).
   Para 5: words in square brackets in sub-para (b) inserted by the Tribunals, Courts and Enforcement Act 2007 (Consequential Amendments) Order 2012, SI 2012/2404, art 3(2), Sch 2, para 6, as from 1 October 2012.

## SCHEDULE 3
## SUBJECT-MATTER OF HEALTH AND SAFETY REGULATIONS

Section 15

**[1.85]**
**1.**   (1)   Regulating or prohibiting—
   (a)   the manufacture, supply or use of any plant;
   (b)   the manufacture, supply, keeping or use of any substance;
   (c)   the carrying on of any process or the carrying out of any operation.

(2)   Imposing requirements with respect to the design, construction, guarding, siting, installation, commissioning, examination, repair, maintenance, alteration, adjustment, dismantling, testing or inspection of any plant.

(3)   Imposing requirements with respect to the marking of any plant or of any articles used or designed for use as components in any plant, and in that connection regulating or restricting the use of specified markings.

(4)   Imposing requirements with respect to the testing, labelling or examination of any substance.

(5)   Imposing requirements with respect to the carrying out of research in connection with any activity mentioned in sub-paragraphs (1) to (4) above.

**2.**   (1)   Prohibiting the importation into the United Kingdom or the landing or unloading there of articles or substances of any specified description, whether absolutely or unless conditions imposed by or under the regulations are complied with.

(2)   Specifying, in a case where an act or omission in relation to such an importation, landing or unloading as is mentioned in the preceding sub-paragraph constitutes an offence under a provision of this Act and of [the Customs and Excise Acts 1979], the Act under which the offence is to be punished.

**3.**   (1)   Prohibiting or regulating the transport of articles or substances of any specified description.

(2)   Imposing requirements with respect to the manner and means of transporting articles or substances of any specified description, including requirements with respect to the construction, testing and marking of containers and means of transport and the packaging and labelling of articles or substances in connection with their transport.

**4.**   (1)   Prohibiting the carrying on of any specified activity or the doing of any specified thing except under the authority and in accordance with the terms and conditions of a licence, or except with the consent or approval of specified authority.

(2)   Providing for the grant, renewal, variation, transfer and revocation of licences (including the variation and revocation of conditions attached to licences).

**5.**   Requiring any person, premises or thing to be registered in any specified circumstances or as a condition of the carrying on of any specified activity or the doing of any specified thing.

**6.**   (1)   Requiring, in specified circumstances, the appointment (whether in a specified capacity or not) of persons (or persons with specified qualifications or experience, or both) to perform specified functions, and imposing duties or conferring powers on persons appointed (whether in pursuance of the regulations or not) to perform specified functions.

(2)   Restricting the performance of specified functions to persons possessing specified qualifications or experience.

**7.** Regulating or prohibiting the employment in specified circumstances of all persons or any class of persons.

**8.** (1) Requiring the making of arrangements for securing the health of persons at work or other persons, including arrangements for medical examinations and health surveys.

(2) Requiring the making of arrangements for monitoring the atmospheric or other conditions in which persons work.

**9.** Imposing requirements with respect to any matter affecting the conditions in which persons work, including in particular such matters as the structural condition and stability of premises, the means of access to and egress from premises, cleanliness, temperature, lighting, ventilation, overcrowding, noise, vibrations, ionising and other radiations, dust and fumes.

**10.** Securing the provision of specified welfare facilities for persons at work, including in particular such things as an adequate water supply, sanitary conveniences, washing and bathing facilities, ambulance and first-aid arrangements, cloakroom accommodation, sitting facilities and refreshment facilities.

**11.** Imposing requirements with respect to the provision and use in specified circumstances of protective clothing or equipment, including affording protection against the weather.

**12.** Requiring in specified circumstances the taking of specified precautions in connection with the risk of fire.

**13.** (1) Prohibiting or imposing requirements in connection with the emission into the atmosphere of any specified gas, smoke or dust or any other specified substance whatsoever.

(2) Prohibiting or imposing requirements in connection with the emission of noise, vibrations or any ionising or other radiations.

(3) Imposing requirements with respect to the monitoring of any such emission as is mentioned in the preceding sub-paragraphs.

**14.** Imposing requirements with respect to the instruction, training and supervision of persons at work.

**15.** (1) Requiring, in specified circumstances, specified matters to be notified in a specified manner to specified persons.

(2) Empowering inspectors in specified circumstances to require persons to submit written particulars of measures proposed to be taken to achieve compliance with any of the relevant statutory provisions.

**16.** Imposing requirements with respect to the keeping and preservation of records and other documents, including plans and maps.

**17.** Imposing requirements with respect to the management of animals.

**18.** The following purposes as regards premises of any specified description where persons work, namely—
    (a) requiring precautions to be taken against dangers to which the premises or persons therein are or may be exposed by reason of conditions (including natural conditions) existing in the vicinity;
    (b) securing that persons in the premises leave them in specified circumstances.

**19.** Conferring, in specified circumstances involving a risk of fire or explosion, power to search a person or any article which a person has with him for the purpose of ascertaining whether he has in his possession any article of a specified kind likely in those circumstances to cause a fire or explosion, and power to seize and dispose of any article of that kind found on such a search.

**20.** Restricting, prohibiting or requiring the doing of any specified thing where any accident or other occurrence of a specified kind has occurred.

**21.** As regards cases of any specified class, being a class such that the variety in the circumstances of particular cases within it calls for the making of special provision for particular cases, any of the following purposes, namely—
    (a) conferring on employers or other persons power to make rules or give directions with respect to matters affecting health or safety;
    (b) requiring employers or other persons to make rules with respect to any such matters;
    (c) empowering specified persons to require employers or other persons either to make rules with respect to any such matters or to modify any such rules previously made by virtue of this paragraph; and

(d)   making admissible in evidence without further proof, in such circumstances and subject to such conditions as may be specified, documents which purport to be copies of rules or rules of any specified class made under this paragraph.

**22.** Conferring on any local or public authority power to make byelaws with respect to any specified matter, specifying the authority or person by whom any byelaws made in the exercise of that power need to be confirmed, and generally providing for the procedure to be followed in connection with the making of any such byelaws.

*Interpretation*

**23.** (1)   In this Schedule "specified" means specified in health and safety regulations.

(2)   It is hereby declared that the mention in this Schedule of a purpose that falls within any more general purpose mentioned therein is without prejudice to the generality of the more general purpose.

**NOTES**

Para 2: words in square brackets in sub-para (2) substituted by the Customs and Excise Management Act 1979, s 177(1), Sch 4, para 12, Table, Pt I.

Regulations: see the note to s 15 at **[1.34]**.

**[SCHEDULE 3A**
**OFFENCES: MODE OF TRIAL AND MAXIMUM PENALTY**

**[1.86]**
**1.** The mode of trial and maximum penalty applicable to each offence listed in the first column of the following table are as set out opposite that offence in the subsequent columns of the table.

| Offence | Mode of trial | Penalty on summary conviction | Penalty on conviction on indictment |
|---|---|---|---|
| An offence under section 33(1)(a) consisting of a failure to discharge a duty to which a person is subject by virtue of sections 2 to 6. | Summarily or on indictment. | Imprisonment for a term not exceeding 12 months, or a fine not exceeding £20,000, or both. | Imprisonment for a term not exceeding two years, or a fine, or both. |
| An offence under section 33(1)(a) consisting of a failure to discharge a duty to which a person is subject by virtue of section 7. | Summarily or on indictment. | Imprisonment for a term not exceeding 12 months, or a fine not exceeding the statutory maximum, or both. | Imprisonment for a term not exceeding two years, or a fine, or both. |
| An offence under section 33(1)(b) consisting of a contravention of section 8. | Summarily or on indictment. | Imprisonment for a term not exceeding 12 months, or a fine not exceeding £20,000, or both. | Imprisonment for a term not exceeding two years, or a fine, or both. |
| An offence under section 33(1)(b) consisting of a contravention of section 9. | Summarily or on indictment. | A fine not exceeding £20,000. | A fine. |
| An offence under section 33(1)(c). | Summarily or on indictment. | Imprisonment for a term not exceeding 12 months, or a fine not exceeding £20,000, or both. | Imprisonment for a term not exceeding two years, or a fine, or both. |
| An offence under section 33(1)(d). | Summarily only. | A fine not exceeding level 5 on the standard scale. | |
| An offence under section 33(1)(e), (f) or (g). | Summarily or on indictment. | Imprisonment for a term not exceeding 12 months, or a fine not exceeding £20,000, or both. | Imprisonment for a term not exceeding two years, or a fine, or both. |

| Offence | Mode of trial | Penalty on summary conviction | Penalty on conviction on indictment |
|---|---|---|---|
| An offence under section 33(1)(h). | Summarily only. | Imprisonment for a term not exceeding 51 weeks (in England and Wales) or 12 months (in Scotland), or a fine not exceeding level 5 on the standard scale, or both. | |
| An offence under section 33(1)(i). | Summarily or on indictment. | A fine not exceeding the statutory maximum. | A fine. |
| An offence under section 33(1)(j). | Summarily or on indictment. | Imprisonment for a term not exceeding 12 months, or a fine not exceeding the statutory maximum, or both. | Imprisonment for a term not exceeding two years, or a fine, or both. |
| An offence under section 33(1)(k), (l) or (m). | Summarily or on indictment. | Imprisonment for a term not exceeding 12 months, or a fine not exceeding £20,000, or both. | Imprisonment for a term not exceeding two years, or a fine, or both. |
| An offence under section 33(1)(n). | Summarily only. | A fine not exceeding level 5 on the standard scale. | |
| An offence under section 33(1)(o). | Summarily or on indictment. | Imprisonment for a term not exceeding 12 months, or a fine not exceeding £20,000, or both. | Imprisonment for a term not exceeding two years, or a fine, or both. |
| An offence under the existing statutory provisions for which no other penalty is specified. | Summarily or on indictment. | Imprisonment for a term not exceeding 12 months, or a fine not exceeding £20,000, or both. | Imprisonment for a term not exceeding two years, or a fine, or both. |

**2.** (1) This paragraph makes transitional modifications of the table as it applies to England and Wales.

(2) In relation to an offence committed before the commencement of section 154(1) of the Criminal Justice Act 2003 (general limit on magistrates' court's powers to imprison), a reference to imprisonment for a term not exceeding 12 months is to be read as a reference to imprisonment for a term not exceeding six months.

(3) In relation to an offence committed before the commencement of section 281(5) of that Act (alteration of penalties for summary offences), a reference to imprisonment for a term not exceeding 51 weeks is to be read as a reference to imprisonment for a term not exceeding six months]

**NOTES**

Commencement: 16 January 2009.

Inserted by the Health and Safety (Offences) Act 2008, s 1(2), Sch 1, as from 16 January 2009, except in relation to offences committed before that date.

The provisions of the Criminal Justice Act 2003 mentioned in paras 2(2), (3) above have not, as of 6 April 2013, come into force.

# SCHEDULES 4–10

*(Sch 4 repealed by the Employment Protection Act 1975, ss 116, 125(3), Sch 15, para 21, Sch 18; Schs 5, 6 repealed by the Building Act 1984, s 133(2), Sch 7; Sch 7 repealed by the Building (Scotland) Act 2003, s 58, Sch 6, para 9; Sch 8 repealed by the Regulatory Reform (Fire Safety) Order 2005, SI 2005/1541 and the Fire (Scotland) Act 2005 (Consequential Modifications and Savings) Order 2006, SSI 2006/475, as from 1 October 2006; Schs 9, 10 repealed by the Statute Law (Repeals) Act 1993.)*

# REHABILITATION OF OFFENDERS ACT 1974

(1974 c 53)

## ARRANGEMENT OF SECTIONS

*An Act to rehabilitate offenders who have not been reconvicted of any serious offence for periods of years, to penalise the unauthorised disclosure of their previous convictions, to amend the law of defamation, and for purposes connected therewith*

[31 July 1974]

**NOTES**
See *Harvey* DI(9)(B)(5).

**[1.87]**
## 1   Rehabilitated persons and spent convictions

(1) Subject to [subsections (2), (5) and (6)] below, where an individual has been convicted, whether before or after the commencement of this Act, of any offence or offences, and the following conditions are satisfied, that is to say—

    (a)   he did not have imposed on him in respect of that conviction a sentence which is excluded from rehabilitation under this Act; and

    (b)   he has not had imposed on him in respect of a subsequent conviction during the rehabilitation period applicable to the first-mentioned conviction in accordance with section 6 below a sentence which is excluded from rehabilitation under this Act;

then, after the end of the rehabilitation period so applicable (including, where appropriate, any extension under section 6(4) below of the period originally applicable to the first-mentioned conviction) or, where that rehabilitation period ended before the commencement of this Act, after the commencement of this Act, that individual shall for the purposes of this Act be treated as a rehabilitated person in respect of the first-mentioned conviction and that conviction shall for those purposes be treated as spent.

(2) A person shall not become a rehabilitated person for the purposes of this Act in respect of a conviction unless he has served or otherwise undergone or complied with any sentence imposed on him in respect of that conviction; but the following shall not, by virtue of this subsection, prevent a person from becoming a rehabilitated person for those purposes—

    (a)   failure to pay a fine or other sum adjudged to be paid by or imposed on a conviction, or breach of a condition of a recognizance or of a bond of caution to keep the peace or be of good behaviour;

    (b)   breach of any condition or requirement applicable in relation to a sentence which renders the person to whom it applies liable to be dealt with for the offence for which the sentence was imposed, or, where the sentence was a suspended sentence of imprisonment, liable to be dealt with in respect of that sentence (whether or not, in any case, he is in fact so dealt with);

    (c)   failure to comply with any requirement of a suspended sentence supervision order;

[(2A)   Where in respect of a conviction a person has been sentenced to imprisonment with an order under section 47(1) of the Criminal Law Act 1977, he is to be treated for the purposes of subsection (2) above as having served the sentence as soon as he completes service of so much of the sentence as was by that order required to be served in prison.]

[(2B)   In subsection (2)(a) above the reference to a fine or other sum adjudged to be paid by or imposed on a conviction does not include a reference to an amount payable under a confiscation order made under Part 2 or 3 of the Proceeds of Crime Act 2002.]

(3)   In this Act "sentence" includes any order made by a court in dealing with a person in respect of his conviction of any offence or offences, other than—

[(za)   a surcharge imposed under section 161A of the Criminal Justice Act 2003;]

(a)   an order for committal or any other order made in default of payment of any fine or other sum adjudged to be paid by or imposed on a conviction, or for want of sufficient distress to satisfy any such fine or other sum;

(b)   an order dealing with a person in respect of a suspended sentence of imprisonment.

[(3A)   In subsection (3)(a), the reference to want of sufficient distress to satisfy a fine or other sum includes a reference to circumstances where—

(a)   there is power to use the procedure in Schedule 12 to the Tribunals, Courts and Enforcement Act 2007 to recover the fine or other sum from a person, but

(b)   it appears, after an attempt has been made to exercise the power, that the person's goods are insufficient to pay the amount outstanding (as defined by paragraph 50(3) of that Schedule).]

(4)   In this Act, references to a conviction, however expressed, include references—

(a)   to a conviction by or before a court outside *Great Britain*; and

(b)   to any finding (other than a finding linked with a finding of insanity [or, as the case may be, a finding that a person is not criminally responsible under section 51A of the Criminal Procedure (Scotland) Act 1995 (c 46)]) in any criminal proceedings . . . that a person has committed an offence or done the act or made the omission charged;

and notwithstanding anything in [section 247 of the Criminal Procedure (Scotland) Act 1995 (c 46)] or [section 14 of the Powers of Criminal Courts (Sentencing) Act 2000] [or section 187 of the Armed Forces Act 2006] (conviction of a person . . . discharged to be deemed not to be a conviction) a conviction in respect of which an order is made [discharging the person concerned] absolutely or conditionally shall be treated as a conviction for the purposes of this Act and the person in question may become a rehabilitated person in respect of that conviction and the conviction a spent conviction for those purposes accordingly.

[(5)   This Act does not apply to any disregarded conviction or caution within the meaning of Chapter 4 of Part 5 of the Protection of Freedoms Act 2012.

(6)   Accordingly, references in this Act to a conviction or caution do not include references to any such disregarded conviction or caution.]

---

**NOTES**

Sub-s (1): words in square brackets substituted by the Protection of Freedoms Act 2012, s 115(1), Sch 9, Pt 9, para 134(1), (2), as from 1 October 2012.

Sub-s (2A): inserted by the Criminal Law Act 1977, s 47, Sch 9, para 11.

Sub-s (2B): inserted by the Proceeds of Crime Act 2002, s 456, Sch 11, paras 1, 7.

Sub-s (3): para (za) inserted by the Domestic Violence, Crime and Victims Act 2004, s 58(1), Sch 10, para 9.

Sub-s (3A): inserted by the Tribunals, Courts and Enforcement Act 2007, s 62(3), Sch 13, para 38, as from a day to be appointed.

Sub-s (4) is amended as follows:

For the words in italics in para (a) there are substituted the words "England and Wales" in relation to England and Wales, and the word "Scotland" is substituted in relation to Scotland, by the Legal Aid, Sentencing and Punishment of Offenders Act 2012, s 141(10), Sch 25, Pt 1, paras 1, 2, 12, 13, as from a day to be appointed.

Words in first pair of square brackets inserted by the Criminal Justice and Licensing (Scotland) Act 2010, s 203, Sch 7, paras 7, 8, as from 25 June 2012 (with effect in relation to criminal proceedings commenced on or after that date).

First words omitted repealed by the Children Act 1989, s 108(7), Sch 15.

Words in second pair of square brackets substituted by the Criminal Justice and Licensing (Scotland) Act 2010, s 24(1), as from 28 March 2011.

Words in third pair of square brackets substituted by the Powers of Criminal Courts (Sentencing) Act 2000, s 165(1), Sch 9, para 47.

Words in fourth pair of square brackets inserted by the Armed Forces Act 2006, s 378(1), Sch 16, para 63, as from 31 October 2009 (for transitional provisions see below).

Second words omitted repealed, and words in final pair of square brackets substituted, by the Criminal Justice Act 1991, ss 100, 101(2), Sch 11, para 20, Sch 13.

Sub-ss (5), (6): added by the Protection of Freedoms Act 2012, s 115(1), Sch 9, Pt 9, para 134(1), (3), as from 1 October 2012.

Amendments by the Armed Forces Act 2006: see also the Armed Forces Act 2006 (Transitional Provisions etc) Order 2009, SI 2009/1059, Sch 1, para 14 which provides as follows:

"No amendment by AFA 2006 of the Rehabilitation of Offenders Act 1974—

(a)   causes a conviction which, immediately before the amendment came into force, was spent (within the meaning of that Act) to cease to be spent; or

(b)   has the effect of increasing the rehabilitation period (within the meaning of that Act) in respect of a conviction which occurred before commencement.".

Criminal Law Act 1977, s 47(1): repealed by the Criminal Justice Act 1991.

**2, 3**   *(S 2 (Rehabilitation of persons dealt with in service disciplinary proceedings), s 3 (Special provision with respect to certain disposals by children's hearings under the Social Work (Scotland) Act 1968) outside the scope of this work. Note that s 3 is also repealed in relation to Scotland by the Children's Hearings (Scotland) Act 2011, s 203(2), Sch 6, as from a day to be appointed and in relation to England and Wales by the Legal Aid, Sentencing and Punishment of Offenders Act 2012, s 141(10), Sch 25, Pt 1, paras 1, 4, as from a day to be appointed.)*

**[1.88]**
## 4   Effect of rehabilitation
(1)   Subject to sections 7 and 8 below, a person who has become a rehabilitated person for the purposes of this Act in respect of a conviction shall be treated for all purposes in law as a person who has not committed or been charged with or prosecuted for or convicted of or sentenced for the offence or offences which were the subject of that conviction; and, notwithstanding the provisions of any other enactment or rule of law to the contrary, but subject as aforesaid—
   (a)   no evidence shall be admissible in any proceedings before a judicial authority exercising its jurisdiction or functions in *Great Britain* to prove that any such person has committed or been charged with or prosecuted for or convicted of or sentenced for any offence which was the subject of a spent conviction; and
   (b)   a person shall not, in any such proceedings, be asked, and, if asked, shall not be required to answer, any question relating to his past which cannot be answered without acknowledging or referring to a spent conviction or spent convictions or any circumstances ancillary thereto.
(2)   Subject to the provisions of any order made under subsection (4) below, where a question seeking information with respect to a person's previous convictions, offences, conduct or circumstances is put to him or to any other person otherwise than in proceedings before a judicial authority—
   (a)   the question shall be treated as not relating to spent convictions or to any circumstances ancillary to spent convictions, and the answer thereto may be framed accordingly; and
   (b)   the person questioned shall not be subjected to any liability or otherwise prejudiced in law by reason of any failure to acknowledge or disclose a spent conviction or any circumstances ancillary to a spent conviction in his answer to the question.
(3)   Subject to the provisions of any order made under subsection (4) below,—
   (a)   any obligation imposed on any person by any rule of law or by the provisions of any agreement or arrangement to disclose any matters to any other person shall not extend to requiring him to disclose a spent conviction or any circumstances ancillary to a spent conviction (whether the conviction is his own or another's); and
   (b)   a conviction which has become spent or any circumstances ancillary thereto, or any failure to disclose a spent conviction or any such circumstances, shall not be a proper ground for dismissing or excluding a person from any office, profession, occupation or employment, or for prejudicing him in any way in any occupation or employment.
(4)   The Secretary of State may by order—
   (a)   make such provision as seems to him appropriate for excluding or modifying the application of either or both of paragraphs (a) and (b) of subsection (2) above in relation to questions put in such circumstances as may be specified in the order;
   (b)   provide for such exceptions from the provisions of subsection (3) above as seem to him appropriate, in such cases or classes of case, and in relation to convictions of such a description, as may be specified in the order.
(5)   For the purposes of this section and section 7 below any of the following are circumstances ancillary to a conviction, that is to say—
   (a)   the offence or offences which were the subject of that conviction;
   (b)   the conduct constituting that offence or those offences; and
   (c)   any process or proceedings preliminary to that conviction, any sentence imposed in respect of that conviction, any proceedings (whether by way of appeal or otherwise) for reviewing that conviction or any such sentence, and anything done in pursuance of or undergone in compliance with any such sentence.
(6)   For the purposes of this section and section 7 below "proceedings before a judicial authority" includes, in addition to proceedings before any of the ordinary courts of law, proceedings before any tribunal, body or person having power—
   (a)   by virtue of any enactment, law, custom or practice;
   (b)   under the rules governing any association, institution, profession, occupation or employment; or
   (c)   under any provision of an agreement providing for arbitration with respect to questions arising thereunder;

to determine any question affecting the rights, privileges, obligations or liabilities of any person, or to receive evidence affecting the determination of any such question.

**NOTES**

Sub-s (1): for the words in italics in para (a) there are substituted the words "England and Wales" in relation to England and Wales, and the word "Scotland" is substituted in relation to Scotland, by the Legal Aid, Sentencing and Punishment of Offenders Act 2012, s 141(10), Sch 25, Pt 1, paras 1, 5, 12, 15, as from a day to be appointed.

Exceptions: for exceptions to this section, see ss 7, 8 and note sub-s (4) above and the Orders listed below. See also, for restrictions on the operation of this section, the National Lottery etc Act 1993, s 19 (repealed by the Police Act 1997, ss 133(d), 134(2), Sch 10, as from a day to be appointed), the Criminal Justice Act 2003, s 327B(8), and the Gambling Act 2005, s 125.

Secretary of State: the functions conferred by sub-s (4) are, in so far as exercisable in relation to Scotland, transferred to the Scottish Ministers, by the Scotland Act 1998 (Transfer of Functions to the Scottish Ministers etc) Order 2003, SI 2003/415, art 2.

Orders: the Rehabilitation of Offenders Act 1974 (Exceptions) Order 1975, SI 1975/1023 at **[2.15]**; the Rehabilitation of Offenders Act 1974 (Exclusions and Exceptions) (Scotland) Order 2013, SSI 2013/50 at **[2.1679]**. Note that many Orders have been made under this section that amend the 1975 Order (which applies to England and Wales); these are not listed here for reasons of space.

**[1.89]**
**5 Rehabilitation periods for particular sentences**
(1) The sentences excluded from rehabilitation under this Act are—
   (a) a sentence of imprisonment for life;
   (b) a sentence of imprisonment[, youth custody] [detention in a young offender institution] or corrective training for a term exceeding *thirty months*;
   (c) a sentence of preventive detention; . . .
   (d) a sentence of detention during Her Majesty's pleasure or for life [under section 90 or 91 of the Powers of Criminal Courts (Sentencing) Act 2000], [or under section 209 or 218 of the Armed Forces Act 2006,] [or under section 205(2) or (3) of the Criminal Procedure (Scotland) Act 1975,] [or a sentence of detention for a term exceeding *thirty months* passed under section 91 of the said Act of 2000] [or section 209 of the said Act of 2006] [(young offenders convicted of grave crimes) or under section 206 of the said Act of 1975 (detention of children convicted on indictment)] [ . . . ];
   [(e) a sentence of custody for life][; and
   (f) a sentence of imprisonment for public protection under section 225 of the Criminal Justice Act 2003, a sentence of detention for public protection under section 226 of that Act or an extended sentence under section [226A, 226B,] 227 or 228 of that Act [(including any sentence within this paragraph passed as a result of any of sections 219 to 222 of the Armed Forces Act 2006)]];
and any other sentence is a sentence subject to rehabilitation under this Act.
[(1A) In *subsection (1)(d)*—
   (a) references to section 209 of the Armed Forces Act 2006 include references to section 71A(4) of the Army Act 1955 or Air Force Act 1955 or section 43A(4) of the Naval Discipline Act 1957;
   (b) the reference to section 218 of the Armed Forces Act 2006 includes a reference to section 71A(3) of the Army Act 1955 or Air Force Act 1955 or section 43A(3) of the Naval Discipline Act 1957.]
(2) For the purposes of this Act—
   (a) the rehabilitation period applicable to a sentence specified in the first column of Table A below is the period specified in the second column of that Table in relation to that sentence, or, where the sentence was imposed on a person who was under [eighteen years of age] at the date of his conviction, half that period; and
   (b) the rehabilitation period applicable to a sentence specified in the first column of Table B below is the period specified in the second column of that Table in relation to that sentence;
reckoned in either case from the date of the conviction in respect of which the sentence was imposed.

*Table A*
*Rehabilitation periods subject to reduction by half for persons [under 18]*

| Sentence | Rehabilitation period |
| --- | --- |
| A sentence of imprisonment [detention in a young offender institution] [or youth custody] or corrective training for a term exceeding six months but not exceeding thirty months. | Ten years |
| A sentence of cashiering, discharge with ignominy or dismissal with disgrace from Her Majesty's service. | Ten years |
| A sentence of imprisonment [detention in a young offender institution] [or youth custody] for a term not exceeding six months. | Seven years |
| A sentence of dismissal from Her Majesty's service. | Seven years |

| Sentence | Rehabilitation period |
|---|---|
| [Any sentence of service detention within the meaning of the Armed Forces Act 2006, or any sentence of detention corresponding to such a sentence,] in respect of a conviction in service disciplinary proceedings. | Five years |
| A fine or any other sentence subject to rehabilitation under this Act, not being a sentence to which Table B below or any of subsections (3) [to (8)] below applies. | Five years |

*Table B*
*Rehabilitation periods for certain sentences confined to young offenders*

| Sentence | Rehabilitation period |
|---|---|
| A sentence of Borstal training. | Seven years |
| [A custodial order under Schedule 5A to the Army Act 1955 or the Air Force Act 1955, or under Schedule 4A to the Naval Discipline Act 1957, where the maximum period of detention specified in the order is more than six months. | Seven years] |
| [A custodial order under section 71AA of the Army Act 1955 or the Air Force Act 1955, or under section 43AA of the Naval Discipline Act 1957, where the maximum period of detention specified in the order is more than six months. | Seven years] |
| A sentence of detention for a term exceeding six months but not exceeding thirty months passed under [section 91 of the Powers of Criminal Courts (Sentencing) Act 2000] [or under section 209 of the Armed Forces Act 2006] or under section [206 of the Criminal Procedure (Scotland) Act 1975.] | Five years |
| A sentence of detention for a term not exceeding six months passed under [any provision mentioned in the fourth entry in this Table]. | Three years |
| An order for detention in a detention centre made under [section 4 of the Criminal Justice Act 1982,] section 4 of the Criminal Justice Act 1961 . . . | Three years |
| [A custodial order under any of the Schedules to the said Acts of 1955 and 1957 mentioned above, where the maximum period of detention specified in the order is six months or less. | Three years] |
| [A custodial order under section 71AA of the said Acts of 1955, or section 43AA of the said Act of 1957, where the maximum period of detention specified in the order is six months or less. | Three years] |

[(2A)　Table B applies in relation to a sentence under section 71A(4) of the Army Act 1955 or Air Force Act 1955 or section 43A(4) of the Naval Discipline Act 1957 as it applies in relation to one under section 209 of the Armed Forces Act 2006.]

(3)　The rehabilitation period applicable—
   (a)　to an order discharging a person absolutely for an offence; *and*
   (b)　*to the discharge by a children's hearing under section [69(1)(b) and (12) of the Children (Scotland) Act 1995] of the referral of a child's case;*
shall be six months from the date of conviction.

(4)　Where in respect of a conviction a person was conditionally discharged, bound over to keep the peace or be of good behaviour, . . . . the rehabilitation period applicable to the sentence shall be one year from the date of conviction or a period beginning with that date and ending when the order for conditional discharge . . . . or (as the case may be) the recognisance or bond of caution to keep the peace or be of good behaviour ceases or ceased to have effect, whichever is the longer.

[(4A)　Where in respect of a conviction [*a probation order* [*or* a community order under section 177 of the Criminal Justice Act 2003] was made], the rehabilitation period applicable to the sentence shall be—
   (a)　in the case of a person aged eighteen years or over at the date of his conviction, five years from the date of conviction;
   (b)　in the case of a person aged under the age of eighteen years at the date of his conviction, two and a half years from the date of conviction or a period beginning with the date of conviction and ending when the [order in question] ceases or ceased to have effect, whichever is the longer.]

[(4B) Where in respect of a conviction a referral order (within the meaning of [the Powers of Criminal Courts (Sentencing) Act 2000]) is made in respect of the person convicted, the rehabilitation period applicable to the sentence shall be—
   (a) if a youth offender contract takes effect under [section 23] of that Act between him and a youth offender panel, the period beginning with the date of conviction and ending on the date when (in accordance with [section 24] of that Act) the contract ceases to have effect;
   (b) if no such contract so takes effect, the period beginning with the date of conviction and having the same length as the period for which such a contract would (ignoring any order under paragraph 11 or 12 of Schedule 1 to that Act) have had effect had one so taken effect.

(4C) Where in respect of a conviction an order is made in respect of the person convicted under paragraph 11 or 12 of Schedule 1 to [the Powers of Criminal Courts (Sentencing) Act 2000] (extension of period for which youth offender contract has effect), the rehabilitation period applicable to the sentence shall be—
   (a) if a youth offender contract takes effect under [section 23] of that Act between the offender and a youth offender panel, the period beginning with the date of conviction and ending on the date when (in accordance with [section 24] of that Act) the contract ceases to have effect;
   (b) if no such contract so takes effect, the period beginning with the date of conviction and having the same length as the period for which, in accordance with the order, such a contract would have had effect had one so taken effect.]

[(4D) The rehabilitation period applicable to an order under section 1(2A) of the Street Offences Act 1959 shall be six months from the date of conviction for the offence in respect of which the order is made.]

(5) Where in respect of a conviction any of the following sentences was imposed, that is to say—
   (a) an order under section 57 of the Children and Young Persons Act 1933 or section 61 of the Children and Young Persons (Scotland) Act 1937 committing the person convicted to the care of a fit person;
   (b) a supervision order under any provision of either of those Acts or of the Children and Young Persons Act 1963;
   [(c) an order under section 413 of the Criminal Procedure (Scotland) Act 1975 committing a child for the purpose of his undergoing residential training;]
   (d) an approved school order under section 61 of the said Act of 1937;
   [(da) a youth rehabilitation order under Part 1 of the Criminal Justice and Immigration Act 2008;]
   (e) . . . a supervision order under [section 63(1) of the Powers of Criminal Courts (Sentencing) Act 2000]; or
   (f) *a supervision requirement under any provision of the [Children (Scotland) Act 1995]*;
   [(g) a community supervision order under Schedule 5A to the Army Act 1955 or the Air Force Act 1955, or under Schedule 4A to the Naval Discipline Act 1957;
   (h) . . . ]
the rehabilitation period applicable to the sentence shall be one year from the date of conviction or a period beginning with that date and ending when the order or requirement ceases or ceased to have effect, whichever is the longer.

(6) Where in respect of a conviction any of the following orders was made, that is to say—
   (a) an order under section 54 of the said Act of 1933 committing the person convicted to custody in a remand home;
   (b) an approved school order under section 57 of the said Act of 1933; or
   (c) an attendance centre order under [section 60 of the Powers of Criminal Courts (Sentencing) Act 2000]; [or
   (d) a secure training order under section 1 of the Criminal Justice and Public Order Act 1994;]
the rehabilitation period applicable to the sentence shall be a period beginning with the date of conviction and ending one year after the date on which the order ceases or ceased to have effect.

[(6A) Where in respect of a conviction a detention and training order was made under [section 100 of the Powers of Criminal Courts (Sentencing) Act 2000][, or an order under section 211 of the Armed Forces Act 2006 was made], the rehabilitation period applicable to the sentence shall be—
   (a) in the case of a person aged fifteen years or over at the date of his conviction, five years if the order was, and three and a half years if the order was not, for a term exceeding six months;
   (b) in the case of a person aged under fifteen years at the date of his conviction, a period beginning with that date and ending one year after the date on which the order ceases to have effect.]

(7) Where in respect of a conviction a hospital order under [Part III of the Mental Health Act 1983] or under [Part VI of the Criminal Procedure (Scotland) Act 1995] (with or without [a restriction order] was made, the rehabilitation period applicable to the sentence shall be the period of five years from the date of conviction or a period beginning with that date and ending two years after the date on which the hospital order ceases or ceased to have effect, whichever is the longer.

(8) Where in respect of a conviction an order was made imposing on the person convicted any disqualification, disability, prohibition or other penalty, the rehabilitation period applicable to the sentence shall be a period beginning with the date of conviction and ending on the date on which the disqualification, disability, prohibition or penalty (as the case may be) ceases or ceased to have effect.

(9) For the purposes of this section—
   (a) "sentence of imprisonment" includes a sentence of detention [under section 207 or 415 of the Criminal Procedure (Scotland) Act 1975] and a sentence of penal servitude, and "term of imprisonment" shall be construed accordingly;
   (b) consecutive terms of imprisonment or of detention under [section 91 of the Powers of Criminal Courts (Sentencing) Act 2000] or [section 206 of the said Act of 1975] and terms which are wholly or partly concurrent (being terms of imprisonment or detention imposed in respect of offences of which a person was convicted in the same proceedings) shall be treated as a single term;
   (c) no account shall be taken of any subsequent variation, made by a court in dealing with a person in respect of a suspended sentence of imprisonment, of the term originally imposed; and
   (d) a sentence imposed by a court outside Great Britain shall be treated as a sentence of that one of the descriptions mentioned in this section which most nearly corresponds to the sentence imposed.

(10) References in this section to the period during which a probation order, or a  . . . supervision order under [the Powers of Criminal Courts (Sentencing) Act 2000], *or a supervision requirement under the [Children (Scotland) Act 1995]*, is or was in force include references to any period during which any order or requirement to which this subsection applies, being an order or requirement made or imposed directly or indirectly in substitution for the first-mentioned order or requirement, is or was in force.
   This subsection applies—
   (a) to any such order or requirement as is mentioned above in this subsection;
   (b) to any order having effect under section 25(2) of [the Children and Young Persons Act 1969] as if it were a training school order in Northern Ireland; and
   (c) to any supervision order made under section 72(2) of the said Act of 1968 and having effect as a supervision order under the Children and Young Persons Act (Northern Ireland) 1950.

*[(10A) The reference in subsection (5) above to the period during which a reception order has effect includes a reference to any subsequent period during which by virtue of the order having been made the Social Work (Scotland) Act 1968 or the Children and Young Persons Act (Northern Ireland) 1968 has effect in relation to the person in respect of whom the order was made and subsection (10) above shall accordingly have effect in relation to any such subsequent period.]*

(11) The Secretary of State may by order—
   (a) substitute different periods or terms for any of the periods or terms mentioned in subsections (1) to (8) above; and
   (b) substitute a different age for the age mentioned in subsection (2)(a) above.

**NOTES**
   Sub-s (1): words in first pair of square brackets in para (b) inserted by the Criminal Justice Act 1982, ss 77, 78, Sch 14, para 36; words in second pair of square brackets in para (b) inserted by the Criminal Justice Act 1988, s 123(6), Sch 8, para 9(a); for the words "thirty months" in italics in paras (b), (d) there are substituted the words "forty eight months" in relation to England and Wales, by the Legal Aid, Sentencing and Punishment of Offenders Act 2012, s 139(1), (2), subject to transitional provisions in s 141(1)–(6), (11), (12) thereof (as noted below) as from a day to be appointed; word omitted from para (c) repealed, and para (e) added, by the Criminal Justice Act 1982, ss 77, 78, Sch 14, para 36, Sch 16; words in first pair of square brackets in para (d) inserted, and words in fourth pair of square brackets substituted, by the Powers of Criminal Courts (Sentencing) Act 2000, s 165(1), Sch 9, para 48(1), (2); words in second and fifth pairs of square brackets inserted by the Armed Forces Act 2006, s 378(1), Sch 16, para 65(1), (2)(a)(i), (ii), as from 31 October 2009; words in third pair of square brackets in para (d) inserted, and words in sixth pair of square brackets substituted, by the Criminal Justice (Scotland) Act 1980, s 83(2), Sch 7, para 24; the words omitted from para (d) were originally inserted by the Armed Forces Act 1976, s 22, Sch 9, para 20(4), and repealed by the Armed Forces Act 2006, s 378(1), Sch 16, para 65(1), (2)(a)(iii), Sch 17, as from 31 October 2009; para (f) and the word immediately preceding it added by the Criminal Justice Act 2003, s 304, Sch 32, Pt 1, para 18(1), (2)(b); references in first pair of square brackets in para (f) inserted by the Legal Aid, Sentencing and Punishment of Offenders Act 2012, s 126, Sch 21, Pt 1, para 2, as from 3 December 2012; words in second pair of square brackets in para (f) added by the Armed Forces Act 2006, s 378(1), Sch 16, para 65(1), (2)(b), as from 31 October 2009.

Sub-s (1A): inserted by the Armed Forces Act 1976, s 22, Sch 9, para 20(5); substituted by the Armed Forces Act 2006, s 378(1), Sch 16, para 65(1), (3), as from 31 October 2009; for the words in italics there are substituted the words "this section" in relation to England and Wales, by the Legal Aid, Sentencing and Punishment of Offenders Act 2012, s 139(1), (3), subject to transitional provisions in s 141(1)–(6), (11), (12) thereof (as noted below) as from a day to be appointed.

**Prospective substitution:** sub-ss (2), (2A), (3), (4), (4A)–(4D), (5), (6), (6A), (7)–(10), (10A), (11) are substituted by new sub-ss (2)–(8), in relation to England and Wales, by the Legal Aid, Sentencing and Punishment of Offenders Act 2012, s 139(1), (4), subject to transitional provisions in s 141(1)–(6), (11), (12) thereof (as noted below), as from a day to be appointed, as follows:

"(2)    For the purposes of this Act and subject to subsections (3) and (4), the rehabilitation period for a sentence is the period—

(a)    beginning with the date of the conviction in respect of which the sentence is imposed, and

(b)    ending at the time listed in the following Table in relation to that sentence:

| Sentence | End of rehabilitation period for adult offenders | End of rehabilitation period for offenders under 18 at date of conviction |
| --- | --- | --- |
| A custodial sentence of more than 30 months and up to, or consisting of, 48 months | The end of the period of 7 years beginning with the day on which the sentence (including any licence period) is completed | The end of the period of 42 months beginning with the day on which the sentence (including any licence period) is completed |
| A custodial sentence of more than 6 months and up to, or consisting of, 30 months | The end of the period of 48 months beginning with the day on which the sentence (including any licence period) is completed | The end of the period of 24 months beginning with the day on which the sentence (including any licence period) is completed |
| A custodial sentence of 6 months or less | The end of the period of 24 months beginning with the day on which the sentence (including any licence period) is completed | The end of the period of 18 months beginning with the day on which the sentence (including any licence period) is completed |
| Removal from Her Majesty's service | The end of the period of 12 months beginning with the date of the conviction in respect of which the sentence is imposed | The end of the period of 6 months beginning with the date of the conviction in respect of which the sentence is imposed |
| A sentence of service detention | The end of the period of 12 months beginning with the day on which the sentence is completed | The end of the period of 6 months beginning with the day on which the sentence is completed |
| A fine | The end of the period of 12 months beginning with the date of the conviction in respect of which the sentence is imposed | The end of the period of 6 months beginning with the date of the conviction in respect of which the sentence is imposed |
| A compensation order | The date on which the payment is made in full | The date on which the payment is made in full |
| A community or youth rehabilitation order | The end of the period of 12 months beginning with the day provided for by or under the order as the last day on which the order is to have effect | The end of the period of 6 months beginning with the day provided for by or under the order as the last day on which the order is to have effect |
| A relevant order | The day provided for by or under the order as the last day on which the order is to have effect | The day provided for by or under the order as the last day on which the order is to have effect |

(3)    Where no provision is made by or under a community or youth rehabilitation order or a relevant order for the last day on which the order is to have effect, the rehabilitation period for the order is to be the period of 24 months beginning with the date of conviction.

(4)    There is no rehabilitation period for—

(a)    an order discharging a person absolutely for an offence, or

(b)    any other sentence in respect of a conviction where the sentence is not dealt with in the Table or under subsection (3),

and, in such cases, references in this Act to any rehabilitation period are to be read as if the period of time were nil.

(5)    See also—

(a)    section 8AA (protection afforded to spent alternatives to prosecution), and

(b)    Schedule 2 (protection for spent cautions).

(6)    The Secretary of State may by order amend column 2 or 3 of the Table or the number of months for the time being specified in subsection (3).

(7)    For the purposes of this section—

(a)    consecutive terms of imprisonment or other custodial sentences are to be treated as a single term,

(b)    terms of imprisonment or other custodial sentences which are wholly or partly concurrent (that is terms of imprisonment or other custodial sentences imposed in respect of offences of which a person was convicted in the same proceedings) are to be treated as a single term,

    (c)    no account is to be taken of any subsequent variation, made by a court dealing with a person in respect of a suspended sentence of imprisonment, of the term originally imposed,

    (d)    no account is to be taken of any subsequent variation of the day originally provided for by or under an order as the last day on which the order is to have effect,

    (e)    no account is to be taken of any detention or supervision ordered by a court under section 104(3) of the Powers of Criminal Courts (Sentencing) Act 2000,

    (f)    a sentence imposed by a court outside England and Wales is to be treated as the sentence mentioned in this section to which it most closely corresponds.

(8)   In this section—

"community or youth rehabilitation order" means—

    (a)    a community order under section 177 of the Criminal Justice Act 2003,

    (b)    a service community order or overseas community order under the Armed Forces Act 2006,

    (c)    a youth rehabilitation order under Part 1 of the Criminal Justice and Immigration Act 2008, or

    (d)    any order of a kind superseded (whether directly or indirectly) by an order mentioned in paragraph (a), (b) or (c),

"custodial sentence" means—

    (a)    a sentence of imprisonment,

    (b)    a sentence of detention in a young offender institution,

    (c)    a sentence of Borstal training,

    (d)    a sentence of youth custody,

    (e)    a sentence of corrective training,

    (f)    a sentence of detention under section 91 of the Powers of Criminal Courts (Sentencing) Act 2000 or section 209 of the Armed Forces Act 2006,

    (g)    a detention and training order under section 100 of the Powers of Criminal Courts (Sentencing) Act 2000 or an order under section 211 of the Armed Forces Act 2006,

    (h)    any sentence of a kind superseded (whether directly or indirectly) by a sentence mentioned in paragraph (f) or (g),

"earlier statutory order" means—

    (a)    an order under section 54 of the Children and Young Persons Act 1933 committing the person convicted to custody in a remand home,

    (b)    an approved school order under section 57 of that Act, or

    (c)    any order of a kind superseded (whether directly or indirectly) by an order mentioned in any of paragraphs (c) to (e) of the definition of "relevant order" or in paragraph (a) or (b) above,

"relevant order" means—

    (a)    an order discharging a person conditionally for an offence,

    (b)    an order binding a person over to keep the peace or be of good behaviour,

    (c)    an order under section 1(2A) of the Street Offences Act 1959,

    (d)    a hospital order under Part 3 of the Mental Health Act 1983 (with or without a restriction order),

    (e)    a referral order under section 16 of the Powers of Criminal Courts (Sentencing) Act 2000,

    (f)    an earlier statutory order, or

    (g)    any order which imposes a disqualification, disability, prohibition or other penalty and is not otherwise dealt with in the Table or under subsection (3),

but does not include a reparation order under section 73 of the Powers of Criminal Courts (Sentencing) Act 2000,

"removal from Her Majesty's service" means a sentence of dismissal with disgrace from Her Majesty's service, a sentence of dismissal from Her Majesty's service or a sentence of cashiering or discharge with ignominy,

"sentence of imprisonment" includes a sentence of penal servitude (and "term of imprisonment" is to be read accordingly),

"sentence of service detention" means—

    (a)    a sentence of service detention (within the meaning given by section 374 of the Armed Forces Act 2006), or a sentence of detention corresponding to such a sentence, in respect of a conviction in service disciplinary proceedings, or

    (b)    any sentence of a kind superseded (whether directly or indirectly) by a sentence mentioned in paragraph (a).".

Sub-s (2): words in square brackets in para (a) and in the heading to Table A substituted by the Criminal Justice Act 1991, ss 68, 101(1), Sch 8, para 5, Sch 12, para 22 (with additional effect in relation to any sentence imposed on any person who was convicted before 1 October 1992 and was aged 17 at the date of his conviction).

In Table A: words in first and third pairs of pairs of square brackets inserted by the Criminal Justice Act 1988, s 123(6), Sch 8, para 9(b); words in second and fourth pairs of square brackets inserted by the Criminal Justice Act 1982, s 77, Sch 14, para 37; words in fifth pair of square brackets substituted by the Armed Forces Act 2006, s 378(1), Sch 16, para 65(1), (4)(a), as from 31 October 2009; words in final pair of square brackets originally inserted by the Criminal Justice and Public Order Act 1994, s 168(1), (3), Sch 9, para 11, and substituted by the Youth Justice and Criminal Evidence Act 1999, s 67, Sch 4, para 6(1), (2).

Table B has been amended as follows—

Entry beginning with the words "A custodial order under Schedule 5A" inserted by the Armed Forces Act 1976, s 22, Sch 9, para 21(1).

Entry beginning with the words "A custodial order under section 71AA" inserted by the Armed Forces Act 1981, s 28, Sch 4, para 2.

In the entry beginning with the words "A sentence of detention for a term exceeding six months" words "section 91 of the Powers of Criminal Courts (Sentencing) Act 2000" in square brackets substituted by the Powers of Criminal Courts (Sentencing) Act 2000, s 165(1), Sch 9, para 48(1), (3); in that entry the words "or under section 209 of the Armed Forces Act 2006" in square brackets inserted by the Armed Forces Act 2006, s 378(1), Sch 16, para 65(1), (4)(b)(i), as from 31 October 2009; in that entry the words "206 of the Criminal Procedure (Scotland) Act 1975" in square brackets substituted by the Criminal Justice (Scotland) Act 1980, s 83(2), Sch 7, para 24.

In the entry beginning with the words "A sentence of detention for a term not exceeding six months" words in square brackets substituted by the Armed Forces Act 2006, s 378(1), Sch 16, para 65(1), (4)(b)(ii), as from 31 October 2009.

In the entry beginning "An order for detention in a detention centre" words "section 4 of the Criminal Justice Act 1982" in square brackets inserted by the Criminal Justice Act 1982, s 77, Sch 14, para 37; words omitted from that entry repealed by the Criminal Justice (Scotland) Act 1980, s 83(2), Sch 7, para 24.

Penultimate entry in square brackets inserted by the Armed Forces Act 1976, s 22, Sch 9, para 21(1).

Final entry in square brackets inserted by the Armed Forces Act 1981, s 28, Sch 4, para 2.

Sub-s (2A): inserted by the Armed Forces Act 2006, s 378(1), Sch 16, para 65(1), (5), as from 31 October 2009.

Sub-s (3): para (b) and the word immediately preceding it repealed by the Children's Hearings (Scotland) Act 2011, s 203(2), Sch 6, as from a day to be appointed; words in square brackets in para (b) substituted by the Children (Scotland) Act 1995, s 105(4), (5), Sch 4, para 23(1), (3).

Sub-s (4): words omitted repealed by the Criminal Justice and Public Order Act 1994, s 168(1), (3), Sch 9, para 11(1)(b), (2), Sch 11.

Sub-s (4A): inserted by the Criminal Justice and Public Order Act 1994, s 168(1), (3), Sch 9, para 11(1)(c), (2); words in first (outer) and fourth pairs of square brackets substituted by the Criminal Justice and Court Services Act 2000, s 74, Sch 7, Pt II, paras 48, 49; words in italics repealed, in relation to Scotland, by the Criminal Justice and Licensing (Scotland) Act 2010, s 1(2), Sch 2, Pt 2, para 32(1), (2), as from 1 February 2011 (see also SSI 2010/413, art 3 which provides that this amendment is of no effect in relation to an offence committed before that date or in relation to any probation order, supervised attendance order or community service order made under the Criminal Procedure (Scotland) Act 1995); words in second (inner) pair of square brackets inserted by the Criminal Justice Act 2003, s 304, Sch 32, Pt 1, para 18(1), (3); words in third (inner) pair of square brackets inserted by the Armed Forces Act 2006, s 378(1), Sch 16, para 65(1), (6), as from 31 October 2009.

Sub-s (4B): inserted, together with sub-s (4C), by the Youth Justice and Criminal Evidence Act 1999, s 67, Sch 4, para 6(1), (3); words in square brackets substituted by the Powers of Criminal Courts (Sentencing) Act 2000, s 165(1), Sch 9, para 48(1), (4).

Sub-s (4C): inserted as noted above; words in square brackets substituted by the Powers of Criminal Courts (Sentencing) Act 2000, s 165(1), Sch 9, para 48(1), (5).

Sub-s (4D): inserted by the Policing and Crime Act 2009, s 18(1), (2), as from 1 April 2010 (note that the coming into force of s 18 of the 2009 Act is of no effect in relation to any person as regards an offence committed by that person contrary to the Street Offences Act 1959, s 1 (loitering or soliciting for purposes of prostitution) during a period which falls wholly or partly before that date (see SI 2010/507, art 6)).

Sub-s (5): para (c) substituted by the Criminal Justice (Scotland) Act 1980, s 83(2), Sch 7, para 24; para (da) inserted by the Criminal Justice and Immigration Act 2008, s 6(2), Sch 4, Pt 1, paras 20, 21, as from 30 November 2009 (subject to savings in relation to (i) any offence committed before the amendment comes into force, and (ii) any failure to comply with an order made in respect of an offence committed before that date: see Sch 27 to the 2008 Act); words omitted from para (e) repealed by the Children Act 1989, s 108(7), Sch 15; words in square brackets in para (e) substituted by the Powers of Criminal Courts (Sentencing) Act 2000, s 165(1), Sch 9, para 48(1), (6); para (f) repealed by the Children's Hearings (Scotland) Act 2011, s 203(2), Sch 6, as from a day to be appointed; words in square brackets in para (f) substituted by the Children (Scotland) Act 1995, s 105(4), (5), Sch 4, para 23(1), (3); paras (g), (h) added by the Armed Forces Act 1976, s 22, Sch 9, para 21(2); para (h) repealed by the Armed Forces Act 1991, s 26, Sch 3.

Sub-s (6): words in square brackets in para (c) substituted by the Powers of Criminal Courts (Sentencing) Act 2000, s 165(1), Sch 9, para 48(1), (7); para (d) and the word immediately preceding it added by the Criminal Justice and Public Order Act 1994, s 168(2), Sch 10, para 30.

Sub-s (6A): inserted by the Crime and Disorder Act 1998, s 119, Sch 8, para 35; words in first pair of square brackets substituted by the Powers of Criminal Courts (Sentencing) Act 2000, s 165(1), Sch 9, para 48(1), (8); words in second pair of square brackets inserted by the Armed Forces Act 2006, s 378(1), Sch 16, para 65(1), (7), as from 31 October 2009.

Sub-s (7): words in first pair of square brackets substituted by the Mental Health Act 1983, s 148, Sch 4, para 39; words in second pair of square brackets substituted by the Mental Health (Care and Treatment) (Scotland) Act 2003 (Modification of Enactments) Order 2005, SSI 2005/465, art 2, Sch 1, para 6; words in third pair of square brackets substituted by the Mental Health (Amendment) Act 1982, s 65(1), Sch 3, para 49.

Sub-s (9): words in first and fourth pairs of square brackets substituted by the Criminal Justice (Scotland) Act 1980, s 83(2), Sch 7, para 24; words in second pair of square brackets substituted by the Powers of Criminal Courts (Sentencing) Act 2000, s 165(1), Sch 9, para 48(1), (9); words in third pair of square brackets inserted by the Armed Forces Act 2006, s 378(1), Sch 16, para 65(1), (8), as from 31 October 2009.

Sub-s (10): words omitted repealed by the Children Act 1989, s 108(7), Sch 15; words in first and third pairs of square brackets substituted by the Powers of Criminal Courts (Sentencing) Act 2000, s 165(1), Sch 9, para 48(1), (10); words in second pair of square brackets substituted by the Children (Scotland) Act 1995, s 105(4), (5), Sch 4, para 23(1), (3), Sch 5; words in italics repealed by the Children's Hearings (Scotland) Act 2011, s 203(2), Sch 6, as from a day to be appointed.

Sub-s (10A): inserted by the Armed Forces Act 1976, s 22, Sch 9, para 21(3); repealed, in relation to Scotland only, by the Children (Scotland) Act 1995, s 105(4), (5), Sch 4, para 23(1), (3), Sch 5.

**Transitional Provisions:** the Legal Aid, Sentencing and Punishment of Offenders Act 2012, s 141 (in force from a day to be appointed) provides as follows:

## "141 Transitional and consequential provision

(1) Section 139 applies in relation to convictions or (as the case may be) cautions before the commencement date (as well as in relation to convictions or cautions on or after that date).

(2) The Rehabilitation of Offenders Act 1974 ("the 1974 Act") applies in relation to convictions or cautions before the commencement date as if the amendments and repeals made by section 139 had always had effect.

(3) Where by virtue of subsection (2)—

(a) a person would, before the commencement date, have been treated for the purposes of the 1974 Act as a rehabilitated person in respect of a conviction, or

(b) a conviction would, before that date, have been treated for the purposes of that Act as spent,

the person or conviction concerned is (subject to any order made by virtue of section 4(4) or 7(4) of that Act) to be so treated on and after that date.

(4) Where by virtue of subsection (2)—

(a)   a person would, before the commencement date, have been treated as mentioned in paragraph 3(1) of Schedule 2 to the 1974 Act in respect of a caution, or

(b)   a caution would, before that date, have been treated for the purposes of that Act as spent,

the person or caution concerned is (subject to any order made by virtue of paragraph 4 or 6(1) and (4) of that Schedule to that Act) to be so treated on and after that date.

(5)   But—

(a)   no person who, immediately before the commencement date—

(i)    is treated as a rehabilitated person for the purposes of the 1974 Act in respect of a conviction, or

(ii)   is treated as mentioned in paragraph 3(1) of Schedule 2 to that Act in respect of a caution, and

(b)   no conviction or caution which, immediately before the commencement date, is treated for the purposes of that Act as spent,

is to cease to be so treated merely because of section 139.

(6)   Section 139 does not apply in relation to alternatives to prosecution given before the commencement date.

(7)–(11)   *(Outside the scope of this work.)*

(12)   In this section "the commencement date" means such day as may be specified by order of the Secretary of State made by statutory instrument; and different days may be specified for different purposes.".

Amendments by the Armed Forces Act 2006: see the note to s 1 at **[1.87]**.

Youth custody; detention in a young offender institution: detention centre orders and youth custody sentences were amalgamated into a single custodial sentence of detention in a young offender institution by the Criminal Justice Act 1982, s 1A (repealed). As to detention in a young offender institution, see the Powers of Criminal Courts (Sentencing) Act 2000, ss 96–98 (repealed by the Criminal Justice and Court Services Act 2000, ss 74, 75, Sch 7, Pt II, paras 160, 182, Sch 8, as from a day to be appointed), and as to the abolition of this sentence, see s 61 of that Act.

Corrective training; preventive detention: these sentences were authorised in certain cases by the Criminal Justice Act 1948, s 21 (repealed) but were abolished by the Criminal Justice Act 1967, s 37(1) (repealed).

Custody for life: as to custody for life, see the Powers of Criminal Courts (Sentencing) Act 2000, ss 93–95 (repealed by the Criminal Justice and Court Services Act 2000, ss 74, 75, Sch 7, Pt II, paras 160, 182, Sch 8, as from a day to be appointed), and as to the abolition of this sentence, see s 61 of that Act.

Borstal training: borstal training was replaced by youth custody (as to which, see the note above).

Order for detention in a detention centre: see the note "Youth custody; detention in a young offender institution" above.

Probation orders: renamed community rehabilitation orders in accordance with the Criminal Justice and Court Services Act 2000, s 43. The power to make community rehabilitation orders was given by the Powers of Criminal Courts (Sentencing) Act 2000, ss 41–45 (repealed subject to savings).

Penal Servitude: the courts no longer have the power to sentence a person to penal servitude (see the Criminal Justice Act 1948, s 1(1), (2)). That section also provides that every enactment conferring power on a court to pass such sentence is to be construed as conferring the power to pass a sentence of imprisonment for a similar term.

Air Force Act 1955, Army Act 1955, Naval Discipline Act 1957: repealed by the Armed Forces Act 2006, s 378, Sch 17.

Children and Young Persons Act 1933: ss 54, 57 repealed by the Children and Young Persons Act 1969, ss 7(6), 72(4), Sch 6.

Criminal Justice Act 1961, s 4: repealed by the Criminal Justice Act 1982, s 78, Sch 16.

Criminal Justice Act 1982, s 4: repealed by the Criminal Justice Act 1988, s 170(2), Sch 16.

Criminal Justice and Public Order Act 1994, s 1: repealed by the Crime and Disorder Act 1998, ss 73(7)(b), 120(2), Sch 10.

Criminal Procedure (Scotland) Act 1975: repealed, subject to transitional provisions and savings, by the Criminal Procedure (Consequential Provisions) Act 1995, ss 4, 6, Schs 3, 5, 6.

Orders: as of 6 April 2013 no Orders had been made under this section.

---

**[1.90]**

## 6   The rehabilitation period applicable to a conviction

(1)   Where only one sentence is imposed in respect of a conviction (not being a sentence excluded from rehabilitation under this Act) the rehabilitation period applicable to the conviction is, subject to the following provisions of this section, the period applicable to the sentence in accordance with section 5 above.

(2)   Where more than one sentence is imposed in respect of a conviction (whether or not in the same proceedings) and none of the sentences imposed is excluded from rehabilitation under this Act, then, subject to the following provisions of this section, if the periods applicable to those sentences in accordance with section 5 above differ, the rehabilitation period applicable to the conviction shall be the longer or the longest (as the case may be) of those periods.

(3)   Without prejudice to subsection (2) above, where in respect of a conviction a person was conditionally discharged *or [a probation order was made]* and after the end of the rehabilitation period applicable to the conviction in accordance with subsection (1) or (2) above he is dealt with, in consequence of a breach of conditional discharge *[or a breach of the order]*, for the offence for which the order for conditional discharge *or probation order* was made, then, if the rehabilitation period applicable to the conviction in accordance with subsection (2) above (taking into account any sentence imposed when he is so dealt with) ends later than the rehabilitation period previously applicable to the conviction, he shall be treated for the purposes of this Act as not having become a rehabilitated person in respect of that conviction, and the conviction shall for those purposes be treated as not having become spent, in relation to any period falling before the end of the new rehabilitation period.

[(3A)   Without prejudice to subsection (2), where—

(a)   an order is made under section 1(2A) of the Street Offences Act 1959 in respect of a conviction,

(b)   after the end of the rehabilitation period applicable to the conviction the offender is dealt with again for the offence for which that order was made, and

(c)    the rehabilitation period applicable to the conviction in accordance with subsection (2) (taking into account any sentence imposed when so dealing with the offender) ends later than the rehabilitation period previously applicable to the conviction,

the offender shall be treated for the purposes of this Act as not having become a rehabilitated person in respect of that conviction, and that conviction shall for those purposes be treated as not having become spent, in relation to any period falling before the end of the new rehabilitation period.]

(4)    Subject to subsection (5) below, where during the rehabilitation period applicable to a conviction—

(a)    the person convicted is convicted of a further offence; and

(b)    no sentence excluded from rehabilitation under this Act is imposed on him in respect of the later conviction;

if the rehabilitation period applicable in accordance with this section to either of the convictions would end earlier than the period so applicable in relation to the other, the rehabilitation period which would (apart from this subsection) end the earlier shall be extended so as to end at the same time as the other rehabilitation period.

(5)    Where the rehabilitation period applicable to a conviction is the rehabilitation period applicable *in accordance with section 5(8) above* to an order imposing on a person any disqualification, disability, prohibition or other penalty, the rehabilitation period applicable to another conviction shall not by virtue of subsection (4) above be extended by reference to that period; but if any other sentence is imposed in respect of the first-mentioned conviction for which a rehabilitation period is prescribed by any other provision of section 5 above, the rehabilitation period applicable to another conviction shall, where appropriate, be extended under subsection (4) above by reference to the rehabilitation period applicable in accordance with that section to that sentence or, where more than one such sentence is imposed, by reference to the longer or longest of the periods so applicable to those sentences, as if the period in question were the rehabilitation period applicable to the first-mentioned conviction.

(6)    . . . , *for the purposes of subsection (4)(a) above there shall be disregarded—*

(a)    *any conviction in England and Wales of [a summary offence or of a scheduled offence (within the meaning of [section 22 of the Magistrates' Courts Act 1980] tried summarily in pursuance of subsection (2) of that section (summary trial where value involved is small),] [or of an offence under section 17 of the Crime (Sentences) Act 1997 (breach of conditions of release supervision order);]*

(b)    *any conviction in Scotland of an offence which is not excluded from the jurisdiction of inferior courts of summary jurisdiction by virtue of section 4 of the Summary Jurisdiction (Scotland) Act 1954 (certain crimes not to be tried in inferior courts of summary jurisdiction);*

[(bb) *any conviction in service disciplinary proceedings for an offence listed in [Schedule 1] to this Act;] and*

(c)    *any conviction by or before a court outside Great Britain of an offence in respect of conduct which, if it had taken place in any part of Great Britain, would not have constituted an offence under the law in force in that part of Great Britain.*

(7)    . . .

**NOTES**

Sub-s (3): words in square brackets substituted by the Criminal Justice and Court Services Act 2000, s 74, Sch 7, Pt II, paras 48, 50; words in italics repealed, in relation to Scotland, by the Criminal Justice and Licensing (Scotland) Act 2010, s 1(2), Sch 2, Pt 2, para 32(1), (3), as from 1 February 2011 (see also SSI 2010/413, art 3 which provides that these amendments are of no effect in relation to an offence committed before that date or in relation to any probation order, supervised attendance order or community service order made under the Criminal Procedure (Scotland) Act 1995).

Sub-s (3A): inserted by the Policing and Crime Act 2009, s 18(1), (3), as from 1 April 2010 (note that the coming into force of s 18 of the 2009 Act is of no effect in relation to any person as regards an offence committed by that person contrary to the Street Offences Act 1959, s 1 (loitering or soliciting for purposes of prostitution) during a period which falls wholly or partly before that date (see SI 2010/507, art 6)).

Sub-s (5): for the words in italics there are substituted the words "by virtue of paragraph (g) of the definition of "relevant order" in section 5(8) above" in relation to England and Wales, by the Legal Aid, Sentencing and Punishment of Offenders Act 2012, s 139(1), (5)(a), subject to transitional provisions in s 141(1)–(6), (11), (12) thereof, as noted in the "Transitional Provisions" note to s 5 of this Act at [**1.89**], as from a day to be appointed.

Sub-s (6): words omitted repealed, and para (bb) inserted, by the Armed Forces Act 1996, ss 13(1), (3)(a), (b), 35(2), Sch 7, Pt III; words in first (outer) pair of square brackets in para (a) substituted by the Criminal Law Act 1977, s 65(4), Sch 12, words in second (inner) square brackets in para (a) substituted by the Magistrates' Courts Act 1980, s 154, Sch 7, para 134, words in final pair of square brackets in that paragraph inserted by the Crime (Sentences) Act 1997, s 55, Sch 4, para 9(2); words in square brackets in para (bb) substituted by the Criminal Justice and Immigration Act 2008, s 49, Sch 10, paras 1, 2, as from 19 December 2008 (in relation to England and Wales), and by the Criminal Justice and Licensing (Scotland) Act 2010, s 203, Sch 7, paras 7, 9, as from 1 November 2011 (in relation to Scotland); subsection repealed (in relation to England and Wales) by the Legal Aid, Sentencing and Punishment of Offenders Act 2012, s 139(1), (5)(b), subject to transitional provisions in s 141(1)–(6), (11), (12) thereof as noted in the "Transitional Provisions" note to s 5 of this Act at [**1.89**].

Sub-s (7): repealed by the Armed Forces Act 1996, s 35(2), Sch 7, Pt III.

Probation orders: see the note to s 5 at [**1.89**].

Summary Jurisdiction (Scotland) Act 1954: repealed by the Criminal Procedure (Scotland) Act 1975, s 461(2), Sch 10, Pt I.

Part 1   Statutes

**[1.91]**

**7   Limitations on rehabilitation under this Act, etc**

(1)   Nothing in section 4(1) above shall affect—

(a)   any right of Her Majesty, by virtue of Her Royal prerogative or otherwise, to grant a free pardon, to quash any conviction or sentence, or to commute any sentence;

(b)   the enforcement by any process or proceedings of any fine or other sum adjudged to be paid by or imposed on a spent conviction;

(c)   the issue of any process for the purpose of proceedings in respect of any breach of a condition or requirement applicable to a sentence imposed in respect of a spent conviction; or

(d)   the operation of any enactment by virtue of which, in consequence of any conviction, a person is subject, otherwise than by way of sentence, to any disqualification, disability, prohibition or other penalty the period of which extends beyond the rehabilitation period applicable in accordance with section 6 above to the conviction.

(2)   Nothing in section 4(1) above shall affect the determination of any issue, or prevent the admission or requirement of any evidence, relating to a person's previous convictions or to circumstances ancillary thereto—

(a)   in any criminal proceedings before a court in *Great Britain* (including any appeal or reference in a criminal matter);

(b)   in any service disciplinary proceedings or in any proceedings on appeal from any service disciplinary proceedings;

[(bb)   in any proceedings under Part 2 of the Sexual Offences Act 2003, or on appeal from any such proceedings;]

[(bc)   in any proceedings on an application under section 2, 4 or 5 of the Protection of Children and Prevention of Sexual Offences (Scotland) Act 2005 (asp 9) or in any appeal under section 6 of that Act;]

[(c)   in any proceedings relating to adoption, the marriage of any minor, [or the formation of a civil partnership by any minor,] the exercise of the inherent jurisdiction of the High Court with respect to minors or the provision by any person of accommodation, care or schooling for minors;

(cc)   in any proceedings brought under the Children Act 1989;]

[(d)   in any proceedings relating to the variation or discharge of a youth rehabilitation order under Part 1 of the Criminal Justice and Immigration Act 2008, or on appeal from any such proceedings;]

(e)   . . .

(f)   in any proceedings in which he is a party or a witness, provided that, on the occasion when the issue or the admission or requirement of the evidence falls to be determined, he consents to the determination of the issue or, as the case may be, the admission or requirement of the evidence notwithstanding the provisions of section 4(1); [ . . .

(g)   . . . ] [or

(h)   in any proceedings brought under Part 7 of the Coroners and Justice Act 2009 (criminal memoirs etc).]

(3)   If at any stage in any proceedings before a judicial authority in *Great Britain* (not being proceedings to which, by virtue of any of paragraphs (a) to (e) of subsection (2) above or of any order for the time being in force under subsection (4) below, section 4(1) above has no application, or proceedings to which section 8 below applies) the authority is satisfied, in the light of any considerations which appear to it to be relevant (including any evidence which has been or may thereafter be put before it), that justice cannot be done in the case except by admitting or requiring evidence relating to a person's spent convictions or to circumstances ancillary thereto, that authority may admit or, as the case may be, require the evidence in question notwithstanding the provisions of subsection (1) of section 4 above, and may determine any issue to which the evidence relates in disregard, so far as necessary, of those provisions.

(4)   The Secretary of State may by order exclude the application of section 4(1) above in relation to any proceedings specified in the order (other than proceedings to which section 8 below applies) to such extent and for such purposes as may be so specified.

(5)   No order made by a court with respect to any person otherwise than on a conviction shall be included in any list or statement of that person's previous convictions given or made to any court which is considering how to deal with him in respect of any offence.

**NOTES**

Sub-s (2) is amended as follows:

For the words in italics in para (a) there are substituted the words "England and Wales" in relation to England and Wales, and the word "Scotland" is substituted in relation to Scotland, by the Legal Aid, Sentencing and Punishment of Offenders Act 2012, s 141(10), Sch 25, Pt 1, paras 1, 6(1), (2), 12, 16(1), (2), as from a day to be appointed.

Para (bb) inserted by the Crime and Disorder Act 1998, s 119, Sch 8, para 36, and substituted by the Sexual Offences Act 2003, s 139, Sch 6, para 19.

Para (bc) inserted, in relation to Scotland, by the Criminal Justice and Licensing (Scotland) Act 2010, s 104, as from 13 December 2010.

Paras (c), (cc) substituted, for the original para (c), in relation to England and Wales only, by the Children Act 1989, s 108(5), Sch 13, para 35(1), (2); words in square brackets in para (c) inserted by the Civil Partnership Act 2004, s 261(1), Sch 27, para 53.

Para (c) also substituted, in relation to Scotland only, by the Children (Scotland) Act 1995, s 105(4), Sch 4, para 23(1), (4)(a), as follows—

"(c)    in any proceedings relating to parental responsibilities or parental rights (within the meaning of section 1(3) and section 2(4) respectively of the Children (Scotland) Act 1995), guardianship, adoption or the provision by any person of accommodation, care or schooling for children under the age of 18 years;

(cc)    in any proceedings under Part II of the Children (Scotland) Act 1995;".

Para (d) substituted by the Criminal Justice and Immigration Act 2008, s 6(2), Sch 4, Pt 1, paras 20, 22, as from 30 November 2009 (subject to savings in relation to (i) any offence committed before the amendment comes into force, and (ii) any failure to comply with an order made in respect of an offence committed before that date: see Sch 27 to the 2008 Act).

Para (e) and final words omitted repealed by the Children (Scotland) Act 1995, s 105(4), (5), Sch 4, para 23(1), (4)(b), (c), Sch 5.

Para (g) repealed by the Banking Act 1987, s 108(2), Sch 7, Pt I.

Para (h) and the word immediately preceding it inserted, in relation to England and Wales, by the Coroners and Justice Act 2009, s 158(1), as from 6 April 2010.

Sub-s (3): for the words in italics there are substituted the words "England and Wales" in relation to England and Wales, and the word "Scotland" is substituted in relation to Scotland, by the Legal Aid, Sentencing and Punishment of Offenders Act 2012, s 141(10), Sch 25, Pt 1, paras 1, 6(1), (3), 12, 16(1), (3), as from a day to be appointed.

Secretary of State: the functions conferred by sub-s (4) are, in so far as exercisable in relation to Scotland, transferred to the Scottish Ministers, by the Scotland Act 1998 (Transfer of Functions to the Scottish Ministers etc) Order 2003, SI 2003/415, art 2.

Orders: the Rehabilitation of Offenders Act 1974 (Exceptions) Order 1975, SI 1975/1023 at **[2.15]**; the Rehabilitation of Offenders Act 1974 (Exclusions and Exceptions) (Scotland) Order 2013, SSI 2013/50 at **[2.1679]**. Note that many Orders have been made under this section that amend the 1975 Order (which applies to England and Wales); these are not listed here for reasons of space.

---

**8**   *((Defamation actions) outside the scope of this work.)*

**[1.92]**
**[8A   Protection afforded to spent cautions**
(1)    Schedule 2 to this Act (protection for spent cautions) shall have effect.
(2)    In this Act "caution" means—
  (a)    a conditional caution, that is to say, a caution given under section 22 of the Criminal Justice Act 2003 (c 44) (conditional cautions for adults) or under section 66A of the Crime and Disorder Act 1998 (c 37) (conditional cautions for children and young persons);
  (b)    any other caution given to a person in England and Wales in respect of an offence which, at the time the caution is given, that person has admitted;
  (c)    *a reprimand or warning given under section 65 of the Crime and Disorder Act 1998 (reprimands and warnings for persons aged under 18);*
  (d)    anything corresponding to a caution, *reprimand or warning* falling within *paragraphs (a) to (c)* (however described) which is given to a person in respect of an offence under the law of a country outside England and Wales [and which is not an alternative to prosecution (within the meaning of section 8AA)].]

---

**NOTES**
Commencement: 19 December 2008.
Inserted, in relation to England and Wales only, by the Criminal Justice and Immigration Act 2008, s 49, Sch 10, paras 1, 3, as from 19 December 2008.
Sub-s (2): para (c) repealed, first words in italics in para (d) repealed, for the second words in italics in para (d) there are substituted the words "paragraph (a) or (b)", and words in square brackets in para (d) inserted by the Legal Aid, Sentencing and Punishment of Offenders Act 2012, ss 135(3), 141(10), Sch 24, paras 1, 2, Sch 25, Pt 1, paras 1, 8, as from a day to be appointed and subject to transitional provisions in s 141(1)–(6), (11), (12) thereof as noted in the "Transitional Provisions" note to s 5 of this Act at **[1.89]**.

---

**[1.93]**
**[8AA   Protection afforded to spent alternatives to prosecution**
(1)    The following provisions of this Act apply, with the modifications specified in subsection (3), to a spent alternative to prosecution as they apply to a spent caution—
  (a)    section 9A (unauthorised disclosure of spent cautions), and
  (b)    paragraphs 2 to 6 of Schedule 2 (protection relating to spent cautions and ancillary circumstances).
(2)    An alternative to prosecution becomes spent for the purposes of this Act when it becomes spent under the law of Scotland.
(3)    The modifications mentioned in subsection (1) are—
  (a)    references to cautions are to be read as references to alternatives to prosecution (and references to cautioned are to be read accordingly),

(b)    references to the offence which was the subject of the caution are to be read as references to the offence in respect of which the alternative to prosecution was given,

(c)    paragraphs (e) and (f) of paragraph 2(1) of Schedule 2 are to be read as if they were—

"(e)    anything done or undergone in pursuance of the terms of the alternative to prosecution,",

(d)    references to cautions for an offence are to be read as references to alternatives to prosecution in respect of an offence, and

(e)    the reference in paragraph 5 of Schedule 2 to the rehabilitation period applicable to the caution is to be read as a reference to the time at which the alternative to prosecution becomes spent.

(4)    In this section "alternative to prosecution" has the same meaning as in section 8B as that section has effect in the law of Scotland but disregarding subsection (1)(f) of that section.]

**NOTES**

Commencement: to be appointed.

Inserted in relation to England and Wales, by the Legal Aid, Sentencing and Punishment of Offenders Act 2012, s 139(1), (6), as from a day to be appointed and subject to transitional provisions in s 141(1)–(6), (11), (12) thereof as noted in the "Transitional Provisions" note to s 5 of this Act at **[1.89]**.

**[1.94]**
**[8B    Protection afforded to spent alternatives to prosecution: Scotland**

(1)    For the purposes of this Act, a person has been given an alternative to prosecution in respect of an offence if the person (whether before or after the commencement of this section)—

(a)    has been given a warning in respect of the offence by—
    (i)    a constable in Scotland, or
    (ii)    a procurator fiscal,

(b)    has accepted, or is deemed to have accepted—
    (i)    a conditional offer issued in respect of the offence under section 302 of the Criminal Procedure (Scotland) Act 1995 (c 46), or
    (ii)    a compensation offer issued in respect of the offence under section 302A of that Act,

(c)    has had a work order made against the person in respect of the offence under section 303ZA of that Act,

[(ca)    has, under subsection (5) of section 20A of the Nature Conservation (Scotland) Act 2004 (asp 6), given notice of intention to comply with a restoration notice given under subsection (4) of that section,]]

(d)    has been given a fixed penalty notice in respect of the offence under section 129 of the Antisocial Behaviour etc (Scotland) Act 2004 (asp 8),

(e)    has accepted an offer made by a procurator fiscal in respect of the offence to undertake an activity or treatment or to receive services or do any other thing as an alternative to prosecution, or

(f)    in respect of an offence under the law of a country or territory outside Scotland, has been given, or has accepted or is deemed to have accepted, anything corresponding to a warning, offer, order or notice falling within paragraphs (a) to (e) under the law of that country or territory.

[(1A)    For the purposes of this Act, a person has also been given an alternative to prosecution in respect of an offence if (whether before or after the commencement of this section) in proceedings before a children's hearing to which subsection (1B) applies—

(a)    a compulsory supervision order (as defined in section 83 of the 2011 Act) has been made or, as the case may be, varied or continued in relation to the person, or

(b)    the referral to the children's hearing has been discharged (whether wholly or in relation to the ground that the person committed the offence).

(1B)    This subsection applies to proceedings if the proceedings were taken in relation to the person on the ground (whether alone or with other grounds) that the person had committed the offence and—

(a)    the ground was accepted for the purposes of the 2011 Act by—
    (i)    the person, and
    (ii)    any person who was a relevant person as respects those proceedings, or

(b)    the ground was established or treated as established for the purposes of the 2011 Act.

(1C)    In subsections (1A) and (1B)—
    "the 2011 Act" means the Children's Hearings (Scotland) Act 2011,
    "relevant person"—
        (a)    has the meaning given by section 200 of the 2011 Act, and
        (b)    includes a person who was deemed to be a relevant person by virtue of section 81(3), 160(4)(b) or 164(6) of that Act.

(1D)    For the purposes of this Act, a person has also been given an alternative to prosecution in respect of an offence if (whether before or after the commencement of this section) in proceedings before a children's hearing to which subsection (1E) applies—

(a)    a supervision requirement has been made or, as the case may be, varied or continued under the Children (Scotland) Act 1995 ("the 1995 Act") in relation to the person, or

(b)    the referral to the children's hearing has been discharged (whether wholly or in relation to the ground that the person committed the offence).

(1E)    This subsection applies to proceedings if the proceedings were taken in relation to the person on the ground (whether alone or with other grounds) that the person had committed the offence and—

(a)    the ground was accepted for the purposes of the 1995 Act by the person and, where necessary, the relevant person (as defined in section 93(2) of that Act), or

(b)    the ground was established, or deemed to have been established, for the purposes of that Act.]

(2)    In this Act, references to an "alternative to prosecution" are to be read in accordance with *subsection (1)*.

(3)    Schedule 3 to this Act (protection for spent alternatives to prosecution: Scotland) has effect.]

**NOTES**

Commencement: 1 November 2011

Inserted by the Criminal Justice and Licensing (Scotland) Act 2010, s 109(1), (2), as from 1 November 2011.

Sub-s (1): para (ca) inserted by the Wildlife and Natural Environment (Scotland) Act 2011, s 40(2), as from 29 June 2011 (though this amendment was of no effect until this section came into force).

Sub-ss (1A)–(1E): inserted by the Children's Hearings (Scotland) Act 2011, s 187(1), (2)(a), as from a day to be appointed.

Sub-s (2): for the words in italics there are substituted the words "subsections (1), (1A) and (1D)" by the Children's Hearings (Scotland) Act 2011, s 187(1), (2)(b), as from a day to be appointed.

**[1.95]**
## 9 Unauthorised disclosure of spent convictions

(1)    In this section—

"official record" means a record kept for the purposes of its functions by any court, police force, Government department, local or other public authority in Great Britain, or a record kept, in Great Britain or elsewhere, for the purposes of any of Her Majesty's forces, being in either case a record containing information about persons convicted of offences; and

"specified information" means information imputing that a named or otherwise identifiable rehabilitated living person has committed or been charged with or prosecuted for or convicted of or sentenced for any offence which is the subject of a spent conviction.

(2)    Subject to the provisions of any order made under subsection (5) below, any person who, in the course of his official duties, has or at any time has had custody of or access to any official record or the information contained therein, shall be guilty of an offence if, knowing or having reasonable cause to suspect that any specified information he has obtained in the course of those duties is specified information, he discloses it, otherwise than in the course of those duties, to another person.

(3)    In any proceedings for an offence under subsection (2) above it shall be a defence for the defendant *(or, in Scotland, the accused person)* to show that the disclosure was made—

(a)    to the rehabilitated person or to another person at the express request of the rehabilitated person; or

(b)    to a person whom he reasonably believed to be the rehabilitated person or to another person at the express request of a person whom he reasonably believed to be the rehabilitated person.

(4)    Any person who obtains any specified information from any official record by means of any fraud, dishonesty or bribe shall be guilty of an offence.

(5)    The Secretary of State may by order make such provision as appears to him to be appropriate for excepting the disclosure of specified information derived from an official record from the provisions of subsection (2) above in such cases or classes of case as may be specified in the order.

(6)    Any person guilty of an offence under subsection (2) above shall be liable on summary conviction to a fine not exceeding [level 4 on the standard scale].

(7)    Any person guilty of an offence under subsection (4) above shall be liable on summary conviction to a fine not exceeding [level 5 on the standard scale] or to imprisonment for a term not exceeding six months, or to both.

(8)    *Proceedings for an offence under subsection (2) above shall not, in England and Wales, be instituted except by or on behalf of the Director of Public Prosecutions.*

**NOTES**

Sub-s (3): words "(or, in Scotland, the accused person)" in italics repealed, in relation to England and Wales, by the Legal Aid, Sentencing and Punishment of Offenders Act 2012, s 141(10), Sch 25, Pt 1, paras 1, 9(1), (2), as from a day to be appointed and subject to transitional provisions in s 141(1)–(6), (11), (12) thereof as noted in the "Transitional Provisions" note to s 5 of this Act at **[1.89]**.

As it applies in relation to Scotland, sub-s (3) is set out below, and for the words "defendant (or, in Scotland, the accused person)" in italics there are substituted the words "accused person", in relation to Scotland, by the Legal Aid, Sentencing and Punishment of Offenders Act 2012, s 141(10), Sch 25, Pt 1, paras 12, 17(1), (2), as from a day to be appointed:

"(3) In any proceedings for an offence under subsection (2) above it shall be a defence for the *defendant (or, in Scotland, the accused person)* to show that the disclosure was made—
(a) to the rehabilitated person or to another person at the express request of the rehabilitated person; or
(b) to a person whom he reasonably believed to be the rehabilitated person or to another person at the express request of a person whom he reasonably believed to be the rehabilitated person.".

Sub-ss (6), (7): maximum fines increased and converted to levels on the standard scale by the Criminal Justice Act 1982, ss 37, 38, 46.

Sub-s (8): the words ", in England and Wales," in italics are repealed, in relation to England and Wales, by the Legal Aid, Sentencing and Punishment of Offenders Act 2012, s 141(10), Sch 25, Pt 1, paras 1, 9(1), (3), as from a day to be appointed and subject to transitional provisions in s 141(1)–(6), (11), (12) thereof as noted in the "Transitional Provisions" note to s 5 of this Act at **[1.89]**. In relation to Scotland, the whole of sub-s (8) is repealed by the Legal Aid, Sentencing and Punishment of Offenders Act 2012, s 141(10), Sch 25, Pt 1, paras 12, 17(1), (3), as from a day to be appointed.

Orders: as of 6 April 2013 no Orders had been made under this section.

---

**[1.96]**
**[9A Unauthorised disclosure of spent cautions**
(1) In this section—
(a) "official record" means a record which—
(i) contains information about persons given a caution for any offence or offences; and
(ii) is kept for the purposes of its functions by any court, police force, Government department or other public authority in England and Wales;
(b) "caution information" means information imputing that a named or otherwise identifiable living person ("the named person") has committed, been charged with or prosecuted or cautioned for any offence which is the subject of a spent caution; and
(c) "relevant person" means any person who, in the course of his official duties (anywhere in the United Kingdom), has or at any time has had custody of or access to any official record or the information contained in it.
(2) Subject to the terms of any order made under subsection (5), a relevant person shall be guilty of an offence if, knowing or having reasonable cause to suspect that any caution information he has obtained in the course of his official duties is caution information, he discloses it, otherwise than in the course of those duties, to another person.
(3) In any proceedings for an offence under subsection (2) it shall be a defence for the defendant to show that the disclosure was made—
(a) to the named person or to another person at the express request of the named person;
(b) to a person whom he reasonably believed to be the named person or to another person at the express request of a person whom he reasonably believed to be the named person.
(4) Any person who obtains any caution information from any official record by means of any fraud, dishonesty or bribe shall be guilty of an offence.
(5) The Secretary of State may by order make such provision as appears to him to be appropriate for excepting the disclosure of caution information derived from an official record from the provisions of subsection (2) in such cases or classes of case as may be specified in the order.
(6) A person guilty of an offence under subsection (2) is liable on summary conviction to a fine not exceeding level 4 on the standard scale.
(7) A person guilty of an offence under subsection (4) is liable on summary conviction to a fine not exceeding level 5 on the standard scale, or to imprisonment for a term not exceeding 51 weeks, or to both.
(8) Proceedings for an offence under subsection (2) shall not be instituted except by or on behalf of the Director of Public Prosecutions.]

---

**NOTES**
Commencement: 19 December 2008.
Inserted, in relation to England and Wales only, by the Criminal Justice and Immigration Act 2008, s 49, Sch 10, paras 1, 4, as from 19 December 2008; for transitional provisions see the note below.
Transitional provisions: Sch 27, Pt 4, para 20 to the Criminal Justice and Immigration Act 2008 provides that in the application of sub-s (7) above to offences committed before the commencement of section 281(5) of the Criminal Justice Act 2003, the reference to 51 weeks is to be read as a reference to 6 months.
Orders: as of 6 April 2013 no Orders had been made under this section.

---

**[1.97]**
**[9B Unauthorised disclosure of spent alternatives to prosecution: Scotland**
(1) In this section—
(a) "official record" means a record that—
(i) contains information about persons given an alternative to prosecution in respect of an offence, and
(ii) is kept for the purposes of its functions by a court, [the Police Service of Scotland or another] police force, Government department, part of the Scottish Administration or other local or public authority in Scotland,

(b)    "relevant information" means information imputing that a named or otherwise identifiable living person has committed, been charged with, prosecuted for or given an alternative to prosecution in respect of an offence which is the subject of an alternative to prosecution which has become spent,

(c)    "subject of the information", in relation to relevant information, means the named or otherwise identifiable living person to whom the information relates.

(2)    Subsection (3) applies to a person who, in the course of the person's official duties (anywhere in the United Kingdom), has or has had custody of or access to an official record or the information contained in an official record.

(3)    The person commits an offence if the person—

(a)    obtains relevant information in the course of the person's official duties,

(b)    knows or has reasonable cause to suspect that the information is relevant information, and

(c)    discloses the information to another person otherwise than in the course of the person's official duties.

(4)    Subsection (3) is subject to the terms of an order under subsection (6).

(5)    In proceedings for an offence under subsection (3), it is a defence for the accused to show that the disclosure was made—

(a)    to the subject of the information or to a person whom the accused reasonably believed to be the subject of the information, or

(b)    to another person at the express request of the subject of the information or of a person whom the accused reasonably believed to be the subject of the information.

(6)    The Scottish Ministers may by order provide for the disclosure of relevant information derived from an official record to be excepted from the provisions of subsection (3) in cases or classes of cases specified in the order.

(7)    A person guilty of an offence under subsection (3) is liable on summary conviction to a fine not exceeding level 4 on the standard scale.

(8)    A person commits an offence if the person obtains relevant information from an official record by means of fraud, dishonesty or bribery.

(9)    A person guilty of an offence under subsection (8) is liable on summary conviction to a fine not exceeding level 5 on the standard scale, or to imprisonment for a term not exceeding 6 months, or to both.]

**NOTES**

Commencement: 1 November 2011.

Inserted by the Criminal Justice and Licensing (Scotland) Act 2010, s 109(1), (3), as from 1 November 2011 (in relation to offences committed on or after that date).

Sub-s (1): words in square brackets in para (a)(ii) inserted by the Police and Fire Reform (Scotland) Act 2012, s 128(1), Sch 7, Pt 1, para 3, as from 1 April 2013.

Orders: as of 6 April 2013 no Orders had been made under this section.

**[1.98]**
**10   Orders**

(1)    Any power of the Secretary of State to make an order under any provision of this Act shall be exercisable by statutory instrument, and an order made under any provision of this Act except section 11 below may be varied or revoked by a subsequent order made under that provision.

[(1A)    Any power of the Secretary of State to make an order under any provision of this Act includes power—

(a)    to make different provision for different purposes, and

(b)    to make incidental, consequential, supplementary, transitional, transitory or saving provision.

(1B)    The power of the Secretary of State to make an order under section 5(6) includes power to make consequential provision which amends or repeals any provision of this Act or any other enactment.]

(2)    No order shall be made by the Secretary of State under any provision of this Act other than section 11 below unless a draft of it has been laid before, and approved by resolution of, each House of Parliament.

**NOTES**

Sub-ss (1A), (1B): inserted, in relation to England and Wales, by the Legal Aid, Sentencing and Punishment of Offenders Act 2012, s 141(10), Sch 25, Pt 1, paras 1, 10, as from a day to be appointed and subject to transitional provisions in s 141(1)–(6), (11), (12) thereof as noted in the "Transitional Provisions" note to s 5 of this Act at **[1.89]**.

Orders: the Rehabilitation of Offenders Act 1974 (Exceptions) (Amendment) (England and Wales) Order 2012, SI 2012/1957.

**[1.99]**
**11   Citation, commencement and extent**

(1)    This Act may be cited as the Rehabilitation of Offenders Act 1974.

(2)    This Act shall come into force on 1st July 1975 or such earlier day as the Secretary of State may by order appoint.

(3)  This Act shall not apply to Northern Ireland.

# SCHEDULES

## [SCHEDULE [1]
### SERVICE DISCIPLINARY CONVICTIONS

*Section 6(4)*

**[1.100]**
*1.  Any conviction for an offence mentioned in this Schedule is a conviction referred to in section 6(6)(bb) of this Act (convictions to be disregarded for the purposes of extending a period of rehabilitation following subsequent conviction).*

### Provisions of the Army Act 1955 and the Air Force Act 1955

*2.  Any offence under any of the provisions of the Army Act 1955 or the Air Force Act 1955 listed in the first column of the following table—*

| Provision | Subject-matter |
|---|---|
| Section 29 | Offences by or in relation to sentries, persons on watch etc. |
| Section 29A | Failure to attend for duty, neglect of duty etc. |
| Section 33 | Insubordinate behaviour. |
| Section 34 | Disobedience to lawful commands. |
| Section 34A | Failure to provide a sample for drug testing. |
| Section 35 | Obstruction of provost officers. |
| Section 36 | Disobedience to standing orders. |
| Section 38 | Absence without leave. |
| Section 39 | Failure to report or apprehend deserters or absentees. |
| Section 42 | Malingering. |
| Section 43 | Drunkenness. |
| Section 43A | Fighting, threatening words etc. |
| Section 44 | Damage to, and loss of, public or service property etc. |
| Section 44A | Damage to, and loss of, Her Majesty's aircraft or aircraft material. |
| Section 44B | Interference etc with equipment, messages or signals. |
| Section 45 | Misapplication and waste of public or service property. |
| Section 46 | Offences relating to issues and decorations. |
| Section 47 | Billeting offences. |
| Section 48 | Offences in relation to requisitioning of vehicles. |
| Section 50 | Inaccurate certification. |
| Section 51 | Low flying. |
| Section 52 | Annoyance by flying. |
| Section 54 | Permitting escape, and unlawful release of prisoners. |
| Section 55 | Resistance to arrest. |
| Section 56 | Escape from confinement. |
| Section 57 | Offences in relation to courts-martial. |
| Section 61 | Making of false statements on enlistment. |
| Section 62 | Making of false documents. |
| Section 63 | Offences against civilian population. |
| Section 69 | Conduct to prejudice of military discipline or air-force discipline. |

*3.  Any offence under section 68 (attempt to commit military offence) or 68A (aiding and abetting etc, and inciting, military offence) of the Army Act 1955 in relation to an offence under any of the provisions of that Act listed in paragraph 2.*

*4.  Any offence under section 68 (attempt to commit air-force offence) or 68A (aiding and abetting etc, and inciting, air-force offence) of the Air Force Act 1955 in relation to an offence under any of the provisions of that Act listed in paragraph 2.*

Provisions of the Naval Discipline Act 1957

**5.** *Any offence under any of the provisions of the Naval Discipline Act 1957 listed in the first column of the following table:—*

| Provision | Subject-matter |
|---|---|
| Section 6 | Offences by or in relation to sentries, persons on watch etc. |
| Section 7 | Failure to attend for duty, neglect of duty etc. |
| Section 11 | Insubordinate behaviour. |
| Section 12 | Disobedience to lawful commands. |
| Section 12A | Failure to provide a sample for drug testing. |
| Section 13 | Fighting, threatening words etc. |
| Section 14 | Obstruction of provost officers. |
| Section 14A | Disobedience to standing orders. |
| Section 17 | Absence without leave etc. |
| Section 18 | Failure to report deserters and absentees. |
| Section 21 | Low flying. |
| Section 22 | Annoyance by flying. |
| Section 25 | Inaccurate certification. |
| Section 27 | Malingering. |
| Section 28 | Drunkenness. |
| Section 29 | Damage to, and loss of, public or service property etc. |
| Section 29A | Damage to, and loss of, Her Majesty's aircraft or aircraft material. |
| Section 29B | Interference etc with equipment, messages or signals. |
| Section 30 | Misapplication and waste of public or service property. |
| Section 31 | Offences relating to issues and decorations. |
| Section 32 | Billeting offences. |
| Section 33 | Offences in relation to the requisitioning of vehicles etc. |
| Section 33A | Permitting escape, and unlawful release of prisoners. |
| Section 33B | Resistance to arrest. |
| Section 33C | Escape from confinement. |
| Section 34A | False statements on entry. |
| Section 35 | Falsification of documents. |
| Section 35A | Offences against civilian population. |
| Section 38 | Offences in relation to courts-martial. |
| Section 39 | Conduct to the prejudice of naval discipline. |

**6.** *Any offence under section 40 (attempt to commit naval offence) or 41 (aiding and abetting etc, and inciting, naval offence) of the Naval Discipline Act 1957 in relation to an offence under any of the provisions of that Act listed in paragraph 5.*

*[Provisions of the Armed Forces Act 2006*

**7.** *Any service offence within the meaning of the Armed Forces Act 2006 except one punishable in the case of an offender aged 18 or over with imprisonment for more than two years.]]*

**NOTES**

Added by the Armed Forces Act 1996, s 13(1), (4), Sch 4.

Numbered as Schedule 1 by the Criminal Justice and Immigration Act 2008, s 49, Sch 10, paras 1, 5, as from 19 December 2008 (in relation to England and Wales), and by the Criminal Justice and Licensing (Scotland) Act 2010, s 203, Sch 7, paras 7, 10, as from 1 November 2011 (in relation to Scotland).

Schedule repealed, in relation to England and Wales, by the Legal Aid, Sentencing and Punishment of Offenders Act 2012, s 141(10), Sch 25, Pt 1, paras 1, 11, as from a day to be appointed and subject to transitional provisions in s 141(1)–(6), (11), (12) thereof as noted in the "Transitional Provisions" note to s 5 of this Act at **[1.89]**.

Para 7: added by the Armed Forces Act 2006, s 378(1), Sch 16, para 66, as from 31 October 2009.

Amendments by the Armed Forces Act 2006: see the note to s 1 at **[1.87]**.

Air Force Act 1955, Army Act 1955, Naval Discipline Act 1957: repealed by the Armed Forces Act 2006, s 378, Sch 17.

**[SCHEDULE 2**
**PROTECTION FOR SPENT CAUTIONS**

*Preliminary*

**[1.101]**
**1.** (1)    For the purposes of this Schedule a caution shall be regarded as a spent caution—
  (a)    in the case of a conditional caution (as defined in section 8A(2)(a)), *at the end of the relevant period for the caution;*
  (b)    in any other case, at the time the caution is given.

(2)    *In sub-paragraph (1)(a) "the relevant period for the caution" means (subject to sub-paragraph (3)) the period of three months from the date on which the conditional caution was given.*

(3)    *If the person concerned is subsequently prosecuted and convicted of the offence in respect of which a conditional caution was given—*
  (a)    *the relevant period for the caution shall end at the same time as the rehabilitation period for the offence; and*
  (b)    *if the conviction occurs after the end of the period mentioned in sub-paragraph (1)(a), the caution shall be treated for the purposes of this Schedule as not having become spent in relation to any period before the end of the rehabilitation period for the offence.*

**2.** (1)    In this Schedule "ancillary circumstances", in relation to a caution, means any circumstances of the following—
  (a)    the offence which was the subject of the caution or the conduct constituting that offence;
  (b)    any process preliminary to the caution (including consideration by any person of how to deal with that offence and the procedure for giving the caution);
  (c)    any proceedings for that offence which take place before the caution is given (including anything which happens after that time for the purpose of bringing the proceedings to an end);
  (d)    any judicial review proceedings relating to the caution;
  (e)    in the case of a *warning under section 65* of the Crime and Disorder Act 1998 (c 37), anything done in pursuance of or undergone in compliance with a requirement to participate in a rehabilitation programme under section *66(2)* of that Act;
  (f)    in the case of a conditional caution, any conditions attached to the caution or anything done in pursuance of or undergone in compliance with those conditions.

(2)    Where the caution relates to two or more offences, references in sub-paragraph (1) to the offence which was the subject of the caution include a reference to each of the offences concerned.

(3)    In this Schedule "proceedings before a judicial authority" has the same meaning as in section 4.

*Protection relating to spent cautions and ancillary circumstances*

**3.** (1)    A person who is given a caution for an offence shall, from the time the caution is spent, be treated for all purposes in law as a person who has not committed, been charged with or prosecuted for, or been given a caution for the offence; and notwithstanding the provisions of any other enactment or rule of law to the contrary—
  (a)    no evidence shall be admissible in any proceedings before a judicial authority exercising its jurisdiction or functions in England and Wales to prove that any such person has committed, been charged with or prosecuted for, or been given a caution for the offence; and
  (b)    a person shall not, in any such proceedings, be asked and, if asked, shall not be required to answer, any question relating to his past which cannot be answered without acknowledging or referring to a spent caution or any ancillary circumstances.

(2)    Nothing in sub-paragraph (1) applies in relation to any proceedings for the offence which are not part of the ancillary circumstances relating to the caution.

(3)    Where a question seeking information with respect to a person's previous cautions, offences, conduct or circumstances is put to him or to any other person otherwise than in proceedings before a judicial authority—
  (a)    the question shall be treated as not relating to spent cautions or to any ancillary circumstances, and the answer may be framed accordingly; and
  (b)    the person questioned shall not be subjected to any liability or otherwise prejudiced in law by reason of any failure to acknowledge or disclose a spent caution or any ancillary circumstances in his answer to the question.

(4)    Any obligation imposed on any person by any rule of law or by the provisions of any agreement or arrangement to disclose any matters to any other person shall not extend to requiring him to disclose a spent caution or any ancillary circumstances (whether the caution is his own or another's).

(5)   A caution which has become spent or any ancillary circumstances, or any failure to disclose such a caution or any such circumstances, shall not be a proper ground for dismissing or excluding a person from any office, profession, occupation or employment, or for prejudicing him in any way in any occupation or employment.

(6)   This paragraph has effect subject to paragraphs 4 to 6.

**4.** The Secretary of State may by order—
(a)   make provision for excluding or modifying the application of either or both of paragraphs (a) or (b) of paragraph 3(3) in relation to questions put in such circumstances as may be specified in the order;
(b)   provide for exceptions from the provisions of sub-paragraphs (4) and (5) of paragraph 3, in such cases or classes of case, and in relation to cautions of such a description, as may be specified in the order.

**5.** Nothing in paragraph 3 affects—
(a)   the operation of the caution in question; or
(b)   the operation of any enactment by virtue of which, in consequence of any caution, a person is subject to any disqualification, disability, prohibition or other restriction or effect, the period of which extends beyond the rehabilitation period applicable to the caution.

**6.** (1)   Section 7(2), (3) and (4) apply for the purposes of this Schedule as follows.

(2)   Subsection (2) (apart from paragraphs (b) and (d)) applies to the determination of any issue, and the admission or requirement of any evidence, relating to a person's previous cautions or to ancillary circumstances as it applies to matters relating to a person's previous convictions and circumstances ancillary thereto.

(3)   Subsection (3) applies to evidence of a person's previous cautions and ancillary circumstances as it applies to evidence of a person's convictions and the circumstances ancillary thereto; and for this purpose subsection (3) shall have effect as if—
(a)   any reference to subsection (2) or (4) of section 7 were a reference to that subsection as applied by this paragraph; and
(b)   the words "or proceedings to which section 8 below applies" were omitted.

(4)   Subsection (4) applies for the purpose of excluding the application of paragraph 3(1); and for that purpose subsection (4) shall have effect as if the words " (other than proceedings to which section 8 below applies)" were omitted.

(5)   References in the provisions applied by this paragraph to section 4(1) are to be read as references to paragraph 3(1).]

**NOTES**

Commencement: 19 December 2008.

Inserted, in relation to England and Wales only, by the Criminal Justice and Immigration Act 2008, s 49, Sch 10, paras 1, 6, as from 19 December 2008.

Para 1 is amended as follows:

in sub-para (1)(a), for the words in italics there are substituted the following words, in relation to England and Wales, by the Legal Aid, Sentencing and Punishment of Offenders Act 2012, s 139(1), (7)(a), as from a day to be appointed and subject to transitional provisions in s 141(1)–(6), (11), (12) thereof as noted in the "Transitional Provisions" note to s 5 of this Act at **[1.89]**:

"—
(i)   at the end of the period of three months from the date on which the caution is given, or
(ii)   if earlier, when the caution ceases to have effect; and";

sub-paras (2), (3), repealed, in relation to England and Wales, by the Legal Aid, Sentencing and Punishment of Offenders Act 2012, s 139(1), (7)(b), as from a day to be appointed and subject to transitional provisions in s 141(1)–(6), (11), (12) thereof as noted in the "Transitional Provisions" note to s 5 of this Act at **[1.89]**.

Para 2: in sub-para (1)(e), for the first words in italics there are substituted the words "youth caution given under section 66ZA" and for the number in italics there is substituted "66ZB(2) or (3)", by the Legal Aid, Sentencing and Punishment of Offenders Act 2012, s 135(3), Sch 24, paras 1, 3, as from 8 April 2013.

Orders: Orders made under this Schedule amend the Rehabilitation of Offenders Act 1974 (Exceptions) Order 1975, SI 1975/1023 at **[2.15]**.

**[SCHEDULE 3**
**PROTECTION FOR SPENT ALTERNATIVES TO PROSECUTION: SCOTLAND**
(introduced by section 8B(3))

*Preliminary*

**[1.102]**
**1.** (1)   For the purposes of this Act, an alternative to prosecution given to any person (whether before or after the commencement of this Schedule) becomes spent—
(a)   in the case of—
(i)   a warning referred to in paragraph (a) of subsection (1) of section 8B, or

      (ii)   a fixed penalty notice referred to in paragraph (d) of that subsection,
          at the time the warning or notice is given,
  [(aa)  in the case of—
      (i)    a compulsory supervision order referred to in paragraph (a) of subsection (1A) of
          that section, the period of 3 months beginning on the day the compulsory supervision
          order is made or, as the case may be, varied or continued, or
      (ii)   a discharge referred to in paragraph (b) of subsection (1A) of that section, the period
          of 3 months beginning on the day of the discharge,
  (ab)  in the case of—
      (i)    a supervision requirement referred to in paragraph (a) of subsection (1D) of that
          section, the period of 3 months beginning on the day the supervision requirement is
          made or, as the case may be, varied or continued, or
      (ii)   a discharge referred to in paragraph (b) of subsection (1D) of that section, the period
          of 3 months beginning on the day of the discharge,]
  (b)   in any other case, at the end of the relevant period.

(2)   The relevant period in relation to an alternative to prosecution is the period of 3 months beginning on the day on which the alternative to prosecution is given.

(3)   Sub-paragraph (1)(a) is subject to sub-paragraph (5).

(4)   Sub-paragraph (2) is subject to sub-paragraph (6).

(5)   If a person who is given a fixed penalty notice referred to in section 8B(1)(d) in respect of an offence is subsequently prosecuted and convicted of the offence, the notice—
  (a)   becomes spent at the end of the rehabilitation period for the offence, and
  (b)   is to be treated as not having become spent in relation to any period before the end of that
       rehabilitation period.

(6)   If a person who is given an alternative to prosecution (other than one to which sub-paragraph (1)(a) applies) in respect of an offence is subsequently prosecuted and convicted of the offence—
  (a)   the relevant period in relation to the alternative to prosecution ends at the same time as the
       rehabilitation period for the offence ends, and
  (b)   if the conviction occurs after the end of the period referred to in sub-paragraph (2), the
       alternative to prosecution is to be treated as not having become spent in relation to any
       period before the end of the rehabilitation period for the offence.

**2.** (1)   In this Schedule, "ancillary circumstances", in relation to an alternative to prosecution, means any circumstances of the following—
  (a)   the offence in respect of which the alternative to prosecution is given or the conduct
       constituting the offence,
  (b)   any process preliminary to the alternative to prosecution being given (including
       consideration by any person of how to deal with the offence and the procedure for giving
       the alternative to prosecution),
  (c)   any proceedings for the offence which took place before the alternative to prosecution was
       given (including anything that happens after that time for the purpose of bringing the
       proceedings to an end),
  (d)   any judicial review proceedings relating to the alternative to prosecution,
  (e)   anything done or undergone in pursuance of the terms of the alternative to prosecution.

(2)   Where an alternative to prosecution is given in respect of two or more offences, references in sub-paragraph (1) to the offence in respect of which the alternative to prosecution is given includes a reference to each of the offences.

(3)   In this Schedule, "proceedings before a judicial authority" has the same meaning as in section 4.

*Protection for spent alternatives to prosecution and ancillary circumstances*

**3.** (1)   A person who is given an alternative to prosecution in respect of an offence is, from the time the alternative to prosecution becomes spent, to be treated for all purposes in law as a person who has not committed, been charged with or prosecuted for, or been given an alternative to prosecution in respect of, the offence.

(2)   Despite any enactment or rule of law to the contrary—
  (a)   where an alternative to prosecution given to a person in respect of an offence has become
       spent, evidence is not admissible in any proceedings before a judicial authority exercising
       its jurisdiction or functions in Scotland to prove that the person has committed, been
       charged with or prosecuted for, or been given an alternative to prosecution in respect of,
       the offence,
  (b)   a person must not, in any such proceedings, be asked any question relating to the
       person's past which cannot be answered without acknowledging or referring to an
       alternative to prosecution that has become spent or any ancillary circumstances, and

    (c)    if a person is asked such a question in any such proceedings, the person is not required to answer it.

(3)   Sub-paragraphs (1) and (2) do not apply in relation to any proceedings—

    (a)   for the offence in respect of which the alternative to prosecution was given, and

    (b)   which are not part of the ancillary circumstances.

**4.** (1)   This paragraph applies where a person ("A") is asked a question, otherwise than in proceedings before a judicial authority, seeking information about—

    (a)   A's or another person's previous conduct or circumstances,

    (b)   offences previously committed by A or the other person, or

    (c)   alternatives to prosecution previously given to A or the other person.

(2)   The question is to be treated as not relating to alternatives to prosecution that have become spent or to any ancillary circumstances and may be answered accordingly.

(3)   A is not to be subjected to any liability or otherwise prejudiced in law because of a failure to acknowledge or disclose an alternative to prosecution that has become spent or any ancillary circumstances in answering the question.

**5.** (1)   An obligation imposed on a person ("A") by a rule of law or by the provisions of an agreement or arrangement to disclose any matter to another person does not extend to requiring A to disclose an alternative to prosecution (whether one given to A or another person) that has become spent or any ancillary circumstances.

(2)   An alternative to prosecution that has become spent or any ancillary circumstances, or any failure to disclose an alternative to prosecution that has become spent or any ancillary circumstances, is not a ground for dismissing or excluding a person from any office, profession, occupation or employment, or for prejudicing the person in any way in any occupation or employment.

**6.**   The Scottish Ministers may by order—

    (a)   exclude or modify the application of either or both of sub-paragraphs (2) and (3) of paragraph 4 in relation to questions put in such circumstances as may be specified in the order,

    (b)   provide for exceptions from any of the provisions of paragraph 5 in such cases or classes of case, or in relation to alternatives to prosecution of such descriptions, as may be specified in the order

**7.**   Paragraphs 3 to 5 do not affect—

    (a)   the operation of an alternative to prosecution, or

    (b)   the operation of an enactment by virtue of which, because of an alternative to prosecution, a person is subject to a disqualification, disability, prohibition or other restriction or effect for a period extending beyond the time at which the alternative to prosecution becomes spent

**8.** (1)   Section 7(2), (3) and (4) apply for the purpose of this Schedule as follows.

(2)   Subsection (2), apart from paragraphs (b) and (d), applies to the determination of any issue, and the admission or requirement of evidence, relating to alternatives to prosecution previously given to a person and to ancillary circumstances as it applies to matters relating to a person's previous convictions and circumstances ancillary thereto.

(3)   Subsection (3) applies to evidence of alternatives to prosecution previously given to a person and ancillary circumstances as it applies to evidence of a person's previous convictions and the circumstances ancillary thereto.

(4)   For that purpose, subsection (3) has effect as if—

    (a)   a reference to subsection (2) or (4) of section 7 were a reference to that subsection as applied by this paragraph, and

    (b)   the words "or proceedings to which section 8 below applies" were omitted.

(5)   Subsection (4) applies for the purpose of excluding the application of paragraph 3.

(6)   For that purpose, subsection (4) has effect as if the words "(other than proceedings to which section 8 below applies)" were omitted.

(7)   References in the provisions applied by this paragraph to section 4(1) are to be read as references to paragraph 3.]

**NOTES**

  Commencement: 1 November 2011.

   Inserted by the Criminal Justice and Licensing (Scotland) Act 2010, s 109(1), (4), as from 1 November 2011.

   Para 1; sub-paras (aa), (ab) inserted by the Children's Hearings (Scotland) Act 2011, s 187(1), (3), as from a day to be appointed.

# SEX DISCRIMINATION ACT 1975 (NOTE)

## (1975 c 65)

**[1.103]**

**NOTES**

In so far as this Act was still in force, the vast majority of it was repealed by the Equality Act 2010, s 211(2), Sch 27, Pt 1, as from 1 October 2010 (see Equality Act 2010 (Commencement No 4, Savings, Consequential, Transitional, Transitory and Incidental Provisions and Revocation) Order 2010, SI 2010/2317 at **[2.1558]**). Sections 76A–76C, and s 81 (in so far as relating to those sections) were also repealed by the 2010 Act, as from 5 April 2011 (see the Equality Act 2010 (Commencement No 6) Order, SI 2011/1066). The commencement of the repeal of this Act by the 2010 Act on 1 October 2010 was provided for by SI 2010/2317 as noted above. That Order provides for numerous transitional provisions and savings in connection with the commencement of the 2010 Act and the repeal of this Act. See, in particular, art 15 (saving where the act complained of occurs wholly before 1 October 2010), Schs 1, 2 (savings in relation to shipping matters), Schs 3, 4 (savings in relation to work on ships, hovercraft and in relation to seafarers), and Schs 5, 6 (savings in relation to existing insurance policies).

Employment Appeal Tribunal: an appeal lies to the Employment Appeal Tribunal on any question of law arising from any decision of, or in any proceedings before, an employment tribunal under or by virtue of this Act; see the Employment Tribunals Act 1996, s 21(1)(b) at **[1.713]** (repealed as from 1 October 2010, but see the savings note above).

# RACE RELATIONS ACT 1976 (NOTE)

## (1976 c 74)

**[1.104]**

**NOTES**

In so far as this Act was still in force, the vast majority of it was repealed by the Equality Act 2010, s 211(2), Sch 27, Pt 1, as from 1 October 2010 (see Equality Act 2010 (Commencement No 4, Savings, Consequential, Transitional, Transitory and Incidental Provisions and Revocation) Order 2010, SI 2010/2317 at **[2.1558]**). Sections 71, 71A, 71B and Sch 1A were also repealed by the 2010 Act, as from 5 April 2011 (see the Equality Act 2010 (Commencement No 6) Order, SI 2011/1066). The commencement of the repeal of this Act by the 2010 Act on 1 October 2010 was provided for by SI 2010/2317 as noted above. That Order provides for numerous transitional provisions and savings in connection with the commencement of the 2010 Act and the repeal of this Act. See, in particular, art 15 (saving where the act complained of occurs wholly before 1 October 2010), Schs 1, 2 (savings in relation to shipping matters), Schs 3, 4 (savings in relation to work on ships, hovercraft and in relation to seafarers), and Schs 5, 6 (savings in relation to existing insurance policies).

Employment Appeal Tribunal: an appeal lies to the Employment Appeal Tribunal on any question of law arising from any decision of, or in any proceedings before, an employment tribunal under or by virtue of this Act; see the Employment Tribunals Act 1996, s 21(1)(c) at **[1.713]** (repealed as from 1 October 2010, but see the savings note above).

# PATENTS ACT 1977

## (1977 c 37)

## ARRANGEMENT OF SECTIONS

### PART I
### NEW DOMESTIC LAW

*Employees' inventions*

### PART III
### MISCELLANEOUS AND GENERAL

*Supplemental*

*An Act to establish a new law of patents applicable to future patents and applications for patents; to amend the law of patents applicable to existing patents and applications for patents; to give effect to certain international conventions on patents; and for connected purposes*

[29 July 1977]

**NOTES**

Only those sections of this Act concerned with inventions made by employees are reproduced here, ie ss 39–43 (and s 132 which makes provision as to the extent, etc of the Act). For definitions within the Act see s 130 (not reproduced). For reasons of space, the subject matter of sections, etc, not printed is not annotated.

## PART I
## NEW DOMESTIC LAW

*Employees' inventions*

**[1.105]**
**39 Right to employees' inventions**
(1) Notwithstanding anything in any rule of law, an invention made by an employee shall, as between him and his employer, be taken to belong to his employer for the purposes of this Act and all other purposes if—
  (a) it was made in the course of the normal duties of the employee or in the course of duties falling outside his normal duties, but specifically assigned to him, and the circumstances in either case were such that an invention might reasonably be expected to result from the carrying out of his duties; or
  (b) the invention was made in the course of the duties of the employee and, at the time of making the invention, because of the nature of his duties and the particular responsibilities arising from the nature of his duties he had a special obligation to further the interests of the employer's undertaking.
(2) Any other invention made by an employee shall, as between him and his employer, be taken for those purposes to belong to the employee.
[(3) Where by virtue of this section an invention belongs, as between him and his employer, to an employee, nothing done—
  (a) by or on behalf of the employee or any person claiming under him for the purposes of pursuing an application for a patent, or
  (b) by any person for the purpose of performing or working the invention,
shall be taken to infringe any copyright or design right to which, as between him and his employer, his employer is entitled in any model or document relating to the invention.]

**NOTES**

Sub-s (3): added by the Copyright, Designs and Patents Act 1988, s 295, Sch 5, para 11(1).

**[1.106]**
**40 Compensation of employees for certain inventions**
[(1) Where it appears to the court or the comptroller on an application made by an employee within the prescribed period that—
  (a) the employee has made an invention belonging to the employer for which a patent has been granted,
  (b) having regard among other things to the size and nature of the employer's undertaking, the invention or the patent for it (or the combination of both) is of outstanding benefit to the employer, and
  (c) by reason of those facts it is just that the employee should be awarded compensation to be paid by the employer,
the court or the comptroller may award him such compensation of an amount determined under section 41 below.]
(2) Where it appears to the court or the comptroller on an application made by an employee within the prescribed period that—
  (a) a patent has been granted for an invention made by and belonging to the employee;
  (b) his rights in the invention, or in any patent or application for a patent for the invention, have since the appointed day been assigned to the employer or an exclusive licence under the patent or application has since the appointed day been granted to the employer;
  (c) the benefit derived by the employee from the contract of assignment, assignation or grant or any ancillary contract ("the relevant contract") is inadequate in relation to the benefit derived by the employer from [the invention or the patent for it (or both)]; and
  (d) by reason of those facts it is just that the employee should be awarded compensation to be paid by the employer in addition to the benefit derived from the relevant contract;
the court or the comptroller may award him such compensation of an amount determined under section 41 below.

(3)   Subsections (1) and (2) above shall not apply to the invention of an employee where a relevant collective agreement provides for the payment of compensation in respect of inventions of the same description as that invention to employees of the same description as that employee.

(4)   Subsection (2) above shall have effect notwithstanding anything in the relevant contract or any agreement applicable to the invention (other than any such collective agreement).

(5)   If it appears to the comptroller on an application under this section that the application involves matters which would more properly be determined by the court, he may decline to deal with it.

(6)   In this section—

"the prescribed period", in relation to proceedings before the court, means the period prescribed by rules of court, and

"relevant collective agreement" means a collective agreement within the meaning of [the Trade Union and Labour Relations (Consolidation) Act 1992], made by or on behalf of a trade union to which the employee belongs, and by the employer or an employers' association to which the employer belongs which is in force at the time of the making of the invention.

(7)   References in this section to an invention belonging to an employer or employee are references to it so belonging as between the employer and the employee.

**NOTES**

Sub-s (1): substituted by the Patents Act 2004, s 10(1), in relation to an invention the patent for which is applied for on or after 1 January 2005.

Sub-s (2): words in square brackets in para (c) substituted by the Patents Act 2004, s 10(2), in relation to an invention the patent for which is applied for on or after 1 January 2005.

Sub-s (6): words in square brackets substituted by the Trade Union and Labour Relations (Consolidation) Act 1992, s 300(2), Sch 2, para 9.

Rules of court: the Patents Rules 2007, SI 2007/3291 (made under ss 14(6), 25(5), 32, 74B, 77(9), 92, 123, 125A and 130(2) of this Act) replacing, as from 17 December 2007, the Patent Rules 1995, SI 1995/2093 (revoked). See r 91 of the 2007 Rules (period prescribed for applications by employee for compensation for the purposes of sub-ss (1), (2)). See also r 73 of, and Sch 3 to, the 2007 Rules in relation to applications under this section and s 41(8) post.

**[1.107]**
## 41   Amount of compensation

[(1)   An award of compensation to an employee under section 40(1) or (2) above shall be such as will secure for the employee a fair share (having regard to all the circumstances) of the benefit which the employer has derived, or may reasonably be expected to derive, from any of the following—

(a)   the invention in question;

(b)   the patent for the invention;

(c)   the assignment, assignation or grant of—

(i)   the property or any right in the invention, or

(ii)   the property in, or any right in or under, an application for the patent,

to a person connected with the employer.]

(2)   For the purposes of subsection (1) above the amount of any benefit derived or expected to be derived by an employer from the assignment, assignation or grant of—

(a)   the property in, or any right in or under, a patent for the invention or an application for such a patent; or

(b)   the property or any right in the invention;

to a person connected with him shall be taken to be the amount which could reasonably be expected to be so derived by the employer if that person had not been connected with him.

(3)   Where the Crown or a Research Council in its capacity as employer assigns or grants the property in, or any right in or under, an invention, patent or application for a patent to a body having among its functions that of developing or exploiting inventions resulting from public research and does so for no consideration or only a nominal consideration, any benefit derived from the invention, patent or application by that body shall be treated for the purposes of the foregoing provisions of this section as so derived by the Crown or, as the case may be, Research Council.

In this subsection "Research Council" means a body which is a Research Council for the purposes of the Science and Technology Act 1965 [or the Arts and Humanities Research Council (as defined by section 1 of the Higher Education Act 2004)].

(4)   In determining the fair share of the benefit to be secured for an employee in respect of . . . an invention which has always belonged to an employer, the court or the comptroller shall, among other things, take the following matters into account, that is to say—

(a)   the nature of the employee's duties, his remuneration and the other advantages he derives or has derived from his employment or has derived in relation to the invention under this Act;

(b)   the effort and skill which the employee has devoted to making the invention;

(c)   the effort and skill which any other person has devoted to making the invention jointly with the employee concerned, and the advice and other assistance contributed by any other employee who is not a joint inventor of the invention; and

(d) the contribution made by the employer to the making, developing and working of the invention by the provision of advice, facilities and other assistance, by the provision of opportunities and by his managerial and commercial skill and activities.

(5) In determining the fair share of the benefit to be secured for an employee in respect of . . . an invention which originally belonged to him, the court or the comptroller shall, among other things, take the following matters into account, that is to say—

(a) any conditions in a licence or licences granted under this Act or otherwise in respect of the invention or the patent [for it];

(b) the extent to which the invention was made jointly by the employee with any other person; and

(c) the contribution made by the employer to the making, developing and working of the invention as mentioned in subsection (4)(d) above.

(6) Any order for the payment of compensation under section 40 above may be an order for the payment of a lump sum or for periodical payment, or both.

(7) Without prejudice to section 32 of the Interpretation Act 1889 (which provides that a statutory power may in general be exercised from time to time), the refusal of the court or the comptroller to make any such order on an application made by an employee under section 40 above shall not prevent a further application being made under that section by him or any successor in title of his.

(8) Where the court or the comptroller has made any such order, the court or he may on the application of either the employer or the employee vary or discharge it or suspend any provision of the order and revive any provision so suspended, and section 40(5) above shall apply to the application as it applies to an application under that section.

(9) In England and Wales any sums awarded by the comptroller under section 40 above shall, if *a county court* so orders, be recoverable *by execution issued from the county court* or otherwise as if they were payable under an order of that court.

(10) In Scotland an order made under section 40 above by the comptroller for the payment of any sums may be enforced in like manner as [an extract registered decree arbitral bearing a warrant for execution issued by the sheriff court of any sheriffdom in Scotland].

(11) In Northern Ireland an order made under section 40 above by the comptroller for the payment of any sums may be enforced as if it were a money judgment.

**NOTES**

Sub-s (1): substituted by the Patents Act 2004, s 10(3), in relation to an invention the patent for which is applied for on or after 1 January 2005.

Sub-s (3): words in square brackets inserted by the Higher Education Act 2004, s 49, Sch 6, para 5.

Sub-s (4): words omitted repealed by the Patents Act 2004, ss 10(4), 16(2), Sch 3, in relation to an invention the patent for which is applied for on or after 1 January 2005.

Sub-s (5): words omitted repealed, and words in square brackets inserted, by the Patents Act 2004, ss 10(4), (5), 16(2), Sch 3, in relation to an invention the patent for which is applied for on or after 1 January 2005.

Sub-s (9): for the first words in italics there are substituted the words "the county court" by the Crime and Courts Act 2013, s 17(5), Sch 9, Pt 3, para 52, as from a day to be appointed; for the second words in italics there are substituted the words "under section 85 of the County Courts Act 1984" by the Tribunals, Courts and Enforcement Act 2007, s 62(3), Sch 13, paras 39, 40, as from a day to be appointed.

Sub-s (10): words in square brackets substituted by the Patents Act 2004, s 16(1), Sch 2, paras 1(1), 11.

Applications under sub-s (8): see the note "Rules" to s 40 at [**1.106**].

Interpretation Act 1889, s 32: repealed and replaced by the Interpretation Act 1978.

[**1.108**]
**42 Enforceability of contracts relating to employees' inventions**

(1) This section applies to any contract (whenever made) relating to inventions made by an employee, being a contract entered into by him—

(a) with the employer (alone or with another); or

(b) with some other person at the request of the employer or in pursuance of the employee's contract of employment.

(2) Any term in a contract to which this section applies which diminishes the employee's rights in inventions of any description made by him after the appointed day and the date of the contract, or in or under patents for those inventions or applications for such patents, shall be unenforceable against him to the extent that it diminishes his rights in an invention of that description so made, or in or under a patent for such an invention or an application for any such patent.

(3) Subsection (2) above shall not be construed as derogating from any duty of confidentiality owed to his employer by an employee by virtue of any rule of law or otherwise.

(4) This section applies to any arrangement made with a Crown employee by or on behalf of the Crown as his employer as it applies to any contract made between an employee and an employer other than the Crown, and for the purposes of this section "Crown employee" means a person employed under or for the purposes of a government department or any officer or body exercising on behalf of the Crown functions conferred by any enactment [or a person serving in the naval, military or air forces of the Crown].

Part 1 Statutes

**NOTES**
Words in square brackets added with retrospective effect by the Armed Forces Act 1981, s 22(1), (2).

**[1.109]**
## 43 Supplementary
(1)   Sections 39 to 42 above shall not apply to an invention made before the appointed day.
(2)   Sections 39 to 42 above shall not apply to an invention made by an employee unless at the time he made the invention one of the following conditions was satisfied in his case, that is to say—
  (a)   he was mainly employed in the United Kingdom; or
  (b)   he was not mainly employed anywhere or his place of employment could not be determined, but his employer had a place of business in the United Kingdom to which the employee was attached, whether or not he was also attached elsewhere.
(3)   In section 39 to 42 above and this section, except so far as the context otherwise requires, references to the making of an invention by an employee are references to his making it alone or jointly with any other person, but do not include references to his merely contributing advice or other assistance in the making of an invention by another employee.
(4)   Any references [in sections 39 to 42] above to a patent and to a patent being granted are respectively references to a patent or other protection and to its being granted whether under the law of the United Kingdom or the law in force in any other country or under any treaty or international convention.
(5)   For the purposes of sections 40 and 41 above the benefit derived or expected to be derived by an employer from [an invention or patent] shall, where he dies before any award is made under section 40 above in respect of [it], include any benefit derived or expected to be derived from [it] by his personal representatives or by any person in whom it was vested by their assent.
[(5A)   For the purposes of sections 40 and 41 above the benefit derived or expected to be derived by an employer from an invention shall not include any benefit derived or expected to be derived from the invention after the patent for it has expired or has been surrendered or revoked.]
(6)   Where an employee dies before an award is made under section 40 above in respect of a patented invention made by him, his personal representatives or their successors in title may exercise his right to make or proceed with an application for compensation under subsection (1) or (2) of that section.
(7)   In sections 40 and 41 above and this section "benefit" means benefit in money or money's worth.
(8)   Section 533 of the Income and Corporation Taxes Act 1970 (definition of connected persons) shall apply for determining for the purposes of section 41(2) above whether one person is connected with another as it applies for determining that question for the purposes of the Tax Acts.

**NOTES**
Sub-s (4): words in square brackets substituted by the Copyright, Designs and Patents Act 1988, s 295, Sch 5, para 11(2).
Sub-s (5): words in square brackets substituted by the Patents Act 2004, s 10(6), in relation to an invention the patent for which is applied for on or after 1 January 2005.
Sub-s (5A): inserted by the Patents Act 2004, s 10(7), in relation to an invention the patent for which is applied for on or after 1 January 2005.
Income and Corporation Taxes Act 1970: repealed and originally replaced by the Income and Corporation Taxes Act 1988, s 839 (also repealed). See now the Corporation Tax Act 2010, s 1122. There has been no amendment to this section to reflect the change.

# PART III
# MISCELLANEOUS AND GENERAL
### Supplemental

**[1.110]**
## 132 Short title, extent, commencement, consequential amendments and repeals
(1)   This Act may be cited as the Patents Act 1977.
(2)   This Act shall extend to the Isle of Man, subject to any modifications contained in an Order made by Her Majesty in Council, and accordingly, subject to any such order, references in this Act to the United Kingdom shall be construed as including references to the Isle of Man.
(3)   For the purposes of this Act the territorial waters of the United Kingdom shall be treated as part of the United Kingdom.
(4)   This Act applies to acts done in an area designated by order under section 1(7) of the Continental Shelf Act 1964, [or specified by Order under [section 10(8) of the Petroleum Act 1998] in connection with any activity falling within [section 11(2)] of that Act], as it applies to acts done in the United Kingdom.
(5)   This Act (except sections 77(6), (7) and (9), 78(7) and (8), this subsection and the repeal of section 41 of the 1949 Act) shall come into operation on such day as may be appointed by the Secretary of State by order, and different days may be appointed under this subsection for different purposes.

(6), (7)   (*Outside the scope of this work.*)

**NOTES**
Sub-s (4): words in first (outer) pair of square brackets substituted by the Oil and Gas (Enterprise) Act 1982, s 37(1), Sch 3, para 39; words in second and third (inner) pairs of square brackets substituted by the Petroleum Act 1998, s 50, Sch 4, para 14.
Orders: the Patents Act 1977 (Commencement No 1) Order 1977, SI 1977/2090; the Patents Act 1977 (Commencement No 2) Order 1978, SI 1978/586; the Patents Act 1977 (Isle of Man) Order 2003, SI 2003/1249.

# STATE IMMUNITY ACT 1978

## (1978 c 33)

### ARRANGEMENT OF SECTIONS

#### PART I
#### PROCEEDINGS IN UNITED KINGDOM BY OR AGAINST OTHER STATES

*Immunity from jurisdiction*

*An Act to make new provision with respect to proceedings in the United Kingdom by or against other States; to provide for the effect of judgments given against the United Kingdom in the courts of States parties to the European Convention on State Immunity; to make new provision with respect to the immunities and privileges of heads of State; and for connected purposes*

[20 July 1978]

**NOTES**
Only sections of this Act relevant to employment law are reproduced here. For reasons of space, the subject matter of sections not printed is not annotated.
See *Harvey* DI(1)(C), PI(C)(4).

#### PART I
#### PROCEEDINGS IN UNITED KINGDOM BY OR AGAINST OTHER STATES

*Immunity from jurisdiction*

**[1.111]**
**1   General immunity from jurisdiction**
(1)   A State is immune from the jurisdiction of the courts of the United Kingdom except as provided in the following provisions of this Part of this Act.
(2)   A court shall give effect to the immunity conferred by this section even though the State does not appear in the proceedings in question.

*Exceptions from immunity*

**[1.112]**
**2   Submission to jurisdiction**
(1)   A State is not immune as respects proceedings in respect of which it has submitted to the jurisdiction of the courts of the United Kingdom.
(2)   A State may submit after the dispute giving rise to the proceedings has arisen or by a prior written agreement; but a provision in any agreement that it is to be governed by the law of the United Kingdom is not to be regarded as a submission.
(3)   A State is deemed to have submitted—
    (a)   if it has instituted the proceedings; or

(b)   subject to subsections (4) and (5) below, if it has intervened or taken any step in the proceedings.

(4)   Subsection (3)(b) above does not apply to intervention or any step taken for the purpose only of—

(a)   claiming immunity; or

(b)   asserting an interest in property in circumstances such that the State would have been entitled to immunity if the proceedings had been brought against it.

(5)   Subsection (3)(b) above does not apply to any step taken by the State in ignorance of facts entitling it to immunity if those facts could not reasonably have been ascertained and immunity is claimed as soon as reasonably practicable.

(6)   A submission in respect of any proceedings extends to any appeal but not to any counter-claim unless it arises out of the same legal relationship or facts as the claim.

(7)   The head of a State's diplomatic mission in the United Kingdom, or the person for the time being performing his functions, shall be deemed to have authority to submit on behalf of the State in respect of any proceedings; and any person who has entered into a contract on behalf of and with the authority of a State shall be deemed to have authority to submit on its behalf in respect of proceedings arising out of the contract.

**[1.113]**
## 4   Contracts of employment

(1)   A State is not immune as respects proceedings relating to a contract of employment between the State and an individual where the contract was made in the United Kingdom or the work is to be wholly or partly performed there.

(2)   Subject to subsections (3) and (4) below, this section does not apply if—

(a)   at the time when the proceedings are brought the individual is a national of the State concerned; or

(b)   at the time when the contract was made the individual was neither a national of the United Kingdom nor habitually resident there; or

(c)   the parties to the contract have otherwise agreed in writing.

(3)   Where the work is for an office, agency or establishment maintained by the State in the United Kingdom for commercial purposes, subsection (2) (a) and (b) above do not exclude the application of this section unless the individual was, at the time when the contract was made, habitually resident in that State.

(4)   Subsection (2)(c) above does not exclude the application of this section where the law of the United Kingdom requires the proceedings to be brought before a court of the United Kingdom.

(5)   In subsection (2)(b) above "national of the United Kingdom" [means—

(a)   a British citizen, a [British overseas territories citizen][, a British National (Overseas)] or a British Overseas citizen; or

(b)   a person who under the British Nationality Act 1981 is a British subject; or

(c)   a British protected person (within the meaning of that Act)].

(6)   In this section "proceedings relating to a contract of employment" includes proceedings between the parties to such a contract in respect of any statutory rights or duties to which they are entitled or subject as employer or employee.

---

**NOTES**

Sub-s (5): words in first (outer) pair of square brackets substituted by the British Nationality Act 1981, s 52(6), Sch 7; words in second (inner) pair of square brackets substituted by virtue of the British Overseas Territories Act 2002, s 2(3); words in third (inner) pair of square brackets inserted by the Hong Kong (British Nationality) Order 1986, SI 1986/948, art 8, Schedule.

---

*Procedure*

**[1.114]**
## 12   Service of process and judgements in default of appearance

(1)   Any writ or other document required to be served for instituting proceedings against a State shall be served by being transmitted through the Foreign and Commonwealth Office to the Ministry of Foreign Affairs of the State and service shall be deemed to have been effected when the writ or document is received at the Ministry.

(2)   Any time for entering an appearance (whether prescribed by rules of court or otherwise) shall begin to run two months after the date on which the writ or document is received as aforesaid.

(3)   A State which appears in proceedings cannot thereafter object that subsection (1) above has not been complied with in the case of those proceedings.

(4)   No judgment in default of appearance shall be given against a State except on proof that subsection (1) above has been complied with and that the time for entering an appearance as extended by subsection (2) above has expired.

(5)   A copy of any judgment given against a State in default of appearance shall be transmitted through the Foreign and Commonwealth Office to the Ministry of Foreign Affairs of that State and any time for applying to have the judgment set aside (whether prescribed by rules of court or otherwise) shall begin to run two months after the date on which the copy of the judgment is received at the Ministry.

(6)   Subsection (1) above does not prevent the service of a writ or other document in any manner to which the State has agreed and subsections (2) and (4) above do not apply where service is effected in any such manner.

(7)   This section shall not be construed as applying to proceedings against a State by way of counter-claim or to an action in rem; and subsection (1) above shall not be construed as affecting any rules of court whereby leave is required for the service of process outside the jurisdiction.

*Supplementary provisions*

**[1.115]**
**16   Excluded matters**
(1)   This Part of this Act does not affect any immunity or privilege conferred by the Diplomatic Privileges Act 1964 or the Consular Relations Act 1968; and—

(a)   section 4 above does not apply to proceedings concerning the employment of the members of a mission within the meaning of the Convention scheduled to the said Act of 1964 or of the members of a consular post within the meaning of the Convention scheduled to the said Act of 1968;

(b)   section 6(1) above does not apply to proceedings concerning a State's title to or its possession of property used for the purposes of a diplomatic mission.

(2)   This Part of this Act does not apply to proceedings relating to anything done by or in relation to the armed forces of a State while present in the United Kingdom and, in particular, has effect subject to the Visiting Forces Act 1952.

(3)   This Part of this Act does not apply to proceedings to which section 17(6) of the Nuclear Installations Act 1965 applies.

(4)   This Part of this Act does not apply to criminal proceedings.

(5)   This Part of this Act does not apply to any proceedings relating to taxation other than those mentioned in section 11 above.

**[1.116]**
**17   Interpretation of Part I**
(1)   In this Part of this Act—

"the Brussels Convention" means the International Convention for the Unification of Certain Rules Concerning the Immunity of State-owned Ships signed in Brussels on 10th April 1926;

"commercial purposes" means purposes of such transactions or activities as are mentioned in section 3(3) above;

"ship" includes hovercraft.

(2)   In sections 2(2) and 13(3) above references to an agreement include references to a treaty, convention or other international agreement.

(3)   For the purposes of sections 3 to 8 above the territory of the United Kingdom shall be deemed to include any [British overseas territory] in respect of which the United Kingdom is a party to the European Convention on State Immunity.

(4)   In sections 3(1), 4(1), 5 and 16(2) above references to the United Kingdom include references to its territorial waters and any area designated under section 1(7) of the Continental Shelf Act 1964.

(5)   In relation to Scotland in this Part of this Act "action in rem" means such an action only in relation to Admiralty proceedings.

**NOTES**

Sub-s (3): words in square brackets substituted by virtue of the British Overseas Territories Act 2002, s 1(2).
Brussels Convention: the text of the Brussels Convention is set out in Cmd 5672.

**PART III**
**MISCELLANEOUS AND SUPPLEMENTARY**

**[1.117]**
**23   Short title, repeals commencement and extent**
(1)   This Act may be cited as the State Immunity Act 1978.

(2)   . . .

(3)   Subject to subsection (4) below, Parts I and II of this Act do not apply to proceedings in respect of matters that occurred before the date of the coming into force of this Act and, in particular—

(a)   sections 2(2) and 13(3) do not apply to any prior agreement, and

(b)   sections 3, 4 and 9 do not apply to any transaction, contract or arbitration agreement, entered into before that date.

(4)   Section 12 above applies to any proceedings instituted after the coming into force of this Act.

(5)   This Act shall come into force on such date as may be specified by an order made by the Lord Chancellor by statutory instrument.

(6)   This Act extends to Northern Ireland.

(7)   Her Majesty may by Order in Council extend any of the provisions of this Act, with or without modification, to any [British overseas territory].

**NOTES**

Sub-s (2): repeals the Administration of Justice (Miscellaneous Provisions) Act 1938, s 13, and the Law Reform (Miscellaneous Provisions) (Scotland) Act 1940, s 7.

Sub-s (7): words in square brackets substituted by virtue of the British Overseas Territories Act 2002, s 1(2).

Orders: the State Immunity Act 1978 (Commencement) Order 1978, SI 1978/1572 (bringing this Act into force on 22 November 1978); the State Immunity (Overseas Territories) Order 1979, SI 1979/458 (extending the provisions of this Act, with modifications, to the following dependent territories: Belize, British Antarctic Territory, British Virgin Islands, Cayman Islands, Falkland Islands and Dependencies, Gilbert Islands, Hong Kong, Montserrat, Pitcairn, Henderson, Ducie and Oeno Islands, Sovereign Base Areas of Akrotiri and Dhekelia, Turks and Caicos Islands); the State Immunity (Guernsey) Order 1980, SI 1980/871 (extending the provisions of this Act, with exceptions, adaptations and modifications, to the Bailiwick of Guernsey); the State Immunity (Isle of Man) Order 1981, SI 1981/1112 (extending the provisions of this Act, with modifications, to the Isle of Man); the State Immunity (Jersey) Order 1985, SI 1985/1642 (extending the provisions of this Act, with modifications, to the Bailiwick of Jersey). There has been no further Order to remove Hong Kong from the application of SI 1979/458 following its cession in 1997.

# LIMITATION ACT 1980

## (1980 c 58)

### ARRANGEMENT OF SECTIONS

#### PART I
#### ORDINARY TIME LIMITS FOR DIFFERENT CLASSES OF ACTION

*An Act to consolidate the Limitation Acts 1939 to 1980*

[13 November 1980]

**NOTES**

Only certain sections of this Act are relevant to employment law, and accordingly, only those sections of most relevance have been included in this work. For reasons of space, the subject matter of the sections and Schedules omitted is not annotated.

Note that this Act does not extend to Scotland; see s 41(4) at **[1.134]**.

Application to arbitral proceedings: this Act applies to arbitral proceedings as it applies to legal proceedings; see the Arbitration Act 1996, s 13(1). As to the commencement of arbitral proceedings for the purposes of this Act, see ss 12 (in particular sub-s (5)), 13(2), (4), 14 of the 1996 Act, and as to when a cause of action accrued, see s 13(3), (4) of the 1996 Act.

# PART I
## ORDINARY TIME LIMITS FOR DIFFERENT CLASSES OF ACTION

*Time limits under Part I subject to extension or exclusion under Part II*

**[1.118]**
**1   Time limits under Part I subject to extension or exclusion under Part II**
(1)   This Part of this Act gives the ordinary time limits for bringing actions of the various classes mentioned in the following provisions of this Part.
(2)   The ordinary time limits given in this Part of this Act are subject to extension or exclusion in accordance with the provisions of Part II of this Act.

*Actions founded on tort*

**[1.119]**
**2   Time limit for actions founded on tort**
An action founded on tort shall not be brought after the expiration of six years from the date on which the cause of action accrued.

**[1.120]**
**[4A   Time limit for actions for defamation or malicious falsehood**
The time limit under section 2 of this Act shall not apply to an action for—
    (a)   libel or slander, or malicious falsehood.
    (b)   slander of title, slander of goods or other malicious falsehood,
but no such action shall be brought after the expiration of one year from the date on which the cause of action accrued.]

**NOTES**

Inserted by the Administration of Justice Act 1985, s 57(2), and substituted by the Defamation Act 1996, s 5(2), (6)

*Actions founded on simple contract*

**[1.121]**
**5   Time limit for actions founded on simple contract**
An action founded on simple contract shall not be brought after the expiration of six years from the date on which the cause of action accrued.

*Actions for sums recoverable by statute*

**[1.122]**
**9   Time limit for actions for sums recoverable by statute**
(1)   An action to recover any sum recoverable by virtue of any enactment shall not be brought after the expiration of six years from the date on which the cause of action accrued.
(2)   Subsection (1) above shall not affect any action to which section 10 of this Act applies.

**[1.123]**
**10   Special time limit for claiming contribution**
(1)   Where under section 1 of the Civil Liability (Contribution) Act 1978 any person becomes entitled to a right to recover contribution in respect of any damage from any other person, no action to recover contribution by virtue of that right shall be brought after the expiration of two years from the date on which that right accrued.
(2)   For the purposes of this section the date on which a right to recover contribution in respect of any damage accrues to any person (referred to below in this section as "the relevant date") shall be ascertained as provided in subsections (3) and (4) below.
(3)   If the person in question is held liable in respect of that damage—
    (a)   by a judgment given in any civil proceedings; or
    (b)   by an award made on any arbitration;
the relevant date shall be the date on which the judgment is given, or the date of the award (as the case may be).
   For the purposes of this subsection no account shall be taken of any judgment or award given or made on appeal in so far as it varies the amount of damages awarded against the person in question.

(4)   If, in any case not within subsection (3) above, the person in question makes or agrees to make any payment to one or more persons in compensation for that damage (whether he admits any liability in respect of the damage or not), the relevant date shall be the earliest date on which the amount to be paid by him is agreed between him (or his representative) and the person (or each of the persons, as the case may be) to whom the payment is to be made.

(5)   An action to recover contribution shall be one to which sections 28, 32[, 33A] and 35 of this Act apply, but otherwise Parts II and III of this Act (except sections 34, 37 and 38) shall not apply for the purposes of this section.

**NOTES**

Sub-s (5): number in square brackets inserted by the Cross-Border Mediation (EU Directive) Regulations 2011, SI 2011/1133, regs 22, 23, as from 20 May 2011.

*Actions in respect of wrongs causing personal injuries or death*

**[1.124]**
**11   Special time limit for actions in respect of personal injuries**
(1)   This section applies to any action for damages for negligence, nuisance or breach of duty (whether the duty exists by virtue of a contract or of provision made by or under a statute or independently of any contract or any such provision) where the damages claimed by the plaintiff for the negligence, nuisance or breach of duty consist of or include damages in respect of personal injuries to the plaintiff or any other person.

[(1A)   This section does not apply to any action brought for damages under section 3 of the Protection from Harassment Act 1997.]

(2)   None of the time limits given in the preceding provisions of this Act shall apply to an action to which this section applies.

(3)   An action to which this section applies shall not be brought after the expiration of the period applicable in accordance with subsection (4) or (5) below.

(4)   Except where subsection (5) below applies, the period applicable is three years from—
    (a)   the date on which the cause of action accrued; or
    (b)   the date of knowledge (if later) of the person injured.

(5)   If the person injured dies before the expiration of the period mentioned in subsection (4) above, the period applicable as respects the cause of action surviving for the benefit of his estate by virtue of section 1 of the Law Reform (Miscellaneous Provisions) Act 1934 shall be three years from—
    (a)   the date of death; or
    (b)   the date of the personal representative's knowledge;
whichever is the later.

(6)   For the purposes of this section "personal representative" includes any person who is or has been a personal representative of the deceased, including an executor who has not proved the will (whether or not he has renounced probate) but not anyone appointed only as a special personal representative in relation to settled land; and regard shall be had to any knowledge acquired by any such person while a personal representative or previously.

(7)   If there is more than one personal representative, and their dates of knowledge are different, subsection (5)(b) above shall be read as referring to the earliest of those dates.

**NOTES**

Sub-s (1A): inserted by the Protection from Harassment Act 1997, s 6.

**[1.125]**
**14   Definition of date of knowledge for purposes of sections 11 and 12**
(1)   [Subject to subsection (1A) below,] In sections 11 and 12 of this Act references to a person's date of knowledge are references to the date on which he first had knowledge of the following facts—
    (a)   that the injury in question was significant; and
    (b)   that the injury was attributable in whole or in part to the act or omission which is alleged to constitute negligence, nuisance or breach of duty; and
    (c)   the identity of the defendant; and
    (d)   if it is alleged that the act or omission was that of a person other than the defendant, the identity of that person and the additional facts supporting the bringing of an action against the defendant;
and knowledge that any acts or omissions did or did not, as a matter of law, involve negligence, nuisance or breach of duty is irrelevant.

[(1A)   In section 11A of this Act and in section 12 of this Act so far as that section applies to an action by virtue of section 6(1)(a) of the Consumer Protection Act 1987 (death caused by defective product) references to a person's date of knowledge are references to the date on which he first had knowledge of the following facts—

(a) such facts about the damage caused by the defect as would lead a reasonable person who had suffered such damage to consider it sufficiently serious to justify his instituting proceedings for damages against a defendant who did not dispute liability and was able to satisfy a judgment; and

(b) that the damage was wholly or partly attributable to the facts and circumstances alleged to constitute the defect; and

(c) the identity of the defendant;

but, in determining the date on which a person first had such knowledge there shall be disregarded both the extent (if any) of that person's knowledge on any date of whether particular facts or circumstances would or would not, as a matter of law, constitute a defect and, in a case relating to loss of or damage to property, any knowledge which that person had on a date on which he had no right of action by virtue of Part I of that Act in respect of the loss or damage.]

(2) For the purposes of this section an injury is significant if the person whose date of knowledge is in question would reasonably have considered it sufficiently serious to justify his instituting proceedings for damages against a defendant who did not dispute liability and was able to satisfy a judgment.

(3) For the purposes of this section a person's knowledge includes knowledge which he might reasonably have been expected to acquire—

(a) from facts observable or ascertainable by him; or

(b) from facts ascertainable by him with the help of medical or other appropriate expert advice which it is reasonable for him to seek;

but a person shall not be fixed under this subsection with knowledge of a fact ascertainable only with the help of expert advice so long as he has taken all reasonable steps to obtain (and, where appropriate, to act on) that advice.

**NOTES**

Words in square brackets in sub-s (1) inserted, and sub-s (1A) inserted, by the Consumer Protection Act 1987, s 6, Sch 1, Pt I, para 3.

*[Actions in respect of latent damage not involving personal injuries*

**[1.126]**
**14A Special time limit for negligence actions where facts relevant to cause of action are not known at date of accrual**

(1) This section applies to any action for damages for negligence, other than one to which section 11 of this Act applies, where the starting date for reckoning the period of limitation under subsection (4)(b) below falls after the date on which the cause of action accrued.

(2) Section 2 of this Act shall not apply to an action to which this section applies.

(3) An action to which this section applies shall not be brought after the expiration of the period applicable in accordance with subsection (4) below.

(4) That period is either—

(a) six years from the date on which the cause of action accrued; or

(b) three years from the starting date as defined by subsection (5) below, if that period expires later than the period mentioned in paragraph (a) above.

(5) For the purposes of this section, the starting date for reckoning the period of limitation under subsection (4)(b) above is the earliest date on which the plaintiff or any person in whom the cause of action was vested before him first had both the knowledge required for bringing an action for damages in respect of the relevant damage and a right to bring such an action.

(6) In subsection (5) above "the knowledge required for bringing an action for damages in respect of the relevant damage" means knowledge both—

(a) of the material facts about the damage in respect of which damages are claimed; and

(b) of the other facts relevant to the current action mentioned in subsection (8) below.

(7) For the purposes of subsection (6)(a) above, the material facts about the damage are such facts about the damage as would lead a reasonable person who had suffered such damage to consider it sufficiently serious to justify his instituting proceedings for damages against a defendant who did not dispute liability and was able to satisfy a judgment.

(8) The other facts referred to in subsection (6)(b) above are—

(a) that the damage was attributable in whole or in part to the act or omission which is alleged to constitute negligence; and

(b) the identity of the defendant; and

(c) if it is alleged that the act or omission was that of a person other than the defendant, the identity of that person and the additional facts supporting the bringing of an action against the defendant.

(9) Knowledge that any acts or omissions did or did not, as a matter of law, involve negligence is irrelevant for the purposes of subsection (5) above.

(10) For the purposes of this section a person's knowledge includes knowledge which he might reasonably have been expected to acquire—

(a) from facts observable or ascertainable by him; or

(b)   from facts ascertainable by him with the help of appropriate expert advice which it is reasonable for him to seek;

but a person shall not be taken by virtue of this subsection to have knowledge of a fact ascertainable only with the help of expert advice so long as he has taken all reasonable steps to obtain (and, where appropriate, to act on) that advice.]

**NOTES**
Inserted, together with the preceding heading and s 14B, by the Latent Damage Act 1986, s 1.

**[1.127]**
**[14B   Overriding time limit for negligence actions not involving personal injuries**
(1)   An action for damages for negligence, other than one to which section 11 of this Act applies, shall not be brought after the expiration of fifteen years from the date (or, if more than one, from the last of the dates) on which there occurred any act or omission—
(a)   which is alleged to constitute negligence; and
(b)   to which the damage in respect of which damages are claimed is alleged to be attributable (in whole or in part).
(2)   This section bars the right of action in a case to which subsection (1) above applies notwithstanding that—
(a)   the cause of action has not yet accrued; or
(b)   where section 14A of this Act applies to the action, the date which is for the purposes of that section the starting date for reckoning the period mentioned in subsection (4)(b) of that section has not yet occurred;
before the end of the period of limitation prescribed by this section.]

**NOTES**
Inserted as noted to s 14A at **[1.126]**.

## PART II
## EXTENSION OR EXCLUSION OF ORDINARY TIME LIMITS

*Disability*

**[1.128]**
**28   Extension of limitation period in case of disability**
(1)   Subject to the following provisions of this section, if on the date when any right of action accrued for which a period of limitation is prescribed by this Act, the person to whom it accrued was under a disability, the action may be brought at any time before the expiration of six years from the date when he ceased to be under a disability or died (whichever first occurred) notwithstanding that the period of limitation has expired.
(2)   This section shall not affect any case where the right of action first accrued to some person (not under a disability) through whom the person under a disability claims.
(3)   When a right of action which has accrued to a person under a disability accrues, on the death of that person while still under a disability, to another person under a disability, no further extension of time shall be allowed by reason of the disability of the second person.
(4)   No action to recover land or money charged on land shall be brought by virtue of this section by any person after the expiration of thirty years from the date on which the right of action accrued to that person or some person through whom he claims.
[(4A)   If the action is one to which section 4A of this Act applies, subsection (1) above shall have effect—
(a)   in the case of an action for libel or slander, as if for the words from "at any time" to "occurred)" there were substituted the words "by him at any time before the expiration of one year from the date on which he ceased to be under a disability"; and
(b)   in the case of an action for slander of title, slander of goods or other malicious falsehood, as if for the words "six years" there were substituted the words "one year".]
(5)   If the action is one to which section 10 of this Act applies, subsection (1) above shall have effect as if for the words "six years" there were substituted the words "two years".
(6)   If the action is one to which section 11 or 12(2) of this Act applies, subsection (1) above shall have effect as if for the words "six years" there were substituted the words "three years".
[(7)   If the action is one to which section 11A of this Act applies or one by virtue of section 6(1)(a) of the Consumer Protection Act 1987 (death caused by defective product), subsection (1) above—
(a)   shall not apply to the time limit prescribed by subsection (3) of the said section 11A or to that time limit as applied by virtue of section 12(1) of this Act; and
(b)   in relation to any other time limit prescribed by this Act shall have effect as if for the word "six years" there were substituted the words "three years".]

**NOTES**
Sub-s (4A): inserted by the Administration of Justice Act 1985, ss 57(3), 69(5), Sch 9, para 14; substituted by the Defamation Act 1996, s 5(3), (6), in relation to causes of action arising on or after 4 September 1996.

Sub-s (7): added by the Consumer Protection Act 1987, s 6, Sch 1, Pt I, para 4.

**[1.129]**
**[28A Extension for cases where the limitation period is the period under section 14A(4)(b)**
(1)   Subject to subsection (2) below, if in the case of any action for which a period of limitation is prescribed by section 14A of this Act—

(a)   the period applicable in accordance with subsection (4) of that section is the period mentioned in paragraph (b) of that subsection;

(b)   on the date which is for the purposes of that section the starting date for reckoning that period the person by reference to whose knowledge that date fell to be determined under subsection (5) of that section was under a disability; and

(c)   section 28 of this Act does not apply to the action;

the action may be brought at any time before the expiration of three years from the date when he ceased to be under a disability or died (whichever first occurred) notwithstanding that the period mentioned above has expired.

(2)   An action may not be brought by virtue of subsection (1) above after the end of the period of limitation prescribed by section 14B of this Act.]

**NOTES**
Inserted by the Latent Damage Act 1986, s 2(1).

*Fraud, concealment and mistake*

**[1.130]**
**32   Postponement of limitation period in case of fraud, concealment or mistake**
(1)   Subject to [subsections (3) and (4A)] below, where in the case of any action for which a period of limitation is prescribed by this Act, either—

(a)   the action is based upon the fraud of the defendant; or

(b)   any fact relevant to the plaintiff's right of action has been deliberately concealed from him by the defendant; or

(c)   the action is for relief from the consequences of a mistake;

the period of limitation shall not begin to run until the plaintiff has discovered the fraud, concealment or mistake (as the case may be) or could with reasonable diligence have discovered it.
   References in this subsection to the defendant include references to the defendant's agent and to any person through whom the defendant claims and his agent.

(2)   For the purposes of subsection (1) above, deliberate commission of a breach of duty in circumstances in which it is unlikely to be discovered for some time amounts to deliberate concealment of the facts involved in that breach of duty.

(3)   Nothing in this section shall enable any action—

(a)   to recover, or recover the value of, any property; or

(b)   to enforce any charge against, or set aside any transaction affecting, any property;

to be brought against the purchaser of the property or any person claiming through him in any case where the property has been purchased for valuable consideration by an innocent third party since the fraud or concealment or (as the case may be) the transaction in which the mistake was made took place.

(4)   A purchaser is an innocent third party for the purposes of this section—

(a)   in the case of fraud or concealment of any fact relevant to the plaintiff's right of action, if he was not a party to the fraud or (as the case may be) to the concealment of that fact and did not at the time of the purchase know or have reason to believe that the fraud or concealment had taken place; and

(b)   in the case of mistake, if he did not at the time of the purchase know or have reason to believe that the mistake had been made.

[(4A)   Subsection (1) above shall not apply in relation to the time limit prescribed by section 11A(3) of this Act or in relation to that time limit as applied by virtue of section 12(1) of this Act].

[(5)   Sections 14A and 14B of this Act shall not apply to any action to which subsection (1)(b) above applies (and accordingly the period of limitation referred to in that subsection, in any case to which either of those sections would otherwise apply, is the period applicable under section 2 of this Act).]

**NOTES**
Sub-s (1): words in square brackets substituted by the Consumer Protection Act 1987, s 6, Sch 1, Pt I, para 5(a).
Sub-s (4A): inserted by the Consumer Protection Act 1987, s 6, Sch 1, Pt I, para 5(b).
Sub-s (5): added by the Latent Damage Act 1986, s 2(2).
   Disapplication of sub-s (1)(c): sub-s (1)(c) is disapplied with respect to certain actions for mistake of law relating to tax brought before 8 September 2003; see the Finance Act 2007, s 107.

*[Discretionary exclusion of time limit for actions for defamation or malicious falsehood*

**[1.131]**
**32A   Discretionary exclusion of time limit for actions for defamation or malicious falsehood**
(1)   If it appears to the court that it would be exclusion of time equitable to allow an action to proceed having regard to limit for actions the degree to which—
   (a)   the operation of section 4A of this Act prejudices the plaintiff or any person whom he represents, and
   (b)   any decision of the court under this subsection would prejudice the defendant or any person whom he represents,
the court may direct that that section shall not apply to the action or shall not apply to any specified cause of action to which the action relates.
(2)   In acting under this section the court shall have regard to all the circumstances of the case and in particular to—
   (a)   the length of, and the reasons for, the delay on the part of the plaintiff;
   (b)   where the reason or one of the reasons for the delay was that all or any of the facts relevant to the cause of action did not become known to the plaintiff until after the end of the period mentioned in section 4A—
      (i)   the date on which any such facts did become known to him, and
      (ii)   the extent to which he acted promptly and reasonably once he knew whether or not the facts in question might be capable of giving rise to an action; and
   (c)   the extent to which, having regard to the delay, relevant evidence is likely—
      (i)   to be unavailable, or
      (ii)   to be less cogent than if the action had been brought within the period mentioned in section 4A.
(3)   In the case of an action for slander of title, slander of goods or other malicious falsehood brought by a personal representative—
   (a)   the references in subsection (2) above to the plaintiff shall be construed as including the deceased person to whom the cause of action accrued and any previous personal representative of that person; and
   (b)   nothing in section 28(3) of this Act shall be construed as affecting the court's discretion under this section.
(4)   In this section "the court" means the court in which the action has been brought.]

**NOTES**
Inserted, together with the preceding heading, by the Administration of Justice Act 1985, s 57(4).
Substituted by the Defamation Act 1996, s 5(4), (6).

*Discretionary exclusion of time limit for actions in respect of personal injuries or death*

**[1.132]**
**33   Discretionary exclusion of time limit for actions in respect of personal injuries or death**
(1)   If it appears to the court that it would be equitable to allow an action to proceed having regard to the degree to which—
   (a)   the provisions of section 11 [or 11A] or 12 of this Act prejudice the plaintiff or any person whom he represents; and
   (b)   any decision of the court under this subsection would prejudice the defendant or any person whom he represents;
the court may direct that those provisions shall not apply to the action, or shall not apply to any specified cause of action to which the action relates.
[(1A)   The court shall not under this section disapply—
   (a)   subsection (3) of section 11A; or
   (b)   where the damages claimed by the plaintiff are confined to damages for loss of or damage to any property, any other provision in its application to an action by virtue of Part I of the Consumer Protection Act 1987.]
(2)   The court shall not under this section disapply section 12(1) except where the reason why the person injured could no longer maintain an action was because of the time limit in section 11 [or subsection (4) of section 11A].
    If, for example, the person injured could at his death no longer maintain an action under the Fatal Accidents Act 1976 because of the time limit in Article 29 in Schedule 1 to the Carriage by Air Act 1961, the court has no power to direct that section 12(1) shall not apply.
(3)   In acting under this section the court shall have regard to all the circumstances of the case and in particular to—
   (a)   the length of, and the reasons for, the delay on the part of the plaintiff;
   (b)   the extent to which, having regard to the delay, the evidence adduced or likely to be adduced by the plaintiff or the defendant is or is likely to be less cogent than if the action had been brought within the time allowed by section 11 [, by section 11A] or (as the case may be) by section 12;

(c)   the conduct of the defendant after the cause of action arose, including the extent (if any) to which he responded to requests reasonably made by the plaintiff for information or inspection for the purpose of ascertaining facts which were or might be relevant to the plaintiff's cause of action against the defendant;

(d)   the duration of any disability of the plaintiff arising after the date of the accrual of the cause of action;

(e)   the extent to which the plaintiff acted promptly and reasonably once he knew whether or not the act or omission of the defendant, to which the injury was attributable, might be capable at that time of giving rise to an action for damages;

(f)   the steps, if any, taken by the plaintiff to obtain medical, legal or other expert advice and the nature of any such advice he may have received.

(4)   In a case where the person injured died when, because of section 11 [or subsection (4) of section 11A], he could no longer maintain an action and recover damages in respect of the injury, the court shall have regard in particular to the length of, and the reasons for, the delay on the part of the deceased.

(5)   In a case under subsection (4) above, or any other case where the time limit, or one of the time limits, depends on the date of knowledge of a person other than the plaintiff, subsection (3) above shall have effect with appropriate modifications, and shall have effect in particular as if references to the plaintiff included references to any person whose date of knowledge is or was relevant in determining a time limit.

(6)   A direction by the court disapplying the provisions of section 12(1) shall operate to disapply the provisions to the same effect in section 1(1) of the Fatal Accidents Act 1976.

(7)   In this section "the court" means the court in which the action has been brought.

(8)   References in this section to section 11 [or 11A] include references to that section as extended by any of the [provisions of this Part of this Act other than this section] or by any provision of Part III of this Act.

**NOTES**

The words in square brackets in sub-ss (1), (3), (4), the words in the first pair of square brackets in sub-s (8), and the whole of sub-s (1A), were inserted, by the Consumer Protection Act 1987, s 6, Sch 1, Pt I, para 6.

Words in second pair of square brackets in sub-s (8) substituted by the Cross-Border Mediation (EU Directive) Regulations 2011, SI 2011/1133, regs 22, 25, as from 20 May 2011.

*[Mediation in certain cross-border disputes*

**[1.133]**

**33A   Extension of time limits because of mediation in certain cross-border disputes**

(1)   In this section—

(a)   "Mediation Directive" means Directive 2008/52/EC of the European Parliament and of the Council of 21 May 2008 on certain aspects of mediation in civil and commercial matters,

(b)   "mediation" has the meaning given by article 3(a) of the Mediation Directive,

(c)   "mediator" has the meaning given by article 3(b) of the Mediation Directive, and

(d)   "relevant dispute" means a dispute to which article 8(1) of the Mediation Directive applies (certain cross-border disputes).

(2)   Subsection (3) applies where—

(a)   a time limit under this Act relates to the subject of the whole or part of a relevant dispute,

(b)   a mediation in relation to the relevant dispute starts before the time limit expires, and

(c)   if not extended by this section, the time limit would expire before the mediation ends or less than eight weeks after it ends.

(3)   For the purposes of initiating judicial proceedings or arbitration, the time limit expires instead at the end of eight weeks after the mediation ends (subject to subsection (4)).

(4)   If a time limit has been extended by this section, subsections (2) and (3) apply to the extended time limit as they apply to a time limit mentioned in subsection (2)(a).

(5)   Where more than one time limit applies in relation to a relevant dispute, the extension by subsection (3) of one of those time limits does not affect the others.

(6)   For the purposes of this section, a mediation starts on the date of the agreement to mediate that is entered into by the parties and the mediator.

(7)   For the purposes of this section, a mediation ends on the date of the first of these to occur—

(a)   the parties reach an agreement in resolution of the relevant dispute,

(b)   a party completes the notification of the other parties that it has withdrawn from the mediation,

(c)   a party to whom a qualifying request is made fails to give a response reaching the other parties within 14 days of the request,

(d)   after the parties are notified that the mediator's appointment has ended (by death, resignation or otherwise), they fail to agree within 14 days to seek to appoint a replacement mediator,

(e)   the mediation otherwise comes to an end pursuant to the terms of the agreement to mediate.

(8) For the purpose of subsection (7), a qualifying request is a request by a party that another (A) confirm to all parties that A is continuing with the mediation.

(9) In the case of any relevant dispute, references in this section to a mediation are references to the mediation so far as it relates to that dispute, and references to a party are to be read accordingly.]

**NOTES**

Commencement: 20 May 2011.

Inserted, together with the preceding heading, by the Cross-Border Mediation (EU Directive) Regulations 2011, SI 2011/1133, regs 22, 26, as from 20 May 2011.

## PART III
## MISCELLANEOUS AND GENERAL

**[1.134]**
**41   Short title, commencement and extent**
(1)   This Act may be cited as the Limitation Act 1980.
(2)   This Act, except section 35, shall come into force on 1st May 1981.
(3)   *(Relates to the commencement of s 35 (outside the scope of this work).)*
(4)   The repeal by this Act of section 14(1) of the Limitation Act 1963 and the corresponding saving in paragraph 2 of Schedule 2 to this Act shall extend to Northern Ireland, but otherwise this Act does not extend to Scotland or to Northern Ireland.

**NOTES**

Orders: the Limitation Act 1980 (Commencement) Order 1981, SI 1981/588.
Limitation Act 1939: repealed by this Act.

# INSOLVENCY ACT 1986

## (1986 c 45)

### ARRANGEMENT OF SECTIONS

#### THE FIRST GROUP OF PARTS
#### COMPANY INSOLVENCY; COMPANIES WINDING UP

#### PART I
#### COMPANY VOLUNTARY ARRANGEMENTS

*The Proposal*

#### PART II
#### ADMINISTRATION

#### PART III
#### RECEIVERSHIP

#### CHAPTER I
#### RECEIVERS AND MANAGERS (ENGLAND AND WALES)

*Receivers and managers appointed out of court*

*Administrative receivers: general*

#### CHAPTER II
#### RECEIVERS (SCOTLAND)

#### PART IV
#### WINDING UP OF COMPANIES REGISTERED UNDER THE COMPANIES ACTS

#### CHAPTER VI
#### WINDING UP BY THE COURT

*Commencement of winding up*

THE SECOND GROUP OF PARTS
INSOLVENCY OF INDIVIDUALS; BANKRUPTCY

PART VIII
INDIVIDUAL VOLUNTARY ARRANGEMENTS

*Moratorium for insolvent debtor*

*Consideration and implementation of debtor's proposal*

PART IX
BANKRUPTCY

CHAPTER II
PROTECTION OF BANKRUPT'S ESTATE AND INVESTIGATION OF HIS AFFAIRS

THE THIRD GROUP OF PARTS
MISCELLANEOUS MATTERS BEARING ON BOTH COMPANY AND INDIVIDUAL INSOLVENCY;
GENERAL INTERPRETATION;
FINAL PROVISIONS

PART XII
PREFERENTIAL DEBTS IN COMPANY AND INDIVIDUAL INSOLVENCY

PART XIX
FINAL PROVISIONS

SCHEDULES

*An Act to consolidate the enactments relating to company insolvency and winding up (including the winding up of companies that are not insolvent, and of unregistered companies); enactments relating to the insolvency and bankruptcy of individuals; and other enactments bearing on those two subject matters, including the functions and qualification of insolvency practitioners, the public administration of insolvency, the penalisation and redress of malpractice and wrongdoing, and the avoidance of certain transactions at an undervalue*

[25 July 1986]

**NOTES**

Most of this Act covers matters outside the scope of this work, and only those provisions most directly relevant to employment law are printed. For reasons of space, the subject matter of sections, etc, not printed is not annotated. All provisions of the Act printed here except ss 37, 44, 57, and the provisions in the Second Group of Parts (ss 252, 254, 260, 285) apply to England, Wales and Scotland. Sections 37 and 44 apply only to England and Wales (by virtue of s 28) and s 57 applies only to Scotland (by virtue of s 50). None of the provisions in the Second Group of Parts (insolvency of individuals) apply to Scotland (by virtue of s 440). For provisions relating to individual insolvency in Scotland, see the Bankruptcy (Scotland) Act 1985 (outside the scope of this work).

For the application of this Act to limited liability partnerships, see the Limited Liability Partnerships Act 2000, the Limited Liability Partnerships Regulations 2001, SI 2001/1090 and the Limited Liability Partnerships (Scotland) Regulations 2001, SSI 2001/128. This Act has also been applied to the insolvency of various types of company and institutions, including the following: (i) special administration regimes (see the note to s 8 at **[1.136]**); (ii) banks (see the Banking (Special Provisions) Act 2008 and the Banking Act 2009 and the Orders and Regulations made under those Acts); (iii) open-ended investment companies (see the Open-Ended Investment Companies Regulations 2001, SI 2001/1228); (iv) insurers (see the Financial Services and Markets Act 2000 (Administration Orders Relating to Insurers) Order 2010, SI 2010/3023, and the Insurers (Reorganisation and Winding Up) Regulations 2004, SI 2004/353); (v) friendly societies (see the Friendly Societies Act 1992); (vi) industrial and provident societies (see the Industrial and Provident Societies Act 1965); (vii) European public limited-liability companies (see the European Public Limited-Liability Company Regulations 2004, SI 2004/2326); (viii) NHS foundation trusts (see the National Health Service Act 2006); (ix) energy companies (see the Energy Act 2004); (x) partnerships (see the Insolvent Partnerships Order 1994, SI 1994/2421); (xi) the Royal Mail (see the Postal Services Act 2011, ss 68–88). See

also the Enterprise Act 2002, ss 254, 255 (power of the Secretary of State and the Treasury to extend the application of this Act to companies incorporated outside Great Britain and to non-companies respectively).
   See *Harvey* G.

# THE FIRST GROUP OF PARTS
# COMPANY INSOLVENCY; COMPANIES WINDING UP

## PART I
## COMPANY VOLUNTARY ARRANGEMENTS

### *The Proposal*

**[1.135]**
**[1A   Moratorium**
(1)   Where the directors of an eligible company intend to make a proposal for a voluntary arrangement, they may take steps to obtain a moratorium for the company.
(2)   The provisions of Schedule A1 to this Act have effect with respect to—
   (a)   companies eligible for a moratorium under this section,
   (b)   the procedure for obtaining such a moratorium,
   (c)   the effects of such a moratorium, and
   (d)   the procedure applicable (in place of sections 1 to 6 and 7) in relation to the approval and implementation of a voluntary arrangement where such a moratorium is or has been in force.]

**NOTES**
   Inserted by the Insolvency Act 2000, s 1, Sch 1, paras 1, 2.

## [PART II
## ADMINISTRATION

**[1.136]**
**8   Administration**
Schedule B1 to this Act (which makes provision about the administration of companies) shall have effect.]

**NOTES**
   This section was substituted for Pt II of this Act (ss 8–27) by the Enterprise Act 2002, s 248(1), except in relation to cases where a petition for an administration order was presented before 15 September 2003, and subject to savings in relation to special administration regimes (as to which see s 249 of the 2002 Act).
   For amendments to the original Part II (ie, as it applies without the amendments made by the Enterprise Act 2002 and, therefore, as it still applies to special administration regimes), see the Companies Act 2006 (Consequential Amendments etc) Order 2008, SI 2008/948, art 3(1), Sch 1, Pt 2, para 101, and the Companies Act 2006 (Consequential Amendments, Transitional Provisions and Savings) Order 2009, SI 2009/1941, art 2(1), Sch 1, para 73.

## PART III
## RECEIVERSHIP

## CHAPTER I
## RECEIVERS AND MANAGERS (ENGLAND AND WALES)

### *Receivers and managers appointed out of court*

**[1.137]**
**37   Liability for contracts, etc**
(1)   A receiver or manager appointed under powers conferred in an instrument (other than an administrative receiver) is, to the same extent as if he had been appointed by order of the court—
   (a)   personally liable on any contract entered into by him in the performance of his functions (except in so far as the contract otherwise provides) and on any contract of employment adopted by him in the performance of those functions, and
   (b)   entitled in respect of that liability to indemnity out of the assets.
(2)   For the purposes of subsection (1)(a), the receiver or manager is not to be taken to have adopted a contract of employment by reason of anything done or omitted to be done within 14 days after his appointment.
(3)   Subsection (1) does not limit any right to indemnity which the receiver or manager would have apart from it, nor limit his liability on contracts entered into without authority, nor confer any right to indemnity in respect of that liability.
(4)   Where at any time the receiver or manager so appointed vacates office—
   (a)   his remuneration and any expenses properly incurred by him, and
   (b)   any indemnity to which he is entitled out of the assets of the company,

shall be charged on and paid out of any property of the company which is in his custody or under his control at that time in priority to any charge or other security held by the person by or on whose behalf he was appointed.

*Administrative receivers: general*

**[1.138]**
**44   Agency and liability for contracts**
(1)   The administrative receiver of a company—
  (a)   is deemed to be the company's agent, unless and until the company goes into liquidation;
  (b)   is personally liable on any contract entered into by him in the carrying out of his functions (except in so far as the contract otherwise provides) and[, to the extent of any qualifying liability,] on any contract of employment adopted by him in the carrying out of those functions; and
  (c)   is entitled in respect of that liability to an indemnity out of the assets of the company.
(2)   For the purposes of subsection (1)(b) the administrative receiver is not to be taken to have adopted a contract of employment by reason of anything done or omitted to be done within 14 days after his appointment.
[(2A)   For the purposes of subsection (1)(b), a liability under a contract of employment is a qualifying liability if—
  (a)   it is a liability to pay a sum by way of wages or salary or contribution to an occupational pension scheme,
  (b)   it is incurred while the administrative receiver is in office, and
  (c)   it is in respect of services rendered wholly or partly after the adoption of the contract.
(2B)   Where a sum payable in respect of a liability which is a qualifying liability for the purposes of subsection (1)(b) is payable in respect of services rendered partly before and partly after the adoption of the contract, liability under subsection (1)(b) shall only extend to so much of the sum as is payable in respect of services rendered after the adoption of the contract.
(2C)   For the purposes of subsections (2A) and (2B)—
  (a)   wages or salary payable in respect of a period of holiday or absence from work through sickness or other good cause are deemed to be wages or (as the case may be) salary in respect of services rendered in that period, and
  (b)   a sum payable in lieu of holiday is deemed to be wages or (as the case may be) salary in respect of services rendered in the period by reference to which the holiday entitlement arose.
(2D)   In subsection (2C)(a), the reference to wages or salary payable in respect of a period of holiday includes any sums which, if they had been paid, would have been treated for the purposes of the enactments relating to social security as earnings in respect of that period.]
(3)   This section does not limit any right to indemnity which the administrative receiver would have apart from it, nor limit his liability on contracts entered into or adopted without authority, nor confer any right to indemnity in respect of that liability.

**NOTES**
Words in square brackets in sub-s (1) inserted, and sub-ss (2A)–(2D) inserted, by the Insolvency Act 1994, s 2.

## CHAPTER II
### RECEIVERS (SCOTLAND)

**[1.139]**
**57   Agency and liability of receiver for contracts**
(1)   A receiver is deemed to be the agent of the company in relation to such property of the company as is attached by the floating charge by virtue of which he was appointed.
[(1A)   Without prejudice to subsection (1), a receiver is deemed to be the agent of the company in relation to any contract of employment adopted by him in the carrying out of his functions.]
(2)   A receiver (including a receiver whose powers are subsequently suspended under section 56) is personally liable on any contract entered into by him in the performance of his functions, except in so far as the contract otherwise provides, and[, to the extent of any qualifying liability,] on any contract of employment adopted by him in the carrying out of those functions.
[(2A)   For the purposes of subsection (2), a liability under a contract of employment is a qualifying liability if—
  (a)   it is a liability to pay a sum by way of wages or salary or contribution to an occupational pension scheme,
  (b)   it is incurred while the receiver is in office, and
  (c)   it is in respect of services rendered wholly or partly after the adoption of the contract.
(2B)   Where a sum payable in respect of a liability which is a qualifying liability for the purposes of subsection (2) is payable in respect of services rendered partly before and partly after the adoption of the contract, liability under that subsection shall only extend to so much of the sum as is payable in respect of services rendered after the adoption of the contract.
(2C)   For the purposes of subsections (2A) and (2B)—

(a)    wages or salary payable in respect of a period of holiday or absence from work through sickness or other good cause are deemed to be wages or (as the case may be) salary in respect of services rendered in that period, and

(b)    a sum payable in lieu of holiday is deemed to be wages or (as the case may be) salary in respect of services rendered in the period by reference to which the holiday entitlement arose.

(2D)   In subsection (2C)(a), the reference to wages or salary payable in respect of a period of holiday includes any sums which, if they had been paid, would have been treated for the purposes of the enactments relating to social security as earnings in respect of that period.]

(3)   A receiver who is personally liable by virtue of subsection (2) is entitled to be indemnified out of the property in respect of which he was appointed.

(4)   Any contract entered into by or on behalf of the company prior to the appointment of a receiver continues in force (subject to its terms) notwithstanding that appointment, but the receiver does not by virtue only of his appointment incur any personal liability on any such contract.

(5)   For the purposes of subsection (2), a receiver is not to be taken to have adopted a contract of employment by reason of anything done or omitted to be done within 14 days after his appointment.

(6)   This section does not limit any right to indemnity which the receiver would have apart from it, nor limit his liability on contracts entered into or adopted without authority, nor confer any right to indemnity in respect of that liability.

(7)   Any contract entered into by a receiver in the performance of his functions continues in force (subject to its terms) although the powers of the receiver are subsequently suspended under section 56.

**NOTES**

Words in square brackets in sub-s (2) inserted, and sub-ss (1A), (2A)–(2D) inserted, by the Insolvency Act 1994, s 3.

## PART IV
## WINDING UP OF COMPANIES REGISTERED UNDER THE COMPANIES ACTS

### CHAPTER VI
### WINDING UP BY THE COURT

#### *Commencement of winding up*

**[1.140]**
### 130   Consequences of winding-up order

(1)   On the making of a winding-up order, a copy of the order must forthwith be forwarded by the company (or otherwise as may be prescribed) to the registrar of companies, who shall enter it in his records relating to the company.

(2)   When a winding-up order has been made or a provisional liquidator has been appointed, no action or proceeding shall be proceeded with or commenced against the company or its property, except by leave of the court and subject to such terms as the court may impose.

(3)   When an order has been made for winding up a company [registered but not formed under the Companies Act 2006], no action or proceeding shall be commenced or proceeded with against the company or its property or any contributory of the company, in respect of any debt of the company, except by leave of the court, and subject to such terms as the court may impose.

(4)   An order for winding up a company operates in favour of all the creditors and of all contributories of the company as if made on the joint petition of a creditor and of a contributory.

**NOTES**

Sub-s (3): words in square brackets substituted by the Companies Act 2006 (Consequential Amendments, Transitional Provisions and Savings) Order 2009, SI 2009/1941, art 2(1), Sch 1, para 75(1), (15), as from 1 October 2009 (for transitional provisions see the note below).

Transitional provisions: the Companies Act 2006 (Consequential Amendments, Transitional Provisions and Savings) Order 2009, SI 2009/1941, art 8 provides as follows—

**"8   Amendments of insolvency legislation**

(1)   The amendments by this Order of the Insolvency Act 1986 ("the 1986 Act") and the Insolvency (Northern Ireland) Order 1989 ("the 1989 Order") apply as follows.

(2)   They apply where, in a company voluntary arrangement, a moratorium comes into force in relation to a company on or after 1st October 2009.

(3)   They apply where a company enters administration on or after 1st October 2009, except where—

    (a)    it enters administration by virtue of an administration order under paragraph 10 of Schedule B1 to the 1986 Act (or paragraph 11 of Schedule B1 to the 1989 Order) on an application made before 1st October 2009,

    (b)    the administration is immediately preceded by a voluntary liquidation in respect of which the resolution to wind up was passed before 1st October 2009, or

    (c)    the administration is immediately preceded by a liquidation on the making of a winding-up order on a petition which was presented before 1st October 2009.

(4)   They apply where, in a receivership, a receiver or manager is appointed in respect of a company on or after 1st October 2009.

(5)   They apply where a company goes into liquidation upon the passing on or after 1st October 2009 of a resolution to

wind up.

(6)    They apply where a company goes into voluntary liquidation under paragraph 83 of Schedule B1 to the 1986 Act (or paragraph 84 of Schedule B1 to the 1989 Order), except where the preceding administration—

(a)    commenced before 1st October 2009, or

(b)    is an administration which commenced by virtue of an administration order under paragraph 10 of Schedule B1 to the 1986 Act (or paragraph 11 of Schedule B1 to the 1989 Order) on an application which was made before 1st October 2009.

(7)    They apply where a company goes into liquidation on the making of a winding-up order on a petition presented on or after 1st October 2009, except where the liquidation is immediately preceded by—

(a)    an administration under paragraph 10 of Schedule B1 to the 1986 Act (or paragraph 11 of Schedule B1 to the 1989 Order) where the administration order was made on an application made before 1st October 2009,

(b)    an administration in respect of which the appointment of an administrator under paragraph 14 or 22 of Schedule B1 to the 1986 Act (or paragraph 15 or 23 of Schedule B1 to the 1989 Order) took effect before 1st October 2009, or

(c)    a voluntary liquidation in respect of which the resolution to wind up was passed before 1st October 2009.".

Application to Scotland: by virtue of the Scotland Act 1998, s 125, Sch 8, para 23, anything directed to be done, or which may be done, to or by the registrar of companies in Scotland by virtue of sub-s (1) above in relation to friendly societies, industrial and provident societies or building societies, shall, or (as the case may be) may, also be done to or by the Accountant in Bankruptcy.

# THE SECOND GROUP OF PARTS
# INSOLVENCY OF INDIVIDUALS; BANKRUPTCY

## PART VIII
## INDIVIDUAL VOLUNTARY ARRANGEMENTS

*Moratorium for insolvent debtor*

**[1.141]**
**252    Interim order of court**

(1)    In the circumstances specified below, the court may in the case of a debtor (being an individual) make an interim order under this section.

(2)    An interim order has the effect that, during the period for which it is in force—

(a)    no bankruptcy petition relating to the debtor may be presented or proceeded with,

[(aa)  no landlord or other person to whom rent is payable may exercise any right of forfeiture by peaceable re-entry in relation to premises let to the debtor in respect of a failure by the debtor to comply with any term or condition of his tenancy of such premises, except with the leave of the court] and

(b)    no other proceedings, and no execution or other legal process, may be commenced or continued [and no distress may be levied] against the debtor or his property except with the leave of the court.

**NOTES**

Sub-s (2): para (aa), and words in square brackets in para (b), inserted by the Insolvency Act 2000, s 3, Sch 3, paras 1, 2, subject to transitional provisions in cases where a proposal (within the meaning of s 253 of this Act) is made before 1 January 2003.

**[1.142]**
**254    Effect of application**

(1)    At any time when an application under section 253 for an interim order is pending,

[(a)    no landlord or other person to whom rent is payable may exercise any right of forfeiture by peaceable re-entry in relation to premises let to the debtor in respect of a failure by the debtor to comply with any term or condition of his tenancy of such premises, except with the leave of the court, and

(b)]    the court may [forbid the levying of any distress on the debtor's property or its subsequent sale, or both, and] stay any action, execution or other legal process against the property or person of the debtor.

(2)    Any court in which proceedings are pending against an individual may, on proof that an application under that section has been made in respect of that individual, either stay the proceedings or allow them to continue on such terms as it thinks fit.

**NOTES**

Sub-s (1): words in square brackets inserted by the Insolvency Act 2000, s 3, Sch 3, paras 1, 4, subject to transitional provisions in cases where a proposal (within the meaning of s 253 of this Act) is made before 1 January 2003.

*Consideration and implementation of debtor's proposal*

**[1.143]**
**260    Effect of approval**

(1)    This section has effect where the meeting summoned under section 257 approves the proposed voluntary arrangement (with or without modifications).

(2)    The approved arrangement—
   (a)    takes effect as if made by the debtor at the meeting, and
   [(b)    binds every person who in accordance with the rules—
      (i)     was entitled to vote at the meeting (whether or not he was present or represented at it), or
      (ii)    would have been so entitled if he had had notice of it,
      as if he were a party to the arrangement.
(2A)   If—
   (a)    when the arrangement ceases to have effect any amount payable under the arrangement to a person bound by virtue of subsection (2)(b)(ii) has not been paid, and
   (b)    the arrangement did not come to an end prematurely,
the debtor shall at that time become liable to pay to that person the amount payable under the arrangement.]
(3)    The Deeds of Arrangement Act 1914 does not apply to the approved voluntary arrangement.
(4)    Any interim order in force in relation to the debtor immediately before the end of the period of 28 days beginning with the day on which the report with respect to the creditors' meeting was made to the court under section 259 ceases to have effect at the end of that period.

    This subsection applies except to such extent as the court may direct for the purposes of any application under section 262 below.
(5)    Where proceedings on a bankruptcy petition have been stayed by an interim order which ceases to have effect under subsection (4), the petition is deemed, unless the court otherwise orders, to have been dismissed.

**NOTES**

    Para (b) of subsection (2), and sub-s (2A), were substituted for the original sub-s (2)(b) by the Insolvency Act 2000, s 3, Sch 3, paras 1, 10, subject to transitional provisions in cases where a proposal (within the meaning of s 253 of this Act) is made before 1 January 2003.

PART IX

BANKRUPTCY

CHAPTER II

PROTECTION OF BANKRUPT'S ESTATE AND INVESTIGATION OF HIS AFFAIRS

**[1.144]**
**285   Restriction on proceedings and remedies**
(1)    At any time when [proceedings on a bankruptcy application are ongoing or] proceedings on a bankruptcy petition are pending or an individual has been *adjudged* bankrupt the court may stay any action, execution or other legal process against the property or person of the debtor or, as the case may be, of the bankrupt.
(2)    Any court in which proceedings are pending against any individual may, on proof that [a bankruptcy application has been made or] a bankruptcy petition has been presented in respect of that individual or that he is an undischarged bankrupt, either stay the proceedings or allow them to continue on such terms as it thinks fit.
(3)    After the making of a bankruptcy order no person who is a creditor of the bankrupt in respect of a debt provable in the bankruptcy shall—
   (a)    have any remedy against the property or person of the bankrupt in respect of that debt, or
   (b)    before the discharge of the bankrupt, commence any action or other legal proceedings against the bankrupt except with the leave of the court and on such terms as the court may impose.

    This is subject to sections 346 (enforcement procedures) and 347 (limited right to distress).
(4)    Subject as follows, subsection (3) does not affect the right of a secured creditor of the bankrupt to enforce his security.
(5)    Where any goods of an undischarged bankrupt are held by any person by way of pledge, pawn or other security, the official receiver may, after giving notice in writing of his intention to do so, inspect the goods.

    Where such a notice has been given to any person, that person is not entitled, without leave of the court, to realise his security unless he has given the trustee of the bankrupt's estate a reasonable opportunity of inspecting the goods and of exercising the bankrupt's right of redemption.
(6)    References in this section to the property or goods of the bankrupt are to any of his property or goods, whether or not comprised in his estate.

**NOTES**

    Sub-s (1): words in square brackets inserted and for the word in italics there is substituted the word "made", by the Enterprise and Regulatory Reform Act 2013, s 71(3), Sch 19, paras 1, 16(1), (2), as from a day to be appointed.
    Sub-s (2): words in square brackets inserted by the Enterprise and Regulatory Reform Act 2013, s 71(3), Sch 19, paras 1, 16(1), (3), as from a day to be appointed.

## THE THIRD GROUP OF PARTS
## MISCELLANEOUS MATTERS BEARING ON BOTH COMPANY AND INDIVIDUAL INSOLVENCY; GENERAL INTERPRETATION; FINAL PROVISIONS

### PART XII
### PREFERENTIAL DEBTS IN COMPANY AND INDIVIDUAL INSOLVENCY

**[1.145]**
**386  Categories of preferential debts**
(1)   A reference in this Act to the preferential debts of a company or an individual is to the debts listed in Schedule 6 to this Act [(contributions to occupational pension schemes; remuneration, &c of employees; levies on coal and steel production)]; and references to preferential creditors are to be read accordingly.
(2)   In that Schedule "the debtor" means the company or the individual concerned.
(3)   Schedule 6 is to be read with [Schedule 4 to the Pension Schemes Act 1993] (occupational pension scheme contributions).

**NOTES**
   Sub-s (1): words in square brackets substituted by the Enterprise Act 2002, s 251(3), subject to transitional provisions in relation to the abolition of preferential status for Crown debts in cases which were started before 15 September 2003.
   Sub-s (3): words in square brackets substituted by the Pension Schemes Act 1993, s 190, Sch 8, para 18.

### PART XIX
### FINAL PROVISIONS

**[1.146]**
**443  Commencement**
This Act comes into force on the day appointed under section 236(2) of the Insolvency Act 1985 for the coming into force of Part III of that Act (individual insolvency and bankruptcy), immediately after that Part of that Act comes into force for England and Wales.

**[1.147]**
**444  Citation**
This Act may be cited as the Insolvency Act 1986.

### SCHEDULES

### [SCHEDULE A1
### MORATORIUM WHERE DIRECTORS PROPOSE VOLUNTARY ARRANGEMENT

**NOTES**
   Only the provisions of this Schedule most directly relevant to employment law are printed; omitted paragraphs are not annotated.

Section 1A

### PART I
### INTRODUCTORY

*Interpretation*

**[1.148]**
**1.**  In this Schedule—
   "the beginning of the moratorium" has the meaning given by paragraph 8(1),
   "the date of filing" means the date on which the documents for the time being referred to in paragraph 7(1) are filed or lodged with the court,
   "hire-purchase agreement" includes a conditional sale agreement, a chattel leasing agreement and a retention of title agreement,
   "market contract" and "market charge" have the meanings given by Part VII of the Companies Act 1989,
   . . .
   "moratorium" means a moratorium under section 1A,
   "the nominee" includes any person for the time being carrying out the functions of a nominee under this Schedule,
   . . .
   "the settlement finality regulations" means the Financial Markets and Insolvency (Settlement Finality) Regulations 1999,
   "system-charge" has the meaning given by the Financial Markets and Insolvency Regulations 1996.

*Eligible companies*

**2.** (1)    A company is eligible for a moratorium if it meets the requirements of paragraph 3, unless—

(a)    it is excluded from being eligible by virtue of paragraph 4, or

(b)    it falls within sub-paragraph (2).

(2)    A company falls within this sub-paragraph if—

[(a)    it effects or carries out contracts of insurance, but is not exempt from the general prohibition, within the meaning of section 19 of the Financial Services and Markets Act 2000, in relation to that activity,

(b)    it has permission under Part IV of that Act to accept deposits,

(bb)    it has a liability in respect of a deposit which it accepted in accordance with the Banking Act 1979 (c 37) or 1987 (c 22),]

(c)    it is a party to a market contract . . . or any of its property is subject to a market charge . . . or a system-charge, or

(d)    it is a participant (within the meaning of the settlement finality regulations) or any of its property is subject to a collateral security charge (within the meaning of those regulations).

[(3)    Paragraphs (a), (b) and (bb) of sub-paragraph (2) must be read with—

(a)    section 22 of the Financial Services and Markets Act 2000;

(b)    any relevant order under that section; and

(c)    Schedule 2 to that Act.]

**3.** (1)    A company meets the requirements of this paragraph if the qualifying conditions are met—

(a)    in the year ending with the date of filing, or

(b)    in the financial year of the company which ended last before that date.

(2)    For the purposes of sub-paragraph (1)—

(a)    the qualifying conditions are met by a company in a period if, in that period, it satisfies two or more of the requirements for being a small company specified for the time being in [section 382(3) of the Companies Act 2006], and

(b)    a company's financial year is to be determined in accordance with that Act.

(3)    [Section 382(4), (5) and (6)] of that Act apply for the purposes of this paragraph as they apply for the purposes of that section.

[(4)    A company does not meet the requirements of this paragraph if it is a [parent company] of a group of companies which does not qualify as a small group or a medium-sized group [in relation to] the financial year of the company which ended last before the date of filing.

[(5)    For the purposes of sub-paragraph (4)—

(a)    "group" has the same meaning as in Part 15 of the Companies Act 2006 (see section 474(1) of that Act); and

(b)    a group qualifies as small in relation to a financial year if it so qualifies under section 383(2) to (7) of that Act, and qualifies as medium-sized in relation to a financial year if it so qualifies under section 466(2) to (7) of that Act.]]

[(6)    Expressions used in this paragraph that are defined expressions in Part 15 of the Companies Act 2006 (accounts and reports) have the same meaning in this paragraph as in that Part.]

**4.** (1)    A company is excluded from being eligible for a moratorium if, on the date of filing—

[(a)    the company is in administration,]

(b)    the company is being wound up,

(c)    there is an administrative receiver of the company,

(d)    a voluntary arrangement has effect in relation to the company,

(e)    there is a provisional liquidator of the company,

(f)    a moratorium has been in force for the company at any time during the period of 12 months ending with the date of filing and—

(i)    no voluntary arrangement had effect at the time at which the moratorium came to an end, or

(ii)    a voluntary arrangement which had effect at any time in that period has come to an end prematurely,

[(fa)    an administrator appointed under paragraph 22 of Schedule B1 has held office in the period of 12 months ending with the date of filing,] or

(g)    a voluntary arrangement in relation to the company which had effect in pursuance of a proposal under section 1(3) has come to an end prematurely and, during the period of 12 months ending with the date of filing, an order under section 5(3)(a) has been made.

(2)    Sub-paragraph (1)(b) does not apply to a company which, by reason of a winding-up order made after the date of filing, is treated as being wound up on that date.

**4A–4K.**    *(Outside the scope of this work.)*

**5.** The Secretary of State may by regulations modify the qualifications for eligibility of a company for a moratorium.]

**NOTES**

This Schedule was inserted by the Insolvency Act 2000, s 1, Sch 1, paras 1, 4.

Para 1: definitions omitted repealed by virtue of the Financial Services and Markets Act 2000 (Consequential Amendments) Order 2002, SI 2002/1555, art 28(1), (2).

Para 2: sub-paras (2)(a)–(bb) substituted for the original sub-paras (2)(a), (b), words omitted from sub-para (2)(c) repealed, and sub-para (3) added, by virtue of SI 2002/1555, arts 28(1), (3), 29.

Para 3 is amended as follows:

Words in square brackets in sub-paras (2), (3) substituted by the Companies Act 2006 (Consequential Amendments etc) Order 2008, SI 2008/948, art 3(1), Sch 1, Pt 2, para 99(1)–(3).

Sub-paras (4), (5) added by the Insolvency Act 1986 (Amendment) (No 3) Regulations 2002, SI 2002/1990, reg 3(1), (2).

Words in square brackets in sub-para (4) substituted by SI 2008/948, art 3(1), Sch 1, Pt 2, para 99(1), (4).

Sub-para (5) substituted by SI 2008/948, art 3(1), Sch 1, Pt 2, para 99(1), (5).

Sub-para (6) added by the Companies Act 2006 (Consequential Amendments, Transitional Provisions and Savings) Order 2009, SI 2009/1941, art 2(1), Sch 1, para 71(1), (4)(a), as from 1 October 2009 (for transitional provisions see the note to s 130 at **[1.140]**).

Para 4: sub-para (1)(a) substituted, and sub-para (1)(fa) inserted, by the Enterprise Act 2002, s 248(3), Sch 17, paras 9, 37(1), (2), except in relation to cases where a petition for an administration order was presented before 15 September 2003, and subject to savings in relation to special administration regimes as noted to s 8 of this Act at **[1.136]**.

Banking Act 1987, Insurance Companies Act 1982: repealed by the Financial Services and Markets Act 2000 (Consequential Amendments and Repeals) Order 2001, SI 2001/3649, art 3(1)(b), (d).

Financial Services and Markets Act 2000 (Financial Promotion) Order 2001, SI 2001/1335: revoked and replaced by the Financial Services and Markets Act 2000 (Financial Promotion) Order 2005, SI 2005/1529.

## [PART II
## OBTAINING A MORATORIUM

### *Nominee's statement*

**[1.149]**

**6.** (1) Where the directors of a company wish to obtain a moratorium, they shall submit to the nominee—

    (a)    a document setting out the terms of the proposed voluntary arrangement,

    (b)    a statement of the company's affairs containing—

        (i)    such particulars of its creditors and of its debts and other liabilities and of its assets as may be prescribed, and

        (ii)    such other information as may be prescribed, and

    (c)    any other information necessary to enable the nominee to comply with sub-paragraph (2) which he requests from them.

(2) The nominee shall submit to the directors a statement in the prescribed form indicating whether or not, in his opinion—

    (a)    the proposed voluntary arrangement has a reasonable prospect of being approved and implemented,

    (b)    the company is likely to have sufficient funds available to it during the proposed moratorium to enable it to carry on its business, and

    (c)    meetings of the company and its creditors should be summoned to consider the proposed voluntary arrangement.

(3) In forming his opinion on the matters mentioned in sub-paragraph (2), the nominee is entitled to rely on the information submitted to him under sub-paragraph (1) unless he has reason to doubt its accuracy.

(4) The reference in sub-paragraph (2)(b) to the company's business is to that business as the company proposes to carry it on during the moratorium.

### *Documents to be submitted to court*

**7.** (1) To obtain a moratorium the directors of a company must file (in Scotland, lodge) with the court—

    (a)    a document setting out the terms of the proposed voluntary arrangement,

    (b)    a statement of the company's affairs containing—

        (i)    such particulars of its creditors and of its debts and other liabilities and of its assets as may be prescribed, and

        (ii)    such other information as may be prescribed,

    (c)    a statement that the company is eligible for a moratorium,

    (d)    a statement from the nominee that he has given his consent to act, and

    (e)    a statement from the nominee that, in his opinion—

        (i)    the proposed voluntary arrangement has a reasonable prospect of being approved and implemented,

        (ii)    the company is likely to have sufficient funds available to it during the proposed moratorium to enable it to carry on its business, and

     (iii)   meetings of the company and its creditors should be summoned to consider the proposed voluntary arrangement.

(2)   Each of the statements mentioned in sub-paragraph (1)(b) to (e), except so far as it contains the particulars referred to in paragraph (b)(i), must be in the prescribed form.

(3)   The reference in sub-paragraph (1)(e)(ii) to the company's business is to that business as the company proposes to carry it on during the moratorium.

(4)   The Secretary of State may by regulations modify the requirements of this paragraph as to the documents required to be filed (in Scotland, lodged) with the court in order to obtain a moratorium.

*Duration of moratorium*

**8.**  (1)   A moratorium comes into force when the documents for the time being referred to in paragraph 7(1) are filed or lodged with the court and references in this Schedule to "the beginning of the moratorium" shall be construed accordingly.

(2)   A moratorium ends at the end of the day on which the meetings summoned under paragraph 29(1) are first held (or, if the meetings are held on different days, the later of those days), unless it is extended under paragraph 32.

(3)   If either of those meetings has not first met before the end of the period of 28 days beginning with the day on which the moratorium comes into force, the moratorium ends at the end of the day on which those meetings were to be held (or, if those meetings were summoned to be held on different days, the later of those days), unless it is extended under paragraph 32.

(4)   If the nominee fails to summon either meeting within the period required by paragraph 29(1), the moratorium ends at the end of the last day of that period.

(5)   If the moratorium is extended (or further extended) under paragraph 32, it ends at the end of the day to which it is extended (or further extended).

(6)   Sub-paragraphs (2) to (5) do not apply if the moratorium comes to an end before the time concerned by virtue of—

    (a)   paragraph 25(4) (effect of withdrawal by nominee of consent to act),

    (b)   an order under paragraph 26(3), 27(3) or 40 (challenge of actions of nominee or directors), or

    (c)   a decision of one or both of the meetings summoned under paragraph 29.

(7)   If the moratorium has not previously come to an end in accordance with sub-paragraphs (2) to (6), it ends at the end of the day on which a decision under paragraph 31 to approve a voluntary arrangement takes effect under paragraph 36.

(8)   The Secretary of State may by order increase or reduce the period for the time being specified in sub-paragraph (3).

*Notification of beginning of moratorium*

**9.**  (1)   When a moratorium comes into force, the directors shall notify the nominee of that fact forthwith.

(2)   If the directors without reasonable excuse fail to comply with sub-paragraph (1), each of them is liable to imprisonment or a fine, or both.

**10.**  (1)   When a moratorium comes into force, the nominee shall, in accordance with the rules—

    (a)   advertise that fact forthwith, and

    (b)   notify the registrar of companies, the company and any petitioning creditor of the company of whose claim he is aware of that fact.

(2)   In sub-paragraph (1)(b), "petitioning creditor" means a creditor by whom a winding-up petition has been presented before the beginning of the moratorium, as long as the petition has not been dismissed or withdrawn.

(3)   If the nominee without reasonable excuse fails to comply with sub-paragraph (1)(a) or (b), he is liable to a fine.

*Notification of end of moratorium*

**11.**  (1)   When a moratorium comes to an end, the nominee shall, in accordance with the rules—

    (a)   advertise that fact forthwith, and

    (b)   notify the court, the registrar of companies, the company and any creditor of the company of whose claim he is aware of that fact.

(2)   If the nominee without reasonable excuse fails to comply with sub-paragraph (1)(a) or (b), he is liable to a fine.]

**NOTES**

Inserted as noted to Pt I of this Schedule at **[1.148]**.

## [PART III
## EFFECTS OF MORATORIUM

*Effect on creditors, etc*

**[1.150]**

**12.** (1) During the period for which a moratorium is in force for a company—

(a) no petition may be presented for the winding up of the company,

(b) no meeting of the company may be called or requisitioned except with the consent of the nominee or the leave of the court and subject (where the court gives leave) to such terms as the court may impose,

(c) no resolution may be passed or order made for the winding up of the company,

[(d) no administration application may be made in respect of the company,

(da) no administrator of the company may be appointed under paragraph 14 or 22 of Schedule B1,]

(e) no administrative receiver of the company may be appointed,

(f) no landlord or other person to whom rent is payable may exercise any right of forfeiture by peaceable re-entry in relation to premises let to the company in respect of a failure by the company to comply with any term or condition of its tenancy of such premises, except with the leave of the court and subject to such terms as the court may impose,

(g) no other steps may be taken to enforce any security over the company's property, or to repossess goods in the company's possession under any hire-purchase agreement, except with the leave of the court and subject to such terms as the court may impose, and

(h) no other proceedings and no execution or other legal process may be commenced or continued, and no distress may be levied, against the company or its property except with the leave of the court and subject to such terms as the court may impose.

(2) Where a petition, other than an excepted petition, for the winding up of the company has been presented before the beginning of the moratorium, section 127 shall not apply in relation to any disposition of property, transfer of shares or alteration in status made during the moratorium or at a time mentioned in paragraph 37(5)(a).

(3) In the application of sub-paragraph (1)(h) to Scotland, the reference to execution being commenced or continued includes a reference to diligence being carried out or continued, and the reference to distress being levied is omitted.

(4) Paragraph (a) of sub-paragraph (1) does not apply to an excepted petition and, where such a petition has been presented before the beginning of the moratorium or is presented during the moratorium, paragraphs (b) and (c) of that sub-paragraph do not apply in relation to proceedings on the petition.

(5) For the purposes of this paragraph, "excepted petition" means a petition under—

(a) section 124A [or 124B] of this Act,

(b) section 72 of the Financial Services Act 1986 on the ground mentioned in subsection (1)(b) of that section, or

(c) section 92 of the Banking Act 1987 on the ground mentioned in subsection (1)(b) of that section,

[(d) section 367 of the Financial Services and Markets Act 2000 on the ground mentioned in subsection (3)(b) of that section.]

*Effect on company*

**15.** (1) Paragraphs 16 to 23 apply in relation to a company for which a moratorium is in force.

(2) The fact that a company enters into a transaction in contravention of any of paragraphs 16 to 22 does not—

(a) make the transaction void, or

(b) make it to any extent unenforceable against the company.

*Company invoices, etc*

**16.** [(1) Every invoice, order for goods or services, business letter or order form (whether in hard copy, electronic or any other form) issued by or on behalf of the company, and all the company's websites, must also contain the nominee's name and a statement that the moratorium is in force for the company.]

(2) If default is made in complying with sub-paragraph (1), the company and (subject to sub-paragraph (3)) any officer of the company is liable to a fine.

(3) An officer of the company is only liable under sub-paragraph (2) if, without reasonable excuse, he authorises or permits the default.

---

**NOTES**

Inserted as noted to Pt I of this Schedule at **[1.148]**.

Para 12: sub-paras (1)(d), (da) substituted, for the original sub-para (1)(d), by the Enterprise Act 2002, s 248(3), Sch 17, paras 9, 37(1), (3), except in relation to cases where a petition for an administration order was presented before 15 September

Part 1   Statutes

2003, and subject to savings in relation to special administration regimes as noted to s 8 of this Act at **[1.136]**; words in square brackets in sub-para (5)(a) inserted by the European Public Limited-Liability Company Regulations 2004, SI 2004/2326, reg 73(4)(b); sub-para (5)(d) inserted by virtue of the Financial Services and Markets Act 2000 (Consequential Amendments) Order 2002, SI 2002/1555.

Para 16: sub-para (1) substituted by the Companies (Trading Disclosures) (Insolvency) Regulations 2008, SI 2008/1897, reg 3(1), as from 1 October 2008.

Banking Act 1987, Financial Services Act 1986: repealed by the Financial Services and Markets Act 2000 (Consequential Amendments and Repeals) Order 2001, SI 2001/3649, art 3(1)(c), (d).

## [PART V
## CONSIDERATION AND IMPLEMENTATION OF VOLUNTARY ARRANGEMENT

### *Summoning of meetings*

**[1.151]**

**29.** (1)   Where a moratorium is in force, the nominee shall summon meetings of the company and its creditors for such a time, date (within the period for the time being specified in paragraph 8(3)) and place as he thinks fit.

(2)   The persons to be summoned to a creditors' meeting under this paragraph are every creditor of the company of whose claim the nominee is aware.

### *Extension of moratorium*

**32.** (1)   Subject to sub-paragraph (2), a meeting summoned under paragraph 29 which resolves that it be adjourned (or further adjourned) may resolve that the moratorium be extended (or further extended), with or without conditions.

(2)   The moratorium may not be extended (or further extended) to a day later than the end of the period of two months which begins—
(a)   where both meetings summoned under paragraph 29 are first held on the same day, with that day,
(b)   in any other case, with the day on which the later of those meetings is first held.

(3)   At any meeting where it is proposed to extend (or further extend) the moratorium, before a decision is taken with respect to that proposal, the nominee shall inform the meeting—
(a)   of what he has done in order to comply with his duty under paragraph 24 and the cost of his actions for the company, and
(b)   of what he intends to do to continue to comply with that duty if the moratorium is extended (or further extended) and the expected cost of his actions for the company.

(4)   Where, in accordance with sub-paragraph (3)(b), the nominee informs a meeting of the expected cost of his intended actions, the meeting shall resolve whether or not to approve that expected cost.

(5)   If a decision not to approve the expected cost of the nominee's intended actions has effect under paragraph 36, the moratorium comes to an end.

(6)   A meeting may resolve that a moratorium which has been extended (or further extended) be brought to an end before the end of the period of the extension (or further extension).

(7)   The Secretary of State may by order increase or reduce the period for the time being specified in sub-paragraph (2).

**NOTES**
Inserted as noted to Pt I of this Schedule at **[1.148]**.

## [SCHEDULE B1
## ADMINISTRATION

Section 8

**NOTES**
Only the provisions of this Schedule most directly relevant to employment law are printed; omitted paragraphs are not annotated.

## NATURE OF ADMINISTRATION

### *Administration*

**[1.152]**

**1.** (1)   For the purposes of this Act "administrator" of a company means a person appointed under this Schedule to manage the company's affairs, business and property.

(2)   For the purposes of this Act—
(a)   a company is "in administration" while the appointment of an administrator of the company has effect,
(b)   a company "enters administration" when the appointment of an administrator takes effect,

(c)    a company ceases to be in administration when the appointment of an administrator of the company ceases to have effect in accordance with this Schedule, and

(d)    a company does not cease to be in administration merely because an administrator vacates office (by reason of resignation, death or otherwise) or is removed from office.

**2.** A person may be appointed as administrator of a company—
    (a)    by administration order of the court under paragraph 10,
    (b)    by the holder of a floating charge under paragraph 14, or
    (c)    by the company or its directors under paragraph 22.

### *Purpose of administration*

**3.** (1)    The administrator of a company must perform his functions with the objective of—
    (a)    rescuing the company as a going concern, or
    (b)    achieving a better result for the company's creditors as a whole than would be likely if the company were wound up (without first being in administration), or
    (c)    realising property in order to make a distribution to one or more secured or preferential creditors.

(2)    Subject to sub-paragraph (4), the administrator of a company must perform his functions in the interests of the company's creditors as a whole.

(3)    The administrator must perform his functions with the objective specified in sub-paragraph (1)(a) unless he thinks either—
    (a)    that it is not reasonably practicable to achieve that objective, or
    (b)    that the objective specified in sub-paragraph (1)(b) would achieve a better result for the company's creditors as a whole.

(4)    The administrator may perform his functions with the objective specified in sub-paragraph (1)(c) only if—
    (a)    he thinks that it is not reasonably practicable to achieve either of the objectives specified in sub-paragraph (1)(a) and (b), and
    (b)    he does not unnecessarily harm the interests of the creditors of the company as a whole.

**4.** The administrator of a company must perform his functions as quickly and efficiently as is reasonably practicable.

### *Status of administrator*

**5.** An administrator is an officer of the court (whether or not he is appointed by the court).

## EFFECT OF ADMINISTRATION

### *Moratorium on other legal process*

**43.** (1)    This paragraph applies to a company in administration.

(2)    No step may be taken to enforce security over the company's property except—
    (a)    with the consent of the administrator, or
    (b)    with the permission of the court.

(3)    No step may be taken to repossess goods in the company's possession under a hire-purchase agreement except—
    (a)    with the consent of the administrator, or
    (b)    with the permission of the court.

(4)    A landlord may not exercise a right of forfeiture by peaceable re-entry in relation to premises let to the company except—
    (a)    with the consent of the administrator, or
    (b)    with the permission of the court.

(5)    In Scotland, a landlord may not exercise a right of irritancy in relation to premises let to the company except—
    (a)    with the consent of the administrator, or
    (b)    with the permission of the court.

(6)    No legal process (including legal proceedings, execution, distress and diligence) may be instituted or continued against the company or property of the company except—
    (a)    with the consent of the administrator, or
    (b)    with the permission of the court.

[(6A)    An administrative receiver of the company may not be appointed.]

(7)    Where the court gives permission for a transaction under this paragraph it may impose a condition on or a requirement in connection with the transaction.

(8)    In this paragraph "landlord" includes a person to whom rent is payable.

*Interim moratorium*

**44.** (1) This paragraph applies where an administration application in respect of a company has been made and—

    (a)    the application has not yet been granted or dismissed, or

    (b)    the application has been granted but the administration order has not yet taken effect.

(2) This paragraph also applies from the time when a copy of notice of intention to appoint an administrator under paragraph 14 is filed with the court until—

    (a)    the appointment of the administrator takes effect, or

    (b)    the period of five business days beginning with the date of filing expires without an administrator having been appointed.

(3) Sub-paragraph (2) has effect in relation to a notice of intention to appoint only if it is in the prescribed form.

(4) This paragraph also applies from the time when a copy of notice of intention to appoint an administrator is filed with the court under paragraph 27(1) until—

    (a)    the appointment of the administrator takes effect, or

    (b)    the period specified in paragraph 28(2) expires without an administrator having been appointed.

(5) The provisions of paragraphs 42 and 43 shall apply (ignoring any reference to the consent of the administrator).

(6) If there is an administrative receiver of the company when the administration application is made, the provisions of paragraphs 42 and 43 shall not begin to apply by virtue of this paragraph until the person by or on behalf of whom the receiver was appointed consents to the making of the administration order.

(7) This paragraph does not prevent or require the permission of the court for—

    (a)    the presentation of a petition for the winding up of the company under a provision mentioned in paragraph 42(4),

    (b)    the appointment of an administrator under paragraph 14,

    (c)    the appointment of an administrative receiver of the company, or

    (d)    the carrying out by an administrative receiver (whenever appointed) of his functions.

## REPLACING ADMINISTRATOR

*Vacation of office: charges and liabilities*

**99.** (1) This paragraph applies where a person ceases to be the administrator of a company (whether because he vacates office by reason of resignation, death or otherwise, because he is removed from office or because his appointment ceases to have effect).

(2) In this paragraph—

    "the former administrator" means the person referred to in sub-paragraph (1), and

    "cessation" means the time when he ceases to be the company's administrator.

(3) The former administrator's remuneration and expenses shall be—

    (a)    charged on and payable out of property of which he had custody or control immediately before cessation, and

    (b)    payable in priority to any security to which paragraph 70 applies.

(4) A sum payable in respect of a debt or liability arising out of a contract entered into by the former administrator or a predecessor before cessation shall be—

    (a)    charged on and payable out of property of which the former administrator had custody or control immediately before cessation, and

    (b)    payable in priority to any charge arising under sub-paragraph (3).

(5) Sub-paragraph (4) shall apply to a liability arising under a contract of employment which was adopted by the former administrator or a predecessor before cessation; and for that purpose—

    (a)    action taken within the period of 14 days after an administrator's appointment shall not be taken to amount or contribute to the adoption of a contract,

    (b)    no account shall be taken of a liability which arises, or in so far as it arises, by reference to anything which is done or which occurs before the adoption of the contract of employment, and

    (c)    no account shall be taken of a liability to make a payment other than wages or salary.

(6) In sub-paragraph (5)(c) "wages or salary" includes—

    (a)    a sum payable in respect of a period of holiday (for which purpose the sum shall be treated as relating to the period by reference to which the entitlement to holiday accrued),

    (b)    a sum payable in respect of a period of absence through illness or other good cause,

    (c)    a sum payable in lieu of holiday,

    (d)    in respect of a period, a sum which would be treated as earnings for that period for the purposes of an enactment about social security, and

    (e)    a contribution to an occupational pension scheme.]

**NOTES**

Inserted by the Enterprise Act 2002, s 248(2), Sch 16, except in relation to cases where a petition for an administration order was presented before 15 September 2003, and subject to savings in relation to special administration regimes (within the meaning of s 249 of the 2002 Act). Note that para 43(6A) was inserted into Sch 16 to the 2002 Act by the Enterprise Act 2002 (Insolvency) Order 2003, SI 2003/2096, art 2(1), (3), as from the same date.

## SCHEDULE 6
## THE CATEGORIES OF PREFERENTIAL DEBTS

Section 386

**[1.153]**

**1–7.** . . .

### Category 4: Contributions to occupational pension schemes, etc

**8.** Any sum which is owed by the debtor and is a sum to which [Schedule 4 to the Pension Schemes Act 1993] applies (contributions to occupational pension schemes and state scheme premiums).

### Category 5: Remuneration, etc, of employees

**9.** So much of any amount which—
  (a)  is owed by the debtor to a person who is or has been an employee of the debtor, and
  (b)  is payable by way of remuneration in respect of the whole or any part of the period of 4 months next before the relevant date,
as does not exceed so much as may be prescribed by order made by the Secretary of State.

**10.** An amount owed by way of accrued holiday remuneration, in respect of any period of employment before the relevant date, to a person whose employment by the debtor has been terminated, whether before, on or after that date.

**11.** So much of any sum owed in respect of money advanced for the purpose as has been applied for the payment of a debt which, if it had not been paid, would have been a debt falling within paragraph 9 or 10.

**12.** So much of any amount which—
  (a)  is ordered (whether before or after the relevant date) to be paid by the debtor under the Reserve Forces (Safeguard of Employment) Act 1985, and
  (b)  is so ordered in respect of a default made by the debtor before that date in the discharge of his obligations under that Act,
as does not exceed such amount as may be prescribed by order made by the Secretary of State.

### Interpretation for Category 5

**13.** (1)  For the purposes of paragraphs 9 to 12, a sum is payable by the debtor to a person by way of remuneration in respect of any period if—
  (a)  it is paid as wages or salary (whether payable for time or for piece work or earned wholly or partly by way of commission) in respect of services rendered to the debtor in that period, or
  (b)  it is an amount falling within the following sub-paragraph and is payable by the debtor in respect of that period.

[(2)  An amount falls within this sub-paragraph if it is—
  (a)  a guarantee payment under Part III of the Employment Rights Act 1996 (employee without work to do);
  (b)  any payment for time off under section 53 (time off to look for work or arrange training) or section 56 (time off for ante-natal care) of that Act or under section 169 of the Trade Union and Labour Relations (Consolidation) Act 1992 (time off for carrying out trade union duties etc);
  (c)  remuneration on suspension on medical grounds, or on maternity grounds, under Part VII of the Employment Rights Act 1996; or
  (d)  remuneration under a protective award under section 189 of the Trade Union and Labour Relations (Consolidation) Act 1992 (redundancy dismissal with compensation).]

**14.** (1)  This paragraph relates to a case in which a person's employment has been terminated by or in consequence of his employer going into liquidation or being *adjudged* bankrupt or (his employer being a company not in liquidation) by or in consequence of—
  (a)  a receiver being appointed as mentioned in section 40 of this Act (debenture-holders secured by floating charge), or
  (b)  the appointment of a receiver under section 53(6) or 54(5) of this Act (Scottish company with property subject to floating charge), or

(c) the taking of possession by debenture-holders (so secured), as mentioned in [section 754 of the Companies Act 2006].

(2) For the purposes of paragraphs 9 to 12, holiday remuneration is deemed to have accrued to that person in respect of any period of employment if, by virtue of his contract of employment or of any enactment that remuneration would have accrued in respect of that period if his employment had continued until he became entitled to be allowed the holiday.

(3) The reference in sub-paragraph (2) to any enactment includes an order or direction made under an enactment.

**15.** Without prejudice to paragraphs 13 and 14—
(a) any remuneration payable by the debtor to a person in respect of a period of holiday or of absence from work through sickness or other good cause is deemed to be wages or (as the case may be) salary in respect of services rendered to the debtor in that period, and
(b) references here and in those paragraphs to remuneration in respect of a period of holiday include any sums which, if they had been paid, would have been treated for the purposes of the enactments to social security as earnings in respect of that period.

*[Category 6: Levies on coal and steel production*

**15A.** (*Outside the scope of this work.*)]

*Orders*

**16.** An order under paragraph 9 or 12—
(a) may contain such transitional provisions as may appear to the Secretary of State necessary or expedient;
(b) shall be made by statutory instrument subject to annulment in pursuance of a resolution of either House of Parliament.

**NOTES**
Paras 1–7: repealed by the Enterprise Act 2002, ss 251(1), 278(2), Sch 26, subject to transitional provisions in relation to the abolition of preferential status for Crown debts in cases which were started before 15 September 2003.
Para 8: words in square brackets substituted by the Pension Schemes Act 1993, s 190, Sch 8, para 18.
Para 13: sub-para (2) substituted by the Employment Rights Act 1996, s 240, Sch 1, para 29.
Para 14: for the word in italics there is substituted the word "made", by the Enterprise and Regulatory Reform Act 2013, s 71(3), Sch 19, paras 1, 64, as from a day to be appointed; words in square brackets in sub-para (1)(c) substituted by the Companies Act 2006 (Consequential Amendments etc) Order 2008, SI 2008/948, arts 3(1)(b), 6, Sch 1, Pt 2, para 104.
Orders: the Insolvency Proceedings (Monetary Limits) Order 1986, SI 1986/1996 (art 4 of which prescribes £800 for the purposes of paras 9, 12 above).

# WAGES ACT 1986 (NOTE)

(1986 c 48)

**[1.154]**

**NOTES**
The whole of this Act has been repealed. Ss 12–26 (Pt II) and Schs 2, 3 were repealed by the Trade Union Reform and Employment Rights Act 1993, ss 35, 51, Sch 10 (see Sch 9 to the 1993 Act for transitional provisions and savings); s 27 was repealed by the Employment Act 1989, s 29(4), Sch 7, Pt II; ss 1–11 (Pt I), 28–33, and Schs 1, 5, were repealed and re-enacted by the Employment Rights Act 1996, s 242, Sch 3 (for the corresponding provisions in the 1996 Act see Destination Table at **[1.1051]**). The remaining provisions of the Act were repealed by a combination of the Coal Industry Act 1992 and the Employment Tribunals Act 1996.

# SEX DISCRIMINATION ACT 1986 (NOTE)

(1986 c 59)

**[1.155]**

**NOTES**
In so far as this Act was still in force, it was repealed by the Equality Act 2010, s 211(2), Sch 27, Pt 1, as from 1 October 2010. The commencement of the repeal of this Act by the 2010 Act was provided for by the Equality Act 2010 (Commencement No 4, Savings, Consequential, Transitional, Transitory and Incidental Provisions and Revocation) Order 2010, SI 2010/2317. That Order (which is at **[2.1558]**) provides for various transitional provisions and savings in connection with the commencement of the 2010 Act and the repeal of this Act. See, in particular, art 15 (saving where the act complained of occurs wholly before 1 October 2010), Sch 1 (savings for s 6 (Collective agreements and rules of undertakings) and s 10 (Short title, commencement and extent) in relation to a shipping matter), and Sch 3 (savings for ss 6, 10 in relation to work on ships, work on hovercraft and seafarers).

# EMPLOYMENT ACT 1988

## (1988 c 19)

*An Act to make provision with respect to trade unions, their members and their property, to things done for the purpose of enforcing membership of a trade union, to trade union ballots and elections and to proceedings involving trade unions; to provide for the Manpower Services Commission to be known as the Training Commission; to amend the law with respect to the constitution and functions of that Commission and with respect to persons to whom facilities for work-experience and training for employment are made available; to enable additional members to be appointed to industrial training boards and to the Agricultural Training Board; and to provide that the terms on which certain persons hold office or employment under the Crown are to be treated for certain purposes as contained in contracts of employment*

[26 May 1988]

**NOTES**

Most of this Act has been repealed by, and re-enacted in, the Trade Union and Labour Relations (Consolidation) Act 1992 at **[1.241]** et seq. The provisions so affected are ss 1–23, 30, Sch 1 and parts of Sch 3. Various other provisions have also been repealed, as noted below. Remaining provisions of the Act are printed in full except as noted below.

**1–23** *((Pt I) repealed by the Trade Union and Labour Relations (Consolidation) Act 1992, s 300(1), Sch 1.)*

## PART II
## EMPLOYMENT AND TRAINING

**24, 25** *(S 24 repealed by the Employment Act 1989, s 29(4), Sch 7, Pt I; s 25 substitutes the Employment and Training Act 1973, ss 2, 3 and introduces Sch 2 (further amendments, etc, to the 1973 Act).)*

**[1.156]**
**26 Status of trainees etc**
(1) Where it appears to the Secretary of State that provision has been made under section 2 of the 1973 Act[, or under section 2(3) [or section 14A] of the Enterprise and New Towns (Scotland) Act 1990,] for persons using facilities provided in pursuance of arrangements under [any of those three sections] to receive payments from any person in connection with their use of those facilities, the Secretary of State may by order provide—
    (a)    that those persons are, for the purposes and in the cases specified or described in or determined under the order, to be treated in respect of their use of those facilities as being or as not being employed;
    (b)    that where those persons are treated as being employed they are to be treated as being the employees of the persons so specified, described or determined and of no others;
    (c)    that where those persons are treated as not being employed they are to be treated as being trained, or are to be treated in such other manner as may be so specified, described or determined; and
    (d)    that those payments are to be treated for the purposes of such enactments and subordinate legislation as may be so specified, described or determined in such manner as may be so specified, described or determined.
[(1A)    The Secretary of State may make an order under subsection (1B) where it appears to the Secretary of State that provision has been made for trainees to receive payments—
    (a)    from the Secretary of State under section 14 of the Education Act 2002,
    (b)    from the Chief Executive of Skills Funding under section 100(1)(c) or (d) of the Apprenticeships, Skills, Children and Learning Act 2009, or
    (c)    from the Welsh Ministers under section 34(1)(c) of the Learning and Skills Act 2000.
(1B)    An order under this subsection may provide—
    (a)    that the trainees are, for the purposes and in the cases specified or described in or determined under the order, to be treated in respect of the training as being or as not being employed;
    (b)    that where the trainees are treated as being employed they are to be treated as being the employees of the persons so specified, described or determined and of no others;
    (c)    that where the trainees are treated as not being employed, they are to be treated in such other manner as may be so specified, described or determined; and
    (d)    that the payments are to be treated for the purposes of such enactments and subordinate legislation as may be so specified, described or determined in such manner as may be so specified, described or determined.
For the purposes of subsection (1A) and this subsection, trainees are persons receiving or proposing to receive training.]

(2)   The power to make an order under this section shall be exercisable by statutory instrument subject to annulment in pursuance of a resolution of either House of Parliament; and such an order may—

   (a)   modify any enactment or subordinate legislation;

   (b)   make different provision for different purposes and for different cases; and

   (c)   contain such incidental, consequential and transitional provision as appears to the Secretary of State to be appropriate.

(3)   The consent of the Treasury shall be required for the making of any order under this section which contains provision for the manner in which any payment is to be treated for the purposes of the Income Tax Acts.

(4)   In this section—

"enactment" includes an enactment contained in this Act or in any Act passed after this Act; and "subordinate legislation" has the same meaning as in the Interpretation Act 1978.

**NOTES**

Sub-s (1): words in first (outer) pair of square brackets inserted by the Enterprise and New Towns (Scotland) Act 1990, s 38(1), Sch 4, para 16; words in second (inner) pair of square brackets inserted, and words in third pair of square brackets substituted, by the Trade Union Reform and Employment Rights Act 1993, s 49(2), Sch 8, para 38.

Sub-ss (1A), (1B): substituted, for sub-s (1A) (as inserted by the Learning and Skills Act 2000, s 149, Sch 9, paras 1, 14), by the Education Act 2011, s 67(1), Sch 16, para 7, as from 1 April 2012.

Orders: the Social Security (Employment Training: Payments) Order 1988, SI 1988/1409; the Employment Action (Miscellaneous Provisions) Order 1991, SI 1991/1995; the North Norfolk Action (Miscellaneous Provisions) Order 1993, SI 1993/1065; the Community Action (Miscellaneous Provisions) Order 1993, SI 1993/1621; the Learning for Work (Miscellaneous Provisions) Order 1993, SI 1993/1949; the Training for Work (Miscellaneous Provisions) Order 1995, SI 1995/1780; the Project Work (Miscellaneous Provisions) Order 1996, SI 1996/1623; the New Deal (Miscellaneous Provisions) Order 1998, SI 1998/217; the New Deal (Miscellaneous Provisions) (Amendment) Order 1998, SI 1998/1425; the Training for Work (Miscellaneous Provisions) (Amendment) Order 1998, SI 1998/1426; the New Deal (25 plus) (Miscellaneous Provisions) Order 1999, SI 1999/779; the New Deal (Miscellaneous Provisions) Order 2001, SI 2001/970; the New Deal (Lone Parents) (Miscellaneous Provisions) Order 2001, SI 2001/2915; the Flexible New Deal (Miscellaneous Provisions) Order 2009, SI 2009/1562; the Community Task Force (Miscellaneous Provisions) Order 2010, SI 2010/349.

**27–29**   (*S 27 repealed by the Social Security (Consequential Provisions) Act 1992, s 3(1), Sch 1; s 28 amends the Employment and Training Act 1973, s 4(3), (5); s 29 (membership of training boards) outside the scope of this work.*)

## PART III
## MISCELLANEOUS AND SUPPLEMENTAL

**30**   (*Repealed by the Trade Union and Labour Relations (Consolidation) Act 1992, s 300(1), Sch 1.*)

*Supplemental*

**[1.157]**
**31   Financial provisions**
There shall be paid out of money provided by Parliament any increases attributable to this Act in the sums payable under any other Act out of money so provided.

**[1.158]**
**32   Interpretation**
(1)   In this Act, except in so far as the context otherwise requires—

. . .

"the 1973 Act" means the Employment and Training Act 1973;

. . .

"modifications" includes additions, alterations and omissions, and cognate expressions shall be construed accordingly;

. . .

(2)   . . .

**NOTES**

Sub-s (1): definitions omitted repealed by the Trade Union and Labour Relations (Consolidation) Act 1992, s 300(1), Sch 1.
Sub-s (2): repealed by the Trade Union and Labour Relations (Consolidation) Act 1992, s 300(1), Sch 1.

**33**   (*Introduces Schs 3 and 4 (minor and consequential amendments, and repeals) outside the scope of this work.*)

**[1.159]**
**34   Short title, commencement and extent**
(1)   This Act may be cited as the Employment Act 1988.
(2), (3)   . . .
(4)–(6)   (*Outside the scope of this work.*)

**NOTES**
Sub-ss (2), (3): repealed by the Trade Union and Labour Relations (Consolidation) Act 1992, s 300(1), Sch 1.

## SCHEDULES

*(Sch 1, Sch 3, Pt I repealed by the Trade Union and Labour Relations (Consolidation) Act 1992, s 300(1), Sch 1; Sch 2 repealed in part by the Employment Act 1989, s 29(4), Sch 7, Pt I, remainder amends the Employment and Training Act 1973, ss 11(3), 12; Sch 3, Pt II contains minor and consequential amendments with regard to employment and training; Sch 4 contains various repeals.)*

# ACCESS TO MEDICAL REPORTS ACT 1988

(1988 c 28)

## ARRANGEMENT OF SECTIONS

*An Act to establish a right of access by individuals to reports relating to themselves provided by medical practitioners for employment or insurance purposes and to make provision for related matters*

[29 July 1988]

**[1.160]**
## 1 Right of access
It shall be the right of an individual to have access, in accordance with the provisions of this Act, to any medical report relating to the individual which is to be, or has been, supplied by a medical practitioner for employment purposes or insurance purposes.

**[1.161]**
## 2 Interpretation
(1)  In this Act—
    "the applicant" means the person referred to in section 3(1) below;
    "care" includes examination, investigation or diagnosis for the purposes of, or in connection with, any form of medical treatment;
    "employment purposes", in the case of any individual, means the purposes in relation to the individual of any person by whom he is or has been, or is seeking to be, employed (whether under a contract of service or otherwise);
    "health professional" has the same meaning as in [the Data Protection Act 1998];
    ["insurance purposes", in a case of any individual who has entered into, or is seeking to enter into, a contract of insurance with an insurer, means the purposes of that insurer in relation to that individual;
    "insurer" means—
      (a)   a person who has permission under [Part 4A] of the Financial Services and Markets Act 2000 to effect or carry out contracts of insurance;
      (b)   an EEA firm of the kind mentioned in paragraph 5(d) of Schedule 3 to that Act, which has permission under paragraph 15 of that Schedule (as a result of qualifying for authorisation under paragraph 12 of that Schedule) to effect or carry out relevant contracts of insurance.]
    "medical practitioner" means a person registered under the Medical Act 1983;
    "medical report", in the case of an individual, means a report relating to the physical or mental health of the individual prepared by a medical practitioner who is or has been responsible for the clinical care of the individual.
[(1A)  The definitions of "insurance purposes" and "insurer" in subsection (1) must be read with—
    (a)   section 22 of the Financial Services and Markets Act 2000;

(b)    any relevant order under that section; and
(c)    Schedule 2 to that Act.]
(2)   Any reference in this Act to the supply of a medical report for employment or insurance purposes shall be construed—
   (a)    as a reference to the supply of such a report for employment or insurance purposes which are purposes of the person who is seeking to be supplied with it; or
   (b)    (in the case of a report that has already been supplied) as a reference to the supply of such a report for employment or insurance purposes which, at the time of its being supplied, were purposes of the person to whom it was supplied.

**NOTES**
   Sub-s (1): in definition "health professional" words in square brackets substituted by the Data Protection Act 1998, s 74(1), Sch 15, para 8; definitions "insurance purposes" and "insurer" substituted for the original definition "insurance purposes" by the Financial Services and Markets Act 2000 (Consequential Amendments and Repeals) Order 2001, SI 2001/3649, art 311(1), (2); words in square brackets in definition "insurer" substituted by the Financial Services Act 2012, s 114(1), Sch 18, Pt 2, para 59, as from 1 April 2013.
   Sub-s (1A): inserted by SI 2001/3649, art 311(1), (3).

**[1.162]**
**3   Consent to applications for medical reports for employment or insurance purposes**
(1)   A person shall not apply to a medical practitioner for a medical report relating to any individual to be supplied to him for employment or insurance purposes unless—
   (a)    that person ("the applicant") has notified the individual that he proposes to make the application; and
   (b)    the individual has notified the applicant that he consents to the making of the application.
(2)   Any notification given under subsection (1)(a) above must inform the individual of his right to withhold his consent to the making of the application, and of the following rights under this Act, namely—
   (a)    the rights arising under sections 4(1) to (3) and 6(2) below with respect to access to the report before or after it is supplied,
   (b)    the right to withhold consent under subsection (1) of section 5 below, and
   (c)    the right to request the amendment of the report under subsection (2) of that section,
as well as of the effect of section 7 below.

**[1.163]**
**4   Access to reports before they are supplied**
(1)   An individual who gives his consent under section 3 above to the making of an application shall be entitled, when giving his consent, to state that he wishes to have access to the report to be supplied in response to the application before it is so supplied; and, if he does so, the applicant shall—
   (a)    notify the medical practitioner of that fact at the time when the application is made, and
   (b)    at the same time notify the individual of the making of the application;
and each such notification shall contain a statement of the effect of subsection (2) below.
(2)   Where a medical practitioner is notified by the applicant under subsection (1) above that the individual in question wishes to have access to the report before it is supplied, the practitioner shall not supply the report unless—
   (a)    he has given the individual access to it and any requirements of section 5 below have been complied with, or
   (b)    the period of 21 days beginning with the date of the making of the application has elapsed without his having received any communication from the individual concerning arrangements for the individual to have access to it.
(3)   Where a medical practitioner—
   (a)    receives an application for a medical report to be supplied for employment or insurance purposes without being notified by the applicant as mentioned in subsection (1) above, but
   (b)    before supplying the report receives a notification from the individual that he wishes to have access to the report before it is supplied,
the practitioner shall not supply the report unless—
   (i)    he has given the individual access to it and any requirements of section 5 below have been complied with, or
   (ii)   the period of 21 days beginning with the date of that notification has elapsed without his having received (either with that notification or otherwise) any communication from the individual concerning arrangements for the individual to have access to it.
(4)   References in this section and section 5 below to giving an individual access to a medical report are references to—
   (a)    making the report or a copy of it available for his inspection; or
   (b)    supplying him with a copy of it;
and where a copy is supplied at the request, or otherwise with the consent, of the individual the practitioner may charge a reasonable fee to cover the costs of supplying it.

**[1.164]**
## 5 Consent to supplying of report and correction of errors
(1) Where an individual has been given access to a report under section 4 above the report shall not be supplied in response to the application in question unless the individual has notified the medical practitioner that he consents to its being so supplied.
(2) The individual shall be entitled, before giving his consent under subsection (1) above, to request the medical practitioner to amend any part of the report which the individual considers to be incorrect or misleading; and, if the individual does so, the practitioner—
    (a) if he is to any extent prepared to accede to the individual's request, shall amend the report accordingly;
    (b) if he is to any extent not prepared to accede to it but the individual requests him to attach to the report a statement of the individual's views in respect of any part of the report which he is declining to amend, shall attach such a statement to the report.
(3) Any request made by an individual under subsection (2) above shall be made in writing.

**[1.165]**
## 6 Retention of reports
(1) A copy of any medical report which a medical practitioner has supplied for employment or insurance purposes shall be retained by him for at least six months from the date on which it was supplied.
(2) A medical practitioner shall, if so requested by an individual, give the individual access to any medical report relating to him which the practitioner has supplied for employment or insurance purposes in the previous six months.
(3) The reference in subsection (2) above to giving an individual access to a medical report is a reference to—
    (a) making a copy of the report available for his inspection; or
    (b) supplying him with a copy of it;
and where a copy is supplied at the request, or otherwise with the consent, of the individual the practitioner may charge a reasonable fee to cover the costs of supplying it.

**[1.166]**
## 7 Exemptions
(1) A medical practitioner shall not be obliged to give an individual access, in accordance with the provisions of section 4(4) or 6(3) above, to any part of a medical report whose disclosure would in the opinion of the practitioner be likely to cause serious harm to the physical or mental health of the individual or others or would indicate the intentions of the practitioner in respect of the individual.
(2) A medical practitioner shall not be obliged to give an individual access, in accordance with those provisions, to any part of a medical report whose disclosure would be likely to reveal information about another person, or to reveal the identity of another person who has supplied information to the practitioner about the individual, unless—
    (a) that person has consented; or
    (b) that person is a health professional who has been involved in the care of the individual and the information relates to or has been provided by the professional in that capacity.
(3) Where it appears to a medical practitioner that subsection (1) or (2) above is applicable to any part (but not the whole) of a medical report—
    (a) he shall notify the individual of that fact; and
    (b) references in the preceding sections of this Act to the individual being given access to the report shall be construed as references to his being given access to the remainder of it;
and other references to the report in sections 4(4), 5(2) and 6(3) above shall similarly be construed as references to the remainder of the report.
(4) Where it appears to a medical practitioner that subsection (1) or (2) above is applicable to the whole of a medical report—
    (a) he shall notify the individual of that fact; but
    (b) he shall not supply the report unless he is notified by the individual that the individual consents to its being supplied;
and accordingly, if he is so notified by the individual, the restrictions imposed by section 4(2) and (3) above on the supply of the report shall not have effect in relation to it.

**[1.167]**
## 8 Application to the court
(1) If a court is satisfied on the application of an individual that any person, in connection with a medical report relating to that individual, has failed or is likely to fail to comply with any requirement of this Act, the court may order that person to comply with that requirement.
(2) The jurisdiction conferred by this section shall be exercisable by *a county court* or, in Scotland, by the sheriff.

Part 1  Statutes

**NOTES**
 Sub-s (2): for the words in italics there are substituted the words "the county court" by the Crime and Courts Act 2013, s 17(5), Sch 9, Pt 3, para 52, as from a day to be appointed.

**[1.168]**
**9   Notifications under this Act**
Any notification required or authorised to be given under this Act—
  (a)   shall be given in writing; and
  (b)   may be given by post.

**[1.169]**
**10   Short title, commencement and extent**
(1)   This Act may be cited as the Access to Medical Reports Act 1988.
(2)   This Act shall come into force on 1st January 1989.
(3)   Nothing in this Act applies to a medical report prepared before the coming into force of this Act.
(4)   This Act does not extend to Northern Ireland.

# EDUCATION REFORM ACT 1988

## (1988 c 40)

*An Act to amend the law relating to education*

[29 July 1988]

**NOTES**
 Most of the provisions of this Act that were within the scope of this work were repealed and re-enacted by the Education Act 1996. Those provisions have in turn been repealed and re-enacted with (relatively minor) amendments by the School Standards and Framework Act 1998: see **[1.1074]** et seq for the 1998 Act. For reasons of space, the subject matter of sections, etc, not printed is not annotated.

## PART IV
## MISCELLANEOUS AND GENERAL
*Miscellaneous provisions*

**[1.170]**
**221   Avoidance of certain contractual terms**
[(1)   This section applies to any contract made after 20th November 1987—
  (a)   for purposes connected with a local authority's education functions, between the authority and a person employed by the authority; or
  (b)   between a governing body of a foundation, voluntary aided or foundation special school and a person employed by the governing body,
other than a contract made in contemplation of the employee's pending dismissal by reason of redundancy.]
and any person employed by them, not being a contract made in contemplation of the employee's pending dismissal by reason of redundancy.
(2)   In so far as a contract to which this section applies provides that the employee—
  (a)   shall not be dismissed by reason of redundancy; or
  (b)   if he is so dismissed, shall be paid a sum in excess of the sum which the employer is liable to pay him under [section 135 of the Employment Rights Act 1996],
the contract shall be void and of no effect.
(3)   In this section—
   "governing body, in relation to an institution, includes a body corporate established for the purpose of conducting that institution;
   . . .

**NOTES**
 Sub-s (1): substituted by the Local Education Authorities and Children's Services Authorities (Integration of Functions) Order 2010, SI 2010/1158, art 5, Sch 2, Pt 1, para 4(1), (4), as from 5 May 2010.
 Sub-s (2): words in square brackets substituted by the Employment Rights Act 1996, s 240, Sch 1, paras 37(1), (4).
 Sub-s (3): definition omitted repealed by the Further and Higher Education Act 1992, s 93, Sch 8, Pt I, paras 27, 52, Sch 9.

**[1.171]**
**238  Citation, extent etc**
(1)  This Act may be cited as the Education Reform Act 1988.
(2)  . . .
(3)  Subject to subsections (4) to (6) below, this Act does not extend to Scotland or Northern Ireland.
(4)–(6)  (*Outside the scope of this work.*)

**NOTES**
Sub-s (2): repealed by the Education Act 1996, s 582(2), Sch 38, Pt I.

# SOCIAL SECURITY ACT 1989

## (1989 c 24)

*An Act to amend the law relating to social security and occupational and personal pension schemes; to make provision with respect to certain employment-related benefit schemes; to provide for the recovery, out of certain compensation payments, of amounts determined by reference to payments of benefit; to make fresh provision with respect to the constitution and functions of war pensions committees; and for connected purposes*

[21 July 1989]

**NOTES**
Only s 23 and Sch 5, which implemented Council Directive 86/378/EEC, and s 33 (short title, etc) are printed here. The Directive itself required implementation by 1 January 1993, but as at 6 April 2013 only those parts of Sch 5 relating to (i) unfair maternity and parental leave provisions, (ii) unfair paternity leave provisions, and (iii) non-compliance – compulsory levelling up (in respect of unfair paternity leave provisions and unfair adoption leave provisions) have been brought into force (as from 23 June 1994, 6 April 2005, and 24 August 2007, respectively); see the first note to Sch 5 for details. Note that the 1986 Directive was repealed and replaced as from 15 August 2009 by the Directive of the European Parliament and of the Council on the implementation of the principle of equal opportunities and equal treatment of men and women in matters of employment and occupation (recast) (Directive 2006/54/EC at **[3.471]** et seq). No provisions of Sch 5, Pt II have been brought into effect, and all have been repealed. Additional provisions relating to paternity and adoption leave were inserted into Sch 5 by the Pensions Act 2004, s 265(1).
See *Harvey* BI(11), L(2).

*Occupational and personal pensions etc*

**[1.172]**
**23  Equal treatment for men and women**
Schedule 5 to this Act shall have effect for the purpose of implementing the directive of the Council of the European Communities, dated 24th July 1986, relating to the principle of equal treatment for men and women in occupational social security schemes, and of making additional, supplemental and consequential provision.

**NOTES**
Commencement: 23 June 1994 and 24 August 2007, in so far as relating to those original provisions of Sch 5 which came into force on those dates (see the note to Sch 5 at **[1.174]** for details); to be appointed (otherwise).

**[1.173]**
**33  Short title, commencement and extent**
(1)  This Act may be cited as the Social Security Act 1989; and this Act, other than section 25, and the Social Security Acts 1975 to 1988 may be cited together as the Social Security Acts 1975 to 1989.
(2)  Apart from the provisions specified in subsection (3) below, this Act shall come into force on such day as the Secretary of State may by order appoint; and different days may be so appointed for different provisions or different purposes of the same provision.
(3)–(7)  (*Outside the scope of this work.*)

**NOTES**
Orders: the commencement orders relevant to the provisions printed here are the Social Security Act 1989 (Commencement No 5) Order 1994, SI 1994/1661 and the Social Security Act 1989 (Commencement No 6) Order 2007, SI 2007/2445.

# SCHEDULES

## SCHEDULE 5
### EMPLOYMENT-RELATED SCHEMES FOR PENSIONS OR OTHER BENEFITS: EQUAL TREATMENT FOR MEN AND WOMEN

Section 23

## PART I
### COMPLIANCE BY SCHEMES

*Schemes to comply with the principle of equal treatment*

**[1.174]**
1. Every employment-related benefit scheme shall comply with the principle of equal treatment.

*The principle*

**2.** (1)   The principle of equal treatment is that persons of the one sex shall not, on the basis of sex, be treated less favourably than persons of the other sex in any respect relating to an employment-related benefit scheme.

(2)   Sub-paragraphs (3) to (6) below have effect, where applicable, for the purpose of determining whether a scheme complies with the principle of equal treatment.

(3)   Where any provision of the scheme imposes on both male and female members a requirement or condition—
   (a)   which is such that the proportion of persons of the one sex ("the sex affected") who can comply with it is considerably smaller than the proportion of persons of the other sex who can do so, and
   (b)   which is not justifiable irrespective of the sex of the members,
the imposition of that requirement or condition shall be regarded as less favourable treatment of persons of the sex affected.

(4)   No account shall be taken of—
   (a)   any difference, on the basis of the sex of members, in the levels of contributions—
      (i)      . . .
      (ii)   which the employer makes, to the extent that the difference is for the purpose of removing or limiting differences, as between men and women, in the amount or value of money purchase benefits;
   (b)   any difference, on the basis of sex, in the amount or value of money purchase benefits, to the extent that the difference is justifiable on actuarial grounds;
   (c)   any special treatment for the benefit of women in connection with pregnancy or childbirth;
   (d)   any permitted age-related differences;
   (e)   any difference of treatment in relation to benefits for a deceased member's surviving husband, wife or other dependants;
   (f)   any difference of treatment in relation to any optional provisions available; or
   (g)   any provisions of a scheme to the extent that they have been specially arranged for the benefit of one particular member of the scheme;
. . . .

(5)   Where the scheme treats persons of the one sex differently according to their marital or family status, that treatment is to be compared with the scheme's treatment of persons of the other sex who have the same status.

(6)   The principle of equal treatment applies in relation to members' dependants as it applies in relation to members.

(7)   If any question arises whether a condition or requirement falling within sub-paragraph (3)(a) above is or is not justifiable irrespective of the sex of the members, it shall be for those who assert that it is so justifiable to prove that fact.

(8)   In this paragraph—
   "money purchase benefits" has the meaning given by *section 84(1) of the 1986 Act*, but with the substitution for references to a personal or occupational pension scheme of references to an employment-related benefit scheme;
   "optional provisions available" means those provisions of a scheme—
      (a)   which apply only in the case of members who elect for them to do so; and
      (b)   whose purpose is to secure for those members—
         (i)   benefits in addition to those otherwise provided under the scheme; or
         (ii)   a choice with respect to the date on which benefits under the scheme are to commence; or
         (iii)   a choice between any two or more benefits;
   "permitted age-related difference" means any difference, on the basis of sex, in the age—
      (a)   at which a service-related benefit in respect of old age or retirement commences; or

    (b)    at which, in consequence of the commencement of such a benefit, any other service-related benefit either ceases to be payable or becomes payable at a reduced rate calculated by reference to the amount of the benefit so commencing.

(9)   For the purposes of this paragraph—

  (a)    any reference to a person's family status is a reference to his having an unmarried partner or any dependants; and

  (b)    a person "has an unmarried partner" if that person and some other person to whom he is not married live together as husband and wife.

*Non-compliance: compulsory levelling up*

**3.**  (1)  To the extent that any provision of an employment-related benefit scheme does not comply with the principle of equal treatment, it shall be overridden by this Schedule and the more favourable treatment accorded to persons of the one sex shall also be accorded to persons of the other sex.

(2)  Where more favourable treatment is accorded to any persons by virtue of sub-paragraph (1) above, that sub-paragraph requires them, in accordance with the principle of equal treatment—

  (a)    to pay contributions at a level appropriate to the treatment so accorded; and

  (b)    to bear any other burden which is an incident of that treatment;

but persons of either sex may instead elect to receive the less favourable treatment and, in accordance with the principle of equal treatment, pay contributions at the level appropriate to that treatment and bear the other burdens incidental to it.

(3)  Where any provision of a scheme is overridden by sub-paragraph (1) above, nothing in this Schedule shall affect any rights accrued or obligations incurred during the period before the date on which that provision is so overridden.

(4)  Sub-paragraph (1) above is without prejudice to the exercise, in compliance with the principle of equal treatment, of any power to amend the scheme.

**4.**  . . .

*Unfair maternity provisions*

**5.**  . . .

*[Unfair paternity leave provisions*

**5A.**  (1)  Where an employment-related benefit scheme includes any unfair paternity leave provisions (irrespective of any differences on the basis of sex in the treatment accorded to members under those provisions), then—

  (a)    the scheme shall be regarded to that extent as not complying with the principle of equal treatment; and

  (b)    subject to sub-paragraph (3), this Schedule shall apply accordingly.

(2)  In this paragraph "unfair paternity leave provisions", in relation to an employment-related benefit scheme, means any provision—

  (a)    which relates to continuing membership of, or the accrual of rights under, the scheme during any period of paid paternity leave in the case of any member who is (or who, immediately before the commencement of such a period, was) an employed earner and which treats such a member otherwise than in accordance with the normal employment requirement; or

  (b)    which requires the amount of any benefit payable under the scheme to or in respect of any such member, to the extent that it falls to be determined by reference to earnings during a period which included a period of paid paternity leave, to be determined otherwise than in accordance with the normal employment requirement.

(3)  In the case of any unfair paternity leave provision—

  (a)    the more favourable treatment required by paragraph 3(1) is treatment no less favourable than would be accorded to the member in accordance with the normal employment requirement; and

  (b)    paragraph 3(2) does not authorise the making of any such election as is there mentioned;

but, in respect of any period of paid paternity leave, a member shall only be required to pay contributions on the amount of contractual remuneration[, ordinary statutory paternity pay or additional statutory paternity pay] actually paid to or for him in respect of that period.

(4)  In this paragraph—

"period of paid paternity leave", in the case of a member, means a period—

  (a)    throughout which the member is absent from work in circumstances where sub-paragraph (5), (6)[, (7) or (8)] applies, and

  (b)    for which the employer (or if he is no longer in his employment, his former employer) pays him any contractual remuneration[, ordinary statutory paternity pay or additional statutory paternity pay]; and "the normal employment requirement" is the requirement that any period of paid paternity leave shall be treated as if it were a period throughout which the member in question works normally and receives the remuneration likely to be paid for doing so.

(5)   This sub-paragraph applies if—
(a)   the member's absence from work is due to the birth or expected birth of a child, and
(b)   the member satisfies the conditions prescribed under section 171ZA(2)(a)(i) and (ii) of the Social Security Contributions and Benefits Act 1992 in relation to that child.

(6)   This sub-paragraph applies if—
(a)   the member's absence from work is due to the placement or expected placement of a child for adoption under the law of any part of the United Kingdom, and
(b)   the member satisfies the conditions prescribed under section 171ZB(2)(a)(i) and (ii) of that Act in relation to that child.

(7)   This sub-paragraph applies if—
(a)   the member's absence from work is due to the adoption or expected adoption of a child who has entered the United Kingdom in connection with or for the purposes of adoption which does not involve the placement of the child for adoption under the law of any part of the United Kingdom, and
(b)   the member satisfies the conditions prescribed under section 171ZB(2)(a)(i) and (ii) of that Act (as applied by virtue of section 171ZK of that Act (adoption cases not involving placement under the law of the United Kingdom)) in relation to that child.

[(8)   This sub-paragraph applies if—
(a)   the member's absence from work is due to the fact that he is caring for a child, and
(b)   in relation to that child, the member satisfies the conditions prescribed—
(i)   under section 171ZEA(2)(a)(i) and (ii) of that Act,
(ii)   under section 171ZEB(2)(a)(i) and (ii) of that Act, or
(iii)   under section 171ZEB(2)(a)(i) and (ii) of that Act as applied by virtue of section 171ZK of that Act (adoption cases not involving placement under the law of the United Kingdom).]

### *Unfair adoption leave provisions*

**5B.** (1)   Where an employment-related benefit scheme includes any unfair adoption leave provisions (irrespective of any differences on the basis of sex in the treatment accorded to members under those provisions), then—
(a)   the scheme shall be regarded to that extent as not complying with the principle of equal treatment; and
(b)   subject to sub-paragraph (3), this Schedule shall apply accordingly.

(2)   In this paragraph "unfair adoption leave provisions", in relation to an employment-related benefit scheme, means any provision—
(a)   which relates to continuing membership of, or the accrual of rights under, the scheme during any period of paid adoption leave in the case of any member who is (or who, immediately before the commencement of such a period, was) an employed earner and which treats such a member otherwise than in accordance with the normal employment requirement; or
(b)   which requires the amount of any benefit payable under the scheme to or in respect of any such member, to the extent that it falls to be determined by reference to earnings during a period which included a period of paid adoption leave, to be determined otherwise than in accordance with the normal employment requirement.

(3)   In the case of any unfair adoption leave provision—
(a)   the more favourable treatment required by paragraph 3(1) is treatment no less favourable than would be accorded to the member in accordance with the normal employment requirement; and
(b)   paragraph 3(2) does not authorise the making of any such election as is there mentioned; but, in respect of any period of paid adoption leave, a member shall only be required to pay contributions on the amount of contractual remuneration or statutory adoption pay actually paid to or for him in respect of that period.

(4)   In this paragraph—
"period of paid adoption leave", in the case of a member, means a period—
(a)   throughout which the member is absent from work in circumstances where sub-paragraph (5) or (6) applies, and
(b)   for which the employer (or, if he is no longer in his employment, his former employer) pays him any contractual remuneration or statutory adoption pay; and
"the normal employment requirement" is the requirement that any period of paid adoption leave shall be treated as if it were a period throughout which the member in question works normally and receives the remuneration likely to be paid for doing so.

(5)   This sub-paragraph applies if—

(a)  the member's absence from work is due to the placement, or expected placement, of a child for adoption under the law of any part of the United Kingdom, and

(b)  the member is a person with whom the child is, or is expected to be, placed for such adoption.

(6)  This sub-paragraph applies if—

(a)  the member's absence from work is due to the adoption or expected adoption of a child who has entered the United Kingdom in connection with or for the purposes of adoption which does not involve the placement of the child for adoption under the law of any part of the United Kingdom, and

(b)  the member is a person by whom the child has been or is expected to be adopted.]

### *Unfair family leave provisions*

**6.** (1)  Where an employment-related benefit scheme includes any unfair family leave provisions (irrespective of any differences on the basis of sex in the treatment accorded to members under those provisions), then—

(a)  the scheme shall be regarded to that extent as not complying with the principle of equal treatment; and

(b)  subject to sub-paragraph (3) below, this Schedule shall apply accordingly.

(2)  In this Schedule "unfair family leave provisions" means any provision—

(a)  which relates to continuing membership of, or the accrual of rights under, the scheme during any period of paid family leave in the case of any member who is an employed earner and which treats such a member otherwise than in accordance with the normal leave requirement; or

(b)  which requires the amount of any benefit payable under the scheme to or in respect of any such member to the extent that it falls to be determined by reference to earnings during a period which included a period of paid family leave, to be determined otherwise than in accordance with the normal leave requirement.

(3)  In the case of any unfair family leave provision—

(a)  the more favourable treatment required by paragraph 3(1) above is treatment no less favourable than would be accorded to the members in accordance with the normal leave requirement;

(b)  paragraph 3(2) above does not authorise the making of any such election as is there mentioned; and

(c)  paragraph 4(1)(a) above does not authorise the making of any modification which does not satisfy the requirements of paragraph (a) above;

but, in respect of a period of paid family leave, a member shall only be required to pay contributions on the amount of contractual remuneration actually paid to or for him in respect of that period.

(4)  In this paragraph—

(a)  "period of paid family leave" means any period—

(i)  throughout which a member is absent from work for family reasons; and

(ii)  for which the employer pays him any contractual remuneration;

(b)  "the normal leave requirement" is the requirement that any period of paid family leave shall be treated as if it were a period throughout which the member in question works normally but only receives the remuneration in fact paid to him for that period.

### *Meaning of "employment-related benefit scheme" etc*

**7.** In this Schedule—

(a)  "employment-related benefit scheme" means any scheme or arrangement which is comprised in one or more instruments or agreements and which has, or is capable of having, effect in relation to one or more descriptions or categories of employments so as to provide service-related benefits to or in respect of employed or self-employed earners—

(i)  who have qualifying service in an employment of any such description or category, or

(ii)  who have made arrangements with the trustees or managers of the scheme to enable them to become members of the scheme,

but does not include a limited scheme;

(b)  "limited scheme" means—

(i)  any personal scheme for employed earners to which the employer does not contribute;

(ii)  any scheme which has only one member, other than a personal scheme for an employed earner to which his employer contributes;

(iii)  any contract of insurance which is made for the benefit of employed earners only and to which the employer is not a party;

(c)     "personal scheme" means any scheme or arrangement which falls within paragraph (a) above by virtue of sub-paragraph (ii) of that paragraph (or which would so fall apart from paragraph (b) above);

(d)     "public service scheme" has *the meaning given by section 51(3)(b) of the 1973 Act*;

(e)     "service-related benefits" means benefits, in the form of pensions or otherwise, payable in money or money's worth in respect of—

    (i)      termination of service;

    (ii)     retirement, old age or death;

    (iii)    interruptions of service by reason of sickness or invalidity;

    (iv)    accidents, injuries or diseases connected with employment;

    (v)     unemployment; or

    (vi)    expenses incurred in connection with children or other dependants;

and includes, in the case of a member who is an employed earner, any other benefit so payable to or in respect of the member in consequence of his employment.

### Extension of ban on compulsory membership

**8.** *Section 15(1) of the 1986 Act* (which renders void any provision making membership of a pension scheme compulsory for an employed earner) shall apply in relation to a self-employed earner as it applies in relation to an employed earner, but with the substitution for references to a personal pension scheme of references to an employment-related benefit scheme which would be such a pension scheme if self-employed earners were regarded as employed earners.

### Jurisdiction

**9.** (1)   The court, on the application of any person interested, shall have jurisdiction to determine any question arising as to—

    (a)     whether any provision of an employment-related benefit scheme does or does not comply with the principle of equal treatment; or

    (b)     whether, and with what effect, any such provision is overridden by paragraph 3 above.

(2)   In sub-paragraph (1) above "the court" means—

    (a)     in England and Wales, the High Court or *a county court*; and

    (b)     in Scotland, the Court of Session or the sheriff court.

(3)   An application under sub-paragraph (1) above may be commenced in *a county court* notwithstanding—

    (a)     any financial limit otherwise imposed on the jurisdiction of *such a* court; or

    (b)     that the only relief claimed is a declaration or an injunction.

### Interpretation

**10.** Expressions other than "benefit" which are used in this Part of this Schedule and in the principal Act have the same meaning in this Part of this Schedule as they have in that Act.

### Supplemental

**11.** . . . . . .

### Future repeal of actuarial provisions

**12.** The Secretary of State may by order repeal paragraph 2(4)(a)(i) above; and if and to the extent that he has not done so before 30th July 1999 it shall cease to have effect on that date.

---

**NOTES**

Commencement: this Schedule has been brought into force as follows (and is to be appointed otherwise)—

(i) on 23 June 1994 in so far as relating to paras 5 (except sub-para (2)(b) and (c)) and 6 (except sub-para (3)(b) and (c)); also paras 1, 2(1), (2), (4)(c), (5), (9), 3 (except sub-para (2)), 7 (except sub-para (d)), 9 and 10, but for the purposes only of giving effect to the provisions of paras 5 and 6 brought into force from that date: see SI 1994/1661, art 2(a), (b), Schedule, Pts I, II.

(ii) on 24 August 2007 in so far as relating to para 3 (except sub-paragraph (2)) for the purposes of paras 5A, 5B: see SI 2007/2445, art 2.

Note that paras 5A, 5B (as inserted by the Pensions Act 2004) came into force on 6 April 2005 (see below).

Para 2: sub-para (4)(a)(i) repealed as from 30 July 1999 by para 12 (qv; no order was made under para 12 prior to the date there stated); final words omitted from sub-para (4) repealed by the Equality Act 2010, s 211(2), Sch 27, Pt 1, as from 1 October 2010; for the words in italics in sub-para (8) there are substituted the words "section 181(1) of the Pension Schemes Act 1993" by the Pension Schemes Act 1993, s 190, Sch 7, para 2(a), as from a day to be appointed.

Para 4: repealed by the Pensions Act 1995, ss 151, 177, Sch 5, para 13(2), Sch 7, Pt III.

Para 5: repealed by the Equality Act 2010, s 211(2), Sch 27, Pt 1, as from 1 October 2010.

Para 5A: inserted, together with para 5B, by the Pensions Act 2004, s 265(1); words in square brackets in sub-paras (3), (4) substituted, and sub-para (8) added, by the Work and Families Act 2006, s 11(1), Sch 1, para 1, as from 6 April 2010.

Para 5B: inserted as noted above.

Para 7: for the words in italics in sub-para (d) there are substituted the words "the same meaning as "public service pension scheme" in section 1 of the Pension Schemes Act 1993" by the Pension Schemes Act 1993, s 190, Sch 7, para 2(b), as from a day to be appointed.

Para 8: for the words in italics there are substituted the words "section 160(1) of the Pension Schemes Act 1993" by the Pension Schemes Act 1993, s 190, Sch 7, para 2(c), as from a day to be appointed.

Para 9: for the words "a county court" in italics in both places they appear, there are substituted the words "the county court" and for the words "such a" in italics in sub-para (3)(a) there is substituted the word "that", by the Crime and Courts Act 2013, s 17(5), Sch 9, Pt 3, paras 52, 128, as from a day to be appointed.

Para 11: repealed by the Pension Schemes Act 1993, s 188(1), Sch 5, Pt I.

1986 Act: ie, the Social Security Act 1986. Section 15(1) and the definition "money purchase benefits" in s 84(1) were repealed and replaced by the Pension Schemes Act 1993 (see now s 160(1) and s 181(1) of that Act respectively).

1973 Act: ie, the Social Security Act 1973. Section 51(3)(b) was repealed by the Pension Schemes Act 1993. The definition "public service scheme" is now replaced by the definition "public service pension scheme" in s 1 of that Act.

Principal Act: ie, the Social Security Act 1975. Repealed by the Social Security (Consequential Provisions) Act 1992 and replaced by the Social Security Administration Act 1992 and the Social Security Contributions and Benefits Act 1992.

*(Sch 5, Pt II: para 13 repealed by the Pension Schemes Act 1993, s 188(1), Sch 5, Pt II; para 14 repealed by the Pensions Act 1995, s 177, Sch 7, Pt I; Sch 5, Pt II, para 15 repealed by the Trade Union Reform and Employment Rights Act 1993, s 51, Sch 10.)*

# EMPLOYMENT ACT 1989

## (1989 c 38)

### ARRANGEMENT OF SECTIONS

*An Act to amend the Sex Discrimination Act 1975 in pursuance of the Directive of the Council of the European Communities, dated 9th February 1976, (No 76/207/EEC) on the implementation of the principle of equal treatment for men and women as regards access to employment, vocational training and promotion, and working conditions; to repeal or amend prohibitions or requirements relating to the employment of young persons and other categories of employees; to make other amendments of the law relating to employment and training; to repeal section 1(1)(a) of the Celluloid and Cinematograph Film Act 1922; to dissolve the Training Commission; to make further provision with respect to industrial training boards; to make provision with respect to the transfer of staff employed in the Skills Training Agency; and for connected purposes*

[16 November 1989]

**NOTES**

Transfer of functions in relation to Wales: as to the transfer of functions under this Act from Ministers of the Crown to the National Assembly for Wales, see the National Assembly for Wales (Transfer of Functions) Order 1999, SI 1999/672.

See *Harvey* L2(E), (F), (G).

**1–6**    *(Ss 1–6 repealed by the Equality Act 2010, s 211(2), Sch 27, Pt 1, as from 1 October 2010. With regard to the repeal of s 1 (overriding of statutory requirements which conflict with certain provisions of the Sex Discrimination Act 1975), see the Equality Act 2010 (Commencement No 4, Savings, Consequential, Transitional, Transitory and Incidental Provisions and Revocation) Order 2010, SI 2010/2317, art 17 at* **[2.1570]** *which provides that despite the repeal of that section, any provision which, immediately before that repeal, is of no effect as a result of that section continues to be of no effect.)*

*Discrimination as respects training*

**7**    *(Repealed by the Equality Act 2010, s 211(2), Sch 27, Pt 1, as from 1 October 2010.)*

**[1.175]**

**8   Power to exempt discrimination in favour of lone parents in connection with training**

(1)   The Secretary of State may by order provide with respect to—

   (a)   any specified arrangements made under section 2 of the Employment and Training Act 1973 (functions of the Secretary of State as respects employment and training) [or under section 2(3) of the Enterprise and New Towns (Scotland) Act 1990 (arrangements by Scottish Enterprise and Highlands and Islands Enterprise in connection with training etc)], or

   (b)   any specified class or description of training for employment provided otherwise than in pursuance of [either of those sections], . . .

   (c)   . . .

that this section shall apply to such special treatment afforded to or in respect of lone parents in connection with their participation in those arrangements, or in that training or scheme, as is specified or referred to in the order.

(2)   Where this section applies to any treatment afforded to or in respect of lone parents, neither the treatment so afforded nor any act done in the implementation of any such treatment shall be regarded [for the purposes of the Equality Act 2010 as giving rise to any contravention of Part 5 of that Act, so far as relating to marriage and civil partnership discrimination (within the meaning of that Act)]

(3)   An order under subsection (1) above may specify or refer to special treatment afforded as mentioned in that subsection—

   (a)   whether it is afforded by the making of any payment or by the fixing of special conditions for participation in the arrangements, training or scheme in question, or otherwise, and

   (b)   whether it is afforded by the Secretary of State or by some other person;

and, without prejudice to the generality of paragraph (b) of that subsection, any class or description of training for employment specified in such an order by virtue of that paragraph may be framed by reference to the person, or the class or description of persons, by whom the training is provided.

(4)   In this section—

   (a)   "employment" and "training" have the same meaning as in the Employment and Training Act 1973; and

   (b)   *"lone parent" has the same meaning as it has for the purposes of any regulations made in pursuance of section 20(1)(a) of the Social Security Act 1986 (income support).*

**NOTES**

Sub-s (1): words in square brackets in para (a) inserted, and words in square brackets in para (b) substituted, by the Enterprise and New Towns (Scotland) Act 1990, s 38(1), Sch 4, para 18; para (c) and word omitted immediately preceding it repealed by the Statute Law (Repeals) Act 2004.

Sub-s (2): words in square brackets substituted by the Equality Act 2010, s 211(1), Sch 26, Pt 1, paras 13, 14, as from 1 October 2010.

Sub-s (4): para (b) substituted by new paras (b), (c), by the Universal Credit (Consequential, Supplementary, Incidental and Miscellaneous Provisions) Regulations 2013, SI 2013/630, reg 7, as from 29 April 2013, as follows:

   "(b)   "couple" has the meaning given by section 39(1) of the Welfare Reform Act 2012; and

   (c)   "lone parent" means a person who—

     (i)   is not a member of a couple, and

     (ii)   is responsible for, and a member of the same household as, a child.".

Orders: the Sex Discrimination Act (Exemption of Special Treatment for Lone Parents) Order 1989, SI 1989/2140 at **[2.117]**; the Sex Discrimination Act (Exemption of Special Treatment for Lone Parents) Order 1991, SI 1991/2813 at **[2.132]**.

*Removal of restrictions and other requirements relating to employment*

**9, 10**   *(S 9 repealed by the Equality Act 2010, s 211(2), Sch 27, Pt 1, as from 1 October 2010; s 10 (Removal of restrictions relating to employment of young persons) outside the scope of this work.)*

**[1.176]**

**11   Exemption of Sikhs from requirements as to wearing of safety helmets on construction sites**

(1)   Any requirement to wear a safety helmet which (apart from this section) would, by virtue of any statutory provision or rule of law, be imposed on a Sikh who is on a construction site shall not apply to him at any time when he is wearing a turban.

(2)   Accordingly, where—

   (a)   a Sikh who is on a construction site is for the time being wearing a turban, and

   (b)   (apart from this section) any associated requirement would, by virtue of any statutory provision or rule of law, be imposed—

     (i)   on the Sikh, or

     (ii)   on any other person,

in connection with the wearing by the Sikh of a safety helmet, that requirement shall not apply to the Sikh or (as the case may be) to that other person.

(3)   In subsection (2) "associated requirement" means any requirement (other than one falling within subsection (1)) which is related to or connected with the wearing, provision or maintenance of safety helmets.

(4)   It is hereby declared that, where a person does not comply with any requirement, being a requirement which for the time being does not apply to him by virtue of subsection (1) or (2)—

(a)   he shall not be liable in tort to any person in respect of any injury, loss or damage caused by his failure to comply with that requirement; and

(b)   in Scotland no action for reparation shall be brought against him by any person in respect of any such injury, loss or damage.

(5)   If a Sikh who is on a construction site—

(a)   does not comply with any requirement to wear a safety helmet, being a requirement which for the time being does not apply to him by virtue of subsection (1), and

(b)   in consequence of any act or omission of some other person sustains any injury, loss or damage which is to any extent attributable to the fact that he is not wearing a safety helmet in compliance with the requirement,

that other person shall, if liable to the Sikh in tort (or, in Scotland, in an action for reparation), be so liable only to the extent that injury, loss or damage would have been sustained by the Sikh even if he had been wearing a safety helmet in compliance with the requirement.

(6)   Where—

(a)   the act or omission referred to in subsection (5) causes the death of the Sikh, and

(b)   the Sikh would have sustained some injury (other than loss of life) in consequence of the act or omission even if he had been wearing a safety helmet in compliance with the requirement in question,

the amount of any damages which, by virtue of that subsection, are recoverable in tort (or, in Scotland, in an action for reparation) in respect of that injury shall not exceed the amount of any damages which would (apart from that subsection) be so recoverable in respect of the Sikh's death.

(7)   In this section—

"building operations" and "works of engineering construction" have the same meaning as in the Factories Act 1961;

"construction site" means any place where any building operations or works of engineering construction are being undertaken;

"injury" includes loss of life, any impairment of a person's physical or mental condition and any disease;

"safety helmet" means any form of protective headgear; and

"statutory provision" means a provision of an Act or of subordinate legislation.

(8)   In this section—

(a)   any reference to a Sikh is a reference to a follower of the Sikh religion; and

(b)   any reference to a Sikh being on a construction site is a reference to his being there whether while at work or otherwise.

(9)   This section shall have effect in relation to any relevant construction site within the territorial sea adjacent to Great Britain as it has effect in relation to any construction site within Great Britain.

(10)   In subsection (9) "relevant construction site" means any construction site where there are being undertaken any building operations or works of engineering construction which are activities falling within Article 7(a) of the Health and Safety at Work etc Act 1974 (Application outside Great Britain) Order 1989.

**NOTES**

Health and Safety at Work etc Act 1974 (Application outside Great Britain) Order 1989: revoked; see now the Health and Safety at Work etc Act 1974 (Application outside Great Britain) Order 2013, SI 2013/240.

**[1.177]**
**12   Protection of Sikhs from racial discrimination in connection with requirements as to wearing of safety helmets**

(1)   Where—

(a)   any person applies to a Sikh any [provision, criterion or practice] relating to the wearing by him of a safety helmet while he is on a construction site, and

(b)   at the time when he so applies the [provision, criterion or practice] that person has no reasonable grounds for believing that the Sikh would not wear a turban at all times when on such a site,

then, for the purpose of determining whether the application of the [provision, criterion or practice] to the Sikh constitutes an act of discrimination falling within [section 19 of the Equality Act 2010 (indirect discrimination), the provision, criterion or practice is to be taken as one in relation to which the condition in subsection (2)(d) of that section (proportionate means of achieving a legitimate aim) is satisfied].

(2)   Any special treatment afforded to a Sikh in consequence of section 11(1) or (2) above shall not be regarded for the purposes of [section 13 of the Equality Act 2010 as giving rise to discrimination against any other person].

(3)   Subsections (7) to (10) of section 11 above shall apply for the purposes of this section as they apply for the purposes of that section.

**NOTES**

Sub-ss (1), (2): words in square brackets substituted by the Equality Act 2010, s 211(1), Sch 26, para 15, as from 1 October 2010 (certain purposes), and as from 15 August 2011 (otherwise). see further the note below.

The Equality Act 2010 (Commencement No 4, Savings, Consequential, Transitional, Transitory and Incidental Provisions and Revocation) Order 2010, SI 2010/2317, art 11(2) (at **[2.1564]**) provides that the amendments made by Sch 26, para 15 to the Equality Act 2010 do not come into force in relation to work on ships, work on hovercraft and seafarers until Regulations under s 81 of the 2010 Act come into force. The Equality Act 2010 (Work on Ships and Hovercraft) Regulations 2011, SI 2011/1771 (at **[2.1611]**) were made under that section and came into force on 15 August 2011.

**13–26**   *(Ss 13–20 amended the Employment Protection (Consolidation) Act 1978, and are repealed as follows: s 13 repealed by the Trade Union Reform and Employment Rights Act 1993, s 51, Sch 10; s 14 repealed by the Trade Union and Labour Relations (Consolidation) Act 1992, s 300(1), Sch 1; ss 15–18 repealed by the Employment Rights Act 1996, s 242, Sch 3, Pt I; s 19 repealed by the Pension Schemes Act 1993, s 188(1), Sch 5, Pt I and the Employment Rights Act 1996, s 242, Sch 3, Pt I; s 20 repealed by the Employment Tribunals Act 1996, s 45, Sch 3, Pt I; s 21 repealed by the Statute Law (Repeals) Act 2004; ss 22 (dissolution of Training Commission), 23–25 (Industrial Training Boards) outside the scope of this work; s 26 repealed by the Education and Inspections Act 2006, s 184, Sch 18, Pt 2.)*

*General*

**27**   *((Power to legislate for Northern Ireland) outside the scope of this work.)*

**[1.178]**
**28   Orders**
(1)   Any power to make an order under this Act shall be exercisable by statutory instrument.
(2), (3)   . . .
(4)   Any statutory instrument containing an order under this Act other than—
   (a), (b). . .
   (c)   an order under section 30,
shall be subject to annulment in pursuance of a resolution of either House of Parliament.
(5)   An order under this Act may contain such consequential or transitional provisions or savings as appear to the Secretary of State to be necessary or expedient.

**NOTES**

Sub-ss (2), (3): repealed by the Equality Act 2010, s 211, Sch 26, Pt 1, paras 13, 16, Sch 27, Pt 1, as from 1 October 2010.

Sub-s (4): para (a) repealed by the Equality Act 2010, s 211, Sch 26, Pt 1, paras 13, 16, Sch 27, Pt 1, as from 1 October 2010; para (b) repealed by the Education and Inspections Act 2006, s 184, Sch 18, Pt 2.

**[1.179]**
**29   Interpretation, minor and consequential amendments, repeals, etc**
(1)   In this Act—
   . . .
   . . .
   "act" includes a deliberate omission;
   "subordinate legislation" has the same meaning as in the Interpretation Act 1978;
   "vocational training" includes advanced vocational training and retraining.
(2)   Any reference in this Act to vocational training shall be construed as including a reference to vocational guidance.
(3)–(6)   *(Introduce Schs 6–9 (minor and consequential amendments, repeals, revocations and transitional provisions).)*

**NOTES**

Sub-s (1): definition "the 1975 Act" (omitted) repealed by the Equality Act 2010, s 211, Sch 26, Pt 1, paras 13, 17, Sch 27, Pt 1, as from 1 October 2010; definition "the 1978 Act" (omitted) repealed by the Employment Rights Act 1996, s 242, Sch 3, Pt I.

**[1.180]**
**30   Short title, commencement and extent**
(1)   This Act may be cited as the Employment Act 1989.
(2)–(4)   . . .
(5), (6)   *(Application to Northern Ireland (outside the scope of this work).)*

**NOTES**

Sub-ss (2)–(4): repealed by the Statute Law (Repeals) Act 2004. Note that sub-s (4) provided that in so far as not brought into force by sub-ss (2), (3), this Act would come into force on a date to be appointed by the Secretary of State. Commencement orders made under sub-s (4) lapsed following the repeal of that subsection.

## SCHEDULES 1–9

*(Sch 1 (Provisions Concerned with Protection of Women at Work) was not specifically repealed by the Equality Act 2010 but it effectively lapsed following the repeal of its enabling provision (ie, s 4 of this Act) on 1 October 2010; Sch 2 (Revocation etc of subordinate legislation requiring different treatment of certain employees); Sch 3 (Removal of restrictions relating to employment of young persons); Schs 4, 5 (dissolution of Training Commission), 6–8 (minor and consequential amendments, repeals and revocations); Sch 9 (transitional provisions and savings): in so far as these provisions are still in force, they are outside the scope of this work.)*

# CONTRACTS (APPLICABLE LAW) ACT 1990

### (1990 c 36)

### ARRANGEMENT OF SECTIONS

*An Act to make provision as to the law applicable to contractual obligations in the case of conflict of laws*

[26 July 1990]

### NOTES

This Act is included for its provisions as to the applicable law of contracts of employment only, and other provisions of the Act and of the Rome Convention are omitted. So far as relevant and except as indicated in the notes below, the Act came into force on 1 April 1991. Note that this Act is disapplied by the effect of s 4A at **[1.184]** (for England and Wales) and by s 4B at **[1.185]** (for Scotland), in cases where the Rome I Regulation of the EU applies, namely, contracts entered into after 17 December 2009 (see Article 28 at **[3.563]**).

See *Harvey* H(3)(B).

**[1.181]**
### 1 Meaning of "the Conventions"
In this Act—
- (a) "the Rome Convention" means the Convention on the law applicable to contractual obligations opened for signature in Rome on 19th June 1980 and signed by the United Kingdom on 7th December 1981;
- (b) "the Luxembourg Convention" means the Convention on the accession of the Hellenic Republic to the Rome Convention signed by the United Kingdom in Luxembourg on 10th April 1984; and
- (c) "the Brussels Protocol" means the first Protocol on the interpretation of the Rome Convention by the European Court signed by the United Kingdom in Brussels on 19th December 1988;
- [(d) "the Funchal Convention" means the Convention on the accession of the Kingdom of Spain and the Portuguese Republic to the Rome Convention and the Brussels Protocol, with adjustments made to the Rome Convention by the Luxembourg Convention, signed by the United Kingdom in Funchal on 18th May 1992;]
- [(e) "the 1996 Accession Convention" means the Convention on the accession of the Republic of Austria, the Republic of Finland and the Kingdom of Sweden to the Rome Convention and the Brussels Protocol, with the adjustments made to the Rome Convention by the Luxembourg Convention and the Funchal Convention, signed by the United Kingdom in Brussels on 29th November 1996;]

and [these Conventions and this Protocol] are together referred to as "the Conventions".

**NOTES**

Para (d) added, and words in final pair of square brackets substituted, by the Contracts (Applicable Law) Act 1990 (Amendment) Order 1994, SI 1994/1900, arts 3, 4; para (e) added by the Contracts (Applicable Law) Act 1990 (Amendment) Order 2000, SI 2000/1825, art 3.

**[1.182]**
## 2   Conventions to have force of law
(1)   Subject to subsections (2) and (3) below, the Conventions shall have the force of law in the United Kingdom.
[(1A)   The internal law for the purposes of Article 1(3) of the Rome Convention is the provisions of the regulations for the time being in force under section 424(3) of the Financial Services and Markets Act 2000.]
(2)   Articles 7(1) and 10(1)(e) of the Rome Convention shall not have the force of law in the United Kingdom.
(3)   Notwithstanding Article 19(2) of the Rome Convention, the Conventions shall apply in the case of conflicts between the laws of different parts of the United Kingdom.
(4)   For ease of reference there are set out in [Schedules 1, 2, 3[, 3A and 3B]] to this Act respectively the English texts of—
    (a)    the Rome Convention;
    (b)    the Luxembourg Convention; . . .
    (c)    the Brussels Protocol[, and
    [(d)    the Funchal Convention; and
    (e)    the 1996 Accession Convention.]]

**NOTES**

Commencement: 1 April 1991 (sub-s (1) in so far as relating to the Rome Convention and Luxembourg Convention, and sub-ss (2)–(4)); 1 March 2005 (sub-s (1) in so far as relating to the Brussels Protocol); to be appointed (sub-s (1) otherwise).

Sub-s (1A): inserted by the Insurance Companies (Amendment) Regulations 1993, SI 1993/174, reg 9; substituted by the Financial Services and Markets Act 2000 (Consequential Amendments and Repeals) Order 2001, SI 2001/3649, art 320.

Sub-s (4): words in first (outer) pair of square brackets substituted, word omitted repealed, and original para (d) and the word immediately preceding it added, by the Contracts (Applicable Law) Act 1990 (Amendment) Order 1994, SI 1994/1900, arts 5, 6; words in second (inner) pair of square brackets substituted, and paras (d), (e) substituted for para (d) (as added as noted above), by the Contracts (Applicable Law) Act 1990 (Amendment) Order 2000, SI 2000/1825, art 4.

**[1.183]**
## 3   Interpretation of Conventions
(1)   Any question as to the meaning or effect of any provision of the Conventions shall, if not referred to the European Court in accordance with the Brussels Protocol, be determined in accordance with the principles laid down by, and any relevant decision of, the European Court.
(2)   Judicial notice shall be taken of any decision of, or expression of opinion by, the European Court on any such question.
(3)   Without prejudice to any practice of the courts as to the matters which may be considered apart from this subsection—
    (a)    the report on the Rome Convention by Professor Mario Giuliano and Professor Paul Lagarde which is reproduced in the Official Journal of the Communities of 31st October 1980 may be considered in ascertaining the meaning or effect of any provision of that Convention; and
    (b)    any report on the Brussels Protocol which is reproduced in the Official Journal of the [European Union] may be considered in ascertaining the meaning or effect of any provision of that Protocol.

**NOTES**

Sub-s (3): words in square brackets substituted by the Treaty of Lisbon (Changes in Terminology) Order 2011, SI 2011/1043, art 4(1), as from 22 April 2011.

**4**   *(S 4 (Revision of Conventions etc) outside the scope of this work.)*

**[1.184]**
## [4A   Disapplication where the rules in the Rome I Regulations apply: England and Wales and Northern Ireland
(1)   Nothing in this Act applies to affect the determination of issues relating to contractual obligations which fall to be determined under the Rome I Regulation.
(2)   In this section the "Rome I Regulation" means Regulation (EC) No 593/2008 of the European Parliament and of the Council on the law applicable to contractual obligations, including that Regulation as applied by regulation 3 of the Law Applicable to Contractual Obligations (England and Wales and Northern Ireland) Regulations 2009 (conflicts falling within Article 22(2) of Regulation (EC) No 593/2008).
(3)   This section extends to England and Wales and Northern Ireland only.]

NOTES

Commencement: 17 December 2009.

Inserted by the Law Applicable to Contractual Obligations (England and Wales and Northern Ireland) Regulations 2009, SI 2009/3064, reg 2, as from 17 December 2009. Note that the Rome I Regulation applies to contracts concluded after 17 December 2009 (see Article 28 at [**3.563**])

**[1.185]**
**[4B   Disapplication where the rules in the Rome I Regulation apply: Scotland**
(1)   Nothing in this Act applies to affect the determination of issues relating to contractual obligations which fall to be determined by the Rome I Regulation.
(2)   In this section "the Rome I Regulation" means Regulation (EC) No 593/2008 of the European Parliament and of the Council on the law applicable to contractual obligations (Rome I), including that Regulation as applied by regulation 4 of the Law Applicable to Contractual Obligations (Scotland) Regulations 2009 (conflicts falling within Article 22(2) of Regulation (EC) No 593/2008).
(3)   This section extends to Scotland only.]

NOTES

Commencement: 17 December 2009.

Inserted by the Law Applicable to Contractual Obligations (Scotland) Regulations 2009, SSI 2009/410, reg 2(a), as from 17 December 2009. Note that the Rome I Regulation applies to contracts concluded after 17 December 2009 (see Article 28 at [**3.563**]).

**5, 6**   *(S 5 (Consequential amendments) outside the scope of this work; s 6 provides that this Act binds the Crown.)*

**[1.186]**
**7   Commencement**
This Act shall come into force on such day as the Lord Chancellor and the Lord Advocate may by order made by statutory instrument appoint; and different days may be appointed for different provisions or different purposes.

NOTES

Orders: the Contracts (Applicable Law) Act 1990 (Commencement No 1) Order 1991, SI 1991/707; the Contracts (Applicable Law) Act 1990 (Commencement No 2) Order 2004, SI 2004/3448.

**8**   *(S 8 (extent) provides, inter alia, that except as provided by virtue of s 4B(3), this Act applies to the whole of the UK (see also s 4A(3) though).)*

**[1.187]**
**9   Short title**
This Act may be cited as the Contracts (Applicable Law) Act 1990.

**SCHEDULES**

**SCHEDULE 1**
**THE ROME CONVENTION**

Section 2

NOTES

Only provisions relevant to employment law are reproduced. Provisions omitted are outside the scope of this work. Article 27 of the Convention has been rescinded and, as included in this Schedule, was repealed by the Contracts (Applicable Law) Act 1990 (Amendment) Order 1994, SI 1994/1900. Articles 22, 30, 31 were also amended by the 1994 Order. The Protocol to the Convention (not reproduced) was substituted by the Contracts (Applicable Law) Act 1990 (Amendment) Order 2000, SI 2000/1825, art 5. The Convention has not otherwise been amended.

The High Contracting Parties to the Treaty establishing the European Economic Community,
Anxious to continue in the field of private international law the work of unification of law which has already been done within the Community, in particular in the field of jurisdiction and enforcement of judgments,
Wishing to establish uniform rules concerning the law applicable to contractual obligations,
Have agreed as follows:

# TITLE I
## SCOPE OF THE CONVENTION

### Article 1
### *Scope of the Convention*

**[1.188]**

**1.** The rules of this Convention shall apply to contractual obligations in any situation involving a choice between the laws of different countries.

**2–4.** . . . .

### Article 2
### *Application of law of non-contracting States*

Any law specified by this Convention shall be applied whether or not it is the law of a Contracting State.

# TITLE II
## UNIFORM RULES

### Article 3
### *Freedom of choice*

**1.** A contract shall be governed by the law chosen by the parties. The choice must be express or demonstrated with reasonable certainty by the terms of the contract or the circumstances of the case. By their choice the parties can select the law applicable to the whole or a part only of the contract.

**2.** The parties may at any time agree to subject the contract to a law other than that which previously governed it, whether as a result of an earlier choice under this Article or of other provisions of this Convention. Any variation by the parties of the law to be applied made after the conclusion of the contract shall not prejudice its formal validity under Article 9 or adversely affect the rights of third parties.

**3.** The fact that the parties have chosen a foreign law, whether or not accompanied by the choice of a foreign tribunal, shall not, where all the other elements relevant to the situation at the time of the choice are connected with one country only, prejudice the application of rules of the law of that country which cannot be derogated from by contract, hereinafter called "mandatory rules".

**4.** The existence and validity of the consent of the parties as to the choice of the applicable law shall be determined in accordance with the provisions of Articles 8, 9 and 11.

### Article 4
### *Applicable law in the absence of choice*

**1.** To the extent that the law applicable to the contract has not been chosen in accordance with Article 3, the contract shall be governed by the law of the country with which it is most closely connected. Nevertheless, a severable part of the contract which has a closer connection with another country may by way of exception be governed by the law of that other country.

**2.** Subject to the provisions of paragraph 5 of this Article, it shall be presumed that the contract is most closely connected with the country where the party who is to effect the performance which is characteristic of the contract has, at the time of conclusion of the contract, his habitual residence, or, in the case of a body corporate or unincorporate, its central administration. However, if the contract is entered into in the course of that party's trade or profession, that country shall be the country in which the principal place of business is situated or, where under the terms of the contract the performance is to be effected through a place of business other than the principal place of business, the country in which that other place of business is situated.

**3, 4.** . . .

**5.** Paragraph 2 shall not apply if the characteristic performance cannot be determined, and the presumptions in paragraphs 2, 3 and 4 shall be disregarded if it appears from the circumstances as a whole that the contract is more closely connected with another country.

## Article 6
### Individual employment contracts

**1.** Notwithstanding the provisions of Article 3, in a contract of employment a choice of law made by the parties shall not have the result of depriving the employee of the protection afforded to him by the mandatory rules of the law which would be applicable under paragraph 2 in the absence of choice.

**2.** Notwithstanding the provisions of Article 4, a contract of employment shall, in the absence of choice in accordance with Article 3, be governed:

    (a)    by the law of the country in which the employee habitually carries out his work in performance of the contract, even if he is temporarily employed in another country; or

    (b)    if the employee does not habitually carry out his work in any one country, by the law of the country in which the place of business through which he was engaged is situated;

unless it appears from the circumstances as a whole that the contract is more closely connected with another country, in which case the contract shall be governed by the law of that country.

## Article 7
### Mandatory rules

**1.** When applying under this Convention the law of a country, effect may be given to the mandatory rules of the law of another country with which the situation has a close connection, if and in so far as, under the law of the latter country, those rules must be applied whatever the law applicable to the contract. In considering whether to give effect to these mandatory rules, regard shall be had to their nature and purpose and to the consequences of their application or non-application.

**2.** Nothing in this Convention shall restrict the application of the rules of the law of the forum in a situation where they are mandatory irrespective of the law otherwise applicable to the contract.

## Article 9
### Formal validity

**1.** A contract concluded between persons who are in the same country is formally valid if it satisfies the formal requirements of the law which governs it under this Convention or of the law of the country where it is concluded.

**2.** A contract concluded between persons who are in different countries is formally valid if it satisfies the formal requirements of the law which governs it under this Convention or of the law of one of those countries.

**3–6.** . . .

## Article 10
### Scope of the applicable law

**1.** The law applicable to a contract by virtue of Articles 3 to 6 and 12 of this Convention shall govern in particular:

    (a)    interpretation;

    (b)    performance;

    (c)    within the limits of the powers conferred on the court by its procedural law, the consequences of breach, including the assessment of damages in so far as it is governed by rules of law;

    (d)    the various ways of extinguishing obligations, and prescription and limitation of actions;

    (e)    the consequences of nullity of the contract.

**2.** In relation to the manner of performance and the steps to be taken in the event of defective performance regard shall be had to the law of the country in which performance takes place.

## Article 14
### Burden of proof, etc

**1.** The law governing the contract under this Convention applies to the extent that it contains, in the law of contract, rules which raise presumptions of law or determine the burden of proof.

**2.** A contract or an act intended to have legal effect may be proved by any mode of proof recognised by the law of the forum or by any of the laws referred to in Article 9 under which that contract or act is formally valid, provided that such mode of proof can be administered by the forum.

*Article 17*
*No retrospective effect*

This Convention shall apply in a Contracting State to contracts made after the date on which this Convention has entered into force with respect to that State.

*Article 18*
*Uniform interpretation*

In the interpretation and application of the preceding uniform rules, regard shall be had to their international character and to the desirability of achieving uniformity in their interpretation and application.

*Article 19*
*States with more than one legal system*

**1.** Where a State comprises several territorial units each of which has its own rules of law in respect of contractual obligations, each territorial unit shall be considered as a country for the purposes of identifying the law applicable under this Convention.

**2.** A State within which different territorial units have their own rules of law in respect of contractual obligations shall not be bound to apply this Convention to conflicts solely between the laws of such units.

**SCHEDULES 2–4**

*(Schs 2–4 outside the scope of this work.)*

# SOCIAL SECURITY CONTRIBUTIONS AND BENEFITS ACT 1992

### (1992 c 4)

### ARRANGEMENT OF SECTIONS

### PART XI
### STATUTORY SICK PAY

*Employer's liability*

*An Act to consolidate certain enactments relating to social security contributions and benefits with amendments to give effect to recommendations of the Law Commission and the Scottish Law Commission*

**[13 February 1992]**

**NOTES**

This consolidating Act re-enacts the statutory provisions as to statutory sick pay (Pt XI) and statutory maternity pay (Pt XII) previously in the Social Security and Housing Benefits Act 1982 and the Social Security Act 1986 respectively. By virtue of the Social Security (Consequential Provisions) Act 1992, s 2 (Continuity of the law), Regulations made under the repealed Acts continue to have effect as if made under the corresponding provision of the consolidating Acts (ie, this Act, the Social Security Administration Act 1992, and the Social Security (Consequential Provisions) Act 1992). Pre-1992 Regulations that continue to have effect (and which are amended by Regulations made under this Act) are noted to the appropriate section/Schedule below. Parts XIIZA and XIIZB, providing respectively for statutory paternity pay and statutory adoption pay, were inserted by the Employment Act 2002, ss 2 and 4 respectively, and ss 171ZEA–171ZEE were inserted therein by the Work and Families Act 2006, ss 6–10, as from 3 March 2010 (see SI 2010/495). These are reproduced here, together with the associated Schedules. Other provisions not printed here are not annotated.

See *Harvey* BI(2)(B), J(2), (8).

# PART XI
# STATUTORY SICK PAY

*Employer's liability*

**[1.189]**
## 151   Employer's liability
(1)   Where an employee has a day of incapacity for work in relation to his contract of service with an employer, that employer shall, if the conditions set out in sections 152 to 154 below are satisfied, be liable to make him, in accordance with the following provisions of this Part of this Act, a payment (to be known as "statutory sick pay") in respect of that day.
(2)   Any agreement shall be void to the extent that it purports—
   (a)   to exclude, limit or otherwise modify any provision of this Part of this Act, or
   (b)   to require an employee to contribute (whether directly or indirectly) towards any costs incurred by his employer under this Part of this Act.
(3)   For the avoidance of doubt, any agreement between an employer and an employee authorising any deductions from statutory sick pay which the employer is liable to pay to the employee in respect of any period shall not be void by virtue of subsection (2)(a) above if the employer—
   (a)   is authorised by that or another agreement to make the same deductions from any contractual remuneration which he is liable to pay in respect of the same period, or
   (b)   would be so authorised if he were liable to pay contractual remuneration in respect of that period.
(4)   For the purposes of this Part of this Act [a day of incapacity for work in relation to a contract of service means a day on which] the employee concerned is, or is deemed in accordance with regulations to be, incapable by reason of some specific disease or bodily or mental disablement of doing work which he can reasonably be expected to do under that contract.
(5)   In any case where an employee has more than one contract of service with the same employer the provisions of this Part of this Act shall, except in such cases as may be prescribed and subject to the following provisions of this Part of this Act, have effect as if the employer were a different employer in relation to each contract of service.
(6)   Circumstances may be prescribed in which, notwithstanding the provisions of subsections (1) to (5) above, the liability to make payments of statutory sick pay is to be a liability of the [Commissioners of Inland Revenue].
[(7)   Regulations under subsection (6) above must be made with the concurrence of the Commissioners of Inland Revenue.]

**NOTES**
   Sub-s (4): words in square brackets substituted by the Social Security (Incapacity for Work) Act 1994, s 11(1), Sch 1, Pt I, para 34.
   Sub-s (6): words in square brackets substituted by the Social Security Contributions (Transfer of Functions, etc) Act 1999, s 1(1), Sch 1, para 9.
   Sub-s (7): added by the Social Security Contributions (Transfer of Functions, etc) Act 1999, s 1(1), Sch 1, para 9.
   Commissioners of Inland Revenue: a reference to the Commissioners of Inland Revenue is now to be taken as a reference to the Commissioners for Her Majesty's Revenue and Customs; see the Commissioners for Revenue and Customs Act 2005, s 50(1), (7).
   Regulations: the Statutory Sick Pay (General) Regulations 1982, SI 1982/894 at **[2.40]**, have effect as if made under this section by virtue of the Social Security (Consequential Provisions) Act 1992, s 2(2); the Statutory Sick Pay (General) Amendment Regulations 2006, SI 2006/799; the Social Security (Miscellaneous Amendments) (No 3) Regulations 2011, SI 2011/2425.

*The qualifying conditions*

**[1.190]**
## 152   Period of incapacity for work
(1)   The first condition is that the day in question forms part of a period of incapacity for work.
(2)   In this Part of this Act "period of incapacity for work" means any period of four or more consecutive days, each of which is a day of incapacity for work in relation to the contract of service in question.
(3)   Any two periods of incapacity for work which are separated by a period of not more than 8 weeks shall be treated as a single period of incapacity for work.

(4)   The Secretary of State may by regulations direct that a larger number of weeks specified in the regulations shall be substituted for the number of weeks for the time being specified in subsection (3) above.

(5)   No day of the week shall be disregarded in calculating any period of consecutive days for the purposes of this section.

(6)   A day may be a day of incapacity for work in relation to a contract of service, and so form part of a period of incapacity for work, notwithstanding that—

(a)   it falls before the making of the contract or after the contract expires or is brought to an end; or

(b)   it is not a day on which the employee concerned would be required by that contract to be available for work.

**NOTES**

Regulations: as of 6 April 2013, no Regulations had been made under sub-s (4).

**[1.191]**
**153   Period of entitlement**

(1)   The second condition is that the day in question falls within a period which is, as between the employee and his employer, a period of entitlement.

(2)   For the purposes of this Part of this Act a period of entitlement, as between an employee and his employer, is a period beginning with the commencement of a period of incapacity for work and ending with whichever of the following first occurs—

(a)   the termination of that period of incapacity for work;

(b)   the day on which the employee reaches, as against the employer concerned, his maximum entitlement to statutory sick pay (determined in accordance with section 155 below);

(c)   the day on which the employee's contract of service with the employer concerned expires or is brought to an end;

(d)   in the case of an employee who is, or has been, pregnant, the day immediately preceding the beginning of the disqualifying period.

(3)   Schedule 11 to this Act has effect for the purpose of specifying circumstances in which a period of entitlement does not arise in relation to a particular period of incapacity for work.

(4)   A period of entitlement as between an employee and an employer of his may also be, or form part of, a period of entitlement as between him and another employer of his.

(5)   The Secretary of State may by regulations—

(a)   specify circumstances in which, for the purpose of determining whether an employee's maximum entitlement to statutory sick pay has been reached in a period of entitlement as between him and an employer of his, days falling within a previous period of entitlement as between the employee and any person who is or has in the past been an employer of his are to be counted; and

(b)   direct that in prescribed circumstances an employer shall provide a person who is about to leave his employment, or who has been employed by him in the past, with a statement in the prescribed form containing such information as may be prescribed in relation to any entitlement of the employee to statutory sick pay.

(6)   Regulations may provide, in relation to prescribed cases, for a period of entitlement to end otherwise than in accordance with subsection (2) above.

(7)   In a case where the employee's contract of service first takes effect on a day which falls within a period of incapacity for work, the period of entitlement begins with that day.

(8)   In a case where the employee's contract of service first takes effect between two periods of incapacity for work which by virtue of section 152(3) above are treated as one, the period of entitlement begins with the first day of the second of those periods.

(9)   In any case where, otherwise than by virtue of section 6(1)(b) above, an employee's earnings under a contract of service in respect of the day on which the contract takes effect do not attract a liability to pay secondary Class 1 contributions, subsections (7) and (8) above shall have effect as if for any reference to the contract first taking effect there were substituted a reference to the first day in respect of which the employee's earnings attract such a liability.

(10)   Regulations shall make provision as to an employer's liability under this Part of this Act to pay statutory sick pay to an employee in any case where the employer's contract of service with that employee has been brought to an end by the employer solely, or mainly, for the purpose of avoiding liability for statutory sick pay.

(11)   Subsection (2)(d) above does not apply in relation to an employee who has been pregnant if her pregnancy terminated, before the beginning of the disqualifying period, otherwise than by confinement.

(12)   In this section—

"confinement" is to be construed in accordance with section 171(1) below;

"disqualifying period" means—

(a)   in relation to a woman entitled to statutory maternity pay, the maternity pay period; and

(b)    in relation to a woman entitled to maternity allowance, the maternity allowance
       period;
"maternity allowance period" has the meaning assigned to it by section 35(2) above, and
"maternity pay period" has the meaning assigned to it by section 165(1) below.

**NOTES**

Regulations: the Statutory Sick Pay (General) Regulations 1982, SI 1982/894 at **[2.40]**, and the Statutory Sick Pay (Mariners, Airmen and Persons Abroad) Regulations 1982, SI 1982/1349, have effect as if made under this section by virtue of the Social Security (Consequential Provisions) Act 1992, s 2(2); the Social Security Maternity Benefits and Statutory Sick Pay (Amendment) Regulations 1994, SI 1994/1367; the Social Security Contributions, Statutory Maternity Pay and Statutory Sick Pay (Miscellaneous Amendments) Regulations 1996, SI 1996/777; the Social Security, Statutory Maternity Pay and Statutory Sick Pay (Miscellaneous Amendments) Regulations 2002, SI 2002/2690; the Statutory Sick Pay (General) (Amendment) Regulations 2008, SI 2008/1735.

**[1.192]**
**154    Qualifying days**
(1)    The third condition is that the day in question is a qualifying day.
(2)    The days which are for the purposes of this Part of this Act to be qualifying days as between an employee and an employer of his (that is to say, those days of the week on which he is required by his contract of service with that employer to be available for work or which are chosen to reflect the terms of that contract) shall be such day or days as may, subject to regulations, be agreed between the employee and his employer or, failing such agreement, determined in accordance with regulations.
(3)    In any case where qualifying days are determined by agreement between an employee and his employer there shall, in each week (beginning with Sunday), be at least one qualifying day.
(4)    A day which is a qualifying day as between an employee and an employer of his may also be a qualifying day as between him and another employer of his.

**NOTES**

Regulations: the Statutory Sick Pay (General) Regulations 1982, SI 1982/894 at **[2.40]**, have effect as if made under this section by virtue of the Social Security (Consequential Provisions) Act 1992, s 2(2).

*Limitations on entitlement, etc*

**[1.193]**
**155    Limitations on entitlement**
(1)    Statutory sick pay shall not be payable for the first three qualifying days in any period of entitlement.
(2)    An employee shall not be entitled, as against any one employer, to an aggregate amount of statutory sick pay in respect of any one period of entitlement which exceeds his maximum entitlement.
(3)    The maximum entitlement as against any one employer is reached on the day on which the amount to which the employee has become entitled by way of statutory sick pay during the period of entitlement in question first reaches or passes the entitlement limit.
(4)    The entitlement limit is an amount equal to 28 times [the weekly rate applicable in accordance with] section 157 below.
(5)    Regulations may make provision for calculating the entitlement limit in any case where an employee's entitlement to statutory sick pay is calculated by reference to different weekly rates in the same period of entitlement.

**NOTES**

Sub-s (4): words in square brackets substituted by the Social Security (Incapacity for Work) Act 1994, s 8(4).
Regulations: the Statutory Sick Pay (General) Regulations 1982, SI 1982/894 at **[2.40]**, have effect as if made under this section by virtue of the Social Security (Consequential Provisions) Act 1992, s 2(2).

**[1.194]**
**156    Notification of incapacity for work**
(1)    Regulations shall prescribe the manner in which, and the time within which, notice of any day of incapacity for work is to be given by or on behalf of an employee to his employer.
(2)    An employer who would, apart from this section, be liable to pay an amount of statutory sick pay to an employee in respect of a qualifying day (the "day in question") shall be entitled to withhold payment of that amount if—
(a)    the day in question is one in respect of which he has not been duly notified in accordance with regulations under subsection (1) above; or
(b)    he has not been so notified in respect of any of the first three qualifying days in a period of entitlement (a "waiting day") and the day in question is the first qualifying day in that period of entitlement in respect of which the employer is not entitled to withhold payment—
       (i)    by virtue of paragraph (a) above; or
       (ii)   in respect of an earlier waiting day by virtue of this paragraph.

(3) Where an employer withholds any amount of statutory sick pay under this section—
  (a) the period of entitlement in question shall not be affected; and
  (b) for the purposes of calculating his maximum entitlement in accordance with section 155 above the employee shall not be taken to have become entitled to the amount so withheld.

**NOTES**

Regulations: the Statutory Sick Pay (General) Regulations 1982, SI 1982/894 at **[2.40]**, have effect as if made under this section by virtue of the Social Security (Consequential Provisions) Act 1992, s 2(2).

*Rates of payment, etc*

**[1.195]**
**157  Rates of payment**
(1) Statutory sick pay shall be payable by an employer at the weekly rate of [£86.70].
(2) The Secretary of State may by order—
  [(a) amend subsection (1) above so as to substitute different provision as to weekly rate or rates of statutory sick pay; and]
  (b) make such consequential amendments as appear to him to be required of any provision contained in this Part of this Act.
(3) The amount of statutory sick pay payable by any one employer in respect of any day shall be the weekly rate applicable on that day divided by the number of days which are, in the week (beginning with Sunday) in which that day falls, qualifying days as between that employer and the employee concerned.

**NOTES**

Sub-s (1): sum in square brackets substituted by the Social Security Benefits Up-rating Order 2013, SI 2013/574, art 8, as from 6 April 2013.

Previous amounts were: £85.85 (as from 6 April 2012, see the Social Security Benefits Up-rating Order 2012, SI 2012/780, art 9); £81.60 (as from 6 April 2011, see the Social Security Benefits Up-rating Order 2011, SI 2011/821, art 9); £79.15 (as from 6 April 2009, see the Social Security Benefits Up-rating Order 2009, SI 2009/497, art 9); £75.40 (as from 6 April 2008, see the Social Security Benefits Up-rating Order 2008, SI 2008/632, art 9); £72.55 (as from 6 April 2007, see the Social Security Benefits Up-rating Order 2007, SI 2007/688, art 9); £70.05 (as from 6 April 2006, see the Social Security Benefits Up-rating Order 2006, SI 2006/645, art 9); £68.20 (as from 6 April 2005, see the Social Security Benefits Up-rating Order 2005, SI 2005/522, art 9).

Sub-s (2): para (a) substituted by the Social Security (Incapacity for Work) Act 1994, s 8(3).

Orders: as of 6 April 2013, no Order had been made under sub-s (2). Note that annual increases in statutory sick pay are effected by Orders made under the Social Security Administration Act 1992, s 150.

**158, 159** *(Repealed by the Statutory Sick Pay Percentage Threshold Order 1995, SI 1995/512, art 5(a).)*

**[1.196]**
**[159A  Power to provide for recovery by employers of sums paid by way of statutory sick pay**
(1) The Secretary of State may by order provide for the recovery by employers, in accordance with the order, of the amount (if any) by which their payments of, or liability incurred for, statutory sick pay in any period exceeds the specified percentage of the amount of their liability for contributions payments in respect of the corresponding period.
(2) An order under subsection (1) above may include provision—
  (a) as to the periods by reference to which the calculation referred to above is to be made,
  (b) for amounts which would otherwise be recoverable but which do not exceed the specified minimum for recovery not to be recoverable,
  (c) for the rounding up or down of any fraction of a pound which would otherwise result from a calculation made in accordance with the order, and
  (d) for any deduction from contributions payments made in accordance with the order to be disregarded for such purposes as may be specified,
and may repeal sections 158 and 159 above and make any amendments of other enactments which are consequential on the repeal of those sections.
(3) In this section—
"contributions payments" means payments which a person is required by or under any enactment to make in discharge of any liability of his as an employer in respect of primary or secondary Class 1 contributions; and
"specified" means specified in or determined in accordance with an order under subsection (1).
(4) The Secretary of State may by regulations make such transitional and consequential provision, and such savings, as he considers necessary or expedient for or in connection with the coming into force of any order under subsection (1) above.]

**NOTES**

Inserted by the Statutory Sick Pay Act 1994, s 3(1).
Orders: the Statutory Sick Pay Percentage Threshold Order 1995, SI 1995/512.

Regulations: the Statutory Sick Pay Percentage Threshold Order 1995 (Consequential) Regulations 1995, SI 1995/513.

*Miscellaneous*

**[1.197]**
## 160    Relationship with benefits and other payments, etc

Schedule 12 to this Act has effect with respect to the relationship between statutory sick pay and certain benefits and payments.

**[1.198]**
## 161    Crown employment—Part XI

(1)    Subject to subsection (2) below, the provisions of this Part of this Act apply in relation to persons employed by or under the Crown as they apply in relation to persons employed otherwise than by or under the Crown.

(2)    The provisions of this Part of this Act do not apply in relation to persons serving as members of Her Majesty's forces, in their capacity as such.

(3)    For the purposes of this section Her Majesty's forces shall be taken to consist of such establishments and organisations as may be prescribed [by regulations made by the Secretary of State with the concurrence of the Treasury], being establishments and organisations in which persons serve under the control of the Defence Council.

**NOTES**

Sub-s (3): words in square brackets inserted by the Social Security Contributions (Transfer of Functions, etc) Act 1999, s 1(1), Sch 1, para 10.

Regulations: as of 6 April 2013, no Regulations had been made under this section.

**[1.199]**
## 162    Special classes of persons

(1)    The Secretary of State may [with the concurrence of the Treasury] make regulations modifying this Part of this Act in such manner as he thinks proper in their application to any person who is, has been or is to be—

   (a)    employed on board any ship, vessel, hovercraft or aircraft;

   (b)    outside Great Britain at any prescribed time or in any prescribed circumstances; or

   (c)    in prescribed employment in connection with continental shelf operations, as defined in section 120(2) above.

(2)    Regulations under subsection (1) above may in particular provide—

   (a)    for any provision of this Part of this Act to apply to any such person, notwithstanding that it would not otherwise apply;

   (b)    for any such provision not to apply to any such person, notwithstanding that it would otherwise apply;

   (c)    for excepting any such person from the application of any such provision where he neither is domiciled nor has a place of residence in any part of Great Britain;

   (d)    for the taking of evidence, for the purposes of the determination of any question arising under any such provision, in a country or territory outside Great Britain, by a British consular official or such other person as may be determined in accordance with the regulations.

**NOTES**

Sub-s (1): words in square brackets inserted by the Social Security Contributions (Transfer of Functions, etc) Act 1999, s 1(1), Sch 1, para 11.

Regulations: the Statutory Sick Pay (Mariners, Airmen and Persons Abroad) Regulations 1982, SI 1982/1349, have effect as if made under this section by virtue of the Social Security (Consequential Provisions) Act 1992, s 2(2); the Social Security Contributions, Statutory Maternity Pay and Statutory Sick Pay (Miscellaneous Amendments) Regulations 1996, SI 1996/777.

**[1.200]**
## 163    Interpretation of Part XI and supplementary provisions

(1)    In this Part of this Act—

"contract of service" (except in paragraph (a) of the definition below of "employee") includes any arrangement providing for the terms of appointment of an employee;

"employee" means a person who is—

   (a)    gainfully employed in Great Britain either under a contract of service or in an office (including elective office) with [general earnings (as defined by section 7 of the Income Tax (Earnings and Pensions) Act 2003)]; . . .

   (b)    . . .

but subject to regulations, which may provide for cases where any such person is not to be treated as an employee for the purposes of this Part of this Act and for cases where any person who would not otherwise be an employee for those purposes is to be treated as an employee for those purposes;

["employer", in relation to an employee and a contract of service of his, means a person who—

    (a)    under section 6 above is liable to pay secondary Class 1 contributions in relation to any earnings of the employee under the contract, or

    (b)    would be liable to pay such contributions but for—

        (i)    the condition in section 6(1)(b), or

        (ii)    the employee being under the age of 16;]

"period of entitlement" has the meaning given by section 153 above;

"period of incapacity for work" has the meaning given by section 152 above;

. . .

"prescribed" means prescribed by regulations;

"qualifying day" has the meaning given by section 154 above;

"week" means any period of 7 days.

(2)  For the purposes of this Part of this Act an employee's normal weekly earnings shall, subject to subsection (4) below, be taken to be the average weekly earnings which in the relevant period have been paid to him or paid for his benefit under his contract of service with the employer in question.

(3)  For the purposes of subsection (2) above, the expressions "earnings" and "relevant period" shall have the meaning given to them by regulations.

(4)  In such cases as may be prescribed an employee's normal weekly earnings shall be calculated in accordance with regulations.

(5)  Without prejudice to any other power to make regulations under this Part of this Act, regulations may specify cases in which, for the purposes of this Part of this Act or such of its provisions as may be prescribed—

    (a)    two or more employers are to be treated as one;

    (b)    two or more contracts of service in respect of which the same person is an employee are to be treated as one.

(6)  Where, in consequence of the establishment of one or more National Health Service trusts under [*the National Health Service Act 2006,* the National Health Service (Wales) Act 2006] or the National Health Service (Scotland) Act 1978, a person's contract of employment is treated by a scheme under [any of those Acts] as divided so as to constitute two or more contracts, [or where an order under [paragraph 26(1) of Schedule 3 to the National Health Service Act 2006] provides that a person's contract of employment is so divided,] regulations may make provision enabling him to elect for all of those contracts to be treated as one contract for the purposes of this Part of this Act or of such provisions of this Part of this Act as may be prescribed; and any such regulations may prescribe—

    (a)    the conditions that must be satisfied if a person is to be entitled to make such an election;

    (b)    the manner in which, and the time within which, such an election is to be made;

    (c)    the persons to whom, and the manner in which, notice of such an election is to be given;

    (d)    the information which a person who makes such an election is to provide, and the persons to whom, and the time within which, he is to provide it;

    (e)    the time for which such an election is to have effect;

    (f)    which one of the person's employers under the two or more contracts is to be regarded for the purposes of statutory sick pay as his employer under the one contract;

and the powers conferred by this subsection are without prejudice to any other power to make regulations under this Part of this Act.

(7)  Regulations may provide for periods of work which begin on one day and finish on the following day to be treated, for the purposes of this Part of this Act, as falling solely within one or other of those days.

---

**NOTES**

Sub-s (1) is amended as follows:

Words in square brackets in definition "employee" substituted by the Income Tax (Earnings and Pensions) Act 2003, s 722, Sch 6, Pt 2, paras 169, 181.

Para (b) of definition "employee" (and the word immediately preceding it) repealed by the Employment Equality (Age) Regulations 2006, SI 2006/1031, reg 49(1), Sch 8, Pt 1, paras 8, 9(1), (2).

Definition "employer" substituted by SI 2006/1031, reg 49(1), Sch 8, Pt 1, paras 8, 9(1), (3).

Definition omitted repealed by the Jobseekers Act 1995, s 41(5), Sch 3.

Sub-s (6): words in first, second and fourth (inner) pairs of square brackets substituted by the National Health Service (Consequential Provisions) Act 2006, s 2, Sch 1, paras 142, 147; words in third (outer) pair of square brackets inserted by the Health Act 1999 (Supplementary, Consequential etc Provisions) Order 2000, SI 2000/90, art 3(1), Sch 1, para 27(1), (2); words in italics repealed by the Health and Social Care Act 2012, s 179, Sch 14, Pt 2, paras 58, 59, as from a day to be appointed.

Regulations: the Statutory Sick Pay Percentage Threshold Order 1995 (Consequential) Regulations 1995, SI 1995/513; the Social Security Contributions, Statutory Maternity Pay and Statutory Sick Pay (Miscellaneous Amendments) Regulations 1996, SI 1996/777; the Social Security Contributions, Statutory Maternity Pay and Statutory Sick Pay (Miscellaneous Amendments) Regulations 1999, SI 1999/567; the Social Security, Statutory Maternity Pay and Statutory Sick Pay (Miscellaneous Amendments) Regulations 2002, SI 2002/2690. Also, by virtue of the Social Security (Consequential Provisions) Act 1992, s 2(2), the Statutory Sick Pay (General) Regulations 1982, SI 1982/894 at **[2.40]**, the Statutory Sick Pay (Mariners, Airmen and Persons Abroad) Regulations 1982, SI 1982/1349, and the Statutory Sick Pay (National Health Service Employees)

Regulations 1991, SI 1991/589, have effect as if made under this section. As of 6 April 2013, no Regulations had been made under sub-s (7).

### PART XII
### STATUTORY MATERNITY PAY

**[1.201]**
**164    Statutory maternity pay—entitlement and liability to pay**
(1)    Where a woman who is or has been an employee satisfies the conditions set out in this section, she shall be entitled, in accordance with the following provisions of this Part of this Act, to payments to be known as "statutory maternity pay".
(2)    The conditions mentioned in subsection (1) above are—
  (a)    that she has been in employed earner's employment with an employer for a continuous period of at least 26 weeks ending with the week immediately preceding the 14th week before the expected week of confinement but has ceased to work for him . . . ;
  [(aa) that at the end of the week immediately preceding that 14th week she was entitled to be in that employment;]
  (b)    that her normal weekly earnings for the period of 8 weeks ending with the week immediately preceding the 14th week before the expected week of confinement are not less than the lower earnings limit in force under section 5(1)(a) above immediately before the commencement of the 14th week before the expected week of confinement; and
  (c)    that she has become pregnant and has reached, or been confined before reaching, the commencement of the 11th week before the expected week of confinement.
(3)    The liability to make payments of statutory maternity pay to a woman is a liability of any person of whom she has been an employee as mentioned in subsection (2)(a) above.
[(4)    A woman shall be entitled to payments of statutory maternity pay only if—
  (a)    she gives the person who will be liable to pay it notice of the date from which she expects his liability to pay her statutory maternity pay to begin; and
  (b)    the notice is given at least 28 days before that date or, if that is not reasonably practicable, as soon as is reasonably practicable.]
(5)    The notice shall be in writing if the person who is liable to pay the woman statutory maternity pay so requests.
(6)    Any agreement shall be void to the extent that it purports—
  (a)    to exclude, limit or otherwise modify any provision of this Part of this Act; or
  (b)    to require an employee or former employee to contribute (whether directly or indirectly) towards any costs incurred by her employer or former employer under this Part of this Act.
(7)    For the avoidance of doubt, any agreement between an employer and an employee authorising any deductions from statutory maternity pay which the employer is liable to pay to the employee in respect of any period shall not be void by virtue of subsection (6)(a) above if the employer—
  (a)    is authorised by that or another agreement to make the same deductions from any contractual remuneration which he is liable to pay in respect of the same period, or
  (b)    would be so authorised if he were liable to pay contractual remuneration in respect of that period.
(8)    Regulations shall make provision as to a former employer's liability to pay statutory maternity pay to a woman in any case where the former employer's contract of service with her has been brought to an end by the former employer solely, or mainly, for the purpose of avoiding liability for statutory maternity pay.
(9)    The Secretary of State may by regulations—
  (a)    specify circumstances in which, notwithstanding subsections (1) to (8) above, there is to be no liability to pay statutory maternity pay in respect of a week;
  (b)    specify circumstances in which, notwithstanding subsections (1) to (8) above, the liability to make payments of statutory maternity pay is to be a liability [of the Commissioners of Inland Revenue];
  (c)    specify in what circumstances employment is to be treated as continuous for the purposes of this Part of this Act;
  (d)    provide that a woman is to be treated as being employed for a continuous period of at least 26 weeks where—
      (i)    she has been employed by the same employer for at least 26 weeks under two or more separate contracts of service; and
      (ii)   those contracts were not continuous;
  [(da) provide for circumstances in which subsection (2)(aa) above does not apply;]
  (e)    provide that any of the provisions specified in subsection (10) below shall have effect subject to prescribed modifications [in such cases as may be prescribed]—
  [(ea) provide that subsection (4) above shall not have effect, or shall have effect subject to prescribed modifications, in such cases as may be prescribed;]
  (f)    provide for amounts earned by a woman under separate contracts of service with the same employer to be aggregated for the purposes of this Part of this Act; and

(g)  provide that—
    (i)  the amount of a woman's earnings for any period, or
    (ii)  the amount of her earnings to be treated as comprised in any payment made to her or for her benefit,
    shall be calculated or estimated in such manner and on such basis as may be prescribed and that for that purpose payments of a particular class or description made or falling to be made to or by a woman shall, to such extent as may be prescribed, be disregarded or, as the case may be, be deducted from the amount of her earnings.

(10)  The provisions mentioned in subsection (9)(e) above are—
    (a)  subsection (2)(a) and (b) above; and
    (b)  [section 166(1) and (2)], . . . below.

[(11)  Any regulations under subsection (9) above which are made by virtue of paragraph (b) of that subsection must be made with the concurrence of the Commissioners of Inland Revenue.]

**NOTES**

Sub-s (2): words omitted repealed by the Employment Act 2002, ss 20(a), 54, Sch 8; para (aa) inserted by the Welfare Reform Act 2012, s 63(1), (3)(a), as from a day to be appointed.

Sub-s (4): substituted by the Employment Act 2002, s 20(b).

Sub-s (9): words in square brackets in para (b) substituted by the Social Security Contributions (Transfer of Functions, etc) Act 1999, s 1(1), Sch 1, para 12(1), (2); para (da) inserted by the Welfare Reform Act 2012, s 63(1), (3)(b), as from a day to be appointed; words in square brackets in para (e) substituted, and para (ea) added, by the Employment Act 2002, s 20(c), (d).

Sub-s (10): words in square brackets substituted by the Employment Act 2002, s 53, Sch 7, paras 2, 6; words omitted repealed by the Maternity Allowance and Statutory Maternity Pay Regulations 1994, SI 1994/1230, regs 1(2), 6(1).

Sub-s (11): added by the Social Security Contributions (Transfer of Functions, etc) Act 1999, s 1(1), Sch 1, para 12(1), (3).

Commissioners of Inland Revenue: a reference to the Commissioners of Inland Revenue is now to be taken as a reference to the Commissioners for Her Majesty's Revenue and Customs; see the Commissioners for Revenue and Customs Act 2005, s 50(1), (7).

Regulations: the Statutory Maternity Pay (General) Regulations 1986, SI 1986/1960 at **[2.70]**, have effect as if made under this section by virtue of the Social Security (Consequential Provisions) Act 1992, s 2(2); the Social Security Maternity Benefits and Statutory Sick Pay (Amendment) Regulations 1994, SI 1994/1367; the Statutory Maternity Pay (General) Amendment Regulations 1996, SI 1996/1335; the Statutory Maternity Pay (General) (Modification and Amendment) Regulations 2000, SI 2000/2883; the Social Security, Statutory Maternity Pay and Statutory Sick Pay (Miscellaneous Amendments) Regulations 2002, SI 2002/2690; the Statutory Maternity Pay (General) and the Statutory Paternity Pay and Statutory Adoption Pay (General) (Amendment) Regulations 2005, SI 2005/358; the Statutory Maternity Pay (General) (Amendment) Regulations 2005 SI 2005/729.

**[1.202]**
**165  The maternity pay period**

(1)  Statutory maternity pay shall be payable, subject to the provisions of this Part of this Act, in respect of each week during a prescribed period ("the maternity pay period") of a duration not exceeding [52 weeks].

[(2)  Subject to subsections (3) and (7), the maternity pay period shall begin with the 11th week before the expected week of confinement.

(3)  Cases may be prescribed in which the first day of the period is to be a prescribed day after the beginning of the 11th week before the expected week of confinement, but not later than the day immediately following the day on which she is confined.]

(4)  [Except in such cases as may be prescribed,] statutory maternity pay shall not be payable to a woman by a person in respect of any week during any part of which she works under a contract of service with him.

(5)  It is immaterial for the purposes of subsection (4) above whether the work referred to in that subsection is work under a contract of service which existed immediately before the maternity pay period or a contract of service which did not so exist.

(6)  Except in such cases as may be prescribed, statutory maternity pay shall not be payable to a woman in respect of any week after she has been confined and during any part of which she works for any employer who is not liable to pay her statutory maternity pay.

(7)  Regulations may provide that this section shall have effect subject to prescribed modifications in relation—
    (a)  to cases in which a woman has been confined before the 11th week before the expected week of confinement; and
    (b)  to cases in which—
        (i)  a woman is confined [at any time after the end of the week immediately preceding the 11th week] before the expected week of confinement; and
        (ii)  the maternity pay period has not then commenced for her.

[(8)  In subsections (1), (4) and (6) "week" means a period of seven days beginning with the day of the week on which the maternity pay period begins.]

**NOTES**

Sub-s (1): words in square brackets substituted by the Work and Families Act 2006, s 1.

Sub-ss (2), (3): substituted by the Work and Families Act 2006, s 11(1), Sch 1, para 7(1), (2).

Sub-s (4): words in square brackets inserted by the Work and Families Act 2006, s 11(1), Sch 1, para 7(1), (3).

Sub-s (7): words in square brackets substituted by the Maternity Allowance and Statutory Maternity Pay Regulations 1994, SI 1994/1230, regs 1(2), 3.

Sub-s (8): inserted by the Work and Families Act 2006, s 11(1), Sch 1, para 7(1), (4).

Regulations: the Statutory Maternity Pay (General) Regulations 1986, SI 1986/1960 at **[2.70]**, have effect as if made under this section by virtue of the Social Security (Consequential Provisions) Act 1992, s 2(2); the Social Security Maternity Benefits and Statutory Sick Pay (Amendment) Regulations 1994, SI 1994/1367; the Statutory Maternity Pay (General) (Modification and Amendment) Regulations 2000, SI 2000/2883; the Social Security, Statutory Maternity Pay and Statutory Sick Pay (Miscellaneous Amendments) Regulations 2002, SI 2002/2690; the Statutory Maternity Pay, Social Security (Maternity Allowance) and Social Security (Overlapping Benefits) (Amendment) Regulations 2006, SI 2006/2379.

**[1.203]**
**[166    Rate of statutory maternity pay**
(1)    Statutory maternity pay shall be payable to a woman—
  (a)    at the earnings-related rate, in respect of the first 6 weeks in respect of which it is payable; and
  (b)    at whichever is the lower of the earnings-related rate and such weekly rate as may be prescribed, in respect of the remaining portion of the maternity pay period.
[(1A)    In subsection (1) "week" means any period of seven days.]
(2)    The earnings-related rate is a weekly rate equivalent to 90 per cent of a woman's normal weekly earnings for the period of 8 weeks immediately preceding the 14th week before the expected week of confinement.
(3)    The weekly rate prescribed under subsection (1)(b) above must not be less than the weekly rate of statutory sick pay for the time being specified in section 157(1) above or, if two or more such rates are for the time being so specified, the higher or highest of those rates.
[(4)    Where for any purpose of this Part of this Act or of regulations it is necessary to calculate the daily rate of statutory maternity pay, the amount payable by way of statutory maternity pay for any day shall be taken as one seventh of the weekly rate.]]

**NOTES**
Substituted by the Employment Act 2002, s 19.
Sub-ss (1A), (4): inserted and added respectively by the Work and Families Act 2006, s 11(1), Sch 1, para 8.
The rate prescribed under sub-s (1)(b) is £136.78 (see the Statutory Maternity Pay (General) Regulations 1986, SI 1986/1960, reg 6, as amended by the Social Security Benefits Up-rating Order 2013, SI 2013/574, art 9, and note that this has effect as from 7 April 2013, except for the purpose of determining the rate of maternity allowance in accordance with s 35A(1) of this Act, for which purpose it comes into force on 8 April 2013).
Previous prescribed rates were: £135.45 (as from 1 and 9 April 2012, see SI 2012/780, art 10); £128.73 (as from 3 and 11 April 2011, see SI 2011/821, art 10); £124.88 (as from 4 and 12 April 2010, see SI 2010/793, art 10); £123.06 (as from 5 and 6 April 2009, see SI 2009/497, art 10); £117.18 (as from 6 and 7 April 2008, see SI 2008/632, art 10); £112.75 (as from 1 and 9 April 2007, see SI 2007/688, art 10); £108.85 (as from 2 and 10 April 2006, see SI 2006/645, art 10); and £106 (as from 3 and 10 April 2005, see SI 2005/522, art 10).
Regulations: the Statutory Maternity Pay (General) Regulations 1986, SI 1986/1960 at **[2.70]**, have effect as if made under this section by virtue of the Social Security (Consequential Provisions) Act 1992, s 2(2); the Social Security Maternity Benefits and Statutory Sick Pay (Amendment) Regulations 1994, SI 1994/1367; the Social Security, Statutory Maternity Pay and Statutory Sick Pay (Miscellaneous Amendments) Regulations 2002, SI 2002/2690.

**[1.204]**
**[167    Funding of employers' liabilities in respect of statutory maternity pay**
(1)    Regulations shall make provision for the payment by employers of statutory maternity pay to be funded by the Commissioners of Inland Revenue to such extent as may be prescribed.
(2)    Regulations under subsection (1) shall—
  (a)    make provision for a person who has made a payment of statutory maternity pay to be entitled, except in prescribed circumstances, to recover an amount equal to the sum of—
    (i)    the aggregate of such of those payments as qualify for small employers' relief; and
    (ii)    an amount equal to 92 per cent of the aggregate of such of those payments as do not so qualify; and
  (b)    include provision for a person who has made a payment of statutory maternity pay qualifying for small employers' relief to be entitled, except in prescribed circumstances, to recover an additional amount, determined in such manner as may be prescribed—
    (i)    by reference to secondary Class 1 contributions paid in respect of statutory maternity pay;
    (ii)    by reference to secondary Class 1 contributions paid in respect of statutory sick pay; or
    (iii)    by reference to the aggregate of secondary Class 1 contributions paid in respect of statutory maternity pay and secondary Class 1 contributions paid in respect of statutory sick pay.
(3)    For the purposes of this section a payment of statutory maternity pay which a person is liable to make to a woman qualifies for small employers' relief if, in relation to that woman's maternity pay period, the person liable to make the payment is a small employer.

(4)  For the purposes of this section "small employer", in relation to a woman's maternity pay period, shall have the meaning assigned to it by regulations, and, without prejudice to the generality of the foregoing, any such regulations—

(a)  may define that expression by reference to the amount of a person's contributions payments for any prescribed period; and

(b)  if they do so, may in that connection make provision for the amount of those payments for that prescribed period—

  (i)   to be determined without regard to any deductions that may be made from them under this section or under any other enactment or instrument; and

  (ii)  in prescribed circumstances, to be adjusted, estimated or otherwise attributed to him by reference to their amount in any other prescribed period.

(5)  Regulations under subsection (1) may, in particular, make provision—

(a)  for funding in advance as well as in arrear;

(b)  for funding, or the recovery of amounts due under provision made by virtue of subsection (2)(b), by means of deductions from such amounts for which employers are accountable to the Commissioners of Inland Revenue as may be prescribed, or otherwise;

(c)  for the recovery by the Commissioners of Inland Revenue of any sums overpaid to employers under the regulations.

(6)  Where in accordance with any provision of regulations under subsection (1) an amount has been deducted from an employer's contributions payments, the amount so deducted shall (except in such cases as may be prescribed) be treated for the purposes of any provision made by or under any enactment in relation to primary or secondary Class 1 contributions—

(a)  as having been paid (on such date as may be determined in accordance with the regulations), and

(b)  as having been received by the Commissioners of Inland Revenue,

towards discharging the employer's liability in respect of such contributions.

(7)  Regulations under this section must be made with the concurrence of the Commissioners of Inland Revenue.

(8)  In this section "contributions payments", in relation to an employer, means any payments which the employer is required, by or under any enactment, to make in discharge of any liability in respect of primary or secondary Class 1 contributions.]

**NOTES**

Substituted by the Employment Act 2002, s 21(1).

Commissioners of Inland Revenue: a reference to the Commissioners of Inland Revenue is now to be taken as a reference to the Commissioners for Her Majesty's Revenue and Customs; see the Commissioners for Revenue and Customs Act 2005, s 50(1), (7).

Regulations: the Statutory Maternity Pay (Compensation of Employers) and Miscellaneous Amendment Regulations 1994, SI 1994/1882; the Statutory Maternity Pay (Compensation of Employers) Amendment Regulations 1995, SI 1995/566; the Statutory Maternity Pay (Compensation of Employers) Amendment Regulations 1999, SI 1999/363; the Statutory Maternity Pay (Compensation of Employers) Amendment Regulations 2003, SI 2003/672; the Statutory Maternity Pay (Compensation of Employers) Amendment Regulations 2004, SI 2004/698; the Statutory Maternity Pay (Compensation of Employers) Amendment Regulations 2011, SI 2011/725.

**[1.205]**
**168   Relationship with benefits and other payments etc**
Schedule 13 to this Act has effect with respect to the relationship between statutory maternity pay and certain benefits and payments.

**[1.206]**
**169   Crown employment—Part XII**
The provisions of this Part of this Act apply in relation to women employed by or under the Crown as they apply in relation to women employed otherwise than by or under the Crown.

**[1.207]**
**170   Special classes of person**
(1)  The Secretary of State may [with the concurrence of the Treasury] make regulations modifying this Part of this Act in such manner as he thinks proper in their application to any person who is, has been or is to be—

(a)  employed on board any ship, vessel, hovercraft or aircraft;

(b)  outside Great Britain at any prescribed time or in any prescribed circumstances; or

(c)  in prescribed employment in connection with continental shelf operations, as defined in section 120(2) above.

(2)  Regulations under subsection (1) above may in particular provide—

(a)  for any provision of this Part of this Act to apply to any such person, notwithstanding that it would not otherwise apply;

(b)  for any such provision not to apply to any such person, notwithstanding that it would otherwise apply;

(c)    for excepting any such person from the application of any such provision where he neither is domiciled nor has a place of residence in any part of Great Britain;

(d)    for the taking of evidence, for the purposes of the determination of any question arising under any such provision, in a country or territory outside Great Britain, by a British consular official or such other person as may be determined in accordance with the regulations.

**NOTES**

Sub-s (1): words in square brackets inserted by the Social Security Contributions (Transfer of Functions, etc) Act 1999, s 1(1), Sch 1, para 14.

Regulations: the Statutory Maternity Pay (Persons Abroad and Mariners) Regulations 1987, SI 1987/418, have effect as if made under this section by virtue of the Social Security (Consequential Provisions) Act 1992, s 2(2); the Social Security Contributions, Statutory Maternity Pay and Statutory Sick Pay (Miscellaneous Amendments) Regulations 1996, SI 1996/777.

**[1.208]**
**171   Interpretation of Part XII and supplementary provisions**
(1)    In this Part of this Act—
"confinement" means—
    (a)    labour resulting in the issue of a living child, or
    (b)    labour after [24 weeks] of pregnancy resulting in the issue of a child whether alive or dead,
and "confined" shall be construed accordingly; and where a woman's labour begun on one day results in the issue of a child on another day she shall be taken to be confined on the day of the issue of the child or, if labour results in the issue of twins or a greater number of children, she shall be taken to be confined on the day of the issue of the last of them;
"dismissed" is to be construed in accordance with [Part X of the Employment Rights Act 1996];
"employee" means a woman who is—
    (a)    gainfully employed in Great Britain either under a contract of service or in an office (including elective office) with [general earnings (as defined by section 7 of the Income Tax (Earnings and Pensions) Act 2003)];  . . .
    (b)    . . .
but subject to regulations [made with the concurrence of [Her Majesty's Revenue and Customs]] which may provide for cases where any such woman is not to be treated as an employee for the purposes of this Part of this Act and for cases where a woman who would not otherwise be an employee for those purposes is to be treated as an employee for those purposes;
["employer", in relation to a woman who is an employee, means a person who—
    (a)    under section 6 above is liable to pay secondary Class 1 contributions in relation to any of her earnings; or
    (b)    would be liable to pay such contributions but for—
        (i)    the condition in section 6(1)(b), or
        (ii)    the employee being under the age of 16;]
"maternity pay period" has the meaning assigned to it by section 165(1) above;
"modifications" includes additions, omissions and amendments, and related expressions shall be construed accordingly;
"prescribed" means specified in or determined in accordance with regulations;
. . .
[(1A)    In this Part, except section 165(1), (4) and (6), section 166(1) and paragraph 3(2) of Schedule 13, "week" means a period of 7 days beginning with Sunday or such other period as may be prescribed in relation to any particular case or class of case.]
(2)    Without prejudice to any other power to make regulations under this Part of this Act, regulations may specify cases in which, for the purposes of this Part of this Act or of such provisions of this Part of this Act as may be prescribed—
    (a)    two or more employers are to be treated as one;
    (b)    two or more contracts of service in respect of which the same woman is an employee are to be treated as one.
(3)    Where, in consequence of the establishment of one or more National Health Service trusts under [the National Health Service Act 2006, the National Health Service (Wales) Act 2006] or the National Health Service (Scotland) Act 1978, a woman's contract of employment is treated by a scheme under [any of those Acts] as divided so as to constitute two or more contracts, [or where an order under [paragraph 26(1) of Schedule 3 to the National Health Service Act 2006] provides that a woman's contract of employment is so divided,] regulations may make provision enabling her to elect for all of those contracts to be treated as one contract for the purposes of this Part of this Act or of such provisions of this Part of this Act as may be prescribed; and any such regulations may prescribe—
    (a)    the conditions that must be satisfied if a woman is to be entitled to make such an election;

(b) the manner in which, and the time within which, such an election is to be made;

(c) the persons to whom, and the manner in which, notice of such an election is to be given;

(d) the information which a woman who makes such an election is to provide, and the persons to whom, and the time within which, she is to provide it;

(e) the time for which such an election is to have effect;

(f) which one of the woman's employers under the two or more contracts is to be regarded for the purposes of statutory maternity pay as her employer under the one contract;

and the powers conferred by this subsection are without prejudice to any other power to make regulations under this Part of this Act.

(4) For the purposes of this Part of this Act a woman's normal weekly earnings shall, subject to subsection (6) below, be taken to be the average weekly earnings which in the relevant period have been paid to her or paid for her benefit under the contract of service with the employer in question.

(5) For the purposes of subsection (4) above "earnings" and "relevant period" shall have the meanings given to them by regulations.

(6) In such cases as may be prescribed a woman's normal weekly earnings shall be calculated in accordance with regulations.

[(7) Regulations under any of subsections (2) to (6) above must be made with the concurrence of the Commissioners of Inland Revenue.]

**NOTES**

Sub-s (1) is amended as follows:

Words in square brackets in definition "confinement" substituted by the Still-Birth (Definition) Act 1992, ss 2(1), 4(2).

Words in square brackets in definition "dismissed" substituted by the Employment Rights Act 1996, s 240, Sch 1, para 51.

Words in first pair of square brackets in definition "employee" substituted by the Income Tax (Earnings and Pensions) Act 2003, s 722, Sch 6, Pt 2, paras 169, 182.

Para (b) of the definition "employee" (and the word omitted immediately preceding it) repealed by the Employment Equality (Age) Regulations 2006, SI 2006/1031, reg 49(1), Sch 8, Pt 1, paras 8, 10(1), (2).

Words in second (outer) pair of square brackets in definition "employee" inserted by the Social Security Contributions (Transfer of Functions, etc) Act 1999, s 1(1), Sch 1, para 15(1), (2).

Words in third (inner) pair of square brackets in definition "employee" substituted by the Commissioners for Revenue and Customs Act 2005, s 50(6), Sch 4, para 43.

Definition "employer" substituted by SI 2006/1031, reg 49(1), Sch 8, Pt 1, paras 8, 10(1), (3).

Definition "week" (omitted) repealed by the Work and Families Act 2006, ss 11(1), 15, Sch 1, para 9(1), (2), Sch 2.

Sub-s (1A): inserted by the Work and Families Act 2006, s 11(1), Sch 1, para 9(1), (3).

Sub-s (3): words in first, second and fourth (inner) pairs of square brackets substituted by the National Health Service (Consequential Provisions) Act 2006, s 2, Sch 1, paras 142, 148; words in third (outer) pair of square brackets inserted by the Health Act 1999 (Supplementary, Consequential etc Provisions) Order 2000, SI 2000/90, art 3(1), Sch 1, para 27(1), (3); words in italics repealed by the Health and Social Care Act 2012, s 179, Sch 14, Pt 2, paras 58, 60, as from a day to be appointed.

Sub-s (7): added by the Social Security Contributions (Transfer of Functions, etc) Act 1999, s 1(1), Sch 1, para 15(1), (3).

Commissioners of Inland Revenue: a reference to the Commissioners of Inland Revenue is now to be taken as a reference to the Commissioners for Her Majesty's Revenue and Customs; see the Commissioners for Revenue and Customs Act 2005, s 50(1), (7).

Regulations: the Statutory Maternity Pay (Compensation of Employers) and Miscellaneous Amendment Regulations 1994, SI 1994/1882. In addition, the Statutory Maternity Pay (General) Regulations 1986, SI 1986/1960 (as amended) at **[2.70]**, the Statutory Maternity Pay (Persons Abroad and Mariners) Regulations 1987, SI 1987/418, and the Statutory Maternity Pay (National Health Service Employees) Regulations 1991, SI 1991/590 have effect as if made under this section by virtue of the Social Security (Consequential Provisions) Act 1992, s 2(2).

**[PART XIIZA**
**[ORDINARY AND ADDITIONAL STATUTORY PATERNITY PAY]**

**NOTES**

Pt XIIZA inserted by the Employment Act 2002, s 2. Sections 171ZEA–171ZEE are inserted into this Part by the Work and Families Act 2006, ss 6–10, as from 3 March 2010.

The Part heading (above) was substituted, and the cross-heading "Ordinary statutory paternity pay" (below) was inserted, by the Work and Families Act 2006, s 11(1), Sch 1, paras 10, 11, as from 6 April 2010.

Adoptions from overseas: this Part is modified in relation to adoptions from overseas as noted to the sections affected. See the Social Security Contributions and Benefits Act 1992 (Application of Parts 12ZA and 12ZB to Adoptions from Overseas) Regulations 2003, SI 2003/499.

*[Ordinary statutory paternity pay]*

**[1.209]**
**171ZA   Entitlement: birth**

(1) Where a person satisfies the conditions in subsection (2) below, he shall be entitled in accordance with the following provisions of this Part to payments to be known as "[ordinary statutory paternity pay".

(2) The conditions are—

(a) that he satisfies prescribed conditions—

(i) as to relationship with a newborn child, and

(ii) as to relationship with the child's mother;

(b)    that he has been in employed earner's employment with an employer for a continuous period of at least 26 weeks ending with the relevant week;

[(ba)  that at the end of the relevant week he was entitled to be in that employment;]

(c)    that his normal weekly earnings for the period of 8 weeks ending with the relevant week are not less than the lower earnings limit in force under section 5(1)(a) above at the end of the relevant week; and

(d)    that he has been in employed earner's employment with the employer by reference to whom the condition in paragraph (b) above is satisfied for a continuous period beginning with the end of the relevant week and ending with the day on which the child is born.

(3)    The references in subsection (2) above to the relevant week are to the week immediately preceding the 14th week before the expected week of the child's birth.

[(3A)  Regulations may provide for circumstances in which subsection (2)(ba) above does not apply.]

(4)    A person's entitlement to [ordinary statutory paternity pay] under this section shall not be affected by the birth, or expected birth, of more than one child as a result of the same pregnancy.

(5)    In this section, "newborn child" includes a child stillborn after twenty-four weeks of pregnancy.]

**NOTES**

Inserted as noted at the beginning of this Part.

Sub-ss (1), (4): words in square brackets substituted by the Work and Families Act 2006, s 11(1), Sch 1, para 12, as from 6 April 2010.

Sub-s (2): para (ba) inserted by the Welfare Reform Act 2012, s 63(1), (4)(a), as from a day to be appointed.

Sub-s (3A): inserted by the Welfare Reform Act 2012, s 63(1), (4)(b), as from a day to be appointed.

Regulations: the Statutory Paternity Pay and Statutory Adoption Pay (General) Regulations 2002, SI 2002/2822 at **[2.668]**.

**[1.210]**
**[171ZB    Entitlement: adoption**

(1)    Where a person satisfies the conditions in subsection (2) below, he shall be entitled in accordance with the following provisions of this Part to payments to be known as "[ordinary statutory paternity pay]".

(2)    The conditions are—

(a)    that he satisfies prescribed conditions—

(i)     as to relationship with a child who is placed for adoption under the law of any part of the United Kingdom, and

(ii)    as to relationship with a person with whom the child is so placed for adoption;

(b)    that he has been in employed earner's employment with an employer for a continuous period of at least 26 weeks ending with the relevant week;

[(ba)  that at the end of the relevant week he was entitled to be in that employment;]

(c)    that his normal weekly earnings for the period of 8 weeks ending with the relevant week are not less than the lower earnings limit in force under section 5(1)(a) at the end of the relevant week;

(d)    that he has been in employed earner's employment with the employer by reference to whom the condition in paragraph (b) above is satisfied for a continuous period beginning with the end of the relevant week and ending with the day on which the child is placed for adoption; and

(e)    where he is a person with whom the child is placed for adoption, that he has elected to receive statutory paternity pay.

(3)    The references in subsection (2) to the relevant week are to the week in which the adopter is notified of being matched with the child for the purposes of adoption.

[(3A)  Regulations may provide for circumstances in which subsection (2)(ba) above does not apply.]

(4)    A person may not elect to receive [ordinary statutory paternity pay] if he has elected in accordance with section 171ZL below to receive statutory adoption pay.

(5)    Regulations may make provision about elections for the purposes of subsection (2)(e) above.

(6)    A person's entitlement to [ordinary statutory paternity pay] under this section shall not be affected by the placement for adoption of more than one child as part of the same arrangement.

(7)    In this section, "adopter", in relation to a person who satisfies the condition under subsection (2)(a)(ii) above, means the person by reference to whom he satisfies that condition.]

**NOTES**

Inserted as noted at the beginning of this Part.

Sub-ss (1), (4), (6): words in square brackets substituted by the Work and Families Act 2006, s 11(1), Sch 1, para 13, as from 6 April 2010.

Sub-s (2): para (ba) inserted by the Welfare Reform Act 2012, s 63(1), (5)(a), as from a day to be appointed.

Sub-s (3A): inserted by the Welfare Reform Act 2012, s 63(1), (5)(b), as from a day to be appointed.

Adoptions from overseas: this section is modified in relation to adoptions from overseas which are adoptions of children who enter Great Britain from outside the United Kingdom in connection with, or for the purposes of, adoption which does not involve the placement of a child for adoption under the law of any part of the United Kingdom; see the Social Security Contributions and Benefits Act 1992 (Application of Parts 12ZA and 12ZB to Adoptions from Overseas) Regulations 2003, SI 2003/499, reg 2, Sch 1.

Regulations: the Statutory Paternity Pay and Statutory Adoption Pay (General) Regulations 2002, SI 2002/2822 at **[2.668]**; the Statutory Paternity Pay (Adoption) and Statutory Adoption Pay (Adoptions from Overseas) (No 2) Regulation 2003, SI 2003/1194; the Statutory Paternity Pay and Statutory Adoption Pay (Amendment) Regulations 2004, SI 2004/488.

## [1.211]
## [171ZC   Entitlement: general

(1)   A person shall be entitled to payments of [ordinary statutory paternity pay] in respect of any period only if—

(a)   he gives the person who will be liable to pay it notice of the date from which he expects the liability to pay him [ordinary statutory paternity pay] to begin; and

(b)   the notice is given at least 28 days before that date or, if that is not reasonably practicable, as soon as is reasonably practicable.

(2)   The notice shall be in writing if the person who is liable to pay the [ordinary statutory paternity pay] so requests.

(3)   The Secretary of State may by regulations—

(a)   provide that subsection (2)(b), (c) or (d) of section 171ZA or 171ZB above shall have effect subject to prescribed modifications in such cases as may be prescribed;

(b)   provide that subsection (1) above shall not have effect, or shall have effect subject to prescribed modifications, in such cases as may be prescribed;

(c)   impose requirements about evidence of entitlement;

(d)   specify in what circumstances employment is to be treated as continuous for the purposes of section 171ZA or 171ZB above;

(e)   provide that a person is to be treated for the purposes of section 171ZA or 171ZB above as being employed for a continuous period of at least 26 weeks where—

  (i)   he has been employed by the same employer for at least 26 weeks under two or more separate contracts of service; and

  (ii)   those contracts were not continuous;

(f)   provide for amounts earned by a person under separate contracts of service with the same employer to be aggregated for the purposes of section 171ZA or 171ZB above;

(g)   provide that—

  (i)   the amount of a person's earnings for any period, or

  (ii)   the amount of his earnings to be treated as comprised in any payment made to him or for his benefit,

shall be calculated or estimated for the purposes of section 171ZA or 171ZB above in such manner and on such basis as may be prescribed and that for that purpose payments of a particular class or description made or falling to be made to or by a person shall, to such extent as may be prescribed, be disregarded or, as the case may be, be deducted from the amount of his earnings.]

### NOTES
Inserted as noted at the beginning of this Part.

Sub-ss (1), (2): words in square brackets substituted by the Work and Families Act 2006, s 11(1), Sch 1, para 14, as from 6 April 2010.

Regulations: the Statutory Paternity Pay and Statutory Adoption Pay (General) Regulations 2002, SI 2002/2822 at **[2.668]**; the Statutory Paternity Pay (Adoption) and Statutory Adoption Pay (Adoptions from Overseas) (No 2) Regulations 2003, SI 2003/1194; the Statutory Maternity Pay (General) and the Statutory Paternity Pay and Statutory Adoption Pay (General) (Amendment) Regulations 2005, SI 2005/358.

## [1.212]
## [171ZD   Liability to make payments

(1)   The liability to make payments of [ordinary] statutory paternity pay under section 171ZA or 171ZB above is a liability of any person of whom the person entitled to the payments has been an employee as mentioned in subsection (2)(b) and (d) of that section.

(2)   Regulations shall make provision as to a former employer's liability to pay [ordinary statutory paternity pay] to a person in any case where the former employee's contract of service with him has been brought to an end by the former employer solely, or mainly, for the purpose of avoiding [liability for ordinary statutory paternity pay or additional statutory paternity pay (or both)].

(3)   The Secretary of State may, with the concurrence of the Board, by regulations specify circumstances in which, notwithstanding this section, liability to make payments of statutory paternity pay is to be a liability of the Board.]

### NOTES
Inserted as noted at the beginning of this Part.

Sub-ss (1), (2): words in square brackets inserted by the Work and Families Act 2006, s 11(1), Sch 1, para 15, as from 6 April 2010.

Regulations: the Statutory Paternity Pay and Statutory Adoption Pay (General) Regulations 2002, SI 2002/2822 at **[2.668]**; the Statutory Paternity Pay (Adoption) and Statutory Adoption Pay (Adoptions from Overseas) (No 2) Regulations 2003, SI 2003/1194.

**[1.213]**
**[171ZE    Rate and period of pay**
(1) [Ordinary statutory paternity pay] shall be payable at such fixed or earnings-related weekly rate as may be prescribed by regulations, which may prescribe different kinds of rate for different cases.
(2) [Ordinary statutory paternity pay] shall be payable in respect of—
  (a) a period of two consecutive weeks within the qualifying period beginning on such date within that period as the person entitled may choose in accordance with regulations, or
  (b) if regulations permit the person entitled to choose to receive [ordinary statutory paternity pay] in respect of—
    (i) a period of a week, or
    (ii) two non-consecutive periods of a week,
such week or weeks within the qualifying period as he may choose in accordance with regulations.
(3) For the purposes of subsection (2) above, the qualifying period shall be determined in accordance with regulations, which shall secure that it is a period of at least 56 days beginning—
  (a) in the case of a person to whom the conditions in section 171ZA(2) above apply, with the date of the child's birth, and
  (b) in the case of a person to whom the conditions in section 171ZB(2) above apply, with the date of the child's placement for adoption.
(4) [Ordinary statutory paternity pay] shall not be payable to a person in respect of a statutory pay week if it is not his purpose at the beginning of the week—
  (a) to care for the child by reference to whom he satisfies the condition in sub-paragraph (i) of section 171ZA(2)(a) or 171ZB(2)(a) above, or
  (b) to support the person by reference to whom he satisfies the condition in sub-paragraph (ii) of that provision.
(5) A person shall not be liable to pay [ordinary statutory paternity pay] to another in respect of a statutory pay week during any part of which the other works under a contract of service with him.
(6) It is immaterial for the purposes of subsection (5) above whether the work referred to in that subsection is work under a contract of service which existed immediately before the statutory pay week or a contract of service which did not so exist.
(7) Except in such cases as may be prescribed, [ordinary statutory paternity pay] shall not be payable to a person in respect of a statutory pay week during any part of which he works for any employer who is not liable to pay him [ordinary statutory paternity pay].
(8) The Secretary of State may by regulations specify circumstances in which there is to be no liability to pay [ordinary statutory paternity pay] in respect of a statutory pay week.
(9) Where more than one child is born as a result of the same pregnancy, the reference in subsection (3)(a) to the date of the child's birth shall be read as a reference to the date of birth of the first child born as a result of the pregnancy.
(10) Where more than one child is placed for adoption as part of the same arrangement, the reference in subsection (3)(b) to the date of the child's placement shall be read as a reference to the date of placement of the first child to be placed as part of the arrangement.
[(10A) Where for any purpose of this Part of this Act or of regulations it is necessary to calculate the daily rate of ordinary statutory paternity pay, the amount payable by way of ordinary statutory paternity pay for any day shall be taken as one seventh of the weekly rate.]
(11) In this section—
  "statutory pay week", in relation to a person entitled to [ordinary statutory paternity pay], means a week chosen by him as a week in respect of which [ordinary statutory paternity pay] shall be payable;
  "week" means any period of seven days.]

**NOTES**
Inserted as noted at the beginning of this Part.
Sub-ss (1), (2), (4), (5), (7), (8), (11): words in square brackets substituted by the Work and Families Act 2006, s 11(1), Sch 1, para 16(1), (2), as from 6 April 2010.
Sub-s (10A): inserted by the Work and Families Act 2006, s 11(1), Sch 1, para 16(1), (3).
The fixed rate, as from 7 April 2013, is £136.78 per week (see the Statutory Paternity Pay and Statutory Adoption Pay (Weekly Rates) Regulations, SI 2002/2818, reg 2 at **[2.651]**, as amended by the Social Security Benefits Up-rating Order 2013, SI 2013/574, art 10(1)(a)). Previous rates were: £135.45 (as from 1 April 2012, see SI 2012/780, art 11(1)(a)); £128.73 (as from 3 April 2011, see SI 2011/821); £124.88 (as from 4 April 2010, see SI 2010/793); £123.06 (as from 5 April 2009, see SI 2009/497); £117.18 (as from 6 April 2008, see SI 2008/632); £112.75 (as from 1 April 2007, see SI 2007/688); £108.85 (as from 2 April 2006, see SI 2006/645); and £106.00 (as from 3 April 2005, see SI 2005/522).
Adoptions from overseas: this section is modified as noted to s 171ZB at **[1.210]**.
Regulations: the Statutory Paternity Pay and Statutory Adoption Pay (Weekly Rates) Regulations 2002, SI 2002/2818 at **[2.650]**; the Statutory Paternity Pay and Statutory Adoption Pay (General) Regulations 2002, SI 2002/2822 at **[2.668]**; the Statutory Paternity Pay (Adoption) and Statutory Adoption Pay (Adoptions from Overseas) (No 2) Regulations 2003,

SI 2003/1194; the Statutory Paternity Pay and Statutory Adoption Pay (Weekly Rates) (Amendment) Regulations 2004, SI 2004/925.

*[Additional statutory paternity pay*

**[1.214]**
**171ZEA   Entitlement to additional statutory paternity pay: birth**
(1)   The Secretary of State may by regulations provide that, where all the conditions in subsection (2) are satisfied in relation to a person ("the claimant"), the claimant shall be entitled in accordance with the following provisions of this Part to payments to be known as "additional statutory paternity pay".
(2)   Those conditions are—
(a)   that the claimant satisfies prescribed conditions—
   (i)   as to relationship with a child, and
   (ii)   as to relationship with the child's mother;
(b)   that the claimant has been in employed earner's employment with an employer for a continuous period of at least the prescribed length ending with a prescribed week;
[(ba) that at the end of that prescribed week the claimant was entitled to be in that employment;]
(c)   that the claimant's normal weekly earnings for a prescribed period ending with a prescribed week are not less than the lower earnings limit in force under section 5(1)(a) at the end of that week;
(d)   if regulations so provide, that the claimant continues in employed earner's employment (whether or not with that employer) until a prescribed time;
(e)   that the mother of the child by reference to whom the condition in paragraph (a) is satisfied became entitled, by reference to the birth of the child—
   (i)   to a maternity allowance, or
   (ii)   to statutory maternity pay;
(f)   that the mother has, in relation to employment as an employed or self-employed earner, taken action that is treated by regulations as constituting for the purposes of this section her return to work;
(g)   that the day on which the mother is treated as returning to work falls—
   (i)   after the end of a prescribed period beginning with the birth of the child, but
   (ii)   at a time when at least a prescribed part of her maternity allowance period or maternity pay period remains unexpired;
(h)   that it is the claimant's intention to care for the child during a period beginning not later than a prescribed time.
(3)   The regulations may—
[(za) exclude the application of the condition mentioned in paragraph (ba) of subsection (2) in prescribed circumstances,]
(a)   exclude the application of the conditions mentioned in paragraphs (f) and (g) of subsection (2) in cases where the child's mother has died, and
(b)   provide that the condition mentioned in paragraph (e) of that subsection shall have effect with prescribed modifications in such cases.
(4)   A person's entitlement to additional statutory paternity pay under this section shall not be affected by the birth of more than one child as a result of the same pregnancy.]

**NOTES**
Commencement: 3 March 2010.
Inserted, together with the preceding heading, by the Work and Families Act 2006, s 6, as from 3 March 2010.
Sub-s (2): para (ba) inserted by the Welfare Reform Act 2012, s 63(1), (6)(a), as from a day to be appointed.
Sub-s (3): para (za) inserted by the Welfare Reform Act 2012, s 63(1), (6)(b), as from a day to be appointed.
Regulations: the Additional Statutory Paternity Pay (General) Regulations 2010, SI 2010/1056 at **[2.1451]**.

**[1.215]**
**[171ZEB   Entitlement to additional statutory paternity pay: adoption**
(1)   The Secretary of State may by regulations provide that, where all the conditions in subsection (2) are satisfied in relation to a person ("the claimant"), the claimant shall be entitled in accordance with the following provisions of this Part to payments to be known as "additional statutory paternity pay".
(2)   Those conditions are—
(a)   that the claimant satisfies prescribed conditions—
   (i)   as to relationship with a child who has been placed for adoption under the law of any part of the United Kingdom, and
   (ii)   as to relationship with a person with whom the child is so placed for adoption ("the adopter");
(b)   that the claimant has been in employed earner's employment with an employer for a continuous period of at least the prescribed length ending with a prescribed week;
[(ba) that at the end of that prescribed week the claimant was entitled to be in that employment;]

(c)   that the claimant's normal weekly earnings for a prescribed period ending with a prescribed week are not less than the lower earnings limit in force under section 5(1)(a) at the end of that week;

(d)   if regulations so provide, that the claimant continues to work in employed earner's employment (whether or not with that employer) until a prescribed time;

(e)   that the adopter became entitled to statutory adoption pay by reference to the placement of the child for adoption;

(f)   that the adopter has, in relation to employment as an employed or self-employed earner, taken action that is treated by regulations as constituting for the purposes of this section the adopter's return to work;

(g)   that the day on which the adopter is treated as returning to work falls—

    (i)   after the end of a prescribed period beginning with the placement of the child for adoption, but

    (ii)   at a time when at least a prescribed part of the adopter's adoption pay period remains unexpired;

(h)   that it is the claimant's intention to care for the child during a period beginning not later than a prescribed time.

(3)   The regulations may—

[(za)   exclude the application of the condition mentioned in paragraph (ba) of subsection (2) in prescribed circumstances,]

(a)   exclude the application of the conditions mentioned in paragraphs (f) and (g) of subsection (2) in cases where the adopter has died, and

(b)   provide that the condition mentioned in paragraph (e) of that subsection shall have effect with prescribed modifications in such cases.

(4)   A person may not elect to receive additional statutory paternity pay if he has elected in accordance with section 171ZL to receive statutory adoption pay.

(5)   A person's entitlement to additional statutory paternity pay under this section shall not be affected by the placement for adoption of more than one child as part of the same arrangement.]

**NOTES**

Commencement: 3 March 2010.

Inserted by the Work and Families Act 2006, s 7, as from 3 March 2010.

Sub-s (2): para (ba) inserted by the Welfare Reform Act 2012, s 63(1), (7)(a), as from a day to be appointed.

Sub-s (3): para (za) inserted by the Welfare Reform Act 2012, s 63(1), (7)(b), as from a day to be appointed.

Adoptions from overseas: this section is modified as noted to s 171ZB at **[1.210]**.

Regulations: the Additional Statutory Paternity Pay (General) Regulations 2010, SI 2010/1056 at **[2.1451]**; the Additional Statutory Paternity Pay (Adoptions from Overseas) Regulations 2010, SI 2010/1057.

**[1.216]**

**[171ZEC   Entitlement to additional statutory paternity pay: general**

(1)   A person shall not be entitled to payments of additional statutory paternity pay in respect of any period unless—

(a)   he gives the person who will be liable to pay it notice of the date from which he expects the liability to pay him additional statutory paternity pay to begin and the date on which he expects that liability to end, and

(b)   the notice is given by such time as may be prescribed.

(2)   The notice shall be in writing if the person who is liable to pay the additional statutory paternity pay so requests.

(3)   The Secretary of State may by regulations—

(a)   provide that the conditions mentioned in subsection (2)(b) or (c) of section 171ZEA or 171ZEB shall have effect subject to prescribed modifications in such cases as may be prescribed;

(b)   provide that subsection (1) of this section shall not have effect, or shall have effect subject to prescribed modifications, in such cases as may be prescribed;

(c)   impose requirements about evidence of entitlement;

(d)   specify in what circumstances employment is to be treated as continuous for the purposes of section 171ZEA or 171ZEB;

(e)   provide that a person is to be treated for the purposes of section 171ZEA or 171ZEB as being employed for a continuous period of the length prescribed under that section where—

    (i)   he has been employed by the same employer for a period of at least that length under two or more contracts of service, and

    (ii)   those contracts were not continuous;

(f)   provide for amounts earned by a person under separate contracts of service with the same employer to be aggregated for the purposes of section 171ZEA or 171ZEB;

(g)   provide that—

    (i)   the amount of a person's earnings for any period, or

(ii)  the amount of his earnings to be treated as comprised in any payment made to him or for his benefit,

shall be calculated or estimated for the purposes of section 171ZEA or 171ZEB in such manner and on such basis as may be prescribed and that for that purpose payments of a particular class or description made or falling to be made to or by a person shall, to such extent as may be prescribed, be disregarded or, as the case may be, be deducted from the amount of his earnings.]

**NOTES**

Commencement: 3 March 2010

Inserted by the Work and Families Act 2006, s 8, as from 3 March 2010.

Regulations: the Additional Statutory Paternity Pay (General) Regulations 2010, SI 2010/1056 at **[2.1451]**; the Additional Statutory Paternity Pay (Adoptions from Overseas) Regulations 2010, SI 2010/1057.

**[1.217]**
**[171ZED    Liability to make payments of additional statutory paternity pay**
(1)   The liability to make payments of additional statutory paternity pay under section 171ZEA or 171ZEB is a liability of any person of whom the person entitled to the payments has been an employee as mentioned in subsection (2)(b) of that section.
(2)   Regulations shall make provision as to a former employer's liability to pay additional statutory paternity pay to a person in any case where the former employee's contract of service with him has been brought to an end solely, or mainly, for the purpose of avoiding liability for additional statutory paternity pay or ordinary statutory paternity pay, or both.
(3)   The Secretary of State may, with the concurrence of the Commissioners for Her Majesty's Revenue and Customs, by regulations specify circumstances in which, notwithstanding this section, liability to make payments of additional statutory paternity pay is to be a liability of the Commissioners.]

**NOTES**

Commencement: 3 March 2010.

Inserted by the Work and Families Act 2006, s 9, as from 3 March 2010.

Regulations: the Additional Statutory Paternity Pay (General) Regulations 2010, SI 2010/1056 at **[2.1451]**; the Additional Statutory Paternity Pay (Adoptions from Overseas) Regulations 2010, SI 2010/1057.

**[1.218]**
**[171ZEE    Rate and period of pay: additional statutory paternity pay**
(1)   Additional statutory paternity pay shall be payable at such fixed or earnings-related weekly rate as may be prescribed by regulations, which may prescribe different kinds of rate for different cases.
(2)   Subject to the following provisions of this section, additional statutory paternity pay shall be payable in respect of a period ("the additional paternity pay period")—
  (a)   beginning with such day as may (subject to subsection (3)) be determined in accordance with regulations, and
  (b)   ending with—
    (i)    the day on which the additional statutory pay period is ended by virtue of subsection (4) or (8), or
    (ii)   such earlier day as the employee may choose in accordance with regulations.
(3)   The first day of the additional paternity pay period must not be earlier than the day on which the child's mother or the person with whom the child is placed for adoption ("the mother or adopter") is treated for the purpose of section 171ZEA or 171ZEB as returning to work; but this subsection does not apply in a case where the mother or adopter has died.
(4)   The additional paternity pay period—
  (a)   shall not last longer than any prescribed number of weeks,
  (b)   shall not continue after the end of the period of 12 months beginning with the relevant date, and
  (c)   shall not continue after the end—
    (i)    in a case falling within section 171ZEA, of the mother's maternity allowance period or maternity pay period, or
    (ii)   in a case falling within section 171ZEB, of the adoption pay period of the person with whom the child is placed for adoption.
(5)   In subsection (4)(b), "the relevant date" means—
  (a)   in the case of a person to whom the conditions in section 171ZEA(2) apply, the date of the child's birth (or, where more than one child is born as a result of the same pregnancy, the date of birth of the first child born as a result of the pregnancy), and
  (b)   in the case of a person to whom the conditions in section 171ZEB(2) apply, the date of the child's placement for adoption (or, where more than one child is placed for adoption as part of the same arrangement, the date of placement of the first child to be placed as part of the arrangement).

(6)   Additional statutory paternity pay shall not be payable to a person in respect of a week if it is not his purpose at the beginning of the week to care for the child by reference to whom he satisfies the condition in sub-paragraph (i) of section 171ZEA(2)(a) or 171ZEB(2)(a).

(7)   Except in such cases as may be prescribed, additional statutory paternity pay shall not be payable to a person in respect of a week during any part of which he works for any employer.

(8)   Where subsection (6) or (7) prevents additional statutory paternity pay being payable to a person in respect of any week, the person's additional paternity pay period shall be taken to have ended at the end of the previous week.

(9)   Where for any purpose of this Part of this Act or of regulations it is necessary to calculate the daily rate of additional statutory paternity pay, the amount payable by way of additional statutory paternity pay for that day shall be taken to be one seventh of the weekly rate.

(10)   In this section "week" means a period of seven days beginning with the day of the week on which the additional paternity pay period began.]

**NOTES**

Commencement: 3 March 2010.

Inserted by the Work and Families Act 2006, s 10, as from 3 March 2010.

Adoptions from overseas: this section is modified as noted to s 171ZB at **[1.210]**.

Regulations: the Additional Statutory Paternity Pay (General) Regulations 2010, SI 2010/1056 at **[2.1451]**; the Additional Statutory Paternity Pay (Adoptions from Overseas) Regulations 2010, SI 2010/1057; the Additional Statutory Paternity Pay (Weekly Rates) Regulations 2010, SI 2010/1060 at **[2.1490]**; the Additional Statutory Paternity Pay (General) (Amendment) Regulations 2011, SI 2011/678.

*[Ordinary and additional statutory paternity pay: supplementary provisions]*

**[1.219]**
**[171ZF   Restrictions on contracting out**
(1)   Any agreement shall be void to the extent that it purports—
   (a)   to exclude, limit or otherwise modify any provision of this Part of this Act, or
   (b)   to require an employee or former employee to contribute (whether directly or indirectly) towards any costs incurred by his employer or former employer under this Part of this Act.

(2)   For the avoidance of doubt, any agreement between an employer and an employee authorising any deductions from [ordinary statutory paternity pay or additional statutory paternity pay] which the employer is liable to pay to the employee in respect of any period shall not be void by virtue of subsection (1)(a) above if the employer—
   (a)   is authorised by that or another agreement to make the same deductions from any contractual remuneration which he is liable to pay in respect of the same period, or
   (b)   would be so authorised if he were liable to pay contractual remuneration in respect of that period.]

**NOTES**

Inserted as noted at the beginning of this Part.

The heading preceding this section was inserted, and the words in square brackets in sub-s (2) were substituted, by the Work and Families Act 2006, s 11(1), Sch 1, paras 17, 18, as from 6 April 2010.

**[1.220]**
**[171ZG   Relationship with contractual remuneration**
(1)   Subject to subsections (2) and (3) below, any entitlement to statutory paternity pay shall not affect any right of a person in relation to remuneration under any contract of service ("contractual remuneration").

(2)   Subject to subsection (3) below—
   (a)   any contractual remuneration paid to a person by an employer of his in respect of any period shall go towards discharging any liability of that employer to pay statutory paternity pay to him in respect of that period; and
   (b)   any statutory paternity pay paid by an employer to a person who is an employee of his in respect of any period shall go towards discharging any liability of that employer to pay contractual remuneration to him in respect of that period.

(3)   Regulations may make provision as to payments which are, and those which are not, to be treated as contractual remuneration for the purposes of subsections (1) and (2) above.

[(4)   In this section "statutory paternity pay" means ordinary statutory paternity pay or additional statutory paternity pay.]]

**NOTES**

Inserted as noted at the beginning of this Part.

Sub-s (4): added by the Work and Families Act 2006, s 11(1), Sch 1, para 19, as from 3 March 2010.

Regulations: the Statutory Paternity Pay and Statutory Adoption Pay (General) Regulations 2002, SI 2002/2822 at **[2.668]**; the Statutory Paternity Pay (Adoption) and Statutory Adoption Pay (Adoptions from Overseas) (No 2) Regulations 2003, SI 2003/1194; the Additional Statutory Paternity Pay (General) Regulations 2010, SI 2010/1056 at **[2.1451]**; the Additional Statutory Paternity Pay (Adoptions from Overseas) Regulations 2010, SI 2010/1057.

**[1.221]**
**[171ZH Crown employment—Part 12ZA**
The provisions of this Part of this Act apply in relation to persons employed by or under the Crown as they apply in relation to persons employed otherwise than by or under the Crown.]

NOTES
Inserted as noted at the beginning of this Part.

**[1.222]**
**[171ZI Special classes of person**
(1) The Secretary of State may with the concurrence of the Treasury make regulations modifying any provision of this Part of this Act in such manner as he thinks proper in its application to any person who is, has been or is to be—
(a) employed on board any ship, vessel, hovercraft or aircraft;
(b) outside Great Britain at any prescribed time or in any prescribed circumstances; or
(c) in prescribed employment in connection with continental shelf operations, as defined in section 120(2) above.
(2) Regulations under subsection (1) above may, in particular, provide—
(a) for any provision of this Part of this Act to apply to any such person, notwithstanding that it would not otherwise apply;
(b) for any such provision not to apply to any such person, notwithstanding that it would otherwise apply;
(c) for excepting any such person from the application of any such provision where he neither is domiciled nor has a place of residence in any part of Great Britain;
(d) for the taking of evidence, for the purposes of the determination of any question arising under any such provision, in a country or territory outside Great Britain, by a British consular official or such other person as may be determined in accordance with the regulations.]

NOTES
Inserted as noted at the beginning of this Part.
Regulations: the Statutory Paternity Pay and Statutory Adoption Pay (Persons Abroad and Mariners) Regulations 2002, SI 2002/2821; the Ordinary Statutory Paternity Pay (Adoption), Additional Statutory Paternity Pay (Adoption) and Statutory Adoption Pay (Adoptions from Overseas) (Persons Abroad and Mariners) Regulations 2010, SI 2010/150; the Statutory Paternity Pay and Statutory Adoption Pay (Persons Abroad and Mariners) Regulations 2002 (Amendment) Regulations 2010, SI 2010/151.

**[1.223]**
**[171ZJ Part 12ZA: supplementary**
(1) In this Part of this Act—
"the Board" means the Commissioners of Inland Revenue;
["employer", in relation to a person who is an employee, means a person who—
(a) under section 6 above is, liable to pay secondary Class 1 contributions in relation to any of the earnings of the person who is an employee; or
(b) would be liable to pay such contributions but for—
(i) the condition in section 6(1)(b), or
(ii) the employee being under the age of 16;]
"modifications" includes additions, omissions and amendments, and related expressions are to be read accordingly;
"prescribed" means prescribed by regulations.
(2) In this Part of this Act, "employee" means a person who is—
(a) gainfully employed in Great Britain either under a contract of service or in an office (including elective office) with [general earnings (as defined by section 7 of the Income Tax (Earnings and Pensions) Act 2003)]; . . .
(b) . . .
(3) Regulations may provide—
(a) for cases where a person who falls within the definition in subsection (2) above is not to be treated as an employee for the purposes of this Part of this Act, and
(b) for cases where a person who would not otherwise be an employee for the purposes of this Part of this Act is to be treated as an employee for those purposes.
(4) Without prejudice to any other power to make regulations under this Part of this Act, regulations may specify cases in which, for the purposes of this Part of this Act or of such provisions of this Part of this Act as may be prescribed—
(a) two or more employers are to be treated as one;
(b) two or more contracts of service in respect of which the same person is an employee are to be treated as one.

(5)   In this Part, except [sections 171ZE and 171ZEE], "week" means a period of 7 days beginning with Sunday or such other period as may be prescribed in relation to any particular case or class of cases.

(6)   For the purposes of this Part of this Act, a person's normal weekly earnings shall, subject to subsection (8) below, be taken to be the average weekly earnings which in the relevant period have been paid to him or paid for his benefit under the contract of service with the employer in question.

(7)   For the purposes of subsection (6) above, "earnings" and "relevant period" shall have the meanings given to them by regulations.

(8)   In such cases as may be prescribed, a person's normal weekly earnings shall be calculated in accordance with regulations.

(9)   Where—

   (a)   in consequence of the establishment of one or more National Health Service trusts under [*the National Health Service Act 2006,* the National Health Service (Wales) Act 2006] or the National Health Service (Scotland) Act 1978 (c 29), a person's contract of employment is treated by a scheme under [any of those Acts] as divided so as to constitute two or more contracts, or

   (b)   an order under [paragraph 26(1) of Schedule 3 to the National Health Service Act 2006] provides that a person's contract of employment is so divided,

regulations may make provision enabling the person to elect for all of those contracts to be treated as one contract for the purposes of this Part of this Act or such provisions of this Part of this Act as may be prescribed.

(10)   Regulations under subsection (9) above may prescribe—

   (a)   the conditions that must be satisfied if a person is to be entitled to make such an election;

   (b)   the manner in which, and the time within which, such an election is to be made;

   (c)   the persons to whom, and the manner in which, notice of such an election is to be given;

   (d)   the information which a person who makes such an election is to provide, and the persons to whom, and the time within which, he is to provide it;

   (e)   the time for which such an election is to have effect;

   (f)   which one of the person's employers under two or more contracts is to be regarded for the purposes of [ordinary statutory paternity pay or additional statutory paternity pay] as his employer under the contract.

(11)   The powers under subsections (9) and (10) are without prejudice to any other power to make regulations under this Part of this Act.

(12)   Regulations under any of subsections (4) to (10) above must be made with the concurrence of the Board.]

---

**NOTES**

Inserted as noted at the beginning of this Part.

Sub-s (1): definition "employer" substituted by the Employment Equality (Age) Regulations 2006, SI 2006/1031, reg 49(1), Sch 8, Pt 1, paras 8, 11(1), (2), (4).

Sub-s (2): words in square brackets in para (a) substituted by the Income Tax (Earnings and Pensions) Act 2003, s 722, Sch 6, Pt 2, paras 169, 183; para (b) (and the word omitted immediately preceding it) repealed by SI 2006/1031, reg 49(1), Sch 8, Pt 1, paras 8, 11(1), (3), (4).

Sub-ss (5), (10): words in square brackets substituted by the Work and Families Act 2006, s 11(1), Sch 1, para 20, as from 3 March 2010.

Sub-s (9): words in square brackets substituted by the National Health Service (Consequential Provisions) Act 2006, s 2, Sch 1, paras 142, 149; words in italics repealed by the Health and Social Care Act 2012, s 179, Sch 14, Pt 2, paras 58, 61, as from a day to be appointed.

Adoptions from overseas: this section is modified as noted to s 171ZB at **[1.210]**.

Commissioners of Inland Revenue: a reference to the Commissioners of Inland Revenue is now to be taken as a reference to the Commissioners for Her Majesty's Revenue and Customs; see the Commissioners for Revenue and Customs Act 2005, s 50(1), (7).

Regulations: the Statutory Paternity Pay and Statutory Adoption Pay (National Health Service Employees) Regulations 2002, SI 2002/2819; the Statutory Paternity Pay and Statutory Adoption Pay (General) Regulations 2002, SI 2002/2822 at **[2.668]**; the Statutory Paternity Pay (Adoption) and Statutory Adoption Pay (Adoptions from Overseas) (No 2) Regulations 2003, SI 2003/1194; the Statutory Paternity Pay and Statutory Adoption Pay (Amendment) Regulations 2004, SI 2004/488; the Ordinary Statutory Paternity Pay (Adoption), Additional Statutory Paternity Pay (Adoption) and Statutory Adoption Pay (Adoptions from Overseas) (Persons Abroad and Mariners) Regulations 2010, SI 2010/150; the Additional Statutory Paternity Pay (National Health Service Employees) Regulations 2010, SI 2010/152; the Additional Statutory Paternity Pay (General) Regulations 2010, SI 2010/1056 at **[2.1451]**; the Additional Statutory Paternity Pay (Adoptions from Overseas) Regulations 2010, SI 2010/1057.

**[1.224]**
**[171ZK   Power to apply Part 12ZA to adoption cases not involving placement**
The Secretary of State may by regulations provide for this Part to have effect in relation to cases which involve adoption, but not the placement of a child for adoption under the law of any part of the United Kingdom, with such modifications as the regulations may prescribe.]

**NOTES**
Inserted as noted at the beginning of this Part.
Regulations: the Social Security Contributions and Benefits Act 1992 (Application of Parts 12ZA and 12ZB to Adoptions from Overseas) Regulations 2003, SI 2003/499; the Statutory Paternity Pay and Statutory Adoption Pay (Amendment) Regulations 2004, SI 2004/488; the Social Security Contributions and Benefits Act 1992 (Application of Parts 12ZA and 12ZB to Adoptions from Overseas) Regulations 2003 (Amendment) Regulations 2010, SI 2010/153.

## [PART XIIZB
## STATUTORY ADOPTION PAY

**NOTES**
Pt XIIZB inserted by the Employment Act 2002, s 4, in relation to a person with whom a child is, or is expected to be placed for adoption on or after 6 April 2003.
Adoptions from overseas: this Part is modified in relation to adoptions from overseas as noted to the sections affected. See the Social Security Contributions and Benefits Act 1992 (Application of Parts 12ZA and 12ZB to Adoptions from Overseas) Regulations 2003, SI 2003/499.

**[1.225]**
**171ZL   Entitlement**
(1)   Where a person who is, or has been, an employee satisfies the conditions in subsection (2) below, he shall be entitled in accordance with the following provisions of this Part to payments to be known as "statutory adoption pay".
(2)   The conditions are—
  (a)   that he is a person with whom a child is, or is expected to be, placed for adoption under the law of any part of the United Kingdom;
  (b)   that he has been in employed earner's employment with an employer for a continuous period of at least 26 weeks ending with the relevant week;
  [(ba) that at the end of the relevant week he was entitled to be in that employment;]
  (c)   that he has ceased to work for the employer;
  (d)   that his normal weekly earnings for the period of 8 weeks ending with the relevant week are not less than the lower earnings limit in force under section 5(1)(a) at the end of the relevant week; and
  (e)   that he has elected to receive statutory adoption pay.
(3)   The references in subsection (2)(b)[, (ba)] and (d) above to the relevant week are to the week in which the person is notified that he has been matched with the child for the purposes of adoption.
(4)   A person may not elect to receive statutory adoption pay if—
  (a)   he has elected in accordance with section 171ZB above to receive statutory paternity pay, or
  [(b)  he falls within subsection (4A)].
[(4A)   A person falls within this subsection if—
  (a)   the child is, or is expected to be, placed for adoption with him as a member of a couple;
  (b)   the other member of the couple is a person to whom the conditions in subsection (2) above apply; and
  (c)   the other member of the couple has elected to receive statutory adoption pay.
(4B)   For the purposes of subsection (4A), a person is a member of a couple if—
  (a)   in the case of an adoption or expected adoption under the law of England and Wales, he is a member of a couple within the meaning of section 144(4) of the Adoption and Children Act 2002;
  (b)   in the case of an adoption or an expected adoption under the law  . . .  of Northern Ireland, he is a member of a married couple.;
  [(c)  in the case of an adoption or expected adoption under the law of Scotland he is a member of a relevant couple within the meaning of section 29(3) of the Adoption and Children (Scotland) Act 2007].]
(5)   A person's entitlement to statutory adoption pay shall not be affected by the placement, or expected placement, for adoption of more than one child as part of the same arrangement.
(6)   A person shall be entitled to payments of statutory adoption pay only if—
  (a)   he gives the person who will be liable to pay it notice of the date from which he expects the liability to pay him statutory adoption pay to begin; and
  (b)   the notice is given at least 28 days before that date or, if that is not reasonably practicable, as soon as is reasonably practicable.
(7)   The notice shall be in writing if the person who is liable to pay the statutory adoption pay so requests.

(8)   The Secretary of State may by regulations—

[(za) exclude the application of subsection (2)(ba) above in prescribed circumstances;]

(a)   provide that subsection (2)(b), (c) or (d) above shall have effect subject to prescribed modifications in such cases as may be prescribed;

(b)   provide that subsection (6) above shall not have effect, or shall have effect subject to prescribed modifications, in such cases as may be prescribed;

(c)   impose requirements about evidence of entitlement;

(d)   specify in what circumstances employment is to be treated as continuous for the purposes of this section;

(e)   provide that a person is to be treated for the purposes of this section as being employed for a continuous period of at least 26 weeks where—

(i)   he has been employed by the same employer for at least 26 weeks under two or more separate contracts of service; and

(ii)   those contracts were not continuous;

(f)   provide for amounts earned by a person under separate contracts of service with the same employer to be aggregated for the purposes of this section;

(g)   provide that—

(i)   the amount of a person's earnings for any period, or

(ii)   the amount of his earnings to be treated as comprised in any payment made to him or for his benefit,

shall be calculated or estimated for the purposes of this section in such manner and on such basis as may be prescribed and that for that purpose payments of a particular class or description made or falling to be made to or by a person shall, to such extent as may be prescribed, be disregarded or, as the case may be, be deducted from the amount of his earnings;

(h)   make provision about elections for statutory adoption pay.]

**NOTES**

Inserted as noted at the beginning of this Part.

Sub-s (2): para (ba) inserted by the Welfare Reform Act 2012, s 63(1), (8)(a), as from a day to be appointed.

Sub-s (3): reference in square brackets inserted by the Welfare Reform Act 2012, s 63(1), (8)(b), as from a day to be appointed.

Sub-s (4): para (b) substituted by the Adoption and Children Act 2002 (Consequential Amendment to Statutory Adoption Pay) Order 2006, SI 2006/2012, art 3(a).

Sub-ss (4A), (4B): inserted by SI 2006/2012, art 3(b); words omitted from sub-s (4B)(b) repealed, and sub-s (4B)(c) inserted, by the Adoption and Children (Scotland) Act 2007 (Consequential Modifications) Order 2011, SI 2011/1740, art 2, Sch 1, Pt 1, para 4, Sch 1, Pt 3, as from 15 July 2011.

Sub-s (8): para (za) inserted by the Welfare Reform Act 2012, s 63(1), (8)(c), as from a day to be appointed.

Adoptions from overseas: this section is modified in relation to adoptions from overseas which are adoptions of children who enter Great Britain from outside the United Kingdom in connection with, or for the purposes of, adoption which does not involve the placement of a child for adoption under the law of any part of the United Kingdom; see the Social Security Contributions and Benefits Act 1992 (Application of Parts 12ZA and 12ZB to Adoptions from Overseas) Regulations 2003, SI 2003/499, reg 3, Sch 2.

Regulations: the Statutory Paternity Pay and Statutory Adoption Pay (General) Regulations 2002, SI 2002/2822 at **[2.668]**; the Statutory Paternity Pay (Adoption) and Statutory Adoption Pay (Adoptions from Overseas) (No 2) Regulations 2003, SI 2003/1194; the Statutory Maternity Pay (General) and the Statutory Paternity Pay and Statutory Adoption Pay (General) (Amendment) Regulations 2005, SI 2005/358.

**[1.226]**
**[171ZM   Liability to make payments**

(1)   The liability to make payments of statutory adoption pay is a liability of any person of whom the person entitled to the payments has been an employee as mentioned in section 171ZL(2)(b) above.

(2)   Regulations shall make provision as to a former employer's liability to pay statutory adoption pay to a person in any case where the former employee's contract of service with him has been brought to an end by the former employer solely, or mainly, for the purpose of avoiding liability for statutory adoption pay.

(3)   The Secretary of State may, with the concurrence of the Board, by regulations specify circumstances in which, notwithstanding this section, liability to make payments of statutory adoption pay is to be a liability of the Board.]

**NOTES**

Inserted as noted at the beginning of this Part.

Regulations: the Statutory Paternity Pay and Statutory Adoption Pay (General) Regulations 2002, SI 2002/2822 at **[2.668]**; the Statutory Paternity Pay (Adoption) and Statutory Adoption Pay (Adoptions from Overseas) (No 2) Regulations 2003, SI 2003/1194.

**[1.227]**
**[171ZN    Rate and period of pay**
(1)    Statutory adoption pay shall be payable at such fixed or earnings-related weekly rate as the Secretary of State may prescribe by regulations, which may prescribe different kinds of rate for different cases.
(2)    Statutory adoption pay shall be payable, subject to the provisions of this Part of this Act, in respect of each week during a prescribed period ("the adoption pay period") of a duration not exceeding [52 weeks].
(3)    [Except in such cases as may be prescribed,] a person shall not be liable to pay statutory adoption pay to another in respect of any week during any part of which the other works under a contract of service with him.
(4)    It is immaterial for the purposes of subsection (3) above whether the work referred to in that subsection is work under a contract of service which existed immediately before the adoption pay period or a contract of service which did not so exist.
(5)    Except in such cases as may be prescribed, statutory adoption pay shall not be payable to a person in respect of any week during any part of which he works for any employer who is not liable to pay him statutory adoption pay.
(6)    The Secretary of State may by regulations specify circumstances in which there is to be no liability to pay statutory adoption pay in respect of a week.
[(6A)    Where for any purpose of this Part of this Act or of regulations it is necessary to calculate the daily rate of statutory adoption pay, the amount payable by way of statutory adoption pay for any day shall be taken as one seventh of the weekly rate.]
(7)    In subsection (2) above, "week" means any period of seven days.
(8)    In subsections (3), (5) and (6) above, "week" means a period of seven days beginning with the day of the week on which the adoption pay period begins.]

**NOTES**
Inserted as noted at the beginning of this Part.
Sub-s (2): words in square brackets substituted by the Work and Families Act 2006, s 2.
Sub-s (3): words in square brackets inserted by the Work and Families Act 2006, s 11(1), Sch 1, para 21(1), (2).
Sub-s (6A): inserted by the Work and Families Act 2006, s 11(1), Sch 1, para 21(1), (3).
The fixed rate, as from 7 April 2013, is £136.78 per week (see the Statutory Paternity Pay and Statutory Adoption Pay (Weekly Rates) Regulations, SI 2002/2818, reg 3 at **[2.652]**, as amended by the Social Security Benefits Up-rating Order 2013, SI 2013/574, art 10(1)(b).)
Previous rates were: £135.45 (as from 1 April 2012, see SI 2012/780); £128.73 (as from 3 April 2011, see SI 2011/821); £124.88 (as from 4 April 2010, see SI 2010/793); £123.06 (as from 5 April 2009, see SI 2009/497); £117.18 (as from 6 April 2008, see SI 2008/632); £112.75 (as from 1 April 2007, see SI 2007/688); £108.85 (as from 2 April 2006, see SI 2006/645); and £106.00 (as from 3 April 2005, see SI 2005/522).
Regulations: the Statutory Paternity Pay and Statutory Adoption Pay (Weekly Rates) Regulations 2002, SI 2002/2818 at **[2.650]**; the Statutory Paternity Pay and Statutory Adoption Pay (General) Regulations 2002, SI 2002/2822 at **[2.668]**; the Statutory Paternity Pay (Adoption) and Statutory Adoption Pay (Adoptions from Overseas) (No 2) Regulations 2003, SI 2003/1194; the Statutory Paternity Pay and Statutory Adoption Pay (General) and the Statutory Paternity Pay and Statutory Adoption Pay (Weekly Rates) (Amendment) Regulations 2006, SI 2006/2236.

**[1.228]**
**[171ZO    Restrictions on contracting out**
(1)    Any agreement shall be void to the extent that it purports—
    (a)    to exclude, limit or otherwise modify any provision of this Part of this Act, or
    (b)    to require an employee or former employee to contribute (whether directly or indirectly) towards any costs incurred by his employer or former employer under this Part of this Act.
(2)    For the avoidance of doubt, any agreement between an employer and an employee authorising any deductions from statutory adoption pay which the employer is liable to pay to the employee in respect of any period shall not be void by virtue of subsection (1)(a) above if the employer—
    (a)    is authorised by that or another agreement to make the same deductions from any contractual remuneration which he is liable to pay in respect of the same period, or
    (b)    would be so authorised if he were liable to pay contractual remuneration in respect of that period.]

**NOTES**
Inserted as noted at the beginning of this Part.

**[1.229]**
**[171ZP    Relationship with benefits and other payments etc**
*(1)    Except as may be prescribed, a day which falls within the adoption pay period shall not be treated as a day of incapacity for work for the purposes of determining, for this Act, whether it forms part of a period of incapacity for work for the purposes of incapacity benefit.*
*(2)    Regulations may provide that in prescribed circumstances a day which falls within the adoption pay period shall be treated as a day of incapacity for work for the purposes of determining entitlement to the higher rate of short-term incapacity benefit or to long-term incapacity benefit.*

(3)   Regulations may provide that an amount equal to a person's statutory adoption pay for a period shall be deducted from any such benefit in respect of the same period and a person shall be entitled to such benefit only if there is a balance after the deduction and, if there is such a balance, at a weekly rate equal to it.

(4)   Subject to subsections (5) and (6) below, any entitlement to statutory adoption pay shall not affect any right of a person in relation to remuneration under any contract of service ("contractual remuneration").

(5)   Subject to subsection (6) below—

   (a)   any contractual remuneration paid to a person by an employer of his in respect of a week in the adoption pay period shall go towards discharging any liability of that employer to pay statutory adoption pay to him in respect of that week; and

   (b)   any statutory adoption pay paid by an employer to a person who is an employee of his in respect of a week in the adoption pay period shall go towards discharging any liability of that employer to pay contractual remuneration to him in respect of that week.

(6)   Regulations may make provision as to payments which are, and those which are not, to be treated as contractual remuneration for the purposes of subsections (4) and (5) above.

(7)   In subsection (5) above, "week" means a period of seven days beginning with the day of the week on which the adoption pay period begins.]

**NOTES**

Inserted as noted at the beginning of this Part.

Sub-ss (1)–(3): repealed by the Welfare Reform Act 2007, s 67, Sch 8, as from a day to be appointed.

Regulations: the Social Security, Statutory Maternity Pay and Statutory Sick Pay (Miscellaneous Amendments) Regulations 2002, SI 2002/2690; the Statutory Paternity Pay and Statutory Adoption Pay (General) Regulations 2002, SI 2002/2822 at **[2.668]**; the Statutory Paternity Pay (Adoption) and Statutory Adoption Pay (Adoptions from Overseas) (No 2) Regulations 2003, SI 2003/1194.

**[1.230]**
**[171ZQ   Crown employment—Part 12ZB**

The provisions of this Part of this Act apply in relation to persons employed by or under the Crown as they apply in relation to persons employed otherwise than by or under the Crown.]

**NOTES**

Inserted as noted at the beginning of this Part.

**[1.231]**
**[171ZR   Special classes of person**

(1)   The Secretary of State may with the concurrence of the Treasury make regulations modifying any provision of this Part of this Act in such manner as he thinks proper in its application to any person who is, has been or is to be—

   (a)   employed on board any ship, vessel, hovercraft or aircraft;

   (b)   outside Great Britain at any prescribed time or in any prescribed circumstances; or

   (c)   in prescribed employment in connection with continental shelf operations, as defined in section 120(2) above.

(2)   Regulations under subsection (1) above may, in particular, provide—

   (a)   for any provision of this Part of this Act to apply to any such person, notwithstanding that it would not otherwise apply;

   (b)   for any such provision not to apply to any such person, notwithstanding that it would otherwise apply;

   (c)   for excepting any such person from the application of any such provision where he neither is domiciled nor has a place of residence in any part of Great Britain;

   (d)   for the taking of evidence, for the purposes of the determination of any question arising under any such provision, in a country or territory outside Great Britain, by a British consular official or such other person as may be determined in accordance with the regulations.]

**NOTES**

Inserted as noted at the beginning of this Part.

Regulations: the Statutory Paternity Pay and Statutory Adoption Pay (Persons Abroad and Mariners) Regulations 2002, SI 2002/2821; the Ordinary Statutory Paternity Pay (Adoption), Additional Statutory Paternity Pay (Adoption) and Statutory Adoption Pay (Adoptions from Overseas) (Persons Abroad and Mariners) Regulations 2010, SI 2010/150; the Statutory Paternity Pay and Statutory Adoption Pay (Persons Abroad and Mariners) Regulations 2002 (Amendment) Regulations 2010, SI 2010/151.

**[1.232]**
**[171ZS   Part 12ZB: supplementary**

(1)   In this Part of this Act—

"adoption pay period" has the meaning given by section 171ZN(2) above;

"the Board" means the Commissioners of Inland Revenue;

["employer", in relation to a person who is an employee, means a person who—

    (a)    under section 6 above is liable to pay secondary Class 1 contributions in relation to any of the earnings of the person who is an employee; or

    (b)    would be liable to pay such contributions but for—

        (ii)   the condition in section 6(1)(b), or

        (ii)   the employee being under the age of 16;]

"modifications" includes additions, omissions and amendments, and related expressions are to be read accordingly;

"prescribed" means prescribed by regulations.

(2)   In this Part of this Act, "employee" means a person who is—

    (a)    gainfully employed in Great Britain either under a contract of service or in an office (including elective office) with [general earnings (as defined by section 7 of the Income Tax (Earnings and Pensions) Act 2003)]; . . .

    (b)    . . .

(3)   Regulations may provide—

    (a)    for cases where a person who falls within the definition in subsection (2) above is not to be treated as an employee for the purposes of this Part of this Act, and

    (b)    for cases where a person who would not otherwise be an employee for the purposes of this Part of this Act is to be treated as an employee for those purposes.

(4)   Without prejudice to any other power to make regulations under this Part of this Act, regulations may specify cases in which, for the purposes of this Part of this Act or of such provisions of this Part of this Act as may be prescribed—

    (a)    two or more employers are to be treated as one;

    (b)    two or more contracts of service in respect of which the same person is an employee are to be treated as one.

(5)   In this Part, except sections 171ZN and 171ZP, "week" means a period of 7 days beginning with Sunday or such other period as may be prescribed in relation to any particular case or class of cases.

(6)   For the purposes of this Part of this Act, a person's normal weekly earnings shall, subject to subsection (8) below, be taken to be the average weekly earnings which in the relevant period have been paid to him or paid for his benefit under the contract of service with the employer in question.

(7)   For the purposes of subsection (6) above, "earnings" and "relevant period" shall have the meanings given to them by regulations.

(8)   In such cases as may be prescribed, a person's normal weekly earnings shall be calculated in accordance with regulations.

(9)   Where—

    (a)    in consequence of the establishment of one or more National Health Service trusts under [*the National Health Service Act 2006,* the National Health Service (Wales) Act 2006] or the National Health Service (Scotland) Act 1978 (c 29), a person's contract of employment is treated by a scheme under [any of those Acts] as divided so as to constitute two or more contracts, or

    (b)    an order under [paragraph 26(1) of Schedule 3 to the National Health Service Act 2006] provides that a person's contract of employment is so divided,

regulations may make provision enabling the person to elect for all of those contracts to be treated as one contract for the purposes of this Part of this Act or such provisions of this Part of this Act as may be prescribed.

(10)   Regulations under subsection (9) above may prescribe—

    (a)    the conditions that must be satisfied if a person is to be entitled to make such an election;

    (b)    the manner in which, and the time within which, such an election is to be made;

    (c)    the persons to whom, and the manner in which, notice of such an election is to be given;

    (d)    the information which a person who makes such an election is to provide, and the persons to whom, and the time within which, he is to provide it;

    (e)    the time for which such an election is to have effect;

    (f)    which one of the person's employers under two or more contracts is to be regarded for the purposes of statutory adoption pay as his employer under the contract.

(11)   The powers under subsections (9) and (10) are without prejudice to any other power to make regulations under this Part of this Act.

(12)   Regulations under any of subsections (4) to (10) above must be made with the concurrence of the Board.]

**NOTES**

Inserted as noted at the beginning of this Part.

Sub-s (1): definition "employer" substituted by the Employment Equality (Age) Regulations 2006, SI 2006/1031, reg 49(1), Sch 8, Pt 1, paras 8, 12(1), (2).

Sub-s (2): words in square brackets in para (a) substituted by the Income Tax (Earnings and Pensions) Act 2003, s 722, Sch 6, Pt 2, paras 169, 184; para (b) (and the word omitted immediately preceding it) repealed by SI 2006/1031, reg 49(1), Sch 8, Pt 1, paras 8, 12(1), (3), (4).

Sub-s (9): words in square brackets substituted by the National Health Service (Consequential Provisions) Act 2006, s 2, Sch 1, paras 142, 150; words in italics repealed by the Health and Social Care Act 2012, s 179, Sch 14, Pt 2, paras 58, 62, as from a day to be appointed.

Adoptions from overseas: this section is modified as noted to s 171ZL at **[1.225]**.

Commissioners of Inland Revenue: a reference to the Commissioners of Inland Revenue is now to be taken as a reference to the Commissioners for Her Majesty's Revenue and Customs; see the Commissioners for Revenue and Customs Act 2005, s 50(1), (7).

Regulations: the Statutory Paternity Pay and Statutory Adoption Pay (National Health Service Employees) Regulations 2002, SI 2002/2819; the Statutory Paternity Pay and Statutory Adoption Pay (General) Regulations 2002, SI 2002/2822 at **[2.668]**; the Statutory Paternity Pay (Adoption) and Statutory Adoption Pay (Adoptions from Overseas) (No 2) Regulations 2003, SI 2003/1194; the Statutory Paternity Pay and Statutory Adoption Pay (Amendment) Regulations 2004, SI 2004/488; the Ordinary Statutory Paternity Pay (Adoption), Additional Statutory Paternity Pay (Adoption) and Statutory Adoption Pay (Adoptions from Overseas) (Persons Abroad and Mariners) Regulations 2010, SI 2010/150.

**[1.233]**
**[171ZT   Power to apply Part 12ZB to adoption cases not involving placement**
The Secretary of State may by regulations provide for this Part to have effect in relation to cases which involve adoption, but not the placement of a child for adoption under the law of any part of the United Kingdom, with such modifications as the regulations may prescribe.]

**NOTES**
Inserted as noted at the beginning of this Part.
Regulations: the Social Security Contributions and Benefits Act 1992 (Application of Parts 12ZA and 12ZB to Adoptions from Overseas) Regulations 2003, SI 2003/499; the Statutory Paternity Pay and Statutory Adoption Pay (Amendment) Regulations 2004, SI 2004/488.

## PART XIII
## GENERAL

*Short title, commencement and extent*

**[1.234]**
**177   Short title, commencement and extent**
(1)   This Act may be cited as the Social Security Contributions and Benefits Act 1992.
(2)   *(Outside the scope of this work.)*
(3)   The enactments consolidated by this Act are repealed, in consequence of the consolidation, by the Consequential Provisions Act.
(4)   Except as provided in Schedule 4 to the Consequential Provisions Act, this Act shall come into force on 1st July 1992.
(5), (6)   *(Outside the scope of this work.)*

## SCHEDULES

### SCHEDULE 11
### CIRCUMSTANCES IN WHICH PERIODS OF ENTITLEMENT
### TO STATUTORY SICK PAY DO NOT ARISE
Section 153(3)

**[1.235]**
**1.** A period of entitlement does not arise in relation to a particular period of incapacity for work in any of the circumstances set out in paragraph 2 below or in such other circumstances as may be prescribed.

**[1A.**   Regulations under paragraph 1 above must be made with the concurrence of the Treasury.]

**2.** The circumstances are that—
    (a), (b) . . .
    (c)   at the relevant date the employee's normal weekly earnings are less than the lower earnings limit then in force under section 5(1)(a) above;
    [(d)   in the period of 57 days ending immediately before the relevant date the employee had at least one day on which—
        (i)   *he was entitled to incapacity benefit (or would have been so entitled had he satisfied the contribution conditions mentioned in section 30A(2)(a) above),* . . .
        (ii), (iii) . . . ]
    [(dd) in the period of 85 days ending immediately before the relevant date the employee had at least one day on which he was entitled to an employment and support allowance (or would have been so entitled had he satisfied the requirements in section 1(2) of the Welfare Reform Act 2007;]
    (f)   the employee has done no work for his employer under his contract of service;
    (g)   on the relevant date there is . . . a stoppage of work due to a trade dispute at the employee's place of employment;

(h)   the employee is, or has been, pregnant and the relevant date falls within the disqualifying period (within the meaning of section 153(12) above);

[(i)   the employee is not entitled to be in his employment on the relevant date].

**3.** In this Schedule "relevant date" means the date on which a period of entitlement would begin in accordance with section 153 above if this Schedule did not prevent it arising.

**4, 5.**   . . .

**[5A.**   (1)   Paragraph 2(d)(i) above does not apply if, at the relevant date, the employee is over pensionable age and is not entitled to incapacity benefit.

(2)   Paragraph 2(d)(i) above ceases to apply if, at any time after the relevant date, the employee is over pensionable age and is not entitled to incapacity benefit.

(3)   In this paragraph "pensionable age" has the meaning given by the rules in paragraph 1 of Schedule 4 to the Pensions Act 1995.]

**6.** For the purposes of paragraph 2(f) above, if an employee enters into a contract of service which is to take effect not more than 8 weeks after the date on which a previous contract of service entered into by him with the same employer ceased to have effect, the two contracts shall be treated as one.

**7.** Paragraph 2(g) above does not apply in the case of an employee who proves that at no time on or before the relevant date did he have a direct interest in the trade dispute in question.

**8.** Paragraph 2(h) above does not apply in relation to an employee who has been pregnant if her pregnancy terminated, before the beginning of the disqualifying period, otherwise than by confinement (as defined for the purposes of statutory maternity pay in section 171(1) above).

**[9.** Paragraph 2(i) above does not apply in prescribed circumstances.]

**NOTES**

Para 1A: inserted by the Social Security Contributions (Transfer of Functions, etc) Act 1999, s 1(1), Sch 1, para 20.

Para 2: sub-para (a) repealed by the Employment Equality (Age) Regulations 2006, SI 2006/1031, reg 49(1), Sch 8, Pt 1, paras 8, 13(1); sub-para (b) repealed by the Fixed-term Employees (Prevention of Less Favourable Treatment) Regulations 2002, SI 2002/2034, reg 11, Sch 2, Pt 1, para 1(a); sub-para (d) substituted, for the original sub-paras (d), (e), by the Social Security (Incapacity for Work) Act 1994, s 11, Sch 1, Pt I, para 43, Sch 2; sub-para (d)(i) repealed by the Welfare Reform Act 2007, s 67, Sch 8, as from a day to be appointed; word omitted from sub-para (d)(i), and sub-para (d)(iii), repealed by the Welfare Reform and Pensions Act 1999, s 88, Sch 13, Pt IV; sub-para (d)(ii) repealed by the Social Security Act 1998, ss 73, 86(2), Sch 8; sub-para (dd) inserted by the Employment and Support Allowance (Consequential Provisions) (No 2) Regulations 2008, SI 2008/1554, reg 44, as from 27 October 2008; words omitted from sub-para (g) repealed by the Jobseekers Act 1995, s 41(5), Sch 3; sub-para (i) added by the Welfare Reform Act 2012, s 63(1), (10)(a), as from a day to be appointed.

Para 4: repealed by SI 2002/2034, reg 11, Sch 2, Pt 1, para 1(b).

Para 5: repealed by the Social Security (Incapacity for Work) Act 1994, s 11, Sch 1, Pt I, para 43, Sch 2.

Para 5A: inserted by the Employment Equality (Age) (Consequential Amendments) Regulations 2007, SI 2007/825, reg 2.

Para 9: added by the Welfare Reform Act 2012, s 63(1), (10)(b), as from a day to be appointed.

Regulations: the Statutory Sick Pay (General) Regulations 1982, SI 1982/894 at **[2.40]**, and the Statutory Sick Pay (Mariners, Airmen and Persons Abroad) Regulations 1982, SI 1982/1349, have effect as if made under this Schedule by virtue of the Social Security (Consequential Provisions) Act 1992, s 2(2); the Social Security (Welfare to Work) Regulations 1998, SI 1998/2231; the Social Security, Statutory Maternity Pay and Statutory Sick Pay (Miscellaneous Amendments) Regulations 2002, SI 2002/2690.

## SCHEDULE 12
## RELATIONSHIP OF STATUTORY SICK PAY WITH BENEFITS
## AND OTHER PAYMENTS, ETC

Section 160

*The general principle*

**[1.236]**

*1.   Any day which—*

(a)   *is a day of incapacity for work in relation to any contract of service; and*

(b)   *falls within a period of entitlement (whether or not it is also a qualifying day),*

*shall not be treated for the purposes of this Act as a day of incapacity for work for the purposes of determining whether a period is  . . .   a period of incapacity for work for the purposes of incapacity benefit].*

*Contractual remuneration*

**2.**   (1)   Subject to sub-paragraphs (2) and (3) below, any entitlement to statutory sick pay shall not affect any right of an employee in relation to remuneration under any contract of service ("contractual remuneration").

(2)   Subject to sub-paragraph (3) below—

(a)   any contractual remuneration paid to an employee by an employer of his in respect of a day of incapacity for work shall go towards discharging any liability of that employer to pay statutory sick pay to that employee in respect of that day; and

(b)   any statutory sick pay paid by an employer to an employee of his in respect of a day of incapacity for work shall go towards discharging any liability of that employer to pay contractual remuneration to that employee in respect of that day.

(3)   Regulations may make provision as to payments which are, and those which are not, to be treated as contractual remuneration for the purposes of sub-paragraph (1) or (2) above.

*[Incapacity benefit*

**3.**  *(1)   This paragraph and paragraph 4 below have effect to exclude, where a period of entitlement as between an employee and an employer of his comes to an end, the provisions by virtue of which short-term incapacity benefit is not paid for the first three days.*

*(2)   If the first day immediately following the day on which the period of entitlement came to an end—*

*(a)   is the day of incapacity for work in relation to that employee, and*

*(b)   is not a day in relation to which paragraph 1 above applies by reason of any entitlement as between the employee and another employer,*

*that day shall, except in prescribed cases, be or form part of a period of incapacity for work notwithstanding section 30C(1)(b) above (by virtue of which a period of incapacity for work must be at least 4 days long).*

*(3)   Where each of the first two consecutive days, or the first three consecutive days, following the day on which the period of entitlement came to an end is a day to which paragraphs (a) and (b) of sub-paragraph (2) above apply, that sub-paragraph has effect in relation to the second day or, as the case may be, in relation to the second and third days, as it has effect in relation to the first.*

**4.**  *(1)   Where a period of entitlement as between an employee and an employer of his comes to an end, section 30A(3) above (exclusion of benefit for first 3 days of period) does not apply in relation to any day which—*

*(a)   is or forms part of a period of incapacity for work (whether by virtue of paragraph 3 above or otherwise), and*

*(b)   falls within the period of 57 days immediately following the day on which the period of entitlement came to an end.*

*(2)   Where sub-paragraph (1) above applies in relation to a day, section 30A(3) above does not apply in relation to any later day in the same period of incapacity for work.*

*Incapacity benefit for widows and widowers*

**5.**  *Paragraph 1 above does not apply for the purpose of determining whether the conditions specified in section 40(3) or (4) or 41(2) or (3) above are satisfied.]*

*Unemployability supplement*

**6.**  *Paragraph 1 above does not apply in relation to paragraph 3 of Schedule 7 to this Act and accordingly the references in paragraph 3 of that Schedule to a period of interruption of employment shall be construed as if the provisions re-enacted in this Part of this Act had not been enacted.*

**NOTES**

Para 1: repealed by the Welfare Reform Act 2007, s 67, Sch 8, as from a day to be appointed; words in square brackets inserted by the Social Security (Incapacity for Work) Act 1994, s 11, Sch 1, Pt I, para 44; words omitted repealed by the Jobseekers Act 1995, s 41(5), Sch 3.

Paras 3–5: substituted by the Social Security (Incapacity for Work) Act 1994, s 11, Sch 1, Pt I, para 44; repealed by the Welfare Reform Act 2007, s 67, Sch 8, as from a day to be appointed.

Para 6: repealed by the Welfare Reform Act 2007, s 67, Sch 8, as from a day to be appointed.

Regulations: the Statutory Sick Pay (General) Regulations 1982, SI 1982/894 at **[2.40]** have effect as if made under this Schedule by virtue of the Social Security (Consequential Provisions) Act 1992, s 2(2).

## SCHEDULE 13
## RELATIONSHIP OF STATUTORY MATERNITY PAY WITH BENEFITS AND OTHER PAYMENTS, ETC

Section 168

*The general principle*

**[1.237]**
*[1. Except as may be prescribed, a day which falls within the maternity pay period shall not be treated as a day of incapacity for work for the purposes of determining, for this Act, whether it forms part of a period of incapacity for work for the purposes of incapacity benefit.]*

*[Incapacity benefit*

**2.** (1) Regulations may provide that in prescribed circumstances a day which falls within the maternity pay period shall be treated as a day of incapacity for work for the purpose of determining entitlement to the higher rate of short-term incapacity benefit or to long-term incapacity benefit.

(2) Regulations may provide that an amount equal to a woman's statutory maternity pay for a period shall be deducted from any such benefit in respect of the same period and a woman shall be entitled to such benefit only if there is a balance after the deduction and, if there is such a balance, at a weekly rate equal to it.]*

*Contractual remuneration*

**3.** (1) Subject to sub-paragraphs (2) and (3) below, any entitlement to statutory maternity pay shall not affect any right of a woman in relation to remuneration under any contract of service ("contractual remuneration").

(2) Subject to sub-paragraph (3) below—
  (a) any contractual remuneration paid to a woman by an employer of hers in respect of a week in the maternity pay period shall go towards discharging any liability of that employer to pay statutory maternity pay to her in respect of that week; and
  (b) any statutory maternity pay paid by an employer to a woman who is an employee of his in respect of a week in the maternity pay period shall go towards discharging any liability of that employer to pay contractual remuneration to her in respect of that week.

[(2A) In sub-paragraph (2) "week" means a period of seven days beginning with the day of the week on which the maternity pay period begins.]

(3) Regulations may make provision as to payments which are, and those which are not, to be treated as contractual remuneration for the purposes of sub-paragraphs (1) and (2) above.

**NOTES**
Para 1: substituted by the Jobseekers Act 1995, s 41(4), Sch 2, para 37; repealed by the Welfare Reform Act 2007, s 67, Sch 8, as from a day to be appointed.
Para 2: substituted by the Social Security (Incapacity for Work) Act 1994, s 11(1), Sch 1, Pt I, para 45(1), (3); repealed by the Welfare Reform Act 2007, s 67, Sch 8, as from a day to be appointed.
Para 3: sub-para (2A) inserted by the Work and Families Act 2006, s 11(1), Sch 1, para 23.
Regulations: the Statutory Maternity Pay (General) Regulations 1986, SI 1986/1960 at **[2.70]** have effect as if made under this Schedule by virtue of the Social Security (Consequential Provisions) Act 1992, s 2(2); Social Security, Statutory Maternity Pay and Statutory Sick Pay (Miscellaneous Amendments) Regulations 2002, SI 2002/2690.

# OFFSHORE SAFETY ACT 1992

(1992 c 15)

*An Act to extend the application of Part I of the Health and Safety at Work etc Act 1974; to increase the penalties for certain offences under that Part; to confer powers for preserving the security of supplies of petroleum and petroleum products; and for connected purposes*

[6 March 1992]

**NOTES**
Regulatory functions: the regulatory functions conferred by, or under, this Act are subject to the Legislative and Regulatory Reform Act 2006, ss 21, 22 at **[1.495]**, **[1.496]**; see the Legislative and Regulatory Reform (Regulatory Functions) Order 2007, SI 2007/3544 (made under s 24(2) of the 2006 Act) for details.

**[1.238]**
**1 Application of Part I of 1974 Act for offshore purposes**
(1) The general purposes of Part I of the Health and Safety at Work etc Act 1974 ("the 1974 Act") shall include—
  (a) securing the safety, health and welfare of persons on offshore installations or engaged on pipe-line works;

(b)    securing the safety of such installations and preventing accidents on or near them;

(c)    securing the proper construction and safe operation of pipe-lines and preventing damage to them; and

(d)    securing the safe dismantling, removal and disposal of offshore installations and pipe-lines;

and that Part shall have effect as if the provisions mentioned in subsection (3) below were existing statutory provisions within the meaning of that Part and, in the case of the enactments there mentioned, were specified in the third column of Schedule 1 to that Act.

(2)    Without prejudice to the generality of subsection (1) of section 15 of the 1974 Act (health and safety regulations), regulations under that section may—

(a)    repeal or modify any of the provisions mentioned in subsection (3) below; and

(b)    make any provision which, but for any such repeal or modification, could be made by regulations or orders made under any enactment there mentioned.

(3)    The provisions referred to in subsections (1) and (2) above are—

(a)    the Mineral Workings (Offshore Installations) Act 1971;

[(b)    sections 10 and 25 of the Petroleum Act 1998;]

(c)    in the Petroleum Act 1987,  . . .  sections 11 to 24 (safety zones); and

(d)    the provisions of any regulations or orders made or having effect under any enactment mentioned in the foregoing paragraphs.

(4)    In this section—

"offshore installation" means any installation which is an offshore installation within the meaning of the Mineral Workings (Offshore Installations) Act 1971, or is to be taken to be an installation for the purposes of sections 11 to 23 of the Petroleum Act 1987;

["pipe-line" means, subject to subsection (4A), a controlled pipeline within the meaning of Part III of the Petroleum Act 1998; and

"pipe-line works" means works of any of the following kinds, namely—

(a)    assembling or placing a pipe-line or length of pipe-line;

(b)    inspecting, testing, maintaining, adjusting, repairing, altering or renewing a pipe-line or length of pipe-line;

(c)    changing the position of or dismantling or removing a pipe-line or length of pipe-line;

(d)    opening the bed of the sea for the purposes of works mentioned in paragraphs (a) to (c), tunnelling or boring for those purposes and other works needed for or incidental to those purposes;

(e)    works for the purpose of determining whether a place is suitable as part of the site of a proposed pipe-line and the carrying out of surveying operations for the purpose of settling the route of a proposed pipe-line.]

[(4A)    In this section "pipe-line" does not include—

(a)    any pipe-line so far as it forms part of the equipment of a vessel or vehicle; or

(b)    any apparatus and works associated with a pipe or system of pipes and prescribed for the purpose of this paragraph by regulations made by the Secretary of State.

(4B)    A statutory instrument containing regulations made by virtue of subsection (4A) shall be subject to annulment in pursuance of a resolution of either House of Parliament; and section 25 of the Petroleum Act 1998 shall apply in relation to any such regulations as it applies in relation to regulations under section 20 of that Act.]

(5)    The provisions mentioned in subsection (3) above and the definitions in subsection (4) above shall have effect as if any reference in—

(a)    section 1(4) of the Mineral Workings (Offshore Installations) Act 1971;

(b)    . . .

(c)    section  . . .  21(7) of the Petroleum Act 1987[; or

(d)    section 14(2) or 45 of the Petroleum Act 1998,]

to tidal waters and parts of the sea in or adjacent to the United Kingdom, or to the territorial sea adjacent to the United Kingdom, were a reference to tidal waters and parts of the sea in or adjacent to Great Britain, or to the territorial sea adjacent to Great Britain.

**NOTES**

Sub-s (3): para (b) substituted, and words omitted from para (c) repealed, by the Petroleum Act 1998, ss 50, 51(1), Sch 4, para 33(1), (2)(a), Sch 5, Pt I.

Sub-s (4): definitions "pipe-line" and "pipe-line works" substituted by the Petroleum Act 1998, s 50, Sch 4, para 33(1), (2)(b).

Sub-ss (4A), (4B): inserted by the Petroleum Act 1998, s 50, Sch 4, para 33(1), (2)(c).

Sub-s (5): para (b) and words omitted from para (c) repealed, and para (d) and word immediately preceding it inserted, by the Petroleum Act 1998, ss 50, 51(1), Sch 4, para 33(1), (2)(d), Sch 5, Pt I.

Regulations: the Offshore Safety (Repeals and Modifications) Regulations 1993, SI 1993/1823; the Reporting of Injuries, Diseases and Dangerous Occurrences Regulations 1995, SI 1995/3163; the Offshore Safety (Miscellaneous Amendments) Regulations 2002, SI 2002/2175; the Offshore Installations (Safety Case) Regulations 2005, SI 2005/3117.

**[1.239]**
**2    Application of Part I for other purposes**
(1)    The general purposes of Part I of the 1974 Act shall include—

(a) securing the proper construction and safe operation of pipe-lines and preventing damage to them;

(b) securing that, in the event of the accidental escape or ignition of anything in a pipe-line, immediate notice of the event is given to persons who will or may have to discharge duties or take steps in consequence of the happening of the event; and

(c) protecting the public from personal injury, fire, explosions and other dangers arising from the transmission, distribution, supply or use of gas;

and that Part shall have effect as if the provisions mentioned in subsection (3) below were existing statutory provisions within the meaning of that Part and, in the case of the enactments there mentioned, were specified in the third column of Schedule 1 to that Act.

(2) Without prejudice to the generality of subsection (1) of section 15 of the 1974 Act (health and safety regulations), regulations under that section may—

(a) repeal or modify any of the provisions mentioned in subsection (3) below; and

(b) make any provision which, but for any such repeal or modification, could be made by regulations made under any enactment mentioned in paragraph (b) of that subsection.

(3) The provisions referred to in subsections (1) and (2) above are—

(a) sections 17 to 32 and 37 (avoidance of damage to pipe-lines and notification of accidents etc) of the Pipe-lines Act 1962;

(b) . . .

(c) the provisions of any regulations made or having effect under any enactment mentioned in paragraph (b) above.

(4) In this section—

"gas" means any substance which is or (if it were in a gaseous state) would be gas within the meaning of Part I of the Gas Act 1986;

"pipe-line" has the same meaning as in the Pipe-lines Act 1962.

**NOTES**

Sub-s (3): para (b) repealed by the Utilities Act 2000, s 108, Sch 8.

**3–6** *(S 3 (Provisions consequential on ss 1, 2) outside the scope of this work; s 4 (Increased penalties under Part I) repealed by the Health and Safety (Offences) Act 2008, s 2(1), Sch 4, as from 16 January 2009, except in relation to offences committed before that date; s 5 (directions by the Secretary of State for preserving the security of petroleum and petroleum products), s 6 (corresponding provisions for Northern Ireland) both outside the scope of this work.)*

**[1.240]**
**7  Short title, repeals, commencement and extent**

(1) This Act may be cited as the Offshore Safety Act 1992.

(2) The enactments mentioned in Schedule 2 to this Act are hereby repealed to the extent specified in the third column of that Schedule.

(3) The following provisions of this Act, namely—

(a) section 2(3)(b) and (c);

(b) section 3(1)(a) and (e), (2) and (3)(b); and

(c) subsection (2) above so far as relating to the repeal in the Continental Shelf Act 1964 and the second repeal in the Gas Act 1986,

shall not come into force until such day as the Secretary of State may by order made by statutory instrument appoint, and different days may be appointed for different provisions or for different purposes.

(4) This Act, except section 6 above, does not extend to Northern Ireland.

**NOTES**

Orders: the Offshore Safety Act 1992 (Commencement No 1) Order 1993, SI 1993/2406; the Offshore Safety Act 1992 (Commencement No 2) Order 1996, SI 1996/487.

## SCHEDULES 1 AND 2

*(Sch 1 (model clauses), Sch 2 (repeals) outside the scope of this work.)*

# TRADE UNION AND LABOUR RELATIONS (CONSOLIDATION) ACT 1992

### (1992 c 52)

## ARRANGEMENT OF SECTIONS

### PART I
### TRADE UNIONS

### CHAPTER I
### INTRODUCTORY

CHAPTER IV
ELECTIONS FOR CERTAIN POSITIONS

*Duty to hold elections*

*Requirements to be satisfied with respect to elections*

*Remedy for failure to comply with requirements*

*Supplementary*

Part 1  Statutes

## CHAPTER VII
## AMALGAMATIONS AND SIMILAR MATTERS

### *Amalgamation or transfer of engagements*

### *Change of name*

### *Supplementary*

## CHAPTER VIIA
## BREACH OF RULES

## CHAPTER IX
## MISCELLANEOUS AND GENERAL PROVISIONS

### *Union modernisation*

### *Exceptions and adaptations for certain bodies*

### *Interpretation*

## PART II
## EMPLOYERS' ASSOCIATIONS

### *Introductory*

### *The list of employers' associations*

### *Status and property of employers' associations*

*An Act to consolidate the enactments relating to collective labour relations, that is to say, to trade unions, employers' associations, industrial relations and industrial action*

[16 July 1992]

**NOTES**
    This Act consolidates the legislation relating to trade unions and industrial relations. It came into force on 16 October 1992.
    The Act is printed in full except for provisions relating to Northern Ireland (ss 294, 301(2), (3), Sch 3, para 12) and repealing and amending provisions (s 300(1), (2), Schs 1, 2), and provisions subsequently repealed. The Act was substantially amended by, inter alia, the Trade Union Reform and Employment Rights Act 1993, the Employment Relations Act 1999, the Employment Act 2002, and the Employment Relations Act 2004 (details are given in notes to each section affected). As to the further power to amend, repeal or modify this Act, see the Employment Relations Act 2004, s 42(1), (4)(d) at **[1.1335]**, the Health and Safety at Work etc Act 1974, s 80 at **[1.78]**, and the Pensions Act 2004, ss 259, 260 at **[1.1345]**, **[1.1346]**.

Employment Appeal Tribunal: an appeal lies to the Employment Appeal Tribunal on any question of law arising from any decision of, or in any proceedings before, an employment tribunal under or by virtue of this Act; see the Employment Tribunals Act 1996, s 21(1)(d) at **[1.713]**.

Ballots or elections under this Act: as to the power of the Secretary of State to provide that any ballot or election authorised or required by this Act should be conducted in a specified permissible manner, see the Employment Relations Act 2004, s 54 at **[1.1336]**.

See *Harvey* M, NI, NII.

# PART I
# TRADE UNIONS

## CHAPTER I
## INTRODUCTORY

### *Meaning of "trade union"*

**[1.241]**
**1   Meaning of "trade union"**
In this Act a "trade union" means an organisation (whether temporary or permanent)—
  (a)   which consists wholly or mainly of workers of one or more descriptions and whose principal purposes include the regulation of relations between workers of that description or those descriptions and employers or employers' associations; or
  (b)   which consists wholly or mainly of—
    (i)    constituent or affiliated organisations which fulfil the conditions in paragraph (a) (or themselves consist wholly or mainly of constituent or affiliated organisations which fulfil those conditions), or
    (ii)   representatives of such constituent or affiliated organisations,
    and whose principal purposes include the regulation of relations between workers and employers or between workers and employers' associations, or the regulation of relations between its constituent or affiliated organisations.

### *The list of trade unions*

**[1.242]**
**2   The list of trade unions**
(1)   The Certification Officer shall keep a list of trade unions containing the names of—
  (a)   the organisations whose names were, immediately before the commencement of this Act, duly entered in the list of trade unions kept by him under section 8 of the Trade Union and Labour Relations Act 1974, and
  (b)   the names of the organisations entitled to have their names entered in the list in accordance with this Part.
(2)   The Certification Officer shall keep copies of the list of trade unions, as for the time being in force, available for public inspection at all reasonable hours free of charge.
(3)   A copy of the list shall be included in his annual report.
(4)   The fact that the name of an organisation is included in the list of trade unions is evidence (in Scotland, sufficient evidence) that the organisation is a trade union.
(5)   On the application of an organisation whose name is included in the list, the Certification Officer shall issue it with a certificate to that effect.
(6)   A document purporting to be such a certificate is evidence (in Scotland, sufficient evidence) that the name of the organisation is entered in the list.

**NOTES**
Trade Union and Labour Relations Act 1974, s 8: repealed by this Act.

**[1.243]**
**3   Application to have name entered on list**
(1)   An organisation of workers, whenever formed, whose name is not entered in the list of trade unions may apply to the Certification Officer to have its name entered in the list.
(2)   The application shall be made in such form and manner as the Certification Officer may require and shall be accompanied by—
  (a)   a copy of the rules of the organisation,
  (b)   a list of its officers,
  (c)   the address of its head or main office, and
  (d)   the name under which it is or is to be known,
and by the prescribed fee.
(3)   If the Certification Officer is satisfied—
  (a)   that the organisation is a trade union,
  (b)   that subsection (2) has been complied with, and
  (c)   that entry of the name in the list is not prohibited by subsection (4),

he shall enter the name of the organisation in the list of trade unions.

(4)   The Certification Officer shall not enter the name of an organisation in the list of trade unions if the name is the same as that under which another organisation—

(a)   was on 30th September 1971 registered as a trade union under the Trade Union Acts 1871 to 1964,

(b)   was at any time registered as a trade union or employers' association under the Industrial Relations Act 1971, or

(c)   is for the time being entered in the list of trade unions or in the list of employers' associations kept under Part II of this Act,

or if the name is one so nearly resembling any such name as to be likely to deceive the public.

**NOTES**

Prescribed fee: the current fee is £150 (see the Certification Officer (Amendment of Fees) Regulations 2005, SI 2005/713, reg 5).

Trade Union Acts 1871 to 1964: the Acts which were cited together under this collective title were: the Trade Union Act 1871 (repealed); the Trade Union Act Amendment Act 1876 (repealed); the Trade Disputes Act 1906 (repealed); the Trade Union Act 1913 (repealed, with a saving, by this Act); the Trade Union (Amalgamation) Act 1917 (repealed); the Trade Disputes and Trade Unions Act 1927 (repealed); the Societies (Miscellaneous Provisions) Act 1940, s 6 (repealed); and the Trade Union (Amalgamations, etc) Act 1964 (repealed by this Act).

Industrial Relations Act 1971: repealed by the Trade Union and Labour Relations Act 1974, ss 1, 25(3), Sch 5.

**[1.244]**
**4   Removal of name from the list**

(1)   If it appears to the Certification Officer, on application made to him or otherwise, that an organisation whose name is entered in the list of trade unions is not a trade union, he may remove its name from the list.

(2)   He shall not do so without giving the organisation notice of his intention and considering any representations made to him by the organisation within such period (of not less than 28 days beginning with the date of the notice) as may be specified in the notice.

(3)   The Certification Officer shall remove the name of an organisation from the list of trade unions if—

(a)   he is requested by the organisation to do so, or

(b)   he is satisfied that the organisation has ceased to exist.

*Certification as independent trade union*

**[1.245]**
**5   Meaning of "independent trade union"**

In this Act an "independent trade union" means a trade union which—

(a)   is not under the domination or control of an employer or group of employers or of one or more employers' associations, and

(b)   is not liable to interference by an employer or any such group or association (arising out of the provision of financial or material support or by any other means whatsoever) tending towards such control;

and references to "independence", in relation to a trade union, shall be construed accordingly.

**[1.246]**
**6   Application for certificate of independence**

(1)   A trade union whose name is entered on the list of trade unions may apply to the Certification Officer for a certificate that it is independent.

The application shall be made in such form and manner as the Certification Officer may require and shall be accompanied by the prescribed fee.

(2)   The Certification Officer shall maintain a record showing details of all applications made to him under this section and shall keep it available for public inspection (free of charge) at all reasonable hours.

(3)   If an application is made by a trade union whose name is not entered on the list of trade unions, the Certification Officer shall refuse a certificate of independence and shall enter that refusal on the record.

(4)   In any other case, he shall not come to a decision on the application before the end of the period of one month after it has been entered on the record; and before coming to his decision he shall make such enquiries as he thinks fit and shall take into account any relevant information submitted to him by any person.

(5)   He shall then decide whether the applicant trade union is independent and shall enter his decision and the date of his decision on the record.

(6)   If he decides that the trade union is independent he shall issue a certificate accordingly; and if he decides that it is not, he shall give reasons for his decision.

**NOTES**

Prescribed fee: the current fee is £4,066 (see the Certification Officer (Amendment of Fees) Regulations 2005, SI 2005/713, reg 7).

**[1.247]**

## 7 Withdrawal or cancellation of certificate

(1)   The Certification Officer may withdraw a trade union's certificate of independence if he is of the opinion that the union is no longer independent.

(2)   Where he proposes to do so he shall notify the trade union and enter notice of the proposal in the record.

(3)   He shall not come to a decision on the proposal before the end of the period of one month after notice of it was entered on the record; and before coming to his decision he shall make such enquiries as he thinks fit and shall take into account any relevant information submitted to him by any person.

(4)   He shall then decide whether the trade union is independent and shall enter his decision and the date of his decision on the record.

(5)   He shall confirm or withdraw the certificate accordingly; and if he decides to withdraw it, he shall give reasons for his decision.

(6)   Where the name of an organisation is removed from the list of trade unions, the Certification Officer shall cancel any certificate of independence in force in respect of that organisation by entering on the record the fact that the organisation's name has been removed from that list and that the certificate is accordingly cancelled.

**[1.248]**

## 8 Conclusive effect of Certification Officer's decision

(1)   A certificate of independence which is in force is conclusive evidence for all purposes that a trade union is independent; and a refusal, withdrawal or cancellation of a certificate of independence, entered on the record, is conclusive evidence for all purposes that a trade union is not independent.

(2)   A document purporting to be a certificate of independence and to be signed by the Certification Officer, or by a person authorised to act on his behalf, shall be taken to be such a certificate unless the contrary is proved.

(3)   A document purporting to be a certified copy of an entry on the record and to be signed by the Certification Officer, or by a person authorised to act on his behalf, shall be taken to be a true copy of such an entry unless the contrary is proved.

(4)   If in any proceedings before a court, the Employment Appeal Tribunal, the Central Arbitration Committee, ACAS or an [employment tribunal] a question arises whether a trade union is independent and there is no certificate of independence in force and no refusal, withdrawal or cancellation of a certificate recorded in relation to that trade union—

  (a)   that question shall not be decided in those proceedings, and

  (b)   the proceedings shall instead be stayed or sisted until a certificate of independence has been issued or refused by the Certification Officer.

(5)   The body before whom the proceedings are stayed or sisted may refer the question of the independence of the trade union to the Certificate Officer who shall proceed in accordance with section 6 as on an application by that trade union.

NOTES

Sub-s (4): words in square brackets substituted by the Employment Rights (Dispute Resolution) Act 1998, s 1(2)(a).

*Supplementary*

**[1.249]**

## 9 Appeal against decision of Certification Officer

(1)   An organisation aggrieved by the refusal of the Certification Officer to enter its name in the list of trade unions, or by a decision of his to remove its name from the list, may appeal to the Employment Appeal Tribunal [on any appealable question].

(2)   A trade union aggrieved by the refusal of the Certification Officer to issue it with a certificate of independence, or by a decision of his to withdraw its certificate, may appeal to the Employment Appeal Tribunal [on any appealable question].

(3)   . . .

(4)   [For the purposes of this section, an appealable question is any question of law] arising in the proceedings before, or arising from the decision of, the Certification Officer.

NOTES

Sub-ss (1), (2): words in square brackets added by the Employment Relations Act 2004, s 51(1)(a).

Sub-s (3): repealed by the Employment Relations Act 2004, ss 51(1)(b), 57(2), Sch 2.

Sub-s (4): words in square brackets substituted by the Employment Relations Act 2004, s 51(1)(c).

CHAPTER II
STATUS AND PROPERTY OF TRADE UNIONS

*General*

**[1.250]**
**10   Quasi-corporate status of trade unions**
(1)   A trade union is not a body corporate but—
  (a)   it is capable of making contracts;
  (b)   it is capable of suing and being sued in its own name, whether in proceedings relating to property or founded on contract or tort or any other cause of action; and
  (c)   proceedings for an offence alleged to have been committed by it or on its behalf may be brought against it in its own name.
(2)   A trade union shall not be treated as if it were a body corporate except to the extent authorised by the provisions of this Part.
(3)   A trade union shall not be registered—
  (a)   as a company under [the Companies Act 2006], or
  (b)   under the Friendly Societies Act 1974 or the Industrial and Provident Societies Act 1965;
and any such registration of a trade union (whenever effected) is void.

**NOTES**
  Sub-s (3): words in square brackets in para (a) substituted by the Companies Act 2006 (Consequential Amendments, Transitional Provisions and Savings) Order 2009, SI 2009/1941, art 2(1), Sch 1, para 134(1), (2), as from 1 October 2009.
  Industrial and Provident Societies Act 1965: see the Co-operative and Community Benefit Societies and Credit Unions Act 2010 which renames this Act as the Co-operative and Community Benefit Societies and Credit Unions Act 1965 (as from a day to be appointed).

**[1.251]**
**11   Exclusion of common law rules as to restraint of trade**
(1)   The purposes of a trade union are not, by reason only that they are in restraint of trade, unlawful so as—
  (a)   to make any member of the trade union liable to criminal proceedings for conspiracy or otherwise, or
  (b)   to make any agreement or trust void or voidable.
(2)   No rule of a trade union is unlawful or unenforceable by reason only that it is in restraint of trade.

*Property of trade union*

**[1.252]**
**12   Property to be vested in trustees**
(1)   All property belonging to a trade union shall be vested in trustees in trust for it.
(2)   A judgment, order or award made in proceedings of any description brought against a trade union is enforceable, by way of execution, diligence, punishment for contempt or otherwise, against any property held in trust for it to the same extent and in the same manner as if it were a body corporate.
(3)   Subsection (2) has effect subject to section 23 (restriction on enforcement of awards against certain property).

**[1.253]**
**13   Vesting of property in new trustees**
(1)   The provisions of this section apply in relation to the appointment or discharge of trustees in whom any property is vested in trust for a trade union whose name is entered in the list of trade unions.
(2)   In the following sections as they apply to such trustees references to a deed shall be construed as references to an instrument in writing—
  (a)   section 39 of the Trustee Act 1925 and section 38 of the Trustee Act (Northern Ireland) 1958 (retirement of trustee without a new appointment), and
  (b)   section 40 of the Trustee Act 1925 and section 39 of the Trustee Act (Northern Ireland) 1958 (vesting of trust property in new or continuing trustees).
(3)   Where such a trustee is appointed or discharged by a resolution taken by or on behalf of the union, the written record of the resolution shall be treated for the purposes of those sections as an instrument in writing appointing or discharging the trustee.
(4)   In section 40 of the Trustee Act 1925 and section 39 of the Trustee Act (Northern Ireland) 1958 as they apply to such trustees, paragraphs (a) and (c) of subsection (4) (which exclude certain property from the section) shall be omitted.

**[1.254]**
**14   Transfer of securities held in trust for trade union**
(1)   In this section—

"instrument of appointment" means an instrument in writing appointing a new trustee of a trade union whose name is entered in the list of trade unions, and

"instrument of discharge" means an instrument in writing discharging a trustee of such a trade union;

and for the purposes of this section where a trustee is appointed or discharged by a resolution taken by or on behalf of such a trade union, the written record of the resolution shall be treated as an instrument in writing appointing or discharging the trustee.

(2)   Where by any enactment or instrument the transfer of securities of any description is required to be effected or recorded by means of entries in a register, then if—

(a)   there is produced to the person authorised or required to keep the register a copy of an instrument of appointment or discharge which contains or has attached to it a list identifying the securities of that description held in trust for the union at the date of the appointment or discharge, and

(b)   it appears to that person that any of the securities so identified are included in the register kept by him,

he shall make such entries as may be necessary to give effect to the instrument of appointment or discharge.

This subsection has effect notwithstanding anything in any enactment or instrument regulating the keeping of the register.

(3)   A document which purports to be a copy of an instrument of appointment or discharge containing or having attached to it such a list, and to be certified in accordance with the following subsection to be a copy of such an instrument, shall be taken to be a copy of such an instrument unless the contrary is proved.

(4)   The certificate shall be given by the president and general secretary of the union and, in the case of an instrument to which a list of securities is attached, shall appear both on the instrument and on the list.

(5)   Nothing done for the purposes of or in pursuance of this section shall be taken to affect any person with notice of any trust or to impose on any person a duty to inquire into any matter.

(6)   In relation to a Scottish trust, references in this section to the appointment and discharge of a trustee shall be construed as including references to, respectively, the assumption and resignation of a trustee; and references to an instrument appointing or discharging a trustee shall be construed accordingly.

**[1.255]**
## 15   Prohibition on use of funds to indemnify unlawful conduct

(1)   It is unlawful for property of a trade union to be applied in or towards—

(a)   the payment for an individual of a penalty which has been or may be imposed on him for an offence or for contempt of court,

(b)   the securing of any such payment, or

(c)   the provision of anything for indemnifying an individual in respect of such a penalty.

(2)   Where any property of a trade union is so applied for the benefit of an individual on whom a penalty has been or may be imposed, then—

(a)   in the case of a payment, an amount equal to the payment is recoverable by the union from him, and

(b)   in any other case, he is liable to account to the union for the value of the property applied.

(3)   If a trade union fails to bring or continue proceedings which it is entitled to bring by virtue of subsection (2), a member of the union who claims that the failure is unreasonable may apply to the court on that ground for an order authorising him to bring or continue the proceedings on the union's behalf and at the union's expense.

(4)   In this section "penalty", in relation to an offence, includes an order to pay compensation and an order for the forfeiture of any property; and references to the imposition of a penalty for an offence shall be construed accordingly.

(5)   The Secretary of State may by order designate offences in relation to which the provisions of this section do not apply.

Any such order shall be made by statutory instrument which shall be subject to annulment in pursuance of a resolution of either House of Parliament.

(6)   This section does not affect—

(a)   any other enactment, any rule of law or any provision of the rules of a trade union which makes it unlawful for the property of a trade union to be applied in a particular way; or

(b)   any other remedy available to a trade union, the trustees of its property or any of its members in respect of an unlawful application of the union's property.

(7)   In this section "member", in relation to a trade union consisting wholly or partly of, or of representatives of, constituent or affiliated organisations, includes a member of any of the constituent or affiliated organisations.

**NOTES**

Orders: as of 6 April 2013 no Orders had been made under this section.

Part 1 Statutes

**[1.256]**
## 16 Remedy against trustees for unlawful use of union property
(1) A member of a trade union who claims that the trustees of the union's property—
(a) have so carried out their functions, or are proposing so to carry out their functions, as to cause or permit an unlawful application of the union's property, or
(b) have complied, or are proposing to comply, with an unlawful direction which has been or may be given, or purportedly given, to them under the rules of the union,
may apply to the court for an order under this section.
(2) In a case relating to property which has already been unlawfully applied, or to an unlawful direction that has already been complied with, an application under this section may be made only by a person who was a member of the union at the time when the property was applied or, as the case may be, the direction complied with.
(3) Where the court is satisfied that the claim is well-founded, it shall make such order as it considers appropriate.
The court may in particular—
(a) require the trustees (if necessary, on behalf of the union) to take all such steps as may be specified in the order for protecting or recovering the property of the union;
(b) appoint a receiver of, or in Scotland a judicial factor on, the property of the union;
(c) remove one or more of the trustees.
(4) Where the court makes an order under this section in a case in which—
(a) property of the union has been applied in contravention of an order of any court, or in compliance with a direction given in contravention of such an order, or
(b) the trustees were proposing to apply property in contravention of such an order or to comply with any such direction,
the court shall by its order remove all the trustees except any trustee who satisfies the court that there is a good reason for allowing him to remain a trustee.
(5) Without prejudice to any other power of the court, the court may on an application for an order under this section grant such interlocutory relief (in Scotland, such interim order) as it considers appropriate.
(6) This section does not affect any other remedy available in respect of a breach of trust by the trustees of a trade union's property.
(7) In this section "member", in relation to a trade union consisting wholly or partly of, or of representatives of, constituent or affiliated organisations, includes a member of any of the constituent or affiliated organisations.

**[1.257]**
## 17 Nomination by members of trade unions
(1) The Secretary of State may make provision by regulations for enabling members of trade unions who are not under 16 years of age to nominate a person or persons to become entitled, on the death of the person making the nomination, to the whole or part of any money payable on his death out of the funds of the trade union.
(2) The regulations may include provision as to the manner in which nominations may be made and as to the manner in which nominations may be varied or revoked.
(3) The regulations may provide that, subject to such exceptions as may be prescribed, no nomination made by a member of a trade union shall be valid if at the date of the nomination the person nominated is an officer or employee of the trade union or is otherwise connected with the trade union in such manner as may be prescribed by the regulations.
(4) The regulations may include such incidental, transitional or supplementary provisions as the Secretary of State may consider appropriate.
(5) They may, in particular, include provision for securing, to such extent and subject to such conditions as may be prescribed in the regulations, that nominations made under the Trade Union Act 1871 Amendment Act 1876 have effect as if made under the regulations and may be varied or revoked accordingly.
(6) Regulations under this section shall be made by statutory instrument which shall be subject to annulment in pursuance of a resolution of either House of Parliament.

**NOTES**
Trade Union Act 1871 Amendment Act 1876: repealed by the Industrial Relations Act 1971.
Regulations: as of 6 April 2013 no Regulations had been made under this section. However, the Trade Union (Nominations) Regulations 1977, SI 1977/789, have effect as if so made by virtue of s 300(3) of, and Sch 3, para 1(2) to, this Act, and the Interpretation Act 1978, s 17(2)(b).

**[1.258]**
## 18 Payments out of union funds on death of member
(1) The Secretary of State may make provision by regulations for enabling money payable out of the funds of a trade union on the death of a member, to an amount not exceeding £5,000, to be paid or distributed on his death without letters of administration, probate of any will or confirmation.

(2)   The regulations may include such incidental, transitional and supplementary provisions as the Secretary of State may consider appropriate.

(3)   Regulations under this section shall be made by statutory instrument which shall be subject to annulment in pursuance of a resolution of either House of Parliament.

(4)   The Treasury may by order under section 6(1) of the Administration of Estates (Small Payments) Act 1965 direct that subsection (1) above shall have effect with the substitution for the reference to £5,000 of a reference to such higher amount as may be specified in the order.

**NOTES**

Regulations: as of 6 April 2013 no Regulations had been made under this section. However, the Trade Union (Nominations) Regulations 1977, SI 1977/789, have effect as if so made by virtue of s 300(3) of, and Sch 3, para 1(2) to, this Act, and the Interpretation Act 1978, s 17(2)(b).

**[1.259]**
**19   Application of certain provisions relating to industrial assurance or friendly societies**
[(1)   Section 99 of the Friendly Societies Act 1992 (insurance of lives of children under 10) applies to a trade union as to [a friendly society].]

(2)   . . .

(3)   Section 52 of the Friendly Societies Act 1974 (charitable subscriptions and contributions to other registered societies) extends to a trade union, or branch of a trade union, as regards contributing to the funds and taking part in the government of a medical society, that is, a society for the purpose of relief in sickness by providing medical attendance and medicine.

A trade union, or branch of a trade union, shall not withdraw from contributing to the funds of such a society except on three months' notice to the society and on payment of all contributions accrued or accruing due to the date of the expiry of the notice.

[(4)   . . . ]

**NOTES**

Sub-s (1): substituted by the Friendly Societies Act 1992 (Transitional and Consequential Provisions) Regulations 1993, SI 1993/3084, reg 7; words in square brackets substituted by the Financial Services and Markets Act 2000 (Consequential Amendments and Repeals) Order 2001, SI 2001/3649, art 332.

Sub-s (2): repealed by SI 1993/3084, reg 8.

Sub-s (4): added by the Financial Services and Markets Act 2000 (Consequential Amendments and Savings) (Industrial Assurance) Order 2001, SI 2001/3647, art 5, Sch 3, Pt I, para 14; repealed by the Employment Relations Act 2004, s 57, Sch 1, para 3, Sch 2.

*Liability of trade unions in proceedings in tort*

**[1.260]**
**20   Liability of trade union in certain proceedings in tort**
(1)   Where proceedings in tort are brought against a trade union—

   (a)   on the ground that an act—

     (i)   induces another person to break a contract or interferes or induces another person to interfere with its performance, or

     (ii)   consists in threatening that a contract (whether one to which the union is a party or not) will be broken or its performance interfered with, or that the union will induce another person to break a contract or interfere with its performance, or

   (b)   in respect of an agreement or combination by two or more persons to do or to procure the doing of an act which, if it were done without any such agreement or combination, would be actionable in tort on such a ground,

then, for the purpose of determining in those proceedings whether the union is liable in respect of the act in question, that act shall be taken to have been done by the union if, but only if, it is to be taken to have been authorised or endorsed by the trade union in accordance with the following provisions.

(2)   An act shall be taken to have been authorised or endorsed by a trade union if it was done, or was authorised or endorsed—

   (a)   by any person empowered by the rules to do, authorise or endorse acts of the kind in question, or

   (b)   by the principal executive committee or the president or general secretary, or

   (c)   by any other committee of the union or any other official of the union (whether employed by it or not).

(3)   For the purposes of paragraph (c) of subsection (2)—

   (a)   any group of persons constituted in accordance with the rules of the union is a committee of the union; and

   (b)   an act shall be taken to have been done, authorised or endorsed by an official if it was done, authorised or endorsed by, or by any member of, any group of persons of which he was at the material time a member, the purposes of which included organising or co-ordinating industrial action.

(4)   The provisions of paragraphs (b) and (c) of subsection (2) apply notwithstanding anything in the rules of the union, or in any contract or rule of law, but subject to the provisions of section 21 (repudiation by union of certain acts).

(5)   Where for the purposes of any proceedings an act is by virtue of this section taken to have been done by a trade union, nothing in this section shall affect the liability of any other person, in those or any other proceedings, in respect of that act.

(6)   In proceedings arising out of an act which is by virtue of this section taken to have been done by a trade union, the power of the court to grant an injunction or interdict includes power to require the union to take such steps as the court considers appropriate for ensuring—

(a)   that there is no, or no further, inducement of persons to take part or to continue to take part in industrial action, and

(b)   that no person engages in any conduct after the granting of the injunction or interdict by virtue of having been induced before it was granted to take part or to continue to take part in industrial action.

The provisions of subsections (2) to (4) above apply in relation to proceedings for failure to comply with any such injunction or interdict as they apply in relation to the original proceedings.

(7)   In this section "rules", in relation to a trade union, means the written rules of the union and any other written provision forming part of the contract between a member and the other members.

**[1.261]**
## 21   Repudiation by union of certain acts

(1)   An act shall not be taken to have been authorised or endorsed by a trade union by virtue only of paragraph (c) of section 20(2) if it was repudiated by the executive, president or general secretary as soon as reasonably practicable after coming to the knowledge of any of them.

(2)   Where an act is repudiated—

(a)   written notice of the repudiation must be given to the committee or official in question, without delay, and

(b)   the union must do its best to give individual written notice of the fact and date of repudiation, without delay—

(i)    to every member of the union who the union has reason to believe is taking part, or might otherwise take part, in industrial action as a result of the act, and

(ii)   to the employer of every such member.

(3)   The notice given to members in accordance with paragraph (b)(i) of subsection (2) must contain the following statement—

"Your union has repudiated the call (or calls) for industrial action to which this notice relates and will give no support to unofficial industrial action taken in response to it (or them). If you are dismissed while taking unofficial industrial action, you will have no right to complain of unfair dismissal."

(4)   If subsection (2) or (3) is not complied with, the repudiation shall be treated as ineffective.

(5)   An act shall not be treated as repudiated if at any time after the union concerned purported to repudiate it the executive, president or general secretary has behaved in a manner which is inconsistent with the purported repudiation.

(6)   The executive, president or general secretary shall be treated as so behaving if, on a request made to any of them within [three months] of the purported repudiation by a person who—

(a)   is a party to a commercial contract whose performance has been or may be interfered with as a result of the act in question, and

(b)   has not been given written notice by the union of the repudiation,

it is not forthwith confirmed in writing that the act has been repudiated.

(7)   In this section "commercial contract" means any contract other than—

(a)   a contract of employment, or

(b)   any other contract under which a person agrees personally to do work or perform services for another.

**NOTES**

Sub-s (6): words in square brackets substituted by the Trade Union Reform and Employment Rights Act 1993, s 49(1), Sch 7, para 17.

**[1.262]**
## 22   Limit on damages awarded against trade unions in actions in tort

(1)   This section applies to any proceedings in tort brought against a trade union, except—

(a)   proceedings for personal injury as a result of negligence, nuisance or breach of duty;

(b)   proceedings for breach of duty in connection with the ownership, occupation, possession, control or use of property;

(c)   proceedings brought by virtue of Part I of the Consumer Protection Act 1987 (product liability).

(2)   In any proceedings in tort to which this section applies the amount which may be awarded against the union by way of damages shall not exceed the following limit—

| Number of members of union | Maximum award of damages |
|---|---|
| Less than 5,000 | £10,000 |
| 5,000 or more but less than 25,000 | £50,000 |
| 25,000 or more but less than 100,000 | £125,000 |
| 100,000 or more | £250,000 |

(3)   The Secretary of State may by order amend subsection (2) so as to vary any of the sums specified; and the order may make such transitional provision as the Secretary of State considers appropriate.

(4)   Any such order shall be made by statutory instrument which shall be subject to annulment in pursuance of a resolution of either House of Parliament.

(5)   In this section—

"breach of duty" means breach of a duty imposed by any rule of law or by or under any enactment;

"personal injury" includes any disease and any impairment of a person's physical or mental condition; and

"property" means any property, whether real or personal (or in Scotland, heritable or moveable).

**NOTES**

Orders: as of 6 April 2013 no Orders had been made under this section.

*Restriction on enforcement against certain property*

**[1.263]**

**23   Restriction on enforcement of awards against certain property**

(1)   Where in any proceedings an amount is awarded by way of damages, costs or expenses—

(a)   against a trade union,

(b)   against trustees in whom property is vested in trust for a trade union, in their capacity as such (and otherwise than in respect of a breach of trust on their part), or

(c)   against members or officials of a trade union on behalf of themselves and all of the members of the union,

no part of that amount is recoverable by enforcement against any protected property.

(2)   The following is protected property—

(a)   property belonging to the trustees otherwise than in their capacity as such;

(b)   property belonging to any member of the union otherwise than jointly or in common with the other members;

(c)   property belonging to an official of the union who is neither a member nor a trustee;

(d)   property comprised in the union's political fund where that fund—

(i)   is subject to rules of the union which prevent property which is or has been comprised in the fund from being used for financing strikes or other industrial action, and

(ii)   was so subject at the time when the act in respect of which the proceedings are brought was done;

(e)   property comprised in a separate fund maintained in accordance with the rules of the union for the purpose only of providing provident benefits.

(3)   For this purpose "provident benefits" includes—

(a)   any payment expressly authorised by the rules of the union which is made—

(i)   to a member during sickness or incapacity from personal injury or while out of work, or

(ii)   to an aged member by way of superannuation, or

(iii)   to a member who has met with an accident or has lost his tools by fire or theft;

(b)   a payment in discharge or aid of funeral expenses on the death of a member or [the spouse or civil partner] of a member or as provision for the children of a deceased member.

**NOTES**

Sub-s (3): words in square brackets in para (b) substituted by the Civil Partnership Act 2004, s 261(1), Sch 27, para 144.

## CHAPTER III
## TRADE UNION ADMINISTRATION

*Register of members' names and addresses*

**[1.264]**

**24   Duty to maintain register of members' names and addresses**

(1)   A trade union shall compile and maintain a register of the names and addresses of its members, and shall secure, so far as is reasonably practicable, that the entries in the register are accurate and are kept up-to-date.

(2)   The register may be kept by means of a computer.

(3)　A trade union shall—

　(a)　allow any member, upon reasonable notice, to ascertain from the register, free of charge and at any reasonable time, whether there is an entry on it relating to him; and

　(b)　if requested to do so by any member, supply him as soon as reasonably practicable, either free of charge or on payment of a reasonable fee, with a copy of any entry on the register relating to him.

(4)　. . .

(5)　For the purposes of this section a member's address means either his home address or another address which he has requested the union in writing to treat as his postal address.

(6)　The remedy for failure to comply with the requirements of this section is by way of application under section 25 (to the Certification Officer) or section 26 (to the court).

. . .

**[1.265]**
**[24A　Securing confidentiality of register during ballots**

(1)　This section applies in relation to a ballot of the members of a trade union on—

　(a)　an election under Chapter IV for a position to which that Chapter applies,

　(b)　a political resolution under Chapter VI, and

　(c)　a resolution to approve an instrument of amalgamation or transfer under Chapter VII.

(2)　Where this section applies in relation to a ballot the trade union shall impose the duty of confidentiality in relation to the register of members' names and addresses on the scrutineer appointed by the union for the purposes of the ballot and on any person appointed by the union as the independent person for the purposes of the ballot.

(3)　The duty of confidentiality in relation to the register of members' names and addresses is, when imposed on a scrutineer or on an independent person, a duty—

　(a)　not to disclose any name or address in the register except in permitted circumstances; and

　(b)　to take all reasonable steps to secure that there is no disclosure of any such name or address by any other person except in permitted circumstances;

and any reference in this Act to "the duty of confidentiality" is a reference to the duty prescribed in this subsection.

(4)　The circumstances in which disclosure of a member's name and address is permitted are—

　(a)　where the member consents;

　(b)　where it is requested by the Certification Officer for the purposes of the discharge of any of his functions or it is required for the purposes of the discharge of any of the functions of an inspector appointed by him;

　(c)　where it is required for the purposes of the discharge of any of the functions of the scrutineer or independent person, as the case may be, under the terms of his appointment;

　(d)　where it is required for the purposes of the investigation of crime or of criminal proceedings.

(5)　Any provision of this Part which incorporates the duty of confidentiality as respects the register into the appointment of a scrutineer or an independent person has the effect of imposing that duty on the scrutineer or independent person as a duty owed by him to the trade union.

(6)　The remedy for failure to comply with the requirements of this section is by way of application under section 25 (to the Certification Officer) or section 26 (to the court).

. . .

**[1.266]**
**25　Remedy for failure: application to Certification Officer**

(1)　A member of a trade union who claims that the union has failed to comply with any of the requirements of section 24 [or 24A] (duties with respect to register of members' names and addresses) may apply to the Certification Officer for a declaration to that effect.

(2)　On an application being made to him, the Certification Officer shall—

　(a)　make such enquiries as he thinks fit, and

　(b)　. . . give the applicant and the trade union an opportunity to be heard,

and may make or refuse the declaration asked for.

(3)　If he makes a declaration he shall specify in it the provisions with which the trade union has failed to comply.

(4)   Where he makes a declaration and is satisfied that steps have been taken by the union with a view to remedying the declared failure, or securing that a failure of the same or any similar kind does not occur in future, or that the union has agreed to take such steps, he shall specify those steps in the declaration.

(5)   Whether he makes or refuses a declaration, he shall give reasons for his decision in writing; and the reasons may be accompanied by written observations on any matter arising from, or connected with, the proceedings.

[(5A)   Where the Certification Officer makes a declaration he shall also, unless he considers that to do so would be inappropriate, make an enforcement order, that is, an order imposing on the union one or both of the following requirements—

    (a)   to take such steps to remedy the declared failure, within such period, as may be specified in the order;

    (b)   to abstain from such acts as may be so specified with a view to securing that a failure of the same or a similar kind does not occur in future.

(5B)   Where an enforcement order has been made, any person who is a member of the union and was a member at the time it was made is entitled to enforce obedience to the order as if he had made the application on which the order was made.]

(6)   In exercising his functions under this section the Certification Officer shall ensure that, so far as is reasonably practicable, an application made to him is determined within six months of being made.

(7)   Where he requests a person to furnish information to him in connection with enquiries made by him under this section, he shall specify the date by which that information is to be furnished and, unless he considers that it would be inappropriate to do so, shall proceed with his determination of the application notwithstanding that the information has not been furnished to him by the specified date.

[(8)   The Certification Officer shall not entertain an application for a declaration as respects an alleged failure to comply with the requirements of section 24A in relation to a ballot to which that section applies unless the application is made before the end of the period of one year beginning with the last day on which votes could be cast in the ballot.]

[(9)   A declaration made by the Certification Officer under this section may be relied on as if it were a declaration made by the court.

(10)   An enforcement order made by the Certification Officer under this section may be enforced in the same way as an order of the court.

(11)   The following paragraphs have effect if a person applies under section 26 in relation to an alleged failure—

    (a)   that person may not apply under this section in relation to that failure;

    (b)   on an application by a different person under this section in relation to that failure, the Certification Officer shall have due regard to any declaration, order, observations or reasons made or given by the court regarding that failure and brought to the Certification Officer's notice.]

**NOTES**

Sub-s (1): words in square brackets inserted by the Trade Union Reform and Employment Rights Act 1993, s 49(2), Sch 8, para 40(a).

Sub-s (2): words omitted repealed by the Employment Relations Act 1999, ss 29, 44, Sch 6, paras 1, 4(1), (2), Sch 9(7).

Sub-ss (5A), (5B), (9)–(11): inserted and added respectively by the Employment Relations Act 1999, s 29, Sch 6, paras 1, 4(1), (3), (4).

Sub-s (8): added by the Trade Union Reform and Employment Rights Act 1993, s 49(2), Sch 8, para 40(b).

**[1.267]**
**26   Remedy for failure: application to court**

(1)   A member of a trade union who claims that the union has failed to comply with any of the requirements of section 24 [or 24A] (duties with respect to register of members' names and addresses) may apply to the court for a declaration to that effect.

(2)   . . .

(3)   If the court makes a declaration it shall specify in it the provisions with which the trade union has failed to comply.

(4)   Where the court makes a declaration it shall also, unless it considers that to do so would be inappropriate, make an enforcement order, that is, an order imposing on the union one or both of the following requirements—

    (a)   to take such steps to remedy the declared failure, within such period, as may be specified in the order;

    (b)   to abstain from such acts as may be so specified with a view to securing that a failure of the same or a similar kind does not occur in future.

(5)   Where an enforcement order has been made, any person who is a member of the union and was a member at the time it was made, is entitled to enforce obedience to the order as if he had made the application on which the order was made.

(6)   Without prejudice to any other power of the court, the court may on an application under this section grant such interlocutory relief (in Scotland, such interim order) as it considers appropriate.

[(7)   The court shall not entertain an application for a declaration as respects an alleged failure to comply with the requirements of section 24A in relation to a ballot to which that section applies unless the application is made before the end of the period of one year beginning with the last day on which votes could be cast in the ballot.]

[(8)   The following paragraphs have effect if a person applies under section 25 in relation to an alleged failure—

  (a)   that person may not apply under this section in relation to that failure;

  (b)   on an application by a different person under this section in relation to that failure, the court shall have due regard to any declaration, order, observations or reasons made or given by the Certification Officer regarding that failure and brought to the court's notice.]

**NOTES**

  Sub-s (1): words in square brackets inserted by the Trade Union Reform and Employment Rights Act 1993, s 49(2), Sch 8, para 41(a).

  Sub-s (2): repealed by the Employment Relations Act 1999, ss 29, 44, Sch 6, paras 1, 5(1), (2), Sch 9(7).

  Sub-s (7): added by the Trade Union Reform and Employment Rights Act 1993, s 49(2), Sch 8, para 41(b).

  Sub-s (8): added by the Employment Relations Act 1999, s 29, Sch 6, paras 1, 5(1), (3).

*Duty to supply copy of rules*

**[1.268]**
**27   Duty to supply copy of rules**
A trade union shall at the request of any person supply him with a copy of its rules either free of charge or on payment of a reasonable charge.

*Accounting records*

**[1.269]**
**28   Duty to keep accounting records**
(1)   A trade union shall—

  (a)   cause to be kept proper accounting records with respect to its transactions and its assets and liabilities, and

  (b)   establish and maintain a satisfactory system of control of its accounting records, its cash holdings and all its receipts and remittances.

(2)   Proper accounting records shall not be taken to be kept with respect to the matters mentioned in subsection (1)(a) unless there are kept such records as are necessary to give a true and fair view of the state of the affairs of the trade union and to explain its transactions.

**[1.270]**
**29   Duty to keep records available for inspection**
(1)   A trade union shall keep available for inspection from their creation until the end of the period of six years beginning with the 1st January following the end of the period to which they relate such of the records of the union, or of any branch or section of the union, as are, or purport to be, records required to be kept by the union under section 28.

  This does not apply to records relating to periods before 1st January 1988.

(2)   In section 30 (right of member to access to accounting records)—

  (a)   references to a union's accounting records are to any such records as are mentioned in subsection (1) above, and

  (b)   references to records available for inspection are to records which the union is required by that subsection to keep available for inspection.

(3)   The expiry of the period mentioned in subsection (1) above does not affect the duty of a trade union to comply with a request for access made under section 30 before the end of that period.

**[1.271]**
**30   Right of access to accounting records**
(1)   A member of a trade union has a right to request access to any accounting records of the union which are available for inspection and relate to periods including a time when he was a member of the union.

  In the case of records relating to a branch or section of the union, it is immaterial whether he was a member of that branch or section.

(2)   Where such access is requested the union shall—

  (a)   make arrangements with the member for him to be allowed to inspect the records requested before the end of the period of twenty-eight days beginning with the day the request was made,

  (b)   allow him and any accountant accompanying him for the purpose to inspect the records at the time and place arranged, and

  (c)   secure that at the time of the inspection he is allowed to take, or is supplied with, any copies of, or of extracts from, records inspected by him which he requires.

(3) The inspection shall be at a reasonable hour and at the place where the records are normally kept, unless the parties to the arrangements agree otherwise.

(4) An "accountant" means a person who is eligible for appointment as a [statutory auditor under Part 42 of the Companies Act 2006].

(5) The union need not allow the member to be accompanied by an accountant if the accountant fails to enter into such agreement as the union may reasonably require for protecting the confidentiality of the records.

(6) Where a member who makes a request for access to a union's accounting records is informed by the union, before any arrangements are made in pursuance of the request—

    (a)   of the union's intention to charge for allowing him to inspect the records to which the request relates, for allowing him to take copies of, or extracts from, those records or for supplying any such copies, and

    (b)   of the principles in accordance with which its charges will be determined,

then, where the union complies with the request, he is liable to pay the union on demand such amount, not exceeding the reasonable administrative expenses incurred by the union in complying with the request, as is determined in accordance with those principles.

(7) In this section "member", in relation to a trade union consisting wholly or partly of, or of representatives of, constituent or affiliated organisations, includes a member of any of the constituent or affiliated organisations.

**NOTES**

Sub-s (4): words in square brackets substituted by the Companies Act 2006 (Consequential Amendments etc) Order 2008, SI 2008/948, art 3(1)(a), Sch 1, Pt 1, para 1(qq)(i).

**[1.272]**
### 31 Remedy for failure to comply with request for access

(1) A person who claims that a trade union has failed in any respect to comply with a request made by him under section 30 may apply to the court [or to the Certification Officer].

(2) Where [on an application to it] the court is satisfied that the claim is well-founded, it shall make such order as it considers appropriate for ensuring that [the applicant]—

    (a)   is allowed to inspect the records requested,

    (b)   is allowed to be accompanied by an accountant when making the inspection of those records, and

    (c)   is allowed to take, or is supplied with, such copies of, or of extracts from, the records as he may require.

[(2A) On an application to him the Certification Officer shall—

    (a)   make such enquiries as he thinks fit, and

    (b)   give the applicant and the trade union an opportunity to be heard.

(2B) Where the Certification Officer is satisfied that the claim is well-founded he shall make such order as he considers appropriate for ensuring that the applicant—

    (a)   is allowed to inspect the records requested,

    (b)   is allowed to be accompanied by an accountant when making the inspection of those records, and

    (c)   is allowed to take, or is supplied with, such copies of, or of extracts from, the records as he may require.

(2C) In exercising his functions under this section the Certification Officer shall ensure that, so far as is reasonably practicable, an application made to him is determined within six months of being made.]

(3) Without prejudice to any other power of the court, the court may on an application [to it] under this section grant such interlocutory relief (in Scotland, such interim order) as it considers appropriate.

[(4) Where the Certification Officer requests a person to furnish information to him in connection with enquiries made by him under this section, he shall specify the date by which that information is to be furnished and, unless he considers that it would be inappropriate to do so, shall proceed with his determination of the application notwithstanding that the information has not been furnished to him by the specified date.

(5) An order made by the Certification Officer under this section may be enforced in the same way as an order of the court.

(6) If a person applies to the court under this section in relation to an alleged failure he may not apply to the Certification Officer under this section in relation to that failure.

(7) If a person applies to the Certification Officer under this section in relation to an alleged failure he may not apply to the court under this section in relation to that failure.]

**NOTES**

Sub-ss (1), (3): words in square brackets inserted by the Employment Relations Act 1999, s 29, Sch 6, paras 1, 6(1), (2), (5).

Sub-s (2): words in first pair of square brackets inserted, and words in second pair of square brackets substituted, by the Employment Relations Act 1999, s 29, Sch 6, paras 1, 6(1), (3).

Sub-ss (2A)–(2C), (4)–(7): inserted and added respectively by the Employment Relations Act 1999, s 29, Sch 6, paras 1, 6(1), (4), (6).

*Annual return, accounts and audit*

**[1.273]**
## 32   Annual return
(1)   A trade union shall send to the Certification Officer as respects each calendar year a return relating to its affairs.

(2)   The annual return shall be in such form and be signed by such persons as the Certification Officer may require and shall be sent to him before 1st June in the calendar year following that to which it relates.

(3)   The annual return shall contain—
  (a)   the following accounts—
     (i)   revenue accounts indicating the income and expenditure of the trade union for the period to which the return relates,
     (ii)   a balance sheet as at the end of that period, and
     (iii)   such other accounts as the Certification Officer may require,
    each of which must give a true and fair view of the matters to which it relates,
  [(aa)   details of the salary paid to and other benefits provided to or in respect of—
     (i)   each member of the executive,
     (ii)   the president, and
     (iii)   the general secretary,
    by the trade union during the period to which the return relates,]
  (b)   a copy of the report made by the auditor or auditors of the trade union on those accounts and such other documents relating to those accounts and such further particulars as the Certification Officer may require, . . .
  (c)   a copy of the rules of the trade union as in force at the end of the period to which the return relates[, and
  (d)   in the case of a trade union required to maintain a register by section 24, a statement of the number of names on the register as at the end of the period to which the return relates and the number of those names which were not accompanied by an address which is a member's address for the purposes of that section;]
and shall have attached to it a note of all the changes in the officers of the union and of any change in the address of the head or main office of the union during the period to which the return relates.

(4)   The Certification Officer may, if in any particular case he considers it appropriate to do so—
  (a)   direct that the period for which a return is to be sent to him shall be a period other than the calendar year last preceding the date on which the return is sent;
  (b)   direct that the date before which a return is to be sent to him shall be such date (whether before or after 1st June) as may be specified in the direction.

(5)   A trade union shall at the request of any person supply him with a copy of its most recent return either free of charge or on payment of a reasonable charge.

(6)   The Certification Officer shall at all reasonable hours keep available for public inspection either free of charge or on payment of a reasonable charge, copies of all annual returns sent to him under this section.

[(7)   For the purposes of this section and section 32A "member of the executive" includes any person who, under the rules or practice of the union, may attend and speak at some or all of the meetings of the executive, otherwise than for the purpose of providing the committee with factual information or with technical or professional advice with respect to matters taken into account by the executive in carrying out its functions.]

**NOTES**
Sub-s (3): para (aa) inserted, word omitted from para (b) repealed, and para (d) and the word immediately preceding it inserted, by the Trade Union Reform and Employment Rights Act 1993, ss 8, 51, Sch 10.
  Sub-s (7): added by the Trade Union Reform and Employment Rights Act 1993, s 49(2), Sch 8, para 42.

**[1.274]**
## [32A   Statement to members following annual return
(1)   A trade union shall take all reasonable steps to secure that, not later than the end of the period of eight weeks beginning with the day on which the annual return of the union is sent to the Certification Officer, all the members of the union are provided with the statement required by this section by any of the methods allowed by subsection (2).

(2)   Those methods are—
  (a)   the sending of individual copies of the statement to members; or
  (b)   any other means (whether by including the statement in a publication of the union or otherwise) which it is the practice of the union to use when information of general interest to all its members needs to be provided to them.

(3)   The statement required by this section shall specify—

(a) the total income and expenditure of the trade union for the period to which the return relates,

(b) how much of the income of the union for that period consisted of payments in respect of membership,

(c) the total income and expenditure for that period of any political fund of the union, and

(d) the salary paid to and other benefits provided to or in respect of—

    (i) each member of the executive,

    (ii) the president, and

    (iii) the general secretary,

    by the trade union during that period.

(4) The requirement imposed by this section is not satisfied if the statement specifies anything inconsistent with the contents of the return.

(5) The statement—

(a) shall also set out in full the report made by the auditor or auditors of the union on the accounts contained in the return and state the name and address of that auditor or of each of those auditors, and

(b) may include any other matter which the union considers may give a member significant assistance in making an informed judgment about the financial activities of the union in the period to which the return relates.

(6) The statement—

(a) shall also include the following statement—

"A member who is concerned that some irregularity may be occurring, or have occurred, in the conduct of the financial affairs of the union may take steps with a view to investigating further, obtaining clarification and, if necessary, securing regularisation of that conduct.

The member may raise any such concern with such one or more of the following as it seems appropriate to raise it with: the officials of the union, the trustees of the property of the union, the auditor or auditors of the union, the Certification Officer (who is an independent officer appointed by the Secretary of State) and the police.

Where a member believes that the financial affairs of the union have been or are being conducted in breach of the law or in breach of rules of the union and contemplates bringing civil proceedings against the union or responsible officials or trustees, he [should] consider obtaining independent legal advice."; and

(b) may include such other details of the steps which a member may take for the purpose mentioned in the statement set out above as the trade union considers appropriate.

(7) A trade union shall send to the Certification Officer a copy of the statement which is provided to its members in pursuance of this section as soon as is reasonably practicable after it is so provided.

(8) Where the same form of statement is not provided to all the members of a trade union, the union shall send to the Certification Officer in accordance with subsection (7) a copy of each form of statement provided to any of them.

(9) If at any time during the period of two years beginning with the day referred to in subsection (1) any member of the trade union requests a copy of the statement required by this section, the union shall, as soon as practicable, furnish him with such a copy free of charge.]

**NOTES**

Inserted by the Trade Union Reform and Employment Rights Act 1993, s 9.

Sub-s (6): word in square brackets substituted by the Employment Relations Act 1999, s 28(3).

---

**[1.275]**
**33 Duty to appoint auditors**

(1) A trade union shall in respect of each accounting period appoint an auditor or auditors to audit the accounts contained in its annual return.

(2) An "accounting period" means any period in relation to which it is required to send a return to the Certification Officer.

**[1.276]**
**34 Eligibility for appointment as auditor**

(1) A person is not qualified to be the auditor or one of the auditors of a trade union unless he is eligible for appointment as a [statutory auditor under Part 42 of the Companies Act 2006].

(2) Two or more persons who are not so qualified may act as auditors of a trade union in respect of an accounting period if—

(a) the receipts and payments in respect of the union's last preceding accounting period did not in the aggregate exceed £5,000,

(b) the number of its members at the end of that period did not exceed 500, and

(c) the value of its assets at the end of that period did not in the aggregate exceed £5,000.

(3)  Where by virtue of subsection (2) persons who are not qualified as mentioned in subsection (1) act as auditors of a trade union in respect of an accounting period, the Certification Officer may (during that period or after it comes to an end) direct the union to appoint a person who is so qualified to audit its accounts for that period.

(4)  The Secretary of State may by regulations—
- (a)  substitute for any sum or number specified in subsection (2) such sum or number as may be specified in the regulations; and
- (b)  prescribe what receipts and payments are to be taken into account for the purposes of that subsection.

Any such regulations shall be made by statutory instrument which shall be subject to annulment in pursuance of a resolution of either House of Parliament.

(5)  None of the following shall act as auditor of a trade union—
- (a)  an officer or employee of the trade union or of any of its branches or sections;
- (b)  a person who is a partner of, or in the employment of, or who employs, such an officer or employee;
- (c)  . . .

. . .

**NOTES**

Sub-s (1): words in square brackets substituted by the Companies Act 2006 (Consequential Amendments etc) Order 2008, SI 2008/948, art 3(1)(a), Sch 1, Pt 1, para 1(qq)(ii).

Sub-s (5): para (c) repealed by the Employment Relations Act 2004, s 53(1), 57(2), Sch 2; final words omitted repealed by the Trade Union Reform and Employment Rights Act 1993, ss 49(1), 51, Sch 7, para 18, Sch 10.

Regulations: as of 6 April 2013 no Regulations had been made under this section.

**[1.277]**
### 35  Appointment and removal of auditors

(1)  The rules of every trade union shall contain provision for the appointment and removal of auditors.

But the following provisions have effect notwithstanding anything in the rules.

(2)  An auditor of a trade union shall not be removed from office except by resolution passed at a general meeting of its members or of delegates of its members.

(3)  An auditor duly appointed to audit the accounts of a trade union shall be re-appointed as auditor for the following accounting period, unless—
- (a)  a resolution has been passed at a general meeting of the trade union appointing somebody instead of him or providing expressly that he shall not be re-appointed, or
- (b)  he has given notice to the trade union in writing of his unwillingness to be re-appointed, or
- (c)  he is ineligible for re-appointment, or
- (d)  he has ceased to act as auditor by reason of incapacity.

(4)  Where notice has been given of an intended resolution to appoint somebody in place of a retiring auditor but the resolution cannot be proceeded with at the meeting because of the death or incapacity of that person, or because he is ineligible for the appointment, the retiring auditor need not automatically be re-appointed.

(5)  The references above to a person being ineligible for appointment as auditor of a trade union are to his not being qualified for the appointment in accordance with [subsections (1) to (4)] of section 34 or being precluded by [subsection (5)] of that section from acting as its auditor.

(6)  The Secretary of State may make provision by regulations as to the procedure to be followed when it is intended to move a resolution—
- (a)  appointing another auditor in place of a retiring auditor, or
- (b)  providing expressly that a retiring auditor shall not be reappointed,

and as to the rights of auditors and members of the trade union in relation to such a motion.

Any such regulations shall be made by statutory instrument which shall be subject to annulment in pursuance of a resolution of either House of Parliament.

(7)  Where regulations under subsection (6)—
- (a)  require copies of any representations made by a retiring auditor to be sent out, or
- (b)  require any such representations to be read out at a meeting,

the court, on the application of the trade union or of any other person, may dispense with the requirement if satisfied that the rights conferred on the retiring auditor by the regulations are being abused to secure needless publicity for defamatory matter.

(8)  On such an application the court may order the costs or expenses of the trade union to be paid, in whole or in part, by the retiring auditor, whether he is a party to the application or not.

**NOTES**

Sub-s (5): words in square brackets substituted by the Trade Union Reform and Employment Rights Act 1993, s 49(1), Sch 7, para 19.

Regulations: as of 6 April 2013 no Regulations had been made under this section.

**[1.278]**
**36 Auditor's report**
(1) The auditor or auditors of a trade union shall make a report to it on the accounts audited by him or them and contained in its annual return.
[(1A) The report shall state the names of, and be signed by, the auditor or auditors.]
(2) The report shall state whether, in the opinion of the auditor or auditors, the accounts give a true and fair view of the matters to which they relate.
(3) It is the duty of the auditor or auditors in preparing their report to carry out such investigations as will enable them to form an opinion as to—
  (a) whether the trade union has kept proper accounting records in accordance with the requirements of section 28,
  (b) whether it has maintained a satisfactory system of control over its transactions in accordance with the requirements of that section, and
  (c) whether the accounts to which the report relates agree with the accounting records.
(4) If in the opinion of the auditor or auditors the trade union has failed to comply with section 28, or if the accounts do not agree with the accounting records, the auditor or auditors shall state that fact in the report.
[(5) Any reference in this section to signature by an auditor is, where the office of auditor is held by a body corporate or partnership, to signature in the name of the body corporate or partnership by an individual authorised to sign on its behalf.]

**NOTES**
Sub-ss (1A), (5): inserted and added respectively by the Employment Relations Act 2004, s 53(2), (3).

**[1.279]**
**37 Rights of auditors**
(1) Every auditor of a trade union—
  (a) has a right of access at all times to its accounting records and to all other documents relating to its affairs, and
  (b) is entitled to require from its officers, or the officers of any of its branches or sections, such information and explanations as he thinks necessary for the performance of his duties as auditor.
(2) If an auditor fails to obtain all the information and explanations which, to the best of his knowledge and belief, are necessary for the purposes of an audit, he shall state that fact in his report.
(3) Every auditor of a trade union is entitled—
  (a) to attend any general meeting of its members, or of delegates of its members, and to receive all notices of and other communications relating to any general meeting which any such member or delegate is entitled to receive, and
  (b) to be heard at any meeting which he attends on any part of the business of the meeting which concerns him as auditor.
[(4) In the case of an auditor which is a body corporate or partnership, its right to attend or be heard at a meeting is exercisable by an individual authorised by it to act as its representative at the meeting.]

**NOTES**
Sub-s (4): added by the Employment Relations Act 2004, s 53(4).

*[Investigation of financial affairs*
**[1.280]**
**37A Power of Certification Officer to require production of documents etc**
(1) The Certification Officer may at any time, if he thinks there is good reason to do so, give directions to a trade union, or a branch or section of a trade union, requiring it to produce such relevant documents as may be specified in the directions; and the documents shall be produced at such time and place as may be so specified.
(2) The Certification Officer may at any time, if he thinks there is good reason to do so, authorise a member of his staff or any other person, on producing (if so required) evidence of his authority, to require a trade union, or a branch or section of a trade union, to produce forthwith to the member of staff or other person such relevant documents as the member of staff or other person may specify.
(3) Where the Certification Officer, or a member of his staff or any other person, has power to require the production of documents by virtue of subsection (1) or (2), the Certification Officer, member of staff or other person has the like power to require production of those documents from any person who appears to the Certification Officer, member of staff or other person to be in possession of them.
(4) Where such a person claims a lien on documents produced by him, the production is without prejudice to the lien.
(5) The power under this section to require the production of documents includes power—

> (a)  if the documents are produced—
>> (i)  to take copies of them or extracts from them, and
>> (ii)  to require the person by whom they are produced, or any person who is or has been an official or agent of the trade union, to provide an explanation of any of them; and
> (b)  if the documents are not produced, to require the person who was required to produce them to state, to the best of his knowledge and belief, where they are.

(6)  In subsections (1) and (2) "relevant documents", in relation to a trade union or a branch or section of a trade union, means accounting documents, and documents of any other description, which may be relevant in considering the financial affairs of the trade union.

(7)  A person shall not be excused from providing an explanation or making a statement in compliance with a requirement imposed under subsection (5) on the ground that to do so would tend to expose him to proceedings for an offence; but an explanation so provided or statement so made may only be used in evidence against the person by whom it is made or provided—

> (a)  on a prosecution for an offence under section 45(9) (false explanations and statements), or
> (b)  on a prosecution for some other offence where in giving evidence the person makes a statement inconsistent with it.]

**NOTES**

Inserted, together with the preceding heading, and ss 37B–37E, by the Trade Union Reform and Employment Rights Act 1993, s 10.

**[1.281]**
**[37B   Investigations by inspectors**

(1)  The Certification Officer may appoint one or more members of his staff or other persons as an inspector or inspectors to investigate the financial affairs of a trade union and to report on them in such manner as he may direct.

(2)  The Certification Officer may only make such an appointment if it appears to him that there are circumstances suggesting—

> (a)  that the financial affairs of the trade union are being or have been conducted for a fraudulent or unlawful purpose,
> (b)  that persons concerned with the management of those financial affairs have, in connection with that management, been guilty of fraud, misfeasance or other misconduct,
> (c)  that the trade union has failed to comply with any duty imposed on it by this Act in relation to its financial affairs, or
> (d)  that a rule of the union relating to its financial affairs has not been complied with.

(3)  Where an inspector is, or inspectors are, appointed under this section it is the duty of all persons who are or have been officials or agents of the trade union—

> (a)  to produce to the inspector or inspectors all relevant documents which are in their possession,
> (b)  to attend before the inspector or inspectors when required to do so, and
> (c)  otherwise to give the inspector or inspectors all assistance in connection with the investigation which they are reasonably able to give.

(4)  Where any person (whether or not within subsection (3)) appears to the inspector or inspectors to be in possession of information relating to a matter which he considers, or they consider, to be relevant to the investigation, the inspector or inspectors may require him—

> (a)  to produce to the inspector or inspectors any relevant documents relating to that matter,
> (b)  to attend before the inspector or inspectors, and
> (c)  otherwise to give the inspector or inspectors all assistance in connection with the investigation which he is reasonably able to give;

and it is the duty of the person to comply with the requirement.

(5)  In subsections (3) and (4) "relevant documents", in relation to an investigation of the financial affairs of a trade union, means accounting documents, and documents of any other description, which may be relevant to the investigation.

(6)  A person shall not be excused from providing an explanation or making a statement in compliance with subsection (3) or a requirement imposed under subsection (4) on the ground that to do so would tend to expose him to proceedings for an offence; but an explanation so provided or statement so made may only be used in evidence against the person by whom it is provided or made—

> (a)  on a prosecution for an offence under section 45(9) (false explanations and statements), or
> (b)  on a prosecution for some other offence where in giving evidence the person makes a statement inconsistent with it.]

**NOTES**

Inserted as noted to s 37A at **[1.280]**.

**[1.282]**
**[37C   Inspectors' reports etc**

(1)  An inspector or inspectors appointed under section 37B—

(a)    may, and if so directed by the Certification Officer shall, make interim reports, and

(b)    on the conclusion of their investigation shall make a final report,

to the Certification Officer.

(2)    Any report under subsection (1) shall be written or printed, as the Certification Officer directs.

(3)    An inspector or inspectors appointed under section 37B may at any time, and if so directed by the Certification Officer shall, inform the Certification Officer of any matters coming to his or their knowledge as a result of the investigation.

(4)    The Certification Officer may direct an inspector or inspectors appointed under section 37B to take no further steps in the investigation, or to take only such further steps as are specified in the direction, if—

(a)    it appears to the Certification Officer that matters have come to light in the course of the investigation which suggest that a criminal offence has been committed and those matters have been referred to the appropriate prosecuting authority, or

(b)    it appears to the Certification Officer appropriate to do so in any other circumstances.

(5)    Where an investigation is the subject of a direction under subsection (4), the inspector or inspectors shall make a final report to the Certification Officer only where the Certification Officer directs him or them to do so at the time of the direction under that subsection or subsequently.

(6)    The Certification Officer shall publish a final report made to him under this section.

(7)    The Certification Officer shall furnish a copy of such a report free of charge—

(a)    to the trade union which is the subject of the report,

(b)    to any auditor of that trade union or of any branch or section of the union, if he requests a copy before the end of the period of three years beginning with the day on which the report is published, and

(c)    to any member of the trade union if—

    (i)    he has complained to the Certification Officer that there are circumstances suggesting any of the states of affairs specified in section 37B(2)(a) to (d),

    (ii)    the Certification Officer considers that the report contains findings which are relevant to the complaint, and

    (iii)    the member requests a copy before the end of the period of three years beginning with the day on which the report is published.

(8)    A copy of any report under this section, certified by the Certification Officer to be a true copy, is admissible in any legal proceedings as evidence of the opinion of the inspector or inspectors in relation to any matter contained in the report; and a document purporting to be a certificate of the Certification Officer under this subsection shall be received in evidence and be deemed to be such a certificate unless the contrary is proved.]

**NOTES**

Inserted as noted to s 37A at **[1.280]**.

**[1.283]**

**[37D    Expenses of investigations**

(1)    The expenses of an investigation under section 37B shall be defrayed in the first instance by the Certification Officer.

(2)    For the purposes of this section there shall be treated as expenses of an investigation, in particular, such reasonable sums as the Certification Officer may determine in respect of general staff costs and overheads.

(3)    A person who is convicted on a prosecution instituted as a result of the investigation may in the same proceedings be ordered to pay the expenses of the investigation to such extent as may be specified in the order.]

**NOTES**

Inserted as noted to s 37A at **[1.280]**.

**[1.284]**

**[37E    Sections 37A and 37B: supplementary**

(1)    Where—

(a)    a report of the auditor or auditors of a trade union, or a branch or section of a trade union, on the accounts audited by him or them and contained in the annual return of the union, or branch or section—

    (i)    does not state without qualification that the accounts give a true and fair view of the matters to which they relate, or

    (ii)    includes a statement in compliance with section 36(4), or

(b)    a member of a trade union has complained to the Certification Officer that there are circumstances suggesting any of the states of affairs specified in section 37B(2)(a) to (d),

the Certification Officer shall consider whether it is appropriate for him to exercise any of the powers conferred on him by sections 37A and 37B.

(2)  If in a case where a member of a trade union has complained as mentioned in subsection (1)(b) the Certification Officer decides not to exercise any of the powers conferred by those sections he shall, as soon as reasonably practicable after making a decision not to do so, notify the member of his decision and, if he thinks fit, of the reasons for it.

(3)  Nothing in section 37A or 37B—

   (a)   requires or authorises anyone to require the disclosure by a person of information which he would in an action in the High Court or the Court of Session be entitled to refuse to disclose on grounds of legal professional privilege except, if he is a lawyer, the name and address of his client, or

   (b)   requires or authorises anyone to require the production by a person of a document which he would in such an action be entitled to refuse to produce on such grounds.

(4)  Nothing in section 37A or 37B requires or authorises anyone to require the disclosure of information or the production of documents in respect of which the person to whom the requirement would relate owes an obligation of confidence by virtue of carrying on the business of banking unless—

   (a)   the person to whom the obligation is owed is the trade union, or any branch or section of the union, concerned or a trustee of any fund concerned, or

   (b)   the person to whom the obligation of confidence is owed consents to the disclosure or production.

(5)  In sections 37A and 37B and this section—

   (a)   references to documents include information recorded in any form, and

   (b)   in relation to information recorded otherwise than in legible form, references to its production are to the production of a copy of the information in legible form.]

**NOTES**

Inserted as noted to s 37A at **[1.280]**.

*Members' superannuation schemes*

**[1.285]**
**38   Members' superannuation schemes: separate fund to be maintained**
(1)  In the following provisions a "members' superannuation scheme" means any scheme or arrangement made by or on behalf of a trade union (including a scheme or arrangement shown in the rules of the union) in so far as it provides—

   (a)   for benefits to be paid by way of pension (including any widows' or children's pensions or dependants' pensions) to or in respect of members or former members of the trade union, and

   (b)   for those benefits to be so paid either out of the funds of the union or under an insurance scheme maintained out of those funds.

(2)  A trade union shall not maintain a members' superannuation scheme unless it maintains a separate fund for the payment of benefits in accordance with the scheme.

   A "separate fund" means a fund separate from the general funds of the trade union.

**[1.286]**
**39   Examination of proposals for new scheme**
(1)  A trade union shall not begin to maintain a members' superannuation scheme unless, before the date on which the scheme begins to be maintained—

   (a)   the proposals for the scheme have been examined by an appropriately qualified actuary, and

   (b)   a copy of a report made to the trade union by the actuary on the results of his examination of the proposals, signed by the actuary, has been sent to the Certification Officer.

(2)  The actuary's report shall state—

   (a)   whether in his opinion the premium or contribution rates will be adequate,

   (b)   whether the accounting or funding arrangements are suitable, and

   (c)   whether in his opinion the fund for the payment of benefits will be adequate.

(3)  A copy of the actuary's report shall, on the application of any of the union's members, be supplied to him free of charge.

**[1.287]**
**40   Periodical re-examination of existing schemes**
(1)  Where a trade union maintains a members' superannuation scheme, it shall arrange for the scheme to be examined periodically by an appropriately qualified actuary and for a report to be made to it by the actuary on the result of his examination.

(2)  The examination shall be of the scheme as it has effect at such date as the trade union may determine, not being more than five years after the date by reference to which the last examination or, as the case may be, the examination of the proposals for the scheme was carried out.

(3)  The examination shall include a valuation (as at the date by reference to which the examination is carried out) of the assets comprised in the fund maintained for the payment of benefits and of the liabilities falling to be discharged out of it.

(4)   The actuary's report shall state—
   (a)   whether in his opinion the premium or contribution rates are adequate,
   (b)   whether the accounting or funding arrangements are suitable, and
   (c)   whether in his opinion the fund for the payment of benefits is adequate.
(5)   A copy of the report, signed by the actuary, shall be sent to the Certification Officer.
(6)   The trade union shall make such arrangements as will enable the report to be sent to the Certification Officer within a year of the date by reference to which the examination was carried out.
(7)   A copy of the actuary's report shall, on the application of any of the union's members, be supplied to him free of charge.

**[1.288]**
**41   Powers of the Certification Officer**
(1)   The Certification Officer may, on the application of a trade union—
   (a)   exempt a members' superannuation scheme which the union proposes to maintain from the requirements of section 39 (examination of proposals for new scheme), or
   (b)   exempt a members' superannuation scheme which the union maintains from the requirements of section 40 (periodical re–examination of scheme),
if he is satisfied that, by reason of the small number of members to which the scheme is applicable or for any other special reasons, it is unnecessary for the scheme to be examined in accordance with those provisions.
(2)   An exemption may be revoked if it appears to the Certification Officer that the circumstances by reason of which it was granted have ceased to exist.
(3)   Where an exemption is revoked under subsection [(2)], the date as at which the next periodical examination is to be carried out under section 40 shall be such as the Certification Officer may direct.
(4)   The Certification Officer may in any case direct that section 40 (periodical re-examination of schemes) shall apply to a trade union with the substitution for the reference to five years of a reference to such shorter period as may be specified in the direction.

**NOTES**
   Sub-s (3): number in square brackets substituted by the Employment Relations Act 2004, s 57(1), Sch 1, para 4.

**[1.289]**
**42   Meaning of "appropriately qualified actuary"**
In sections 39 and 40 an "appropriately qualified actuary" means a person who is either—
   (a)   a Fellow of the Institute of Actuaries, or
   (b)   a Fellow of the Faculty of Actuaries,
or is approved by the Certification Officer on the application of the trade union as a person having actuarial knowledge.

*Supplementary*

**[1.290]**
**43   Newly-formed trade unions**
(1)   The following provisions of this Chapter do not apply to a trade union which has been in existence for less than twelve months—
   (a)   section 27 (duty to supply copy of rules),
   (b)   sections 32 to 37 (annual return, [statement for members,] accounts and audit),   . . .
   [(ba) sections 37A to 37E (investigation of financial affairs), and]
   (c)   sections 38 to 42 (members' superannuation schemes).
(2)   Sections 24 to 26 (register of members' names and addresses) do not apply to a trade union until more than one year has elapsed since its formation (by amalgamation or otherwise).
   For this purpose the date of formation of a trade union formed otherwise than by amalgamation shall be taken to be the date on which the first members of the executive of the union are first appointed or elected.

**NOTES**
   Sub-s (1): words in square brackets in para (b) inserted, word omitted repealed, and para (ba) inserted, by the Trade Union Reform and Employment Rights Act 1993, ss 49(2), 51, Sch 8, para 43, Sch 10.

**[1.291]**
**44   Discharge of duties in case of union having branches or sections**
(1)   The following provisions apply where a trade union consists of or includes branches or sections.
(2)   Any duty falling upon the union in relation to a branch or section under the provisions of—
   section 28 (duty to keep accounting records),
   [sections 32 and 33 to 37] (annual return, accounts and audit), or
   sections 38 to 42 (members' superannuation schemes),

shall be treated as discharged to the extent to which a branch or section discharges it instead of the union.

(3)   In sections 29 to 31 (right of member to access to accounting records) references to a branch or section do not include a branch or section which is itself a trade union.

(4)   Any duty falling upon a branch or section by reason of its being a trade union under—

section 24 (register of members' names and addresses),

section 28 (duty to keep accounting records),

[sections 32 and 33 to 37] (annual return, accounts and audit), or

sections 38 to 42 (members' superannuation schemes),

shall be treated as discharged to the extent to which the union of which it is a branch or section discharges the duty instead of it.

[(5)   Where the duty falling on a trade union under section 32 to send to the Certification Officer a return relating to its affairs is treated as discharged by the union by virtue of subsection (2) or (4) of this section, the duties imposed by section 32A in relation to the return shall be treated as duties of the branch or section of the union, or the trade union of which it is a branch or section, by which that duty is in fact discharged.]

**NOTES**

Sub-ss (2), (4): words in square brackets substituted by the Trade Union Reform and Employment Rights Act 1993, s 49(2), Sch 8, para 44(a).

Sub-s (5): added by the Trade Union Reform and Employment Rights Act 1993, s 49(2), Sch 8, para 44(b).

**[1.292]**
**45   Offences**

(1)   If a trade union refuses or wilfully neglects to perform a duty imposed on it by or under any of the provisions of—

section 27 (duty to supply copy of rules),

sections 28 to 30 (accounting records),

sections 32 to 37 (annual return, [statement for members,] accounts and audit), or

sections 38 to 42 (members' superannuation schemes),

it commits an offence.

(2)   The offence shall be deemed to have been also committed by—

(a)   every officer of the trade union who is bound by the rules of the union to discharge on its behalf the duty breach of which constitutes the offence, or

(b)   if there is no such officer, every member of the general committee of management of the union.

(3)   In any proceedings brought against an officer or member by virtue of subsection (2) in respect of a breach of duty, it is a defence for him to prove that he had reasonable cause to believe, and did believe, that some other person who was competent to discharge that duty was authorised to discharge it instead of him and had discharged it or would do so.

(4)   A person who wilfully alters or causes to be altered a document which is required for the purposes of any of the provisions mentioned in subsection (1), with intent to falsify the document or to enable a trade union to evade any of those provisions, commits an offence.

[(5)   If a person contravenes any duty, or requirement imposed, under section 37A (power of Certification officer to require production of documents etc) or 37B (investigations by inspectors) he commits an offence.

(6)   In any proceedings brought against a person in respect of a contravention of a requirement imposed under section 37A(3) or 37B(4) to produce documents it is a defence for him to prove—

(a)   that the documents were not in his possession, and

(b)   that it was not reasonably practicable for him to comply with the requirement.

(7)   If an official or agent of a trade union—

(a)   destroys, mutilates or falsifies, or is privy to the destruction, mutilation or falsification of, a document relating to the financial affairs of the trade union, or

(b)   makes, or is privy to the making of, a false entry in any such document,

he commits an offence unless he proves that he had no intention to conceal the financial affairs of the trade union or to defeat the law.

(8)   If such a person fraudulently—

(a)   parts with, alters or deletes anything in any such document, or

(b)   is privy to the fraudulent parting with, fraudulent alteration of or fraudulent deletion in, any such document,

he commits an offence.

(9)   If a person in purported compliance with a duty, or requirement imposed, under section 37A or 37B to provide an explanation or make a statement—

(a)   provides or makes an explanation or statement which he knows to be false in a material particular, or

(b)   recklessly provides or makes an explanation or statement which is false in a material particular,

he commits an offence.]

NOTES

Sub-s (1): words in square brackets inserted by the Trade Union Reform and Employment Rights Act 1993, s 49(2), Sch 8, para 45.

Sub-ss (5)–(9): substituted, for the original sub-s (5), by the Trade Union Reform and Employment Rights Act 1993, s 11(1).

**[1.293]**

**[45A Penalties and prosecution time limits**

(1)   A person guilty of an offence under section 45 is liable on summary conviction—

(a)   in the case of an offence under subsection (1) or (5), to a fine not exceeding level 5 on the standard scale;

(b)   in the case of an offence under subsection (4), (7), (8) or (9), to imprisonment for a term not exceeding six months or to a fine not exceeding level 5 on the standard scale or to both.

(2)   Proceedings for an offence under section 45(1) relating to the duty imposed by section 32 (duty to send annual return to Certification Officer) may be commenced at any time before the end of the period of three years beginning with the date when the offence was committed.

(3)   Proceedings for any other offence under section 45(1) may be commenced—

(a)   at any time before the end of the period of six months beginning with the date when the offence was committed, or

(b)   at any time after the end of that period but before the end of the period of twelve months beginning with the date when evidence sufficient in the opinion of the Certification Officer or, in Scotland, the procurator fiscal, to justify the proceedings came to his knowledge;

but no proceedings may be commenced by virtue of paragraph (b) after the end of the period of three years beginning with the date when the offence was committed.

(4)   For the purposes of subsection (3)(b), a certificate signed by or on behalf of the Certification Officer or the procurator fiscal which states the date on which evidence sufficient in his opinion to justify the proceedings came to his knowledge shall be conclusive evidence of that fact.

(5)   A certificate stating that matter and purporting to be so signed shall be deemed to be so signed unless the contrary is proved.

(6)   For the purposes of this section—

(a)   in England and Wales, proceedings are commenced when an information is laid, and

(b)   in Scotland, subsection (3) of [section 136 of the Criminal Procedure (Scotland) Act 1995] (date of commencement of proceedings) applies as it applies for the purposes of that section.]

NOTES

Inserted by the Trade Union Reform and Employment Rights Act 1993, s 11(2).

Sub-s (6): words in square brackets substituted by the Criminal Procedure (Consequential Provisions) (Scotland) Act 1995, s 5, Sch 4, para 85.

**[1.294]**

**[45B Duty to secure positions not held by certain offenders**

(1)   A trade union shall secure that a person does not at any time hold a position in the union to which this section applies if—

(a)   within the period of five years immediately preceding that time he has been convicted of an offence under subsection (1) or (5) of section 45, or

(b)   within the period of ten years immediately preceding that time he has been convicted of an offence under subsection (4), (7), (8) or (9) of that section.

(2)   Subject to subsection (4), the positions to which this section applies are—

(a)   member of the executive,

(b)   any position by virtue of which a person is a member of the executive,

(c)   president, and

(d)   general secretary.

(3)   For the purposes of subsection (2)(a) "member of the executive" includes any person who, under the rules or practice of the union, may attend and speak at some or all of the meetings of the executive, otherwise than for the purpose of providing the committee with factual information or with technical or professional advice with respect to matters taken into account by the executive in carrying out its functions.

(4)   This section does not apply to the position of president or general secretary if the holder of that position—

(a)   is not, in respect of that position, either a voting member of the executive or an employee of the union,

(b)   holds that position for a period which under the rules of the union cannot end more than thirteen months after he took it up, and

(c)   has not held either position at any time in the period of twelve months ending with the day before he took up that position.

(5)   In subsection (4)(a) "a voting member of the executive" means a person entitled in his own right to attend meetings of the executive and to vote on matters on which votes are taken by the executive (whether or not he is entitled to attend all such meetings or to vote on all such matters or in all circumstances).]

**NOTES**

Inserted, together with s 45C, by the Trade Union Reform and Employment Rights Act 1993, s 12.

**[1.295]**
**[45C   Remedies and enforcement**
(1)   A member of a trade union who claims that the union has failed to comply with the requirement of section 45B may apply to the Certification Officer or to the court for a declaration to that effect.
(2)   On an application being made to him, the Certification Officer—
   [(aa) shall make such enquiries as he thinks fit,]
   (a)   shall   .   .   .   give the applicant and the trade union an opportunity to be heard,
   (b)   shall ensure that, so far as is reasonably practicable, the application is determined within six months of being made,
   (c)   may make or refuse the declaration asked for, and
   (d)   shall, whether he makes or refuses the declaration, give reasons for his decision in writing.
(3), (4)   .   .   .
(5)   Where the court makes a declaration it shall also, unless it considers that it would be inappropriate, make an order imposing on the trade union a requirement to take within such period as may be specified in the order such steps to remedy the declared failure as may be so specified.
[(5A)   Where the Certification Officer makes a declaration he shall also, unless he considers that it would be inappropriate, make an order imposing on the trade union a requirement to take within such period as may be specified in the order such steps to remedy the declared failure as may be so specified.
(5B)   The following paragraphs have effect if a person applies to the Certification Officer under this section in relation to an alleged failure—
   (a)   that person may not apply to the court under this section in relation to that failure;
   (b)   on an application by a different person to the court under this section in relation to that failure, the court shall have due regard to any declaration, order, observations or reasons made or given by the Certification Officer regarding that failure and brought to the court's notice.
(5C)   The following paragraphs have effect if a person applies to the court under this section in relation to an alleged failure—
   (a)   that person may not apply to the Certification Officer under this section in relation to that failure;
   (b)   on an application by a different person to the Certification Officer under this section in relation to that failure, the Certification Officer shall have regard to any declaration, order, observations or reasons made or given by the court regarding that failure and brought to the Certification Officer's notice.]
(6)   Where an order has been made [under subsection (5) or (5A)], any person who is a member of the trade union and was a member at the time the order was made is entitled to enforce the order as if he had made the application on which the order was made.
[(7)   Where the Certification Officer requests a person to furnish information to him in connection with enquiries made by him under this section, he shall specify the date by which that information is to be furnished and, unless he considers that it would be inappropriate to do so, shall proceed with his determination of the application notwithstanding that the information has not been furnished to him by the specified date.
(8)   A declaration made by the Certification Officer under this section may be relied on as if it were a declaration made by the court.
(9)   An order made by the Certification Officer under this section may be enforced in the same way as an order of the court.]]

**NOTES**

Inserted as noted to s 45B at **[1.294]**.

Sub-s (2): para (aa) inserted, and words omitted from para (a) repealed, by the Employment Relations Act 1999, ss 29, 44, Sch 6, paras 1, 7(1)–(3), Sch 9(7).

Sub-ss (3), (4): repealed by the Employment Relations Act 1999, ss 29, 44, Sch 6, paras 1, 7(1), (4), Sch 9(7).

Sub-ss (5A)–(5C), (7)–(9): inserted and added respectively by the Employment Relations Act 1999, s 29, Sch 6, paras 1, 7(1), (5), (7).

Sub-s (6): words in square brackets inserted by the Employment Relations Act 1999, s 29, Sch 6, paras 1, 7(1), (6).

**[1.296]**
**[45D Appeals from Certification Officer**
An appeal lies to the Employment Appeal Tribunal on any question of law arising in proceedings before or arising from any decision of the Certification Officer under section 25, 31 or 45C.]

NOTES
Inserted by the Employment Relations Act 1999, s 29, Sch 6, paras 1, 8.

CHAPTER IV
ELECTIONS FOR CERTAIN POSITIONS
*Duty to hold elections*

**[1.297]**
**46 Duty to hold elections for certain positions**
(1)   A trade union shall secure—
  (a)   that every person who holds a position in the union to which this Chapter applies does so by virtue of having been elected to it at an election satisfying the requirements of this Chapter, and
  (b)   that no person continues to hold such a position for more than five years without being re-elected at such an election.
(2)   The positions to which this Chapter applies (subject as mentioned below) are—
  (a)   member of the executive,
  (b)   any position by virtue of which a person is a member of the executive,
  (c)   president, and
  (d)   general secretary;
. . .
(3)   In this Chapter "member of the executive" includes any person who, under the rules or practice of the union, may attend and speak at some or all of the meetings of the executive, otherwise than for the purpose of providing the committee with factual information or with technical or professional advice with respect to matters taken into account by the executive in carrying out its functions.
(4)   This Chapter does not apply to the position of president or general secretary if the holder of that position—
  (a)   is not, in respect of that position, either a voting member of the executive or an employee of the union,
  (b)   holds that position for a period which under the rules of the union cannot end more than 13 months after he took it up, and
  (c)   has not held either position at any time in the period of twelve months ending with the day before he took up that position.
[(4A)   This Chapter also does not apply to the position of president if—
  (a)   the holder of that position was elected or appointed to it in accordance with the rules of the union,
  (b)   at the time of his election or appointment as president he held a position mentioned in paragraph (a), (b) or (d) of subsection (2) by virtue of having been elected to it at a qualifying election,
  (c)   it is no more than five years since—
    (i)   he was elected, or re-elected, to the position mentioned in paragraph (b) which he held at the time of his election or appointment as president, or
    (ii)   he was elected to another position of a kind mentioned in that paragraph at a qualifying election held after his election or appointment as president of the union, and
  (d)   he has, at all times since his election or appointment as president, held a position mentioned in paragraph (a), (b) or (d) of subsection (2) by virtue of having been elected to it at a qualifying election.]
(5)   [In subsection (4)] a "voting member of the executive" means a person entitled in his own right to attend meetings of the executive and to vote on matters on which votes are taken by the executive (whether or not he is entitled to attend all such meetings or to vote on all such matters or in all circumstances).
[(5A)   In subsection (4A) "qualifying election" means an election satisfying the requirements of this Chapter.
(5B)   The "requirements of this Chapter" referred to in subsections (1) and (5A) are those set out in sections 47 to 52 below.]
(6)   The provisions of this Chapter apply notwithstanding anything in the rules or practice of the union; and the terms and conditions on which a person is employed by the union shall be disregarded in so far as they would prevent the union from complying with the provisions of this Chapter.

**NOTES**

Sub-s (2): words omitted repealed by the Employment Relations Act 2004, ss 52(1), (2), 57(2), Sch 2.

Sub-ss (4A), (5A), (5B): inserted by the Employment Relations Act 2004, s 52(1), (3), (5).

Sub-s (5): words in square brackets inserted by the Employment Relations Act 2004, s 52(1), (4).

*Requirements to be satisfied with respect to elections*

**[1.298]**

## 47   Candidates

(1)   No member of the trade union shall be unreasonably excluded from standing as a candidate.

(2)   No candidate shall be required, directly or indirectly, to be a member of a political party.

(3)   A member of a trade union shall not be taken to be unreasonably excluded from standing as a candidate if he is excluded on the ground that he belongs to a class of which all the members are excluded by the rules of the union.

But a rule which provides for such a class to be determined by reference to whom the union chooses to exclude shall be disregarded.

**[1.299]**

## 48   Election addresses

(1)   The trade union shall—

    (a)   provide every candidate with an opportunity of preparing an election address in his own words and of submitting it to the union to be distributed to the persons accorded entitlement to vote in the election; and

    (b)   secure that, so far as reasonably practicable, copies of every election address submitted to it in time are distributed to each of those persons by post along with the voting papers for the election.

(2)   The trade union may determine the time by which an election address must be submitted to it for distribution; but the time so determined must not be earlier than the latest time at which a person may become a candidate in the election.

(3)   The trade union may provide that election addresses submitted to it for distribution—

    (a)   must not exceed such length, not being less than one hundred words, as may be determined by the union, and

    (b)   may, as regards photographs and other matter not in words, incorporate only such matter as the union may determine.

(4)   The trade union shall secure that no modification of an election address submitted to it is made by any person in any copy of the address to be distributed except—

    (a)   at the request or with the consent of the candidate, or

    (b)   where the modification is necessarily incidental to the method adopted for producing that copy.

(5)   The trade union shall secure that the same method of producing copies is applied in the same way to every election address submitted and, so far as reasonably practicable, that no such facility or information as would enable a candidate to gain any benefit from—

    (a)   the method by which copies of the election addresses are produced, or

    (b)   the modifications which are necessarily incidental to that method,

is provided to any candidate without being provided equally to all the others.

(6)   The trade union shall, so far as reasonably practicable, secure that the same facilities and restrictions with respect to the preparation, submission, length or modification of an election address, and with respect to the incorporation of photographs or other matter not in words, are provided or applied equally to each of the candidates.

(7)   The arrangements made by the trade union for the production of the copies to be so distributed must be such as to secure that none of the candidates is required to bear any of the expense of producing the copies.

(8)   No-one other than the candidate himself shall incur any civil or criminal liability in respect of the publication of a candidate's election address or of any copy required to be made for the purposes of this section.

**[1.300]**

## 49   Appointment of independent scrutineer

(1)   The trade union shall, before the election is held, appoint a qualified independent person ("the scrutineer") to carry out—

    (a)   the functions in relation to the election which are required under this section to be contained in his appointment; and

    (b)   such additional functions in relation to the election as may be specified in his appointment.

(2)   A person is a qualified independent person in relation to an election if—

    (a)   he satisfies such conditions as may be specified for the purposes of this section by order of the Secretary of State or is himself so specified; and

(b) the trade union has no grounds for believing either that he will carry out any functions conferred on him in relation to the election otherwise than competently or that his independence in relation to the union, or in relation to the election, might reasonably be called into question.

An order under paragraph (a) shall be made by statutory instrument which shall be subject to annulment in pursuance of a resolution of either House of Parliament.

(3) The scrutineer's appointment shall require him—

(a) to be the person who supervises the production [of the voting papers and (unless he is appointed under section 51A to undertake the distribution of the voting papers) their distribution] and to whom the voting papers are returned by those voting;

[(aa) to—

(i) inspect the register of names and addresses of the members of the trade union, or

(ii) examine the copy of the register as at the relevant date which is supplied to him in accordance with subsection (5A)(a),

whenever it appears to him appropriate to do so and, in particular, when the conditions specified in subsection (3A) are satisfied;]

(b) to take such steps as appear to him to be appropriate for the purpose of enabling him to make his report (see section 52);

(c) to make his report to the trade union as soon as reasonably practicable after the last date for the return of voting papers; and

(d) to retain custody of all voting papers returned for the purposes of the election [and the copy of the register supplied to him in accordance with subsection (5A)(a)]—

(i) until the end of the period of one year beginning with the announcement by the union of the result of the election; and

(ii) if within that period an application is made under section 54 (complaint of failure to comply with election requirements), until the Certification Officer or the court authorises him to dispose of the papers [or copy].

[(3A) The conditions referred to in subsection (3)(aa) are—

(a) that a request that the scrutineer inspect the register or examine the copy is made to him during the appropriate period by a member of the trade union or candidate who suspects that the register is not, or at the relevant date was not, accurate and up-to-date, and

(b) that the scrutineer does not consider that the suspicion of the member or candidate is ill-founded.

(3B) In subsection (3A) "the appropriate period" means the period—

(a) beginning with the first day on which a person may become a candidate in the election or, if later, the day on which the scrutineer is appointed, and

(b) ending with the day before the day on which the scrutineer makes his report to the trade union.

(3C) The duty of confidentiality as respects the register is incorporated in the scrutineer's appointment.]

(4) The trade union shall ensure that nothing in the terms of the scrutineer's appointment (including any additional functions specified in the appointment) is such as to make it reasonable for any person to call the scrutineer's independence in relation to the union into question.

(5) The trade union shall, before the scrutineer begins to carry out his functions, either—

(a) send a notice stating the name of the scrutineer to every member of the union to whom it is reasonably practicable to send such a notice, or

(b) take all such other steps for notifying members of the name of the scrutineer as it is the practice of the union to take when matters of general interest to all its members need to be brought to their attention.

[(5A) The trade union shall—

(a) supply to the scrutineer as soon as is reasonably practicable after the relevant date a copy of the register of names and addresses of its members as at that date, and

(b) comply with any request made by the scrutineer to inspect the register.

(5B) Where the register is kept by means of a computer the duty imposed on the trade union by subsection (5A)(a) is either to supply a legible printed copy or (if the scrutineer prefers) to supply a copy of the computer data and allow the scrutineer use of the computer to read it at any time during the period when he is required to retain custody of the copy.]

(6) The trade union shall ensure that the scrutineer duly carries out his functions and that there is no interference with his carrying out of those functions which would make it reasonable for any person to call the scrutineer's independence in relation to the union into question.

(7) The trade union shall comply with all reasonable requests made by the scrutineer for the purposes of, or in connection with, the carrying out of his functions.

[(8) In this section "the relevant date" means—

(a) where the trade union has rules determining who is entitled to vote in the election by reference to membership on a particular date, that date, and

(b) otherwise, the date, or the last date, on which voting papers are distributed for the purposes of the election.]

**NOTES**

Sub-s (3): words in square brackets in para (a) substituted, and para (aa) and the words in square brackets in para (d) inserted, by the Trade Union Reform and Employment Rights Act 1993, ss 1(1)(a), (b), 49(2), Sch 8, para 46.

Sub-ss (3A)–(3C), (5A), (5B), (8): inserted and added respectively by the Trade Union Reform and Employment Rights Act 1993, s 1(1)(c)–(e).

Orders: the Trade Union Ballots and Elections (Independent Scrutineer Qualifications) Order 1993, SI 1993/1909 at **[2.135]**; the Trade Union Ballots and Elections (Independent Scrutineer Qualifications) (Amendment) Order 2010, SI 2010/436.

**[1.301]**
## 50  Entitlement to vote
(1)   Subject to the provisions of this section, entitlement to vote shall be accorded equally to all members of the trade union.

(2)   The rules of the union may exclude entitlement to vote in the case of all members belonging to one of the following classes, or to a class falling within one of the following—
- (a)   members who are not in employment;
- (b)   members who are in arrears in respect of any subscription or contribution due to the union;
- (c)   members who are apprentices, trainees or students or new members of the union.

(3)   The rules of the union may restrict entitlement to vote to members who fall within—
- (a)   a class determined by reference to a trade or occupation,
- (b)   a class determined by reference to a geographical area, or
- (c)   a class which is by virtue of the rules of the union treated as a separate section within the union,

or to members who fall within a class determined by reference to any combination of the factors mentioned in paragraphs (a), (b) and (c).

The reference in paragraph (c) to a section of a trade union includes a part of the union which is itself a trade union.

(4)   Entitlement may not be restricted in accordance with subsection (3) if the effect is that any member of the union is denied entitlement to vote at all elections held for the purposes of this Chapter otherwise than by virtue of belonging to a class excluded in accordance with subsection (2).

**[1.302]**
## 51  Voting
(1)   The method of voting must be by the marking of a voting paper by the person voting.

(2)   Each voting paper must—
- (a)   state the name of the independent scrutineer and clearly specify the address to which, and the date by which, it is to be returned,
- (b)   be given one of a series of consecutive whole numbers every one of which is used in giving a different number in that series to each voting paper printed or otherwise produced for the purposes of the election, and
- (c)   be marked with its number.

(3)   Every person who is entitled to vote at the election must—
- (a)   be allowed to vote without interference from, or constraint imposed by, the union or any of its members, officials or employees, and
- (b)   so far as is reasonably practicable, be enabled to do so without incurring any direct cost to himself.

(4)   So far as is reasonably practicable, every person who is entitled to vote at the election must—
- (a)   have sent to him by post, at his home address or another address which he has requested the trade union in writing to treat as his postal address, a voting paper which either lists the candidates at the election or is accompanied by a separate list of those candidates; and
- (b)   be given a convenient opportunity to vote by post.

(5)   The ballot shall be conducted so as to secure that—
- (a)   so far as is reasonably practicable, those voting do so in secret, and
- (b)   the votes given at the election are fairly and accurately counted.

For the purposes of paragraph (b) an inaccuracy in counting shall be disregarded if it is accidental and on a scale which could not affect the result of the election.

(6)   The ballot shall be so conducted as to secure that the result of the election is determined solely by counting the number of votes cast directly for each candidate.

(7)   Nothing in subsection (6) shall be taken to prevent the system of voting used for the election being the single transferable vote, that is, a vote capable of being given so as to indicate the voter's order of preference for the candidates and of being transferred to the next choice—
- (a)   when it is not required to give a prior choice the necessary quota of votes, or
- (b)   when, owing to the deficiency in the number of votes given for a prior choice, that choice is eliminated from the list of candidates.

**[1.303]**
**[51A Counting of votes etc by independent person**
(1)   The trade union shall ensure that—
  (a)   the storage and distribution of the voting papers for the purposes of the election, and
  (b)   the counting of the votes cast in the election,
are undertaken by one or more independent persons appointed by the union.
(2)   A person is an independent person in relation to an election if—
  (a)   he is the scrutineer, or
  (b)   he is a person other than the scrutineer and the trade union has no grounds for believing either that he will carry out any functions conferred on him in relation to the election otherwise than competently or that his independence in relation to the union, or in relation to the election, might reasonably be called into question.
(3)   An appointment under this section shall require the person appointed to carry out his functions so as to minimise the risk of any contravention of requirements imposed by or under any enactment or the occurrence of any unfairness or malpractice.
(4)   The duty of confidentiality as respects the register is incorporated in an appointment under this section.
(5)   Where the person appointed to undertake the counting of votes is not the scrutineer, his appointment shall require him to send the voting papers back to the scrutineer as soon as reasonably practicable after the counting has been completed.
(6)   The trade union—
  (a)   shall ensure that nothing in the terms of an appointment under this section is such as to make it reasonable for any person to call into question the independence of the person appointed in relation to the union,
  (b)   shall ensure that a person appointed under this section duly carries out his functions and that there is no interference with his carrying out of those functions which would make it reasonable for any person to call into question the independence of the person appointed in relation to the union, and
  (c)   shall comply with all reasonable requests made by a person appointed under this section for the purposes of, or in connection with, the carrying out of his functions.]

**NOTES**
Inserted by the Trade Union Reform and Employment Rights Act 1993, s 2(1).

**[1.304]**
**52   Scrutineer's report**
(1)   The scrutineer's report on the election shall state—
  (a)   the number of voting papers distributed for the purposes of the election,
  (b)   the number of voting papers returned to the scrutineer,
  (c)   the number of valid votes cast in the election for each candidate,  . . .
  (d)   the number of spoiled or otherwise invalid voting papers returned[, and
  (e)   the name of the person (or of each of the persons) appointed under section 51A or, if no person was so appointed, that fact.]
(2)   The report shall also state whether the scrutineer is satisfied—
  (a)   that there are no reasonable grounds for believing that there was any contravention of a requirement imposed by or under any enactment in relation to the election,
  (b)   that the arrangements made [(whether by him or any other person)] with respect to the production, storage, distribution, return or other handling of the voting papers used in the election, and the arrangements for the counting of the votes, included all such security arrangements as were reasonably practicable for the purpose of minimising the risk that any unfairness or malpractice might occur, and
  (c)   that he has been able to carry out his functions without such interference as would make it reasonable for any person to call his independence in relation to the union into question;
and if he is not satisfied as to any of those matters, the report shall give particulars of his reasons for not being satisfied as to that matter.
[(2A)   The report shall also state—
  (a)   whether the scrutineer—
    (i)   has inspected the register of names and addresses of the members of the trade union, or
    (ii)   has examined the copy of the register as at the relevant date which is supplied to him in accordance with section 49(5A)(a),
  (b)   if he has, whether in the case of each inspection or examination he was acting on a request by a member of the trade union or candidate or at his own instance,
  (c)   whether he declined to act on any such request, and
  (d)   whether any inspection of the register, or any examination of the copy of the register, has revealed any matter which he considers should be drawn to the attention of the trade union in order to assist it in securing that the register is accurate and up-to-date,

but shall not state the name of any member or candidate who has requested such an inspection or examination.]

[(2B)   Where one or more persons other than the scrutineer are appointed under section 51A, the statement included in the scrutineer's report in accordance with subsection (2)(b) shall also indicate—

   (a)   whether he is satisfied with the performance of the person, or each of the persons, so appointed, and

   (b)   if he is not satisfied with the performance of the person, or any of them, particulars of his reasons for not being so satisfied.]

(3)   The trade union shall not publish the result of the election until it has received the scrutineer's report.

(4)   The trade union shall within the period of three months after it receives the report either—

   (a)   send a copy of the report to every member of the union to whom it is reasonably practicable to send such a copy; or

   (b)   take all such other steps for notifying the contents of the report to the members of the union (whether by publishing the report or otherwise) as it is the practice of the union to take when matters of general interest to all its members need to be brought to their attention.

(5)   Any such copy or notification shall be accompanied by a statement that the union will, on request, supply any member of the union with a copy of the report, either free of charge or on payment of such reasonable fee as may be specified in the notification.

(6)   The trade union shall so supply any member of the union who makes such a request and pays the fee (if any) notified to him.

**NOTES**

   Sub-s (1): word omitted from para (c) repealed, and para (e) and the word immediately preceding it added, by the Trade Union Reform and Employment Rights Act 1993, ss 2(2)(a), 51, Sch 10.

   Sub-s (2): words in square brackets in para (b) inserted by the Trade Union Reform and Employment Rights Act 1993, s 2(2)(b).

   Sub-ss (2A), (2B): inserted by the Trade Union Reform and Employment Rights Act 1993, ss 1(2), 2(2)(c).

**[1.305]**
**53   Uncontested elections**
Nothing in this Chapter shall be taken to require a ballot to be held at an uncontested election.

*Remedy for failure to comply with requirements*

**[1.306]**
**54   Remedy for failure to comply with requirements: general**
(1)   The remedy for a failure on the part of a trade union to comply with the requirements of this Chapter is by way of application under section 55 (to the Certification Officer) or section 56 (to the court).

   . . .

(2)   An application under those sections may be made—

   (a)   by a person who is a member of the trade union (provided, where the election has been held, he was also a member at the time when it was held), or

   (b)   by a person who is or was a candidate at the election;

and the references in those sections to a person having a sufficient interest are to such a person.

(3)   [Where an election has been held, no application under those sections with respect to that election] may be made after the end of the period of one year beginning with the day on which the union announced the result of the election.

**NOTES**

   Sub-s (1): words omitted repealed by the Employment Relations Act 1999, ss 29, 44, Sch 6, paras 1, 9, Sch 9(7).

   Sub-s (3): words in square brackets substituted by the Employment Relations Act 2004, s 57(1), Sch 1, para 5.

**[1.307]**
**55   Application to Certification Officer**
(1)   A person having a sufficient interest (see section 54(2)) who claims that a trade union has failed to comply with any of the requirements of this Chapter may apply to the Certification Officer for a declaration to that effect.

(2)   On an application being made to him, the Certification Officer shall—

   (a)   make such enquiries as he thinks fit, and

   (b)   . . .   give the applicant and the trade union an opportunity to be heard,

and may make or refuse the declaration asked for.

(3)   If he makes a declaration he shall specify in it the provisions with which the trade union has failed to comply.

(4)   Where he makes a declaration and is satisfied that steps have been taken by the union with a view to remedying the declared failure, or securing that a failure of the same or any similar kind does not occur in future, or that the union has agreed to take such steps, he shall specify those steps in the declaration.

(5)   Whether he makes or refuses a declaration, he shall give reasons for his decision in writing; and the reasons may be accompanied by written observations on any matter arising from, or connected with, the proceedings.

[(5A)   Where the Certification Officer makes a declaration he shall also, unless he considers that to do so would be inappropriate, make an enforcement order, that is, an order imposing on the union one or more of the following requirements—

(a)   to secure the holding of an election in accordance with the order;

(b)   to take such other steps to remedy the declared failure as may be specified in the order;

(c)   to abstain from such acts as may be so specified with a view to securing that a failure of the same or a similar kind does not occur in future.

The Certification Officer shall in an order imposing any such requirement as is mentioned in paragraph (a) or (b) specify the period within which the union is to comply with the requirements of the order.

(5B)   Where the Certification Officer makes an order requiring the union to hold a fresh election, he shall (unless he considers that it would be inappropriate to do so in the particular circumstances of the case) require the election to be conducted in accordance with the requirements of this Chapter and such other provisions as may be made by the order.

(5C)   Where an enforcement order has been made—

(a)   any person who is a member of the union and was a member at the time the order was made, or

(b)   any person who is or was a candidate in the election in question,

is entitled to enforce obedience to the order as if he had made the application on which the order was made.]

(6)   In exercising his functions under this section the Certification Officer shall ensure that, so far as is reasonably practicable, an application made to him is determined within six months of being made.

(7)   Where he requests a person to furnish information to him in connection with enquiries made by him under this section, he shall specify the date by which that information is to be furnished and, unless he considers that it would be inappropriate to do so, shall proceed with his determination of the application notwithstanding that the information has not been furnished to him by the specified date.

[(8)   A declaration made by the Certification Officer under this section may be relied on as if it were a declaration made by the court.

(9)   An enforcement order made by the Certification Officer under this section may be enforced in the same way as an order of the court.

(10)   The following paragraphs have effect if a person applies under section 56 in relation to an alleged failure—

(a)   that person may not apply under this section in relation to that failure;

(b)   on an application by a different person under this section in relation to that failure, the Certification Officer shall have due regard to any declaration, order, observations or reasons made or given by the court regarding that failure and brought to the Certification Officer's notice.]

**NOTES**

Sub-s (2): words omitted from para (b) repealed by the Employment Relations Act 1999, ss 29, 44, Sch 6, paras 1, 10(1), (2), Sch 9(7).

Sub-ss (5A)–(5C), (8)–(10): inserted and added respectively by the Employment Relations Act 1999, s 29, Sch 6, paras 1, 10(1), (3), (4).

[1.308]
### 56   Application to court

(1)   A person having a sufficient interest (see section 54(2)) who claims that a trade union has failed to comply with any of the requirements of this Chapter may apply to the court for a declaration to that effect.

(2)   . . .

(3)   If the court makes the declaration asked for, it shall specify in the declaration the provisions with which the trade union has failed to comply.

(4)   Where the court makes a declaration it shall also, unless it considers that to do so would be inappropriate, make an enforcement order, that is, an order imposing on the union one or more of the following requirements—

(a)   to secure the holding of an election in accordance with the order;

(b)   to take such other steps to remedy the declared failure as may be specified in the order;

(c)   to abstain from such acts as may be so specified with a view to securing that a failure of the same or a similar kind does not occur in future.

The court shall in an order imposing any such requirement as is mentioned in paragraph (a) or (b) specify the period within which the union is to comply with the requirements of the order.

(5)   Where the court makes an order requiring the union to hold a fresh election, the court shall (unless it considers that it would be inappropriate to do so in the particular circumstances of the case) require the election to be conducted in accordance with the requirements of this Chapter and such other provisions as may be made by the order.

(6)   Where an enforcement order has been made—

(a)    any person who is a member of the union and was a member at the time the order was made, or

(b)    any person who is or was a candidate in the election in question,

is entitled to enforce obedience to the order as if he had made the application on which the order was made.

(7)   Without prejudice to any other power of the court, the court may on an application under this section grant such interlocutory relief (in Scotland, such interim order) as it considers appropriate.

[(8)   The following paragraphs have effect if a person applies under section 55 in relation to an alleged failure—

(a)    that person may not apply under this section in relation to that failure;

(b)    on an application by a different person under this section in relation to that failure, the court shall have due regard to any declaration, order, observations or reasons made or given by the Certification Officer regarding that failure and brought to the court's notice.]

**NOTES**

Sub-s (2): repealed by the Employment Relations Act 1999, ss 29, 44, Sch 6, paras 1, 11(1), (2), Sch 9(7).
Sub-s (8): added by the Employment Relations Act 1999, s 29, Sch 6, paras 1, 11(1), (3).

**[1.309]**
**[56A   Appeals from Certification Officer**
An appeal lies to the Employment Appeal Tribunal on any question of law arising in proceedings before or arising from any decision of the Certification Officer under section 55.]

**NOTES**

Inserted by the Employment Relations Act 1999, s 29, Sch 6, paras 1, 12.

*Supplementary*

**[1.310]**
**57   Exemption of newly-formed trade unions, &c**
(1)   The provisions of this Chapter do not apply to a trade union until more than one year has elapsed since its formation (by amalgamation or otherwise).

For this purpose the date of formation of a trade union formed otherwise than by amalgamation shall be taken to be the date on which the first members of the executive of the union are first appointed or elected.

(2)   Where a trade union is formed by amalgamation, the provisions of this Chapter do not apply in relation to a person who—

(a)    by virtue of an election held a position to which this Chapter applies in one of the amalgamating unions immediately before the amalgamation, and

(b)    becomes the holder of a position to which this Chapter applies in the amalgamated union in accordance with the instrument of transfer,

until after the end of the period for which he would have been entitled in accordance with this Chapter to continue to hold the first-mentioned position without being re-elected.

(3)   Where a trade union transfers its engagements to another trade union, the provisions of this Chapter do not apply in relation to a person who—

(a)    held a position to which this Chapter applies in the transferring union immediately before the transfer, and

(b)    becomes the holder of a position to which this Chapter applies in the transferee union in accordance with the instrument of transfer,

until after the end of the period of one year beginning with the date of the transfer or, if he held the first-mentioned position by virtue of an election, any longer period for which he would have been entitled in accordance with this Chapter to continue to hold that position without being re-elected.

**[1.311]**
**58   Exemption of certain persons nearing retirement**
(1)   Section 46(1)(b) (requirement of re-election) does not apply to a person holding a position to which this Chapter applies if the following conditions are satisfied.

(2)   The conditions are that—

(a)    he holds the position by virtue of having been elected at an election in relation to which the requirements of this Chapter were satisfied,

(b)    he is a full-time employee of the union by virtue of the position,

(c)    he will reach retirement age within five years,

(d) he is entitled under the rules of the union to continue as the holder of the position until retirement age without standing for re-election,

(e) he has been a full-time employee of the union for a period (which need not be continuous) of at least ten years, and

(f) the period between the day on which the election referred to in paragraph (a) took place and the day immediately preceding that on which paragraph (c) is first satisfied does not exceed five years.

(3) For the purposes of this section "retirement age", in relation to any person, means the earlier of—

(a) the age fixed by, or in accordance with, the rules of the union for him to retire from the position in question, or

(b) the age which is for the time being pensionable age [within the meaning given by the rules in paragraph 1 of Schedule 4 to the Pensions Act 1995].

**NOTES**

Sub-s (3): words in square brackets substituted by the Pensions Act 1995, s 126(c), Sch 4, Pt III, para 15.

**[1.312]**
**59 Period for giving effect to election**
Where a person holds a position to which this Chapter applies immediately before an election at which he is not re-elected to that position, nothing in this Chapter shall be taken to require the union to prevent him from continuing to hold that position for such period (not exceeding six months) as may reasonably be required for effect to be given to the result of the election.

**[1.313]**
**60 Overseas members**
(1) A trade union which has overseas members may choose whether or not to accord any of those members entitlement to vote at an election for a position to which this Chapter applies.

(2) An "overseas member" means a member of the union (other than a merchant seaman or offshore worker) who is outside Great Britain throughout the period during which votes may be cast.

For this purpose—

"merchant seaman" means a person whose employment, or the greater part of it, is carried out on board sea-going ships; and

"offshore worker" means a person in offshore employment, other than one who is in such employment in an area where the law of Northern Ireland applies.

(3) Where the union chooses to accord an overseas member entitlement to vote, section 51 (requirements as to voting) applies in relation to him; but nothing in section 47 (candidates) or section 50 (entitlement to vote) applies in relation to an overseas member or in relation to a vote cast by such a member.

**[1.314]**
**61 Other supplementary provisions**
(1) For the purposes of this Chapter the date on which a contested election is held shall be taken, in the case of an election in which votes may be cast on more than one day, to be the last of those days.

(2) Nothing in this Chapter affects the validity of anything done by a person holding a position to which this Chapter applies.

## CHAPTER V
## RIGHTS OF TRADE UNION MEMBERS

*Right to a ballot before industrial action*

**[1.315]**
**62 Right to ballot before industrial action**
(1) A member of a trade union who claims that members of the union, including himself, are likely to be or have been induced by the union to take part or to continue to take part in industrial action which does not have the support of a ballot may apply to the court for an order under this section.

[In this section "the relevant time" means the time when the application is made.]

(2) For this purpose industrial action shall be regarded as having the support of a ballot only if—

[(a) the union has held a ballot in respect of the action—

(i) in relation to which the requirements of section 226B so far as applicable before and during the holding of the ballot were satisfied,

(ii) in relation to which the requirements of sections 227 to 231 were satisfied, and

(iii) in which the majority voting in the ballot answered "Yes" to the question applicable in accordance with section 229(2) to industrial action of the kind which the applicant has been or is likely to be induced to take part in;

(b)    such of the requirements of the following sections as have fallen to be satisfied at the relevant time have been satisfied, namely—
    (i)    section 226B so far as applicable after the holding of the ballot, and
    (ii)   section 231B;  . . .
[(bb) section 232A does not prevent the industrial action from being regarded as having the support of the ballot; and]
(c)    the requirements of section 233 (calling of industrial action with support of ballot) are satisfied.
Any reference in this subsection to a requirement of a provision which is disapplied or modified by section 232 has effect subject to that section.]
(3)    Where on an application under this section the court is satisfied that the claim is well-founded, it shall make such order as it considers appropriate for requiring the union to take steps for ensuring—
(a)    that there is no, or no further, inducement of members of the union to take part or to continue to take part in the industrial action to which the application relates, and
(b)    that no member engages in conduct after the making of the order by virtue of having been induced before the making of the order to take part or continue to take part in the action.
(4)    Without prejudice to any other power of the court, the court may on an application under this section grant such interlocutory relief (in Scotland, such interim order) as it considers appropriate.
(5)    For the purposes of this section an act shall be taken to be done by a trade union if it is authorised or endorsed by the union; and the provisions of section 20(2) to (4) apply for the purpose of determining whether an act is to be taken to be so authorised or endorsed.
Those provisions also apply in relation to proceedings for failure to comply with an order under this section as they apply in relation to the original proceedings.
(6)    In this section—
"inducement" includes an inducement which is or would be ineffective, whether because of the member's unwillingness to be influenced by it or for any other reason; and
"industrial action" means a strike or other industrial action by persons employed under contracts of employment.
(7)    Where a person holds any office or employment under the Crown on terms which do not constitute a contract of employment between that person and the Crown, those terms shall nevertheless be deemed to constitute such a contract for the purposes of this section.
(8)    References in this section to a contract of employment include any contract under which one person personally does work or performs services for another; and related expressions shall be construed accordingly.
(9)    Nothing in this section shall be construed as requiring a trade union to hold separate ballots for the purposes of this section and sections 226 to 234 (requirement of ballot before action by trade union).

**NOTES**
Sub-s (1): words in square brackets added by the Trade Union Reform and Employment Rights Act 1993, s 49(2), Sch 8, para 47(a).
Sub-s (2): paras (a), (b), (c) substituted by the Trade Union Reform and Employment Rights Act 1993, s 49(2), Sch 8, para 47(b); word omitted from para (b) repealed, and para (bb) inserted, by the Employment Relations Act 2004, ss 24(2), 57(2), Sch 2.

*Right not to be denied access to the courts*

**[1.316]**
**63    Right not to be denied access to the courts**
(1)    This section applies where a matter is under the rules of a trade union required or allowed to be submitted for determination or conciliation in accordance with the rules of the union, but a provision of the rules purporting to provide for that to be a person's only remedy has no effect (or would have no effect if there were one).
(2)    Notwithstanding anything in the rules of the union or in the practice of any court, if a member or former member of the union begins proceedings in a court with respect to a matter to which this section applies, then if—
(a)    he has previously made a valid application to the union for the matter to be submitted for determination or conciliation in accordance with the union's rules, and
(b)    the court proceedings are begun after the end of the period of six months beginning with the day on which the union received the application,
the rules requiring or allowing the matter to be so submitted, and the fact that any relevant steps remain to be taken under the rules, shall be regarded for all purposes as irrelevant to any question whether the court proceedings should be dismissed, stayed or sisted, or adjourned.
(3)    An application shall be deemed to be valid for the purposes of subsection (2)(a) unless the union informed the applicant, before the end of the period of 28 days beginning with the date on which the union received the application, of the respects in which the application contravened the requirements of the rules.

(4)   If the court is satisfied that any delay in the taking of relevant steps under the rules is attributable to unreasonable conduct of the person who commenced the proceedings, it may treat the period specified in subsection (2)(b) as extended by such further period as it considers appropriate.

(5)   In this section—

(a)   references to the rules of a trade union include any arbitration or other agreement entered into in pursuance of a requirement imposed by or under the rules; and

(b)   references to the relevant steps under the rules, in relation to any matter, include any steps falling to be taken in accordance with the rules for the purposes of or in connection with the determination or conciliation of the matter, or any appeal, review or reconsideration of any determination or award.

(6)   This section does not affect any enactment or rule of law by virtue of which a court would apart from this section disregard any such rules of a trade union or any such fact as is mentioned in subsection (2).

*Right not to be unjustifiably disciplined*

**[1.317]**
**64   Right not to be unjustifiably disciplined**
(1)   An individual who is or has been a member of a trade union has the right not to be unjustifiably disciplined by the union.

(2)   For this purpose an individual is "disciplined" by a trade union if a determination is made, or purportedly made, under the rules of the union or by an official of the union or a number of persons including an official that—

(a)   he should be expelled from the union or a branch or section of the union,

(b)   he should pay a sum to the union, to a branch or section of the union or to any other person;

(c)   sums tendered by him in respect of an obligation to pay subscriptions or other sums to the union, or to a branch or section of the union, should be treated as unpaid or paid for a different purpose,

(d)   he should be deprived to any extent of, or of access to, any benefits, services or facilities which would otherwise be provided or made available to him by virtue of his membership of the union, or a branch or section of the union,

(e)   another trade union, or a branch or section of it, should be encouraged or advised not to accept him as a member, or

(f)   he should be subjected to some other detriment;

and whether an individual is "unjustifiably disciplined" shall be determined in accordance with section 65.

(3)   Where a determination made in infringement of an individual's right under this section requires the payment of a sum or the performance of an obligation, no person is entitled in any proceedings to rely on that determination for the purpose of recovering the sum or enforcing the obligation.

(4)   Subject to that, the remedies for infringement of the right conferred by this section are as provided by sections 66 and 67, and not otherwise.

(5)   The right not to be unjustifiably disciplined is in addition to (and not in substitution for) any right which exists apart from this section; [and, subject to section 66(4), nothing] in this section or sections 65 to 67 affects any remedy for infringement of any such right.

**NOTES**

Sub-s (5): words in square brackets substituted by the Trade Union Reform and Employment Rights Act 1993, s 49(2), Sch 8, para 48.

Conciliation: employment tribunal proceedings and claims which could be the subject of employment tribunal proceedings arising out of a contravention, or alleged contravention, of this section are proceedings to which the Employment Tribunals Act 1996, s 18 applies; see s 18(1)(b) of that Act at **[1.706]**.

**[1.318]**
**65   Meaning of "unjustifiably disciplined"**
(1)   An individual is unjustifiably disciplined by a trade union if the actual or supposed conduct which constitutes the reason, or one of the reasons, for disciplining him is—

(a)   conduct to which this section applies, or

(b)   something which is believed by the union to amount to such conduct;

but subject to subsection (6) (cases of bad faith in relation to assertion of wrongdoing).

(2)   This section applies to conduct which consists in—

(a)   failing to participate in or support a strike or other industrial action (whether by members of the union or by others), or indicating opposition to or a lack of support for such action;

(b)   failing to contravene, for a purpose connected with such a strike or other industrial action, a requirement imposed on him by or under a contract of employment;

(c)     asserting (whether by bringing proceedings or otherwise) that the union, any official or representative of it or a trustee of its property has contravened, or is proposing to contravene, a requirement which is, or is thought to be, imposed by or under the rules of the union or any other agreement or by or under any enactment (whenever passed) or any rule of law;

(d)     encouraging or assisting a person
       (i)     to perform an obligation imposed on him by a contract of employment, . . .
       (ii)     to make or attempt to vindicate any such assertion as is mentioned in paragraph (c); . . .

(e)     contravening a requirement imposed by or in consequence of a determination which infringes the individual's or another individual's right not to be unjustifiably disciplined,

[(f)     failing to agree, or withdrawing agreement, to the making from his wages (in accordance with arrangements between his employer and the union) of deductions representing payments to the union in respect of his membership,

(g)     resigning or proposing to resign from the union or from another union, becoming or proposing to become a member of another union, refusing to become a member of another union, or being a member of another union,

(h)     working with, or proposing to work with, individuals who are not members of the union or who are or are not members of another union,

(i)     working for, or proposing to work for, an employer who employs or who has employed individuals who are not members of the union or who are or are not members of another union, or

(j)     requiring the union to do an act which the union is, by any provision of this Act, required to do on the requisition of a member].

(3)     This section applies to conduct which involves . . . the Certification Officer being consulted or asked to provide advice or assistance with respect to any matter whatever, or which involves any person being consulted or asked to provide advice or assistance with respect to a matter which forms, or might form, the subject-matter of any such assertion as is mentioned in subsection (2)(c) above.

(4)     This section also applies to conduct which consists in proposing to engage in, or doing anything preparatory or incidental to, conduct falling within subsection (2) or (3).

(5)     This section does not apply to an act, omission or statement comprised in conduct falling within subsection (2), (3) or (4) above if it is shown that the act, omission or statement is one in respect of which individuals would be disciplined by the union irrespective of whether their acts, omissions or statements were in connection with conduct within subsection (2) or (3) above.

(6)     An individual is not unjustifiably disciplined if it is shown—
    (a)     that the reason for disciplining him, or one of them, is that he made such an assertion as is mentioned in subsection (2)(c), or encouraged or assisted another person to make or attempt to vindicate such an assertion,
    (b)     that the assertion was false, and
    (c)     that he made the assertion, or encouraged or assisted another person to make or attempt to vindicate it, in the belief that it was false or otherwise in bad faith,
and that there was no other reason for disciplining him or that the only other reasons were reasons in respect of which he does not fall to be treated as unjustifiably disciplined.

(7)     In this section—
"conduct" includes statements, acts and omissions;
"contract of employment", in relation to an individual, includes any agreement between that individual and a person for whom he works or normally works[, "employer" includes such a person and related expressions shall be construed accordingly;] . . .
"representative", in relation to a union, means a person acting or purporting to act—
    (a)     in his capacity as a member of the union, or
    (b)     on the instructions or advice of a person acting or purporting to act in that capacity or in the capacity of an official of the union;
["require" (on the part of an individual) includes request or apply for, and "requisition" shall be construed accordingly; and
"wages" shall be construed in accordance with the definitions of "contract of employment", "employer" and related expressions.]

(8)     Where a person holds any office or employment under the Crown on terms which do not constitute a contract of employment between him and the Crown, those terms shall nevertheless be deemed to constitute such a contract for the purposes of this section.

**NOTES**

Sub-s (2): word omitted from para (d) repealed, and paras (f)–(j) added, by the Trade Union Reform and Employment Rights Act 1993, ss 16(1), 51, Sch 10.

Sub-s (3): words omitted repealed by the Employment Relations Act 1999, s 44, Sch 9(6).

Sub-s (7): in definition "contract of employment", words in square brackets added, and word omitted repealed, and definitions "require" and "wages" added, by the Trade Union Reform and Employment Rights Act 1993, ss 16(2), 49(2), 51, Sch 8, para 49, Sch 10.

**[1.319]**
**66 Complaint of infringement of right**
(1)   An individual who claims that he has been unjustifiably disciplined by a trade union may present a complaint against the union to an [employment tribunal].
(2)   The tribunal shall not entertain such a complaint unless it is presented—
   (a)   before the end of the period of three months beginning with the date of the making of the determination claimed to infringe the right, or
   (b)   where the tribunal is satisfied—
      (i)   that it was not reasonably practicable for the complaint to be presented before the end of that period, or
      (ii)   that any delay in making the complaint is wholly or partly attributable to a reasonable attempt to appeal against the determination or to have it reconsidered or reviewed,
      within such further period as the tribunal considers reasonable.
[(2A)   Section 292A (extension of time limits to facilitate conciliation before institution of proceedings) applies for the purposes of subsection (2)(a).]
(3)   Where the tribunal finds the complaint well-founded, it shall make a declaration to that effect.
[(4)   Where a complaint relating to an expulsion which is presented under this section is declared to be well-founded, no complaint in respect of the expulsion shall be presented or proceeded with under section 174 (right not to be excluded or expelled from trade union).]

**NOTES**
Sub-s (1): words in square brackets substituted by the Employment Rights (Dispute Resolution) Act 1998, s 1(2)(a).
Sub-s (2A): inserted by the Enterprise and Regulatory Reform Act 2013, s 8, Sch 2, paras 1, 2, as from a day to be appointed.
Sub-s (4): substituted by the Trade Union Reform and Employment Rights Act 1993, s 49(2), Sch 8, para 50.

**[1.320]**
**67 Further remedies for infringement of right**
(1)   An individual whose complaint under section 66 has been declared to be well-founded may make an application [to an employment tribunal] for one or both of the following—
   (a)   an award of compensation to be paid to him by the union;
   (b)   an order that the union pay him an amount equal to any sum which he has paid in pursuance of any such determination as is mentioned in section 64(2)(b).
(2)   . . .
(3)   An application under this section shall not be entertained if made before the end of the period of four weeks beginning with the date of the declaration or after the end of the period of six months beginning with that date.
(4)   . . .
(5)   The amount of compensation awarded shall, subject to the following provisions, be such as the  . . .  [employment tribunal] considers just and equitable in all the circumstances.
(6)   In determining the amount of compensation to be awarded, the same rule shall be applied concerning the duty of a person to mitigate his loss as applies to damages recoverable under the common law in England and Wales or Scotland.
(7)   Where the  . . .  [employment tribunal] finds that the infringement complained of was to any extent caused or contributed to by the action of the applicant, it shall reduce the amount of the compensation by such proportion as it considers just and equitable having regard to that finding.
(8)   The amount of compensation [calculated in accordance with subsections (5) to (7)] shall not exceed the aggregate of—
   (a)   an amount equal to 30 times the limit for the time being imposed by [section 227(1)(a) of the Employment Rights Act 1996] (maximum amount of a week's pay for basic award in unfair dismissal cases), and
   (b)   an amount equal to the limit for the time being imposed by [section 124(1)] of that Act (maximum compensatory award in such cases);
. . .
[(8A)   If on the date on which the application was made—
   (a)   the determination infringing the applicant's right not to be unjustifiably disciplined has not been revoked, or
   (b)   the union has failed to take all the steps necessary for securing the reversal of anything done for the purpose of giving effect to the determination,
the amount of compensation shall be not less than the amount for the time being specified in section 176(6A).]
(9)   . . .

**NOTES**
Sub-s (1): words in square brackets inserted by the Employment Relations Act 2004, s 34(1), (2).
Sub-ss (2), (4): repealed by the Employment Relations Act 2004, ss 34(1), (3), 57(2), Sch 2.
Sub-ss (5), (7): words omitted repealed by the Employment Relations Act 2004, ss 34(1), (4), 57(2), Sch 2; words in square brackets substituted by the Employment Rights (Dispute Resolution) Act 1998, s 1(2)(a).

Sub-s (8): words in first pair of square brackets substituted by the Trade Union Reform and Employment Rights Act 1993, s 49(2), Sch 8, para 51(a); words in second and third pairs of square brackets substituted by the Employment Rights Act 1996, s 240, Sch 1, para 56(1), (2); words omitted repealed by the Employment Relations Act 2004, ss 34(1), (5), 57(2), Sch 2.

Sub-s (8A): inserted by the Employment Relations Act 2004, s 34(1), (6).

Sub-s (9): repealed by the Trade Union Reform and Employment Rights Act 1993, ss 49(2), 51, Sch 8, para 51(b), Sch 10.

*[Right not to suffer deduction of unauthorised or excessive union subscriptions*

**[1.321]**

**[68   Right not to suffer deduction of unauthorised subscriptions**

(1)   Where arrangements ("subscription deduction arrangements") exist between the employer of a worker and a trade union relating to the making from workers' wages of deductions representing payments to the union in respect of the workers' membership of the union ("subscription deductions"), the employer shall ensure that no subscription deduction is made from wages payable to the worker on any day unless—

   (a)   the worker has authorised in writing the making from his wages of subscription deductions; and

   (b)   the worker has not withdrawn the authorisation.

(2)   A worker withdraws an authorisation given for the purposes of subsection (1), in relation to a subscription deduction which falls to be made from wages payable to him on any day, if a written notice withdrawing the authorisation has been received by the employer in time for it to be reasonably practicable for the employer to secure that no such deduction is made.

(3)   A worker's authorisation of the making of subscription deductions from his wages shall not give rise to any obligation on the part of the employer to the worker to maintain or continue to maintain subscription deduction arrangements.

(4)   In this section and section 68A, "employer", "wages" and "worker" have the same meanings as in the Employment Rights Act 1996.]]

**NOTES**

Substituted, together with the preceding heading and s 68A, for the original s 68, by the Trade Union Reform and Employment Rights Act 1993, s 15; this section was further substituted by the Deregulation (Deduction from Pay of Union Subscriptions) Order 1998, SI 1998/1529, art 2(1).

Conciliation: employment tribunal proceedings and claims which could be the subject of employment tribunal proceedings arising out of a contravention, or alleged contravention, of this section are proceedings to which the Employment Tribunals Act 1996, s 18 applies; see s 18(1)(b) of that Act at **[1.706]**.

The rights conferred by this section are "relevant statutory rights" for the purposes of the Employment Rights Act 1996, s 104 (dismissal on grounds of assertion of statutory right); see s 104(4)(c) of that Act at **[1.907]**.

**[1.322]**

**[68A   Complaint of infringement of rights**

(1)   A worker may present a complaint to an [employment tribunal] that his employer has made a deduction from his wages in contravention of section 68—

   (a)   within the period of three months beginning with the date of the payment of the wages from which the deduction, or (if the complaint relates to more than one deduction) the last of the deductions, was made, or

   (b)   where the tribunal is satisfied that it was not reasonably practicable for the complaint to be presented within that period, within such further period as the tribunal considers reasonable.

[(1A)   Section 292A (extension of time limits to facilitate conciliation before institution of proceedings) applies for the purposes of subsection (1)(a).]

[(2)   Where a tribunal finds that a complaint under this section is well founded, it shall make a declaration to that effect and shall order the employer to pay to the worker the whole amount of the deduction, less any such part of the amount as has already been paid to the worker by the employer.]

(3)   Where the making of a deduction from the wages of a worker both contravenes section 68(1) and involves one or more of the contraventions specified in subsection (4) of this section, the aggregate amount which may be ordered by an [employment tribunal] or court (whether on the same occasion or on different occasions) to be paid in respect of the contraventions shall not exceed the amount, or (where different amounts may be ordered to be paid in respect of different contraventions) the greatest amount, which may be ordered to be paid in respect of any one of them.

(4)   The contraventions referred to in subsection (3) are—

   (a)   a contravention of the requirement not to make a deduction without having given the particulars required by section 8 (itemised pay statements) or 9(1) (standing statements of fixed deductions) of [the Employment Rights Act 1996],

   (b)   a contravention of [section 13 of that Act] (requirement not to make unauthorised deductions), and

   (c)   a contravention of section 86(1) or 90(1) of this Act (requirements not to make deductions of political fund contributions in certain circumstances).]

*Right to terminate membership of union*

**[1.323]**
## 69   Right to terminate membership of union
In every contract of membership of a trade union, whether made before or after the passing of this Act, a term conferring a right on the member, on giving reasonable notice and complying with any reasonable conditions, to terminate his membership of the union shall be implied.

*Supplementary*

**[1.324]**
## 70   Membership of constituent or affiliated organisation
In this Chapter "member", in relation to a trade union consisting wholly or partly of, or of representatives of, constituent or affiliated organisations, includes a member of any of the constituent or affiliated organisations.

[CHAPTER VA
COLLECTIVE BARGAINING: RECOGNITION

**[1.325]**
## 70A   Recognition of trade unions
Schedule A1 shall have effect.]

**[1.326]**
## [70B   Training
(1)   This section applies where—
  (a)   a trade union is recognised, in accordance with Schedule A1, as entitled to conduct collective bargaining on behalf of a bargaining unit (within the meaning of Part I of that Schedule), and
  (b)   a method for the conduct of collective bargaining is specified by the Central Arbitration Committee under paragraph 31(3) of that Schedule (and is not the subject of an agreement under paragraph 31(5)(a) or (b)).
(2)   The employer must from time to time invite the trade union to send representatives to a meeting for the purpose of—
  (a)   consulting about the employer's policy on training for workers within the bargaining unit,
  (b)   consulting about his plans for training for those workers during the period of six months starting with the day of the meeting, and
  (c)   reporting about training provided for those workers since the previous meeting.
(3)   The date set for a meeting under subsection (2) must not be later than—
  (a)   in the case of a first meeting, the end of the period of six months starting with the day on which this section first applies in relation to a bargaining unit, and
  (b)   in the case of each subsequent meeting, the end of the period of six months starting with the day of the previous meeting.
(4)   The employer shall, before the period of two weeks ending with the date of a meeting, provide to the trade union any information—
  (a)   without which the union's representatives would be to a material extent impeded in participating in the meeting, and
  (b)   which it would be in accordance with good industrial relations practice to disclose for the purposes of the meeting.
[(4A)   If the information mentioned in subjection (4) includes information relating to the employment situation the employer must (so far as not required by subsection (4)) also provide at the same time to the trade union the following information—
  (a)   the number of agency workers working temporarily for and under the supervision and direction of the employer,
  (b)   the parts of the employer's undertaking in which those agency workers are working, and
  (c)   the type of work those agency workers are carrying out.]
(5)   Section 182(1) shall apply in relation to the provision of information under subsection (4) [or (4A)] as it applies in relation to the disclosure of information under section 181.

(6)　The employer shall take account of any written representations about matters raised at a meeting which he receives from the trade union within the period of four weeks starting with the date of the meeting.

(7)　Where more than one trade union is recognised as entitled to conduct collective bargaining on behalf of a bargaining unit, a reference in this section to "the trade union" is a reference to each trade union.

(8)　Where at a meeting under this section (Meeting 1) an employer indicates his intention to convene a subsequent meeting (Meeting 2) before the expiry of the period of six months beginning with the date of Meeting 1, for the reference to a period of six months in subsection (2)(b) there shall be substituted a reference to the expected period between Meeting 1 and Meeting 2.

(9)　The Secretary of State may by order made by statutory instrument amend any of subsections (2) to (6).

(10)　No order shall be made under subsection (9) unless a draft has been laid before, and approved by resolution of, each House of Parliament.]

**NOTES**

Inserted, together with s 70C, by the Employment Relations Act 1999, s 5.

Sub-s (4A): inserted by the Agency Workers Regulations 2010, SI 2010/93, reg 25, Sch 2, Pt 1, paras 1, 2(a), as from 1 October 2011.

Sub-s (5): words in square brackets inserted by SI 2010/93, reg 25, Sch 2, Pt 1, paras 1, 2(b), as from 1 October 2011.

Conciliation: employment tribunal proceedings and claims which could be the subject of employment tribunal proceedings under or arising out of a contravention, or alleged contravention, of this section are proceedings to which the Employment Tribunals Act 1996, s 18 applies; see s 18(1)(f) of that Act at **[1.706]**, and the Employment Tribunals Act 1996 (Application of Conciliation Provisions) Order 2000, SI 2000/1337 (made under s 18(8)(a), (b)).

Orders: as of 6 April 2013 no Orders had been made under this section.

**[1.327]**
**[70C　Section 70B: complaint to employment tribunal**

(1)　A trade union may present a complaint to an employment tribunal that an employer has failed to comply with his obligations under section 70B in relation to a bargaining unit.

(2)　An employment tribunal shall not consider a complaint under this section unless it is presented—

(a)　before the end of the period of three months beginning with the date of the alleged failure, or

(b)　within such further period as the tribunal considers reasonable in a case where it is satisfied that it was not reasonably practicable for the complaint to be presented before the end of that period of three months.

[(2A)　Section 292A (extension of time limits to facilitate conciliation before institution of proceedings) applies for the purposes of subsection (2)(a).]

(3)　Where an employment tribunal finds a complaint under this section well-founded it—

(a)　shall make a declaration to that effect, and

(b)　may make an award of compensation to be paid by the employer to each person who was, at the time when the failure occurred, a member of the bargaining unit.

(4)　The amount of the award shall not, in relation to each person, exceed two weeks' pay.

(5)　For the purpose of subsection (4) a week's pay—

(a)　shall be calculated in accordance with Chapter II of Part XIV of the Employment Rights Act 1996 (taking the date of the employer's failure as the calculation date), and

(b)　shall be subject to the limit in section 227(1) of that Act.

(6)　Proceedings for enforcement of an award of compensation under this section—

(a)　may, in relation to each person to whom compensation is payable, be commenced by that person, and

(b)　may not be commenced by a trade union.]

**NOTES**

Inserted as noted to s 70B at **[1.326]**.

Sub-s (2A): inserted by the Enterprise and Regulatory Reform Act 2013, s 8, Sch 2, paras 1, 4, as from a day to be appointed.

CHAPTER VI
APPLICATION OF FUNDS FOR POLITICAL OBJECTS

*Restriction on use of funds for certain political objects*

**[1.328]**
**71　Restriction on use of funds for certain political objects**

(1)　The funds of a trade union shall not be applied in the furtherance of the political objects to which this Chapter applies unless—

(a)　there is in force in accordance with this Chapter a resolution (a "political resolution") approving the furtherance of those objects as an object of the union (see sections 73 to 81), and

  (b)  there are in force rules of the union as to—
     (i)   the making of payments in furtherance of those objects out of a separate fund, and
     (ii)  the exemption of any member of the union objecting to contribute to that fund,
     which comply with this Chapter (see sections 82, 84 and 85) and have been approved by
     the Certification Officer.

(2)  This applies whether the funds are so applied directly, or in conjunction with another trade union, association or body, or otherwise indirectly.

**[1.329]**
**72  Political objects to which restriction applies**
(1)  The political objects to which this Chapter applies are the expenditure of money—
  (a)  on any contribution to the funds of, or on the payment of expenses incurred directly or indirectly by, a political party;
  (b)  on the provision of any service or property for use by or on behalf of any political party;
  (c)  in connection with the registration of electors, the candidature of any person, the selection of any candidate or the holding of any ballot by the union in connection with any election to a political office;
  (d)  on the maintenance of any holder of a political office;
  (e)  on the holding of any conference or meeting by or on behalf of a political party or of any other meeting the main purpose of which is the transaction of business in connection with a political party;
  (f)  on the production, publication or distribution of any literature, document, film, sound recording or advertisement the main purpose of which is to persuade people to vote for a political party or candidate or to persuade them not to vote for a political party or candidate.

(2)  Where a person attends a conference or meeting as a delegate or otherwise as a participator in the proceedings, any expenditure incurred in connection with his attendance as such shall, for the purposes of subsection (1)(e), be taken to be expenditure incurred on the holding of the conference or meeting.

(3)  In determining for the purposes of subsection (1) whether a trade union has incurred expenditure of a kind mentioned in that subsection, no account shall be taken of the ordinary administrative expenses of the union.

(4)  In this section—
  "candidate" means a candidate for election to a political office and includes a prospective candidate;
  "contribution", in relation to the funds of a political party, includes any fee payable for affiliation to, or membership of, the party and any loan made to the party;
  "electors" means electors at an election to a political office;
  "film" includes any record, however made, of a sequence of visual images, which is capable of being used as a means of showing that sequence as a moving picture;
  "local authority" means a local authority within the meaning of section 270 of the Local Government Act 1972 or section 235 of the Local Government (Scotland) Act 1973; and
  "political office" means the office of member of Parliament, member of the European Parliament or member of a local authority or any position within a political party.

**[1.330]**
**[72A  Application of funds in breach of section 71**
(1)  A person who is a member of a trade union and who claims that it has applied its funds in breach of section 71 may apply to the Certification Officer for a declaration that it has done so.

(2)  On an application under this section the Certification Officer—
  (a)  shall make such enquiries as he thinks fit,
  (b)  shall give the applicant and the union an opportunity to be heard,
  (c)  shall ensure that, so far as is reasonably practicable, the application is determined within six months of being made,
  (d)  may make or refuse the declaration asked for,
  (e)  shall, whether he makes or refuses the declaration, give reasons for his decision in writing, and
  (f)  may make written observations on any matter arising from, or connected with, the proceedings.

(3)  If he makes a declaration he shall specify in it—
  (a)  the provisions of section 71 breached, and
  (b)  the amount of the funds applied in breach.

(4)  If he makes a declaration and is satisfied that the union has taken or agreed to take steps with a view to—
  (a)  remedying the declared breach, or
  (b)  securing that a breach of the same or any similar kind does not occur in future,
he shall specify those steps in making the declaration.

(5) If he makes a declaration he may make such order for remedying the breach as he thinks just under the circumstances.

(6) Where the Certification Officer requests a person to furnish information to him in connection with enquiries made by him under this section, he shall specify the date by which that information is to be furnished and, unless he considers that it would be inappropriate to do so, shall proceed with his determination of the application notwithstanding that the information has not been furnished to him by the specified date.

(7) A declaration made by the Certification Officer under this section may be relied on as if it were a declaration made by the court.

(8) Where an order has been made under this section, any person who is a member of the union and was a member at the time it was made is entitled to enforce obedience to the order as if he had made the application on which the order was made.

(9) An order made by the Certification Officer under this section may be enforced in the same way as an order of the court.

(10) If a person applies to the Certification Officer under this section in relation to an alleged breach he may not apply to the court in relation to the breach; but nothing in this subsection shall prevent such a person from exercising any right to appeal against or challenge the Certification Officer's decision on the application to him.

(11) If—

   (a) a person applies to the court in relation to an alleged breach, and

   (b) the breach is one in relation to which he could have made an application to the Certification Officer under this section,

he may not apply to the Certification Officer under this section in relation to the breach.]

**NOTES**

   Inserted by the Employment Relations Act 1999, s 29, Sch 6, paras 1, 13.

*Political resolution*

**[1.331]**
**73 Passing and effect of political resolution**

(1) A political resolution must be passed by a majority of those voting on a ballot of the members of the trade union held in accordance with this Chapter.

(2) A political resolution so passed shall take effect as if it were a rule of the union and may be rescinded in the same manner and subject to the same provisions as such a rule.

(3) If not previously rescinded, a political resolution shall cease to have effect at the end of the period of ten years beginning with the date of the ballot on which it was passed.

(4) Where before the end of that period a ballot is held on a new political resolution, then—

   (a) if the new resolution is passed, the old resolution shall be treated as rescinded, and

   (b) if it is not passed, the old resolution shall cease to have effect at the end of the period of two weeks beginning with the date of the ballot.

**[1.332]**
**74 Approval of political ballot rules**

(1) A ballot on a political resolution must be held in accordance with rules of the trade union (its "political ballot rules") approved by the Certification Officer.

(2) Fresh approval is required for the purposes of each ballot which it is proposed to hold, notwithstanding that the rules have been approved for the purposes of an earlier ballot.

(3) The Certification Officer shall not approve a union's political ballot rules unless he is satisfied that the requirements set out in—

   section 75 (appointment of independent scrutineer),

   section 76 (entitlement to vote),

   section 77 (voting), . . .

   [section 77A (counting of votes etc. by independent person), and]

   section 78 (scrutineer's report),

would be satisfied in relation to a ballot held by the union in accordance with the rules.

**NOTES**

   Sub-s (3): word omitted repealed, and words in square brackets inserted, by the Trade Union Reform and Employment Rights Act 1993, ss 3, 51, Sch 1, para 1, Sch 10.

**[1.333]**
**75 Appointment of independent scrutineer**

(1) The trade union shall, before the ballot is held, appoint a qualified independent person ("the scrutineer") to carry out—

   (a) the functions in relation to the ballot which are required under this section to be contained in his appointment; and

   (b) such additional functions in relation to the ballot as may be specified in his appointment.

(2) A person is a qualified independent person in relation to a ballot if—

(a) he satisfies such conditions as may be specified for the purposes of this section by order of the Secretary of State or is himself so specified; and

(b) the trade union has no grounds for believing either that he will carry out any functions conferred on him in relation to the ballot otherwise than competently or that his independence in relation to the union, or in relation to the ballot, might reasonably be called into question.

An order under paragraph (a) shall be made by statutory instrument which shall be subject to annulment in pursuance of a resolution of either House of Parliament.

(3) The scrutineer's appointment shall require him—

(a) to be the person who supervises the production [of the voting papers and (unless he is appointed under section 77A to undertake the distribution of the voting papers) their distribution] and to whom the voting papers are returned by those voting;

[(aa) to—

(i) inspect the register of names and addresses of the members of the trade union, or

(ii) examine the copy of the register as at the relevant date which is supplied to him in accordance with subsection (5A)(a),

whenever it appears to him appropriate to do so and, in particular, when the conditions specified in subsection (3A) are satisfied;]

(b) to take such steps as appear to him to be appropriate for the purpose of enabling him to make his report (see section 78);

(c) to make his report to the trade union as soon as reasonably practicable after the last date for the return of voting papers; and

(d) to retain custody of all voting papers returned for the purposes of the ballot [and the copy of the register supplied to him in accordance with subsection (5A)(a)]—

(i) until the end of the period of one year beginning with the announcement by the union of the result of the ballot; and

(ii) if within that period an application is made under section 79 (complaint of failure to comply with ballot rules), until the Certification Officer or the court authorises him to dispose of the papers [or copy].

[(3A) The conditions referred to in subsection (3)(aa) are—

(a) that a request that the scrutineer inspect the register or examine the copy is made to him during the appropriate period by a member of the trade union who suspects that the register is not, or at the relevant date was not, accurate and up-to-date, and

(b) that the scrutineer does not consider that the member's suspicion is ill-founded.

(3B) In subsection (3A) "the appropriate period" means the period—

(a) beginning with the day on which the scrutineer is appointed, and

(b) ending with the day before the day on which the scrutineer makes his report to the trade union.

(3C) The duty of confidentiality as respects the register is incorporated in the scrutineer's appointment.]

(4) The trade union shall ensure that nothing in the terms of the scrutineer's appointment (including any additional functions specified in the appointment) is such as to make it reasonable for any person to call the scrutineer's independence in relation to the union into question.

(5) The trade union shall, before the scrutineer begins to carry out his functions, either—

(a) send a notice stating the name of the scrutineer to every member of the union to whom it is reasonably practicable to send such a notice, or

(b) take all such other steps for notifying members of the name of the scrutineer as it is the practice of the union to take when matters of general interest to all its members need to be brought to their attention.

[(5A) The trade union shall—

(a) supply to the scrutineer as soon as is reasonably practicable after the relevant date a copy of the register of names and addresses of its members as at that date, and

(b) comply with any request made by the scrutineer to inspect the register.

(5B) Where the register is kept by means of a computer the duty imposed on the trade union by subsection (5A)(a) is either to supply a legible printed copy or (if the scrutineer prefers) to supply a copy of the computer data and allow the scrutineer use of the computer to read it at any time during the period when he is required to retain custody of the copy.]

(6) The trade union shall ensure that the scrutineer duly carries out his functions and that there is no interference with his carrying out of those functions which would make it reasonable for any person to call the scrutineer's independence in relation to the union into question.

(7) The trade union shall comply with all reasonable requests made by the scrutineer for the purposes of, or in connection with, the carrying out of his functions.

[(8) In this section "the relevant date" means—

(a) where the trade union has rules determining who is entitled to vote in the ballot by reference to membership on a particular date, that date, and

(b) otherwise, the date, or the last date, on which voting papers are distributed for the purposes of the ballot.]

**NOTES**

Sub-s (3): words in square brackets in para (a) substituted, para (aa) inserted, and words in square brackets in para (d) inserted, by the Trade Union Reform and Employment Rights Act 1993, s 3, Sch 1, para 2(a)–(c).

Sub-ss (3A)–(3C), (5A), (5B), (8): inserted and added respectively by the Trade Union Reform and Employment Rights Act 1993, s 3, Sch 1, para 2(d)–(f).

Orders: the Trade Union Ballots and Elections (Independent Scrutineer Qualifications) Order 1993, SI 1993/1909 at **[2.135]**; the Trade Union Ballots and Elections (Independent Scrutineer Qualifications) (Amendment) Order 2010, SI 2010/436.

**[1.334]**
**76　Entitlement to vote**
Entitlement to vote in the ballot shall be accorded equally to all members of the trade union.

**[1.335]**
**77　Voting**
(1)　The method of voting must be by the marking of a voting paper by the person voting.
(2)　Each voting paper must—
　(a)　state the name of the independent scrutineer and clearly specify the address to which, and the date by which, it is to be returned, and
　(b)　be given one of a series of consecutive whole numbers every one of which is used in giving a different number in that series to each voting paper printed or otherwise produced for the purposes of the ballot, and
　(c)　be marked with its number.
(3)　Every person who is entitled to vote in the ballot must—
　(a)　be allowed to vote without interference from, or constraint imposed by, the union or any of its members, officials or employees, and
　(b)　so far as is reasonably practicable, be enabled to do so without incurring any direct cost to himself.
(4)　So far as is reasonably practicable, every person who is entitled to vote in the ballot must—
　(a)　have a voting paper sent to him by post at his home address or another address which he has requested the trade union in writing to treat as his postal address, and
　(b)　be given a convenient opportunity to vote by post.
(5)　The ballot shall be conducted so as to secure that—
　(a)　so far as is reasonably practicable, those voting do so in secret, and
　(b)　the votes given in the ballot are fairly and accurately counted.
For the purposes of paragraph (b) an inaccuracy in counting shall be disregarded if it is accidental and on a scale which could not affect the result of the ballot.

**[1.336]**
**[77A　Counting of votes etc by independent person**
(1)　The trade union shall ensure that—
　(a)　the storage and distribution of the voting papers for the purposes of the ballot, and
　(b)　the counting of the votes cast in the ballot,
are undertaken by one or more independent persons appointed by the union.
(2)　A person is an independent person in relation to a ballot if—
　(a)　he is the scrutineer, or
　(b)　he is a person other than the scrutineer and the trade union has no grounds for believing either that he will carry out any functions conferred on him in relation to the ballot otherwise than competently or that his independence in relation to the union, or in relation to the ballot, might reasonably be called into question.
(3)　An appointment under this section shall require the person appointed to carry out his functions so as to minimise the risk of any contravention of requirements imposed by or under any enactment or the occurrence of any unfairness or malpractice.
(4)　The duty of confidentiality as respects the register is incorporated in an appointment under this section.
(5)　Where the person appointed to undertake the counting of votes is not the scrutineer, his appointment shall require him to send the voting papers back to the scrutineer as soon as reasonably practicable after the counting has been completed.
(6)　The trade union—
　(a)　shall ensure that nothing in the terms of an appointment under this section is such as to make it reasonable for any person to call into question the independence of the person appointed in relation to the union,
　(b)　shall ensure that a person appointed under this section duly carries out his functions and that there is no interference with his carrying out of those functions which would make it reasonable for any person to call into question the independence of the person appointed in relation to the union, and
　(c)　shall comply with all reasonable requests made by a person appointed under this section for the purposes of, or in connection with, the carrying out of his functions.]

NOTES

Inserted by the Trade Union Reform and Employment Rights Act 1993, s 3, Sch 1, para 3.

**[1.337]**
## 78  Scrutineer's report

(1)  The scrutineer's report on the ballot shall state—

(a)  the number of voting papers distributed for the purposes of the ballot,

(b)  the number of voting papers returned to the scrutineer,

(c)  the number of valid votes cast in the ballot for and against the resolution,  . . .

(d)  the number of spoiled or otherwise invalid voting papers returned[; and

(e)  the name of the person (or of each of the persons) appointed under section 77A or, if no person was so appointed, that fact.]

(2)  The report shall also state whether the scrutineer is satisfied—

(a)  that there are no reasonable grounds for believing that there was any contravention of a requirement imposed by or under any enactment in relation to the ballot,

(b)  that the arrangements made [(whether by him or any other person)] with respect to the production, storage, distribution, return or other handling of the voting papers used in the ballot, and the arrangements for the counting of the votes, included all such security arrangements as were reasonably practicable for the purpose of minimising the risk that any unfairness or malpractice might occur, and

(c)  that he has been able to carry out his functions without such interference as would make it reasonable for any person to call his independence in relation to the union into question;

and if he is not satisfied as to any of those matters, the report shall give particulars of his reasons for not being satisfied as to that matter.

[(2A)  The report shall also state—

(a)  whether the scrutineer—

(i)  has inspected the register of names and addresses of the members of the trade union, or

(ii)  has examined the copy of the register as at the relevant date which is supplied to him in accordance with section 75(5A)(a),

(b)  if he has, whether in the case of each inspection or examination he was acting on a request by a member of the trade union or at his own instance,

(c)  whether he declined to act on any such request, and

(d)  whether any inspection of the register, or any examination of the copy of the register, has revealed any matter which he considers should be drawn to the attention of the trade union in order to assist it in securing that the register is accurate and up-to-date,

but shall not state the name of any member who has requested such an inspection or examination.

(2B)  Where one or more persons other than the scrutineer are appointed under section 77A, the statement included in the scrutineer's report in accordance with subsection (2)(b) shall also indicate—

(a)  whether he is satisfied with the performance of the person, or each of the persons, so appointed, and

(b)  if he is not satisfied with the performance of the person, or any of them, particulars of his reasons for not being so satisfied.]

(3)  The trade union shall not publish the result of the ballot until it has received the scrutineer's report.

(4)  The trade union shall within the period of three months after it receives the report—

(a)  send a copy of the report to every member of the union to whom it is reasonably practicable to send such a copy; or

(b)  take all such other steps for notifying the contents of the report to the members of the union (whether by publishing the report or otherwise) as it is the practice of the union to take when matters of general interest to all its members need to be brought to their attention.

(5)  Any such copy or notification shall be accompanied by a statement that the union will, on request, supply any member of the union with a copy of the report, either free of charge or on payment of such reasonable fee as may be specified in the notification.

(6)  The trade union shall so supply any member of the union who makes such a request and pays the fee (if any) notified to him.

NOTES

Sub-s (1): word omitted from para (c) repealed, and para (e) and the word immediately preceding it added, by the Trade Union Reform and Employment Rights Act 1993, ss 3, 51, Sch 1, para 4(a), Sch 10.

Sub-s (2): words in square brackets inserted by the Trade Union Reform and Employment Rights Act 1993, s 3, Sch 1, para 4(b).

Sub-ss (2A), (2B): inserted by the Trade Union Reform and Employment Rights Act 1993, s 3, Sch 1, para 4(c).

**[1.338]**
## 79  Remedy for failure to comply with ballot rules: general
(1)  The remedy for—
  (a)    the taking by a trade union of a ballot on a political resolution otherwise than in accordance with political ballot rules approved by the Certification Officer, or
  (b)    the failure of a trade union, in relation to a proposed ballot on a political resolution, to comply with the political ballot rules so approved,
is by way of application under section 80 (to the Certification Officer) or 81 (to the court).
. . .
(2)  An application under those sections may be made only by a person who is a member of the trade union and, where the ballot has been held, was a member at the time when it was held.
  References in those sections to a person having a sufficient interest are to such a person.
(3)  No such application may be made after the end of the period of one year beginning with the day on which the union announced the result of the ballot.

**NOTES**
  Sub-s (1): words omitted repealed by the Employment Relations Act 1999, ss 29, 44, Sch 6, paras 1, 14, Sch 9(7).

**[1.339]**
## 80  Application to Certification Officer
(1)  A person having a sufficient interest (see section 79(2)) who claims that a trade union—
  (a)    has held a ballot on a political resolution otherwise than in accordance with political ballot rules approved by the Certification Officer, or
  (b)    has failed in relation to a proposed ballot on a political resolution to comply with political ballot rules so approved,
may apply to the Certification Officer for a declaration to that effect.
(2)  On an application being made to him, the Certification Officer shall—
  (a)    make such enquiries as he thinks fit, and
  (b)    . . .  give the applicant and the trade union an opportunity to be heard,
and may make or refuse the declaration asked for.
(3)  If he makes a declaration he shall specify in it the provisions with which the trade union has failed to comply.
(4)  Where he makes a declaration and is satisfied that steps have been taken by the union with a view to remedying the declared failure, or securing that a failure of the same or any similar kind does not occur in future, or that the union has agreed to take such steps, he shall in making the declaration specify those steps.
(5)  Whether he makes or refuses a declaration, he shall give reasons for his decision in writing; and the reasons may be accompanied by written observations on any matter arising from, or connected with, the proceedings.
[(5A)  Where the Certification Officer makes a declaration he shall also, unless he considers that to do so would be inappropriate, make an enforcement order, that is, an order imposing on the union one or more of the following requirements—
  (a)    to secure the holding of a ballot in accordance with the order;
  (b)    to take such other steps to remedy the declared failure as may be specified in the order;
  (c)    to abstain from such acts as may be so specified with a view to securing that a failure of the same or a similar kind does not occur in future.
  The Certification Officer shall in an order imposing any such requirement as is mentioned in paragraph (a) or (b) specify the period within which the union must comply with the requirements of the order.
(5B)  Where the Certification Officer makes an order requiring the union to hold a fresh ballot, he shall (unless he considers that it would be inappropriate to do so in the particular circumstances of the case) require the ballot to be conducted in accordance with the union's political ballot rules and such other provisions as may be made by the order.
(5C)  Where an enforcement order has been made, any person who is a member of the union and was a member at the time the order was made is entitled to enforce obedience to the order as if he had made the application on which the order was made.]
(6)  In exercising his functions under this section the Certification Officer shall ensure that, so far as is reasonably practicable, an application made to him is determined within six months of being made.
(7)  Where he requests a person to furnish information to him in connection with enquiries made by him under this section, he shall specify the date by which that information is to be furnished and shall, unless he considers that it would be inappropriate to do so, proceed with his determination of the application notwithstanding that the information has not been furnished to him by the specified date.
[(8)  A declaration made by the Certification Officer under this section may be relied on as if it were a declaration made by the court.]

(9) An enforcement order made by the Certification Officer under this section may be enforced in the same way as an order of the court.

(10) The following paragraphs have effect if a person applies under section 81 in relation to a matter—

    (a)   that person may not apply under this section in relation to that matter;

    (b)   on an application by a different person under this section in relation to that matter, the Certification Officer shall have due regard to any declaration, order, observations, or reasons made or given by the court regarding that matter and brought to the Certification Officer's notice.]

**NOTES**

Sub-s (2): words omitted from para (b) repealed by the Employment Relations Act 1999, ss 29, 44, Sch 6, paras 1, 15(1), (2), Sch 9(7).

Sub-ss (5A)–(5C), (8)–(10): inserted and added respectively by the Employment Relations Act 1999, s 29, Sch 6, paras 1, 15(1), (3), (4).

**[1.340]**

## 81  Application to court

(1) A person having a sufficient interest (see section 79(2)) who claims that a trade union—

    (a)   has held a ballot on a political resolution otherwise than in accordance with political ballot rules approved by the Certification Officer, or

    (b)   has failed in relation to a proposed ballot on a political resolution to comply with political ballot rules so approved,

may apply to the court for a declaration to that effect.

(2)   . . .

(3) If the court makes the declaration asked for, it shall specify in the declaration the provisions with which the trade union has failed to comply.

(4) Where the court makes a declaration it shall also, unless it considers that to do so would be inappropriate, make an enforcement order, that is, an order imposing on the union one or more of the following requirements—

    (a)   to secure the holding of a ballot in accordance with the order;

    (b)   to take such other steps to remedy the declared failure as may be specified in the order;

    (c)   to abstain from such acts as may be so specified with a view to securing that a failure of the same or a similar kind does not occur in future.

The court shall in an order imposing any such requirement as is mentioned in paragraph (a) or (b) specify the period within which the union must comply with the requirements of the order.

(5) Where the court makes an order requiring the union to hold a fresh ballot, the court shall (unless it considers that it would be inappropriate to do so in the particular circumstances of the case) require the ballot to be conducted in accordance with the union's political ballot rules and such other provisions as may be made by the order.

(6) Where an enforcement order has been made, any person who is a member of the union and was a member at the time the order was made is entitled to enforce obedience to the order as if he had made the application on which the order was made.

(7) Without prejudice to any other power of the court, the court may on an application under this section grant such interlocutory relief (in Scotland, such interim order) as it considers appropriate.

[(8) The following paragraphs have effect if a person applies under section 80 in relation to a matter—

    (a)   that person may not apply under this section in relation to that matter;

    (b)   on an application by a different person under this section in relation to that matter, the court shall have due regard to any declaration, order, observations or reasons made or given by the Certification Officer regarding that matter and brought to the court's notice.]

**NOTES**

Sub-s (2): repealed by the Employment Relations Act 1999, ss 29, 44, Sch 6, paras 1, 16(1), (2), Sch 9(7).

Sub-s (8): added by the Employment Relations Act 1999, s 29, Sch 6, paras 1, 16(1), (3).

*The political fund*

**[1.341]**

## 82  Rules as to political fund

(1) The trade union's rules must provide—

    (a)   that payments in the furtherance of the political objects to which this Chapter applies shall be made out of a separate fund (the "political fund" of the union);

    (b)   that a member of the union who gives notice in accordance with section 84 that he objects to contributing to the political fund shall be exempt from any obligation to contribute to it;

    (c)   that a member shall not by reason of being so exempt—

        (i)   be excluded from any benefits of the union, or

   (ii)    be placed in any respect either directly or indirectly under a disability or at a disadvantage as compared with other members of the union (except in relation to the control or management of the political fund); and

  (d)    that contribution to the political fund shall not be made a condition for admission to the union.

(2)   A member of a trade union who claims that he is aggrieved by a breach of any rule made in pursuance of this section may complain to the Certification Officer.

[(2A)   On a complaint being made to him the Certification Officer shall make such enquiries as he thinks fit.]

(3)   Where, after giving the member and a representative of the union an opportunity of being heard, the Certification Officer considers that a breach has been committed, he may make such order for remedying the breach as he thinks just under the circumstances.

[(3A)   Where the Certification Officer requests a person to furnish information to him in connection with enquiries made by him under this section, he shall specify the date by which that information is to be furnished and, unless he considers that it would be inappropriate to do so, shall proceed with his determination of the application notwithstanding that the information has not been furnished to him by the specified date.]

[(4A)   Where an order has been made under this section, any person who is a member of the union and was a member at the time it was made is entitled to enforce obedience to the order as if he had made the complaint on which it was made.

(4B)   An order made by the Certification Officer under this section may be enforced—

  (a)    in England and Wales, in the same way as an order of the county court;

  (b)    in Scotland, in the same way as an order of the sheriff.]

---

**NOTES**

Sub-ss (2A), (3A): inserted by the Employment Relations Act 1999, s 29, Sch 6, paras 1, 17.

Sub-ss (4A), (4B): substituted, for the original sub-s (4), by the Employment Relations Act 2004, s 57(1), Sch 1, para 6.

---

**[1.342]**
### 83   Assets and liabilities of political fund

(1)   There may be added to a union's political fund only—

  (a)    sums representing contributions made to the fund by members of the union or by any person other than the union itself, and

  (b)    property which accrues to the fund in the course of administering the assets of the fund.

(2)   The rules of the union shall not be taken to require any member to contribute to the political fund at a time when there is no political resolution in force in relation to the union.

(3)   No liability of a union's political fund shall be discharged out of any other fund of the union.

   This subsection applies notwithstanding any term or condition on which the liability was incurred or that an asset of the other fund has been charged in connection with the liability.

**[1.343]**
### 84   Notice of objection to contributing to political fund

(1)   A member of a trade union may give notice in the following form, or in a form to the like effect, that he objects to contribute to the political fund—

---

Name of Trade Union

**POLITICAL FUND (EXEMPTION NOTICE)**

I give notice that I object to contributing to the Political Fund of the Union, and am in consequence exempt, in manner provided by Chapter VI of Part I of the Trade Union and Labour Relations (Consolidation) Act 1992, from contributing to that fund.

A.B.

Address. . . . . . . . . . .

day of. . . . . . . . . . . . . . . . . . . . . 19. . . . . .

---

(2)   On the adoption of a political resolution, notice shall be given to members of the union acquainting them—

  (a)    that each member has a right to be exempted from contributing to the union's political fund, and

  (b)    that a form of exemption notice can be obtained by or on behalf of a member either by application at or by post from—

     (i)    the head office or any branch office of the union, or

    (ii)    the office of the Certification Officer.

(3)   The notice to members shall be given in accordance with rules of the union approved for the purpose by the Certification Officer, who shall have regard in each case to the existing practice and character of the union.

(4)   On giving an exemption notice in accordance with this section, a member shall be exempt from contributing to the union's political fund—

(a)    where the notice is given within one month of the giving of notice to members under subsection (2) following the passing of a political resolution on a ballot held at a time when no such resolution is in force, as from the date on which the exemption notice is given;

(b)    in any other case, as from the 1st January next after the exemption notice is given.

(5)    An exemption notice continues to have effect until it is withdrawn.

**[1.344]**

**85    Manner of giving effect to exemptions**

(1)    Effect may be given to the exemption of members from contributing to the political fund of a union either—

(a)    by a separate levy of contributions to that fund from the members who are not exempt, or

(b)    by relieving members who are exempt from the payment of the whole or part of any periodical contribution required from members towards the expenses of the union.

(2)    In the latter case, the rules shall provide—

(a)    that relief shall be given as far as possible to all members who are exempt on the occasion of the same periodical payment, and

(b)    for enabling each member of the union to know what portion (if any) of any periodical contribution payable by him is a contribution to the political fund.

*Duties of employer who deducts union contributions*

**[1.345]**

**86    Certificate of exemption or objection to contributing to political fund**

(1)    If a member of a trade union which has a political fund certifies in writing to his employer that, or to the effect that—

(a)    he is exempt from the obligation to contribute to the fund, or

(b)    he has, in accordance with section 84, notified the union in writing of his objection to contributing to the fund,

the employer shall ensure that no amount representing a contribution to the political fund is deducted by him from emoluments payable to the member.

(2)    The employer's duty under subsection (1) applies from the first day, following the giving of the certificate, on which it is reasonably practicable for him to comply with that subsection, until the certificate is withdrawn.

(3)    An employer may not refuse to deduct any union dues from emoluments payable to a person who has given a certificate under this section if he continues to deduct union dues from emoluments payable to other members of the union, unless his refusal is not attributable to the giving of the certificate or otherwise connected with the duty imposed by subsection (1).

---

**NOTES**

No complaint is to be presented under the Employment Rights Act 1996, s 23 in respect of any deduction made in contravention of this section; see sub-s (5) of that section at **[1.767]**.

The rights conferred by this section are "relevant statutory rights" for the purposes of the Employment Rights Act 1996, s 104 (dismissal on grounds of assertion of statutory right); see s 104(4)(c) of that Act at **[1.907]**.

Conciliation: employment tribunal proceedings and claims which could be the subject of employment tribunal proceedings arising out of a contravention, or alleged contravention, of this section are proceedings to which the Employment Tribunals Act 1996, s 18 applies; see s 18(1)(b) of that Act at **[1.706]**.

---

**[1.346]**

**[87    Complaint in respect of employer's failure**

(1)    A person who claims his employer has failed to comply with section 86 in deducting or refusing to deduct any amount from emoluments payable to him may present a complaint to an employment tribunal.

(2)    A tribunal shall not consider a complaint under subsection (1) unless it is presented—

(a)    within the period of three months beginning with the date of the payment of the emoluments or (if the complaint relates to more than one payment) the last of the payments, or

(b)    where the tribunal is satisfied that it was not reasonably practicable for the complaint to be presented within that period, within such further period as the tribunal considers reasonable.

[(2A)    Section 292A (extension of time limits to facilitate conciliation before institution of proceedings) applies for the purposes of subsection (2)(a).]

(3)    Where on a complaint under subsection (1) arising out of subsection (3) (refusal to deduct union dues) of section 86 the question arises whether the employer's refusal to deduct an amount was attributable to the giving of the certificate or was otherwise connected with the duty imposed by subsection (1) of that section, it is for the employer to satisfy the tribunal that it was not.

(4)    Where a tribunal finds that a complaint under subsection (1) is well-founded—

(a)   it shall make a declaration to that effect and, where the complaint arises out of subsection (1) of section 86, order the employer to pay to the complainant the amount deducted in contravention of that subsection less any part of that amount already paid to him by the employer, and

(b)   it may, if it considers it appropriate to do so in order to prevent a repetition of the failure, make an order requiring the employer to take, within a specified time, the steps specified in the order in relation to emoluments payable by him to the complainant.

(5)   A person who claims his employer has failed to comply with an order made under subsection (4)(b) on a complaint presented by him may present a further complaint to an employment tribunal; but only one complaint may be presented under this subsection in relation to any order.

(6)   A tribunal shall not consider a complaint under subsection (5) unless it is presented—

(a)   after the end of the period of four weeks beginning with the date of the order, but

(b)   before the end of the period of six months beginning with that date.

(7)   Where on a complaint under subsection (5) a tribunal finds that an employer has, without reasonable excuse, failed to comply with an order made under subsection (4)(b), it shall order the employer to pay to the complainant an amount equal to two weeks pay.

(8)   Chapter II of Part XIV of the Employment Rights Act 1996 (calculation of a week's pay) applies for the purposes of subsection (7) with the substitution for section 225 of the following—

"For the purposes of this Chapter in its application to subsection (7) of section 87 of the Trade Union and Labour Relations (Consolidation) Act 1992, the calculation date is the date of the payment, or (if more than one) the last of the payments, to which the complaint related."]

---

**NOTES**

Substituted by the Employment Rights (Dispute Resolution) Act 1998, s 6.

Sub-s (2A): inserted by the Enterprise and Regulatory Reform Act 2013, s 8, Sch 2, paras 1, 5, as from a day to be appointed.

**88**   ((*Application of provisions of Wages Act 1986*) *repealed by the Employment Rights (Dispute Resolution) Act 1998, s 15, Sch 2.*)

*Position where political resolution ceases to have effect*

**[1.347]**
**89   Administration of political fund where no resolution in force**
(1)   The following provisions have effect with respect to the political fund of a trade union where there ceases to be any political resolution in force in relation to the union.
(2)   If the resolution ceases to have effect by reason of a ballot being held on which a new political resolution is not passed, the union may continue to make payments out of the fund as if the resolution had continued in force for six months beginning with the date of the ballot.

But no payment shall be made which causes the fund to be in deficit or increases a deficit in it.
(3)   There may be added to the fund only—

(a)   contributions to the fund paid to the union (or to a person on its behalf) before the resolution ceased to have effect, and

(b)   property which accrues to the fund in the course of administering the assets of the fund.

(4)   The union may, notwithstanding any of its rules or any trusts on which the fund is held, transfer the whole or part of the fund to such other fund of the union as it thinks fit.
(5)   If a new political resolution is subsequently passed, no property held immediately before the date of the ballot by or on behalf of the union otherwise than in its political fund, and no sums representing such property, may be added to the fund.

**[1.348]**
**90   Discontinuance of contributions to political fund**
(1)   Where there ceases to be any political resolution in force in relation to a trade union, the union shall take such steps as are necessary to ensure that the collection of contributions to its political fund is discontinued as soon as is reasonably practicable.
(2)   The union may, notwithstanding any of its rules, pay into any of its other funds any such contribution which is received by it after the resolution ceases to have effect.
(3)   If the union continues to collect contributions, it shall refund to a member who applies for a refund the contributions made by him collected after the resolution ceased to have effect.
(4)   A member of a trade union who claims that the union has failed to comply with subsection (1) may apply to the court for a declaration to that effect.
(5)   Where the court is satisfied that the complaint is well-founded, it may, if it considers it appropriate to do so in order to secure that the collection of contributions to the political fund is discontinued, make an order requiring the union to take, within such time as may be specified in the order, such steps as may be so specified.

Such an order may be enforced by a person who is a member of the union and was a member at the time the order was made as if he had made the application.

(6)   The remedy for failure to comply with subsection (1) is in accordance with subsections (4) and (5), and not otherwise; but this does not affect any right to recover sums payable to a person under subsection (3).

**[1.349]**
## 91   Rules to cease to have effect
(1)   If there ceases to be any political resolution in force in relation to a trade union, the rules of the union made for the purpose of complying with this Chapter also cease to have effect, except so far as they are required to enable the political fund to be administered at a time when there is no such resolution in force.
(2)   If the resolution ceases to have effect by reason of a ballot being held on which a new political resolution is not passed, the rules cease to have effect at the end of the period of six months beginning with the date of the ballot.
   In any other case the rules cease to have effect when the resolution ceases to have effect.
(3)   Nothing in this section affects the operation of section 82(2) (complaint to Certification Officer in respect of breach of rules) in relation to a breach of a rule occurring before the rule in question ceased to have effect.
(4)   No member of a trade union who has at any time been exempt from the obligation to contribute to its political fund shall by reason of his having been exempt—
   (a)   be excluded from any benefits of the union, or
   (b)   be placed in any respect either directly or indirectly under a disability or at a disadvantage as compared with other members (except in relation to the control or management of the political fund).

*Supplementary*

**[1.350]**
## 92   Manner of making union rules
If the Certification Officer is satisfied, and certifies, that rules of a trade union made for any of the purposes of this Chapter and requiring approval by him have been approved—
   (a)   by a majority of the members of the union voting for the purpose, or
   (b)   by a majority of delegates of the union at a meeting called for the purpose,
the rules shall have effect as rules of the union notwithstanding that the rules of the union as to the alteration of rules or the making of new rules have not been complied with.

**[1.351]**
## 93   Effect of amalgamation
(1)   Where on an amalgamation of two or more trade unions—
   (a)   there is in force in relation to each of the amalgamating unions a political resolution and such rules as are required by this Chapter, and
   (b)   the rules of the amalgamated union in force immediately after the amalgamation include such rules as are required by this Chapter,
the amalgamated union shall be treated for the purposes of this Chapter as having passed a political resolution.
(2)   That resolution shall be treated as having been passed on the date of the earliest of the ballots on which the resolutions in force immediately before the amalgamation with respect to the amalgamating unions were passed.
(3)   Where one of the amalgamating unions is a Northern Ireland union, the references above to the requirements of this Chapter shall be construed as references to the requirements of the corresponding provisions of the law of Northern Ireland.

**[1.352]**
## 94   Overseas members of trade unions
(1)   Where a political resolution is in force in relation to the union—
   (a)   rules made by the union for the purpose of complying with section 74 (political ballot rules) in relation to a proposed ballot may provide for overseas members of the union not to be accorded entitlement to vote in the ballot, and
   (b)   rules made by the union for the purpose of complying with section 84 (notice of right to object to contribute to political fund to be given where resolution passed) may provide for notice not to be given by the union to its overseas members.
(2)   Accordingly, where provision is made in accordance with subsection (1)(a), the Certification Officer shall not on that ground withhold his approval of the rules; and where provision is made in accordance with subsection (1)(b), section 84(2) (duty to give notice) shall not be taken to require notice to be given to overseas members.
(3)   An "overseas member" means a member of the trade union (other than a merchant seaman or offshore worker) who is outside Great Britain throughout the period during which votes may be cast.
   For this purpose—

"merchant seaman" means a person whose employment, or the greater part of it, is carried out on board sea-going ships; and

"offshore worker" means a person in offshore employment, other than one who is in such employment in an area where the law of Northern Ireland applies.

**[1.353]**
## 95   Appeals from Certification Officer
An appeal lies to the Employment Appeal Tribunal on any question of law arising in proceedings before or arising from any decision of the Certification Officer under this Chapter.

**[1.354]**
## 96   Meaning of "date of the ballot"
In this Chapter the "date of the ballot" means, in the case of a ballot in which votes may be cast on more than one day, the last of those days.

## CHAPTER VII
## AMALGAMATIONS AND SIMILAR MATTERS

**NOTES**
  Regulations: for Regulations supplementing the provisions of this Chapter, see the Trade Unions and Employers' Associations (Amalgamations etc) Regulations 1975, SI 1975/536 at **[2.1]**.

*Amalgamation or transfer of engagements*

**[1.355]**
## 97   Amalgamation or transfer of engagements
(1)   Two or more trade unions may amalgamate and become one trade union, with or without a division or dissolution of the funds of any one or more of the amalgamating unions, but shall not do so unless—
    (a)   the instrument of amalgamation is approved in accordance with section 98, and
    (b)   the requirements of [section 99 (notice to members) and section 100 (resolution to be passed by required majority in ballot held in accordance with sections 100A to 100E)] are complied with in respect of each of the amalgamating unions.
(2)   A trade union may transfer its engagements to another trade union which undertakes to fulfil those engagements, but shall not do so unless—
    (a)   the instrument of transfer is approved in accordance with section 98, and
    (b)   the requirements of [section 99 (notice to members) and section 100 (resolution to be passed by required majority in ballot held in accordance with sections 100A to 100E)] are complied with in respect of the transferor union.
(3)   An amalgamation or transfer of engagements does not prejudice any right of any creditor of any trade union party to the amalgamation or transfer.
(4)   The above provisions apply to every amalgamation or transfer of engagements notwithstanding anything in the rules of any of the trade unions concerned.

**NOTES**
  Sub-ss (1), (2): words in square brackets substituted by the Trade Union Reform and Employment Rights Act 1993, s 49(2), Sch 8, para 52.

**[1.356]**
## 98   Approval of instrument of amalgamation or transfer
(1)   The instrument of amalgamation or transfer must be approved by the Certification Officer and shall be submitted to him for approval before [a ballot of the members of any amalgamating union, or (as the case may be) of the transferor union, is held on the resolution to approve the instrument].
[(2)   If the Certification Officer is satisfied—
    (a)   that an instrument of amalgamation complies with the requirements of any regulations in force under this Chapter, and
    (b)   that he is not prevented from approving the instrument of amalgamation by subsection (3),
he shall approve the instrument.
(3)   The Certification Officer shall not approve an instrument of amalgamation if it appears to him that the proposed name of the amalgamated union is the same as the name under which another organisation—
    (a)   was on 30th September 1971 registered as a trade union under the Trade Union Acts 1871 to 1964,
    (b)   was at any time registered as a trade union or employers' association under the Industrial Relations Act 1971, or
    (c)   is for the time being entered in the list of trade unions or in the list of employers' associations,
or if the proposed name is one so nearly resembling any such name as to be likely to deceive the public.

(4) Subsection (3) does not apply if the proposed name is the name of one of the amalgamating unions.

(5) If the Certification Officer is satisfied that an instrument of transfer complies with the requirements of any regulations in force under this Chapter, he shall approve the instrument.]

**NOTES**

Sub-s (1): words in square brackets substituted by the Trade Union Reform and Employment Rights Act 1993, s 49(2), Sch 8, para 53.

Sub-ss (2)–(5): substituted, for the original sub-s (2), by the Employment Relations Act 2004, s 50(1).

Trade Union Acts 1871 to 1964: repealed, see the note to s 3 at **[1.243]**.

Industrial Relations Act 1971: repealed by the Trade Union and Labour Relations Act 1974, ss 1, 25(3), Sch 5.

**[1.357]**
**99 Notice to be given to members**

(1) The trade union shall take all reasonable steps to secure [that every voting paper which is supplied for voting in the ballot on the resolution to approve the instrument of amalgamation or transfer is accompanied by] a notice in writing approved for the purpose by the Certification Officer.

(2) The notice shall be in writing and shall either—
  (a) set out in full the instrument of amalgamation or transfer to which the resolution relates, or
  (b) give an account of it sufficient to enable those receiving the notice to form a reasonable judgment of the main effects of the proposed amalgamation or transfer.

(3) If the notice does not set out the instrument in full it shall state where copies of the instrument may be inspected by those receiving the notice.

[(3A) The notice shall not contain any statement making a recommendation or expressing an opinion about the proposed amalgamation or transfer.]

(4) The notice shall also comply with the requirements of any regulations in force under this Chapter.

(5) The notice proposed to be supplied to members of the union under this section shall be submitted to the Certification Officer for approval; and he shall approve it if he is satisfied that it meets the requirements of this section.

**NOTES**

Sub-s (1): words in square brackets substituted by the Trade Union Reform and Employment Rights Act 1993, s 49(2), Sch 8, para 54.

Sub-s (3A): inserted by the Trade Union Reform and Employment Rights Act 1993, s 5.

**[1.358]**
**[100 Requirement of ballot on resolution**

(1) A resolution approving the instrument of amalgamation or transfer must be passed on a ballot of the members of the trade union held in accordance with sections 100A to 100E.

(2) A simple majority of those voting is sufficient to pass such a resolution unless the rules of the trade union expressly require it to be approved by a greater majority or by a specified proportion of the members of the union.]

**NOTES**

Substituted, together with ss 100A–100E for the original s 100, by the Trade Union Reform and Employment Rights Act 1993, s 4.

**[1.359]**
**[100A Appointment of independent scrutineer**

(1) The trade union shall, before the ballot is held, appoint a qualified independent person ("the scrutineer") to carry out—
  (a) the functions in relation to the ballot which are required under this section to be contained in his appointment; and
  (b) such additional functions in relation to the ballot as may be specified in his appointment.

(2) A person is a qualified independent person in relation to a ballot if—
  (a) he satisfies such conditions as may be specified for the purposes of this section by order of the Secretary of State or is himself so specified; and
  (b) the trade union has no grounds for believing either that he will carry out any functions conferred on him in relation to the ballot otherwise than competently or that his independence in relation to the union, or in relation to the ballot, might reasonably be called into question.

An order under paragraph (a) shall be made by statutory instrument which shall be subject to annulment in pursuance of a resolution of either House of Parliament.

(3) The scrutineer's appointment shall require him—
  (a) to be the person who supervises the production of the voting papers and (unless he is appointed under section 100D to undertake the distribution of the voting papers) their distribution and to whom the voting papers are returned by those voting;

(b)   to—
  (i)   inspect the register of names and addresses of the members of the trade union, or
  (ii)   examine the copy of the register as at the relevant date which is supplied to him in accordance with subsection (9)(a),
  whenever it appears to him appropriate to do so and, in particular, when the conditions specified in subsection (4) are satisfied;
(c)   to take such steps as appear to him to be appropriate for the purpose of enabling him to make his report (see section 100E);
(d)   to make his report to the trade union as soon as reasonably practicable after the last date for the return of voting papers; and
(e)   to retain custody of all voting papers returned for the purposes of the ballot and the copy of the register supplied to him in accordance with subsection (9)(a)—
  (i)   until the end of the period of one year beginning with the announcement by the union of the result of the ballot; and
  (ii)   if within that period a complaint is made under section 103 (complaint as regards passing of resolution), until the Certification Officer or Employment Appeal Tribunal authorises him to dispose of the papers or copy.

(4)   The conditions referred to in subsection (3)(b) are—
(a)   that a request that the scrutineer inspect the register or examine the copy is made to him during the appropriate period by a member of the trade union who suspects that the register is not, or at the relevant date was not, accurate and up-to-date, and
(b)   that the scrutineer does not consider that the member's suspicion is ill-founded.

(5)   In subsection (4) "the appropriate period" means the period—
(a)   beginning with the day on which the scrutineer is appointed, and
(b)   ending with the day before the day on which the scrutineer makes his report to the trade union.

(6)   The duty of confidentiality as respects the register is incorporated in the scrutineer's appointment.

(7)   The trade union shall ensure that nothing in the terms of the scrutineer's appointment (including any additional functions specified in the appointment) is such as to make it reasonable for any person to call the scrutineer's independence in relation to the union into question.

(8)   The trade union shall, before the scrutineer begins to carry out his functions, either—
(a)   send a notice stating the name of the scrutineer to every member of the union to whom it is reasonably practicable to send such a notice, or
(b)   take all such other steps for notifying members of the name of the scrutineer as it is the practice of the union to take when matters of general interest to all its members need to be brought to their attention.

(9)   The trade union shall—
(a)   supply to the scrutineer as soon as is reasonably practicable after the relevant date a copy of the register of names and addresses of its members as at that date, and
(b)   comply with any request made by the scrutineer to inspect the register.

(10)   Where the register is kept by means of a computer the duty imposed on the trade union by subsection (9)(a) is either to supply a legible printed copy or (if the scrutineer prefers) to supply a copy of the computer data and allow the scrutineer use of the computer to read it at any time during the period when he is required to retain custody of the copy.

(11)   The trade union shall ensure that the scrutineer duly carries out his functions and that there is no interference with his carrying out of those functions which would make it reasonable for any person to call the scrutineer's independence in relation to the union into question.

(12)   The trade union shall comply with all reasonable requests made by the scrutineer for the purposes of, or in connection with, the carrying out of his functions.

(13)   In this section "the relevant date" means—
(a)   where the trade union has rules determining who is entitled to vote in the ballot by reference to membership on a particular date, that date, and
(b)   otherwise, the date, or the last date, on which voting papers are distributed for the purposes of the ballot.]

**NOTES**

Substituted as noted to s 100 at **[1.358]**.

Orders: the Trade Union Ballots and Elections (Independent Scrutineer Qualifications) Order 1993, SI 1993/1909 at **[2.135]**; the Trade Union Ballots and Elections (Independent Scrutineer Qualifications) (Amendment) Order 2010, SI 2010/436.

**[1.360]**
**[100B  Entitlement to vote**
Entitlement to vote in the ballot shall be accorded equally to all members of the trade union.]

**NOTES**

Substituted as noted to s 100 at **[1.358]**.

**[1.361]**
**[100C    Voting**
(1)   The method of voting must be by the marking of a voting paper by the person voting.
(2)   Each voting paper must—
  (a)   state the name of the independent scrutineer and clearly specify the address to which, and the date by which, it is to be returned, and
  (b)   be given one of a series of consecutive whole numbers every one of which is used in giving a different number in that series to each voting paper printed or otherwise produced for the purposes of the ballot, and
  (c)   be marked with its number.
(3)   Every person who is entitled to vote in the ballot must—
  (a)   be allowed to vote without interference or constraint, and
  (b)   so far as is reasonably practicable, be enabled to do so without incurring any direct cost to himself.
(4)   So far as is reasonably practicable, every person who is entitled to vote in the ballot must—
  (a)   have a voting paper sent to him by post at his home address or another address which he has requested the trade union in writing to treat as his postal address, and
  (b)   be given a convenient opportunity to vote by post.
(5)   No voting paper which is sent to a person for voting shall have enclosed with it any other document except—
  (a)   the notice which, under section 99(1), is to accompany the voting paper,
  (b)   an addressed envelope, and
  (c)   a document containing instructions for the return of the voting paper,
without any other statement.
(6)   The ballot shall be conducted so as to secure that—
  (a)   so far as is reasonably practicable, those voting do so in secret, and
  (b)   the votes given in the ballot are fairly and accurately counted.
For the purposes of paragraph (b) an inaccuracy in counting shall be disregarded if it is accidental and on a scale which could not affect the result of the ballot.]

NOTES
Substituted as noted to s 100 at **[1.358]**.

**[1.362]**
**[100D    Counting of votes etc by independent person**
(1)   The trade union shall ensure that—
  (a)   the storage and distribution of the voting papers for the purposes of the ballot, and
  (b)   the counting of the votes cast in the ballot,
are undertaken by one or more independent persons appointed by the trade union.
(2)   A person is an independent person in relation to a ballot if—
  (a)   he is the scrutineer, or
  (b)   he is a person other than the scrutineer and the trade union has no grounds for believing either that he will carry out any functions conferred on him in relation to the ballot otherwise than competently or that his independence in relation to the union, or in relation to the ballot, might reasonably be called into question.
(3)   An appointment under this section shall require the person appointed to carry out his functions so as to minimise the risk of any contravention of requirements imposed by or under any enactment or the occurrence of any unfairness or malpractice.
(4)   The duty of confidentiality as respects the register is incorporated in the scrutineer's appointment.
(5)   Where the person appointed to undertake the counting of votes is not the scrutineer, his appointment shall require him to send the voting papers back to the scrutineer as soon as reasonably practicable after the counting has been completed.
(6)   The trade union—
  (a)   shall ensure that nothing in the terms of an appointment under this section is such as to make it reasonable for any person to call into question the independence of the person appointed in relation to the union,
  (b)   shall ensure that a person appointed under this section duly carries out his functions and that there is no interference with his carrying out of those functions which would make it reasonable for any person to call into question the independence of the person appointed in relation to the union, and
  (c)   shall comply with all reasonable requests made by a person appointed under this section for the purposes of, or in connection with, the carrying out of his functions.]

NOTES
Substituted as noted to s 100 at **[1.358]**.

**[1.363]**
**[100E   Scrutineer's report**
(1)   The scrutineer's report on the ballot shall state—
   (a)   the number of voting papers distributed for the purposes of the ballot,
   (b)   the number of voting papers returned to the scrutineer,
   (c)   the number of valid votes cast in the ballot for and against the resolution,
   (d)   the number of spoiled or otherwise invalid voting papers returned, and
   (e)   the name of the person (or of each of the persons) appointed under section 100D or, if no
         person was so appointed, that fact.
(2)   The report shall also state whether the scrutineer is satisfied—
   (a)   that there are no reasonable grounds for believing that there was any contravention of a
         requirement imposed by or under any enactment in relation to the ballot,
   (b)   that the arrangements made (whether by him or any other person) with respect to the
         production, storage, distribution, return or other handling of the voting papers used in the
         ballot, and the arrangements for the counting of the votes, included all such security
         arrangements as were reasonably practicable for the purpose of minimising the risk that
         any unfairness or malpractice might occur, and
   (c)   that he has been able to carry out his functions without any such interference as would
         make it reasonable for any person to call his independence in relation to the union into
         question;
and if he is not satisfied as to any of those matters, the report shall give particulars of his reasons
for not being satisfied as to that matter.
(3)   The report shall also state—
   (a)   whether the scrutineer—
         (i)    has inspected the register of names and addresses of the members of the trade union,
                or
         (ii)   has examined the copy of the register as at the relevant date which is supplied to him
                in accordance with section 100A(9)(a),
   (b)   if he has, whether in the case of each inspection or examination he was acting on a request
         by a member of the trade union or at his own instance,
   (c)   whether he declined to act on any such request, and
   (d)   whether any inspection of the register, or any examination of the copy of the register, has
         revealed any matter which he considers should be drawn to the attention of the trade union
         in order to assist it in securing that the register is accurate and up-to-date,
but shall not state the name of any member who has requested such an inspection or examination.
(4)   Where one or more persons other than the scrutineer are appointed under section 100D, the
statement included in the scrutineer's report in accordance with subsection (2)(b) shall also
indicate—
   (a)   whether he is satisfied with the performance of the person, or each of the persons, so
         appointed, and
   (b)   if he is not satisfied with the performance of the person, or any of them, particulars of his
         reasons for not being so satisfied.
(5)   The trade union shall not publish the result of the ballot until it has received the
scrutineer's report.
(6)   The trade union shall within the period of three months after it receives the report—
   (a)   send a copy of the report to every member of the union to whom it is reasonably
         practicable to send such a copy; or
   (b)   take all such other steps for notifying the contents of the report to the members of the union
         (whether by publishing the report or otherwise) as it is the practice of the union to take
         when matters of general interest to all its members need to be brought to their attention.
(7)   Any such copy or notification shall be accompanied by a statement that the union will, on
request, supply any member of the trade union with a copy of the report, either free of charge or on
payment of such reasonable fee as may be specified in the notification.
(8)   The trade union shall so supply any member of the union who makes such a request and pays
the fee (if any) notified to him.]

**NOTES**
Substituted as noted to s 100 at **[1.358]**.

**[1.364]**
**101   Registration of instrument of amalgamation or transfer**
(1)   An instrument of amalgamation or transfer shall not take effect before it has been registered
by the Certification Officer under this Chapter.
(2)   It shall not be so registered before the end of the period of six weeks beginning with the date
on which an application for its registration is sent to the Certification Officer.

[(3) An application for registration of an instrument of amalgamation or transfer shall not be sent to the Certification Officer until section 100E(6) has been complied with in relation to the scrutineer's report on the ballot held on the resolution to approve the instrument.]

**NOTES**

Sub-s (3): added by the Trade Union Reform and Employment Rights Act 1993, s 49(2), Sch 8, para 55.

**[1.365]**
**[101A Listing and certification after amalgamation**
(1) Subsection (2) applies if when an instrument of amalgamation is registered by the Certification Officer under this Chapter each of the amalgamating unions is entered in the list of trade unions.
(2) The Certification Officer shall—
  (a) enter, with effect from the amalgamation date, the name of the amalgamated union in the list of trade unions, and
  (b) remove, with effect from that date, the names of the amalgamating unions from that list.
(3) Subsection (4) applies if when an instrument of amalgamation is registered by the Certification Officer under this Chapter each of the amalgamating unions has a certificate of independence which is in force.
(4) The Certification Officer shall issue to the amalgamated trade union, with effect from the amalgamation date, a certificate that the union is independent.
(5) In this section "the amalgamation date" means the date on which the instrument of amalgamation takes effect.]

**NOTES**

Inserted, together with s 101B, by the Employment Relations Act 2004, s 50(2).

**[1.366]**
**[101B Supply of information by amalgamated union**
(1) If an instrument of amalgamation is registered under this Chapter by the Certification Officer and the amalgamated union is entered in the list of trade unions in accordance with section 101A, that union shall send to him, in such manner and form as he may require—
  (a) a copy of the rules of the union,
  (b) a list of its officers, and
  (c) the address of its head or main office.
(2) The information required to be sent under subsection (1) must be accompanied by any fee prescribed for the purpose under section 108.
(3) The information must be sent—
  (a) before the end of the period of six weeks beginning with the date on which the instrument of amalgamation takes effect, or
  (b) if the Certification Officer considers that it is not reasonably practicable for the amalgamated union to send it in that period, before the end of such longer period, beginning with that date, as he may specify to the amalgamated union.
(4) If any of subsections (1) to (3) are not complied with by the amalgamated union, the Certification Officer shall remove its name from the list of trade unions.]

**NOTES**

Inserted as noted to s 101A at **[1.365]**.

Prescribed fee: the fee of £41 is prescribed for the purposes of sub-s (2) above in circumstances where, at the time the instrument of amalgamation was registered by the Certification Officer, the condition in s 101A(3) was satisfied and the Certification Officer was, accordingly, under the duty in sub-s (4) of that section to issue a certificate of independence to the amalgamated union (see the Certification Officer (Amendment of Fees) Regulations 2005, SI 2005/713, reg 8).

**[1.367]**
**102 Power to alter rules of transferee union for purposes of transfer**
(1) Where a trade union proposes to transfer its engagements to another trade union and an alteration of the rules of the transferee union is necessary to give effect to provisions in the instrument of transfer, the committee of management or other governing body of that union may by memorandum in writing alter the rules of that union so far as is necessary to give effect to those provisions.
  This subsection does not apply if the rules of the trade union expressly provide that this section is not to apply to that union.
(2) An alteration of the rules of a trade union under subsection (1) shall not take effect unless or until the instrument of transfer takes effect.
(3) The provisions of subsection (1) have effect, where they apply, notwithstanding anything in the rules of the union.

**[1.368]**
### 103  Complaints as regards passing of resolution
[(1)  A member of a trade union who claims that the union—
  (a)  has failed to comply with any of the requirements of sections 99 to 100E, or
  (b)  has, in connection with a resolution approving an instrument of amalgamation or transfer, failed to comply with any rule of the union relating to the passing of the resolution,
may complain to the Certification Officer.]
(2)  Any complaint must be made before the end of the period of six weeks beginning with the date on which an application for registration of the instrument of amalgamation or transfer is sent to the Certification Officer.
  Where a complaint is made, the Certification Officer shall not register the instrument before the complaint is finally determined or is withdrawn.
[(2A)  On a complaint being made to him the Certification Officer shall make such enquiries as he thinks fit].
(3)  If the Certification Officer, after giving the complainant and the trade union an opportunity of being heard, finds the complaint to be justified—
  (a)  he shall make a declaration to that effect, and
  (b)  he may make an order specifying the steps which must be taken before he will entertain any application to register the instrument of amalgamation or transfer;
and where he makes such an order, he shall not entertain any application to register the instrument unless he is satisfied that the steps specified in the order have been taken.
  An order under this subsection may be varied by the Certification Officer by a further order.
(4)  The Certification Officer shall furnish a statement, orally or in writing, of the reasons for his decision on a complaint under this section.
(5)  The validity of a resolution approving an instrument of amalgamation or transfer shall not be questioned in any legal proceedings whatsoever (except proceedings before the Certification Officer under this section or proceedings arising out of such proceedings) on any ground on which a complaint could be, or could have been, made to the Certification Officer under this section.
[(6)  Where the Certification Officer requests a person to furnish information to him in connection with enquiries made by him under this section, he shall specify the date by which that information is to be furnished and, unless he considers that it would be inappropriate to do so, shall proceed with his determination of the application notwithstanding that the information has not been furnished to him by the specified date.
(7)  A declaration made by the Certification Officer under this section may be relied on as if it were a declaration made by the court.
(8)  Where an order has been made under this section, any person who is a member of the union and was a member at the time it was made is entitled to enforce obedience to the order as if he had made the [complaint] on which the order was made.
(9)  An order made by the Certification Officer under this section may be enforced in the same way as an order of the court].

---

**NOTES**
  Sub-s (1): substituted by the Trade Union Reform and Employment Rights Act 1993, s 49(2), Sch 8, para 56.
  Sub-ss (2A), (6), (7), (9): inserted and added respectively by the Employment Relations Act 1999, s 29, Sch 6, paras 1, 18.
  Sub-s (8): added by the Employment Relations Act 1999, s 29, Sch 6, paras 1, 18; word in square brackets substituted by the Employment Relations Act 2004, s 57(1), Sch 1, para 7.

**[1.369]**
### 104  Appeal from decision of Certification Officer
An appeal lies to the Employment Appeal Tribunal, at the instance of the complainant or the trade union, on any question of law arising in any proceedings before, or arising from any decision of, the Certification Officer under section 103.

**[1.370]**
### 105  Transfer of property on amalgamation or transfer
(1)  Where an instrument of amalgamation or transfer takes effect, the property held—
  (a)  for the benefit of any of the amalgamating unions, or for the benefit of a branch of any of those unions, by the trustees of the union or branch, or
  (b)  for the benefit of the transferor trade union, or for the benefit of a branch of the transferor trade union, by the trustees of the union or branch,
shall without any conveyance, assignment or assignation vest, on the instrument taking effect, or on the appointment of the appropriate trustees, whichever is the later, in the appropriate trustees.
(2)  In the case of property to be held for the benefit of a branch of the amalgamated union, or of the transferee union, "the appropriate trustees" means the trustees of that branch, unless the rules of the amalgamated or transferee union provide that the property to be so held is to be held by the trustees of the union.
(3)  In any other case "the appropriate trustees" means the trustees of the amalgamated or transferee union.

(4)  This section does not apply—
  (a)  to property excepted from the operation of this section by the instrument of amalgamation or transfer, or
  (b)  to stocks and securities in the public funds of the United Kingdom or Northern Ireland.

**[1.371]**
**106  Amalgamation or transfer involving Northern Ireland**
(1)  This Chapter has effect subject to the following modifications in the case of an amalgamation or transfer of engagements to which a trade union and a Northern Ireland union are party.
(2)  The requirements of sections [98 to 100E and 101(3) (approval of instrument, notice to members and ballot on resolution)] do not apply in relation to the Northern Ireland union; but the Certification Officer shall not register the instrument under section 101 unless he is satisfied that it will be effective under the law of Northern Ireland.
(3)  The instrument of amalgamation or transfer submitted to the Certification Officer for his approval under section 98 shall state which of the bodies concerned is a Northern Ireland union and, in the case of an amalgamation, whether the amalgamated body is to be a Northern Ireland union; and the Certification Officer shall withhold his approval if the instrument does not contain that information.
(4)  Nothing in section 102 (alteration of rules) or [sections 103 and 104] (complaint as to passing of resolution) applies in relation to the Northern Ireland union.
(5)  Subject to the exceptions specified above, the provisions of this Chapter as to amalgamations or transfers of engagements apply in relation to the Northern Ireland union.

---

**NOTES**
Sub-ss (2), (4): words in square brackets substituted by the Trade Union Reform and Employment Rights Act 1993, s 49(2), Sch 8, para 57(a), (b).

---

*Change of name*
**[1.372]**
**107  Change of name of trade union**
(1)  A trade union may change its name by any method expressly provided for by its rules or, if its rules do not expressly provide for a method of doing so, by adopting in accordance with its rules an alteration of the provision in them which gives the union its name.
(2)  If the name of the trade union is entered in the list of trade unions a change of name shall not take effect until approved by the Certification Officer.
(3)  The Certification Officer shall not approve a change of name if it appears to him that the proposed new name—
  (a)  is the same as one entered in the list as the name of another trade union, or
  (b)  is the same as one entered in the list of employers' associations kept under Part II of this Act,
or is a name so nearly resembling such a name as to be likely to deceive the public.
(4)  A change of name by a trade union does not affect any right or obligation of the union or any of its members; and any pending legal proceedings may be continued by or against the union, the trustees of the union or any other officer of the union who can sue or be sued on its behalf notwithstanding its change of name.

*Supplementary*
**[1.373]**
**108  General powers to make regulations**
(1)  The Secretary of State may make regulations as respects—
  (a)  applications to the Certification Officer under this Chapter,
  (b)  the registration under this Chapter of any document or matter,
  (c)  the inspection of documents kept by the Certification Officer under this Chapter,
  (d)  the charging of fees in respect of such matters, and of such amounts, as may with the approval of the Treasury be prescribed by the regulations,
and generally for carrying this Chapter into effect.
(2)  Provision may in particular be made—
  (a)  requiring an application for the registration of an instrument of amalgamation or transfer, or of a change of name, to be accompanied by such statutory declarations or other documents as may be specified in the regulations;
  (b)  as to the form or content of any document required by this Chapter, or by the regulations, to be sent or submitted to the Certification Officer and as to the manner in which any such document is to be signed or authenticated;
  (c)  authorising the Certification Officer to require notice to be given or published in such manner as he may direct of the fact that an application for registration of an instrument of amalgamation or transfer has been or is to be made to him.
(3)  Regulations under this section may make different provision for different circumstances.

(4)   Regulations under this section shall be made by statutory instrument which shall be subject to annulment in pursuance of a resolution of either House of Parliament.

**NOTES**

Regulations: the Certification Officer (Amendment of Fees) Regulations 2005, SI 2005/713. By virtue of s 300(3) of, and Sch 3, para 1(2) to, this Act, and the Interpretation Act 1978, s 17(2)(b), the Trade Union and Employers' Associations (Amalgamations, etc) Regulations 1975, SI 1975/536 (at **[2.1]**), have effect as if made under this section.

[CHAPTER VIIA
BREACH OF RULES

**[1.374]**
**108A   Right to apply to Certification Officer**
(1)   A person who claims that there has been a breach or threatened breach of the rules of a trade union relating to any of the matters mentioned in subsection (2) may apply to the Certification Officer for a declaration to that effect, subject to subsections (3) to (7).
(2)   The matters are—
  (a)   the appointment or election of a person to, or the removal of a person from, any office;
  (b)   disciplinary proceedings by the union (including expulsion);
  (c)   the balloting of members on any issue other than industrial action;
  (d)   the constitution or proceedings of any executive committee or of any decision-making meeting;
  (e)   such other matters as may be specified in an order made by the Secretary of State.
(3)   The applicant must be a member of the union, or have been one at the time of the alleged breach or threatened breach.
(4)   A person may not apply under subsection (1) in relation to a claim if he is entitled to apply under section 80 in relation to the claim.
(5)   No application may be made regarding—
  (a)   the dismissal of an employee of the union;
  (b)   disciplinary proceedings against an employee of the union.
(6)   An application must be made—
  (a)   within the period of six months starting with the day on which the breach or threatened breach is alleged to have taken place, or
  (b)   if within that period any internal complaints procedure of the union is invoked to resolve the claim, within the period of six months starting with the earlier of the days specified in subsection (7).
(7)   Those days are—
  (a)   the day on which the procedure is concluded, and
  (b)   the last day of the period of one year beginning with the day on which the procedure is invoked.
(8)   The reference in subsection (1) to the rules of a union includes references to the rules of any branch or section of the union.
(9)   In subsection (2)(c) "industrial action" means a strike or other industrial action by persons employed under contracts of employment.
(10)   For the purposes of subsection (2)(d) a committee is an executive committee if—
  (a)   it is a committee of the union concerned and has power to make executive decisions on behalf of the union or on behalf of a constituent body,
  (b)   it is a committee of a major constituent body and has power to make executive decisions on behalf of that body, or
  (c)   it is a sub-committee of a committee falling within paragraph (a) or (b).
(11)   For the purposes of subsection (2)(d) a decision-making meeting is—
  (a)   a meeting of members of the union concerned (or the representatives of such members) which has power to make a decision on any matter which, under the rules of the union, is final as regards the union or which, under the rules of the union or a constituent body, is final as regards that body, or
  (b)   a meeting of members of a major constituent body (or the representatives of such members) which has power to make a decision on any matter which, under the rules of the union or the body, is final as regards that body.
(12)   For the purposes of subsections (10) and (11), in relation to the trade union concerned—
  (a)   a constituent body is any body which forms part of the union, including a branch, group, section or region;
  (b)   a major constituent body is such a body which has more than 1,000 members.
(13)   Any order under subsection (2)(e) shall be made by statutory instrument; and no such order shall be made unless a draft of it has been laid before and approved by resolution of each House of Parliament.

(14)   If a person applies to the Certification Officer under this section in relation to an alleged breach or threatened breach he may not apply to the court in relation to the breach or threatened breach; but nothing in this subsection shall prevent such a person from exercising any right to appeal against or challenge the Certification Officer's decision on the application to him.

(15)   If—

(a)   a person applies to the court in relation to an alleged breach or threatened breach, and

(b)   the breach or threatened breach is one in relation to which he could have made an application to the Certification Officer under this section,

he may not apply to the Certification Officer under this section in relation to the breach or threatened breach.]

**NOTES**

Inserted, together with the preceding heading and ss 108B, 108C, by the Employment Relations Act 1999, s 29, Sch 6, paras 1, 19.

Orders: as of 6 April 2013 no Orders had been made under this section.

**[1.375]**
**[108B   Declarations and orders**

(1)   The Certification Officer may refuse to accept an application under section 108A unless he is satisfied that the applicant has taken all reasonable steps to resolve the claim by the use of any internal complaints procedure of the union.

(2)   If he accepts an application under section 108A the Certification Officer—

(a)   shall make such enquiries as he thinks fit,

(b)   shall give the applicant and the union an opportunity to be heard,

(c)   shall ensure that, so far as is reasonably practicable, the application is determined within six months of being made,

(d)   may make or refuse the declaration asked for, and

(e)   shall, whether he makes or refuses the declaration, give reasons for his decision in writing.

(3)   Where the Certification Officer makes a declaration he shall also, unless he considers that to do so would be inappropriate, make an enforcement order, that is, an order imposing on the union one or both of the following requirements—

(a)   to take such steps to remedy the breach, or withdraw the threat of a breach, as may be specified in the order;

(b)   to abstain from such acts as may be so specified with a view to securing that a breach or threat of the same or a similar kind does not occur in future.

(4)   The Certification Officer shall in an order imposing any such requirement as is mentioned in subsection (3)(a) specify the period within which the union is to comply with the requirement.

(5)   Where the Certification Officer requests a person to furnish information to him in connection with enquiries made by him under this section, he shall specify the date by which that information is to be furnished and, unless he considers that it would be inappropriate to do so, shall proceed with his determination of the application notwithstanding that the information has not been furnished to him by the specified date.

(6)   A declaration made by the Certification Officer under this section may be relied on as if it were a declaration made by the court.

(7)   Where an enforcement order has been made, any person who is a member of the union and was a member at the time it was made is entitled to enforce obedience to the order as if he had made the application on which the order was made.

(8)   An enforcement order made by the Certification Officer under this section may be enforced in the same way as an order of the court.

(9)   An order under section 108A(2)(e) may provide that, in relation to an application under section 108A with regard to a prescribed matter, the preceding provisions of this section shall apply with such omissions or modifications as may be specified in the order; and a prescribed matter is such matter specified under section 108A(2)(e) as is prescribed under this subsection].

**NOTES**

Inserted as noted to s 108A at **[1.374]**.

**[1.376]**
**[108C   Appeals from Certification Officer**

An appeal lies to the Employment Appeal Tribunal on any question of law arising in proceedings before or arising from any decision of the Certification Officer under this Chapter.]

**NOTES**

Inserted as noted to s 108A at **[1.374]**.

**109–114**   *((Chapter VIII) repealed by the Employment Relations Act 1999, ss 28(2)(a), 44, Sch 9(6).)*

CHAPTER IX
MISCELLANEOUS AND GENERAL PROVISIONS

**115, 116**   *(Repealed by the Trade Union Reform and Employment Rights Act 1993, ss 7(1), (4), 51, Sch 10.)*

*[Union modernisation*

**[1.377]**
**116A   Provision of money for union modernisation**
(1)   The Secretary of State may provide money to a trade union to enable or assist it to do any or all of the following—
  (a)   improve the carrying out of any of its existing functions;
  (b)   prepare to carry out any new function;
  (c)   increase the range of services it offers to persons who are or may become members of it;
  (d)   prepare for an amalgamation or the transfer of any or all of its engagements;
  (e)   ballot its members (whether as a result of a requirement imposed by this Act or otherwise).
(2)   No money shall be provided to a trade union under this section unless at the time when the money is provided the union has a certificate of independence.
(3)   Money may be provided in such a way as the Secretary of State thinks fit (whether as grants or otherwise) and on such terms as he thinks fit (whether as to repayment or otherwise).
(4)   If money is provided to a trade union under this section, the terms on which it is so provided shall be deemed to include a prohibition ("a political fund prohibition") on any of it being added to the political fund of the union.
(5)   If a political fund prohibition is contravened, the Secretary of State—
  (a)   is entitled to recover from the trade union as a debt due to him an amount equal to the amount of money added to the union's political fund in contravention of the prohibition (whether or not that money continues to form part of the political fund); and
  (b)   must take such steps as are reasonably practicable to recover that amount.
(6)   An amount recoverable under subsection (5) is a liability of the trade union's political fund.
(7)   Subsection (5) does not prevent money provided to a trade union under this section from being provided on terms containing further sanctions for a contravention of the political fund prohibition.]

**NOTES**
Inserted, together with the preceding heading, by the Employment Relations Act 2004, s 55(1).

*Exceptions and adaptations for certain bodies*

**[1.378]**
**117   Special register bodies**
(1)   In this section a "special register body" means an organisation whose name appeared in the special register maintained under section 84 of the Industrial Relations Act 1971 immediately before 16 September 1974, and which is a company [registered under the Companies Act 2006] or is incorporated by charter or letters patent.
(2)   The provisions of this Part apply to special register bodies as to other trade unions, subject to the following exceptions and adaptations.
(3)   In Chapter II (status and property of trade unions)—
  (a)   in section 10 (quasi-corporate status of trade unions)—
    (i)   subsections (1) and (2) (prohibition on trade union being incorporated) do not apply, and
    (ii)   subsection (3) (prohibition on registration under certain Acts) does not apply so far as it relates to registration as a company under [the Companies Act 2006];
  (b)   section 11 (exclusion of common law rules as to restraint of trade) applies to the purposes or rules of a special register body only so far as they relate to the regulation of relations between employers or employers' associations and workers;
  (c)   sections 12 to 14 (vesting of property in trustees; transfer of securities) do not apply; and
  (d)   in section 20 (liability of trade union in certain proceedings in tort) in subsection (7) the reference to the contract between a member and the other members shall be construed as a reference to the contract between a member and the body.
(4)   Sections 33 to 35 (appointment and removal of auditors) do not apply to a special register body which is registered as a company under the [Companies Act 2006]; and sections 36 and 37 (rights and duties of auditors) apply to the auditors appointed by such a body under [Chapter 2 of Part 16 of that Act].
(5)   [Sections 45B and 45C (disqualification) and Chapter IV (elections) apply only] to—
  (a)   the position of voting member of the executive, and
  (b)   any position by virtue of which a person is a voting member of the executive.
In this subsection "voting member of the executive" has the meaning given by section 46(5).

## NOTES

Sub-ss (1), (3), (4): words in square brackets substituted by the Companies Act 2006 (Consequential Amendments, Transitional Provisions and Savings) Order 2009, SI 2009/1941, art 2(1), Sch 1, para 134(1), (3), as from 1 October 2009.

Sub-s (5): words in square brackets substituted by the Trade Union Reform and Employment Rights Act 1993, s 49(3), Sch 8, para 61.

Industrial Relations Act 1971: repealed by the Trade Union and Labour Relations Act 1974, ss 1, 25(3), Sch 5.

**[1.379]**
## 118 Federated trade unions

(1) In this section a "federated trade union" means a trade union which consists wholly or mainly of constituent or affiliated organisations, or representatives or such organisations, as described in paragraph (b) of the definition of "trade union" in section 1.

(2) The provisions of this Part apply to federated trade unions subject to the following exceptions and adaptations.

(3) For the purposes of section 22 (limit on amount of damages) as it applies to a federated trade union, the members of such of its constituent or affiliated organisations as have their head or main office in Great Britain shall be treated as members of the union.

(4) The following provisions of Chapter III (trade union administration) do not apply to a federated trade union which consists wholly or mainly of representatives of constituent or affiliated organisations—
- (a) section 27 (duty to supply copy of rules),
- (b) section 28 (duty to keep accounting records),
- (c) sections 32 to 37 (annual return, [statement for members,] accounts and audit), . . .
- [(ca) sections 37A to 37E (investigation of financial affairs), and]
- (d) sections 38 to 42 (members' superannuation schemes).

(5) Sections 29 to 31 (right of member to access to accounting records) do not apply to a federated trade union which has no members other than constituent or affiliated organisations or representatives of such organisations.

(6) Sections 24 to 26 (register of members' names and addresses) and Chapter IV (elections for certain trade union positions) do not apply to a federated trade union—
- (a) if it has no individual members other than representatives of constituent or affiliated organisations, or
- (b) if its individual members (other than such representatives) are all merchant seamen and a majority of them are ordinarily resident outside the United Kingdom.

For this purpose "merchant seaman" means a person whose employment, or the greater part of it, is carried out on board sea-going ships.

(7) The provisions of Chapter VI (application of funds for political objects) apply to a trade union which is in whole or part an association or combination of other unions as if the individual members of the component unions were members of that union and not of the component unions.

But nothing in that Chapter prevents a component union from collecting contributions on behalf of the association or combination from such of its members as are not exempt from the obligation to contribute to the political fund of the association or combination.

[(8) In the application of section 116A to a federated trade union, subsection (2) of that section shall be omitted.]

## NOTES

Sub-s (4): words in square brackets in para (c) inserted, word omitted from that paragraph repealed, and para (ca) inserted, by the Trade Union Reform and Employment Rights Act 1993, ss 49(3), 51, Sch 8, para 62, Sch 10.

Sub-s (8): added by the Employment Relations Act 2004, s 55(2).

*Interpretation*

**[1.380]**
## 119 Expressions relating to trade unions

In this Act, in relation to a trade union—
- ["agent" means a banker or solicitor of, or any person employed as an auditor by, the union or any branch or section of the union;]
- "branch or section", except where the context otherwise requires, includes a branch or section which is itself a trade union;
- "executive" means the principal committee of the union exercising executive functions, by whatever name it is called;
- ["financial affairs" means affairs of the union relating to any fund which is applicable for the purposes of the union (including any fund of a branch or section of the union which is so applicable);]
- "general secretary" means the official of the union who holds the office of general secretary or, where there is no such office, holds an office which is equivalent, or (except in section 14(4)) the nearest equivalent, to that of general secretary;
- "officer" includes—

    (a)   any member of the governing body of the union, and

    (b)   any trustee of any fund applicable for the purposes of the union;

"official" means—

    (a)   an officer of the union or of a branch or section of the union, or

    (b)   a person elected or appointed in accordance with the rules of the union to be a representative of its members or of some of them,

and includes a person so elected or appointed who is an employee of the same employer as the members or one or more of the members whom he is to represent;

"president" means the official of the union who holds the office of president or, where there is no such office, who holds an office which is equivalent, or (except in section 14(4) or Chapter IV) the nearest equivalent, to that of president; and

"rules", except where the context otherwise requires, includes the rules of any branch or section of the union.

**NOTES**

  Definitions "agent" and "financial affairs" inserted by the Trade Union Reform and Employment Rights Act 1993, s 49(2), Sch 8, para 63.

**[1.381]**
## 120   Northern Ireland unions

In this Part a "Northern Ireland union" means a trade union whose principal office is situated in Northern Ireland.

**[1.382]**
## 121   Meaning of "the court"

In this Part "the court" (except where the reference is expressed to be to the county court or sheriff court) means the High Court or the Court of Session.

## PART II
## EMPLOYERS' ASSOCIATIONS

*Introductory*

**[1.383]**
## 122   Meaning of "employers' association"

(1)   In this Act an "employers' association" means an organisation (whether temporary or permanent)—

    (a)   which consists wholly or mainly of employers or individual owners of undertakings of one or more descriptions and whose principal purposes include the regulation of relations between employers of that description or those descriptions and workers or trade unions; or

    (b)   which consists wholly or mainly of—

        (i)   constituent or affiliated organisations which fulfil the conditions in paragraph (a) (or themselves consist wholly or mainly of constituent or affiliated organisations which fulfil those conditions), or

        (ii)   representatives of such constituent or affiliated organisations,

and whose principal purposes include the regulation of relations between employers and workers or between employers and trade unions, or the regulation of relations between its constituent or affiliated organisations.

(2)   References in this Act to employers' associations include combinations of employers and employers' associations.

*The list of employers' associations*

**[1.384]**
## 123   The list of employers' associations

(1)   The Certification Officer shall keep a list of employers' associations containing the names of—

    (a)   the organisations whose names were, immediately before the commencement of this Act, duly entered in the list of employers' associations kept by him under section 8 of the Trade Union and Labour Relations Act 1974, and

    (b)   the names of the organisations entitled to have their names entered in the list in accordance with this Part.

(2)   The Certification Officer shall keep copies of the list of employers' associations, as for the time being in force, available for public inspection at all reasonable hours free of charge.

(3)   A copy of the list shall be included in his annual report.

(4)   The fact that the name of an organisation is included in the list of employers' associations is evidence (in Scotland, sufficient evidence) that the organisation is an employers' association.

(5)   On the application of an organisation whose name is included in the list, the Certification Officer shall issue it with a certificate to that effect.

(6)   A document purporting to be such a certificate is evidence (in Scotland, sufficient evidence) that the name of the organisation is entered in the list.

NOTES
   Trade Union and Labour Relations Act 1974, s 8: repealed by this Act.

**[1.385]**
**124   Application to have name entered in the list**
(1)   An organisation of employers, whenever formed, whose name is not entered in the list of employers' associations may apply to the Certification Officer to have its name entered in the list.
(2)   The application shall be made in such form and manner as the Certification Officer may require and shall be accompanied by—
   (a)   a copy of the rules of the organisation,
   (b)   a list of its officers,
   (c)   the address of its head or main office, and
   (d)   the name under which it is or is to be known,
and by the prescribed fee.
(3)   If the Certification Officer is satisfied—
   (a)   that the organisation is an employers' association,
   (b)   that subsection (2) has been complied with, and
   (c)   that entry of the name in the list is not prohibited by subsection (4),
he shall enter the name of the organisation in the list of employers' associations.
(4)   The Certification Officer shall not enter the name of an organisation in the list of employers' associations if the name is the same as that under which another organisation—
   (a)   was on 30th September 1971 registered as a trade union under the Trade Union Acts 1871 to 1964,
   (b)   was at any time registered as an employers' association or trade union under the Industrial Relations Act 1971, or
   (c)   is for the time being entered in the list of employers' associations or in the list of trade unions kept under Chapter I of Part I of this Act,
or if the name is one so nearly resembling any such name as to be likely to deceive the public.

NOTES
   Trade Union Acts 1871 to 1964: repealed, see the note to s 3 at **[1.243]**.
   Industrial Relations Act 1971: repealed by the Trade Union and Labour Relations Act 1974, ss 1, 25(3), Sch 5.
   Prescribed fee: the current fee is £150 (see the Certification Officer (Amendment of Fees) Regulations 2005, SI 2005/713, reg 6).

**[1.386]**
**125   Removal of name from the list**
(1)   If it appears to the Certification Officer, on application made to him or otherwise, that an organisation whose name is entered in the list of employers' associations is not an employers' association, he may remove its name from the list.
(2)   He shall not do so without giving the organisation notice of his intention and considering any representations made to him by the organisation within such period (of not less than 28 days beginning with the date of the notice) as may be specified in the notice.
(3)   The Certification Officer shall remove the name of an organisation from the list of employers' associations if—
   (a)   he is requested by the organisation to do so, or
   (b)   he is satisfied that the organisation has ceased to exist.

**[1.387]**
**126   Appeal against decision of Certification Officer**
(1)   An organisation aggrieved by the refusal of the Certification Officer to enter its name in the list of employers' associations, or by a decision of his to remove its name from the list, may appeal to the Employment Appeal Tribunal [on any appealable question].
(2)   . . .
(3)   [For the purposes of this section, an appealable question is any question of law] arising in the proceedings before, or arising from the decision of, the Certification Officer.

NOTES
   Sub-s (1): words in square brackets added by the Employment Relations Act 2004, s 51(2)(a).
   Sub-s (2): repealed by the Employment Relations Act 2004, ss 51(2)(b), 57(2), Sch 2.
   Sub-s (3): words in square brackets substituted by the Employment Relations Act 2004, s 51(2)(c).

*Status and property of employers' associations*

**[1.388]**
### 127 Corporate or quasi-corporate status of employers' associations
(1)   An employers' association may be either a body corporate or an unincorporated association.
(2)   Where an employers' association is unincorporated—
  (a)   it is capable of making contracts;
  (b)   it is capable of suing and being sued in its own name, whether in proceedings relating to property or founded on contract or tort or any other cause of action; and
  (c)   proceedings for an offence alleged to have been committed by it or on its behalf may be brought against it in its own name.
(3)   . . .

**NOTES**
Sub-s (3): repealed by the Regulatory Reform (Removal of 20 Member Limit in Partnerships etc) Order 2002, SI 2002/3203, art 4.

**[1.389]**
### 128 Exclusion of common law rules as to restraint of trade
(1)   The purposes of an unincorporated employers' association and, so far as they relate to the regulation of relations between employers and workers or trade unions, the purposes of an employers' association which is a body corporate are not, by reason only that they are in restraint of trade, unlawful so as—
  (a)   to make any member of the association liable to criminal proceedings for conspiracy or otherwise, or
  (b)   to make any agreement or trust void or voidable.
(2)   No rule of an unincorporated employers' association or, so far as it relates to the regulation of relations between employers and workers or trade unions, of an employers' association which is a body corporate, is unlawful or unenforceable by reason only that it is in restraint of trade.

**[1.390]**
### 129 Property of unincorporated employers' associations, &c
(1)   The following provisions of Chapter II of Part I of this Act apply to an unincorporated employers' association as in relation to a trade union—
  (a)   section 12(1) and (2) (property to be vested in trustees),
  (b)   section 13 (vesting of property in new trustees), and
  (c)   section 14 (transfer of securities held in trust for trade union).
(2)   In sections 13 and 14 as they apply by virtue of subsection (1) the reference to entry in the list of trade unions shall be construed as a reference to entry in the list of employers' associations.
(3)   Section 19 (application of certain provisions relating to . . . friendly societies) applies to any employers' association as in relation to a trade union.

**NOTES**
Sub-s (3): words omitted repealed by the Financial Services and Markets Act 2000 (Consequential Amendments and Repeals) Order 2001, SI 2001/3649, art 333.

**[1.391]**
### 130 Restriction on enforcement of awards against certain property
(1)   Where in any proceedings an amount is awarded by way of damages, costs or expenses—
  (a)   against an employers' association,
  (b)   against trustees in whom property is vested in trust for an employers' association, in their capacity as such (and otherwise than in respect of a breach of trust on their part), or
  (c)   against members or officials of an employers' association on behalf of themselves and all of the members of the association,
no part of that amount is recoverable by enforcement against any protected property.
(2)   The following is protected property—
  (a)   property belonging to the trustees otherwise than in their capacity as such;
  (b)   property belonging to any member of the association otherwise than jointly or in common with the other members;
  (c)   property belonging to an official of the association who is neither a member nor a trustee.

*Administration of employers' associations*

**[1.392]**
### 131 Administrative provisions applying to employers' associations
(1)   The following provisions of Chapter III of Part I of this Act apply to an employers' association as in relation to a trade union—
    section 27 (duty to supply copy of rules),
    section 28 (duty to keep accounting records),

[section 32(1), (2), (3)(a), (b) and (c) and (4) to (6) and sections 33 to 37] (annual return, accounts and audit),
[sections 37A to 37E (investigation of financial affairs),]
sections 38 to 42 (members' superannuation schemes),
section 43(1) (exemption for newly-formed organisations),
section 44(1), (2) and (4) (discharge of duties in case of organisation having branches or sections), and
[sections 45 and 45A] (offences).
(2)   Sections 33 to 35 (appointment and removal of auditors) do not apply to an employers' association which is registered as a company under [the Companies Act 2006]; and sections 36 and 37 (rights and duties of auditors) apply to the auditors appointed by such an association under . . . [ . . . Chapter 2 of Part 16 of that Act]].

**NOTES**
 Sub-s (1): words in first and third pairs of square brackets substituted, and words in second pair of square brackets inserted, by the Trade Union Reform and Employment Rights Act 1993, s 49(2), Sch 8, para 64.
 Sub-s (2): words in first pair of square brackets substituted by the Companies Act 2006 (Consequential Amendments, Transitional Provisions and Savings) Order 2009, SI 2009/1941, art 2(1), Sch 1, para 134(1), (4), as from 1 October 2009; words omitted repealed by the Companies Act 2006 (Consequential Amendments etc) Order 2008, SI 2008/948, art 3(1)(b), (2), Sch 1, Pt 2, para 188, Sch 2; words in second (outer) pair of square brackets added by the Companies Act 2006 (Commencement No 3, Consequential Amendments, Transitional Provisions and Savings) Order 2007, SI 2007/2194, art 10(1), (2), Sch 4, Pt 3, para 74.

*Application of funds for political objects*

**[1.393]**
**132   Application of funds for political objects**
[(1)]   [Subject to subsections (2) to (5), the] provisions of Chapter VI of Part I of this Act (application of funds for political objects) apply to an unincorporated employers' association as in relation to a trade union.
[(2)   Subsection (1) does not apply to these provisions—
  (a)   section 72A;
  (b)   in section 80, subsections (5A) to (5C) and (8) to (10);
  (c)   in section 81, subsection (8).
(3)   In its application to an unincorporated employers' association, section 79 shall have effect as if at the end of subsection (1) there were inserted—

  "The making of an application to the Certification Officer does not prevent the applicant, or any other person, from making an application to the court in respect of the same matter."

(4)   In its application to an unincorporated employers' association, section 80(2)(b) shall have effect as if the words "where he considers it appropriate," were inserted at the beginning.
(5)   In its application to an unincorporated employers' association, section 81 shall have effect as if after subsection (1) there were inserted—

  "(2)   If an application in respect of the same matter has been made to the Certification Officer, the court shall have due regard to any declaration, reasons or observations of his which are brought to its notice."]

**NOTES**
 Original text of this section numbered sub-s (1), words in square brackets therein substituted, and sub-ss (2)–(5) added by the Employment Relations Act 1999, s 29, Sch 6, paras 1, 20.

*Amalgamations and similar matters*

**[1.394]**
**[133   Amalgamations and transfers of engagements**
(1)   Subject to subsection (2), the provisions of Chapter VII of Part I of this Act (amalgamations and similar matters) apply to unincorporated employers' associations as in relation to trade unions.
(2)   In its application to such associations that Chapter shall have effect—
  (a)   as if in section 99(1) for the words from "that every" to "accompanied by" there were substituted the words "that, not less than seven days before the ballot on the resolution to approve the instrument of amalgamation or transfer is held, every member is supplied with",
  (b)   as if the requirements imposed by sections 100A to 100E consisted only of those specified in sections 100B and 100C(1) and (3)(a) together with the requirement that every member must, so far as is reasonably possible, be given a fair opportunity of voting,  . . .
  [(ba) as if the references in sections 101A and 101B to the list of trade unions were to the list of employers' associations, and]
  (c)   with the omission of sections 101(3)[, 101A(3) and (4)][, 103(2A) and (6) to (9)] and 107.]

NOTES
Substituted by the Trade Union Reform and Employment Rights Act 1993, s 49(2), Sch 8, para 65.
Sub-s (2): word omitted from para (b) repealed, para (ba) inserted, and words in first pair of square brackets in para (c) inserted, by the Employment Relations Act 2004, ss 50(3), 57(2), Sch 2; words in second pair of square brackets in para (c) inserted by the Employment Relations Act 1999, s 29, Sch 6, paras 1, 21.

**[1.395]**
## 134   Change of name of employers' association
(1)   An unincorporated employers' association may change its name by any method expressly provided for by its rules or, if its rules do not expressly provide for a method of doing so, by adopting in accordance with its rules an alteration of the provision in them which gives the association its name.

(2)   If the name of an employers' association, whether incorporated or unincorporated, is entered in the list of employers' associations a change of name shall not take effect until approved by the Certification Officer.

(3)   The Certification Officer shall not approve a change of name if it appears to him that the proposed new name—

    (a)   is the same as one entered in the list as the name of another employers' association, or

    (b)   is the same as one entered in the list of trade unions kept under Part I of this Act,

or is a name so nearly resembling such a name as to be likely to deceive the public.

(4)   A change of name by an unincorporated employers' association does not affect any right or obligation of the association or any of its members; and any pending legal proceedings may be continued by or against the association, the trustees of the association or any other officer of the association who can sue or be sued on its behalf notwithstanding its change of name.

(5)   The power conferred by section 108 (power to make regulations for carrying provisions into effect) applies in relation to this section as in relation to a provision of Chapter VII of Part I.

*General*

**[1.396]**
## 135   Federated employers' associations
(1)   In this section a "federated employers' association" means an employers' association which consists wholly or mainly of constituent or affiliated organisations, or representatives or such organisations, as described in paragraph (b) of the definition of "employers' association" in section 122.

(2)   The provisions of Part I applied by this Part to employers' associations apply to federated employers' associations subject to the following exceptions and adaptations.

(3)   The following provisions of Chapter III of Part I (administration) do not apply to a federated employers' association which consists wholly or mainly of representatives of constituent or affiliated organisations—

    (a)   section 27 (duty to supply copy of rules),

    (b)   section 28 (duty to keep accounting records),

    (c)   [section 32(1), (2), (3)(a), (b) and (c) and (4) to (6) and sections 33 to 37] (annual return, accounts and audit),  . . .

    [(ca) sections 37A to 37E (investigation of financial affairs), and]

    (d)   sections 38 to 42 (members' superannuation schemes).

(4)   The provisions of Chapter VI of Part I (application of funds for political objects) apply to a employers' association which is in whole or part an association or combination of other associations as if the individual members of the component associations were members of that association and not of the component associations.

But nothing in that Chapter prevents a component association from collecting contributions on behalf of the association or combination from such of its members as are not exempt from the obligation to contribute to the political fund of the association or combination.

NOTES
Sub-s (3): words in square brackets in para (c) substituted, word omitted from that paragraph repealed, and para (ca) inserted, by the Trade Union Reform and Employment Rights Act 1993, ss 49(2), 51, Sch 8, para 66, Sch 10.

**[1.397]**
## 136   Meaning of "officer" of employers' association
In this Act "officer", in relation to an employers' association, includes—

    (a)   any member of the governing body of the association, and

    (b)   any trustee of any fund applicable for the purposes of the association.

## PART III
## RIGHTS IN RELATION TO UNION MEMBERSHIP AND ACTIVITIES

*Access to employment*

**[1.398]**

**137 Refusal of employment on grounds related to union membership**

(1) It is unlawful to refuse a person employment—
  (a) because he is, or is not, a member of a trade union, or
  (b) because he is unwilling to accept a requirement—
      (i) to take steps to become or cease to be, or to remain or not to become, a member of a trade union, or
      (ii) to make payments or suffer deductions in the event of his not being a member of a trade union.

(2) A person who is thus unlawfully refused employment has a right of complaint to an [employment tribunal].

(3) Where an advertisement is published which indicates, or might reasonably be understood as indicating—
  (a) that employment to which the advertisement relates is open only to a person who is, or is not, a member of a trade union, or
  (b) that any such requirement as is mentioned in subsection (1)(b) will be imposed in relation to employment to which the advertisement relates,

a person who does not satisfy that condition or, as the case may be, is unwilling to accept that requirement, and who seeks and is refused employment to which the advertisement relates, shall be conclusively presumed to have been refused employment for that reason.

(4) Where there is an arrangement or practice under which employment is offered only to persons put forward or approved by a trade union, and the trade union puts forward or approves only persons who are members of the union, a person who is not a member of the union and who is refused employment in pursuance of the arrangement or practice shall be taken to have been refused employment because he is not a member of the trade union.

(5) A person shall be taken to be refused employment if he seeks employment of any description with a person and that person—
  (a) refuses or deliberately omits to entertain and process his application or enquiry, or
  (b) causes him to withdraw or cease to pursue his application or enquiry, or
  (c) refuses or deliberately omits to offer him employment of that description, or
  (d) makes him an offer of such employment the terms of which are such as no reasonable employer who wished to fill the post would offer and which is not accepted, or
  (e) makes him an offer of such employment but withdraws it or causes him not to accept it.

(6) Where a person is offered employment on terms which include a requirement that he is, or is not, a member of a trade union, or any such requirement as is mentioned in subsection (1)(b), and he does not accept the offer because he does not satisfy or, as the case may be, is unwilling to accept that requirement, he shall be treated as having been refused employment for that reason.

(7) Where a person may not be considered for appointment or election to an office in a trade union unless he is a member of the union, or of a particular branch or section of the union or of one of a number of particular branches or sections of the union, nothing in this section applies to anything done for the purpose of securing compliance with that condition although as holder of the office he would be employed by the union.

  For this purpose an "office" means any position—
  (a) by virtue of which the holder is an official of the union, or
  (b) to which Chapter IV of Part I applies (duty to hold elections).

(8) The provisions of this section apply in relation to an employment agency acting, or purporting to act, on behalf of an employer as in relation to an employer.

**NOTES**

Sub-s (2): words in square brackets substituted by the Employment Rights (Dispute Resolution) Act 1998, s 1(2)(a).

Conciliation: employment tribunal proceedings and claims which could be the subject of employment tribunal proceedings arising out of a contravention, or alleged contravention, of this section are proceedings to which the Employment Tribunals Act 1996, s 18 applies; see s 18(1)(b) of that Act at **[1.706]**.

**[1.399]**

**138 Refusal of service of employment agency on grounds related to union membership**

(1) It is unlawful for an employment agency to refuse a person any of its services—
  (a) because he is, or is not, a member of a trade union, or
  (b) because he is unwilling to accept a requirement to take steps to become or cease to be, or to remain or not to become, a member of a trade union.

(2) A person who is thus unlawfully refused any service of an employment agency has a right of complaint to an [employment tribunal].

[(2A)  Section 12A of the Employment Tribunals Act 1996 (financial penalties) applies in relation to a complaint under this section as it applies in relation to a claim involving an employer and a worker (reading references to an employer as references to the employment agency and references to a worker as references to the complainant).]

(3)  Where an advertisement is published which indicates, or might reasonably be understood as indicating—

(a)    that any service of an employment agency is available only to a person who is, or is not, a member of a trade union, or

(b)    that any such requirement as is mentioned in subsection (1)(b) will be imposed in relation to a service to which the advertisement relates,

a person who does not satisfy that condition or, as the case may be, is unwilling to accept that requirement, and who seeks to avail himself of and is refused that service, shall be conclusively presumed to have been refused it for that reason.

(4)  A person shall be taken to be refused a service if he seeks to avail himself of it and the agency—

(a)    refuses or deliberately omits to make the service available to him, or

(b)    causes him not to avail himself of the service or to cease to avail himself of it, or

(c)    does not provide the same service, on the same terms, as is provided to others.

(5)  Where a person is offered a service on terms which include a requirement that he is, or is not, a member of a trade union, or any such requirement as is mentioned in subsection (1)(b), and he does not accept the offer because he does not satisfy or, as the case may be, is unwilling to accept that requirement, he shall be treated as having been refused the service for that reason.

**NOTES**

Sub-s (2): words in square brackets substituted by the Employment Rights (Dispute Resolution) Act 1998, s 1(2)(a).

Sub-s (2A): inserted by the Enterprise and Regulatory Reform Act 2013, s 16(2), Sch 3, para 1, as from a day to be appointed.

Conciliation: employment tribunal proceedings and claims which could be the subject of employment tribunal proceedings arising out of a contravention, or alleged contravention, of this section are proceedings to which the Employment Tribunals Act 1996, s 18 applies; see s 18(1)(b) of that Act at **[1.706]**.

**[1.400]**
### 139  Time limit for proceedings

(1)  An [employment tribunal] shall not consider a complaint under section 137 or 138 unless it is presented to the tribunal—

(a)    before the end of the period of three months beginning with the date of the conduct to which the complaint relates, or

(b)    where the tribunal is satisfied that it was not reasonably practicable for the complaint to be presented before the end of that period, within such further period as the tribunal considers reasonable.

(2)  The date of the conduct to which a complaint under section 137 relates shall be taken to be—

(a)    in the case of an actual refusal, the date of the refusal;

(b)    in the case of a deliberate omission—

(i)    to entertain and process the complainant's application or enquiry, or

(ii)    to offer employment,

the end of the period within which it was reasonable to expect the employer to act;

(c)    in the case of conduct causing the complainant to withdraw or cease to pursue his application or enquiry, the date of that conduct;

(d)    in a case where an offer was made but withdrawn, the date when it was withdrawn;

(e)    in any other case where an offer was made but not accepted, the date on which it was made.

(3)  The date of the conduct to which a complaint under section 138 relates shall be taken to be—

(a)    in the case of an actual refusal, the date of the refusal;

(b)    in the case of a deliberate omission to make a service available, the end of the period within which it was reasonable to expect the employment agency to act;

(c)    in the case of conduct causing the complainant not to avail himself of a service or to cease to avail himself of it, the date of that conduct;

(d)    in the case of failure to provide the same service, on the same terms, as is provided to others, the date or last date on which the service in fact provided was provided.

[(4)  Section 292A (extension of time limits to facilitate conciliation before institution of proceedings) applies for the purposes of subsection (1)(a).]

**NOTES**

Sub-s (1): words in square brackets substituted by the Employment Rights (Dispute Resolution) Act 1998, s 1(2)(a).

Sub-s (4): added by the Enterprise and Regulatory Reform Act 2013, s 8, Sch 2, paras 1, 6, as from a day to be appointed.

**[1.401]**
**140 Remedies**
(1)  Where the [employment tribunal] finds that a complaint under section 137 or 138 is well-founded, it shall make a declaration to that effect and may make such of the following as it considers just and equitable—
(a)  an order requiring the respondent to pay compensation to the complainant of such amount as the tribunal may determine;
(b)  a recommendation that the respondent take within a specified period action appearing to the tribunal to be practicable for the purpose of obviating or reducing the adverse effect on the complainant of any conduct to which the complaint relates.
(2)  Compensation shall be assessed on the same basis as damages for breach of statutory duty and may include compensation for injury to feelings.
(3)  If the respondent fails without reasonable justification to comply with a recommendation to take action, the tribunal may increase its award of compensation or, if it has not made such an award, make one.
(4)  The total amount of compensation shall not exceed the limit for the time being imposed by [section 124(1) of the Employment Rights Act 1996] (limit on compensation for unfair dismissal).

**NOTES**
Sub-s (1): words in square brackets substituted by the Employment Rights (Dispute Resolution) Act 1998, s 1(2)(a).
Sub-s (4): words in square brackets substituted by the Employment Rights Act 1996, s 240, Sch 1, para 56(1), (6).

**[1.402]**
**141  Complaint against employer and employment agency**
(1)  Where a person has a right of complaint against a prospective employer and against an employment agency arising out of the same facts, he may present a complaint against either of them or against them jointly.
(2)  If a complaint is brought against one only, he or the complainant may request the tribunal to join or sist the other as a party to the proceedings.
   The request shall be granted if it is made before the hearing of the complaint begins, but may be refused if it is made after that time; and no such request may be made after the tribunal has made its decision as to whether the complaint is well-founded.
(3)  Where a complaint is brought against an employer and an employment agency jointly, or where it is brought against one and the other is joined or sisted as a party to the proceedings, and the tribunal—
(a)  finds that the complaint is well-founded as against the employer and the agency, and
(b)  makes an award of compensation,
it may order that the compensation shall be paid by the one or the other, or partly by one and partly by the other, as the tribunal may consider just and equitable in the circumstances.

**[1.403]**
**142  Awards against third parties**
(1)  If in proceedings on a complaint under section 137 or 138 either the complainant or the respondent claims that the respondent was induced to act in the manner complained of by pressure which a trade union or other person exercised on him by calling, organising, procuring or financing a strike or other industrial action, or by threatening to do so, the complainant or the respondent may request the [employment tribunal] to direct that the person who he claims exercised the pressure be joined or sisted as a party to the proceedings.
(2)  The request shall be granted if it is made before the hearing of the complaint begins, but may be refused if it is made after that time; and no such request may be made after the tribunal has made its decision as to whether the complaint is well-founded.
(3)  Where a person has been so joined or sisted as a party to the proceedings and the tribunal—
(a)  finds that the complaint is well-founded,
(b)  makes an award of compensation, and
(c)  also finds that the claim in subsection (1) above is well-founded,
it may order that the compensation shall be paid by the person joined instead of by the respondent, or partly by that person and partly by the respondent, as the tribunal may consider just and equitable in the circumstances.
(4)  Where by virtue of section 141 (complaint against employer and employment agency) there is more than one respondent, the above provisions apply to either or both of them.

**NOTES**
Sub-s (1): words in square brackets substituted by the Employment Rights (Dispute Resolution) Act 1998, s 1(2)(a).

**[1.404]**
**143  Interpretation and other supplementary provisions**
(1)  In sections 137 to 143—

"advertisement" includes every form of advertisement or notice, whether to the public or not, and references to publishing an advertisement shall be construed accordingly;

"employment" means employment under a contract of employment, and related expressions shall be construed accordingly; and

"employment agency" means a person who, for profit or not, provides services for the purpose of finding employment for workers or supplying employers with workers, but subject to subsection (2) below.

(2)   For the purposes of sections 137 to 143 as they apply to employment agencies—

(a)    services other than those mentioned in the definition of "employment agency" above shall be disregarded, and

(b)    a trade union shall not be regarded as an employment agency by reason of services provided by it only for, or in relation to, its members.

(3)   References in sections 137 to 143 to being or not being a member of a trade union are to being or not being a member of any trade union, of a particular trade union or of one of a number of particular trade unions.

Any such reference includes a reference to being or not being a member of a particular branch or section of a trade union or of one of a number of particular branches or sections of a trade union.

(4)   The remedy of a person for conduct which is unlawful by virtue of section 137 or 138 is by way of a complaint to an [employment tribunal] in accordance with this Part, and not otherwise.

No other legal liability arises by reason that conduct is unlawful by virtue of either of those sections.

---

**NOTES**

Sub-s (4): words in square brackets substituted by the Employment Rights (Dispute Resolution) Act 1998, s 1(2)(a).

*Contracts for supply of goods or services*

**[1.405]**
**144   Union membership requirement in contract for goods or services void**
A term or condition of a contract for the supply of goods or services is void in so far as it purports to require that the whole, or some part, of the work done for the purposes of the contract is done only by persons who are, or are not, members of trade unions or of a particular trade union.

**[1.406]**
**145   Refusal to deal on union membership grounds prohibited**
(1)   A person shall not refuse to deal with a supplier or prospective supplier of goods or services on union membership grounds.

"Refuse to deal" and "union membership grounds" shall be construed as follows.

(2)   A person refuses to deal with a person if, where he maintains (in whatever form) a list of approved suppliers of goods or services, or of persons from whom tenders for the supply of goods or services may be invited, he fails to include the name of that person in that list.

He does so on union membership grounds if the ground, or one of the grounds, for failing to include his name is that if that person were to enter into a contract with him for the supply of goods or services, work to be done for the purposes of the contract would, or would be likely to, be done by persons who were, or who were not, members of trade unions or of a particular trade union.

(3)   A person refuses to deal with a person if, in relation to a proposed contract for the supply of goods or services—

(a)    he excludes that person from the group of persons from whom tenders for the supply of the goods or services are invited, or

(b)    he fails to permit that person to submit such a tender, or

(c)    he otherwise determines not to enter into a contract with that person for the supply of the goods or services.

He does so on union membership grounds if the ground, or one of the grounds, on which he does so is that if the proposed contract were entered into with that person, work to be done for the purposes of the contract would, or would be likely to, be done by persons who were, or who were not, members of trade unions or of a particular trade union.

(4)   A person refuses to deal with a person if he terminates a contract with him for the supply of goods or services.

He does so on union membership grounds if the ground, or one of the grounds, on which he does so is that work done, or to be done, for the purposes of the contract has been, or is likely to be, done by persons who are or are not members of trade unions or of a particular trade union.

(5)   The obligation to comply with this section is a duty owed to the person with whom there is a refusal to deal and to any other person who may be adversely affected by its contravention; and a breach of the duty is actionable accordingly (subject to the defences and other incidents applying to actions for breach of statutory duty).

*[Inducements*

**[1.407]**
**145A  Inducements relating to union membership or activities**
(1)   A worker has the right not to have an offer made to him by his employer for the sole or main purpose of inducing the worker—
  (a)   not to be or seek to become a member of an independent trade union,
  (b)   not to take part, at an appropriate time, in the activities of an independent trade union,
  (c)   not to make use, at an appropriate time, of trade union services, or
  (d)   to be or become a member of any trade union or of a particular trade union or of one of a number of particular trade unions.
(2)   In subsection (1) "an appropriate time" means—
  (a)   a time outside the worker's working hours, or
  (b)   a time within his working hours at which, in accordance with arrangements agreed with or consent given by his employer, it is permissible for him to take part in the activities of a trade union or (as the case may be) make use of trade union services.
(3)   In subsection (2) "working hours", in relation to a worker, means any time when, in accordance with his contract of employment (or other contract personally to do work or perform services), he is required to be at work.
(4)   In subsections (1) and (2)—
  (a)   "trade union services" means services made available to the worker by an independent trade union by virtue of his membership of the union, and
  (b)   references to a worker's "making use" of trade union services include his consenting to the raising of a matter on his behalf by an independent trade union of which he is a member.
(5)   A worker or former worker may present a complaint to an employment tribunal on the ground that his employer has made him an offer in contravention of this section.]

NOTES
  Inserted, together with the preceding heading and ss 145B–145F, by the Employment Relations Act 2004, s 29.
  Conciliation: employment tribunal proceedings and claims which could be the subject of employment tribunal proceedings arising out of a contravention, or alleged contravention, of this section and ss 145B, 146 are proceedings to which the Employment Tribunals Act 1996, s 18 applies; see s 18(1)(b) of that Act at **[1.706]**.
  Tribunal jurisdiction: the Employment Act 2002, s 38 applies to proceedings before the employment tribunal relating to a claim under this section and ss 145B, 146; see s 38(1) of, and Sch 5 to, the 2002 Act at **[1.1228]**, **[1.1236]**. See also s 207A of this Act at **[1.474]** (as inserted by the Employment Act 2008). That section provides that in proceedings before an employment tribunal relating to a claim by an employee under any of the jurisdictions listed in Sch A2 to this Act at **[1.648]** (which includes this section) the tribunal may adjust any award given if the employer or the employee has unreasonably failed to comply with the relevant Code of Practice as defined by s 207A(4). See also the revised Acas Code of Practice 1 – Disciplinary and Grievance Procedures (2009) at **[4.1]**.
  National security: for the effect of national security considerations on a complaint under this section and ss 145B, 146, see the Employment Tribunals Act 1996, s 10(1) at **[1.694]**.
  The rights conferred by this section are "relevant statutory rights" for the purposes of the Employment Rights Act 1996, s 104 (dismissal on grounds of assertion of statutory right); see s 104(4)(c) of that Act at **[1.907]**.

**[1.408]**
**[145B  Inducements relating to collective bargaining**
(1)   A worker who is a member of an independent trade union which is recognised, or seeking to be recognised, by his employer has the right not to have an offer made to him by his employer if—
  (a)   acceptance of the offer, together with other workers' acceptance of offers which the employer also makes to them, would have the prohibited result, and
  (b)   the employer's sole or main purpose in making the offers is to achieve that result.
(2)   The prohibited result is that the workers' terms of employment, or any of those terms, will not (or will no longer) be determined by collective agreement negotiated by or on behalf of the union.
(3)   It is immaterial for the purposes of subsection (1) whether the offers are made to the workers simultaneously.
(4)   Having terms of employment determined by collective agreement shall not be regarded for the purposes of section 145A (or section 146 or 152) as making use of a trade union service.
(5)   A worker or former worker may present a complaint to an employment tribunal on the ground that his employer has made him an offer in contravention of this section.]

NOTES
  Inserted as noted to s 145A at **[1.407]**.
  Conciliation: see the note to s 145A at **[1.407]**.
  Tribunal jurisdiction: see the note to s 145A at **[1.407]**.
  National security: see the note to s 145A at **[1.407]**.
  The rights conferred by this section are "relevant statutory rights" for the purposes of the Employment Rights Act 1996, s 104 (dismissal on grounds of assertion of statutory right); see s 104(4)(c) of that Act at **[1.907]**.

**[1.409]**
**[145C    Time limit for proceedings**
[(1)]    An employment tribunal shall not consider a complaint under section 145A or 145B unless it is presented—
- (a)    before the end of the period of three months beginning with the date when the offer was made or, where the offer is part of a series of similar offers to the complainant, the date when the last of them was made, or
- (b)    where the tribunal is satisfied that it was not reasonably practicable for the complaint to be presented before the end of that period, within such further period as it considers reasonable.

[(2)    Section 292A (extension of time limits to facilitate conciliation before institution of proceedings) applies for the purposes of subsection (1)(a).]

NOTES
Inserted as noted to s 145A at **[1.407]**.
The existing provision is numbered as sub-s (1) and sub-s (2) is added, by the Enterprise and Regulatory Reform Act 2013, s 8, Sch 2, paras 1, 7, as from a day to be appointed.

**[1.410]**
**[145D    Consideration of complaint**
(1)    On a complaint under section 145A it shall be for the employer to show what was his sole or main purpose in making the offer.
(2)    On a complaint under section 145B it shall be for the employer to show what was his sole or main purpose in making the offers.
(3)    On a complaint under section 145A or 145B, in determining any question whether the employer made the offer (or offers) or the purpose for which he did so, no account shall be taken of any pressure which was exercised on him by calling, organising, procuring or financing a strike or other industrial action, or by threatening to do so; and that question shall be determined as if no such pressure had been exercised.
(4)    In determining whether an employer's sole or main purpose in making offers was the purpose mentioned in section 145B(1), the matters taken into account must include any evidence—
- (a)    that when the offers were made the employer had recently changed or sought to change, or did not wish to use, arrangements agreed with the union for collective bargaining,
- (b)    that when the offers were made the employer did not wish to enter into arrangements proposed by the union for collective bargaining, or
- (c)    that the offers were made only to particular workers, and were made with the sole or main purpose of rewarding those particular workers for their high level of performance or of retaining them because of their special value to the employer.]

NOTES
Inserted as noted to s 145A at **[1.407]**.

**[1.411]**
**[145E    Remedies**
(1)    Subsections (2) and (3) apply where the employment tribunal finds that a complaint under section 145A or 145B is well-founded.
(2)    The tribunal—
- (a)    shall make a declaration to that effect, and
- (b)    shall make an award to be paid by the employer to the complainant in respect of the offer complained of.

(3)    The amount of the award shall be [£3,600] (subject to any adjustment of the award that may fall to be made under Part 3 of the Employment Act 2002).
(4)    Where an offer made in contravention of section 145A or 145B is accepted—
- (a)    if the acceptance results in the worker's agreeing to vary his terms of employment, the employer cannot enforce the agreement to vary, or recover any sum paid or other asset transferred by him under the agreement to vary;
- (b)    if as a result of the acceptance the worker's terms of employment are varied, nothing in section 145A or 145B makes the variation unenforceable by either party.

(5)    Nothing in this section or sections 145A and 145B prejudices any right conferred by section 146 or 149.
(6)    In ascertaining any amount of compensation under section 149, no reduction shall be made on the ground—
- (a)    that the complainant caused or contributed to his loss, or to the act or failure complained of, by accepting or not accepting an offer made in contravention of section 145A or 145B, or
- (b)    that the complainant has received or is entitled to an award under this section.]

**NOTES**
Inserted as noted to s 145A at **[1.407]**.

Sub-s (3): sum in square brackets substituted by the Employment Rights (Increase of Limits) Order 2012, SI 2012/3007, art 3, Schedule, as from 1 February 2013, in relation to any case where the appropriate date (as defined in the order) falls on or after that date (see SI 2012/3007, art 4 at **[2.1636]**). The previous sum was £3,500 as from 1 February 2012 (see SI 2011/3006). This sum may be further varied by the Secretary of State, see the Employment Relations Act 1999, s 34(1)(ea), (3)(b) at **[1.1202]**.

**[1.412]**
**[145F    Interpretation and other supplementary provisions**
(1)   References in sections 145A to 145E to being or becoming a member of a trade union include references—
  (a)    to being or becoming a member of a particular branch or section of that union, and
  (b)    to being or becoming a member of one of a number of particular branches or sections of that union.
(2)   References in those sections—
  (a)    to taking part in the activities of a trade union, and
  (b)    to services made available by a trade union by virtue of membership of the union,
shall be construed in accordance with subsection (1).
(3)   In sections 145A to 145E—
  "worker" means an individual who works, or normally works, as mentioned in paragraphs (a) to
       (c) of section 296(1), and
  "employer" means—
       (a)    in relation to a worker, the person for whom he works;
       (b)    in relation to a former worker, the person for whom he worked.
(4)   The remedy of a person for infringement of the right conferred on him by section 145A or 145B is by way of a complaint to an employment tribunal in accordance with this Part, and not otherwise.]

**NOTES**
Inserted as noted to s 145A at **[1.407]**.

*[Detriment]*

**[1.413]**
**146   [Detriment] on grounds related to union membership or activities**
(1)   [A worker] has the right not to [be subjected to any detriment as an individual by any act, or any deliberate failure to act, by his employer if the act or failure takes place] for [the sole or main purpose] of—
  (a)    preventing or deterring him from being or seeking to become a member of an independent trade union, or penalising him for doing so,
  (b)    preventing or deterring him from taking part in the activities of an independent trade union at an appropriate time, or penalising him for doing so,  . . .
  [(ba)  preventing or deterring him from making use of trade union services at an appropriate time, or penalising him for doing so, or]
  (c)    compelling him to be or become a member of any trade union or of a particular trade union or of one of a number of particular trade unions.
(2)   In subsection [(1)] "an appropriate time" means—
  (a)    a time outside the [worker's] working hours, or
  (b)    a time within his working hours at which, in accordance with arrangements agreed with or consent given by his employer, it is permissible for him to take part in the activities of a trade union [or (as the case may be) make use of trade union services];
and for this purpose "working hours", in relation to [a worker], means any time when, in accordance with his contract of employment [(or other contract personally to do work or perform services)], he is required to be at work.
[(2A)   In this section—
  (a)    "trade union services" means services made available to the worker by an independent trade union by virtue of his membership of the union, and
  (b)    references to a worker's "making use" of trade union services include his consenting to the raising of a matter on his behalf by an independent trade union of which he is a member.
(2B)   If an independent trade union of which a worker is a member raises a matter on his behalf (with or without his consent), penalising the worker for that is to be treated as penalising him as mentioned in subsection (1)(ba).
(2C)   A worker also has the right not to be subjected to any detriment as an individual by any act, or any deliberate failure to act, by his employer if the act or failure takes place because of the worker's failure to accept an offer made in contravention of section 145A or 145B.

(2D)   For the purposes of subsection (2C), not conferring a benefit that, if the offer had been accepted by the worker, would have been conferred on him under the resulting agreement shall be taken to be subjecting him to a detriment as an individual (and to be a deliberate failure to act).]

(3)   [A worker] also has the right not to [be subjected to any detriment as an individual by any act, or any deliberate failure to act, by his employer if the act or failure takes place] for [the sole or main purpose] of enforcing a requirement (whether or not imposed by [a contract of employment] or in writing) that, in the event of his not being a member of any trade union or of a particular trade union or of one of a number of particular trade unions, he must make one or more payments.

(4)   For the purposes of subsection (3) any deduction made by an employer from the remuneration payable to [a worker] in respect of his employment shall, if it is attributable to his not being a member of any trade union or of a particular trade union or of one of a number of particular trade unions, be treated as [a detriment to which he has been subjected as an individual by an act of his employer taking place] for [the sole or main purpose] of enforcing a requirement of a kind mentioned in that subsection.

(5)   [A worker or former worker] may present a complaint to an [employment tribunal] on the ground that [he has been subjected to a detriment] by his employer in contravention of this section.

[(5A)   This section does not apply where—
   (a)   the worker is an employee; and
   (b)   the detriment in question amounts to dismissal.]

**NOTES**

   The heading preceding this section and the words in square brackets in the section heading were substituted by the Employment Relations Act 2004, s 30(7).

   Sub-s (1): words in first and third pairs of square brackets substituted, word omitted from para (b) repealed, and para (ba) inserted, by the Employment Relations Act 2004, ss 30(1), (2), 31(1), (2), 57, Sch 1, para 8, Sch 2; words in second pair of square brackets substituted by the Employment Relations Act 1999, s 2, Sch 2, paras 1, 2(1), (2).

   Sub-s (2): words in first, second and fourth pairs of square brackets substituted, and words in third and fifth pairs of square brackets inserted, by the Employment Relations Act 2004, ss 30(1)–(3), 31(1), (3).

   Sub-ss (2A)–(2D): inserted by the Employment Relations Act 2004, s 31(1), (4).

   Sub-s (3): words in first, third and fourth pairs of square brackets substituted by the Employment Relations Act 2004, ss 30(1), (2), (4), 57(1), Sch 1, para 8; words in second pair of square brackets substituted by the Employment Relations Act 1999, s 2, Sch 2, paras 1, 2(1), (3).

   Sub-s (4): words in first and third pairs of square brackets substituted by the Employment Relations Act 2004, ss 30(1), (2), 57(1), Sch 1, para 8; words in second pair of square brackets substituted by the Employment Relations Act 1999, s 2, Sch 2, paras 1, 2(1), (4).

   Sub-s (5): words in first pair of square brackets substituted by the Employment Relations Act 2004, s 30(1), (5); words in second pair of square brackets substituted by the Employment Rights (Dispute Resolution) Act 1998, s 1(2)(a); words in third pair of square brackets substituted by the Employment Relations Act 1999, s 2, Sch 2, paras 1, 2(1), (5).

   Sub-s (5A): added (as sub-s (6)) by the Employment Relations Act 1999, s 2, Sch 2, paras 1, 2(1), (6); substituted (and renumbered) by the Employment Relations Act 2004, s 30(1), (6).

   This section and ss 147, 152–154 and 181–185 are modified, in relation to governing bodies with delegated budgets, by the Education (Modification of Enactments Relating to Employment) (England) Order 2003, SI 2003/1964, art 3, Schedule at **[2.746]**, **[2.750]** and the Education (Modification of Enactments Relating to Employment) (Wales) Order 2006, SI 2006/1073, art 3, Schedule at **[2.1043]**, **[2.1046]**.

   Conciliation: see the note to s 145A at **[1.407]**.

   Tribunal jurisdiction: see the note to s 145A at **[1.407]**.

   National security: see the fifth note to s 145A at **[1.407]**.

   The rights conferred by this section are "relevant statutory rights" for the purposes of the Employment Rights Act 1996, s 104 (dismissal on grounds of assertion of statutory right); see s 104(4)(c) of that Act at **[1.907]**.

**[1.414]**
## 147   Time limit for proceedings

[(1)]   An [employment tribunal] shall not consider a complaint under section 146 unless it is presented—
   (a)   before the end of the period of three months beginning with the date of the [act or failure to which the complaint relates or, where that act or failure is part of a series of similar acts or failures (or both) the last of them], or
   (b)   where the tribunal is satisfied that it was not reasonably practicable for the complaint to be presented before the end of that period, within such further period as it considers reasonable.

[(2)   For the purposes of subsection (1)—
   (a)   where an act extends over a period, the reference to the date of the act is a reference to the last day of that period;
   (b)   a failure to act shall be treated as done when it was decided on.

(3)   For the purposes of subsection (2), in the absence of evidence establishing the contrary an employer shall be taken to decide on a failure to act—
   (a)   when he does an act inconsistent with doing the failed act, or
   (b)   if he has done no such inconsistent act, when the period expires within which he might reasonably have been expected to do the failed act if it was to be done.]

[(4)   Section 292A (extension of time limits to facilitate conciliation before institution of proceedings) applies for the purposes of subsection (1)(a).]

**NOTES**

Sub-s (1): original text renumbered as sub-s (1) and words in second pair of square brackets substituted by the Employment Relations Act 1999, s 2, Sch 2, paras 1, 3(1)–(3); words in first pair of square brackets substituted by the Employment Rights (Dispute Resolution) Act 1998, s 1(2)(a).

Sub-ss (2), (3): added by the Employment Relations Act 1999, s 2, Sch 2, paras 1, 3(1), (4).

Sub-s (4): added by the Enterprise and Regulatory Reform Act 2013, s 8, Sch 2, paras 1, 8, as from a day to be appointed. Modified as noted to s 146 at **[1.413]**.

**[1.415]**
**148   Consideration of complaint**
(1)   On a complaint under section 146 it shall be for the employer to show [what was the sole or main purpose] for which [he acted or failed to act].
(2)   In determining any question whether [the employer acted or failed to act, or the purpose for which he did so], no account shall be taken of any pressure which was exercised on him by calling, organising, procuring or financing a strike or other industrial action, or by threatening to do so; and that question shall be determined as if no such pressure had been exercised.
[(3)–(5)   . . .   ]

**NOTES**

Sub-s (1): words in first pair of square brackets substituted by the Employment Relations Act 2004, s 57(1), Sch 1, para 9; words in second pair of square brackets substituted by the Employment Relations Act 1999, s 2, Sch 2, paras 1, 4(1), (2).

Sub-s (2): words in square brackets substituted by the Employment Relations Act 1999, s 2, Sch 2, paras 1, 4(1), (3).

Sub-ss (3)–(5): added by the Trade Union Reform and Employment Rights Act 1993, s 13; repealed by the Employment Relations Act 2004, ss 31, 57(2), Sch 2.

**[1.416]**
**149   Remedies**
(1)   Where the [employment tribunal] finds that a complaint under section 146 is well-founded, it shall make a declaration to that effect and may make an award of compensation to be paid by the employer to the complainant in respect of the [act or failure] complained of.
(2)   The amount of the compensation awarded shall be such as the tribunal considers just and equitable in all the circumstances having regard to the infringement complained of and to any loss sustained by the complainant which is attributable to the [act or failure] which infringed his right.
(3)   The loss shall be taken to include—
   (a)   any expenses reasonably incurred by the complainant in consequence of the [act or failure] complained of, and
   (b)   loss of any benefit which he might reasonably be expected to have had but for that [act or failure].
(4)   In ascertaining the loss, the tribunal shall apply the same rule concerning the duty of a person to mitigate his loss as applies to damages recoverable under the common law of England and Wales or Scotland.
(5)   In determining the amount of compensation to be awarded no account shall be taken of any pressure which was exercised on the employer by calling, organising, procuring or financing a strike or other industrial action, or by threatening to do so; and that question shall be determined as if no such pressure had been exercised.
(6)   Where the tribunal finds that the [act or failure] complained of was to any extent caused or contributed to by action of the complainant, it shall reduce the amount of the compensation by such proportion as it considers just and equitable having regard to that finding.

**NOTES**

Sub-s (1): words in first pair of square brackets substituted by the Employment Rights (Dispute Resolution) Act 1998, s 1(2)(a); words in second pair of square brackets substituted by the Employment Relations Act 1999, s 2, Sch 2, paras 1, 5(a).

Sub-ss (2), (3), (6): words in square brackets substituted by the Employment Relations Act 1999, s 2, Sch 2, paras 1, 5(a), (b).

**[1.417]**
**150   Awards against third parties**
(1)   If in proceedings on a complaint under section 146—
   (a)   the complaint is made on the ground that [the complainant has been subjected to detriment by an act or failure by his employer taking place] for [the sole or main purpose] of compelling him to be or become a member of any trade union or of a particular trade union or of one of a number of particular trade unions, and
   (b)   either the complainant or the employer claims in proceedings before the tribunal that the employer was induced to [act or fail to act in the way] complained of by pressure which a trade union or other person exercised on him by calling, organising, procuring or financing a strike or other industrial action, or by threatening to do so,

the complainant or the employer may request the tribunal to direct that the person who he claims exercised the pressure be joined or sisted as a party to the proceedings.

(2)   The request shall be granted if it is made before the hearing of the complaint begins, but may be refused if it is made after that time; and no such request may be made after the tribunal has made a declaration that the complaint is well-founded.

(3)   Where a person has been so joined or sisted as a party to proceedings and the tribunal—

    (a)   makes an award of compensation, and

    (b)   finds that the claim mentioned in subsection (1)(b) is well-founded,

it may order that the compensation shall be paid by the person joined instead of by the employer, or partly by that person and partly by the employer, as the tribunal may consider just and equitable in the circumstances.

**NOTES**

    Sub-s (1): words in first pair of square brackets in para (a) and words in square brackets in para (b) substituted by the Employment Relations Act 1999, s 2, Sch 2, paras 1, 6; words in second pair of square brackets in para (a) substituted by the Employment Relations Act 2004, s 57(1), Sch 1, para 10.

**[1.418]**
### 151   Interpretation and other supplementary provisions

(1)   References in sections 146 to 150 to being, becoming or ceasing to remain a member of a trade union include references to being, becoming or ceasing to remain a member of a particular branch or section of that union and to being, becoming or ceasing to remain a member of one of a number of particular branches or sections of that union   . . .

[(1A)   References in those sections—

    (a)   to taking part in the activities of a trade union, and

    (b)   to services made available by a trade union by virtue of membership of the union,

shall be construed in accordance with subsection (1).]

[(1B)   In sections 146 to 150—

    "worker" means an individual who works, or normally works, as mentioned in paragraphs (a) to

        (c) of section 296(1), and

    "employer" means—

        (a)   in relation to a worker, the person for whom he works;

        (b)   in relation to a former worker, the person for whom he worked.]

(2)   The remedy of [a person] for infringement of the right conferred on him by section 146 is by way of a complaint to an [employment tribunal] in accordance with this Part, and not otherwise.

**NOTES**

    Sub-s (1): words omitted repealed by the Employment Relations Act 2004, ss 31(6), 57(2), Sch 2.

    Sub-ss (1A), (1B): inserted by the Employment Relations Act 2004, s 31(7), (8).

    Sub-s (2): words in first pair of square brackets substituted by the Employment Relations Act 2004, s 30(9); words in second pair of square brackets substituted by the Employment Rights (Dispute Resolution) Act 1998, s 1(2)(a).

*Dismissal [of employee]*

**[1.419]**
### 152   Dismissal [of employee] on grounds related to union membership or activities

(1)   For purposes of [Part X of the Employment Rights Act 1996] (unfair dismissal) the dismissal of an employee shall be regarded as unfair if the reason for it (or, if more than one, the principal reason) was that the employee—

    (a)   was, or proposed to become, a member of an independent trade union,   . . .

    (b)   had taken part, or proposed to take part, in the activities of an independent trade union at an appropriate time,   . . .

    [(ba) had made use, or proposed to make use, of trade union services at an appropriate time,

    (bb) had failed to accept an offer made in contravention of section 145A or 145B, or]

    (c)   was not a member of any trade union, or of a particular trade union, or of one of a number of particular trade unions, or had refused, or proposed to refuse, to become or remain a member.

(2)   In subsection [(1)] "an appropriate time" means—

    (a)   a time outside the employee's working hours, or

    (b)   a time within his working hours at which, in accordance with arrangements agreed with or consent given by his employer, it is permissible for him to take part in the activities of a trade union [or (as the case may be) make use of trade union services];

and for this purpose "working hours", in relation to an employee, means any time when, in accordance with his contract of employment, he is required to be at work.

[(2A)   In this section—

    (a)   "trade union services" means services made available to the employee by an independent trade union by virtue of his membership of the union, and

(b)  references to an employee's "making use" of trade union services include his consenting to the raising of a matter on his behalf by an independent trade union of which he is a member.

(2B)  Where the reason or one of the reasons for the dismissal was that an independent trade union (with or without the employee's consent) raised a matter on behalf of the employee as one of its members, the reason shall be treated as falling within subsection (1)(ba).]

(3)  Where the reason, or one of the reasons, for the dismissal was—

(a)  the employee's refusal, or proposed refusal, to comply with a requirement (whether or not imposed by his contract of employment or in writing) that, in the event of his not being a member of any trade union, or of a particular trade union, or of one of a number of particular trade unions, he must make one or more payments, or

(b)  his objection, or proposed objection, (however expressed) to the operation of a provision (whether or not forming part of his contract of employment or in writing) under which, in the event mentioned in paragraph (a), his employer is entitled to deduct one or more sums from the remuneration payable to him in respect of his employment,

the reason shall be treated as falling within subsection (1)(c).

(4)  References in this section to being, becoming or ceasing to remain a member of a trade union include references to being, becoming or ceasing to remain a member of a particular branch or section of that union or of one of a number of particular branches or sections of that trade union . . .

[(5)  References in this section—

(a)  to taking part in the activities of a trade union, and

(b)  to services made available by a trade union by virtue of membership of the union,

shall be construed in accordance with subsection (4).]

**NOTES**

The words in square brackets in the heading preceding this section and in the section heading were substituted by the Employment Relations Act 2004, s 30(10).

Sub-s (1): words in first pair of square brackets substituted by the Employment Rights Act 1996, s 240, Sch 1, para 56(1), (7); words omitted from paras (a), (b) repealed, and paras (ba), (bb) inserted, by the Employment Relations Act 2004, ss 32(1), (2), 57(2), Sch 2.

Sub-s (2): number in square brackets substituted, and words in square brackets inserted, by the Employment Relations Act 2004, s 32(1), (3).

Sub-ss (2A), (2B), (5): inserted and added respectively by the Employment Relations Act 2004, s 32(1), (4), (6).

Sub-s (4): words omitted repealed by the Employment Relations Act 2004, ss 32(1), (5), 57(2), Sch 2.

Modified as noted to s 146 at [**1.413**].

**[1.420]**
**153  Selection for redundancy on grounds related to union membership or activities**
Where the reason or principal reason for the dismissal of an employee was that he was redundant, but it is shown—

(a)  that the circumstances constituting the redundancy applied equally to one or more other employees in the same undertaking who held positions similar to that held by him and who have not been dismissed by the employer, and

(b)  that the reason (or, if more than one, the principal reason) why he was selected for dismissal was one of those specified in section 152(1),

the dismissal shall be regarded as unfair for the purposes of [Part X of the Employment Rights Act 1996] (unfair dismissal).

**NOTES**

Words in square brackets substituted by the Employment Rights Act 1996, s 240, Sch 1, para 56(1), (7).

Modified as noted to s 146 at [**1.413**].

**[1.421]**
**[154  Disapplication of qualifying period and upper age limit for unfair dismissal**
Sections 108(1) and 109(1) of the Employment Rights Act 1996 (qualifying period and upper age limit for unfair dismissal protection) do not apply to a dismissal which by virtue of section 152 or 153 is regarded as unfair for the purposes of Part 10 of that Act.]

**NOTES**

Substituted by the Employment Relations Act 2004, s 35.

Modified as noted to s 146 at [**1.413**].

Section 109 of the Employment Rights Act 1996 was repealed by the Employment Equality (Age) Regulations 2006, SI 2006/1031, reg 49(1), Sch 8, Pt 1, paras 21, 25, as from 1 October 2006, but there has been no corresponding amendment to this section.

**[1.422]**
**155  Matters to be disregarded in assessing contributory fault**
(1)   Where an [employment tribunal] makes an award of compensation for unfair dismissal in a case where the dismissal is unfair by virtue of section 152 or 153, the tribunal shall disregard, in considering whether it would be just and equitable to reduce, or further reduce, the amount of any part of the award, any such conduct or action of the complainant as is specified below.
(2)   Conduct or action of the complainant shall be disregarded in so far as it constitutes a breach or proposed breach of a requirement—
(a)    to be or become a member of any trade union or of a particular trade union or of one of a number of particular trade unions,
(b)    to cease to be, or refrain from becoming, a member of any trade union or of a particular trade union or of one of a number of particular trade unions, . . .
(c)    not to take part in the activities of any trade union or of a particular trade union or of one of a number of particular trade unions[, or
(d)    not to make use of services made available by any trade union or by a particular trade union or by one of a number of particular trade unions].
For the purposes of this subsection a requirement means a requirement imposed on the complainant by or under an arrangement or contract of employment or other agreement.
[(2A)   Conduct or action of the complainant shall be disregarded in so far as it constitutes acceptance of or failure to accept an offer made in contravention of section 145A or 145B.]
(3)   Conduct or action of the complainant shall be disregarded in so far as it constitutes a refusal, or proposed refusal, to comply with a requirement of a kind mentioned in section 152(3)(a) (payments in lieu of membership) or an objection, or proposed, objection, (however expressed) to the operation of a provision of a kind mentioned in section 152(3)(b) (deductions in lieu of membership).

NOTES
Sub-s (1): words in square brackets substituted by the Employment Rights (Dispute Resolution) Act 1998, s 1(2)(a).
Sub-s (2): word omitted from para (b) repealed, and para (d) and the word immediately preceding it inserted, by the Employment Relations Act 2004, s 57, Sch 1, para 11(1), (2), Sch 2.
Sub-s (2A): inserted by the Employment Relations Act 2004, s 57(1), Sch 1, para 11(1), (3).

**[1.423]**
**156  Minimum basic award**
(1)   Where a dismissal is unfair by virtue of section 152(1) or 153, the amount of the basic award of compensation, before any reduction is made under [section 122 of the Employment Rights Act 1996], shall be not less than [£5,500].
(2)   But where the dismissal is unfair by virtue of section 153, [subsection (2)] of that section (reduction for contributory fault) applies in relation to so much of the basic award as is payable because of subsection (1) above.

NOTES
Sub-s (1): words in first pair of square brackets substituted by the Employment Rights Act 1996, s 240, Sch 1, para 56(1), (9); sum in second pair of square brackets substituted by the Employment Rights (Increase of Limits) Order 2012, SI 2012/3007, art 3, Schedule, as from 1 February 2013, in relation to any case where the appropriate date (as defined in the order) falls on or after that date (see SI 2012/3007, art 4 at **[2.1636]**). The previous sum was £5,300 as from 1 February 2012 (see SI 2011/3006). This sum may be further varied by the Secretary of State, see the Employment Relations Act 1999, s 34(1)(f), (3)(b) at **[1.1202]**.
Sub-s (2): words in square brackets substituted by the Employment Rights Act 1996, s 240, Sch 1, para 56(1), (9).

**157–159**   *(Ss 157, 158 repealed by the Employment Relations Act 1999, ss 33(1)(b), 36(1)(b), 44, Sch 9(10); s 159 repealed by the Employment Relations Act 1999, ss 36(1)(b), (3), 44, Sch 9(10).)*

**[1.424]**
**160  Awards against third parties**
(1)   If in proceedings before an [employment tribunal] on a complaint of unfair dismissal either the employer or the complainant claims—
(a)    that the employer was induced to dismiss the complainant by pressure which a trade union or other person exercised on the employer by calling, organising, procuring or financing a strike or other industrial action, or by threatening to do so, and
(b)    that the pressure was exercised because the complainant was not a member of any trade union or of a particular trade union or of one of a number of particular trade unions,
the employer or the complainant may request the tribunal to direct that the person who he claims exercised the pressure be joined or sisted as a party to the proceedings.
(2)   The request shall be granted if it is made before the hearing of the complaint begins, but may be refused after that time; and no such request may be made after the tribunal has made an award of compensation for unfair dismissal or an order for reinstatement or re-engagement.
(3)   Where a person has been so joined or sisted as a party to the proceedings and the tribunal—
(a)    makes an award of compensation for unfair dismissal, and

(b)    finds that the claim mentioned in subsection (1) is well-founded,

the tribunal may order that the compensation shall be paid by that person instead of the employer, or partly by that person and partly by the employer, as the tribunal may consider just and equitable.

**NOTES**

Sub-s (1): words in square brackets substituted by the Employment Rights (Dispute Resolution) Act 1998, s 1(2)(a).

**[1.425]**
**161    Application for interim relief**
(1)    An employee who presents a complaint of unfair dismissal alleging that the dismissal is unfair by virtue of section 152 may apply to the tribunal for interim relief.

(2)    The tribunal shall not entertain an application for interim relief unless it is presented to the tribunal before the end of the period of seven days immediately following the effective date of termination (whether before, on or after that date).

(3)    In a case where the employee relies on [section 152(1)(a), (b) or (ba), or on section 152(1)(bb) otherwise than in relation to an offer made in contravention of section 145A(1)(d),] the tribunal shall not entertain an application for interim relief unless before the end of that period there is also so presented a certificate in writing signed by an authorised official of the independent trade union of which the employee was or proposed to become a member stating—

(a)    that on the date of the dismissal the employee was or proposed to become a member of the union, and

(b)    that there appear to be reasonable grounds for supposing that the reason for his dismissal (or, if more than one, the principal reason) was one alleged in the complaint.

(4)    An "authorised official" means an official of the trade union authorised by it to act for the purposes of this section.

(5)    A document purporting to be an authorisation of an official by a trade union to act for the purposes of this section and to be signed on behalf of the union shall be taken to be such an authorisation unless the contrary is proved; and a document purporting to be a certificate signed by such an official shall be taken to be signed by him unless the contrary is proved.

(6)    For the purposes of subsection (3) the date of dismissal shall be taken to be—

(a)    where the employee's contract of employment was terminated by notice (whether given by his employer or by him), the date on which the employer's notice was given, and

(b)    in any other case, the effective date of termination.

**NOTES**

Sub-s (3): words in square brackets substituted by the Employment Relations Act 2004, s 57(1), Sch 1, para 12.

**[1.426]**
**162    Application to be promptly determined**
(1)    An [employment tribunal] shall determine an application for interim relief as soon as practicable after receiving the application and, where appropriate, the requisite certificate.

(2)    The tribunal shall give to the employer, not later than seven days before the hearing, a copy of the application and of any certificate, together with notice of the date, time and place of the hearing.

(3)    If a request under section 160 (awards against third parties) is made three days or more before the date of the hearing, the tribunal shall also give to the person to whom the request relates, as soon as reasonably practicable, a copy of the application and of any certificate, together with notice of the date, time and place of the hearing.

(4)    The tribunal shall not exercise any power it has of postponing the hearing of an application for interim relief except where it is satisfied that special circumstances exist which justify it in doing so.

**NOTES**

Sub-s (1): words in square brackets substituted by the Employment Rights (Dispute Resolution) Act 1998, s 1(2)(a).

**[1.427]**
**163    Procedure on hearing of application and making of order**
(1)    If on hearing an application for interim relief it appears to the tribunal that it is likely that on determining the complaint to which the application relates that it will find that, by virtue of section 152, the complainant has been unfairly dismissed, the following provisions apply.

(2)    The tribunal shall announce its findings and explain to both parties (if present) what powers the tribunal may exercise on the application and in what circumstances it will exercise them, and shall ask the employer (if present) whether he is willing, pending the determination or settlement of the complaint—

(a)    to reinstate the employee, that is to say, to treat him in all respects as if he had not been dismissed, or

(b)    if not, to re-engage him in another job on terms and conditions not less favourable than those which would have been applicable to him if he had not been dismissed.

(3)  For this purpose "terms and conditions not less favourable than those which would have been applicable to him if he had not been dismissed" means as regards seniority, pension rights and other similar rights that the period prior to the dismissal shall be regarded as continuous with his employment following the dismissal.

(4)  If the employer states that he is willing to reinstate the employee, the tribunal shall make an order to that effect.

(5)  If the employer states that he is willing to re-engage the employee in another job, and specifies the terms and conditions on which he is willing to do so, the tribunal shall ask the employee whether he is willing to accept the job on those terms and conditions; and—

(a)    if the employee is willing to accept the job on those terms and conditions, the tribunal shall make an order to that effect, and

(b)    if he is not, then, if the tribunal is of the opinion that the refusal is reasonable, the tribunal shall make an order for the continuation of his contract of employment, and otherwise the tribunal shall make no order.

(6)  If on the hearing of an application for interim relief the employer fails to attend before the tribunal, or states that he is unwilling either to reinstate the employee or re-engage him as mentioned in subsection (2), the tribunal shall make an order for the continuation of the employee's contract of employment.

**[1.428]**
## 164   Order for continuation of contract of employment

(1)  An order under section 163 for the continuation of a contract of employment is an order that the contract of employment continue in force—

(a)    for the purposes of pay or [any other benefit] derived from the employment, seniority, pension rights and other similar matters, and

(b)    for the purpose of determining for any purpose the period for which the employee has been continuously employed,

from the date of its termination (whether before or after the making of the order) until the determination or settlement of the complaint.

(2)  Where the tribunal makes such an order it shall specify in the order the amount which is to be paid by the employer to the employee by way of pay in respect of each normal pay period, or part of any such period, falling between the date of dismissal and the determination or settlement of the complaint.

(3)  Subject as follows, the amount so specified shall be that which the employee could reasonably have been expected to earn during that period, or part, and shall be paid—

(a)    in the case of payment for any such period falling wholly or partly after the making of the order, on the normal pay day for that period, and

(b)    in the case of a payment for any past period, within such time as may be specified in the order.

(4)  If an amount is payable in respect only of part of a normal pay period, the amount shall be calculated by reference to the whole period and reduced proportionately.

(5)  Any payment made to an employee by an employer under his contract of employment, or by way of damages for breach of that contract, in respect of a normal pay period or part of any such period shall go towards discharging the employer's liability in respect of that period under subsection (2); and conversely any payment under that subsection in respect of a period shall go towards discharging any liability of the employer under, or in respect of the breach of, the contract of employment in respect of that period.

(6)  If an employee, on or after being dismissed by his employer, receives a lump sum which, or part of which, is in lieu of wages but is not referable to any normal pay period, the tribunal shall take the payment into account in determining the amount of pay to be payable in pursuance of any such order.

(7)  For the purposes of this section the amount which an employee could reasonably have been expected to earn, his normal pay period and the normal pay day for each such period shall be determined as if he had not been dismissed.

**NOTES**

Sub-s (1): words in square brackets substituted by the Trade Union Reform and Employment Rights Act 1993, s 49(2), Sch 8, para 69.

**[1.429]**
## 165   Application for variation or revocation of order

(1)  At any time between the making of an order under section 163 and the determination or settlement of the complaint, the employer or the employee may apply to an [employment tribunal] for the revocation or variation of the order on the ground of a relevant change of circumstances since the making of the order.

(2)  Sections 161 to 163 apply in relation to such an application as in relation to an original application for interim relief, except that—

(a)    no certificate need be presented to the tribunal under section 161(3), and

(b) in the case of an application by the employer, section 162(2) (service of copy of application and notice of hearing) has effect with the substitution of a reference to the employee for the reference to the employer.

**[1.430]**
## 166 Consequences of failure to comply with order
(1) If on the application of an employee an [employment tribunal] is satisfied that the employer has not complied with the terms of an order for the reinstatement or re-engagement of the employee under section 163(4) or [(5)], the tribunal shall—
   (a) make an order for the continuation of the employee's contract of employment, and
   (b) order the employer to pay the employee such compensation as the tribunal considers just and equitable in all the circumstances having regard—
      (i) to the infringement of the employee's right to be reinstated or re-engaged in pursuance of the order, and
      (ii) to any loss suffered by the employee in consequence of the non-compliance.
(2) Section 164 applies to an order under subsection (1)(a) as in relation to an order under section 163.
(3) If on the application of an employee an [employment tribunal] is satisfied that the employer has not complied with the terms of an order for the continuation of a contract of employment, the following provisions apply.
(4) If the non-compliance consists of a failure to pay an amount by way of pay specified in the order, the tribunal shall determine the amount owed by the employer on the date of the determination.
   If on that date the tribunal also determines the employee's complaint that he has been unfairly dismissed, it shall specify that amount separately from any other sum awarded to the employee.
(5) In any other case, the tribunal shall order the employer to pay the employee such compensation as the tribunal considers just and equitable in all the circumstances having regard to any loss suffered by the employee in consequence of the non-compliance.

**[1.431]**
## 167 Interpretation and other supplementary provisions
(1) [Part X of the Employment Rights Act 1996] (unfair dismissal) has effect subject to the provisions of sections 152 to 166 above.
(2) Those sections shall be construed as one with that Part; and in those sections—
   "complaint of unfair dismissal" means a complaint under [section 111 of the Employment Rights Act 1996];
   "award of compensation for unfair dismissal" means an award of compensation for unfair dismissal under [section 112(4) or 117(3)(a)] of that Act; and
   "order for reinstatement or re-engagement" means an order for reinstatement or re-engagement under [section 113] of that Act.
(3) Nothing in those sections shall be construed as conferring a right to complain of unfair dismissal from employment of a description to which that Part does not otherwise apply.

*Time off for trade union duties and activities*
**[1.432]**
## 168 Time off for carrying out trade union duties
(1) An employer shall permit an employee of his who is an official of an independent trade union recognised by the employer to take time off during his working hours for the purpose of carrying out any duties of his, as such an official, concerned with—
   (a) negotiations with the employer related to or connected with matters falling within section 178(2) (collective bargaining) in relation to which the trade union is recognised by the employer, or
   (b) the performance on behalf of employees of the employer of functions related to or connected with matters falling within that provision which the employer has agreed may be so performed by the trade union[, or

(c)   receipt of information from the employer and consultation by the employer under section 188 (redundancies) or under the [Transfer of Undertakings (Protection of Employment) Regulations 2006]][, or

(d)   negotiations with a view to entering into an agreement under regulation 9 of the Transfer of Undertakings (Protection of Employment) Regulations 2006 that applies to employees of the employer, or

(e)   the performance on behalf of employees of the employer of functions related to or connected with the making of an agreement under that regulation.]

(2)   He shall also permit such an employee to take time off during his working hours for the purpose of undergoing training in aspects of industrial relations—

(a)   relevant to the carrying out of such duties as are mentioned in subsection (1), and

(b)   approved by the Trades Union Congress or by the independent trade union of which he is an official.

(3)   The amount of time off which an employee is to be permitted to take under this section and the purposes for which, the occasions on which and any conditions subject to which time off may be so taken are those that are reasonable in all the circumstances having regard to any relevant provisions of a Code of Practice issued by ACAS.

(4)   An employee may present a complaint to an [employment tribunal] that his employer has failed to permit him to take time off as required by this section.

---

**NOTES**

Sub-s (1): para (c) and the word immediately preceding it added by the Collective Redundancies and Transfer of Undertakings (Protection of Employment) (Amendment) Regulations 1999, SI 1999/1925, reg 14; words in square brackets in para (c) substituted, and paras (d), (e) and the word immediately preceding them added, by the Transfer of Undertakings (Protection of Employment) Regulations 2006, SI 2006/246, regs 9(4), 20, Sch 2, para 1(e).

Sub-s (4): words in square brackets substituted by the Employment Rights (Dispute Resolution) Act 1998, s 1(2)(a).

Conciliation: employment tribunal proceedings and claims which could be the subject of employment tribunal proceedings arising out of a contravention, or alleged contravention, of this section are proceedings to which the Employment Tribunals Act 1996, s 18 applies; see s 18(1)(b) of that Act at **[1.706]**.

The relevant code is ACAS Code of Practice 3: Time off for Trade Union Duties and Activities (2010) at **[4.98]**.

The rights conferred by this section are "relevant statutory rights" for the purposes of the Employment Rights Act 1996, s 104 (dismissal on grounds of assertion of statutory right); see s 104(4)(c) of that Act at **[1.907]**.

---

**[1.433]**
**[168A   Time off for union learning representatives**

(1)   An employer shall permit an employee of his who is—

(a)   a member of an independent trade union recognised by the employer, and

(b)   a learning representative of the trade union,

to take time off during his working hours for any of the following purposes.

(2)   The purposes are—

(a)   carrying on any of the following activities in relation to qualifying members of the trade union—

(i)   analysing learning or training needs,

(ii)   providing information and advice about learning or training matters,

(iii)   arranging learning or training, and

(iv)   promoting the value of learning or training,

(b)   consulting the employer about carrying on any such activities in relation to such members of the trade union,

(c)   preparing for any of the things mentioned in paragraphs (a) and (b).

(3)   Subsection (1) only applies if—

(a)   the trade union has given the employer notice in writing that the employee is a learning representative of the trade union, and

(b)   the training condition is met in relation to him.

(4)   The training condition is met if—

(a)   the employee has undergone sufficient training to enable him to carry on the activities mentioned in subsection (2), and the trade union has given the employer notice in writing of that fact,

(b)   the trade union has in the last six months given the employer notice in writing that the employee will be undergoing such training, or

(c)   within six months of the trade union giving the employer notice in writing that the employee will be undergoing such training, the employee has done so, and the trade union has given the employer notice of that fact.

(5)   Only one notice under subsection (4)(b) may be given in respect of any one employee.

(6)   References in subsection (4) to sufficient training to carry out the activities mentioned in subsection (2) are to training that is sufficient for those purposes having regard to any relevant provision of a Code of Practice issued by ACAS or the Secretary of State.

(7)   If an employer is required to permit an employee to take time off under subsection (1), he shall also permit the employee to take time off during his working hours for the following purposes—

(a)   undergoing training which is relevant to his functions as a learning representative, and

(b)   where the trade union has in the last six months given the employer notice under subsection (4)(b) in relation to the employee, undergoing such training as is mentioned in subsection (4)(a).

(8)   The amount of time off which an employee is to be permitted to take under this section and the purposes for which, the occasions on which and any conditions subject to which time off may be so taken are those that are reasonable in all the circumstances having regard to any relevant provision of a Code of Practice issued by ACAS or the Secretary of State.

(9)   An employee may present a complaint to an employment tribunal that his employer has failed to permit him to take time off as required by this section.

(10)   In subsection (2)(a), the reference to qualifying members of the trade union is to members of the trade union—

(a)   who are employees of the employer of a description in respect of which the union is recognised by the employer, and

(b)   in relation to whom it is the function of the union learning representative to act as such.

(11)   For the purposes of this section, a person is a learning representative of a trade union if he is appointed or elected as such in accordance with its rules.]

**NOTES**

Inserted by the Employment Act 2002, s 43(1), (2).

Conciliation: employment tribunal proceedings and claims which could be the subject of employment tribunal proceedings arising out of a contravention, or alleged contravention, of this section are proceedings to which the Employment Tribunals Act 1996, s 18 applies; see s 18(1)(b) of that Act at **[1.706]**.

The relevant code is ACAS Code of Practice 3: Time off for Trade Union Duties and Activities (2010) at **[4.98]**.

The rights conferred by this section are "relevant statutory rights" for the purposes of the Employment Rights Act 1996, s 104 (dismissal on grounds of assertion of statutory right); see s 104(4)(c) of that Act at **[1.907]**.

Note: the Employment Act 2002 (Commencement No 4 and Transitional Provisions) Order 2003, SI 2003/1190, art 3 provides that the requirements of sub-s (3) above shall be treated as being satisfied in relation to an employee if (a) immediately before 27 April 2003 he has the function of carrying on any or all of the activities mentioned in sub-s (2) above in relation to qualifying members of the union and has had that function for a continuous period of six months or more, and (b) he acquired that function by reason of being appointed or elected, in accordance with the rules of the union, to carry it on.

**[1.434]**
**169   Payment for time off under section 168**

(1)   An employer who permits an employee to take time off under section 168 [or 168A] shall pay him for the time taken off pursuant to the permission.

(2)   Where the employee's remuneration for the work he would ordinarily have been doing during that time does not vary with the amount of work done, he shall be paid as if he had worked at that work for the whole of that time.

(3)   Where the employee's remuneration for the work he would ordinarily have been doing during that time varies with the amount of work done, he shall be paid an amount calculated by reference to the average hourly earnings for that work.

The average hourly earnings shall be those of the employee concerned or, if no fair estimate can be made of those earnings, the average hourly earnings for work of that description of persons in comparable employment with the same employer or, if there are no such persons, a figure of average hourly earnings which is reasonable in the circumstances.

(4)   A right to be paid an amount under this section does not affect any right of an employee in relation to remuneration under his contract of employment, but—

(a)   any contractual remuneration paid to an employee in respect of a period of time off to which this section applies shall go towards discharging any liability of the employer under this section in respect of that period, and

(b)   any payment under this section in respect of a period shall go towards discharging any liability of the employer to pay contractual remuneration in respect of that period.

(5)   An employee may present a complaint to an [employment tribunal] that his employer has failed to pay him in accordance with this section.

**NOTES**

Sub-s (1): words in square brackets inserted by the Employment Act 2002, s 43(1), (3).

Sub-s (5): words in square brackets substituted by the Employment Rights (Dispute Resolution) Act 1998, s 1(2)(a).

Conciliation: employment tribunal proceedings and claims which could be the subject of employment tribunal proceedings arising out of a contravention, or alleged contravention, of this section are proceedings to which the Employment Tribunals Act 1996, s 18 applies; see s 18(1)(b) of that Act at **[1.706]**.

The rights conferred by this section are "relevant statutory rights" for the purposes of the Employment Rights Act 1996, s 104 (dismissal on grounds of assertion of statutory right); see s 104(4)(c) of that Act at **[1.907]**.

**[1.435]**
**170   Time off for trade union activities**
(1)   An employer shall permit an employee of his who is a member of an independent trade union recognised by the employer in respect of that description of employee to take time off during his working hours for the purpose of taking part in—
    (a)   any activities of the union, and
    (b)   any activities in relation to which the employee is acting as a representative of the union.
(2)   The right conferred by subsection (1) does not extent to activities which themselves consist of industrial action, whether or not in contemplation or furtherance of a trade dispute.
[(2A)   The right conferred by subsection (1) does not extend to time off for the purpose of acting as, or having access to services provided by, a learning representative of a trade union.
(2B)   An employer shall permit an employee of his who is a member of an independent trade union recognised by the employer in respect of that description of employee to take time off during his working hours for the purpose of having access to services provided by a person in his capacity as a learning representative of the trade union.
(2C)   Subsection (2B) only applies if the learning representative would be entitled to time off under subsection (1) of section 168A for the purpose of carrying on in relation to the employee activities of the kind mentioned in subsection (2) of that section.]
(3)   The amount of time off which an employee is to be permitted to take under this section and the purposes for which, the occasions on which and any conditions subject to which time off may be so taken are those that are reasonable in all the circumstances having regard to any relevant provisions of a Code of Practice issued by ACAS.
(4)   An employee may present a complaint to an [employment tribunal] that his employer has failed to permit him to take time off as required by this section.
[(5)   For the purposes of this section—
    (a)   a person is a learning representative of a trade union if he is appointed or elected as such in accordance with its rules, and
    (b)   a person who is a learning representative of a trade union acts as such if he carries on the activities mentioned in section 168A(2) in that capacity.]

**NOTES**
Sub-ss (2A)–(2C), (5): inserted and added respectively by the Employment Act 2002, s 43(1), (4), (5).
Sub-s (4): words in square brackets substituted by the Employment Rights (Dispute Resolution) Act 1998, s 1(2)(a).
Code of Practice under sub-s (3): the code under the provisions contained in this subsection is ACAS Code of Practice 3: Time off for Trade Union Duties and Activities (2010) at **[4.98]**.
Conciliation: employment tribunal proceedings and claims which could be the subject of employment tribunal proceedings arising out of a contravention, or alleged contravention, of this section are proceedings to which the Employment Tribunals Act 1996, s 18 applies; see s 18(1)(b) of that Act at **[1.706]**.
The rights conferred by this section are "relevant statutory rights" for the purposes of the Employment Rights Act 1996, s 104 (dismissal on grounds of assertion of statutory right); see s 104(4)(c) of that Act at **[1.907]**.

**[1.436]**
**171   Time limit for proceedings**
[(1)]   An [employment tribunal] shall not consider a complaint under section 168, [168A,] 169 or 170 unless it is presented to the tribunal—
    (a)   within three months of the date when the failure occurred, or
    (b)   where the tribunal is satisfied that it was not reasonably practicable for the complaint to be presented within that period, within such further period as the tribunal considers reasonable.
[(2)   Section 292A (extension of time limits to facilitate conciliation before institution of proceedings) applies for the purposes of subsection (1)(a).]

**NOTES**
The existing provision is numbered as sub-s (1) and sub-s (2) is added, by the Enterprise and Regulatory Reform Act 2013, s 8, Sch 2, paras 1, 9, as from a day to be appointed; in sub-s (1), words in first pair of square brackets substituted by the Employment Rights (Dispute Resolution) Act 1998, s 1(2)(a) and number in second pair of square brackets inserted by the Employment Act 2002, s 53, Sch 7, paras 18, 19.

**[1.437]**
**172   Remedies**
(1)   Where the tribunal finds a complaint under section 168[, 168A] or 170 is well-founded, it shall make a declaration to that effect and may make an award of compensation to be paid by the employer to the employee.
(2)   The amount of the compensation shall be such as the tribunal considers just and equitable in all the circumstances having regard to the employer's default in failing to permit time off to be taken by the employee and to any loss sustained by the employee which is attributable to the matters complained of.

(3)   Where on a complaint under section 169 the tribunal finds that the employer has failed to pay the employee in accordance with that section, it shall order him to pay the amount which it finds to be due.

**NOTES**

Sub-s (1): number in square brackets inserted by the Employment Act 2002, s 53, Sch 7, paras 18, 20.

**[1.438]**
**173   Interpretation and other supplementary provisions**
(1)   For the purposes of sections 168[, 168A] and 170 the working hours of an employee shall be taken to be any time when in accordance with his contract of employment he is required to be at work.
(2)   The remedy of an employee for infringement of the rights conferred on him by section 168, [168A,] 169 or 170 is by way of complaint to an [employment tribunal] in accordance with this Part, and not otherwise.
[(3)   The Secretary of State may by order made by statutory instrument amend section 168A for the purpose of changing the purposes for which an employee may take time off under that section.
(4)   No order may be made under subsection (3) unless a draft of the order has been laid before and approved by resolution of each House of Parliament.]

**NOTES**

Sub-s (1): number in square brackets inserted by the Employment Act 2002, s 53, Sch 7, paras 18, 21(a).
Sub-s (2): number in first pair of square brackets inserted by the Employment Act 2002, s 53, Sch 7, paras 18, 21(b); words in second pair of square brackets substituted by the Employment Rights (Dispute Resolution) Act 1998, s 1(2)(a).
Sub-ss (3), (4): added by the Employment Act 2002, s 43(1), (6).
Orders: as of 6 April 2013, no Orders had been made under this section.

*[Right to membership of trade union*

**[1.439]**
**174   Right not to be excluded or expelled from union**
(1)   An individual shall not be excluded or expelled from a trade union unless the exclusion or expulsion is permitted by this section.
(2)   The exclusion or expulsion of an individual from a trade union is permitted by this section if (and only if)—
    (a)   he does not satisfy, or no longer satisfies, an enforceable membership requirement contained in the rules of the union,
    (b)   he does not qualify, or no longer qualifies, for membership of the union by reason of the union operating only in a particular part or particular parts of Great Britain,
    (c)   in the case of a union whose purpose is the regulation of relations between its members and one particular employer or a number of particular employers who are associated, he is not, or is no longer, employed by that employer or one of those employers, or
    (d)   the exclusion or expulsion is entirely attributable to [conduct of his (other than excluded conduct) and the conduct to which it is wholly or mainly attributable is not protected conduct].
(3)   A requirement in relation to membership of a union is "enforceable" for the purposes of subsection (2)(a) if it restricts membership solely by reference to one or more of the following criteria—
    (a)   employment in a specified trade, industry or profession,
    (b)   occupational description (including grade, level or category of appointment), and
    (c)   possession of specified trade, industrial or professional qualifications or work experience.
[(4)   For the purposes of subsection (2)(d) "excluded conduct", in relation to an individual, means—
    (a)   conduct which consists in his being or ceasing to be, or having been or ceased to be, a member of another trade union,
    (b)   conduct which consists in his being or ceasing to be, or having been or ceased to be, employed by a particular employer or at a particular place, or
    (c)   conduct to which section 65 (conduct for which an individual may not be disciplined by a union) applies or would apply if the references in that section to the trade union which is relevant for the purposes of that section were references to any trade union.
(4A)   For the purposes of subsection (2)(d) "protected conduct" is conduct which consists in the individual's being or ceasing to be, or having been or ceased to be, a member of a political party.
(4B)   Conduct which consists of activities undertaken by an individual as a member of a political party is not conduct falling within subsection (4A).]
[(4C)   Conduct which consists in an individual's being or having been a member of a political party is not conduct falling within subsection (4A) if membership of that political party is contrary to—
    (a)   a rule of the trade union, or
    (b)   an objective of the trade union.

(4D)  For the purposes of subsection (4C)(b) in the case of conduct consisting in an individual's being a member of a political party, an objective is to be disregarded—
- (a)   in relation to an exclusion, if it is not reasonably practicable for the objective to be ascertained by a person working in the same trade, industry or profession as the individual;
- (b)   in relation to an expulsion, if it is not reasonably practicable for the objective to be ascertained by a member of the union.

(4E)  For the purposes of subsection (4C)(b) in the case of conduct consisting in an individual's having been a member of a political party, an objective is to be disregarded—
- (a)   in relation to an exclusion, if at the time of the conduct it was not reasonably practicable for the objective to be ascertained by a person working in the same trade, industry or profession as the individual;
- (b)   in relation to an expulsion, if at the time of the conduct it was not reasonably practicable for the objective to be ascertained by a member of the union.

(4F)  Where the exclusion or expulsion of an individual from a trade union is wholly or mainly attributable to conduct which consists of an individual's being or having been a member of a political party but which by virtue of subsection (4C) is not conduct falling within subsection (4A), the exclusion or expulsion is not permitted by virtue of subsection (2)(d) if any one or more of the conditions in subsection (4G) apply.

(4G)  Those conditions are—
- (a)   the decision to exclude or expel is taken otherwise than in accordance with the union's rules;
- (b)   the decision to exclude or expel is taken unfairly;
- (c)   the individual would lose his livelihood or suffer other exceptional hardship by reason of not being, or ceasing to be, a member of the union.

(4H)  For the purposes of subsection (4G)(b) a decision to exclude or expel an individual is taken unfairly if (and only if)—
- (a)   before the decision is taken the individual is not given—
    - (i)   notice of the proposal to exclude or expel him and the reasons for that proposal, and
    - (ii)   a fair opportunity to make representations in respect of that proposal, or
- (b)   representations made by the individual in respect of that proposal are not considered fairly.]

(5)  An individual who claims that he has been excluded or expelled from a trade union in contravention of this section may present a complaint to an [employment tribunal].]

**NOTES**

Substituted, together with the preceding heading, by the Trade Union Reform and Employment Rights Act 1993, s 14.

Sub-s (2): words in square brackets in para (d) substituted by the Employment Relations Act 2004, s 33(1), (2), (7).

Sub-ss (4), (4A), (4B): substituted, for the original sub-s (4), by the Employment Relations Act 2004, s 33(1), (3), (7).

Sub-ss (4C)–(4H): inserted by the Employment Act 2008, s 19(1), (2), as from 6 April 2009, except in the case of any decision by a union to exclude or expel an individual which is taken before that date (see SI 2009/603, Schedule).

Sub-s (5): words in square brackets substituted by the Employment Rights (Dispute Resolution) Act 1998, s 1(2)(a).

Conciliation: employment tribunal proceedings and claims which could be the subject of employment tribunal proceedings arising out of a contravention, or alleged contravention, of this section are proceedings to which the Employment Tribunals Act 1996, s 18 applies; see s 18(1)(b) of that Act at **[1.706]**.

**[1.440]**
**[175    Time limit for proceedings**
[(1)    An [employment tribunal] shall not entertain a complaint under section 174 unless it is presented—
- (a)   before the end of the period of six months beginning with the date of the exclusion or expulsion, or
- (b)   where the tribunal is satisfied that it was not reasonably practicable for the complaint to be presented before the end of that period, within such further period as the tribunal considers reasonable.

[(2)    Section 292A (extension of time limits to facilitate conciliation before institution of proceedings) applies for the purposes of subsection (1)(a).]]

**NOTES**

Substituted by the Trade Union Reform and Employment Rights Act 1993, s 14.

The existing provision is numbered as sub-s (1) and sub-s (2) is added, by the Enterprise and Regulatory Reform Act 2013, s 8, Sch 2, paras 1, 10, as from a day to be appointed; words in square brackets in sub-s (1) substituted by the Employment Rights (Dispute Resolution) Act 1998, s 1(2)(a).

**[1.441]**
**[176    Remedies**
(1)    Where the [employment tribunal] finds a complaint under section 174 is well-founded, it shall make a declaration to that effect.

[(1A)    If a tribunal makes a declaration under subsection (1) and it appears to the tribunal that the exclusion or expulsion was mainly attributable to conduct falling within section 174(4A) it shall make a declaration to that effect.

(1B)  If a tribunal makes a declaration under subsection (1A) and it appears to the tribunal that the other conduct to which the exclusion or expulsion was attributable consisted wholly or mainly of conduct of the complainant which was contrary to—
   (a)  a rule of the union, or
   (b)  an objective of the union,
it shall make a declaration to that effect.
(1C)  For the purposes of subsection (1B), it is immaterial whether the complainant was a member of the union at the time of the conduct contrary to the rule or objective.
(1D)  A declaration by virtue of subsection (1B)(b) shall not be made unless the union shows that, at the time of the conduct of the complainant which was contrary to the objective in question, it was reasonably practicable for that objective to be ascertained—
   (a)  if the complainant was not at that time a member of the union, by [a person working in the same trade, industry or profession as the complainant], and
   (b)  if he was at that time a member of the union, by a member of the union.]
(2)  An individual whose complaint has been declared to be well-founded may make an application [to an employment tribunal] for an award of compensation to be paid to him by the union.
  . . .
(3)  The application shall not be entertained if made—
   (a)  before the end of the period of four weeks beginning with the date of the declaration [under subsection (1)], or
   (b)  after the end of the period of six months beginning with that date.
(4)  The amount of compensation awarded shall, subject to the following provisions, be such as the [employment tribunal]  . . .  considers just and equitable in all the circumstances.
(5)  Where the [employment tribunal]  . . .  finds that the exclusion or expulsion complained of was to any extent caused or contributed to by the action of the applicant, it shall reduce the amount of the compensation by such proportion as it considers just and equitable having regard to that finding.
(6)  The amount of compensation calculated in accordance with subsections (4) and (5) shall not exceed the aggregate of—
   (a)  an amount equal to thirty times the limit for the time being imposed by [section 227(1)(a) of the Employment Rights Act 1996] (maximum amount of a week's pay for basic award in unfair dismissal cases), and
   (b)  an amount equal to the limit for the time being imposed by [section 113] of that Act (maximum compensatory award in such cases);
  . . .
[(6A)  If on the date on which the application was made the applicant had not been admitted or re-admitted to the union, the award shall not be less than [£8,400].
(6B)  Subsection (6A) does not apply in a case where the tribunal which made the declaration under subsection (1) also made declarations under subsections (1A) and (1B).]
(7), (8)  . . . ]

**NOTES**

Substituted by the Trade Union Reform and Employment Rights Act 1993, s 14.

Sub-s (1): words in square brackets substituted by the Employment Rights (Dispute Resolution) Act 1998, s 1(2)(a).

Sub-ss (1A)–(1C): inserted, together with sub-s (1D), by the Employment Relations Act 2004, s 33(1), (4), (7).

Sub-s (1D): inserted as noted above; words in square brackets in para (a) substituted by the Employment Act 2008, s 19(1), (3), as from 6 April 2009, except in relation to any complaint presented by an individual under s 174 of this Act that relates to a decision to exclude or expel the individual which was taken before that date (see SI 2009/603, Schedule).

Sub-s (2): words in square brackets inserted, and words omitted repealed, by the Employment Relations Act 2004, ss 34(7), (8)(b), 57(2), Sch 2.

Sub-s (3): words in square brackets in para (a) inserted by the Employment Relations Act 2004, s 33(1), (5), (7).

Sub-ss (4), (5): words in square brackets substituted by the Employment Rights (Dispute Resolution) Act 1998, s 1(2)(a); words omitted repealed by the Employment Relations Act 2004, ss 34(7), (9), (10), 57(2).

Sub-s (6): words in square brackets substituted by the Employment Rights Act 1996, s 240, Sch 1, para 56(1), (13); words omitted repealed by the Employment Relations Act 2004, ss 34(7), (11), 57(2), Sch 2.

Sub-s (6A): inserted, together with sub-s (6B), by the Employment Relations Act 2004, s 33(1), (6), (7); sum in square brackets substituted by the Employment Rights (Increase of Limits) Order 2012, SI 2012/3007, art 3, Schedule, as from 1 February 2013, in relation to any case where the appropriate date (as defined in the order) falls on or after that date (see SI 2012/3007, art 4 at [**2.1636**]). The previous sum was £8,100 as from 1 February 2012 (see SI 2011/3006). This sum may be further varied by the Secretary of State, see the Employment Relations Act 1999, s 34(1)(g), (3)(b) at [**1.1202**].

Sub-s (6B): inserted as noted above.

Sub-ss (7), (8): repealed by the Employment Relations Act 1999, ss 36(1)(b), 44, Sch 9(10).

**[1.442]**
**[177  Interpretation and other supplementary provisions**
(1)  For the purposes of section 174—
   (a)  "trade union" does not include an organisation falling within paragraph (b) of section 1,
   (b)  "conduct" includes statements, acts and omissions, and

(c)   "employment" includes any relationship whereby an individual personally does work or performs services for another person (related expressions being construed accordingly).

(2)   For the purposes of sections 174 to 176—

(a)   if an individual's application for membership of a trade union is neither granted nor rejected before the end of the period within which it might reasonably have been expected to be granted if it was to be granted, he shall be treated as having been excluded from the union on the last day of that period, and

(b)   an individual who under the rules of a trade union ceases to be a member of the union on the happening of an event specified in the rules shall be treated as having been expelled from the union.

(3)   The remedy of an individual for infringement of the rights conferred by section 174 is by way of a complaint to an [employment tribunal] in accordance with that section, sections 175 and 176 and this section, and not otherwise.

(4)   Where a complaint relating to an expulsion which is presented under section 174 is declared to be well-founded, no complaint in respect of the expulsion shall be presented or proceeded with under section 66 (complaint of infringement of right not to be unjustifiably disciplined).

(5)   The rights conferred by section 174 are in addition to, and not in substitution for, any right which exists apart from that section; and, subject to subsection (4), nothing in that section, section 175 or 176 or this section affects any remedy for infringement of any such right.]

**NOTES**

Substituted by the Trade Union Reform and Employment Rights Act 1993, s 14.

Sub-s (3): words in square brackets substituted by the Employment Rights (Dispute Resolution) Act 1998, s 1(2)(a).

## PART IV
## INDUSTRIAL RELATIONS

### CHAPTER I
### COLLECTIVE BARGAINING

*Introductory*

**[1.443]**
### 178   Collective agreements and collective bargaining
(1)   In this Act "collective agreement" means any agreement or arrangement made by or on behalf of one or more trade unions and one or more employers or employers' associations and relating to one or more of the matters specified below; and "collective bargaining" means negotiations relating to or connected with one or more of those matters.

(2)   The matters referred to above are—

(a)   terms and conditions of employment, or the physical conditions in which any workers are required to work;

(b)   engagement or non-engagement, or termination or suspension of employment or the duties of employment, of one or more workers;

(c)   allocation of work or the duties of employment between workers or groups of workers;

(d)   matters of discipline;

(e)   a worker's membership or non-membership of a trade union;

(f)   facilities for officials of trade unions; and

(g)   machinery for negotiation or consultation, and other procedures, relating to any of the above matters, including the recognition by employers or employers' associations of the right of a trade union to represent workers in such negotiation or consultation or in the carrying out of such procedures.

(3)   In this Act "recognition", in relation to a trade union, means the recognition of the union by an employer, or two or more associated employers, to any extent, for the purpose of collective bargaining; and "recognised" and other related expressions shall be construed accordingly.

*Enforceability of collective agreements*

**[1.444]**
### 179   Whether agreement intended to be a legally enforceable contract
(1)   A collective agreement shall be conclusively presumed not to have been intended by the parties to be a legally enforceable contract unless the agreement—

(a)   is in writing, and

(b)   contains a provision which (however expressed) states that the parties intend that the agreement shall be a legally enforceable contract.

(2)   A collective agreement which does satisfy those conditions shall be conclusively presumed to have been intended by the parties to be a legally enforceable contract.

(3)   If a collective agreement is in writing and contains a provision which (however expressed) states that the parties intend that one or more parts of the agreement specified in that provision, but not the whole of the agreement, shall be a legally enforceable contract, then—

(a)   the specified part or parts shall be conclusively presumed to have been intended by the parties to be a legally enforceable contract, and

(b)   the remainder of the agreement shall be conclusively presumed not to have been intended by the parties to be such a contract.

(4)   A part of a collective agreement which by virtue of subsection (3)(b) is not a legally enforceable contract may be referred to for the purpose of interpreting a party of the agreement which is such a contract.

**[1.445]**
**180   Effect of provisions restricting right to take industrial action**
(1)   Any terms of a collective agreement which prohibit or restrict the right of workers to engage in a strike or other industrial action, or have the effect of prohibiting or restricting that right, shall not form part of any contract between a worker and the person for whom he works unless the following conditions are met.

(2)   The conditions are that the collective agreement—
(a)   is in writing,
(b)   contains a provision expressly stating that those terms shall or may be incorporated in such a contract,
(c)   is reasonably accessible at his place of work to the worker to whom it applies and is available for him to consult during working hours, and
(d)   is one where each trade union which is a party to the agreement is an independent trade union;

and that the contract with the worker expressly or impliedly incorporates those terms in the contract.

(3)   The above provisions have effect notwithstanding anything in section 179 and notwithstanding any provision to the contrary in any agreement (including a collective agreement or a contract with any worker).

*Disclosure of information for purposes of collective bargaining*

**[1.446]**
**181   General duty of employers to disclose information**
(1)   An employer who recognises an independent trade union shall, for the purposes of all stages of collective bargaining about matters, and in relation to descriptions of workers, in respect of which the union is recognised by him, disclose to representatives of the union, on request, the information required by this section.

In this section and sections 182 to 185 "representative", in relation to a trade union, means an official or other person authorised by the union to carry on such collective bargaining.

(2)   The information to be disclosed is all information relating to the employer's undertaking [(including information relating to use of agency workers in that undertaking)] which is in his possession, or that of an associated employer, and is information—
(a)   without which the trade union representatives would be to a material extent impeded in carrying on collective bargaining with him, and
(b)   which it would be in accordance with good industrial relations practice that he should disclose to them for the purposes of collective bargaining.

(3)   A request by trade union representatives for information under this section shall, if the employer so requests, be in writing or be confirmed in writing.

(4)   In determining what would be in accordance with good industrial relations practice, regard shall be had to the relevant provisions of any Code of Practice issued by ACAS, but not so as to exclude any other evidence of what that practice is.

(5)   Information which an employer is required by virtue of this section to disclose to trade union representatives shall, if they so request, be disclosed or confirmed in writing.

**NOTES**
Sub-s (2): words in square brackets inserted by the Agency Workers Regulations 2010, SI 2010/93, reg 25, Sch 2, Pt 1, paras 1, 3, as from 1 October 2011.
Code of Practice for the purposes of sub-s (4): see ACAS Code of Practice 2: Disclosure of Information to Trade Unions for Collective Bargaining Purposes (1998) at **[4.90]**.
Modified as noted to s 146 at **[1.413]**.

**[1.447]**
**182   Restrictions on general duty**
(1)   An employer is not required by section 181 to disclose information—
(a)   the disclosure of which would be against the interests of national security, or
(b)   which he could not disclose without contravening a prohibition imposed by or under an enactment, or
(c)   which has been communicated to him in confidence, or which he has otherwise obtained in consequence of the confidence reposed in him by another person, or

(d)   which relates specifically to an individual (unless that individual has consented to its being disclosed), or

(e)   the disclosure of which would cause substantial injury to his undertaking for reasons other than its effect on collective bargaining, or

(f)   obtained by him for the purpose of bringing, prosecuting or defending any legal proceedings.

In formulating the provisions of any Code of Practice relating to the disclosure of information, ACAS shall have regard to the provisions of this subsection.

(2)   In the performance of his duty under section 181 an employer is not required—

(a)   to produce, or allow inspection of, any document (other than a document prepared for the purpose of conveying or confirming the information) or to make a copy of or extracts from any document, or

(b)   to compile or assemble any information where the compilation or assembly would involve an amount of work or expenditure out of reasonable proportion to the value of the information in the conduct of collective bargaining.

**NOTES**
Modified as noted to s 146 at **[1.413]**.

**[1.448]**
**183   Complaint of failure to disclose information**
(1)   A trade union may present a complaint to the Central Arbitration Committee that an employer has failed—

(a)   to disclose to representatives of the union information which he was required to disclose to them by section 181, or

(b)   to confirm such information in writing in accordance with that section.

The complaint must be in writing and in such form as the Committee may require.

(2)   If on receipt of a complaint the Committee is of the opinion that it is reasonably likely to be settled by conciliation, it shall refer the complaint to ACAS and shall notify the trade union and employer accordingly, whereupon ACAS shall seek to promote a settlement of the matter.

If a complaint so referred is not settled or withdrawn and ACAS is of the opinion that further attempts at conciliation are unlikely to result in a settlement, it shall inform the Committee of its opinion.

(3)   If the complaint is not referred to ACAS or, if it is so referred, on ACAS informing the Committee of its opinion that further attempts at conciliation are unlikely to result in a settlement, the Committee shall proceed to hear and determine the complaint and shall make a declaration stating whether it finds the complaint well-founded, wholly or in part, and stating the reasons for its findings.

(4)   On the hearing of a complaint any person who the Committee considers has a proper interest in the complaint is entitled to be heard by the Committee, but a failure to accord a hearing to a person other than the trade union and employer directly concerned does not affect the validity of any decision of the Committee in those proceedings.

(5)   If the Committee finds the complaint wholly or partly well founded, the declaration shall specify—

(a)   the information in respect of which the Committee finds that the complaint is well founded,

(b)   the date (or, if more than one, the earliest date) on which the employer refused or failed to disclose or, as the case may be, to confirm in writing, any of the information in question, and

(c)   a period (not being less than one week from the date of the declaration) within which the employer ought to disclose that information, or, as the case may be, to confirm it in writing.

(6)   On a hearing of a complaint under this section a certificate signed by or on behalf of a Minister of the Crown and certifying that a particular request for information could not be complied with except by disclosing information the disclosure of which would have been against the interests of national security shall be conclusive evidence of that fact.

A document which purports to be such a certificate shall be taken to be such a certificate unless the contrary is proved.

**NOTES**
Modified as noted to s 146 at **[1.413]**.

**[1.449]**
**184   Further complaint of failure to comply with declaration**
(1)   After the expiration of the period specified in a declaration under section 183(5)(c) the trade union may present a further complaint to the Central Arbitration Committee that the employer has failed to disclose or, as the case may be, to confirm in writing to representatives of the union information specified in the declaration.

The complaint must be in writing and in such form as the Committee may require.

(2) On receipt of a further complaint the Committee shall proceed to hear and determine the complaint and shall make a declaration stating whether they find the complaint well-founded, wholly or in part, and stating the reasons for their finding.

(3) On the hearing of a further complaint any person who the Committee consider has a proper interest in that complaint shall be entitled to be heard by the Committee, but a failure to accord a hearing to a person other than the trade union and employer directly concerned shall not affect the validity of any decision of the Committee in those proceedings.

(4) If the Committee find the further complaint wholly or partly well-founded the declaration shall specify the information in respect of which the Committee find that that complaint is well-founded.

**NOTES**
Modified as noted to s 146 at **[1.413]**.

**[1.450]**
**185 Determination of claim and award**

(1) On or after presenting a further complaint under section 184 the trade union may present to the Central Arbitration Committee a claim, in writing, in respect of one or more descriptions of employees (but not workers who are not employees) specified in the claim that their contracts should include the terms and conditions specified in the claim.

(2) The right to present a claim expires if the employer discloses or, as the case may be, confirms in writing, to representatives of the trade union the information specified in the declaration under section 183(5) or 184(4); and a claim presented shall be treated as withdrawn if the employer does so before the Committee make an award on the claim.

(3) If the Committee find, or have found, the further complaint wholly or partly well-founded, they may, after hearing the parties, make an award that in respect of any description of employees specified in the claim the employer shall, from a specified date, observe either—

    (a)   the terms and conditions specified in the claim; or

    (b)   other terms and conditions which the Committee consider appropriate.

The date specified may be earlier than that on which the award is made but not earlier than the date specified in accordance with section 183(5)(b) in the declaration made by the Committee on the original complaint.

(4) An award shall be made only in respect of a description of employees, and shall comprise only terms and conditions relating to matters in respect of which the trade union making the claim is recognised by the employer.

(5) Terms and conditions which by an award under this section an employer is required to observe in respect of an employee have effect as part of the employee's contract of employment as from the date specified in the award, except in so far as they are superseded or varied—

    (a)   by a subsequent award under this section,

    (b)   by a collective agreement between the employer and the union for the time being representing that employee, or

    (c)   by express or implied agreement between the employee and the employer so far as that agreement effects an improvement in terms and conditions having effect by virtue of the award.

(6) Where—

    (a)   by virtue of any enactment, other than one contained in this section, providing for minimum remuneration or terms and conditions, a contract of employment is to have effect as modified by an award, order or other instrument under that enactment, and

    (b)   by virtue of an award under this section any terms and conditions are to have effect as part of that contract,

that contract shall have effect in accordance with that award, order or other instrument or in accordance with the award under this section, whichever is the more favourable, in respect of any terms and conditions of that contract, to the employee.

(7) No award may be made under this section in respect of terms and conditions of employment which are fixed by virtue of any enactment.

**NOTES**
Modified as noted to s 146 at **[1.413]**.

*Prohibition of union recognition requirements*

**[1.451]**
**186 Recognition requirement in contract for goods or services void**

A term or condition of a contract for the supply of goods or services is void in so far as it purports to require a party to the contract—

    (a)   to recognise one or more trade unions (whether or not named in the contract) for the purpose of negotiating on behalf of workers, or any class of worker, employed by him, or

    (b)   to negotiate or consult with, or with an official of, one or more trade unions (whether or not so named).

**[1.452]**
**187   Refusal to deal on grounds of union exclusion prohibited**
(1)   A person shall not refuse to deal with a supplier or prospective supplier of goods or services if the ground or one of the grounds for his action is that the person against whom it is taken does not, or is not likely to—
  (a)   recognise one or more trade unions for the purpose of negotiating on behalf of workers, or any class of worker, employed by him, or
  (b)   negotiate or consult with, or with an official of, one or more trade unions.
(2)   A person refuses to deal with a person if—
  (a)   where he maintains (in whatever form) a list of approved suppliers of goods or services, or of persons from whom tenders for the supply of goods or services may be invited, he fails to include the name of that person in that list; or
  (b)   in relation to a proposed contract for the supply of goods or services—
    (i)    he excludes that person from the group of persons from whom tenders for the supply of the goods or services are invited, or
    (ii)   he fails to permit that person to submit such a tender; or
    [(iii)] he otherwise determines not to enter into a contract with that person for the supply of the goods or services [or
  (c)   he terminates a contract with that person for the supply of goods or services.]
(3)   The obligation to comply with this section is a duty owed to the person with whom there is a refusal to deal and to any other person who may be adversely affected by its contravention; and a breach of the duty is actionable accordingly (subject to the defences and other incidents applying to actions for breach of statutory duty).

**NOTES**
  Sub-s (2): original para (c) renumbered as sub-para (iii) of para (b), and new para (c) and the word immediately preceding it added, by the Trade Union Reform and Employment Rights Act 1993, s 49(1), Sch 7, para 23.

CHAPTER II
PROCEDURE FOR HANDLING REDUNDANCIES

*Duty of employer to consult   . . .   representatives*

**[1.453]**
**188   Duty of employer to consult   . . .   representatives**
[(1)   Where an employer is proposing to dismiss as redundant 20 or more employees at one establishment within a period of 90 days or less, the employer shall consult about the dismissals all the persons who are appropriate representatives of any of the employees who may be [affected by the proposed dismissals or may be affected by measures taken in connection with those dismissals.]
(1A)   The consultation shall begin in good time and in any event—
  (a)   where the employer is proposing to dismiss 100 or more employees as mentioned in subsection (1), at least [45 days], and
  (b)   otherwise, at least 30 days,
before the first of the dismissals takes effect.
[(1B)   For the purposes of this section the appropriate representatives of any affected employees are—
  (a)   if the employees are of a description in respect of which an independent trade union is recognised by their employer, representatives of the trade union, or
  (b)   in any other case, whichever of the following employee representatives the employer chooses:—
    (i)    employee representatives appointed or elected by the affected employees otherwise than for the purposes of this section, who (having regard to the purposes for and the method by which they were appointed or elected) have authority from those employees to receive information and to be consulted about the proposed dismissals on their behalf;
    (ii)   employee representatives elected by the affected employees, for the purposes of this section, in an election satisfying the requirements of section 188A(1).]
(2)   The consultation shall include consultation about ways of—
  (a)   avoiding the dismissals,
  (b)   reducing the numbers of employees to be dismissed, and
  (c)   mitigating the consequences of the dismissals,
and shall be undertaken by the employer with a view to reaching agreement with the appropriate representatives.]
(3)   In determining how many employees an employer is proposing to dismiss as redundant no account shall be taken of employees in respect of whose proposed dismissals consultation has already begun.
(4)   For the purposes of the consultation the employer shall disclose in writing to the [appropriate] representatives—

(a)   the reasons for his proposals,

(b)   the numbers and descriptions of employees whom it is proposed to dismiss as redundant,

(c)   the total number of employees of any such description employed by the employer at the establishment in question,

(d)   the proposed method of selecting the employees who may be dismissed, . . .

(e)   the proposed method of carrying out the dismissals, with due regard to any agreed procedure, including the period over which the dismissals are to take effect [ . . .

(f)   the proposed method of calculating the amount of any redundancy payments to be made (otherwise than in compliance with an obligation imposed by or by virtue of any enactment) to employees who may be dismissed],

[(g)   the number of agency workers working temporarily for and under the supervision and direction of the employer,

(h)   the parts of the employer's undertaking in which those agency workers are working, and

(i)   the type of work those agency workers are carrying out].

(5)   That information shall be [given to each of the appropriate representatives by being delivered to them], or sent by post to an address notified by them to the employer, or [in the case of representatives of a trade union)] sent by post to the union at the address of its head or main office.

[(5A)   The employer shall allow the appropriate representatives access to [the affected employees] and shall afford to those representatives such accommodation and other facilities as may be appropriate.]

(6)   . . .

(7)   If in any case there are special circumstances which render it not reasonably practicable for the employer to comply with a requirement of subsection [(1A), (2) or (4)], the employer shall take all such steps towards compliance with that requirement as are reasonably practicable in those circumstances.

[Where the decision leading to the proposed dismissals is that of a person controlling the employer (directly or indirectly), a failure on the part of that person to provide information to the employer shall not constitute special circumstances rendering it not reasonably practicable for the employer to comply with such a requirement.]

[(7A)   Where—

[(a)   the employer has invited any of the affected employees to elect employee representatives, and]

(b)   the invitation was issued long enough before the time when the consultation is required by subsection (1A)(a) or (b) to begin to allow them to elect representatives by that time,

the employer shall be treated as complying with the requirements of this section in relation to those employees if he complies with those requirements as soon as is reasonably practicable after the election of the representatives.]

[(7B)   If, after the employer has invited affected employees to elect representatives, the affected employees fail to do so within a reasonable time, he shall give to each affected employee the information set out in subsection (4).]

(8)   This section does not confer any rights on a trade union[, a representative] or an employee except as provided by sections 189 to 192 below.

---

NOTES

In the section-heading and the heading preceding this section, words omitted repealed by the Collective Redundancies and Transfer of Undertakings (Protection of Employment) (Amendment) Regulations 1995, SI 1995/2587, reg 3(1), (10).

Sub-s (1): substituted, together with sub-ss (1A), (1B), (2), for the original sub-ss (1), (2), by SI 1995/2587, reg 3(1), (2); words in square brackets substituted by the Collective Redundancies and Transfer of Undertakings (Protection of Employment) (Amendment) Regulations 1999, SI 1999/1925, regs 2(1), (2), 3(1), (2).

Sub-s (1A): substituted as noted above; words in square brackets substituted for original words "90 days" by the Trade Union and Labour Relations (Consolidation) Act 1992 (Amendment) Order 2013, SI 2013/763, art 3(1), (2), as from 6 April 2013, in relation to proposals to dismiss as redundant 100 or more employees at one establishment within a period of 90 days or less which are made on or after 6 April 2013 (see art 2(1) of the 2013 Order at **[2.1678]**).

Sub-s (1B): substituted as noted above; further substituted by SI 1999/1925, regs 2(1), (2), 3(1), (3).

Sub-s (2): substituted as noted above.

Sub-s (4): word in first pair of square brackets substituted by SI 1995/2587, reg 3(1), (3); word omitted from para (d) repealed, and para (f) and the word immediately preceding it added, by the Trade Union Reform and Employment Rights Act 1993, ss 34(1), (2)(a), 51, Sch 10; word omitted from para (e) repealed, and paras (g)–(i) added, by the Agency Workers Regulations 2010, SI 2010/93, reg 25, Sch 2, Pt 1, paras 1, 4(1), (3), as from 1 October 2011.

Sub-s (5): words in square brackets substituted or inserted by SI 1995/2587, reg 3(1), (4).

Sub-s (5A): inserted by SI 1995/2587, reg 3(1), (5); words in square brackets substituted by SI 1999/1925, regs 2(1), (2), 3(1), (4).

Sub-s (6): repealed by SI 1995/2587, reg 3(1), (6).

Sub-s (7): words in first pair of square brackets substituted by SI 1995/2587, reg 3(1), (7); words in second pair of square brackets added by the Trade Union Reform and Employment Rights Act 1993, s 34(1), (2)(c).

Sub-s (7A): inserted by SI 1995/2587, reg 3(1), (8); para (a) substituted by SI 1999/1925, regs 2(1), (2), 3(1), (5).

Sub-s (7B): inserted by SI 1999/1925, regs 2(1), (2), 3(1), (6).

Sub-s (8): words in square brackets inserted by SI 1995/2587, reg 3(1), (9).

Conciliation: employment tribunal proceedings and claims which could be the subject of employment tribunal proceedings arising out of a contravention, or alleged contravention, of this section are proceedings to which the Employment Tribunals Act 1996, s 18 applies; see s 18(1)(b) of that Act at **[1.706]**.

**[1.454]**
**[188A**
(1)   The requirements for the election of employee representatives under section 188(1B)(b)(ii) are that—

(a)   the employer shall make such arrangements as are reasonably practical to ensure that the election is fair;

(b)   the employer shall determine the number of representatives to be elected so that there are sufficient representatives to represent the interests of all the affected employees having regard to the number and classes of those employees;

(c)   the employer shall determine whether the affected employees should be represented either by representatives of all the affected employees or by representatives of particular classes of those employees;

(d)   before the election the employer shall determine the term of office as employee representatives so that it is of sufficient length to enable information to be given and consultations under section 188 to be completed;

(e)   the candidates for election as employee representatives are affected employees on the date of the election;

(f)   no affected employee is unreasonably excluded from standing for election;

(g)   all affected employees on the date of the election are entitled to vote for employee representatives;

(h)   the employees entitled to vote may vote for as many candidates as there are representatives to be elected to represent them or, if there are to be representatives for particular classes of employees, may vote for as many candidates as there are representatives to be elected to represent their particular class of employee;

(i)   the election is conducted so as to secure that—

   (i)   so far as is reasonably practicable, those voting do so in secret, and

   (ii)   the votes given at the election are accurately counted.

(2)   Where, after an election of employee representatives satisfying the requirements of subsection (1) has been held, one of those elected ceases to act as an employee representative and any of those employees are no longer represented, they shall elect another representative by an election satisfying the requirements of subsection (1)(a), (e), (f) and (i).]

**NOTES**
Inserted by the Collective Redundancies and Transfer of Undertakings (Protection of Employment) (Amendment) Regulations 1999, SI 1999/1925, regs 2(1), (2), 4.

**[1.455]**
**189   Complaint . . . and protective award**
[(1)   Where an employer has failed to comply with a requirement of section 188 or section 188A, a complaint may be presented to an employment tribunal on that ground—

(a)   in the case of a failure relating to the election of employee representatives, by any of the affected employees or by any of the employees who have been dismissed as redundant;

(b)   in the case of any other failure relating to employee representatives, by any of the employee representatives to whom the failure related,

(c)   in the case of failure relating to representatives of a trade union, by the trade union, and

(d)   in any other case, by any of the affected employees or by any of the employees who have been dismissed as redundant.]

[(1A)   If on a complaint under subsection (1) a question arises as to whether or not any employee representative was an appropriate representative for the purposes of section 188, it shall be for the employer to show that the employee representative had the authority to represent the affected employees.

(1B)   On a complaint under subsection (1)(a) it shall be for the employer to show that the requirements in section 188A have been satisfied.]

(2)   If the tribunal finds the complaint well-founded it shall make a declaration to that effect and may also make a protective award.

(3)   A protective award is an award in respect of one or more descriptions of employees—

(a)   who have been dismissed as redundant, or whom it is proposed to dismiss as redundant, and

(b)   in respect of whose dismissal or proposed dismissal the employer has failed to comply with a requirement of section 188,

ordering the employer to pay remuneration for the protected period.

(4)   The protected period—

(a)   begins with the date on which the first of the dismissals to which the complaint relates takes effect, or the date of the award, whichever is the earlier, and

(b) is of such length as the tribunal determines to be just and equitable in all the circumstances having regard to the seriousness of the employer's default in complying with any requirement of section 188;

but shall not exceed 90 days . . .

(5) An [employment tribunal] shall not consider a complaint under this section unless it is presented to the tribunal—

(a) before the [date on which the last of the dismissals to which the complaint relates] takes effect, or

(b) [during] the period of three months beginning with [that date], or

(c) where the tribunal is satisfied that it was not reasonably practicable for the complaint to be presented [during the] period of three months, within such further period as it considers reasonable.

[(5A) Where the complaint concerns a failure to comply with a requirement of section 188, section 292A (extension of time limits to facilitate conciliation before institution of proceedings) applies for the purposes of subsection (5)(b).]

(6) If on a complaint under this section a question arises—

(a) whether there were special circumstances which rendered it not reasonably practicable for the employer to comply with any requirement of section 188, or

(b) whether he took all such steps towards compliance with that requirement as were reasonably practicable in those circumstances,

it is for the employer to show that there were and that he did.

**NOTES**

Section heading: words omitted repealed by the Collective Redundancies and Transfer of Undertakings (Protection of Employment) (Amendment) Regulations 1995, SI 1995/2587, reg 4(1), (5).

Sub-s (1): substituted by the Collective Redundancies and Transfer of Undertakings (Protection of Employment) (Amendment) Regulations 1999, SI 1999/1925, regs 2(1), (2), 5(1), (2).

Sub-ss (1A), (1B): inserted by SI 1999/1925, regs 2(1), (2), 5(1), (3).

Sub-s (4): words omitted repealed by SI 1999/1925, regs 2(1), (2), 5(1), (4).

Sub-s (5): words in first pair of square brackets substituted by the Employment Rights (Dispute Resolution) Act 1998, s 1(2)(a); other words in square brackets substituted by SI 1995/2587, reg 4(1), (4).

Sub-s (5A): inserted by the Enterprise and Regulatory Reform Act 2013, s 8, Sch 2, paras 1, 11, as from a day to be appointed.

**[1.456]**
**190  Entitlement under protective award**

(1) Where an [employment tribunal] has made a protective award, every employee of a description to which the award relates is entitled, subject to the following provisions and to section 191, to be paid remuneration by his employer for the protected period.

(2) The rate of remuneration payable is a week's pay for each week of the period; and remuneration in respect of a period less than one week shall be calculated by reducing proportionately the amount of a week's pay.

(3)    . . .

(4) An employee is not entitled to remuneration under a protective award in respect of a period during which he is employed by the employer unless he would be entitled to be paid by the employer in respect of that period—

(a) by virtue of his contract of employment, or

(b) by virtue of [sections 87 to 91 of the Employment Rights Act 1996] (rights of employee in period of notice),

if that period fell within the period of notice required to be given by [section 86(1)] of that Act.

(5) [Chapter II of Part XIV of the Employment Rights Act 1996] applies with respect to the calculation of a week's pay for the purposes of this section.

The calculation date for the purposes of [that Chapter] is the date on which the protective award was made or, in the case of an employee who was dismissed before the date on which the protective award was made, the date which by virtue of [section 226(5)] is the calculation date for the purpose of computing the amount of a redundancy payment in relation to that dismissal (whether or not the employee concerned is entitled to any such payment).

(6) If an employee of a description to which a protective award relates dies during the protected period, the award has effect in his case as if the protected period ended on his death.

**NOTES**

Sub-s (1): words in square brackets substituted by the Employment Rights (Dispute Resolution) Act 1998, s 1(2)(a).

Sub-s (3): repealed by the Trade Union Reform and Employment Rights Act 1993, ss 34(1), (3), 51, Sch 10.

Sub-ss (4), (5): words in square brackets substituted by the Employment Rights Act 1996, s 240, Sch 1, para 56(1), (14).

Conciliation: employment tribunal proceedings and claims which could be the subject of employment tribunal proceedings arising out of a contravention, or alleged contravention, of this section are proceedings to which the Employment Tribunals Act 1996, s 18 applies; see s 18(1)(b) of that Act at **[1.706]**.

**[1.457]**
**191   Termination of employment during protected period**
(1)   Where the employee is employed by the employer during the protected period and—
  (a)   he is fairly dismissed by his employer [otherwise than as redundant], or
  (b)   he unreasonably terminates the contract of employment,
then, subject to the following provisions, he is not entitled to remuneration under the protective award in respect of any period during which but for that dismissal or termination he would have been employed.
(2)   If an employer makes an employee an offer (whether in writing or not and whether before or after the ending of his employment under the previous contract) to renew his contract of employment, or to re-engage him under a new contract, so that the renewal or re-engagement would take effect before or during the protected period, and either—
  (a)   the provisions of the contract as renewed, or of the new contract, as to the capacity and place in which he would be employed, and as to the other terms and conditions of his employment, would not differ from the corresponding provisions of the previous contract, or
  (b)   the offer constitutes an offer of suitable employment in relation to the employee,
the following subsections have effect.
(3)   If the employee unreasonably refuses the offer, he is not entitled to remuneration under the protective award in respect of a period during which but for that refusal he would have been employed.
(4)   If the employee's contract of employment is renewed, or he is re-engaged under a new contract of employment, in pursuance of such an offer as is referred to in subsection (2)(b), there shall be a trial period in relation to the contract as renewed, or the new contract (whether or not there has been a previous trial period under this section).
(5)   The trial period begins with the ending of his employment under the previous contract and ends with the expiration of the period of four weeks beginning with the date on which he starts work under the contract as renewed, or the new contract, or such longer period as may be agreed in accordance with subsection (6) for the purpose of retraining the employee for employment under that contract.
(6)   Any such agreement—
  (a)   shall be made between the employer and the employee or his representative before the employee starts work under the contract as renewed or, as the case may be, the new contract,
  (b)   shall be in writing,
  (c)   shall specify the date of the end of the trial period, and
  (d)   shall specify the terms and conditions of employment which will apply in the employee's case after the end of that period.
(7)   If during the trial period—
  (a)   the employee, for whatever reason, terminates the contract, or gives notice to terminate it and the contract is thereafter, in consequence, terminated, or
  (b)   the employer, for a reason connected with or arising out of the change to the renewed, or new, employment, terminates the contract, or gives notice to terminate it and the contract is thereafter, in consequence, terminated,
the employee remains entitled under the protective award unless, in a case falling within paragraph (a), he acted unreasonably in terminating or giving notice to terminate the contract.

**NOTES**
  Sub-s (1): words in square brackets substituted by the Trade Union Reform and Employment Rights Act 1993, s 49(2), Sch 8, para 70.

**[1.458]**
**192   Complaint by employee to [employment tribunal]**
(1)   An employee may present a complaint to an [employment tribunal] on the ground that he is an employee of a description to which a protective award relates and that his employer has failed, wholly or in part, to pay him remuneration under the award.
(2)   An [employment tribunal] shall not entertain a complaint under this section unless it is presented to the tribunal—
  (a)   before the end of the period of three months beginning with the day (or, if the complaint relates to more than one day, the last of the days) in respect of which the complaint is made of failure to pay remuneration, or
  (b)   where the tribunal is satisfied that it was not reasonably practicable for the complaint to be presented within the period of three months, within such further period as it may consider reasonable.
[(2A)   Section 292A (extension of time limits to facilitate conciliation before institution of proceedings) applies for the purposes of subsection (2)(a).]
(3)   Where the tribunal finds a complaint under this section well founded it shall order the employer to pay the complainant the amount of remuneration which it finds is due to him.

(4)   The remedy of an employee for infringement of his right to remuneration under a protective award is by way of complaint under this section, and not otherwise.

*Duty of employer to notify Secretary of State*

[1.459]
**193   Duty of employer to notify Secretary of State of certain redundancies**
(1)   An employer proposing to dismiss as redundant 100 or more employees at one establishment within a period of 90 days or less shall notify the Secretary of State, in writing, of his proposal[—
   (a)   before giving notice to terminate an employee's contract of employment in respect of any of those dismissals, and
   (b)]   at least [45 days] before the first of those dismissals takes effect.
(2)   An employer proposing to dismiss as redundant [20] or more employees at one establishment within [such a period] shall notify the Secretary of State, in writing, of his proposal[—
   (a)   before giving notice to terminate an employee's contract of employment in respect of any of those dismissals, and
   (b)]   at least 30 days before the first of those dismissals takes effect.
(3)   In determining how many employees an employer is proposing to dismiss as redundant within the period mentioned in subsection (1) or (2), no account shall be taken of employees in respect of whose proposed dismissal notice has already been given to the Secretary of State.
(4)   A notice under this section shall—
   (a)   be given to the Secretary of State by delivery to him or by sending it by post to him, at such address as the Secretary of State may direct in relation to the establishment where the employees proposed to be dismissed are employed,
   [(b)   where there are representatives to be consulted under section 188, identify them and state the date when consultation with them under that section began,] and
   (c)   be in such form and contain such particulars, in addition to those required by paragraph (b), as the Secretary of State may direct.
(5)   After receiving a notice under this section from an employer the Secretary of State may by written notice require the employer to give him such further information as may be specified in the notice.
(6)   [Where there are representatives to be consulted under section 188 the employer shall give to each of them a copy of any notice given under section (1) or (2).]
   The copy shall be delivered to them or sent by post to an address notified by them to the employer, or [(in the case of representatives of a trade union)] sent by post to the union at the address of its head or main office.
(7)   If in any case there are special circumstances rendering it not reasonably practicable for the employer to comply with any of the requirements of subsections (1) to (6), he shall take all such steps towards compliance with that requirement as are reasonably practicable in the circumstances.
   [Where the decision leading to the proposed dismissals is that of a person controlling the employer (directly or indirectly), a failure on the part of that person to provide information to the employer shall not constitute special circumstances rendering it not reasonably practicable for the employer to comply with any of those requirements.]

[1.460]
**194   Offence of failure to notify**
(1)   An employer who fails to give notice to the Secretary of State in accordance with section 193 commits an offence and is liable on summary conviction to a fine not exceeding level 5 on the standard scale.

(2)   Proceedings in England or Wales for such an offence shall be instituted only by or with the consent of the Secretary of State or by an officer authorised for that purpose by special or general directions of the Secretary of State.

An officer so authorised may . . . prosecute or conduct proceedings for such an offence before a magistrates' court.

(3)   Where an offence under this section committed by a body corporate is proved to have been committed with the consent or connivance of, or to be attributable to neglect on the part of, any director, manager, secretary or other similar officer of the body corporate, or any person purporting to act in any such capacity, he as well as the body corporate is guilty of the offence and liable to be proceeded against and punished accordingly.

(4)   Where the affairs of a body corporate are managed by its members, subsection (3) applies in relation to the acts and defaults of a member in connection with his functions of management as if he were a director of the body corporate.

**NOTES**

Sub-s (2): words omitted repealed by the Legal Services Act 2007, ss 208(1), 210, Sch 21, paras 104, 105, Sch 23, as from 1 January 2010.

*Supplementary provisions*

**[1.461]**
**[195   Construction of references to dismissal as redundant etc**
(1)   In this Chapter references to dismissal as redundant are references to dismissal for a reason not related to the individual concerned or for a number of reasons all of which are not so related.
(2)   For the purposes of any proceedings under this Chapter, where an employee is or is proposed to be dismissed it shall be presumed, unless the contrary is proved, that he is or is proposed to be dismissed as redundant.]

**NOTES**

Substituted by the Trade Union Reform and Employment Rights Act 1993, s 34(1), (5).

**[1.462]**
**[196   Construction of references to representatives**
(1)   For the purposes of this Chapter persons are employee representatives if—
   (a)   they have been elected by employees for the specific purpose of being consulted by their employer about dismissals proposed by him, or
   (b)   having been elected [or appointed] by employees (whether before or after dismissals have been proposed by their employer) otherwise than for that specific purpose, it is appropriate (having regard to the purposes for which they were elected) for the employer to consult them about dismissals proposed by him,
and (in either case) they are employed by the employer at the time when they are elected [or appointed].
(2)   References in this Chapter to representatives of a trade union, in relation to an employer, are to officials or other persons authorised by the trade union to carry on collective bargaining with the employer.]
[(3)   References in this Chapter to affected employees are to employees who may be affected by the proposed dismissals or who may be affected by measures taken in connection with such dismissals.]

**NOTES**

Substituted by the Collective Redundancies and Transfer of Undertakings (Protection of Employment) (Amendment) Regulations 1995, SI 1995/2587, reg 6.
Sub-s (1): words in square brackets inserted by the Collective Redundancies and Transfer of Undertakings (Protection of Employment) (Amendment) Regulations 1999, SI 1999/1925, regs 2(1), (2), 6(1)–(3).
Sub-s (3): added by SI 1999/1925, regs 2(1), (2), 6(1), (4).

**[1.463]**
**197   Power to vary provisions**
(1)   The Secretary of State may by order made by statutory instrument vary—
   (a)   the provisions of sections 188(2) and 193(1) (requirements as to consultation and notification), and
   (b)   the periods referred to at the end of section 189(4) (maximum protected period);
but no such order shall be made which has the effect of reducing to less than 30 days the periods referred to in sections 188(2) and 193(1) as the periods which must elapse before the first of the dismissals takes effect.
(2)   No such order shall be made unless a draft of the order has been laid before Parliament and approved by a resolution of each House of Parliament.

"The periods referred to in sections 188(2) and 193(1)": the provisions referred to in s 188(2) as originally enacted now appear in s 188(1A), but there has been no corresponding amendment to the reference to s 188(2) here.

Orders: the Trade Union and Labour Relations (Consolidation) Act 1992 (Amendment) Order 2013, SI 2013/763 at **[2.1677]**.

**[1.464]**
## 198 Power to adapt provisions in case of collective agreement
(1) This section applies where there is in force a collective agreement which establishes—
- (a) arrangements for providing alternative employment for employees to whom the agreement relates if they are dismissed as redundant by an employer to whom it relates, or
- (b) arrangements for [handling the dismissal of employees as redundant].

(2) On the application of all the parties to the agreement the Secretary of State may, if he is satisfied having regard to the provisions of the agreement that the arrangements are on the whole at least as favourable to those employees as the foregoing provisions of this Chapter, by order made by statutory instrument adapt, modify or exclude any of those provisions both in their application to all or any of those employees and in their application to any other employees of any such employer.

(3) The Secretary of State shall not make such an order unless the agreement—
- (a) provides for procedures to be followed (whether by arbitration or otherwise) in cases where an employee to whom the agreement relates claims that any employer or other person to whom it relates has not complied with the provisions of the agreement, and
- (b) provides that those procedures include a right to arbitration or adjudication by an independent referee or body in cases where (by reason of an equality of votes or otherwise) a decision cannot otherwise be reached,

or indicates that any such employee may present a complaint to an [employment tribunal] that any such employer or other person has not complied with those provisions.

(4) An order under this section may confer on an [employment tribunal] to whom a complaint is presented as mentioned in subsection (3) such powers and duties as the Secretary of State considers appropriate.

(5) An order under this section may be varied or revoked by a subsequent order thereunder either in pursuance of an application made by all or any of the parties to the agreement in question or without any such application.

Sub-s (1): words in square brackets in para (b) substituted by the Trade Union Reform and Employment Rights Act 1993, s 49(2), Sch 8, para 71.

Sub-ss (3), (4): words in square brackets substituted by the Employment Rights (Dispute Resolution) Act 1998, s 1(2)(a).
Orders: as of 6 April 2013, no Orders had been made under this section.

# CHAPTER III
# CODES OF PRACTICE
## *Codes of Practice issued by ACAS*

**[1.465]**
## 199 Issue of Codes of Practice by ACAS
(1) ACAS may issue Codes of Practice containing such practical guidance as it thinks fit for the purpose of promoting the improvement of industrial relations [or for purposes connected with trade union learning representatives].

(2) In particular, ACAS shall in one or more Codes of Practice provide practical guidance on the following matters—
- (a) the time off to be permitted by an employer to a trade union official in accordance with section 168 (time off for carrying out trade union duties);
- (b) the time off to be permitted by an employer to a trade union member in accordance with section 170 (time off for trade union activities); and
- (c) the information to be disclosed by employers to trade union representatives in accordance with sections 181 and 182 (disclosure of information for purposes of collective bargaining).

(3) The guidance mentioned in subsection (2)(a) shall include guidance on the circumstances in which a trade union official is to be permitted to take time off under section 168 in respect of duties connected with industrial action; and the guidance mentioned in subsection (2)(b) shall include guidance on the question whether, and the circumstances in which, a trade union member is to be permitted to take time off under section 170 for trade union activities connected with industrial action.

(4) ACAS may from time to time revise the whole or any part of a Code of Practice issued by it and issue that revised Code.

**NOTES**

Sub-s (1): words in square brackets added by the Employment Act 2002, s 43(1), (7).

Codes made under this section: the current codes are: ACAS Code of Practice 1–Disciplinary and Grievance Procedures (2009) at **[4.1]**; ACAS Code of Practice 2–Disclosure of information to trade unions for collective bargaining purposes (1998) at **[4.90]**; ACAS Code of Practice 3–Time off for trade union duties and activities (2010) at **[4.98]**.

**[1.466]**
## 200   Procedure for issue of Code by ACAS

(1)   Where ACAS proposes to issue a Code of Practice, or a revised Code, it shall prepare and publish a draft of the Code, shall consider any representations made to it about the draft and may modify the draft accordingly.

(2)   If ACAS determines to proceed with the draft, it shall transmit the draft to the Secretary of State who—

(a)   if he approves of it, shall lay it before both Houses of Parliament, and

(b)   if he does not approve of it, shall publish details of his reasons for withholding approval.

[(3)   A Code containing practical guidance—

(a)   on the time off to be permitted to a trade union learning representative in accordance with section 168A (time off for training and carrying out functions as a learning representative),

(b)   on the training that is sufficient to enable a trade union learning representative to carry on the activities mentioned in section 168A(2) (activities for which time off is to be permitted), or

(c)   on any of the matters referred to in section 199(2),

shall not be issued unless the draft has been approved by a resolution of each House of Parliament; and if it is so approved, ACAS shall issue the Code in the form of the draft.]

(4)   In any other case the following procedure applies—

(a)   if, within the period of 40 days beginning with the day on which the draft is laid before Parliament, (or, if copies are laid before the two Houses on different days, with the later of the two days) either House so resolves, no further proceedings shall be taken thereon, but without prejudice to the laying before Parliament of a new draft;

(b)   if no such resolution is passed, ACAS shall issue the Code in the form of the draft.

In reckoning the period of 40 days no account shall be taken of any period during which Parliament is dissolved or prorogued or during which both Houses are adjourned for more than four days.

(5)   A Code issued in accordance with this section shall come into effect on such day as the Secretary of State may appoint by order made by statutory instrument.

The order may contain such transitional provisions or savings as appear to him to be necessary or expedient.

**NOTES**

Sub-s (3): substituted by the Employment Act 2002, s 43(1), (8).

The current codes are as noted to s 199 at **[1.465]**.

Orders: the Employment Code of Practice (Disciplinary and Grievance Procedures) Order 2009, SI 2009/771; the Employment Protection Code of Practice (Time Off for Trade Union Duties and Activities) Order 2009, SI 2009/3223. Note that new Orders made under this section (upon the revision of an existing Code of Practice) effectively supersede previous Orders.

**[1.467]**
## 201   Consequential revision of Code issued by ACAS

(1)   A Code of Practice issued by ACAS may be revised by it in accordance with this section for the purpose of bringing it into conformity with subsequent statutory provisions by the making of consequential amendments and the omission of obsolete passages.

"Subsequent statutory provisions" means provisions made by or under an Act of Parliament and coming into force after the Code was issued (whether before or after the commencement of this Act).

(2)   Where ACAS proposes to revise a Code under this section, it shall transmit a draft of the revised Code to the Secretary of State who—

(a)   if he approves of it, shall lay the draft before each House of Parliament, and

(b)   if he does not approve of it, shall publish details of his reasons for withholding approval.

(3)   If within the period of 40 days beginning with the day on which the draft is laid before Parliament, (or, if copies are laid before the two Houses on different days, with the later of the two days) either House so resolves, no further proceedings shall be taken thereon, but without prejudice to the laying before Parliament of a new draft.

In reckoning the period of 40 days no account shall be taken of any period during which Parliament is dissolved or prorogued or during which both Houses are adjourned for more than four days.

(4)   If no such resolution is passed ACAS shall issue the Code in the form of the draft and it shall come into effect on such day as the Secretary of State may appoint by order made by statutory instrument.

The order may contain such transitional provisions or savings as appear to the Secretary of State to be necessary or expedient.

**NOTES**

Orders: the Employment Protection Code of Practice (Disclosure of Information) Order 1998, SI 1998/45.

**[1.468]**
## 202  Revocation of Code issued by ACAS

(1)  A Code of Practice issued by ACAS may, at the request of ACAS, be revoked by the Secretary of State by order made by statutory instrument.

The order may contain such transitional provisions and savings as appear to him to be appropriate.

(2)  If ACAS requests the Secretary of State to revoke a Code and he decides not to do so, he shall publish details of his reasons for his decision.

(3)  An order shall not be made under this section unless a draft of it has been laid before and approved by resolution of each House of Parliament.

**NOTES**

Orders: as of 6 April 2013 no Orders had been made under this section, but by virtue of s 300(3) of, and Sch 3, para 1(2) to, this Act, and the Interpretation Act 1978, s 17(2)(b), the Employment Codes of Practice (Revocation) Order 1991, SI 1991/1264 has effect as if made under this section.

### *Codes of Practice issued by the Secretary of State*

**[1.469]**
## 203  Issue of Codes of Practice by the Secretary of State

(1)  The Secretary of State may issue Codes of Practice containing such practical guidance as he thinks fit for the purpose—

(a)  of promoting the improvement of industrial relations, or

(b)  of promoting what appear to him to be to be desirable practices in relation to the conduct by trade unions of ballots and elections [or for purposes connected with trade union learning representatives].

(2)  The Secretary of State may from time to time revise the whole or any part of a Code of Practice issued by him and issue that revised Code.

**NOTES**

Sub-s (1): words in square brackets in para (b) added by the Employment Act 2002, s 43(1), (7).

Codes issued under this section: Access and unfair practices during recognition and derecognition ballots (2005) at **[4.220]**; Industrial Action Ballots and Notice to Employers (2005) at **[4.228]**. In addition, the Code of Practice on Picketing (1992) at **[4.211]** has effect as if made under this section by virtue of s 300(3) of, and Sch 3, para 1(2) to, this Act and the Interpretation Act 1978, s 17(2)(b)

**[1.470]**
## 204  Procedure for issue of Code by Secretary of State

(1)  When the Secretary of State proposes to issue a Code of Practice, or a revised Code, he shall after consultation with ACAS prepare and publish a draft of the Code, shall consider any representations made to him about the draft and may modify the draft accordingly.

(2)  If he determines to proceed with the draft, he shall lay it before both Houses of Parliament and, if it is approved by resolution of each House, shall issue the Code in the form of the draft.

(3)  A Code issued under this section shall come into effect on such day as the Secretary of State may by order appoint.

The order may contain such transitional provisions or savings as appear to him to be necessary or expedient.

(4)  An order under subsection (3) shall be made by statutory instrument, which shall be subject to annulment in pursuance of a resolution of either House of Parliament.

**NOTES**

Orders: the Employment Code of Practice (Industrial Action Ballots and Notice to Employers) Order 2005, SI 2005/2420; the Employment Code of Practice (Access and Unfair Practices during Recognition and Derecognition Ballots) Order 2005, SI 2005/2421. Note that new Orders made under this section (upon the revision of an existing Code of Practice) effectively supersede previous Orders. Also, by virtue of s 300(3) of, and Sch 3, para 1(2) to, this Act, and the Interpretation Act 1978, s 17(2)(b), the Employment Code of Practice (Picketing) Order 1992, SI 1992/476, has effect as if made under this section.

**[1.471]**
## 205  Consequential revision of Code issued by Secretary of State

(1)  A Code of Practice issued by the Secretary of State may be revised by him in accordance with this section for the purpose of bringing it into conformity with subsequent statutory provisions by the making of consequential amendments and the omission of obsolete passages.

"Subsequent statutory provisions" means provisions made by or under an Act of Parliament and coming into force after the Code was issued (whether before or after the commencement of this Act).

(2) Where the Secretary of State proposes to revise a Code under this section, he shall lay a draft of the revised Code before each House of Parliament.

(3) If within the period of 40 days beginning with the day on which the draft is laid before Parliament, or, if copies are laid before the two Houses on different days, with the later of the two days, either House so resolves, no further proceedings shall be taken thereon, but without prejudice to the laying before Parliament of a new draft.

In reckoning the period of 40 days no account shall be taken of any period during which Parliament is dissolved or prorogued or during which both Houses are adjourned for more than four days.

(4) If no such resolution is passed the Secretary of State shall issue the Code in the form of the draft and it shall come into effect on such day as he may appoint by order made by statutory instrument.

The order may contain such transitional provisions and savings as appear to him to be appropriate.

**[1.472]**
## 206    Revocation of Code issued by Secretary of State
(1) A Code of Practice issued by the Secretary of State may be revoked by him by order made by statutory instrument.

The order may contain such transitional provisions and savings as appear to him to be appropriate.

(2) An order shall not be made under this section unless a draft of it has been laid before and approved by resolution of each House of Parliament.

*Supplementary provisions*

**[1.473]**
## 207    Effect of failure to comply with Code
(1) A failure on the part of any person to observe any provision of a Code of Practice issued under this Chapter shall not of itself render him liable to any proceedings.

(2) In any proceedings before an [employment tribunal] or the Central Arbitration Committee any Code of Practice issued under this Chapter by ACAS shall be admissible in evidence, and any provision of the Code which appears to the tribunal or Committee to be relevant to any question arising in the proceedings shall be taken into account in determining that question.

(3) In any proceedings before a court or [employment tribunal] or the Central Arbitration Committee any Code of Practice issued under this Chapter by the Secretary of State shall be admissible in evidence, and any provision of the Code which appears to the court, tribunal or Committee to be relevant to any question arising in the proceedings shall be taken into account in determining that question.

**NOTES**
Sub-ss (2), (3): words in square brackets substituted by the Employment Rights (Dispute Resolution) Act 1998, s 1(2)(a).

**[1.474]**
## [207A    Effect of failure to comply with Code: adjustment of awards
(1) This section applies to proceedings before an employment tribunal relating to a claim by an employee under any of the jurisdictions listed in Schedule A2.

(2) If, in the case of proceedings to which this section applies, it appears to the employment tribunal that—
  (a) the claim to which the proceedings relate concerns a matter to which a relevant Code of Practice applies,
  (b) the employer has failed to comply with that Code in relation to that matter, and
  (c) that failure was unreasonable,
the employment tribunal may, if it considers it just and equitable in all the circumstances to do so, increase any award it makes to the employee by no more than 25%.

(3) If, in the case of proceedings to which this section applies, it appears to the employment tribunal that—
  (a) the claim to which the proceedings relate concerns a matter to which a relevant Code of Practice applies,
  (b) the employee has failed to comply with that Code in relation to that matter, and
  (c) that failure was unreasonable,
the employment tribunal may, if it considers it just and equitable in all the circumstances to do so, reduce any award it makes to the employee by no more than 25%.

(4) In subsections (2) and (3), "relevant Code of Practice" means a Code of Practice issued under this Chapter which relates exclusively or primarily to procedure for the resolution of disputes.

(5) Where an award falls to be adjusted under this section and under section 38 of the Employment Act 2002, the adjustment under this section shall be made before the adjustment under that section.

(6) The Secretary of State may by order amend Schedule A2 for the purpose of—

(a) adding a jurisdiction to the list in that Schedule, or

(b) removing a jurisdiction from that list.

(7) The power of the Secretary of State to make an order under subsection (6) includes power to make such incidental, supplementary, consequential or transitional provision as the Secretary of State thinks fit.

(8) An order under subsection (6) shall be made by statutory instrument.

(9) No order shall be made under subsection (6) unless a draft of the statutory instrument containing it has been laid before Parliament and approved by a resolution of each House.]

**NOTES**

Commencement: 6 April 2009.

Inserted by the Employment Act 2008, s 3(1), (2), as from 6 April 2009 (subject to transitional provisions and savings in the Employment Act 2008 (Commencement No 1, Transitional Provisions and Savings) Order 2008, SI 2008/3232, Schedule, Pt 1, paras 1(c), 2, 3).

"A relevant Code": see ACAS Code of Practice 1: Disciplinary and grievance procedures (2009) at **[4.1]**.

Orders: as of 6 April 2013 no Orders had been made under this section.

Where an award of compensation for unfair dismissal falls to be reduced or increased under this section, the adjustment is to be in the amount awarded under the Employment Rights Act 1996, s 118(1)(b), and is to be applied immediately before any reduction under s 123(6), (7) of that Act; see s 124A of the 1996 Act at **[1.935]**.

**[1.475]**
**208  Provisions of earlier Code superseded by later**

(1) If ACAS is of the opinion that the provisions of a Code of Practice to be issued by it under this Chapter will supersede the whole or part of a Code previously issued under this Chapter, by it or by the Secretary of State, it shall in the new Code state that on the day on which the new Code comes into effect the old Code or a specified part of it shall cease to have effect.

(2) If the Secretary of State is of the opinion that the provisions of a Code of Practice to be issued by him under this Chapter will supersede the whole or part of a Code previously issued under this Chapter by him or by ACAS, he shall in the new Code state that on the day on which the new Code comes into effect the old Code or a specified part of it shall cease to have effect.

(3) The above provisions do not affect any transitional provisions or savings made by the order bringing the new Code into effect.

CHAPTER IV
GENERAL

*Functions of ACAS*

**[1.476]**
**209  General duty to promote improvement of industrial relations**

It is the general duty of ACAS to promote the improvement of industrial relations  . . .

**NOTES**

Words omitted repealed by the Employment Relations Act 1999, ss 26, 44, Sch 9(5).

**[1.477]**
**210  Conciliation**

(1) Where a trade dispute exists or is apprehended ACAS may, at the request of one or more parties to the dispute or otherwise, offer the parties to the dispute its assistance with a view to bringing about a settlement.

(2) The assistance may be by way of conciliation or by other means, and may include the appointment of a person other than an officer or servant of ACAS to offer assistance to the parties to the dispute with a view to bringing about a settlement.

(3) In exercising its functions under this section ACAS shall have regard to the desirability of encouraging the parties to a dispute to use any appropriate agreed procedures for negotiation or the settlement of disputes.

**[1.478]**
**[210A  Information required by ACAS for purpose of settling recognition disputes**

(1) This section applies where ACAS is exercising its functions under section 210 with a view to bringing about a settlement of a recognition dispute.

(2) The parties to the recognition dispute may jointly request ACAS or a person nominated by ACAS to do either or both of the following—

(a) hold a ballot of the workers involved in the dispute;

(b) ascertain the union membership of the workers involved in the dispute.

(3)   In the following provisions of this section references to ACAS include references to a person nominated by ACAS; and anything done by such a person under this section shall be regarded as done in the exercise of the functions of ACAS mentioned in subsection (1).

(4)   At any time after ACAS has received a request under subsection (2), it may require any party to the recognition dispute—

   (a)   to supply ACAS with specified information concerning the workers involved in the dispute, and

   (b)   to do so within such period as it may specify.

(5)   ACAS may impose a requirement under subsection (4) only if it considers that it is necessary to do so—

   (a)   for the exercise of the functions mentioned in subsection (1); and

   (b)   in order to enable or assist it to comply with the request.

(6)   The recipient of a requirement under this section must, within the specified period, supply ACAS with such of the specified information as is in the recipient's possession.

(7)   A request under subsection (2) may be withdrawn by any party to the recognition dispute at any time and, if it is withdrawn, ACAS shall take no further steps to hold the ballot or to ascertain the union membership of the workers involved in the dispute.

(8)   If a party to a recognition dispute fails to comply with subsection (6), ACAS shall take no further steps to hold the ballot or to ascertain the union membership of the workers involved in the dispute.

(9)   Nothing in this section requires ACAS to comply with a request under subsection (2).

(10)   In this section—

"party", in relation to a recognition dispute, means each of the employers, employers' associations and trade unions involved in the dispute;

"a recognition dispute" means a trade dispute between employers and workers which is connected wholly or partly with the recognition by employers or employers' associations of the right of a trade union to represent workers in negotiations, consultations or other procedures relating to any of the matters mentioned in paragraphs (a) to (f) of section 218(1);

"specified" means specified in a requirement under this section; and

"workers" has the meaning given in section 218(5).]

**NOTES**
Inserted by the Employment Relations Act 2004, s 21.

**[1.479]**
### 211   Conciliation officers
(1)   ACAS shall designate some of its officers to perform the functions of conciliation officers under any enactment (whenever passed) relating to matters which are or could be the subject of proceedings before an [employment tribunal].

(2)   References in any such enactment to a conciliation officer are to an officer designated under this section.

**NOTES**
Sub-s (1): words in square brackets substituted by the Employment Rights (Dispute Resolution) Act 1998, s 1(2)(a).

**[1.480]**
### 212   Arbitration
(1)   Where a trade dispute exists or is apprehended ACAS may, at the request of one or more of the parties to the dispute and with the consent of all the parties to the dispute, refer all or any of the matters to which the dispute relates for settlement to the arbitration of—

   (a)   one or more persons appointed by ACAS for that purpose (not being officers or employees of ACAS), or

   (b)   the Central Arbitration Committee.

(2)   In exercising its functions under this section ACAS shall consider the likelihood of the dispute being settled by conciliation.

(3)   Where there exist appropriate agreed procedures for negotiation or the settlement of disputes, ACAS shall not refer a matter for settlement to arbitration under this section unless—

   (a)   those procedures have been used and have failed to result in a settlement, or

   (b)   there is, in ACAS's opinion, a special reason which justifies arbitration under this section as an alternative to those procedures.

(4)   Where a matter is referred to arbitration under subsection (1)(a)—

   (a)   if more than one arbitrator or arbiter is appointed, ACAS shall appoint one of them to act as chairman; and

   (b)   the award may be published if ACAS so decides and all the parties consent.

(5)   [Nothing in any of sections 1 to 15 of and schedule 1 to the Arbitration (Scotland) Act 2010 or] [Part I of the Arbitration Act 1996] (general provisions as to arbitration) [applies] to an arbitration under this section.

**[1.481]**
**[212A    Arbitration scheme for unfair dismissal cases etc**
(1)    ACAS may prepare a scheme providing for arbitration in the case of disputes involving proceedings, or claims which could be the subject of proceedings, before an employment tribunal [under, or] arising out of a contravention or alleged contravention of—
　　[(zza) section 63F(4), (5) or (6) or 63I(1)(b) of the Employment Rights Act 1996 (study and training);]
　　[(za) section 80G(1) or 80H(1)(b) of *the Employment Rights Act 1996* (flexible working),]
　　(a)　　Part X of [that Act] (unfair dismissal), or
　　(b)　　any enactment specified in an order made by the Secretary of State.
(2)    When ACAS has prepared such a scheme it shall submit a draft of the scheme to the Secretary of State who, if he approves it, shall make an order—
　　(a)　　setting out the scheme, and
　　(b)　　making provision for it to come into effect.
(3)    ACAS may from time to time prepare a revised version of such a scheme and, when it has done so, shall submit a draft of the revised scheme to the Secretary of State who, if he approves it, shall make an order—
　　(a)　　setting out the revised scheme, and
　　(b)　　making provision for it to come into effect.
(4)    ACAS may take any steps appropriate for promoting awareness of a scheme prepared under this section.
(5)    Where the parties to any dispute within subsection (1) agree in writing to submit the dispute to arbitration in accordance with a scheme having effect by virtue of an order under this section, ACAS shall refer the dispute to the arbitration of a person appointed by ACAS for the purpose (not being an officer or employee of ACAS).
(6)    Nothing in the Arbitration Act 1996 shall apply to an arbitration conducted in accordance with a scheme having effect by virtue of an order under this section except to the extent that the order provides for any provision of Part I of that Act so to apply; and the order may provide for any such provision so to apply subject to modifications.
(7)    A scheme set out in an order under this section may, in relation to an arbitration conducted in accordance with the law of Scotland, make provision—
　　(a)　　that a reference on a preliminary point may be made, or
　　(b)　　conferring a right of appeal which shall lie,
to the relevant court on such grounds and in respect of such matters as may be specified in the scheme; and in this subsection "relevant court" means such court, being the Court of Session or the Employment Appeal Tribunal, as may be specified in the scheme, and a different court may be specified as regards different grounds or matters.
(8)    Where a scheme set out in an order under this section includes provision for the making of re-employment orders in arbitrations conducted in accordance with the scheme, the order setting out the scheme may require employment tribunals to enforce such orders—
　　(a)　　in accordance with section 117 of the Employment Rights Act 1996 (enforcement by award of compensation), or
　　(b)　　in accordance with that section as modified by the order.
For this purpose "re-employment orders" means orders requiring that persons found to have been unfairly dismissed be reinstated, re-engaged or otherwise re-employed.
(9)    An order under this section setting out a scheme may provide that, in the case of disputes within subsection (1)(a), such part of an award made in accordance with the scheme as is specified by the order shall be treated as a basic award of compensation for unfair dismissal for the purposes of section 184(1)(d) of the Employment Rights Act 1996 (which specifies such an award as a debt which the Secretary of State must satisfy if the employer has become insolvent).
(10)    An order under this section shall be made by statutory instrument.
(11)    No order shall be made under subsection (1)(b) unless a draft of the statutory instrument containing it has been laid before Parliament and approved by a resolution of each House.
(12)    A statutory instrument containing an order under this section (other than one of which a draft has been approved by resolution of each House of Parliament) shall be subject to annulment in pursuance of a resolution of either House of Parliament.]

Para (zza) inserted, and for the words in italics in para (za) there are substituted the words "that Act", by the Apprenticeships, Skills, Children and Learning Act 2009, s 40(5), Sch 1, paras 12, 13, as from 6 April 2010 (except in relation to small employers and their employees), and as from a day to be appointed (otherwise) (as to the meaning of "small employers" etc, see further the notes at **[1.840]**).

Orders: the ACAS Arbitration Scheme (Great Britain) Order 2004, SI 2004/753 at **[2.778]**; the ACAS (Flexible Working) Arbitration Scheme (Great Britain) Order 2004, SI 2004/2333.

**[1.482]**
**[212B   Dismissal procedures agreements**
ACAS may, in accordance with any dismissal procedures agreement (within the meaning of the Employment Rights Act 1996), refer any matter to the arbitration of a person appointed by ACAS for the purpose (not being an officer or employee of ACAS).]

**NOTES**
Inserted by the Employment Rights (Dispute Resolution) Act 1998, s 15, Sch 1, para 7.

**[1.483]**
**[213   Advice**
(1)   ACAS may, on request or otherwise, give employers, employers' associations, workers and trade unions such advice as it thinks appropriate on matters concerned with or affecting or likely to affect industrial relations.
(2)   ACAS may also publish general advice on matters concerned with or affecting or likely to affect industrial relations.]

**NOTES**
Substituted by the Trade Union Reform and Employment Rights Act 1993, s 43(2).

**[1.484]**
**214   Inquiry**
(1)   ACAS may, if it thinks fit, inquire into any question relating to industrial relations generally or to industrial relations in any particular industry or in any particular undertaking or part of an undertaking.
(2)   The findings of an inquiry under this section, together with any advice given by ACAS in connection with those findings, may be published by ACAS if—
   (a)   it appears to ACAS that publication is desirable for the improvement of industrial relations, either generally or in relation to the specific question inquired into, and
   (b)   after sending a draft of the findings to all parties appearing to be concerned and taking account of their views, it thinks fit.

*Courts of inquiry*

**[1.485]**
**215   Inquiry and report by court of inquiry**
(1)   Where a trade dispute exists or is apprehended, the Secretary of State may inquire into the causes and circumstances of the dispute, and, if he thinks fit, appoint a court of inquiry and refer to it any matters appearing to him to be connected with or relevant to the dispute.
(2)   The court shall inquire into the matters referred to it and report on them to the Secretary of State; and it may make interim reports if it thinks fit.
(3)   Any report of the court, and any minority report, shall be laid before both Houses of Parliament as soon as possible.
(4)   The Secretary of State may, before or after the report has been laid before Parliament, publish or cause to be published from time to time, in such manner as he thinks fit, any information obtained or conclusions arrived at by the court as the result or in the course of its inquiry.
(5)   No report or publication made or authorised by the court or the Secretary of State shall include any information obtained by the court of inquiry in the course of its inquiry—
   (a)   as to any trade union, or
   (b)   as to any individual business (whether carried on by a person, firm, or company),
which is not available otherwise than through evidence given at the inquiry, except with the consent of the secretary of the trade union or of the person, firm, or company in question.
   Nor shall any individual member of the court or any person concerned in the inquiry disclose such information without such consent.
(6)   The Secretary of State shall from time to time present to Parliament a report of his proceedings under this section.

**[1.486]**
**216   Constitution and proceedings of court of inquiry**
(1)   A court of inquiry shall consist of—
   (a)   a chairman and such other persons as the Secretary of State thinks fit to appoint, or
   (b)   one person appointed by the Secretary of State,

as the Secretary of State thinks fit.

(2) A court may act notwithstanding any vacancy in its number.

(3) A court may conduct its inquiry in public or. in private, at its discretion.

(4) The Secretary of State may make rules regulating the procedure of a court of inquiry, including rules as to summoning of witnesses, quorum, and the appointment of committees and enabling the court to call for such documents as the court may determine to be relevant to the subject matter of the inquiry.

(5) A court of inquiry may, if and to such extent as may be authorised by rules under this section, by order require any person who appears to the court to have knowledge of the subject-matter of the inquiry—

(a) to supply (in writing or otherwise) such particulars in relation thereto as the court may require, and

(b) where necessary, to attend before the court and give evidence on oath;

and the court may administer or authorise any person to administer an oath for that purpose.

(6) Provision shall be made by rules under this section with respect to the cases in which persons may appear by [a relevant lawyer] in proceedings before a court of inquiry, and except as provided by those rules no person shall be entitled to appear in any such proceedings by [a relevant lawyer].

[(7) In subsection (6) "relevant lawyer" means—

(a) a person who, for the purposes of the Legal Services Act 2007, is an authorised person in relation to an activity which constitutes the exercise of a right of audience or the conduct of litigation within the meaning of that Act, or

(b) an advocate or solicitor in Scotland.]

**NOTES**

Sub-s (6): words in square brackets substituted by the Legal Services Act 2007, s 208(1), Sch 21, paras 104, 106(a), as from 1 January 2010.

Sub-s (7): added by the Legal Services Act 2007, s 208(1), Sch 21, paras 104, 106(b), as from 1 January 2010.

Rules: as of 6 April 2013 no Rules had been made under this section.

*Supplementary provisions*

**[1.487]**

**217 Exclusion of power of arbiter to state case to Court of Session**

Section 3 of the Administration of Justice (Scotland) Act 1972 (power of arbiter to state case for opinion of Court of Session) does not apply to—

(a) any form of arbitration relating to a trade dispute, or

(b) any other arbitration arising from a collective agreement.

**[1.488]**

**218 Meaning of "trade dispute" in Part IV**

(1) In this Part "trade dispute" means a dispute between employers and workers, or between workers and workers, which is connected with one or more of the following matters—

(a) terms and conditions of employment, or the physical conditions in which any workers are required to work;

(b) engagement or non-engagement, or termination or suspension of employment or the duties of employment, of one or more workers;

(c) allocation of work or the duties of employment as between workers or groups of workers;

(d) matters of discipline;

(e) the membership or non-membership of a trade union on the part of a worker;

(f) facilities for officials of trade unions; and

(g) machinery for negotiation or consultation, and other procedures, relating to any of the foregoing matters, including the recognition by employers or employers' associations of the right of a trade union to represent workers in any such negotiation or consultation or in the carrying out of such procedures.

(2) A dispute between a Minister of the Crown and any workers shall, notwithstanding that he is not the employer of those workers, be treated for the purposes of this Part as a dispute between an employer and those workers if the dispute relates—

(a) to matters which have been referred for consideration by a joint body on which, by virtue of any provision made by or under any enactment, that Minister is represented, or

(b) to matters which cannot be settled without that Minister exercising a power conferred on him by or under an enactment.

(3) There is a trade dispute for the purpose of this Part even though it relates to matters occurring outside Great Britain.

(4) A dispute to which a trade union or employer's association is a party shall be treated for the purposes of this Part as a dispute to which workers or, as the case may be, employers are parties.

(5) In this section—

"employment" includes any relationship whereby one person personally does work or performs services for another; and "worker", in relation to a dispute to which an employer is a party, includes any worker even if not employed by that employer.

# PART V
# INDUSTRIAL ACTION

*Protection of acts in contemplation or furtherance of trade dispute*

**[1.489]**
## 219   Protection from certain tort liabilities

(1)   An act done by a person in contemplation or furtherance of a trade dispute is not actionable in tort on the ground only—

    (a)   that it induces another person to break a contract or interferes or induces another person to interfere with its performance, or

    (b)   that it consists in his threatening that a contract (whether one to which he is a party or not) will be broken or its performance interfered with, or that he will induce another person to break a contract or interfere with its performance.

(2)   An agreement or combination by two or more persons to do or procure the doing of an act in contemplation or furtherance of a trade dispute is not actionable in tort if the act is one which if done without any such agreement or combination would not be actionable in tort.

(3)   Nothing in subsections (1) and (2) prevents an act done in the course of picketing from being actionable in tort unless it is done in the course of attendance declared lawful by section 220 (peaceful picketing).

(4)   Subsections (1) and (2) have effect subject to sections 222 to 225 (action excluded from protection) and [to sections 226 (requirement of ballot before action by trade union) and 234A (requirement of notice to employer of industrial action); and in those sections "not protected" means excluded from the protection afforded by this section or, where the expression is used with reference to a particular person, excluded from that protection as respects that person.]

**NOTES**
   Sub-s (4): words in square brackets substituted by the Trade Union Reform and Employment Rights Act 1993, s 49(2), Sch 8, para 72.

**[1.490]**
## 220   Peaceful picketing

(1)   It is lawful for a person in contemplation or furtherance of a trade dispute to attend—

    (a)   at or near his own place of work, or

    (b)   if he is an official of a trade union, at or near the place of work of a member of the union whom he is accompanying and whom he represents,

for the purpose only of peacefully obtaining or communicating information, or peacefully persuading any person to work or abstain from working.

(2)   If a person works or normally works—

    (a)   otherwise than at any one place, or

    (b)   at a place the location of which is such that attendance there for a purpose mentioned in subsection (1) is impracticable,

his place of work for the purposes of that subsection shall be any premises of his employer from which he works or from which his work is administered.

(3)   In the case of a worker not in employment where—

    (a)   his last employment was terminated in connection with a trade dispute, or

    (b)   the termination of his employment was one of the circumstances giving rise to a trade dispute,

in relation to that dispute his former place of work shall be treated for the purposes of subsection (1) as being his place of work.

(4)   A person who is an official of a trade union by virtue only of having been elected or appointed to be a representative of some of the members of the union shall be regarded for the purposes of subsection (1) as representing only those members; but otherwise an official of a union shall be regarded for those purposes as representing all its members.

**[1.491]**
## 221   Restrictions on grant of injunctions and interdicts

(1)   Where—

    (a)   an application for an injunction or interdict is made to a court in the absence of the party against whom it is sought or any in representative of his, and

    (b)   he claims, or in the opinion of the court would be likely to claim, that he acted in contemplation or furtherance of a trade dispute,

the court shall not grant the injunction or interdict unless satisfied that all steps which in the circumstances were reasonable have been taken with a view to securing that notice of the application and an opportunity of being heard with respect to the application have been given to him.

(2)  Where—
- (a)  an application for an interlocutory injunction is made to a court pending the trial of an action, and
- (b)  the party against whom it is sought claims that he acted in contemplation or furtherance of a trade dispute,

the court shall, in exercising its discretion whether or not to grant the injunction, have regard to the likelihood of that party's succeeding at the trial of the action in establishing any matter which would afford a defence to the action under section 219 (protection from certain tort liabilities) or section 220 (peaceful picketing).

This subsection does not extend to Scotland.

*Action excluded from protection*

**[1.492]**

## 222  Action to enforce trade union membership

(1)  An act is not protected if the reason, or one of the reasons, for which it is done is the fact or belief that a particular employer—
- (a)  is employing, has employed or might employ a person who is not a member of a trade union, or
- (b)  is failing, has failed or might fail to discriminate against such a person.

(2)  For the purposes of subsection (1)(b) an employer discriminates against a person if, but only if, he ensures that his conduct in relation to—
- (a)  persons, or persons of any description, employed by him, or who apply to be, or are, considered by him for employment, or
- (b)  the provision of employment for such persons,

is different, in some or all cases, according to whether or not they are members of a trade union, and is more favourable to those who are.

(3)  An act is not protected if it constitutes, or is one of a number of acts which together constitute, an inducement or attempted inducement of a person—
- (a)  to incorporate in a contract to which that person is a party, or a proposed contract to which he intends to be a party, a term or condition which is or would be void by virtue of section 144 (union membership requirement in contract for goods or services), or
- (b)  to contravene section 145 (refusal to deal with person on grounds relating to union membership).

(4)  References in this section to an employer employing a person are to a person acting in the capacity of the person for whom a worker works or normally works.

(5)  References in this section to not being a member of a trade union are to not being a member of any trade union, of a particular trade union or of one of a number of particular trade unions.

Any such reference includes a reference to not being a member of a particular branch or section of a trade union or of one of a number of particular branches or sections of a trade union.

**[1.493]**

## 223  Action taken because of dismissal for taking unofficial action

An act is not protected if the reason, or one of the reasons, for doing it is the fact or belief that an employer has dismissed one or more employees in circumstances such that by virtue of section 237 (dismissal in connection with unofficial action) they have no right to complain of unfair dismissal.

**[1.494]**

## 224  Secondary action

(1)  An act is not protected if one of the facts relied on for the purpose of establishing liability is that there has been secondary action which is not lawful picketing.

(2)  There is secondary action in relation to a trade dispute when, and only when, a person—
- (a)  induces another to break a contract of employment or interferes or induces another to interfere with its performance, or
- (b)  threatens that a contract of employment under which he or another is employed will be broken or its performance interfered with, or that he will induce another to break a contract of employment or to interfere with its performance,

and the employer under the contract of employment is not the employer party to the dispute.

(3)  Lawful picketing means acts done in the course of such attendance as is declared lawful by section 220 (peaceful picketing)—
- (a)  by a worker employed (or, in the case of a worker not in employment, last employed) by the employer party to the dispute, or
- (b)  by a trade union official whose attendance is lawful by virtue of subsection (1)(b) of that section.

(4)  For the purposes of this section an employer shall not be treated as party to a dispute between another employer and workers of that employer; and where more than one employer is in dispute with his workers, the dispute between each employer and his workers shall be treated as a separate dispute.

In this subsection "worker" has the same meaning as in section 244 (meaning of "trade dispute").

(5)   An act in contemplation or furtherance of a trade dispute which is primary action in relation to that dispute may not be relied on as secondary action in relation to another trade dispute.

Primary action means such action as is mentioned in paragraph (a) or (b) of subsection (2) where the employer under the contract of employment is the employer party to the dispute.

(6)   In this section "contract of employment" includes any contract under which one person personally does work or performs services for another, and related expressions shall be construed accordingly.

**[1.495]**
**225   Pressure to impose union recognition requirement**
(1)   An act is not protected if it constitutes, or is one of a number of acts which together constitute, an inducement or attempted inducement of a person—
  (a)   to incorporate in a contract to which that person is a party, or a proposed contract to which he intends to be a party, a term or condition which is or would be void by virtue of section 186 (recognition requirement in contract for goods or services), or
  (b)   to contravene section 187 (refusal to deal with person on grounds of union exclusion).
(2)   An act is not protected if—
  (a)   it interferes with the supply (whether or not under a contract) of goods or services, or can reasonably be expected to have that effect, and
  (b)   one of the facts relied upon for the purpose of establishing liability is that a person has—
      (i)   induced another to break a contract of employment or interfered or induced another to interfere with its performance, or
      (ii)   threatened that a contract of employment under which he or another is employed will be broken or its performance interfered with, or that he will induce another to break a contract of employment or to interfere with its performance, and
  (c)   the reason, or one of the reasons, for doing the act is the fact or belief that the supplier (not being the employer under the contract of employment mentioned in paragraph (b)) does not, or might not—
      (i)   recognise one or more trade unions for the purpose of negotiating on behalf of workers, or any class of worker, employed by him, or
      (ii)   negotiate or consult with, or with an official of, one or more trade unions.

*Requirement of ballot before action by trade union*

**[1.496]**
**226   Requirement of ballot before action by trade union**
(1)   An act done by a trade union to induce a person to take part, or continue to take part, in industrial action—
  [(a)   is not protected unless the industrial action has the support of a ballot, and
  (b)   where section 226A falls to be complied with in relation to the person's employer, is not protected as respects the employer unless the trade union has complied with section 226A in relation to him.]
[In this section "the relevant time", in relation to an act by a trade union to induce a person to take part, or continue to take part, in industrial action, means the time at which proceedings are commenced in respect of the act.]
(2)   Industrial action shall be regarded as having the support of a ballot only if—
  [(a)   the union has held a ballot in respect of the action—
      (i)   in relation to which the requirements of section 226B so far as applicable before and during the holding of the ballot were satisfied,
      (ii)   in relation to which the requirements of sections 227 to [231] were satisfied, and
      (iii)   in which the majority voting in the ballot answered "Yes" to the question applicable in accordance with section 229(2) to industrial action of the kind to which the act of inducement relates;
  (b)   such of the requirements of the following sections as have fallen to be satisfied at the relevant time have been satisfied, namely—
      (i)   section 226B so far as applicable after the holding of the ballot, and
      (ii)   section 231B; . . . .
  [(bb)   section 232A does not prevent the industrial action from being regarded as having the support of the ballot; and]
  (c)   the requirements of section 233 (calling of industrial action with support of ballot) are satisfied.
Any reference in this subsection to a requirement of a provision which is disapplied or modified by section 232 has effect subject to that section.]
(3)   Where separate workplace ballots are held by virtue of [section 228(1)—
  (a)   industrial action shall be regarded as having the support of a ballot if the conditions specified in subsection (2) are satisfied, and
  (b)   the trade union shall be taken to have complied with the requirements relating to a ballot imposed by section 226A if those requirements are complied with,

in relation] to the ballot for the place of work of the person induced to take part, or continue to take part, in the industrial action.

[(3A)   If the requirements of section 231A fall to be satisfied in relation to an employer, as respects that employer industrial action shall not be regarded as having the support of a ballot unless those requirements are satisfied in relation to that employer.]

(4)   For the purposes of this section an inducement, in relation to a person, includes an inducement which is or would be ineffective, whether because of his unwillingness to be influenced by it or for any other reason.

**NOTES**

Sub-s (1): words in first pair of square brackets substituted, and words in second pair of square brackets added, by the Trade Union Reform and Employment Rights Act 1993, ss 18(1), 49(2), Sch 8, para 73(a).

Sub-s (2): paras (a)–(c) substituted by the Trade Union Reform and Employment Rights Act 1993, s 49(2), Sch 8, para 73(b); number in square brackets in para (a)(ii) substituted, word omitted from para (b) repealed, and para (bb) inserted, by the Employment Relations Act 1999, ss 4, 44, Sch 3, paras 1, 2(1), (2), Sch 9(1).

Sub-s (3): words in square brackets substituted by the Trade Union Reform and Employment Rights Act 1993, s 49(2), Sch 8, para 73(c).

Sub-s (3A): inserted by the Employment Relations Act 1999, s 4, Sch 3, paras 1, 2(1), (3).

**[1.497]**
**[226A   Notice of ballot and sample voting paper for employers**
[(1)   The trade union must take such steps as are reasonably necessary to ensure that—
  (a)   not later than the seventh day before the opening day of the ballot, the notice specified in subsection (2), and
  (b)   not later than the third day before the opening day of the ballot, the sample voting paper specified in [subsection (2F)],
is received by every person who it is reasonable for the union to believe (at the latest time when steps could be taken to comply with paragraph (a)) will be the employer of persons who will be entitled to vote in the ballot.
(2)   The notice referred to in paragraph (a) of subsection (1) is a notice in writing—
  (a)   stating that the union intends to hold the ballot,
  (b)   specifying the date which the union reasonably believes will be the opening day of the ballot, and
  [(c)   containing—
    (i)    the lists mentioned in subsection (2A) and the figures mentioned in subsection (2B), together with an explanation of how those figures were arrived at, or
    (ii)   where some or all of the employees concerned are employees from whose wages the employer makes deductions representing payments to the union, either those lists and figures and that explanation or the information mentioned in subsection (2C)].
[(2A)   The lists are—
  (a)   a list of the categories of employee to which the employees concerned belong, and
  (b)   a list of the workplaces at which the employees concerned work.
(2B)   The figures are—
  (a)   the total number of employees concerned,
  (b)   the number of the employees concerned in each of the categories in the list mentioned in subsection (2A)(a), and
  (c)   the number of the employees concerned who work at each workplace in the list mentioned in subsection (2A)(b).
(2C)   The information referred to in subsection (2)(c)(ii) is such information as will enable the employer readily to deduce—
  (a)   the total number of employees concerned,
  (b)   the categories of employee to which the employees concerned belong and the number of the employees concerned in each of those categories, and
  (c)   the workplaces at which the employees concerned work and the number of them who work at each of those workplaces.
(2D)   The lists and figures supplied under this section, or the information mentioned in subsection (2C) that is so supplied, must be as accurate as is reasonably practicable in the light of the information in the possession of the union at the time when it complies with subsection (1)(a).
(2E)   For the purposes of subsection (2D) information is in the possession of the union if it is held, for union purposes—
  (a)   in a document, whether in electronic form or any other form, and
  (b)   in the possession or under the control of an officer or employee of the union.
(2F)   The sample voting paper referred to in paragraph (b) of subsection (1) is—
  (a)   a sample of the form of voting paper which is to be sent to the employees concerned, or
  (b)   where the employees concerned are not all to be sent the same form of voting paper, a sample of each form of voting paper which is to be sent to any of them.
(2G)   Nothing in this section requires a union to supply an employer with the names of the employees concerned.

(2H)    In this section references to the "employees concerned" are references to those employees of the employer in question who the union reasonably believes will be entitled to vote in the ballot.
(2I)    For the purposes of this section, the workplace at which an employee works is—
  (a)    in relation to an employee who works at or from a single set of premises, those premises, and
  (b)    in relation to any other employee, the premises with which his employment has the closest connection.]
(3), [(3A), (3B)]    . . .
(4)    In this section references to the opening day of the ballot are references to the first day when a voting paper is sent to any person entitled to vote in the ballot.
(5)    This section, in its application to a ballot in which merchant seamen to whom section 230(2A) applies are entitled to vote, shall have effect with the substitution in [subsection (2F)], for references to the voting paper which is to be sent to the employees, of references to the voting paper which is to be sent or otherwise provided to them.]

**NOTES**
Inserted by the Trade Union Reform and Employment Rights Act 1993, s 18(2).
Sub-ss (1), (5): words in square brackets substituted by the Employment Relations Act 2004, s 22(1), (2), (6).
Sub-s (2): para (c) substituted by the Employment Relations Act 2004, s 22(1), (3).
Sub-ss (2A)–(2I): inserted by the Employment Relations Act 2004, s 22(1), (4).
Sub-s (3): repealed by the Employment Relations Act 2004, ss 22(1), (5), 57(2), Sch 2.
Sub-ss (3A), (3B): inserted by the Employment Relations Act 1999, s 4, Sch 3, paras 1, 3(1), (3), and repealed by the Employment Relations Act 2004, ss 22(1), (5), 57(2), Sch 2.

**[1.498]**
**[226B    Appointment of scrutineer**
(1)    The trade union shall, before the ballot in respect of the industrial action is held, appoint a qualified person ("the scrutineer") whose terms of appointment shall require him to carry out in relation to the ballot the functions of—
  (a)    taking such steps as appear to him to be appropriate for the purpose of enabling him to make a report to the trade union (see section 231B); and
  (b)    making the report as soon as reasonably practicable after the date of the ballot and, in any event, not later than the end of the period of four weeks beginning with that date.
(2)    A person is a qualified person in relation to a ballot if—
  (a)    he satisfies such conditions as may be specified for the purposes of this section by order of the Secretary of State or is himself so specified; and
  (b)    the trade union has no grounds for believing either that he will carry out the functions conferred on him under subsection (1) otherwise than competently or that his independence in relation to the union, or in relation to the ballot, might reasonably be called into question.
An order under paragraph (a) shall be made by statutory instrument which shall be subject to annulment in pursuance of a resolution of either House of Parliament.
(3)    The trade union shall ensure that the scrutineer duly carries out the functions conferred on him under subsection (1) and that there is no interference with the carrying out of those functions from the union or any of its members, officials or employees.
(4)    The trade union shall comply with all reasonable requests made by the scrutineer for the purposes of, or in connection with, the carrying out of those functions.]

**NOTES**
Inserted by the Trade Union Reform and Employment Rights Act 1993, s 20(1).
Orders: the Trade Union Ballots and Elections (Independent Scrutineer Qualifications) Order 1993, SI 1993/1909 at **[2.135]**; the Trade Union Ballots and Elections (Independent Scrutineer Qualifications) (Amendment) Order 2010, SI 2010/436.

**[1.499]**
**[226C    Exclusion for small ballots**
Nothing in section 226B, section 229(1A)(a) or section 231B shall impose a requirement on a trade union unless—
  (a)    the number of members entitled to vote in the ballot, or
  (b)    where separate workplace ballots are held in accordance with section 228(1), the aggregate of the number of members entitled to vote in each of them,
exceeds 50.]

**NOTES**
Inserted by the Trade Union Reform and Employment Rights Act 1993, s 20(4).

**[1.500]**
**227   Entitlement to vote in ballot**
(1)   Entitlement to vote in the ballot must be accorded equally to all the members of the trade union who it is reasonable at the time of the ballot for the union to believe will be induced [by the union] to take part or, as the case may be, to continue to take part in the industrial action in question, and to no others.
(2)   . . .

**NOTES**
Sub-s (1): words in square brackets inserted by the Employment Relations Act 2004, s 23.
Sub-s (2): repealed by the Employment Relations Act 1999, ss 4, 44, Sch 3, paras 1, 4, Sch 9(1).

**[1.501]**
**[228   Separate workplace ballots**
(1)   Subject to subsection (2), this section applies if the members entitled to vote in a ballot by virtue of section 227 do not all have the same workplace.
(2)   This section does not apply if the union reasonably believes that all those members have the same workplace.
(3)   Subject to section 228A, a separate ballot shall be held for each workplace; and entitlement to vote in each ballot shall be accorded equally to, and restricted to, members of the union who—
   (a)   are entitled to vote by virtue of section 227, and
   (b)   have that workplace.
(4)   In this section and section 228A "workplace" in relation to a person who is employed means—
   (a)   if the person works at or from a single set of premises, those premises, and
   (b)   in any other case, the premises with which the person's employment has the closest connection.]

**NOTES**
Substituted, together with s 228A for the original s 228, by the Employment Relations Act 1999, s 4, Sch 3, paras 1, 5.

**[1.502]**
**[228A   Separate workplaces: single and aggregate ballots**
(1)   Where section 228(3) would require separate ballots to be held for each workplace, a ballot may be held in place of some or all of the separate ballots if one of subsections (2) to (4) is satisfied in relation to it.
(2)   This subsection is satisfied in relation to a ballot if the workplace of each member entitled to vote in the ballot is the workplace of at least one member of the union who is affected by the dispute.
(3)   This subsection is satisfied in relation to a ballot if entitlement to vote is accorded to, and limited to, all the members of the union who—
   (a)   according to the union's reasonable belief have an occupation of a particular kind or have any of a number of particular kinds of occupation, and
   (b)   are employed by a particular employer, or by any of a number of particular employers, with whom the union is in dispute.
(4)   This subsection is satisfied in relation to a ballot if entitlement to vote is accorded to, and limited to, all the members of the union who are employed by a particular employer, or by any of a number of particular employers, with whom the union is in dispute.
(5)   For the purposes of subsection (2) the following are members of the union affected by a dispute—
   (a)   if the dispute relates (wholly or partly) to a decision which the union reasonably believes the employer has made or will make concerning a matter specified in subsection (1)(a), (b) or (c) of section 244 (meaning of "trade dispute"), members whom the decision directly affects,
   (b)   if the dispute relates (wholly or partly) to a matter specified in subsection (1)(d) of that section, members whom the matter directly affects,
   (c)   if the dispute relates (wholly or partly) to a matter specified in subsection (1)(e) of that section, persons whose membership or non-membership is in dispute,
   (d)   if the dispute relates (wholly or partly) to a matter specified in subsection (1)(f) of that section, officials of the union who have used or would use the facilities concerned in the dispute.]

**NOTES**
Substituted as noted to s 228 at **[1.501]**.

**[1.503]**
## 229  Voting paper
(1)   The method of voting in a ballot must be by the marking of a voting paper by the person voting.
[(1A)   Each voting paper must—
   (a)   state the name of the independent scrutineer,
   (b)   clearly specify the address to which, and the date by which, it is to be returned,
   (c)   be given one of a series of consecutive whole numbers every one of which is used in giving a different number in that series to each voting paper printed or otherwise produced for the purposes of the ballot, and
   (d)   be marked with its number.
This subsection, in its application to a ballot in which merchant seamen to whom section 230(2A) applies are entitled to vote, shall have effect with the substitution, for the reference to the address to which the voting paper is to be returned, of a reference to the ship to which the seamen belong.]
(2)   The voting paper must contain at least one of the following questions—
   (a)   a question (however framed) which requires the person answering it to say, by answering "Yes" or "No", whether he is prepared to take part or, as the case may be, to continue to take part in a strike;
   (b)   a question (however framed) which requires the person answering it to say, by answering "Yes" or "No", whether he is prepared to take part or, as the case may be, to continue to take part in industrial action short of a strike.
[(2A)   For the purposes of subsection (2) an overtime ban and a call-out ban constitute industrial action short of a strike.]
(3)   The voting paper must specify who, in the event of a vote in favour of industrial action, is authorised for the purposes of section 233 to call upon members to take part or continue to take part in the industrial action.
The person or description of persons so specified need not be authorised under the rules of the union but must be within section [20(2)] (persons for whose acts the union is taken to be responsible).
(4)   The following statement must (without being qualified or commented upon by anything else on the voting paper) appear on every voting paper—

   "If you take part in a strike or other industrial action, you may be in breach of your contract of employment.
   [However, if you are dismissed for taking part in strike or other industrial action which is called officially and is otherwise lawful, the dismissal will be unfair if it takes place fewer than [twelve] weeks after you started taking part in the action, and depending on the circumstances may be unfair if it takes place later.]".

---

NOTES
   Sub-s (1A): inserted by the Trade Union Reform and Employment Rights Act 1993, s 20(2).
   Sub-s (2A): inserted by the Employment Relations Act 1999, s 4, Sch 3, paras 1, 6(1), (2).
   Sub-s (3): number in square brackets substituted by the Trade Union Reform and Employment Rights Act 1993, s 49(1), Sch 7, para 25.
   Sub-s (4): words in first (outer) pair of square brackets added by the Employment Relations Act 1999, s 4, Sch 3, paras 1, 6(1), (3); word in second (inner) pair of square brackets substituted by the Employment Relations Act 2004, s 57(1), Sch 1, para 13.

**[1.504]**
## 230  Conduct of ballot
(1)   Every person who is entitled to vote in the ballot must—
   (a)   be allowed to vote without interference from, or constraint imposed by, the union or any of its members, officials or employees, and
   (b)   so far as is reasonably practicable, be enabled to do so without incurring any direct cost to himself.
[(2)   Except as regards persons falling within subsection (2A), so far as is reasonably practicable, every person who is entitled to vote in the ballot must—
   (a)   have a voting paper sent to him by post at his home address or any other address which he has requested the trade union in writing to treat as his postal address; and
   (b)   be given a convenient opportunity to vote by post.
[(2A)   Subsection (2B) applies to a merchant seaman if the trade union reasonably believes that—
   (a)   he will be employed in a ship either at sea or at a place outside Great Britain at some time in the period during which votes may be cast, and
   (b)   it will be convenient for him to receive a voting paper and to vote while on the ship or while at a place where the ship is rather than in accordance with subsection (2).
(2B)   Where this subsection applies to a merchant seaman he shall, if it is reasonably practicable—
   (a)   have a voting paper made available to him while on the ship or while at a place where the ship is, and
   (b)   be given an opportunity to vote while on the ship or while at a place where the ship is.]

[(2C)   In subsections (2A) and (2B) "merchant seaman" means a person whose employment, or the greater part of it, is carried out on board sea-going ships.]
(4)   A ballot shall be conducted so as to secure that—
  (a)   so far as is reasonably practicable, those voting do so in secret, and
  (b)   the votes given in the ballot are fairly and accurately counted.
  For the purposes of paragraph (b) an inaccuracy in counting shall be disregarded if it is accidental and on a scale which could not affect the result of the ballot.

**NOTES**
  Sub-ss (2)–(2C): substituted, for the original sub-ss (2), (3), by the Trade Union Reform and Employment Rights Act 1993, s 17; sub-ss (2A), (2B) further substituted by the Employment Relations Act 1999, s 4, Sch 3, paras 1, 7.

**[1.505]**
**231   Information as to result of ballot**
As soon as is reasonably practicable after the holding of the ballot, the trade union shall take such steps as are reasonably necessary to ensure that all persons entitled to vote in the ballot are informed of the number of—
  (a)   votes cast in the ballot,
  (b)   individuals answering "Yes" to the question, or as the case may be, to each question,
  (c)   individuals answering "No" to the question, or, as the case may be, to each question, and
  (d)   spoiled voting papers.

**[1.506]**
**[231A   Employers to be informed of ballot result**
(1)   As soon as reasonably practicable after the holding of the ballot, the trade union shall take such steps as are reasonably necessary to ensure that every relevant employer is informed of the matters mentioned in section 231.
(2)   In subsection (1) "relevant employer" means a person who it is reasonable for the trade union to believe (at the time when the steps are taken) was at the time of the ballot the employer of any persons entitled to vote.]

**NOTES**
  Inserted by the Trade Union Reform and Employment Rights Act 1993, s 19.

**[1.507]**
**[231B   Scrutineer's report**
(1)   The scrutineer's report on the ballot shall state whether the scrutineer is satisfied—
  (a)   that there are no reasonable grounds for believing that there was any contravention of a requirement imposed by or under any enactment in relation to the ballot,
  (b)   that the arrangements made with respect to the production, storage, distribution, return or other handling of the voting papers used in the ballot, and the arrangements for the counting of the votes, included all such security arrangements as were reasonably practicable for the purpose of minimising the risk that any unfairness or malpractice might occur, and
  (c)   that he has been able to carry out the functions conferred on him under section 226B(1) without any interference from the trade union or any of its members, officials or employees;
and if he is not satisfied as to any of those matters, the report shall give particulars of his reason for not being satisfied as to that matter.
(2)   If at any time within six months from the date of the ballot—
  (a)   any person entitled to vote in the ballot, or
  (b)   the employer of any such person,
requests a copy of the scrutineer's report, the trade union must, as soon as practicable, provide him with one either free of charge or on payment of such reasonable fee as may be specified by the trade union.]

**NOTES**
  Inserted by the Trade Union Reform and Employment Rights Act 1993, s 20(3).

**[1.508]**
**232   Balloting of overseas members**
(1)   A trade union which has overseas members may choose whether or not to accord any of those members entitlement to vote in a ballot; and nothing in section [226B to 230 and 231B] applies in relation to an overseas member or a vote cast by such a member.
[(2)   Where overseas members have voted in the ballot—
  (a)   the references in sections 231 and 231A to persons entitled to vote in the ballot do not include overseas members, and

(b)    those sections shall be read as requiring the information mentioned in section 231 to distinguish between overseas members and other members.]

(3)    An "overseas member" of a trade union means a member (other than a merchant seaman or offshore worker) who is outside Great Britain throughout the period during which votes may be cast.

For this purpose—

"merchant seaman" means a person whose employment, or the greater part of it, is carried out on board sea-going ships; and

"offshore worker" means a person in offshore employment, other than one who is in such employment in an area where the law of Northern Ireland applies.

(4)    A member who throughout the period during which votes may be cast is in Northern Ireland shall not be treated as an overseas member—

(a)    where the ballot is one to which section 228(1) or (2) applies (workplace ballots) and his place of work is in Great Britain, or

(b)    where the ballot is one to which section 228(3) applies (general ballots) and relates to industrial action involving members both in Great Britain and in Northern Ireland.

(5)    In relation to offshore employment the references in subsection (4) to Northern Ireland include any area where the law of Northern Ireland applies and the references to Great Britain include any area where the law of England and Wales or Scotland applies.

**NOTES**

Sub-s (1): words in square brackets substituted by the Trade Union Reform and Employment Rights Act 1993, s 49(2), Sch 8, para 74(a).

Sub-s (2): substituted by the Trade Union Reform and Employment Rights Act 1993, s 49(2), Sch 8, para 74(b).

**[1.509]**
**[232A    Inducement of member denied entitlement to vote**

Industrial action shall not be regarded as having the support of a ballot if the following conditions apply in the case of any person—

(a)    he was a member of the trade union at the time when the ballot was held,

(b)    it was reasonable at that time for the trade union to believe he would be induced to take part or, as the case may be, to continue to take part in the industrial action,

(c)    he was not accorded entitlement to vote in the ballot, and

(d)    he was induced by the trade union to take part or, as the case may be, to continue to take part in the industrial action.]

**NOTES**

Inserted by the Employment Relations Act 1999, s 4, Sch 3, paras 1, 8.

**[1.510]**
**[232B    Small accidental failures to be disregarded**

(1)    If—

(a)    in relation to a ballot there is a failure (or there are failures) to comply with a provision mentioned in subsection (2) or with more than one of those provisions, and

(b)    the failure is accidental and on a scale which is unlikely to affect the result of the ballot or, as the case may be, the failures are accidental and taken together are on a scale which is unlikely to affect the result of the ballot,

the failure (or failures) shall be disregarded [for all purposes (including, in particular, those of section 232A(c))].

(2)    The provisions are section 227(1), section 230(2) and section [230(2B)].]

**NOTES**

Inserted by the Employment Relations Act 1999, s 4, Sch 3, paras 1, 9.

Words in square brackets inserted by the Employment Relations Act 2004, s 24(1).

**[1.511]**
**233    Calling of industrial action with support of ballot**

(1)    Industrial action shall not be regarded as having the support of a ballot unless it is called by a specified person and the conditions specified below are satisfied.

(2)    A "specified person" means a person specified or of a description specified in the voting paper for the ballot in accordance with section 229(3).

(3)    The conditions are that—

(a)    there must have been no call by the trade union to take part or continue to take part in industrial action to which the ballot relates, or any authorisation or endorsement by the union of any such industrial action, before the date of the ballot;

(b)    there must be a call for industrial action by a specified person, and industrial action to which it relates must [begin], before the ballot ceases to be effective in accordance with section 234.

(4)   For the purposes of this section a call shall be taken to have been made by a trade union if it was authorised or endorsed by the union; and the provisions of section 20(2) to (4) apply for the purpose of determining whether a call, or industrial action, is to be taken to have been so authorised or endorsed.

**NOTES**

Sub-s (3): word in square brackets substituted by the Employment Relations Act 2004, s 57(1), Sch 1, para 14.

**[1.512]**
**234   Period after which ballot ceases to be effective**
[(1)   Subject to the following provisions, a ballot ceases to be effective for the purposes of section 233(3)(b) in relation to industrial action by members of a trade union at the end of the period, beginning with the date of the ballot—
   (a)   of four weeks, or
   (b)   of such longer duration not exceeding eight weeks as is agreed between the union and the members' employer.]
(2)   Where for the whole or part of that period the calling or organising of industrial action is prohibited—
   (a)   by virtue of a court order which subsequently lapses or is discharged, recalled or set aside, or
   (b)   by virtue of an undertaking given to a court by any person from which he is subsequently released or by which he ceases to be bound,
the trade union may apply to the court for an order that the period during which the prohibition had effect shall not count towards the period referred to in subsection (1).
(3)   The application must be made forthwith upon the prohibition ceasing to have effect—
   (a)   to the court by virtue of whose decision it ceases to have effect, or
   (b)   where an order lapses or an undertaking ceases to bind without any such decision, to the court by which the order was made or to which the undertaking was given;
and no application may be made after the end of the period of eight weeks beginning with the date of the ballot.
(4)   The court shall not make an order if it appears to the court—
   (a)   that the result of the ballot no longer represents the views of the union members concerned, or
   (b)   that an event is likely to occur as a result of which those members would vote against industrial action if another ballot were to be held.
(5)   No appeal lies from the decision of the court to make or refuse an order under this section.
(6)   The period between the making of an application under this section and its determination does not count towards the period referred to in subsection (1).
   But a ballot shall not by virtue of this subsection (together with any order of the court) be regarded as effective for the purposes of section 233(3)(b) after the end of the period of twelve weeks beginning with the date of the ballot.

**NOTES**

Sub-s (1): substituted by the Employment Relations Act 1999, s 4, Sch 3, paras 1, 10.

*[Requirement on trade union to give notice of industrial action*

**[1.513]**
**234A   Notice to employers of industrial action**
(1)   An act done by a trade union to induce a person to take part, or continue to take part, in industrial action is not protected as respects his employer unless the union has taken or takes such steps as are reasonably necessary to ensure that the employer receives within the appropriate period a relevant notice covering the act.
(2)   Subsection (1) imposes a requirement in the case of an employer only if it is reasonable for the union to believe, at the latest time when steps could be taken to ensure that he receives such a notice, that he is the employer of persons who will be or have been induced to take part, or continue to take part, in the industrial action.
(3)   For the purposes of this section a relevant notice is a notice in writing which—
   [(a)   contains—
      (i)   the lists mentioned in subsection (3A) and the figures mentioned in subsection (3B), together with an explanation of how those figures were arrived at, or
      (ii)   where some or all of the affected employees are employees from whose wages the employer makes deductions representing payments to the union, either those lists and figures and that explanation or the information mentioned in subsection (3C), and]
   (b)   states whether industrial action is intended to be continuous or discontinuous and specifies—
      (i)   where it is to be continuous, the intended date for any of the affected employees to begin to take part in the action,

     (ii)   where it is to be discontinuous, the intended dates for any of the affected employees to take part in the action, . . .

  (c)  . . .

[(3A)   The lists referred to in subsection (3)(a) are—

  (a)   a list of the categories of employee to which the affected employees belong, and

  (b)   a list of the workplaces at which the affected employees work.

(3B)   The figures referred to in subsection (3)(a) are—

  (a)   the total number of the affected employees,

  (b)   the number of the affected employees in each of the categories in the list mentioned in subsection (3A)(a), and

  (c)   the number of the affected employees who work at each workplace in the list mentioned in subsection (3A)(b).

(3C)   The information referred to in subsection (3)(a)(ii) is such information as will enable the employer readily to deduce—

  (a)   the total number of the affected employees,

  (b)   the categories of employee to which the affected employees belong and the number of the affected employees in each of those categories, and

  (c)   the workplaces at which the affected employees work and the number of them who work at each of those workplaces.

(3D)   The lists and figures supplied under this section, or the information mentioned in subsection (3C) that is so supplied, must be as accurate as is reasonably practicable in the light of the information in the possession of the union at the time when it complies with subsection (1).

(3E)   For the purposes of subsection (3D) information is in the possession of the union if it is held, for union purposes—

  (a)   in a document, whether in electronic form or any other form, and

  (b)   in the possession or under the control of an officer or employee of the union.

(3F)   Nothing in this section requires a union to supply an employer with the names of the affected employees.]

(4)   For the purposes of subsection (1) the appropriate period is the period—

  (a)   beginning with the day when the union satisfies the requirement of section 231A in relation to the ballot in respect of the industrial action, and

  (b)   ending with the seventh day before the day, or before the first of the days, specified in the relevant notice.

(5)   For the purposes of subsection (1) a relevant notice covers an act done by the union if the person induced [falls within a notified category of employee and the workplace at which he works is a notified workplace] and—

  (a)   where he is induced to take part or continue to take part in industrial action which the union intends to be continuous, if—

     (i)   the notice states that the union intends the industrial action to be continuous, and

     (ii)   there is no participation by him in the industrial action before the date specified in the notice in consequence of any inducement by the union not covered by a relevant notice; and

  (b)   where he is induced to take part or continue to take part in industrial action which the union intends to be discontinuous, if there is no participation by him in the industrial action on a day not so specified in consequence of any inducement by the union not covered by a relevant notice.

[(5B)   In subsection (5)—

  (a)   a "notified category of employee" means—

     (i)   a category of employee that is listed in the notice, or

     (ii)   where the notice contains the information mentioned in subsection (3C), a category of employee that the employer (at the time he receives the notice) can readily deduce from the notice is a category of employee to which some or all of the affected employees belong, and

  (b)   a "notified workplace" means—

     (i)   a workplace that is listed in the notice, or

     (ii)   where the notice contains the information mentioned in subsection (3C), a workplace that the employer (at the time he receives the notice) can readily deduce from the notice is the workplace at which some or all of the affected employees work.

(5C)   In this section references to the "affected employees" are references to those employees of the employer who the union reasonably believes will be induced by the union, or have been so induced, to take part or continue to take part in the industrial action.

(5D)   For the purposes of this section, the workplace at which an employee works is—

  (a)   in relation to an employee who works at or from a single set of premises, those premises, and

  (b)   in relation to any other employee, the premises with which his employment has the closest connection.]

(6)   For the purposes of this section—

(a)    a union intends industrial action to be discontinuous if it intends it to take place only on some days on which there is an opportunity to take the action, and

(b)    a union intends industrial action to be continuous if it intends it to be not so restricted.

(7)    [Subject to subsections (7A) and (7B),] where—

(a)    continuous industrial action which has been authorised or endorsed by a union ceases to be so authorised or endorsed . . . , and

(b)    the industrial action has at a later date again been authorised or endorsed by the union (whether as continuous or discontinuous action),

no relevant notice covering acts done to induce persons to take part in the earlier action shall operate to cover acts done to induce persons to take part in the action authorised or endorsed at the later date and this section shall apply in relation to an act to induce a person to take part, or continue to take part, in the industrial action after that date as if the references in subsection (3)(b)(i) to the industrial action were to the industrial action taking place after that date.

[(7A)    Subsection (7) shall not apply where industrial action ceases to be authorised or endorsed in order to enable the union to comply with a court order or an undertaking given to a court.

(7B)    Subsection (7) shall not apply where—

(a)    a union agrees with an employer, before industrial action ceases to be authorised or endorsed, that it will cease to be authorised or endorsed with effect from a date specified in the agreement ("the suspension date") and that it may again be authorised or endorsed with effect from a date not earlier than a date specified in the agreement ("the resumption date"),

(b)    the action ceases to be authorised or endorsed with effect from the suspension date, and

(c)    the action is again authorised or endorsed with effect from a date which is not earlier than the resumption date or such later date as may be agreed between the union and the employer.]

(8)    The requirement imposed on a trade union by subsection (1) shall be treated as having been complied with if the steps were taken by other relevant persons or committees whose acts were authorised or endorsed by the union and references to the belief or intention of the union in subsection (2) or, as the case may be, subsections (3), (5)[, (5C)] and (6) shall be construed as references to the belief or the intention of the person or committee taking the steps.

(9)    The provisions of section 20(2) to (4) apply for the purpose of determining for the purposes of subsection (1) who are relevant persons or committees and whether the trade union is to be taken to have authorised or endorsed the steps the person or committee took and for the purposes of [subsections (7) to (7B)] whether the trade union is to be taken to have authorised or endorsed the industrial action.]

**NOTES**

Inserted, together with the preceding heading, by the Trade Union Reform and Employment Rights Act 1993, s 21.

Sub-s (3): para (a) substituted, and para (c) and the word immediately preceding it repealed, by the Employment Relations Act 2004, ss 25(1), (2), 57(2), Sch 2,.

Sub-ss (3A)–(3F): inserted by the Employment Relations Act 2004, s 25(1), (3).

Sub-s (5): words in square brackets substituted by the Employment Relations Act 2004, s 25(1), (4).

Sub-ss (5B)–(5D): substituted (for the original sub-s (5A) as inserted by the Employment Relations Act 1999, s 4, Sch 3, paras 1, 11(1), (3)) by the Employment Relations Act 2004, s 25(1), (5).

Sub-s (7): words in square brackets inserted, and words omitted repealed, by the Employment Relations Act 1999, ss 4, 44, Sch 3, paras 1, 11(1), (4), Sch 9(1).

Sub-ss (7A), (7B): inserted by the Employment Relations Act 1999, s 4, Sch 3, paras 1, 11(1), (5).

Sub-s (8): number in square brackets inserted by the Employment Relations Act 2004, s 25(1), (6).

Sub-s (9): words in square brackets substituted by the Employment Relations Act 1999, s 4, Sch 3, paras 1, 11(1), (6).

**[1.514]**
### 235    Construction of references to contract of employment

In sections 226 to [234A] (requirement of ballot before action by trade union) references to a contract of employment include any contract under which one person personally does work or performs services for another; [and "employer" and other related expressions] shall be construed accordingly.

**NOTES**

Number and words in square brackets substituted by the Trade Union Reform and Employment Rights Act 1993, s 49(2), Sch 8, para 75.

*[Industrial action affecting supply of goods or services to an individual*

**[1.515]**
### 235A    Industrial action affecting supply of goods or services to an individual

(1)    Where an individual claims that—

(a)    any trade union or other person has done, or is likely to do, an unlawful act to induce any person to take part, or to continue to take part, in industrial action, and

(b)    an effect, or a likely effect, of the industrial action is or will be to—

(i)    prevent or delay the supply of goods or services, or

(ii)    reduce the quality of goods or services supplied,

to the individual making the claim,
he may apply to the High Court or the Court of Session for an order under this section.
(2)   For the purposes of this section an act to induce any person to take part, or to continue to take part, in industrial action is unlawful—

- (a)   if it is actionable in tort by any one or more persons, or
- (b)   (where it is or would be the act of a trade union) if it could form the basis of an application by a member under section 62.

(3)   In determining whether an individual may make an application under this section it is immaterial whether or not the individual is entitled to be supplied with the goods or services in question.

(4)   Where on an application under this section the court is satisfied that the claim is well-founded, it shall make such order as it considers appropriate for requiring the person by whom the act of inducement has been, or is likely to be, done to take steps for ensuring—

- (a)   that no, or no further, act is done by him to induce any persons to take part or to continue to take part in the industrial action, and
- (b)   that no person engages in conduct after the making of the order by virtue of having been induced by him before the making of the order to take part or continue to take part in the industrial action.

(5)   Without prejudice to any other power of the court, the court may on an application under this section grant such interlocutory relief (in Scotland, such interim order) as it considers appropriate.

(6)   For the purposes of this section an act of inducement shall be taken to be done by a trade union if it is authorised or endorsed by the union; and the provisions of section 20(2) to (4) apply for the purposes of determining whether such an act is to be taken to be so authorised or endorsed.

Those provisions also apply in relation to proceedings for failure to comply with an order under this section as they apply in relation to the original proceedings.]

**NOTES**
Inserted, together with the preceding heading and ss 235B, 235C, by the Trade Union Reform and Employment Rights Act 1993, s 22.

**235B, 235C**   (*Inserted by the Trade Union Reform and Employment Rights Act 1993, s 22; repealed by the Employment Relations Act 1999, ss 28(2)(b), 44, Sch 9(6).*)

*No compulsion to work*

**[1.516]**
**236  No compulsion to work**
No court shall, whether by way of—

- (a)   an order for specific performance or specific implement of a contract of employment, or
- (b)   an injunction or interdict restraining a breach or threatened breach of such a contract,

compel an employee to do any work or attend at any place for the doing of any work.

*Loss of unfair dismissal protection*

**[1.517]**
**237  Dismissal of those taking part in unofficial industrial action**
(1)   An employee has no right to complain of unfair dismissal if at the time of dismissal he was taking part in an unofficial strike or other unofficial industrial action.

[(1A)   Subsection (1) does not apply to the dismissal of the employee if it is shown that the reason (or, if more than one, the principal reason) for the dismissal or, in a redundancy case, for selecting the employee for dismissal was one of those specified in [or under—

- (a)   section [98B,] 99, 100, 101A(d), 103[, 103A, 104C *or 104D*] of the Employment Rights Act 1996 (dismissal in [jury service,] family, health and safety, working time, employee representative, [protected disclosure, flexible working *and pension scheme membership*] cases),
- (b)   section 104 of that Act in its application in relation to time off under section 57A of that Act (dependants)].]

In this subsection "redundancy case" has the meaning given in [section 105(9)] of that Act[; and a reference to a specified reason for dismissal includes a reference to specified circumstances of dismissal].]

(2)   A strike or other industrial action is unofficial in relation to an employee unless—

- (a)   he is a member of a trade union and the action is authorised or endorsed by that union, or
- (b)   he is not a member of a trade union but there are among those taking part in the industrial action members of a trade union by which the action has been authorised or endorsed.

Provided that, a strike or other industrial action shall not be regarded as unofficial if none of those taking part in it are members of a trade union.

(3)   The provisions of section 20(2) apply for the purpose of determining whether industrial action is to be taken to have been authorised or endorsed by a trade union.

(4)   The question whether industrial action is to be so taken in any case shall be determined by reference to the facts as at the time of dismissal.

Provided that, where an act is repudiated as mentioned in section 21, industrial action shall not thereby be treated as unofficial before the end of the next working day after the day on which the repudiation takes place.

(5) In this section the "time of dismissal" means—

(a) where the employee's contract of employment is terminated by notice, when the notice is given,

(b) where the employee's contract of employment is terminated without notice, when the termination takes effect, and

(c) where the employee is employed under a contract for a fixed term which expires without being renewed under the same contract, when that term expires;

and a "working day" means any day which is not a Saturday or Sunday, Christmas Day, Good Friday or a bank holiday under the Banking and Financial Dealings Act 1971.

(6) For the purposes of this section membership of a trade union for purposes unconnected with the employment in question shall be disregarded; but an employee who was a member of a trade union when he began to take part in industrial action shall continue to be treated as a member for the purpose of determining whether that action is unofficial in relation to him or another notwithstanding that he may in fact have ceased to be a member.

---

**NOTES**

Sub-s (1A): inserted by the Trade Union Reform and Employment Rights Act 1993, s 49(2), Sch 8, para 76, and subsequently amended as follows—

Words in first (outer) pair of square brackets substituted by the Employment Relations Act 1999, s 9, Sch 4, Pt III, paras 1, 2(a).

Number "98B," in square brackets inserted by the Employment Relations Act 2004, s 40(8)(a).

Words ", 103A, 104C or 104D" in square brackets substituted by the Pensions Act 2008, s 57(1), (6)(a), as from 30 June 2012, and for the words "or 104D" in italics there is substituted ", 104D or 104E", by the Apprenticeships, Skills, Children and Learning Act 2009, s 40(5), Sch 1, paras 12, 14(a), as from 6 April 2010 (except in relation to small employers and their employees), and as from a day to be appointed (otherwise). As to the meaning of "small employers" see the note at **[1.840]**.

Words "jury service," in square brackets inserted by the Employment Relations Act 2004, s 40(8)(b).

Words "protected disclosure, flexible working and pension scheme membership" in square brackets substituted by the Pensions Act 2008, s 57(1), (6)(b), as from 30 June 2012, and for the words in italics within those square brackets there are substituted the words ", pension scheme membership, and study and training", by the Apprenticeships, Skills, Children and Learning Act 2009, s 40(5), Sch 1, paras 12, 14(b), as from 6 April 2010 (except in relation to small employers and their employees), and as from a day to be appointed (otherwise). As to the meaning of "small employers" see the note at **[1.840]**.

Words "section 105(9)" in square brackets substituted by the Employment Rights Act 1996, s 240, Sch 1, para 56(1), (15).

Words "; and a reference to a specified reason for dismissal includes a reference to specified circumstances of dismissal" in square brackets inserted by the Employment Relations Act 1999, s 9, Sch 4, Pt III, paras 1, 2(b).

**[1.518]**
**238 Dismissals in connection with other industrial action**

(1) This section applies in relation to an employee who has a right to complain of unfair dismissal (the "complainant") and who claims to have been unfairly dismissed, where at the date of the dismissal—

(a) the employer was conducting or instituting a lock-out, or

(b) the complainant was taking part in a strike or other industrial action.

(2) In such a case an [employment tribunal] shall not determine whether the dismissal was fair or unfair unless it is shown—

(a) that one or more relevant employees of the same employer have not been dismissed, or

(b) that a relevant employee has before the expiry of the period of three months beginning with the date of his dismissal been offered re-engagement and that the complainant has not been offered re-engagement.

[(2A) Subsection (2) does not apply to the dismissal of the employee if it is shown that the reason (or, if more than one, the principal reason) for the dismissal or, in a redundancy case, for selecting the employee for dismissal was one of those specified in [or under—

(a) section [98B,] 99, 100, 101A(d)[, 103, 104C *or 104D*] of the Employment Rights Act 1996 (dismissal in [jury service,] family, health and safety, working time[, employee representative, flexible working *and pension scheme membership*] cases),

(b) section 104 of that Act in its application in relation to time off under section 57A of that Act (dependants);]

In this subsection "redundancy case" has the meaning given in [section 105(9)] of that Act[; and a reference to a specified reason for dismissal includes a reference to specified circumstances of dismissal].]

[(2B) Subsection (2) does not apply in relation to an employee who is regarded as unfairly dismissed by virtue of section 238A below.]

(3) For this purpose "relevant employees" means—

(a) in relation to a lock-out, employees who were directly interested in the dispute in contemplation or furtherance of which the lock-out occurred, and

Part 1  Statutes

(b)   in relation to a strike or other industrial action, those employees at the establishment of the employer at or from which the complainant works who at the date of his dismissal were taking part in the action.

Nothing in section 237 (dismissal of those taking part in unofficial industrial action) affects the question who are relevant employees for the purposes of this section.

(4)   An offer of re-engagement means an offer (made either by the original employer or by a successor of that employer or an associated employer) to re-engage an employee, either in the job which he held immediately before the date of dismissal or in a different job which would be reasonably suitable in his case.

(5)   In this section "date of dismissal" means—

(a)   where the employee's contract of employment was terminated by notice, the date on which the employer's notice was given, and

(b)   in any other case, the effective date of termination.

**NOTES**

Sub-s (2): words in square brackets substituted by the Employment Rights (Dispute Resolution) Act 1998, s 1(2)(a).

Sub-s (2A): inserted by the Trade Union Reform and Employment Rights Act 1993, s 49(2), Sch 8, para 77, and subsequently amended as follows—

Words in first (outer) pair of square brackets substituted by the Employment Relations Act 1999, s 9, Sch 4, Pt III, paras 1, 3(a).

Number "98B," in square brackets inserted by the Employment Relations Act 2004, s 40(9)(a).

Words ", 103, 104C or 104D" in square brackets substituted by the Pensions Act 2008, s 57(1), (7)(a), as from 30 June 2012, and for the words "or 104D" in italics there are substituted the words ", 104D or 104E" by the Apprenticeships, Skills, Children and Learning Act 2009, s 40(5), Sch 1, paras 12, 15(a), as from 6 April 2010 (except in relation to small employers and their employees), and as from a day to be appointed (otherwise). As to the meaning of "small employers" see the note at **[1.840]**.

Words "jury service," in square brackets inserted by the Employment Relations Act 2004, s 40(9)(b).

Words ", employee representative, flexible working and pension scheme membership" in square brackets substituted by the Pensions Act 2008, s 57(1), (7)(b), as from 30 June 2012, and for the words in italics within those square brackets there are substituted the words ", pension scheme membership, and study and training", by the Apprenticeships, Skills, Children and Learning Act 2009, s 40(5), Sch 1, paras 12, 15(b), as from 6 April 2010 (except in relation to small employers and their employees), and as from a day to be appointed (otherwise). As to the meaning of "small employers" see the note at **[1.840]**.

Words "section 105(9)" in square brackets substituted by the Employment Rights Act 1996, s 240, Sch 1, para 56(1), (15).

Words "; and a reference to a specified reason for dismissal includes a reference to specified circumstances of dismissal" in square brackets inserted by the Employment Relations Act 1999, s 9, Sch 4, Pt III, paras 1, 3(b).

Sub-s (2B): inserted by the Employment Relations Act 1999, s 16, Sch 5, paras 1, 2.

**[1.519]**
**[238A  Participation in official industrial action**

(1)   For the purposes of this section an employee takes protected industrial action if he commits an act which, or a series of acts each of which, he is induced to commit by an act which by virtue of section 219 is not actionable in tort.

(2)   An employee who is dismissed shall be regarded for the purposes of Part X of the Employment Rights Act 1996 (unfair dismissal) as unfairly dismissed if—

(a)   the reason (or, if more than one, the principal reason) for the dismissal is that the employee took protected industrial action, and

(b)   subsection (3), (4) or (5) applies to the dismissal.

(3)   This subsection applies to a dismissal if [the date of the dismissal is] [within the protected period].

(4)   This subsection applies to a dismissal if—

(a)   [the date of the dismissal is] after the end of that period, and

(b)   the employee had stopped taking protected industrial action before the end of that period.

(5)   This subsection applies to a dismissal if—

(a)   [the date of the dismissal is] after the end of that period,

(b)   the employee had not stopped taking protected industrial action before the end of that period, and

(c)   the employer had not taken such procedural steps as would have been reasonable for the purposes of resolving the dispute to which the protected industrial action relates.

(6)   In determining whether an employer has taken those steps regard shall be had, in particular, to—

(a)   whether the employer or a union had complied with procedures established by any applicable collective or other agreement;

(b)   whether the employer or a union offered or agreed to commence or resume negotiations after the start of the protected industrial action;

(c)   whether the employer or a union unreasonably refused, after the start of the protected industrial action, a request that conciliation services be used;

(d)   whether the employer or a union unreasonably refused, after the start of the protected industrial action, a request that mediation services be used in relation to procedures to be adopted for the purposes of resolving the dispute;

[(e)   where there was agreement to use either of the services mentioned in paragraphs (c) and (d), the matters specified in section 238B].

(7)   In determining whether an employer has taken those steps no regard shall be had to the merits of the dispute.

[(7A)   For the purposes of this section "the protected period", in relation to the dismissal of an employee, is the sum of the basic period and any extension period in relation to that employee.

(7B)   The basic period is twelve weeks beginning with the first day of protected industrial action.

(7C)   An extension period in relation to an employee is a period equal to the number of days falling on or after the first day of protected industrial action (but before the protected period ends) during the whole or any part of which the employee is locked out by his employer.

(7D)   In subsections (7B) and (7C), the "first day of protected industrial action" means the day on which the employee starts to take protected industrial action (even if on that day he is locked out by his employer).]

(8)   For the purposes of this section no account shall be taken of the repudiation of any act by a trade union as mentioned in section 21 in relation to anything which occurs before the end of the next working day (within the meaning of section 237) after the day on which the repudiation takes place.

[(9)   In this section "date of dismissal" has the meaning given by section 238(5).]]

**NOTES**

Inserted by the Employment Relations Act 1999, s 16, Sch 5, paras 1, 3.

Sub-ss (3)–(5): words in square brackets substituted by the Employment Relations Act 2004, ss 26(1), (2), 27(1)–(4).

Sub-s (6): para (e) inserted by the Employment Relations Act 2004, s 28(1).

Sub-ss (7A)–(7D), (9): inserted and added respectively by the Employment Relations Act 2004, ss 26(1), (3), 27(1), (5)).

"Locked out": this expression is not defined for the purposes of this Act, but for a definition of "lock-out" see the Employment Rights Act 1996, s 235(4) at **[1.1042]**.

**[1.520]**

**[238B   Conciliation and mediation: supplementary provisions**

(1)   The matters referred to in subsection (6)(e) of section 238A are those specified in subsections (2) to (5); and references in this section to "the service provider" are to any person who provided a service mentioned in subsection (6)(c) or (d) of that section.

(2)   The first matter is: whether, at meetings arranged by the service provider, the employer or, as the case may be, a union was represented by an appropriate person.

(3)   The second matter is: whether the employer or a union, so far as requested to do so, co-operated in the making of arrangements for meetings to be held with the service provider.

(4)   The third matter is: whether the employer or a union fulfilled any commitment given by it during the provision of the service to take particular action.

(5)   The fourth matter is: whether, at meetings arranged by the service provider between the parties making use of the service, the representatives of the employer or a union answered any reasonable question put to them concerning the matter subject to conciliation or mediation.

(6)   For the purposes of subsection (2) an "appropriate person" is—

(a)   in relation to the employer—

(i)   a person with the authority to settle the matter subject to conciliation or mediation on behalf of the employer, or

(ii)   a person authorised by a person of that type to make recommendations to him with regard to the settlement of that matter, and

(b)   in relation to a union, a person who is responsible for handling on the union's behalf the matter subject to conciliation or mediation.

(7)   For the purposes of subsection (4) regard may be had to any timetable which was agreed for the taking of the action in question or, if no timetable was agreed, to how long it was before the action was taken.

(8)   In any proceedings in which regard must be had to the matters referred to in section 238A(6)(e)—

(a)   notes taken by or on behalf of the service provider shall not be admissible in evidence;

(b)   the service provider must refuse to give evidence as to anything communicated to him in connection with the performance of his functions as a conciliator or mediator if, in his opinion, to give the evidence would involve his making a damaging disclosure; and

(c)   the service provider may refuse to give evidence as to whether, for the purposes of subsection (5), a particular question was or was not a reasonable one.

(9)   For the purposes of subsection (8)(b) a "damaging disclosure" is—

(a)   a disclosure of information which is commercially sensitive, or

(b)   a disclosure of information that has not previously been disclosed which relates to a position taken by a party using the conciliation or mediation service on the settlement of the matter subject to conciliation or mediation,

to which the person who communicated the information to the service provider has not consented.]

**NOTES**

Inserted by the Employment Relations Act 2004, s 28(2).

**[1.521]**
**239 Supplementary provisions relating to unfair dismissal**
(1) [Sections 237 to 238A] (loss of unfair dismissal protection in connection with industrial action) shall be construed as one with [Part X of the Employment Rights Act 1996][; but sections 108 and 109 of that Act (qualifying period and age limit) shall not apply in relation to section 238A of this Act].
(2) In relation to a complaint to which section 238 [or 238A] applies, [section 111(2)] of that Act (time limit for complaint) does not apply, but an [employment tribunal] shall not consider the complaint unless it is presented to the tribunal—
    (a)   before the end of the period of six months beginning with the date of the complainant's dismissal (as defined by section 238(5)), or
    (b)   where the tribunal is satisfied that it was not reasonably practicable for the complaint to be presented before the end of that period, within such further period as the tribunal considers reasonable.
(3) Where it is shown that the condition referred to in section 238(2)(b) is fulfilled (discriminatory re-engagement), the references in—
    (a)   [sections 98 to 106 of the Employment Rights Act 1996], and
    (b)   sections 152 and 153 of this Act,
to the reason or principal reason for which the complainant was dismissed shall be read as references to the reason or principal reason he has not been offered re-engagement.
[(4) In relation to a complaint under section 111 of the 1996 Act (unfair dismissal: complaint to employment tribunal) that a dismissal was unfair by virtue of section 238A of this Act—
    (a)   no order shall be made under section 113 of the 1996 Act (reinstatement or re-engagement) until after the conclusion of protected industrial action by any employee in relation to the relevant dispute,
    (b)   regulations under section 7 of the Employment Tribunals Act 1996 may make provision about the adjournment and renewal of applications (including provision requiring adjournment in specified circumstances), and
    (c)   regulations under section 9 of that Act may require a pre-hearing review to be carried out in specified circumstances.]

**NOTES**

Sub-s (1): words in first pair of square brackets substituted, and words in third pair of square brackets added, by the Employment Relations Act 1999, s 16, Sch 5, paras 1, 4(1)–(3); words in second pair of square brackets substituted by the Employment Rights Act 1996, s 240, Sch 1, para 56(1), (16).

Sub-s (2): words in first pair of square brackets inserted by the Employment Relations Act 1999, s 16, Sch 5, paras 1, 4(1), (4); words in second pair of square brackets substituted by the Employment Rights Act 1996, s 240, Sch 1, para 56(1), (16); words in final pair of square brackets substituted by the Employment Rights (Dispute Resolution) Act 1998, s 1(2)(a).

Sub-s (3): words in square brackets substituted by the Employment Rights Act 1996, s 240, Sch 1, para 56(1), (16).

Sub-s (4): added by the Employment Relations Act 1999, s 16, Sch 5, paras 1, 4(1), (5).

*Criminal offences*

**[1.522]**
**240 Breach of contract involving injury to persons or property**
(1) A person commits an offence who wilfully and maliciously breaks a contract of service or hiring, knowing or having reasonable cause to believe that the probable consequences of his so doing, either alone or in combination with others, will be—
    (a)   to endanger human life or cause serious bodily injury, or
    (b)   to expose valuable property, whether real or personal, to destruction or serious injury.
(2) Subsection (1) applies equally whether the offence is committed from malice conceived against the person endangered or injured or, as the case may be, the owner of the property destroyed or injured, or otherwise.
(3) A person guilty of an offence under this section is liable on summary conviction *to imprisonment for a term not exceeding three months or* to a fine not exceeding level 2 on the standard scale *or both*.
(4) This section does not apply to seamen.

**NOTES**

Sub-s (3): words in italics repealed by the Criminal Justice Act 2003, s 332, Sch 37, Pt 9, in relation to England and Wales, as from a day to be appointed.

By virtue of the Criminal Justice Act 2003, s 280(1), Sch 25, para 95, a summary offence under this section is not punishable with imprisonment (as from a day to be appointed).

**[1.523]**
**241 Intimidation or annoyance by violence or otherwise**
(1)  A person commits an offence who, with a view to compelling another person to abstain from doing or to do any act which that person has a legal right to do or abstain from doing, wrongfully and without legal authority—
  (a)  uses violence to or intimidates that person or his [spouse or civil partner] or children, or injures his property,
  (b)  persistently follows that person about from place to place,
  (c)  hides any tools, clothes or other property owned or used by that person, or deprives him of or hinders him in the use thereof,
  (d)  watches or besets the house or other place where that person resides, works, carries on business or happens to be, or the approach to any such house or place, or
  (e)  follows that person with two or more other persons in a disorderly manner in or through any street or road.
(2)  A person guilty of an offence under this section is liable on summary conviction to imprisonment for a term not exceeding six months or a fine not exceeding level 5 on the standard scale, or both.
(3)  . . .

**NOTES**
Sub-s (1): words in square brackets substituted by the Civil Partnership Act 2004, s 261(1), Sch 27, para 145.
Sub-s (3): repealed by the Serious Organised Crime and Police Act 2005, ss 111, 174(2), Sch 7, Pt 1, para 30, Sch 17, Pt 2.

**[1.524]**
**242 Restriction of offence of conspiracy: England and Wales**
(1)  Where in pursuance of any such agreement as is mentioned in section 1(1) of the Criminal Law Act 1977 (which provides for the offence of conspiracy) the acts in question in relation to an offence are to be done in contemplation or furtherance of a trade dispute, the offence shall be disregarded for the purposes of that subsection if it is a summary offence which is not punishable with imprisonment.
(2)  This section extends to England and Wales only.

**[1.525]**
**243 Restriction of offence of conspiracy: Scotland**
(1)  An agreement or combination by two or more persons to do or procure to be done an act in contemplation or furtherance of a trade dispute is not indictable as a conspiracy if that act committed by one person would not be punishable as a crime.
(2)  A crime for this purpose means an offence punishable on indictment, or an offence punishable on summary conviction, and for the commission of which the offender is liable under the statute making the offence punishable to be imprisoned either absolutely or at the discretion of the court as an alternative for some other punishment.
(3)  Where a person is convicted of any such agreement or combination as is mentioned above to do or procure to be done an act which is punishable only on summary conviction, and is sentenced to imprisonment, the imprisonment shall not exceed three months or such longer time as may be prescribed by the statute for the punishment of the act when committed by one person.
(4)  Nothing in this section—
  (a)  exempts from punishment a person guilty of a conspiracy for which a punishment is awarded by an Act of Parliament, or
  (b)  affects the law relating to riot, unlawful assembly, breach of the peace, . . . or any offence against the State or the Sovereign.
(5)  This section extends to Scotland only.

**NOTES**
Sub-s (4): words omitted from para (b) repealed by the Criminal Justice and Licensing (Scotland) Act 2010, s 203, Sch 7, para 19, as from 28 March 2011.

*Supplementary*

**[1.526]**
**244 Meaning of "trade dispute" in Part V**
(1)  In this Part a "trade dispute" means a dispute between workers and their employer which relates wholly or mainly to one or more of the following—
  (a)  terms and conditions of employment, or the physical conditions in which any workers are required to work;
  (b)  engagement or non-engagement, or termination or suspension of employment or the duties of employment, of one or more workers;
  (c)  allocation of work or the duties of employment between workers or groups of workers;
  (d)  matters of discipline;
  (e)  a worker's membership or non-membership of a trade union;

  (f)    facilities for officials of trade unions; and

  (g)   machinery for negotiation or consultation, and other procedures, relating to any of the above matters, including the recognition by employers or employers' associations of the right of a trade union to represent workers in such negotiation or consultation or in the carrying out of such procedures.

(2)   A dispute between a Minister of the Crown and any workers shall, notwithstanding that he is not the employer of those workers, be treated as a dispute between those workers and their employer if the dispute relates to matters which—

  (a)   have been referred for consideration by a joint body on which, by virtue of provision made by or under any enactment, he is represented, or

  (b)   cannot be settled without him exercising a power conferred on him by or under an enactment.

(3)   There is a trade dispute even though it relates to matters occurring outside the United Kingdom, so long as the person or persons whose actions in the United Kingdom are said to be in contemplation or furtherance of a trade dispute relating to matters occurring outside the United Kingdom are likely to be affected in respect of one or more of the matters specified in subsection (1) by the outcome of the dispute.

(4)   An act, threat or demand done or made by one person or organisation against another which, if resisted, would have led to a trade dispute with that other, shall be treated as being done or made in contemplation of a trade dispute with that other, notwithstanding that because that other submits to the act or threat or accedes to the demand no dispute arises.

(5)   In this section—

"employment" includes any relationship whereby one person personally does work or performs services for another; and

"worker", in relation to a dispute with an employer, means—

  (a)   a worker employed by that employer; or

  (b)   a person who has ceased to be so employed if his employment was terminated in connection with the dispute or if the termination of his employment was one of the circumstances giving rise to the dispute.

**[1.527]**
**245  Crown employees and contracts**
Where a person holds any office or employment under the Crown on terms which do not constitute a contract of employment between that person and the Crown, those terms shall nevertheless be deemed to constitute such a contract for the purposes of—

  (a)   the law relating to liability in tort of a person who commits an act which—

    (i)   induces another person to break a contract, interferes with the performance of a contract or induces another person to interfere with its performance, or

    (ii)   consists in a threat that a contract will be broken or its performance interfered with, or that any person will be induced to break a contract or interfere with its performance, and

  (b)   the provisions of this or any other Act which refer (whether in relation to contracts generally or only in relation to contracts of employment) to such an act.

**[1.528]**
**246  Minor definitions**
In this Part—

"date of the ballot" means, in the case of a ballot in which votes may be cast on more than one day, the last of those days;

. . . ,

"strike" means [(except for the purposes of section 229(2))] any concerted stoppage of work;

"working hours", in relation to a person, means any time when under his contract of employment, or other contract personally to do work or perform services, he is required to be at work.

NOTES

   Definition "place of work" (omitted) repealed by the Trade Union Reform and Employment Rights Act 1993, ss 49(1), 51, Sch 7, para 26, Sch 10; words in square brackets in definition "strike" inserted by the Employment Relations Act 1999, s 4, Sch 3, paras 1, 6(4).

# PART VI
## ADMINISTRATIVE PROVISIONS

*ACAS*

**[1.529]**
**247  ACAS**
(1)   There shall continue to be a body called the Advisory, Conciliation and Arbitration Service (referred to in this Act as "ACAS").

(2)   ACAS is a body corporate of which the corporators are the members of its Council.

(3)   Its functions, and those of its officers and servants, shall be performed on behalf of the Crown, but not so as to make it subject to directions of any kind from any Minister of the Crown as to the manner in which it is to exercise its functions under any enactment.

(4)   For the purposes of civil proceedings arising out of those functions the Crown Proceedings Act 1947 applies to ACAS as if it were a government department and the Crown Suits (Scotland) Act 1857 applies to it as if it were a public department.

(5)   Nothing in section 9 of the Statistics of Trade Act 1947 (restriction on disclosure of information obtained under that Act) shall prevent or penalise the disclosure to ACAS, for the purposes of the exercise of any of its functions, of information obtained under that Act by a government department.

(6)   ACAS shall maintain offices in such of the major centres of employment in Great Britain as it thinks fit for the purposes of discharging its functions under any enactment.

**[1.530]**
**248   The Council of ACAS**
(1)   ACAS shall be directed by a Council which, subject to the following provisions, shall consist of a chairman and nine ordinary members appointed by the Secretary of State.

(2)   Before appointing those ordinary members of the Council, the Secretary of State shall—
   (a)   as to three of them, consult such organisations representing employers as he considers appropriate, and
   (b)   as to three of them, consult such organisations representing workers as he considers appropriate.

(3)   The Secretary of State may, if he thinks fit, appoint a further two ordinary members of the Council (who shall be appointed so as to take office at the same time); and before making those appointments he shall—
   (a)   as to one of them, consult such organisations representing employers as he considers appropriate, and
   (b)   as to one of them, consult such organisations representing workers as he considers appropriate.

(4)   The Secretary of State may appoint up to three deputy chairman who may be appointed from the ordinary members, or in addition to those members.

(5)   The Council shall determine its own procedure, including the quorum necessary for its meetings.

(6)   If the Secretary of State has not appointed a deputy chairman, the Council may choose a member to act as chairman in the absence or incapacity of the chairman.

(7)   The validity of proceedings of the Council is not affected by any vacancy among the members of the Council or by any defect in the appointment of any of them.

**[1.531]**
**249   Terms of appointment of members of Council**
(1)   The members of the Council shall hold and vacate office in accordance with their terms of appointment, subject to the following provisions.

(2)   . . .

Appointment as [chairman, or as] deputy chairman, or as an ordinary member of the Council, may be a full-time or part-time appointment; and the Secretary of State may, with the consent of the member concerned, vary the terms of his appointment as to whether his appointment is full-time or part-time.

(3)   A person shall not be appointed to the Council for a term exceeding five years, but previous membership does not affect eligibility for re-appointment.

(4)   A member may at any time resign his membership, and the chairman or a deputy chairman may at any time resign his office as such, by notice in writing to the Secretary of State.

A deputy chairman appointed in addition to the ordinary members of the Council shall on resigning his office as deputy chairman cease to be a member of the Council.

(5)   If the Secretary of State is satisfied that a member—
   (a)   has been absent from meetings of the Council for a period longer than six consecutive months without the permission of the Council, or
   (b)   has become bankrupt or [has had a debt relief order (under Part 7A of the Insolvency Act 1986) made in respect of him or has] made an arrangement with his creditors (or, in Scotland, has had his estate sequestrated or has made a trust deed for his creditors or has made and had accepted a composition contract), or
   (c)   is incapacitated by physical or mental illness, or
   (d)   is otherwise unable or unfit to discharge the functions of a member,
the Secretary of State may declare his office as a member to be vacant and shall notify the declaration in such manner as he thinks fit, whereupon the office shall become vacant.

If the chairman or a deputy chairman ceases to be a member of the Council, he shall also cease to be chairman or, as the case may be, a deputy chairman.

**NOTES**

Sub-s (2): words omitted repealed, and words in square brackets inserted, by the Trade Union Reform and Employment Rights Act 1993, ss 43(3), 51, Sch 10.

Sub-s (5): words in square brackets in para (b) inserted by the Tribunals, Courts and Enforcement Act 2007 (Consequential Amendments) Order 2012, SI 2012/2404, art 3(2), Sch 2, para 28(1), (2), as from 1 October 2012.

**[1.532]**
## 250 Remuneration, &c of members of Council

(1)   ACAS shall pay to the members of its Council such remuneration and travelling and other allowances as may be determined by the Secretary of State.

(2)   The Secretary of State may pay, or make provision for payment, to or in respect of a member of the Council such pension, allowance or gratuity on death or retirement as he may determine.

(3)   Where a person ceases to be the holder of the Council otherwise than on the expiry of his term of office and it appears to the Secretary of State that there are special circumstances which make it right for him to receive compensation, he may make him a payment of such amount he may determine.

(4)   The approval of the Treasury is required for any determination by the Secretary of State under this section.

**NOTES**

Transfer of Functions: by the Transfer of Functions (Treasury and Minister for the Civil Service) Order 1995, SI 1995/269, arts 3, 5(2), Schedule, para 21, the function of the Treasury under this section was transferred to the Minister for the Civil Service, and accordingly the reference to the Treasury in sub-s (4) above is to be read as if it were a reference to the Minister for the Civil Service.

**[1.533]**
## 251 Secretary, officers and staff of ACAS

(1)   ACAS may, with the approval of the Secretary of State, appoint a secretary.

The consent of the Secretary of State is required as to his terms and conditions of service.

(2)   ACAS may appoint such other officers and staff as it may determine.

The consent of the Secretary of State is required as to their numbers, manner of appointment and terms and conditions of service.

(3)   The Secretary of State shall not give his consent under subsection (1) or (2) without the approval of the Treasury.

(4)   ACAS shall pay to the Treasury, at such times in each accounting year as may be determined by the Treasury, sums of such amounts as may be so determined as being equivalent to the increase in that year of such liabilities of his as are attributable to the provision of pensions, allowances or gratuities to or in respect of persons who are or have been in the service of ACAS in so far as that increase results from the service of those persons during that accounting year and to the expense to be incurred in administering those pensions, allowances or gratuities.

(5)   The fixing of the common seal of ACAS shall be authenticated by the signature of the secretary of ACAS or some other person authorised by ACAS to act for that purpose.

A document purporting to be duly executed under the seal of ACAS shall be received in evidence and shall, unless the contrary is proved, be deemed to be so executed.

**[1.534]**
## [251A Fees for exercise of functions by ACAS

(1)   ACAS may, in any case in which it thinks it appropriate to do so, but subject to any directions under subsection (2) below, charge a fee for exercising a function in relation to any person.

(2)   The Secretary of State may direct ACAS to charge fees, in accordance with the direction, for exercising any function specified in the direction, but the Secretary of State shall not give a direction under this subsection without consulting ACAS.

(3)   A direction under subsection (2) above may require ACAS to charge fees in respect of the exercise of a function only in specified descriptions of case.

(4)   A direction under subsection (2) above shall specify whether fees are to be charged in respect of the exercise of any specified function—

    (a)   at the full economic cost level, or

    (b)   at a level less than the full economic cost but not less than a specified proportion or percentage of the full economic cost.

(5)   Where a direction requires fees to be charged at the full economic cost level ACAS shall fix the fee for the case at an amount estimated to be sufficient to cover the administrative costs of ACAS of exercising the function including an appropriate sum in respect of general staff costs and overheads.

(6)   Where a direction requires fees to be charged at a level less than the full economic cost ACAS shall fix the fee for the case at such amount, not being less than the proportion or percentage of the full economic cost specified under subsection (4)(b) above, as it thinks appropriate (computing that cost in the same way as under subsection (5) above).

(7) No liability to pay a fee charged under this section shall arise on the part of any person unless ACAS has notified that person that a fee may or will be charged.

(8) For the purposes of this section—

(a) a function is exercised "in relation to" a person who avails himself of the benefit of its exercise, whether or not he requested its exercise and whether the function is such as to be exercisable in relation to particular persons only or in relation to persons generally; and

(b) where a function is exercised in relation to two or more persons the fee chargeable for its exercise shall be apportioned among them as ACAS thinks appropriate.]

**NOTES**

Inserted by the Trade Union Reform and Employment Rights Act 1993, s 44.

**[1.535]**
**[251B  Prohibition on disclosure of information**

(1) Information held by ACAS shall not be disclosed if the information—

(a) relates to a worker, an employer of a worker or a trade union (a "relevant person"), and

(b) is held by ACAS in connection with the provision of a service by ACAS or its officers.

This is subject to subsection (2).

(2) Subsection (1) does not prohibit the disclosure of information if—

(a) the disclosure is made for the purpose of enabling or assisting ACAS to carry out any of its functions under this Act,

(b) the disclosure is made for the purpose of enabling or assisting an officer of ACAS to carry out the functions of a conciliation officer under any enactment,

(c) the disclosure is made for the purpose of enabling or assisting—

(i) a person appointed by ACAS under section 210(2), or

(ii) an arbitrator or arbiter appointed by ACAS under any enactment,

to carry out functions specified in the appointment,

(3) Subsection (2) does not authorise the making of a disclosure which contravenes the Data Protection Act 1998.

(4) A person who discloses information in contravention of this section commits an offence and is liable on summary conviction to a fine not exceeding level 5 on the standard scale.

(5) Proceedings in England and Wales for an offence under this section may be instituted only with the consent of the Director of Public Prosecutions.

(6) For the purposes of this section information held by—

(a) a person appointed by ACAS under section 210(2) in connection with functions specified in the appointment, or

(b) an arbitrator or arbiter appointed by ACAS under any enactment in connection with functions specified in the appointment,

is information that is held by ACAS in connection with the provision of a service by ACAS.]

**NOTES**

Commencement: 25 April 2013.

Inserted by the Enterprise and Regulatory Reform Act 2013, s 10, as from 25 April 2013, except in relation to a disclosure, or a request for information, made before that date (see s 24(1) of the 2013 Act at **[1.1855]**).

**[1.536]**
**252  General financial provisions**

(1) The Secretary of State shall pay to ACAS such sums as are approved by the Treasury and as he considers appropriate for the purpose of enabling ACAS to perform its functions.

(2) ACAS may pay to—

(a) persons appointed under section 210(2) (conciliation) who are not officers or servants of ACAS, and

(b) arbitrators or arbiters appointed by ACAS under any enactment,

such fees and travelling and other allowances as may be determined by the Secretary of State with the approval of the Treasury.

**[1.537]**
**253  Annual report and accounts**

(1) ACAS shall as soon as practicable after the end of each [financial year] make a report to the Secretary of State on its activities during that year.

The Secretary of State shall lay a copy of the report before each House of Parliament and arrange for it to be published.

(2) ACAS shall keep proper accounts and proper records in relation to the accounts and shall prepare in respect of each financial year a statement of accounts, in such form as the Secretary of State may, with the approval of the Treasury, direct.

(3) ACAS shall not later than 30th November following the end of the financial year to which the statement relates, send copies of the statement to the Secretary of State and to the Comptroller and Auditor General.

(4)    The Comptroller and Auditor General shall examine, certify and report on each such statement and shall lay a copy of the statement and of his report before each House of Parliament.

**NOTES**

Sub-s (1): words in square brackets substituted by the Employment Relations Act 1999, s 27(1).

*The Certification Officer*

**[1.538]**
**254    The Certification Officer**
(1)    There shall continue to be an officer called the Certification Officer.
(2)    The Certification Officer shall be appointed by the Secretary of State after consultation with ACAS.
(3)    The Certification Officer may appoint one or more assistant certification officers and shall appoint an assistant certification officer for Scotland.
(4)    The Certification Officer may delegate to an assistant certification officer such functions as he thinks appropriate, and in particular may delegate to the assistant certification officer for Scotland such functions as he thinks appropriate in relation to organisations whose principal office is in Scotland.
    References to the Certification Officer in enactments relating to his functions shall be construed accordingly.
(5)    ACAS shall provide for the Certification Officer the requisite staff (from among the officers and servants of ACAS) and the requisite accommodation, equipment and other facilities.
[(5A)    Subject to subsection (6), ACAS shall pay to the Certification Officer such sums as he may require for the performance of any of his functions.]
(6)    The Secretary of State shall pay to the Certification Officer such sums as he may require for making payments under the scheme under section 115 (payments towards expenditure in connection with secret ballots).

**NOTES**

Sub-s (5A): inserted by the Trade Union Reform and Employment Rights Act 1993, s 49(2), Sch 8, para 78.

**[1.539]**
**255    Remuneration, &c of Certification Officer and assistants**
(1)    ACAS shall pay to the Certification Officer and any assistant certification officer such remuneration and travelling and other allowances as may be determined by the Secretary of State.
(2)    The Secretary of State may pay, or make provision for payment, to or in respect of the Certification Officer and any assistant certification officer such pension, allowance or gratuity on death or retirement as he may determine.
(3)    Where a person ceases to be the Certification Officer or an assistant certification officer otherwise than on the expiry of his term of office and it appears to the Secretary of State that there are special circumstances which make it right for him to receive compensation, he may make him a payment of such amount as he may determine.
(4)    The approval of the Treasury is required for any determination by the Secretary of State under this section.

**[1.540]**
**256    Procedure before the Certification Officer**
(1)    Except in relation to matters as to which express provision is made by or under an enactment, the Certification Officer may regulate the procedure to be followed—
    (a)    on any application or complaint made to him, or
    (b)    where his approval is sought with respect to any matter.
[(2)    He shall in particular make provision about the disclosure, and restriction of the disclosure, of the identity of an individual who has made or is proposing to make any such application or complaint.
(2A)    Provision under subsection (2) shall be such that if the application or complaint relates to a trade union—
    (a)    the individual's identity is disclosed to the union unless the Certification Officer thinks the circumstances are such that it should not be so disclosed;
    (b)    the individual's identity is disclosed to such other persons (if any) as the Certification Officer thinks fit.]
(3)    The Secretary of State may, with the consent of the Treasury, make a scheme providing for the payment by the Certification Officer to persons of such sums as may be specified in or determined under the scheme in respect of expenses incurred by them for the purposes of, or in connection with, their attendance at hearings held by him in the course of carrying out his functions.
(4)    . . .

**NOTES**

Sub-ss (2), (2A): substituted, for the original sub-s (2), by the Employment Relations Act 1999, s 29, Sch 6, paras 1, 22.

Sub-s (4): repealed by the Trade Union Reform and Employment Rights Act 1993, s 51, Sch 10.

**[1.541]**
**[256ZA   Striking out**
(1)   At any stage of proceedings on an application or complaint made to the Certification Officer, he may—
   (a)   order the application or complaint, or any response, to be struck out on the grounds that it is scandalous, vexatious, has no reasonable prospect of success or is otherwise misconceived,
   (b)   order anything in the application or complaint, or in any response, to be amended or struck out on those grounds, or
   (c)   order the application or complaint, or any response, to be struck out on the grounds that the manner in which the proceedings have been conducted by or on behalf of the applicant or complainant or (as the case may be) respondent has been scandalous, vexatious, or unreasonable.
(2)   The Certification Officer may order an application or complaint made to him to be struck out for excessive delay in proceeding with it.
(3)   An order under this section may be made on the Certification Officer's own initiative and may also be made—
   (a)   if the order sought is to strike out an application or complaint, or to amend or strike out anything in an application or complaint, on an application by the respondent, or
   (b)   if the order sought is to strike out any response, or to amend or strike out anything in any response, on an application by the person who made the application or complaint mentioned in subsection (1).
(4)   Before making an order under this section, the Certification Officer shall send notice to the party against whom it is proposed that the order should be made giving him an opportunity to show cause why the order should not be made.
(5)   Subsection (4) shall not be taken to require the Certification Officer to send a notice under that subsection if the party against whom it is proposed that the order under this section should be made has been given an opportunity to show cause orally why the order should not be made.
(6)   Nothing in this section prevents the Certification Officer from making further provision under section 256(1) about the striking out of proceedings on any application or complaint made to him.
(7)   An appeal lies to the Employment Appeal Tribunal on any question of law arising from a decision of the Certification Officer under this section.
(8)   In this section—
   "response" means any response made by a trade union or other body in the exercise of a right to be heard, or to make representations, in response to the application or complaint;
   "respondent" means any trade union, or other body, that has such a right.]

**NOTES**
Inserted by the Employment Relations Act 2004, s 48.

**[1.542]**
**[256A   Vexatious litigants**
(1)   The Certification Officer may refuse to entertain any application or complaint made to him under a provision of Chapters III to VIIA of Part I by a vexatious litigant.
(2)   The Certification Officer must give reasons for such a refusal.
(3)   Subsection (1) does not apply to a complaint under section 37E(1)(b) or to an application under section 41.
(4)   For the purposes of subsection (1) a vexatious litigant is a person who is the subject of—
   (a)   . . .
   (b)   a civil proceedings order or an all proceedings order which is made under section 42(1) of the [Senior Courts Act 1981] and which remains in force,
   (c)   an order which is made under section 1 of the Vexatious Actions (Scotland) Act 1898, or
   (d)   an order which is made under section 32 of the Judicature (Northern Ireland) Act 1978.]

**NOTES**
Inserted by the Employment Relations Act 1999, s 29, Sch 6, paras 1, 23.
Sub-s (4): para (a) repealed by the Employment Relations Act 2004, ss 49(1), (9), 57(2), Sch 2; words in square brackets in para (b) substituted by the Constitutional Reform Act 2005, s 59(5), Sch 11, Pt 1, para 1(2), as from 1 October 2009.

**[1.543]**
**[256B   Vexatious litigants: applications disregarded**
(1)   For the purposes of a relevant enactment an application to the Certification Officer shall be disregarded if—
   (a)   it was made under a provision mentioned in the relevant enactment, and
   (b)   it was refused by the Certification Officer under section 256A(1).

(2) The relevant enactments are sections 26(8), 31(7), 45C(5B), 56(8), 72A(10), 81(8) and 108A(13).]

**NOTES**
   Inserted by the Employment Relations Act 1999, s 29, Sch 6, paras 1, 23.

**[1.544]**
**257   Custody of documents submitted under earlier legislation**
(1) The Certification Officer shall continue to have custody of the annual returns, accounts, copies of rules and other documents submitted for the purposes of—
   (a)   the Trade Union Acts 1871 to 1964,
   (b)   the Industrial Relations Act 1971, or
   (c)   the Trade Union and Labour Relations Act 1974,
of which he took custody under section 9 of the Employment Protection Act 1975.
(2) He shall keep available for public inspection (either free of charge or on payment of a reasonable charge) at all reasonable hours such of those documents as were available for public inspection in pursuance of any of those Acts.

**NOTES**
   Trade Union Acts 1871 to 1964: repealed, see the note to s 3 at **[1.243]**.
   Industrial Relations Act 1971: repealed by the Trade Union and Labour Relations Act 1974, ss 1, 25(3), Sch 5.
   Trade Union and Labour Relations Act 1974; Employment Protection Act 1975, s 9: repealed by this Act.

**[1.545]**
**258   Annual report and accounts**
(1) The Certification Officer shall, as soon as practicable after the end of each [financial year], make a report of his activities during that year to ACAS and to the Secretary of State.
   The Secretary of State shall lay a copy of the report before each House of Parliament and arrange for it to be published.
(2) The accounts prepared by ACAS in respect of any financial year shall show separately any sums disbursed to or on behalf of the Certification Officer in consequence of the provisions of this Part.

**NOTES**
   Sub-s (1): words in square brackets substituted by the Employment Relations Act 1999, s 29, Sch 6, paras 1, 24.

*Central Arbitration Committee*

**[1.546]**
**259   The Central Arbitration Committee**
(1) There shall continue to be a body called the Central Arbitration Committee.
(2) The functions of the Committee shall be performed on behalf of the Crown, but not so as to make it subject to directions of any kind from any Minister of the Crown as to the manner in which it is to exercise its functions.
(3) ACAS shall provide for the Committee the requisite staff (from among the officers and servants of ACAS) and the requisite accommodation, equipment and other facilities.

**[1.547]**
**260   The members of the Committee**
[(1) The Central Arbitration Committee shall consist of members appointed by the Secretary of State.
(2) The Secretary of State shall appoint a member as chairman, and may appoint a member as deputy chairman or members as deputy chairmen.
(3) The Secretary of State may appoint as members only persons experienced in industrial relations, and they shall include some persons whose experience is as representatives of employers and some whose experience is as representatives of workers.
(3A) Before making an appointment under subsection (1) or (2) the Secretary of State shall consult ACAS and may consult other persons.]
(4) At any time when the chairman of the Committee is absent or otherwise incapable of acting, or there is a vacancy in the office of chairman, and the Committee has a deputy chairman or deputy chairmen—
   (a)   the deputy chairman, if there is only one, or
   (b)   if there is more than one, such of the deputy chairmen as they may agree or in default of
         agreement as the Secretary of State may direct,
may perform any of the functions of chairman of the Committee.
(5) At any time when every person who is chairman or deputy chairman is absent or otherwise incapable of acting, or there is no such person, such member of the Committee as the Secretary of State may direct may perform any of the functions of the chairman of the Committee.

(6)   The validity of any proceedings of the Committee shall not be affected by any vacancy among the members of the Committee or by any defect in the appointment of a member of the Committee.

**NOTES**

Sub-ss (1)–(3A): substituted, for the original sub-ss (1)–(3), by the Employment Relations Act 1999, s 24.

**[1.548]**
**261   Terms of appointment of members of Committee**
(1)   The members of the Central Arbitration Committee shall hold and vacate office in accordance with their terms of appointment, subject to the following provisions.
(2)   A person shall not be appointed to the Committee for a term exceeding five years, but previous membership does not affect eligibility for re-appointment.
(3)   The Secretary of State may, with the consent of the member concerned, vary the terms of his appointment as to whether he is a full-time or part-time member.
(4)   A member may at any time resign his membership, and the chairman or a deputy chairman may at any time resign his office as such, by notice in writing to the Secretary of State.
(5)   If the Secretary of State is satisfied that a member—
   (a)   has become bankrupt or [has had a debt relief order (under Part 7A of the Insolvency Act 1986) made in respect of him or has] made an arrangement with his creditors (or, in Scotland, has had his estate sequestrated or has made a trust deed for his creditors or has made and had accepted a composition contract), or
   (b)   is incapacitated by physical or mental illness, or
   (c)   is otherwise unable or unfit to discharge the functions of a member,
the Secretary of State may declare his office as a member to be vacant and shall notify the declaration in such manner as he thinks fit, whereupon the office shall become vacant.
(6)   If the chairman or a deputy chairman ceases to be a member of the Committee, he shall also cease to be chairman or, as the case may be, a deputy chairman.

**NOTES**

Sub-s (5): words in square brackets in para (a) inserted by the Tribunals, Courts and Enforcement Act 2007 (Consequential Amendments) Order 2012, SI 2012/2404, art 3(2), Sch 2, para 28(1), (3), as from 1 October 2012.

**[1.549]**
**262   Remuneration, &c of members of Committee**
(1)   ACAS shall pay to the members of the Central Arbitration Committee such remuneration and travelling and other allowances as may be determined by the Secretary of State.
(2)   The Secretary of State may pay, or make provision for payment, to or in respect of a member of the Committee such pension, allowance or gratuity on death or retirement as he may determine.
(3)   Where a person ceases to be the holder of the Committee otherwise than on the expiry of his term of office and it appears to the Secretary of State that there are special circumstances which make it right for him to receive compensation, he may make him a payment of such amount he may determine.
(4)   The approval of the Treasury is required for any determination by the Secretary of State under this section.

**[1.550]**
**263   Proceedings of the Committee**
(1)   For the purpose of discharging its functions in any particular case the Central Arbitration Committee shall consist of the chairman and such other members as the chairman may direct:
   Provided that, it may sit in two or more divisions constituted of such members as the chairman may direct, and in a division in which the chairman does not sit the functions of the chairman shall be performed by a deputy chairman.
(2)   The Committee may, at the discretion of the chairman, where it appears expedient to do so, call in the aid of one or more assessors, and may settle the matter wholly or partly with their assistance.
(3)   The Committee may at the discretion of the chairman sit in private where it appears expedient to do so.
(4)   If in any case the Committee cannot reach a unanimous decision on its award, the chairman shall decide the matter acting with the full powers of an umpire or, in Scotland, an oversman.
(5)   Subject to the above provisions, the Committee shall determine its own procedure.
(6)   [Part I of the Arbitration Act 1996] (general provisions as to arbitration) and [sections 1 to 15 of and schedule 1 to the Arbitration (Scotland) Act 2010] do not apply to proceedings before the Committee.
[(7)   In relation to the discharge of the Committee's functions under Schedule A1—
   (a)   section 263A and subsection (6) above shall apply, and
   (b)   subsections (1) to (5) above shall not apply.]

**NOTES**

Sub-s (6): words in first pair of square brackets substituted by the Arbitration Act 1996, s 107(1), Sch 3, para 6; words in second pair of square brackets substituted by the Arbitration (Scotland) Act 2010 (Consequential Amendments) Order 2010, SSI 2010/220, art 2, Schedule, para 6(1), (3), as from 5 June 2010.

Sub-s (7): added by the Employment Relations Act 1999, s 25(1), (2).

**[1.551]**
**[263A   Proceedings of the Committee under Schedule A1**
(1)   For the purpose of discharging its functions under Schedule A1 in any particular case, the Central Arbitration Committee shall consist of a panel established under this section.
(2)   The chairman of the Committee shall establish a panel or panels, and a panel shall consist of these three persons appointed by him—
    (a)   the chairman or a deputy chairman of the Committee, who shall be chairman of the panel;
    (b)   a member of the Committee whose experience is as a representative of employers;
    (c)   a member of the Committee whose experience is as a representative of workers.
(3)   The chairman of the Committee shall decide which panel is to deal with a particular case.
(4)   A panel may at the discretion of its chairman sit in private where it appears expedient to do so.
(5)   If—
    (a)   a panel cannot reach a unanimous decision on a question arising before it, and
    (b)   a majority of the panel have the same opinion,
the question shall be decided according to that opinion.
(6)   If—
    (a)   a panel cannot reach a unanimous decision on a question arising before it, and
    (b)   a majority of the panel do not have the same opinion,
the chairman of the panel shall decide the question acting with the full powers of an umpire or, in Scotland, an oversman.
(7)   Subject to the above provisions, a panel shall determine its own procedure.
[(8)   The reference in subsection (1) to the Committee's functions under Schedule A1 does not include a reference to its functions under paragraph 166 of that Schedule.]]

**NOTES**

Inserted by the Employment Relations Act 1999, s 25(1), (3).

Sub-s (8): added by the Employment Relations Act 2004, s 57(1), Sch 1, para 15.

**[1.552]**
**264   Awards of the Committee**
(1)   The Central Arbitration Committee may correct in any award[, or in any decision or declaration of the Committee under Schedule A1] any clerical mistake or error arising from an accidental slip or omission.
(2)   If a question arises as to the interpretation of an award of the Committee, [or of a decision or declaration of the Committee under Schedule A1] any party may apply to the Committee for a decision; and the Committee shall decide the question after hearing the parties or, if the parties consent, without a hearing, and shall notify the parties.
(3)   Decisions of the Committee in the exercise of any of its functions shall be published.

**NOTES**

Sub-ss (1), (2): words in square brackets inserted by the Employment Relations Act 1999, s 25(1), (4).

**[1.553]**
**265   Annual report and accounts**
(1)   ACAS shall, as soon as practicable after the end of each [financial year], make a report to the Secretary of State on the activities of the Central Arbitration Committee during that year.
    For that purpose the Committee shall, as soon as practicable after the end of each [financial year], transmit to ACAS an account of its activities during that year.
(2)   The accounts prepared by ACAS in respect of any financial year shall show separately any sums disbursed to or on behalf of the Committee in consequence of the provisions of this Part.

**NOTES**

Sub-s (1): words in square brackets substituted by the Employment Relations Act 1999, s 27(2).

**266–271**   *(Repealed by the Employment Relations Act 1999, ss 28(2)(c), 44, Sch 9(6).)*

*Supplementary*

**[1.554]**
**272   Meaning of "financial year"**
In this Part "financial year" means the twelve months ending with 31st March.

## PART VII
## MISCELLANEOUS AND GENERAL

*Crown employment, etc*

**[1.555]**
### 273 Crown employment
(1)  The provisions of this Act have effect (except as mentioned below) in relation to Crown employment and persons in Crown employment as in relation to other employment and other workers or employees.
(2)  The following provisions are excepted from subsection (1)—
  [section 87(4)(b) (power of tribunal] to make order in respect of employer's failure to comply with duties as to union contributions);
  sections 184 and 185 (remedy for failure to comply with declaration as to disclosure of information);
  Chapter II of Part IV (procedure for handling redundancies).
(3)  In this section "Crown employment" means employment under or for the purposes of a government department or any officer or body exercising on behalf of the Crown functions conferred by an enactment.
(4)  For the purposes of the provisions of this Act as they apply in relation to Crown employment or persons in Crown employment—
  (a)  "employee" and "contract of employment" mean a person in Crown employment and the terms of employment of such a person (but subject to subsection (5) below);
  (b)  "dismissal" means the termination of Crown employment;
  (c)  . . .
  (d)  the reference in 182(1)(e) (disclosure of information for collective bargaining: restrictions on general duty) to the employer's undertaking shall be construed as a reference to the national interest; and
  (e)  any other reference to an undertaking shall be construed, in relation to a Minister of the Crown, as a reference to his functions or (as the context may require) to the department of which he is in charge, and in relation to a government department, officer or body shall be construed as a reference to the functions of the department, officer or body or (as the context may require) to the department, officer or body.
(5)  Sections 137 to 143 (rights in relation to trade union membership: access to employment) apply in relation to Crown employment otherwise than under a contract only where the terms of employment correspond to those of a contract of employment.
(6)  This section has effect subject to section 274 (armed forces) and section 275 (exemption on grounds of national security).

**NOTES**
Sub-s (2): words in square brackets substituted by the Employment Rights (Dispute Resolution) Act 1998, s 15, Sch 1, para 8.
Sub-s (4): para (c) repealed by the Trade Union Reform and Employment Rights Act 1993, s 51, Sch 10.

**[1.556]**
### 274 Armed forces
(1)  Section 273 (application of Act to Crown employment) does not apply to service as a member of the naval, military or air forces of the Crown.
(2)  But that section applies to employment by an association established for the purposes of [Part XI of the Reserve Forces Act 1996] (territorial, auxiliary and reserve forces associations) as it applies to employment for the purposes of a government department.

**NOTES**
Sub-s (2): words in square brackets substituted by the Reserve Forces Act 1996, s 131(1), Sch 10, para 24.

**[1.557]**
### 275 Exemption on grounds of national security
(1)  Section 273 (application of Act to Crown employment) does not apply to employment in respect of which there is in force a certificate issued by or on behalf of a Minister of the Crown certifying that employment of a description specified in the certificate, or the employment of a particular person so specified, is (or, at a time specified in the certificate, was) required to be excepted from that section for the purpose of safeguarding national security.
(2)  A document purporting to be such a certificate shall, unless the contrary is proved, be deemed to be such a certificate.

**[1.558]**
### 276  Further provision as to Crown application
(1)  Section 138 (refusal of service of employment agency on grounds related to union membership), and the other provisions of Part III applying in relation to that section, bind the Crown so far as they relate to the activities of an employment agency in relation to employment to which those provisions apply.

This does not affect the operation of those provisions in relation to Crown employment by virtue of section 273.

(2)  Sections 144 and 145 (prohibition of union membership requirements) and sections 186 and 187 (prohibition of union recognition requirements) bind the Crown.

*House of Lords and House of Commons staff*

**[1.559]**
### 277  House of Lords staff
(1)  [The provisions of this Act (except those specified below)] apply in relation to employment as a relevant member of the House of Lords staff as in relation to other employment.

[(1A)  The following provisions are excepted from subsection (1)—
> sections 184 and 185 (remedy for failure to comply with declaration as to disclosure of information),
> Chapter II of Part IV (procedure for handling redundancies).]

(2)  Nothing in any rule of law or the law or practice of Parliament prevents a person from bringing [a civil employment claim before the court or from bringing] before an [employment tribunal] proceedings of any description  . . .  which could be brought before such a tribunal in relation to other employment.

[(2A)  For the purposes of the application of the other provisions of this Act as they apply by virtue of this section—
> (a)   the reference in section 182(1)(e) (disclosure of information for collective bargaining: restrictions) to a person's undertaking shall be construed as a reference to the national interest or, if the case so requires, the interests of the House of Lords; and
> (b)   any other reference to an undertaking shall be construed as a reference to the House of Lords.]

[(3)  In this section—
> "relevant member of the House of Lords staff" means any person who is employed under a contract of employment with the Corporate Officer of the House of Lords;
> "civil employment claim" means a claim arising out of or relating to a contract of employment or any other contract connected with employment, or a claim in tort arising in connection with a person's employment; and
> "the court" means the High Court or *a county court*.]

---

**NOTES**

Sub-s (1): words in square brackets substituted by the Trade Union Reform and Employment Rights Act 1993, s 49(1), Sch 7, para 12(a).

Sub-s (1A): inserted by the Trade Union Reform and Employment Rights Act 1993, s 49(1), Sch 7, para 12(b).

Sub-s (2): words in first pair of square brackets inserted, and words omitted repealed, by the Trade Union Reform and Employment Rights Act 1993, ss 49(1), 51, Sch 7, para 12(c), Sch 10; words in second pair of square brackets substituted by the Employment Rights (Dispute Resolution) Act 1998, s 1(2)(a).

Sub-s (2A): inserted by the Trade Union Reform and Employment Rights Act 1993, s 49(1), Sch 7, para 12(d).

Sub-s (3): substituted, for the original sub-ss (3)–(6), by the Trade Union Reform and Employment Rights Act 1993, s 49(1), Sch 7, para 12(e); for the words in italics there are substituted the words "the county court" by the Crime and Courts Act 2013, s 17(5), Sch 9, Pt 3, para 52, as from a day to be appointed.

---

**[1.560]**
### 278  House of Commons staff
(1)  The provisions of this Act (except those specified below) apply in relation to employment as a relevant member of the House of Commons staff as in relation to other employment.

(2)  The following provisions are excepted from subsection (1)—
> sections 184 and 185 (remedy for failure to comply with declaration as to disclosure of information),
> Chapter II of Part IV (procedure for handling redundancies).

[(2A)  Nothing in any rule of law or the law or practice of Parliament prevents a relevant member of the House of Commons staff from bringing a civil employment claim before the court or from bringing before an [employment tribunal] proceedings of any description which could be brought before such a tribunal by any person who is not such a member.]

(3)  In this section "relevant member of the House of Commons staff" has the same meaning as in section 139 of the Employment Protection (Consolidation) Act 1978.

> ["civil employment claim" means a claim arising out of or relating to a contract of employment or any other contract connected with employment, or a claim in tort arising in connection with a person's employment; and

"the court" means the High Court or the county court.]

(4)   For the purposes of the other provisions of this Act as they apply by virtue of this section—

(a)   "employee" and "contract of employment" include a relevant member of the House of Commons staff and the terms of employment of any such member (but subject to subsection (5) below);

(b)   "dismissal" includes the termination of any such member's employment;

(c)   the reference in [section] 182(1)(e) (disclosure of information for collective bargaining: restrictions on general duty) to the employer's undertaking shall be construed as a reference to the national interest or, if the case so requires, the interests of the House of Commons; and

(d)   any other reference to an undertaking shall be construed as a reference to the House of Commons.

(5)   Sections 137 to 143 (access to employment) apply by virtue of this section in relation to employment otherwise than under a contract only where the terms of employment correspond to those of a contract of employment.

(6)   [Subsections (6) to (12) of section 195 of the Employment Rights Act 1996] (person to be treated as employer of House of Commons staff) apply, with any necessary modifications, for the purposes of this section.

---

**NOTES**

Sub-s (2A): inserted by the Trade Union Reform and Employment Rights Act 1993, s 49(2), Sch 8, para 85(a); words in square brackets substituted by the Employment Rights (Dispute Resolution) Act 1998, s 1(2)(a).

Sub-s (3): definitions "civil employment claim" and "the court" inserted by the Trade Union Reform and Employment Rights Act 1993, s 49(2), Sch 8, para 85(b). See further note to sub-s (6) below.

Sub-s (4): word in square brackets in para (c) inserted by the Trade Union Reform and Employment Rights Act 1993, s 49(1), Sch 7, para 27.

Sub-s (6): words in square brackets substituted by the Employment Rights Act 1996, s 240, Sch 1, para 56(1), (17). The 1996 Act does not provide for the equivalent substitution of s 195 for the reference to s 139 of the 1978 Act in sub-s (3) of this section; this is presumably a drafting error.

Employment Protection (Consolidation) Act 1978, s 139: repealed so far as relevant by the Employment Rights Act 1996, s 242, Sch 3, Pt I; for the meaning of "relevant member of the House of Commons staff", see now s 195(5) of the 1996 Act at **[1.1002]**.

---

*Health service practitioners*

**[1.561]**

### 279   Health service practitioners

[(1)]   In this Act "worker" includes an individual regarded in his capacity as one who works or normally works or seeks to work as a person [performing . . . personal dental services or] providing . . . general dental services, general ophthalmic services or pharmaceutical services in accordance with arrangements made—

(a)   by [the National Health Service Commissioning Board] [[under section 126 of the National Health Service Act 2006] or] [a] [Local Health Board] under section [ . . . ] . . . , [71 or 80 of the National Health Service (Wales) Act 2006] of the National Health Service Act 1977, or

(b)   by a Health Board under section [17C,] . . . , 25, *26, or 27* of the National Health Service (Scotland) Act 1978 [or as a person providing local pharmaceutical services under a pilot scheme [established under section 134 of the National Health Service Act 2006 or section 92 of the National Health Service (Wales) Act 2006, or under an LPS scheme established under Schedule 12 to the National Health Service Act 2006 or Schedule 7 to the National Health Service (Wales) Act 2006]];

and "employer", in relation to such an individual, regarded in that capacity, means that . . . board.

[(2)   In this Act "worker" also includes an individual regarded in his capacity as one who works or normally works or seeks to work as a person performing primary medical services *or primary dental services*—

(a)   in accordance with arrangements made by [the National Health Service Commissioning Board or a] Local Health Board under [section 92 or 107 of the National Health Service Act 2006, or section 50 or 64 of the National Health Service (Wales) Act 2006]; or

(b)   under a contract under [section 84 or 100 of the National Health Service Act 2006 or section 42 or 57 of the National Health Service (Wales) Act 2006] entered into by him with [the National Health Service Commissioning Board or a] Local Health Board, [or under a contract under section 117 of the National Health Service Act 2006 [entered into by him with the National Health Service Commissioning Board],]

and "employer" in relation to such an individual, regarded in that capacity, means that Trust, . . . Board.]

[(3)   In this Act "worker" also includes an individual regarded in his capacity as one who works or normally works or seeks to work as a person performing primary medical services—

   (a)   in accordance with arrangements made by a Health Board under section 17C of the National Health Service (Scotland) Act 1978; or

   (b)   under a contract under section 17J of that Act entered into by him with a Health Board, and "employer" in relation to such an individual, regarded in that capacity, means that Health Board.]

[(4)   In this Act—

   (a)   "worker" also includes an individual regarded in his capacity as one who works or normally works or seeks to work as a person performing pharmaceutical care services under a contract entered into by him with a Health Board under section 17Q of the National Health Service (Scotland) Act 1978; and

   (b)   "employer" in relation to such a person, regarded in that capacity, means that Health Board.]

**NOTES**

This section has been amended as follows:

Sub-s (1): numbered as such by the Health and Social Care (Community Health and Standards) Act 2003, s 184, Sch 11, para 59(1), (3).

Sub-s (1) (opening paragraph): words in square brackets inserted by the National Health Service (Primary Care) Act 1997, s 41(10), Sch 2, Pt I, para 67(a); words omitted repealed by the Primary Medical Services (Scotland) Act 2004 (Consequential Modifications) Order 2004, SI 2004/957, art 2, Schedule, para 7(a)(i).

Sub-s (1)(a): words in first pair of square brackets substituted and word in fourth pair of square brackets inserted by the Health and Social Care Act 2012, s 55(2), Sch 5, para 66(a), (b), as from 1 April 2013; words in second (outer) pair of square brackets inserted by the National Health Service Reform and Health Care Professions Act 2002, s 2(5), Sch 2, Pt 2, para 60; words in third (inner) pair of square brackets inserted by the National Health Service (Consequential Provisions) Act 2006, s 2, Sch 1, paras 153, 154(a)(ii); words in fifth pair of square brackets substituted by the References to Health Authorities Order 2007, SI 2007/961, art 3, Schedule, para 22; reference in sixth pair of square brackets originally inserted by the National Health Service (Primary Care) Act 1997, s 41(10), Sch 2, Pt I, para 67(b), and repealed by the Health and Social Care (Community Health and Standards) Act 2003, ss 184, 196, Sch 11, para 59(1), (2), Sch 14, Pt 4; second reference omitted repealed by the Health and Social Care (Community Health and Standards) Act 2003, ss 184, 196, Sch 11, para 59(1), (2), Sch 14, Pt 4; final words in square brackets substituted by the National Health Service (Consequential Provisions) Act 2006, s 2, Sch 1, paras 153, 154(a)(iii) (it is assumed that a drafting error has occurred in this paragraph, as references to specific provisions of the National Health Service Act 1977 have been repealed, but the (redundant) reference to that Act has not been repealed).

Sub-s (1)(b): reference in first pair of square brackets inserted by the National Health Service (Primary Care) Act 1997, s 41(10), Sch 2, Pt I, para 67(c); reference omitted repealed by the Primary Medical Services (Scotland) Act 2004 (Consequential Modifications) Order 2004, SI 2004/957, art 2, Schedule, para 7(a)(ii); for the words in italics there are substituted the words "or 26" by the Smoking, Health and Social Care (Scotland) Act 2005 (Consequential Modifications) (England, Wales and Northern Ireland) Order 2006, SI 2006/1056, art 2, Schedule, Pt 1, para 6(a), as from a day to be appointed; words in second (outer) pair of square brackets inserted by the Health and Social Care Act 2001, s 67(1), Sch 5, Pt I, para 9; words in third (inner) pair of square brackets substituted by the National Health Service (Consequential Provisions) Act 2006, s 2, Sch 1, paras 153, 154(b); final words omitted repealed by the Health and Social Care Act 2012, s 55(2), Sch 5, para 66(c), as from 1 April 2013.

Sub-s (2): added by the Health and Social Care (Community Health and Standards) Act 2003, s 184, Sch 11, para 59(1), (4); for the words in italics in the opening paragraph there are substituted the words ", primary dental services or primary ophthalmic services" by the Health Act 2006, s 80(1), Sch 8, para 30(a), as from a day to be appointed; words in first pair of square brackets in para (a) substituted by the Health and Social Care Act 2012, s 55(2), Sch 5, para 66(d), as from 1 April 2013; words in second pair of square brackets in para (a) and words in first pair of square brackets in para (b) substituted by the National Health Service (Consequential Provisions) Act 2006, s 2, Sch 1, paras 153, 155; words in second and fourth (inner) pairs of square brackets in para (b) substituted, and final words omitted repealed by the Health and Social Care Act 2012, s 55(2), Sch 5, para 66(e)–(g), as from 1 April 2013; words in third (outer) pair of square brackets in para (b) inserted by the Health Act 2006, s 80(1), Sch 8, para 30(b) (as amended by the National Health Service (Consequential Provisions) Act 2006, s 2, Sch 1, paras 281, 291), as from a day to be appointed.

Sub-s (3): added by the Primary Medical Services (Scotland) Act 2004 (Consequential Modifications) Order 2004, SI 2004/957, art 2, Schedule, para 7(b).

Sub-s (4): added by SI 2006/1056, art 2, Schedule, Pt 1, para 6(b), as from a day to be appointed.

Transitional provisions and miscellaneous:

Note that notwithstanding the coming into force of the amendments to the definition of worker in this section made by the Health and Social Care (Community Health and Standards) Act 2003, Sch 11, para 59, in relation to any complaint arising in respect of a matter which occurred before 1 April 2004, this section has effect as if those amendments had not been brought into force; see the General Medical Services and Personal Medical Services Transitional and Consequential Provisions Order 2004, SI 2004/865, art 112, and the General Medical Services Transitional and Consequential Provisions (Wales) (No 2) Order 2004, SI 2004/1016, art 88.

The General Medical Services and Personal Medical Services Transitional and Consequential Provisions Order 2004, SI 2004/865, art 109(1), (2)(d), and the General Medical Services Transitional and Consequential Provisions (Wales) (No 2) Order 2004, SI 2004/1016, art 85(1), (2)(d) (both made under the Health and Social Care (Community Health and Standards) Act 2003, ss 176, 195(1), 200, 201) provide that until such time as default contracts entered into pursuant s 176(3) of the 2003 Act cease to exist, any reference to a general medical services contract or to a contract under the National Health Service Act 1977, s 28Q includes a reference to a default contract.

*Police service*

**[1.562]**
**280 Police service**
(1) In this Act "employee" or "worker" does not include a person in police service; and the provisions of sections 137 and 138 (rights in relation to trade union membership: access to employment) do not apply in relation to police service.
(2) "Police service" means service as a member of any constabulary maintained by virtue of an enactment, or in any other capacity by virtue of which a person has the powers or privileges of a constable.

**NOTES**
Meaning of "police service":
An individual who as a member of the prison service acts in a capacity in which he has the powers or privileges of a constable is not, by virtue of his having those powers or privileges, to be regarded as in police service for the purposes of any provision of this Act; see the Criminal Justice and Public Order Act 1994, s 126(1), (2).
A member of the Independent Police Complaints Commission's staff, who is not a constable, is not treated as being in police service for the purposes of this section; see the Police Reform Act 2002, s 13, Sch 3, Pt 3, para 19(5).
A constable or cadet of the British Transport Police Force may not be a member of a trade union, except for the British Transport Police Federation, although the Chief Constable of the British Transport Police Force may allow an officer to continue membership of a trade union acquired before joining the Force; see the Railways and Transport Safety Act 2003, s 30.
A member of staff of the Serious Organised Crime Agency who is designated under the Serious Organised Crime and Police Act 2005, s 43, as a person having the powers of a constable, is not treated as being in police service for the purpose of this section; see s 53(1), (2)(a) of the 2005 Act.

*Excluded classes of employment*

**281** *(Repealed by the Employment Protection (Part-time Employees) Regulations 1995, SI 1995/31, regs 5, 6, Schedule.)*

**[1.563]**
**[282 Fixed term employment**
(1) In this section, "fixed term contract" means a contract of employment that, under its provisions determining how it will terminate in the normal course, will terminate—
(a) on the expiry of a specific term,
(b) on the completion of a particular task, or
(c) on the occurrence or non-occurrence of any other specific event other than the attainment by the employee of any normal and bona fide retiring age in the establishment for an employee holding the position held by him.
(2) The provisions of Chapter II of Part IV (procedure for handling redundancies) do not apply to employment under a fixed term contract unless—
(a) the employer is proposing to dismiss the employee as redundant; and
(b) the dismissal will take effect before the expiry of the specific term, the completion of the particular task or the occurrence or non-occurrence of the specific event (as the case may be).]

**NOTES**
Commencement: 6 April 2013.
Substituted by the Trade Union and Labour Relations (Consolidation) Act 1992 (Amendment) Order 2013, SI 2013/763, art 3(1), (4), as from 6 April 2013, in relation to proposals to dismiss as redundant 20 or more employees at one establishment within a period of 90 days or less which are made on or after that date (see art 2(2) of the 2013 Order at **[2.1678]**).
This section and the notes relating to it previously read as follows—

"**282 Short-term employment**
(1) The provisions of Chapter II of Part IV (procedure for handling redundancies) do not apply to employment—
(a) under a contract for a fixed term of three months or less, or
(b) under a contract made in contemplation of the performance of a specific task which is not expected to last for more than three months,
where the employee has not been continuously employed for a period of more than three months.
[(2) Chapter I of Part XIV of the Employment Rights Act 1996 (computation of period of continuous employment), and any provision modifying or supplementing that Chapter for the purposes of that Act, apply for the purposes of this section.]
Notes
Sub-s (2): substituted by the Employment Rights Act 1996, s 240, Sch 1, para 56(1), (18).".

**283** *(Repealed by the Trade Union Reform and Employment Rights Act 1993, ss 34(1), (6), 51, Sch 10.)*

**[1.564]**
**284 Share fishermen**
The following provisions of this Act do not apply to employment as master or as member of the crew of a fishing vessel where the employee [(or, in the case of sections 145A to 151, the worker)] is remunerated only by a share in the profits or gross earnings of the vessel—
In Part III (rights in relation to trade union membership and activities)—

Part 1 Statutes

sections 137 to 143 (access to employment),
[sections 145A to 151 (inducements and detriment)], and
sections 168 to 173 (time off for trade union duties and activities);
In Part IV, Chapter II (procedure for handling redundancies).

**NOTES**
Words in first pair of square brackets inserted, and words in second pair of square brackets substituted, by the Employment Relations Act 2004, s 57(1), Sch 1, para 16.

**[1.565]**
**285   Employment outside Great Britain**
(1)   The following provisions of this Act do not apply to employment where under his contract of employment an employee works, or in the case of a prospective employee would ordinarily work, outside Great Britain—
In Part III (rights in relation to trade union membership and activities)—
sections 137 to 143 (access to employment),
[sections 145A to 151 (inducements and detriment)], and
sections 168 to 173 (time off for trade union duties and activities);
In Part IV, [sections 193 and 194 (duty to notify Secretary of State of certain redundancies)].
[(1A)   Sections 145A to 151 do not apply to employment where under his contract personally to do work or perform services a worker who is not an employee works outside Great Britain.]
(2)   For the purposes of [subsections (1) and (1A)] employment on board a ship registered in the United Kingdom shall be treated as employment where under his contract a person ordinarily works in Great Britain unless—
(a)   the ship is registered at a port outside Great Britain, or
(b)   the employment is wholly outside Great Britain, or
(c)   the employee or, as the case may be, [the worker or] the person seeking employment or seeking to avail himself of a service of an employment agency, is not ordinarily resident in Great Britain.

**NOTES**
Sub-s (1): words in first pair of square brackets substituted by the Employment Relations Act 2004, s 57(1), Sch 1, para 17(1), (2); words in second pair of square brackets substituted by the Employment Relations Act 1999, s 32(1).
Sub-s (1A): inserted by the Employment Relations Act 2004, s 57(1), Sch 1, para 17(1), (3).
Sub-s (2): words in first pair of square brackets substituted, and words in square brackets in para (c) inserted, by the Employment Relations Act 2004, s 57(1), Sch 1, para 17(1), (4).

**[1.566]**
**286   Power to make further provision as to excluded classes of employment**
(1)   This section applies in relation to the following provisions—
In Part III (rights in relation to trade union membership and activities), [sections 145A to 151 (inducements and detriment)],
In Part IV, Chapter II (procedure for handling redundancies), and
In Part V (industrial action), section 237 (dismissal of those taking part in unofficial industrial action).
(2)   The Secretary of State may by order made by statutory instrument provide that any of those provisions—
(a)   shall not apply to persons or to employment of such classes as may be prescribed by the order, or
(b)   shall apply to persons or employments of such classes as may be prescribed by the order subject to such exceptions and modifications as may be so prescribed,
and may vary or revoke any of the provisions of sections 281 to 285 above (excluded classes of employment) so far as they relate to any such provision.
(3)   Any such order shall be made by statutory instrument and may contains such incidental, supplementary or transitional provisions as appear to the Secretary of State to be necessary or expedient.
(4)   No such order shall be made unless a draft of the order has been laid before Parliament and approved by a resolution of each House of Parliament.

**NOTES**
Sub-s (1): words in square brackets substituted by the Employment Relations Act 2004, s 57(1), Sch 1, para 18.
Orders: the Trade Union and Labour Relations (Consolidation) Act 1992 (Amendment) Order 2013, SI 2013/763 at **[2.1677]**.

*Offshore employment*

**[1.567]**
**287   Offshore employment**
*(1)   In this Act "offshore employment" means employment for the purposes of activities—*
*(a)   in the territorial waters of the United Kingdom, or*

    (b)    *connected with the exploration of the sea-bed or subsoil, or the exploitation of their natural resources, in the United Kingdom sector of the continental shelf, or*

    (c)    *connected with the exploration or exploitation, in a foreign sector of the continental shelf, of a cross-boundary petroleum field.*

(2)   Her Majesty may by Order in Council provide that—

    (a)    the provisions of this Act, and

    (b)    any Northern Ireland legislation making provision for purposes corresponding to any of the purposes of this Act,

apply, to such extent and for such purposes as may be specified in the Order and with or without modification, to or in relation to a person in offshore employment or, in relation to sections 137 to 143 (access to employment), a person seeking such employment.

(3)   An Order in Council under this section—

    (a)    may make different provision for different cases;

    (b)    may provide that the enactments to which this section applies, as applied, apply—

        (i)    to individuals whether or not they are British subjects, and

        (ii)   to bodies corporate whether or not they are incorporated under the law of a part of the United Kingdom,

    and apply notwithstanding that the application may affect the activities of such an individual or body outside the United Kingdom;

    (c)    may make provision for conferring jurisdiction on any court or class of court specified in the Order, or on [employment tribunals], in respect of offences, causes of action or other matters arising in connection with offshore employment;

    (d)    may provide that the enactments to which this section applies apply in relation to a person in offshore employment in a part of the areas referred to in subsection (1)(a) and (b);

    (e)    may exclude from the operation of section 3 of the Territorial Waters Jurisdiction Act 1878 (consents required for prosecutions) proceedings for offences under the enactments to which this section applies in connection with offshore employment;

    (f)    may provide that such proceedings shall not be brought without such consent as may be required by the Order;

    (g)    may modify or exclude any of sections 281 to 285 (excluded classes of employment) or any corresponding provision of Northern Ireland legislation.

[(3A)   An Order in Council under this section shall be subject to annulment in pursuance of a resolution of either House of Parliament.]

(4)   Any jurisdiction conferred on a court or tribunal under this section is without prejudice to jurisdiction exercisable apart from this section, by that or any other court or tribunal.

(5)   *In this section—*

    *"cross-boundary petroleum field" means a petroleum field that extends across the boundary between the United Kingdom sector of the continental shelf and a foreign sector;*

    *"foreign sector of the continental shelf" means an area outside the territorial waters of any state, within which rights with respect to the sea-bed and subsoil and their natural resources are exercisable by a state other than the United Kingdom;*

    *"petroleum field" means a geological structure identified as an oil or gas field by the Order in Council concerned; and*

    *"United Kingdom sector of the continental shelf" means the areas designated under section 1(7) of the Continental Shelf Act 1964.*

**NOTES**

Sub-s (1): substituted by the Petroleum Act 1998, s 50, Sch 4, para 34(2), as from a day to be appointed, as follows—

    "(1)   In this Act "offshore employment" means employment for the purposes of—

      (a)   any activities in the territorial sea adjacent to the United Kingdom, and

      (b)   any such activities as are mentioned in section 11(2) of the Petroleum Act 1998 in waters within subsection (8)(b) or (c) of that section.".

Sub-s (3): words in square brackets in para (c) substituted by the Employment Rights (Dispute Resolution) Act 1998, s 1(2)(a).

Sub-s (3A): inserted by the Employment Relations Act 1999, s 32(2).

Sub-s (5): repealed by the Petroleum Act 1998, ss 50, 51, Sch 4, para 34(3), Sch 5, Pt I, as from a day to be appointed.

Orders: the Employment Relations (Offshore Employment) Order 2000, SI 2000/1828. Also, by virtue of s 300(3) of, and Sch 3, para 1(2) to, this Act, and the Interpretation Act 1978, s 17(2)(b), the Employment Protection (Offshore Employment) Order 1976, SI 1976/766, has effect as if made under this section.

*Contracting out, &c*

**[1.568]**
**288  Restriction on contracting out**

(1)   Any provision in an agreement (whether a contract of employment or not) is void in so far as it purports—

    (a)    to exclude or limit the operation of any provision of this Act, or

    (b)    to preclude a person from bringing—

(i)    proceedings before an [employment tribunal] or the Central Arbitration Committee under any provision of this Act, . . .

(ii)    . . .

(2)    Subsection (1) does not apply to an agreement to refrain from instituting or continuing proceedings where a conciliation officer has taken action under [*section 18* of [the Employment Tribunals Act 1996] (conciliation).]

[(2A)    Subsection (1) does not apply to an agreement to refrain from instituting or continuing any proceedings, other than excepted proceedings, specified in [subsection (1)(b) of that section] before an [employment tribunal] if the conditions regulating *compromise* agreements under this Act are satisfied in relation to the agreement.

(2B)    The conditions regulating *compromise* agreements under this Act are that—

(a)    the agreement must be in writing;

(b)    the agreement must relate to the particular [proceedings];

(c)    the complainant must have received [advice from a relevant independent adviser] as to the terms and effect of the proposed agreement and in particular its effect on his ability to pursue his rights before an [employment tribunal];

(d)    there must be in force, when the adviser gives the advice, a [contract of insurance, or an indemnity provided for members of a professional body] covering the risk of a claim by the complainant in respect of loss arising in consequence of the advice;

(e)    the agreement must identify the adviser; and

(f)    the agreement must state that the conditions regulating compromise agreements under this Act are satisfied.

(2C)    The proceedings excepted from subsection (2A) are proceedings on a complaint of non-compliance with section 188.]

(3)    Subsection (1) does not apply—

(a)    to such an agreement as is referred to in section 185(5)(b) or (c) to the extent that it varies or supersedes an award under that section;

(b)    to any provision in a collective agreement excluding rights under Chapter II of Part IV (procedure for handling redundancies), if an order under section 198 is in force in respect of it.

[(4)    A person is a relevant independent adviser for the purposes of subsection (2B)(c)—

(a)    if he is a qualified lawyer,

(b)    if he is an officer, official, employee or member of an independent trade union who has been certified in writing by the trade union as competent to give advice and as authorised to do so on behalf of the trade union,

(c)    if he works at an advice centre (whether as an employee or a volunteer) and has been certified in writing by the centre as competent to give advice and as authorised to do so on behalf of the centre, or

(d)    if he is a person of a description specified in an order made by the Secretary of State.

(4A)    But a person is not a relevant independent adviser for the purposes of subsection (2B)(c) in relation to the complainant—

(a)    if he is, is employed by or is acting in the matter for the other party or a person who is connected with the other party,

(b)    in the case of a person within subsection (4)(b) or (c), if the trade union or advice centre is the other party or a person who is connected with the other party,

(c)    in the case of a person within subsection (4)(c), if the complainant makes a payment for the advice received from him, or

(d)    in the case of a person of a description specified in an order under subsection (4)(d), if any condition specified in the order in relation to the giving of advice by persons of that description is not satisfied.

(4B)    In subsection (4)(a) "qualified lawyer" means—

(a)    as respects England and Wales, a [a person who, for the purposes of the Legal Services Act 2007, is an authorised person in relation to an activity which constitutes the exercise of a right of audience or the conduct of litigation (within the meaning of that Act), and]

(b)    as respects Scotland, an advocate (whether in practice as such or employed to give legal advice), or a solicitor who holds a practising certificate.

(4C)    An order under subsection (4)(d) shall be made by statutory instrument which shall be subject to annulment in pursuance of a resolution of either House of Parliament.

(5)    For the purposes of subsection (4A) any two persons are to be treated as connected—

(a)    if one is a company of which the other (directly or indirectly) has control, or

(b)    if both are companies of which a third person (directly or indirectly) has control.]

[(6)    An agreement under which the parties agree to submit a dispute to arbitration—

(a)    shall be regarded for the purposes of subsections (2) and (2A) as being an agreement to refrain from instituting or continuing proceedings if—

(i)    the dispute is covered by a scheme having effect by virtue of an order under section 212A, and

(ii)    the agreement is to submit it to arbitration in accordance with the scheme, but

(b)    shall be regarded for those purposes as neither being nor including such an agreement in any other case.]

**NOTES**
Sub-s (1): words in square brackets in para (b)(i) substituted by the Employment Rights (Dispute Resolution) Act 1998, s 1(2)(a); para (b)(ii) and the word immediately preceding it repealed by the Employment Relations Act 2004, s 57, Sch 1, para 19, Sch 2.

Sub-s (2): words in first (outer) pair of square brackets substituted by the Employment Tribunals Act 1996, s 43, Sch 1, para 8(a); words in second (inner) pair of square brackets substituted by the Employment Rights (Dispute Resolution) Act 1998, s 1(2)(c); for the words in italics there are substituted the words "any of sections 18A to 18C" by the Enterprise and Regulatory Reform Act 2013, s 7(2), Sch 1, para 1, as from a day to be appointed.

Sub-s (2A): inserted, together with sub-ss (2B), (2C), by the Trade Union Reform and Employment Rights Act 1993, s 39(2), Sch 6, para 4(a); for the word in italics there is substituted the word "settlement" by the Enterprise and Regulatory Reform Act 2013, s 23(1)(a), as from a day to be appointed; words in first pair of square brackets substituted by the Employment Tribunals Act 1996, s 43, Sch 1, para 8(b); words in second pair of square brackets substituted by the Employment Rights (Dispute Resolution) Act 1998, s 1(2)(a).

Sub-s (2B): inserted as noted above; for the word in italics there is substituted the word "settlement" by the Enterprise and Regulatory Reform Act 2013, s 23(1)(a), as from a day to be appointed; words in square brackets substituted by the Employment Rights (Dispute Resolution) Act 1998, ss 1(2)(a), 9(1), (2)(c), 10(1), (2)(c), 15, Sch 1, para 9(1), (2).

Sub-s (2C): inserted as noted above.

Sub-ss (4), (4A)–(4C), (5): substituted, for the original sub-ss (4), (5) (as added by the Trade Union Reform and Employment Rights Act 1993, s 39(2), Sch 6, para 4(b)), by the Employment Rights (Dispute Resolution) Act 1998, s 15, Sch 1, para 9(1), (3).

Sub-s (4B): substituted as noted above; words square brackets substituted by the Legal Services Act 2007, s 208(1), Sch 21, paras 104, 107, as from 1 January 2010.

Sub-s (6): added by the Employment Rights (Dispute Resolution) Act 1998, s 8(3).

Orders: the Compromise Agreements (Description of Person) Order 2004, SI 2004/754 at **[2.786]**; the Compromise Agreements (Description of Person) Order 2004 (Amendment) Order 2004, SI 2004/2515.

**[1.569]**
## 289   Employment governed by foreign law
For the purposes of this Act it is immaterial whether the law which (apart from this Act) governs any person's employment is the law of the United Kingdom, or of a part of the United Kingdom, or not.

**290, 291**    *(Repealed by the Employment Tribunals Act 1996, s 45, Sch 3, Pt I. S 291(1) had been repealed by the Trade Union Reform and Employment Rights Act 1993. S 290 and s 291(2) and (3) are re-enacted respectively as ss 18(1) and 21(1) and (2) of the 1996 Act, at* **[1.706]**, **[1.713]**.)

*Other supplementary provisions*

**[1.570]**
## 292   Death of employee or employer
(1)    This section has effect in relation to the following provisions so far as they confer rights on employees or make provision in connection therewith—

(a)    . . .

(b)    sections 168 to 173 (time off for trade union duties and activities);

(c)    sections 188 to 198 (procedure for handling redundancies).

[(1A)    This section also has effect in relation to sections 145A to 151 so far as those sections confer rights on workers or make provision in connection therewith.]

(2)    Where the employee [or worker] or employer dies, tribunal proceedings may be instituted or continued by a personal representative of the deceased employee [or worker] or, as the case may be, defended by a personal representative of the deceased employer.

(3)    If there is no personal representative of a deceased employee [or worker], tribunal proceedings or proceedings to enforce a tribunal award may be instituted or continued on behalf of his estate by such other person as the [employment tribunal] may appoint, being either—

(a)    a person authorised by the employee [or worker] to act in connection with the proceedings before his death, or

(b)    the widower, widow, [surviving civil partner,] child, father, mother, brother or sister of the employee [or worker].

In such a case any award made by the [employment tribunal] shall be in such terms and shall be enforceable in such manner as may be prescribed.

(4)    Any right arising under any of the provisions mentioned in subsection (1) [or (1A)] which by virtue of this section accrues after the death of the employee [or worker] in question shall devolve as if it had accrued before his death.

(5)    Any liability arising under any of those provisions which by virtue of this section accrues after the death of the employer in question shall be treated for all purposes as if it had accrued immediately before his death.

**NOTES**

Sub-s (1): para (a) repealed by the Employment Relations Act 2004, s 57, Sch 1, para 20(1), (2), Sch 2.

Sub-s (1A): inserted by the Employment Relations Act 2004, s 57(1), Sch 1, para 20(1), (3).

Sub-ss (2), (4): words in square brackets inserted by the Employment Relations Act 2004, s 57(1), Sch 1, para 20(1), (4), (5).

Sub-s (3): words in first, third and fifth pairs of square brackets inserted by the Employment Relations Act 2004, s 57(1), Sch 1, para 20(1), (4); words in second and final pairs of square brackets substituted by the Employment Rights (Dispute Resolution) Act 1998, s 1(1), (2)(a); words in fourth pair of square brackets inserted by the Civil Partnership Act 2004, s 261(1), Sch 27, para 146.

Regulations: by virtue of s 300(3) of, and Sch 3, para 1(2) to, this Act, and the Interpretation Act 1978, s 17(2)(b), the Employment Tribunal Awards (Enforcement in case of death) Regulations 1976, SI 1976/663, have effect as if made under this section.

**[1.571]**

**[292A  Extension of time limits to facilitate conciliation before institution of proceedings**

(1)  This section applies where this Act provides for it to apply for the purposes of a provision of this Act (a "relevant provision").

(2)  In this section—

  (a)   Day A is the day on which the complainant concerned complies with the requirement in subsection (1) of section 18A of the Employment Tribunals Act 1996 (requirement to contact ACAS before instituting proceedings) in relation to the matter in respect of which the proceedings are brought, and

  (b)   Day B is the day on which the complainant concerned receives or, if earlier, is treated as receiving (by virtue of regulations made under subsection (11) of that section) the certificate issued under subsection (4) of that section.

(3)  In working out when a time limit set by a relevant provision expires the period beginning with the day after Day A and ending with Day B is not to be counted.

(4)  If a time limit set by a relevant provision would (if not extended by this subsection) expire during the period beginning with Day A and ending one month after Day B, the time limit expires instead at the end of that period.

(5)  Where an employment tribunal has power under this Act to extend a time limit set by a relevant provision, the power is exercisable in relation to the time limit as extended by this section.]

**NOTES**

Commencement: to be appointed.

Inserted by the Enterprise and Regulatory Reform Act 2013, s 8, Sch 2, paras 1, 13, as from a day to be appointed.

**[1.572]**

**293  Regulations**

(1)  The Secretary of State may by regulations prescribe anything authorised or required to be prescribed for the purposes of this Act.

(2)  The regulations may contain such incidental, supplementary or transitional provisions as appear to the Secretary of State to be necessary or expedient.

(3)  Regulations under this section shall be made by statutory instrument which shall be subject to annulment in pursuance of a resolution of either House of Parliament.

**294**  *(Reciprocal arrangements with Northern Ireland: outside the scope of this work.)*

*Interpretation*

**[1.573]**

**295  Meaning of "employee" and related expressions**

(1)  In this Act—

    "contract of employment" means a contract of service or of apprenticeship,

    "employee" means an individual who has entered into or works under (or, where the employment has ceased, worked under) a contract of employment, and

    "employer", in relation to an employee, means the person by whom the employee is (or, where the employment has ceased, was) employed.

(2)  Subsection (1) has effect subject to section 235 and other provisions conferring a wider meaning on "contract of employment" or related expressions.

**[1.574]**

**296  Meaning of "worker" and related expressions**

(1)  In this Act "worker" means an individual who works, or normally works or seeks to work—

  (a)   under a contract of employment, or

  (b)   under any other contract whereby he undertakes to do or perform personally any work or services for another party to the contract who is not a professional client of his, or

  (c)   in employment under or for the purposes of a government department (otherwise than as a member of the naval, military or air forces of the Crown) in so far as such employment does not fall within paragraph (a) or (b) above.

(2)   In this Act "employer", in relation to a worker, means a person for whom one or more workers work, or have worked or normally work or seek to work.

[(3)   This section has effect subject to [sections 68(4), 145F(3) and 151(1B)].]

**NOTES**

Sub-s (3): added by the Trade Union Reform and Employment Rights Act 1993, s 49(2), Sch 8, para 88; words in square brackets substituted by the Employment Relations Act 2004, s 57(1), Sch 1, para 21.

**[1.575]**
**297   Associated employers**
For the purposes of this Act any two employers shall be treated as associated if—
   (a)   one is a company of which the other (directly or indirectly) has control, or
   (b)   both are companies of which a third person (directly or indirectly) has control;
and "associated employer" shall be construed accordingly.

**[1.576]**
**298   Minor definitions: general**
In this Act, unless the context otherwise requires—
   "act" and "action" each includes omission, and references to doing an act or taking action shall
      be construed accordingly;
   ["agency worker" has the meaning given in regulation 3 of the Agency Workers
      Regulations 2010;]
   ["certificate of independence" means a certificate issued under—
      (a)   section 6(6), or
      (b)   section 101A(4);]
   "contravention" includes a failure to comply, and cognate expressions shall be construed
      accordingly;
   "dismiss", "dismissal" and "effective date of termination", in relation to an employee, shall be
      construed in accordance with [Part X of the Employment Rights Act 1996];
      . . .
   "tort", as respects Scotland, means delict, and cognate expressions shall be construed
      accordingly.

**NOTES**

Definition "agency worker" inserted by the Agency Workers Regulations 2010, SI 2010/93, reg 25, Sch 2, Pt 1, paras 1, 5, as from 1 October 2011; definition "certificate of independence" inserted by the Employment Relations Act 2004, s 50(4); words in square brackets in definitions "dismiss", "dismissal", and "effective date of termination" substituted by the Employment Rights Act 1996, s 240, Sch 1, para 56(1), (19); definition "post" (omitted) repealed by the Postal Services Act 2000 (Consequential Modifications No 1) Order 2001, SI 2001/1149, art 3(2), Sch 2.

**[1.577]**
**299   Index of defined expressions**
In this Act the expressions listed below are defined by or otherwise fall to be construed in accordance with the provisions indicated—

| | |
|---|---|
| ACAS | section 247(1) |
| act and action | section 298 |
| advertisement (in sections 137 to 143) | section 143(1) |
| [affected employees (in Part IV, Chapter II) | section 196(3)] |
| [agency worker | section 298] |
| [agent (of trade union) | section 119] |
| appropriately qualified actuary (in sections 38 to 41) | section 42 |
| associated employer | section 297 |
| branch or section (of trade union) | section 119 |
| [certificate of independence | section 298] |
| collective agreement and collective bargaining | section 178(1) |
| . . . | . . . |
| contract of employment | |
| —generally | section 295(1) |
| —in sections 226 to 234 | section 235 |
| —in relation to Crown employment | section 273(4)(a) |
| —in relation to House of Lords or House of Commons staff | section 277(4) and 278(4)(a) |

| | |
|---|---|
| contravention | section 298 |
| the court (in Part I) | section 121 |
| date of the ballot (in Part V) | section 246 |
| dismiss and dismissal | |
| —generally | section 298 |
| —in relation to Crown employment | section 273(4)(c) |
| —in relation to House of Commons staff | section 278(4)(b) |
| [the duty of confidentiality | section 24A(3)] |
| effective date of termination | section 298 |
| employee | |
| —generally | section 295(1) |
| —in relation to Crown employment | section 273(4)(a) |
| —in relation to House of Commons staff | section 278(4)(a) |
| —excludes police service | section 280 |
| [employee representatives (in Part IV, Chapter II) | section 196(1)] |
| employer | |
| —in relation to an employee | section 295(1) |
| —in relation to a worker | section 296(2) |
| —in relation to health service practitioners | section 279 |
| employment and employment agency (in sections 137 to 143) | section 143(1) |
| executive (of trade union) | section 119 |
| [financial affairs (of trade union) | section 119] |
| financial year (in Part VI) | section 72 |
| general secretary | section 119 |
| independent trade union (and related expressions) | section 5 |
| list | |
| —of trade unions | section 2 |
| —of employers' associations | section 123 |
| Northern Ireland union (in Part I) | section 120 |
| not protected (in sections 222 to 226) | section 219(4) |
| officer | |
| —of trade union | section 119 |
| —of employers' association | section 136 |
| official (of trade union) | section 119 |
| offshore employment | section 287 |
| . . . | . . . |
| political fund | section 82(1)(a) |
| political resolution | section 82(1)(a) |
| . . . | . . . |
| prescribed | section 293(1) |
| president | section 119 |
| recognised, recognition and related expressions | section 178(3) |
| . . . | . . . |
| [representatives of a trade union (in Part IV, Chapter II) | section 196(2)] |
| rules (of trade union) | section 119 |
| strike (in Part V) | section 246 |
| tort (as respects Scotland) | section 298 |
| trade dispute | |
| —in Part IV | section 218 |
| —in Part V | section 244 |

| trade union | section 1 |
|---|---|
| undertaking (of employer) | |
| —in relation to Crown employment | section 273(4)(e) and (f) |
| —in relation to House of Commons staff | section 278(4)(c) and (d) |
| worker | |
| —generally | section 296(1) |
| —includes health service practitioners | section 279 |
| —excludes police service | section 280 |
| working hours (in Part V) | section 246 |

**NOTES**

Entry "affected employees" inserted by the Collective Redundancies and Transfer of Undertakings (Protection of Employment) (Amendment) Regulations 1999, SI 1999/1925, regs 2(1), (2), 7.

Entry "agency worker" inserted by the Agency Workers Regulations 2010, SI 2010/93, reg 25, Sch 2, Pt 1, paras 1, 6, as from 1 October 2011.

Entries "agent (of trade union)", "the duty of confidentiality" and "financial affairs (of trade union)" inserted by the Trade Union Reform and Employment Rights Act 1993, s 49(2), Sch 8, para 89.

Entry "certificate of independence" inserted by the Employment Relations Act 2004, s 50(5).

Entries "the Commissioner" and "redundancy" (omitted) repealed by the Trade Union Reform and Employment Rights Act 1993, s 51, Sch 10.

Entry "employee representatives" inserted, and entry "representatives of a trade union" substituted, by the Collective Redundancies and Transfer of Undertakings (Protection of Employment) (Amendment) Regulations 1995, SI 1995/2587, reg 7.

Entry relating to "place of work (in Part V)" (omitted) repealed by the Employment Relations Act 2004, s 57, Sch 1, para 22, Sch 2.

Entry "post" (omitted) repealed by the Postal Services Act 2000 (Consequential Modifications No 1) 2001, SI 2001/1149, art 3(2), Sch 2.

*Final provisions*

**[1.578]**
**300 Repeals, consequential amendments, transitional provisions and savings**
(1), (2) (*Introduce Sch 1 (repeals), and Sch 2 (amendments) respectively.*)
(3) Schedule 3 contains transitional provisions and savings.

**[1.579]**
**301 Extent**
(1) This Act extends to England and Wales and [(apart from section 212A(6)) to] Scotland.
(2), (3) (*Application to Northern Ireland (outside the scope of this work).*)

**NOTES**

Sub-s (1): words in square brackets inserted by the Employment Rights (Dispute Resolution) Act 1998, s 15, Sch 1, para 10.

**[1.580]**
**302 Commencement**
This Act comes into force at the end of the period of three months beginning with the day on which it is passed.

**[1.581]**
**303 Short title**
This Act may be cited as the Trade Union and Labour Relations (Consolidation) Act 1992.

# SCHEDULES

## [SCHEDULE A1
## COLLECTIVE BARGAINING: RECOGNITION

Section 70A

**NOTES**

This Schedule was inserted by the Employment Relations Act 1999, s 1(1), (3), Sch 1.

## PART I
## RECOGNITION

*Introduction*

**[1.582]**
**1.** A trade union (or trade unions) seeking recognition to be entitled to conduct collective bargaining on behalf of a group or groups of workers may make a request in accordance with this Part of this Schedule.

**2.** (1)   This paragraph applies for the purposes of this Part of this Schedule.

(2)   References to the bargaining unit are to the group of workers concerned (or the groups taken together).

(3)   References to the proposed bargaining unit are to the bargaining unit proposed in the request for recognition.

[(3A)   References to an appropriate bargaining unit's being decided by the CAC are to a bargaining unit's being decided by the CAC to be appropriate under paragraph 19(2) or (3) or 19A(2) or (3).]

(4)   References to the employer are to the employer of the workers constituting the bargaining unit concerned.

(5)   References to the parties are to the union (or unions) and the employer.

**3.** (1)   This paragraph applies for the purposes of this Part of this Schedule.

(2)   The meaning of collective bargaining given by section 178(1) shall not apply.

(3)   References to collective bargaining are to negotiations relating to pay, hours and holidays; but this has effect subject to sub-paragraph (4).

(4)   If the parties agree matters as the subject of collective bargaining, references to collective bargaining are to negotiations relating to the agreed matters; and this is the case whether the agreement is made before or after the time when the CAC issues a declaration, or the parties agree, that the union is (or unions are) entitled to conduct collective bargaining on behalf of a bargaining unit.

(5)   Sub-paragraph (4) does not apply in construing paragraph 31(3).

(6)   Sub-paragraphs (2) to (5) do not apply in construing paragraph 35 or 44.

**NOTES**

Inserted as noted at the beginning of this Schedule.
Para 2: sub-para (3A) inserted by the Employment Relations Act 2004, s 57(1), Sch 1, para 23(1), (2).

*Request for recognition*

**[1.583]**
**4.** (1)   The union or unions seeking recognition must make a request for recognition to the employer.

(2)   Paragraphs 5 to 9 apply to the request.

**5.** The request is not valid unless it is received by the employer.

**6.** The request is not valid unless the union (or each of the unions) has a certificate [of independence].

**7.** (1)   The request is not valid unless the employer, taken with any associated employer or employers, employs—
    (a)   at least 21 workers on the day the employer receives the request, or
    (b)   an average of at least 21 workers in the 13 weeks ending with that day.

(2)   To find the average under sub-paragraph (1)(b)—
    (a)   take the number of workers employed in each of the 13 weeks (including workers not employed for the whole of the week);
    (b)   aggregate the 13 numbers;
    (c)   divide the aggregate by 13.

(3)  For the purposes of sub-paragraph (1)(a) any worker employed by an associated company incorporated outside Great Britain must be ignored unless the day the request was made fell within a period during which he ordinarily worked in Great Britain.

(4)  For the purposes of sub-paragraph (1)(b) any worker employed by an associated company incorporated outside Great Britain must be ignored in relation to a week unless the whole or any part of that week fell within a period during which he ordinarily worked in Great Britain.

(5)  For the purposes of sub-paragraphs (3) and (4) a worker who is employed on board a ship registered in the register maintained under section 8 of the Merchant Shipping Act 1995 shall be treated as ordinarily working in Great Britain unless—
  (a)  the ship's entry in the register specifies a port outside Great Britain as the port to which the vessel is to be treated as belonging,
  (b)  the employment is wholly outside Great Britain, or
  (c)  the worker is not ordinarily resident in Great Britain.

[(5A)  Sub-paragraph (5B) applies to an agency worker whose contract within regulation 3(1)(b) of the Agency Workers Regulations 2010 (contract with the temporary work agency) is not a contract of employment.

(5B)  For the purposes of sub-paragraphs (1) and (2), the agency worker is to be treated as having a contract of employment with the temporary work agency for the duration of the assignment with the employer (and "assignment" has the same meaning as in those Regulations).]

(6)  The Secretary of State may by order—
  (a)  provide that sub-paragraphs (1) to (5) are not to apply, or are not to apply in specified circumstances, or
  (b)  vary the number of workers for the time being specified in sub-paragraph (1);
and different provision may be made for different circumstances.

(7)  An order under sub-paragraph (6)—
  (a)  shall be made by statutory instrument, and
  (b)  may include supplementary, incidental, saving or transitional provisions.

(8)  No such order shall be made unless a draft of it has been laid before Parliament and approved by a resolution of each House of Parliament.

**8.**  The request is not valid unless it—
  (a)  is in writing,
  (b)  identifies the union or unions and the bargaining unit, and
  (c)  states that it is made under this Schedule.

**9.**  The Secretary of State may by order made by statutory instrument prescribe the form of requests and the procedure for making them; and if he does so the request is not valid unless it complies with the order.

**NOTES**
Inserted as noted at the beginning of this Schedule.
Para 6: words in square brackets substituted by the Employment Relations Act 2004, s 50(6).
Para 7: sub-paras (5A), (5B) inserted by the Agency Workers Regulations 2010, SI 2010/93, reg 25, Sch 2, Pt 1, paras 1, 7(1), (2), as from 1 October 2011.
Orders: as of 6 April 2013 no Orders had been made under para 7 or 9.

*Parties agree*

**[1.584]**
**10.**  (1)  If before the end of the first period the parties agree a bargaining unit and that the union is (or unions are) to be recognised as entitled to conduct collective bargaining on behalf of the unit, no further steps are to be taken under this Part of this Schedule.

(2)  If before the end of the first period the employer informs the union (or unions) that the employer does not accept the request but is willing to negotiate, sub-paragraph (3) applies.

(3)  The parties may conduct negotiations with a view to agreeing a bargaining unit and that the union is (or unions are) to be recognised as entitled to conduct collective bargaining on behalf of the unit.

(4)  If such an agreement is made before the end of the second period no further steps are to be taken under this Part of this Schedule.

(5)  The employer and the union (or unions) may request ACAS to assist in conducting the negotiations.

(6)  The first period is the period of 10 working days starting with the day after that on which the employer receives the request for recognition.

(7)  The second period is—
  (a)  the period of 20 working days starting with the day after that on which the first period ends, or
  (b)  such longer period (so starting) as the parties may from time to time agree.

**NOTES**
Inserted as noted at the beginning of this Schedule.

*Employer rejects request*

**[1.585]**
**11.** (1)  This paragraph applies if—
   (a)  before the end of the first period the employer fails to respond to the request, or
   (b)  before the end of the first period the employer informs the union (or unions) that the employer does not accept the request (without indicating a willingness to negotiate).

(2)  The union (or unions) may apply to the CAC to decide both these questions—
   [(a)  whether the proposed bargaining unit is appropriate;]
   (b)  whether the union has (or unions have) the support of a majority of the workers constituting the appropriate bargaining unit.

**NOTES**
Inserted as noted at the beginning of this Schedule.
Para 11: sub-para (2)(a) substituted by the Employment Relations Act 2004, s 1(1).

*Negotiations fail*

**[1.586]**
**12.** (1)  Sub-paragraph (2) applies if—
   (a)  the employer informs the union (or unions) under paragraph 10(2), and
   (b)  no agreement is made before the end of the second period.

(2)  The union (or unions) may apply to the CAC to decide both these questions—
   [(a)  whether the proposed bargaining unit is appropriate;]
   (b)  whether the union has (or unions have) the support of a majority of the workers constituting the appropriate bargaining unit.

(3)  Sub-paragraph (4) applies if—
   (a)  the employer informs the union (or unions) under paragraph 10(2), and
   (b)  before the end of the second period the parties agree a bargaining unit but not that the union is (or unions are) to be recognised as entitled to conduct collective bargaining on behalf of the unit.

(4)  The union (or unions) may apply to the CAC to decide the question whether the union has (or unions have) the support of a majority of the workers constituting the bargaining unit.

(5)  But no application may be made under this paragraph if within the period of 10 working days starting with the day after that on which the employer informs the union (or unions) under paragraph 10(2) the employer proposes that ACAS be requested to assist in conducting the negotiations and—
   (a)  the union rejects (or unions reject) the proposal, or
   (b)  the union fails (or unions fail) to accept the proposal within the period of 10 working days starting with the day after that on which the employer makes the proposal.

**NOTES**
Inserted as noted at the beginning of this Schedule.
Para 12: sub-para (2)(a) substituted by the Employment Relations Act 2004, s 1(2).

*Acceptance of applications*

**[1.587]**
**13.** The CAC must give notice to the parties of receipt of an application under paragraph 11 or 12.

**14.** (1)  This paragraph applies if—
   (a)  two or more relevant applications are made,
   (b)  at least one worker falling within one of the relevant bargaining units also falls within the other relevant bargaining unit (or units), and
   (c)  the CAC has not accepted any of the applications.

(2)  A relevant application is an application under paragraph 11 or 12.

(3)  In relation to a relevant application, the relevant bargaining unit is—
   (a)  the proposed bargaining unit, where the application is under paragraph 11(2) or 12(2);
   (b)  the agreed bargaining unit, where the application is under paragraph 12(4).

(4)  Within the acceptance period the CAC must decide, with regard to each relevant application, whether the 10 per cent test is satisfied.

(5)  The 10 per cent test is satisfied if members of the union (or unions) constitute at least 10 per cent of the workers constituting the relevant bargaining unit.

(6)  The acceptance period is—

(a)   the period of 10 working days starting with the day after that on which the CAC receives the last relevant application, or

(b)   such longer period (so starting) as the CAC may specify to the parties by notice containing reasons for the extension.

(7)   If the CAC decides that—

(a)   the 10 per cent test is satisfied with regard to more than one of the relevant applications, or

(b)   the 10 per cent test is satisfied with regard to none of the relevant applications,

the CAC must not accept any of the relevant applications.

(8)   If the CAC decides that the 10 per cent test is satisfied with regard to one only of the relevant applications the CAC—

(a)   must proceed under paragraph 15 with regard to that application, and

(b)   must not accept any of the other relevant applications.

(9)   The CAC must give notice of its decision to the parties.

(10)   If by virtue of this paragraph the CAC does not accept an application, no further steps are to be taken under this Part of this Schedule in relation to that application.

**15.**  (1)   This paragraph applies to these applications—

(a)   any application with regard to which no decision has to be made under paragraph 14;

(b)   any application with regard to which the CAC must proceed under this paragraph by virtue of paragraph 14.

(2)   Within the acceptance period the CAC must decide whether—

(a)   the request for recognition to which the application relates is valid within the terms of paragraphs 5 to 9, and

(b)   the application is made in accordance with paragraph 11 or 12 and admissible within the terms of paragraphs 33 to 42.

(3)   In deciding those questions the CAC must consider any evidence which it has been given by the employer or the union (or unions).

(4)   If the CAC decides that the request is not valid or the application is not made in accordance with paragraph 11 or 12 or is not admissible—

(a)   the CAC must give notice of its decision to the parties,

(b)   the CAC must not accept the application, and

(c)   no further steps are to be taken under this Part of this Schedule.

(5)   If the CAC decides that the request is valid and the application is made in accordance with paragraph 11 or 12 and is admissible it must—

(a)   accept the application, and

(b)   give notice of the acceptance to the parties.

(6)   The acceptance period is—

(a)   the period of 10 working days starting with the day after that on which the CAC receives the application, or

(b)   such longer period (so starting) as the CAC may specify to the parties by notice containing reasons for the extension.

**NOTES**
Inserted as noted at the beginning of this Schedule.

*Withdrawal of application*

**[1.588]**
**16.**  (1)   If an application under paragraph 11 or 12 is accepted by the CAC, the union (or unions) may not withdraw the application—

(a)   after the CAC issues a declaration under paragraph [19F(5) or] 22(2), or

(b)   after the union (or the last of the unions) receives notice under paragraph 22(3) or 23(2).

(2)   If an application is withdrawn by the union (or unions)—

(a)   the CAC must give notice of the withdrawal to the employer, and

(b)   no further steps are to be taken under this Part of this Schedule.

**NOTES**
Inserted as noted at the beginning of this Schedule.
Para 16: words in square brackets in sub-para (1) inserted by the Employment Relations Act 2004, s 57(1), Sch 1, para 23(1), (3).

*Notice to cease consideration of application*

**[1.589]**
**17.**  (1)   This paragraph applies if the CAC has received an application under paragraph 11 or 12 and—

(a)   it has not decided whether the application is admissible, or

(b)   it has decided that the application is admissible.

(2)  No further steps are to be taken under this Part of this Schedule if, before the final event occurs, the parties give notice to the CAC that they want no further steps to be taken.

(3)  The final event occurs when the first of the following occurs—
  (a)   the CAC issues a declaration under paragraph [19F(5) or] 22(2) in consequence of the application;
  (b)   the last day of the notification period ends;
and the notification period is that defined by paragraph [24(6)] and arising from the application.

---

**NOTES**

Inserted as noted at the beginning of this Schedule.

Para 17: words in square brackets in sub-para (3) inserted, and number in square brackets in that sub-paragraph substituted, by the Employment Relations Act 2004, s 57(1), Sch 1, para 23(1), (4).

---

*Appropriate bargaining unit*

**[1.590]**
**18.**  (1)   If the CAC accepts an application under paragraph 11(2) or 12(2) it must try to help the parties to reach within the appropriate period an agreement as to what the appropriate bargaining unit is.

(2)   The appropriate period is [(subject to any notice under sub-paragraph (3), (4) or (5))]—
  (a)   the period of 20 working days starting with the day after that on which the CAC gives notice of acceptance of the application, or
  (b)   such longer period (so starting) as the CAC may specify to the parties by notice containing reasons for the extension.

[(3)   If, during the appropriate period, the CAC concludes that there is no reasonable prospect of the parties' agreeing an appropriate bargaining unit before the time when (apart from this sub-paragraph) the appropriate period would end, the CAC may, by a notice given to the parties, declare that the appropriate period ends with the date of the notice.

(4)   If, during the appropriate period, the parties apply to the CAC for a declaration that the appropriate period is to end with a date (specified in the application) which is earlier than the date with which it would otherwise end, the CAC may, by a notice given to the parties, declare that the appropriate period ends with the specified date.

(5)   If the CAC has declared under sub-paragraph (4) that the appropriate period ends with a specified date, it may before that date by a notice given to the parties specify a later date with which the appropriate period ends.

(6)   A notice under sub-paragraph (3) must contain reasons for reaching the conclusion mentioned in that sub-paragraph.

(7)   A notice under sub-paragraph (5) must contain reasons for the extension of the appropriate period.]

**[18A.**  (1)   This paragraph applies if the CAC accepts an application under paragraph 11(2) or 12(2).

(2)   Within 5 working days starting with the day after that on which the CAC gives the employer notice of acceptance of the application, the employer must supply the following information to the union (or unions) and the CAC—
  (a)   a list of the categories of worker in the proposed bargaining unit,
  (b)   a list of the workplaces at which the workers in the proposed bargaining unit work, and
  (c)   the number of workers the employer reasonably believes to be in each category at each workplace.

(3)   The lists and numbers supplied under this paragraph must be as accurate as is reasonably practicable in the light of the information in the possession of the employer at the time when he complies with sub-paragraph (2).

(4)   The lists and numbers supplied to the union (or unions) and to the CAC must be the same.

(5)   For the purposes of this paragraph, the workplace at which a worker works is—
  (a)   if the person works at or from a single set of premises, those premises, and
  (b)   in any other case, the premises with which the worker's employment has the closest connection.]

**[19.**  (1)   This paragraph applies if—
  (a)   the CAC accepts an application under paragraph 11(2) or 12(2),
  (b)   the parties have not agreed an appropriate bargaining unit at the end of the appropriate period (defined by paragraph 18), and
  (c)   at the end of that period either no request under paragraph 19A(1)(b) has been made or such a request has been made but the condition in paragraph 19A(1)(c) has not been met.

(2)   Within the decision period, the CAC must decide whether the proposed bargaining unit is appropriate.

(3)  If the CAC decides that the proposed bargaining unit is not appropriate, it must also decide within the decision period a bargaining unit which is appropriate.

(4)  The decision period is—
  (a)  the period of 10 working days starting with the day after that with which the appropriate period ends, or
  (b)  such longer period (so starting) as the CAC may specify to the parties by notice containing reasons for the extension.

**19A.**  (1)  This paragraph applies if—
  (a)  the CAC accepts an application under paragraph 11(2) or 12(2),
  (b)  during the appropriate period (defined by paragraph 18), the CAC is requested by the union (or unions) to make a decision under this paragraph, and
  (c)  the CAC is, either at the time the request is made or at a later time during the appropriate period, of the opinion that the employer has failed to comply with the duty imposed by paragraph 18A.

(2)  Within the decision period, the CAC must decide whether the proposed bargaining unit is appropriate.

(3)  If the CAC decides that the proposed bargaining unit is not appropriate, it must also decide within the decision period a bargaining unit which is appropriate.

(4)  The decision period is—
  (a)  the period of 10 working days starting with the day after the day on which the request is made, or
  (b)  such longer period (so starting) as the CAC may specify to the parties by notice containing reasons for the extension.

**19B.**  (1)  This paragraph applies if the CAC has to decide whether a bargaining unit is appropriate for the purposes of paragraph 19(2) or (3) or 19A(2) or (3).

(2)  The CAC must take these matters into account—
  (a)  the need for the unit to be compatible with effective management;
  (b)  the matters listed in sub-paragraph (3), so far as they do not conflict with that need.

(3)  The matters are—
  (a)  the views of the employer and of the union (or unions);
  (b)  existing national and local bargaining arrangements;
  (c)  the desirability of avoiding small fragmented bargaining units within an undertaking;
  (d)  the characteristics of workers falling within the bargaining unit under consideration and of any other employees of the employer whom the CAC considers relevant;
  (e)  the location of workers.

(4)  In taking an employer's views into account for the purpose of deciding whether the proposed bargaining unit is appropriate, the CAC must take into account any view the employer has about any other bargaining unit that he considers would be appropriate.

(5)  The CAC must give notice of its decision to the parties.]

---

**NOTES**

Inserted as noted at the beginning of this Schedule.

Para 18: words in square brackets in sub-para (2) inserted, and sub-paras (3)–(7) added, by the Employment Relations Act 2004, s 2(1), (2).

Para 18A: inserted by the Employment Relations Act 2004, s 3.

Paras 19, 19A, 19B: substituted, for the original para 19, by the Employment Relations Act 2004, s 4.

---

*[Union communications with workers after acceptance of application*

**[1.591]**
**19C.**  (1)  This paragraph applies if the CAC accepts an application under paragraph 11(2) or 12(2) or (4).

(2)  The union (or unions) may apply to the CAC for the appointment of a suitable independent person to handle communications during the initial period between the union (or unions) and the relevant workers.

(3)  In the case of an application under paragraph 11(2) or 12(2), the relevant workers are—
  (a)  in relation to any time before an appropriate bargaining unit is agreed by the parties or decided by the CAC, those falling within the proposed bargaining unit, and
  (b)  in relation to any time after an appropriate bargaining unit is so agreed or decided, those falling within the bargaining unit agreed or decided upon.

(4)  In the case of an application under paragraph 12(4), the relevant workers are those falling within the bargaining unit agreed by the parties.

(5)  The initial period is the period starting with the day on which the CAC informs the parties under sub-paragraph (7)(b) and ending with the first day on which any of the following occurs—
  (a)  the application under paragraph 11 or 12 is withdrawn;

   (b)   the CAC gives notice to the union (or unions) of a decision under paragraph 20 that the application is invalid;

   (c)   the CAC notifies the union (or unions) of a declaration issued under paragraph 19F(5) or 22(2);

   (d)   the CAC informs the union (or unions) under paragraph 25(9) of the name of the person appointed to conduct a ballot.

(6)   A person is a suitable independent person if—

   (a)   he satisfies such conditions as may be specified for the purposes of paragraph 25(7)(a) by an order under that provision, or is himself specified for those purposes by such an order, and

   (b)   there are no grounds for believing either that he will carry out any functions arising from his appointment otherwise than competently or that his independence in relation to those functions might reasonably be called into question.

(7)   On an application under sub-paragraph (2) the CAC must as soon as reasonably practicable—

   (a)   make such an appointment as is mentioned in that sub-paragraph, and

   (b)   inform the parties of the name of the person appointed and the date of his appointment.

(8)   The person appointed by the CAC is referred to in paragraphs 19D and 19E as "the appointed person".

**19D.**   (1)   An employer who is informed by the CAC under paragraph 19C(7)(b) must comply with the following duties (so far as it is reasonable to expect him to do so).

(2)   The duties are—

   (a)   to give to the CAC, within the period of 10 working days starting with the day after that on which the employer is informed under paragraph 19C(7)(b), the names and home addresses of the relevant workers;

   (b)   if the relevant workers change as a result of an appropriate bargaining unit being agreed by the parties or decided by the CAC, to give to the CAC, within the period of 10 working days starting with the day after that on which the bargaining unit is agreed or the CAC's decision is notified to the employer, the names and home addresses of those who are now the relevant workers;

   (c)   to give to the CAC, as soon as reasonably practicable, the name and home address of any worker who joins the bargaining unit after the employer has complied with paragraph (a) or (b);

   (d)   to inform the CAC, as soon as reasonably practicable, of any worker whose name has been given to the CAC under paragraph (a), (b) or (c) and who ceases to be a relevant worker (otherwise than by reason of a change mentioned in paragraph (b)).

(3)   Nothing in sub-paragraph (2) requires the employer to give information to the CAC after the end of the initial period.

(4)   As soon as reasonably practicable after the CAC receives any information under sub-paragraph (2), it must pass it on to the appointed person.

**19E.**   (1)   During the initial period, the appointed person must if asked to do so by the union (or unions) send to any worker—

   (a)   whose name and home address have been passed on to him under paragraph 19D(4), and

   (b)   who is (so far as the appointed person is aware) still a relevant worker,

any information supplied by the union (or unions) to the appointed person.

(2)   The costs of the appointed person shall be borne—

   (a)   if the application under paragraph 19C was made by one union, by the union, and

   (b)   if that application was made by more than one union, by the unions in such proportions as they jointly indicate to the appointed person or, in the absence of such an indication, in equal shares.

(3)   The appointed person may send to the union (or each of the unions) a demand stating his costs and the amount of those costs to be borne by the recipient.

(4)   In such a case the recipient must pay the amount stated to the person sending the demand and must do so within the period of 15 working days starting with the day after that on which the demand is received.

(5)   In England and Wales, if the amount stated is not paid in accordance with sub-paragraph (4) it shall, if *a county court* so orders, be recoverable *by execution issued from that court* or otherwise as if it were payable under an order of that court.

(6)   *Where an amount is recoverable under sub-paragraph (5) execution may be carried out*, to the same extent and in the same manner as if the union were a body corporate, against any property held in trust for the union other than protected property as defined in section 23(2).

(7)   References to the costs of the appointed person are to—

(a)   the costs wholly, exclusively and necessarily incurred by the appointed person in connection with handling during the initial period communications between the union (or unions) and the relevant workers,

(b)   such reasonable amount as the appointed person charges for his services, and

(c)   such other costs as the union (or unions) agree.

**19F.** (1)   If the CAC is satisfied that the employer has failed to fulfil a duty mentioned in paragraph 19D(2), and the initial period has not yet ended, the CAC may order the employer—

(a)   to take such steps to remedy the failure as the CAC considers reasonable and specifies in the order, and

(b)   to do so within such period as the CAC considers reasonable and specifies in the order; and in this paragraph a "remedial order" means an order under this sub-paragraph.

(2)   If the CAC is satisfied that the employer has failed to comply with a remedial order and the initial period has not yet ended, the CAC must as soon as reasonably practicable notify the employer and the union (or unions) that it is satisfied that the employer has failed to comply.

(3)   A remedial order and a notice under sub-paragraph (2) must draw the recipient's attention to the effect of sub-paragraphs (4) and (5).

(4)   Sub-paragraph (5) applies if—

(a)   the CAC is satisfied that the employer has failed to comply with a remedial order,

(b)   the parties have agreed an appropriate bargaining unit or the CAC has decided an appropriate bargaining unit,

(c)   in the case of an application under paragraph 11(2) or 12(2), the CAC, if required to do so, has decided under paragraph 20 that the application is not invalid, and

(d)   the initial period has not yet ended.

(5)   The CAC may issue a declaration that the union is (or unions are) recognised as entitled to conduct collective bargaining on behalf of the workers constituting the bargaining unit.]

**NOTES**

This Schedule was inserted as noted at the beginning of this Schedule.

Paras 19C–19F: inserted by the Employment Relations Act 2004, s 5(1).

Para 19E: inserted as noted above; for the first words in italics in sub-para (5) there are substituted the words "the county court" by the Crime and Courts Act 2013, s 17(5), Sch 9, Pt 3, para 52, as from a day to be appointed; for the second words in italics in sub-para (5) there are substituted the words "under section 85 of the County Courts Act 1984" and for the words in italics in sub-para (6) there are substituted the words "Where a warrant of control is issued under section 85 of the 1984 Act to recover an amount in accordance with sub-paragraph (5), the power conferred by the warrant is exercisable" by the Tribunals, Courts and Enforcement Act 2007, s 62(3), Sch 13, paras 108, 109, as from a day to be appointed.

*Union recognition*

**[1.592]**
**20.** (1)   This paragraph applies if—

(a)   the CAC accepts an application under paragraph 11(2) or 12(2),

(b)   the parties have agreed an appropriate bargaining unit at the end of the appropriate period [(defined by paragraph 18)], or the CAC has decided an appropriate bargaining unit, and

(c)   that bargaining unit differs from the proposed bargaining unit.

(2)   Within the decision period the CAC must decide whether the application is invalid within the terms of paragraphs 43 to 50.

(3)   In deciding whether the application is invalid, the CAC must consider any evidence which it has been given by the employer or the union (or unions).

(4)   If the CAC decides that the application is invalid—

(a)   the CAC must give notice of its decision to the parties,

(b)   the CAC must not proceed with the application, and

(c)   no further steps are to be taken under this Part of this Schedule.

(5)   If the CAC decides that the application is not invalid it must—

(a)   proceed with the application, and

(b)   give notice to the parties that it is so proceeding.

(6)   The decision period is—

(a)   the period of 10 working days starting with the day after that on which the parties agree an appropriate bargaining unit or the CAC decides an appropriate bargaining unit, or

(b)   such longer period (so starting) as the CAC may specify to the parties by notice containing reasons for the extension.

**21.** (1)   This paragraph applies if—

(a)   the CAC accepts an application under paragraph 11(2) or 12(2),

(b)   the parties have agreed an appropriate bargaining unit at the end of the appropriate period [(defined by paragraph 18)], or the CAC has decided an appropriate bargaining unit, and

(c)   that bargaining unit is the same as the proposed bargaining unit.

(2)   This paragraph also applies if the CAC accepts an application under paragraph 12(4).

(3)   The CAC must proceed with the application.

**22.** (1)   This paragraph applies if—
   (a)   the CAC proceeds with an application in accordance with paragraph 20 or 21 [(and makes no declaration under paragraph 19F(5))], and
   (b)   the CAC is satisfied that a majority of the workers constituting the bargaining unit are members of the union (or unions).

(2)   The CAC must issue a declaration that the union is (or unions are) recognised as entitled to conduct collective bargaining on behalf of the workers constituting the bargaining unit.

(3)   But if any of the three qualifying conditions is fulfilled, instead of issuing a declaration under sub-paragraph (2) the CAC must give notice to the parties that it intends to arrange for the holding of a secret ballot in which the workers constituting the bargaining unit are asked whether they want the union (or unions) to conduct collective bargaining on their behalf.

(4)   These are the three qualifying conditions—
   (a)   the CAC is satisfied that a ballot should be held in the interests of good industrial relations;
   [(b)   the CAC has evidence, which it considers to be credible, from a significant number of the union members within the bargaining unit that they do not want the union (or unions) to conduct collective bargaining on their behalf;]
   (c)   membership evidence is produced which leads the CAC to conclude that there are doubts whether a significant number of the union members within the bargaining unit want the union (or unions) to conduct collective bargaining on their behalf.

(5)   For the purposes of sub-paragraph (4)(c) membership evidence is—
   (a)   evidence about the circumstances in which union members became members;
   (b)   evidence about the length of time for which union members have been members, in a case where the CAC is satisfied that such evidence should be taken into account.

**23.** (1)   This paragraph applies if—
   (a)   the CAC proceeds with an application in accordance with paragraph 20 or 21 [(and makes no declaration under paragraph 19F(5))], and
   (b)   the CAC is not satisfied that a majority of the workers constituting the bargaining unit are members of the union (or unions).

(2)   The CAC must give notice to the parties that it intends to arrange for the holding of a secret ballot in which the workers constituting the bargaining unit are asked whether they want the union (or unions) to conduct collective bargaining on their behalf.

**24.** (1)   This paragraph applies if the CAC gives notice under paragraph 22(3) or 23(2).

(2)   Within the notification period—
   (a)   the union (or unions), or
   (b)   the union (or unions) and the employer,
may notify the CAC that the party making the notification does not (or the parties making the notification do not) want the CAC to arrange for the holding of the ballot.

(3)   If the CAC is so notified—
   (a)   it must not arrange for the holding of the ballot,
   (b)   it must inform the parties that it will not arrange for the holding of the ballot, and why, and
   (c)   no further steps are to be taken under this Part of this Schedule.

(4)   If the CAC is not so notified it must arrange for the holding of the ballot.

[(5)   The notification period is, in relation to notification by the union (or unions)—
   (a)   the period of 10 working days starting with the day on which the union (or last of the unions) receives the CAC's notice under paragraph 22(3) or 23(2), or
   (b)   such longer period so starting as the CAC may specify to the parties by notice.

(6)   The notification period is, in relation to notification by the union (or unions) and the employer—
   (a)   the period of 10 working days starting with the day on which the last of the parties receives the CAC's notice under paragraph 22(3) or 23(2), or
   (b)   such longer period so starting as the CAC may specify to the parties by notice.

(7)   The CAC may give a notice under sub-paragraph (5)(b) or (6)(b) only if the parties have applied jointly to it for the giving of such a notice.]

**25.** (1)   This paragraph applies if the CAC arranges under paragraph 24 for the holding of a ballot.

(2)   The ballot must be conducted by a qualified independent person appointed by the CAC.

(3)   The ballot must be conducted within—
   (a)   the period of 20 working days starting with the day after that on which the qualified independent person is appointed, or

    (b)   such longer period (so starting) as the CAC may decide.

(4)  The ballot must be conducted—
    (a)   at a workplace or workplaces decided by the CAC,
    (b)   by post, or
    (c)   by a combination of the methods described in sub-paragraphs (a) and (b),

depending on the CAC's preference.

(5)  In deciding how the ballot is to be conducted the CAC must take into account—
    (a)   the likelihood of the ballot being affected by unfairness or malpractice if it were conducted at a workplace or workplaces;
    (b)   costs and practicality;
    (c)   such other matters as the CAC considers appropriate.

(6)  The CAC may not decide that the ballot is to be conducted as mentioned in sub-paragraph (4)(c) unless there are special factors making such a decision appropriate; and special factors include—
    (a)   factors arising from the location of workers or the nature of their employment;
    (b)   factors put to the CAC by the employer or the union (or unions).

[(6A)  If the CAC decides that the ballot must (in whole or in part) be conducted at a workplace (or workplaces), it may require arrangements to be made for workers—
    (a)   who (but for the arrangements) would be prevented by the CAC's decision from voting by post, and
    (b)   who are unable, for reasons relating to those workers as individuals, to cast their votes in the ballot at the workplace (or at any of them),

to be given the opportunity (if they request it far enough in advance of the ballot for this to be practicable) to vote by post; and the CAC's imposing such a requirement is not to be treated for the purposes of sub-paragraph (6) as a decision that the ballot be conducted as mentioned in sub-paragraph (4)(c).]

(7)  A person is a qualified independent person if—
    (a)   he satisfies such conditions as may be specified for the purposes of this paragraph by order of the Secretary of State or is himself so specified, and
    (b)   there are no grounds for believing either that he will carry out any functions conferred on him in relation to the ballot otherwise than competently or that his independence in relation to the ballot might reasonably be called into question.

(8)  An order under sub-paragraph (7)(a) shall be made by statutory instrument subject to annulment in pursuance of a resolution of either House of Parliament.

(9)  As soon as is reasonably practicable after the CAC is required under paragraph 24 to arrange for the holding of a ballot it must inform the parties—
    (a)   that it is so required;
    (b)   of the name of the person appointed to conduct the ballot and the date of his appointment;
    (c)   of the period within which the ballot must be conducted;
    (d)   whether the ballot is to be conducted by post or at a workplace or workplaces;
    (e)   of the workplace or workplaces concerned (if the ballot is to be conducted at a workplace or workplaces).

**26.**  (1)  An employer who is informed by the CAC under paragraph 25(9) must comply with the following [five] duties.

(2)  The first duty is to co-operate generally, in connection with the ballot, with the union (or unions) and the person appointed to conduct the ballot; and the second and third duties are not to prejudice the generality of this.

(3)  The second duty is to give to the union (or unions) such access to the workers constituting the bargaining unit as is reasonable to enable the union (or unions) to inform the workers of the object of the ballot and to seek their support and their opinions on the issues involved.

(4)  The third duty is to do the following (so far as it is reasonable to expect the employer to do so)—
    (a)   to give to the CAC, within the period of 10 working days starting with the day after that on which the employer is informed under paragraph 25(9), the names and home addresses of the workers constituting the bargaining unit;
    (b)   to give to the CAC, as soon as is reasonably practicable, the name and home address of any worker who joins the unit after the employer has complied with paragraph (a);
    (c)   to inform the CAC, as soon as is reasonably practicable, of any worker whose name has been given to the CAC under paragraph [19D or paragraph (a) or (b) of this sub-paragraph and] who ceases to be within the unit.

[(4A)  The fourth duty is to refrain from making any offer to any or all of the workers constituting the bargaining unit which—

(a)    has or is likely to have the effect of inducing any or all of them not to attend any relevant meeting between the union (or unions) and the workers constituting the bargaining unit, and

(b)    is not reasonable in the circumstances.

(4B)    The fifth duty is to refrain from taking or threatening to take any action against a worker solely or mainly on the grounds that he—

(a)    attended or took part in any relevant meeting between the union (or unions) and the workers constituting the bargaining unit, or

(b)    indicated his intention to attend or take part in such a meeting.

(4C)    A meeting is a relevant meeting in relation to a worker for the purposes of sub-paragraphs (4A) and (4B) if—

(a)    it is organised in accordance with any agreement reached concerning the second duty or as a result of a step ordered to be taken under paragraph 27 to remedy a failure to comply with that duty, and

(b)    it is one which the employer is, by such an agreement or order as is mentioned in paragraph (a), required to permit the worker to attend.

(4D)    Without prejudice to the generality of the second duty imposed by this paragraph, an employer is to be taken to have failed to comply with that duty if—

(a)    he refuses a request for a meeting between the union (or unions) and any or all of the workers constituting the bargaining unit to be held in the absence of the employer or any representative of his (other than one who has been invited to attend the meeting) and it is not reasonable in the circumstances for him to do so,

(b)    he or a representative of his attends such a meeting without having been invited to do so,

(c)    he seeks to record or otherwise be informed of the proceedings at any such meeting and it is not reasonable in the circumstances for him to do so, or

(d)    he refuses to give an undertaking that he will not seek to record or otherwise be informed of the proceedings at any such meeting unless it is reasonable in the circumstances for him to do either of those things.

(4E)    The fourth and fifth duties do not confer any rights on a worker; but that does not affect any other right which a worker may have.]

[(4F)    Sub-paragraph (4)(a) does not apply to names and addresses that the employer has already given to the CAC under paragraph 19D.

(4G)    Where (because of sub-paragraph (4F)) the employer does not have to comply with sub-paragraph (4)(a), the reference in sub-paragraph (4)(b) to the time when the employer complied with sub-paragraph (4)(a) is to be read as a reference to the time when the employer is informed under paragraph 25(9).

(4H)    If—

(a)    a person was appointed on an application under paragraph 19C, and

(b)    the person appointed to conduct the ballot is not that person,

the CAC must, as soon as is reasonably practicable, pass on to the person appointed to conduct the ballot the names and addresses given to it under paragraph 19D.]

(5)    As soon as is reasonably practicable after the CAC receives any information under sub-paragraph (4) it must pass it on to the person appointed to conduct the ballot.

(6)    If asked to do so by the union (or unions) the person appointed to conduct the ballot must send to any worker—

(a)    whose name and home address have been [passed on to him under paragraph 19D or this paragraph], and

(b)    who is still within the unit (so far as the person so appointed is aware),

any information supplied by the union (or unions) to the person so appointed.

(7)    The duty under sub-paragraph (6) does not apply unless the union bears (or unions bear) the cost of sending the information.

[(8)    Each of the powers specified in sub-paragraph (9) shall be taken to include power to issue Codes of Practice—

(a)    about reasonable access for the purposes of sub-paragraph (3), and

(b)    about the fourth duty imposed by this paragraph.

(9)    The powers are—

(a)    the power of ACAS under section 199(1);

(b)    the power of the Secretary of State under section 203(1)(a).]

**27.**    (1)    If the CAC is satisfied that the employer has failed to fulfil any of the [duties imposed on him] by paragraph 26, and the ballot has not been held, the CAC may order the employer—

(a)    to take such steps to remedy the failure as the CAC considers reasonable and specifies in the order, and

(b)    to do so within such period as the CAC considers reasonable and specifies in the order.

(2)  If the CAC is satisfied that the employer has failed to comply with an order under sub-paragraph (1), and the ballot has not been held, the CAC may issue a declaration that the union is (or unions are) recognised as entitled to conduct collective bargaining on behalf of the bargaining unit.

(3)  If the CAC issues a declaration under sub-paragraph (2) it shall take steps to cancel the holding of the ballot; and if the ballot is held it shall have no effect.

[27A.  (1)  Each of the parties informed by the CAC under paragraph 25(9) must refrain from using any unfair practice.

(2)  A party uses an unfair practice if, with a view to influencing the result of the ballot, the party—
- (a)  offers to pay money or give money's worth to a worker entitled to vote in the ballot in return for the worker's agreement to vote in a particular way or to abstain from voting,
- (b)  makes an outcome-specific offer to a worker entitled to vote in the ballot,
- (c)  coerces or attempts to coerce a worker entitled to vote in the ballot to disclose—
  - (i)  whether he intends to vote or to abstain from voting in the ballot, or
  - (ii)  how he intends to vote, or how he has voted, in the ballot,
- (d)  dismisses or threatens to dismiss a worker,
- (e)  takes or threatens to take disciplinary action against a worker,
- (f)  subjects or threatens to subject a worker to any other detriment, or
- (g)  uses or attempts to use undue influence on a worker entitled to vote in the ballot.

(3)  For the purposes of sub-paragraph (2)(b) an "outcome-specific offer" is an offer to pay money or give money's worth which—
- (a)  is conditional on the issuing by the CAC of a declaration that—
  - (i)  the union is (or unions are) recognised as entitled to conduct collective bargaining on behalf of the bargaining unit, or
  - (ii)  the union is (or unions are) not entitled to be so recognised, and
- (b)  is not conditional on anything which is done or occurs as a result of the declaration in question.

(4)  The duty imposed by this paragraph does not confer any rights on a worker; but that does not affect any other right which a worker may have.

(5)  Each of the following powers shall be taken to include power to issue Codes of Practice about unfair practices for the purposes of this paragraph—
- (a)  the power of ACAS under section 199(1);
- (b)  the power of the Secretary of State under section 203(1)(a).

**27B.**  (1)  A party may complain to the CAC that another party has failed to comply with paragraph 27A.

(2)  A complaint under sub-paragraph (1) must be made on or before the first working day after—
- (a)  the date of the ballot, or
- (b)  if votes may be cast in the ballot on more than one day, the last of those days.

(3)  Within the decision period the CAC must decide whether the complaint is well-founded.

(4)  A complaint is well-founded if—
- (a)  the CAC finds that the party complained against used an unfair practice, and
- (b)  the CAC is satisfied that the use of that practice changed or was likely to change, in the case of a worker entitled to vote in the ballot—
  - (i)  his intention to vote or to abstain from voting,
  - (ii)  his intention to vote in a particular way, or
  - (iii)  how he voted.

(5)  The decision period is—
- (a)  the period of 10 working days starting with the day after that on which the complaint under sub-paragraph (1) was received by the CAC, or
- (b)  such longer period (so starting) as the CAC may specify to the parties by a notice containing reasons for the extension.

(6)  If, at the beginning of the decision period, the ballot has not begun, the CAC may by notice to the parties and the qualified independent person postpone the date on which it is to begin until a date which falls after the end of the decision period.

**27C.**  (1)  This paragraph applies if the CAC decides that a complaint under paragraph 27B is well-founded.

(2)  The CAC must, as soon as is reasonably practicable, issue a declaration to that effect.

(3)  The CAC may do either or both of the following—
- (a)  order the party concerned to take any action specified in the order within such period as may be so specified, or

(b)   give notice to the employer and to the union (or unions) that it intends to arrange for the holding of a secret ballot in which the workers constituting the bargaining unit are asked whether they want the union (or unions) to conduct collective bargaining on their behalf.

(4)   The CAC may give an order or a notice under sub-paragraph (3) either at the same time as it issues the declaration under sub-paragraph (2) or at any other time before it acts under paragraph 29.

(5)   The action specified in an order under sub-paragraph (3)(a) shall be such as the CAC considers reasonable in order to mitigate the effect of the failure of the party concerned to comply with the duty imposed by paragraph 27A.

(6)   The CAC may give more than one order under sub-paragraph (3)(a).

**27D.**   (1)   This paragraph applies if the CAC issues a declaration under paragraph 27C(2) and the declaration states that the unfair practice used consisted of or included—
(a)   the use of violence, or
(b)   the dismissal of a union official.

(2)   This paragraph also applies if the CAC has made an order under paragraph 27C(3)(a) and—
(a)   it is satisfied that the party subject to the order has failed to comply with it, or
(b)   it makes another declaration under paragraph 27C(2) in relation to a complaint against that party.

(3)   If the party concerned is the employer, the CAC may issue a declaration that the union is (or unions are) recognised as entitled to conduct collective bargaining on behalf of the bargaining unit.

(4)   If the party concerned is a union, the CAC may issue a declaration that the union is (or unions are) not entitled to be so recognised.

(5)   The powers conferred by this paragraph are in addition to those conferred by paragraph 27C(3).

**27E.**   (1)   This paragraph applies if the CAC issues a declaration that a complaint under paragraph 27B is well-founded and—
(a)   gives a notice under paragraph 27C(3)(b), or
(b)   issues a declaration under paragraph 27D.

(2)   If the ballot in connection with which the complaint was made has not been held, the CAC shall take steps to cancel it.

(3)   If that ballot is held, it shall have no effect.

**27F.** (1)   This paragraph applies if the CAC gives a notice under paragraph 27C(3)(b).

(2)   Paragraphs 24 to 29 apply in relation to that notice as they apply in relation to a notice given under paragraph 22(3) or 23(2) but with the modifications specified in sub-paragraphs (3) to (6).

(3)   In each of sub-paragraphs (5)(a) and (6)(a) of paragraph 24 for "10 working days" substitute "5 working days".

(4)   An employer's duty under paragraph (a) of paragraph 26(4) is limited to—
(a)   giving the CAC the names and home addresses of any workers in the bargaining unit which have not previously been given to it in accordance with that duty;
(b)   giving the CAC the names and home addresses of those workers who have joined the bargaining unit since he last gave the CAC information in accordance with that duty;
(c)   informing the CAC of any change to the name or home address of a worker whose name and home address have previously been given to the CAC in accordance with that duty; and
(d)   informing the CAC of any worker whose name had previously been given to it in accordance with that duty who has ceased to be within the bargaining unit.

(5)   Any order given under paragraph 27(1) or 27C(3)(a) for the purposes of the cancelled or ineffectual ballot shall have effect (to the extent that the CAC specifies in a notice to the parties) as if it were made for the purposes of the ballot to which the notice under paragraph 27C(3)(b) relates.

(6)   The gross costs of the ballot shall be borne by such of the parties and in such proportions as the CAC may determine and, accordingly, sub-paragraphs (2) and (3) of paragraph 28 shall be omitted and the reference in sub-paragraph (4) of that paragraph to the employer and the union (or each of the unions) shall be construed as a reference to the party or parties which bear the costs in accordance with the CAC's determination.]

**28.**   (1)   This paragraph applies if the holding of a ballot has been arranged under paragraph 24 whether or not it has been cancelled.

(2)   The gross costs of the ballot shall be borne—
(a)   as to half, by the employer, and
(b)   as to half, by the union (or unions).

(3)   If there is more than one union they shall bear their half of the gross costs—
(a)   in such proportions as they jointly indicate to the person appointed to conduct the ballot, or

(b)   in the absence of such an indication, in equal shares.

(4)   The person appointed to conduct the ballot may send to the employer and the union (or each of the unions) a demand stating—

(a)   the gross costs of the ballot, and

(b)   the amount of the gross costs to be borne by the recipient.

(5)   In such a case the recipient must pay the amount stated to the person sending the demand, and must do so within the period of 15 working days starting with the day after that on which the demand is received.

(6)   In England and Wales, if the amount stated is not paid in accordance with sub-paragraph (5) it shall, if *a county court* so orders, be recoverable *by execution issued from that court* or otherwise as if it were payable under an order of that court.

[(6A)   *Where an amount is recoverable from a union under sub-paragraph (6) execution may be carried out*, to the same extent and in the same manner as if the union were a body corporate, against any property held in trust for the union other than protected property as defined in section 23(2).]

(7)   References to the costs of the ballot are to—

(a)   the costs wholly, exclusively and necessarily incurred in connection with the ballot by the person appointed to conduct it,

(b)   such reasonable amount as the person appointed to conduct the ballot charges for his services, and

(c)   such other costs as the employer and the union (or unions) agree.

**29.** (1)   As soon as is reasonably practicable after the CAC is informed of the result of a ballot by the person conducting it, the CAC must act under this paragraph.

[(1A)   The duty in sub-paragraph (1) does not apply if the CAC gives a notice under paragraph 27C(3)(b).]

(2)   The CAC must inform the employer and the union (or unions) of the result of the ballot.

(3)   If the result is that the union is (or unions are) supported by—

(a)   a majority of the workers voting, and

(b)   at least 40 per cent of the workers constituting the bargaining unit,

the CAC must issue a declaration that the union is (or unions are) recognised as entitled to conduct collective bargaining on behalf of the bargaining unit.

(4)   If the result is otherwise the CAC must issue a declaration that the union is (or unions are) not entitled to be so recognised.

(5)   The Secretary of State may by order amend sub-paragraph (3) so as to specify a different degree of support; and different provision may be made for different circumstances.

(6)   An order under sub-paragraph (5) shall be made by statutory instrument.

(7)   No such order shall be made unless a draft of it has been laid before Parliament and approved by a resolution of each House of Parliament.

---

**NOTES**

Inserted as noted at the beginning of this Schedule.

Paras 20, 21: words in square brackets inserted by the Employment Relations Act 2004, s 57(1), Sch 1, para 23(1), (5).

Para 22: words in square brackets in sub-para (1)(a) inserted, and sub-para (4)(b) substituted, by the Employment Relations Act 2004, ss 5(2), 6(1).

Para 23: words in square brackets in sub-para (1)(a) inserted by the Employment Relations Act 2004, s 5(2).

Para 24: sub-paras (5)–(7) substituted, for the original sub-para (5), by the Employment Relations Act 2004, s 7.

Para 25: sub-para (6A) inserted by the Employment Relations Act 2004, s 8(1).

Para 26: word in square brackets in sub-para (1) substituted, sub-paras (4A)–(4E) inserted, and sub-paras (8), (9) substituted (for the original sub-para (8)), by the Employment Relations Act 2004, s 9(1)–(4); words in square brackets in sub-paras (4)(c), (6)(a) substituted, and sub-paras (4F)–(4H) inserted, by s 5(3)–(5) of the 2004 Act.

Para 27: words in square brackets substituted by the Employment Relations Act 2004, s 9(5).

Paras 27A–27F: inserted by the Employment Relations Act 2004, s 10(1).

Para 28: for the first words in italics in sub-para (6) there are substituted the words "the county court" by the Crime and Courts Act 2013, s 17(5), Sch 9, Pt 3, para 52, as from a day to be appointed; for the second words in italics in sub-para (6) there are substituted the words "under section 85 of the County Courts Act 1984" by the Tribunals, Courts and Enforcement Act 2007, s 62(3), Sch 13, paras 108, 110(1), (2), as from a day to be appointed; sub-para (6A) inserted by the Employment Relations Act 2004, s 57(1), Sch 1, para 23(1), (6); for the words in italics in sub-para (6A) there are substituted the words "Where a warrant of control is issued under section 85 of the 1984 Act to recover an amount in accordance with sub-paragraph (6), the power conferred by the warrant is exercisable" by the Tribunals, Courts and Enforcement Act 2007, s 62(3), Sch 13, paras 108, 110(1), (3), as from a day to be appointed.

Para 29: sub-para (1A) inserted by the Employment Relations Act 2004, s 10(2).

Orders: the Recognition and Derecognition Ballots (Qualified Persons) Order 2000, SI 2000/1306 at [**2.569**]; the Recognition and Derecognition Ballots (Qualified Persons) (Amendment) Order 2010, SI 2010/437 (both made under para 25). As of 6 April 2013, no Orders had been made under para 29.

*Consequences of recognition*

**[1.593]**

**30.** (1)   This paragraph applies if the CAC issues a declaration under this Part of this Schedule that the union is (or unions are) recognised as entitled to conduct collective bargaining on behalf of a bargaining unit.

(2)   The parties may in the negotiation period conduct negotiations with a view to agreeing a method by which they will conduct collective bargaining.

(3)   If no agreement is made in the negotiation period the employer or the union (or unions) may apply to the CAC for assistance.

(4)   The negotiation period is—
(a)   the period of 30 working days starting with the start day, or
(b)   such longer period (so starting) as the parties may from time to time agree.

(5)   The start day is the day after that on which the parties are notified of the declaration.

**31.** (1)   This paragraph applies if an application for assistance is made to the CAC under paragraph 30.

(2)   The CAC must try to help the parties to reach in the agreement period an agreement on a method by which they will conduct collective bargaining.

(3)   If at the end of the agreement period the parties have not made such an agreement the CAC must specify to the parties the method by which they are to conduct collective bargaining.

(4)   Any method specified under sub-paragraph (3) is to have effect as if it were contained in a legally enforceable contract made by the parties.

(5)   But if the parties agree in writing—
(a)   that sub-paragraph (4) shall not apply, or shall not apply to particular parts of the method specified by the CAC, or
(b)   to vary or replace the method specified by the CAC,
the written agreement shall have effect as a legally enforceable contract made by the parties.

(6)   Specific performance shall be the only remedy available for breach of anything which is a legally enforceable contract by virtue of this paragraph.

(7)   If at any time before a specification is made under sub-paragraph (3) the parties jointly apply to the CAC requesting it to stop taking steps under this paragraph, the CAC must comply with the request.

(8)   The agreement period is—
(a)   the period of 20 working days starting with the day after that on which the CAC receives the application under paragraph 30, or
(b)   such longer period (so starting) as the CAC may decide with the consent of the parties.

**NOTES**

Inserted as noted at the beginning of this Schedule.

*Method not carried out*

**[1.594]**

**32.** (1)   This paragraph applies if—
(a)   the CAC issues a declaration under this Part of this Schedule that the union is (or unions are) recognised as entitled to conduct collective bargaining on behalf of a bargaining unit,
(b)   the parties agree a method by which they will conduct collective bargaining, and
(c)   one or more of the parties fails to carry out the agreement.

(2)   The [employer or the union (or unions)] may apply to the CAC for assistance.

(3)   Paragraph 31 applies as if "paragraph 30" (in each place) read "paragraph 30 or paragraph 32".

**NOTES**

Inserted as noted at the beginning of this Schedule.

Para 32: words in square brackets in sub-para (2) substituted by the Employment Relations Act 2004, s 57(1), Sch 1, para 23(1), (7).

*General provisions about admissibility*

**[1.595]**

**33.**   An application under paragraph 11 or 12 is not admissible unless—
(a)   it is made in such form as the CAC specifies, and
(b)   it is supported by such documents as the CAC specifies.

**34.**   An application under paragraph 11 or 12 is not admissible unless the union gives (or unions give) to the employer—
(a)   notice of the application, and

(b)    a copy of the application and any documents supporting it.

**35.** (1)    An application under paragraph 11 or 12 is not admissible if the CAC is satisfied that there is already in force a collective agreement under which a union is (or unions are) recognised as entitled to conduct collective bargaining on behalf of any workers falling within the relevant bargaining unit.

(2)    But sub-paragraph (1) does not apply to an application under paragraph 11 or 12 if—
    (a)    the union (or unions) recognised under the collective agreement and the union (or unions) making the application under paragraph 11 or 12 are the same, and
    (b)    the matters in respect of which the union is (or unions are) entitled to conduct collective bargaining do not include [all of the following: pay, hours and holidays ("the core topics")].

(3)    A declaration of recognition which is the subject of a declaration under paragraph 83(2) must for the purposes of sub-paragraph (1) be treated as ceasing to have effect to the extent specified in paragraph 83(2) on the making of the declaration under paragraph 83(2).

(4)    In applying sub-paragraph (1) an agreement for recognition (the agreement in question) must be ignored if—
    (a)    the union does not have (or none of the unions has) a certificate [of independence],
    (b)    at some time there was an agreement (the old agreement) between the employer and the union under which the union (whether alone or with other unions) was recognised as entitled to conduct collective bargaining on behalf of a group of workers which was the same or substantially the same as the group covered by the agreement in question, and
    (c)    the old agreement ceased to have effect in the period of three years ending with the date of the agreement in question.

(5)    It is for the CAC to decide whether one group of workers is the same or substantially the same as another, but in deciding the CAC may take account of the views of any person it believes has an interest in the matter.

(6)    The relevant bargaining unit is—
    (a)    the proposed bargaining unit, where the application is under paragraph 11(2) or 12(2);
    (b)    the agreed bargaining unit, where the application is under paragraph 12(4).

**36.** (1)    An application under paragraph 11 or 12 is not admissible unless the CAC decides that—
    (a)    members of the union (or unions) constitute at least 10 per cent of the workers constituting the relevant bargaining unit, and
    (b)    a majority of the workers constituting the relevant bargaining unit would be likely to favour recognition of the union (or unions) as entitled to conduct collective bargaining on behalf of the bargaining unit.

(2)    The relevant bargaining unit is—
    (a)    the proposed bargaining unit, where the application is under paragraph 11(2) or 12(2);
    (b)    the agreed bargaining unit, where the application is under paragraph 12(4).

(3)    The CAC must give reasons for the decision.

**37.** (1)    This paragraph applies to an application made by more than one union under paragraph 11 or 12.

(2)    The application is not admissible unless—
    (a)    the unions show that they will co-operate with each other in a manner likely to secure and maintain stable and effective collective bargaining arrangements, and
    (b)    the unions show that, if the employer wishes, they will enter into arrangements under which collective bargaining is conducted by the unions acting together on behalf of the workers constituting the relevant bargaining unit.

(3)    The relevant bargaining unit is—
    (a)    the proposed bargaining unit, where the application is under paragraph 11(2) or 12(2);
    (b)    the agreed bargaining unit, where the application is under paragraph [12(4)].

**38.** (1)    This paragraph applies if—
    (a)    the CAC accepts a relevant application relating to a bargaining unit or proceeds under paragraph 20 with an application relating to a bargaining unit,
    (b)    the application has not been withdrawn,
    (c)    no notice has been given under paragraph 17(2),
    (d)    the CAC has not issued a declaration under paragraph [19F(5), 22(2), 27(2), 27D(3), 27D(4),] 29(3) or 29(4) in relation to that bargaining unit, and
    (e)    no notification has been made under paragraph 24(2).

(2)    Another relevant application is not admissible if—
    (a)    at least one worker falling within the relevant bargaining unit also falls within the bargaining unit referred to in sub-paragraph (1), and

(b)   the application is made by a union (or unions) other than the union (or unions) which made the application referred to in sub-paragraph (1).

(3)   A relevant application is an application under paragraph 11 or 12.

(4)   The relevant bargaining unit is—
   (a)   the proposed bargaining unit, where the application is under paragraph 11(2) or 12(2);
   (b)   the agreed bargaining unit, where the application is under paragraph 12(4).

**39.**   (1)   This paragraph applies if the CAC accepts a relevant application relating to a bargaining unit or proceeds under paragraph 20 with an application relating to a bargaining unit.

(2)   Another relevant application is not admissible if—
   (a)   the application is made within the period of 3 years starting with the day after that on which the CAC gave notice of acceptance of the application mentioned in sub-paragraph (1),
   (b)   the relevant bargaining unit is the same or substantially the same as the bargaining unit mentioned in sub-paragraph (1), and
   (c)   the application is made by the union (or unions) which made the application mentioned in sub-paragraph (1).

(3)   A relevant application is an application under paragraph 11 or 12.

(4)   The relevant bargaining unit is—
   (a)   the proposed bargaining unit, where the application is under paragraph 11(2) or 12(2);
   (b)   the agreed bargaining unit, where the application is under paragraph 12(4).

(5)   This paragraph does not apply if paragraph 40 or 41 applies.

**40.**   (1)   This paragraph applies if the CAC issues a declaration under paragraph [27D(4) or] 29(4) that a union is (or unions are) not entitled to be recognised as entitled to conduct collective bargaining on behalf of a bargaining unit; and this is so whether the ballot concerned is [arranged] under this Part or Part III of this Schedule.

(2)   An application under paragraph 11 or 12 is not admissible if—
   (a)   the application is made within the period of 3 years starting with the day after that on which the declaration was issued,
   (b)   the relevant bargaining unit is the same or substantially the same as the bargaining unit mentioned in sub-paragraph (1), and
   (c)   the application is made by the union (or unions) which made the application leading to the declaration.

(3)   The relevant bargaining unit is—
   (a)   the proposed bargaining unit, where the application is under paragraph 11(2) or 12(2);
   (b)   the agreed bargaining unit, where the application is under paragraph 12(4).

**41.**   (1)   This paragraph applies if the CAC issues a declaration under paragraph [119D(4), 119H(5) or] 121(3) that bargaining arrangements are to cease to have effect; and this is so whether the ballot concerned is [arranged] under Part IV or Part V of this Schedule.

(2)   An application under paragraph 11 or 12 is not admissible if—
   (a)   the application is made within the period of 3 years starting with the day after that on which the declaration was issued,
   (b)   the relevant bargaining unit is the same or substantially the same as the bargaining unit to which the bargaining arrangements mentioned in sub-paragraph (1) relate, and
   (c)   the application is made by the union which was a party (or unions which were parties) to the proceedings leading to the declaration.

(3)   The relevant bargaining unit is—
   (a)   the proposed bargaining unit, where the application is under paragraph 11(2) or 12(2);
   (b)   the agreed bargaining unit, where the application is under paragraph 12(4).

**42.**   (1)   This paragraph applies for the purposes of paragraphs 39 to 41.

(2)   It is for the CAC to decide whether one bargaining unit is the same or substantially the same as another, but in deciding the CAC may take account of the views of any person it believes has an interest in the matter.

**NOTES**
   Inserted as noted at the beginning of this Schedule.
   Para 35: words in square brackets in sub-para (2)(b) substituted by the Employment Relations Act 2004, s 11; words in square brackets in sub-para (4)(a) substituted by s 50(6) of the 2004 Act.
   Paras 37, 38: numbers in square brackets substituted by the Employment Relations Act 2004, s 57(1), Sch 1, para 23(1), (8), (9).
   Paras 40, 41: words in first pair of square brackets in sub-para (1) inserted, and word in second pair of square brackets in that sub-paragraph substituted, by the Employment Relations Act 2004, s 57(1), Sch 1, para 23(1), (10), (11).

*General provisions about validity*

**[1.596]**

**43.** (1) Paragraphs 44 to 50 apply if the CAC has to decide under paragraph 20 whether an application is valid.

(2) In those paragraphs—
- (a) references to the application in question are to that application, and
- (b) references to the relevant bargaining unit are to the bargaining unit agreed by the parties or decided by the CAC.

**44.** (1) The application in question is invalid if the CAC is satisfied that there is already in force a collective agreement under which a union is (or unions are) recognised as entitled to conduct collective bargaining on behalf of any workers falling within the relevant bargaining unit.

(2) But sub-paragraph (1) does not apply to the application in question if—
- (a) the union (or unions) recognised under the collective agreement and the union (or unions) making the application in question are the same, and
- (b) the matters in respect of which the union is (or unions are) entitled to conduct collective bargaining do not include [all of the following: pay, hours and holidays ("the core topics")].

(3) A declaration of recognition which is the subject of a declaration under paragraph 83(2) must for the purposes of sub-paragraph (1) be treated as ceasing to have effect to the extent specified in paragraph 83(2) on the making of the declaration under paragraph 83(2).

(4) In applying sub-paragraph (1) an agreement for recognition (the agreement in question) must be ignored if—
- (a) the union does not have (or none of the unions has) a certificate [of independence],
- (b) at some time there was an agreement (the old agreement) between the employer and the union under which the union (whether alone or with other unions) was recognised as entitled to conduct collective bargaining on behalf of a group of workers which was the same or substantially the same as the group covered by the agreement in question, and
- (c) the old agreement ceased to have effect in the period of three years ending with the date of the agreement in question.

(5) It is for the CAC to decide whether one group of workers is the same or substantially the same as another, but in deciding the CAC may take account of the views of any person it believes has an interest in the matter.

**45.** The application in question is invalid unless the CAC decides that—
- (a) members of the union (or unions) constitute at least 10 per cent of the workers constituting the relevant bargaining unit, and
- (b) a majority of the workers constituting the relevant bargaining unit would be likely to favour recognition of the union (or unions) as entitled to conduct collective bargaining on behalf of the bargaining unit.

**46.** (1) This paragraph applies if—
- (a) the CAC accepts an application under paragraph 11 or 12 relating to a bargaining unit or proceeds under paragraph 20 with an application relating to a bargaining unit,
- (b) the application has not been withdrawn,
- (c) no notice has been given under paragraph 17(2),
- (d) the CAC has not issued a declaration under paragraph [19F(5), 22(2), 27(2), 27D(3), 27D(4),] 29(3) or 29(4) in relation to that bargaining unit, and
- (e) no notification has been made under paragraph 24(2).

(2) The application in question is invalid if—
- (a) at least one worker falling within the relevant bargaining unit also falls within the bargaining unit referred to in sub-paragraph (1), and
- (b) the application in question is made by a union (or unions) other than the union (or unions) which made the application referred to in sub-paragraph (1).

**47.** (1) This paragraph applies if the CAC accepts an application under paragraph 11 or 12 relating to a bargaining unit or proceeds under paragraph 20 with an application relating to a bargaining unit.

(2) The application in question is invalid if—
- (a) the application is made within the period of 3 years starting with the day after that on which the CAC gave notice of acceptance of the application mentioned in sub-paragraph (1),
- (b) the relevant bargaining unit is the same or substantially the same as the bargaining unit mentioned in sub-paragraph (1), and
- (c) the application is made by the union (or unions) which made the application mentioned in sub-paragraph (1).

(3)   This paragraph does not apply if paragraph 48 or 49 applies.

**48.** (1)   This paragraph applies if the CAC issues a declaration under paragraph [27D(4) or] 29(4) that a union is (or unions are) not entitled to be recognised as entitled to conduct collective bargaining on behalf of a bargaining unit; and this is so whether the ballot concerned is [arranged] under this Part or Part III of this Schedule.

(2)   The application in question is invalid if—
  (a)   the application is made within the period of 3 years starting with the date of the declaration,
  (b)   the relevant bargaining unit is the same or substantially the same as the bargaining unit mentioned in sub-paragraph (1), and
  (c)   the application is made by the union (or unions) which made the application leading to the declaration.

**49.** (1)   This paragraph applies if the CAC issues a declaration under paragraph [119D(4), 119H(5) or] 121(3) that bargaining arrangements are to cease to have effect; and this is so whether the ballot concerned is [arranged] under Part IV or Part V of this Schedule.

(2)   The application in question is invalid if—
  (a)   the application is made within the period of 3 years starting with the day after that on which the declaration was issued,
  (b)   the relevant bargaining unit is the same or substantially the same as the bargaining unit to which the bargaining arrangements mentioned in sub-paragraph (1) relate, and
  (c)   the application is made by the union which was a party (or unions which were parties) to the proceedings leading to the declaration.

**50.** (1)   This paragraph applies for the purposes of paragraphs 47 to 49.

(2)   It is for the CAC to decide whether one bargaining unit is the same or substantially the same as another, but in deciding the CAC may take account of the views of any person it believes has an interest in the matter.

**NOTES**
Inserted as noted at the beginning of this Schedule.
Para 44: words in square brackets in sub-para (2)(b) substituted by the Employment Relations Act 2004, s 11; words in square brackets in sub-para (4)(a) substituted by s 50(6) of the 2004 Act.
Para 46: numbers in square brackets substituted by the Employment Relations Act 2004, s 57(1), Sch 1, para 23(1), (12).
Paras 48, 49: words in first pair of square brackets in sub-para (1) inserted, and word in second pair of square brackets in that sub-paragraph substituted, by the Employment Relations Act 2004, s 57(1), Sch 1, para 23(1), (13), (14).

*Competing applications*

**[1.597]**
**51.** (1)   For the purposes of this paragraph—
  (a)   the original application is the application referred to in paragraph 38(1) or 46(1), and
  (b)   the competing application is the other application referred to in paragraph 38(2) or the application in question referred to in paragraph 46(2);
but an application cannot be an original application unless it was made under paragraph 11(2) or 12(2).

(2)   This paragraph applies if—
  (a)   the CAC decides that the competing application is not admissible by reason of paragraph 38 or is invalid by reason of paragraph 46,
  (b)   at the time the decision is made the parties to the original application have not agreed the appropriate bargaining unit under paragraph 18, and the CAC has not decided the appropriate bargaining unit under paragraph 19 [or 19A], in relation to the application, and
  (c)   the 10 per cent test (within the meaning given by paragraph 14) is satisfied with regard to the competing application.

(3)   In such a case—
  (a)   the CAC must cancel the original application,
  (b)   the CAC must give notice to the parties to the application that it has been cancelled,
  (c)   no further steps are to be taken under this Part of this Schedule in relation to the application, and
  (d)   the application shall be treated as if it had never been admissible.

**NOTES**
Inserted as noted at the beginning of this Schedule.
Para 51: words in square brackets in sub-para (2)(b) inserted by the Employment Relations Act 2004, s 57(1), Sch 1, para 23(1), (15).

## PART II
## VOLUNTARY RECOGNITION

*Agreements for recognition*

**[1.598]**

**52.** (1)   This paragraph applies for the purposes of this Part of this Schedule.

(2)   An agreement is an agreement for recognition if the following conditions are fulfilled in relation to it—

(a)   the agreement is made in the permitted period between a union (or unions) and an employer in consequence of a request made under paragraph 4 and valid within the terms of paragraphs 5 to 9;

(b)   under the agreement the union is (or unions are) recognised as entitled to conduct collective bargaining on behalf of a group or groups of workers employed by the employer;

(c)   if sub-paragraph (5) applies to the agreement, it is satisfied.

(3)   The permitted period is the period which begins with the day on which the employer receives the request and ends when the first of the following occurs—

(a)   the union withdraws (or unions withdraw) the request;

(b)   the union withdraws (or unions withdraw) any application under paragraph 11 or 12 made in consequence of the request;

(c)   the CAC gives notice of a decision under paragraph 14(7) which precludes it from accepting such an application under paragraph 11 or 12;

(d)   the CAC gives notice under paragraph 15(4)(a) or 20(4)(a) in relation to such an application under paragraph 11 or 12;

(e)   the parties give notice to the CAC under paragraph 17(2) in relation to such an application under paragraph 11 or 12;

(f)   the CAC issues a declaration under paragraph [19F(5) or] 22(2) in consequence of such an application under paragraph 11 or 12;

(g)   the CAC is notified under paragraph 24(2) in relation to such an application under paragraph 11 or 12;

(h)   the last day of the notification period ends (the notification period being that defined by paragraph [24(6)]) and arising from such an application under paragraph 11 or 12);

(i)   the CAC is required under paragraph 51(3) to cancel such an application under paragraph 11 or 12.

(4)   Sub-paragraph (5) applies to an agreement if—

(a)   at the time it is made the CAC has received an application under paragraph 11 or 12 in consequence of the request mentioned in sub-paragraph (2), and

(b)   the CAC has not decided whether the application is admissible or it has decided that it is admissible.

(5)   This sub-paragraph is satisfied if, in relation to the application under paragraph 11 or 12, the parties give notice to the CAC under paragraph 17 before the final event (as defined in paragraph 17) occurs.

**NOTES**

Inserted as noted at the beginning of this Schedule.

Para 52: words in square brackets in sub-para (3)(f) inserted, and number in square brackets in sub-para (3)(h) substituted, by the Employment Relations Act 2004, s 57(1), Sch 1, para 23(1), (16).

*Other interpretation*

**[1.599]**

**53.** (1)   This paragraph applies for the purposes of this Part of this Schedule.

(2)   In relation to an agreement for recognition, references to the bargaining unit are to the group of workers (or the groups taken together) to which the agreement for recognition relates.

(3)   In relation to an agreement for recognition, references to the parties are to the union (or unions) and the employer who are parties to the agreement.

**54.** (1)   This paragraph applies for the purposes of this Part of this Schedule.

(2)   The meaning of collective bargaining given by section 178(1) shall not apply.

(3)   Except in paragraph 63(2), in relation to an agreement for recognition references to collective bargaining are to negotiations relating to the matters in respect of which the union is (or unions are) recognised as entitled to conduct negotiations under the agreement for recognition.

(4)   In paragraph 63(2) the reference to collective bargaining is to negotiations relating to pay, hours and holidays.

**NOTES**

Inserted as noted at the beginning of this Schedule.

## Determination of type of agreement

**[1.600]**

**55.** (1)   This paragraph applies if one or more of the parties to an agreement applies to the CAC for a decision whether or not the agreement is an agreement for recognition.

(2)   The CAC must give notice of receipt of an application under sub-paragraph (1) to any parties to the agreement who are not parties to the application.

(3)   The CAC must within the decision period decide whether the agreement is an agreement for recognition.

(4)   If the CAC decides that the agreement is an agreement for recognition it must issue a declaration to that effect.

(5)   If the CAC decides that the agreement is not an agreement for recognition it must issue a declaration to that effect.

(6)   The decision period is—
- (a)   the period of 10 working days starting with the day after that on which the CAC receives the application under sub-paragraph (1), or
- (b)   such longer period (so starting) as the CAC may specify to the parties to the agreement by notice containing reasons for the extension.

**NOTES**
Inserted as noted at the beginning of this Schedule.

## Termination of agreement for recognition

**[1.601]**

**56.** (1)   The employer may not terminate an agreement for recognition before the relevant period ends.

(2)   After that period ends the employer may terminate the agreement, with or without the consent of the union (or unions).

(3)   The union (or unions) may terminate an agreement for recognition at any time, with or without the consent of the employer.

(4)   Sub-paragraphs (1) to (3) have effect subject to the terms of the agreement or any other agreement of the parties.

(5)   The relevant period is the period of three years starting with the day after the date of the agreement.

**57.** (1)   If an agreement for recognition is terminated, as from the termination the agreement and any provisions relating to the collective bargaining method shall cease to have effect.

(2)   For this purpose provisions relating to the collective bargaining method are—
- (a)   any agreement between the parties as to the method by which collective bargaining is to be conducted with regard to the bargaining unit, or
- (b)   anything effective as, or as if contained in, a legally enforceable contract and relating to the method by which collective bargaining is to be conducted with regard to the bargaining unit.

**NOTES**
Inserted as noted at the beginning of this Schedule.

## Application to CAC to specify method

**[1.602]**

**58.** (1)   This paragraph applies if the parties make an agreement for recognition.

(2)   The parties may in the negotiation period conduct negotiations with a view to agreeing a method by which they will conduct collective bargaining.

(3)   If no agreement is made in the negotiation period the employer or the union (or unions) may apply to the CAC for assistance.

(4)   The negotiation period is—
- (a)   the period of 30 working days starting with the start day, or
- (b)   such longer period (so starting) as the parties may from time to time agree.

(5)   The start day is the day after that on which the agreement is made.

**59.** (1)   This paragraph applies if—
- (a)   the parties to an agreement for recognition agree a method by which they will conduct collective bargaining, and
- (b)   one or more of the parties fails to carry out the agreement as to a method.

(2)   The employer or the union (or unions) may apply to the CAC for assistance.

**60.** (1) This paragraph applies if an application for assistance is made to the CAC under paragraph 58 or 59.

(2) The application is not admissible unless the conditions in sub-paragraphs (3) and (4) are satisfied.

(3) The condition is that the employer, taken with any associated employer or employers, must—
(a) employ at least 21 workers on the day the application is made, or
(b) employ an average of at least 21 workers in the 13 weeks ending with that day.

(4) The condition is that the union (or every union) has a certificate [of independence].

(5) To find the average under sub-paragraph (3)(b)—
(a) take the number of workers employed in each of the 13 weeks (including workers not employed for the whole of the week);
(b) aggregate the 13 numbers;
(c) divide the aggregate by 13.

(6) For the purposes of sub-paragraph (3)(a) any worker employed by an associated company incorporated outside Great Britain must be ignored unless the day the application was made fell within a period during which he ordinarily worked in Great Britain.

(7) For the purposes of sub-paragraph (3)(b) any worker employed by an associated company incorporated outside Great Britain must be ignored in relation to a week unless the whole or any part of that week fell within a period during which he ordinarily worked in Great Britain.

(8) For the purposes of sub-paragraphs (6) and (7) a worker who is employed on board a ship registered in the register maintained under section 8 of the Merchant Shipping Act 1995 shall be treated as ordinarily working in Great Britain unless—
(a) the ship's entry in the register specifies a port outside Great Britain as the port to which the vessel is to be treated as belonging,
(b) the employment is wholly outside Great Britain, or
(c) the worker is not ordinarily resident in Great Britain.

(9) An order made under paragraph 7(6) may also—
(a) provide that sub-paragraphs (2), (3) and (5) to (8) of this paragraph are not to apply, or are not to apply in specified circumstances, or
(b) vary the number of workers for the time being specified in sub-paragraph (3).

**61.** (1) An application to the CAC is not admissible unless—
(a) it is made in such form as the CAC specifies, and
(b) it is supported by such documents as the CAC specifies.

(2) An application which is made by a union (or unions) to the CAC is not admissible unless the union gives (or unions give) to the employer—
(a) notice of the application, and
(b) a copy of the application and any documents supporting it.

(3) An application which is made by an employer to the CAC is not admissible unless the employer gives to the union (or each of the unions)—
(a) notice of the application, and
(b) a copy of the application and any documents supporting it.

---

**NOTES**
Inserted as noted at the beginning of this Schedule.
Para 60: words in square brackets in sub-para (4) substituted by the Employment Relations Act 2004, s 50(6).

*CAC's response to application*

**[1.603]**
**62.** (1) The CAC must give notice to the parties of receipt of an application under paragraph 58 or 59.

(2) Within the acceptance period the CAC must decide whether the application is admissible within the terms of paragraphs 60 and 61.

(3) In deciding whether an application is admissible the CAC must consider any evidence which it has been given by the employer or the union (or unions).

(4) If the CAC decides that the application is not admissible—
(a) the CAC must give notice of its decision to the parties,
(b) the CAC must not accept the application, and
(c) no further steps are to be taken under this Part of this Schedule.

(5) If the CAC decides that the application is admissible it must—
(a) accept the application, and
(b) give notice of the acceptance to the parties.

(6) The acceptance period is—

(a)   the period of 10 working days starting with the day after that on which the CAC receives the application, or

(b)   such longer period (so starting) as the CAC may specify to the parties by notice containing reasons for the extension.

**63.** (1)   If the CAC accepts an application it must try to help the parties to reach in the agreement period an agreement on a method by which they will conduct collective bargaining.

(2)   If at the end of the agreement period the parties have not made such an agreement the CAC must specify to the parties the method by which they are to conduct collective bargaining.

(3)   Any method specified under sub-paragraph (2) is to have effect as if it were contained in a legally enforceable contract made by the parties.

(4)   But if the parties agree in writing—

(a)   that sub-paragraph (3) shall not apply, or shall not apply to particular parts of the method specified by the CAC, or

(b)   to vary or replace the method specified by the CAC,

the written agreement shall have effect as a legally enforceable contract made by the parties.

(5)   Specific performance shall be the only remedy available for breach of anything which is a legally enforceable contract by virtue of this paragraph.

(6)   If the CAC accepts an application, the applicant may not withdraw it after the end of the agreement period.

(7)   If at any time before a specification is made under sub-paragraph (2) the parties jointly apply to the CAC requesting it to stop taking steps under this paragraph, the CAC must comply with the request.

(8)   The agreement period is—

(a)   the period of 20 working days starting with the day after that on which the CAC gives notice of acceptance of the application, or

(b)   such longer period (so starting) as the parties may from time to time agree.

**NOTES**

Inserted as noted at the beginning of this Schedule.

## PART III
## CHANGES AFFECTING BARGAINING UNIT

### *Introduction*

**[1.604]**

**64.** (1)   This Part of this Schedule applies if—

(a)   the CAC has issued a declaration that a union is (or unions are) recognised as entitled to conduct collective bargaining on behalf of a bargaining unit, and

(b)   provisions relating to the collective bargaining method apply in relation to the unit.

(2)   In such a case, in this Part of this Schedule—

(a)   references to the original unit are to the bargaining unit on whose behalf the union is (or unions are) recognised as entitled to conduct collective bargaining, and

(b)   references to the bargaining arrangements are to the declaration and to the provisions relating to the collective bargaining method which apply in relation to the original unit.

(3)   For this purpose provisions relating to the collective bargaining method are—

(a)   the parties' agreement as to the method by which collective bargaining is to be conducted with regard to the original unit,

(b)   anything effective as, or as if contained in, a legally enforceable contract and relating to the method by which collective bargaining is to be conducted with regard to the original unit, or

(c)   any provision of this Part of this Schedule that a method of collective bargaining is to have effect with regard to the original unit.

**65.**   References in this Part of this Schedule to the parties are to the employer and the union (or unions) concerned.

**NOTES**

Inserted as noted at the beginning of this Schedule.

### *Either party believes unit no longer appropriate*

**[1.605]**

**66.** (1)   This paragraph applies if the employer believes or the union believes (or unions believe) that the original unit is no longer an appropriate bargaining unit.

(2)   The employer or union (or unions) may apply to the CAC to make a decision as to what is an appropriate bargaining unit.

**67.** (1) An application under paragraph 66 is not admissible unless the CAC decides that it is likely that the original unit is no longer appropriate by reason of any of the matters specified in sub-paragraph (2).

(2) The matters are—
- (a) a change in the organisation or structure of the business carried on by the employer;
- (b) a change in the activities pursued by the employer in the course of the business carried on by him;
- (c) a substantial change in the number of workers employed in the original unit.

**68.** (1) The CAC must give notice to the parties of receipt of an application under paragraph 66.

(2) Within the acceptance period the CAC must decide whether the application is admissible within the terms of paragraphs 67 and 92.

(3) In deciding whether the application is admissible the CAC must consider any evidence which it has been given by the employer or the union (or unions).

(4) If the CAC decides that the application is not admissible—
- (a) the CAC must give notice of its decision to the parties,
- (b) the CAC must not accept the application, and
- (c) no further steps are to be taken under this Part of this Schedule.

(5) If the CAC decides that the application is admissible it must—
- (a) accept the application, and
- (b) give notice of the acceptance to the parties.

(6) The acceptance period is—
- (a) the period of 10 working days starting with the day after that on which the CAC receives the application, or
- (b) such longer period (so starting) as the CAC may specify to the parties by notice containing reasons for the extension.

**69.** (1) This paragraph applies if—
- (a) the CAC gives notice of acceptance of the application, and
- (b) before the end of the first period the parties agree a bargaining unit or units (the new unit or units) differing from the original unit and inform the CAC of their agreement.

(2) If in the CAC's opinion the new unit (or any of the new units) contains at least one worker falling within an outside bargaining unit no further steps are to be taken under this Part of this Schedule.

(3) If sub-paragraph (2) does not apply—
- (a) the CAC must issue a declaration that the union is (or unions are) recognised as entitled to conduct collective bargaining on behalf of the new unit or units;
- (b) so far as it affects workers in the new unit (or units) who fall within the original unit, the declaration shall have effect in place of any declaration that the union is (or unions are) recognised as entitled to conduct collective bargaining on behalf of the original unit;
- (c) the method of collective bargaining relating to the original unit shall have effect in relation to the new unit or units, with any modifications which the CAC considers necessary to take account of the change of bargaining unit and specifies in the declaration.

(4) The first period is—
- (a) the period of 10 working days starting with the day after that on which the CAC gives notice of acceptance of the application, or
- (b) such longer period (so starting) as the parties may from time to time agree and notify to the CAC.

(5) An outside bargaining unit is a bargaining unit which fulfils these conditions—
- (a) it is not the original unit;
- (b) a union is (or unions are) recognised as entitled to conduct collective bargaining on its behalf;
- (c) the union (or at least one of the unions) is not a party referred to in paragraph 64.

**70.** (1) This paragraph applies if—
- (a) the CAC gives notice of acceptance of the application, and
- (b) the parties do not inform the CAC before the end of the first period that they have agreed a bargaining unit or units differing from the original unit.

(2) During the second period—
- (a) the CAC must decide whether or not the original unit continues to be an appropriate bargaining unit;
- (b) if the CAC decides that the original unit does not so continue, it must decide what other bargaining unit is or units are appropriate;
- (c) the CAC must give notice to the parties of its decision or decisions under paragraphs (a) and (b).

(3)   In deciding whether or not the original unit continues to be an appropriate bargaining unit the CAC must take into account only these matters—
- (a)   any change in the organisation or structure of the business carried on by the employer;
- (b)   any change in the activities pursued by the employer in the course of the business carried on by him;
- (c)   any substantial change in the number of workers employed in the original unit.

(4)   In deciding what other bargaining unit is or units are appropriate the CAC must take these matters into account—
- (a)   the need for the unit or units to be compatible with effective management;
- (b)   the matters listed in sub-paragraph (5), so far as they do not conflict with that need.

(5)   The matters are—
- (a)   the views of the employer and of the union (or unions);
- (b)   existing national and local bargaining arrangements;
- (c)   the desirability of avoiding small fragmented bargaining units within an undertaking;
- (d)   the characteristics of workers falling within the original unit and of any other employees of the employer whom the CAC considers relevant;
- (e)   the location of workers.

(6)   If the CAC decides that two or more bargaining units are appropriate its decision must be such that no worker falls within more than one of them.

(7)   The second period is—
- (a)   the period of 10 working days starting with the day after that on which the first period ends, or
- (b)   such longer period (so starting) as the CAC may specify to the parties by notice containing reasons for the extension.

**71.** If the CAC gives notice under paragraph 70 of a decision that the original unit continues to be an appropriate bargaining unit no further steps are to be taken under this Part of this Schedule.

**72.** Paragraph 82 applies if the CAC gives notice under paragraph 70 of—
- (a)   a decision that the original unit is no longer an appropriate bargaining unit, and
- (b)   a decision as to the bargaining unit which is (or units which are) appropriate.

**73.** (1)   This paragraph applies if—
- (a)   the parties agree under paragraph 69 a bargaining unit or units differing from the original unit,
- (b)   paragraph 69(2) does not apply, and
- (c)   at least one worker falling within the original unit does not fall within the new unit (or any of the new units).

(2)   In such a case—
- (a)   the CAC must issue a declaration that the bargaining arrangements, so far as relating to the worker or workers mentioned in sub-paragraph (1)(c), are to cease to have effect on a date specified by the CAC in the declaration, and
- (b)   the bargaining arrangements shall cease to have effect accordingly.

---

NOTES
Inserted as noted at the beginning of this Schedule.

---

*Employer believes unit has ceased to exist*

**[1.606]**
**74.** (1)   If the employer—
- (a)   believes that the original unit has ceased to exist, and
- (b)   wishes the bargaining arrangements to cease to have effect,

he must give the union (or each of the unions) a notice complying with sub-paragraph (2) and must give a copy of the notice to the CAC.

(2)   A notice complies with this sub-paragraph if it—
- (a)   identifies the unit and the bargaining arrangements,
- (b)   states the date on which the notice is given,
- (c)   states that the unit has ceased to exist, and
- (d)   states that the bargaining arrangements are to cease to have effect on a date which is specified in the notice and which falls after the end of the period of 35 working days starting with the day after that on which the notice is given.

(3)   Within the validation period the CAC must decide whether the notice complies with sub-paragraph (2).

(4)   If the CAC decides that the notice does not comply with sub-paragraph (2)—
- (a)   the CAC must give the parties notice of its decision, and
- (b)   the employer's notice shall be treated as not having been given.

(5) If the CAC decides that the notice complies with sub-paragraph (2) it must give the parties notice of the decision.

(6) The bargaining arrangements shall cease to have effect on the date specified under sub-paragraph (2)(d) if—
- (a) the CAC gives notice under sub-paragraph (5), and
- (b) the union does not (or unions do not) apply to the CAC under paragraph 75.

(7) The validation period is—
- (a) the period of 10 working days starting with the day after that on which the CAC receives the copy of the notice, or
- (b) such longer period (so starting) as the CAC may specify to the parties by notice containing reasons for the extension.

**75.** (1) Paragraph 76 applies if—
- (a) the CAC gives notice under paragraph 74(5), and
- (b) within the period of 10 working days starting with the day after that on which the notice is given the union makes (or unions make) an application to the CAC for a decision on the questions specified in sub-paragraph (2).

(2) The questions are—
- (a) whether the original unit has ceased to exist;
- (b) whether the original unit is no longer appropriate by reason of any of the matters specified in sub-paragraph (3).

(3) The matters are—
- (a) a change in the organisation or structure of the business carried on by the employer;
- (b) a change in the activities pursued by the employer in the course of the business carried on by him;
- (c) a substantial change in the number of workers employed in the original unit.

**76.** (1) The CAC must give notice to the parties of receipt of an application under paragraph 75.

(2) Within the acceptance period the CAC must decide whether the application is admissible within the terms of paragraph 92.

(3) In deciding whether the application is admissible the CAC must consider any evidence which it has been given by the employer or the union (or unions).

(4) If the CAC decides that the application is not admissible—
- (a) the CAC must give notice of its decision to the parties,
- (b) the CAC must not accept the application, and
- (c) no further steps are to be taken under this Part of this Schedule.

(5) If the CAC decides that the application is admissible it must—
- (a) accept the application, and
- (b) give notice of the acceptance to the parties.

(6) The acceptance period is—
- (a) the period of 10 working days starting with the day after that on which the CAC receives the application, or
- (b) such longer period (so starting) as the CAC may specify to the parties by notice containing reasons for the extension.

**77.** (1) If the CAC accepts an application it—
- (a) must give the employer and the union (or unions) an opportunity to put their views on the questions in relation to which the application was made;
- (b) must decide the questions before the end of the decision period.

(2) If the CAC decides that the original unit has ceased to exist—
- (a) the CAC must give the parties notice of its decision, and
- (b) the bargaining arrangements shall cease to have effect on the termination date.

(3) If the CAC decides that the original unit has not ceased to exist, and that it is not the case that the original unit is no longer appropriate by reason of any of the matters specified in paragraph 75(3)—
- (a) the CAC must give the parties notice of its decision, and
- (b) the employer's notice shall be treated as not having been given.

(4) If the CAC decides that the original unit has not ceased to exist, and that the original unit is no longer appropriate by reason of any of the matters specified in paragraph 75(3), the CAC must give the parties notice of its decision.

(5) The decision period is—
- (a) the period of 10 working days starting with the day after that on which the CAC gives notice of acceptance of the application, or
- (b) such longer period (so starting) as the CAC may specify to the parties by notice containing reasons for the extension.

(6)   The termination date is the later of—
  (a)   the date specified under paragraph 74(2)(d), and
  (b)   the day after the last day of the decision period.

**78.** (1)   This paragraph applies if—
  (a)   the CAC gives notice under paragraph 77(4), and
  (b)   before the end of the first period the parties agree a bargaining unit or units (the new unit or units) differing from the original unit and inform the CAC of their agreement.

(2)   If in the CAC's opinion the new unit (or any of the new units) contains at least one worker falling within an outside bargaining unit no further steps are to be taken under this Part of this Schedule.

(3)   If sub-paragraph (2) does not apply—
  (a)   the CAC must issue a declaration that the union is (or unions are) recognised as entitled to conduct collective bargaining on behalf of the new unit or units;
  (b)   so far as it affects workers in the new unit (or units) who fall within the original unit, the declaration shall have effect in place of any declaration that the union is (or unions are) recognised as entitled to conduct collective bargaining on behalf of the original unit;
  (c)   the method of collective bargaining relating to the original unit shall have effect in relation to the new unit or units, with any modifications which the CAC considers necessary to take account of the change of bargaining unit and specifies in the declaration.

(4)   The first period is—
  (a)   the period of 10 working days starting with the day after that on which the CAC gives notice under paragraph 77(4), or
  (b)   such longer period (so starting) as the parties may from time to time agree and notify to the CAC.

(5)   An outside bargaining unit is a bargaining unit which fulfils these conditions—
  (a)   it is not the original unit;
  (b)   a union is (or unions are) recognised as entitled to conduct collective bargaining on its behalf;
  (c)   the union (or at least one of the unions) is not a party referred to in paragraph 64.

**79.** (1)   This paragraph applies if—
  (a)   the CAC gives notice under paragraph 77(4), and
  (b)   the parties do not inform the CAC before the end of the first period that they have agreed a bargaining unit or units differing from the original unit.

(2)   During the second period the CAC—
  (a)   must decide what other bargaining unit is or units are appropriate;
  (b)   must give notice of its decision to the parties.

(3)   In deciding what other bargaining unit is or units are appropriate, the CAC must take these matters into account—
  (a)   the need for the unit or units to be compatible with effective management;
  (b)   the matters listed in sub-paragraph (4), so far as they do not conflict with that need.

(4)   The matters are—
  (a)   the views of the employer and of the union (or unions);
  (b)   existing national and local bargaining arrangements;
  (c)   the desirability of avoiding small fragmented bargaining units within an undertaking;
  (d)   the characteristics of workers falling within the original unit and of any other employees of the employer whom the CAC considers relevant;
  (e)   the location of workers.

(5)   If the CAC decides that two or more bargaining units are appropriate its decision must be such that no worker falls within more than one of them.

(6)   The second period is—
  (a)   the period of 10 working days starting with the day after that on which the first period ends, or
  (b)   such longer period (so starting) as the CAC may specify to the parties by notice containing reasons for the extension.

**80.**   Paragraph 82 applies if the CAC gives notice under paragraph 79 of a decision as to the bargaining unit which is (or units which are) appropriate.

**81.** (1)   This paragraph applies if—
  (a)   the parties agree under paragraph 78 a bargaining unit or units differing from the original unit,
  (b)   paragraph 78(2) does not apply, and
  (c)   at least one worker falling within the original unit does not fall within the new unit (or any of the new units).

(2)   In such a case—
  (a)   the CAC must issue a declaration that the bargaining arrangements, so far as relating to the worker or workers mentioned in sub-paragraph (1)(c), are to cease to have effect on a date specified by the CAC in the declaration, and
  (b)   the bargaining arrangements shall cease to have effect accordingly.

**NOTES**
Inserted as noted at the beginning of this Schedule.

*Position where CAC decides new unit*

**[1.607]**
**82.** (1)   This paragraph applies if the CAC gives notice under paragraph 70 of—
  (a)   a decision that the original unit is no longer an appropriate bargaining unit, and
  (b)   a decision as to the bargaining unit which is (or units which are) appropriate.

(2)   This paragraph also applies if the CAC gives notice under paragraph 79 of a decision as to the bargaining unit which is (or units which are) appropriate.

(3)   The CAC—
  (a)   must proceed as stated in paragraphs 83 to 89 with regard to the appropriate unit (if there is one only), or
  (b)   must proceed as stated in paragraphs 83 to 89 with regard to each appropriate unit separately (if there are two or more).

(4)   References in those paragraphs to the new unit are to the appropriate unit under consideration.

**83.** (1)   This paragraph applies if in the CAC's opinion the new unit contains at least one worker falling within a statutory outside bargaining unit.

(2)   In such a case—
  (a)   the CAC must issue a declaration that the relevant bargaining arrangements, so far as relating to workers falling within the new unit, are to cease to have effect on a date specified by the CAC in the declaration, and
  (b)   the relevant bargaining arrangements shall cease to have effect accordingly.

(3)   The relevant bargaining arrangements are—
  (a)   the bargaining arrangements relating to the original unit, and
  (b)   the bargaining arrangements relating to each statutory outside bargaining unit containing workers who fall within the new unit.

(4)   The bargaining arrangements relating to the original unit are the bargaining arrangements as defined in paragraph 64.

(5)   The bargaining arrangements relating to an outside unit are—
  (a)   the declaration recognising a union (or unions) as entitled to conduct collective bargaining on behalf of the workers constituting the outside unit, and
  (b)   the provisions relating to the collective bargaining method.

(6)   For this purpose the provisions relating to the collective bargaining method are—
  (a)   any agreement by the employer and the union (or unions) as to the method by which collective bargaining is to be conducted with regard to the outside unit,
  (b)   anything effective as, or as if contained in, a legally enforceable contract and relating to the method by which collective bargaining is to be conducted with regard to the outside unit, or
  (c)   any provision of this Part of this Schedule that a method of collective bargaining is to have effect with regard to the outside unit.

(7)   A statutory outside bargaining unit is a bargaining unit which fulfils these conditions—
  (a)   it is not the original unit;
  (b)   a union is (or unions are) recognised as entitled to conduct collective bargaining on its behalf by virtue of a declaration of the CAC;
  (c)   the union (or at least one of the unions) is not a party referred to in paragraph 64.

(8)   The date specified under sub-paragraph [(2)(a)] must be—
  (a)   the date on which the relevant period expires, or
  (b)   if the CAC believes that to maintain the relevant bargaining arrangements would be impracticable or contrary to the interests of good industrial relations, the date after the date on which the declaration is issued;
and the relevant period is the period of 65 working days starting with the day after that on which the declaration is issued.

**84.** (1)   This paragraph applies if in the CAC's opinion the new unit contains—
  (a)   at least one worker falling within a voluntary outside bargaining unit, but
  (b)   no worker falling within a statutory outside bargaining unit.

(2)   In such a case—

(a)   the CAC must issue a declaration that the original bargaining arrangements, so far as relating to workers falling within the new unit, are to cease to have effect on a date specified by the CAC in the declaration, and

(b)   the original bargaining arrangements shall cease to have effect accordingly.

(3)   The original bargaining arrangements are the bargaining arrangements as defined in paragraph 64.

(4)   A voluntary outside bargaining unit is a bargaining unit which fulfils these conditions—

(a)   it is not the original unit;

(b)   a union is (or unions are) recognised as entitled to conduct collective bargaining on its behalf by virtue of an agreement with the employer;

(c)   the union (or at least one of the unions) is not a party referred to in paragraph 64.

(5)   The date specified under sub-paragraph (2)(a) must be—

(a)   the date on which the relevant period expires, or

(b)   if the CAC believes that to maintain the original bargaining arrangements would be impracticable or contrary to the interests of good industrial relations, the date after the date on which the declaration is issued;

and the relevant period is the period of 65 working days starting with the day after that on which the declaration is issued.

**85.** (1)   If the CAC's opinion is not that mentioned in paragraph 83(1) or 84(1) it must—

(a)   decide whether the difference between the original unit and the new unit is such that the support of the union (or unions) within the new unit needs to be assessed, and

(b)   inform the parties of its decision.

(2)   If the CAC's decision is that such support does not need to be assessed—

(a)   the CAC must issue a declaration that the union is (or unions are) recognised as entitled to conduct collective bargaining on behalf of the new unit;

(b)   so far as it affects workers in the new unit who fall within the original unit, the declaration shall have effect in place of any declaration that the union is (or unions are) recognised as entitled to conduct collective bargaining on behalf of the original unit;

(c)   the method of collective bargaining relating to the original unit shall have effect in relation to the new unit, with any modifications which the CAC considers necessary to take account of the change of bargaining unit and specifies in the declaration.

**86.** (1)   This paragraph applies if the CAC decides under paragraph 85(1) that the support of the union (or unions) within the new unit needs to be assessed.

(2)   The CAC must decide these questions—

(a)   whether members of the union (or unions) constitute at least 10 per cent of the workers constituting the new unit;

(b)   whether a majority of the workers constituting the new unit would be likely to favour recognition of the union (or unions) as entitled to conduct collective bargaining on behalf of the new unit.

(3)   If the CAC decides one or both of the questions in the negative—

(a)   the CAC must issue a declaration that the bargaining arrangements, so far as relating to workers falling within the new unit, are to cease to have effect on a date specified by the CAC in the declaration, and

(b)   the bargaining arrangements shall cease to have effect accordingly.

**87.** (1)   This paragraph applies if—

(a)   the CAC decides both the questions in paragraph 86(2) in the affirmative, and

(b)   the CAC is satisfied that a majority of the workers constituting the new unit are members of the union (or unions).

(2)   The CAC must issue a declaration that the union is (or unions are) recognised as entitled to conduct collective bargaining on behalf of the workers constituting the new unit.

(3)   But if any of the three qualifying conditions is fulfilled, instead of issuing a declaration under sub-paragraph (2) the CAC must give notice to the parties that it intends to arrange for the holding of a secret ballot in which the workers constituting the new unit are asked whether they want the union (or unions) to conduct collective bargaining on their behalf.

(4)   These are the three qualifying conditions—

(a)   the CAC is satisfied that a ballot should be held in the interests of good industrial relations;

[(b)   the CAC has evidence, which it considers to be credible, from a significant number of the union members within the new bargaining unit that they do not want the union (or unions) to conduct collective bargaining on their behalf;]

(c)   membership evidence is produced which leads the CAC to conclude that there are doubts whether a significant number of the union members within the new unit want the union (or unions) to conduct collective bargaining on their behalf.

(5)   For the purposes of sub-paragraph (4)(c) membership evidence is—

(a)  evidence about the circumstances in which union members became members;
(b)  evidence about the length of time for which union members have been members, in a case where the CAC is satisfied that such evidence should be taken into account.

(6)  If the CAC issues a declaration under sub-paragraph (2)—
(a)  so far as it affects workers in the new unit who fall within the original unit, the declaration shall have effect in place of any declaration that the union is (or unions are) recognised as entitled to conduct collective bargaining on behalf of the original unit;
(b)  the method of collective bargaining relating to the original unit shall have effect in relation to the new unit, with any modifications which the CAC considers necessary to take account of the change of bargaining unit and specifies in the declaration.

**88.**  (1)  This paragraph applies if—
(a)  the CAC decides both the questions in paragraph 86(2) in the affirmative, and
(b)  the CAC is not satisfied that a majority of the workers constituting the new unit are members of the union (or unions).

(2)  The CAC must give notice to the parties that it intends to arrange for the holding of a secret ballot in which the workers constituting the new unit are asked whether they want the union (or unions) to conduct collective bargaining on their behalf.

**89.**  (1)  If the CAC gives notice under paragraph 87(3) or 88(2) the union (or unions) may within the notification period notify the CAC that the union does not (or unions do not) want the CAC to arrange for the holding of the ballot; and the notification period is the period of 10 working days starting with the day after that on which the union (or last of the unions) receives the CAC's notice.

(2)  If the CAC is so notified—
(a)  it must not arrange for the holding of the ballot,
(b)  it must inform the parties that it will not arrange for the holding of the ballot, and why,
(c)  it must issue a declaration that the bargaining arrangements, so far as relating to workers falling within the new unit, are to cease to have effect on a date specified by it in the declaration, and
(d)  the bargaining arrangements shall cease to have effect accordingly.

(3)  If the CAC is not so notified it must arrange for the holding of the ballot.

(4)  Paragraph 25 applies if the CAC arranges under this paragraph for the holding of a ballot (as well as if the CAC arranges under paragraph 24 for the holding of a ballot).

(5)  Paragraphs 26 to 29 apply accordingly, [but as if—
(a)  references to the bargaining unit were references to the new unit, and
(b)  paragraph 26(4F) to (4H), and the references in paragraph 26(4) and (6) to paragraph 19D, were omitted].

(6)  If as a result of the ballot the CAC issues a declaration that the union is (or unions are) recognised as entitled to conduct collective bargaining on behalf of the new unit—
(a)  so far as it affects workers in the new unit who fall within the original unit, the declaration shall have effect in place of any declaration that the union is (or unions are) recognised as entitled to conduct collective bargaining on behalf of the original unit;
(b)  the method of collective bargaining relating to the original unit shall have effect in relation to the new unit, with any modifications which the CAC considers necessary to take account of the change of bargaining unit and specifies in the declaration.

(7)  If as a result of the ballot the CAC issues a declaration that the union is (or unions are) not entitled to be recognised as entitled to conduct collective bargaining on behalf of the new unit—
(a)  the CAC must state in the declaration the date on which the bargaining arrangements, so far as relating to workers falling within the new unit, are to cease to have effect, and
(b)  the bargaining arrangements shall cease to have effect accordingly.

(8)  Paragraphs (a) and (b) of sub-paragraph (6) also apply if the CAC issues a declaration under paragraph 27(2) [or 27D(3)].

[(9)  Paragraphs (a) and (b) of sub-paragraph (7) also apply if the CAC issues a declaration under paragraph 27D(4).]

---

**NOTES**
Inserted as noted at the beginning of this Schedule.
Para 83: number in square brackets substituted by the Employment Relations Act 2004, s 57(1), Sch 1, para 23(1), (17).
Para 87: sub-para (4)(b) substituted by the Employment Relations Act 2004, s 6(2).
Para 89: words in square brackets in sub-para (5) substituted, words in square brackets in sub-para (8) inserted, and sub-para (9) added, by the Employment Relations Act 2004, s 57(1), Sch 1, para 23(1), (18)–(20).

---

*Residual workers*

**[1.608]**
**90.**  (1)  This paragraph applies if—
(a)  the CAC decides an appropriate bargaining unit or units under paragraph 70 or 79, and

    (b)   at least one worker falling within the original unit does not fall within the new unit (or any of the new units).

(2)   In such a case—

    (a)   the CAC must issue a declaration that the bargaining arrangements, so far as relating to the worker or workers mentioned in sub-paragraph (1)(b), are to cease to have effect on a date specified by the CAC in the declaration, and

    (b)   the bargaining arrangements shall cease to have effect accordingly.

**91.**  (1)  This paragraph applies if—

    (a)   the CAC has proceeded as stated in paragraphs 83 to 89 with regard to the new unit (if there is one only) or with regard to each new unit (if there are two or more), and

    (b)   in so doing the CAC has issued one or more declarations under paragraph 83.

(2)   The CAC must—

    (a)   consider each declaration issued under paragraph 83, and

    (b)   in relation to each declaration, identify each statutory outside bargaining unit which contains at least one worker who also falls within the new unit to which the declaration relates;

and in this paragraph each statutory outside bargaining unit so identified is referred to as a parent unit.

(3)   The CAC must then—

    (a)   consider each parent unit, and

    (b)   in relation to each parent unit, identify any workers who fall within the parent unit but who do not fall within the new unit (or any of the new units);

and in this paragraph the workers so identified in relation to a parent unit are referred to as a residual unit.

(4)   In relation to each residual unit, the CAC must issue a declaration that the outside union is (or outside unions are) recognised as entitled to conduct collective bargaining on its behalf.

(5)   But no such declaration shall be issued in relation to a residual unit if the CAC has received an application under paragraph 66 or 75 in relation to its parent unit.

(6)   In this paragraph references to the outside union (or to outside unions) in relation to a residual unit are to the union which is (or unions which are) recognised as entitled to conduct collective bargaining on behalf of its parent unit.

(7)   If the CAC issues a declaration under sub-paragraph (4)—

    (a)   the declaration shall have effect in place of the existing declaration that the outside union is (or outside unions are) recognised as entitled to conduct collective bargaining on behalf of the parent unit, so far as the existing declaration relates to the residual unit;

    (b)   if there is a method of collective bargaining relating to the parent unit, it shall have effect in relation to the residual unit with any modifications which the CAC considers necessary to take account of the change of bargaining unit and specifies in the declaration.

**NOTES**

Inserted as noted at the beginning of this Schedule.

*Applications under this Part*

**[1.609]**

**92.**  (1)  An application to the CAC under this Part of this Schedule is not admissible unless—

    (a)   it is made in such form as the CAC specifies, and

    (b)   it is supported by such documents as the CAC specifies.

(2)   An application which is made by a union (or unions) to the CAC under this Part of this Schedule is not admissible unless the union gives (or unions give) to the employer—

    (a)   notice of the application, and

    (b)   a copy of the application and any documents supporting it.

(3)   An application which is made by an employer to the CAC under this Part of this Schedule is not admissible unless the employer gives to the union (or each of the unions)—

    (a)   notice of the application, and

    (b)   a copy of the application and any documents supporting it.

**NOTES**

Inserted as noted at the beginning of this Schedule.

*Withdrawal of application*

**[1.610]**

**93.**  (1)  If an application under paragraph 66 or 75 is accepted by the CAC, the applicant (or applicants) may not withdraw the application—

    (a)   after the CAC issues a declaration under paragraph 69(3) or 78(3),

    (b)   after the CAC decides under paragraph 77(2) or 77(3),

(c)  after the CAC issues a declaration under paragraph [83(2)], 85(2), 86(3) or 87(2) in relation to the new unit (where there is only one) or a declaration under any of those paragraphs in relation to any of the new units (where there is more than one),

(d)  after the union has (or unions have) notified the CAC under paragraph 89(1) in relation to the new unit (where there is only one) or any of the new units (where there is more than one), or

(e)  after the end of the notification period referred to in paragraph 89(1) and relating to the new unit (where there is only one) or any of the new units (where there is more than one).

(2)  If an application is withdrawn by the applicant (or applicants)—

(a)  the CAC must give notice of the withdrawal to the other party (or parties), and

(b)  no further steps are to be taken under this Part of this Schedule.

**NOTES**

Inserted as noted at the beginning of this Schedule.

Para 93: number in square brackets in sub-para (1)(c) substituted by the Employment Relations Act 2004, s 57(1), Sch 1, para 23(1), (21).

*Meaning of collective bargaining*

**[1.611]**

**94.**  (1)  This paragraph applies for the purposes of this Part of this Schedule.

(2)  Except in relation to paragraphs 69(5), 78(5) and 83(6), the meaning of collective bargaining given by section 178(1) shall not apply.

(3)  In relation to a new unit references to collective bargaining are to negotiations relating to the matters which were the subject of collective bargaining in relation to the corresponding original unit; and the corresponding original unit is the unit which was the subject of an application under paragraph 66 or 75 in consequence of which the new unit was agreed by the parties or decided by the CAC.

(4)  But if the parties agree matters as the subject of collective bargaining in relation to the new unit, references to collective bargaining in relation to that unit are to negotiations relating to the agreed matters; and this is the case whether the agreement is made before or after the time when the CAC issues a declaration that the union is (or unions are) recognised as entitled to conduct collective bargaining on behalf of the new unit.

(5)  In relation to a residual unit in relation to which a declaration is issued under paragraph 91, references to collective bargaining are to negotiations relating to the matters which were the subject of collective bargaining in relation to the corresponding parent unit.

(6)  In construing paragraphs 69(3)(c), 78(3)(c), 85(2)(c), 87(6)(b) and 89(6)(b)—

(a)  sub-paragraphs (3) and (4) do not apply, and

(b)  references to collective bargaining are to negotiations relating to pay, hours and holidays.

**NOTES**

Inserted as noted at the beginning of this Schedule.

*Method of collective bargaining*

**[1.612]**

**95.**  (1)  This paragraph applies for the purposes of this Part of this Schedule.

(2)  Where a method of collective bargaining has effect in relation to a new unit, that method shall have effect as if it were contained in a legally enforceable contract made by the parties.

(3)  But if the parties agree in writing—

(a)  that sub-paragraph (2) shall not apply, or shall not apply to particular parts of the method, or

(b)  to vary or replace the method,

the written agreement shall have effect as a legally enforceable contract made by the parties.

(4)  Specific performance shall be the only remedy available for breach of anything which is a legally enforceable contract by virtue of this paragraph.

**NOTES**

Inserted as noted at the beginning of this Schedule.

# PART IV
# DERECOGNITION: GENERAL

*Introduction*

**[1.613]**

**96.**  (1)  This Part of this Schedule applies if the CAC has issued a declaration that a union is (or unions are) recognised as entitled to conduct collective bargaining on behalf of a bargaining unit.

(2)    In such a case references in this Part of this Schedule to the bargaining arrangements are to the declaration and to the provisions relating to the collective bargaining method.

(3)    For this purpose the provisions relating to the collective bargaining method are—
(a)    the parties' agreement as to the method by which collective bargaining is to be conducted,
(b)    anything effective as, or as if contained in, a legally enforceable contract and relating to the method by which collective bargaining is to be conducted, or
(c)    any provision of Part III of this Schedule that a method of collective bargaining is to have effect.

**97.**    For the purposes of this Part of this Schedule the relevant date is the date of the expiry of the period of 3 years starting with the date of the CAC's declaration.

**98.**    References in this Part of this Schedule to the parties are to the employer and the union (or unions) concerned.

---

**NOTES**
Inserted as noted at the beginning of this Schedule.

---

*Employer employs fewer than 21 workers*
**[1.614]**
**99.**    (1)    This paragraph applies if—
(a)    the employer believes that he, taken with any associated employer or employers, employed an average of fewer than 21 workers in any period of 13 weeks, and
(b)    that period ends on or after the relevant date.

(2)    If the employer wishes the bargaining arrangements to cease to have effect, he must give the union (or each of the unions) a notice complying with sub-paragraph (3) and must give a copy of the notice to the CAC.

(3)    A notice complies with this sub-paragraph if it—
[(za)    is not invalidated by paragraph 99A,]
(a)    identifies the bargaining arrangements,
(b)    specifies the period of 13 weeks in question,
(c)    states the date on which the notice is given,
(d)    is given within the period of 5 working days starting with the day after the last day of the specified period of 13 weeks,
(e)    states that the employer, taken with any associated employer or employers, employed an average of fewer than 21 workers in the specified period of 13 weeks, and
(f)    states that the bargaining arrangements are to cease to have effect on a date which is specified in the notice and which falls after the end of the period of 35 working days starting with the day after that on which the notice is given.

(4)    To find the average number of workers employed by the employer, taken with any associated employer or employers, in the specified period of 13 weeks—
(a)    take the number of workers employed in each of the 13 weeks (including workers not employed for the whole of the week);
(b)    aggregate the 13 numbers;
(c)    divide the aggregate by 13.

(5)    For the purposes of sub-paragraph (1)(a) any worker employed by an associated company incorporated outside Great Britain must be ignored in relation to a week unless the whole or any part of that week fell within a period during which he ordinarily worked in Great Britain.

[(5A)    Sub-paragraph (5B) applies to an agency worker whose contract within regulation 3(1)(b) of the Agency Workers Regulations 2010 (contract with the temporary work agency) is not a contract of employment.

(5B)    For the purposes of sub-paragraphs (1) and (4), the agency worker is to be treated as having a contract of employment with the temporary work agency for the duration of the assignment with the employer (and "assignment" has the same meaning as in those Regulations).]

(6)    For the purposes of sub-paragraph (5) a worker who is employed on board a ship registered in the register maintained under section 8 of the Merchant Shipping Act 1995 shall be treated as ordinarily working in Great Britain unless—
(a)    the ship's entry in the register specifies a port outside Great Britain as the port to which the vessel is to be treated as belonging,
(b)    the employment is wholly outside Great Britain, or
(c)    the worker is not ordinarily resident in Great Britain.

(7)    An order made under paragraph 7(6) may also—
(a)    provide that sub-paragraphs (1) to (6) of this paragraph and paragraphs [99A] to 103 are not to apply, or are not to apply in specified circumstances, or
(b)    vary the number of workers for the time being specified in sub-paragraphs (1)(a) and (3)(e).

**[99A.** (1)  A notice given for the purposes of paragraph 99(2) ("the notice in question") is invalidated by this paragraph if—

(a)  a relevant application was made, or an earlier notice under paragraph 99(2) was given, within the period of 3 years prior to the date when the notice in question was given,

(b)  the relevant application, or that earlier notice, and the notice in question relate to the same bargaining unit, and

(c)  the CAC accepted the relevant application or (as the case may be) decided under paragraph 100 that the earlier notice under paragraph 99(2) complied with paragraph 99(3).

(2)  A relevant application is an application made to the CAC—

(a)  by the employer under paragraph 106, 107 or 128, or

(b)  by a worker (or workers) under paragraph 112.]

**100.** (1)  [If an employer gives notice for the purposes of paragraph 99(2),] within the validation period the CAC must decide whether the notice complies with paragraph 99(3).

(2)  If the CAC decides that the notice does not comply with paragraph 99(3)—

(a)  the CAC must give the parties notice of its decision, and

(b)  the employer's notice shall be treated as not having been given.

(3)  If the CAC decides that the notice complies with paragraph 99(3) it must give the parties notice of the decision.

(4)  The bargaining arrangements shall cease to have effect on the date specified under paragraph 99(3)(f) if—

(a)  the CAC gives notice under sub-paragraph (3), and

(b)  the union does not (or unions do not) apply to the CAC under paragraph 101.

(5)  The validation period is—

(a)  the period of 10 working days starting with the day after that on which the CAC receives the copy of the notice, or

(b)  such longer period (so starting) as the CAC may specify to the parties by notice containing reasons for the extension.

**101.** (1)  This paragraph applies if—

(a)  the CAC gives notice under paragraph 100(3), and

(b)  within the period of 10 working days starting with the day after that on which the notice is given, the union makes (or unions make) an application to the CAC for a decision whether the period of 13 weeks specified under paragraph 99(3)(b) ends on or after the relevant date and whether the statement made under paragraph 99(3)(e) is correct.

(2)  An application is not admissible unless—

(a)  it is made in such form as the CAC specifies, and

(b)  it is supported by such documents as the CAC specifies.

(3)  An application is not admissible unless the union gives (or unions give) to the employer—

(a)  notice of the application, and

(b)  a copy of the application and any documents supporting it.

(4), (5)   . . .

**102.** (1)  The CAC must give notice to the parties of receipt of an application under paragraph 101.

(2)  Within the acceptance period the CAC must decide whether the application is admissible within the terms of paragraph 101.

(3)  In deciding whether an application is admissible the CAC must consider any evidence which it has been given by the employer or the union (or unions).

(4)  If the CAC decides that the application is not admissible—

(a)  the CAC must give notice of its decision to the parties,

(b)  the CAC must not accept the application,

(c)  no further steps are to be taken under this Part of this Schedule, and

(d)  the bargaining arrangements shall cease to have effect on the date specified under paragraph 99(3)(f).

(5)  If the CAC decides that the application is admissible it must—

(a)  accept the application, and

(b)  give notice of the acceptance to the parties.

(6)  The acceptance period is—

(a)  the period of 10 working days starting with the day after that on which the CAC receives the application, or

(b)  such longer period (so starting) as the CAC may specify to the parties by notice containing reasons for the extension.

**103.** (1)  If the CAC accepts an application it—

(a)   must give the employer and the union (or unions) an opportunity to put their views on the questions whether the period of 13 weeks specified under paragraph 99(3)(b) ends on or after the relevant date and whether the statement made under paragraph 99(3)(e) is correct;

(b)   must decide the questions within the decision period and must give reasons for the decision.

(2)   If the CAC decides that the period of 13 weeks specified under paragraph 99(3)(b) ends on or after the relevant date and that the statement made under paragraph 99(3)(e) is correct the bargaining arrangements shall cease to have effect on the termination date.

(3)   If the CAC decides that the period of 13 weeks specified under paragraph 99(3)(b) does not end on or after the relevant date or that the statement made under paragraph 99(3)(e) is not correct, the notice under paragraph 99 shall be treated as not having been given.

[(3A)   Sub-paragraph (3) does not prevent the notice from being treated for the purposes of the provisions mentioned in sub-paragraph (3B) as having been given.

(3B)   Those provisions are—
(a)   paragraphs 109(1), 113(1) and 130(1);
(b)   paragraph 99A(1) in its application to a later notice given for the purposes of paragraph 99(2).]

(4)   The decision period is—
(a)   the period of 10 working days starting with the day after that on which the CAC gives notice of acceptance of the application, or
(b)   such longer period (so starting) as the CAC may specify to the parties by notice containing reasons for the extension.

(5)   The termination date is the later of—
(a)   the date specified under paragraph 99(3)(f), and
(b)   the day after the last day of the decision period.

---

**NOTES**

Inserted as noted at the beginning of this Schedule.

Para 99: sub-para (3)(za) inserted, and number in square brackets in sub-para (7)(a) substituted, by the Employment Relations Act 2004, s 12(1)–(3); sub-paras (5A), (5B) inserted by the Agency Workers Regulations 2010, SI 2010/93, reg 25, Sch 2, Pt 1, paras 1, 7(1), (3), s from 1 October 2011.

Para 99A: inserted by the Employment Relations Act 2004, s 12(4).

Para 100: words in square brackets in sub-para (1) inserted by the Employment Relations Act 2004, s 12(5).

Para 101: sub-paras (4), (5) repealed by the Employment Relations Act 2004, ss 12(6), 57(2), Sch 2.

Para 103: sub-paras (3A), (3B) inserted by the Employment Relations Act 2004, s 12(7).

---

*Employer's request to end arrangements*

**[1.615]**
**104.** (1)   This paragraph and paragraphs 105 to 111 apply if after the relevant date the employer requests the union (or each of the unions) to agree to end the bargaining arrangements.

(2)   The request is not valid unless it—
(a)   is in writing,
(b)   is received by the union (or each of the unions),
(c)   identifies the bargaining arrangements, and
(d)   states that it is made under this Schedule.

**105.** (1)   If before the end of the first period the parties agree to end the bargaining arrangements no further steps are to be taken under this Part of this Schedule.

(2)   Sub-paragraph (3) applies if before the end of the first period—
(a)   the union informs the employer that the union does not accept the request but is willing to negotiate, or
(b)   the unions inform the employer that the unions do not accept the request but are willing to negotiate.

(3)   The parties may conduct negotiations with a view to agreeing to end the bargaining arrangements.

(4)   If such an agreement is made before the end of the second period no further steps are to be taken under this Part of this Schedule.

(5)   The employer and the union (or unions) may request ACAS to assist in conducting the negotiations.

(6)   The first period is the period of 10 working days starting with the day after—
(a)   the day on which the union receives the request, or
(b)   the last day on which any of the unions receives the request.

(7)   The second period is—
(a)   the period of 20 working days starting with the day after that on which the first period ends, or

(b)    such longer period (so starting) as the parties may from time to time agree.

**106.** (1)    This paragraph applies if—
(a)    before the end of the first period the union fails (or unions fail) to respond to the request, or
(b)    before the end of the first period the union informs the employer that it does not (or unions inform the employer that they do not) accept the request (without indicating a willingness to negotiate).

(2)    The employer may apply to the CAC for the holding of a secret ballot to decide whether the bargaining arrangements should be ended.

**107.** (1)    This paragraph applies if—
(a)    the union informs (or unions inform) the employer under paragraph 105(2), and
(b)    no agreement is made before the end of the second period.

(2)    The employer may apply to the CAC for the holding of a secret ballot to decide whether the bargaining arrangements should be ended.

(3)    But no application may be made if within the period of 10 working days starting with the day after that on which the union informs (or unions inform) the employer under paragraph 105(2) the union proposes (or unions propose) that ACAS be requested to assist in conducting the negotiations and—
(a)    the employer rejects the proposal, or
(b)    the employer fails to accept the proposal within the period of 10 working days starting with the day after that on which the union makes (or unions make) the proposal.

**108.** (1)    An application under paragraph 106 or 107 is not admissible unless—
(a)    it is made in such form as the CAC specifies, and
(b)    it is supported by such documents as the CAC specifies.

(2)    An application under paragraph 106 or 107 is not admissible unless the employer gives to the union (or each of the unions)—
(a)    notice of the application, and
(b)    a copy of the application and any documents supporting it.

**109.** (1)    An application under paragraph 106 or 107 is not admissible if—
(a)    a relevant application was made[, or a notice under paragraph 99(2) was given,] within the period of 3 years prior to the date of the application under paragraph 106 or 107,
(b)    the relevant application[, or notice under paragraph 99(2),] and the application under paragraph 106 or 107 relate to the same bargaining unit, and
(c)    the CAC accepted the relevant application [or (as the case may be) decided under paragraph 100 that the notice complied with paragraph 99(3)].

(2)    A relevant application is an application made to the CAC—
(a)    . . .
(b)    by the employer under paragraph 106, 107 or 128, or
(c)    by a worker (or workers) under paragraph 112.

**110.** (1)    An application under paragraph 106 or 107 is not admissible unless the CAC decides that—
(a)    at least 10 per cent of the workers constituting the bargaining unit favour an end of the bargaining arrangements, and
(b)    a majority of the workers constituting the bargaining unit would be likely to favour an end of the bargaining arrangements.

(2)    The CAC must give reasons for the decision.

**111.** (1)    The CAC must give notice to the parties of receipt of an application under paragraph 106 or 107.

(2)    Within the acceptance period the CAC must decide whether—
(a)    the request is valid within the terms of paragraph 104, and
(b)    the application is made in accordance with paragraph 106 or 107 and admissible within the terms of paragraphs 108 to 110.

(3)    In deciding those questions the CAC must consider any evidence which it has been given by the employer or the union (or unions).

(4)    If the CAC decides that the request is not valid or the application is not made in accordance with paragraph 106 or 107 or is not admissible—
(a)    the CAC must give notice of its decision to the parties,
(b)    the CAC must not accept the application, and
(c)    no further steps are to be taken under this Part of this Schedule.

(5)    If the CAC decides that the request is valid and the application is made in accordance with paragraph 106 or 107 and is admissible it must—

(a)    accept the application, and

(b)    give notice of the acceptance to the parties.

(6)   The acceptance period is—

(a)    the period of 10 working days starting with the day after that on which the CAC receives the application, or

(b)    such longer period (so starting) as the CAC may specify to the parties by notice containing reasons for the extension.

---

**NOTES**

Inserted as noted at the beginning of this Schedule.

Para 109: words in square brackets in sub-para (1) inserted, and sub-para (2)(a) repealed, by the Employment Relations Act 2004, ss 12(8), (9), 57(2).

---

*Workers' application to end arrangements*

**[1.616]**

**112.** (1)    A worker or workers falling within the bargaining unit may after the relevant date apply to the CAC to have the bargaining arrangements ended.

(2)   An application is not admissible unless—

(a)    it is made in such form as the CAC specifies, and

(b)    it is supported by such documents as the CAC specifies.

(3)   An application is not admissible unless the worker gives (or workers give) to the employer and to the union (or each of the unions)—

(a)    notice of the application, and

(b)    a copy of the application and any documents supporting it.

**113.** (1)   An application under paragraph 112 is not admissible if—

(a)    a relevant application was made[, or a notice under paragraph 99(2) was given,] within the period of 3 years prior to the date of the application under paragraph 112,

(b)    the relevant application[, or notice under paragraph 99(2),] and the application under paragraph 112 relate to the same bargaining unit, and

(c)    the CAC accepted the relevant application [or (as the case may be) decided under paragraph 100 that the notice complied with paragraph 99(3)].

(2)   A relevant application is an application made to the CAC—

(a)    . . .

(b)    by the employer under paragraph 106, 107 or 128, or

(c)    by a worker (or workers) under paragraph 112.

**114.** (1)   An application under paragraph 112 is not admissible unless the CAC decides that—

(a)    at least 10 per cent of the workers constituting the bargaining unit favour an end of the bargaining arrangements, and

(b)    a majority of the workers constituting the bargaining unit would be likely to favour an end of the bargaining arrangements.

(2)   The CAC must give reasons for the decision.

**115.** (1)   The CAC must give notice to the worker (or workers), the employer and the union (or unions) of receipt of an application under paragraph 112.

(2)   Within the acceptance period the CAC must decide whether the application is admissible within the terms of paragraphs 112 to 114.

(3)   In deciding whether the application is admissible the CAC must consider any evidence which it has been given by the employer, the union (or unions) or any of the workers falling within the bargaining unit.

(4)   If the CAC decides that the application is not admissible—

(a)    the CAC must give notice of its decision to the worker (or workers), the employer and the union (or unions),

(b)    the CAC must not accept the application, and

(c)    no further steps are to be taken under this Part of this Schedule.

(5)   If the CAC decides that the application is admissible it must—

(a)    accept the application, and

(b)    give notice of the acceptance to the worker (or workers), the employer and the union (or unions).

(6)   The acceptance period is—

(a)    the period of 10 working days starting with the day after that on which the CAC receives the application, or

(b)    such longer period (so starting) as the CAC may specify to the worker (or workers), the employer and the union (or unions) by notice containing reasons for the extension.

**116.** (1)  If the CAC accepts the application, in the negotiation period the CAC must help the employer, the union (or unions) and the worker (or workers) with a view to—
    (a)   the employer and the union (or unions) agreeing to end the bargaining arrangements, or
    (b)   the worker (or workers) withdrawing the application.

(2)  The negotiation period is—
    (a)   the period of 20 working days starting with the day after that on which the CAC gives notice of acceptance of the application, or
    (b)   such longer period (so starting) as the CAC may decide with the consent of the worker (or workers), the employer and the union (or unions).

**NOTES**

Inserted as noted at the beginning of this Schedule.

Para 113: words in square brackets in sub-para (1) inserted, and sub-para (2)(a) repealed, by the Employment Relations Act 2004, ss 12(8), (9), 57(2), Sch 2.

*Ballot on derecognition*

**[1.617]**
**117.** (1)  This paragraph applies if the CAC accepts an application under paragraph 106 or 107.

(2)  This paragraph also applies if—
    (a)   the CAC accepts an application under paragraph 112, and
    (b)   in the period mentioned in paragraph 116(1) there is no agreement or withdrawal as there described.

(3)  The CAC must arrange for the holding of a secret ballot in which the workers constituting the bargaining unit are asked whether the bargaining arrangements should be ended.

(4)  The ballot must be conducted by a qualified independent person appointed by the CAC.

(5)  The ballot must be conducted within—
    (a)   the period of 20 working days starting with the day after that on which the qualified independent person is appointed, or
    (b)   such longer period (so starting) as the CAC may decide.

(6)  The ballot must be conducted—
    (a)   at a workplace or workplaces decided by the CAC,
    (b)   by post, or
    (c)   by a combination of the methods described in sub-paragraphs (a) and (b),
depending on the CAC's preference.

(7)  In deciding how the ballot is to be conducted the CAC must take into account—
    (a)   the likelihood of the ballot being affected by unfairness or malpractice if it were conducted at a workplace or workplaces;
    (b)   costs and practicality;
    (c)   such other matters as the CAC considers appropriate.

(8)  The CAC may not decide that the ballot is to be conducted as mentioned in sub-paragraph (6)(c) unless there are special factors making such a decision appropriate; and special factors include—
    (a)   factors arising from the location of workers or the nature of their employment;
    (b)   factors put to the CAC by the employer or the union (or unions).

[(8A)  If the CAC decides that the ballot must (in whole or in part) be conducted at a workplace (or workplaces), it may require arrangements to be made for workers—
    (a)   who (but for the arrangements) would be prevented by the CAC's decision from voting by post, and
    (b)   who are unable, for reasons relating to those workers as individuals, to cast their votes in the ballot at the workplace (or at any of them),
to be given the opportunity (if they request it far enough in advance of the ballot for this to be practicable) to vote by post; and the CAC's imposing such a requirement is not to be treated for the purposes of sub-paragraph (8) as a decision that the ballot be conducted as mentioned in sub-paragraph (6)(c).]

(9)  A person is a qualified independent person if—
    (a)   he satisfies such conditions as may be specified for the purposes of this paragraph by order of the Secretary of State or is himself so specified, and
    (b)   there are no grounds for believing either that he will carry out any functions conferred on him in relation to the ballot otherwise than competently or that his independence in relation to the ballot might reasonably be called into question.

(10)  An order under sub-paragraph (9)(a) shall be made by statutory instrument subject to annulment in pursuance of a resolution of either House of Parliament.

(11)  As soon as is reasonably practicable after the CAC is required under sub-paragraph (3) to arrange for the holding of a ballot it must inform the employer and the union (or unions)—
    (a)   that it is so required;

  (b)    of the name of the person appointed to conduct the ballot and the date of his appointment;

  (c)    of the period within which the ballot must be conducted;

  (d)    whether the ballot is to be conducted by post or at a workplace or workplaces;

  (e)    of the workplace or workplaces concerned (if the ballot is to be conducted at a workplace or workplaces).

**118.** (1)   An employer who is informed by the CAC under paragraph 117(11) must comply with the following [five] duties.

(2)   The first duty is to co-operate generally, in connection with the ballot, with the union (or unions) and the person appointed to conduct the ballot; and the second and third duties are not to prejudice the generality of this.

(3)   The second duty is to give to the union (or unions) such access to the workers constituting the bargaining unit as is reasonable to enable the union (or unions) to inform the workers of the object of the ballot and to seek their support and their opinions on the issues involved.

(4)   The third duty is to do the following (so far as it is reasonable to expect the employer to do so)—

  (a)    to give to the CAC, within the period of 10 working days starting with the day after that on which the employer is informed under paragraph 117(11), the names and home addresses of the workers constituting the bargaining unit;

  (b)    to give to the CAC, as soon as is reasonably practicable, the name and home address of any worker who joins the unit after the employer has complied with paragraph (a);

  (c)    to inform the CAC, as soon as is reasonably practicable, of any worker whose name has been given to the CAC under paragraph (a) or (b) but who ceases to be within the unit.

[(4A)   The fourth duty is to refrain from making any offer to any or all of the workers constituting the bargaining unit which—

  (a)    has or is likely to have the effect of inducing any or all of them not to attend any relevant meeting between the union (or unions) and the workers constituting the bargaining unit, and

  (b)    is not reasonable in the circumstances.

(4B)   The fifth duty is to refrain from taking or threatening to take any action against a worker solely or mainly on the grounds that he—

  (a)    attended or took part in any relevant meeting between the union (or unions) and the workers constituting the bargaining unit, or

  (b)    indicated his intention to attend or take part in such a meeting.

(4C)   A meeting is a relevant meeting in relation to a worker for the purposes of sub-paragraph (4A) and (4B) if—

  (a)    it is organised in accordance with any agreement reached concerning the second duty or as a result of a step ordered to be taken under paragraph 119 to remedy a failure to comply with that duty, and

  (b)    it is one which the employer is, by such an agreement or order as is mentioned in paragraph (a), required to permit the worker to attend.

(4D)   Without prejudice to the generality of the second duty imposed by this paragraph, an employer is to be taken to have failed to comply with that duty if—

  (a)    he refuses a request for a meeting between the union (or unions) and any or all of the workers constituting the bargaining unit to be held in the absence of the employer or any representative of his (other than one who has been invited to attend the meeting) and it is not reasonable in the circumstances for him to do so,

  (b)    he or a representative of his attends such a meeting without having been invited to do so,

  (c)    he seeks to record or otherwise be informed of the proceedings at any such meeting and it is not reasonable in the circumstances for him to do so, or

  (d)    he refuses to give an undertaking that he will not seek to record or otherwise be informed of the proceedings at any such meeting unless it is reasonable in the circumstances for him to do either of those things.

(4E)   The fourth and fifth duties do not confer any rights on a worker; but that does not affect any other right which a worker may have.]

(5)   As soon as is reasonably practicable after the CAC receives any information under sub-paragraph (4) it must pass it on to the person appointed to conduct the ballot.

(6)   If asked to do so by the union (or unions) the person appointed to conduct the ballot must send to any worker—

  (a)    whose name and home address have been given under sub-paragraph (5), and

  (b)    who is still within the unit (so far as the person so appointed is aware),

any information supplied by the union (or unions) to the person so appointed.

(7)   The duty under sub-paragraph (6) does not apply unless the union bears (or unions bear) the cost of sending the information.

[(8) Each of the powers specified in sub-paragraph (9) shall be taken to include power to issue Codes of Practice—
   (a)   about reasonable access for the purposes of sub-paragraph (3), and
   (b)   about the fourth duty imposed by this paragraph.
(9)   The powers are—
   (a)   the power of ACAS under section 199(1);
   (b)   the power of the Secretary of State under section 203(1)(a).]

**119.** (1)   If the CAC is satisfied that the employer has failed to fulfil any of the [duties imposed on him] by paragraph 118, and the ballot has not been held, the CAC may order the employer—
   (a)   to take such steps to remedy the failure as the CAC considers reasonable and specifies in the order, and
   (b)   to do so within such period as the CAC considers reasonable and specifies in the order.
(2)   If—
   (a)   the ballot has been arranged in consequence of an application under paragraph 106 or 107,
   (b)   the CAC is satisfied that the employer has failed to comply with an order under sub-paragraph (1), and
   (c)   the ballot has not been held,
the CAC may refuse the application.
(3)   . . . .
(4)   If the CAC refuses an application under sub-paragraph (2) it shall take steps to cancel the holding of the ballot; and if the ballot is held it shall have no effect.

[**119A.** (1)   Each of the parties informed by the CAC under paragraph 117(11) must refrain from using any unfair practice.
(2)   A party uses an unfair practice if, with a view to influencing the result of the ballot, the party—
   (a)   offers to pay money or give money's worth to a worker entitled to vote in the ballot in return for the worker's agreement to vote in a particular way or to abstain from voting,
   (b)   makes an outcome-specific offer to a worker entitled to vote in the ballot,
   (c)   coerces or attempts to coerce a worker entitled to vote in the ballot to disclose—
      (i)   whether he intends to vote or to abstain from voting in the ballot, or
      (ii)   how he intends to vote, or how he has voted, in the ballot,
   (d)   dismisses or threatens to dismiss a worker,
   (e)   takes or threatens to take disciplinary action against a worker,
   (f)   subjects or threatens to subject a worker to any other detriment, or
   (g)   uses or attempts to use undue influence on a worker entitled to vote in the ballot.
(3)   For the purposes of sub-paragraph (2)(b) an "outcome-specific offer" is an offer to pay money or give money's worth which—
   (a)   is conditional on—
      (i)   the issuing by the CAC of a declaration that the bargaining arrangements are to cease to have effect, or
      (ii)   the refusal by the CAC of an application under paragraph 106, 107 or 112, and
   (b)   is not conditional on anything which is done or occurs as a result of that declaration or, as the case may be, of that refusal.
(4)   The duty imposed by this paragraph does not confer any rights on a worker; but that does not affect any other right which a worker may have.
(5)   Each of the following powers shall be taken to include power to issue Codes of Practice about unfair practices for the purposes of this paragraph—
   (a)   the power of ACAS under section 199(1);
   (b)   the power of the Secretary of State under section 203(1)(a).

**119B.** (1)   A party may complain to the CAC that another party has failed to comply with paragraph 119A.
(2)   A complaint under sub-paragraph (1) must be made on or before the first working day after—
   (a)   the date of the ballot, or
   (b)   if votes may be cast in the ballot on more than one day, the last of those days.
(3)   Within the decision period the CAC must decide whether the complaint is well-founded.
(4)   A complaint is well-founded if—
   (a)   the CAC finds that the party complained against used an unfair practice, and
   (b)   the CAC is satisfied that the use of that practice changed or was likely to change, in the case of a worker entitled to vote in the ballot—
      (i)   his intention to vote or to abstain from voting,
      (ii)   his intention to vote in a particular way, or
      (iii)   how he voted.

(5)   The decision period is—
  (a)   the period of 10 working days starting with the day after that on which the complaint under sub-paragraph (1) was received by the CAC, or
  (b)   such longer period (so starting) as the CAC may specify to the parties by a notice containing reasons for the extension.

(6)   If, at the beginning of the decision period, the ballot has not begun, the CAC may by notice to the parties and the qualified independent person postpone the date on which it is to begin until a date which falls after the end of the decision period.

**119C.**   (1)   This paragraph applies if the CAC decides that a complaint under paragraph 119B is well-founded.

(2)   The CAC must, as soon as is reasonably practicable, issue a declaration to that effect.

(3)   The CAC may do either or both of the following—
  (a)   order the party concerned to take any action specified in the order within such period as may be so specified, or
  (b)   make arrangements for the holding of a secret ballot in which the workers constituting the bargaining unit are asked whether the bargaining arrangements should be ended.

(4)   The CAC may give an order or make arrangements under sub-paragraph (3) either at the same time as it issues the declaration under sub-paragraph (2) or at any other time before it acts under paragraph 121.

(5)   The action specified in an order under sub-paragraph (3)(a) shall be such as the CAC considers reasonable in order to mitigate the effect of the failure of the party complained against to comply with the duty imposed by paragraph 119A.

(6)   The CAC may give more than one order under sub-paragraph (3)(a).

**119D.**   (1)   This paragraph applies if the CAC issues a declaration under paragraph 119C(2) and the declaration states that the unfair practice used consisted of or included—
  (a)   the use of violence, or
  (b)   the dismissal of a union official.

(2)   This paragraph also applies if the CAC has made an order under paragraph 119C(3)(a) and—
  (a)   it is satisfied that the party subject to the order has failed to comply with it, or
  (b)   it makes another declaration under paragraph 119C(2) in relation to a complaint against that party.

(3)   If the party concerned is the employer, the CAC may refuse the employer's application under paragraph 106 or 107.

(4)   If the party concerned is a union, the CAC may issue a declaration that the bargaining arrangements are to cease to have effect on a date specified by the CAC in the declaration.

(5)   If a declaration is issued under sub-paragraph (4) the bargaining arrangements shall cease to have effect accordingly.

(6)   The powers conferred by this paragraph are in addition to those conferred by paragraph 119C(3).

**119E.**   (1)   This paragraph applies if the CAC issues a declaration that a complaint under paragraph 119B is well-founded and—
  (a)   makes arrangements under paragraph 119C(3)(b),
  (b)   refuses under paragraph 119D(3) or 119H(6) an application under paragraph 106, 107 or 112, or
  (c)   issues a declaration under paragraph 119D(4) or 119H(5).

(2)   If the ballot in connection with which the complaint was made has not been held, the CAC shall take steps to cancel it.

(3)   If that ballot is held, it shall have no effect.

**119F.**   (1)   This paragraph applies if the CAC makes arrangements under paragraph 119C(3)(b).

(2)   Paragraphs 117(4) to (11) and 118 to 121 apply in relation to those arrangements as they apply in relation to arrangements made under paragraph 117(3) but with the modifications specified in sub-paragraphs (3) to (5).

(3)   An employer's duty under paragraph (a) of paragraph 118(4) is limited to—
  (a)   giving the CAC the names and home addresses of any workers in the bargaining unit which have not previously been given to it in accordance with that duty;
  (b)   giving the CAC the names and home addresses of those workers who have joined the bargaining unit since he last gave the CAC information in accordance with that duty;
  (c)   informing the CAC of any change to the name or home address of a worker whose name and home address have previously been given to the CAC in accordance with that duty; and

(d)   informing the CAC of any worker whose name had previously been given to it in accordance with that duty who has ceased to be within the bargaining unit.

(4)   Any order given under paragraph 119(1) or 119C(3)(a) for the purposes of the cancelled or ineffectual ballot shall have effect (to the extent that the CAC specifies in a notice to the parties) as if it were made for the purposes of the ballot for which arrangements are made under paragraph 119C(3)(b).

(5)   The gross costs of the ballot shall be borne by such of the parties and in such proportions as the CAC may determine and, accordingly, sub-paragraphs (2) and (3) of paragraph 120 shall be omitted and the reference in sub-paragraph (4) of that paragraph to the employer and the union (or each of the unions) shall be construed as a reference to the party or parties which bear the costs in accordance with the CAC's determination.

**119G.**   (1)   Paragraphs 119A to 119C, 119E and 119F apply in relation to an application under paragraph 112 as they apply in relation to an application under paragraph 106 or 107 but with the modifications specified in this paragraph.

(2)   References in those paragraphs (and, accordingly, in paragraph 119H(3)) to a party shall be read as including references to the applicant worker or workers; but this is subject to sub-paragraph (3).

(3)   The reference in paragraph 119A(1) to a party informed under paragraph 117(11) shall be read as including a reference to the applicant worker or workers.

**119H.**   (1)   This paragraph applies in relation to an application under paragraph 112 in the cases specified in sub-paragraphs (2) and (3).

(2)   The first case is where the CAC issues a declaration under paragraph 119C(2) and the declaration states that the unfair practice used consisted of or included—
(a)   the use of violence, or
(b)   the dismissal of a union official.

(3)   The second case is where the CAC has made an order under paragraph 119C(3)(a) and—
(a)   it is satisfied that the party subject to the order has failed to comply with it, or
(b)   it makes another declaration under paragraph 119C(2) in relation to a complaint against that party.

(4)   If the party concerned is the employer, the CAC may order him to refrain from further campaigning in relation to the ballot.

(5)   If the party concerned is a union, the CAC may issue a declaration that the bargaining arrangements are to cease to have effect on a date specified by the CAC in the declaration.

(6)   If the party concerned is the applicant worker (or any of the applicant workers), the CAC may refuse the application under paragraph 112.

(7)   If a declaration is issued under sub-paragraph (5) the bargaining arrangements shall cease to have effect accordingly.

(8)   The powers conferred by this paragraph are in addition to those conferred by paragraph 119C(3).

**119I.**   (1)   This paragraph applies if—
(a)   a ballot has been arranged in consequence of an application under paragraph 112,
(b)   the CAC has given the employer an order under paragraph 119(1), 119C(3) or 119H(4), and
(c)   the ballot for the purposes of which the order was made (or any other ballot for the purposes of which it has effect) has not been held.

(2)   The applicant worker (or each of the applicant workers) and the union (or each of the unions) is entitled to enforce obedience to the order.

(3)   The order may be enforced—
(a)   in England and Wales, in the same way as an order of the county court;
(b)   in Scotland, in the same way as an order of the sheriff.]

**120.** (1)   This paragraph applies if the holding of a ballot has been arranged under paragraph 117(3), whether or not it has been cancelled.

(2)   The gross costs of the ballot shall be borne—
(a)   as to half, by the employer, and
(b)   as to half, by the union (or unions).

(3)   If there is more than one union they shall bear their half of the gross costs—
(a)   in such proportions as they jointly indicate to the person appointed to conduct the ballot, or
(b)   in the absence of such an indication, in equal shares.

(4)   The person appointed to conduct the ballot may send to the employer and the union (or each of the unions) a demand stating—
(a)   the gross costs of the ballot, and

(b)    the amount of the gross costs to be borne by the recipient.

(5)    In such a case the recipient must pay the amount stated to the person sending the demand, and must do so within the period of 15 working days starting with the day after that on which the demand is received.

(6)    In England and Wales, if the amount stated is not paid in accordance with sub-paragraph (5) it shall, if *a county court* so orders, be recoverable *by execution issued from that court* or otherwise as if it were payable under an order of that court.

[(6A)    *Where an amount is recoverable from a union under sub-paragraph (6) execution may be carried out*, to the same extent and in the same manner as if the union were a body corporate, against any property held in trust for the union other than protected property as defined in section 23(2).]

(7)    References to the costs of the ballot are to—
   (a)    the costs wholly, exclusively and necessarily incurred in connection with the ballot by the person appointed to conduct it,
   (b)    such reasonable amount as the person appointed to conduct the ballot charges for his services, and
   (c)    such other costs as the employer and the union (or unions) agree.

**121.** (1)    As soon as is reasonably practicable after the CAC is informed of the result of a ballot by the person conducting it, the CAC must act under this paragraph.

[(1A)    The duty in sub-paragraph (1) does not apply if the CAC makes arrangements under paragraph 119C(3)(b).]

(2)    The CAC must inform the employer and the union (or unions) of the result of the ballot.

(3)    If the result is that the proposition that the bargaining arrangements should be ended is supported by—
   (a)    a majority of the workers voting, and
   (b)    at least 40 per cent of the workers constituting the bargaining unit,
the CAC must issue a declaration that the bargaining arrangements are to cease to have effect on a date specified by the CAC in the declaration.

(4)    If the result is otherwise the CAC must refuse the application under paragraph 106, 107 or 112.

(5)    If a declaration is issued under sub-paragraph (3) the bargaining arrangements shall cease to have effect accordingly.

(6)    The Secretary of State may by order amend sub-paragraph (3) so as to specify a different degree of support; and different provision may be made for different circumstances.

(7)    An order under sub-paragraph (6) shall be made by statutory instrument.

(8)    No such order shall be made unless a draft of it has been laid before Parliament and approved by a resolution of each House of Parliament.

---

**NOTES**

Inserted as noted at the beginning of this Schedule.

Para 117: sub-para (8A) inserted by the Employment Relations Act 2004, s 8(2).

Para 118: word in square brackets in sub-para (1) substituted, sub-paras (4A)–(4E) inserted, and sub-paras (8), (9) substituted (for the original sub-para (8)), by the Employment Relations Act 2004, s 9(6)–(9).

Para 119: words in square brackets in sub-para (1) substituted, and sub-para (3) repealed, by the Employment Relations Act 2004, ss 9(10), 57, Sch 1, paras 23(1), (22), Sch 2.

Paras 119A–119I: inserted by the Employment Relations Act 2004, s 13(1).

Para 120: for the first words in italics in sub-para (6) there are substituted the words "the county court" by the Crime and Courts Act 2013, s 17(5), Sch 9, Pt 3, para 52, as from a day to be appointed; for the second words in italics in sub-para (6) there are substituted the words "under section 85 of the County Courts Act 1984" by the Tribunals, Courts and Enforcement Act 2007, s 62(3), Sch 13, paras 108, 111(1), (2), as from a day to be appointed; sub-para (6A) inserted by the Employment Relations Act 2004, s 57(1), Sch 1, para 23(1), (23); for the words in italics in sub-para (6A) there are substituted the words "Where a warrant of control is issued under section 85 of the 1984 Act to recover an amount in accordance with sub-paragraph (6), the power conferred by the warrant is exercisable" by the Tribunals, Courts and Enforcement Act 2007, s 62(3), Sch 13, paras 108, 111(1), (3), as from a day to be appointed.

Para 121: sub-para (1A) inserted by the Employment Relations Act 2004, s 13(2).

Code of Practice: Access and unfair practices during recognition and derecognition ballots (2005) at **[4.220]**.

Orders: the Recognition and Derecognition Ballots (Qualified Persons) Order 2000, SI 2000/1306 at **[2.569]**; the Recognition and Derecognition Ballots (Qualified Persons) (Amendment) Order 2010, SI 2010/437.

# PART V
## DERECOGNITION WHERE RECOGNITION AUTOMATIC

*Introduction*

**[1.618]**

**122.** (1)  This Part of this Schedule applies if—
  (a)  the CAC has issued a declaration under paragraph [19F(5), 22(2), 27(2) or 27D(3)] that a union is (or unions are) recognised as entitled to conduct collective bargaining on behalf of a bargaining unit, and
  (b)  the parties have agreed under paragraph 30 or 31 a method by which they will conduct collective bargaining.

(2)  In such a case references in this Part of this Schedule to the bargaining arrangements are to—
  (a)  the declaration, and
  (b)  the parties' agreement.

**123.** (1)  This Part of this Schedule also applies if—
  (a)  the CAC has issued a declaration under paragraph [19F(5), 22(2), 27(2) or 27D(3)] that a union is (or unions are) recognised as entitled to conduct collective bargaining on behalf of a bargaining unit, and
  (b)  the CAC has specified to the parties under paragraph 31(3) the method by which they are to conduct collective bargaining.

(2)  In such a case references in this Part of this Schedule to the bargaining arrangements are to—
  (a)  the declaration, and
  (b)  anything effective as, or as if contained in, a legally enforceable contract by virtue of paragraph 31.

**124.** (1)  This Part of this Schedule also applies if the CAC has issued a declaration under paragraph 87(2) that a union is (or unions are) recognised as entitled to conduct collective bargaining on behalf of a bargaining unit.

(2)  In such a case references in this Part of this Schedule to the bargaining arrangements are to—
  (a)  the declaration, and
  (b)  paragraph 87(6)(b).

**125.** For the purposes of this Part of this Schedule the relevant date is the date of the expiry of the period of 3 years starting with the date of the CAC's declaration.

**126.** References in this Part of this Schedule to the parties are to the employer and the union (or unions) concerned.

---

**NOTES**

Inserted as noted at the beginning of this Schedule.

Paras 122, 123: words in square brackets substituted by the Employment Relations Act 2004, s 57(1), Sch 1, para 23(1), (24), (25).

---

*Employer's request to end arrangements*

**[1.619]**

**127.** (1)  The employer may after the relevant date request the union (or each of the unions) to agree to end the bargaining arrangements.

(2)  The request is not valid unless it—
  (a)  is in writing,
  (b)  is received by the union (or each of the unions),
  (c)  identifies the bargaining arrangements,
  (d)  states that it is made under this Schedule, and
  (e)  states that fewer than half of the workers constituting the bargaining unit are members of the union (or unions).

**128.** (1)  If before the end of the negotiation period the parties agree to end the bargaining arrangements no further steps are to be taken under this Part of this Schedule.

(2)  If no such agreement is made before the end of the negotiation period, the employer may apply to the CAC for the holding of a secret ballot to decide whether the bargaining arrangements should be ended.

(3)  The negotiation period is the period of 10 working days starting with the day after—
  (a)  the day on which the union receives the request, or
  (b)  the last day on which any of the unions receives the request;
or such longer period (so starting) as the parties may from time to time agree.

**129.** (1)  An application under paragraph 128 is not admissible unless—
  (a)  it is made in such form as the CAC specifies, and

(b)   it is supported by such documents as the CAC specifies.

(2)   An application under paragraph 128 is not admissible unless the employer gives to the union (or each of the unions)—

(a)   notice of the application, and

(b)   a copy of the application and any documents supporting it.

**130.** (1)   An application under paragraph 128 is not admissible if—

(a)   a relevant application was made[, or a notice under paragraph 99(2) was given,] within the period of 3 years prior to the date of the application under paragraph 128,

(b)   the relevant application[, or notice under paragraph 99(2),] and the application under paragraph 128 relate to the same bargaining unit, and

(c)   the CAC accepted the relevant application [or (as the case may be) decided under paragraph 100 that the notice complied with paragraph 99(3)].

(2)   A relevant application is an application made to the CAC—

(a)     . . .

(b)   by the employer under paragraph 106, 107 or 128, or

(c)   by a worker (or workers) under paragraph 112.

**131.** (1)   An application under paragraph 128 is not admissible unless the CAC is satisfied that fewer than half of the workers constituting the bargaining unit are members of the union (or unions).

(2)   The CAC must give reasons for the decision.

**132.** (1)   The CAC must give notice to the parties of receipt of an application under paragraph 128.

(2)   Within the acceptance period the CAC must decide whether—

(a)   the request is valid within the terms of paragraph 127, and

(b)   the application is admissible within the terms of paragraphs 129 to 131.

(3)   In deciding those questions the CAC must consider any evidence which it has been given by the parties.

(4)   If the CAC decides that the request is not valid or the application is not admissible—

(a)   the CAC must give notice of its decision to the parties,

(b)   the CAC must not accept the application, and

(c)   no further steps are to be taken under this Part of this Schedule.

(5)   If the CAC decides that the request is valid and the application is admissible it must—

(a)   accept the application, and

(b)   give notice of the acceptance to the parties.

(6)   The acceptance period is—

(a)   the period of 10 working days starting with the day after that on which the CAC receives the application, or

(b)   such longer period (so starting) as the CAC may specify to the parties by notice containing reasons for the extension.

**NOTES**

Inserted as noted at the beginning of this Schedule.

Para 130: words in square brackets in sub-para (1) inserted, and sub-para (2)(a) repealed, by the Employment Relations Act 2004, ss 12(8), (9), 57(2), Sch 2.

*Ballot on derecognition*

**[1.620]**

**133.** (1)   Paragraph 117 applies if the CAC accepts an application under paragraph 128 (as well as in the cases mentioned in paragraph 117(1) and (2)).

(2)   Paragraphs 118 to 121 apply accordingly, but as if—

(a)   the [references in paragraphs 119(2)(a) and 119D(3)] to paragraph 106 or 107 were to paragraph 106, 107 or 128;

(b)   the [references in paragraphs 119A(3)(a)(ii), 119E(1)(b) and 121(4)] to paragraph 106, 107 or 112 were to paragraph 106, 107, 112 or 128.

**NOTES**

Inserted as noted at the beginning of this Schedule.

Para 133: words in square brackets in sub-para (2) substituted by the Employment Relations Act 2004, s 57(1), Sch 1, para 23(1), (26).

## PART VI
## DERECOGNITION WHERE UNION NOT INDEPENDENT

*Introduction*

**[1.621]**
**134.** (1) This Part of this Schedule applies if—
    (a) an employer and a union (or unions) have agreed that the union is (or unions are) recognised as entitled to conduct collective bargaining on behalf of a group or groups of workers, and
    (b) the union does not have (or none of the unions has) a certificate [of independence].
(2) In such a case references in this Part of this Schedule to the bargaining arrangements are to—
    (a) the parties' agreement mentioned in sub-paragraph (1)(a), and
    (b) any agreement between the parties as to the method by which they will conduct collective bargaining.

**135.** In this Part of this Schedule—
    (a) references to the parties are to the employer and the union (or unions);
    (b) references to the bargaining unit are to the group of workers referred to in paragraph 134(1)(a) (or the groups taken together).

**136.** The meaning of collective bargaining given by section 178(1) shall not apply in relation to this Part of this Schedule.

---

**NOTES**
Inserted as noted at the beginning of this Schedule.
Para 134: words in square brackets in sub-para (1)(b) substituted by the Employment Relations Act 2004, s 50(6).

---

*Workers' application to end arrangements*

**[1.622]**
**137.** (1) A worker or workers falling within the bargaining unit may apply to the CAC to have the bargaining arrangements ended.
(2) An application is not admissible unless—
    (a) it is made in such form as the CAC specifies, and
    (b) it is supported by such documents as the CAC specifies.
(3) An application is not admissible unless the worker gives (or workers give) to the employer and to the union (or each of the unions)—
    (a) notice of the application, and
    (b) a copy of the application and any documents supporting it.

**138.** An application under paragraph 137 is not admissible if the CAC is satisfied that any of the unions has a certificate [of independence].

**139.** (1) An application under paragraph 137 is not admissible unless the CAC decides that—
    (a) at least 10 per cent of the workers constituting the bargaining unit favour an end of the bargaining arrangements, and
    (b) a majority of the workers constituting the bargaining unit would be likely to favour an end of the bargaining arrangements.
(2) The CAC must give reasons for the decision.

**140.** An application under paragraph 137 is not admissible if the CAC is satisfied that—
    (a) the union (or any of the unions) has made an application to the Certification Officer under section 6 for a certificate that it is independent, and
    (b) the Certification Officer has not come to a decision on the application (or each of the applications).

**141.** (1) The CAC must give notice to the worker (or workers), the employer and the union (or unions) of receipt of an application under paragraph 137.
(2) Within the acceptance period the CAC must decide whether the application is admissible within the terms of paragraphs 137 to 140.
(3) In deciding whether the application is admissible the CAC must consider any evidence which it has been given by the employer, the union (or unions) or any of the workers falling within the bargaining unit.
(4) If the CAC decides that the application is not admissible—
    (a) the CAC must give notice of its decision to the worker (or workers), the employer and the union (or unions),
    (b) the CAC must not accept the application, and
    (c) no further steps are to be taken under this Part of this Schedule.
(5) If the CAC decides that the application is admissible it must—

   (a)   accept the application, and

   (b)   give notice of the acceptance to the worker (or workers), the employer and the union (or unions).

(6)   The acceptance period is—

   (a)   the period of 10 working days starting with the day after that on which the CAC receives the application, or

   (b)   such longer period (so starting) as the CAC may specify to the worker (or workers), the employer and the union (or unions) by notice containing reasons for the extension.

**142.** (1)   If the CAC accepts the application, in the negotiation period the CAC must help the employer, the union (or unions) and the worker (or workers) with a view to—

   (a)   the employer and the union (or unions) agreeing to end the bargaining arrangements, or

   (b)   the worker (or workers) withdrawing the application.

(2)   The negotiation period is—

   (a)   the period of 20 working days starting with the day after that on which the CAC gives notice of acceptance of the application, or

   (b)   such longer period (so starting) as the CAC may decide with the consent of the worker (or workers), the employer and the union (or unions).

**143.** (1)   This paragraph applies if—

   (a)   the CAC accepts an application under paragraph 137,

   (b)   during the period mentioned in paragraph 142(1) or 145(3) the CAC is satisfied that the union (or each of the unions) has made an application to the Certification Officer under section 6 for a certificate that it is independent, that the application (or each of the applications) to the Certification Officer was made before the application under paragraph 137 and that the Certification Officer has not come to a decision on the application (or each of the applications), and

   (c)   at the time the CAC is so satisfied there has been no agreement or withdrawal as described in paragraph 142(1) or 145(3).

(2)   In such a case paragraph 142(1) or 145(3) shall cease to apply from the time when the CAC is satisfied as mentioned in sub-paragraph (1)(b).

**144.** (1)   This paragraph applies if the CAC is subsequently satisfied that—

   (a)   the Certification Officer has come to a decision on the application (or each of the applications) mentioned in paragraph 143(1)(b), and

   (b)   his decision is that the union (or any of the unions) which made an application under section 6 is independent.

(2)   In such a case—

   (a)   the CAC must give the worker (or workers), the employer and the union (or unions) notice that it is so satisfied, and

   (b)   the application under paragraph 137 shall be treated as not having been made.

**145.** (1)   This paragraph applies if the CAC is subsequently satisfied that—

   (a)   the Certification Officer has come to a decision on the application (or each of the applications) mentioned in paragraph 143(1)(b), and

   (b)   his decision is that the union (or each of the unions) which made an application under section 6 is not independent.

(2)   The CAC must give the worker (or workers), the employer and the union (or unions) notice that it is so satisfied.

(3)   In the new negotiation period the CAC must help the employer, the union (or unions) and the worker (or workers) with a view to—

   (a)   the employer and the union (or unions) agreeing to end the bargaining arrangements, or

   (b)   the worker (or workers) withdrawing the application.

(4)   The new negotiation period is—

   (a)   the period of 20 working days starting with the day after that on which the CAC gives notice under sub-paragraph (2), or

   (b)   such longer period (so starting) as the CAC may decide with the consent of the worker (or workers), the employer and the union (or unions).

**146.** (1)   This paragraph applies if—

   (a)   the CAC accepts an application under paragraph 137,

   (b)   paragraph 143 does not apply, and

   (c)   during the relevant period the CAC is satisfied that a certificate of independence has been issued to the union (or any of the unions) under section 6.

(2)   In such a case the relevant period is the period starting with the first day of the negotiation period (as defined in paragraph 142(2)) and ending with the first of the following to occur—

(a) any agreement by the employer and the union (or unions) to end the bargaining arrangements;

(b) any withdrawal of the application by the worker (or workers);

(c) the CAC being informed of the result of a relevant ballot by the person conducting it;

and a relevant ballot is a ballot held by virtue of this Part of this Schedule.

(3) This paragraph also applies if—

(a) the CAC gives notice under paragraph 145(2), and

(b) during the relevant period the CAC is satisfied that a certificate of independence has been issued to the union (or any of the unions) under section 6.

(4) In such a case, the relevant period is the period starting with the first day of the new negotiation period (as defined in paragraph 145(4)) and ending with the first of the following to occur—

(a) any agreement by the employer and the union (or unions) to end the bargaining arrangements;

(b) any withdrawal of the application by the worker (or workers);

(c) the CAC being informed of the result of a relevant ballot by the person conducting it;

and a relevant ballot is a ballot held by virtue of this Part of this Schedule.

(5) If this paragraph applies—

(a) the CAC must give the worker (or workers), the employer and the union (or unions) notice that it is satisfied as mentioned in sub-paragraph (1)(c) or (3)(b), and

(b) the application under paragraph 137 shall be treated as not having been made.

**NOTES**

Inserted as noted at the beginning of this Schedule.

Para 138: words in square brackets substituted by the Employment Relations Act 2004, s 50(6).

*Ballot on derecognition*

**[1.623]**

**147.** (1) Paragraph 117 applies if—

(a) the CAC accepts an application under paragraph 137, and

(b) in the period mentioned in paragraph 142(1) or 145(3) there is no agreement or withdrawal as there described,

(as well as in the cases mentioned in paragraph 117(1) and (2)).

(2) Paragraphs 118 to 121 apply accordingly, but as if—

(a) the [references in paragraphs 119H(1) and 119I(1)(a)] to paragraph 112 were to paragraph 112 or 137;

(b) the [references in paragraphs 119A(3)(a)(ii), 119E(1)(b) and 121(4)] to paragraph 106, 107 or 112 were to paragraph 106, 107, 112 or 137;

(c) the reference in paragraph 119(4) to the CAC refusing an application under paragraph 119(2) included a reference to it being required to give notice under paragraph 146(5).

**NOTES**

Inserted as noted at the beginning of this Schedule.

Para 147: words in square brackets in sub-para (2) substituted by the Employment Relations Act 2004, s 57(1), Sch 1, para 23(1), (27).

*Derecognition: other cases*

**[1.624]**

**148.** (1) This paragraph applies if as a result of a declaration by the CAC another union is (or other unions are) recognised as entitled to conduct collective bargaining on behalf of a group of workers at least one of whom falls within the bargaining unit.

(2) The CAC must issue a declaration that the bargaining arrangements are to cease to have effect on a date specified by the CAC in the declaration.

(3) If a declaration is issued under sub-paragraph (2) the bargaining arrangements shall cease to have effect accordingly.

(4) It is for the CAC to decide whether sub-paragraph (1) is fulfilled, but in deciding the CAC may take account of the views of any person it believes has an interest in the matter.

**NOTES**

Inserted as noted at the beginning of this Schedule.

# PART VII
## LOSS OF INDEPENDENCE

### Introduction

**[1.625]**
**149.** (1)   This Part of this Schedule applies if the CAC has issued a declaration that a union is (or unions are) recognised as entitled to conduct collective bargaining on behalf of a bargaining unit.

(2)   In such a case references in this Part of this Schedule to the bargaining arrangements are to the declaration and to the provisions relating to the collective bargaining method.

(3)   For this purpose the provisions relating to the collective bargaining method are—
- (a)   the parties' agreement as to the method by which collective bargaining is to be conducted,
- (b)   anything effective as, or as if contained in, a legally enforceable contract and relating to the method by which collective bargaining is to be conducted, or
- (c)   any provision of Part III of this Schedule that a method of collective bargaining is to have effect.

**150.** (1)   This Part of this Schedule also applies if—
- (a)   the parties have agreed that a union is (or unions are) recognised as entitled to conduct collective bargaining on behalf of a bargaining unit,
- (b)   the CAC has specified to the parties under paragraph 63(2) the method by which they are to conduct collective bargaining, and
- (c)   the parties have not agreed in writing to replace the method or that paragraph 63(3) shall not apply.

(2)   In such a case references in this Part of this Schedule to the bargaining arrangements are to—
- (a)   the parties' agreement mentioned in sub-paragraph (1)(a), and
- (b)   anything effective as, or as if contained in, a legally enforceable contract by virtue of paragraph 63.

**151.** References in this Part of this Schedule to the parties are to the employer and the union (or unions) concerned.

---

**NOTES**
Inserted as noted at the beginning of this Schedule.

### Loss of certificate

**[1.626]**
**152.** (1)   This paragraph applies if—
- (a)   only one union is a party, and
- (b)   under section 7 the Certification Officer withdraws the union's certificate of independence.

(2)   This paragraph also applies if—
- (a)   more than one union is a party, and
- (b)   under section 7 the Certification Officer withdraws the certificate of independence of each union (whether different certificates are withdrawn on the same or on different days).

(3)   Sub-paragraph (4) shall apply on the day after—
- (a)   the day on which the Certification Officer informs the union (or unions) of the withdrawal (or withdrawals), or
- (b)   if there is more than one union, and he informs them on different days, the last of those days.

(4)   The bargaining arrangements shall cease to have effect; and the parties shall be taken to agree that the union is (or unions are) recognised as entitled to conduct collective bargaining on behalf of the bargaining unit concerned.

---

**NOTES**
Inserted as noted at the beginning of this Schedule.

### Certificate re-issued

**[1.627]**
**153.** (1)   This paragraph applies if—
- (a)   only one union is a party,
- (b)   paragraph 152 applies, and
- (c)   as a result of an appeal under section 9 against the decision to withdraw the certificate, the Certification Officer issues a certificate that the union is independent.

(2)   This paragraph also applies if—
- (a)   more than one union is a party,
- (b)   paragraph 152 applies, and
- (c)   as a result of an appeal under section 9 against a decision to withdraw a certificate, the Certification Officer issues a certificate that any of the unions concerned is independent.

(3)   Sub-paragraph (4) shall apply, beginning with the day after—
  (a)   the day on which the Certification Officer issues the certificate, or
  (b)   if there is more than one union, the day on which he issues the first or only certificate.
(4)   The bargaining arrangements shall have effect again; and paragraph 152 shall cease to apply.

**NOTES**
  Inserted as noted at the beginning of this Schedule.

*Miscellaneous*

**[1.628]**
**154.** Parts III to VI of this Schedule shall not apply in the case of the parties at any time when, by virtue of this Part of this Schedule, the bargaining arrangements do not have effect.

**155.** If—
  (a)   by virtue of paragraph 153 the bargaining arrangements have effect again beginning with a particular day, and
  (b)   in consequence section 70B applies in relation to the bargaining unit concerned,
for the purposes of section 70B(3) that day shall be taken to be the day on which section 70B first applies in relation to the unit.

**NOTES**
  Inserted as noted at the beginning of this Schedule.

# PART VIII
# DETRIMENT

*Detriment*

**[1.629]**
**156.** (1)   A worker has a right not to be subjected to any detriment by any act, or any deliberate failure to act, by his employer if the act or failure takes place on any of the grounds set out in sub-paragraph (2).
(2)   The grounds are that—
  (a)   the worker acted with a view to obtaining or preventing recognition of a union (or unions) by the employer under this Schedule;
  (b)   the worker indicated that he supported or did not support recognition of a union (or unions) by the employer under this Schedule;
  (c)   the worker acted with a view to securing or preventing the ending under this Schedule of bargaining arrangements;
  (d)   the worker indicated that he supported or did not support the ending under this Schedule of bargaining arrangements;
  (e)   the worker influenced or sought to influence the way in which votes were to be cast by other workers in a ballot arranged under this Schedule;
  (f)   the worker influenced or sought to influence other workers to vote or to abstain from voting in such a ballot;
  (g)   the worker voted in such a ballot;
  (h)   the worker proposed to do, failed to do, or proposed to decline to do, any of the things referred to in paragraphs (a) to (g).
(3)   A ground does not fall within sub-paragraph (2) if it constitutes an unreasonable act or omission by the worker.
(4)   This paragraph does not apply if the worker is an employee and the detriment amounts to dismissal within the meaning of the Employment Rights Act 1996.
(5)   A worker may present a complaint to an employment tribunal on the ground that he has been subjected to a detriment in contravention of this paragraph.
(6)   Apart from the remedy by way of complaint as mentioned in sub-paragraph (5), a worker has no remedy for infringement of the right conferred on him by this paragraph.

**157.** (1)   An employment tribunal shall not consider a complaint under paragraph 156 unless it is presented—
  (a)   before the end of the period of 3 months starting with the date of the act or failure to which the complaint relates or, if that act or failure is part of a series of similar acts or failures (or both), the last of them, or
  (b)   where the tribunal is satisfied that it was not reasonably practicable for the complaint to be presented before the end of that period, within such further period as it considers reasonable.
(2)   For the purposes of sub-paragraph (1)—
  (a)   where an act extends over a period, the reference to the date of the act is a reference to the last day of that period;

(b)    a failure to act shall be treated as done when it was decided on.

(3)    For the purposes of sub-paragraph (2), in the absence of evidence establishing the contrary an employer must be taken to decide on a failure to act—

(a)    when he does an act inconsistent with doing the failed act, or

(b)    if he has done no such inconsistent act, when the period expires within which he might reasonably have been expected to do the failed act if it was to be done.

[(4)    Section 292A (extension of time limits to facilitate conciliation before institution of proceedings) applies for the purposes of sub-paragraph (1)(a).]

**158.** On a complaint under paragraph 156 it shall be for the employer to show the ground on which he acted or failed to act.

**159.** (1)    If the employment tribunal finds that a complaint under paragraph 156 is well-founded it shall make a declaration to that effect and may make an award of compensation to be paid by the employer to the complainant in respect of the act or failure complained of.

(2)    The amount of the compensation awarded shall be such as the tribunal considers just and equitable in all the circumstances having regard to the infringement complained of and to any loss sustained by the complainant which is attributable to the act or failure which infringed his right.

(3)    The loss shall be taken to include—

(a)    any expenses reasonably incurred by the complainant in consequence of the act or failure complained of, and

(b)    loss of any benefit which he might reasonably be expected to have had but for that act or failure.

(4)    In ascertaining the loss, the tribunal shall apply the same rule concerning the duty of a person to mitigate his loss as applies to damages recoverable under the common law of England and Wales or Scotland.

(5)    If the tribunal finds that the act or failure complained of was to any extent caused or contributed to by action of the complainant, it shall reduce the amount of the compensation by such proportion as it considers just and equitable having regard to that finding.

**160.** (1)    If the employment tribunal finds that a complaint under paragraph 156 is well-founded and—

(a)    the detriment of which the worker has complained is the termination of his worker's contract, but

(b)    that contract was not a contract of employment,

any compensation awarded under paragraph 159 must not exceed the limit specified in sub-paragraph (2).

(2)    The limit is the total of—

(a)    the sum which would be the basic award for unfair dismissal, calculated in accordance with section 119 of the Employment Rights Act 1996, if the worker had been an employee and the contract terminated had been a contract of employment, and

(b)    the sum for the time being specified in section 124(1) of that Act which is the limit for a compensatory award to a person calculated in accordance with section 123 of that Act.

NOTES

Inserted as noted at the beginning of this Schedule.

Para 157: sub-para (4) added by the Enterprise and Regulatory Reform Act 2013, s 8, Sch 2, paras 1, 14, as from a day to be appointed.

Conciliation: employment tribunal proceedings and claims which could be the subject of employment tribunal proceedings under or arising out of a contravention, or alleged contravention, of para 156 are proceedings to which the Employment Tribunals Act 1996, s 18 applies; see s 18(1)(f) of that Act at **[1.706]**, and the Employment Tribunals Act 1996 (Application of Conciliation Provisions) Order 2000, SI 2000/1337 (made under s 18(8)(a), (b)).

Tribunal jurisdiction: the Employment Act 2002, s 38 applies to proceedings before the employment tribunal relating to a claim under this section; see s 38(1) of, and Sch 5 to, the 2002 Act at **[1.1228]**, **[1.1236]**. See also s 207A of this Act at **[1.474]** (as inserted by the Employment Act 2008). That section provides that in proceedings before an employment tribunal relating to a claim by an employee under any of the jurisdictions listed in Sch A2 to the 1992 Act at **[1.648]** (which includes this section) the tribunal may adjust any award given if the employer or the employee has unreasonably failed to comply with the relevant Code of Practice as defined by s 207A(4). See also the revised Acas Code of Practice 1 – Disciplinary and Grievance Procedures (2009) at **[4.1]**.

*Dismissal*

**[1.630]**

**161.** (1)    For the purposes of Part X of the Employment Rights Act 1996 (unfair dismissal) the dismissal of an employee shall be regarded as unfair if the dismissal was made—

(a)    for a reason set out in sub-paragraph (2), or

(b)    for reasons the main one of which is one of those set out in sub-paragraph (2).

(2)    The reasons are that—

(a)  the employee acted with a view to obtaining or preventing recognition of a union (or unions) by the employer under this Schedule;

(b)  the employee indicated that he supported or did not support recognition of a union (or unions) by the employer under this Schedule;

(c)  the employee acted with a view to securing or preventing the ending under this Schedule of bargaining arrangements;

(d)  the employee indicated that he supported or did not support the ending under this Schedule of bargaining arrangements;

(e)  the employee influenced or sought to influence the way in which votes were to be cast by other workers in a ballot arranged under this Schedule;

(f)  the employee influenced or sought to influence other workers to vote or to abstain from voting in such a ballot;

(g)  the employee voted in such a ballot;

(h)  the employee proposed to do, failed to do, or proposed to decline to do, any of the things referred to in paragraphs (a) to (g).

(3)  A reason does not fall within sub-paragraph (2) if it constitutes an unreasonable act or omission by the employee.

**NOTES**
Inserted as noted at the beginning of this Schedule.

### *Selection for redundancy*

**[1.631]**
**162.** For the purposes of Part X of the Employment Rights Act 1996 (unfair dismissal) the dismissal of an employee shall be regarded as unfair if the reason or principal reason for the dismissal was that he was redundant but it is shown—

(a)  that the circumstances constituting the redundancy applied equally to one or more other employees in the same undertaking who held positions similar to that held by him and who have not been dismissed by the employer, and

(b)  that the reason (or, if more than one, the principal reason) why he was selected for dismissal was one falling within paragraph 161(2).

**NOTES**
Inserted as noted at the beginning of this Schedule.

### *Employees with fixed-term contracts*

**[1.632]**
*163. Section 197(1) of the Employment Rights Act 1996 (fixed-term contracts) does not prevent Part X of that Act from applying to a dismissal which is regarded as unfair by virtue of paragraph 161 or 162.*

**NOTES**
Inserted as noted at the beginning of this Schedule.
Para 163: repealed by the Employment Relations Act 1999, s 44, Sch 9(3), as from a day to be appointed.
Note that s 197(1) of the 1996 Act was itself repealed by s 44 of, and Sch 9(3) to, the 1999 Act.

### *Exclusion of requirement as to qualifying period*

**[1.633]**
**164.** Sections 108 and 109 of the Employment Rights Act 1996 (qualifying period and upper age limit for unfair dismissal protection) do not apply to a dismissal which by virtue of paragraph 161 or 162 is regarded as unfair for the purposes of Part X of that Act.

**NOTES**
Inserted as noted at the beginning of this Schedule.
Section 109 of the Employment Rights Act 1996 was repealed by the Employment Equality (Age) Regulations 2006, SI 2006/1031, reg 49(1), Sch 8, Pt 1, paras 21, 25, but there has been no corresponding amendment to this paragraph.

### *Meaning of worker's contract*

**[1.634]**
**165.** References in this Part of this Schedule to a worker's contract are to the contract mentioned in paragraph (a) or (b) of section 296(1) or the arrangements for the employment mentioned in paragraph (c) of section 296(1).

**NOTES**
Inserted as noted at the beginning of this Schedule.

## PART IX
## GENERAL

*[Rights of appeal against demands for costs*

**[1.635]**
**165A.** (1)   This paragraph applies where a demand has been made under paragraph 19E(3), 28(4) or 120(4).

(2)   The recipient of the demand may appeal against the demand within 4 weeks starting with the day after receipt of the demand.

(3)   An appeal under this paragraph lies to an employment tribunal.

(4)   On an appeal under this paragraph against a demand under paragraph 19E(3), the tribunal shall dismiss the appeal unless it is shown that—
  (a)   the amount specified in the demand as the costs of the appointed person is too great, or
  (b)   the amount specified in the demand as the amount of those costs to be borne by the recipient is too great.

(5)   On an appeal under this paragraph against a demand under paragraph 28(4) or paragraph 120(4), the tribunal shall dismiss the appeal unless it is shown that—
  (a)   the amount specified in the demand as the gross costs of the ballot is too great, or
  (b)   the amount specified in the demand as the amount of the gross costs to be borne by the recipient is too great.

(6)   If an appeal is allowed, the tribunal shall rectify the demand and the demand shall have effect as if it had originally been made as so rectified.

(7)   If a person has appealed under this paragraph against a demand and the appeal has not been withdrawn or finally determined, the demand—
  (a)   is not enforceable until the appeal has been withdrawn or finally determined, but
  (b)   as from the withdrawal or final determination of the appeal shall be enforceable as if paragraph (a) had not had effect.]

**NOTES**
  This Schedule was inserted as noted at the beginning of this Schedule.
  Para 165A: inserted by the Employment Relations Act 2004, s 14.

*Power to amend*

**[1.636]**
**166.** [(1)   This paragraph applies if the CAC represents to the Secretary of State that a provision of this Schedule has an unsatisfactory effect and should be amended.

(2)   The Secretary of State, with a view to rectifying the effect—
  (a)   may amend the provision by exercising (if applicable) any of the powers conferred on him by paragraphs 7(6), 29(5), 121(6), 166A, 166B, 169A, 169B and 171A, or
  (b)   may amend the provision by order in such other way as he thinks fit.

(2A)   The Secretary of State need not proceed in a way proposed by the CAC (if it proposes one).

(2B)   Nothing in this paragraph prevents the Secretary of State from exercising any of the powers mentioned in sub-paragraph (2)(a) in the absence of a representation from the CAC.]

(3)   An order under [sub-paragraph (2)(b)] shall be made by statutory instrument.

(4)   No such order shall be made unless a draft of it has been laid before Parliament and approved by a resolution of each House of Parliament.

**[166A.**   (1)   This paragraph applies in relation to any provision of paragraph 19D(2), 26(4) or 118(4) which requires the employer to give to the CAC a worker's home address.

(2)   The Secretary of State may by order provide that the employer must give to the CAC (in addition to the worker's home address) an address of a specified kind for the worker.

(3)   In this paragraph "address" includes any address or number to which information may be sent by any means.

(4)   An order under this paragraph may—
  (a)   amend this Schedule;
  (b)   include supplementary or incidental provision (including, in particular, provision amending paragraph 19E(1)(a), 26(6)(a) or 118(6)(a));
  (c)   make different provision for different cases or circumstances.

(5)   An order under this paragraph shall be made by statutory instrument.

(6)   No such order shall be made unless a draft of it has been laid before Parliament and approved by a resolution of each House of Parliament.]

**[166B.** (1)   The Secretary of State may by order provide that, during any period beginning and ending with the occurrence of specified events, employers and unions to which the order applies are prohibited from using such practices as are specified as unfair practices in relation to an application under this Schedule of a specified description.

(2)   An order under this paragraph may make provision about the consequences of a contravention of any prohibition imposed by the order (including provision modifying the effect of any provision of this Schedule in the event of such a contravention).

(3)   An order under this paragraph may confer functions on the CAC

(4)   An order under this paragraph may contain provision extending for the purposes of the order either or both of the following powers to issue Codes of Practice—
   (a)   the power of ACAS under section 199(1);
   (b)   the power of the Secretary of State under section 203(1)(a).

(5)   An order under this paragraph may—
   (a)   include supplementary or incidental provisions (including provision amending this Schedule), and
   (b)   make different provision for different cases or circumstances.

(6)   An order under this paragraph shall be made by statutory instrument.

(7)   No such order shall be made unless a draft of it has been laid before and approved by a resolution of each House of Parliament.

(8)   In this paragraph "specified" means specified in an order under this paragraph.]

**NOTES**
Inserted as noted at the beginning of this Schedule.
Para 166: sub-paras (1), (2), (2A), (2B) substituted, for the original sub-paras (1), (2), and words in square brackets in sub-para (3) substituted, by the Employment Relations Act 2004, s 15.
Paras 166A, 166B: inserted by the Employment Relations Act 2004, ss 16, 17.

*Guidance*

**[1.637]**
**167.** (1)   The Secretary of State may issue guidance to the CAC on the way in which it is to exercise its functions under paragraph 22 or 87.

(2)   The CAC must take into account any such guidance in exercising those functions.

(3)   However, no guidance is to apply with regard to an application made to the CAC before the guidance in question was issued.

(4)   The Secretary of State must—
   (a)   lay before each House of Parliament any guidance issued under this paragraph, and
   (b)   arrange for any such guidance to be published by such means as appear to him to be most appropriate for drawing it to the attention of persons likely to be affected by it.

**NOTES**
Inserted as noted at the beginning of this Schedule.

*Method of conducting collective bargaining*

**[1.638]**
**168.** (1)   After consulting ACAS the Secretary of State may by order specify for the purposes of paragraphs 31(3) and 63(2) a method by which collective bargaining might be conducted.

(2)   If such an order is made the CAC—
   (a)   must take it into account under paragraphs 31(3) and 63(2), but
   (b)   may depart from the method specified by the order to such extent as the CAC thinks it is appropriate to do so in the circumstances.

(3)   An order under this paragraph shall be made by statutory instrument subject to annulment in pursuance of a resolution of either House of Parliament.

**NOTES**
Inserted as noted at the beginning of this Schedule.
Orders: the Trade Union Recognition (Method of Collective Bargaining) Order 2000, SI 2000/1300 at **[2.566]**.

*Directions about certain applications*

**[1.639]**
**169.** (1)   The Secretary of State may make to the CAC directions as described in sub-paragraph (2) in relation to any case where—
   (a)   two or more applications are made to the CAC,
   (b)   each application is a relevant application,
   (c)   each application relates to the same bargaining unit, and
   (d)   the CAC has not accepted any of the applications.

(2)   The directions are directions as to the order in which the CAC must consider the admissibility of the applications.

(3)   The directions may include—
   (a)   provision to deal with a case where a relevant application is made while the CAC is still considering the admissibility of another one relating to the same bargaining unit;
   (b)   other incidental provisions.

(4)   A relevant application is an application under paragraph 101, 106, 107, 112 or 128.

**NOTES**
Inserted as noted at the beginning of this Schedule.

*[Rights of appeal against demands for costs]*

**[1.640]**
**169A.**  (1)   The Secretary of State may by order make provision for any case where—
   (a)   an application has been made, a declaration has been issued, or any other thing has been done under or for the purposes of this Schedule by, to or in relation to a union, or
   (b)   anything has been done in consequence of anything so done,
and the union amalgamates or transfers all or any of its engagements.

(2)   An order under this paragraph may, in particular, make provision for cases where an amalgamated union, or union to which engagements are transferred, does not have a certificate of independence.]

**NOTES**
This Schedule was inserted as noted at the beginning of this Schedule.
Para 169A: inserted, together with paras 169B, 169C, by the Employment Relations Act 2004, s 18.

*[Effect of change of identity of employer]*

**[1.641]**
**169B.**  (1)   The Secretary of State may by order make provision for any case where—
   (a)   an application has been made, a declaration has been issued, or any other thing has been done under or for the purposes of this Schedule in relation to a group of workers, or
   (b)   anything has been done in consequence of anything so done,
and the person who was the employer of the workers constituting that group at the time the thing was done is no longer the employer of all of the workers constituting that group (whether as a result of a transfer of the whole or part of an undertaking or business or otherwise).

(2)   In this paragraph "group" includes two or more groups taken together.]

**NOTES**
This Schedule was inserted as noted at the beginning of this Schedule.
Para 169B: inserted as noted to para 169A at **[1.640]**.

*[Orders under paragraphs 169A and 169B: supplementary]*

**[1.642]**
**169C.**  (1)   An order under paragraph 169A or 169B may—
   (a)   amend this Schedule;
   (b)   include supplementary, incidental, saving or transitional provisions;
   (c)   make different provision for different cases or circumstances.

(2)   An order under paragraph 169A or 169B shall be made by statutory instrument.

(3)   No such order shall be made unless a draft of it has been laid before Parliament and approved by a resolution of each House of Parliament.]

**NOTES**
This Schedule was inserted as noted at the beginning of this Schedule.
Para 169C: inserted as noted to para 169A at **[1.640]**.

*Notice of declarations*

**[1.643]**
**170.** (1)   If the CAC issues a declaration under this Schedule it must notify the parties of the declaration and its contents.

(2)   The reference here to the parties is to—
   (a)   the union (or unions) concerned and the employer concerned, and
   (b)   if the declaration is issued in consequence of an application by a worker or workers, the worker or workers making it.

**NOTES**
Inserted as noted at the beginning of this Schedule.

*[Supply of information to CAC*

**[1.644]**
**170A.** (1)   The CAC may, if it considers it necessary to do so to enable or assist it to exercise any of its functions under this Schedule, exercise any or all of the powers conferred in sub-paragraphs (2) to (4).

(2)   The CAC may require an employer to supply the CAC case manager, within such period as the CAC may specify, with specified information concerning either or both of the following—

(a)   the workers in a specified bargaining unit who work for the employer;

(b)   the likelihood of a majority of those workers being in favour of the conduct by a specified union (or specified unions) of collective bargaining on their behalf.

(3)   The CAC may require a union to supply the CAC case manager, within such period as the CAC may specify, with specified information concerning either or both of the following—

(a)   the workers in a specified bargaining unit who are members of the union;

(b)   the likelihood of a majority of the workers in a specified bargaining unit being in favour of the conduct by the union (or by it and other specified unions) of collective bargaining on their behalf.

(4)   The CAC may require an applicant worker to supply the CAC case manager, within such period as the CAC may specify, with specified information concerning the likelihood of a majority of the workers in his bargaining unit being in favour of having bargaining arrangements ended.

(5)   The recipient of a requirement under this paragraph must, within the specified period, supply the CAC case manager with such of the specified information as is in the recipient's possession.

(6)   From the information supplied to him under this paragraph, the CAC case manager must prepare a report and submit it to the CAC.

(7)   If an employer, a union or a worker fails to comply with sub-paragraph (5), the report under sub-paragraph (6) must mention that failure; and the CAC may draw an inference against the party concerned.

(8)   The CAC must give a copy of the report under sub-paragraph (6) to the employer, to the union (or unions) and, in the case of an application under paragraph 112 or 137, to the applicant worker (or applicant workers).

(9)   In this paragraph—

"applicant worker" means a worker who—

(a)   falls within a bargaining unit ("his bargaining unit") and

(b)   has made an application under paragraph 112 or 137 to have bargaining arrangements ended;

"the CAC case manager" means the member of the staff provided to the CAC by ACAS who is named in the requirement (but the CAC may, by notice given to the recipient of a requirement under this paragraph, change the member of that staff who is to be the CAC case manager for the purposes of that requirement);

"collective bargaining" is to be construed in accordance with paragraph 3; and

"specified" means specified in a requirement under this paragraph.]

**NOTES**
This Schedule was inserted as noted at the beginning of this Schedule.
Para 170A: inserted by the Employment Relations Act 2004, s 19.

*CAC's general duty*

**[1.645]**
**171.** In exercising functions under this Schedule in any particular case the CAC must have regard to the object of encouraging and promoting fair and efficient practices and arrangements in the workplace, so far as having regard to that object is consistent with applying other provisions of this Schedule in the case concerned.

**NOTES**
Inserted as noted at the beginning of this Schedule.

*["Pay" and other matters subject to collective bargaining*

**[1.646]**
**171A.** (1)   In this Schedule "pay" does not include terms relating to a person's membership of or rights under, or his employer's contributions to—

(a)   an occupational pension scheme (as defined by section 1 of the Pension Schemes Act 1993), or

(b)   a personal pension scheme (as so defined).

(2)   The Secretary of State may by order amend sub-paragraph (1).

(3)   The Secretary of State may by order—

    (a)   amend paragraph 3(3), 54(4) or 94(6)(b) by adding specified matters relating to pensions to the matters there specified to which negotiations may relate;

    (b)   amend paragraph 35(2)(b) or 44(2)(b) by adding specified matters relating to pensions to the core topics there specified.

(4)  An order under this paragraph may—

    (a)   include supplementary, incidental, saving or transitional provisions including provision amending this Schedule, and

    (b)   make different provision for different cases.

(5)  An order under this paragraph may make provision deeming—

    (a)   the matters to which any pre-commencement declaration of recognition relates, and

    (b)   the matters to which any pre-commencement method of collective bargaining relates,

to include matters to which a post-commencement declaration of recognition or method of collective bargaining could relate.

(6)  In sub-paragraph (5)—

"pre-commencement declaration of recognition" means a declaration of recognition issued by the CAC before the coming into force of the order,

"pre-commencement method of collective bargaining" means a method of collective bargaining specified by the CAC before the coming into force of the order,

and references to a post-commencement declaration of recognition or method of collective bargaining shall be construed accordingly.

(7)  An order under this paragraph shall be made by statutory instrument; and no such order shall be made unless a draft of it has been laid before Parliament and approved by a resolution of each House of Parliament.]

**NOTES**

This Schedule was inserted as noted at the beginning of this Schedule.

Para 171A: inserted by the Employment Relations Act 2004, s 20.

*General interpretation*

**[1.647]**

**172.** (1)   References in this Schedule to the CAC are to the Central Arbitration Committee.

(2)  For the purposes of this Schedule in its application to a part of Great Britain a working day is a day other than—

    (a)   a Saturday or a Sunday,

    (b)   Christmas day or Good Friday, or

    (c)   a day which is a bank holiday under the Banking and Financial Dealings Act 1971 in that part of Great Britain.]

**NOTES**

Inserted as noted at the beginning of this Schedule.

# SCHEDULE A2
## TRIBUNAL JURISDICTIONS TO WHICH SECTION 207A APPLIES

**[1.648]**

. . .

. . .

. . .

Section 145A of this Act (inducements relating to union membership or activities)

Section 145B of this Act (inducements relating to collective bargaining)

Section 146 of this Act (detriment in relation to union membership and activities)

Paragraph 156 of Schedule A1 to this Act (detriment in relation to union recognition rights)

. . .

Section 23 of the Employment Rights Act 1996 (c 18) (unauthorised deductions and payments)

Section 48 of that Act (detriment in employment)

Section 111 of that Act (unfair dismissal)

Section 163 of that Act (redundancy payments)

Section 24 of the National Minimum Wage Act 1998 (c 39) (detriment in relation to national minimum wage)

[Sections 120 and 127 of the Equality Act 2010 (discrimination etc in work cases)]

The Employment Tribunal Extension of Jurisdiction (England and Wales) Order 1994 (SI 1994/1623) (breach of employment contract and termination)

The Employment Tribunal Extension of Jurisdiction (Scotland) Order 1994 (SI 1994/1624) (corresponding provision for Scotland)

Regulation 30 of the Working Time Regulations 1998 (SI 1998/1833) (breach of regulations)

Regulation 32 of the Transnational Information and Consultation of Employees Regulations 1999 (SI 1999/3323) (detriment relating to European Works Councils)

. . .

Regulation 45 of the European Public Limited-Liability Company Regulations 2004 (SI 2004/2326) (detriment in employment)

Regulation 33 of the Information and Consultation of Employees Regulations 2004 (SI 2004/3426) (detriment in employment)

Paragraph 8 of the Schedule to the Occupational and Personal Pension Schemes (Consultation by Employers and Miscellaneous Amendment) Regulations 2006 (SI 2006/349) (detriment in employment)

. . .

Regulation 34 of the European Cooperative Society (Involvement of Employees) Regulations 2006 (SI 2006/2059) (detriment in relation to involvement in a European Cooperative Society)

Regulation 17 of the Cross-border Railway Services (Working Time) Regulations 2008 (SI 2008/1660) (breach of regulations).]

[Regulation 9 of the Employment Relations Act 1999 (Blacklists) Regulations 2010 (SI 2010/493) (detriment connected with prohibited list)].]

**NOTES**

Commencement: 6 April 2009.

Inserted by the Employment Act 2008, s 3(1), (3), as from 6 April 2009 (subject to transitional provisions and savings in the Employment Act 2008 (Commencement No 1, Transitional Provisions and Savings) Order 2008, SI 2008/3232, Schedule, Pt 1, paras 1(c), 2, 3).

Entries relating to "Section 2 of the Equal Pay Act 1970", "Section 63 of the Sex Discrimination Act 1975", "Section 54 of the Race Relation Act 1976", "section 17A of the Disability Discrimination Act 1995", "Regulation 28 of the Employment Equality (Sexual Orientation) Regulations 2003", "Regulation 28 of the Employment Equality (Religion or Belief) Regulations 2003", and "Regulation 36 of the Employment Equality (Age) Regulations 2006" (all omitted) repealed by the Equality Act 2010, s 211, Sch 26, Pt 1, para 24(1), (2), Sch 27, Pt 1, as from 1 October 2010. Note that the Equality Act 2010 (Commencement No 4, Savings, Consequential, Transitional, Transitory and Incidental Provisions and Revocation) Order 2010, SI 2010/2317 (at **[2.1558]** et seq) provides for various transitional provisions and savings in connection with the commencement of the 2010 Act and the repeal of these entries. See, in particular, art 15 (saving where the act complained of occurs wholly before 1 October 2010).

Entry relating to "Sections 120 and 127 of the Equality Act 2010" inserted by the Equality Act 2010, s 211, Sch 26, Pt 1, paras 24(1), (3), as from 1 October 2010 (as to transitional provisions and savings, see the note immediately above).

Entry relating to the Employment Relations Act 1999 (Blacklists) Regulations 2010 inserted by the Employment Relations Act 1999 (Blacklists) Regulations 2010, SI 2010/493, reg 17(1), (6), as from 2 March 2010.

## SCHEDULES 1 AND 2

*(Schs 1, 2 contain repeals and consequential amendments; in so far as relevant, these have been incorporated at the appropriate place.)*

## SCHEDULE 3
## TRANSITIONAL PROVISIONS AND SAVINGS

Section 300(3)

*Continuity of the law*

**[1.649]**

**1.** (1)  The repeal and re-enactment of provisions in this Act does not affect the continuity of the law.

(2)  Anything done (including subordinate legislation made), or having effect as done, under a provision reproduced in this Act has effect as if done under the corresponding provision of this Act.

(3)    References (express or implied) in this Act or any other enactment, instrument or document to a provision of this Act shall, so far as the context permits, be construed as including, in relation to times, circumstances and purposes before the commencement of this Act, a reference to corresponding earlier provisions.

(4)    A reference (express or implied) in any enactment, instrument or other document to a provision reproduced in this Act shall be construed, so far as is required for continuing its effect, and subject to any express amendment made by this Act, as being, or as the case may required including, a reference to the corresponding provision of this Act.

### General saving for old transitional provisions and savings

**2.** (1)    The repeal by this Act of a transitional provision or saving relating to the coming into force of a provision reproduced in this Act does not affect the operation of the transitional provision or saving, in so far as it is not specifically reproduced in this Act but remains capable of having effect in relation to the corresponding provision of this Act.

(2)    The repeal by this Act of an enactment previously repealed subject to savings does not affect the continued operation of those savings.

(3)    The repeal by this Act of a saving on the previous repeal of an enactment does not affect the operation of the saving in so far as it is not specifically reproduced in this Act but remains capable of having effect.

### Effect of repeal of 1946 Act

**3.**    The repeal by this Act of the Trade Disputes and Trade Unions Act 1946 shall not be construed as reviving in any respect the effect of the Trade Disputes and Trade Unions Act 1927.

### Pre-1974 references to registered trade unions or employers' associations

**4.** (1)    Any reference in an enactment passed, or instrument made under an enactment, before 16th September 1974—
    (a)    to a trade union or employers' association registered under—
        (i)    the Trade Union Acts 1871 to 1964, or
        (ii)    the Industrial Relations Act 1971, or
    (b)    to an organisation of workers or an organisation of employers within the meaning of the Industrial Relations Act 1971,
shall be construed as a reference to a trade union or employers' association within the meaning of this Act.

(2)    Subsection (1) does not apply to any enactment relating to income tax or corporation tax.

### Enforceability of collective agreements

**5.**    Section 179 of this Act (enforceability of collective agreements) does not apply to a collective agreement made on or after 1st December 1971 and before 16th September 1974.

### Trade unions and employers' associations ceasing to be incorporated by virtue of 1974 Act

**6.** (1)    The repeal by this Act of section 19 of the Trade Union and Labour Relations Act 1974 (transitional provisions for trade unions and employers' associations ceasing to be incorporated) does not affect—
    (a)    the title to property which by virtue of that section vested on 16th September 1974 in "the appropriate trustees" as defined by that section, or
    (b)    any liability, obligation or right affecting such property which by virtue of that section became a liability, obligation or right of those trustees.

(2)    A certificate given by the persons who on that date were the president and general secretary of a trade union or employers' association, or occupied positions equivalent to that of president and general secretary, that the persons named in the certificate are the appropriate trustees of the union or association for the purposes of section 19(2) of the Trade Union and Labour Relations Act 1974 is conclusive evidence that those persons were the appropriate trustees for those purposes.

(3)    A document which purports to be such a certificate shall be taken to be such a certificate unless the contrary is proved.

### References to former Industrial Arbitration Board

**7.**    Any reference to the former Industrial Arbitration Board in relation to which section 10(2) of the Employment Protection Act 1975 applied immediately before the commencement of this Act shall continue to be construed as a reference to the Central Arbitration Committee.

*Effect of political resolution passed before 1984 amendments*

**8.** A resolution under section 3 of the Trade Union Act 1913, or rule made for the purposes of that section, in relation to which section 17(2) of the Trade Union Act 1984 applied immediately before the commencement of this Act shall continue to have effect as if for any reference to the political objects to which section 3 of the 1913 Act formerly applied there were substituted a reference to the objects to which that section applied as amended by the 1984 Act.

*Persons elected to trade union office before 1988 amendments*

**9, 10.** (*Spent.*)

*Qualification to act as auditor of trade union or employers' association*

**11.** (1) Nothing in section 34 (eligibility for appointment as auditor) affects the validity of any appointment as auditor of a trade union or employers' association made before 1st October 1991 (when section 389 of the Companies Act 1985 was repealed and replaced by the provisions of Part II of the Companies Act 1989).

(2) A person who is not qualified as mentioned in section 34(1) may act as auditor of a trade union in respect of an accounting period if—

(a) the union was registered under the Trade Union Acts 1871 to 1964 on 30th September 1971,

(b) he acted as its auditor in respect of the last period in relation to which it was required to make an annual return under section 16 of the Trade Union Act 1871,

(c) he has acted as its auditor in respect of every accounting period since that period, and

(d) he retains an authorisation formerly granted by the Board of Trade or the Secretary of State under section 16(1)(b) of the Companies Act 1948 (adequate knowledge and experience, or pre-1947 practice).

**12.** . . .

*Use of existing forms, &c*

**13.** Any document made, served or issued on or after the commencement of this Act which contains a reference to an enactment repealed by this Act shall be construed, except so far as a contrary intention appears, as referring or, as the context may require, including a reference to the corresponding provision of this Act.

*Saving for power to vary or revoke*

**14.** The power of the Secretary of State by further order to vary or revoke the Funds for Trade Union Ballots Order 1982 extends to so much of section 115(2)(a) as reproduces the effect of Article 2 of that order.

**NOTES**

Para 12: applied to Northern Ireland only and was repealed by the Trade Union and Labour Relations (Northern Ireland) Order 1995, SI 1995/1980.

Note: it is assumed that the word "required" in the second place it occurs in para 1 should read "require".

Companies Act 1948: repealed (see now the Companies Act 1985 and the Companies Act 2006). Note that most of the 1985 Act was repealed by the 2006 Act as from 1 October 2009 (subject to a variety of savings and transitional provisions).

Companies Act 1985: see the note above.

Companies Act 1989: Part II of the 1989 Act was repealed by the Companies Act 2006.

Employment Act 1988: ss 12(1), 13–15 of that Act are repealed by s 300(1) of, and Sch 1 to, this Act.

Employment Protection Act 1975: s 10(2) of that Act is repealed by s 300(1) of, and Sch 1 to, this Act.

Industrial Relations Act 1971: repealed by the Trade Union and Labour Relations Act 1974, ss 1, 25(3), Sch 5.

Trade Disputes and Trade Unions Act 1927: repealed by the Trade Disputes and Trade Unions Act 1946, s 1.

Trade Disputes and Trade Unions Act 1946: repealed by s 300(1) of, and Sch 1 to, this Act.

Trade Union Act 1913: s 3 of that Act is repealed by s 300(1) of, and Sch 1 to, this Act.

Trade Union Acts 1871 to 1964: repealed, see the note to s 3 at **[1.243]**.

Trade Union Act 1984: s 3 was repealed by the Employment Act 1988, ss 14(2), 33(2), Sch 4. The whole Act is repealed by s 300(1) of, and Sch 1 to, this Act.

Trade Union and Labour Relations Act 1974: repealed by s 300(1) of, and Sch 1 to, this Act.

Part 1   Statutes

# TRADE UNION REFORM AND EMPLOYMENT RIGHTS ACT 1993 (NOTE)

### (1993 c 19)

*An Act to make further reforms of the law relating to trade unions and industrial relations; to make amendments of the law relating to employment rights and to abolish the right to statutory minimum remuneration; to amend the law relating to the constitution and jurisdiction of industrial tribunals and the Employment Appeal Tribunal; to amend section 56A of the Sex Discrimination Act 1975; to provide for the Secretary of State to have functions of securing the provision of careers services; to make further provision about employment and training functions of Scottish Enterprise and of Highlands and Islands Enterprise; and for connected purposes*

1 July 1993

**[1.650]**

NOTES

Almost all of this major Act either amends other legislation (principally the Trade Union and Labour Relations (Consolidation) Act 1992) or has since been repealed and re-enacted by the Employment Tribunals Act 1996 and the Employment Rights Act 1996. It is therefore not necessary to reproduce provisions of the Act here. Instead this note summarises the position under the two major categories indicated above, in the following tables.

**1 PROVISIONS AMENDING THE 1992 ACT**

| Section/Schedule | Amendments |
|---|---|
| 1 | Amends ss 49, 52 |
| 2 | Inserts s 51A, amends s 52 |
| 3 | Introduces Sch 1 (which amends ss 74, 75 and 78 and inserts s 77A) |
| 4 | Substitutes s 100 with new ss 100–100E |
| 5 | Amends s 99 |
| 6 | Inserts s 24A |
| 7 | Repeals ss 115, 116 |
| 8 | Amends s 32 |
| 9 | Inserts s 32A |
| 10 | Inserts ss 37A–37E |
| 11 | Amends s 45 and inserts s 45A |
| 12 | Inserts ss 45B, 45C |
| 13 | Amends s 148 |
| 14 | Substitutes ss 174–177 |
| 15 | Substitutes s 68 with new ss 68 and 68A |
| 16 | Amends s 65 |
| 17 | Amends s 230 |
| 18 | Amends s 226 and inserts s 226A |
| 19 | Inserts s 231A |
| 20 | Amends s 229 and inserts ss 226B, 226C, 231B |
| 21 | Inserts s 234A |
| 22 | Inserts ss 235A–235C (ss 235B, 235C repealed by the Employment Relations Act 1999) |
| 34 | Amends ss 188, 190, 193, substitutes s 195, repeals s 283 (repealed in part by SI 1995/2587 and the Statute Law (Repeals) Act 2004) |
| 43 | Amends ss 209, 249, substitutes s 213 (repealed in part by the Employment Relations Act 1999) |
| 44 | Inserts s 251A |
| Sch 1 | Amends ss 74, 75, 78, inserts s 77A |
| Sch 6 (part) | Amends s 288 (repealed in part by the Employment Rights (Dispute Resolution) Act 1998) |

**2 PROVISIONS REPEALED BY THE EMPLOYMENT TRIBUNALS ACT 1996**

| Section/Schedule | Effect of provision | Provisions as re-enacted |
|---|---|---|
| 36 | Amended the Employment Protection (Consolidation) Act 1978, s 128 | 4(1)–(7), 41(2) |
| 37 | Substituted Sch 11, Pt I, para 16 to the 1978 Act | 28(2)–(5) |
| 38 | Amended s 131 of the 1978 Act | 3(1), (3), (5), 8(2), (4) |
| 40 | Amended Sch 9, para 1 to the 1978 Act | 7(5), 11(1)–(6) |

| Section/Schedule | Effect of provision | Provisions as re-enacted |
| --- | --- | --- |
| 41 | Inserted Sch 11, Pt I, para 18A to the 1978 Act | 31 |
| 42 | Inserted s 136A of the 1978 Act | 33, 37(3) |

## 3 PROVISIONS REPEALED BY THE EMPLOYMENT RIGHTS ACT 1996

| Section/Schedule | Effect of provision | Provisions as re-enacted |
| --- | --- | --- |
| 23 | Substituted the Employment Protection (Consolidation) Act 1978, Pt III with ss 33–38A and ss 39–44 (enacted by Sch 2) | 71–78, 236(3), 79–83, 85, 236(3) |
| 24 | Substituted s 60, amended ss 53, 59, 64 of the 1978 Act | 99(1)–(3), 105(1), (2), 108(3), 109(2), 92(4) |
| 25 | Introduced Sch 3 (inserted ss 45–47 of the 1978 Act) | 66–70, 106(3) |
| 26 | Introduced Sch 4 (substituted ss 1–6 of the 1978 Act) | 1–7, 198 |
| 28 | Introduced Sch 5 (inserted ss 22A–C, 57A, 75A, 77–79 and amended ss 57(3), 59(2), 64(4), 71–73 of the 1978 Act) | 44, 48, 49, 98(6), 100, 105(3), 108(3), 109(2), 117(3), (4), 118, 119(1), 120, 122(3), 125, 128–132, 236(3). |
| 29 | Inserted s 60A, amended ss 59(2), 64(4) of the 1978 Act | 104, 105(7), 108(3), 109(2) |
| 30 | Amended ss 71, 74, 75 of the 1978 Act | 117(2), 123(1), 124(3),(4) |
| 31 | Amended s 138, inserted s 138A of the 1978 Act | 192(1)–(8), 236(3) |
| 39(1) | Amended s 140 of the 1978 Act | 203(2)–(4) |
| Sch 2 | Substituted ss 39–44 of the 1978 Act | 79–83, 85, 236(3) |
| Sch 3 | Inserted ss 45–47 of the 1978 Act | 66–70, 106(3) |
| Sch 4 | Substituted ss 1–6 of the 1978 Act | 1–7, 198 |
| Sch 5 | Inserted ss 22A–C, 57A, 75A, 77–79 and amended ss 57(3), 59(2), 64(4), 71–73 of the 1978 Act | 44, 48, 49, 98(6), 100, 105(3), 108(3), 109(2), 117(3), (4), 118, 119(1), 120, 122(3), 125, 128–132, 236(3) |
| Sch 6 (part) | Amended the Wages Act 1986, s 6 | 203(2)–(4), 231 |

## 4 OTHER PROVISIONS NOT REPRODUCED

| Section/Schedule | Effect of provision | Provisions as re-enacted |
| --- | --- | --- |
| 27 | Inserted the Employment Protection (Consolidation) Act 1978, s146(4A)–(4C) | Repealed by SI 1995/31 |
| 32 | Inserted the Sex Discrimination Act 1986, s 6(4A)–(4D) | Repealed by the Equality Act 2010 |
| 33 | Amended SI 1981/1794 | Repealed by SI 2006/246 |
| 35 | Repealed the Wages Act 1986, Pt II | Repealed by the Statute Law (Repeals) Act 2004 |
| 39(2) | Introduces Sch 6 | See Sch 6 below |
| 45–47 | Amend the Employment and Training Act 1973, Enterprise and the New Towns (Scotland) Act 1990 | Outside the scope of this work |
| 48 | Interpretation | Unnecessary |
| 49 | Introduces Schs 7 and 8 | See Schs 7 and 8 below |
| 50 | Introduces Sch 9 | See Sch 9 below |
| 51 | Introduces Sch 10 | See Sch 10 below |
| 52 | Commencement | Unnecessary |
| 53 | Financial provision | Unnecessary |
| 54 | Application to Northern Ireland | Outside the scope of this work |
| 55 | Short title | Unnecessary |
| Sch 6 (part) | Amended the Sex Discrimination Act 1975, s 77 and the Race Relations Act 1976, s 72 | Repealed by the Equality Act 2010 |
| Sch 7 | Miscellaneous amendments | Unnecessary (in so far as relevant to this work such amendments have been incorporated) |
| Schs 8 | Consequential amendments | Unnecessary (in so far as relevant to this work such amendments have been incorporated) |
| Sch 9 | Transitional provisions and savings | Spent |
| Sch 10 | Repeals | Unnecessary (in so far as relevant to this work such repeals have been incorporated) |

# PENSION SCHEMES ACT 1993

### (1993 c 48)

## ARRANGEMENT OF SECTIONS

### PART III
### CERTIFICATION OF PENSION SCHEMES AND EFFECTS ON MEMBERS' STATE SCHEME RIGHTS AND DUTIES

### CHAPTER I
### CERTIFICATION

*General requirements for certification*

### PART VII
### INSOLVENCY OF EMPLOYERS

### CHAPTER II
### PAYMENT BY SECRETARY OF STATE OF UNPAID SCHEME CONTRIBUTIONS

### PART X
### INVESTIGATIONS: THE PENSIONS OMBUDSMAN

### PART XI
### GENERAL AND MISCELLANEOUS PROVISIONS

*Avoidance of certain transactions and provisions*

### PART XII
### SUPPLEMENTARY PROVISIONS

*Interpretation*

*An Act to consolidate certain enactments relating to pension schemes with amendments to give effect to recommendations of the Law Commission and the Scottish Law Commission*

[5 November 1993]

### NOTES

Only certain parts of this Act most relevant to employment law are reproduced. Provisions omitted are not annotated. The provisions reproduced have been extensively amended by the Pensions Acts 1995 and 2004, and the Child Support, Pensions and Social Security Act 2000, and are printed as so amended.

Bank insolvency or administration: in so far as any provision of this Act applies to liquidation or administration, it applies with specified modifications in the case of a bank insolvency or administration; see the Banking Act 2009 (Parts 2 and 3 Consequential Amendments) Order 2009, SI 2009/317.

See *Harvey* BI(9), G(1)(E).

## PART III
## CERTIFICATION OF PENSION SCHEMES AND EFFECTS ON MEMBERS' STATE SCHEME RIGHTS AND DUTIES

### CHAPTER I
### CERTIFICATION

*General requirements for certification*

**[1.651]**
**11   Elections as to employments covered by contracting-out certificates**
(1)   Subject to the provisions of this Part, an employment otherwise satisfying the conditions for inclusion in a contracting-out certificate shall be so included if and so long as the employer so elects and not otherwise.
(2)   Subject to subsections (3) and (4), an election may be so made, and an employment so included, either generally or in relation only to a particular description of earners.
(3)   Except in such cases as may be prescribed, an employer shall not, in making or abstaining from making any election under this section, discriminate between different earners on any grounds other than the nature of their employment.
(4)   If the [Inland Revenue consider] that an employer is contravening subsection (3) in relation to any scheme, [they] may—
   (a)   refuse to give effect to any election made by him in relation to that scheme; or
   (b)   cancel any contracting-out certificate held by him in respect of it.
(5)   Regulations may make provision—
   (a)   for regulating the manner in which an employer is to make an election with a view to the issue, variation or surrender of a contracting-out certificate;
   (b)   for requiring an employer to give a notice of his intentions in respect of making or abstaining from making any such election in relation to any existing or proposed scheme—
      (i)    to employees in any employment to which the scheme applies or to which it is proposed that it should apply;
      (ii)   to any independent trade union recognised to any extent for the purpose of collective bargaining in relation to those employees;
      (iii)  to the trustees and managers of the scheme; and
      (iv)   to such other persons as may be prescribed;
   (c)   for requiring an employer, in connection with any such notice, to furnish such information as may be prescribed and to undertake such consultations as may be prescribed with any such trade union as is mentioned in paragraph (b)(ii);
   (d)   for empowering the [Inland Revenue] to refuse to give effect to an election made by an employer unless [they are] satisfied that he has complied with the requirements of the regulations;
   (e)   for referring to an [employment tribunal] any question—
      (i)    whether an organisation is such a trade union as is mentioned in paragraph (b)(ii), or
      (ii)   whether the requirements of the regulations as to consultation have been complied with.

---

**NOTES**
   Sub-s (4): words in square brackets substituted by the Social Security Contributions (Transfer of Functions, etc) Act 1999, s 1(1), Sch 1, para 37.
   Sub-s (5): words in first and second pairs of square brackets substituted by the Social Security Contributions (Transfer of Functions, etc) Act 1999, s 1(1), Sch 1, para 37; words in final pair of square brackets substituted by the Employment Rights (Dispute Resolution) Act 1998, s 1(2)(a).
   Inland Revenue: a reference to the Inland Revenue is now to be taken as a reference to Her Majesty's Revenue and Customs; see the Commissioners for Revenue and Customs Act 2005, s 50(1), (7).
   Regulations: the Occupational Pension Schemes (Contracting-out) Regulations 1996, SI 1996/1172; the Personal and Occupational Pension Schemes (Miscellaneous Amendments) Regulations 1999, SI 1999/3198; the Occupational and Personal Pension Schemes (Contracting-out) (Miscellaneous Amendments) Regulations 2002, SI 2002/681; the Occupational, Personal and Stakeholder Pensions (Miscellaneous Amendments) Regulations 2009, SI 2009/615.

---

## PART VII
## INSOLVENCY OF EMPLOYERS

### CHAPTER II
### PAYMENT BY SECRETARY OF STATE OF UNPAID SCHEME CONTRIBUTIONS

**[1.652]**
**123   Interpretation of Chapter II**
(1)   For the purposes of this Chapter, an employer shall be taken to be insolvent if, but only if, in England and Wales—
   (a)   he has been adjudged bankrupt or has made a composition or arrangement with his creditors;

  (b)    he has died and his estate falls to be administered in accordance with an order under section 421 of the Insolvency Act 1986; or

  (c)    where the employer is a company—

      (i)    a winding-up order . . . is made or a resolution for voluntary winding up is passed with respect to it [or the company enters administration],

      (ii)    a receiver or manager of its undertaking is duly appointed,

      (iii)    possession is taken, by or on behalf of the holders of any debentures secured by a floating charge, of any property of the company comprised in or subject to the charge, or

      (iv)    a voluntary arrangement proposed for the purpose of Part I of the Insolvency Act 1986 is approved under that Part.

(2)    For the purposes of this Chapter, an employer shall be taken to be insolvent if, but only if, in Scotland—

  (a)    sequestration of his estate is awarded or he executes a trust deed for his creditors or enters into a composition contract;

  (b)    he has died and a judicial factor appointed under section 11A of the Judicial Factors (Scotland) Act 1889 is required by this section to divide his insolvent estate among his creditors; or

  (c)    where the employer is a company—

      (i)    a winding-up order . . . is made or a resolution for voluntary winding up is passed with respect to it [or the company enters administration],

      (ii)    a receiver of its undertaking is duly appointed, or

      (iii)    a voluntary arrangement proposed for the purpose of Part I of the Insolvency Act 1986 is approved under that Part.

(3)    In this Chapter—

"contract of employment", "employee", "employer" and "employment" and other expressions which are defined in [the Employment Rights Act 1996] have the same meaning as in that Act;

"holiday pay" means—

  (a)    pay in respect of holiday actually taken; or

  (b)    any accrued holiday pay which under the employee's contract of employment would in the ordinary course have become payable to him in respect of the period of a holiday if his employment with the employer had continued until he became entitled to a holiday;

   . . .

(4)    . . .

(5)    Any reference in this Chapter to the resources of a scheme is a reference to the funds out of which the benefits provided by the scheme are from time to time payable.

**NOTES**

  Sub-ss (1), (2): words omitted from sub-para (c)(i) repealed, and words in square brackets added, by the Enterprise Act 2002 (Insolvency) Order 2003, SI 2003/2096, art 4, Schedule, para 22, except in relation to cases where a petition for an administration order was presented before 15 September 2003.

  Sub-s (3): words in square brackets substituted by the Employment Rights Act 1996, s 240, Sch 1, para 61(1), (3); definition "occupational pension scheme" (omitted) repealed by the Pensions Act 2004, ss 319(1), 320, Sch 12, paras 9, 19(a), Sch 13, Pt 1.

  Sub-s (4): repealed by the Pensions Act 2004, ss 319(1), 320, Sch 12, paras 9, 19(b), Sch 13, Pt 1.

**[1.653]**

**124   Duty of Secretary of State to pay unpaid contributions to schemes**

(1)    If, on an application made to him in writing by the persons competent to act in respect of an occupational pension scheme or a personal pension scheme, the Secretary of State is satisfied—

  (a)    that an employer has become insolvent; and

  (b)    that at the time he did so there remained unpaid relevant contributions falling to be paid by him to the scheme,

then, subject to the provisions of this section and section 125, the Secretary of State shall pay into the resources of the scheme the sum which in his opinion is payable in respect of the unpaid relevant contributions.

(2)    In this section and section 125 "relevant contributions" means contributions falling to be paid by an employer to an occupational pension scheme or a personal pension scheme, either on his own account or on behalf of an employee; and for the purposes of this section a contribution shall not be treated as falling to be paid on behalf of an employee unless a sum equal to that amount has been deducted from the pay of the employee by way of a contribution from him.

(3)    [Subject to subsection (3A),] the sum payable under this section in respect of unpaid contributions of an employer on his own account to an occupational pension scheme or a personal pension scheme shall be the least of the following amounts—

(a) the balance of relevant contributions remaining unpaid on the date when he became insolvent and payable by the employer on his own account to the scheme in respect of the 12 months immediately preceding that date;

(b) the amount certified by an actuary to be necessary for the purpose of meeting the liability of the scheme on dissolution to pay the benefits provided by the scheme to or in respect of the employees of the employer;

(c) an amount equal to 10 per cent. of the total amount of remuneration paid or payable to those employees in respect of the 12 months immediately preceding the date on which the employer became insolvent.

[(3A) Where the scheme in question is a money purchase scheme, the sum payable under this section by virtue of subsection (3) shall be the lesser of the amounts mentioned in paragraphs (a) and (c) of that subsection.]

(4) For the purposes of subsection (3)(c), "remuneration" includes holiday pay, statutory sick pay, statutory maternity pay under Part V of the Social Security Act 1986 or Part XII of the Social Security Contributions and Benefits Act 1992 [and any payment such as is referred to in section 184(2) of the Employment Rights Act 1996].

(5) Any sum payable under this section in respect of unpaid contributions on behalf of an employee shall not exceed the amount deducted from the pay of the employee in respect of the employee's contributions to the scheme during the 12 months immediately preceding the date on which the employer became insolvent.

[(6) In this section "on his own account", in relation to an employer, means on his own account but to fund benefits for, or in respect of, one or more employees.]

**NOTES**
Sub-s (3): words in square brackets inserted by the Pensions Act 1995, s 90.
Sub-s (3A): inserted by the Pensions Act 1995, s 90.
Sub-s (4): words in square brackets substituted by the Employment Rights Act 1996, s 240, Sch 1, para 61(1), (3).
Sub-s (6): added by the Pensions Act 2004, s 319(1), Sch 12, paras 9, 20.
Social Security Act 1986, Pt V: repealed by the Social Security (Consequential Provisions) Act 1992. The relevant provisions of that Part relating to maternity pay were re-enacted in the Social Security Contributions and Benefits Act 1992, Pt XII.

**[1.654]**
**125 Certification of amounts payable under s 124 by insolvency officers**
(1) This section applies where one of the officers mentioned in subsection (2) ("the relevant officer") has been or is required to be appointed in connection with an employer's insolvency.
(2) The officers referred to in subsection (1) are—
(a) a trustee in bankruptcy;
(b) a liquidator;
(c) an administrator;
(d) a receiver or manager; or
(e) a trustee under a composition or arrangement between the employer and his creditors or under a trust deed for his creditors executed by the employer;
and in this subsection "trustee", in relation to a composition or arrangement, includes the supervisor of a voluntary arrangement proposed for the purposes of and approved under Part I or VIII of the Insolvency Act 1986.
(3) Subject to subsection (5), where this section applies the Secretary of State shall not make any payment under section 124 in respect of unpaid relevant contributions until he has received a statement from the relevant officer of the amount of relevant contributions which appear to have been unpaid on the date on which the employer became insolvent and to remain unpaid; and the relevant officer shall on request by the Secretary of State provide him as soon as reasonably practicable with such a statement.
(4) Subject to subsection (5), an amount shall be taken to be payable, paid or deducted as mentioned in subsection (3)(a) or (c) or (5) of section 124 only if it is so certified by the relevant officer.
(5) If the Secretary of State is satisfied—
(a) that he does not require a statement under subsection (3) in order to determine the amount of relevant contributions that was unpaid on the date on which the employer became insolvent and remains unpaid, or
(b) that he does not require a certificate under subsection (4) in order to determine the amounts payable, paid or deducted as mentioned in subsection (3)(a) or (c) or (5) of section 124,
he may make a payment under that section in respect of the contributions in question without having received such a statement or, as the case may be, such a certificate.

**[1.655]**
**126 Complaint to [employment tribunal]**
(1) Any persons who are competent to act in respect of an occupational pension scheme or a personal pension scheme and who have applied for a payment to be made under section 124 into the resources of the scheme may present a complaint to an [employment tribunal] that—

(a)    the Secretary of State has failed to make any such payment; or

(b)    any such payment made by him is less than the amount which should have been paid.

(2)    Such a complaint must be presented within the period of three months beginning with the date on which the decision of the Secretary of State on that application was communicated to the persons presenting it or, if that is not reasonably practicable, within such further period as is reasonable.

(3)    Where an [employment tribunal] finds that the Secretary of State ought to make a payment under section 124, it shall make a declaration to that effect and shall also declare the amount of any such payment which it finds that the Secretary of State ought to make.

**NOTES**

Section heading, sub-ss (1), (3): words in square brackets substituted by the Employment Rights (Dispute Resolution) Act 1998, s 1(2)(a).

**[1.656]**
**127    Transfer to Secretary of State of rights and remedies**
(1)    Where in pursuance of section 124 the Secretary of State makes any payment into the resources of an occupational pension scheme or a personal pension scheme in respect of any contributions to the scheme, any rights and remedies in respect of those contributions belonging to the persons competent to act in respect of the scheme shall, on the making of the payment, become rights and remedies of the Secretary of State.

(2)    Where the Secretary of State makes any such payment as is mentioned in subsection (1) and the sum (or any part of the sum) falling to be paid by the employer on account of the contributions in respect of which the payment is made constitutes—

(a)    a preferential debt within the meaning of the Insolvency Act 1986 for the purposes of any provision of that Act (including any such provision as applied by an order made under that Act) or any provision of [the Companies Acts (as defined in section 2(1) of the Companies Act 2006)]; or

(b)    a preferred debt within the meaning of the Bankruptcy (Scotland) Act 1985 for the purposes of any provision of that Act (including any such provision as applied by section 11A of the Judicial Factors (Scotland) Act 1889,

then, without prejudice to the generality of subsection (1), there shall be included among the rights and remedies which become rights and remedies of the Secretary of State in accordance with that subsection any right arising under any such provision by reason of the status of that sum (or that part of it) as a preferential or preferred debt.

(3)    In computing for the purposes of any provision referred to in subsection (2)(a) or (b) the aggregate amount payable in priority to other creditors of the employer in respect of—

(a)    any claim of the Secretary of State to be so paid by virtue of subsection (2); and

(b)    any claim by the persons competent to act in respect of the scheme,

any claim falling within paragraph (a) shall be treated as if it were a claim of those persons; but the Secretary of State shall be entitled, as against those persons, to be so paid in respect of any such claim of his (up to the full amount of the claim) before any payment is made to them in respect of any claim falling within paragraph (b).

**NOTES**

Sub-s (2): words in square brackets in para (a) substituted by the Companies Act 2006 (Consequential Amendments, Transitional Provisions and Savings) Order 2009, SI 2009/1941, art 2(1), Sch 1, para 144(1), (2), as from 1 October 2009.

## PART X
## INVESTIGATIONS: THE PENSIONS OMBUDSMAN

**[1.657]**
**145    The Pensions Ombudsman**
(1)    For the purpose of conducting investigations in accordance with this Part or any corresponding legislation having effect in Northern Ireland there shall be a commissioner to be known as the Pensions Ombudsman.

[(1A)    Provisions conferring power on the Pensions Ombudsman to conduct investigations as mentioned in subsection (1) are to be read as conferring power that—

(a)    in a case of a prescribed description, or

(b)    in a case involving a scheme that is prescribed or is of a prescribed description,

may be exercised whatever the extent of any connections with places outside the United Kingdom.

(1B)    In subsection (1A) "scheme" means occupational pension scheme or personal pension scheme.

(1C)    Subsection (1A) shall not be taken to prejudice any power of the Pensions Ombudsman apart from that subsection to conduct investigations in a case having connections with places outside the United Kingdom.]

(2)    The Pensions Ombudsman shall be appointed by the Secretary of State and shall hold [and vacate] office upon such terms and conditions as the Secretary of State may think fit.

[(3)   The Pensions Ombudsman may resign or be removed from office in accordance with those terms and conditions.]

[(4A)   The Pensions Ombudsman may (with the approval of the Secretary of State as to numbers) appoint such persons to be employees of his as he thinks fit, on such terms and conditions as to remuneration and other matters as the Pensions Ombudsman may with the approval of the Secretary of State determine.

(4B)   The Secretary of State may, on such terms as to payment by the Pensions Ombudsman as the Secretary of State thinks fit, make available to the Pensions Ombudsman such additional staff and such other facilities as he thinks fit.

(4C)   Any function of the Pensions Ombudsman, other than the determination of complaints made and disputes referred under this Part, may be performed by any—

(a)   employee appointed by the Pensions Ombudsman under subsection (4A), or

(b)   member of staff made available to him by the Secretary of State under subsection (4B),

who is authorised for that purpose by the Pensions Ombudsman.]

(5)   The Secretary of State may—

(a)   pay to or in respect of the Pensions Ombudsman such amounts by way of remuneration, compensation for loss of office, pension, allowances and gratuities, or by way of provision for any such benefits, as the Secretary of State may determine  . . .  ; and

(b)   reimburse him in respect of any expenses incurred by him in the performance of his functions.

(6)   The Pensions Ombudsman shall prepare a report on the discharge of his functions for each financial year, and shall submit it to the Secretary of State as soon as practicable afterwards.

(7)   The Secretary of State shall arrange for the publication of each report submitted to him under subsection (6).

[(8)   As soon as is reasonably practicable, the Pensions Ombudsman shall send to the Comptroller and Auditor General a statement of the Pensions Ombudsman's accounts in respect of a financial year.

(9)   The Comptroller and Auditor General shall—

(a)   examine, certify and report on a statement received under this section; and

(b)   send a copy of the statement and the report to the Secretary of State who shall lay them before Parliament.

(10)   In this section "financial year" means a period of 12 months ending with 31st March.]

---

**NOTES**

Sub-ss (1A)–(1C): inserted by the Pensions Act 2004, s 319(1), Sch 12, paras 9, 23, as from a day to be appointed.

Sub-s (2): words in square brackets inserted by the Pensions Act 2004, s 274(1).

Sub-s (3): substituted by the Pensions Act 2004, s 274(2).

Sub-ss (4A)–(4C): substituted, for the original sub-s (4), by the Pensions Act 1995, s 156.

Sub-s (5): words omitted repealed by the Pensions Act 1995, ss 173, 177, Sch 6, paras 2, 7, Sch 7, Pt IV.

Sub-ss (8)–(10): added by the Government Resources and Accounts Act 2000 (Audit of Public Bodies) Order 2008, SI 2008/817, arts 9, 10.

---

**[1.658]**

**[145A   Deputy Pensions Ombudsman**

(1)   The Secretary of State may appoint one or more persons to act as a deputy to the Pensions Ombudsman ("a Deputy Pensions Ombudsman").

(2)   Any such appointment is to be upon such terms and conditions as the Secretary of State thinks fit.

(3)   A Deputy Pensions Ombudsman—

(a)   is to hold and vacate office in accordance with the terms and conditions of his appointment, and

(b)   may resign or be removed from office in accordance with those terms and conditions.

(4)   A Deputy Pensions Ombudsman may perform the functions of the Pensions Ombudsman—

(a)   during any vacancy in that office,

(b)   at any time when the Pensions Ombudsman is for any reason unable to discharge his functions, or

(c)   at any other time, with the consent of the Secretary of State.

(5)   References to the Pensions Ombudsman in relation to the performance of his functions are accordingly to be construed as including references to a Deputy Pensions Ombudsman in relation to the performance of those functions.

(6)   The Secretary of State may—

(a)   pay to or in respect of a Deputy Pensions Ombudsman such amounts—

(i)   by way of remuneration, compensation for loss of office, pension, allowances and gratuities, or

(ii)   by way of provision for any such benefits,

as the Secretary of State may determine, and

(b)   reimburse the Pensions Ombudsman in respect of any expenses incurred by a Deputy Pensions Ombudsman in the performance of any of the Pensions Ombudsman's functions.]

Part 1 Statutes

**[1.659]**
## 146 Functions of the Pensions Ombudsman
[(1)  The Pensions Ombudsman may investigate and determine the following [matters]—

(a)  a complaint made to him by or on behalf of an actual or potential beneficiary of an occupational or personal pension scheme who alleges that he has sustained injustice in consequence of maladministration in connection with any act or omission of a person responsible for the management of the scheme,

(b)  a complaint made to him—

(i)  by or on behalf of a person responsible for the management of an occupational pension scheme who in connection with any act or omission of another person responsible for the management of the scheme, alleges maladministration of the scheme, or

(ii)  by or on behalf of the trustees or managers or an occupational pension scheme who in connection with any act or omission of any trustee or manager of another such scheme, allege maladministration of the other scheme,

and in any case falling within sub-paragraph (ii) references in this Part to the scheme to which the complaint relates [are references to the other scheme referred to in that sub-paragraph],

[(ba)  a complaint made to him by or on behalf of an independent trustee of a trust scheme who, in connection with any act or omission which is an act or omission either—

(i)  of trustees of the scheme who are not independent trustees, or

(ii)  of former trustees of the scheme who were not independent trustees,

alleges maladministration of the scheme,]

(c)  any dispute of fact or law  . . .  in relation to an occupational or personal pension scheme between—

(i)  a person responsible for the management of the scheme, and

(ii)  an actual or potential beneficiary,

and which is referred to him by or on behalf of the actual or potential beneficiary, and

(d)  any dispute of fact or law  . . .  between the trustees or managers of an occupational pension scheme and—

(i)  another person responsible for the management of the scheme, or

(ii)  any trustee or manager of another such scheme, [and in a case falling within sub-paragraph (ii) references in this Part to the scheme to which the reference relates are references to each of the schemes,

(e)  any dispute not falling within paragraph (f) between different trustees of the same occupational pension scheme,

[(f)  any dispute, in relation to a time while section 22 of the Pensions Act 1995 (circumstances in which Regulatory Authority may appoint an independent trustee) applies in relation to an occupational pension scheme, between an independent trustee of the scheme appointed under section 23(1) of that Act and either—

(i)  other trustees of the scheme, or

(ii)  former trustees of the scheme who were not independent trustees appointed under section 23(1) of that Act, and]

(g)  any question relating, in the case of an occupational pension scheme with a sole trustee, to the carrying out of the functions of that trustee.]

[(1A)  The Pensions Ombudsman shall not investigate or determine any dispute or question falling within subsection (1)(c) to (g) unless it is referred to him—

(a)  in the case of a dispute falling within subsection (1)(c), by or on behalf of the actual or potential beneficiary who is a party to the dispute,

(b)  in the case of a dispute falling within subsection (1)(d), by or on behalf of any of the parties to the dispute,

(c)  in the case of a dispute falling within subsection (1)(e), by or on behalf of at least half the trustees of the scheme,

(d)  in the case of a dispute falling within subsection (1)(f), by or on behalf of the independent trustee who is a party to the dispute,

(e)  in the case of a question falling within subsection (1)(g), by or on behalf of the sole trustee.

(1B)  For the purposes of this Part, any reference to or determination by the Pensions Ombudsman of a question falling within subsection (1)(g) shall be taken to be the reference or determination of a dispute.]

(2)  Complaints and references made to the Pensions Ombudsman must be made to him in writing.

(3)  For the purposes of this Part, the following persons (subject to subsection (4)) are responsible for the management of an occupational pension scheme [or a personal pension scheme]—

(a)   the trustees or managers, and

(b)   the employer;

but, in relation to a person falling within one of those paragraphs, references in this Part to another person responsible for the management of the same scheme are to a person falling within the other paragraph.

(3A)   . . .

(4)   Regulations may provide that, subject to any prescribed modifications or exceptions, this Part shall apply in the case of an occupational or personal pension scheme in relation to any prescribed person or body of persons where the person or body—

(a)   is not a trustee or manager of employer, but

(b)   is concerned with the financing or administration of, or the provision or benefits under, the scheme,

as if for the purposes of this Part he were a person responsible for the management of the scheme.]

[(4A)   For the purposes of subsection (4) a person or body of persons is concerned with the administration of an occupational or personal pension scheme where the person or body is responsible for carrying out an act of administration concerned with the scheme.]

(5)   The Pensions Ombudsman may investigate a complaint or dispute notwithstanding that it arose, or relates to a matter which arose, before 1st October 1990 (the date on which the provisions under which his office was constituted came into force).

(6)   The Pensions Ombudsman shall not investigate or determine a complaint or dispute—

[(a)   if, before the making of the complaint or the reference of the dispute—

(i)    proceedings in respect of the matters which would be the subject of the investigation have been begun in any court or employment tribunal, and

(ii)   those proceedings are proceedings which have not been discontinued or which have been discontinued on the basis of a settlement or compromise binding all the persons by or on whose behalf the complaint or reference is made;]

(b)   if the scheme is of a description which is excluded from the jurisdiction of the Pensions Ombudsman by regulations under this subsection; or

(c)   if and to the extent that the complaint or dispute, or any matter arising in connection with the complaint or dispute, is of a description which is excluded from the jurisdiction of the Pensions Ombudsman by regulations under this subsection.

[(6A)   For the purposes of subsection (6)(c)—

(a)   a description of complaint may be framed (in particular) by reference to the person making the complaint or to the scheme concerned (or to both), and

(b)   a description of dispute may be framed (in particular) by reference to the person referring the dispute or to the scheme concerned (or to both).]

(7)   The persons who, for the purposes of this Part are [actual or potential beneficiaries] in relation to a scheme are—

(a)   a member of the scheme,

(b)   the [widow, widower or surviving civil partner], or any surviving dependant, of a deceased member of the scheme;

[(ba) a person who is entitled to a pension credit as against the trustees or managers of the scheme;]

[(bb) a person who has given notice in accordance with section 8 of the Pensions Act 2008 (right to opt out of membership of an automatic enrolment scheme);]

(c)   where the complaint or dispute relates to the question—

(i)    whether a person who claims to be such a person as is mentioned in [paragraph (a), (b)[, (ba) or (bb)]] is such a person, or

(ii)   whether a person who claims to be entitled to become a member of the scheme is so entitled,

the person so claiming.

(8)   In this Part—

"employer", in relation to a pension scheme, includes a person—

(a)   who is or has been an employer in relation to the scheme, or

(b)   who is or has been treated under section 181(2) as an employer in relation to the scheme for the purposes of any provision of this Act, or under section 176(2) of the Pension Schemes (Northern Ireland) Act 1993 as an employer in relation to the scheme for the purposes of any provision of that Act;

["independent trustee", in relation to a scheme, means—

(a)   a trustee of the scheme appointed under [section 23(1) of the Pensions Act 1995 (appointment of independent trustee by the Regulatory Authority)],

(b)   a person appointed under section 7(1) of that Act to replace a trustee falling within paragraph (a) or this paragraph;]

"member", in relation to a pension scheme, includes a person—

(a)   who is or has been in pensionable service under the scheme, or

(b)   who is or has been treated under section 181(4) as a member in relation to the scheme for the purposes of any provision of this Act or under section 176(3) of the

Pension Schemes (Northern Ireland) Act 1993 as a member in relation to the scheme for the purposes of any provision of that Act;

"Northern Ireland public service pension scheme" means a public service pension scheme within the meaning of section 176(1) of that Act;

"pensionable service" in this subsection includes pensionable service as defined in section 176(1) of that Act;

"trustees or managers", in relation to a pension scheme which is a public service pension scheme or a Northern Ireland public service pension scheme, includes the scheme's administrators.

NOTES

Sub-s (1): substituted, together with sub-ss (2), (3), (3A), (4) for the original sub-ss (1)–(4), by the Pensions Act 1995, s 157(1), (2); word in first pair of square brackets and words in square brackets in paras (b), (d) substituted, para (ba) inserted, and words omitted repealed, by the Child Support, Pensions and Social Security Act 2000, s 53(1), (2), (9)(a)–(c), Sch 9, Pt III(3); para (f) substituted by the Pensions Act 2004, s 319(1), Sch 12, paras 9, 24(a).

Sub-ss (1A), (1B): inserted by the Child Support, Pensions and Social Security Act 2000, s 53(1), (4).

Sub-ss (2), (4): substituted as noted above.

Sub-s (3): substituted as noted above; words in square brackets inserted by the Child Support, Pensions and Social Security Act 2000, s 53(1), (5).

Sub-s (3A): substituted as noted above; repealed by the Child Support, Pensions and Social Security Act 2000, s 85, Sch 9, Pt III(3).

Sub-s (4A): inserted by the Pensions Act 2004, s 275.

Sub-s (6): para (a) substituted by the Child Support, Pensions and Social Security Act 2000, s 53(1), (6), (10).

Sub-s (6A): inserted by the Pensions Act 2004, s 319(1), Sch 12, paras 9, 24(b), as from a day to be appointed.

Sub-s (7): words in first pair of square brackets substituted by the Pensions Act 1995, s 157(1), (3); words in square brackets in para (b) substituted by the Civil Partnership (Pensions and Benefit Payments) (Consequential, etc Provisions) Order 2005, SI 2005/2053, art 2, Schedule, Pt 3, para 16; para (ba) inserted, and words in first (outer) pair of square brackets in para (c)(i) substituted, by the Child Support, Pensions and Social Security Act 2000, s 53(1), (7); para (bb) inserted, and words in second (inner) pair of square brackets in para (c)(i) substituted, by the Pensions Act 2008, s 66, as from 30 June 2012.

Sub-s (8): definition "independent trustee" inserted by the Child Support, Pensions and Social Security Act 2000, s 53(1), (8); words in square brackets in that definition substituted by the Pensions Act 2004, s 319(1), Sch 12, paras 9, 24(c).

Regulations: the Personal and Occupational Pension Schemes (Pensions Ombudsman) Regulations 1996, SI 1996/2475.

**[1.660]**
## 147 Death, insolvency or disability of authorised complainant
(1) Where an [actual or potential beneficiary] dies or is a minor or is otherwise unable to act for himself, then, unless subsection (3) applies—
  (a) any complaint or dispute (whenever arising) which the [actual or potential beneficiary] might otherwise have made or referred under this Part may be made or referred by the appropriate person, and
  (b) anything in the process of being done by or in relation to the [actual or potential beneficiary] under or by virtue of this Part may be continued by or in relation to the appropriate person,
and any reference in this Part, except this section, to an [actual or potential beneficiary] shall be construed as including a reference to the appropriate person.
(2) For the purposes of subsection (1) "the appropriate person" means—
  (a) where the [actual or potential beneficiary] has died, his personal representatives; or
  (b) in any other case, a member of [his] family, or some body or individual suitable to represent him.
(3) Where a person is acting as an insolvency practitioner in relation to [a person by whom, or on whose behalf, a complaint or reference has been made under this Part], investigations under this Part shall be regarded for the purposes of the Insolvency Act 1986 and the Bankruptcy (Scotland) Act 1985 as legal proceedings.
(4) In this section "acting as an insolvency practitioner" shall be construed in accordance with section 388 of the Insolvency Act 1986, but disregarding subsection (5) of that section (exclusion of official receiver).

NOTES

Sub-ss (1)–(3): words in square brackets substituted by the Pensions Act 1995, s 157(1), (4), (5).

**[1.661]**
## 148 Staying court proceedings where a complaint is made or a dispute is referred
(1) This section applies where—
  (a) complaint has been made or a dispute referred to the Pensions Ombudsman; and
  (b) any party to the investigation subsequently commences any legal proceedings in any court against any other party to the investigation in respect of any of the matters which are the subject of the complaint or dispute.
(2) In England and Wales, where this section applies any party to the legal proceedings may at any time after acknowledgement of service, and before delivering any pleadings or taking any other step in the proceedings, apply to that court to stay the proceedings.
(3) In Scotland, where this section applies any party to the legal proceedings may—

(a)    if the proceedings are in the Court of Session, at any time—
   (i)    after appearance has been entered but before defences have been lodged or any other step in the proceedings has been taken; or
   (ii)   (in procedure by petition) after intimation and service but before answers have been lodged or any other step in the proceedings has been taken; and
(b)    if the proceedings are in the sheriff court, at any time—
   (i)    after notice has been given of intention to defend but before defences have been lodged or any other step in the proceedings has been taken; or
   (ii)   (in summary cause procedure) after appearance has been made, or notice of intention to appear has been lodged, but before any defence has been stated or any other step in the proceedings has been taken,
apply to the court for a sist of process.
(4)   On an application under subsection (2) or (3) the court may make an order staying or, in Scotland, sisting the proceedings if it is satisfied—
(a)    that there is no sufficient reason why the matter should not be investigated by the Pensions Ombudsman; and
(b)    that the applicant was at the time when the legal proceedings were commenced and still remains ready and willing to do all things necessary to the proper conduct of the investigation.
(5)   For the purposes of this section the parties to an investigation are—
   [(a)   to the person by whom, or on whose behalf, the complaint or reference was made, and
   (b)    to any person (if different) responsible for the management of the scheme to which the complaint or reference relates;]
      [(ba), (bb) . . . ]
(c)    any person against whom allegations are made in the complaint or reference; and
(d)    any person claiming under a person falling within paragraphs (a) to (c).

___

**NOTES**
Sub-s (5): paras (a), (b) substituted by the Pensions Act 1995, s 157(1), (6); paras (ba), (bb) inserted by the Child Support, Pensions and Social Security Act 2000, s 54(1), (2)(a), and repealed by the Pensions Act 2004, ss 276(2)(a), 320, Sch 13, Pt 1.

**[1.662]**
**149    Procedure on an investigation**
(1)   Where the Pensions Ombudsman proposes to conduct an investigation into a complaint made or dispute referred under this Part, he shall give—
(a)    [any person (other than the person by whom, or on whose behalf, the complaint or reference was made) responsible for the management of the scheme to which the complaint or reference relates], and
(b)    any other person against whom allegations are made in the complaint or reference,
an opportunity to comment on any allegations contained in the complaint or reference.
(2)   The Secretary of State may make rules with respect to the procedure which is to be adopted in connection with the making of complaints, the reference of disputes, and the investigation of complaints made and disputes referred, under this Part.
(3)   The rules may include provision—
(a)    requiring any oral hearing held in connection with such an investigation to take place in public, except in such cases as may be specified in the rules;  . . .
(b)    as to the persons entitled to appear and be heard on behalf of parties to an investigation, as defined in section 148(5);
   [(ba)  . . . ]
(c)    for the payment by the Ombudsman of such travelling and other allowances (including compensation for loss of remunerative time) as the Secretary of State may determine, to—
   (i)    actual or potential beneficiaries of a scheme to which a complaint or reference relates, or
   (ii)   person appearing and being heard on behalf of such actual or potential beneficiaries, who attend at the request of the Ombudsman any oral hearing held in connection with an investigation into the complaint or dispute][;  . . .
(d)    . . . ]
(4)   Subject to any provision made by the rules, the procedure for conducting such an investigation shall be such as the Pensions Ombudsman considers appropriate in the circumstances of the case; and he may, in particular, obtain information from such persons and in such manner, and make such inquiries, as he thinks fit.
[(5)   The Pensions Ombudsman may disclose any information which he obtains for the purposes of an investigation under this Part to any person to whom subsection (6) applies, if the Ombudsman considers that the disclosure would enable or assist that person to discharge any of his functions.
(6)   This subsection applies to the following—
(a)    the Regulatory Authority,
[(b)   the Board of the Pension Protection Fund,

(ba) the Ombudsman for the Board of the Pension Protection Fund,]

(c) . . .

(d) any department of the Government (including the government of Northern Ireland),

[(e) the Financial Conduct Authority,

(ea) the Prudential Regulation Authority,

(eb) the Bank of England,]

(f), (g) . . .

[(h) a person appointed under—

  (i) Part 14 of the Companies Act 1985,

  (ii) section 167 of the Financial Services and Markets Act 2000,

  (iii) subsection (3) or (5) of section 168 of that Act, or

  (iv) section 284 of that Act,

  to conduct an investigation;]

(j) . . .

[(k) a body designated under section 326(1) of the Financial Services and Markets Act 2000; . . .

(l) a recognised investment exchange[, recognised clearing house, EEA central counterparty or third country central counterparty] (as defined by section 285 of that Act)];

[(n) a person who, in a member State other than the United Kingdom, has functions corresponding to functions of the Pensions Ombudsman]'

[(o) [the body corporate mentioned in paragraph 2] of Schedule 17 to the Financial Services and Markets Act 2000 (the scheme operator of the ombudsman scheme);

(p) an ombudsman as defined in paragraph 1 of that Schedule (interpretation)].

(7) The Secretary of State may by order—

  (a) amend subsection (6) by adding any person or removing any person for the time being specified in that subsection, or

  (b) restrict the circumstances in which, or impose conditions subject to which, disclosure may be made to any person for the time being specified in that subsection.]

[(8) . . . ]

---

**NOTES**

Sub-s (1): words in square brackets in para (a) substituted by the Pensions Act 1995, s 157(7). Note that this subsection was substituted (by new sub-ss (1), (1A), (1B)) by the Child Support, Pensions and Social Security Act 2000, s 54(1), (3), (9). This amendment was brought into force on 1 March 2002 for the purposes of making rules and regulations only (see SI 2002/437). However, section 54 of the 2000 Act was subsequently repealed by the Pensions Act 2004, ss 276(2)(b), 320, Sch 13, Pt 1 without being brought into force for the remaining purposes.

Sub-s (3): word omitted from para (a) repealed, and para (c) inserted, by the Pensions Act 1995, ss 158, 177, Sch 7, Pt IV; paras (ba), (d) and the word immediately preceding para (d) inserted, by the Child Support, Pensions and Social Security Act 2000, s 54(1), (4), (5), (9), and repealed by the Pensions Act 2004, ss 276(2)(c), (d), 320, Sch 13, Pt 1.

Sub-ss (5), (7): added, together with sub-s (6), by the Pensions Act 1995, s 159(1).

Sub-s (6): added as noted above and is amended as follows:

paras (b), (ba) substituted for the original para (b), and para (n) added, by the Pensions Act 2004, s 319(1), Sch 12, paras 9, 25;

para (c) and the word omitted from para (k) repealed by the Pensions Act 2004, s 320, Sch 13, Pt 1;

paras (e), (ea), (eb) substituted for original para (e), by the Financial Services Act 2012, s 114(1), Sch 18, Pt 2, para 78(1), (2)(a), as from 1 April 2013;

paras (f), (g) repealed, para (h) substituted, and paras (k), (l) substituted for the original paras (k)–(m), by the Financial Services and Markets Act 2000 (Consequential Amendments and Repeals) Order 2001, SI 2001/3649, art 123;

para (j) repealed by the Companies Act 2006 (Consequential Amendments, Transitional Provisions and Savings) Order 2009, SI 2009/1941, art 2(1), Sch 1, para 144(1), (3), as from 1 October 2009;

words in square brackets in para (l) substituted by the Financial Services and Markets Act 2000 (Over the Counter Derivatives, Central Counterparties and Trade Repositories) Regulations 2013, SI 2013/504, reg 21, as from 1 April 2013;

paras (o), (p) added by the Pensions Ombudsman (Disclosure of Information) (Amendment of Specified Persons) Order 2005, SI 2005/2743, art 2; words in square brackets in para (o) substituted by the Financial Services Act 2012, s 114(1), Sch 18, Pt 2, para 78(1), (2)(b), as from 1 April 2013.

Sub-s (8): added by the Child Support, Pensions and Social Security Act 2000, s 54(1), (6), and repealed by the Pensions Act 2004, ss 276(2)(e), 320, Sch 13, Pt 1.

Rules: the Personal and Occupational Pensions (Pensions Ombudsman) Procedure Rules 1995, SI 1995/1053; the Personal and Occupational Pension Schemes (Pensions Ombudsman) (Procedure) Amendment Rules 1996, SI 1996/2638.

Orders: the Pensions Ombudsman (Disclosure of Information) (Amendment of Specified Persons) Order 2005, SI 2005/2743.

---

**[1.663]**
**150 Investigations: further provisions**

(1) For the purposes of an investigation under this Part or under any corresponding legislation having effect in Northern Ireland, the Pensions Ombudsman may require—

  (a) [any person responsible for the management of the scheme to which the complaint or reference relates], or

  (b) any other person who, in his opinion is able to furnish information or produce documents relevant to the investigation,

to furnish any such information or produce any such documents.

(2)   For the purposes of any such investigation the Pensions Ombudsman shall have the same powers as the court in respect of the attendance and examination of witnesses (including the administration of oaths and affirmations and the examination of witnesses abroad) and in respect of the production of documents.

(3)   No person shall be compelled for the purposes of any such investigation to give any evidence or produce any document which he could not be compelled to give or produce in civil proceedings before the court.

(4)   If any person without lawful excuse obstructs the Pensions Ombudsman in the performance of his functions or is guilty of any act or omission in relation to an investigation under this Part which, if that investigation were a proceeding in the court, would constitute contempt of court, the Pensions Ombudsman may certify the offence to the court.

(5)   Where an offence is certified under subsection (4) the court may inquire into the matter and, after hearing any witnesses who may be produced against or on behalf of the person charged with the offence and hearing any statement that may be offered in defence, deal with him in any manner in which the court could deal with him if he had committed the like offence in relation to the court.

(6)   To assist him in an investigation, the Pensions Ombudsman may obtain advice from any person who in his opinion is qualified to give it and may pay to any such person such fees or allowances as he may with the approval of the Treasury determine.

(7)   The Pensions Ombudsman may refer any question of law arising for determination in connection with a complaint or dispute to the High Court or, in Scotland, the Court of Session.

(8)   In this section "the court" means—
   (a)   in England and Wales, *a county court*;
   (b)   in Scotland, the sheriff.

(9)   Subsections (4) and (5) shall be construed, in their application to Scotland, as if contempt of court were categorised as an offence in Scots law.

**NOTES**

Sub-s (1): words in square brackets substituted by the Pensions Act 1995, s 157(1), (8).

Sub-s (8): for the words in italics there are substituted the words "the county court" by the Crime and Courts Act 2013, s 17(5), Sch 9, Pt 3, para 52, as from a day to be appointed.

**[1.664]**
**151   Determinations of the Pensions Ombudsman**
(1)   Where the Pensions Ombudsman has conducted an investigation under this Part he shall send a written statement of his determination of the complaint or dispute in question—
   [(a)   to the person by whom, or on whose behalf, the complaint or reference was made, and
   (b)   to any person (if different) responsible for the management of the scheme to which the complaint or reference relates][ . . .
   (c)   . . . ]
and any such statement shall contain the reasons for his determination.

(2)   Where the Pensions Ombudsman makes a determination under this Part or under any corresponding legislation having effect in Northern Ireland, he may direct [any person responsible for the management of the scheme to which the complaint or reference relates] to take, or refrain from taking, such steps as he may specify in the statement referred to in subsection (1) or otherwise in writing.

(3)   Subject to subsection (4), the determination by the Pensions Ombudsman of a complaint or dispute, and any direction given by him under subsection (2), shall be final and binding on—
   [(a)   the person by whom, or on whose behalf, the complaint or reference was made,
   (b)   any person (if different) responsible for the management of the scheme to which the complaint or reference relates,
   [(ba), (bb)  . . . ]
   (c)   any person claiming under a person falling within paragraph (a) or (b).]

(4)   An appeal on a point of law shall lie to the High Court or, in Scotland, the Court of Session from a determination or direction of the Pensions Ombudsman at the instance of any person falling within paragraphs (a) to (c) of subsection (3).

(5)   Any determination or direction of the Pensions Ombudsman shall be enforceable—
   (a)   in England and Wales, in *a county court* as if it were a judgment or order of that court, and
   (b)   in Scotland, [in like manner as an extract registered decree arbitral bearing warrant for execution issued by the sheriff court of any sheriffdom in Scotland].

(6)   If the Pensions Ombudsman considers it appropriate to do so in any particular case, he may publish in such form and manner as he thinks fit a report of any investigation under this Part and of the result of that investigation.

(7)   For the purposes of the law of defamation, the publication of any matter by the Pensions Ombudsman—
   (a)   in submitting or publishing a report under section 145(6) or subsection (6) of this section, or
   [(aa)  in disclosing any information under s 149(5)]

(b)   in sending to any person a statement under subsection (1) or a direction under subsection (2),

shall be absolutely privileged.

**NOTES**

Sub-s (1): paras (a), (b) substituted by the Pensions Act 1995, s 157(1), (9); para (c) and the word immediately preceding it inserted by the Child Support, Pensions and Social Security Act 2000, s 54(1), (7), (9), and repealed by the Pensions Act 2004, ss 276(2)(f), 320, Sch 13, Pt 1.

Sub-s (2): words in square brackets substituted by the Pensions Act 1995, s 157(1), (10).

Sub-s (3): paras (a)–(c) substituted by the Pensions Act 1995, s 157(1), (11); paras (ba), (bb) substituted for the original word "and" at the end of para (b) by the Child Support, Pensions and Social Security Act 2000, s 54(1), (8), (9), and repealed by the Pensions Act 2004, ss 276(2)(g), 320, Sch 13, Pt 1.

Sub-s (5): for the words in italics in para (a) there are substituted the words "the county court" by the Crime and Courts Act 2013, s 17(5), Sch 9, Pt 3, para 52, as from a day to be appointed; words in square brackets in para (b) substituted by the Pensions Act 1995, s 173, Sch 6, paras 2, 8.

Sub-s (7): para (aa) inserted by the Pensions Act 1995, s 159(2).

**[1.665]**
**[151A   Interest on late payment of benefit**
Where under this Part the Pensions Ombudsman directs a person responsible for the management of an occupational or personal pension scheme to make any payment in respect of benefit under the scheme which, in his opinion, ought to have been paid earlier, his direction may also require the payment of interest at the prescribed rate.]

**NOTES**

Inserted by the Pensions Act 1995, s 160.

Regulations: the Personal and Occupational Pension Schemes (Pensions Ombudsman) Regulations 1996, SI 1996/2475.

# PART XI
# GENERAL AND MISCELLANEOUS PROVISIONS
*Avoidance of certain transactions and provisions*

**[1.666]**
**160   Terms of contracts of service or schemes restricting choice to be void**
(1)   Subject to such exceptions as may be prescribed—
   (a)   any term of a contract of service (whenever made) or any rule of a personal or occupational pension scheme to the effect that an employed earner must be a member—
      (i)    of a personal or occupational pension scheme,
      (ii)   of a particular personal or occupational pension scheme, or
      (iii)  of one or other of a number of particular personal or occupational pension schemes, shall be void; and
   (b)   any such term or rule to the effect that contributions shall be paid by or in respect of an employed earner—
      (i)    to a particular personal or occupational pension scheme of which the earner is not a member, or
      (ii)   to one or other of a number of personal or occupational pension schemes of none of which he is a member,
      shall be unenforceable for so long as he is not a member of the scheme or any of the schemes.
(2)   Subsection (1) shall not be construed so as to have the effect that an employer is required, when he would not otherwise be—
   (a)   to make contributions to a personal or occupational pension scheme; or
   (b)   to increase an employed earner's pay in lieu of making contributions to a personal or occupational pension scheme.

**NOTES**

Regulations: by virtue of s 189(1) of, and Sch 6, Pt I, para 2(2) to, this Act, the Pension Schemes (Voluntary Contributions Requirements and Voluntary and Compulsory Membership) Regulations 1987, SI 1987/1108 have effect as if made under this section.

**[1.667]**
**161   Provisions excluding Chapter II of Part VII to be void**
Any provision in an agreement (whether a contract of employment or not) shall be void in so far as it purports—
   (a)   to exclude or limit the operation of any provision of Chapter II of Part VII of this Act; or
   (b)   to preclude any person from presenting a complaint to, or bringing any proceedings before, an [employment tribunal] under that Chapter.

**NOTES**
Words in square brackets substituted by the Employment Rights (Dispute Resolution) Act 1998, s 1(2)(a).

## PART XII
## SUPPLEMENTARY PROVISIONS

*Interpretation*

**[1.668]**
**181   General interpretation**
(1)   In this Act, unless the context otherwise requires—
   ["abolition date" means the day appointed for the commencement of section 15(1) of the Pensions Act 2007;]

   . . .

   "age", in relation to any person, shall be construed so that—
      (a)   he is over or under a particular age if he has or, as the case may be, has not attained that age;
      (b)   he is between two particular ages if he has attained the first but not the second;
   ["appropriate scheme" and "appropriate scheme certificate" are to be construed in accordance with section 181A;]

   . . .

   "Category A retirement pension" and "Category B retirement pension" mean the retirement pensions of those descriptions payable under Part II of the Social Security Contributions and Benefits Act 1992;
   ["civil recovery order" means an order under section 266 of the Proceeds of Crime Act 2002 or an order under section 276 imposing the requirement mentioned in section 277(3);]
   "contract of service" has the same meaning as in section 122(1) of the Social Security Contributions and Benefits Act 1992;
   "contracted-out employment" shall be construed in accordance with section 8;

   . . .

   "contracting-out certificate" and references to a contracted-out scheme and to contracting-out shall be construed in accordance with section 7 [and section 181A];
   "contributions equivalent premium" has the meaning given in [section 55(2)];
   "earner" and "earnings" shall be construed in accordance with sections 3, 4 and 112 of the Social Security Contributions and Benefits Act 1992;
   "earnings factors" shall be construed in accordance with sections 22 and 23 of the Social Security Contributions and Benefits Act 1992;
   ["employed earner" and "self-employed earner" have the meanings given by section 2 of the Social Security Contributions and Benefits Act 1992;]
   "employee" means a person gainfully employed in Great Britain either under a contract of service or in an office (including an elective office) with [general earnings (as defined by section 7 of the Income Tax (Earnings and Pensions) Act 2003)];
   "employer" means—
      (a)   in the case of an employed earner employed under a contract of service, his employer;
      (b)   in the case of an employed earner employed in an office with emoluments—
         (i)   such person as may be prescribed in relation to that office; or
         (ii)   if no person is prescribed, the government department, public authority or body of persons responsible for paying the emoluments of the office;
   "employment" includes any trade, business, profession, office or vocation and "employed" shall be construed accordingly except in the expression "employed earner";

   . . .

   ["Financial Services Compensation Scheme" means the Financial Services Compensation Scheme referred to in section 213(2) of the Financial Services and Markets Act 2000;]
   [ . . . ]
   "guaranteed minimum pension" has the meaning given in section 8(2);
   "independent trade union" has the same meaning as in the Trade Union and Labour Relations (Consolidation) Act 1992;
   "[employment tribunal]" means a tribunal established or having effect as if established under [section 1(1) of [the Employment Tribunals Act 1996]];
   ["HMRC" means the Commissioners for Her Majesty's Revenue and Customs;]
   "the Inland Revenue" means the Commissioners of Inland Revenue;

   . . .

   "linked qualifying service" has the meaning given in section 179;
   "long-term benefit" has the meaning given in section 20(2) of the Social Security Contributions and Benefits Act 1992;

"lower earnings limit" and "upper earnings limit" shall be construed in accordance with section 5
    of the Social Security Contributions and Benefits Act 1992 and "current", in relation to
    those limits, means for the time being in force;

*"minimum contributions" shall be construed in accordance with sections 43 to 45;*

"minimum payment" has the meaning given in section 8(2);

"modifications" includes additions, omissions and amendments, and related expressions shall be
    construed accordingly;

"money purchase benefits", in relation to a member of a personal or occupational pension
    scheme or the [widow, widower or surviving civil partner] of a member of such a scheme,
    means benefits the rate or amount of which is calculated by reference to a payment or
    payments made by the member or by any other person in respect of the member and [which
    fall within section 181B];

["money purchase contracted-out scheme" is to be construed in accordance with section 181A;]

"money purchase scheme" means a pension scheme under which all the benefits that may be
    provided are money purchase benefits;

"normal pension age" has the meaning given in section 180;

"occupational pension scheme" has the meaning given in section 1;

["overseas arrangement" means a scheme or arrangement which—
    (a)    has effect, or is capable of having effect, so as to provide benefits on termination of
        employment or on death or retirement to or in respect of earners;
    (b)    is administered wholly or primarily outside Great Britain;
    (c)    is not an appropriate scheme; and
    (d)    is not an occupational pension scheme;]

["pension credit" means a credit under section 29(1)(b) of the Welfare Reform and Pensions Act
    1999 or under corresponding Northern Ireland legislation;]

["pension debit" means a debit under section 29(1)(a) of the Welfare Reform and Pensions Act
    1999;]

["pensionable age"—
    (a)    so far as any provisions (other than sections 46 to 48) relate to guaranteed minimum
        pensions, means the age of 65 in the case of a man and the age of 60 in the case of
        a woman, and
    (b)    in any other case, has the meaning given by the rules in paragraph 1 of Schedule 4
        to the Pensions Act 1995];

"pensionable service" has the meaning given in section 70(2);

. . .

"personal pension scheme" has the meaning given in section 1;

"prescribe" means prescribe by regulations and "prescribed" shall be construed accordingly;

. . .

"the preservation requirements" has the meaning given in section 69(2);

"primary Class 1 contributions" and "secondary Class 1 contributions" have the same meanings
    as in the Social Security Contributions and Benefits Act 1992;

"protected rights" has the meaning given in section 10[, as it had effect immediately prior to the
    abolition date];

"public service pension scheme" has the meaning given in section 1;

. . .

"regulations" means regulations made by the Secretary of State under this Act;

["the Regulatory Authority" means the Pensions Regulator;]

"resources", in relation to an occupational pension scheme, means the funds out of which the
    benefits provided by the scheme are payable from time to time, including the proceeds of
    any policy of insurance taken out, or annuity contract entered into, for the purposes of the
    scheme;

"rights", in relation to accrued rights (within the meaning of section 73, 136 or 179) or transfer
    credits, includes rights to benefit and also options to have benefits paid in a particular form
    or at a particular time;

[ . . . ]

. . .

"short service benefit" has the meaning given in section 71(2);

. . .

"tax week" means one of the successive periods in a tax year beginning with the first day of that
    year and every seventh day thereafter, the last day of a tax year (or, in a leap year, the last
    two days) being treated accordingly as a separate tax week;

"tax year" means the 12 months beginning with 6th April in any year;

"trade or business", in relation to a public or local authority, includes the exercise and
    performance of the powers and duties of the authority;

"transfer credits" means rights allowed to an earner under the rules of an occupational pension scheme by reference to[—

(a) a transfer to the scheme of, or transfer payment to the trustees or managers of the scheme in respect of, any of his rights (including transfer credits allowed) under another occupational pension scheme or a personal pension scheme, other than rights attributable (directly or indirectly) to a pension credit, or

(b) a cash transfer sum paid under Chapter 5 of Part 4 in respect of him, to the trustees or managers of the scheme;]

. . .

["the upper accrual point" has the meaning given by section 122 of the Social Security Contributions and Benefits Act 1992;]

. . .

"week" means a period of seven days beginning with Sunday;

["working life", in relation to a person, means the period beginning with the tax year in which the person attains the age of 16 and ending with—

(a) the tax year before the one in which the person attains the age of 65 in the case of a man or 60 in the case of a woman, or

(b) if earlier, the tax year before the one in which the person dies].

(2) References to employers in the provisions of this Act (other than sections 123 to 127, 157, [and 160] ("the excluded provisions")) are to be treated, in relation to persons within the application of an occupational pension scheme and qualifying or prospectively qualifying for its benefits, as including references to persons who in relation to them and their employment are treated by regulations as being employers for the purposes of those provisions.

(3) Subject to any such regulations, references to an employer in any of the provisions of this Act (other than the excluded provisions or . . . , Chapter I of Part IV, Part VIII so far as it applies for the purposes of Chapter I of Part IV, sections . . . 153(2), 158(1) to (5), 162, 163, . . . and 176 and . . . ) shall, in relation to an earner employed in an office with emoluments, be construed as references to—

(a) such person as may be prescribed in relation to that office; or

(b) if no person is prescribed, the government department, public authority or body of persons responsible for paying the emoluments of that office.

(4) Regulations may for any purpose of any provision of this Act (other than the excluded provisions or section . . . *31,* . . . *43,* . . . 111, 160, 164, 165 or 169) prescribe the persons who are to be regarded as members or prospective members of an occupational pension scheme and as to the times at which and the circumstances in which a person is to be treated as becoming, or as ceasing to be, a member or prospective member.

(5) In sections 165 and 166—

(a) references to the United Kingdom include references to the territorial waters of the United Kingdom; and

(b) references to Great Britain include references to the territorial waters of the United Kingdom adjacent to Great Britain.

(6) Any reference in section 185 or 186 to an order or regulations under this Act includes a reference to an order or regulations made under any provision of an enactment passed after this Act and directed to be construed as one with it; but this subsection applies only so far as a contrary intention is not expressed in the enactment so passed, and shall be without prejudice to the generality of any such direction.

(7) In the application of section 158 . . . to Northern Ireland any reference to a government department is to be taken to be, or to include (as the context may require), a Northern Ireland department.

---

**NOTES**

Sub-s (1) has been amended as follows:

Definition "abolition date" inserted by the Pensions Act 2007, s 15(3)(a), Sch 4, Pt 1, paras 1, 34(1), (2)(a), as from 6 April 2012.

Definitions "accrued rights premium", "the Board", "contracted-out protected rights premium", "limited revaluation premium", "pensioner's rights premium", "personal pension protected rights premium", "state scheme premium", "transfer premium" (omitted) repealed by the Pensions Act 1995, ss 151, 177, Sch 5, para 77(a)(i), Sch 7, Pt III.

Definitions "appropriate scheme" and "appropriate scheme certificate" substituted by the Pensions Act 2007, s 15(3)(a), Sch 4, Pt 1, paras 1, 34(1), (2)(b), as from 6 April 2012.

Definition "civil recovery order" inserted by the Proceeds of Crime Act 2002, s 456, Sch 11, paras 1, 22(1), (6).

In definition "contracting-out certificate" words in square brackets inserted by the Pensions Act 2007, s 15(3)(a), Sch 4, Pt 1, paras 1, 34(1), (2)(c), as from 6 April 2012.

In definition "contributions equivalent premium" words in square brackets substituted by the Pensions Act 1995, ss 151, Sch 5, para 77(a).

Definitions "employed earner" and "self-employed earner" substituted, for the original definition "employed earner", by the Welfare Reform and Pensions Act 1999, Sch 2, para 3(1)(b).

In definition "employee" words in square brackets substituted by the Income Tax (Earnings and Pensions) Act 2003, s 722, Sch 6, Pt 2, paras 207.

In definition "employment tribunal" (formerly "industrial tribunal") words in first and third (inner) pairs of square brackets substituted by the Employment Rights (Dispute Resolution) Act 1998, s 1(2)(a), (c); words in second (outer) pair of square brackets substituted by the Employment Tribunals Act 1996, s 43, Sch 1, para 11.

Definition "equal access requirements" (omitted) repealed for certain purposes by the Pension Schemes Act 1993, ss 188, 190, Sch 5, Pt II, Sch 7, para 3(i), and repealed for remaining purposes by the Pensions Act 1995, ss 122, 177, Sch 3, para 44(a)(i), Sch 7, Pt I.

Definition "Financial Services Compensation Scheme" inserted by the Financial Services and Markets Act 2000 (Consequential Amendments and Repeals) Order 2001, SI 2001/3649, art 127(a).

Definition "the flat rate introduction year" (omitted) originally inserted by the Pensions Act 2007, s 12(4), Sch 1, Pt 7, para 38, and repealed by the National Insurance Contributions Act 2008, s 4(2), Sch 2, in relation to 2009–10 and subsequent tax years.

Definition "HMRC" inserted by the Pensions Act 2007, s 15(3)(a), Sch 4, Pt 1, paras 1, 34(1), (2)(a), as from 6 April 2012.

Definition "insurance company" (omitted) repealed by SI 2001/3649, art 127(b).

Definition "minimum contributions" repealed by the Pensions Act 2007, ss 15(3)(a), 27(2), Sch 4, Pt 2, paras 46, 58(1), (2), Sch 7, Pt 7, as from a day to be appointed.

In definition "money purchase benefits" words in first pair of square brackets substituted by the Civil Partnership (Pensions and Benefit Payments) (Consequential, etc Provisions) Order 2005, SI 2005/2053, art 2, Schedule, Pt 3, para 18; words in second pair of square brackets substituted by the Pensions Act 2011, s 29(1), (7), with retrospective effect as from 1 January 1997.

Definition "money purchase contracted-out scheme" substituted by the Pensions Act 2007, s 15(3)(a), Sch 4, Pt 1, paras 1, 34(1), (2)(d), as from 6 April 2012.

Definition "overseas arrangement" inserted by the Child Support, Pensions and Social Security Act 2000, s 56, Sch 5, Pt I, para 2(3).

Definition "pension credit" inserted by the Welfare Reform and Pensions Act 1999, s 84(1), Sch 12, Pt I, paras 28, 41(a).

Definition "pension debit" inserted by the Welfare Reform and Pensions Act 1999, s 32(1), (5).

Definition "pensionable age" substituted by the Pensions Act 1995, s 126, Sch 4, para 17.

Definition "the prescribed equivalent" (omitted) repealed by the Welfare Reform and Pensions Act 1999, s 88, Sch 13, Pt VI.

In definition "protected rights" words in square brackets inserted by the Pensions Act 2008 (Abolition of Protected Rights) (Consequential Amendments) (No 2) Order 2011, SI 2011/1730, art 5(1), (22)(a), as from 6 April 2012.

Definitions "the Register" and "the Registrar" (omitted) repealed by the Pensions Act 2004, s 320, Sch 13, Pt 1.

Definition "the Regulatory Authority" inserted by the Pensions Act 1995, s 122, Sch 3, para 44(a)(ii), and substituted by the Pensions Act 2004, s 7(2)(a).

Definition "safeguarded rights" (omitted) originally inserted by the Welfare Reform and Pensions Act 1999, s 84(1), Sch 12, Pt I, paras 28, 41(b), and repealed by the Pensions Act 2008, s 148, Sch 11, Pt 2, as from 6 April 2009.

Definition "self-employed pension arrangement" (omitted) repealed by the Welfare Reform and Pensions Act 1999, ss 18, 88, Sch 2, para 3(2)(c), Sch 13, Pt I.

Definitions "tax-exemption" and "tax-approval" (omitted) repealed by the Taxation of Pension Schemes (Consequential Amendments) Order 2006, SI 2006/745, art 7.

In definition "transfer credits" words in square brackets substituted by the Pensions Act 2004, s 319(1), Sch 12, paras 9, 31.

Definition "the upper accrual point" inserted by the Pensions Act 2007, s 12(4), Sch 1, Pt 7, para 38.

Definition "voluntary contributions requirements" (omitted) repealed by the Pensions Act 2004, ss 267(3), 320, Sch 13, Pt 1.

Definition "working life" substituted by the Pensions Act 2004, s 282.

Sub-s (2): words in square brackets substituted by the Pensions Act 1995, s 122, Sch 3, paras 22, 44(b).

Sub-s (3): first words omitted repealed by the Pensions Act 2004, s 320, Sch 13, Pt 1; other words omitted repealed by the Pensions Act 1995, ss 151, 173, 177, Sch 5, paras 18, 77(b), Sch 6, paras 2, 14, Sch 7, Pts III, IV.

Sub-s (4) is amended as follows:

Section reference "6" (omitted) repealed by the Pensions Act 2004, s 320, Sch 13, Pt 1.

Section references "27", "28", "29," and "32" (omitted) repealed by SI 2011/1730, art 5(1), (22)(b), as from 6 April 2012.

Section reference "31," in italics repealed by SI 2011/1730, art 9(1), (7), as from 6 April 2015.

Section reference "43" in italics repealed by the Pensions Act 2007, ss 15(3)(a), 27(2), Sch 4, Pt 2, paras 46, 58(1), (3), Sch 7, Pt 7, as from a day to be appointed.

Section reference "44" (omitted) repealed by the Pensions Act 2007, ss 15(3)(a), 27(2), Sch 4, Pt 1, paras 1, 34(1), (3), Sch 4, Pt 2, paras 46, 58(1), (3), Sch 7, Pt 7, as from 6 April 2012.

Sub-s (7): words omitted repealed by the Pensions Act 1995, ss 151, 177, Sch 5, paras 18, 77(c), Sch 7, Pt III.

Commissioners of Inland Revenue: a reference to the Commissioners of Inland Revenue is now to be taken as a reference to the Commissioners for Her Majesty's Revenue and Customs; see the Commissioners for Revenue and Customs Act 2005, s 50(1), (7).

Regulations: Regulations made under this section are generally outside the scope of this work.

**[1.669]**
## 193 Short title and commencement

(1) This Act may be cited as the Pension Schemes Act 1993.

(2) Subject to the provisions of Schedule 9, this Act shall come into force on such day as the Secretary of State may by order appoint.

(3) As respects the coming into force of—

    (a) Part II of Schedule 5 and section 188(1) so far as it relates to it; or

    (b) Schedule 7 and section 190 so far as it relates to it,

an order under subsection (2) may appoint different days from the day appointed for the other provisions of this Act or different days for different purposes.

**NOTES**

Orders: the Pension Schemes Act 1993 (Commencement No 1) Order 1994, SI 1994/86.

# PENSIONS ACT 1995

## (1995 c 26)

### ARRANGEMENT OF SECTIONS

#### PART I
#### OCCUPATIONAL PENSIONS

*Resolution of disputes*

#### PART IV
#### MISCELLANEOUS AND SUPPLEMENTAL

*General*

*An Act to amend the law about pensions and for connected purposes*

[19 July 1995]

#### NOTES

This major Act covers a wide range of aspects of pension law. Only those areas of most direct relevance to employment law are reproduced here. Provisions omitted are not annotated.

Sections 62–66 (Equal treatment) were included in earlier editions of this work; those provisions were repealed by the Equality Act 2010, s 211(2), Sch 27, Pt 1, as from 1 October 2010. The Equality Act 2010 (Commencement No 4, Savings, Consequential, Transitional, Transitory and Incidental Provisions and Revocation) Order 2010, SI 2010/2317 (at **[2.1558]** et seq) provides for various transitional provisions and savings in connection with the commencement of the 2010 Act and the repeal of previous legislation. See, in particular, art 15 (savings for various enactments (including the Equal Pay Act 1970) in cases where the act complained of occurs wholly before 1 October 2010). There are no specific transitional provisions in the 2010 Order relating to ss 62–66 but, in so far as they apply to the 1970 Act, the transitional provisions relating to the repeal of that Act would appear to apply to those sections.

See *Harvey* BI(9) (11).

## PART I
## OCCUPATIONAL PENSIONS

*Resolution of disputes*

**[1.670]**
**[50  Requirement for dispute resolution arrangements**
(1)  The trustees or managers of an occupational pension scheme must secure that dispute resolution arrangements [complying with the requirements of this section] are made and implemented.
(2)  Dispute resolution arrangements are [arrangements] for the resolution of pension disputes.
(3)  For this purpose a pension dispute is a dispute which—
   (a)  is between—
      (i)  the trustees or managers of a scheme, and
      (ii)  one or more persons with an interest in the scheme (see section 50A),
   (b)  is about matters relating to the scheme, and
   (c)  is not an exempted dispute (see subsection (9)).
(4)  The dispute resolution arrangements must provide a procedure—
   (a)  for any of the parties to the dispute mentioned in subsection (3)(a)(ii) to make an application for a decision to be taken on the matters in dispute ("an application for the resolution of a pension dispute"), and
   (b)  for the trustees or managers to take that decision.
[(4A)  The dispute resolution arrangements may make provision for securing that an application for the resolution of a pension dispute may not be made to the trustees or managers unless—
   (a)  the matters in dispute have been previously referred to a person of a description specified in the arrangements ("the specified person") in order for him to consider those matters, and
   (b)  the specified person has given his decision on those matters,

and for enabling the specified person's decision to be confirmed or replaced by the decision taken by the trustees or managers on the application, after reconsidering those matters.]

(5) Where an application for the resolution of a pension dispute is made in accordance with the dispute resolution arrangements, the trustees or managers must—

(a) take the decision required on the matters in dispute within a reasonable period of the receipt of the application by them, and

(b) notify the applicant of the decision within a reasonable period of it having been taken.

[(5A) In a case where a reference is made to the specified person in accordance with provision made under subsection (4A), subsection (5) applies in relation to the specified person as it applies in relation to the trustees or managers in a case where an application for the resolution of a pension dispute is made to them.]

(6) The procedure provided for by the dispute resolution arrangements [in pursuance of subsection (4)] must include the provision required by section 50B.

(7) Dispute resolution arrangements under subsection (1) must, in the case of existing schemes, have effect on and after the date of commencement of this section in relation to applications made on or after that date.

(8) This section does not apply in relation to an occupational pension scheme if—

(a) every member of the scheme is a trustee of the scheme,

(b) the scheme has no more than one member, or

(c) the scheme is of a prescribed description.

(9) For the purposes of this section a dispute is an exempted dispute if—

(a) proceedings in respect of it have been commenced in any court or tribunal,

(b) the Pensions Ombudsman has commenced an investigation in respect of it as a result of a complaint made or a dispute referred to him, or

(c) it is of a prescribed description.

(10) If, in the case of an occupational pension scheme, the dispute resolution arrangements required by this section to be made—

(a) have not been made, or

(b) are not being implemented,

section 10 applies to any of the trustees or managers who have failed to take all reasonable steps to secure that such arrangements are made or implemented.]

**NOTES**

The original section 50 was substituted by new ss 50, 50A, 50B by the Pensions Act 2004, s 273 (as amended as noted below).

The amendments made to this section, ie, the insertion of the words in square brackets in sub-ss (1), (6), the substitution of the word in square brackets in sub-s (2), and the insertion of sub-ss (4A), (5A), were amendments made to the Pensions Act 2004, s 273 by the Pensions Act 2007, s 16(1)–(6).

Regulations: the Personal and Occupational Pension Schemes (Miscellaneous Amendments) Regulations 1999, SI 1999/3198; the Stakeholder Pension Schemes Regulations 2000, SI 2000/1403; the Occupational Pension Schemes (Republic of Ireland Schemes Exemption (Revocation) and Tax Exempt Schemes (Miscellaneous Amendments)) Regulations 2006, SI 2006/467; the Occupational Pension Schemes (Internal Dispute Resolution Procedures Consequential and Miscellaneous Amendments) Regulations 2008, SI 2008/649 at **[2.1137]**.

**[1.671]**
**[50A Meaning of "person with an interest in the scheme"**

(1) For the purposes of section 50 a person is a person with an interest in an occupational pension scheme if—

(a) he is a member of the scheme,

(b) he is a widow, widower[, surviving civil partner] or surviving dependant of a deceased member of the scheme,

(c) he is a surviving non-dependant beneficiary of a deceased member of the scheme,

(d) he is a prospective member of the scheme,

(e) he has ceased to be within any of the categories of persons referred to in paragraphs (a) to (d), or

(f) he claims to be such a person as is mentioned in paragraphs (a) to (e) and the dispute relates to whether he is such a person.

(2) In subsection (1)(c) a "non-dependant beneficiary", in relation to a deceased member of an occupational pension scheme, means a person who, on the death of the member, is entitled to the payment of benefits under the scheme.

(3) In subsection (1)(d) a "prospective member" means any person who, under the terms of his contract of service or the rules of the scheme—

(a) is able, at his own option, to become a member of the scheme,

(b) will become so able if he continues in the same employment for a sufficiently long period,

(c) will be admitted to the scheme automatically unless he makes an election not to become a member, or

(d) may be admitted to it subject to the consent of his employer.]

**[1.672]**
**[50B   The dispute resolution procedure**
(1)   The procedure provided for by the dispute resolution arrangements [in pursuance of section 50(4) must (in accordance with section 50(6))] include the following provision.
(2)   The procedure must provide that an application for the resolution of a pension dispute under section 50(4) may be made or continued on behalf of a person who is a party to the dispute mentioned in section 50(3)(a)(ii)—
   (a)   where the person dies, by his personal representative,
   (b)   where the person is a minor or is otherwise incapable of acting for himself, by a member of his family or some other person suitable to represent him, and
   (c)   in any other case, by a representative nominated by him.
[(3)   The procedure—
   (a)   must include provision requiring an application to which subsection (3A) applies to be made by the end of such reasonable period as is specified;
   (b)   may include provision about the time limits for making such other applications for the resolution of pension disputes as are specified.
(3A)   This subsection applies to—
   (a)   any application by a person with an interest in a scheme as mentioned in section 50A(1)(e), and
   (b)   any application by a person with an interest in a scheme as mentioned in section 50A(1)(f) who is claiming to be such a person as is mentioned in section 50A(1)(e).]
(4)   The procedure must include provision about—
   (a)   the manner in which an application for the resolution of a pension dispute is to be made,
   (b)   the particulars which must be included in such an application, and
   (c)   the manner in which any decisions required [in relation to such an application] are to be reached and given.
[(4A)   The provision made under subsection (4)(c) may include provision for decisions of the trustees or managers to be taken on their behalf by one or more of their number.]
(5)   The procedure must provide that if, after an application for the resolution of a pension dispute has been made, the dispute becomes an exempted dispute within the meaning of section 50(9)(a) or (b), the resolution of the dispute under the procedure ceases.]

*General*

**[1.673]**
**124   Interpretation of Part I**
(1)   In this Part—
   "active member", in relation to an occupational pension scheme, means a person who is in pensionable service under the scheme,
   "the actuary" and "the auditor", in relation to an occupational pension scheme, have the meanings given by section 47,
   ["the Authority" means the Pensions Regulator,]
   ["civil partnership status", in relation to a person, means whether that person has previously formed a civil partnership and, if so, whether that civil partnership has ended,]
   "the Compensation Board" has the meaning given by section 78(1),
   "the compensation provisions" has the meaning given by section 81(3),
   "contravention" includes failure to comply,
   "deferred member", in relation to an occupational pension scheme, means a person (other than an active or pensioner member) who has accrued rights under the scheme,
   "employer", in relation to an occupational pension scheme, means the employer of persons in the description *or category* of employment to which the scheme in question relates (but see section 125(3)),
   "equal treatment rule" has the meaning given by section 62,
   "firm" means a body corporate or a partnership,
   "fund manager", in relation to an occupational pension scheme, means a person who manages the investments held for the purposes of the scheme,
   "independent trustee" has the meaning given by section 23(3),

"managers", in relation to an occupational pension scheme other than a trust scheme, means the persons responsible for the management of the scheme,

"member", in relation to an occupational pension scheme, means any active, deferred[, pensioner or pension credit] member (but see section 125(4)),

. . .

. . .

. . .

"normal pension age" has the meaning given by section 180 of the Pension Schemes Act 1993,

"payment schedule" has the meaning given by section 87(2),

["pension credit" means a credit under section 29(1)(b) of the Welfare Reform and Pensions Act 1999" or under corresponding Northern Ireland legislation,

"pension credit member", in relation to an occupational pension scheme, means a person who has rights under the scheme which are attributable (directly or indirectly) to a pension credit,

"pension credit rights", in relation to an occupational pension scheme, means rights to future benefits under the scheme which are attributable (directly or indirectly) to a pension credit,]

"pensionable service", in relation to a member of an occupational pension scheme, means service in any description *or category* of employment to which the scheme relates which qualifies the member (on the assumption that it continues for the appropriate period) for pension or other benefits under the scheme,

"pensioner member", in relation to an occupational pension scheme, means a person who in respect of his pensionable service under the scheme or by reason of transfer credits, is entitled to the present payment of pension or other benefits [ . . . ],

"prescribed" means prescribed by regulations,

"professional adviser", in relation to a scheme, has the meaning given by section 47,

"public service pension scheme" has the meaning given by section 1 of the Pension Schemes Act 1993,

"regulations" means regulations made by the Secretary of State,

"resources", in relation to an occupational pension scheme, means the funds out of which the benefits provided by the scheme are payable from time to time, including the proceeds of any policy of insurance taken out, or annuity contract entered into, for the purposes of the scheme,

"Scottish partnership" means a partnership constituted under the law of Scotland,

"the Taxes Act 1988" means the Income and Corporation Taxes Act 1988,

"transfer credits" means rights allowed to a member under the rules of an occupational pension scheme by reference to[—

    (a)    a transfer to the scheme of, or transfer payment to the trustees or managers of the scheme in respect of, any of his rights (including transfer credits allowed) under another occupational pension scheme or a personal pension scheme, other than pension credit rights, or

    (b)    a cash transfer sum paid under Chapter 5 of Part 4 of the Pension Schemes Act 1993 (early leavers) in respect of him, to the trustees or managers of the scheme,]

"trustees or managers", in relation to an occupational pension scheme, means—

    (a)    in the case of a trust scheme, the trustees of the scheme, and

    (b)    in any other case, the managers of the scheme,

"trust scheme" means an occupational pension scheme established under a trust.

(2)    For the purposes of this Part—

    (a)    the accrued rights of a member of an occupational pension scheme at any time are the rights which have accrued to or in respect of him at that time to future benefits under the scheme, and

    (b)    at any time when the pensionable service of a member of an occupational pension scheme is continuing, his accrued rights are to be determined as if he had opted, immediately before that time, to terminate that service;

and references to accrued pension or accrued benefits are to be interpreted accordingly.

[(2A)    In subsection (2)(a), the reference to rights which have accrued to or in respect of the member does not include any rights which are pension credit rights.]

(3)    In determining what is "pensionable service" for the purposes of this Part—

    (a)    service notionally attributable for any purpose of the scheme is to be disregarded, and

    (b)    no account is to be taken of any rules of the scheme by which a period of service can be treated for any purpose as being longer or shorter than it actually is

[but, in its application for the purposes of section 51, paragraph (b) does not affect the operation of any rules of the scheme by virtue of which a period of service is to be rounded up or down by a period of less than a month].

[(3A)    In a case of the winding-up of an occupational pension scheme in pursuance of an order of the Authority under section 11 or of an order of a court, the winding-up shall (subject to subsection (3E) [and to sections 28, 154 and 219 of the Pensions Act 2004]) be taken for the purposes of this Part to begin—

    (a)   if the order provides for a time to be the time when the winding-up begins, at that time; and

    (b)   in any other case, at the time when the order comes into force.

(3B)  In a case of the winding-up of an occupational pension scheme in accordance with a requirement or power contained in the rules of the scheme, the winding-up shall (subject to subsections (3C) to (3E) [and to sections 154 and 219 of the Pensions Act 2004]) be taken for the purposes of this Part to begin—

    (a)   at the time (if any) which under those rules is the time when the winding-up begins; and

    (b)   if paragraph (a) does not apply, at the earliest time which is a time fixed by the trustees or managers as the time from which steps for the purposes of the winding-up are to be taken.

(3C)  Subsection (3B) shall not require a winding-up of a scheme to be treated as having begun at any time before the end of any period during which effect is being given—

    (a)   to a determination under section 38 that the scheme is not for the time being to be wound up; or

    (b)   to a determination in accordance with the rules of the scheme to postpone the commencement of a winding-up.

(3D)  In subsection (3B)(b) the reference to the trustees or managers of the scheme shall have effect in relation to any scheme the rules of which provide for a determination that the scheme is to be wound up to be made by persons other than the trustees or managers as including a reference to those other persons.

(3E)  Subsections (3A) to (3D) above do not apply for such purposes as may be prescribed.]

(4)  In the application of this Part to Scotland, in relation to conviction on indictment, references to imprisonment are to be read as references to imprisonment for a term not exceeding two years.

(5)  Subject to the provisions of this Act, expressions used in this Act and in the Pension Schemes Act 1993 have the same meaning in this Act as in that.

**NOTES**

Sub-s (1) is amended as follows:

Definition "the Authority" substituted by the Pensions Act 2004, s 7(2)(b).

Definition "civil partnership status" inserted by the Civil Partnership (Pensions and Benefit Payments) (Consequential, etc Provisions) Order 2005, SI 2005/2053, art 2, Schedule, Pt 4, para 25.

In definition "employer" words in italics repealed by the Pensions Act 2004, s 320, Sch 13, Pt 1, as from a day to be appointed.

In definition "member" words in square brackets substituted by the Welfare Reform and Pensions Act 1999, s 84(1), Sch 12, Pt I, paras 43, 61(1), (2).

Definitions "member-nominated director", "member-nominated trustee" and "the minimum funding requirement" (omitted) repealed by the Pensions Act 2004, s 320, Sch 13, Pt 1.

Definitions "pension credit", "pension credit member", "pension credit rights" inserted by the Welfare Reform and Pensions Act 1999, s 84(1), Sch 12, Pt I, paras 43, 61(1),(3).

In definition "pensionable service" words in italics repealed by the Pensions Act 2004, s 320, Sch 13, Pt 1, as from a day to be appointed.

In definition "pensioner member" the words omitted were originally inserted by the Child Support, Pensions and Social Security Act 2000, s 56, Sch 5, Pt I, para 8(3), and repealed by the Taxation of Pension Schemes (Consequential Amendments) Order 2006, SI 2006/745, art 10(1), (7).

In definition "transfer credits" words in square brackets substituted by the Pensions Act 2004, s 319(1), Sch 12, paras 34, 69(1), (2).

Sub-s (2A): inserted by the Welfare Reform and Pensions Act 1999, s 84(1), Sch 12, Pt I, paras 43, 61(1), (4).

Sub-s (3): words in square brackets added by the Welfare Reform and Pensions Act 1999, s 18, Sch 2, Pt I, para 18.

Sub-ss (3A), (3B): inserted, together with sub-ss (3C)–(3E), by the Child Support, Pensions and Social Security Act 2000, s 49(2); words in square brackets inserted by the Pensions Act 2004, s 319(1), Sch 12, paras 34, 69(1), (3), (4).

Sub-ss (3C)–(3E): inserted as noted above.

Transitional provisions: for transitional provisions in connection with the continuity of functions, etc, following the transfer of functions from the Authority to the Regulator, see SI 2005/695, arts 5, 6, Sch 3.

Regulations: the Occupational Pension Schemes (Winding Up Notices and Reports etc) Regulations 2002, SI 2002/459; the Occupational Pension Schemes (Winding Up) (Amendment) Regulations 2004, SI 2004/1140; the Occupational Pension Schemes (Winding up etc) Regulations 2005, SI 2005/706 (all made under sub-s (3E)).

**[1.674]**

**125  Section 124: supplementary**

(1)  For the purposes of this Part, an occupational pension scheme is salary related if—

    (a)   the scheme is not a money purchase scheme, and

    (b)   the scheme does not fall within a prescribed class or description,

and "salary related trust scheme" is to be read accordingly.

(2)  Regulations may apply this Part with prescribed modifications to occupational pension schemes—

    (a)   which are not money purchase schemes, but

    (b)   where some of the benefits that may be provided are money purchase benefits.

(3)  Regulations may, in relation to occupational pension schemes, extend for the purposes of this Part the meaning of "employer" to include[—

    (a)]  persons who have been the employer in relation to the scheme[;

    (b)   such other persons as may be prescribed].

(4)   For any of the purposes of this Part, regulations may in relation to occupational pension schemes—

(a)   extend or restrict the meaning of "member",
(b)   determine who is to be treated as a prospective member, and
(c)   determine the times at which a person is to be treated as becoming, or as ceasing to be, a member or prospective member.

**NOTES**

Sub-s (3): words in square brackets inserted by the Pensions Act 2004, s 240(1), as from a day to be appointed.
Regulations: regulations made under this section are outside the scope of this work.

## PART IV
## MISCELLANEOUS AND SUPPLEMENTAL
### *General*

**[1.675]**
**180   Commencement**
(1)   Subject to the following provisions, this Act shall come into force on such day as the Secretary of State may by order made by statutory instrument appoint and different days may be appointed for different purposes.
(2)–(4)   (*Outside the scope of this work.*)

**NOTES**

Orders: the commencement orders relevant to the sections of the Act reproduced here are the Pensions Act 1995 (Commencement No 2) Order 1995, SI 1995/3104; the Pensions Act 1995 (Commencement No 3) Order 1996, SI 1996/778; the Pensions Act 1995 (Commencement No 8) Order 1996, SI 1996/2637; the Pensions Act 1995 (Commencement No 10) Order 1997, SI 1997/664.

**[1.676]**
**181   Short title**
This Act may be cited as the Pensions Act 1995.

# DISABILITY DISCRIMINATION ACT 1995 (NOTE)

### (1995 c 50)

**[1.677]**

**NOTES**

In so far as this Act was still in force, the vast majority of it was repealed by the Equality Act 2010, s 211(2), Sch 27, Pt 1, as from 1 October 2010 (see the Equality Act 2010 (Commencement No 4, Savings, Consequential, Transitional, Transitory and Incidental Provisions and Revocation) Order 2010, SI 2010/2317 at **[2.1558]**). Sections 49A–49D were repealed by the 2010 Act, as from 5 April 2011 (see the Equality Act 2010 (Commencement No 6) Order, SI 2011/1066). The commencement of the repeal of this Act by the 2010 Act on 1 October 2010 was provided for by SI 2010/2317 as noted above. That Order provides for numerous transitional provisions and savings in connection with the commencement of the 2010 Act and the repeal of this Act. See, in particular, art 13 (transitional provisions with regard to guidance issued under s 3), art 15 (saving where the act complained of occurs wholly before 1 October 2010), Schs 1, 2 (savings in relation to shipping matters), Schs 3, 4 (savings in relation to work on ships, hovercraft and in relation to seafarers), and Schs 5, 6 (savings in relation to existing insurance policies).
Employment Appeal Tribunal: an appeal lies to the Employment Appeal Tribunal on any question of law arising from any decision of, or in any proceedings before, an employment tribunal under or by virtue of this Act; see the Employment Tribunals Act 1996, s 21(1)(e) at **[1.713]** (repealed as from 1 October 2010, but see the savings note above).

# [EMPLOYMENT TRIBUNALS ACT 1996]

### (1996 c 17)

### ARRANGEMENT OF SECTIONS

### PART I
### EMPLOYMENT TRIBUNALS

#### *Introductory*

*An Act to consolidate enactments relating to [employment tribunals] and the Employment Appeal Tribunal*

[22 May 1996]

**NOTES**

Title: substituted by the Employment Rights (Dispute Resolution) Act 1998, s 1(2)(c).

Long title: words in square brackets substituted by virtue of the Employment Rights (Dispute Resolution) Act 1998, s 1(2)(b).

This Act is the first separate legislation devoted to the constitution, powers and procedure of Employment Tribunals and the Employment Appeal Tribunal. It consolidates provisions mainly in the Employment Protection (Consolidation) Act 1978 but also widely scattered in other Acts. A Destination Table, showing where previous statutory provisions consolidated by this Act are now to be found, is printed after the Act.

As to the further power to amend this Act, see s 40 *post*, the Employment Relations Act 2004, s 42(1), (4)(d) at **[1.1335]**, and the Pensions Act 2004, ss 259, 260.

Employment Appeal Tribunal: an appeal lies to the Employment Appeal Tribunal on any question of law arising from any decision of, or in any proceedings before, an employment tribunal under or by virtue of this Act; see s 21(1)(g) at **[1.713]**.

Employment Judges: a person who is a member of a panel of chairmen of employment tribunals which is appointed in accordance with regulations under s 1(1) of this Act may be referred to as an Employment Judge; see s 3A at **[1.681]** (as inserted by the Tribunals, Courts and Enforcement Act 2007, s 48(1), Sch 8, paras 35, 36).

By the Tribunals, Courts and Enforcement Act 2007 (Commencement No 6 and Transitional Provisions) Order 2008, SI 2008/2696, art 3, staff appointed to employment tribunals or the Employment Appeal Tribunal before 3 November 2008 are to be treated, for the purpose of any enactment, as if they had been appointed by the Lord Chancellor under the Tribunals, Courts and Enforcement Act 2007, s 40(1) (tribunal staff and services).

The Tribunals, Courts and Enforcement Act 2007, s 2 (at **[1.1526]**) makes provision for the appointment of a Senior President of Tribunals who has certain functions with respect to employment tribunals, the Employment Appeal Tribunal, and the representation of their members; see also Sch 1, Pt 4 to that Act.

By the Tribunals, Courts and Enforcement Act 2007, Sch 6, Pt 6, an employment tribunal is a scheduled tribunal for the purposes of s 35 of that Act, under which the Lord Chancellor has powers relating to the transfer of Ministerial responsibilities for scheduled tribunals.

By the Tribunals, Courts and Enforcement Act 2007, Sch 6, Pt 5, the Employment Appeal Tribunal is a scheduled tribunal for the purposes of ss 35, 36 of that Act. For the powers of the Lord Chancellor relating to the transfer of Ministerial responsibilities for scheduled tribunals and the transfer of powers to make procedural rules, see ss 35, 36, respectively of that Act.

For the power of the Lord Chancellor to provide for a function of a scheduled tribunal (as specified in Sch 6, Pts 1–4 to the 2007 Act) to be transferred to an employment tribunal or the Employment Appeals Tribunal, see the Tribunals, Courts and Enforcement Act 2007, s 30(1)(f)–(i), (2)–(9).

See *Harvey* PI.

# PART I
# [EMPLOYMENT TRIBUNALS]

**NOTES**

The Part heading was substituted by the Employment Rights (Dispute Resolution) Act 1998, s 1(2)(b).

*Introductory*

**[1.678]**
## 1 [Employment tribunals]
(1)   The Secretary of State may by regulations make provision for the establishment of tribunals to be known as [employment tribunals].
(2)   Regulations made wholly or partly under section 128(1) of the Employment Protection (Consolidation) Act 1978 and in force immediately before this Act comes into force shall, so far as made under that provision, continue to have effect (until revoked) as if made under subsection (1);  . . .

**NOTES**

Section heading, sub-s (1): words in square brackets substituted by the Employment Rights (Dispute Resolution) Act 1998, s 1(2)(b).

Sub-s (2): words omitted repealed by the Employment Rights (Dispute Resolution) Act 1998, s 15, Sch 2.

Employment Protection (Consolidation) Act 1978, s 128(1): repealed by this Act.

Regulations: the Employment Tribunals (Constitution and Rules of Procedure) Regulations 2004, SI 2004/1861 at **[2.809]** (as subsequently amended by, *inter alia*, the Employment Tribunals (Constitution and Rules of Procedure) (Amendment) Regulations 2008, SI 2008/2771 which was also made under this section) which revoke and replace (subject to transitional provisions in reg 20 of the 2004 Regulations at **[2.854]**) the Employment Tribunals (Constitution and Rules of Procedure) Regulations 2001, SI 2001/1171, and the Employment Tribunals (Constitution and Rules of Procedure) (Scotland) Regulations 2001, SI 2001/1170 (the Regulations continued in force by sub-s (2) were revoked and replaced by the 2001 Regulations).

**Stop Press:** see the Employment Tribunals (Constitution and Rules of Procedure) Regulations 2013, SI 2013/1237 at **[2.1689]**.

*Jurisdiction*

**[1.679]**
## 2   Enactments conferring jurisdiction on [employment tribunals]
[Employment tribunals] shall exercise the jurisdiction conferred on them by or by virtue of this Act or any other Act, whether passed before or after this Act.

**NOTES**

Words in square brackets substituted by the Employment Rights (Dispute Resolution) Act 1998, s 1(2)(b).

**[1.680]**
## 3  Power to confer further jurisdiction on [employment tribunals]
(1)   The appropriate Minister may by order provide that proceedings in respect of—
   (a)   any claim to which this section applies, or
   (b)   any claim to which this section applies and which is of a description specified in the order, may, subject to such exceptions (if any) as may be so specified, be brought before an [employment tribunal].
(2)   Subject to subsection (3), this section applies to—
   (a)   a claim for damages for breach of a contract of employment or other contract connected with employment,
   (b)   a claim for a sum due under such a contract, and
   (c)   a claim for the recovery of a sum in pursuance of any enactment relating to the terms or performance of such a contract,
if the claim is such that a court in England and Wales or Scotland would under the law for the time being in force have jurisdiction to hear and determine an action in respect of the claim.
(3)   This section does not apply to a claim for damages, or for a sum due, in respect of personal injuries.
(4)   Any jurisdiction conferred on an [employment tribunal] by virtue of this section in respect of any claim is exercisable concurrently with any court in England and Wales or in Scotland which has jurisdiction to hear and determine an action in respect of the claim.
(5)   In this section—
   "appropriate Minister", as respects a claim in respect of which an action could be heard and determined by a court in England and Wales, means the Lord Chancellor and, as respects a claim in respect of which an action could be heard and determined by a court in Scotland, means the [Secretary of State], and
   "personal injuries" includes any disease and any impairment of a person's physical or mental condition.
(6)   In this section a reference to breach of a contract includes a reference to breach of—
   (a)   a term implied in a contract by or under any enactment or otherwise,

(b)    a term of a contract as modified by or under any enactment or otherwise, and

(c)    a term which, although not contained in a contract, is incorporated in the contract by another term of the contract.

**NOTES**

Section heading, sub-ss (1), (4): words in square brackets substituted by the Employment Rights (Dispute Resolution) Act 1998, s 1(2)(a), (b).

Sub-s (5): words in square brackets in definition "appropriate Minister" substituted by virtue of the Transfer of Functions (Lord Advocate and Secretary of State) Order 1999, SI 1999/678, art 2(1), Schedule.

Transfer of functions: functions under this section are transferred, in so far as they are exercisable in or as regards Scotland, to the Scottish Ministers, by the Scotland Act 1998 (Transfer of Functions to the Scottish Ministers etc) Order 1999, SI 1999/1750, art 2, Sch 1.

Conciliation: employment tribunal proceedings and claims which could be the subject of employment tribunal proceedings which are proceedings in respect of which an employment tribunal has jurisdiction by virtue of this section are proceedings to which s 18(1)(e) of this Act at **[1.706]** applies.

Orders: as of 6 April 2013 no Orders had been made under this section but, by virtue of s 44 of, and Sch 2, Pt I, paras 1–4 to, this Act, the Employment Tribunals Extension of Jurisdiction (England and Wales) Order 1994, SI 1994/1623 at **[2.211]**, and the Employment Tribunals Extension of Jurisdiction (Scotland) Order 1994, SI 1994/1624 at **[2.222]**, have effect as if made under this section.

**[1.681]**
**[3A  Meaning of "Employment Judge"**
A person who is a member of a panel of *chairmen of employment tribunals* which is appointed in accordance with regulations under section 1(1) may be referred to as an Employment Judge.]

**NOTES**

Inserted by the Tribunals, Courts and Enforcement Act 2007, s 48(1), Sch 8, paras 35, 36.

For the words in italics there are substituted the words "Employment Judges" by the Crime and Courts Act 2013, s 21(4), Sch 14, Pt 7, para 13(1), as from a day to be appointed.

*Membership etc*

**[1.682]**
**4  Composition of a tribunal**
(1)   Subject to the following provisions of this section [and to section 7(3A)], proceedings before an [employment tribunal] shall be heard by—
    (a)    the person who, in accordance with regulations made under section 1(1), is the chairman, and
    *(b)    two other members, or (with the consent of the parties) one other member, selected as the other members (or member) in accordance with regulations so made.*
(2)   Subject to subsection (5), the proceedings specified in subsection (3) shall be heard by the person mentioned in subsection (1)(a) alone [or alone by any Employment Judge who, in accordance with regulations made under section 1(1), is a member of the tribunal].
(3)   The proceedings referred to in subsection (2) are—
    (a)    proceedings [on a complaint under section 68A[, 87] or 192 of the Trade Union and Labour Relations (Consolidation) Act 1992 or] on an application under section 161, 165 or 166 of [that Act],
    (b)    proceedings on a complaint under section 126 of the Pension Schemes Act 1993,
    (c)    proceedings [on a reference under section 11, 163 or 170 of the Employment Rights Act 1996,] on a complaint under section 23[, 34][, 111] or 188 of [that Act, on a complaint under section 70(1) of that Act relating to section 64 of that Act,] on an application under section 128, 131 or 132 of that [Act or for an appointment under section 206(4) of that] Act,
    [(ca)  proceedings on a complaint under [regulation 15(10) of the Transfer of Undertakings (Protection of Employment) Regulations 2006],]
    [(cc)  proceedings on a complaint under section 11 of the National Minimum Wage Act 1998;
    (cd)  proceedings on an appeal under [section 19C] of the National Minimum Wage Act 1998;]
    [(ce)  proceedings on a complaint under regulation 30 of the Working Time Regulations 1998 relating to an amount due under regulation 14(2) or 16(1) of those Regulations,
    (cf)   proceedings on a complaint under regulation 18 of the Merchant Shipping (Working Time: Inland Waterways) Regulations 2003 relating to an amount due under regulation 11 of those Regulations,
    (cg)  proceedings on a complaint under regulation 18 of the Civil Aviation (Working Time) Regulations 2004 relating to an amount due under regulation 4 of those Regulations,
    (ch)  proceedings on a complaint under regulation 19 of the Fishing Vessels (Working Time: Sea-fishermen) Regulations 2004 relating to an amount due under regulation 11 of those Regulations,]
    (d)    proceedings in respect of which an [employment tribunal] has jurisdiction by virtue of section 3 of this Act,

(e)    proceedings in which the parties have given their written consent to the proceedings being heard in accordance with subsection (2) (whether or not they have subsequently withdrawn it),

(f)    . . . and

(g)    proceedings in which the person (or, where more than one, each of the persons) against whom the proceedings are brought does not, or has ceased to, contest the case.

(4)    The Secretary of State [and the Lord Chancellor, acting jointly,] may by order amend the provisions of subsection (3).

(5)    Proceedings specified in subsection (3) shall be heard in accordance with subsection (1) if a person who, in accordance with regulations made under section 1(1), may be the chairman of an [employment tribunal], having regard to—

(a)    whether there is a likelihood of a dispute arising on the facts which makes it desirable for the proceedings to be heard in accordance with subsection (1),

(b)    whether there is a likelihood of an issue of law arising which would make it desirable for the proceedings to be heard in accordance with subsection (2),

(c)    any views of any of the parties as to whether or not the proceedings ought to be heard in accordance with either of those subsections, and

(d)    whether there are other proceedings which might be heard concurrently but which are not proceedings specified in subsection (3),

decides at any stage of the proceedings that the proceedings are to be heard in accordance with subsection (1).

(6)    Where (in accordance with the following provisions of this Part) the Secretary of State makes [employment tribunal] procedure regulations, the regulations may provide that [any act which is required or authorised by the regulations to be done by an employment tribunal and is of a description specified by the regulations for the purposes of this subsection may] be done by the person mentioned in subsection (1)(a) alone [or alone by any Employment Judge who, in accordance with regulations made under section 1(1), is a member of the tribunal].

[(6A)    Subsection (6) in particular enables employment tribunal procedure regulations to provide that—

(a)    the determination of proceedings in accordance with regulations under section 7(3A), (3B) or (3C)(a),

(b)    the carrying-out of pre-hearing reviews in accordance with regulations under subsection (1) of section 9 (including the exercise of powers in connection with such reviews in accordance with regulations under paragraph (b) of that subsection), or

(c)    the hearing and determination of a preliminary issue in accordance with regulations under section 9(4) (where it involves hearing witnesses other than the parties or their representatives as well as where, in accordance with regulations under section 7(3C)(b), it does not),

may be done by the person mentioned in subsection (1)(a) alone [or alone by any Employment Judge who, in accordance with regulations made under section 1(1), is a member of the tribunal].]

[(6B)    Employment tribunal procedure regulations may (subject to subsection (6C)) also provide that any act which—

(a)    by virtue of subsection (6) may be done by the person mentioned in subsection (1)(a) alone [or alone by any Employment Judge who, in accordance with regulations made under section 1(1), is a member of the tribunal], and

(b)    is of a description specified by the regulations for the purposes of this subsection,

may be done by a person appointed as a legal officer in accordance with regulations under section 1(1); and any act so done shall be treated as done by an employment tribunal.

(6C)    But regulations under subsection (6B) may not specify—

(a)    the determination of any proceedings, other than proceedings in which the parties have agreed the terms of the determination or in which the person bringing the proceedings has given notice of the withdrawal of the case, or

(b)    the carrying-out of pre-hearing reviews in accordance with regulations under section 9(1).]

[(6D)    A person appointed as a legal officer in accordance with regulations under section 1(1) may determine proceedings in respect of which an employment tribunal has jurisdiction, or make a decision falling to be made in the course of such proceedings, if—

(a)    the proceedings are of a description specified in an order under this subsection made by the Secretary of State and the Lord Chancellor acting jointly, and

(b)    all the parties to the proceedings consent in writing;

and any determination or decision made under this subsection shall be treated as made by an employment tribunal.]

(7)    . . .

**NOTES**

Sub-s (1): words in square brackets substituted by the Employment Rights (Dispute Resolution) Act 1998, ss 1(2)(a), 15, Sch 1, para 12(1), (2); para (b) substituted by s 4 of the 1998 Act, as from a day to be appointed, as follows—

"(b)    two other members selected as the other members in accordance with regulations so made or, with appropriate consent, one other member selected as the other member in accordance with regulations so made;

and in paragraph (b) "appropriate consent" means either consent given at the beginning of the hearing by such of the parties as are then present in person or represented, or consent given by each of the parties.".

Sub-s (2): words in square brackets inserted by the Tribunals, Courts and Enforcement Act 2007, s 48(1), Sch 8, paras 35, 37.

Sub-s (3) is amended as follows:

All words and numbers in square brackets in paras (a), (c) (with the exception of the number ", 111") were inserted or substituted by the Employment Rights (Dispute Resolution) Act 1998, ss 3(1)–(3), 15, Sch 1, para 12.

Number ", 111" in square brackets in para (c) inserted by the Employment Tribunals Act 1996 (Tribunal Composition) Order 2012, SI 2012/988, art 2, as from 6 April 2012.

Para (ca) inserted, words in square brackets in para (d) substituted, and para (f) repealed, by the Employment Rights (Dispute Resolution) Act 1998, ss 1(2)(a), 3(1), (4), (5), 15, Sch 1, para 12, Sch 2.

Words in square brackets in para (ca) substituted by the Transfer of Undertakings (Protection of Employment) Regulations 2006, SI 2006/246, reg 20, Sch 2, para 8.

Paras (cc), (cd) inserted by the National Minimum Wage Act 1998, s 27(1).

Words in square brackets in para (cd) substituted by the Employment Act 2008, s 9(4).

Paras (ce)–(ch) inserted by the Employment Tribunals Act 1996 (Tribunal Composition) Order 2009, SI 2009/789, art 2, as from 6 April 2009.

Sub-s (4): words in square brackets inserted by the Tribunals, Courts and Enforcement Act 2007, s 48(1), Sch 8, paras 35, 38.

Sub-s (5): words in square brackets substituted by the Employment Rights (Dispute Resolution) Act 1998, ss 1(2)(a), 15, Sch 1, para 12(1), (4).

Sub-s (6): words in first and second pairs of square brackets substituted by the Employment Rights (Dispute Resolution) Act 1998, ss 1(2)(a), 15, Sch 1, para 12(1), (4); words in final pair of square brackets inserted by the Tribunals, Courts and Enforcement Act 2007, s 48(1), Sch 8, paras 35, 37.

Sub-ss (6A)–(6C): inserted by the Employment Rights (Dispute Resolution) Act 1998, ss 3(6), 5; words in square brackets in sub-ss (6A), (6B) inserted by the Tribunals, Courts and Enforcement Act 2007, s 48(1), Sch 8, paras 35, 37.

Sub-s (6D): inserted by the Enterprise and Regulatory Reform Act 2013, s 11(1), as from 25 April 2013 (so far as is necessary for enabling the exercise of any power to make orders) and as from a day to be appointed (otherwise).

Sub-s (7): repealed by the Employment Relations Act 1999, ss 41, 44, Sch 8, para 2, Sch 9(12).

This section is modified for the purposes of national security proceedings by the Employment Tribunals (Constitution and Rules of Procedure) Regulations 2004, SI 2004/1861, reg 12 at **[2.820]**.

Regulations: the Employment Tribunals (Constitution and Rules of Procedure) Regulations 2004, SI 2004/1861 at **[2.809]**; the Employment Tribunals (Constitution and Rules of Procedure) (Amendment) Regulations 2004, SI 2004/2351; the Employment Tribunals (Constitution and Rules of Procedure) (Amendment) Regulations 2005, SI 2005/435; the Employment Tribunals (Constitution and Rules of Procedure) (Amendment) (No 2) Regulations 2005, SI 2005/1865; the Employment Tribunals (Constitution and Rules of Procedure) Regulations 2013, SI 2013/1237 at **[2.1689]** (all made under sub-ss (6), (6A)).

Orders: the Employment Tribunals Act 1996 (Tribunal Composition) Order 2009, SI 2009/789; the Employment Tribunals Act 1996 (Tribunal Composition) Order 2012, SI 2012/988 (which was made under sub-s (4) and which amends sub-s (3) above).

---

**[1.683]**

## 5   Remuneration, fees and allowances

(1)   The Secretary of State may pay to—

(a)    the [President of the Employment Tribunals (England and Wales)],

(b)    the [President of the Employment Tribunals (Scotland)],   . . .

[(c)    any person who is an Employment Judge on a full-time basis, and]

[(d)    any person who is a legal officer appointed in accordance with such regulations,]

such remuneration as he may with the consent of the Treasury determine.

(2)   The Secretary of State may pay to—

(a)    members of [employment tribunals],

(b)    any assessors appointed for the purposes of proceedings before [employment tribunals], and

(c)    any persons required for the purposes of section [131(2) of the Equality Act 2010] to prepare reports,,

such fees and allowances as he may with the consent of the Treasury determine.

(3)   The Secretary of State may pay to any other persons such allowances as he may with the consent of the Treasury determine for the purposes of, or in connection with, their attendance at [employment tribunals].

---

NOTES

Sub-s (1): words in first and second pairs of square brackets substituted, word omitted from para (b) repealed, and para (d) inserted, by the Employment Rights (Dispute Resolution) Act 1998, ss 1(2)(d), (e), 15, Sch 1, para 13, Sch 2; para (c) substituted by the Tribunals, Courts and Enforcement Act 2007, s 48(1), Sch 8, paras 35, 39.

Sub-s (2): words in square brackets in para (c) substituted by the Equality Act 2010, s 211(1), Sch 26, Pt 1, paras 27, 28, as from 1 October 2010; other words in square brackets substituted by the Employment Rights (Dispute Resolution) Act 1998, s 1(2)(b).

Sub-s (3): words in square brackets substituted by the Employment Rights (Dispute Resolution) Act 1998, s 1(2)(b).

**[1.684]**
**[5A    Training etc**
The Senior President of Tribunals is responsible, within the resources made available by the Lord Chancellor, for the maintenance of appropriate arrangements for the training, guidance and welfare of members of panels of members of employment tribunals (in their capacities as members of such panels, whether or not panels of *chairmen*).]

**NOTES**
Commencement: 3 November 2008.
Inserted, together with ss 5B–5D, by the Tribunals, Courts and Enforcement Act 2007, s 48(1), Sch 8, paras 35, 40, as from 3 November 2008.
For the word in italics there are substituted the words "Employment Judges" by the Crime and Courts Act 2013, s 21(4), Sch 14, Pt 7, para 13(1), as from a day to be appointed.

**[1.685]**
**[5B    Members of employment tribunals: removal from office**
(1)    Any power by which the President of the Employment Tribunals (England and Wales) may be removed from that office may be exercised only with the concurrence of the Lord Chief Justice of England and Wales.
(2)    Any power by which the President of the Employment Tribunals (Scotland) may be removed from that office may be exercised only with the concurrence of the Lord President of the Court of Session.
(3)    Any power by which a member of a panel may be removed from membership of the panel—
    (a)    may, if the person exercises functions wholly or mainly in Scotland, be exercised only with the concurrence of the Lord President of the Court of Session;
    (b)    may, if paragraph (a) does not apply, be exercised only with the concurrence of the Lord Chief Justice of England and Wales.
(4)    In subsection (3) "panel" means—
    (a)    a panel of *chairmen of employment tribunals,* or
    (b)    any other panel of members of employment tribunals,
which is appointed in accordance with regulations made under section 1(1).
(5)    The Lord Chief Justice of England and Wales may nominate a judicial office holder (as defined in section 109(4) of the Constitutional Reform Act 2005) to exercise his functions under this section.
(6)    The Lord President of the Court of Session may nominate a judge of the Court of Session who is a member of the First or Second Division of the Inner House of that Court to exercise his functions under this section.]

**NOTES**
Commencement: 3 November 2008.
Inserted as noted to s 5A at **[1.684]**.
Sub-s (4): for the words in italics there are substituted the words "Employment Judges" by the Crime and Courts Act 2013, s 21(4), Sch 14, Pt 7, para 13(1), as from a day to be appointed.

**[1.686]**
**[5C    Oaths**
(1)    Subsection (2) applies to a person ("the appointee")—
    (a)    who is appointed—
        (i)    as President of the Employment Tribunals (England and Wales),
        (ii)    as President of the Employment Tribunals (Scotland), or
        (iii)    as a member of a panel (as defined in section 5B(4)), and
    (b)    who has not previously taken the required oaths after accepting another office.
(2)    The appointee must take the required oaths before—
    (a)    the Senior President of Tribunals, or
    (b)    an eligible person who is nominated by the Senior President of Tribunals for the purpose of taking the oaths from the appointee.
(3)    If the appointee is a President or panel member appointed before the coming into force of this section, the requirement in subsection (2) applies in relation to the appointee from the coming into force of this section.
(4)    A person is eligible for the purposes of subsection (2)(b) if one or more of the following paragraphs applies to him—
    (a)    he holds high judicial office (as defined in section 60(2) of the Constitutional Reform Act 2005);
    (b)    he holds judicial office (as defined in section 109(4) of that Act);
    (c)    he holds (in Scotland) the office of sheriff.
(5)    In this section "the required oaths" means—
    (a)    the oath of allegiance, and
    (b)    the judicial oath,

as set out in the Promissory Oaths Act 1868.]

**NOTES**
Commencement: 3 November 2008.
Inserted as noted to s 5A at **[1.684]**.

**[1.687]**
**[5D Judicial assistance**
(1) Subsection (2) applies where regulations under section 1(1) make provision for a relevant tribunal judge, or a relevant judge, to be able by virtue of his office to act as a member of a panel of members of employment tribunals.
(2) The provision has effect only if—
  (a) the persons in relation to whom the provision operates have to be persons nominated for the purposes of the provision by the Senior President of Tribunals,
  (b) its operation in relation to a panel established for England and Wales in any particular case requires the consent of the President of Employment Tribunals (England and Wales),
  (c) its operation in relation to a panel established for Scotland in any particular case requires the consent of the President of Employment Tribunals (Scotland),
  (d) its operation as respects a particular relevant judge requires—
    (i) the consent of the relevant judge, and
    (ii) the appropriate consent (see subsection (3)) [except where the relevant judge is the Lord Chief Justice of England and Wales], and
  (e) it operates as respects a relevant tribunal judge or a relevant judge only for the purpose of enabling him to act as a member of a panel of *chairmen of employment tribunals*.
(3) In subsection (2)(d)(ii) "the appropriate consent" means—
  (a) the consent of the Lord Chief Justice of England and Wales where the relevant judge is—
    (i) [the Master of the Rolls or] an ordinary judge of the Court of Appeal in England and Wales,
    [(ia) within subsection (4)(b)(ia),]
    (ii) a puisne judge of the High Court in England and Wales,
    (iii) a circuit judge,
    (iv) a district judge in England and Wales, *or*
    (v) a District Judge (Magistrates' Courts); [or
    (vi) within subsection (4)(b)(x) to (xvi);]
  (b) the consent of the Lord President of the Court of Session where the relevant judge is—
    (i) a judge of the Court of Session, or
    (ii) a sheriff;
  (c) the consent of the Lord Chief Justice of Northern Ireland where the relevant judge is—
    (i) a Lord Justice of Appeal in Northern Ireland,
    (ii) a puisne judge of the High Court in Northern Ireland,
    (iii) a county court judge in Northern Ireland, or
    (iv) a district judge in Northern Ireland.
(4) In this section—
  (a) "relevant tribunal judge" means—
    (i) a person who is a judge of the First-tier Tribunal by virtue of appointment under paragraph 1(1) of Schedule 2 to the Tribunals, Courts and Enforcement Act 2007,
    (ii) a transferred-in judge of the First-tier Tribunal,
    (iii) a person who is a judge of the Upper Tribunal by virtue of appointment under paragraph 1(1) of Schedule 3 to that Act,
    (iv) a transferred-in judge of the Upper Tribunal,
    (v) a deputy judge of the Upper Tribunal, *or*
    (vi) a person who is the Chamber President of a chamber of the First-tier Tribunal, or of a chamber of the Upper Tribunal, and does not fall within any of sub-paragraphs (i) to (v)[, or
    (vii) is the Senior President of Tribunals;]
  (b) "relevant judge" means a person who—
    (i) is [the Lord Chief Justice of England and Wales, the Master of the Rolls or] an ordinary judge of the Court of Appeal in England and Wales (including the vice-president, if any, of either division of that Court),
    [(ia) is the President of the Queen's Bench Division or Family Division, or the Chancellor, of the High Court in England and Wales,]
    (ii) is a Lord Justice of Appeal in Northern Ireland,
    (iii) is a judge of the Court of Session,
    (iv) is a puisne judge of the High Court in England and Wales or Northern Ireland,
    (v) is a circuit judge,
    (vi) is a sheriff in Scotland,
    (vii) is a county court judge in Northern Ireland,

(viii) is a district judge in England and Wales or Northern Ireland, *or*

(ix) is a District Judge (Magistrates' Courts),

[(x) is a deputy judge of the High Court in England and Wales,

(xi) is a Recorder,

(xii) is a Deputy District Judge (Magistrates' Courts),

(xiii) is a deputy district judge appointed under section 8 of the County Courts Act 1984 or section 102 of the Senior Courts Act 1981,

(xiv) holds an office listed in the first column of the table in section 89(3C) of the Senior Courts Act 1981 (senior High Court Masters etc),

(xv) holds an office listed in column 1 of Part 2 of Schedule 2 to that Act (High Court Masters etc), or

(xvi) is the Judge Advocate General or a person appointed under section 30(1)(a) or (b) of the Courts-Martial (Appeals) Act 1951 (assistants to the Judge Advocate General).]

(5) References in subsection (4)(b)(iii) to (ix) to office-holders do not include deputies or temporary office-holders.]

**NOTES**

Commencement: 3 November 2008.

Inserted as noted to s 5A at **[1.684]**.

Sub-s (2): words in square brackets in para (d)(ii) inserted by the Crime and Courts Act 2013, s 21(4), Sch 14, Pt 6, para 12(1), (2), as from a day to be appointed; for the words in italics in para (e) there are substituted the words "Employment Judges" by the Crime and Courts Act 2013, s 21(4), Sch 14, Pt 7, para 13(1), as from a day to be appointed.

Sub-s (3): words in square brackets inserted and word in italics repealed by the Crime and Courts Act 2013, s 21(4), Sch 14, Pt 6, para 12(1), (3), as from a day to be appointed.

Sub-s (4): words in square brackets inserted and words in italics repealed by the Crime and Courts Act 2013, s 21(4), Sch 14, Pt 6, para 12(1), (4)–(7), as from a day to be appointed.

*Procedure*

**[1.688]**
**6 Conduct of hearings**

(1) A person may appear before an [employment tribunal] in person or be represented by—

(a) counsel or a solicitor,

(b) a representative of a trade union or an employers' association, or

(c) any other person whom he desires to represent him.

(2) [Nothing in any of sections 1 to 15 of and schedule 1 to the Arbitration (Scotland) Act 2010 or] [Part I of the Arbitration Act 1996] [applies] to any proceedings before an [employment tribunal].

**NOTES**

Sub-s (1): words in square brackets substituted by the Employment Rights (Dispute Resolution) Act 1998, s 1(2)(a).

Sub-s (2): words in first pair of square brackets inserted, and word in third pair of square brackets substituted, by the Arbitration (Scotland) Act 2010 (Consequential Amendments) Order 2010, SSI 2010/220, art 2, Schedule, para 7, as from 5 June 2010; words in second pair of square brackets substituted by the Arbitration Act 1996, s 107(1), Sch 3, para 62; words in final pair of square brackets substituted by the Employment Rights (Dispute Resolution) Act 1998, s 1(2)(a).

**[1.689]**
**7 [Employment tribunal] procedure regulations**

(1) The Secretary of State may by regulations ("[employment tribunal] procedure regulations") make such provision as appears to him to be necessary or expedient with respect to proceedings before [employment tribunals].

(2) Proceedings before [employment tribunals] shall be instituted in accordance with [employment tribunal] procedure regulations.

(3) [Employment tribunal] procedure regulations may, in particular, include provision—

(a) for determining by which tribunal any proceedings are to be determined,

(b) for enabling an [employment tribunal] to hear and determine proceedings brought by virtue of section 3 concurrently with proceedings brought before the tribunal otherwise than by virtue of that section,

(c) for treating the Secretary of State (either generally or in such circumstances as may be prescribed by the regulations) as a party to any proceedings before an [employment tribunal] (where he would not otherwise be a party to them) and entitling him to appear and to be heard accordingly,

(d) for requiring persons to attend to give evidence and produce documents and for authorising the administration of oaths to witnesses,

(e) for enabling an [employment tribunal], on the application of any party to the proceedings before it or of its own motion, to order—

(i) in England and Wales, such discovery or inspection of documents, or the furnishing of such further particulars, as might be ordered by *a county court* on application by a party to proceedings before it, or

      (ii)   in Scotland, such recovery or inspection of documents as might be ordered by a sheriff,

  (f)   for prescribing the procedure to be followed in any proceedings before an [employment tribunal], including provision—

      (i)   . . .

    [(ia)  for postponing fixing a time and place for a hearing, or postponing a time fixed for a hearing, for such period as may be determined in accordance with the regulations for the purpose of giving an opportunity for the proceedings to be settled by way of conciliation and withdrawn, and]

      (ii)  for enabling an [employment tribunal] to review its decisions, and revoke or vary its orders and awards, in such circumstances as may be determined in accordance with the regulations,

  (g)   for the appointment of one or more assessors for the purposes of any proceedings before an [employment tribunal], where the proceedings are brought under an enactment which provides for one or more assessors to be appointed,

  (h)   for authorising an [employment tribunal] to require persons to furnish information and produce documents to a person required for the purposes of section [131(2) of the Equality Act 2010] to prepare a report, and

  (j)   for the registration and proof of decisions, orders and awards of [employment tribunals].

[(3ZA)  Employment tribunal procedure regulations may—

  (a)   authorise the Secretary of State to prescribe, or prescribe requirements in relation to, any form which is required by such regulations to be used for the purpose of instituting, or entering an appearance to, proceedings before employment tribunals,

  (b)   authorise the Secretary of State to prescribe requirements in relation to documents to be supplied with any such form [(including certificates issued under section 18A(4))], and

  (c)   make provision about the publication of anything prescribed under authority conferred by virtue of this subsection.]

[(3A)  Employment tribunal procedure regulations may authorise the determination of proceedings without any hearing in such circumstances as the regulations may prescribe.]

[(3AA)  Employment tribunal procedure regulations under subsection (3A) may only authorise the determination of proceedings without any hearing in circumstances where—

  (a)   all the parties to the proceedings consent in writing to the determination without a hearing, or

  (b)   the person (or, where more than one, each of the persons) against whom the proceedings are brought—

      (i)   has presented no response in the proceedings, or

      (ii)  does not contest the case.

(3AB)  For the purposes of subsection (3AA)(b), a person does not present a response in the proceedings if he presents a response but, in accordance with provision made by the regulations, it is not accepted.]

(3B)  Employment tribunal procedure regulations may authorise the determination of proceedings without hearing anyone other than the person or persons by whom the proceedings are brought (or his or their representatives) where—

  (a)   the person (or, where more than one, each of the persons) against whom the proceedings are brought has done nothing to contest the case, or

  (b)   it appears from the application made by the person (or, where more than one, each of the persons) bringing the proceedings that he is not (or they are not) seeking any relief which an employment tribunal has power to give or that he is not (or they are not) entitled to any such relief.

(3C)  Employment tribunal procedure regulations may authorise the determination of proceedings without hearing anyone other than the person or persons by whom, and the person or persons against whom, the proceedings are brought (or his or their representatives) where—

  (a)   an employment tribunal is on undisputed facts bound by the decision of a court in another case to dismiss the case of the person or persons by whom, or of the person or persons against whom, the proceedings are brought, or

  (b)   the proceedings relate only to a preliminary issue which may be heard and determined in accordance with regulations under section 9(4).]

(4)  A person who without reasonable excuse fails to comply with—

  (a)   any requirement imposed by virtue of subsection (3)(d) or (h), or

  (b)   any requirement with respect to the discovery, recovery or inspection of documents imposed by virtue of subsection (3)(e)[, or

  (c)   any requirement imposed by virtue of employment tribunal procedure regulations to give written answers for the purpose of facilitating the determination of proceedings as mentioned in subsection (3A), (3B) or (3C),]

is guilty of an offence and liable on summary conviction to a fine not exceeding level 3 on the standard scale.

(5) Subject to any regulations under section 11(1)(a), [employment tribunal] procedure regulations may include provision authorising or requiring an [employment tribunal], in circumstances specified in the regulations, to send notice or a copy of—

(a) any document specified in the regulations which relates to any proceedings before the tribunal, or

(b) any decision, order or award of the tribunal,

to any government department or other person or body so specified.

(6) Where in accordance with [employment tribunal] procedure regulations an [employment tribunal] determines in the same proceedings—

(a) a complaint presented under section 111 of the Employment Rights Act 1996, and

(b) a question referred under section 163 of that Act,

subsection (2) of that section has no effect for the purposes of the proceedings in so far as they relate to the complaint under section 111.

**NOTES**

Section heading, sub-ss (1), (2), (5), (6): words in square brackets substituted by the Employment Rights (Dispute Resolution) Act 1998, s 1(2)(a), (b).

Sub-s (3): for the words in italics in para (e) there are substituted the words "the county court" by the Crime and Courts Act 2013, s 17(5), Sch 9, Pt 3, para 52, as from a day to be appointed; sub-para (f)(ia) inserted by the Employment Act 2002, s 24(1); words in square brackets in para (h) substituted by the Equality Act 2010, s 211(1), Sch 26, Pt 1, paras 27, 29, as from 1 October 2010; other words in square brackets substituted, and sub-para (f)(i) repealed, by the Employment Rights (Dispute Resolution) Act 1998, ss 1(2)(a), (b), 15, Sch 1, para 14(1), (2), Sch 2.

Sub-s (3ZA): inserted by the Employment Act 2002, s 25; words in square brackets in para (b) inserted by the Enterprise and Regulatory Reform Act 2013, s 7(2), Sch 1, paras 2, 3, as from a day to be appointed.

Sub-ss (3A), (3B): inserted, together with sub-s (3C), by the Employment Rights (Dispute Resolution) Act 1998, s 2.

Sub-ss (3AA), (3AB): inserted by the Employment Act 2008, s 4, as from 6 April 2009.

Sub-s (3C): inserted as noted above; substituted by the Employment Act 2002, s 26.

Sub-s (4): para (c) and the word immediately preceding it inserted by the Employment Rights (Dispute Resolution) Act 1998, s 15, Sch 1, para 14(1), (3).

Note: sub-s (3) did not contain a para (i) in the Queen's Printer's copy of this Act.

Regulations: the Employment Tribunals (Enforcement of Orders in Other Jurisdictions) (Scotland) Regulations 2002, SI 2002/2972; the Employment Tribunals (Constitution and Rules of Procedure) Regulations 2004, SI 2004/1861 at **[2.809]**; the Employment Tribunals (Constitution and Rules of Procedure) (Amendment) Regulations 2004, SI 2004/2351; the Employment Tribunals (Constitution and Rules of Procedure) (Amendment) Regulations 2005, SI 2005/435; the Employment Tribunals (Constitution and Rules of Procedure) (Amendment) (No 2) Regulations 2005, SI 2005/1865; the Employment Tribunals (Constitution and Rules of Procedure) (Amendment) Regulations 2010, SI 2010/131; the Employment Tribunals (Constitution and Rules of Procedure) (Amendment) Regulations 2012, SI 2012/468; the Employment Tribunals (Constitution and Rules of Procedure) Regulations 2013, SI 2013/1237 at **[2.1689]**.

**[1.690]**
**[7A Practice directions**
[(A1) The Senior President of Tribunals may make directions about the procedure of employment tribunals.]

(1) Employment tribunal procedure regulations may include provision—

(a) enabling the [territorial] President to make directions about the procedure of employment tribunals, including directions about the exercise by tribunals of powers under such regulations,

(b) for securing compliance with [directions under subsection (A1) or paragraph (a)], and

(c) about the publication of [directions under subsection (A1) or paragraph (a)].

(2) Employment tribunal procedure regulations may, instead of providing for any matter, refer to provision made or to be made about that matter by directions made [under subsection (A1) or (1)(a)].

[(2A) The power under subsection (A1) includes—

(a) power to vary or revoke directions made in exercise of the power, and

(b) power to make different provision for different purposes (including different provision for different areas).

(2B) Directions under subsection (A1) may not be made without the approval of the Lord Chancellor.

(2C) Directions under subsection (1)(a) may not be made without the approval of—

(a) the Senior President of Tribunals, and

(b) the Lord Chancellor.

(2D) Subsections (2B) and (2C)(b) do not apply to directions to the extent that they consist of guidance about any of the following—

(a) the application or interpretation of the law;

(b) the making of decisions by members of an employment tribunal.

(2E) Subsections (2B) and (2C)(b) do not apply to directions to the extent that they consist of criteria for determining which members of employment tribunals may be selected to decide particular categories of matter; but the directions may, to that extent, be made only after consulting the Lord Chancellor.]

Part 1 Statutes

(3) In this section, references to the [territorial] President are to a person appointed in accordance with regulations under section 1(1) as—

(a) President of the Employment Tribunals (England and Wales), or

(b) President of the Employment Tribunals (Scotland).]

**NOTES**

Inserted by the Employment Act 2002, s 27.

Sub-ss (A1), (2A)–(2E): inserted by the Tribunals, Courts and Enforcement Act 2007, s 48(1), Sch 8, paras 35, 41(1), (2), (5), as from 3 November 2008.

Sub-s (1): word in square brackets in para (a) inserted, and words in square brackets in paras (b), (c) substituted, by the Tribunals, Courts and Enforcement Act 2007, s 48(1), Sch 8, paras 35, 41(1), (3), as from 3 November 2008.

Sub-s (2): words in square brackets substituted by the Tribunals, Courts and Enforcement Act 2007, s 48(1), Sch 8, paras 35, 41(1), (4), as from 3 November 2008.

Sub-s (3): word in square brackets inserted by the Tribunals, Courts and Enforcement Act 2007, s 48(1), Sch 8, paras 35, 41(1), (6), as from 3 November 2008.

Regulations: the Employment Tribunals (Constitution and Rules of Procedure) Regulations 2004, SI 2004/1861 at **[2.809]**; the Employment Tribunals (Constitution and Rules of Procedure) Regulations 2013, SI 2013/1237 at **[2.1689]**.

**[1.691]**

**[7B    Mediation**

(1) Employment tribunal procedure regulations may include provision enabling practice directions to provide for members to act as mediators in relation to disputed matters in a case that is the subject of proceedings.

(2) The provision that may be included in employment tribunal procedure regulations by virtue of subsection (1) includes provision for enabling practice directions to provide for a member to act as mediator in relation to disputed matters in a case even though the member has been selected to decide matters in the case.

(3) Once a member has begun to act as mediator in relation to a disputed matter in a case that is the subject of proceedings, the member may decide matters in the case only with the consent of the parties.

(4) Staff appointed under section 40(1) of the Tribunals, Courts and Enforcement Act 2007 (staff for employment and other tribunals) may, subject to their terms of appointment, act as mediators in relation to disputed matters in a case that is the subject of proceedings.

(5) Before making a practice direction that makes provision in relation to mediation, the person making the direction must consult *the Advisory, Conciliation and Arbitration Service.*

(6) In this section—

"member" means a member of a panel of members of employment tribunals (whether or not a panel of *chairmen)*;

"practice direction" means a direction under section 7A;

"proceedings" means proceedings before an employment tribunal.]

**NOTES**

Commencement: 3 November 2008.

Inserted by the Tribunals, Courts and Enforcement Act 2007, s 48(1), Sch 8, paras 35, 42, as from 3 November 2008.

Sub-s (5): for the words in italics there is substituted "ACAS" by the Enterprise and Regulatory Reform Act 2013, s 7(2), Sch 1, paras 2, 4, as from a day to be appointed.

Sub-s (6): for the word in italics there are substituted the words "Employment Judges" by the Crime and Courts Act 2013, s 21(4), Sch 14, Pt 7, para 13(1), as from a day to be appointed.

Regulations: the Employment Tribunals (Constitution and Rules of Procedure) Regulations 2013, SI 2013/1237 at **[2.1689]**.

**[1.692]**

**8    Procedure in contract cases**

(1) Where in proceedings brought by virtue of section 3 an [employment tribunal] finds that the whole or part of a sum claimed in the proceedings is due, the tribunal shall order the respondent to the proceedings to pay the amount which it finds due.

(2) An order under section 3 may provide that an [employment tribunal] shall not in proceedings in respect of a claim, or a number of claims relating to the same contract, order the payment of an amount exceeding such sum as may be specified in the order as the maximum amount which an [employment tribunal] may order to be paid in relation to a claim or in relation to a contract.

(3) An order under section 3 may include provisions—

(a) as to the manner in which and time within which proceedings are to be brought by virtue of that section, and

(b) modifying any other enactment.

(4) An order under that section may make different provision in relation to proceedings in respect of different descriptions of claims.

**NOTES**

Sub-ss (1), (2): words in square brackets substituted by the Employment Rights (Dispute Resolution) Act 1998, s 1(2)(a).

The sum specified for the purposes of sub-s (2) is £25,000, see the Employment Tribunals Extension of Jurisdiction (England and Wales) Order 1994, SI 1994/1623, art 10 at **[2.221]**, and the Employment Tribunals Extension of Jurisdiction (Scotland) Order 1994, SI 1994/1624, art 10 at **[2.231]**.

---

**[1.693]**
## 9   Pre-hearing reviews and preliminary matters

(1)   [Employment tribunal] procedure regulations may include provision—
- (a)   *for authorising the carrying-out by an [employment tribunal] of a preliminary consideration of any proceedings before it (a "pre-hearing review"), and*
- (b)   for enabling such powers to be exercised in connection with a pre-hearing review as may be prescribed by the regulations.

(2)   Such regulations may in particular include provision—
- (a)   for authorising any tribunal carrying out a pre-hearing review under the regulations to make, in circumstances specified in the regulations, an order requiring a party to the proceedings in question, *if he wishes to continue to participate in those proceedings,* to pay a deposit of an amount not exceeding [£1,000] [as a condition of
  - (i)   continuing to participate in those proceedings, or
  - (ii)   pursuing any specified allegations or arguments], and
- (b)   for prescribing—
  - (i)   the manner in which the amount of any such deposit is to be determined in any particular case,
  - (ii)   the consequences of non-payment of any such deposit, and
  - (iii)   the circumstances in which any such deposit, or any part of it, may be refunded to the party who paid it or be paid over to another party to the proceedings.

[(2A)   Regulations under subsection (1)(b), so far as relating to striking out, may not provide for striking out on a ground which does not apply outside a pre-hearing review.]

(3)   The Secretary of State may from time to time by order substitute for the sum specified in subsection (2)(a) such other sum as is specified in the order.

(4)   [Employment tribunal] procedure regulations may also include provision for authorising an [employment tribunal] to hear and determine [separately any preliminary issue of a description prescribed by the regulations which is raised by any case].

**NOTES**

Sub-s (1): words in square brackets substituted by the Employment Rights (Dispute Resolution) Act 1998, s 1(2)(a); para (a) substituted by the Employment Act 2002, s 28(1), (2), as from a day to be appointed, as follows—

"(a)   for authorising an employment tribunal to carry out a review of any proceedings before it at any time before a hearing held for the purpose of determining them (a "pre-hearing review"),".

Sub-s (2): sum in first pair of square brackets in para (a) substituted by the Employment Tribunals (Increase of Maximum Deposit) Order 2012, SI 2012/149, art 2, as from 15 February 2012; words in italics repealed and words in second pair of square brackets inserted by the Enterprise and Regulatory Reform Act 2013, s 21(1), (2), as from 25 June 2013.

Sub-s (2A): inserted by the Employment Act 2002, s 28(1), (3).

Sub-s (4): words in square brackets substituted by the Employment Rights (Dispute Resolution) Act 1998, ss 1(2)(a), 15, Sch 1, para 15.

Regulations: the Employment Tribunals (Constitution and Rules of Procedure) Regulations 2004, SI 2004/1861 at **[2.809]**; the Employment Tribunals (Constitution and Rules of Procedure) (Amendment) Regulations 2004, SI 2004/2351; the Employment Tribunals (Constitution and Rules of Procedure) (Amendment) Regulations 2005, SI 2005/435; the Employment Tribunals (Constitution and Rules of Procedure) Regulations 2013, SI 2013/1237 at **[2.1689]**.

Orders: the Employment Tribunals (Increase of Maximum Deposit) Order 2012, SI 2012/149 (which supersedes previous Orders made under sub-s (3) above).

---

**[1.694]**
## [10   National security

(1)   If on a complaint under—
- [(a)   section 145A, 145B or 146 of the Trade Union and Labour Relations (Consolidation) Act 1992 (inducements and detriments in respect of trade union membership etc),]   . . . .
- (b)   section 111 of the Employment Rights Act 1996 (unfair dismissal), [or
- (c)   regulation 9 of the Employment Relations Act 1999 (Blacklists) Regulations 2010 (detriment connected with prohibited list)],

it is shown that the action complained of was taken for the purpose of safeguarding national security, the employment tribunal shall dismiss the complaint.

(2)   Employment tribunal procedure regulations may make provision about the composition of the tribunal (including provision disapplying or modifying section 4) for the purposes of proceedings in relation to which—
- (a)   a direction is given under subsection (3), or
- (b)   an order is made under subsection (4).

(3)   A direction may be given under this subsection by a Minister of the Crown if—
- (a)   it relates to particular Crown employment proceedings, and
- (b)   the Minister considers it expedient in the interests of national security.

(4)   An order may be made under this subsection by the President or a Regional *Chairman* in relation to particular proceedings if he considers it expedient in the interests of national security.

(5)   Employment tribunal procedure regulations may make provision enabling a Minister of the Crown, if he considers it expedient in the interests of national security—

(a)   to direct a tribunal to sit in private for all or part of particular Crown employment proceedings;

(b)   to direct a tribunal to exclude the applicant from all or part of particular Crown employment proceedings;

(c)   to direct a tribunal to exclude the applicant's representatives from all or part of particular Crown employment proceedings;

(d)   to direct a tribunal to take steps to conceal the identity of a particular witness in particular Crown employment proceedings;

(e)   to direct a tribunal to take steps to keep secret all or part of the reasons for its decision in particular Crown employment proceedings.

[(6)   Employment tribunal procedure regulations may enable a tribunal, if it considers it expedient in the interests of national security, to do in relation to particular proceedings before it anything of a kind which, by virtue of subsection (5), employment tribunal procedure regulations may enable a Minister of the Crown to direct a tribunal to do in relation to particular Crown employment proceedings.]

(7)   In relation to cases where a person has been excluded by virtue of subsection (5)(b) or (c) or (6), employment tribunal procedure regulations may make provision—

(a)   for the appointment by the Attorney General, or by the Advocate General for Scotland, of a person to represent the interests of the applicant;

(b)   about the publication and registration of reasons for the tribunal's decision;

(c)   permitting an excluded person to make a statement to the tribunal before the commencement of the proceedings, or the part of the proceedings, from which he is excluded.

(8)   Proceedings are Crown employment proceedings for the purposes of this section if the employment to which the complaint relates—

(a)   is Crown employment, or

(b)   is connected with the performance of functions on behalf of the Crown.

(9)   The reference in subsection (4) to the President or a Regional Chairman is to a person appointed in accordance with regulations under section 1(1) as—

(a)   a Regional Chairman,

(b)   President of the Employment Tribunals (England and Wales), or

(c)   President of the Employment Tribunals (Scotland).]

**NOTES**

Substituted, together with ss 10A, 10B for the original s 10, by the Employment Relations Act 1999, s 41, Sch 8, para 3.

Sub-s (1): para (a) substituted by the Employment Relations Act 2004, s 57(1), Sch 1, para 24; word omitted from para (a) repealed, and para (c) (and the word immediately preceding it) inserted, by the Employment Relations Act 1999 (Blacklists) Regulations 2010, SI 2010/493, reg 17(1), (2), as from 2 March 2010.

Sub-s (4): for the word in italics there are substituted the words "Employment Judge" by the Crime and Courts Act 2013, s 21(4), Sch 14, Pt 7, para 13(3), as from a day to be appointed.

Sub-s (6): substituted by the Employment Relations Act 2004, s 36.

Attorney General: the functions of the Attorney General may be discharged by the Solicitor General; see the Law Officers Act 1997, s 1.

Regulations: the Employment Tribunals (Constitution and Rules of Procedure) Regulations 2004, SI 2004/1861 at **[2.809]**; the Employment Tribunals (Constitution and Rules of Procedure) (Amendment) Regulations 2004, SI 2004/2351; the Employment Tribunals (Constitution and Rules of Procedure) (Amendment) Regulations 2005, SI 2005/435; the Employment Tribunals (Constitution and Rules of Procedure) (Amendment) (No 2) Regulations 2005, SI 2005/1865; the Employment Tribunals (Constitution and Rules of Procedure) Regulations 2013, SI 2013/1237 at **[2.1689]**.

**[1.695]**
**[10A   Confidential information**

(1)   Employment tribunal procedure regulations may enable an employment tribunal to sit in private for the purpose of hearing evidence from any person which in the opinion of the tribunal is likely to consist of—

(a)   information which he could not disclose without contravening a prohibition imposed by or by virtue of any enactment,

(b)   information which has been communicated to him in confidence or which he has otherwise obtained in consequence of the confidence reposed in him by another person, or

(c)   information the disclosure of which would, for reasons other than its effect on negotiations with respect to any of the matters mentioned in section 178(2) of the Trade Union and Labour Relations (Consolidation) Act 1992, cause substantial injury to any undertaking of his or in which he works.

(2)   The reference in subsection (1)(c) to any undertaking of a person or in which he works shall be construed—

(a)   in relation to a person in Crown employment, as a reference to the national interest,

(b)    in relation to a person who is a relevant member of the House of Lords staff, as a reference to the national interest or (if the case so requires) the interests of the House of Lords, and

(c)    in relation to a person who is a relevant member of the House of Commons staff, as a reference to the national interest or (if the case so requires) the interests of the House of Commons.]

**NOTES**

Substituted as noted to s 10 at **[1.694]**.

Regulations: the Employment Tribunals (Constitution and Rules of Procedure) Regulations 2004, SI 2004/1861 at **[2.809]**; the Employment Tribunals (Constitution and Rules of Procedure) Regulations 2013, SI 2013/1237 at **[2.1689]**.

**[1.696]**
**[10B    Restriction of publicity in cases involving national security**

(1)    This section applies where a tribunal has been directed under section 10(5) or has determined under section 10(6)—

(a)    to take steps to conceal the identity of a particular witness, or

(b)    to take steps to keep secret all or part of the reasons for its decision.

(2)    It is an offence to publish—

(a)    anything likely to lead to the identification of the witness, or

(b)    the reasons for the tribunal's decision or the part of its reasons which it is directed or has determined to keep secret.

(3)    A person guilty of an offence under this section is liable on summary conviction to a fine not exceeding level 5 on the standard scale.

(4)    Where a person is charged with an offence under this section it is a defence to prove that at the time of the alleged offence he was not aware, and neither suspected nor had reason to suspect, that the publication in question was of, or included, the matter in question.

(5)    Where an offence under this section committed by a body corporate is proved to have been committed with the consent or connivance of, or to be attributable to any neglect on the part of—

(a)    a director, manager, secretary or other similar officer of the body corporate, or

(b)    a person purporting to act in any such capacity,

he as well as the body corporate is guilty of the offence and liable to be proceeded against and punished accordingly.

(6)    A reference in this section to publication includes a reference to inclusion in a programme which is included in a programme service, within the meaning of the Broadcasting Act 1990.]

**NOTES**

Substituted as noted to s 10 at **[1.694]**.

**[1.697]**
**11    Restriction of publicity in cases involving sexual misconduct**

(1)    [Employment tribunal] procedure regulations may include provision—

(a)    for cases involving allegations of the commission of sexual offences, for securing that the registration or other making available of documents or decisions shall be so effected as to prevent the identification of any person affected by or making the allegation, and provision—

(b)    for cases involving allegations of sexual misconduct, enabling an [employment tribunal], on the application of any party to proceedings before it or of its own motion, to make a restricted reporting order having effect (if not revoked earlier) until the promulgation of the decision of the tribunal.

(2)    If any identifying matter is published or included in a relevant programme in contravention of a restricted reporting order—

(a)    in the case of publication in a newspaper or periodical, any proprietor, any editor and any publisher of the newspaper or periodical,

(b)    in the case of publication in any other form, the person publishing the matter, and

(c)    in the case of matter included in a relevant programme—

(i)    any body corporate engaged in providing the service in which the programme is included, and

(ii)    any person having functions in relation to the programme corresponding to those of an editor of a newspaper,

shall be guilty of an offence and liable on summary conviction to a fine not exceeding level 5 on the standard scale.

(3)    Where a person is charged with an offence under subsection (2) it is a defence to prove that at the time of the alleged offence he was not aware, and neither suspected nor had reason to suspect, that the publication or programme in question was of, or included, the matter in question.

(4)    Where an offence under subsection (2) committed by a body corporate is proved to have been committed with the consent or connivance of, or to be attributable to any neglect on the part of—

(a)    a director, manager, secretary or other similar officer of the body corporate, or

(b)    a person purporting to act in any such capacity,

he as well as the body corporate is guilty of the offence and liable to be proceeded against and punished accordingly.

(5)   In relation to a body corporate whose affairs are managed by its members "director", in subsection (4), means a member of the body corporate.

(6)   In this section—

"identifying matter", in relation to a person, means any matter likely to lead members of the public to identify him as a person affected by, or as the person making, the allegation,

"relevant programme" has the same meaning as in the Sexual Offences (Amendment) Act 1992,

"restricted reporting order" means an order—

(a)   made in exercise of a power conferred by regulations made by virtue of this section, and

(b)   prohibiting the publication in Great Britain of identifying matter in a written publication available to the public or its inclusion in a relevant programme for reception in Great Britain,

"sexual misconduct" means the commission of a sexual offence, sexual harassment or other adverse conduct (of whatever nature) related to sex, and conduct is related to sex whether the relationship with sex lies in the character of the conduct or in its having reference to the sex or sexual orientation of the person at whom the conduct is directed,

"sexual offence" means any offence to which section 4 of the Sexual Offences (Amendment) Act 1976, the Sexual Offences (Amendment) Act 1992 or section 274(2) of the Criminal Procedure (Scotland) Act 1995 applies (offences under the Sexual Offences Act 1956, Part I of the Criminal Law (Consolidation) (Scotland) Act 1995 and certain other enactments), and

"written publication" has the same meaning as in the Sexual Offences (Amendment) Act 1992.

---

**NOTES**

Sub-s (1): words in square brackets substituted by the Employment Rights (Dispute Resolution) Act 1998, s 1(2)(a).

Sexual Offences (Amendment) Act 1976, s 4: repealed by Youth Justice and Criminal Evidence Act 1999, ss 48, 67(3), Sch 2, para 4, Sch 6.

Sexual Offences (Amendment) Act 1992: the definition "written publication" in that Act was repealed by the Youth Justice and Criminal Evidence Act 1999, ss 48, 67(3), Sch 2, paras 6, 12(1), (2), Sch 6.

Regulations: the Employment Tribunals (Constitution and Rules of Procedure) Regulations 2004, SI 2004/1861 at **[2.809]**; the Employment Tribunals (Constitution and Rules of Procedure) Regulations 2013, SI 2013/1237 at **[2.1689]**.

---

**[1.698]**

## 12   Restriction of publicity in disability cases

(1)   This section applies to proceedings on a complaint under [section 120 of the Equality Act 2010, where the complaint relates to disability] in which evidence of a personal nature is likely to be heard by the [employment tribunal] hearing the complaint.

(2)   [Employment tribunal] procedure regulations may include provision in relation to proceedings to which this section applies for—

(a)   enabling an [employment tribunal], on the application of the complainant or of its own motion, to make a restricted reporting order having effect (if not revoked earlier) until the promulgation of the decision of the tribunal, and

(b)   where a restricted reporting order is made in relation to a complaint which is being dealt with by the tribunal together with any other proceedings, enabling the tribunal to direct that the order is to apply also in relation to those other proceedings or such part of them as the tribunal may direct.

(3)   If any identifying matter is published or included in a relevant programme in contravention of a restricted reporting order—

(a)   in the case of publication in a newspaper or periodical, any proprietor, any editor and any publisher of the newspaper or periodical,

(b)   in the case of publication in any other form, the person publishing the matter, and

(c)   in the case of matter included in a relevant programme—

(i)   any body corporate engaged in providing the service in which the programme is included, and

(ii)   any person having functions in relation to the programme corresponding to those of an editor of a newspaper,

shall be guilty of an offence and liable on summary conviction to a fine not exceeding level 5 on the standard scale.

(4)   Where a person is charged with an offence under subsection (3), it is a defence to prove that at the time of the alleged offence he was not aware, and neither suspected nor had reason to suspect, that the publication or programme in question was of, or included, the matter in question.

(5)   Where an offence under subsection (3) committed by a body corporate is proved to have been committed with the consent or connivance of, or to be attributable to any neglect on the part of—

(a)   a director, manager, secretary or other similar officer of the body corporate, or

(b)   a person purporting to act in any such capacity,

he as well as the body corporate is guilty of the offence and liable to be proceeded against and punished accordingly.

(6)   In relation to a body corporate whose affairs are managed by its members "director", in subsection (5), means a member of the body corporate.

(7)   In this section—

"evidence of a personal nature" means any evidence of a medical, or other intimate, nature which might reasonably be assumed to be likely to cause significant embarrassment to the complainant if reported,

"identifying matter" means any matter likely to lead members of the public to identify the complainant or such other persons (if any) as may be named in the order,

"promulgation" has such meaning as may be prescribed by regulations made by virtue of this section,

"relevant programme" means a programme included in a programme service, within the meaning of the Broadcasting Act 1990,

"restricted reporting order" means an order—

(a)   made in exercise of a power conferred by regulations made by virtue of this section, and

(b)   prohibiting the publication in Great Britain of identifying matter in a written publication available to the public or its inclusion in a relevant programme for reception in Great Britain, and

"written publication" includes a film, a sound track and any other record in permanent form but does not include an indictment or other document prepared for use in particular legal proceedings.

**NOTES**

Sub-s (1): words in first pair of square brackets substituted by the Equality Act 2010, s 211(1), Sch 26, Pt 1, paras 27, 30, as from 1 October 2010; words in second pair of square brackets substituted by the Employment Rights (Dispute Resolution) Act 1998, s 1(2)(a).

Sub-s (2): words in square brackets substituted by the Employment Rights (Dispute Resolution) Act 1998, s 1(2)(a).

Regulations: the Employment Tribunals (Constitution and Rules of Procedure) Regulations 2004, SI 2004/1861 at **[2.809]**; the Employment Tribunals (Constitution and Rules of Procedure) Regulations 2013, SI 2013/1237 at **[2.1689]**.

*[Financial penalties*

**[1.699]**
**12A   Financial penalties**

(1)   Where an employment tribunal determining a claim involving an employer and a worker—

(a)   concludes that the employer has breached any of the worker's rights to which the claim relates, and

(b)   is of the opinion that the breach has one or more aggravating features,

the tribunal may order the employer to pay a penalty to the Secretary of State (whether or not it also makes a financial award against the employer on the claim).

(2)   The tribunal shall have regard to an employer's ability to pay—

(a)   in deciding whether to order the employer to pay a penalty under this section;

(b)   (subject to subsections (3) to (7)) in deciding the amount of a penalty.

(3)   The amount of a penalty under this section shall be—

(a)   at least £100;

(b)   no more than £5,000.

This subsection does not apply where subsection (5) or (7) applies.

(4)   Subsection (5) applies where an employment tribunal—

(a)   makes a financial award against an employer on a claim, and

(b)   also orders the employer to pay a penalty under this section in respect of the claim.

(5)   In such a case, the amount of the penalty under this section shall be 50% of the amount of the award, except that—

(a)   if the amount of the financial award is less than £200, the amount of the penalty shall be £100;

(b)   if the amount of the financial award is more than £10,000, the amount of the penalty shall be £5,000.

(6)   Subsection (7) applies, instead of subsection (5), where an employment tribunal—

(a)   considers together two or more claims involving different workers but the same employer, and

(b)   orders the employer to pay a penalty under this section in respect of any of those claims.

(7)   In such a case—

(a)   the amount of the penalties in total shall be at least £100;

(b)   the amount of a penalty in respect of a particular claim shall be—

(i)   no more than £5,000, and

(ii)   where the tribunal makes a financial award against the employer on the claim, no more than 50% of the amount of the award.

But where the tribunal makes a financial award on any of the claims and the amount awarded is less than £200 in total, the amount of the penalties in total shall be £100 (and paragraphs (a) and (b) shall not apply).

(8)  Two or more claims in respect of the same act and the same worker shall be treated as a single claim for the purposes of this section.

(9)  Subsection (5) or (7) does not require or permit an order under subsection (1) (or a failure to make such an order) to be reviewed where the tribunal subsequently awards compensation under—

(a)  section 140(3) of the Trade Union and Labour Relations (Consolidation) Act 1992 (failure to comply with tribunal's recommendation),

(b)  section 117 of the Employment Rights Act 1996 (failure to reinstate etc),

(c)  section 124(7) of the Equality Act 2010 (failure to comply with tribunal's recommendation), or

(d)  any other provision empowering the tribunal to award compensation, or further compensation, for a failure to comply (or to comply fully) with an order or recommendation of the tribunal.

(10)  An employer's liability to pay a penalty under this section is discharged if 50% of the amount of the penalty is paid no later than 21 days after the day on which notice of the decision to impose the penalty is sent to the employer.

(11)  In this section—

"claim"—

(a)  means anything that is referred to in the relevant legislation as a claim, a complaint or a reference, other than a reference made by virtue of section 122(2) or 128(2) of the Equality Act 2010 (reference by court of question about a non-discrimination or equality rule etc), and

(b)  also includes an application, under regulations made under section 45 of the Employment Act 2002, for a declaration that a person is a permanent employee;

"employer" has the same meaning as in Part 4A of the Employment Rights Act 1996, and also—

(a)  in relation to an individual seeking to be employed by a person as a worker, includes that person;

(b)  in relation to a right conferred by section 47A or 63A of the Employment Rights Act 1996 (right to time off for young person for study or training), includes the principal within the meaning of section 63A(3) of that Act;

(c)  in relation to a right conferred by the Agency Workers Regulations 2010 (SI 2010/93), includes the hirer within the meaning of those Regulations and (where the worker is not actually employed by the temporary work agency) the temporary work agency within that meaning;

"financial award" means an award of a sum of money, but does not including anything payable by virtue of section 13;

"worker" has the same meaning as in Part 4A of the Employment Rights Act 1996, and also includes an individual seeking to be employed by a person as a worker.

(12)  The Secretary of State may by order—

(a)  amend subsection (3), (5) or (7) by substituting a different amount;

(b)  amend subsection (5), (7) or (10) by substituting a different percentage;

(c)  amend this section so as to alter the meaning of "claim".

(13)  The Secretary of State shall pay sums received under this section into the Consolidated Fund.]

**NOTES**

Commencement: to be appointed.

Inserted, together with preceding cross-heading, by the Enterprise and Regulatory Reform Act 2013, s 16(1), as from a day to be appointed, subject to s 24(5) of the 2013 Act at **[1.1855]**.

*[Costs etc, interest and enforcement]*

**NOTES**

The words in square brackets in the heading above are inserted by the Enterprise and Regulatory Reform Act 2013, s 16(2), Sch 3, paras 2, 3, as from a day to be appointed.

**[1.700]**

**13  Costs and expenses**

[(1)  Employment tribunal procedure regulations may include provision—

(a)  for the award of costs or expenses;

(b)  for the award of any allowances payable under section 5(2)(c) or (3).

(1A)  Regulations under subsection (1) may include provision authorising an employment tribunal to have regard to a person's ability to pay when considering the making of an award against him under such regulations.

(1B) Employment tribunal procedure regulations may include provision for authorising an employment tribunal—

(a)   to disallow all or part of the costs or expenses of a representative of a party to proceedings before it by reason of that representative's conduct of the proceedings;

(b)   to order a representative of a party to proceedings before it to meet all or part of the costs or expenses incurred by a party by reason of the representative's conduct of the proceedings;

(c)   to order a representative of a party to proceedings before it to meet all or part of any allowances payable by the Secretary of State under section 5(2)(c) or (3) by reason of the representative's conduct of the proceedings.

(1C) Employment tribunal procedure regulations may also include provision for taxing or otherwise settling the costs or expenses referred to in subsection (1)(a) or (1B)(b) (and, in particular in England and Wales, for enabling the amount of such costs to be assessed by way of detailed assessment in *a county court*).]

(2)   In relation to proceedings under section 111 of the Employment Rights Act 1996—

(a)   where the employee has expressed a wish to be reinstated or re-engaged which has been communicated to the employer at least seven days before the hearing of the complaint,

      . . .

(b)   . . .

[employment tribunal] procedure regulations shall include provision for requiring the employer to pay the costs or expenses of any postponement or adjournment of the hearing caused by his failure, without a special reason, to adduce reasonable evidence as to the availability of the job from which the complainant was dismissed   . . .   or of comparable or suitable employment.

**NOTES**

Sub-ss (1), (1A)–(1C): substituted, for the original sub-s (1), by the Employment Act 2002, s 22(1); for the words in italics in sub-s (1C) there are substituted the words "the county court" by the Crime and Courts Act 2013, s 17(5), Sch 9, Pt 3, para 52, as from a day to be appointed.

Sub-s (2): words in square brackets substituted by the Employment Rights (Dispute Resolution) Act 1998, s 1(2)(a); words omitted repealed by the Employment Relations Act 1999, ss 9, 44, Sch 4, Pt III, paras 1, 4, Sch 9(2).

Regulations: the Employment Tribunals (Constitution and Rules of Procedure) Regulations 2004, SI 2004/1861 at **[2.809]**; the Employment Tribunals (Constitution and Rules of Procedure) Regulations 2013, SI 2013/1237 at **[2.1689]**.

**[1.701]**
**[13A   Payments in respect of preparation time**

(1)   Employment tribunal procedure regulations may include provision for authorising an employment tribunal to order a party to proceedings before it to make a payment to any other party in respect of time spent in preparing that other party's case.

(2)   Regulations under subsection (1) may include provision authorising an employment tribunal to have regard to a person's ability to pay when considering the making of an order against him under such regulations.

(3)   If employment tribunal procedure regulations include—

(a)   provision of the kind mentioned in subsection (1), and

(b)   provision of the kind mentioned in section 13(1)(a),

they shall also[, subject to subsection (4),] include provision to prevent an employment tribunal exercising its powers under both kinds of provision in favour of the same person in the same proceedings.

[(4)   Subsection (3) does not require the regulations to include provision to prevent an employment tribunal from making—

(a)   an order of the kind mentioned in subsection (1), and

(b)   an award of the kind mentioned in section 13(1)(a) that is limited to witnesses' expenses.]]

**NOTES**

Inserted by the Employment Act 2002, s 22(2).

Sub-s (3): words in square brackets inserted by the Enterprise and Regulatory Reform Act 2013, s 21(1), (3)(a), as from 25 June 2013.

Sub-s (4): added by the Enterprise and Regulatory Reform Act 2013, s 21(1), (3)(b), as from 25 April 2013 (so far as is necessary for enabling the exercise of any power to make regulations) and as from 25 June 2013 (otherwise).

Regulations: the Employment Tribunals (Constitution and Rules of Procedure) Regulations 2004, SI 2004/1861 at **[2.809]**; the Employment Tribunals (Constitution and Rules of Procedure) Regulations 2013, SI 2013/1237 at **[2.1689]**.

**[1.702]**
**14   Interest**

(1)   The Secretary of State may by order made with the approval of the Treasury provide that sums payable in pursuance of decisions of [employment tribunals] shall carry interest at such rate and between such times as may be prescribed by the order.

(2)   Any interest due by virtue of such an order shall be recoverable as a sum payable in pursuance of the decision.

(3)   The power conferred by subsection (1) includes power—

(a)   to specify cases or circumstances in which interest is not payable,
(b)   to provide that interest is payable only on sums exceeding a specified amount or falling
      between specified amounts,
(c)   to make provision for the manner in which and the periods by reference to which interest
      is to be calculated and paid,
(d)   to provide that any enactment—
      (i)    does or does not apply in relation to interest payable by virtue of subsection (1), or
      (ii)   applies to it with such modifications as may be specified in the order,
(e)   to make provision for cases where sums are payable in pursuance of decisions or awards
      made on appeal from [employment tribunals],
(f)   to make such incidental or supplemental provision as the Secretary of State considers
      necessary.
(4)   In particular, an order under subsection (1) may provide that the rate of interest shall be the
rate specified in section 17 of the Judgments Act 1838 as that enactment has effect from time
to time.

**NOTES**

Sub-ss (1), (3): words in square brackets substituted by the Employment Rights (Dispute Resolution) Act 1998, s 1(2)(b).
Orders: as of 6 April 2013 no Orders had been made under this section but, by virtue of s 44 of, and Sch 2, Pt I, paras 1–4
to, this Act, the Employment Tribunals (Interest) Order 1990, SI 1990/479 at **[2.120]** has effect as if made under this section.

**[1.703]**
**15   Enforcement**
(1)   Any sum payable in pursuance of a decision of an [employment tribunal] in England and
Wales which has been registered in accordance with [employment tribunal] procedure regulations
[shall be recoverable by execution issued from *a county court* or otherwise as if it were payable
under an order of *a county court*].
(2)   Any order for the payment of any sum made by an [employment tribunal] in Scotland (or any
copy of such an order certified by the Secretary of the Tribunals) may be enforced as if it were an
extract registered decree arbitral bearing a warrant for execution issued by the sheriff court of any
sheriffdom in Scotland.
(3)   In this section a reference to a decision or order of an [employment tribunal]—
(a)   does not include a decision or order which, on being reviewed, has been revoked by the
      tribunal, and
(b)   in relation to a decision or order which on being reviewed, has been varied by the tribunal,
      shall be construed as a reference to the decision or order as so varied.

**NOTES**

Sub-s (1): words in first and second pairs of square brackets substituted by the Employment Rights (Dispute Resolution) Act
1998, s 1(2)(a); words in third pair of square brackets substituted by the Tribunals, Courts and Enforcement Act 2007, s 48(1),
Sch 8, paras 35, 43, as from 1 April 2009; for the words "a county court" in italics there are substituted the words "the county
court" by the Crime and Courts Act 2013, s 17(5), Sch 9, Pt 3, para 52, as from a day to be appointed.
Note: the Tribunals, Courts and Enforcement Act 2007, s 62(3), Sch 13, para 125 (in force from a day to be appointed)
provides that in sub-s (1) for the words "by execution issued from the county court" there are substituted the words "under
section 85 of the County Courts Act 1984". Para 125 of the 2007 Act is amended by the Crime and Courts Act 2013, s 25(9)(d)
(as from a day to be appointed) so that it reads as follows:

"In section 15 of the Employment Tribunals Act 1996 (enforcement), in subsection (1) for the words from "by execution",
to "court" in the first place after "by execution", substitute "under section 85 of the County Courts Act 1984".".

Sub-ss (2), (3): words in square brackets substituted by the Employment Rights (Dispute Resolution) Act 1998, s 1(2)(a).

*Recoupment of social security benefits*

**[1.704]**
**16   Power to provide for recoupment of benefits**
(1)   This section applies to payments which are the subject of proceedings before [employment
tribunals] and which are—
(a)   payments of wages or compensation for loss of wages,
(b)   payments by employers to employees under sections 146 to 151, sections 168 to 173 or
      section 192 of the Trade Union and Labour Relations (Consolidation) Act 1992,
(c)   payments by employers to employees under—
      (i)    Part III, V, VI or VII,
      (ii)   section 93, or
      (iii)  Part X,
      of the Employment Rights Act 1996, . . .
(d)   payments by employers to employees of a nature similar to, or for a purpose corresponding
      to the purpose of, payments within paragraph (b) or (c), [or
(e)   payments by employers to employees under regulation 5, 6 or 9 of the Employment
      Relations Act 1999 (Blacklists) Regulations 2010,]

and to payments of remuneration under a protective award under section 189 of the Trade Union and Labour Relations (Consolidation) Act 1992.

(2)   The Secretary of State may by regulations make with respect to payments to which this section applies provision for any or all of the purposes specified in subsection (3).

(3)   The purposes referred to in subsection (2) are—

(a)   enabling the Secretary of State to recover from an employer, by way of total or partial recoupment of [universal credit,] jobseeker's allowance, [*income support* or income-related employment and support allowance]—

  (i)   a sum not exceeding the amount of the prescribed element of the monetary award, or

  (ii)   in the case of a protective award, the amount of the remuneration,

(b)   requiring or authorising an [employment tribunal] to order the payment of such a sum, by way of total or partial recoupment of [universal credit,] [jobseeker's allowance, *income support* or income-related employment and support allowance], to the Secretary of State instead of to an employee, and

(c)   requiring an [employment tribunal] to order the payment to an employee of only the excess of the prescribed element of the monetary award over the amount of any [universal credit,] jobseeker's allowance, [*income support* or income-related employment and support allowance] shown to the tribunal to have been paid to the employee and enabling the Secretary of State to recover from the employer, by way of total or partial recoupment of the benefit, a sum not exceeding that amount.

(4)   Regulations under this section may be framed—

(a)   so as to apply to all payments to which this section applies or to one or more classes of those payments, and

[(b)   so as to apply to all or any of the benefits mentioned in subsection (3)].

(5)   Regulations under this section may—

(a)   confer powers and impose duties on [employment tribunals] or  . . . .  other persons,

(b)   impose on an employer to whom a monetary award or protective award relates a duty—

  (i)   to furnish particulars connected with the award, and

  (ii)   to suspend payments in pursuance of the award during any period prescribed by the regulations,

(c)   provide for an employer who pays a sum to the Secretary of State in pursuance of this section to be relieved from any liability to pay the sum to another person,

[(cc)   provide for the determination by the Secretary of State of any issue arising as to the total or partial recoupment in pursuance of the regulations of [universal credit,] a jobseeker's allowance, unemployment benefit, [income support or income-related employment and support allowance],

(d)   confer on an employee a right of appeal to an appeal tribunal constituted under Chapter I of Part I of the Social Security Act 1998 against any decision of the Secretary of State on any such issue, and]

(e)   provide for the proof in proceedings before [employment tribunals] (whether by certificate or in any other manner) of any amount of [universal credit,] jobseeker's allowance, [*income support* or income-related employment and support allowance] paid to an employee.

(6)   Regulations under this section may make different provision for different cases.

NOTES

Sub-s (1): words in square brackets substituted by the Employment Rights (Dispute Resolution) Act 1998, s 1(2)(b); word omitted from para (c) repealed, and para (e) (and the word immediately preceding it) inserted, by the Employment Relations Act 1999 (Blacklists) Regulations 2010, SI 2010/493, reg 17(1), (3), as from 2 March 2010.

Sub-s (3): words "employment tribunal" in square brackets substituted by the Employment Rights (Dispute Resolution) Act 1998, s 1(2)(a); words "universal credit," in square brackets in paras (a), (b) and (c) inserted by the Universal Credit (Consequential, Supplementary, Incidental and Miscellaneous Provisions) Regulations 2013, SI 2013/630, reg 11(1), (2)(a), as from 29 April 2013; other words in square brackets substituted by the Welfare Reform Act 2007, s 28, Sch 3, Pt 1, para 15(1), (2)(a), (b); the words ", income support" in italics in paras (a), (b), (c) are repealed by the Welfare Reform Act 2009, ss 9(3)(b), 58(1), Sch 7, Pt 1, as from a day to be appointed (for further provisions in relation to the abolition of income support, see s 9(1), (2), (4)–(10) of that Act).

Sub-s (4): para (b) substituted by the Welfare Reform Act 2007, s 28, Sch 3, Pt 1, para 15(1), (2)(c).

Sub-s (5): words in square brackets in para (a), and words in first pair of square brackets in para (e), substituted by the Employment Rights (Dispute Resolution) Act 1998, s 1(2)(b); words omitted from para (a) repealed, and paras (cc), (d) substituted for the original para (d), by the Social Security Act 1998, s 86, Sch 7, para 147, Sch 8; words in second pair of square brackets in para (cc), and words in third pair of square brackets in para (e), substituted by the Welfare Reform Act 2007, s 28, Sch 3, Pt 1, para 15(1), (2)(a); words in first pair of square brackets in para (cc) and words in second pair of square brackets in para (e) inserted by SI 2013/630, reg 11(1), (2)(b), (3), as from 29 April 2013; the words ", income support" in italics in para (e) repealed by the Welfare Reform Act 2009, ss 9(3)(b), 58(1), Sch 7, Pt 1, as from a day to be appointed (for further provisions in relation to the abolition of income support, see s 9(1), (2), (4)–(10) of that Act, and note that the 2009 Act does not provide for the repeal of these words in para (cc) of this subsection).

Regulations: the Employment Protection (Recoupment of Benefits) Regulations 1996, SI 1996/2349 at **[2.246]**.

**[1.705]**

**17 Recoupment: further provisions**

(1) Where in pursuance of any regulations under section 16 a sum has been recovered by or paid to the Secretary of State by way of total or partial recoupment of [universal credit,] jobseeker's allowance[, *income support* or income-related employment and support allowance]—

    (a) no sum shall be recoverable under Part III *or V* of the Social Security Administration Act 1992, and

    (b) no abatement, payment or reduction shall be made by reference to the [universal credit,] jobseeker's allowance[, *income support* or income-related employment and support allowance] recouped.

(2) Any amount found to have been duly recovered by or paid to the Secretary of State in pursuance of regulations under section 16 by way of total or partial recoupment of jobseeker's allowance shall be paid into the National Insurance Fund.

(3) In section 16—

"monetary award" means the amount which is awarded, or ordered to be paid, to the employee by the tribunal or would be so awarded or ordered apart from any provision of regulations under that section, and

"the prescribed element", in relation to any monetary award, means so much of that award as is attributable to such matters as may be prescribed by regulations under that section.

(4) In section 16 "income-based jobseeker's allowance" has the same meaning as in the Jobseekers Act 1995.

[(5) In this section and section 16 "income-related employment and support allowance" means an income-related allowance under Part 1 of the Welfare Reform Act 2007 (employment and support allowance).]

**NOTES**

Sub-s (1): words "universal credit," inserted by the Universal Credit (Consequential, Supplementary, Incidental and Miscellaneous Provisions) Regulations 2013, SI 2013/630, reg 11(1), (4), as from 29 April 2013; other words in square brackets substituted by the Welfare Reform Act 2007, s 28, Sch 3, Pt 1, para 15(1), (3), as from 27 October 2008; words ", income support" in italics in both places they occur and words "or V" in italics repealed by the Welfare Reform Act 2009, ss 9(3)(b), 58(1), Sch 7, Pt 1, as from a day to be appointed (for further provisions in relation to the abolition of income support, see s 9(1), (2), (4)–(10) of that Act).

Sub-s (5): added by the Welfare Reform Act 2007, s 28, Sch 3, Pt 1, para 15(1), (4), as from 18 March 2008 (for the purpose of making regulations), and as from 27 October 2008 (otherwise).

*Conciliation*

**[1.706]**

**18 Conciliation[: relevant proceedings etc]**

(1) *This section applies in the case of [employment tribunal] proceedings and claims which could be the subject of [employment tribunal] proceedings—*

    [(a) under section 120 or 127 of the Equality Act 2010,]

    (b) arising out of a contravention, or alleged contravention, of section 64, 68[, 70B] [, 86], 137, 138, [145A, 145B,] 146, 168, [168A,] 169, 170, 174, 188 or 190 of the Trade Union and Labour Relations (Consolidation) Act 1992 [or paragraph 156 of Schedule A1 to that Act],

    (c) . . .

    (d) [under or] arising out of a contravention, or alleged contravention, of section 8, 13, 15, 18(1), 21(1), 28[, [63F(4), (5) or (6), 63I(1)(b),] [80G(1), 80H(1)(b),] 80(1)][, 92 or 135,] or of Part V, VI, VII or X, of the Employment Rights Act 1996,

    [(dd) under or by virtue of section 11, 18, *20(1)(a)* or 24 of the National Minimum Wage Act 1998;]

    (e) which are proceedings in respect of which an [employment tribunal] has jurisdiction by virtue of section 3 of this Act, . . .

    (f) *[under or] arising out of a contravention, or alleged contravention, of a provision specified by an order under subsection (8)(b) as a provision to which this paragraph applies [* . . .

    (ff) under regulation 30 of the Working Time Regulations 1998,] [ . . .

    (g) under regulation 27 or 32 of the Transnational Information and Consultation of Employees Regulations 1999,][ . . .

    (h) arising out of a contravention, or alleged contravention of regulation [5(1) or] 7(2) of the Part-time Workers (Prevention of Less Favourable Treatment) Regulations 2000,]

    [(i) arising out of a contravention, or alleged contravention, of regulation 3 or 6(2) of the Fixed-term Employees (Prevention of Less Favourable Treatment) Regulations 2002; . . .

    (j) under regulation 9 of those Regulations], [ . . .

    (k), (l)] . . .

    [(m) under regulation 18 of the Merchant Shipping (Working Time: Inland Waterways) Regulations 2003] [ . . .

    (n) *under regulation 41 or 45 of the European Public Limited-Liability Company Regulations 2004,]* [[(o)] under regulation 19 of the Fishing Vessels (Working Time: Sea-fishermen) Regulations 2004], [ . . .

(p) under regulation 29 or 33 of the Information and Consultation of Employees Regulations 2004], [ . . .

(q) under paragraph 4 or 8 of the Schedule to the Occupational and Personal Pension Schemes (Consultation by Employers and Miscellaneous Amendment) Regulations 2006], [ . . .

(r) . . .

[(s) under regulation 30 or 34 of the European Cooperative Society (Involvement of Employees) Regulations 2006], [ . . .

(t) under regulation 45 or 51 of the Companies (Cross-Border Mergers) Regulations 2007][, . . .

(u) under regulation 17 of the Cross-border Railway Services (Working Time) Regulations 2008][, . . .

(v) under section 56 of the Pensions Act 2008][, or

(v) under regulation 28 or 32 of the European Public Limited-Liability Company (Employee Involvement) (Great Britain) Regulations 2009(SI 2009/2401)][, . . .

(w) under regulation 5, 6 or 9 of the Employment Relations Act 1999 (Blacklists) Regulations 2010][, or

(x) arising out of a contravention, or alleged contravention of regulation 5, 12, 13 or 17(2) of the Agency Workers Regulations 2010].

[(1A) Sections 18A and 18B apply in the case of matters which could be the subject of relevant proceedings, and section 18C applies in the case of relevant proceedings themselves.]

*(2) Where an application has been presented to an [employment tribunal], and a copy of it has been sent to a conciliation officer, it is the duty of the conciliation officer—*

*(a) if he is requested to do so by the person by whom and the person against whom the proceedings are brought, or*

*(b) if, in the absence of any such request, the conciliation officer considers that he could act under this subsection with a reasonable prospect of success,*

*to endeavour to promote a settlement of the proceedings without their being determined by an [employment tribunal].*

[(2A) . . . ]

*(3) Where at any time—*

*(a) a person claims that action has been taken in respect of which proceedings could be brought by him before an [employment tribunal], but*

*(b) before any application relating to that action has been presented by him a request is made to a conciliation officer (whether by that person or by the person against whom the proceedings could be instituted) to make his services available to them,*

the conciliation officer [may endeavour to promote a settlement between the parties without proceedings being instituted].

*(4) Where a person who has presented a complaint to an [employment tribunal] under section 111 of the Employment Rights Act 1996 has ceased to be employed by the employer against whom the complaint was made, the conciliation officer shall (for the purpose of promoting a settlement of the complaint in accordance with subsection (2)) in particular—*

*(a) seek to promote the reinstatement or re-engagement of the complainant by the employer, or by a successor of the employer or by an associated employer, on terms appearing to the conciliation officer to be equitable, or*

*(b) where the complainant does not wish to be reinstated or re-engaged, or where reinstatement or re-engagement is not practicable, and the parties desire the conciliation officer to act, seek to promote agreement between them as to a sum by way of compensation to be paid by the employer to the complainant.*

*[(5) Where a conciliation officer acts pursuant to subsection (3) in a case where the person claiming as specified in paragraph (a) of that subsection has ceased to be employed by the employer and the proceedings which he claims could be brought by him are proceedings under section 111 of the Employment Rights Act 1996, the conciliation officer may in particular—*

*(a) seek to promote the reinstatement or re-engagement of that person by the employer, or by a successor of the employer or by an associated employer, on terms appearing to the conciliation officer to be equitable, or*

*(b) where the person does not wish to be reinstated or re-engaged, or where reinstatement or re-engagement is not practicable, seek to promote agreement between them as to a sum by way of compensation to be paid by the employer to that person.]*

(6) In proceeding under *this section* a conciliation officer shall, where appropriate, have regard to the desirability of encouraging the use of other procedures available for the settlement of grievances.

(7) Anything communicated to a conciliation officer in connection with the performance of his functions under *this section* shall not be admissible in evidence in any proceedings before an [employment tribunal], except with the consent of the person who communicated it to that officer.

(8) The Secretary of State [and the Lord Chancellor, acting jointly,] may by order—

(a)    direct that further provisions of the Employment Rights Act 1996 be added to the list in
       subsection (1)(d), or

(b)    specify a provision of any other Act as a provision to which subsection (1)(f) applies.

[(9)   An order under subsection (8) that adds employment tribunal proceedings to the list in
subsection (1) may amend an enactment so as to extend the time limit for instituting those
proceedings in such a way as appears necessary or expedient in order to facilitate the conciliation
process provided for by section 18A.

(10)   An order under subsection (8) that removes employment tribunal proceedings from the list in
subsection (1) may—

(a)    repeal or revoke any provision of an enactment that, for the purpose mentioned in
       subsection (9), extends the time limit for instituting those proceedings;

(b)    make further amendments which are consequential on that repeal or revocation.]

**NOTES**

Section heading: words in square brackets inserted by the Enterprise and Regulatory Reform Act 2013, s 7(2), Sch 1, paras 2, 5(1), (2), as from a day to be appointed.

Sub-s (1) has been amended as follows:

For the first words in italics there are substituted the words "In this section and sections 18A to 18C "relevant proceedings" means employment tribunal proceedings—" by the Enterprise and Regulatory Reform Act 2013, s 7(2), Sch 1, paras 2, 5(1), (3), as from a day to be appointed.

Words "employment tribunal" in square brackets (in every place they occur) substituted by the Employment Rights (Dispute Resolution) Act 1998, s 1(2)(a).

Para (a) substituted by the Equality Act 2010, s 211(1), Sch 26, Pt 1, paras 27, 31(a), as from 1 October 2010.

In para (b) figure ", 70B" and final words in square brackets inserted by the Enterprise and Regulatory Reform Act 2013, s 7(2), Sch 1, paras 2, 5(1), (4), as from a day to be appointed.

In para (b) figure ", 86" in square brackets inserted by the Employment Rights (Dispute Resolution) Act 1998, s 15, Sch 1, para 16.

In para (b) figures "145A, 145B," in square brackets inserted by the Employment Relations Act 2004, s 57(1), Sch 1, para 25.

In para (b) figure "168A," in square brackets inserted by the Employment Act 2002, s 53, Sch 7, para 23(1), (2)(a).

Para (c) repealed by the Equality Act 2010, s 211, Sch 26, Pt 1, paras 27, 31(b), Sch 27, Pt 1, as from 1 October 2010.

In para (d) words "under or" and reference to "80G(1), 80H(1)(b)," in square brackets inserted by the Employment Act 2002, s 53, Sch 7, para 23(1), (2)(b).

In para (d) words "63F(4), (5) or (6), 63I(1)(b)," in square brackets inserted by the Apprenticeships, Skills, Children and Learning Act 2009, s 40(5), Sch 1, para 16, as from 6 April 2010 (except in relation to small employers and their employees), and as from a day to be appointed (otherwise) (as to the meaning of "small employers" etc, see further the notes at **[1.481]**).

In para (d) figure ", 80(1)" in square brackets inserted by virtue of the Employment Tribunals (Application of Conciliation Provisions) Order 2000, SI 2000/1337, art 2.

In para (d) words ", 92 or 135," in square brackets substituted by the Employment Rights (Dispute Resolution) Act 1998, s 11(1).

Para (dd) inserted by the National Minimum Wage Act 1998, s 30(1); for the reference in italics there is substituted "19D(1)(a)" by the Enterprise and Regulatory Reform Act 2013, s 7(2), Sch 1, paras 2, 5(1), (5), as from a day to be appointed. Note that new ss 19, 19A–19H were substituted for ss 19–22, 22A–22F of the 1998 Act by the Employment Act 2008, s 9(1), as from 6 April 2009. It is therefore believed that the reference to s 20(1)(a) of the 1998 Act in this paragraph should (as from 6 April 2009) be read as a reference to s 19D(1)(a) of the 1998 Act but no amendment to this effect was made by the 2008 Act.

Word omitted from para (e) repealed by the Working Time Regulations 1998, SI 1998/1833, reg 33(a).

In para (f), words in square brackets inserted by the Employment Act 2002, s 53, Sch 7, para 23(1), (2)(c) and words omitted repealed by the Transnational Information and Consultation of Employees Regulations 1999, SI 1999/3323, reg 33(1)(a). Para (f) is repealed by the Enterprise and Regulatory Reform Act 2013, s 7(2), Sch 1, paras 2, 5(1), (6), as from a day to be appointed.

Para (ff) inserted by SI 1998/1833, reg 33(b).

Word omitted from para (ff) repealed by the Part-time Workers (Prevention of Less Favourable Treatment) Regulations 2000, SI 2000/1551, reg 10, Schedule, para 1(a)(i).

Para (g) and the word immediately preceding it added by SI 1999/3323, reg 33(1)(b).

Word omitted from para (g) repealed by the Fixed-term Employees (Prevention of Less Favourable Treatment) Regulations 2002, SI 2002/2034, reg 11, Sch 2, Pt 1, para 2(a)(i).

Para (h) and the word immediately preceding it added by SI 2000/1551, reg 10, Schedule, para 1(a)(ii).

In para (h) words "5(1) or" in square brackets inserted by the Part-time Workers (Prevention of Less Favourable Treatment) Regulations 2001, SI 2001/1107, reg 2.

Para (i) added by SI 2002/2034, reg 11, Sch 2, Pt 1, para 2(a)(ii).

Word omitted from para (i) repealed by the Employment Equality (Sexual Orientation) Regulations 2003, SI 2003/1661, reg 39, Sch 5, para 1(a)(i).

Para (j) added by SI 2002/2034, reg 11, Sch 2, Pt 1, para 2(a)(ii).

Word omitted from para (j) repealed by the Employment Equality (Religion or Belief) Regulations 2003, SI 2003/1660, reg 39(2), Sch 5, para 1(a)(i).

Para (k) (and the word immediately preceding it) added by SI 2003/1661, reg 39, Sch 5, para 1(a)(ii); repealed by the Equality Act 2010, s 211, Sch 26, Pt 1, paras 27, 31(b), Sch 27, Pt 1, as from 1 October 2010.

Para (l) added by SI 2003/1660, reg 39(5), Sch 5, para 1(a)(ii); repealed by the Equality Act 2010, s 211, Sch 26, Pt 1, paras 27, 31(b), Sch 27, Pt 1, as from 1 October 2010.

Para (m) added by SI 2003/3049, reg 20, Sch 2, para 2(1), (2).

Word omitted from para (m) repealed by the Information and Consultation of Employees Regulations 2004, SI 2004/3426, reg 34(a).

Para (n) and the word immediately preceding it added by the European Public Limited-Liability Company Regulations 2004, SI 2004/2326, reg 46. Para (n) is repealed by the Enterprise and Regulatory Reform Act 2013, s 7(2), Sch 1, paras 2, 5(1), (6), as from a day to be appointed.

Para (o) added by the Fishing Vessels (Working Time: Sea-fishermen) Regulations 2004, SI 2004/1713, reg 21, Sch 2, para 1(1), (2). Note that this paragraph was originally added as para (n) and was redesignated as para (o) by SI 2004/3426, reg 34(b).

Para (p) and the word immediately preceding it added by SI 2004/3426, reg 34(c).

Para (q) and the word immediately preceding it added, and word omitted from para (o) repealed, by the Occupational and Personal Pension Schemes (Consultation by Employers and Miscellaneous Amendment) Regulations 2006, SI 2006/349, reg 17, Schedule, para 9.

Para (r) (and the word immediately preceding it) added, and word omitted from para (p) repealed, by the Employment Equality (Age) Regulations 2006, SI 2006/1031, reg 49(1), Sch 8, Pt 1, paras 18, 19(1), (2); repealed by the Equality Act 2010, s 211, Sch 26, Pt 1, paras 27, 31(b), Sch 27, Pt 1, as from 1 October 2010.

Para (s) added, and word omitted from para (q) repealed, by the European Cooperative Society (Involvement of Employees) Regulations 2006, SI 2006/2059, reg 35.

Para (t) (and the word immediately preceding it) added by the Companies (Cross-Border Mergers) Regulations 2007, SI 2007/2974, reg 52.

Para (u) and the word immediately preceding it added, and word omitted from para (s) repealed, by the Cross-border Railway Services (Working Time) Regulations 2008, SI 2008/1660, reg 19, Sch 3, para 1(a), as from 27 July 2008

First para (v) and the word immediately preceding it added by the Pensions Act 2008, s 56(6), as from 30 June 2012.

Second para (v) and the word immediately preceding it added, and word omitted from para (t) repealed, by the European Public Limited-Liability Company (Employee Involvement) (Great Britain) Regulations 2009, SI 2009/2401, reg 33, as from 1 October 2009.

Para (w) and the word immediately preceding it added, and word omitted from para (u) repealed, by the Employment Relations Act 1999 (Blacklists) Regulations 2010, SI 2010/493, reg 17(1), (4), as from 2 March 2010.

Para (x) and the word immediately preceding it added, and word omitted from the second para (v) repealed, by the Agency Workers Regulations 2010, SI 2010/93, reg 25, Sch 2, Pt 1, para 8(a), as from 1 October 2011.

Sub-s (1A): inserted by the Enterprise and Regulatory Reform Act 2013, s 7(2), Sch 1, paras 2, 5(1), (7), as from a day to be appointed.

Sub-ss (2), (4): words in square brackets substituted by the Employment Rights (Dispute Resolution) Act 1998, s 1(2)(a); repealed by the Enterprise and Regulatory Reform Act 2013, s 7(2), Sch 1, paras 2, 5(1), (8), as from a day to be appointed.

Sub-s (2A): originally inserted by the Employment Act 2002, s 24(2), and repealed by the Employment Act 2008, ss 6(1), 20, Schedule, Pt 1, as from 6 April 2009.

Sub-s (3): words in first pair of square brackets substituted by the Employment Rights (Dispute Resolution) Act 1998, s 1(2)(a); words in second pair of square brackets substituted by the Employment Act 2008, s 5(1), (2), as from 6 April 2009; repealed by the Enterprise and Regulatory Reform Act 2013, s 7(2), Sch 1, paras 2, 5(1), (8), as from a day to be appointed.

Sub-s (5): substituted by the Employment Act 2008, s 5(1), (3), as from 6 April 2009; repealed by the Enterprise and Regulatory Reform Act 2013, s 7(2), Sch 1, paras 2, 5(1), (8), as from a day to be appointed.

Sub-s (6): for the words in italics there are substituted the words "any of sections 18A to 18C", by the Enterprise and Regulatory Reform Act 2013, s 7(2), Sch 1, paras 2, 5(1), (9), as from a day to be appointed.

Sub-s (7): for the words in italics there are substituted the words "any of sections 18A to 18C", by the Enterprise and Regulatory Reform Act 2013, s 7(2), Sch 1, paras 2, 5(1), (9), as from a day to be appointed; words in square brackets substituted by the Employment Rights (Dispute Resolution) Act 1998, s 1(2)(a).

Sub-s (8): words in square brackets inserted by the Tribunals, Courts and Enforcement Act 2007, s 48(1), Sch 8, paras 35, 38; for paras (a), (b) in italics there are substituted the words "amend the definition of "relevant proceedings" in subsection (1) by adding to or removing from the list in that subsection particular types of employment tribunal proceedings.", by the Enterprise and Regulatory Reform Act 2013, s 9(1), (2), as from a day to be appointed.

Sub-ss (9), (10): added by the Enterprise and Regulatory Reform Act 2013, s 9(1), (3), as from 25 April 2013 (so far as is necessary for enabling the exercise of any power to make orders) and as from a day to be appointed (otherwise).

Note: the Employment Relations Act 1999, ss 10–13, are to be treated as provisions of the Employment Rights Act 1996, Pt V, for the purposes of sub-s (1)(d) above; see s 14 of the 1999 Act at **[1.1195]**.

Orders: the Employment Tribunals Act (Application of Conciliation Provisions) Order 2000, SI 2000/1299 (revoked by SI 2000/1336 without coming into force); the Employment Tribunals Act (Application of Conciliation Provisions) Order 2000 (Revocation) Order 2000, SI 2000/1336; the Employment Tribunals Act 1996 (Application of Conciliation Provisions) Order 2000, SI 2000/1337 (which amends sub-s (1)(d) as noted above and specifies that the Trade Union and Labour Relations (Consolidation) Act 1992, s 70B, Sch 1, para 156 are provisions to which sub-s (1)(f) above applies).

**[1.707]**
**[18A   Requirement to contact ACAS before instituting proceedings**
(1)   Before a person ("the prospective claimant") presents an application to institute relevant proceedings relating to any matter, the prospective claimant must provide to ACAS prescribed information, in the prescribed manner, about that matter.
This is subject to subsection (7).
(2)   On receiving the prescribed information in the prescribed manner, ACAS shall send a copy of it to a conciliation officer.
(3)   The conciliation officer shall, during the prescribed period, endeavour to promote a settlement between the persons who would be parties to the proceedings.
(4)   If—
   (a)   during the prescribed period the conciliation officer concludes that a settlement is not possible, or
   (b)   the prescribed period expires without a settlement having been reached,
the conciliation officer shall issue a certificate to that effect, in the prescribed manner, to the prospective claimant.
(5)   The conciliation officer may continue to endeavour to promote a settlement after the expiry of the prescribed period.

(6)   In subsections (3) to (5) "settlement" means a settlement that avoids proceedings being instituted.

(7)   A person may institute relevant proceedings without complying with the requirement in subsection (1) in prescribed cases.

The cases that may be prescribed include (in particular)—

cases where the requirement is complied with by another person instituting relevant proceedings relating to the same matter;

cases where proceedings that are not relevant proceedings are instituted by means of the same form as proceedings that are;

cases where section 18B applies because ACAS has been contacted by a person against whom relevant proceedings are being instituted.

(8)   A person who is subject to the requirement in subsection (1) may not present an application to institute relevant proceedings without a certificate under subsection (4).

(9)   Where a conciliation officer acts under this section in a case where the prospective claimant has ceased to be employed by the employer and the proposed proceedings are proceedings under section 111 of the Employment Rights Act 1996, the conciliation officer may in particular—

(a)   seek to promote the reinstatement or re-engagement of the prospective claimant by the employer, or by a successor of the employer or by an associated employer, on terms appearing to the conciliation officer to be equitable, or

(b)   where the prospective claimant does not wish to be reinstated or re-engaged, or where reinstatement or re-engagement is not practicable, seek to promote agreement between them as to a sum by way of compensation to be paid by the employer to the prospective claimant.

(10)   In subsections (1) to (7) "prescribed" means prescribed in employment tribunal procedure regulations.

(11)   The Secretary of State may by employment tribunal procedure regulations make such further provision as appears to the Secretary of State to be necessary or expedient with respect to the conciliation process provided for by subsections (1) to (8).

(12)   Employment tribunal procedure regulations may (in particular) make provision—

(a)   authorising the Secretary of State to prescribe, or prescribe requirements in relation to, any form which is required by such regulations to be used for the purpose of providing information to ACAS under subsection (1) or issuing a certificate under subsection (4);

(b)   requiring ACAS to give a person any necessary assistance to comply with the requirement in subsection (1);

(c)   for the extension of the period prescribed for the purposes of subsection (3);

(d)   treating the requirement in subsection (1) as complied with, for the purposes of any provision extending the time limit for instituting relevant proceedings, by a person who is relieved of that requirement by virtue of subsection (7)(a).]

**NOTES**

Commencement: 25 April 2013 (so far as is necessary for enabling the exercise of any power to make regulations); to be appointed (otherwise).

Inserted, together with s 18B, by the Enterprise and Regulatory Reform Act 2013, s 7(1), as from 25 April 2013 (so far as is necessary for enabling the exercise of any power to make regulations) and as from a day to be appointed (otherwise).

**[1.708]**
**[18B   Conciliation before institution of proceedings: other ACAS duties**

(1)   This section applies where—

(a)   a person contacts ACAS requesting the services of a conciliation officer in relation to a matter that (if not settled) is likely to give rise to relevant proceedings against that person, and

(b)   ACAS has not received information from the prospective claimant under section 18A(1).

(2)   This section also applies where—

(a)   a person contacts ACAS requesting the services of a conciliation officer in relation to a matter that (if not settled) is likely to give rise to relevant proceedings by that person, and

(b)   the requirement in section 18A(1) would apply to that person but for section 18A(7).

(3)   Where this section applies a conciliation officer shall endeavour to promote a settlement between the persons who would be parties to the proceedings.

(4)   If at any time—

(a)   the conciliation officer concludes that a settlement is not possible, or

(b)   a conciliation officer comes under the duty in section 18A(3) to promote a settlement between the persons who would be parties to the proceedings,

the duty in subsection (3) ceases to apply at that time.

(5)   In subsections (3) and (4) "settlement" means a settlement that avoids proceedings being instituted.

(6)   Subsection (9) of section 18A applies for the purposes of this section as it applies for the purposes of that section.]

NOTES
Commencement: to be appointed.
Inserted as noted to s 18A at [**1.707**].

**[1.709]**
**[18C  Conciliation after institution of proceedings**
(1)  Where an application instituting relevant proceedings has been presented to an employment tribunal, and a copy of it has been sent to a conciliation officer, the conciliation officer shall endeavour to promote a settlement—
    (a)    if requested to do so by the person by whom and the person against whom the proceedings are brought, or
    (b)    if, in the absence of any such request, the conciliation officer considers that the officer could act under this section with a reasonable prospect of success.
(2)  Where a person who has presented a complaint to an employment tribunal under section 111 of the Employment Rights Act 1996 has ceased to be employed by the employer against whom the complaint was made, the conciliation officer may in particular—
    (a)    seek to promote the reinstatement or re-engagement of the complainant by the employer, or by a successor of the employer or by an associated employer, on terms appearing to the conciliation officer to be equitable, or
    (b)    where the complainant does not wish to be reinstated or re-engaged, or where reinstatement or re-engagement is not practicable, and the parties desire the conciliation officer to act, seek to promote agreement between them as to a sum by way of compensation to be paid by the employer to the complainant.
(3)  In subsection (1) "settlement" means a settlement that brings proceedings to an end without their being determined by an employment tribunal.]

NOTES
Commencement: to be appointed.
Inserted by the Enterprise and Regulatory Reform Act 2013, s 7(2), Sch 1, paras 2, 6, as from a day to be appointed.

**[1.710]**
**19  Conciliation procedure**
[(1)]  [Employment tribunal] procedure regulations shall include in relation to [employment tribunal] proceedings in the case of which any enactment makes provision for conciliation—
    (a)    provisions requiring a copy of the application by which the proceedings are instituted, and a copy of any notice relating to it which is lodged by or on behalf of the person against whom the proceedings are brought, to be sent to a conciliation officer, [and]
    (b)    provisions securing that the applicant and the person against whom the proceedings are brought are notified that the services of a conciliation officer are available to them,  . . .
    (c)    . . .
[(2)  . . . ]

NOTES
Sub-s (1): numbered as such by the Employment Act 2002, s 24(4); word omitted from para (b) and the whole of para (c) repealed by ss 24(3), 54 of, and Sch 8 to, the 2002 Act; word "and" in square brackets inserted by s 53 of, and Sch 7, para 23(1), (3) to, the 2002 Act; other words in square brackets substituted by the Employment Rights (Dispute Resolution) Act 1998, s 1(2)(a).
Sub-s (2): originally added by the Employment Act 2002, s 24(4), and repealed by the Employment Act 2008, ss 6(2), 20, Schedule, Pt 1, as from 6 April 2009.
Regulations: the Employment Tribunals (Constitution and Rules of Procedure) Regulations 2004, SI 2004/1861 at [**2.809**]; the Employment Tribunals (Constitution and Rules of Procedure) Regulations 2013, SI 2013/1237 at [**2.1689**].

**[1.711]**
**[19A  Conciliation: recovery of sums payable under *compromises***
(1)  Subsections (3) to (6) apply if—
    (a)    a conciliation officer—
        (i)    has taken action under *section 18* in a case, and
        (ii)    issues a certificate in writing stating that a *compromise* has been reached in the case, and
    (b)    all of the terms of the *compromise* are set out—
        (i)    in a single relevant document, or
        (ii)    in a combination of two or more relevant documents.
(2)  A document is a "relevant document" for the purposes of subsection (1) if—
    (a)    it is the certificate, or
    (b)    it is a document that is referred to in the certificate or that is referred to in a document that is within this paragraph.

(3)   Any sum payable by a person under the terms of the *compromise* (a "*compromise* sum") shall, subject to subsections (4) to (7), be recoverable—

(a)   in England and Wales, by execution issued from *a county court* or otherwise as if the sum were payable under an order of that court;

(b)   in Scotland, by diligence as if the certificate were an extract registered decree arbitral bearing a warrant for execution issued by the sheriff court of any sheriffdom in Scotland.

(4)   A *compromise* sum is not recoverable under subsection (3) if—

(a)   the person by whom it is payable applies for a declaration that the sum would not be recoverable from him under the general law of contract, and

(b)   that declaration is made.

(5)   If rules of court so provide, a *compromise* sum is not recoverable under subsection (3) during the period—

(a)   beginning with the issue of the certificate, and

(b)   ending at such time as may be specified in, or determined under, rules of court.

(6)   If the terms of the *compromise* provide for the person to whom a *compromise* sum is payable to do anything in addition to discontinuing or not starting proceedings, that sum is recoverable by him under subsection (3)—

(a)   in England and Wales, only if *a county court* so orders;

(b)   in Scotland, only if the sheriff so orders.

(7)   Once an application has been made for a declaration under subsection (4) in relation to a sum, no further reliance may be placed on subsection (3) for the recovery of the sum while the application is pending.

(8)   An application for a declaration under subsection (4) may be made to an employment tribunal, *a county court* or the sheriff.

(9)   Employment tribunal procedure regulations may (in particular) make provision as to the time within which an application to an employment tribunal for a declaration under subsection (4) is to be made.

(10)   Rules of court may make provision as to—

(a)   the time within which an application to *a county court* for a declaration under subsection (4) is to be made;

(b)   the time within which an application to the sheriff for a declaration under subsection (4) is to be made;

(c)   when an application (whether made to *a county court*, the sheriff or an employment tribunal) for a declaration under subsection (4) is pending for the purposes of subsection (7).

(11)   Nothing in this section shall be taken to prejudice any rights or remedies that a person has apart from this section.

(12)   In this section "*compromise*" (except in the phrase "*compromise* sum") means a settlement, *or compromise,* to avoid proceedings or bring proceedings to an end.]

**NOTES**

Commencement: 1 April 2009.

Inserted by the Tribunals, Courts and Enforcement Act 2007, s 142, as from 1 April 2009.

Section heading: for the word in italics there is substituted the word "settlements" by the Enterprise and Regulatory Reform Act 2013, s 23(2)(c), as from a day to be appointed.

For the words "a county court" in each place they appear in italics there are substituted the words "the county court" by the Crime and Courts Act 2013, s 17(5), Sch 9, Pt 3, para 52, as from a day to be appointed.

For the word "compromise" in each place it appears in italics in sub-ss (1), (3)–(6), there is substituted the word "settlement" by the Enterprise and Regulatory Reform Act 2013, s 23(2)(a), as from a day to be appointed.

Sub-s (1): for the words "section 18" in italics there are substituted the words "any of sections 18A to 18C" by the Enterprise and Regulatory Reform Act 2013, s 7(2), Sch 1, paras 2, 7, as from a day to be appointed.

Subordinate Legislation: the Act of Sederunt (Summary Applications, Statutory Applications and Appeals etc Rules) Amendment (Employment Tribunals Act 1996) 2009, SSI 2009/109.

Sub-s (12): for the word "compromise" in the first two places it appears in italics, there is substituted the word "settlement", and the words ", or compromise," are repealed, by the Enterprise and Regulatory Reform Act 2013, s 23(2)(b), as from a day to be appointed.

# PART II
# THE EMPLOYMENT APPEAL TRIBUNAL

*Introductory*

**[1.712]**
## 20   The Appeal Tribunal

(1)   The Employment Appeal Tribunal ("the Appeal Tribunal") shall continue in existence.

(2)   The Appeal Tribunal shall have a central office in London but may sit at any time and in any place in Great Britain.

(3)   The Appeal Tribunal shall be a superior court of record and shall have an official seal which shall be judicially noticed.

[(4) Subsection (2) is subject to regulation 34 of the Transnational Information and Consultation of Employees Regulations [1999,] [regulation 46(1) of the European Public Limited-Liability Company Regulations] [2004,] [regulation 36(1) of the Information and Consultation of Employees Regulations] [2004,] [regulation 37(1) of the European Cooperative Society (Involvement of Employees) Regulations] [2006,] [regulation 58(1) of the Companies (Cross-Border Mergers) Regulations 2007] [and regulation 33(1) of the European Public Limited-Liability Company (Employee Involvement) (Great Britain) Regulations 2009 (SI 2009/2401)].]

**NOTES**

Sub-s (4): added by the Transnational Information and Consultation of Employees Regulations 1999, SI 1999/3323, reg 35(1), (2), and subsequently amended as follows:

Entry relating to the European Public Limited-Liability Company Regulations inserted by the European Public Limited-Liability Company Regulations 2004, SI 2004/2326, reg 48(2).

Entry relating to the Information and Consultation of Employees Regulations inserted by the Information and Consultation of Employees Regulations 2004, SI 2004/3426, reg 36(2).

Entry relating to the European Cooperative Society (Involvement of Employees) Regulations inserted by the European Cooperative Society (Involvement of Employees) Regulations 2006, SI 2006/2059, reg 37.

Entry relating to the Companies (Cross-Border Mergers) Regulations inserted by the Companies (Cross-Border Mergers) Regulations 2007, SI 2007/2974, reg 58(2)(b).

Entry relating to the European Public Limited-Liability Company (Employee Involvement) (Great Britain) Regulations 2009 inserted by the European Public Limited-Liability Company (Employee Involvement) (Great Britain) Regulations 2009, SI 2009/2401, reg 35(2)(b), as from 1 October 2009.

The other amendments in sub-s (4) are purely grammatical changes made by the same Regulations noted above, ie, the substitution of a particular year and the word "and", with the same year and a comma.

*Jurisdiction*

**[1.713]**
**21 Jurisdiction of Appeal Tribunal**
(1) An appeal lies to the Appeal Tribunal on any question of law arising from any decision of, or arising in any proceedings before, an [employment tribunal] under or by virtue of—
(a)–(c). . .
(d) the Trade Union and Labour Relations (Consolidation) Act 1992,
(e) . . .
(f) the Employment Rights Act 1996, [ . . .
[(ff) . . . ]
[(fg) . . . ]
[(g) this Act,
(ga) the National Minimum Wage Act 1998,
(gb) the Employment Relations Act 1999],
[(gc) the Equality Act 2006,]
[(gd) the Pensions Act 2008,]
[(gd) the Equality Act 2010,]]
[(h) the Working Time Regulations 1998, . . .
(i) the Transnational Information and Consultation of Employees Regulations 1999]; [ . . .
(j) the Part-time Workers (Prevention of Less Favourable Treatment) Regulations 2000,][ . . .
(k) the Fixed-term Employees (Prevention of Less Favourable Treatment) Regulations 2002,][ . . .
(l) . . . ][ . . .
(m) . . . ],
[(n) the Merchant Shipping (Working Time: Inland Waterways) Regulations 2003], [ . . .
(o) the European Public Limited-Liability Company Regulations 2004],
[[(p)] the Fishing Vessels (Working Time: Sea-fishermen) Regulations 2004], [ . . .
(q) the Information and Consultation of Employees Regulations 2004], [ . . .
(r) the Schedule to the Occupational and Personal Pension Schemes (Consultation by Employers and Miscellaneous Amendment) Regulations 2006], [ . . .
(s) . . . ][, . . .
(t) the European Cooperative Society (Involvement of Employees) Regulations 2006], [ . . .
(u) the Companies (Cross-Border Mergers) Regulations 2007][, . . .
(v) the Cross-border Railway Services (Working Time) Regulations 2008][, . . .
(w) the European Public Limited-Liability Company (Employee Involvement) (Great Britain) Regulations 2009 (SI 2009/2401)][, . . .
(x) the Employment Relations Act 1999 (Blacklists) Regulations 2010][, or
(y) the Agency Workers Regulations 2010].
(2) No appeal shall lie except to the Appeal Tribunal from any decision of an [employment tribunal] under or by virtue of the Acts listed [or the Regulations referred to] in subsection (1).

(3)   Subsection (1) does not affect any provision contained in, or made under, any Act which provides for an appeal to lie to the Appeal Tribunal (whether from an [employment tribunal], the Certification Officer or any other person or body) otherwise than on a question to which that subsection applies.

[(4)   The Appeal Tribunal also has any jurisdiction in respect of matters other than appeals which is conferred on it by or under—

   (a)   the Trade Union and Labour Relations (Consolidation) Act 1992,

   (b)   this Act, or

   (c)   any other Act].

**NOTES**

Sub-s (1) has been amended as follows:

Words in first pair of square brackets substituted by the Employment Rights (Dispute Resolution) Act 1998, s 1(2)(a).

Paras (a)–(c), (e) repealed by the Equality Act 2010, s 211, Sch 26, Pt 1, paras 27, 32(a), Sch 27, Pt 1, as from 1 October 2010 (see further the savings note below).

Word omitted from para (f) repealed by the National Minimum Wage Act 1998, s 53, Sch 3.

Para (ff) originally inserted by the National Minimum Wage Act 1998, s 29 (see further the notes below).

Para (fg) originally inserted by the Tax Credits Act 1999, s 7, Sch 3, para 5, and repealed by the Tax Credits Act 2002, s 60, Sch 6.

Para (g) added by the Employment Rights (Dispute Resolution) Act 1998, s 15, Sch 1, para 17(1), (2) (see further the notes below).

Paras (g), (ga), (gb) substituted, for the original para (ff) (as inserted as noted above) and the original para (g) (as inserted as noted above), by the Employment Relations Act 2004, s 38.

Para (gc) inserted by the Equality Act 2006, s 40, Sch 3, para 57.

Para (gd) inserted by the Pensions Act 2008, s 59, as from 30 June 2012.

Para (ge) inserted by the Equality Act 2010, s 211(1), Sch 26, Pt 1, paras 27, 32(b), as from 1 October 2010.

Paras (h), (i) substituted (for words that appeared in the original para (g) (as inserted as noted above)) by the Transnational Information and Consultation of Employees Regulations 1999, SI 1999/3323, reg 35(1), (3).

Word omitted from para (h) repealed, and para (j) and the word immediately preceding it added, by the Part-time Workers (Prevention of Less Favourable Treatment) Regulations 2000, SI 2000/1551, reg 10, Schedule, para 1(b).

Word omitted from para (i) repealed, and para (k) and the word immediately preceding it added, by the Fixed-term Employees (Prevention of Less Favourable Treatment) Regulations 2002, SI 2002/2034, reg 11, Sch 2, Pt 1, para 2(b).

Word omitted from para (j) repealed, and para (l) and the word immediately preceding it added, by the Employment Equality (Sexual Orientation) Regulations 2003, SI 2003/1661, reg 39, Sch 5, para 1(b); para (l) subsequently repealed by the Equality Act 2010, s 211, Sch 26, Pt 1, paras 27, 32(a), Sch 27, Pt 1, as from 1 October 2010 (see further the savings note below).

Word omitted from para (k) repealed, and para (m) and the word immediately preceding it added, by the Employment Equality (Religion or Belief) Regulations 2003, SI 2003/1660, reg 39(2), Sch 5, para 1(b); para (m) subsequently repealed by the Equality Act 2010, s 211, Sch 26, Pt 1, paras 27, 32(a), Sch 27, Pt 1, as from 1 October 2010 (see further the savings note below).

Word omitted from para (l) repealed, and para (n) added, by the Merchant Shipping (Working Time: Inland Waterways) Regulations 2003, SI 2003/3049, reg 20, Sch 2, para 2(1), (3).

Word omitted from para (n) repealed by the Information and Consultation of Employees Regulations 2004, SI 2004/3426, reg 37(a).

Para (o) and the word immediately preceding it added by the European Public Limited-Liability Company Regulations 2004, SI 2004/2326, reg 49.

Para (p) inserted by the Fishing Vessels (Working Time: Sea-fishermen) Regulations 2004, SI 2004/1713, reg 21, Sch 2, para 1(1), (3). Note that this paragraph was originally added as para (o) and was redesignated as para (p) by SI 2004/3426, reg 37(b).

Para (q) and the word immediately preceding it added by SI 2004/3426, reg 37(c).

Para (r) and the word immediately preceding it added, and word omitted from para (p) repealed, by the Occupational and Personal Pension Schemes (Consultation by Employers and Miscellaneous Amendment) Regulations 2006, SI 2006/349, reg 17, Schedule, para 10.

Para (s) and the word immediately preceding it added, and word omitted from para (q) repealed, by the Employment Equality (Age) Regulations 2006, SI 2006/1031, reg 49(1), Sch 8, Pt 1, paras 18, 20; para (s) subsequently repealed by the Equality Act 2010, s 211, Sch 26, Pt 1, paras 27, 32(a), Sch 27, Pt 1, as from 1 October 2010 (see further the savings note below).

Para (t) and the word immediately preceding it added, and word omitted from para (r) repealed, by the European Cooperative Society (Involvement of Employees) Regulations 2006, SI 2006/2059, reg 38.

Para (u) and the word immediately preceding it added, and word omitted from para (s) repealed, by the Companies (Cross-Border Mergers) Regulations 2007, SI 2007/2974, reg 59.

Para (v) and the word immediately preceding it added, and word omitted from para (t) repealed, by the Cross-border Railway Services (Working Time) Regulations 2008, SI 2008/1660, reg 19, Sch 3, para 1(b), as from 27 July 2008.

Para (w) and the word immediately preceding it added, and word omitted from para (u) repealed, by the European Public Limited-Liability Company (Employee Involvement) (Great Britain) Regulations 2009, SI 2009/2401, reg 36, as from 1 October 2009.

Para (x) and the word immediately preceding it added, and word omitted from para (v) repealed, by the Employment Relations Act 1999 (Blacklists) Regulations 2010, SI 2010/493, reg 17(1), (5), as from 2 March 2010.

Para (y) and the word immediately preceding it added, and word omitted from para (w) repealed, by the Agency Workers Regulations 2010, SI 2010/93, reg 25, Sch 2, Pt 1, para 8(b)(i), as from 1 October 2011.

Sub-s (2): words in first pair of square brackets substituted by the Employment Rights (Dispute Resolution) Act 1998, s 1(2)(a); words in second pair of square brackets inserted by SI 1998/1833, reg 34(b).

Sub-s (3): words square brackets substituted by the Employment Rights (Dispute Resolution) Act 1998, s 1(2)(a).

Sub-s (4): added by the Employment Rights (Dispute Resolution) Act 1998, s 15, Sch 1, para 17(1), (3).

Savings: sub-s (1)(a)–(c), (e), (l), (m) and (s) related to the EAT's jurisdiction under the Equal Pay Act 1970, the Sex Discrimination Act 1975, the Race Relations Act 1976, the Disability Discrimination Act 1995, the Employment Equality

(Sexual Orientation) Regulations 2003, the Employment Equality (Religion or Belief) Regulations 2003, and the Employment Equality (Age) Regulations 2006 respectively (all of which were repealed or revoked by the Equality Act 2010, as from 1 October 2010). The Equality Act 2010 (Commencement No 4, Savings, Consequential, Transitional, Transitory and Incidental Provisions and Revocation) Order 2010, SI 2010/2317, art 15 at **[2.1568]** provides that the 2010 Act does not apply where the act complained of occurs wholly before 1 October 2010 so that (a) nothing in the 2010 Act affects (i) the operation of a previous enactment or anything duly done or suffered under a previous enactment; (ii) any right, obligation or liability acquired or incurred under a previous enactment; (iii) any penalty incurred in relation to any unlawful act under a previous enactment; (iv) any investigation, legal proceeding or remedy in respect of any such right, obligation, liability or penalty; and (b) any such investigation, legal proceeding or remedy may be instituted, continued or enforced, and any such penalty may be imposed, as if the 2010 Act had not been commenced. By art 1 of the 2010 Order "previous enactment" includes the six enactments listed *ante*.

Appeal Tribunal: the Tribunals and Inquiries Act 1992, s 11 (appeals from certain tribunals) does not apply in relation to proceedings before employment tribunals which arise under or by virtue of any of the enactments mentioned in sub-s (1) above; see s 11(2) of the 1992 Act.

See also as a source of authority to hear appeals, the Transfer of Undertakings (Protection of Employment) Regulations 2006, SI 2006/246, reg 16(2) at **[2.1012]**.

*Membership etc*

**[1.714]**

## 22 Membership of Appeal Tribunal

(1)  The Appeal Tribunal shall consist of—

(a)  such number of judges as may be nominated from time to time [by the Lord Chief Justice, after consulting the Lord Chancellor,] from the judges  . . .  of the High Court and the Court of Appeal [and the judges within subsection (2A)],

(b)  at least one judge of the Court of Session nominated from time to time by the Lord President of the Court of Session, and

(c)  such number of other members as may be appointed from time to time by Her Majesty on the joint recommendation of the Lord Chancellor and the Secretary of State ("appointed members").

(2)  The appointed members shall be persons who appear to the Lord Chancellor and the Secretary of State to have special knowledge or experience of industrial relations either—

(a)  as representatives of employers, or

(b)  as representatives of workers (within the meaning of the Trade Union and Labour Relations (Consolidation) Act 1992).

[(2A)  A person is a judge within this subsection if the person—

(a)  is the Senior President of Tribunals,

(b)  is a deputy judge of the High Court,

(c)  is the Judge Advocate General,

(d)  is a Circuit judge,

(e)  is a Chamber President, or a Deputy Chamber President, of a chamber of the Upper Tribunal or of a chamber of the First-tier Tribunal,

(f)  is a judge of the Upper Tribunal by virtue of appointment under paragraph 1(1) of Schedule 3 to the Tribunals, Courts and Enforcement Act 2007,

(g)  is a transferred-in judge of the Upper Tribunal (see section 31(2) of that Act),

(h)  is a deputy judge of the Upper Tribunal (whether under paragraph 7 of Schedule 3 to, or section 31(2) of, that Act),

(i)  is a district judge, which here does not include a deputy district judge, or

(j)  is a District Judge (Magistrates' Courts), which here does not include a Deputy District Judge (Magistrates' Courts).]

(3)  The [Lord Chief Justice shall] appoint one of the judges nominated under subsection (1) to be the President of the Appeal Tribunal.

[(3A)  The Lord Chief Justice must not make an appointment under subsection (3) unless—

(a)  he has consulted the Lord Chancellor, and

(b)  the Lord President of the Court of Session agrees.]

(4)  No judge shall be nominated a member of the Appeal Tribunal [under subsection (1)(b)] except with his consent.

[(5)  The Lord Chief Justice may nominate a judicial office holder (as defined in section 109(4) of the Constitutional Reform Act 2005) to exercise his functions under this section.

(6)  The Lord President of the Court of Session may nominate a judge of the Court of Session who is a member of the First or Second Division of the Inner House of that Court to exercise his functions under subsection (3A)(b).]

**NOTES**

Sub-s (1): words in first pair of square brackets substituted, and words omitted repealed, by the Constitutional Reform Act 2005, ss 15, 146, Sch 4, Pt 1, paras 245, 246(1), (2), Sch 18, Pt 2; words in second pair of square brackets inserted by the Crime and Courts Act 2013, s 21(4), Sch 14, Pt 5, para 11(1), (2), as from a day to be appointed.

Sub-s (2A): inserted by the Crime and Courts Act 2013, s 21(4), Sch 14, Pt 5, para 11(1), (3), as from a day to be appointed.

Sub-s (3): words in square brackets substituted by the Constitutional Reform Act 2005, s 15, Sch 4, Pt 1, paras 245, 246(1), (3).

Sub-ss (3A), (5), (6): inserted and added respectively by the Constitutional Reform Act 2005, s 15, Sch 4, Pt 1, paras 245, 246(1), (4), (5).

Sub-s (4): words in square brackets inserted by the Crime and Courts Act 2013, s 21(4), Sch 14, Pt 5, para 11(1), (4), as from a day to be appointed.

---

**[1.715]**
## 23   Temporary membership

(1)   At any time when—
    (a)    the office of President of the Appeal Tribunal is vacant, or
    (b)    the person holding that office is temporarily absent or otherwise unable to act as the President of the Appeal Tribunal,
the [Lord Chief Justice] may nominate another judge nominated under section 22(1)(a) to act temporarily in his place.

(2)   At any time when a judge of the Appeal Tribunal nominated under paragraph (a) or (b) of subsection (1) of section 22 is temporarily absent or otherwise unable to act as a member of the Appeal Tribunal—
    (a)    in the case of a judge nominated under paragraph (a) of that subsection, the [Lord Chief Justice] may nominate another judge who is qualified to be nominated under that paragraph to act temporarily in his place, and
    (b)    in the case of a judge nominated under paragraph (b) of that subsection, the Lord President of the Court of Session may nominate another judge who is qualified to be nominated under that paragraph to act temporarily in his place.

(3)   At any time when an appointed member of the Appeal Tribunal is temporarily absent or otherwise unable to act as a member of the Appeal Tribunal, the Lord Chancellor and the Secretary of State may jointly appoint a person appearing to them to have the qualifications for appointment as an appointed member to act temporarily in his place.

(4)   A person nominated or appointed to act temporarily in place of the President or any other member of the Appeal Tribunal, when so acting, has all the functions of the person in whose place he acts.

(5)   No judge shall be nominated to act temporarily as a member of the Appeal Tribunal except with his consent.

[(6)   The functions conferred on the Lord Chief Justice by the preceding provisions of this section may be exercised only after consulting the Lord Chancellor.

(7)   The functions conferred on the Lord Chancellor by subsection (3) may be exercised only after consultation with the Lord Chief Justice.

(8)   The Lord Chief Justice may nominate a judicial office holder (as defined in section 109(4) of the Constitutional Reform Act 2005) to exercise his functions under this section.]

---

**NOTES**
Sub-ss (1), (2): words in square brackets substituted by the Constitutional Reform Act 2005, s 15, Sch 4, Pt 1, paras 245, 247(1)–(3).

Sub-ss (6)–(8): added by the Constitutional Reform Act 2005, s 15, Sch 4, Pt 1, paras 245, 247(1), (4).

**[1.716]**
## 24   Temporary additional judicial membership

[(1)   This section applies if both of the following conditions are met—
    (a)    the Lord Chancellor thinks that it is expedient, after consulting the Lord Chief Justice, for a qualified person to be appointed to be a temporary additional judge of the Appeal Tribunal in order to facilitate in England and Wales the disposal of business in the Appeal Tribunal;
    (b)    the Lord Chancellor requests the Lord Chief Justice to make such an appointment.

(1A)   The Lord Chief Justice may, after consulting the Lord Chancellor, appoint a qualified person as mentioned in subsection (1)(a).

(1B)   An appointment under this section is—
    (a)    for such period, or
    (b)    on such occasions,
as the Lord Chief Justice determines, after consulting the Lord Chancellor.]

(2)   In [this section] "qualified person" means a person who—
    (a)    is qualified for appointment as a judge of the High Court under section 10 of the [Senior Courts Act 1981], or
    (b)    has held office as a judge of the High Court or the Court of Appeal.

(3)   A person appointed to be a temporary additional judge of the Appeal Tribunal has all the functions of a judge nominated under section 22(1)(a).

[(4)   The Lord Chief Justice may nominate a judicial office holder (as defined in section 109(4) of the Constitutional Reform Act 2005) to exercise his functions under this section.]

**NOTES**

Sub-ss (1), (1A), (1B): substituted, for the original sub-s (1), by the Constitutional Reform Act 2005, s 15, Sch 4, Pt 1, paras 245, 248(1), (2).

Sub-s (2): words in first pair of square brackets substituted by the Constitutional Reform Act 2005, s 15, Sch 4, Pt 1, paras 245, 248(1), (3); words in second pair of square brackets substituted by the Constitutional Reform Act 2005, s 59, Sch 11, Pt 1, para 1(2), as from October 2009.

Sub-s (4): added by the Constitutional Reform Act 2005, s 15, Sch 4, Pt 1, paras 245, 248(1), (4).

**[1.717]**
**[24A   Training etc of members of Appeal Tribunal**
The Senior President of Tribunals is responsible, within the resources made available by the Lord Chancellor, for the maintenance of appropriate arrangements for the training, guidance and welfare of judges, and other members, of the Appeal Tribunal (in their capacities as members of the Appeal Tribunal).]

**NOTES**

Commencement: 3 November 2008.

Inserted, together with s 24B, by the Tribunals, Courts and Enforcement Act 2007, s 48(1), Sch 8, paras 35, 44, as from 3 November 2008.

**[1.718]**
**[24B   Oaths**
(1)   Subsection (2) applies to a person ("the appointee")—
   (a)   who is appointed under section 22(1)(c) or 23(3), or
   (b)   who is appointed under section 24(1A) and—
      (i)   falls when appointed within paragraph (a), but not paragraph (b), of section 24(2), and
      (ii)   has not previously taken the required oaths after accepting another office.
(2)   The appointee must take the required oaths before—
   (a)   the Senior President of Tribunals, or
   (b)   an eligible person who is nominated by the Senior President of Tribunals for the purpose of taking the oaths from the appointee.
(3)   If the appointee is a member of the Appeal Tribunal appointed before the coming into force of this section, the requirement in subsection (2) applies in relation to the appointee from the coming into force of this section.
(4)   A person is eligible for the purposes of subsection (2)(b) if one or more of the following paragraphs applies to him—
   (a)   he holds high judicial office (as defined in section 60(2) of the Constitutional Reform Act 2005);
   (b)   he holds judicial office (as defined in section 109(4) of that Act);
   (c)   he holds (in Scotland) the office of sheriff.
(5)   In this section "the required oaths" means—
   (a)   the oath of allegiance, and
   (b)   the judicial oath,
as set out in the Promissory Oaths Act 1868.]

**NOTES**

Commencement: 3 November 2008.

Inserted as noted to s 24A at [1.717].

**[1.719]**
**25   Tenure of appointed members**
(1)   Subject to subsections (2) to (4), an appointed member shall hold and vacate office in accordance with the terms of his appointment.
(2)   An appointed member—
   (a)   may at any time resign his membership by notice in writing addressed to the Lord Chancellor and the Secretary of State, and
   (b)   shall vacate his office on the day on which he attains the age of seventy.
(3)   Subsection (2)(b) is subject to section 26(4) to (6) of the Judicial Pensions and Retirement Act 1993 (Lord Chancellor's power to authorise continuance of office up to the age of seventy-five).
(4)   If the Lord Chancellor, after consultation with the Secretary of State, is satisfied that an appointed member—
   (a)   has been absent from sittings of the Appeal Tribunal for a period longer than six consecutive months without the permission of the President of the Appeal Tribunal,

    (b)    has become bankrupt or [had a debt relief order (under Part 7A of the Insolvency Act 1986) made in respect of him or has] made an arrangement with his creditors, or has had his estate sequestrated or made a trust deed for behoof of his creditors or a composition contract,

    (c)    is incapacitated by physical or mental illness, or

    (d)    is otherwise unable or unfit to discharge the functions of a member,

the Lord Chancellor may declare his office as a member to be vacant and shall notify the declaration in such manner as the Lord Chancellor thinks fit; and when the Lord Chancellor does so, the office becomes vacant.

[(5)    The Lord Chancellor may declare an appointed member's office vacant under subsection (4) only with the concurrence of the appropriate senior judge.

(6)    The appropriate senior judge is the Lord Chief Justice of England and Wales, unless the member whose office is to be declared vacant exercises functions wholly or mainly in Scotland, in which case it is the Lord President of the Court of Session.]

**NOTES**

    Sub-s (4): words in square brackets in para (b) inserted by the Tribunals, Courts and Enforcement Act 2007 (Consequential Amendments) Order 2012, SI 2012/2404, arts 3(2), 5, Sch 2, para 35, as from 1 October 2012, in relation to a debt relief order the application for which is made after that date.

    Sub-ss (5), (6): added by the Constitutional Reform Act 2005, s 15, Sch 4, Pt 1, paras 245, 249.

---

**26**   *(Repealed by the Tribunals, Courts and Enforcement Act 2007, s 146, Sch 23, Pt 1, as from 3 November 2008.)*

**[1.720]**
**27   Remuneration, pensions and allowances**

(1)    The Secretary of State shall pay—

    (a)    the appointed members, [and]

    (b)    any person appointed to act temporarily in the place of an appointed member, . . .

    (c)    . . .

such remuneration and such travelling and other allowances as he may, with the relevant approval, determine; and for this purpose the relevant approval is that of the Treasury in the case of persons within paragraph (a) or (b) . . .

(2)    A person appointed to be a temporary additional judge of the Appeal Tribunal shall be paid such remuneration and allowances as the Lord Chancellor may, with the approval of the Treasury, determine.

(3)    If the Secretary of State determines, with the approval of the Treasury, that this subsection applies in the case of an appointed member, the Secretary of State shall—

    (a)    pay such pension, allowance or gratuity to or in respect of that person on his retirement or death, or

    (b)    make to the member such payments towards the provision of a pension, allowance or gratuity for his retirement or death,

as the Secretary of State may, with the approval of the Treasury, determine.

(4)    Where—

    (a)    a person ceases to be an appointed member otherwise than on his retirement or death, and

    (b)    it appears to the Secretary of State that there are special circumstances which make it right for him to receive compensation,

the Secretary of State may make to him a payment of such amount as the Secretary of State may, with the approval of the Treasury, determine.

**NOTES**

    Sub-s (1): word in square brackets inserted, and words omitted repealed, by the Tribunals, Courts and Enforcement Act 2007, ss 48(1), 146, Sch 8, paras 35, 45, Sch 23, Pt 1, as from 3 November 2008.

---

**[1.721]**
**28   Composition of Appeal Tribunal**

(1)    The Appeal Tribunal may sit, in accordance with directions given by the President of the Appeal Tribunal, either as a single tribunal or in two or more divisions concurrently.

(2)    *Subject to subsections (3) to (5), proceedings before the Appeal Tribunal shall be heard by a judge and either two or four appointed members, so that in either case there is an equal number—*

    (a)    *of persons whose knowledge or experience of industrial relations is as representatives of employers, and*

    (b)    *of persons whose knowledge or experience of industrial relations is as representatives of workers.*

(3)    *With the consent of the parties, proceedings before the Appeal Tribunal may be heard by a judge and one appointed member or by a judge and three appointed members.*

(4)    *Proceedings on an appeal on a [chairman-alone question] shall be heard by a judge alone unless a judge directs that the proceedings shall be heard in accordance with subsections (2) and (3).*

*[(4A)    In subsection (4) "chairman-alone question" means—*
*(a)    a question arising from any decision of an employment tribunal that is a decision of—*
*(i)    the person mentioned in section 4(1)(a) acting alone, or*
*(ii)    any Employment Judge acting alone, or*
*(b)    a question arising in any proceedings before an employment tribunal that are proceedings before—*
*(i)    the person mentioned in section 4(1)(a) alone, or*
*(ii)    any Employment Judge alone.]*
(5)    . . .

---

**NOTES**

Sub-ss (2)–(4A): substituted by new sub-ss (2)–(7), by the Enterprise and Regulatory Reform Act 2013, s 12(1), (2), as from 25 June 2013, subject to savings in s 24(2) of the 2013 Act at **[1.1855]**, as follows:

"(2)    Proceedings before the Appeal Tribunal are to be heard by a judge alone.
This is subject to subsections (3) to (6) and to any provision made by virtue of section 30(2)(f) or (2A).
(3)    A judge may direct that proceedings are to be heard by a judge and either two or four appointed members.
(4)    A judge may, with the consent of the parties, direct that proceedings are to be heard by a judge and either one or three appointed members.
(5)    The Lord Chancellor may by order provide for proceedings of a description specified in the order to be heard by a judge and either two or four appointed members.
(6)    In proceedings heard by a judge and two or four appointed members, there shall be an equal number of—
(a)    employer-representative members, and
(b)    worker-representative members.
(7)    In this section—
"employer-representative members" means appointed members whose knowledge or experience of industrial relations is as representatives of employers;
"worker-representative members" means appointed members whose knowledge or experience of industrial relations is as representatives of workers.".

Sub-s (4): words in square brackets substituted by the Tribunals, Courts and Enforcement Act 2007, s 48(1), Sch 8, paras 35, 46(1), (2), as from 3 November 2008.
Sub-s (4A): inserted by the Tribunals, Courts and Enforcement Act 2007, s 48(1), Sch 8, paras 35, 46(1), (3), as from 3 November 2008.
Sub-s (5): repealed by the Employment Relations Act 1999, ss 41, 44, Sch 8, para 4, Sch 9(12). There has been no corresponding amendment to sub-s (2).

---

*Procedure*

**[1.722]**
**29    Conduct of hearings**
(1)    A person may appear before the Appeal Tribunal in person or be represented by—
(a)    counsel or a solicitor,
(b)    a representative of a trade union or an employers' association, or
(c)    any other person whom he desires to represent him.
(2)    The Appeal Tribunal has in relation to—
(a)    the attendance and examination of witnesses,
(b)    the production and inspection of documents, and
(c)    all other matters incidental to its jurisdiction,
the same powers, rights, privileges and authority (in England and Wales) as the High Court and (in Scotland) as the Court of Session.

**[1.723]**
**[29A    Practice directions**
(1)    Directions about the procedure of the Appeal Tribunal may be given—
(a)    by the Senior President of Tribunals, or
(b)    by the President of the Appeal Tribunal.
(2)    A power under subsection (1) includes—
(a)    power to vary or revoke directions given in exercise of the power, and
(b)    power to make different provision for different purposes.
(3)    Directions under subsection (1)(a) may not be given without the approval of the Lord Chancellor.
(4)    Directions under subsection (1)(b) may not be given without the approval of—
(a)    the Senior President of Tribunals, and
(b)    the Lord Chancellor.
(5)    Subsection (1) does not prejudice any power apart from that subsection to give directions about the procedure of the Appeal Tribunal.
(6)    Directions may not be given in exercise of any such power as is mentioned in subsection (5) without the approval of—
(a)    the Senior President of Tribunals, and
(b)    the Lord Chancellor.

(7)   Subsections (3), (4)(b) and (6)(b) do not apply to directions to the extent that they consist of guidance about any of the following—
   (a)   the application or interpretation of the law;
   (b)   the making of decisions by members of the Appeal Tribunal.
(8)   Subsections (3), (4)(b) and (6)(b) do not apply to directions to the extent that they consist of criteria for determining which members of the Appeal Tribunal may be chosen to decide particular categories of matter; but the directions may, to that extent, be given only after consulting the Lord Chancellor.
(9)   Subsections (4) and (6) do not apply to directions given in a particular case for the purposes of that case only.
(10)   Subsection (6) does not apply to directions under section 28(1).]

**NOTES**
Commencement: 3 November 2008.
Inserted by the Tribunals, Courts and Enforcement Act 2007, s 48(1), Sch 8, paras 35, 47, as from 3 November 2008.

**[1.724]**
## 30   Appeal Tribunal procedure rules
(1)   The Lord Chancellor, after consultation with the Lord President of the Court of Session, shall make rules ("Appeal Tribunal procedure rules") with respect to proceedings before the Appeal Tribunal.
(2)   Appeal Tribunal procedure rules may, in particular, include provision—
   (a)   with respect to the manner in which, and the time within which, an appeal may be brought,
   (b)   with respect to the manner in which any application [or complaint] to the Appeal Tribunal may be made,
   (c)   for requiring persons to attend to give evidence and produce documents and for authorising the administration of oaths to witnesses,
   (d)   for requiring or enabling the Appeal Tribunal to sit in private in circumstances in which an [employment tribunal] is required or empowered to sit in private by virtue of [section 10A] of this Act,
   (e)   . . . and
   (f)   for interlocutory matters arising on any appeal or application to the Appeal Tribunal to be dealt with *otherwise than in accordance with section 28(2) to (5) of this Act.*
[(2A)   Appeal Tribunal procedure rules may make provision of a kind which may be made by employment tribunal procedure regulations under section 10(2), (5), (6) or (7).
(2B)   For the purposes of subsection (2A)—
   (a)   the reference in section 10(2) to section 4 shall be treated as a reference to section 28, and
   (b)   the reference in section 10(4) to the President or a Regional *Chairman* shall be treated as a reference to a judge of the Appeal Tribunal.
(2C)   Section 10B shall have effect in relation to a direction to or determination of the Appeal Tribunal as it has effect in relation to a direction to or determination of an employment tribunal.]
(3)   Subject to Appeal Tribunal procedure rules [and directions under section 28(1) or 29A(1)], the Appeal Tribunal has power to regulate its own procedure.

**NOTES**
Sub-s (2): words in square brackets in para (b) inserted by the Transnational Information and Consultation of Employees Regulations 1999, SI 1999/3323, reg 35(1), (4); words in first pair of square brackets in para (d) substituted by the Employment Rights (Dispute Resolution) Act 1998, s 1(2)(a), and words in second pair of square brackets substituted by the Employment Relations Act 1999, s 41, Sch 8, para (1), (2); para (e) repealed by the Employment Relations Act 2004, s 57, Sch 1, para 26, Sch 2; for the words in italics in para (f) there are substituted the words "by an officer of the Appeal Tribunal" by the Enterprise and Regulatory Reform Act 2013, s 12(1), (3), as from 25 June 2013, subject to savings in s 24(2) of the 2013 Act at **[1.1855]**.
Sub-ss (2A)–(2C): inserted by the Employment Relations Act 1999, s 41, Sch 8, para 5(1), (3); for the word in italics in sub-s (2B) there are substituted the words "Employment Judge" by the Crime and Courts Act 2013, s 21(4), Sch 14, Pt 7, para 13(3), as from a day to be appointed.
Sub-s (3): words in square brackets inserted by the Tribunals, Courts and Enforcement Act 2007, s 48(1), Sch 8, paras 35, 48, as from 3 November 2008.
Rules: by virtue of s 44 of, and Sch 2, Pt I, paras 1–4 to, this Act, the Employment Appeal Tribunal Rules 1993, SI 1993/2854 at **[2.142]** have effect as if made under this section. These Rules have subsequently been amended by Rules made under this section; ie, the Employment Appeal Tribunal (Amendment) Rules 1996, SI 1996/3216; the Employment Appeal Tribunal (Amendment) Rules 2001, SI 2001/1128; the Employment Appeal Tribunal (Amendment) Rules 2001 (Amendment) Rules 2001, SI 2001/1476; the Employment Appeal Tribunal (Amendment) Rules 2004, SI 2004/2526; the Employment Appeal Tribunal (Amendment) Rules 2005, SI 2005/1871.

**[1.725]**
## 31   Restriction of publicity in cases involving sexual misconduct
(1)   Appeal Tribunal procedure rules may, as respects proceedings to which this section applies, include provision—

(a) for cases involving allegations of the commission of sexual offences, for securing that the registration or other making available of documents or divisions shall be so effected as to prevent the identification of any person affected by or making the allegation, and

(b) for cases involving allegations of sexual misconduct, enabling the Appeal Tribunal, on the application of any party to the proceedings before it or of its own motion, to make a restricted reporting order having effect (if not revoked earlier) until the promulgation of the decision of the Appeal Tribunal.

(2) This section applies to—

(a) proceedings on an appeal against a decision of an [employment tribunal] to make, or not to make, a restricted reporting order, and

(b) proceedings on an appeal against any interlocutory decision of an [employment tribunal] in proceedings in which the [employment tribunal] has made a restricted reporting order which it has not revoked.

(3) If any identifying matter is published or included in a relevant programme in contravention of a restricted reporting order—

(a) in the case of publication in a newspaper or periodical, any proprietor, any editor and any publisher of the newspaper or periodical,

(b) in the case of publication in any other form, the person publishing the matter, and

(c) in the case of matter included in a relevant programme—

(i) any body corporate engaged in providing the service in which the programme is included, and

(ii) any person having functions in relation to the programme corresponding to those of an editor of a newspaper,

shall be guilty of an offence and liable on summary conviction to a fine not exceeding level 5 on the standard scale.

(4) Where a person is charged with an offence under subsection (3) it is a defence to prove that at the time of the alleged offence he was not aware, and neither suspected nor had reason to suspect, that the publication or programme in question was of, or included, the matter in question.

(5) Where an offence under subsection (3) committed by a body corporate is proved to have been committed with the consent or connivance of, or to be attributable to any neglect on the part of—

(a) a director, manager, secretary or other similar officer of the body corporate, or

(b) a person purporting to act in any such capacity,

he as well as the body corporate is guilty of the offence and liable to be proceeded against and punished accordingly.

(6) In relation to a body corporate whose affairs are managed by its members "director", in subsection (5), means a member of the body corporate.

(7) "Restricted reporting order" means—

(a) in subsections (1) and (3), an order—

(i) made in exercise of a power conferred by rules made by virtue of this section, and

(ii) prohibiting the publication in Great Britain of identifying matter in a written publication available to the public or its inclusion in a relevant programme for reception in Great Britain, and

(b) in subsection (2), an order which is a restricted reporting order for the purposes of section 11.

(8) In this section—

"identifying matter", in relation to a person, means any matter likely to lead members of the public to identify him as a person affected by, or as the person making, the allegation,

"relevant programme" has the same meaning as in the Sexual Offences (Amendment) Act 1992,

"sexual misconduct" means the commission of a sexual offence, sexual harassment or other adverse conduct (of whatever nature) related to sex, and conduct is related to sex whether the relationship with sex lies in the character of the conduct or in its having reference to the sex or sexual orientation of the person at whom the conduct is directed,

"sexual offence" means any offence to which section 4 of the Sexual Offences (Amendment) Act 1976, the Sexual Offences (Amendment) Act 1992 or section 274(2) of the Criminal Procedure (Scotland) Act 1995 applies (offences under the Sexual Offences Act 1956, Part I of the Criminal Law (Consolidation) (Scotland) Act 1995 and certain other enactments), and

"written publication" has the same meaning as in the Sexual Offences (Amendment) Act 1992.

**NOTES**

Sub-s (2): words in square brackets substituted by the Employment Rights (Dispute Resolution) Act 1998, s 1(2)(a).

Sexual Offences (Amendment) Act 1976, s 4: repealed by Youth Justice and Criminal Evidence Act 1999, ss 48, 67(3), Sch 2, para 4, Sch 6.

Sexual Offences (Amendment) Act 1992: the definition "written publication" in that Act was repealed by the Youth Justice and Criminal Evidence Act 1999, ss 48, 67(3), Sch 2, paras 6, 12(1), (2), Sch 6.

Rules: see the note to s 30 at **[1.724]**.

**[1.726]**
## 32   Restriction of publicity in disability cases
(1)   This section applies to proceedings—
-   (a)   on an appeal against a decision of an [employment tribunal] to make, or not to make, a restricted reporting order, or
-   (b)   on an appeal against any interlocutory decision of an [employment tribunal] in proceedings in which the [employment tribunal] has made a restricted reporting order which it has not revoked.

(2)   Appeal Tribunal procedure rules may, as respects proceedings to which this section applies, include provision for—
-   (a)   enabling the Appeal Tribunal, on the application of the complainant or of its own motion, to make a restricted reporting order having effect (if not revoked earlier) until the promulgation of the decision of the Appeal Tribunal, and
-   (b)   where a restricted reporting order is made in relation to an appeal which is being dealt with by the Appeal Tribunal together with any other proceedings, enabling the Appeal Tribunal to direct that the order is to apply also in relation to those other proceedings or such part of them as the Appeal Tribunal may direct.

(3)   If any identifying matter is published or included in a relevant programme in contravention of a restricted reporting order—
-   (a)   in the case of publication in a newspaper or periodical, any proprietor, any editor and any publisher of the newspaper or periodical,
-   (b)   in the case of publication in any other form, the person publishing the matter, and
-   (c)   in the case of matter included in a relevant programme—
    -   (i)   any body corporate engaged in providing the service in which the programme is included, and
    -   (ii)   any person having functions in relation to the programme corresponding to those of an editor of a newspaper,

shall be guilty of an offence and liable on summary conviction to a fine not exceeding level 5 on the standard scale.

(4)   Where a person is charged with an offence under subsection (3), it is a defence to prove that at the time of the alleged offence he was not aware, and neither suspected nor had reason to suspect, that the publication or programme in question was of, or included, the matter in question.

(5)   Where an offence under subsection (3) committed by a body corporate is proved to have been committed with the consent or connivance of, or to be attributable to any neglect on the part of—
-   (a)   a director, manager, secretary or other similar officer of the body corporate, or
-   (b)   a person purporting to act in any such capacity,

he as well as the body corporate is guilty of the offence and liable to be proceeded against and punished accordingly.

(6)   In relation to a body corporate whose affairs are managed by its members "director", in subsection (5), means a member of the body corporate.

(7)   "Restricted reporting order" means—
-   (a)   in subsection (1), an order which is a restricted reporting order for the purposes of section 12, and
-   (b)   in subsections (2) and (3), an order—
    -   (i)   made in exercise of a power conferred by rules made by virtue of this section, and
    -   (ii)   prohibiting the publication in Great Britain of identifying matter in a written publication available to the public or its inclusion in a relevant programme for reception in Great Britain.

(8)   In this section—
"complainant" means the person who made the complaint to which the proceedings before the Appeal Tribunal relate,
"identifying matter" means any matter likely to lead members of the public to identify the complainant or such other persons (if any) as may be named in the order,
"promulgation" has such meaning as may be prescribed by rules made by virtue of this section,
"relevant programme" means a programme included in a programme service, within the meaning of the Broadcasting Act 1990, and
"written publication" includes a film, a sound track and any other record in permanent form but does not include an indictment or other document prepared for use in particular legal proceedings.

---

**NOTES**

Sub-s (1): words in square brackets substituted by the Employment Rights (Dispute Resolution) Act 1998, s 1(2)(a).
Rules: see the note to s 30 at **[1.724]**.

**[1.727]**
## 33   Restriction of vexatious proceedings

(1)   If, on an application made by the Attorney General or the Lord Advocate under this section, the Appeal Tribunal is satisfied that a person has habitually and persistently and without any reasonable ground—

(a)   instituted vexatious proceedings, whether [before the Certification Officer,] in an [employment tribunal] or before the Appeal Tribunal, and whether against the same person or against different persons, or

(b)   made vexatious applications in any proceedings, whether [before the Certification Officer,] in an [employment tribunal] or before the Appeal Tribunal,

the Appeal Tribunal may, after hearing the person or giving him an opportunity of being heard, make a restriction of proceedings order.

(2)   A "restriction of proceedings order" is an order that—

(a)   no proceedings shall without the leave of the Appeal Tribunal be instituted [before the Certification Officer,] in any [employment tribunal] or before the Appeal Tribunal by the person against whom the order is made,

(b)   any proceedings instituted by him [before the Certification Officer,] in any [employment tribunal] or before the Appeal Tribunal before the making of the order shall not be continued by him without the leave of the Appeal Tribunal, and

(c)   no application (other than one for leave under this section) is to be made by him in any proceedings [before the Certification Officer,] in any [employment tribunal] or before the Appeal Tribunal without the leave of the Appeal Tribunal.

(3)   A restriction of proceedings order may provide that it is to cease to have effect at the end of a specified period, but otherwise it remains in force indefinitely.

(4)   Leave for the institution or continuance of, or for the making of an application in, any proceedings [before the Certification Officer,] in an [employment tribunal] or before the Appeal Tribunal by a person who is the subject of a restriction of proceedings order shall not be given unless the Appeal Tribunal is satisfied—

(a)   that the proceedings or application are not an abuse of [process], and

(b)   that there are reasonable grounds for the proceedings or application.

(5)   A copy of a restriction of proceedings order shall be published in the London Gazette and the Edinburgh Gazette.

**NOTES**

Sub-s (1): words in first pair of square brackets in paras (a), (b) inserted by the Employment Relations Act 2004, s 49(1)–(3); words in second pair of square brackets in those paragraphs substituted by the Employment Rights (Dispute Resolution) Act 1998, s 1(2)(a).

Sub-s (2): words in first pair of square brackets in paras (a)–(c) inserted by the Employment Relations Act 2004, s 49(1), (4)–(6); words in second pair of square brackets in those paragraphs substituted by the Employment Rights (Dispute Resolution) Act 1998, s 1(2)(a).

Sub-s (4): words in first pair of square brackets inserted, and word in third pair of square brackets substituted, by the Employment Relations Act 2004, s 49(1), (7); words in second pair of square brackets substituted by the Employment Rights (Dispute Resolution) Act 1998, s 1(2)(a).

**[1.728]**
## [34   Costs and expenses

(1)   Appeal Tribunal procedure rules may include provision for the award of costs or expenses.

(2)   Rules under subsection (1) may include provision authorising the Appeal Tribunal to have regard to a person's ability to pay when considering the making of an award against him under such rules.

(3)   Appeal Tribunal procedure rules may include provision for authorising the Appeal Tribunal—

(a)   to disallow all or part of the costs or expenses of a representative of a party to proceedings before it by reason of that representative's conduct of the proceedings;

(b)   to order a representative of a party to proceedings before it to meet all or part of the costs or expenses incurred by a party by reason of the representative's conduct of the proceedings.

(4)   Appeal Tribunal procedure rules may also include provision for taxing or otherwise settling the costs or expenses referred to in subsection (1) or (3)(b) (and, in particular in England and Wales, for enabling the amount of such costs to be assessed by way of detailed assessment in the High Court).]

**NOTES**

Substituted by the Employment Act 2002, s 23.

Rules: see the note to s 30 at **[1.724]**.

*Decisions and further appeals*

**[1.729]**
## 35 Powers of Appeal Tribunal
(1)   For the purpose of disposing of an appeal, the Appeal Tribunal may—
   (a)   exercise any of the powers of the body or officer from whom the appeal was brought, or
   (b)   remit the case to that body or officer.
(2)   Any decision or award of the Appeal Tribunal on an appeal has the same effect, and may be enforced in the same manner, as a decision or award of the body or officer from whom the appeal was brought.

**[1.730]**
## 36 Enforcement of decisions etc
(1)–(3)   . . .
(4)   No person shall be punished for contempt of the Appeal Tribunal except by, or with the consent of, a judge.
(5)   A magistrates' court shall not remit the whole or part of a fine imposed by the Appeal Tribunal unless it has the consent of a judge who is a member of the Appeal Tribunal.

**NOTES**
  Sub-ss (1)–(3): repealed by the Employment Relations Act 2004, s 57, Sch 1, para 27, Sch 2.

**[1.731]**
## 37 Appeals from Appeal Tribunal
(1)   Subject to subsection (3), an appeal on any question of law lies from any decision or order of the Appeal Tribunal to the relevant appeal court with the leave of the Appeal Tribunal or of the relevant appeal court.
(2)   In subsection (1) the "relevant appeal court" means—
   (a)   in the case of proceedings in England and Wales, the Court of Appeal, and
   (b)   in the case of proceedings in Scotland, the Court of Session.
(3)   No appeal lies from a decision of the Appeal Tribunal refusing leave for the institution or continuance of, or for the making of an application in, proceedings by a person who is the subject of a restriction of proceedings order made under section 33.
(4)   This section is without prejudice to section 13 of the Administration of Justice Act 1960 (appeal in case of contempt of court).

## PART III
## SUPPLEMENTARY

*Crown employment and Parliamentary staff*

**[1.732]**
## 38 Crown employment
(1)   This Act has effect in relation to Crown employment and persons in Crown employment as it has effect in relation to other employment and other employees.
(2)   In this Act "Crown employment" means employment under or for the purposes of a government department or any officer or body exercising on behalf of the Crown functions conferred by a statutory provision.
(3)   For the purposes of the application of this Act in relation to Crown employment in accordance with subsection (1)—
   (a)   references to an employee shall be construed as references to a person in Crown employment, and
   (b)   references to a contract of employment shall be construed as references to the terms of employment of a person in Crown employment.
*(4)   Subsection (1) applies to—*
   *(a)   service as a member of the naval, military or air forces of the Crown, and*
   *(b)   employment by an association established for the purposes of Part XI of the Reserve Forces Act 1996;*
*but Her Majesty may by Order in Council make any provision of this Act apply to service as a member of the naval, military or air forces of the Crown subject to such exceptions and modifications as may be specified in the Order in Council.*

**NOTES**
  Sub-s (4) has effect, by virtue of Sch 2, Pt II, para 9, and until the relevant commencement date as defined in para 9(2), as if the subsection set out in para 9(1) were substituted for sub-s (4) of this section: see Sch 2, Pt II, para 9 at **[1.741]** and the notes thereto.

**[1.733]**
**39 Parliamentary staff**
(1)   This Act has effect in relation to employment as a relevant member of the House of Lords staff or a relevant member of the House of Commons staff as it has effect in relation to other employment.
(2)   Nothing in any rule of law or the law or practice of Parliament prevents a relevant member of the House of Lords staff or a relevant member of the House of Commons staff from bringing before an [employment tribunal] proceedings of any description which could be brought before such a tribunal by a person who is not a relevant member of the House of Lords staff or a relevant member of the House of Commons staff.
(3)   For the purposes of the application of this Act in relation to a relevant member of the House of Commons staff—
   (a)   references to an employee shall be construed as references to a relevant member of the House of Commons staff, and
   (b)   references to a contract of employment shall be construed as including references to the terms of employment of a relevant member of the House of Commons staff.
(4)   In this Act "relevant member of the House of Lords staff" means any person who is employed under a contract of employment with the Corporate Officer of the House of Lords.
(5)   In this Act "relevant member of the House of Commons staff" has the same meaning as in section 195 of the Employment Rights Act 1996; and (subject to an Order in Council under subsection (12) of that section)—
   (a)   subsections (6) and (7) of that section have effect for determining who is the employer of a relevant member of the House of Commons staff for the purposes of this Act, and
   (b)   subsection (8) of that section applies in relation to proceedings brought by virtue of this section.

**NOTES**
Sub-s (2): words in square brackets substituted by the Employment Rights (Dispute Resolution) Act 1998, s 1(2)(a).

*General*
**[1.734]**
**40 Power to amend Act**
(1)   The Secretary of State [and the Lord Chancellor, acting jointly,] may by order—
   (a)   provide that any provision of this Act to which this section applies and which is specified in the order shall not apply to persons, or to employments, of such classes as may be prescribed in the order, or
   (b)   provide that any provision of this Act to which this section applies shall apply to persons or employments of such classes as may be prescribed in the order subject to such exceptions and modifications as may be so prescribed.
(2)   This section applies to sections 3, 8, 16 and 17 *and to section 18 so far as deriving from section 133 of the Employment Protection (Consolidation) Act 1978.*

**NOTES**
Sub-s (1): words in square brackets inserted by the Tribunals, Courts and Enforcement Act 2007, s 48(1), Sch 8, paras 35, 38.
Sub-s (2): words in italics repealed by the Enterprise and Regulatory Reform Act 2013, s 7(2), Sch 1, paras 2, 8, as from a day to be appointed.
Employment Protection (Consolidation) Act 1978: s 133 of that Act is repealed by s 45 of, and Sch 3, Pt I to, this Act.
Orders: as of 6 April 2013 no Orders had been made under this section but, by virtue of s 44 of, and Sch 2, Pt I, paras 1–4 to, this Act, the Redundancy Payments (National Health Service) (Modification) Order 1993, SI 1993/3167, and the Employment Protection (Continuity of Employment of National Health Service Employees) (Modification) Order 1996, SI 1996/1023, have effect as if made under this section.

**[1.735]**
**41 Orders, regulations and rules**
(1)   Any power conferred by this Act on a Minister of the Crown to make an order, and any power conferred by this Act to make regulations or rules, is exercisable by statutory instrument.
(2)   No recommendation shall be made to Her Majesty to make an Order in Council under section 38(4), and no order shall be made under section 3, 4(4) [or (6D)] [,12A(12)], [28(5)] or 40, unless a draft of the Order in Council or order has been laid before Parliament and approved by a resolution of each House of Parliament.
(3)   A statutory instrument containing—
   (a)   an order made by a Minister of the Crown under any other provision of this Act except Part II of Schedule 2, or
   (b)   regulations or rules made under this Act,
is subject to annulment in pursuance of a resolution of either House of Parliament.
(4)   Any power conferred by this Act which is exercisable by statutory instrument includes power to make such incidental, supplementary or transitional provision as appears to the Minister exercising the power to be necessary or expedient.

**NOTES**

Sub-s (2) is amended as follows:

words "or (6D)" in square brackets inserted by the Enterprise and Regulatory Reform Act 2013, s 11(2), as from a day to be appointed;

figure ",12A(12)" in square brackets inserted by the Enterprise and Regulatory Reform Act 2013, s 16(2), Sch 3, paras 2, 4, as from a day to be appointed;

figure "28(5)" in square brackets inserted by the Enterprise and Regulatory Reform Act 2013, s 12(1), (4), as from 25 June 2013, subject to savings in s 24(2) of the 2013 Act at **[1.1855]**.

**[1.736]**

## 42   Interpretation

(1)   In this Act—

["ACAS" means the Advisory, Conciliation and Arbitration Service,]

"the Appeal Tribunal" means the Employment Appeal Tribunal,

"Appeal Tribunal procedure rules" shall be construed in accordance with section 30(1),

"appointed member" shall be construed in accordance with section 22(1)(c),

["Certification Officer" shall be construed in accordance with section 254 of the Trade Union and
   Labour Relations (Consolidation) Act 1992,]

"conciliation officer" means an officer designated by *the Advisory, Conciliation and Arbitration
   Service* under section 211 of the Trade Union and Labour Relations (Consolidation) Act
   1992,

"contract of employment" means a contract of service or apprenticeship, whether express or
   implied, and (if it is express) whether oral or in writing,

"employee" means an individual who has entered into or works under (or, where the employment
   has ceased, worked under) a contract of employment,

"employer", in relation to an employee, means the person by whom the employee is (or, where
   the employment has ceased, was) employed,

"employers' association" has the same meaning as in the Trade Union and Labour Relations
   (Consolidation) Act 1992,

"employment" means employment under a contract of employment and "employed" shall be
   construed accordingly,

"[employment tribunal] procedure regulations" shall be construed in accordance with
   section 7(1),

["representative" shall be construed in accordance with section 6(1) (in Part 1) or section 29(1)
   (in Part 2),]

"statutory provision" means a provision, whether of a general or a special nature, contained in,
   or in any document made or issued under, any Act, whether of a general or special nature,

"successor", in relation to the employer of an employee, means (subject to subsection (2)) a
   person who in consequence of a change occurring (whether by virtue of a sale or other
   disposition or by operation of law) in the ownership of the undertaking, or of the part of the
   undertaking, for the purposes of which the employee was employed, has become the owner
   of the undertaking or part, and

"trade union" has the meaning given by section 1 of the Trade Union and Labour Relations
   (Consolidation) Act 1992.

(2)   The definition of "successor" in subsection (1) has effect (subject to the necessary
modifications) in relation to a case where—

(a)   the person by whom an undertaking or part of an undertaking is owned immediately before
      a change is one of the persons by whom (whether as partners, trustees or otherwise) it is
      owned immediately after the change, or

(b)   the persons by whom an undertaking or part of an undertaking is owned immediately
      before a change (whether as partners, trustees or otherwise) include the persons by whom,
      or include one or more of the persons by whom, it is owned immediately after the change,

as it has effect where the previous owner and the new owner are wholly different persons.

(3)   For the purposes of this Act any two employers shall be treated as associated if—

(a)   one is a company of which the other (directly or indirectly) has control, or

(b)   both are companies of which a third person (directly or indirectly) has control;

and "associated employer" shall be construed accordingly.

**NOTES**

Sub-s (1): definition "ACAS" inserted and for the words in italics in definition "conciliation officer" there is substituted "ACAS", by the Enterprise and Regulatory Reform Act 2013, s 7(2), Sch 1, paras 2, 9, as from a day to be appointed; definition "Certification Officer" inserted by the Employment Relations Act 2004, s 49(8); in definition "employment tribunal procedure regulations" words in square brackets substituted by the Employment Rights (Dispute Resolution) Act 1998, s 1(2)(a); definition "representative" inserted by the Enterprise and Regulatory Reform Act 2013, s 21(1), (4), as from 25 June 2013.

*Final provisions*

**43–45** *(S 43 introduces Sch 1 (consequential amendments), s 44 introduces Sch 2 (transitional provisions, savings and transitory provisions), s 45 introduces Sch 3 (repeals and revocations).)*

**[1.737]**
**46 Commencement**
This Act shall come into force at the end of the period of three months beginning with the day on which it is passed.

**[1.738]**
**47 Extent**
This Act does not extend to Northern Ireland.

**[1.739]**
**48 Short title**
This Act may be cited as the [Employment Tribunals Act 1996].

NOTES
  Words in square brackets substituted by the Employment Rights (Dispute Resolution) Act 1998, s 1(2)(c).

## SCHEDULES
## SCHEDULE 1

*(Sch 1 (Consequential amendments; in so far as relevant to this work, these amendments have been incorporated at the appropriate place).)*

## SCHEDULE 2
## TRANSITIONAL PROVISIONS, SAVINGS AND TRANSITORY PROVISIONS
Section 44

## PART I
## TRANSITIONAL PROVISIONS AND SAVINGS

**[1.740]**
**1.** The substitution of this Act for the provisions repealed or revoked by this Act does not affect the continuity of the law.

**2.** Anything done, or having effect as done, (including the making of subordinate legislation) under or for the purposes of any provision repealed or revoked by this Act has effect as if done under or for the purposes of any corresponding provision of this Act.

**3.** Any reference (express or implied) in this Act or any other enactment, or in any instrument or document, to a provision of this Act is (so far as the context permits) to be read as (according to the context) being or including in relation to times, circumstances and purposes before the commencement of this Act a reference to the corresponding provision repealed or revoked by this Act.

**4.** (1) Any reference (express or implied) in any enactment, or in any instrument or document, to a provision repealed or revoked by this Act is (so far as the context permits) to be read as (according to the context) being or including in relation to times, circumstances and purposes after the commencement of this Act a reference to the corresponding provision of this Act.

(2) In particular, where a power conferred by an Act is expressed to be exercisable in relation to enactments contained in Acts passed before or in the same Session as the Act conferring the power, the power is also exercisable in relation to provisions of this Act which reproduce such enactments.

**5.** Paragraphs 1 to 4 have effect in place of section 17(2) of the Interpretation Act 1978 (but are without prejudice to any other provision of that Act).

**6.** The repeal by the Act of section 130 of, and Schedule 10 to, the Employment Protection (Consolidation) Act 1978 (jurisdiction of referees under specified provisions to be exercised by [employment tribunals]) does not affect—
  (a)  the operation of those provisions in relation to any question which may arise after the commencement of this Act, or
  (b)  the continued operation of those provisions after the commencement of this Act in relation to any question which has arisen before that commencement.

NOTES
  Para 6: words in square brackets substituted by the Employment Rights (Dispute Resolution) Act 1998, s 1(2)(b).

## PART II
## TRANSITORY PROVISIONS

**[1.741]**
**7, 8.** *(Para 7 (transitory provisions – disability discrimination) and para 8 (transitory provisions – jobseeker's allowance) are spent. Note that para 7 was also repealed by the Equality Act 2010, s 211(2), Sch 27, Pt 1, as from 1 October 2010.)*

### *Armed forces*

**9.** (1)   If section 31 of the Trade Union Reform and Employment Rights Act 1993 has not come into force before the commencement of this Act, section 38 shall have effect until the relevant commencement date as if for subsection (4) there were substituted—

"(4)   Subsection (1)—
  (a)   does not apply to service as a member of the naval, military or air forces of the Crown, but
  (b)   does apply to employment by an association established for the purposes of Part XI of the Reserve Forces Act 1996.".

(2)   The reference in sub-paragraph (1) to the relevant commencement date is a reference—
  (a)   if an order has been made before the commencement of this Act appointing a day after that commencement as the day on which section 31 of the Trade Union Reform and Employment Rights Act 1993 is to come into force, to the day so appointed, and
  (b)   otherwise, to such day as the Secretary of State may by order appoint.

**10.**   *(Para 10 (further transitory provisions – armed forces) is spent.)*

**NOTES**
  Para 9: the Trade Union Reform and Employment Rights Act 1993, s 31 was repealed (never having been brought into force) by the Employment Rights Act 1996, s 242, Sch 3, Pt I, and replaced by s 192 of that Act at **[1.999]**. The said s 192 had not been brought into force as of 6 April 2013, and is the subject of transitional provisions as noted to that section.
  "Relevant commencement date": no such Order as is mentioned in para 9(2)(a) was made, and as of 6 April 2013 no Order had been made under para 9(2)(b).

## SCHEDULE 3

*(Sch 3 (repeals and revocations) in so far as relevant to this work, these have been incorporated at the appropriate place.)*

# EMPLOYMENT TRIBUNALS ACT 1996; DESTINATION TABLE

**[1.742]**

## DESTINATION TABLE

This table shows in column (1) the enactments repealed by the Employment Tribunals Act 1996 and in column (2) the provisions of that Act corresponding thereto.

In certain cases the enactment in column (1), though having a corresponding provision in column (2) is not, or not wholly, repealed as it is still required, or partly required, for the purposes of other legislation.

A "dash" in the right hand column means that the repealed provision to which it corresponds in the left hand column is spent, unnecessary or for some other reason not specifically reproduced.

| (1) | (2) | (1) | (2) |
|---|---|---|---|
| **Betting, Gaming and Lotteries Act 1963 (c 2)** | **Employment Tribunals Act 1996 (c 17)** | **Employment Protection (Consolidation) Act 1978 (c 44)** | **Employment Tribunals Act 1996 (c 17)** |
| Sch 5A, para 21 ............ | s 18(1) | s 132(4) ...................... | s 17(1) |
| **Sex Discrimination Act 1975 (c 65)** | **Employment Tribunals Act 1996 (c 17)** | s 132(5) ...................... | s 17(2) |
| | | s 132(6) ...................... | s 17(3), (4) |
| s 64(1) ......................... | s 18(2) | s 133(1) ...................... | s 18(1) |
| s 64(2) ......................... | s 18(3) | s 133(2) ...................... | s 18(2) |
| s 64(3) ......................... | s 18(6) | s 133(3) ...................... | s 18(3) |
| s 64(4) ......................... | s 18(7) | s 133(4) ...................... | s 18(2), (3) |
| **Race Relations Act 1976 (c 74)** | **Employment Tribunals Act 1996 (c 17)** | s 133(5) ...................... | s 18(6) |
| | | s 133(6) ...................... | s 18(7) |
| s 55(1) ......................... | s 18(2) | s 133(7) ...................... | s 18(8) |
| s 55(2) ......................... | s 18(3) | s 134(1) ...................... | s 18(1), (2) |
| s 55(3) ......................... | s 18(6) | s 134(2) ...................... | s 18(4) |
| s 55(4) ......................... | s 18(7) | s 134(3) ...................... | s 18(3), (5) |
| **Employment Protection (Consolidation) Act 1978 (c 44)** | **Employment Tribunals Act 1996 (c 17)** | s 134(4) ...................... | s 18(6) |
| | | s 134(5) ...................... | s 18(7) |
| | | s 135(1) ...................... | s 20(1) |
| s 128(1) ....................... | ss 1(1), 2 | s 135(2)–(5) ................ | s 22 |
| s 128(2) ....................... | Spent | s 135(6) ...................... | Spent |
| s 128(2A), (2B) ........... | s 4(1), (2) | s 136(1) ...................... | s 21(1) |
| s 128(2C) ..................... | s 4(3) | s 136(2), (3) ................ | Rep 1992 c 52, s 300(1), Sch 1 |
| s 128(2D), (2F) ............ | s 4(4), (5) | | |
| s 128(2E) ..................... | s 41(2) | s 136(4) ...................... | s 37(1), (2), (4) |
| s 128(4) ....................... | s 7(2) | s 136(5) ...................... | s 21(2) |
| s 128(5), (6) ................. | s 4(6), (7) | s 136A(1)–(4) .............. | s 33(1)–(4) |
| s 130 ........................... | Sch 2, para 6 | s 136A(5) .................... | s 37(3) |
| s 131(1) ....................... | s 3(1) | s 136A(6) .................... | s 33(5) |
| s 131(2) ....................... | s 3(2) | s 138(1)† ..................... | s 38(1) |
| s 131(3)† ...................... | s 3(3) | s 138(2)† ..................... | s 38(2) |
| s 131(4) ....................... | s 8(1) | s 138(3)† ..................... | s 38(4) |
| s 131(4A) ..................... | s 8(2) | s 138(7)(a), (b)† ........... | s 38(3) |
| s 131(5) ....................... | s 8(3) | s 138(7)(c)† ................. | s 10(6) |
| s 131(5A) ..................... | s 8(4) | s 138(7)(e) .................. | s 10(3)(a) |
| s 131(6) ....................... | s 3(4) | s 138A(2)(b)† .............. | s 38(4) |
| s 131(7) ....................... | s 3(5), (6) | s 138A(6)† ................... | s 41(2) |
| s 131(8) ....................... | s 41(2) | s 139(1)* ..................... | ss 10(3), (6), 39(1), (3) |
| s 132(1) ....................... | s 16(1) | s 139(2)† ..................... | s 39(2) |
| s 132(2) ....................... | s 16(2), (3) | s 139A(1)† ................... | s 39(1) |
| s 132(3) ....................... | s 16(4)–(6) | s 139A(2)† ................... | s 39(2) |

† Not repealed (provisions of the 1978 Act not repealed by this Act were repealed by the Employment Rights Act 1996 (qv below)      * Repealed in part

| (1) | (2) | (1) | (2) |
|---|---|---|---|
| Employment Protection (Consolidation) Act 1978 (c 44) | Employment Tribunals Act 1996 (c 17) | Employment Protection (Consolidation) Act 1978 (c 44) | Employment Tribunals Act 1996 (c 17) |
| s 139A(3)(a) ................. | s 10(3)(b) | Sch 11, para 7 .............. | s 23(3) |
| s 139A(5)† ................... | s 39(4) | Sch 11, para 8(1), (2).... | s 24(1), (2) |
| s 149(1), (2)† ............... | s 40(1), (2) | Sch 11, para 9 .............. | s 23(4) |
| s 149(4)† ..................... | s 41(2) | Sch 11, para 10 ............ | s 24(3) |
| s 153(1)† ..................... | s 42(1) | Sch 11, para 11 ............ | s 23(5) |
| s 153(4)† ..................... | s 42(3) | Sch 11, para 12 ............ | s 20(3) |
| s 153(4A)† ................... | s 42(2) | Sch 11, paras 13, 14 ..... | s 20(2) |
| s 154(1)† ..................... | s 41(1) | Sch 11, para 15 ............ | s 28(1) |
| s 154(2), (3)† ............... | s 41(3), (4) | Sch 11, para 16 ............ | s 28(2)–(5) |
| Sch 9, para 1(1) ........... | s 7(1) | Sch 11, para 17(1), (2).. | s 30(1), (3) |
| Sch 9, para 1(2)(a)–(g), (j) | s 7(3)(a)–(g), (j) | Sch 11, para 18 ............ | s 30(2) |
| Sch 9, para 1(2)(h), (i).... | s 13(1) | Sch 11, para 18A .......... | s 31 |
| Sch 9, para 1(2)(ga) ..... | s 7(3)(h) | Sch 11, para 19 ............ | s 34 |
| Sch 9, para 1(3) ........... | s 19 | Sch 11, para 20 ............ | s 29(1) |
| Sch 9, para 1(4) ........... | s 13(2) | Sch 11, para 21 ............ | s 35 |
| Sch 9, para 1(4A) ......... | s 10(1) | Sch 11, para 21A .......... | s 36(1)–(3) |
| Sch 9, para 1(5) ........... | s 10(2) | Sch 11, para 22(1) ........ | s 29(2) |
| Sch 9, para 1(5A) ......... | s 11(1), (6) | Sch 11, para 22(2) ........ | s 36(4) |
| Sch 9, para 1(6) ........... | s 7(5) | Sch 11, para 23(1) ........ | Rep 1981 c 49, s 16(6) |
| Sch 9, para 1(7) ........... | s 7(4) | Sch 11, para 23(2) ........ | s 36(5) |
| Sch 9, para 1(8)–(11) ... | s 11(2)–(5) | Sch 11, para 23(3) ........ | Spent |
| Sch 9, para 1A(1) ......... | s 9(1) | Sch 11, para 24 ............ | s 26 |
| Sch 9, para 1A(2) ......... | s 9(2) | Sch 11, para 25 ............ | s 27(1) |
| Sch 9, para 1A(3) ......... | s 9(3) | Sch 11, paras 26–28 ..... | s 27(2)–(4) |
| Sch 9, para 1B .............. | s 9(4) | Sch 15, para 18 ............ | Spent |
| Sch 9, para 2(1) ........... | s 10(4) | Sch 16* ....................... | Spent (so far as relevant) |
| Sch 9, para 2(2) ........... | s 10(5) | Social Security Act 1980 (c 30) | Employment Tribunals Act 1996 (c 17) |
| Sch 9, para 3 ................. | Rep 1990 c 38, s 16(2), Sch 3 | Sch 4, para 13 .............. | s 16(5) |
| Sch 9, para 4 ................. | s 6(2) | Employment Act 1980 (c 42) | Employment Tribunals Act 1996 (c 17) |
| Sch 9, para 5 ................. | s 7(6) | | |
| Sch 9, para 6 ................. | s 6(1) | Sch 1, para 16 .............. | s 7(2) |
| Sch 9, para 6A .............. | s 14 | Sch 1, para 17 .............. | s 18(1) |
| Sch 9, para 7(1)–(3) ..... | s 15(1)–(3) | Sch 1, para 18 .............. | s 18(3), (5) |
| Sch 9, para 8 ................. | Rep 1993 c 19, s 51, Sch 10 | Sch 1, para 19† ............ | s 21(2) |
| | | Sch 1, para 26 .............. | s 7(3)(a) |
| Sch 9, para 9 ................. | s 5(1) | Sch 1, para 27 .............. | s 15(2) |
| Sch 9, para 10 .............. | s 5(2), (3) | Sch 1, para 28 .............. | s 30(2) |
| Sch 9, para 11 .............. | Rep 1981 c 20, s 36, Sch 4 | Sch 1, para 29 .............. | s 36(1), (2) |
| Sch 10 ......................... | Sch 2, para 6 | Contempt of Court Act 1981 (c 49) | Employment Tribunals Act 1996 (c 17) |
| Sch 11, para 1 .............. | s 25(1) | | |
| Sch 11, para 2 .............. | s 25(2), (3) | s 16(6) ......................... | — |
| Sch 11, para 3 .............. | s 25(4) | Supreme Court Act 1981 (c 54) | Employment Tribunals Act 1996 (c 17) |
| Sch 11, para 4 .............. | s 23(1) | | |
| Sch 11, paras 5, 6 ........ | s 23(2) | Sch 5* ......................... | s 24(2) |

† Not repealed (provisions of the 1978 Act not repealed by this Act were repealed by the Employment Rights Act 1996 (qv below)    * Repealed in part

| (1) | (2) | (1) | (2) |
|---|---|---|---|
| Employment Act 1982 (c 46) | Employment Tribunals Act 1996 (c 17) | Trade Union Reform and Employment Rights Act 1993 (c 19) | Employment Tribunals Act 1996 (c 17) |
| Sch 3, Pt I, para 7 ........ | s 14 | | |
| Sch 3, Pt I, para 8(1) .... | s 30(2) | s 31(2)† ...................... | ss 38(4), 41(2) |
| Sch 3, Pt I, para 8(2) .... | Spent | s 36(1) ........................... | Unnecessary |
| Sch 3, Pt I, para 9 ........ | s 36(3) | s 36(2) .......................... | ss 4(1)–(5), 41(2) |
| Wages Act 1986 (c 48) | Employment Tribunals Act 1996 (c 17) | s 36(3) .......................... | s 4(6), (7) |
| | | s 37 .............................. | s 28(2)–(5) |
| Sch 4, para 9 ................ | s 18(1) | s 38(a) ........................... | s 3(1) |
| Sch 4, para 10 .............. | s 21(1) | s 38(b) ........................... | s 3(3) |
| Social Security Act 1986 (c 50) | Employment Tribunals Act 1996 (c 17) | s 38(c) ........................... | s 8(2) |
| | | s 38(d) ........................... | s 8(4) |
| Sch 10, Pt II, para 50(a).. | s 16(3) | s 38(e) ........................... | s 3(5) |
| Sch 10, Pt II, para 50(b).. | s 16(4), (5) | s 40(1) ........................... | Unnecessary |
| Sch 10, Pt II, para 50(c).. | s 17(1) | s 40(2) ........................... | s 11(1), (6) |
| Employment Act 1988 (c 19)† | Employment Tribunals Act 1996 (c 17) | s 40(3) ........................... | s 7(5) |
| | | s 40(4) ........................... | s 11(2)–(6) |
| Sch 3, Pt I, para 2(3) .... | s 18(1) | s 41 .............................. | s 31 |
| Sch 3, Pt I, para 2(4) .... | s 21(2) | s 42 .............................. | ss 33, 37(3) |
| Sch 3, Pt I, para 2(5) .... | s 36(1) | Sch 7, para 6(a) ............ | s 10(1) |
| Employment Act 1989 (c 38) | Employment Tribunals Act 1996 (c 17) | Sch 7, para 6(b) ............ | s 10(5) |
| | | Sch 7, para 7 ................ | s 30(2) |
| s 20 .............................. | s 9(1)–(3) | Sch 7, para 11† ............. | ss 10(3), 39(1), (2), (4) |
| Sch 6, para 26 .............. | s 7(3)(e) | Sch 8, para 19 .............. | s 16(1) |
| Social Security (Consequential Provisions) Act 1992 (c 6) | Employment Tribunals Act 1996 (c 17) | Sch 8, para 20 .............. | s 18(1) |
| | | Sch 8, para 28(a) ........... | s 13(2) |
| | | Sch 8, para 28(b) .......... | s 9(1) |
| Sch 2, para 50(1) .......... | s 17(1) | Sch 8, para 28(c) ........... | s 9(4) |
| Sch 2, para 50(2) .......... | Spent | Sch 8, paras 29, 30 ........ | s 30(2) |
| Trade Union and Labour Relations (Consolidation) Act 1992 (c 52) | Employment Tribunals Act 1996 (c 17) | Sch 8, para 86 .............. | s 18(1) |
| | | Sch 8, para 87 .............. | Spent |
| s 290 ............................ | s 18(1) | Pension Schemes Act 1993 (c 48) | Employment Tribunals Act 1996 (c 17) |
| s 291(2), (3) ................. | s 21(1), (2) | | |
| Sch 2, para 19 .............. | s 16(1) | Sch 8, para 11(2) ........... | s 4(3)(b) |
| Sch 2, para 20 .............. | s 22(2) | Sunday Trading Act 1994 (c 20) | Employment Tribunals Act 1996 (c 17) |
| Sch 2, para 21(1)† ....... | — | | |
| Sch 2, para 21(2)(b)†, (d)†, (f)† ................... | s 42(1) | Sch 4, para 21 ................ | s 18(1) |
| Sch 2, para 21(3)† ........ | s 42(2) | Deregulation and Contracting Out Act 1994 (c 40) | Employment Tribunals Act 1996 (c 17) |
| Sch 2, para 24(1), (2) ... | s 10(4) | | |
| Sch 2, para 25(a) .......... | s 30(2) | Sch 8† ........................... | s 18(1) |
| Sch 2, para 25(b) .......... | s 36(1), (3) | Jobseekers Act 1995 (c 18) | Employment Tribunals Act 1996 (c 17) |
| Sch 3, para 1(4)† .......... | s 10(2) | | |
| Judicial Pensions and Retirement Act 1993 (c 8) | Employment Tribunals Act 1996 (c 17) | Sch 2, para 2(1) ............. | Unnecessary |
| | | Sch 2, para 2(2) ............. | ss 16(3), (4), 17(2) |
| Sch 6, para 30 .............. | s 25(2), (3) | Sch 2, para 2(3) ............. | s 16(5) |
| Trade Union Reform and Employment Rights Act 1993 (c 19) | Employment Tribunals Act 1996 (c 17) | Sch 2, para 2(4) ............. | s 17(1) |
| | | Sch 2, para 2(5) ............. | s 17(3), (4) |
| s 31(1)† ....................... | s 38(4) | | |

† Not repealed            * Repealed in part

| (1) | (2) | (1) | (2) |
|---|---|---|---|
| Pensions Act 1995 (c 26) | Employment Tribunals Act 1996 (c 17) | Reserve Forces Act 1996 (c 14) | Employment Rights Act 1996 (c 18) |
| Sch 3, para 8.................. | s 18(1) | | |
| Sch 3, para 9.................. | s 21(1) | Sch 10, para 17† .......... | s 38(4) |
| Disability Discrimination Act 1995 (c 50) | Employment Tribunals Act 1996 (c 17) | Equal Pay (Amendment) Regulations 1983, SI 1983/1794 | Employment Tribunals Act 1996 (c 17) |
| s 62.............................. | s 12 | Reg 3 ........................... | ss 5(2), 7(3)(h), (4) |
| s 63(1), (2).................... | s 32(1), (2) | Collective Redundancies and Transfer of Undertakings (Protection of Employment) (Amendment) Regulations 1995, SI 1995/2587 | Employment Tribunals Act 1996 (c 17) |
| s 63(3) .......................... | s 32(3)–(6) | | |
| s 63(4), (5)................... | s 32(7) | | |
| s 63(6) ......................... | s 32(8) | | |
| Sch 3, Pt I, para 1(1) .... | s 18(2) | | |
| Sch 3, Pt I, para 1(2) .... | s 18(3) | | |
| Sch 3, Pt I, para 1(3) .... | s 18(6) | | |
| Sch 3, Pt I, para 1(4) .... | s 18(7) | Regs 12(3), 13(3)......... | s 18(1) |
| Sch 6, para 2.................. | s 21(1) | Reg 14(4)*................... | s 10(5) |

† Not repealed

* Repealed in part

# EMPLOYMENT RIGHTS ACT 1996

## (1996 c 18)

### ARRANGEMENT OF SECTIONS

#### PART I
#### EMPLOYMENT PARTICULARS

*Right to statements of employment particulars*

*Right to itemised pay statement*

*Enforcement*

#### PART II
#### PROTECTION OF WAGES

*Deductions by employer*

*Payments to employer*

*Cash shortages and stock deficiencies in retail employment*

*Enforcement*

*Supplementary*

#### PART III
#### GUARANTEE PAYMENTS

## PART IV
## SUNDAY WORKING FOR SHOP AND BETTING WORKERS

## PART IVA
## PROTECTED DISCLOSURES

## PART V
## PROTECTION FROM SUFFERING DETRIMENT IN EMPLOYMENT

## PART VI
## TIME OFF WORK

## CHAPTER II
## REMEDIES FOR UNFAIR DISMISSAL

## CHAPTER III
## SUPPLEMENTARY

PART XI
REDUNDANCY PAYMENTS ETC

CHAPTER I
RIGHT TO REDUNDANCY PAYMENT

CHAPTER II
RIGHT ON DISMISSAL BY REASON OF REDUNDANCY

*Dismissal by reason of redundancy*

*Exclusions*

*Supplementary*

CHAPTER III
RIGHT BY REASON OF LAY-OFF OR SHORT-TIME

*Lay-off and short-time*

*Exclusions*

*Supplementary*

CHAPTER IV
GENERAL EXCLUSIONS FROM RIGHT

CHAPTER V
OTHER PROVISIONS ABOUT REDUNDANCY PAYMENTS

CHAPTER VI
PAYMENTS BY SECRETARY OF STATE

CHAPTER VII
SUPPLEMENTARY

*Application of Part to particular cases*

SCHEDULES

Schedule 2—Transitional provisions, savings and transitory provisions

Part I—Transitional provisions and savings . . . . . . . . . . . . . . . . . . . . . . . . . [1.1049]

Part II—Transitory provisions . . . . . . . . . . . . . . . . . . . . . . . . . . . . . . . . [1.1050]

*An Act to consolidate enactments relating to employment rights*

[22 May 1996]

**NOTES**

This Act consolidates the individual employment legislation contained principally in the Employment Protection (Consolidation) Act 1978 (as extensively and repeatedly amended) and unrepealed provisions of the Wages Act 1986. It also incorporates relevant provisions in a number of other Acts as detailed in the Destination Table printed immediately following the text of the Act at **[1.1051]**. Provisions of the 1978 Act relating to employment tribunals and the Employment Appeal Tribunal were separately consolidated into the Employment Tribunals Act 1996 at **[1.678]** et seq.

The Act came into force on 22 August 1996, subject to transitional provisions in Sch 2, Pt II relating to consolidation of legislation not yet in force. Commencement details are not given for individual sections unless affected by Sch 2 or subsequently inserted by other legislation with effect on or after 6 April 2008. The whole of the Act is printed (as in force on 6 April 2013) except for ss 238 and 239, which apply to Northern Ireland and the Isle of Man, Schedules 1 and 3, which enact consequential amendments and repeals, and the sections (240 and 242) introducing them. Other provisions omitted are those repealed by subsequent legislation (as noted to each such provision). Provisions prospectively added to, and amendments prospectively made by, the Enterprise and Regulatory Reform Act 2013, the Growth and Infrastructure Act 2013 and the Crime and Courts Act 2013, each of which received Royal Assent on 25 April 2013, have been incorporated into the text of this Act at the appropriate places. As to the further power to amend this Act, see s 209 of this Act *post*, the Employment Relations Act 2004, s 42(1), (4)(d) at **[1.1335]**, the Health and Safety at Work etc Act 1974, s 80 at **[1.78]**, and the Pensions Act 2004, ss 259, 260.

Employment Appeal Tribunal: an appeal lies to the Employment Appeal Tribunal on any question of law arising from any decision of, or in any proceedings before, an employment tribunal under or by virtue of this Act; see the Employment Tribunals Act 1996, s 21(1)(f) at **[1.713]**.

See *Harvey* CII, DI, DII, E, H, J.

# PART I
# EMPLOYMENT PARTICULARS

*Right to statements of employment particulars*

**[1.743]**
## 1   Statement of initial employment particulars

(1)   Where an employee begins employment with an employer, the employer shall give to the employee a written statement of particulars of employment.

(2)   The statement may (subject to section 2(4)) be given in instalments and (whether or not given in instalments) shall be given not later than two months after the beginning of the employment.

(3)   The statement shall contain particulars of—

  (a)   the names of the employer and employee,

  (b)   the date when the employment began, and

  (c)   the date on which the employee's period of continuous employment began (taking into account any employment with a previous employer which counts towards that period).

(4)   The statement shall also contain particulars, as at a specified date not more than seven days before the statement (or the instalment containing them) is given, of—

  (a)   the scale or rate of remuneration or the method of calculating remuneration,

  (b)   the intervals at which remuneration is paid (that is, weekly, monthly or other specified intervals),

  (c)   any terms and conditions relating to hours of work (including any terms and conditions relating to normal working hours),

  (d)   any terms and conditions relating to any of the following—

    (i)   entitlement to holidays, including public holidays, and holiday pay (the particulars given being sufficient to enable the employee's entitlement, including any entitlement to accrued holiday pay on the termination of employment, to be precisely calculated),

    (ii)   incapacity for work due to sickness or injury, including any provision for sick pay, and

    (iii)   pensions and pension schemes,

  (e)   the length of notice which the employee is obliged to give and entitled to receive to terminate his contract of employment,

  (f)   the title of the job which the employee is employed to do or a brief description of the work for which he is employed,

  (g)   where the employment is not intended to be permanent, the period for which it is expected to continue or, if it is for a fixed term, the date when it is to end,

(h) either the place of work or, where the employee is required or permitted to work at various places, an indication of that and of the address of the employer,

(j) any collective agreements which directly affect the terms and conditions of the employment including, where the employer is not a party, the persons by whom they were made, and

(k) where the employee is required to work outside the United Kingdom for a period of more than one month—

    (i) the period for which he is to work outside the United Kingdom,

    (ii) the currency in which remuneration is to be paid while he is working outside the United Kingdom,

    (iii) any additional remuneration payable to him, and any benefits to be provided to or in respect of him, by reason of his being required to work outside the United Kingdom, and

    (iv) any terms and conditions relating to his return to the United Kingdom.

(5) Subsection (4)(d)(iii) does not apply to an employee of a body or authority if—

(a) the employee's pension rights depend on the terms of a pension scheme established under any provision contained in or having effect under any Act, and

(b) any such provision requires the body or authority to give to a new employee information concerning the employee's pension rights or the determination of questions affecting those rights.

**NOTES**

Failure to give statement: as to penalties for the failure to give a statement of employer particulars under sub-s (1) above or s 4(1) *post*, in relation to proceedings to which the Employment Act 2002, s 38, Sch 5 applies, see s 38 of that Act at **[1.1228]**.

Note: sub-s (4) did not contain a para (i) in the Queen's Printer's copy of this Act.

**[1.744]**

## 2 Statement of initial particulars: supplementary

(1) If, in the case of a statement under section 1, there are no particulars to be entered under any of the heads of paragraph (d) or (k) of subsection (4) of that section, or under any of the other paragraphs of subsection (3) or (4) of that section, that fact shall be stated.

(2) A statement under section 1 may refer the employee for particulars of any of the matters specified in subsection (4)(d)(ii) and (iii) of that section to the provisions of some other document which is reasonably accessible to the employee.

(3) A statement under section 1 may refer the employee for particulars of either of the matters specified in subsection (4)(e) of that section to the law or to the provisions of any collective agreement directly affecting the terms and conditions of the employment which is reasonably accessible to the employee.

(4) The particulars required by section 1(3) and (4)(a) to (c), (d)(i), (f) and (h) shall be included in a single document.

(5) Where before the end of the period of two months after the beginning of an employee's employment the employee is to begin to work outside the United Kingdom for a period of more than one month, the statement under section 1 shall be given to him not later than the time when he leaves the United Kingdom in order to begin so to work.

(6) A statement shall be given to a person under section 1 even if his employment ends before the end of the period within which the statement is required to be given.

**[1.745]**

## 3 Note about disciplinary procedures and pensions

(1) A statement under section 1 shall include a note—

(a) specifying any disciplinary rules applicable to the employee or referring the employee to the provisions of a document specifying such rules which is reasonably accessible to the employee,

[(aa) specifying any procedure applicable to the taking of disciplinary decisions relating to the employee, or to a decision to dismiss the employee, or referring the employee to the provisions of a document specifying such a procedure which is reasonably accessible to the employee,]

(b) specifying (by description or otherwise)—

    (i) a person to whom the employee can apply if dissatisfied with any disciplinary decision relating to him [or any decision to dismiss him], and

    (ii) a person to whom the employee can apply for the purpose of seeking redress of any grievance relating to his employment, and the manner in which any such application should be made, and

(c) where there are further steps consequent on any such application, explaining those steps or referring to the provisions of a document explaining them which is reasonably accessible to the employee.

(2) Subsection (1) does not apply to rules, disciplinary decisions, [decisions to dismiss,] grievances or procedures relating to health or safety at work.

(3), (4)   . . .

(5)   The note shall also state whether there is in force a contracting-out certificate (issued in accordance with Chapter 1 of Part III of the Pension Schemes Act 1993) stating that the employment is contracted-out employment (for the purposes of that Part of that Act).

**NOTES**

Sub-ss (1), (2): words in square brackets inserted by the Employment Act 2002, s 35.
Sub-ss (3), (4): repealed by the Employment Act 2002, ss 36, 54, Sch 8.

**[1.746]**
**4   Statement of changes**
(1)   If, after the material date, there is a change in any of the matters particulars of which are required by sections 1 to 3 to be included or referred to in a statement under section 1, the employer shall give to the employee a written statement containing particulars of the change.
(2)   For the purposes of subsection (1)—
  (a)   in relation to a matter particulars of which are included or referred to in a statement given under section 1 otherwise than in instalments, the material date is the date to which the statement relates,
  (b)   in relation to a matter particulars of which—
    (i)   are included or referred to in an instalment of a statement given under section 1, or
    (ii)   are required by section 2(4) to be included in a single document but are not included in an instalment of a statement given under section 1 which does include other particulars to which that provision applies,
    the material date is the date to which the instalment relates, and
  (c)   in relation to any other matter, the material date is the date by which a statement under section 1 is required to be given.
(3)   A statement under subsection (1) shall be given at the earliest opportunity and, in any event, not later than—
  (a)   one month after the change in question, or
  (b)   where that change results from the employee being required to work outside the United Kingdom for a period of more than one month, the time when he leaves the United Kingdom in order to begin so to work, if that is earlier.
(4)   A statement under subsection (1) may refer the employee to the provisions of some other document which is reasonably accessible to the employee for a change in any of the matters specified in sections 1(4)(d)(ii) and (iii) and 3(1)(a) and (c).
(5)   A statement under subsection (1) may refer the employee for a change in either of the matters specified in section 1(4)(e) to the law or to the provisions of any collective agreement directly affecting the terms and conditions of the employment which is reasonably accessible to the employee.
(6)   Where, after an employer has given to an employee a statement under section 1, either—
  (a)   the name of the employer (whether an individual or a body corporate or partnership) is changed without any change in the identity of the employer, or
  (b)   the identity of the employer is changed in circumstances in which the continuity of the employee's period of employment is not broken,
and subsection (7) applies in relation to the change, the person who is the employer immediately after the change is not required to give to the employee a statement under section 1; but the change shall be treated as a change falling within subsection (1) of this section.
(7)   This subsection applies in relation to a change if it does not involve any change in any of the matters (other than the names of the parties) particulars of which are required by sections 1 to 3 to be included or referred to in the statement under section 1.
(8)   A statement under subsection (1) which informs an employee of a change such as is referred to in subsection (6)(b) shall specify the date on which the employee's period of continuous employment began.

**NOTES**

Failure to give statement: see the note to s 1 at **[1.743]**.

**[1.747]**
**5   Exclusion from rights to statements**
(1)   Sections 1 to 4 apply to an employee who at any time comes or ceases to come within the exceptions from those sections provided by [section] 199, and under section 209, as if his employment with his employer terminated or began at that time.
(2)   The fact that section 1 is directed by subsection (1) to apply to an employee as if his employment began on his ceasing to come within the exceptions referred to in that subsection does not affect the obligation under section 1(3)(b) to specify the date on which his employment actually began.

**[1.748]**
**6 Reasonably accessible document or collective agreement**
In sections 2 to 4 references to a document or collective agreement which is reasonably accessible to an employee are references to a document or collective agreement which—
(a) the employee has reasonable opportunities of reading in the course of his employment, or
(b) is made reasonably accessible to the employee in some other way.

**[1.749]**
**7 Power to require particulars of further matters**
The Secretary of State may by order provide that section 1 shall have effect as if particulars of such further matters as may be specified in the order were included in the particulars required by that section; and, for that purpose, the order may include such provisions amending that section as appear to the Secretary of State to be expedient.

**[1.750]**
**[7A Use of alternative documents to give particulars**
(1) Subsections (2) and (3) apply where—
(a) an employer gives an employee a document in writing in the form of a contract of employment or letter of engagement,
(b) the document contains information which, were the document in the form of a statement under section 1, would meet the employer's obligation under that section in relation to the matters mentioned in subsections (3) and (4)(a) to (c), (d)(i), (f) and (h) of that section, and
(c) the document is given after the beginning of the employment and before the end of the period for giving a statement under that section.
(2) The employer's duty under section 1 in relation to any matter shall be treated as met if the document given to the employee contains information which, were the document in the form of a statement under that section, would meet the employer's obligation under that section in relation to that matter.
(3) The employer's duty under section 3 shall be treated as met if the document given to the employee contains information which, were the document in the form of a statement under section 1 and the information included in the form of a note, would meet the employer's obligation under section 3.
(4) For the purposes of this section a document to which subsection (1)(a) applies shall be treated, in relation to information in respect of any of the matters mentioned in section 1(4), as specifying the date on which the document is given to the employee as the date as at which the information applies.
(5) Where subsection (2) applies in relation to any matter, the date on which the document by virtue of which that subsection applies is given to the employee shall be the material date in relation to that matter for the purposes of section 4(1).
(6) Where subsection (3) applies, the date on which the document by virtue of which that subsection applies is given to the employee shall be the material date for the purposes of section 4(1) in relation to the matters of which particulars are required to be given under section 3.
(7) The reference in section 4(6) to an employer having given a statement under section 1 shall be treated as including his having given a document by virtue of which his duty to give such a statement is treated as met.]

**[1.751]**
**[7B Giving of alternative documents before start of employment**
A document in the form of a contract of employment or letter of engagement given by an employer to an employee before the beginning of the employee's employment with the employer shall, when the employment begins, be treated for the purposes of section 7A as having been given at that time.]

*Right to itemised pay statement*

**[1.752]**

## 8   Itemised pay statement

(1)   An employee has the right to be given by his employer, at or before the time at which any payment of wages or salary is made to him, a written itemised pay statement.

(2)   The statement shall contain particulars of—

    (a)   the gross amount of the wages or salary,

    (b)   the amounts of any variable, and (subject to section 9) any fixed, deductions from that gross amount and the purposes for which they are made,

    (c)   the net amount of wages or salary payable, and

    (d)   where different parts of the net amount are paid in different ways, the amount and method of payment of each part-payment.

**NOTES**

Conciliation: employment tribunal proceedings and claims which could be the subject of employment tribunal proceedings under this section are proceedings to which the Employment Tribunals Act 1996, s 18 applies; see s 18(1)(d) of that Act at **[1.706]**.

National minimum wage statement: a statement required to be given under the National Minimum Wage Act 1998, s 12 (national minimum wage statement) to a worker by his employer may, if the worker is an employee, be included in the written itemised pay statement required to be given to him by his employer under this section; see s 12(3) of the 1998 Act at **[1.1127]**.

Contravention of this section: for restrictions on the amount which may be ordered by an employment tribunal or court to be paid under the Trade Union and Labour Relations (Consolidation) Act 1992, s 68A, where the making of a deduction from the wages of a worker both contravenes s 68(1) of that Act and involves a contravention of the requirement not to make a deduction without having given the particulars required by this section, see s 68A(3), (4) of the 1992 Act at **[1.322]**.

**[1.753]**

## 9   Standing statement of fixed deductions

(1)   A pay statement given in accordance with section 8 need not contain separate particulars of a fixed deduction if—

    (a)   it contains instead an aggregate amount of fixed deductions, including that deduction, and

    (b)   the employer has given to the employee, at or before the time at which the pay statement is given, a standing statement of fixed deductions which satisfies subsection (2).

(2)   A standing statement of fixed deductions satisfies this subsection if—

    (a)   it is in writing,

    (b)   it contains, in relation to each deduction comprised in the aggregate amount of deductions, particulars of—

        (i)   the amount of the deduction,

        (ii)   the intervals at which the deduction is to be made, and

        (iii)   the purpose for which it is made, and

    (c)   it is (in accordance with subsection (5)) effective at the date on which the pay statement is given.

(3)   A standing statement of fixed deductions may be amended, whether by—

    (a)   addition of a new deduction,

    (b)   a change in the particulars, or

    (c)   cancellation of an existing deduction,

by notice in writing, containing particulars of the amendment, given by the employer to the employee.

(4)   An employer who has given to an employee a standing statement of fixed deductions shall—

    (a)   within the period of twelve months beginning with the date on which the first standing statement was given, and

    (b)   at intervals of not more than twelve months afterwards,

re-issue it in a consolidated form incorporating any amendments notified in accordance with subsection (3).

(5)   For the purposes of subsection (2)(c) a standing statement of fixed deductions—

    (a)   becomes effective on the date on which it is given to the employee, and

    (b)   ceases to be effective at the end of the period of twelve months beginning with that date or, where it is re-issued in accordance with subsection (4), with the end of the period of twelve months beginning with the date of the last re-issue.

**NOTES**

Contravention of this section: for restrictions on the amount which may be ordered by an employment tribunal or court to be paid under the Trade Union and Labour Relations (Consolidation) Act 1992, s 68A, where the making of a deduction from the wages of a worker both contravenes s 68(1) of that Act and involves a contravention of the requirement not to make a deduction without having given the particulars required by sub-s (1) above, see s 68A(3), (4) of the 1992 Act at **[1.322]**.

**[1.754]**

## 10   Power to amend provisions about pay and standing statements

The Secretary of State may by order—

(a)    vary the provisions of sections 8 and 9 as to the particulars which must be included in a pay statement or a standing statement of fixed deductions by adding items to, or removing items from, the particulars listed in those sections or by amending any such particulars, and

(b)    vary the provisions of subsections (4) and (5) of section 9 so as to shorten or extend the periods of twelve months referred to in those subsections, or those periods as varied from time to time under this section.

**NOTES**

Orders: as of 6 April 2013 no Orders had been made under this section.

*Enforcement*

**[1.755]**

**11  References to [employment tribunals]**

(1)  Where an employer does not give an employee a statement as required by section 1, 4 or 8 (either because he gives him no statement or because the statement he gives does not comply with what is required), the employee may require a reference to be made to an [employment tribunal] to determine what particulars ought to have been included or referred to in a statement so as to comply with the requirements of the section concerned.

(2)  Where—

(a)    a statement purporting to be a statement under section 1 or 4, or a pay statement or a standing statement of fixed deductions purporting to comply with section 8 or 9, has been given to an employee, and

(b)    a question arises as to the particulars which ought to have been included or referred to in the statement so as to comply with the requirements of this Part,

either the employer or the employee may require the question to be referred to and determined by an [employment tribunal].

(3)  For the purposes of this section—

(a)    a question as to the particulars which ought to have been included in the note required by section 3 to be included in the statement under section 1 does not include any question whether the employment is, has been or will be contracted-out employment (for the purposes of Part III of the Pension Schemes Act 1993), and

(b)    a question as to the particulars which ought to have been included in a pay statement or standing statement of fixed deductions does not include a question solely as to the accuracy of an amount stated in any such particulars.

(4)  An [employment tribunal] shall not consider a reference under this section in a case where the employment to which the reference relates has ceased unless an application requiring the reference to be made was made—

(a)    before the end of the period of three months beginning with the date on which the employment ceased, or

(b)    within such further period as the tribunal considers reasonable in a case where it is satisfied that it was not reasonably practicable for the application to be made before the end of that period of three months.

[(5)  Section 207A(3) (extension because of mediation in certain European cross-border disputes) applies for the purposes of subsection (4)(a).].

[(6)  Where the reference concerns compliance with section 8, section 207B (extension of time limits to facilitate conciliation before institution of proceedings) also applies for the purposes of subsection (4)(a).]

**NOTES**

Section heading, sub-ss (1), (2), (4): words in square brackets substituted by the Employment Rights (Dispute Resolution) Act 1998, s 1(2)(a), (b).

Sub-s (5): added by the Cross-Border Mediation (EU Directive) Regulations 2011, SI 2011/1133, regs 30, 31, as from 20 May 2011.

Sub-s (6): added by the Enterprise and Regulatory Reform Act 2013, s 8, Sch 2, paras 15, 16, as from a day to be appointed.

**[1.756]**

**12  Determination of references**

(1)  Where, on a reference under section 11(1), an [employment tribunal] determines particulars as being those which ought to have been included or referred to in a statement given under section 1 or 4, the employer shall be deemed to have given to the employee a statement in which those particulars were included, or referred to, as specified in the decision of the tribunal.

(2)  On determining a reference under section 11(2) relating to a statement purporting to be a statement under section 1 or 4, an [employment tribunal] may—

(a)    confirm the particulars as included or referred to in the statement given by the employer,

(b)    amend those particulars, or

(c)    substitute other particulars for them,

as the tribunal may determine to be appropriate; and the statement shall be deemed to have been given by the employer to the employee in accordance with the decision of the tribunal.

(3)   Where on a reference under section 11 an [employment tribunal] finds—

(a)    that an employer has failed to give an employee any pay statement in accordance with section 8, or

(b)    that a pay statement or standing statement of fixed deductions does not, in relation to a deduction, contain the particulars required to be included in that statement by that section or section 9,

the tribunal shall make a declaration to that effect.

(4)   Where on a reference in the case of which subsection (3) applies the tribunal further finds that any unnotified deductions have been made (from the pay of the employee during the period of thirteen weeks immediately preceding the date of the application for the reference (whether or not the deductions were made in breach of the contract of employment), the tribunal may order the employer to pay the employee a sum not exceeding the aggregate of the unnotified deductions so made.

(5)   For the purposes of subsection (4) a deduction is an unnotified deduction if it is made without the employer giving the employee, in any pay statement or standing statement of fixed deductions, the particulars of the deduction required by section 8 or 9.

**NOTES**

  Sub-ss (1)–(3): words in square brackets substituted by the Employment Rights (Dispute Resolution) Act 1998, s 1(2)(a). See further, as to remedies following a reference under s 11(1) or (2), the notes to s 1 at **[1.743]**.

## PART II
## PROTECTION OF WAGES

### *Deductions by employer*

**[1.757]**
### 13   Right not to suffer unauthorised deductions

(1)   An employer shall not make a deduction from wages of a worker employed by him unless—

(a)    the deduction is required or authorised to be made by virtue of a statutory provision or a relevant provision of the worker's contract, or

(b)    the worker has previously signified in writing his agreement or consent to the making of the deduction.

(2)   In this section "relevant provision", in relation to a worker's contract, means a provision of the contract comprised—

(a)    in one or more written terms of the contract of which the employer has given the worker a copy on an occasion prior to the employer making the deduction in question, or

(b)    in one or more terms of the contract (whether express or implied and, if express, whether oral or in writing) the existence and effect, or combined effect, of which in relation to the worker the employer has notified to the worker in writing on such an occasion.

(3)   Where the total amount of wages paid on any occasion by an employer to a worker employed by him is less than the total amount of the wages properly payable by him to the worker on that occasion (after deductions), the amount of the deficiency shall be treated for the purposes of this Part as a deduction made by the employer from the worker's wages on that occasion.

(4)   Subsection (3) does not apply in so far as the deficiency is attributable to an error of any description on the part of the employer affecting the computation by him of the gross amount of the wages properly payable by him to the worker on that occasion.

(5)   For the purposes of this section a relevant provision of a worker's contract having effect by virtue of a variation of the contract does not operate to authorise the making of a deduction on account of any conduct of the worker, or any other event occurring, before the variation took effect.

(6)   For the purposes of this section an agreement or consent signified by a worker does not operate to authorise the making of a deduction on account of any conduct of the worker, or any other event occurring, before the agreement or consent was signified.

(7)   This section does not affect any other statutory provision by virtue of which a sum payable to a worker by his employer but not constituting "wages" within the meaning of this Part is not to be subject to a deduction at the instance of the employer.

**NOTES**

  Conciliation: employment tribunal proceedings and claims which could be the subject of employment tribunal proceedings under this section are proceedings to which the Employment Tribunals Act 1996, s 18 applies; see s 18(1)(d) of that Act at **[1.706]**.

  Contravention of this section: for restrictions on the amount which may be ordered by an employment tribunal or court to be paid under the Trade Union and Labour Relations (Consolidation) Act 1992, s 68A, where the making of a deduction from the wages of a worker both contravenes s 68(1) of that Act and involves a contravention of this section, see s 68A(3), (4) of the 1992 Act at **[1.322]**.

**[1.758]**
## 14 Excepted deductions
(1)   Section 13 does not apply to a deduction from a worker's wages made by his employer where the purpose of the deduction is the reimbursement of the employer in respect of—
   (a)   an overpayment of wages, or
   (b)   an overpayment in respect of expenses incurred by the worker in carrying out his employment,
made (for any reason) by the employer to the worker.
(2)   Section 13 does not apply to a deduction from a worker's wages made by his employer in consequence of any disciplinary proceedings if those proceedings were held by virtue of a statutory provision.
(3)   Section 13 does not apply to a deduction from a worker's wages made by his employer in pursuance of a requirement imposed on the employer by a statutory provision to deduct and pay over to a public authority amounts determined by that authority as being due to it from the worker if the deduction is made in accordance with the relevant determination of that authority.
(4)   Section 13 does not apply to a deduction from a worker's wages made by his employer in pursuance of any arrangements which have been established—
   (a)   in accordance with a relevant provision of his contract to the inclusion of which in the contract the worker has signified his agreement or consent in writing, or
   (b)   otherwise with the prior agreement or consent of the worker signified in writing,
and under which the employer is to deduct and pay over to a third person amounts notified to the employer by that person as being due to him from the worker, if the deduction is made in accordance with the relevant notification by that person.
(5)   Section 13 does not apply to a deduction from a worker's wages made by his employer where the worker has taken part in a strike or other industrial action and the deduction is made by the employer on account of the worker's having taken part in that strike or other action.
(6)   Section 13 does not apply to a deduction from a worker's wages made by his employer with his prior agreement or consent signified in writing where the purpose of the deduction is the satisfaction (whether wholly or in part) of an order of a court or tribunal requiring the payment of an amount by the worker to the employer.

*Payments to employer*

**[1.759]**
## 15 Right not to have to make payments to employer
(1)   An employer shall not receive a payment from a worker employed by him unless—
   (a)   the payment is required or authorised to be made by virtue of a statutory provision or a relevant provision of the worker's contract, or
   (b)   the worker has previously signified in writing his agreement or consent to the making of the payment.
(2)   In this section "relevant provision", in relation to a worker's contract, means a provision of the contract comprised—
   (a)   in one or more written terms of the contract of which the employer has given the worker a copy on an occasion prior to the employer receiving the payment in question, or
   (b)   in one or more terms of the contract (whether express or implied and, if express, whether oral or in writing) the existence and effect, or combined effect, of which in relation to the worker the employer has notified to the worker in writing on such an occasion.
(3)   For the purposes of this section a relevant provision of a worker's contract having effect by virtue of a variation of the contract does not operate to authorise the receipt of a payment on account of any conduct of the worker, or any other event occurring, before the variation took affect.
(4)   For the purposes of this section an agreement or consent signified by a worker does not operate to authorise the receipt of a payment on account of any conduct of the worker, or any other event occurring, before the agreement or consent was signified.
(5)   Any reference in this Part to an employer receiving a payment from a worker employed by him is a reference to his receiving such a payment in his capacity as the worker's employer.

**NOTES**
   Conciliation: employment tribunal proceedings and claims which could be the subject of employment tribunal proceedings under this section are proceedings to which the Employment Tribunals Act 1996, s 18 applies; see s 18(1)(d) of that Act at **[1.706]**.

**[1.760]**
## 16 Excepted payments
(1)   Section 15 does not apply to a payment received from a worker by his employer where the purpose of the payment is the reimbursement of the employer in respect of—
   (a)   an overpayment of wages, or
   (b)   an overpayment in respect of expenses incurred by the worker in carrying out his employment,
made (for any reason) by the employer to the worker.

(2)    Section 15 does not apply to a payment received from a worker by his employer in consequence of any disciplinary proceedings if those proceedings were held by virtue of a statutory provision.

(3)    Section 15 does not apply to a payment received from a worker by his employer where the worker has taken part in a strike or other industrial action and the payment has been required by the employer on account of the worker's having taken part in that strike or other action.

(4)    Section 15 does not apply to a payment received from a worker by his employer where the purpose of the payment is the satisfaction (whether wholly or in part) of an order of a court or tribunal requiring the payment of an amount by the worker to the employer.

*Cash shortages and stock deficiencies in retail employment*

**[1.761]**
**17    Introductory**
(1)    In the following provisions of this Part—
   "cash shortage" means a deficit arising in relation to amounts received in connection with retail transactions, and
   "stock deficiency" means a stock deficiency arising in the course of retail transactions.

(2)    In the following provisions of this Part "retail employment", in relation to a worker, means employment involving (whether or not on a regular basis)—
   (a)    the carrying out by the worker of retail transactions directly with members of the public or with fellow workers or other individuals in their personal capacities, or
   (b)    the collection by the worker of amounts payable in connection with retail transactions carried out by other persons directly with members of the public or with fellow workers or other individuals in their personal capacities.

(3)    References in this section to a "retail transaction" are to the sale or supply of goods or the supply of services (including financial services).

(4)    References in the following provisions of this Part to a deduction made from wages of a worker in retail employment, or to a payment received from such a worker by his employer, on account of a cash shortage or stock deficiency include references to a deduction or payment so made or received on account of—
   (a)    any dishonesty or other conduct on the part of the worker which resulted in any such shortage or deficiency, or
   (b)    any other event in respect of which he (whether or not together with any other workers) has any contractual liability and which so resulted,
in each case whether or not the amount of the deduction or payment is designed to reflect the exact amount of the shortage or deficiency.

(5)    References in the following provisions of this Part to the recovery from a worker of an amount in respect of a cash shortage or stock deficiency accordingly include references to the recovery from him of an amount in respect of any such conduct or event as is mentioned in subsection (4)(a) or (b).

(6)    In the following provisions of this Part "pay day", in relation to a worker, means a day on which wages are payable to the worker.

**[1.762]**
**18    Limits on amount and time of deductions**
(1)    Where (in accordance with section 13) the employer of a worker in retail employment makes, on account of one or more cash shortages or stock deficiencies, a deduction or deductions from wages payable to the worker on a pay day, the amount or aggregate amount of the deduction or deductions shall not exceed one-tenth of the gross amount of the wages payable to the worker on that day.

(2)    Where the employer of a worker in retail employment makes a deduction from the worker's wages on account of a cash shortage or stock deficiency, the employer shall not be treated as making the deduction in accordance with section 13 unless (in addition to the requirements of that section being satisfied with respect to the deduction)—
   (a)    the deduction is made, or
   (b)    in the case of a deduction which is one of a series of deductions relating to the shortage or deficiency, the first deduction in the series was made,
not later than the end of the relevant period.

(3)    In subsection (2) "the relevant-period" means the period of twelve months beginning with the date when the employer established the existence of the shortage or deficiency or (if earlier) the date when he ought reasonably to have done so.

---

**NOTES**
   Conciliation: employment tribunal proceedings and claims which could be the subject of employment tribunal proceedings under sub-s (1) are proceedings to which the Employment Tribunals Act 1996, s 18 applies; see s 18(1)(d) of that Act at **[1.706]**.

**[1.763]**
**19 Wages determined by reference to shortages etc**
(1)   This section applies where—
  (a)   by virtue of an agreement between a worker in retail employment and his employer, the amount of the worker's wages or any part of them is or may be determined by reference to the incidence of cash shortages or stock deficiencies, and
  (b)   the gross amount of the wages payable to the worker on any pay day is, on account of any such shortages or deficiencies, less than the gross amount of the wages that would have been payable to him on that day if there had been no such shortages or deficiencies.
(2)   The amount representing the difference between the two amounts referred to in subsection (1)(b) shall be treated for the purposes of this Part as a deduction from the wages payable to the worker on that day made by the employer on account of the cash shortages or stock deficiencies in question.
(3)   The second of the amounts referred to in subsection (1)(b) shall be treated for the purposes of this Part (except subsection (1)) as the gross amount of the wages payable to him on that day.
(4)   Accordingly—
  (a)   section 13, and
  (b)   if the requirements of section 13 and subsection (2) of section 18 are satisfied, subsection (1) of section 18,
have effect in relation to the amount referred to in subsection (2) of this section.

**[1.764]**
**20 Limits on method and timing of payments**
(1)   Where the employer of a worker in retail employment receives from the worker a payment on account of a cash shortage or stock deficiency, the employer shall not be treated as receiving the payment in accordance with section 15 unless (in addition to the requirements of that section being satisfied with respect to the payment) he has previously—
  (a)   notified the worker in writing of the worker's total liability to him in respect of that shortage or deficiency, and
  (b)   required the worker to make the payment by means of a demand for payment made in accordance with the following provisions of this section.
(2)   A demand for payment made by the employer of a worker in retail employment in respect of a cash shortage or stock deficiency—
  (a)   shall be made in writing, and
  (b)   shall be made on one of the worker's pay days.
(3)   A demand for payment in respect of a particular cash shortage or stock deficiency, or (in the case of a series of such demands) the first such demand, shall not be made—
  (a)   earlier than the first pay day of the worker following the date when he is notified of his total liability in respect of the shortage or deficiency in pursuance of subsection (1)(a) or, where he is so notified on a pay day, earlier than that day, or
  (b)   later than the end of the period of twelve months beginning with the date when the employer established the existence of the shortage or deficiency or (if earlier) the date when he ought reasonably to have done so.
(4)   For the purposes of this Part a demand for payment shall be treated as made by the employer on one of a worker's pay days if it is given to the worker or posted to, or left at, his last known address—
  (a)   on that pay day, or
  (b)   in the case of a pay day which is not a working day of the employer's business, on the first such working day following that pay day.
(5)   Legal proceedings by the employer of a worker in retail employment for the recovery from the worker of an amount in respect of a cash shortage or stock deficiency shall not be instituted by the employer after the end of the period referred to in subsection (3)(b) unless the employer has within that period made a demand for payment in respect of that amount in accordance with this section.

**[1.765]**
**21 Limit on amount of payments**
(1)   Where the employer of a worker in retail employment makes on any pay day one or more demands for payment in accordance with section 20, the amount or aggregate amount required to be paid by the worker in pursuance of the demand or demands shall not exceed—
  (a)   one-tenth of the gross amount of the wages payable to the worker on that day, or
  (b)   where one or more deductions falling within section 18(1) are made by the employer from those wages, such amount as represents the balance of that one-tenth after subtracting the amount or aggregate amount of the deduction or deductions.
(2)   Once an amount has been required to be paid by means of a demand for payment made in accordance with section 20 on any pay day, that amount shall not be taken into account under subsection (1) as it applies to any subsequent pay day, even though the employer is obliged to make further requests for it to be paid.

(3)   Where in any legal proceedings the court finds that the employer of a worker in retail employment is (in accordance with section 15 as it applies apart from section 20(1)) entitled to recover an amount from the worker in respect of a cash shortage or stock deficiency, the court shall, in ordering the payment by the worker to the employer of that amount, make such provision as appears to the court to be necessary to ensure that it is paid by the worker at a rate not exceeding that at which it could be recovered from him by the employer in accordance with this section.

**NOTES**

Conciliation: employment tribunal proceedings and claims which could be the subject of employment tribunal proceedings under sub-s (1) are proceedings to which the Employment Tribunals Act 1996, s 18 applies; see s 18(1)(d) of that Act at **[1.706]**.

**[1.766]**
**22   Final instalments of wages**
(1)   In this section "final instalment of wages", in relation to a worker, means—
  (a)   the amount of wages payable to the worker which consists of or includes an amount payable by way of contractual remuneration in respect of the last of the periods for which he is employed under his contract prior to its termination for any reason (but excluding any wages referable to any earlier such period), or
  (b)   where an amount in lieu of notice is paid to the worker later than the amount referred to in paragraph (a), the amount so paid,
in each case whether the amount in question is paid before or after the termination of the worker's contract.
(2)   Section 18(1) does not operate to restrict the amount of any deductions which may (in accordance with section 13(1)) be made by the employer of a worker in retail employment from the worker's final instalment of wages.
(3)   Nothing in section 20 or 21 applies to a payment falling within section 20(1) which is made on or after the day on which any such worker's final instalment of wages is paid; but (even if the requirements of section 15 would otherwise be satisfied with respect to it) his employer shall not be treated as receiving any such payment in accordance with that section if the payment was first required to be made after the end of the period referred to in section 20(3)(b).
(4)   Section 21(3) does not apply to an amount which is to be paid by a worker on or after the day on which his final instalment of wages is paid.

*Enforcement*

**[1.767]**
**23   Complaints to [employment tribunals]**
(1)   A worker may present a complaint to an [employment tribunal]—
  (a)   that his employer has made a deduction from his wages in contravention of section 13 (including a deduction made in contravention of that section as it applies by virtue of section 18(2)),
  (b)   that his employer has received from him a payment in contravention of section 15 (including a payment received in contravention of that section as it applies by virtue of section 20(1)),
  (c)   that his employer has recovered from his wages by means of one or more deductions falling within section 18(1) an amount or aggregate amount exceeding the limit applying to the deduction or deductions under that provision, or
  (d)   that his employer has received from him in pursuance of one or more demands for payment made (in accordance with section 20) on a particular pay day, a payment or payments of an amount or aggregate amount exceeding the limit applying to the demand or demands under section 21(1).
(2)   Subject to subsection (4), an [employment tribunal] shall not consider a complaint under this section unless it is presented before the end of the period of three months beginning with—
  (a)   in the case of a complaint relating to a deduction by the employer, the date of payment of the wages from which the deduction was made, or
  (b)   in the case of a complaint relating to a payment received by the employer, the date when the payment was received.
(3)   Where a complaint is brought under this section in respect of—
  (a)   a series of deductions or payments, or
  (b)   a number of payments falling within subsection (1)(d) and made in pursuance of demands for payment subject to the same limit under section 21(1) but received by the employer on different dates,
the references in subsection (2) to the deduction or payment are to the last deduction or payment in the series or to the last of the payments so received.
[(3A)   Section 207A(3) (extension because of mediation in certain European cross-border disputes) *applies* for the purposes of subsection (2).]

(4)   Where the [employment tribunal] is satisfied that it was not reasonably practicable for a complaint under this section to be presented before the end of the relevant period of three months, the tribunal may consider the complaint if it is presented within such further period as the tribunal considers reasonable.

[(5)   No complaint shall be presented under this section in respect of any deduction made in contravention of section 86 of the Trade Union and Labour Relations (Consolidation) Act 1992 (deduction of political fund contribution where certificate of exemption or objection has been given).]

**NOTES**

Section heading, sub-ss (1), (2), (4): words in square brackets substituted by the Employment Rights (Dispute Resolution) Act 1998, s 1(2)(a), (b).

Sub-s (3A): inserted by the Cross-Border Mediation (EU Directive) Regulations 2011, SI 2011/1133, regs 30, 32, as from 20 May 2011; for the word in italics there are substituted the words "and section 207B (extension of time limits to facilitate conciliation before institution of proceedings) apply" by the Enterprise and Regulatory Reform Act 2013, s 8, Sch 2, paras 15, 17, as from a day to be appointed.

Sub-s (5): added by the Employment Rights (Dispute Resolution) Act 1998, s 15, Sch 1, para 18.

Tribunal jurisdiction: the Employment Act 2002, s 38 applies to proceedings before the employment tribunal relating to a claim under this section; see s 38(1) of, and Sch 5 to, the 2002 Act at **[1.1228]**, **[1.1236]**. See also the Trade Union and Labour Relations (Consolidation) Act 1992, s 207A at **[1.474]** (as inserted by the Employment Act 2008). That section provides that in proceedings before an employment tribunal relating to a claim by an employee under any of the jurisdictions listed in Sch A2 to the 1992 Act at **[1.648]** (which includes this section) the tribunal may adjust any award given if the employer or the employee has unreasonably failed to comply with the relevant Code of Practice as defined by s 207A(4). See also the revised Acas Code of Practice 1 – Disciplinary and Grievance Procedures (2009) at **[4.1]**.

As to the power of an officer acting for the purposes of the National Minimum Wage Act 1998 to present a complaint under sub-s (1)(a) above where a notice of underpayment served under s 19 of the 1998 Act has not been complied with, see s 19D(1)(a) of that Act at **[1.1139]**. As to the reversal of the burden of proof where such a complaint is made, see s 28(2) of that Act at **[1.1146]**.

**[1.768]**
## 24   Determination of complaints

[(1)]   Where a tribunal finds a complaint under section 23 well-founded, it shall make a declaration to that effect and shall order the employer—
  (a)   in the case of a complaint under section 23(1)(a), to pay to the worker the amount of any deduction made in contravention of section 13,
  (b)   in the case of a complaint under section 23(1)(b), to repay to the worker the amount of any payment received in contravention of section 15,
  (c)   in the case of a complaint under section 23(1)(c), to pay to the worker any amount recovered from him in excess of the limit mentioned in that provision, and
  (d)   in the case of a complaint under section 23(1)(d), to repay to the worker any amount received from him in excess of the limit mentioned in that provision.

[(2)   Where a tribunal makes a declaration under subsection (1), it may order the employer to pay to the worker (in addition to any amount ordered to be paid under that subsection) such amount as the tribunal considers appropriate in all the circumstances to compensate the worker for any financial loss sustained by him which is attributable to the matter complained of.]

**NOTES**

Sub-s (1) numbered as such, and sub-s (2) added, by the Employment Act 2008, s 7(1), as from 6 April 2009, except where the complaint has been presented to the employment tribunal before that date (see SI 2008/3232, Schedule, Pt 1, para 5).

**[1.769]**
## 25   Determinations: supplementary

(1)   Where, in the case of any complaint under section 23(1)(a), a tribunal finds that, although neither of the conditions set out in section 13(1)(a) and (b) was satisfied with respect to the whole amount of the deduction, one of those conditions was satisfied with respect to any lesser amount, the amount of the deduction shall for the purposes of section 24(a) be treated as reduced by the amount with respect to which that condition was satisfied.

(2)   Where, in the case of any complaint under section 23(1)(b), a tribunal finds that, although neither of the conditions set out in section 15(1)(a) and (b) was satisfied with respect to the whole amount of the payment, one of those conditions was satisfied with respect to any lesser amount, the amount of the payment shall for the purposes of section 24(b) be treated as reduced by the amount with respect to which that condition was satisfied.

(3)   An employer shall not under section 24 be ordered by a tribunal to pay or repay to a worker any amount in respect of a deduction or payment, or in respect of any combination of deductions or payments, in so far as it appears to the tribunal that he has already paid or repaid any such amount to the worker.

(4) Where a tribunal has under section 24 ordered an employer to pay or repay to a worker any amount in respect of a particular deduction or payment falling within section 23(1)(a) to (d), the amount which the employer is entitled to recover (by whatever means) in respect of the matter in relation to which the deduction or payment was originally made or received shall be treated as reduced by that amount.

(5) Where a tribunal has under section 24 ordered an employer to pay or repay to a worker any amount in respect of any combination of deductions or payments falling within section 23(1)(c) or (d), the aggregate amount which the employer is entitled to recover (by whatever means) in respect of the cash shortages or stock deficiencies in relation to which the deductions or payments were originally made or required to be made shall be treated as reduced by that amount.

**[1.770]**
**26  Complaints and other remedies**
Section 23 does not affect the jurisdiction of an [employment tribunal] to consider a reference under section 11 in relation to any deduction from the wages of a worker; but the aggregate of any amounts ordered by an [employment tribunal] to be paid under section 12(4) and under section 24 (whether on the same or different occasions) in respect of a particular deduction shall not exceed the amount of the deduction.

**NOTES**
Words in square brackets substituted by the Employment Rights (Dispute Resolution) Act 1998, s 1(2)(a).

*Supplementary*

**[1.771]**
**27  Meaning of "wages" etc**
(1) In this Part "wages", in relation to a worker, means any sums payable to the worker in connection with his employment, including—
  (a)  any fee, bonus, commission, holiday pay or other emolument referable to his employment, whether payable under his contract or otherwise,
  (b)  statutory sick pay under Part XI of the Social Security Contributions and Benefits Act 1992,
  (c)  statutory maternity pay under Part XII of that Act,
  [(ca)  [ordinary statutory paternity pay or additional statutory paternity pay] under Part 12ZA of that Act,
  (cb)  statutory adoption pay under Part 12ZB of that Act,]
  (d)  a guarantee payment (under section 28 of this Act),
  (e)  any payment for time off under Part VI of this Act or section 169 of the Trade Union and Labour Relations (Consolidation) Act 1992 (payment for time off for carrying out trade union duties etc),
  (f)  remuneration on suspension on medical grounds under section 64 of this Act and remuneration on suspension on maternity grounds under section 68 of this Act,
  [(fa)  remuneration on ending the supply of an agency worker on maternity grounds under section 68C of this Act,]
  (g)  any sum payable in pursuance of an order for reinstatement or re-engagement under section 113 of this Act,
  (h)  any sum payable in pursuance of an order for the continuation of a contract of employment under section 130 of this Act or section 164 of the Trade Union and Labour Relations (Consolidation) Act 1992, and
  (j)  remuneration under a protective award under section 189 of that Act,
but excluding any payments within subsection (2).
(2) Those payments are—
  (a)  any payment by way of an advance under an agreement for a loan or by way of an advance of wages (but without prejudice to the application of section 13 to any deduction made from the worker's wages in respect of any such advance),
  (b)  any payment in respect of expenses incurred by the worker in carrying out his employment,
  (c)  any payment by way of a pension, allowance or gratuity in connection with the worker's retirement or as compensation for loss of office,
  (d)  any payment referable to the worker's redundancy, and
  (e)  any payment to the worker otherwise than in his capacity as a worker.
(3) Where any payment in the nature of a non-contractual bonus is (for any reason) made to a worker by his employer, the amount of the payment shall for the purposes of this Part—
  (a)  be treated as wages of the worker, and
  (b)  be treated as payable to him as such on the day on which the payment is made.
(4) In this Part "gross amount", in relation to any wages payable to a worker, means the total amount of those wages before deductions of whatever nature.

(5)   For the purposes of this Part any monetary value attaching to any payment or benefit in kind furnished to a worker by his employer shall not be treated as wages of the worker except in the case of any voucher, stamp or similar document which is—

(a)   of a fixed value expressed in monetary terms, and

(b)   capable of being exchanged (whether on its own or together with other vouchers, stamps or documents, and whether immediately or only after a time) for money, goods or services (or for any combination of two or more of those things).

**NOTES**

Sub-s (1): paras (ca), (cb) inserted by the Employment Act 2002, s 53, Sch 7, paras 24, 25; words in square brackets in para (ca) substituted by the Work and Families Act 2006, s 11(1), Sch 1, para 29, as from 6 April 2010; para (fa) inserted by the Agency Workers Regulations 2010, SI 2010/93, reg 25, Sch 2, Pt 1, paras 9, 10, as from 1 October 2011.

Note: sub-s (1) did not contain a para (i) in the Queen's Printer's copy of this Act.

# PART III
# GUARANTEE PAYMENTS

**NOTES**

Recoupment of social security benefits: as to the power to provide for recoupment of social security benefits in relation to payments by employers to employees under this Part, that are the subject of proceedings before employment tribunals, see the Employment Tribunals Act 1996, s 16 at [**1.704**].

## [1.772]
## 28   Right to guarantee payment

(1)   Where throughout a day during any part of which an employee would normally be required to work in accordance with his contract of employment the employee is not provided with work by his employer by reason of—

(a)   a diminution in the requirements of the employer's business for work of the kind which the employee is employed to do, or

(b)   any other occurrence affecting the normal working of the employer's business in relation to work of the kind which the employee is employed to do,

the employee is entitled to be paid by his employer an amount in respect of that day.

(2)   In this Act a payment to which an employee is entitled under subsection (1) is referred to as a guarantee payment.

(3)   In this Part—

(a)   a day falling within subsection (1) is referred to as a "workless day", and

(b)   "workless period" has a corresponding meaning.

(4)   In this Part "day" means the period of twenty-four hours from midnight to midnight.

(5)   Where a period of employment begun on any day extends, or would normally extend, over midnight into the following day—

(a)   if the employment before midnight is, or would normally be, of longer duration than that after midnight, the period of employment shall be treated as falling wholly on the first day, and

(b)   in any other case, the period of employment shall be treated as falling wholly on the second day.

**NOTES**

Conciliation: employment tribunal proceedings and claims which could be the subject of employment tribunal proceedings under this section are proceedings to which the Employment Tribunals Act 1996, s 18 applies; see s 18(1)(d) of that Act at [**1.706**].

## [1.773]
## 29   Exclusions from right to guarantee payment

(1)   An employee is not entitled to a guarantee payment unless he has been continuously employed for a period of not less than one month ending with the day before that in respect of which the guarantee payment is claimed.

(2)   . . .

(3)   An employee is not entitled to a guarantee payment in respect of a workless day if the failure to provide him with work for that day occurs in consequence of a strike, lock-out or other industrial action involving any employee of his employer or of an associated employer.

(4)   An employee is not entitled to a guarantee payment in respect of a workless day if—

(a)   his employer has offered to provide alternative work for that day which is suitable in all the circumstances (whether or not it is work which the employee is under his contract employed to perform), and

(b)   the employee has unreasonably refused that offer.

(5)   An employee is not entitled to a guarantee payment if he does not comply with reasonable requirements imposed by his employer with a view to ensuring that his services are available.

Part 1   Statutes

**NOTES**

Sub-s (2): repealed by the Fixed-term Employees (Prevention of Less Favourable Treatment) Regulations 2002, SI 2002/2034, reg 11, Sch 2, Pt 1, para 3(1), (2) (except in relation to Government training schemes, agency workers or apprentices; see regs 18–20 of the 2002 Regulations at **[2.614]** et seq).

**[1.774]**
**30   Calculation of guarantee payment**
(1)   Subject to section 31, the amount of a guarantee payment payable to an employee in respect of any day is the sum produced by multiplying the number of normal working hours on the day by the guaranteed hourly rate; and, accordingly, no guarantee payment is payable to an employee in whose case there are no normal working hours on the day in question.
(2)   The guaranteed hourly rate, in relation to an employee, is the amount of one week's pay divided by the number of normal working hours in a week for that employee when employed under the contract of employment in force on the day in respect of which the guarantee payment is payable.
(3)   But where the number of normal working hours differs from week to week or over a longer period, the amount of one week's pay shall be divided instead by—
    (a)   the average number of normal working hours calculated by dividing by twelve the total number of the employee's normal working hours during the period of twelve weeks ending with the last complete week before the day in respect of which the guarantee payment is payable, or
    (b)   where the employee has not been employed for a sufficient period to enable the calculation to be made under paragraph (a), a number which fairly represents the number of normal working hours in a week having regard to such of the considerations specified in subsection (4) as are appropriate in the circumstances.
(4)   The considerations referred to in subsection (3)(b) are—
    (a)   the average number of normal working hours in a week which the employee could expect in accordance with the terms of his contract, and
    (b)   the average number of normal working hours of other employees engaged in relevant comparable employment with the same employer.
(5)   If in any case an employee's contract has been varied, or a new contract has been entered into, in connection with a period of short-time working, subsections (2) and (3) have effect as if for the references to the day in respect of which the guarantee payment is payable there were substituted references to the last day on which the original contract was in force.

**[1.775]**
**31   Limits on amount of and entitlement to guarantee payment**
(1)   The amount of a guarantee payment payable to an employee in respect of any day shall not exceed [£24.20].
(2)   An employee is not entitled to guarantee payments in respect of more than the specified number of days in any period of three months.
(3)   The specified number of days for the purposes of subsection (2) is the number of days, not exceeding five, on which the employee normally works in a week under the contract of employment in force on the day in respect of which the guarantee payment is claimed.
(4)   But where that number of days varies from week to week or over a longer period, the specified number of days is instead—
    (a)   the average number of such days, not exceeding five, calculated by dividing by twelve the total number of such days during the period of twelve weeks ending with the last complete week before the day in respect of which the guarantee payment is claimed, and rounding up the resulting figure to the next whole number, or
    (b)   where the employee has not been employed for a sufficient period to enable the calculation to be made under paragraph (a), a number which fairly represents the number of the employee's normal working days in a week, not exceeding five, having regard to such of the considerations specified in subsection (5) as are appropriate in the circumstances.
(5)   The considerations referred to in subsection (4)(b) are—
    (a)   the average number of normal working days in a week which the employee could expect in accordance with the terms of his contract, and
    (b)   the average number of such days of other employees engaged in relevant comparable employment with the same employer.
(6)   If in any case an employee's contract has been varied, or a new contract has been entered into, in connection with a period of short-time working, subsections (3) and (4) have effect as if for the references to the day in respect of which the guarantee payment is claimed there were substituted references to the last day on which the original contract was in force.
[(7)   The Secretary of State may by order vary—
    (a)   the length of the period specified in subsection (2);
    (b)   a limit specified in subsection (3) or (4).]

NOTES
Sub-s (1): sum in square brackets substituted by the Employment Rights (Increase of Limits) Order 2012, SI 2012/3007, art 3, Schedule, as from 1 February 2013, in relation to any case where the appropriate date (as defined in the order) falls on or after that date (see SI 2012/3007, art 4 at **[2.1636]**).
The previous sum was £23.50 (see SI 2011/3006). This sum may be varied by the Secretary of State, see the Employment Relations Act 1999, s 34(1)(a), (3)(a) at **[1.1202]**.
Sub-s (7): substituted by the Employment Relations Act 1999, s 35.

**[1.776]**
## 32 Contractual remuneration
(1)   A right to a guarantee payment does not affect any right of an employee in relation to remuneration under his contract of employment ("contractual remuneration").
(2)   Any contractual remuneration paid to an employee in respect of a workless day goes towards discharging any liability of the employer to pay a guarantee payment in respect of that day; and, conversely, any guarantee payment paid in respect of a day goes towards discharging any liability of the employer to pay contractual remuneration in respect of that day.
(3)   For the purposes of subsection (2), contractual remuneration shall be treated as paid in respect of a workless day—
  (a)   where it is expressed to be calculated or payable by reference to that day or any part of that day, to the extent that it is so expressed, and
  (b)   in any other case, to the extent that it represents guaranteed remuneration, rather than remuneration for work actually done, and is referable to that day when apportioned rateably between that day and any other workless period falling within the period in respect of which the remuneration is paid.

**[1.777]**
## 33 Power to modify provisions about guarantee payments
The Secretary of State may by order provide that in relation to any description of employees the provisions of—
  (a)   sections 28(4) and (5), 30, 31(3) to (5) (as originally enacted or as varied under section 31(7)) and 32, and
  (b)   so far as they apply for the purposes of those provisions, Chapter II of Part XIV and section 234,
shall have effect subject to such modifications and adaptations as may be prescribed by the order.

NOTES
Orders: as of 6 April 2013 no Orders had been made under this section.

**[1.778]**
## 34 Complaints to [employment tribunals]
(1)   An employee may present a complaint to an [employment tribunal] that his employer has failed to pay the whole or any part of a guarantee payment to which the employee is entitled.
(2)   An [employment tribunal] shall not consider a complaint relating to a guarantee payment in respect of any day unless the complaint is presented to the tribunal—
  (a)   before the end of the period of three months beginning with that day, or
  (b)   within such further period as the tribunal considers reasonable in a case where it is satisfied that it was not reasonably practicable for the complaint to be presented before the end of that period of three months.
[(2A)   Section 207A(3) (extension because of mediation in certain European cross-border disputes) *applies* for the purposes of subsection (2)(a).]
(3)   Where an [employment tribunal] finds a complaint under this section well-founded, the tribunal shall order the employer to pay to the employee the amount of guarantee payment which it finds is due to him.

NOTES
Words in square brackets substituted by the Employment Rights (Dispute Resolution) Act 1998, s 1(2)(a), (b).
Sub-s (2A): inserted by the Cross-Border Mediation (EU Directive) Regulations 2011, SI 2011/1133, regs 30, 33, as from 20 May 2011; for the word in italics there are substituted the words "and section 207B (extension of time limits to facilitate conciliation before institution of proceedings) apply", by the Enterprise and Regulatory Reform Act 2013, s 8, Sch 2, paras 15, 18, as from a day to be appointed.

**[1.779]**
## 35 Exemption orders
(1)   Where—
  (a)   at any time there is in force a collective agreement, or an agricultural wages order, under which employees to whom the agreement or order relates have a right to guaranteed remuneration, and

Part 1    Statutes

(b)   on the application of all the parties to the agreement, or of the Board making the order, the appropriate Minister (having regard to the provisions of the agreement or order) is satisfied that section 28 should not apply to those employees,

he may make an order under this section excluding those employees from the operation of that section.

(2)   In subsection (1) "agricultural wages order" means an order made under—

    *(a)*   *section 3 of the Agricultural Wages Act 1948, or*

    (b)   section 3 of the Agricultural Wages (Scotland) Act 1949.

(3)   In subsection (1) "the appropriate Minister" means—

    (a)   in relation to a collective agreement or to an order such as is referred to in subsection (2)(b), the Secretary of State, *and*

    *(b)*   *in relation to an order such as is referred to in subsection (2)(a), the [Secretary of State].*

(4)   The Secretary of State shall not make an order under this section in respect of an agreement unless—

    (a)   the agreement provides for procedures to be followed (whether by arbitration or otherwise) in cases where an employee claims that his employer has failed to pay the whole or any part of any guaranteed remuneration to which the employee is entitled under the agreement and those procedures include a right to arbitration or adjudication by an independent referee or body in cases where (by reason of an equality of votes or otherwise) a decision cannot otherwise be reached, or

    (b)   the agreement indicates that an employee to whom the agreement relates may present a complaint to an [employment tribunal] that his employer has failed to pay the whole or any part of any guaranteed remuneration to which the employee is entitled under the agreement.

(5)   Where an order under this section is in force in respect of an agreement indicating as described in paragraph (b) of subsection (4) an [employment tribunal] shall have jurisdiction over a complaint such as is mentioned in that paragraph as if it were a complaint falling within section 34.

(6)   An order varying or revoking an earlier order under this section may be made in pursuance of an application by all or any of the parties to the agreement in question, or the Board which made the order in question, or in the absence of such an application.

---

**NOTES**

Sub-s (2): para (a) repealed by the Enterprise and Regulatory Reform Act 2013, s 72(4), Sch 20, as from a day to be appointed.

Sub-s (3): words in square brackets in para (b) substituted by the Ministry of Agriculture, Fisheries and Food (Dissolution) Order 2002, SI 2002/794, art 5(1), Sch 1, para 37; para (b) and word immediately preceding it repealed by the Enterprise and Regulatory Reform Act 2013, s 72(4), Sch 20, as from a day to be appointed.

Sub-ss (4), (5): words in square brackets substituted by the Employment Rights (Dispute Resolution) Act 1998, s 1(2)(a).

Orders: as of 6 April 2013 no Orders had been made under this section. However, the following Guarantee Payments Exemption Orders in force at that date and not subsequently revoked have effect as if made hereunder by virtue of s 241 of, and Sch 2, Pt I, paras 1–4 to, this Act: No 1 (SI 1977/156) Federation of Civil Engineering Contracts; No 2 (SI 1977/157) National Federation of Demolition Contractors; No 5 (SI 1977/902) British Footwear Manufacturers' Federation; No 6 (SI 1977/1096) Steeplejacks and Lightning Conductor Engineers; No 7 (SI 1977/1158) Paper and Board Industry; No 8 (SI 1977/1322) Smiths Food Group; No 9 (SI 1977/1349) British Leather Federation; No 10 (SI 1977/1522) Fibreboard Packing Case Industry; No 11 (SI 1977/1523) Henry Wiggin & Co Ltd; No 12 (SI 1977/1583) Refractory Users Federation; No 13 (SI 1977/1601) Multiwall Sack Manufacturers; No 14 (SI 1977/2032) Tudor Food Products; No 15 (SI 1978/153) British Carton Association; No 16 (SI 1978/429) Henry Wiggin & Co; No 17 (SI 1978/737) NJC for Workshops for the Blind; No 18 (SI 1978/826) Employers' Federation of Card Clothing Manufacturers; No 19 (SI 1979/1403) NJC for the Motor Vehicle Repair Industry; No 21 (SI 1981/6) Plant Hire Working Rule Agreement; No 23 (SI 1987/1757) National Agreement for Wire and Wire Rope Industries (revoking No 4); No 24 (SI 1989/1326) Rowntree Mackintosh Confectionery Ltd (revoking No 22 as amended); No 25 (SI 1989/1575) Building and Allied Trades Joint Industrial Council (revoking No 20); No 26 (SI 1989/2163) Airflow Streamlines; No 27 (SI 1990/927) G & G Kynock plc; No 28 (SI 1990/2330) Bridon Ropes Ltd; No 30 (SI 1996/2132) National Joint Council for the Building Industry.

---

## PART IV
## SUNDAY WORKING FOR SHOP AND BETTING WORKERS

*Protected shop workers and betting workers*

**[1.780]**

### 36 Protected shop workers and betting workers

(1)   Subject to subsection (5), a shop worker or betting worker is to be regarded as "protected" for the purposes of any provision of this Act if (and only if) subsection (2) or (3) applies to him.

(2)   This subsection applies to a shop worker or betting worker if—

    (a)   on the day before the relevant commencement date he was employed as a shop worker or a betting worker but not to work only on Sunday,

    (b)   he has been continuously employed during the period beginning with that day and ending with the day which, in relation to the provision concerned, is the appropriate date, and

(c)   throughout that period, or throughout every part of it during which his relations with his employer were governed by a contract of employment, he was a shop worker or a betting worker.

(3)   This subsection applies to any shop worker or betting worker whose contract of employment is such that under it he—

(a)   is not, and may not be, required to work on Sunday, and

(b)   could not be so required even if the provisions of this Part were disregarded.

(4)   Where on the day before the relevant commencement date an employee's relations with his employer had ceased to be governed by a contract of employment, he shall be regarded as satisfying subsection (2)(a) if—

(a)   that day fell in a week which counts as a period of employment with that employer under section 212(2) or (3) or under regulations under section 219, and

(b)   on the last day before the relevant commencement date on which his relations with his employer were governed by a contract of employment, the employee was employed as a shop worker or a betting worker but not to work only on Sunday.

(5)   A shop worker is not a protected shop worker, and a betting worker is not a protected betting worker, if—

(a)   he has given his employer an opting-in notice on or after the relevant commencement date, and

(b)   after giving the notice, he has expressly agreed with his employer to do shop work, or betting work, on Sunday or on a particular Sunday.

(6)   In this Act "opting-in notice", in relation to a shop worker or a betting worker, means written notice, signed and dated by the shop worker or betting worker, in which the shop worker or betting worker expressly states that he wishes to work on Sunday or that he does not object to Sunday working.

(7)   [Subject to subsection (8),] in this Act "the relevant commencement date" means—

(a)   in relation to a shop worker, 26th August 1994, and

(b)   in relation to a betting worker, 3rd January 1995.

[(8)   In any provision of this Act which applies to Scotland by virtue of section 1(5) of the Sunday Working (Scotland) Act 2003 (extension to Scotland of provisions which refer to shop workers and betting workers), "the relevant commencement date" means, in relation to Scotland, the date on which that section came into force.]

**NOTES**

Sub-s (7): words in square brackets inserted by the Sunday Working (Scotland) Act 2003, s 1(1), (2)(a).

Sub-s (8): added by the Sunday Working (Scotland) Act 2003, s 1(1), (2)(b).

Relevant commencement date: the Sunday Working (Scotland) Act 2003, s 1 came into force on 6 April 2004 (see SI 2004/958).

**[1.781]**
**37   Contractual requirements relating to Sunday work**

(1)   Any contract of employment under which a shop worker or betting worker who satisfies section 36(2)(a) was employed on the day or before the relevant commencement date is unenforceable to the extent that it—

(a)   requires the shop worker to do shop work, or the betting worker to do betting work, on Sunday on or after that date, or

(b)   requires the employer to provide the shop worker with shop work, or the betting worker with betting work, on Sunday on or after that date.

(2)   Subject to subsection (3), any agreement entered into after the relevant commencement date between a protected shop worker, or a protected betting worker, and his employer is unenforceable to the extent that it—

(a)   requires the shop worker to do shop work, or the betting worker to do betting work, on Sunday, or

(b)   requires the employer to provide the shop worker with shop work, or the betting worker with betting work, on Sunday.

(3)   Where, after giving an opting-in notice, a protected shop worker or a protected betting worker expressly agrees with his employer to do shop work or betting work on Sunday or on a particular Sunday (and so ceases to be protected), his contract of employment shall be taken to be varied to the extent necessary to give effect to the terms of the agreement.

(4)   . . .

(5)   For the purposes of section 36(2)(b), the appropriate date—

(a)   in relation to subsections (2) and (3) of this section, is the day on which the agreement is entered into,   . . .

(b)   . . .

**NOTES**

Sub-s (4): repealed by the Employment Relations Act 1999, ss 9, 44, Sch 4, Pt III, paras 1, 5, 6(a), Sch 9(2).

Sub-s (5): word omitted from para (a), and para (b) repealed, by the Employment Relations Act 1999, ss 9, 44, Sch 4, Pt III, paras 1, 5, 6(b), (c), Sch 9(2).

---

**[1.782]**
## 38 Contracts with guaranteed hours
(1) This section applies where—
   (a)    under the contract of employment under which a shop worker or betting worker who satisfies section 36(2)(a) was employed on the day before the relevant commencement date, the employer is, or may be, required to provide him with shop work, or betting work, for a specified number of hours each week,
   (b)    under the contract the shop worker or betting worker was, or might have been, required to work on Sunday before that date, and
   (c)    the shop worker has done shop work, or the betting worker betting work, on Sunday in that employment (whether or not before that day) but has, on or after that date, ceased to do so.
(2)   So long as the shop worker remains a protected shop worker, or the betting worker remains a protected betting worker, the contract shall not be regarded as requiring the employer to provide him with shop work, or betting work, on weekdays in excess of the hours normally worked by the shop worker or betting worker on weekdays before he ceased to do shop work, or betting work, on Sunday.
(3)   For the purposes of section 36(2)(b), the appropriate date in relation to this section is any time in relation to which the contract is to be enforced.

**[1.783]**
## 39 Reduction of pay etc
(1)   This section applies where—
   (a)    under the contract of employment under which a shop worker or betting worker who satisfies section 36(2)(a) was employed on the day before the relevant commencement date, the shop worker or betting worker was, or might have been, required to work on Sunday before the relevant commencement date,
   (b)    the shop worker has done shop work, or the betting worker has done betting work, on Sunday in that employment (whether or not before that date) but has, on or after that date, ceased to do so, and
   (c)    it is not apparent from the contract what part of the remuneration payable, or of any other benefit accruing, to the shop worker or betting worker was intended to be attributable to shop work, or betting work, on Sunday.
(2)   So long as the shop worker remains a protected shop worker, or the betting worker remains a protected betting worker, the contract shall be regarded as enabling the employer to reduce the amount of remuneration paid, or the extent of the other benefit provided, to the shop worker or betting worker in respect of any period by the relevant proportion.
(3)   In subsection (2) "the relevant proportion" means the proportion which the hours of shop work, or betting work, which (apart from this Part) the shop worker, or betting worker, could have been required to do on Sunday in the period ("the contractual Sunday hours") bears to the aggregate of those hours and the hours of work actually done by the shop worker, or betting worker, in the period.
(4)   Where, under the contract of employment, the hours of work actually done on weekdays in any period would be taken into account determining the contractual Sunday hours, they shall be taken into account in determining the contractual Sunday hours for the purposes of subsection (3).
(5)   For the purposes of section 36(2)(b), the appropriate date in relation to this section is the end of the period in respect of which the remuneration is paid or the benefit accrues.

*Opting-out of Sunday work*

**[1.784]**
## 40 Notice of objection to Sunday working
(1)   A shop worker or betting worker to whom this section applies may at any time give his employer written notice, signed and dated by the shop worker or betting worker, to the effect that he objects to Sunday working.
(2)   In this Act "opting-out notice" means a notice given under subsection (1) by a shop worker or betting worker to whom this section applies.
(3)   This section applies to any shop worker or betting worker under his contract of employment—
   (a)    is or may be required to work on Sunday (whether or not a result of previously giving an opting-in notice), but
   (b)    is not employed to work only on Sunday.

**[1.785]**
## 41 Opted-out shop workers and betting workers
(1)   Subject to subsection (2), a shop worker or betting worker is regarded as "opted-out" for the purposes of any provision of this (and only if)—
   (a)    he has given his employer an opting-out notice,

(b)    he has been continuously employed during the period beginning with the day on which the notice was given and ending with the day which, in relation to the provision concerned, is the appropriate date, and

(c)    throughout that period, or throughout every part of it during which his relations with his employer were governed by a contract of employment, he was a shop worker or a betting worker.

(2)   A shop worker is not an opted-out shop worker, and a betting worker is not an opted out betting worker, if—

(a)    after giving the opting-out notice concerned, he has given his employer an opting-in notice, and

(b)    after giving the opting-in notice, he has expressly agreed with his employer to do shop work, or betting work, on Sunday or on a particular Sunday.

(3)   In this Act "notice period", in relation to an opted-out shop worker or an opted-out betting worker, means, subject to section 42(2), the period of three months beginning with the day on which the opting-out notice concerned was given.

**[1.786]**
## 42  Explanatory statement

(1)  Where a person becomes a shop worker or betting worker to whom section 40 applies, his employer shall, before the end of the period two months beginning with the day on which that person becomes such worker, give him a written statement in the prescribed form.

(2)  If—

(a)    an employer fails to comply with subsection (1) in relation to any shop worker or betting worker, and

(b)    the shop worker or betting worker, on giving the employer an opting-out notice, becomes an opted-out shop worker or an opted-out betting worker,

section 41(3) has effect in relation to the shop worker or betting worker with the substitution for "three months" of "one month".

(3)  An employer shall not be regarded as failing to comply with subsection (1) in any case where, before the end of the period referred to that subsection, the shop worker or betting worker has given him an opting-out notice.

(4)  Subject to subsection (6), the prescribed form in the case of a shop worker is as follows—

### "STATUTORY RIGHTS IN RELATION TO SUNDAY SHOP WORK

You have become employed as a shop worker and are or can be required under your contract of employment to do the Sunday work your contract provides for.

However, if you wish, you can give a notice, as described in the next paragraph, to your employer and you will then have the right not to work in or about a shop on any Sunday on which the shop is open once three months have passed from the date on which you gave the notice.

Your notice must—
> be in writing;
> be signed and dated by you;
> say that you object to Sunday working.

For three months after you give the notice, your employer can still require you to do all the Sunday work your contract provides for. After the three month period has ended, you have the right to complain to an [employment tribunal] if, because of your refusal to work on Sundays on which the shop is open, your employer—
> dismisses you, or
> does something else detrimental to you, for example, failing to promote you.

Once you have the rights described, you can surrender them only by giving your employer a further notice, signed and dated by you, saying that you wish to work on Sunday or that you do not object to Sunday working and then agreeing with your employer to work on Sundays or on a particular Sunday.".

(5)  Subject to subsection (6), the prescribed form in the case of betting worker is as follows—

### "STATUTORY RIGHTS IN RELATION TO SUNDAY BETTING WORK

You have become employed under a contract of employment under which you are or can be required to do Sunday betting work that is to say, work—
> at a track on a Sunday on which your employer is taking bets at the track, or
> in a licensed betting office on a Sunday on which it is open for business.

However, if you wish, you can give a notice, as described in the next paragraph, to your employer and you will then have the right not to do Sunday betting work once three months have passed from the date on which you gave the notice.

Your notice must—

be in writing;

be signed and dated by you;

say that you object to doing Sunday betting work.

For three months after you give the notice, your employer can still require you to do all the Sunday betting work your contract provides for. After the three month period has ended, you have the right to complain to an [employment tribunal] if, because of your refusal to do Sunday betting work, your employer—

dismisses you, or

does something else detrimental to you, for example, failing to promote you.

Once you have the rights described, you can surrender them only by giving your employer a further notice, signed and dated by you, saying that you wish to do Sunday betting work or that you do not object to doing Sunday betting work and then agreeing with your employer to do such work on Sundays or on a particular Sunday.".

(6)   The Secretary of State may by order amend the prescribed forms set out in subsections (4) and (5).

**NOTES**

Sub-ss (4), (5): words in square brackets substituted by the Employment Rights (Dispute Resolution) Act 1998, s 1(2)(a).
Orders: as of 6 April 2013 no Orders had been made under this section.

**[1.787]**
**43   Contractual requirements relating to Sunday work**
(1)   Where a shop worker or betting worker gives his employer an opting-out notice, the contract of employment under which he was employed immediately before he gave that notice becomes unenforceable to the extent that it—
  (a)   requires the shop worker to do shop work, or the betting worker to do betting work, on Sunday after the end of the notice period, or
  (b)   requires the employer to provide the shop worker with shop work, or the betting worker with betting work, on Sunday after the end of that period.
(2)   Subject to subsection (3), any agreement entered into between an opted-out shop worker, or an opted-out betting worker, and his employer is unenforceable to the extent that it—
  (a)   requires the shop worker to do shop work, or the betting worker to do betting work, on Sunday after the end of the notice period, or
  (b)   requires the employer to provide the shop worker with shop work, or the betting worker with betting work, on Sunday after the end of that period.
(3)   Where, after giving an opting-in notice, an opted-out shop worker an opted-out betting worker expressly agrees with his employer to do shop work or betting work on Sunday or on a particular Sunday (and so ceases to be opted-out), his contract of employment shall be taken to be varied to the extent necessary to give effect to the terms of the agreement.
(4)   . . .
(5)   For the purposes of section 41(1)(b), the appropriate date—
  (a)   in relation to subsections (2) and (3) of this section, is the day on which the agreement is entered into,   . . .
  (b)   . . .

**NOTES**

Sub-s (4): repealed by the Employment Relations Act 1999, ss 9, 44, Sch 4, Pt III, paras 1, 5, 7(a), Sch 9(2).
Sub-s (5): word omitted from para (a), and para (b), repealed by the Employment Relations Act 1999, ss 9, Sch 4, Pt III, paras 1, 5, 7(b), (c), Sch 9(2).

**[PART IVA**
**PROTECTED DISCLOSURES**

**[1.788]**
**43A   Meaning of "protected disclosure"**
In this Act a "protected disclosure" means a qualifying disclosure (as defined by section 43B) which is made by a worker in accordance with any of sections 43C to 43H.]

**NOTES**

Inserted, together with ss 43A–43L, by the Public Interest Disclosure Act 1998, s 1.

**[1.789]**
**[43B Disclosures qualifying for protection**
(1) In this Part a "qualifying disclosure" means any disclosure of information which, in the reasonable belief of the worker making the disclosure, [is made in the public interest and] tends to show one or more of the following—
(a) that a criminal offence has been committed, is being committed or is likely to be committed,
(b) that a person has failed, is failing or is likely to fail to comply with any legal obligation to which he is subject,
(c) that a miscarriage of justice has occurred, is occurring or is likely to occur,
(d) that the health or safety of any individual has been, is being or is likely to be endangered,
(e) that the environment has been, is being or is likely to be damaged, or
(f) that information tending to show any matter falling within any one of the preceding paragraphs has been, or is likely to be deliberately concealed.
(2) For the purposes of subsection (1), it is immaterial whether the relevant failure occurred, occurs or would occur in the United Kingdom or elsewhere, and whether the law applying to it is that of the United Kingdom or of any other country or territory.
(3) A disclosure of information is not a qualifying disclosure if the person making the disclosure commits an offence by making it.
(4) A disclosure of information in respect of which a claim to legal professional privilege (or, in Scotland, to confidentiality as between client and professional legal adviser) could be maintained in legal proceedings is not a qualifying disclosure if it is made by a person to whom the information had been disclosed in the course of obtaining legal advice.
(5) In this Part "the relevant failure", in relation to a qualifying disclosure, means the matter falling within paragraphs (a) to (f) of subsection (1).]

**NOTES**
Inserted as noted to s 43A at **[1.788]**.
Sub-s (1): words in square brackets inserted by the Enterprise and Regulatory Reform Act 2013, s 17, as from 25 June 2013, subject to savings in s 24(6) of the 2013 Act at **[1.1855]**.

**[1.790]**
**[43C Disclosure to employer or other responsible person**
(1) A qualifying disclosure is made in accordance with this section if the worker makes the disclosure *in good faith*—
(a) to his employer, or
(b) where the worker reasonably believes that the relevant failure relates solely or mainly to—
(i) the conduct of a person other than his employer, or
(ii) any other matter for which a person other than his employer has legal responsibility, to that other person.
(2) A worker who, in accordance with a procedure whose use by him is authorised by his employer, makes a qualifying disclosure to a person other than his employer, is to be treated for the purposes of this Part as making the qualifying disclosure to his employer.]

**NOTES**
Inserted as noted to s 43A at **[1.788]**.
Sub-s (1): words in italics repealed by the Enterprise and Regulatory Reform Act 2013, s 18(1)(a), as from 25 June 2013, subject to savings in s 24(6) of the 2013 Act at **[1.1855]**.

**[1.791]**
**[43D Disclosure to legal adviser**
A qualifying disclosure is made in accordance with this section if it is made in the course of obtaining legal advice.]

**NOTES**
Inserted as noted to s 43A at **[1.788]**.

**[1.792]**
**[43E Disclosure to Minister of the Crown**
A qualifying disclosure is made in accordance with this section if—
(a) the worker's employer is—
(i) an individual appointed under any enactment [(including any enactment comprised in, or in an instrument made under, an Act of the Scottish Parliament)] by a Minister of the Crown [or a member of the Scottish Executive], or
(ii) a body any of whose members are so appointed, and
(b) the disclosure is made *in good faith* to a Minister of the Crown [or a member of the Scottish Executive].]

Part 1 Statutes

**NOTES**

Inserted as noted to s 43A at **[1.788]**.

Words in square brackets inserted by the Scotland Act 1998 (Consequential Modifications) Order 2000, SI 2000/2040, arts 1(1), 2(1), Schedule, Pt I, para 19.

Words in italics repealed by the Enterprise and Regulatory Reform Act 2013, s 18(1)(b), as from 25 June 2013, subject to savings in s 24(6) of the 2013 Act at **[1.1855]**.

---

**[1.793]**

**[43F  Disclosure to prescribed person**

(1)  A qualifying disclosure is made in accordance with this section if the worker—

   (a)  makes the disclosure *in good faith* to a person prescribed by an order made by the Secretary of State for the purposes of this section, and

   (b)  reasonably believes—

      (i)  that the relevant failure falls within any description of matters in respect of which that person is so prescribed, and

      (ii)  that the information disclosed, and any allegation contained in it, are substantially true.

(2)  An order prescribing persons for the purposes of this section may specify persons or descriptions of persons, and shall specify the descriptions of matters in respect of which each person, or persons of each description, is or are prescribed.]

---

**NOTES**

Inserted as noted to s 43A at **[1.788]**.

Sub-s (1): words in italics repealed by the Enterprise and Regulatory Reform Act 2013, s 18(1)(c), as from 25 June 2013, subject to savings in s 24(6) of the 2013 Act at **[1.1855]**.

Orders: the Public Interest Disclosure (Prescribed Persons) Order 1999, SI 1999/1549 at **[2.443]**; the Public Interest Disclosure (Prescribed Persons) (Amendment) Order 2003, SI 2003/1993; the Public Interest Disclosure (Prescribed Persons) (Amendment) Order 2004, SI 2004/3265; the Public Interest Disclosure (Prescribed Persons) (Amendment) Order 2005, SI 2005/2464; the Public Interest Disclosure (Prescribed Persons) (Amendment) Order 2008, SI 2008/531; the Public Interest Disclosure (Prescribed Persons) (Amendment) Order 2009, SI 2009/2457; the Public Interest Disclosure (Prescribed Persons) (Amendment) Order 2010, SI 2010/7; the Public Interest Disclosure (Prescribed Persons) (Amendment) Order 2012, SI 2012/462.

---

**[1.794]**

**[43G  Disclosure in other cases**

(1)  A qualifying disclosure is made in accordance with this section if—

   *(a)  the worker makes the disclosure in good faith,*

   (b)  *he* reasonably believes that the information disclosed, and any allegation contained in it, are substantially true,

   (c)  he does not make the disclosure for purposes of personal gain,

   (d)  any of the conditions in subsection (2) is met, and

   (e)  in all the circumstances of the case, it is reasonable for him to make the disclosure.

(2)  The conditions referred to in subsection (1)(d) are—

   (a)  that, at the time he makes the disclosure, the worker reasonably believes that he will be subjected to a detriment by his employer if he makes a disclosure to his employer or in accordance with section 43F,

   (b)  that, in a case where no person is prescribed for the purposes of section 43F in relation to the relevant failure, the worker reasonably believes that it is likely that evidence relating to the relevant failure will be concealed or destroyed if he makes a disclosure to his employer, or

   (c)  that the worker has previously made a disclosure of substantially the same information—

      (i)  to his employer, or

      (ii)  in accordance with section 43F.

(3)  In determining for the purposes of subsection (1)(e) whether it is reasonable for the worker to make the disclosure, regard shall be had, in particular, to—

   (a)  the identity of the person to whom the disclosure is made,

   (b)  the seriousness of the relevant failure,

   (c)  whether the relevant failure is continuing or is likely to occur in the future,

   (d)  whether the disclosure is made in breach of a duty of confidentiality owed by the employer to any other person,

   (e)  in a case falling within subsection (2)(c)(i) or (ii), any action which the employer or the person to whom the previous disclosure in accordance with section 43F was made has taken or might reasonably be expected to have taken as a result of the previous disclosure, and

   (f)  in a case falling within subsection (2)(c)(i), whether in making the disclosure to the employer the worker complied with any procedure whose use by him was authorised by the employer.

(4)   For the purposes of this section a subsequent disclosure may be regarded as a disclosure of substantially the same information as that disclosed by a previous disclosure as mentioned in subsection (2)(c) even though the subsequent disclosure extends to information about action taken or not taken by any person as a result of the previous disclosure.]

### NOTES

Inserted as noted to s 43A at **[1.788]**.

Sub-s (1): para (a) repealed and for the word in italics in para (b) there are substituted the words "the worker", by the Enterprise and Regulatory Reform Act 2013, s 18(2), as from 25 June 2013, subject to savings in s 24(6) of the 2013 Act at **[1.1855]**.

## [1.795]
## [43H   Disclosure of exceptionally serious failure
(1)   A qualifying disclosure is made in accordance with this section if—
  (a)   *the worker makes the disclosure in good faith,*
  (b)   *he* reasonably believes that the information disclosed, and any allegation contained in it, are substantially true,
  (c)   he does not make the disclosure for purposes of personal gain,
  (d)   the relevant failure is of an exceptionally serious nature, and
  (e)   in all the circumstances of the case, it is reasonable for him to make the disclosure.
(2)   In determining for the purposes of subsection (1)(e) whether it is reasonable for the worker to make the disclosure, regard shall be had, in particular, to the identity of the person to whom the disclosure is made.]

### NOTES

Inserted as noted to s 43A at **[1.788]**.

Sub-s (1): para (a) repealed and for the word in italics in para (b) there are substituted the words "the worker", by the Enterprise and Regulatory Reform Act 2013, s 18(3), as from 25 June 2013, subject to savings in s 24(6) of the 2013 Act at **[1.1855]**.

## [1.796]
## [43J   Contractual duties of confidentiality
(1)   Any provision in an agreement to which this section applies is void in so far as it purports to preclude the worker from making a protected disclosure.
(2)   This section applies to any agreement between a worker and his employer (whether a worker's contract or not), including an agreement to refrain from instituting or continuing any proceedings under this Act or any proceedings for breach of contract.]

### NOTES

Inserted as noted to s 43A at **[1.788]**.

## [1.797]
## [43K   Extension of meaning of "worker" etc for Part IVA
(1)   For the purposes of this Part "worker" includes an individual who is not a worker as defined by section 230(3) but who—
  (a)   works or worked for a person in circumstances in which—
    (i)   he is or was introduced or supplied to do that work by a third person, and
    (ii)   the terms on which he is or was engaged to do the work are or were in practice substantially determined not by him but by the person for whom he works or worked, by the third person or by both of them,
  (b)   contracts or contracted with a person, for the purposes of that person's business, for the execution of work to be done in a place not under the control or management of that person and would fall within section 230(3)(b) if for "personally" in that provision there were substituted "(whether personally or otherwise)",
  [(ba)   works or worked as a person performing services under a contract entered into by him with [the National Health Service Commissioning Board] [under *section 84 or 100 of the* National Health Service Act 2006 or with a Local Health Board under *section 42 or 57 of* the National Health Service (Wales) Act 2006] *[or with [the National Health Service Commissioning Board] under section 117 of that Act],]*
  [(bb)   works or worked as a person performing services under a contract entered into by him with a Health Board under section 17J [or 17Q] of the National Health Service (Scotland) Act 1978,]
  (c)   *works or worked as a person providing . . . general dental services, general ophthalmic services or pharmaceutical services* in accordance with arrangements made—
    (i)   by [the National Health Service Commissioning Board] [[under section 126 of the National Health Service Act 2006,] or] [Local Health Board] under [section 71 or 80 of the National Health Service (Wales) Act 2006], or

     (ii)    by a Health Board under section [2C, 17AA, 17C,] . . . 25, *26 or 27* of the National Health Service (Scotland) Act 1978, *or*

*[(ca) works or worked as a person performing services under a contract entered into by him with a Health Board under section 17Q of the National Health Service (Scotland) Act 1978,]*

   (d)    is or was provided with work experience provided pursuant to a training course or programme or with training for employment (or with both) otherwise than—
     (i)    under a contract of employment, or
     (ii)    by an educational establishment on a course run by that establishment;

and any reference to a worker's contract, to employment or to a worker being "employed" shall be construed accordingly.

(2)    For the purposes of this Part "employer" includes—
   (a)    in relation to a worker falling within paragraph (a) of subsection (1), the person who substantially determines or determined the terms on which he is or was engaged,
  [(aa)  in relation to a worker falling within paragraph (ba) of that subsection, [the National Health Service Commissioning Board, or the] Local Health Board referred to in that paragraph,]
  [(ab)  in relation to a worker falling within paragraph (bb) of that subsection, the Health Board referred to in that paragraph,]
   (b)    in relation to a worker falling within paragraph (c) of that subsection, the authority or board referred to in that paragraph, and
  *[(ba) in relation to a worker falling within paragraph (ca) of that subsection, the Health Board referred to in that paragraph, and]*
   (c)    in relation to a worker falling within paragraph (d) of that subsection, the person providing the work experience or training.

(3)    In this section "educational establishment" includes any university, college, school or other educational establishment.

[(4)    The Secretary of State may by order make amendments to this section as to what individuals count as "workers" for the purposes of this Part (despite not being within the definition in section 230(3)).

(5)    An order under subsection (4) may not make an amendment that has the effect of removing a category of individual unless the Secretary of State is satisfied that there are no longer any individuals in that category.]]

**NOTES**

Inserted as noted to s 43A at **[1.788]**.

Sub-s (1) is amended as follows:

Para (ba): inserted by the Health and Social Care (Community Health and Standards) Act 2003, s 184, Sch 11, para 65(1), (2); words in first and fourth (inner) pairs of square brackets substituted by the Health and Social Care Act 2012, s 55(2), Sch 5, paras 72, 73(a), as from 1 April 2013; words in second pair of square brackets substituted by the National Health Service (Consequential Provisions) Act 2006, s 2, Sch 1, paras 177, 178(a); words in third (outer) pair of square brackets inserted by the Health Act 2006, s 80(1), Sch 8, para 37 (as amended by the National Health Service (Consequential Provisions) Act 2006, s 2, Sch 1, paras 281, 294), as from a day to be appointed; for the first and second words in italics there are substituted the words "section 83(2), 84, 92, 100, 107, 115(4), 117 or 134 of, or Schedule 12 to," and "section 41(2)(b), 42, 50, 57, 64 or 92 of, or Schedule 7 to," respectively, and third words in italics repealed by the Enterprise and Regulatory Reform Act 2013, s 20(1), (2), as from 25 June 2013, subject to savings in s 24(6) of the 2013 Act at **[1.1855]**.

Para (bb): inserted by the Primary Medical Services (Scotland) Act 2004 (Consequential Modifications) Order 2004, SI 2004/957, art 2, Schedule, para 8(a)(i); words in square brackets inserted by the Enterprise and Regulatory Reform Act 2013, s 20(1), (3), as from 25 June 2013, subject to savings in s 24(6) of the 2013 Act at **[1.1855]**.

Para (c): for the first words in italics there are substituted the words "works or worked as a person providing services" by the Enterprise and Regulatory Reform Act 2013, s 20(1), (4)(a), as from 25 June 2013, subject to savings in s 24(6) of the 2013 Act at **[1.1855]**; first words omitted repealed by SI 2004/957, art 2, Schedule, para 8(a)(ii); words in first pair of square brackets in para (c)(i) substituted by the Health and Social Care Act 2012, s 55(2), Sch 5, paras 72, 73(b), as from 1 April 2013; words in second (outer) pair of square brackets in para (c)(i) inserted by the National Health Service Reform and Health Care Professions Act 2002, s 2(5), Sch 2, Pt 2, para 63; words in third (inner) pair of square brackets in para (c)(i) inserted, and words in fifth pair of square brackets in that paragraph substituted, by the National Health Service (Consequential Provisions) Act 2006, s 2, Sch 1, paras 177, 178(b); words in fourth pair of square brackets in para (c)(i) substituted by the References to Health Authorities Order 2007, SI 2007/961, art 3, Schedule, para 27(1), (2); figures in square brackets in para (c)(ii) inserted by the Enterprise and Regulatory Reform Act 2013, s 20(1), (4)(b), as from 25 June 2013, subject to savings in s 24(6) of the 2013 Act at **[1.1855]**; figure omitted from para (c)(ii) repealed by SI 2004/957, art 2, Schedule, para 8(a)(iii); for the words in italics in para (c)(ii) there are substituted the words "or 26", by the Smoking, Health and Social Care (Scotland) Act 2005 (Consequential Modifications) (England, Wales and Northern Ireland) Order 2006, SI 2006/1056, art 2, Schedule, Pt 1, para 7(a)(i), as from a day to be appointed.

Para (ca): inserted by SI 2006/1056, art 2, Schedule, Pt 1, para 7(a)(ii), as from a day to be appointed and repealed, together with word immediately preceding it, by the Enterprise and Regulatory Reform Act 2013, s 20(1), (5), as from 25 June 2013, subject to savings in s 24(6) of the 2013 Act at **[1.1855]**.

Sub-s (2) is amended as follows:

Para (aa): inserted by the Health and Social Care (Community Health and Standards) Act 2003, s 184, Sch 11, para 65(1), (3) and words in square brackets therein substituted by the Health and Social Care Act 2012, s 55(2), Sch 5, paras 72, 73(c), as from 1 April 2013.

Para (ab): inserted by SI 2004/957, art 2, Schedule, para 8(b).

Para (ba): inserted by SI 2006/1056, art 2, Schedule, Pt 1, para 7(b), as from a day to be appointed and repealed by the Enterprise and Regulatory Reform Act 2013, s 20(1), (6), as from 25 June 2013, subject to savings in s 24(6) of the 2013 Act at **[1.1855]**.

Sub-ss (4), (5): added by the Enterprise and Regulatory Reform Act 2013, s 20(1), (7), as from 25 April 2013 (so far as is necessary for enabling the exercise of any power to make orders) and as from 25 June 2013 (otherwise), subject to savings in s 24(6) of the 2013 Act at **[1.1855]**.

Transitional provisions and miscellaneous: the General Medical Services and Personal Medical Services Transitional and Consequential Provisions Order 2004, SI 2004/865, art 109(1), (2)(d), and the General Medical Services Transitional and Consequential Provisions (Wales) (No 2) Order 2004, SI 2004/1016, art 85(1), (2)(d) (both made under the Health and Social Care (Community Health and Standards) Act 2003, ss 176, 195(1), 200, 201) provide that until such time as default contracts entered into pursuant s 176(3) of the 2003 Act cease to exist, any reference to a general medical services contract or to a contract under the National Health Service Act 1977, s 28Q shall include a reference to a default contract.

See further the Enterprise and Regulatory Reform Act 2013, s 20(10) at **[1.1854]**.

**[1.798]**
**[43KA   Application of this Part and related provisions to police**
(1)   For the purposes of—
   (a)   this Part,
   (b)   section 47B and sections 48 and 49 so far as relating to that section, and
   (c)   section 103A and the other provisions of Part 10 so far as relating to the right not to be unfairly dismissed in a case where the dismissal is unfair by virtue of section 103A,
a person who holds, otherwise than under a contract of employment, the office of constable or an appointment as a police cadet shall be treated as an employee employed by the relevant officer under a contract of employment; and any reference to a worker being "employed" and to his "employer" shall be construed accordingly.
(2)   In this section "the relevant officer" means—
   (a)   in relation to a member of a police force or a special constable appointed for a police area, the chief officer of police;
   [(b)   in relation to a member of a police force seconded to the *Serious Organised Crime Agency to serve as a member of its staff*, that Agency; and]
   (d)   in relation to any other person holding the office of constable or an appointment as police cadet, the person who has the direction and control of the body of constables or cadets in question.]

NOTES
Inserted by the Police Reform Act 2002, s 37(1).
Sub-s (2): para (b) substituted, for the original paras (b), (c), by the Serious Organised Crime and Police Act 2005, s 59, Sch 4, paras 84, 85; for the words in italics in para (b) there are substituted the words "National Crime Agency to serve as a National Crime Agency officer" by the Crime and Courts Act 2013, s 15(3), Sch 8, Pt 2, paras 49, 50, as from a day to be appointed.

**[1.799]**
**[43L   Other interpretative provisions**
(1)   In this Part—
   "qualifying disclosure" has the meaning given by section 43B;
   "the relevant failure", in relation to a qualifying disclosure, has the meaning given by section 43B(5).
(2)   In determining for the purposes of this Part whether a person makes a disclosure for purposes of personal gain, there shall be disregarded any reward payable by or under any enactment.
(3)   Any reference in this Part to the disclosure of information shall have effect, in relation to any case where the person receiving the information is already aware of it, as a reference to bringing the information to his attention.]

NOTES
Inserted as noted to s 43A at **[1.788]**.

# PART V
## PROTECTION FROM SUFFERING DETRIMENT IN EMPLOYMENT

NOTES
Conciliation: employment tribunal proceedings and claims which could be the subject of employment tribunal proceedings under this Part are proceedings to which the Employment Tribunals Act 1996, s 18 applies; see s 18(1)(d) of that Act at **[1.706]**.
Recoupment of social security benefits: as to the power to provide for recoupment of social security benefits in relation to payments by employers to employees under this Part, that are the subject of proceedings before employment tribunals, see the Employment Tribunals Act 1996, s 16 at **[1.704]**.

*Rights not to suffer detriment*

**[1.800]**
**[43M   Jury service**
(1)   An employee has the right not to be subjected to any detriment by any act, or any deliberate failure to act, by his employer on the ground that the employee—

(a) has been summoned under the Juries Act 1974, *the Coroners Act 1988*, the Court of Session Act 1988 or the Criminal Procedure (Scotland) Act 1995 to attend for service as a juror, or

(b) has been absent from work because he attended at any place in pursuance of being so summoned.

(2) This section does not apply where the detriment in question amounts to dismissal within the meaning of Part 10.

(3) For the purposes of this section, an employee is not to be regarded as having been subjected to a detriment by a failure to pay remuneration in respect of a relevant period unless under his contract of employment he is entitled to be paid that remuneration.

(4) In subsection (3) "a relevant period" means any period during which the employee is absent from work because of his attendance at any place in pursuance of being summoned as mentioned in subsection (1)(a).]

**NOTES**

Inserted by the Employment Relations Act 2004, s 40(1).

Sub-s (1): for the words in italics in para (a) there are substituted the words "Part 1 of the Coroners and Justice Act 2009" by the Coroners and Justice Act 2009, s 177(1), Sch 21, Pt 1, para 36(1), (2), as from a day to be appointed.

Conciliation: see the note following the Part heading *ante*.

**[1.801]**
**44 Health and safety cases**
(1) An employee has the right not to be subjected to any detriment by any act, or any deliberate failure to act, by his employer done on the ground that—

(a) having been designated by the employer to carry out activities in connection with preventing or reducing risks to health and safety at work, the employee carried out (or proposed to carry out) any such activities,

(b) being a representative of workers on matters of health and safety at work or member of a safety committee—
  (i) in accordance with arrangements established under or by virtue of any enactment, or
  (ii) by reason of being acknowledged as such by the employer,
  the employee performed (or proposed to perform) any functions as such a representative or a member of such committee,

[(ba) the employee took part (or proposed to take part) in consultation with the employer pursuant to the Health and Safety (Consultation with Employees) Regulations 1996 or in an election of representatives of employee safety within the meaning of those Regulations (whether as a candidate or otherwise),]

(c) being an employee at a place where—
  (i) there was no such representative or safety committee, or
  (ii) there was such a representative or safety committee but it was not reasonably practicable for the employee to raise the matter by those means,
  he brought to his employer's attention, by reasonable means, circumstances connected with his work which he reasonably believed were harmful or potentially harmful to health or safety,

(d) in circumstances of danger which the employee reasonable believed to be serious and imminent and which he could no reasonably have been expected to avert, he left (or proposed to leave) or (while the danger persisted) refused to return to his place of work or any dangerous part of his place of work, or

(e) in circumstances of danger which the employee reasonably believed to be serious and imminent, he took (or proposed to take) appropriate steps to protect himself or other persons from the danger.

(2) For the purposes of subsection (1)(e) whether steps which employee took (or proposed to take) were appropriate is to be judged by reference to all the circumstances including, in particular, his knowledge and the facilities and advice available to him at the time.

(3) An employee is not to be regarded as having been subjected to a detriment on the ground specified in subsection (1)(e) if the employer shows that it was (or would have been) so negligent for the employee to take the steps which he took (or proposed to take) that a reasonable employer might have treated him as the employer did.

(4) . . . this section does not apply where the detriment in question amounts to dismissal (within the meaning of [Part X]).

**NOTES**

Sub-s (1): para (ba) inserted by the Health and Safety (Consultation with Employees) Regulations 1996, SI 1996/1513, reg 8.

Sub-s (4): words omitted repealed, and words in square brackets substituted, by the Employment Relations Act 1999, ss 18(2), 44, Sch 9(3).

Conciliation: see the note following the Part heading *ante*.

**[1.802]**
**45  Sunday working for shop and betting workers**
(1)  An employee who is—
  (a)  a protected shop worker or an opted-out shop worker, or
  (b)  a protected betting worker or an opted-out betting worker,
has the right not to be subjected to any detriment by any act, or any deliberate failure to act, by his employer done on the ground that he employee refused (or proposed to refuse) to do shop work, or betting work, on Sunday or on a particular Sunday.
(2)  Subsection (1) does not apply to anything done in relation to an opted-out shop worker or an opted-out betting worker on the ground that he refused (or proposed to refuse) to do shop work, or betting work, on any Sunday or Sundays falling before the end of the notice period.
(3)  An employee who is a shop worker or a betting worker has the right not to be subjected to any detriment by any act, or any deliberate failure to act, by his employer done on the ground that the employee gave (or proposed to give) an opting-out notice to his employer.
(4)  Subsections (1) and (3) do not apply where the detriment in question amounts to dismissal (within the meaning of Part X).
(5)  For the purposes of this section a shop worker or betting worker who does not work on Sunday or on a particular Sunday is not to be regarded as having been subjected to any detriment by—
  (a)  a failure to pay remuneration in respect of shop work, or betting work, on a Sunday which he has not done,
  (b)  a failure to provide him with any other benefit, where that failure results from the application (in relation to a Sunday on which the employee has not done shop work, or betting work) of a contractual term under which the extent of that benefit varies according to the number of hours worked by the employee or the remuneration of the employee, or
  (c)  a failure to provide him with any work, remuneration or other benefit which by virtue of section 38 or 39 the employer is not obliged to provide.
(6)  Where an employer offers to pay a sum specified in the offer to any or more employees—
  (a)  who are protected shop workers or opted-out shop workers or protected betting workers or opted-out betting workers, or
  (b)  who under their contracts of employment are not obliged to do shop work, or betting work, on Sunday,
if they agree to do shop work, or betting work, on Sunday or on a particular Sunday subsections (7) and (8) apply.
(7)  An employee to whom the offer is not made is not to be regarded for the purposes of this section as having been subjected to any detriment by any failure to make the offer to him or to pay him the sum specified in the offer.
(8)  An employee who does not accept the offer is not to be regarded for the purposes of this section as having been subjected to any detriment by any failure to pay him the sum specified in the offer.
(9)  For the purposes of section 36(2)(b) or 41(1)(b), the appropriate date in relation to this section is the date of the act or failure to act.
(10)  For the purposes of subsection (9)—
  (a)  where an act extends over a period, the "date of the act" means the first day of that period, and
  (b)  a deliberate failure to act shall be treated as done when it was decided on;
and, in the absence of evidence establishing the contrary, an employee shall be taken to decide on a failure to act when he does an act inconsistent with doing the failed act or, if he has done no such inconsistent act, when the period expires within which he might reasonably have been expected to do the failed act if it was to be done.

**NOTES**
Conciliation: see the note following the Part heading *ante*.

**[1.803]**
**[45A  Working time cases**
(1)  A worker has the right not to be subjected to any detriment by any act, or any deliberate failure to act, by his employer done on the ground that the worker—
  (a)  refused (or proposed to refuse) to comply with a requirement which the employer imposed (or proposed to impose) in contravention of the Working Time Regulations 1998,
  (b)  refused (or proposed to refuse) to forgo a right conferred on him by those Regulations,
  (c)  failed to sign a workforce agreement for the purposes of those Regulations, or to enter into, or agree to vary or extend, any other agreement with his employer which is provided for in those Regulations,
  (d)  being—
    (i)  a representative of members of the workforce for the purposes of Schedule 1 to those Regulations, or

(ii)    a candidate in an election in which any person elected will, on being elected, be such
      a representative,
    performed (or proposed to perform) any functions or activities as such a representative or
    candidate,
  (e)   brought proceedings against the employer to enforce a right conferred on him by those
      Regulations, or
  (f)   alleged that the employer had infringed such a right.
(2)   It is immaterial for the purposes of subsection (1)(e) or (f)—
  (a)   whether or not the worker has the right, or
  (b)   whether or not the right has been infringed,
but, for those provisions to apply, the claim to the right and that it has been infringed must be made
in good faith.
(3)   It is sufficient for subsection (1)(f) to apply that the worker, without specifying the right, made
it reasonably clear to the employer what the right claimed to have been infringed was.
(4)   This section does not apply where a worker is an employee and the detriment in question
amounts to dismissal within the meaning of Part X . . . ]
[(5)   A reference in this section to the Working Time Regulations 1998 includes a reference to—
  [(a)]  the Merchant Shipping (Working Time: Inland Waterways) Regulations 2003;
  [(b)  the Fishing Vessels (Working Time: Sea-fishermen) Regulations 2004];
  [(c)  the Cross-border Railway Services (Working Time) Regulations 2008].]]

**NOTES**

Inserted by the Working Time Regulations 1998, SI 1998/1833, regs 2(1), 31(1).

Sub-s (4): words omitted repealed by the Employment Relations Act 1999, ss 18(3), 44, Sch 9(3).

Sub-s (5): added by the Merchant Shipping (Working Time: Inland Waterways) Regulations 2003, SI 2003/3049, reg 20, Sch 2, para 3(1), (2); the letter "(a)" and para (b) were inserted by the Fishing Vessels (Working Time: Sea-fishermen) Regulations 2004, SI 2004/1713, reg 21, Sch 2, para 2(1), (2)(b); para (c) inserted by the Cross-border Railway Services (Working Time) Regulations 2008, SI 2008/1660, reg 19, Sch 3, para 2(1), (2), as from 27 July 2008.

Conciliation: see the note following the Part heading *ante*.

**[1.804]**
**46   Trustees of occupational pension schemes**
(1)   An employee has the right not to be subjected to any detriment by any act, or any deliberate
failure to act, by his employer done on the ground that, being a trustee of a relevant occupational
pension scheme which relates to his employment, the employee performed (or propose to perform)
any functions as such a trustee.
(2)   . . . this section does not apply where the detriment in question amounts to dismissal
(within the meaning of [Part X]).
[(2A)   This section applies to an employee who is a director of a company which is a trustee of a
relevant occupational pension scheme as it applies to an employee who is a trustee of such a
scheme (references to such a trustee being read for this purpose as references to such a director).]
(3)   In this section "relevant occupational pension scheme" means an occupational pension scheme
(as defined in section 1 of the Pension Schemes Act 1993) established under a trust.

**NOTES**

Sub-s (2): words omitted repealed, and words in square brackets substituted, by the Employment Relations Act 1999, ss 18(2), 44, Sch 9(3).

Sub-s (2A): inserted by the Welfare Reform and Pensions Act 1999, s 18, Sch 2, para 19(1), (2).

Conciliation: see the note following the Part heading *ante*.

**[1.805]**
**47   Employee representatives**
(1)   An employee has the right not to be subjected to any detriment by any act, or any deliberate
failure to act, by his employer done on the ground that, being—
  (a)   an employee representative for the purposes of Chapter II of Part IV of the Trade Union
      and Labour Relation (Consolidation) Act 1992 (redundancies) or [regulations 9, 13 and 15
      of the Transfer of Undertakings (Protection of Employment) Regulations 2006], or
  (b)   a candidate in an election in which any person elected will, on being elected, be such an
      employee representative,
he performed (or proposed to perform) any functions or activities as such an employee
representative or candidate.
[(1A)   An employee has the right not to be subjected to any detriment by any act, or by any
deliberate failure to act, by his employer done on the ground of his participation in an election of
employee representatives for the purposes of Chapter II of Part IV of the Trade Union and Labour
Relations (Consolidation) Act 1992 (redundancies) or [regulations 9, 13 and 15 of the Transfer of
Undertakings (Protection of Employment) Regulations 2006].]
(2)   . . . this section does not apply where the detriment in question amounts to dismissal
(within the meaning of [Part X]).

**NOTES**

Sub-s (1): words in square brackets in para (a) substituted by the Transfer of Undertakings (Protection of Employment) Regulations 2006, SI 2006/246, reg 20, Sch 2, para 10.

Sub-s (1A): inserted by the Collective Redundancies and Transfer of Undertakings (Protection of Employment) (Amendment) Regulations 1999, SI 1999/1925, reg 12; words in square brackets substituted by SI 2006/246, reg 20, Sch 2, para 10.

Sub-s (2): words omitted repealed, and words in square brackets substituted, by the Employment Relations Act 1999, ss 18(2), 44, Sch 9(3).

Conciliation: see the note following the Part heading *ante*.

## [1.806]
## [47A  Employees exercising the right to time off work for study or training

(1)  An employee has the right not to be subjected to any detriment by any act, or any deliberate failure to act, by his employer or the principal (within the meaning of section 63A(3)) done on the ground that, being a person entitled to—

(a)   time off under section 63A(1) or (3), and

(b)   remuneration under section 63B(1) in respect of that time taken off,

the employee exercised (or proposed to exercise) that right or received (or sought to receive) such remuneration.

(2)   . . .   this section does not apply where the detriment in question amounts to dismissal (within the meaning of [Part X]).]

**NOTES**

Inserted by the Teaching and Higher Education Act 1998, s 44(1), Sch 3, para 10.

Sub-s (2): words omitted repealed, and words in square brackets substituted, by the Employment Relations Act 1999, ss 18(2), 44, Sch 9(3).

Conciliation: see the note following the Part heading *ante*.

## [1.807]
## [47AA  Employees in England aged 16 or 17 participating in education or training

(1)   An employee has the right not to be subjected to any detriment by any act, or any deliberate failure to act, by his employer done on the ground that, being a person entitled to be permitted to participate in education or training by section 27 or 28 of the Education and Skills Act 2008, the employee exercised, or proposed to exercise, that right.

(2)   This section does not apply where the detriment in question amounts to dismissal (within the meaning of Part 10).]

**NOTES**

Commencement: to be appointed.

Inserted by the Education and Skills Act 2008, s 37, as from a day to be appointed.

Corresponding provision for Wales: where a Measure of the National Assembly for Wales includes provision that appears to the Secretary of State to correspond to provision made by the Education and Skills Act 2008, s 2 (duty to participate in education or training), the Secretary of State may make provision, by order, in relation to Wales that corresponds to any provision inserted by ss 37–39 of the 2008 Act; see 67 of the 2008 Act.

Conciliation: see the note following the Part heading *ante*.

## [1.808]
## [47B  Protected disclosures

(1)   A worker has the right not to be subjected to any detriment by any act, or any deliberate failure to act, by his employer done on the ground that the worker has made a protected disclosure.

[(1A)   A worker ("W") has the right not to be subjected to any detriment by any act, or any deliberate failure to act, done—

(a)   by another worker of W's employer in the course of that other worker's employment, or

(b)   by an agent of W's employer with the employer's authority,

on the ground that W has made a protected disclosure.

(1B)   Where a worker is subjected to detriment by anything done as mentioned in subsection (1A), that thing is treated as also done by the worker's employer.

(1C)   For the purposes of subsection (1B), it is immaterial whether the thing is done with the knowledge or approval of the worker's employer.

(1D)   In proceedings against W's employer in respect of anything alleged to have been done as mentioned in subsection (1A)(a), it is a defence for the employer to show that the employer took all reasonable steps to prevent the other worker—

(a)   from doing that thing, or

(b)   from doing anything of that description.

(1E)   A worker or agent of W's employer is not liable by reason of subsection (1A) for doing something that subjects W to detriment if—

(a)   the worker or agent does that thing in reliance on a statement by the employer that doing it does not contravene this Act, and

(b)  it is reasonable for the worker or agent to rely on the statement.
But this does not prevent the employer from being liable by reason of subsection (1B).]
(2)  . . . this section does not apply where—
(a)  the worker is an employee, and
(b)  the detriment in question amounts to dismissal (within the meaning of [Part X]).
(3)  For the purposes of this section, and of sections 48 and 49 so far as relating to this section, "worker", "worker's contract", "employment" and "employer" have the extended meaning given by section 43K.]

**NOTES**
Inserted by the Public Interest Disclosure Act 1998, ss 2, 18(2).
Sub-ss (1A)–(1E): inserted by the Enterprise and Regulatory Reform Act 2013, s 19(1), as from a day to be appointed, subject to savings in s 24(6) of the 2013 Act at **[1.1855]**.
Sub-s (2): words omitted repealed, and words in square brackets substituted, by the Employment Relations Act 1999, ss 18(2), Sch 9(3).
Conciliation: see the note following the Part heading *ante*.

**[1.809]**
**[47C  Leave for family and domestic reasons**
(1)  An employee has the right not to be subjected to any detriment by any act, or any deliberate failure to act, by his employer done for a prescribed reason.
(2)  A prescribed reason is one which is prescribed by regulations made by the Secretary of State and which relates to—
(a)  pregnancy, childbirth or maternity,
(b)  ordinary, compulsory or additional maternity leave,
[(ba) ordinary or additional adoption leave,]
(c)  parental leave,
[(ca) ordinary or additional paternity leave, or]
(d)  time off under section 57A.
(3)  A reason prescribed under this section in relation to parental leave may relate to action which an employee takes, agrees to take or refuses to take under or in respect of a collective or workforce agreement.
(4)  Regulations under this section may make different provision for different cases or circumstances.]

**NOTES**
Inserted by the Employment Relations Act 1999, s 9, Sch 4, Pt III, paras 1, 5, 8.
Sub-s (2): para (ba) inserted, and para (ca) substituted for the original word "or" at the end of para (c), by the Employment Act 2002, s 53, Sch 7, paras 24, 26; para (ca) further substituted by the Work and Families Act 2006, s 11(1), Sch 1, para 30, as from 3 March 2010.
Regulations: the Maternity and Parental Leave etc Regulations 1999, SI 1999/3312 at **[2.484]**; the Paternity and Adoption Leave Regulations 2002, SI 2002/2788 at **[2.619]**; the Maternity and Parental Leave (Amendment) Regulations 2002, SI 2002/2789; the Paternity and Adoption Leave (Adoptions from Overseas) Regulations 2003, SI 2003/921; the Maternity and Parental Leave etc and the Paternity and Adoption Leave (Amendment) Regulations 2006, SI 2006/2014; the Maternity and Parental Leave etc and the Paternity and Adoption Leave (Amendment) Regulations 2008, SI 2008/1966; the Additional Paternity Leave Regulations 2010, SI 2010/1055 at **[2.1415]**; the Additional Paternity Leave (Adoptions from Overseas) Regulations 2010, SI 2010/1059.
Conciliation: see the note following the Part heading *ante*.

**[1.810]**
**[47D  Tax credits**
(1)  An employee has the right not to be subjected to any detriment by any act, or any deliberate failure to act, by his employer, done on the ground that—
(a)  any action was taken, or was proposed to be taken, by or on behalf of the employee with a view to enforcing, or otherwise securing the benefit of, a right conferred on the employee by regulations under section 25 of the Tax Credits Act 2002,
(b)  a penalty was imposed on the employer, or proceedings for a penalty were brought against him, under that Act, as a result of action taken by or on behalf of the employee for the purpose of enforcing, or otherwise securing the benefit of, such a right, or
(c)  the employee is entitled, or will or may be entitled, to working tax credit.
(2)  It is immaterial for the purposes of subsection (1)(a) or (b)—
(a)  whether or not the employee has the right, or
(b)  whether or not the right has been infringed,
but, for those provisions to apply, the claim to the right and (if applicable) the claim that it has been infringed must be made in good faith.
(3)  Subsections (1) and (2) apply to a person who is not an employee within the meaning of this Act but who is an employee within the meaning of section 25 of the Tax Credits Act 2002, with references to his employer in those subsections (and sections 48(2) and (4) and 49(1)) being construed in accordance with that section.

(4) Subsections (1) and (2) do not apply to an employee if the detriment in question amounts to dismissal (within the meaning of Part 10).]

**NOTES**
Inserted by the Tax Credits Act 2002, s 27, Sch 1, paras 1(1), (2).
Conciliation: see the note following the Part heading *ante*.

**[1.811]**
**[47E   Flexible working**
(1)   An employee has the right not to be subjected to any detriment by any act, or any deliberate failure to act, by his employer done on the ground that the employee—
   (a)   made (or proposed to make) an application under section 80F,
   (b)   exercised (or proposed to exercise) a right conferred on him under section 80G,
   (c)   brought proceedings against the employer under section 80H, or
   (d)   alleged the existence of any circumstance which would constitute a ground for bringing such proceedings.
(2)   This section does not apply where the detriment in question amounts to dismissal within the meaning of Part 10.]

**NOTES**
Inserted by the Employment Act 2002, s 47(1), (3).
Note: in the Queen's Printer's copy of the Employment Act 2002, this section was originally numbered as s 47D. In a correction slip, issued in December 2002, the section number was changed to s 47E to take account of the fact that a s 47D had already been inserted by the Tax Credits Act 2002.
Conciliation: see the note following the Part heading *ante*.

**[1.812]**
**[47F   Study and training**
(1)   An employee has the right not to be subjected to any detriment by any act, or any deliberate failure to act, by the employee's employer done on the ground that the employee—
   (a)   made (or proposed to make) a section 63D application,
   (b)   exercised (or proposed to exercise) a right conferred on the employee under section 63F,
   (c)   brought proceedings against the employer under section 63I, or
   (d)   alleged the existence of any circumstance which would constitute a ground for bringing such proceedings.
(2)   This section does not apply if the detriment in question amounts to dismissal within the meaning of Part 10.]

**NOTES**
Commencement: 6 April 2010 (except in relation to small employers and their employees); to be appointed (otherwise).
Inserted by the Apprenticeships, Skills, Children and Learning Act 2009, s 40(1), (3), as from 6 April 2010 (except in relation to small employers and their employees), and as from a day to be appointed (otherwise) (as to the meaning of "small employers" etc, see further the notes at **[1.840]**).
Conciliation: see the note following the Part heading *ante*.

**[1.813]**
**[47G   Employee shareholder status**
(1)   An employee has the right not to be subjected to a detriment by any act, or any deliberate failure to act, by the employee's employer done on the ground that the employee refused to accept an offer by the employer for the employee to become an employee shareholder (within the meaning of section 205A).
(2)   This section does not apply if the detriment in question amounts to dismissal within the meaning of Part 10.]

**NOTES**
Commencement: to be appointed.
Inserted by the Growth and Infrastructure Act 2013, s 31(2), as from a day to be appointed.

*Enforcement*

**[1.814]**
**48   Complaints to [employment tribunals]**
(1)   An employee may present a complaint to an [employment tribunal] that he has been subjected to a detriment in contravention of section [43M,] 44, 45, [46, 47[, 47A[, 47C *or* 47E]]].
[(1ZA)   A worker may present a complaint to an employment tribunal that he has been subjected to a detriment in contravention of section 45A.]
[(1A)   A worker may present a complaint to an employment tribunal that he has been subjected to a detriment in contravention of section 47B.]
[(1B)   A person may present a complaint to an employment tribunal that he has been subjected to a detriment in contravention of section 47D.]

(2) On such a complaint it is for the employer to show the ground on which any act, or deliberate failure to act, was done.

(3) An [employment tribunal] shall not consider a complaint under this section unless it is presented—

(a) before the end of the period of three months beginning with the date of the act or failure to act to which the complaint relates or, where that act or failure is part of a series of similar acts or failures, the last of them, or

(b) within such further period as the tribunal considers reasonable in a case where it is satisfied that it was not reasonably practicable for the complaint to be presented before the end of that period of three months.

(4) For the purposes of subsection (3)—

(a) where an act extends over a period, the "date of the act" means the last day of that period, and

(b) a deliberate failure to act shall be treated as done when it was decided on;

and, in the absence of evidence establishing the contrary, an employer shall be taken to decide on a failure to act when he does an act inconsistent with doing the failed act or, if he has done no such inconsistent act, when the period expires within which he might reasonably have been expected do the failed act if it was to be done.

[(4A) Section 207A(3) (extension because of mediation in certain European cross-border disputes) *applies* for the purposes of subsection (3)(a).]

[(5) In this section and section 49 any reference to the employer *includes, where* a person complains that he has been subjected to a detriment in contravention of section 47A, the principal (within the meaning of section 63A(3)).]

**NOTES**

Section heading, sub-s (3): words in square brackets substituted by the Employment Rights (Dispute Resolution) Act 1998, s 1(2)(a), (b).

Sub-s (1) is amended as follows:

Words in first pair of square brackets substituted by the Employment Rights (Dispute Resolution) Act 1998, s 1(2)(a).

Figure "43M," in square brackets inserted by the Employment Relations Act 2004, s 40(2).

Figures "46, 47" in square brackets substituted by the Teaching and Higher Education Act 1998, s 44(1), Sch 3, para 11(a).

Figure ", 47A" in square brackets substituted by the Employment Relations Act 1999, s 9, Sch 4, Pt III, paras 5, 9.

Words in square brackets beginning ", 47C or" substituted by the Employment Act 2002, s 53, Sch 7, paras 24, 27.

For the words "or 47E" in italics there are substituted the words ", 47E or 47F" by the Apprenticeships, Skills, Children and Learning Act 2009, s 40(5), Sch 1, paras 1, 2, as from 6 April 2010 (except in relation to small employers and their employees), and as from a day to be appointed (otherwise) (as to the meaning of "small employers" etc, see further the notes at **[1.840]**), and for the words "or 47F" there is substituted ", 47F or 47G" by the Growth and Infrastructure Act 2013, s 31(3), as from a day to be appointed.

Sub-s (1ZA): inserted by the Working Time Regulations 1998, SI 1998/1833, regs 2(1), 31(2).

Sub-s (1A): inserted by the Public Interest Disclosure Act 1998, ss 3, 18(2).

Sub-s (1B): inserted by the Tax Credits Act 2002, s 27, Sch 1, para 1(1), (3).

Sub-s (4A): inserted by the Cross-Border Mediation (EU Directive) Regulations 2011, SI 2011/1133, regs 30, 34, as from 20 May 2011; for the word in italics there are substituted the words "and section 207B (extension of time limits to facilitate conciliation before institution of proceedings) apply", by the Enterprise and Regulatory Reform Act 2013, s 8, Sch 2, paras 15, 19, as from a day to be appointed.

Sub-s (5): added by the Teaching and Higher Education Act 1998, s 44(1), Sch 3, para 11(b); for the words in italics there are substituted the words "(a) where", and para (b) is added, by the Enterprise and Regulatory Reform Act 2013, s 19(2), as from a day to be appointed, subject to savings in s 24(6) of the 2013 Act at **[1.1855]**, as follows:

"(b)   in the case of proceedings against a worker or agent under section 47B(1A), the worker or agent.".

Conciliation: see the note following the Part heading *ante*.

Tribunal jurisdiction: the Employment Act 2002, s 38 applies to proceedings before the employment tribunal relating to a claim under this section; see s 38(1) of, and Sch 5 to, the 2002 Act at **[1.1228]**, **[1.1236]**. See also the Trade Union and Labour Relations (Consolidation) Act 1992, s 207A at **[1.474]** (as inserted by the Employment Act 2008). That section provides that in proceedings before an employment tribunal relating to a claim by an employee under any of the jurisdictions listed in Sch A2 to the 1992 Act at **[1.648]** (which includes this section) the tribunal may adjust any award given if the employer or the employee has unreasonably failed to comply with the relevant Code of Practice as defined by s 207A(4). See also the revised Acas Code of Practice 1 – Disciplinary and Grievance Procedures (2009) at **[4.1]**.

**[1.815]**
**49   Remedies**

(1) Where an [employment tribunal] finds a complaint under section 48 well-founded, the tribunal—

(a) shall make a declaration to that effect, and

(b) may make an award of compensation to be paid by the employer to the complainant in respect of the act or failure to act to which the complaint relates.

(2) [Subject to [subsections (5A) and (6)]] The amount of the compensation awarded shall be such as the tribunal considers just and equitable in all the circumstances having regard to—

(a) the infringement to which the complaint relates, and

(b) any loss which is attributable to the act, or failure to act, which infringed the complainant's right.

(3)   The loss shall be taken to include—
(a)   any expenses reasonably incurred by the complainant in consequence of the act, or failure to act, to which the complaint relates, and
(b)   loss of any benefit which he might reasonably be expected to have had but for that act or failure to act.

(4)   In ascertaining the loss the tribunal shall apply the same rule concerning the duty of a person to mitigate his loss as applies to damages recoverable under the common law of England and Wales or (as the case may be) Scotland.

(5)   Where the tribunal finds that the act, or failure to act, to which the complaint relates was to any extent caused or contributed to by action of the complainant, it shall reduce the amount of the compensation by such proportion as it considers just and equitable having regard to that finding.

[(5A)   Where—
(a)   the complaint is made under section 48(1ZA),
(b)   the detriment to which the worker is subjected is the termination of his worker's contract, and
(c)   that contract is not a contract of employment,
any compensation must not exceed the compensation that would be payable under Chapter II of Part X if the worker had been an employee and had been dismissed for the reason specified in section 101A.]

[(6)   Where—
(a)   the complaint is made under section 48(1A),
(b)   the detriment to which the worker is subjected is the termination of his worker's contract, and
(c)   that contract is not a contract of employment,
any compensation must not exceed the compensation that would be payable under Chapter II of Part X if the worker had been an employee and had been dismissed for the reason specified in section 103A.]

[(6A)   Where—
(a)   the complaint is made under section 48(1A), and
(b)   it appears to the tribunal that the protected disclosure was not made in good faith,
the tribunal may, if it considers it just and equitable in all the circumstances to do so, reduce any award it makes to the worker by no more than 25%.]

[(7)   Where—
(a)   the complaint is made under section 48(1B) by a person who is not an employee, and
(b)   the detriment to which he is subjected is the termination of his contract with the person who is his employer for the purposes of section 25 of the Tax Credits Act 2002,
any compensation must not exceed the compensation that would be payable under Chapter 2 of Part 10 if the complainant had been an employee and had been dismissed for the reason specified in section 104B.]

**NOTES**
Sub-s (1): words in square brackets substituted by the Employment Rights (Dispute Resolution) Act 1998, s 1(2)(a).
Sub-s (2): words in first (outer) pair of square brackets inserted by the Public Interest Disclosure Act 1998, ss 4(1), (2), 18(2); words in second (inner) pair of square brackets substituted by the Working Time Regulations 1998, SI 1998/1833, regs 2(1), 31(3)(a).
Sub-s (5A): inserted by the Working Time Regulations 1998, SI 1998/1833, regs 2(1), 31(3)(b).
Sub-s (6): added by the Public Interest Disclosure Act 1998, ss 4(1), (3), 18(2).
Sub-s (6A): inserted by the Enterprise and Regulatory Reform Act 2013, s 18(4), as from 25 June 2013, subject to savings in s 24(6) of the 2013 Act at [**1.1855**].
Sub-s (7): added by the Tax Credits Act 2002, s 27, Sch 1, para 1(1), (4).
Conciliation: see the note following the Part heading *ante*.

*[Application to police of rights relating to health and safety*

**[1.816]**
**49A   Application to police of section 44 and related provisions**
(1)   For the purposes of section 44, and of sections 48 and 49 so far as relating to that section, the holding, otherwise than under a contract of employment, of the office of constable or an appointment as police cadet shall be treated as employment by the relevant officer under a contract of employment.

[(2)   In this section "the relevant officer", in relation to—
(a)   a person holding the office of constable, or
(b)   a person holding an appointment as a police cadet,
means the person who under section 51A of the Health and Safety at Work etc Act 1974 is to be treated as his employer for the purposes of Part 1 of that Act.]

**NOTES**
Inserted by the Police (Health and Safety) Act 1997, s 3.
Sub-s (2): substituted by the Serious Organised Crime and Police Act 2005, s 158(1), (2)(a), (3), (5).
Conciliation: see the note following the Part heading *ante*.

Note: this section was amended by the Police Reform Act 2002, s 95, as from a day to be appointed. Those amendments lapsed following the repeal of that section without being brought into force, by the Serious Organised Crime and Police Act 2005, ss 158(4)(a), 174(2), Sch 17, Pt 1.

## PART VI
## TIME OFF WORK

**NOTES**

Conciliation: employment tribunal proceedings and claims which could be the subject of employment tribunal proceedings under this Part are proceedings to which the Employment Tribunals Act 1996, s 18 applies; see s 18(1)(d) of that Act at **[1.706]**.

*Public duties*

**[1.817]**
### 50   Right to time off for public duties
(1)   An employer shall permit an employee of his who is a justice of the peace to take time off during the employee's working hours for the purpose of performing any of the duties of his office.
(2)   An employer shall permit an employee of his who is a member of—
  (a)   a local authority,
  (b)   a statutory tribunal,
  [(c)   . . . ]
  [(ca)  . . . . ]
  (d)   [an independent monitoring board for a prison] or a prison visiting committee,
  (e)   a relevant health body,
  (f)   a relevant education body,   . . .
  (g)   the Environment Agency or the Scottish Environment Protection Agency, [or
  [(h)   Scottish Water   . . . ,]]
to take time off during the employee's working hours for the purposes specified in subsection (3).
(3)   The purposes referred to in subsection (2) are—
  (a)   attendance at a meeting of the body or any of its committees or sub-committees, and
  (b)   the doing of any other thing approved by the body, or anything of a class so approved, for the purpose of the discharge of the functions of the body or of any of its committees or sub-committees[, and
  (c)   in the case of a local authority which are operating executive arrangements—
    (i)   attendance at a meeting of the executive of that local authority or committee of that executive; and
    (ii)   the doing of any other thing, by an individual member of that executive, for the purposes of the discharge of any function which is to any extent the responsibility of that executive.]
(4)   The amount of time off which an employee is to be permitted to take under this section, and the occasions on which and any condition subject to which time off may be so taken, are those that are reasonable in all the circumstances having regard, in particular, to—
  (a)   how much time off is required for the performance of the duties of the office or as a member of the body in question, and how much time off is required for the performance of the particular duty,
  (b)   how much time off the employee has already been permitted under this section or sections 168 and 170 of the Trade Union and Labour Relations (Consolidation) Act 1992 (time off trade union duties and activities), and
  (c)   the circumstances of the employer's business and the effect of the employee's absence on the running of that business.
(5)   In subsection (2)(a) "a local authority" means—
  (a)   a local authority within the meaning of the Local Government Act 1972,
  (b)   a council constituted under section 2 of the Local Government etc (Scotland) Act 1994,
  (c)   the Common Council of the City of London,
  (d)   a National Park authority, or
  (e)   the Broads Authority.
(6)   . . .
(7)   In subsection (2)(d)—
  (a)   ["independent monitoring board" means a board] appointed under section 6(2) of the Prison Act 1952, and
  (b)   "a prison visiting committee" means a visiting committee appointed under section 19(3) of the Prisons (Scotland) Act 1989 or constituted by virtue of rules made under section 39 (as read with section 8(1)) of that Act.
(8)   In subsection (2)(e) "a relevant health body" means—
  [(za)  the National Health Service Commissioning Board,
  (zb)  a clinical commissioning group established under section 14D of the National Health Service Act 2006,]

(a)  a National Health Service trust established under [*section 25 of the National Health Service Act 2006,* section 18 of the National Health Service (Wales) Act 2006] or the National Health Service (Scotland) Act 1978,

[(ab)  an NHS foundation trust,]

[(ac)  the National Institute for Health and Care Excellence,]

[(ad)  the Health and Social Care Information Centre,]

(b)  a [*Strategic Health Authority established under section 13 of the National Health Service Act 2006,* a] [Local Health Board established under section 11 of the National Health Service (Wales) Act 2006] . . . [, a Special Health Authority established under [section 28 of the National Health Service Act 2006 or section 22 of the National Health Service (Wales) Act 2006] *or a Primary Care Trust established under] [section 18 of the National Health Service Act 2006],* or

(c)  a Health Board constituted under section 2 of the National Health Service (Scotland) Act 1978.

(9)  In subsection (2)(f) "a relevant education body" means—

(a)  a managing or governing body of an educational establishment maintained by a [local authority (as defined in section 579(1) of the Education Act 1996)],

[(b)  a further education corporation, sixth form college corporation or higher education corporation,]

(c)  a school council appointed under section 125(1) of the Local Government (Scotland) Act 1973,

[(d)  a parent council within the meaning of section 5(2) of the Scottish Schools (Parental Involvement) Act 2006,]

(e)  . . .

(f)  a board of management of a college of further education within the meaning of section 36(1) of the Further and Higher Education (Scotland) Act 1992,

(g)  a governing body of a central institution within the meaning of section 135(1) of the Education (Scotland) Act 1980, . . .

(h)  a governing body of a designated institution within the meaning of Part II of the Further and Higher Education (Scotland) Act 1992,

[(i)  . . .

(j)  the General Teaching Council for Wales.]

[(9A)  In subsection (3)(c) of this section "executive" and "executive arrangements" have the same meaning as in Part II of the Local Government Act 2000.]

[(9B)  In subsection (9)(b) "further education corporation", "sixth form college corporation" and "higher education corporation" have the same meanings as in the Further and Higher Education Act 1992.]

(10)  The Secretary of State may by order—

(a)  modify the provisions of subsections (1) and (2) and (5) to (9) by adding any office or body, removing any office or body or altering the description of any office or body, or

(b)  modify the provisions of subsection (3).

(11)  For the purposes of this section the working hours of an employee shall be taken to be any time when, in accordance with his contract of employment, the employee is required to be at work.

---

**NOTES**

Sub-s (2) is amended as follows:

Para (c) substituted by the Police and Justice Act 2006, s 52, Sch 14, para 31, and repealed by the Police Reform and Social Responsibility Act 2011, s 99, Sch 16, Pt 3, para 219, as from 22 November 2012 (for general transitional provisions relating to police reform and the abolition of existing police authorities, see Sch 15 to the 2011 Act).

Para (ca) inserted by the Police Act 1997, s 134(1), Sch 9, para 88, and repealed by the Serious Organised Crime and Police Act 2005, ss 59, 174(2), Sch 4, paras 84, 86, Sch 17, Pt 2.

Words in square brackets in para (d) substituted by the Offender Management Act 2007, s 39, Sch 3, Pt 2, para 8(a), as from 1 November 2007.

Word omitted from para (f) repealed, and para (h) and the word immediately preceding it added, by the Time Off for Public Duties Order 2000, SI 2000/1737, art 2.

Para (h) substituted by the Water Industry (Scotland) Act 2002 (Consequential Modifications) Order 2004, SI 2004/1822, art 2, Schedule, Pt 1, para 18; words omitted from para (h) repealed by Public Services Reform (Scotland) Act 2010 (Consequential Modifications of Enactments) Order 2011, SI 2011/2581, art 2, Sch 3, Pt 1, para 2, as from 28 October 2011.

Sub-s (3): para (c) and the word immediately preceding it inserted, in relation to England, by the Local Authorities (Executive and Alternative Arrangements) (Modification of Enactments and Other Provisions) (England) Order 2001, SI 2001/2237, art 30(a), and in relation to Wales, by the Local Authorities (Executive and Alternative Arrangements) (Modification of Enactments and Other Provisions) (Wales) Order 2002, SI 2002/808, arts 2(o), 29(a).

Sub-s (6): repealed by the Police and Justice Act 2006, s 52, Sch 15, Pt 1.

Sub-s (7): words in square brackets in para (a) substituted by the Offender Management Act 2007, s 39, Sch 3, Pt 2, para 8(b).

Sub-s (8) is amended as follows:

Paras (za), (zb) inserted by the Health and Social Care Act 2012, s 55(2), Sch 5, paras 72, 74(a), as from 1 October 2012.

Words in square brackets in para (a) substituted by the National Health Service (Consequential Provisions) Act 2006, s 2, Sch 1, paras 177, 179(a).

Words in italics in para (a) repealed by the Health and Social Care Act 2012, s 179, Sch 14, paras 68, 69, as from a day to be appointed.

Para (ab) inserted by the Health and Social Care (Community Health and Standards) Act 2003, s 34, Sch 4, paras 99, 100.

Para (ac) inserted by the Health and Social Care Act 2012, s 249, Sch 17, para 6(1), (2), as from a day to be appointed.

Para (ad) inserted by the Health and Social Care Act 2012, s 277, Sch 19, para 6(1), (2), as from a day to be appointed.

Words in italics in para (b) repealed by the Health and Social Care Act 2012, s 55(2), Sch 5, paras 72, 74(b), as from a day to be appointed.

Words in first, fourth (inner), and fifth pairs of square brackets in para (b) substituted, and words omitted from that paragraph repealed, by the National Health Service (Consequential Provisions) Act 2006, s 2, Sch 1, paras 177, 179(b); words in second pair of square brackets in para (b) substituted by the References to Health Authorities Order 2007, SI 2007/961, art 3, Schedule, para 27(1), (3); words in third (outer) pair of square brackets in para (b) substituted by the Health Act 1999 (Supplementary, Consequential etc Provisions) Order 2000, SI 2000/90, art 3(1), Sch 1, para 30(1), (2).

Sub-s (9): words in square brackets in para (a) substituted by the Local Education Authorities and Children's Services Authorities (Integration of Functions) Order 2010, SI 2010/1158, art 5, Sch 2, Pt 2, para 41(1), (2), as from 5 May 2010; para (b) substituted by the Apprenticeships, Skills, Children and Learning Act 2009 (Consequential Amendments) (England and Wales) Order 2010, SI 2010/1080, art 2, Sch 1, Pt 1, para 96(a), as from 1 April 2010; para (d) substituted by the Time Off for Public Duties (Parent Councils) Order 2007, SI 2007/1837, art 2; para (e) repealed by the Standards in Scotland's Schools etc Act 2000, s 60(2), Sch 3; word omitted from para (g) repealed, and paras (i), (j) added, by the Time Off for Public Duties (No 2) Order 2000, SI 2000/2463, art 2; para (i) repealed by the Education Act 2011, s 11(1), Sch 2, para 24, as from 1 April 2012.

Sub-s (9A): inserted, in relation to England, by SI 2001/2237, art 30(b), and in relation to Wales, by SI 2002/808, arts 2(o), 29(b).

Sub-s (9B): inserted by SI 2010/1080, art 2, Sch 1, Pt 1, para 96(b), as from 1 April 2010.

Conciliation: see the note following the Part heading *ante*.

Local Government (Scotland) Act 1973, s 125: repealed by the Self-Governing Schools etc (Scotland) Act 1989, s 82(2), Sch 11.

Orders: the Time Off for Public Duties Order 2000, SI 2000/1737; the Time Off for Public Duties (No 2) Order 2000, SI 2000/2463; the Time Off for Public Duties (Parent Councils) Order 2007, SI 2007/1837.

---

**[1.818]**
**51 Complaints to [employment tribunals]**
(1)   An employee may present a complaint to an [employment tribunal] that his employer has failed to permit him to take time off as required by section 50.
(2)   An [employment tribunal] shall not consider a complaint under this section that an employer has failed to permit an employee to take time off unless it is presented—
  (a)   before the end of the period of three months beginning with the date on which the failure occurred, or
  (b)   within such further period as the tribunal considers reasonable in a case where it is satisfied that it was not reasonably practicable for the complaint to be presented before the end of that period of three months.
[(2A)   Section 207A(3) (extension because of mediation in certain European cross-border disputes) *applies* for the purposes of subsection (2)(a).]
(3)   Where an [employment tribunal] finds a complaint under this section well-founded, the tribunal—
  (a)   shall make a declaration to that effect, and
  (b)   may make an award of compensation to be paid by the employer to the employee.
(4)   The amount of the compensation shall be such as the tribunal considers just and equitable in all the circumstances having regard to—
  (a)   the employer's default in failing to permit time off to be taken by the employee, and
  (b)   any loss sustained by the employee which is attributable to the matters to which the complaint relates.

**NOTES**

Section heading, sub-ss (1)–(3): words in square brackets substituted by the Employment Rights (Dispute Resolution) Act 1998, s 1(2)(a), (b).

Sub-s (2A): inserted by the Cross-Border Mediation (EU Directive) Regulations 2011, SI 2011/1133, regs 30, 35, as from 20 May 2011; for the word in italics there are substituted the words "and section 207B (extension of time limits to facilitate conciliation before institution of proceedings) apply", by the Enterprise and Regulatory Reform Act 2013, s 8, Sch 2, paras 15, 20, as from a day to be appointed.

Conciliation: see the note following the Part heading *ante*.

*Looking for work and making arrangements for training*

**[1.819]**
**52 Right to time off to look for work or arrange training**
(1)   An employee who is given notice of dismissal by reason of redundancy is entitled to be permitted by his employer to take reasonable time off during the employee's working hours before the end of his notice in order to—
  (a)   look for new employment, or
  (b)   make arrangements for training for future employment.
(2)   An employee is not entitled to take time off under this section unless, on whichever is the later of—
  (a)   the date on which the notice is due to expire, and
  (b)   the date on which it would expire were it the notice required to be given by section 86(1),

he will have been (or would have been) continuously employed for period of two years or more.
(3) For the purposes of this section the working hours of an employee shall be taken to be any time when, in accordance with his contract of employment, the employee is required to be at work.

**NOTES**
  Conciliation: see the note following the Part heading *ante*.

**[1.820]**
## 53 Right to remuneration for time off under section 52
(1) An employee who is permitted to take time off under section 52 is entitled to be paid remuneration by his employer for the period of absence at the appropriate hourly rate.
(2) The appropriate hourly rate, in relation to an employee, is the amount of one week's pay divided by the number of normal working hours in a week for that employee when employed under the contract of employment in force on the day when the notice of dismissal was given.
(3) But where the number of normal working hours differs from week to week or over a longer period, the amount of one week's pay shall be divided instead by the average number of normal working hours calculated by dividing by twelve the total number of the employee's normal working hours during the period of twelve weeks ending with the last complete week before the day on which the notice was given.
(4) If an employer unreasonably refuses to permit an employee to take time off from work as required by section 52, the employee is entitled to be paid an amount equal to the remuneration to which he would have been entitled under subsection (1) if he had been permitted to take the time off.
(5) The amount of an employer's liability to pay remuneration under subsection (1) shall not exceed, in respect of the notice period of any employee, forty per cent of a week's pay of that employee.
(6) A right to any amount under subsection (1) or (4) does not affect any right of an employee in relation to remuneration under his contract of employment ("contractual remuneration").
(7) Any contractual remuneration paid to an employee in respect of a period of time off under section 52 goes towards discharging any liability of the employer to pay remuneration under subsection (1) in respect of that period; and, conversely, any payment of remuneration under subsection (1) in respect of a period goes towards discharging any liability the employer to pay contractual remuneration in respect of that period.

**NOTES**
  Conciliation: see the note following the Part heading *ante*.

**[1.821]**
## 54 Complaints to [employment tribunals]
(1) An employee may present a complaint to an [employment tribunal] that his employer—
  (a)  has unreasonably refused to permit him to take time off as required by section 52, or
  (b)  has failed to pay the whole or any part of any amount to which the employee is entitled under section 53(1) or (4).
(2) An [employment tribunal] shall not consider a complaint under this section unless it is presented—
  (a)  before the end of the period of three months beginning with the date on which it is alleged that the time off should have been permitted, or
  (b)  within such further period as the tribunal considers reasonable in a case where it is satisfied that it was not reasonably practicable for the complaint to be presented before the end of that period of three months.
[(2A) Section 207A(3) (extension because of mediation in certain European cross-border disputes) *applies* for the purposes of subsection (2)(a).]
(3) Where an [employment tribunal] finds a complaint under this section well-founded, the tribunal shall—
  (a)  make a declaration to that effect, and
  (b)  order the employer to pay to the employee the amount which it finds due to him.
(4) The amount which may be ordered by a tribunal to be paid by an employer under subsection (3) (or, where the employer is liable to pay remuneration under section 53, the aggregate of that amount and the amount of that liability) shall not exceed, in respect of the notice period of any employee, forty per cent of a week's pay of that employee.

**NOTES**
  Section heading, sub-ss (1)–(3): words in square brackets substituted by the Employment Rights (Dispute Resolution) Act 1998, s 1(2)(a), (b).
  Sub-s (2A): inserted by the Cross-Border Mediation (EU Directive) Regulations 2011, SI 2011/1133, regs 30, 36, as from 20 May 2011; for the word in italics there are substituted the words "and section 207B (extension of time limits to facilitate conciliation before institution of proceedings) apply", by the Enterprise and Regulatory Reform Act 2013, s 8, Sch 2, paras 15, 21, as from a day to be appointed.

Part 1   Statutes

Conciliation: see the note following the Part heading *ante*.

*Ante-natal care*

**[1.822]**
**55   Right to time off for ante-natal care**
(1)   An employee who—
   (a)   is pregnant, and
   (b)   has, on the advice of a registered medical practitioner, registered midwife or [registered nurse], made an appointment to attend at any place for the purpose of receiving ante-natal care,
is entitled to be permitted by her employer to take time off during the employee's working hours in order to enable her to keep the appointment.
(2)   An employee is not entitled to take time off under this section to keep an appointment unless, if her employer requests her to do so, she produces for his inspection—
   (a)   a certificate from a registered medical practitioner, registered midwife or [registered nurse] stating that the employee is pregnant, and
   (b)   an appointment card or some other document showing that the appointment has been made.
(3)   Subsection (2) does not apply where the employee's appointment is the first appointment during her pregnancy for which she seek permission to take time off in accordance with subsection (1).
(4)   For the purposes of this section the working hours of an employee shall be taken to be any time when, in accordance with her contract of employment, the employee is required to be at work.
[(5)   References in this section to a registered nurse are to such a nurse—
   (a)   who is also registered in the Specialist Community Public Health Nurses' Part of the register maintained under article 5 of the Nursing and Midwifery Order 2001, and
   (b)   whose entry in that Part of the register is annotated to show that he holds a qualification in health visiting.]

**NOTES**
Sub-ss (1), (2): words in square brackets substituted by the Nursing and Midwifery Order 2001, SI 2002/253, art 54(3), Sch 5, para 13.
Sub-s (5): added by the Health Act 1999 (Consequential Amendments) (Nursing and Midwifery) Order 2004, SI 2004/1771, art 3, Schedule, Pt 1, para 3.
Conciliation: see the note following the Part heading *ante*.

**[1.823]**
**56   Right to remuneration for time off under section 55**
(1)   An employee who is permitted to take time off under section 55 is entitled to be paid remuneration by her employer for the period of absence at the appropriate hourly rate.
(2)   The appropriate hourly rate, in relation to an employee, is the amount of one week's pay divided by the number of normal working hours in a week for that employee when employed under the contract of employment in force on the day when the time off is taken.
(3)   But where the number of normal working hours differs from week to week or over a longer period, the amount of one week's pay shall be divided instead by—
   (a)   the average number of normal working hours calculated by dividing by twelve the total number of the employee's normal working hours during the period of twelve weeks ending with the last complete week before the day on which the time off taken, or
   (b)   where the employee has not been employed for a sufficient period to enable the calculation to be made under paragraph (a), a number which fairly represents the number of normal working hours in a week having regard to such of the considerations specified in subsection (4) as are appropriate in the circumstances.
(4)   The considerations referred to in subsection (3)(b) are—
   (a)   the average number of normal working hours in a week which the employee could expect in accordance with the terms of her contract, and
   (b)   the average number of normal working hours of other employees engaged in relevant comparable employment with the same employer.
(5)   A right to any amount under subsection (1) does not affect any right of an employee in relation to remuneration under her contract of employment ("contractual remuneration").
(6)   Any contractual remuneration paid to an employee in respect of a period of time off under section 55 goes towards discharging any liability of the employer to pay remuneration under subsection (1) in respect of that period; and, conversely, any payment of remuneration under subsection (1) in respect of a period goes towards discharging any liability of the employer to pay contractual remuneration in respect of that period.

**NOTES**
Conciliation: see the note following the Part heading *ante*.

**[1.824]**
**57   Complaints to [employment tribunals]**
(1)   An employee may present a complaint to an [employment tribunal] that her employer—
   (a)   has unreasonably refused to permit her to take time off as required by section 55, or
   (b)   has failed to pay the whole or any part of any amount to which the employee is entitled under section 56.
(2)   An [employment tribunal] shall not consider a complaint under this action unless it is presented—
   (a)   before the end of the period of three months beginning with the date of the appointment concerned, or
   (b)   within such further period as the tribunal considers reasonable in a case where it is satisfied that it was not reasonably practicable for the complaint to be presented before the end of that period of three months.
[(2A)   Section 207A(3) (extension because of mediation in certain European cross-border disputes) *applies for the purposes of subsection (3)(a).*]
(3)   Where an [employment tribunal] finds a complaint under this section well-founded, the tribunal shall make a declaration to that effect.
(4)   If the complaint is that the employer has unreasonably refused to permit the employee to take time off, the tribunal shall also order the employer to pay to the employee an amount equal to the remuneration to which she would have been entitled under section 56 if the employer had not refused.
(5)   If the complaint is that the employer has failed to pay the employee the whole or part of any amount to which she is entitled under section 56, the tribunal shall also order the employer to pay to the employee the amount which it finds due to her.

**NOTES**
   Section heading, sub-ss (1)–(3): words in square brackets substituted by the Employment Rights (Dispute Resolution) Act 1998, s 1(2)(a), (b).
   Sub-s (2A): inserted by the Cross-Border Mediation (EU Directive) Regulations 2011, SI 2011/1133, regs 30, 37, as from 20 May 2011; for the words in italics there are substituted the words "and section 207B (extension of time limits to facilitate conciliation before institution of proceedings) apply for the purposes of subsection (2)(a)", by the Enterprise and Regulatory Reform Act 2013, s 8, Sch 2, paras 15, 22, as from a day to be appointed.
   Conciliation: see the note following the Part heading *ante*.

*[Ante-natal care: agency workers*

**[1.825]**
**57ZA   Right to time off for ante-natal care (agency workers)**
(1)   An agency worker who—
   (a)   is pregnant, and
   (b)   has, on the advice of a registered medical practitioner, registered midwife or registered nurse, made an appointment to attend at any place for the purpose of receiving ante-natal care,
is entitled to be permitted, by the temporary work agency and the hirer, to take time off during the agency worker's working hours in order to enable her to keep the appointment.
(2)   An agency worker is not entitled to be permitted by either of those persons to take time off under this section to keep an appointment unless, if that person requests her to do so, she produces for that person's inspection—
   (a)   a certificate from a registered medical practitioner, registered midwife or registered nurse stating that the agency worker is pregnant, and
   (b)   an appointment card or some other document showing that the appointment has been made.
(3)   Subsection (2) does not apply where the agency worker's appointment is the first appointment during her pregnancy for which she seeks permission to take time off in accordance with subsection (1).
(4)   For the purposes of this section the working hours of an agency worker shall be taken to be any time when, in accordance with the terms under which the agency worker works temporarily for and under the supervision and direction of the hirer, the agency worker is required to be at work.
(5)   In this section references to a registered nurse have the same meaning as in section 55.]

**NOTES**
   Commencement: 1 October 2011.
   Inserted, together with the preceding heading and ss 57ZB–57ZD, by the Agency Workers Regulations 2010, SI 2010/93, reg 25, Sch 2, Pt 1, paras 9, 11, as from 1 October 2011.
   Conciliation: see the note following the Part heading *ante*.

**[1.826]**
**[57ZB   Right to remuneration for time off under section 57ZA**
(1)   An agency worker who is permitted to take time off under section 57ZA is entitled to be paid remuneration by the temporary work agency for the period of absence at the appropriate hourly rate.

(2) The appropriate hourly rate, in relation to an agency worker, is the amount of one week's pay divided by the number of normal working hours in a week for that agency worker in accordance with the terms under which the agency worker works temporarily for and under the supervision and direction of the hirer that are in force on the day when the time off is taken.

(3) But where the number of normal working hours during the assignment differs from week to week or over a longer period, the amount of one week's pay shall be divided instead by the average number of normal working hours calculated by dividing by twelve the total number of the agency worker's normal working hours during the period of twelve weeks ending with the last complete week before the day on which the time off is taken.

(4) A right to any amount under subsection (1) does not affect any right of an agency worker in relation to remuneration under her contract with the temporary work agency ("contractual remuneration").

(5) Any contractual remuneration paid to an agency worker in respect of a period of time off under section 57ZA goes towards discharging any liability of the temporary work agency to pay remuneration under subsection (1) in respect of that period; and, conversely, any payment of remuneration under subsection (1) in respect of a period goes towards discharging any liability of the temporary work agency to pay contractual remuneration in respect of that period.]

---

**NOTES**

Commencement: 1 October 2011.

Inserted as noted to s 57ZA at **[1.825]**.

Conciliation: see the note following the Part heading *ante*.

---

**[1.827]**

**[57ZC Complaint to employment tribunal: agency workers**

(1) An agency worker may present a complaint to an employment tribunal that the temporary work agency—
  (a) has unreasonably refused to permit her to take time off as required by section 57ZA, or
  (b) has failed to pay the whole or any part of any amount to which she is entitled under section 57ZB.

(2) An agency worker may present a complaint to an employment tribunal that the hirer has unreasonably refused to permit her to take time off as required by section 57ZA.

(3) An employment tribunal shall not consider a complaint under subsection (1) or (2) unless it is presented—
  (a) before the end of the period of three months beginning with the date of the appointment concerned, or
  (b) within such further period as the tribunal considers reasonable in a case where it is satisfied that it was not reasonably practicable for the complaint to be presented before the end of that period of three months.

[(3A) Section 207A(3) (extension because of mediation in certain European cross-border disputes) and section 207B (extension of time limits to facilitate conciliation before institution of proceedings) apply for the purposes of subsection (3)(a).]

(4) Where an employment tribunal finds a complaint under this section well-founded, the tribunal shall make a declaration to that effect.

(5) If the complaint is that the temporary work agency or hirer has unreasonably refused to permit the agency worker to take time off, the tribunal shall also order payment to the agency worker of an amount equal to the remuneration to which she would have been entitled under section 57ZB if she had not been refused the time off.

(6) Where the tribunal orders payment under subsection (5), the amount payable by each party shall be such as may be found by the tribunal to be just and equitable having regard to the extent of each respondent's responsibility for the infringement to which the complaint relates.

(7) If the complaint is that the temporary work agency has failed to pay the agency worker the whole or part of any amount to which she is entitled under section 57ZB, the tribunal shall also order the temporary work agency to pay to the agency worker the amount which it finds due to her.]

---

**NOTES**

Commencement: 1 October 2011.

Inserted as noted to s 57ZA at **[1.825]**.

Sub-s (3A): inserted by the Enterprise and Regulatory Reform Act 2013, s 8, Sch 2, paras 15, 23, as from a day to be appointed.

Conciliation: see the note following the Part heading *ante*.

---

**[1.828]**

**[57ZD Agency workers: supplementary**

(1) Without prejudice to any other duties of the hirer or temporary work agency under any enactment or rule of law sections 57ZA to 57ZC do not apply where the agency worker—
  (a) has not completed the qualifying period, or

(b)    is no longer entitled to the rights conferred by regulation 5 of the Agency Workers
       Regulations 2010 pursuant to regulation 8(a) or (b) of those Regulations.
(2)    Nothing in those sections imposes a duty on the hirer or temporary work agency beyond the
original intended duration, or likely duration of the assignment, whichever is the longer.
(3)    Those sections do not apply where sections 55 to 57 apply.
(4)    In this section and sections 57ZA to 57ZC the following have the same meaning as in the
Agency Workers Regulations 2010—
       "agency worker";
       "assignment";
       "hirer";
       "qualifying period";
       "temporary work agency".]

NOTES
   Commencement: 1 October 2011.
   Inserted as noted to s 57ZA at [**1.825**].
   Conciliation: see the note following the Part heading *ante*.

*[Dependants*

**[1.829]**
**57A    Time off for dependants**
(1)    An employee is entitled to be permitted by his employer to take a reasonable amount of time
off during the employee's working hours in order to take action which is necessary—
       (a)    to provide assistance on an occasion when a dependant falls ill, gives birth or is injured or
              assaulted,
       (b)    to make arrangements for the provision of care for a dependant who is ill or injured,
       (c)    in consequence of the death of a dependant,
       (d)    because of the unexpected disruption or termination of arrangements for the care of a
              dependant, or
       (e)    to deal with an incident which involves a child of the employee and which occurs
              unexpectedly in a period during which an educational establishment which the child
              attends is responsible for him.
(2)    Subsection (1) does not apply unless the employee—
       (a)    tells his employer the reason for his absence as soon as reasonably practicable, and
       (b)    except where paragraph (a) cannot be complied with until after the employee has returned
              to work, tells his employer for how long he expects to be absent.
(3)    Subject to subsections (4) and (5), for the purposes of this section "dependant" means, in
relation to an employee—
       (a)    a spouse [or civil partner],
       (b)    a child,
       (c)    a parent,
       (d)    a person who lives in the same household as the employee, otherwise than by reason of
              being his employee, tenant, lodger or boarder.
(4)    For the purposes of subsection (1)(a) or (b) "dependant" includes, in addition to the persons
mentioned in subsection (3), any person who reasonably relies on the employee—
       (a)    for assistance on an occasion when the person falls ill or is injured or assaulted, or
       (b)    to make arrangements for the provision of care in the event of illness or injury.
(5)    For the purposes of subsection (1)(d) "dependant" includes, in addition to the persons
mentioned in subsection (3), any person who reasonably relies on the employee to make
arrangements for the provision of care.
(6)    A reference in this section to illness or injury includes a reference to mental illness or injury.]

NOTES
   Inserted, together with preceding heading and s 57B, by the Employment Relations Act 1999, s 8, Sch 4, Pt II.
   Sub-s (3): words in square brackets in para (a) inserted by the Civil Partnership Act 2004, s 261(1), Sch 27, para 151.
   Conciliation: see the note following the Part heading *ante*.

**[1.830]**
**[57B    Complaint to employment tribunal**
(1)    An employee may present a complaint to an employment tribunal that his employer has
unreasonably refused to permit him to take time off as required by section 57A.
(2)    An employment tribunal shall not consider a complaint under this section unless it is
presented—
       (a)    before the end of the period of three months beginning with the date when the refusal
              occurred, or
       (b)    within such further period as the tribunal considers reasonable in a case where it is satisfied
              that it was not reasonably practicable for the complaint to be presented before the end of
              that period of three months.

[(2A) Section 207A(3) (extension because of mediation in certain European cross-border disputes) *applies* for the purposes of subsection (2)(a).]

(3) Where an employment tribunal finds a complaint under subsection (1) well-founded, it—

    (a) shall make a declaration to that effect, and

    (b) may make an award of compensation to be paid by the employer to the employee.

(4) The amount of compensation shall be such as the tribunal considers just and equitable in all the circumstances having regard to—

    (a) the employer's default in refusing to permit time off to be taken by the employee, and

    (b) any loss sustained by the employee which is attributable to the matters complained of.]

**NOTES**

Inserted as noted to s 57A at **[1.829]**.

Sub-s (2A): inserted by the Cross-Border Mediation (EU Directive) Regulations 2011, SI 2011/1133, regs 30, 38, as from 20 May 2011; for the word in italics there are substituted the words "and section 207B (extension of time limits to facilitate conciliation before institution of proceedings) apply", by the Enterprise and Regulatory Reform Act 2013, s 8, Sch 2, paras 15, 24, as from a day to be appointed.

Conciliation: see the note following the Part heading *ante*.

*Occupational pension scheme trustees*

**[1.831]**

**58 Right to time off for pension scheme trustees**

(1) The employer in relation to a relevant occupational pension scheme shall permit an employee of his who is a trustee of the scheme to the time off during the employee's working hours for the purpose of—

    (a) performing any of his duties as such a trustee, or

    (b) undergoing training relevant to the performance of those duties.

(2) The amount of time off which an employee is to be permitted to take under this section and the purposes for which, the occasions on which and any conditions subject to which time off may be so taken are those that are reasonable in all the circumstances having regard, in particular, to—

    (a) how much time off is required for the performance of the duties of a trustee of the scheme and the undergoing of relevant training, and how much time off is required for performing the particular duty or for undergoing the particular training, and

    (b) the circumstances of the employer's business and the effect of the employee's absence on the running of that business.

[(2A) This section applies to an employee who is a director of a company which is a trustee of a relevant occupational pension scheme as it applies to an employee who is a trustee of such a scheme (references to such a trustee being read for this purpose as references to such a director).]

(3) In this section—

    (a) "relevant occupational pension scheme" means an occupational pension scheme (as defined in section 1 of the Pension Schemes Act 1993) established under a trust, and

    (b) references to the employer, in relation to such a scheme, are to an employer of persons in the description *or category* of employment to which the scheme relates[, and

    (c) references to training are to training on the employer's premises or elsewhere.]

(4) For the purposes of this section the working hours of an employee shall be taken to be any time when, in accordance with his contract of employment, the employee is required to be at work.

**NOTES**

Sub-s (2A): inserted by the Welfare Reform and Pensions Act 1999, s 18, Sch 2, para 19(1), (3).

Sub-s (3): words in italics in para (b) repealed by the Pensions Act 2004, s 320, Sch 13, Pt 1, as from a day to be appointed; para (c) and word immediately preceding it added by the Teaching and Higher Education Act 1998, s 44(1), Sch 3, para 12.

Conciliation: see the note following the Part heading *ante*.

**[1.832]**

**59 Right to payment for time off under section 58**

(1) An employer who permits an employee to take time off under section 58 shall pay him for the time taken off pursuant to the permission.

(2) Where the employee's remuneration for the work he would ordinarily have been doing during that time does not vary with the amount of work done, he must be paid as if he had worked at that work for the whole of that time.

(3) Where the employee's remuneration for the work he would ordinarily have been doing during that time varies with the amount of work done, he must be paid an amount calculated by reference to the average hourly earnings for that work.

(4) The average hourly earnings mentioned in subsection (3) are—

    (a) those of the employee concerned, or

    (b) if no fair estimate can be made of those earnings, the average hourly earnings for work of that description of persons in comparable employment with the same employer or, if there are no such persons, a figure of average hourly earnings which is reasonable in the circumstances.

(5)   A right to be paid an amount under subsection (1) does not affect any right of an employee in relation to remuneration under his contract of employment ("contractual remuneration").

(6)   Any contractual remuneration paid to an employee in respect of a period of time off under section 58 goes towards discharging any liability of the employer under subsection (1) in respect of that period; and, conversely, any payment under subsection (1) in respect of a period goes towards discharging any liability of the employer to pay contractual remuneration in respect of that period.

**NOTES**

   Conciliation: see the note following the Part heading *ante*.

**[1.833]**
**60   Complaints to [employment tribunals]**
(1)   An employee may present a complaint to an [employment tribunal] that his employer—
   (a)   has failed to permit him to take time off as required by section 58, or
   (b)   has failed to pay him in accordance with section 59.
(2)   An [employment tribunal] shall not consider a complaint under this section unless it is presented—
   (a)   before the end of the period of three months beginning with the date when the failure occurred, or
   (b)   within such further period as the tribunal considers reasonable in a case where it is satisfied that it was not reasonably practicable for the complaint to be presented before the end of that period of three months.
[(2A)   Section 207A(3) (extension because of mediation in certain European cross-border disputes) *applies* for the purposes of subsection (2)(a).]
(3)   Where an [employment tribunal] finds a complaint under subsection (1)(a) well-founded, the tribunal—
   (a)   shall make a declaration to that effect, and
   (b)   may make an award of compensation to be paid by the employer to the employee.
(4)   The amount of the compensation shall be such as the tribunal considers just and equitable in all the circumstances having regard to—
   (a)   the employer's default in failing to permit time off to be taken by the employee, and
   (b)   any loss sustained by the employee which is attributable to the matters complained of.
(5)   Where on a complaint under subsection (1)(b) an [employment tribunal] finds that an employer has failed to pay an employee in accordance with section 59, it shall order the employer to pay the amount which it finds to be due.

**NOTES**

   Section heading, sub-ss (1)–(3), (5): words in square brackets substituted by the Employment Rights (Dispute Resolution) Act 1998, s 1(2)(a), (b).
   Sub-s (2A): inserted by the Cross-Border Mediation (EU Directive) Regulations 2011, SI 2011/1133, regs 30, 39, as from 20 May 2011; for the word in italics there are substituted the words "and section 207B (extension of time limits to facilitate conciliation before institution of proceedings) apply", by the Enterprise and Regulatory Reform Act 2013, s 8, Sch 2, paras 15, 25, as from a day to be appointed.
   Conciliation: see the note following the Part heading *ante*.

*Employee representatives*

**[1.834]**
**61   Right to time off for employee representatives**
(1)   An employee who is—
   (a)   an employee representative for the purposes of Chapter II of Part IV of the Trade Union and Labour Relations (Consolidation) Act 1992 (redundancies) or [regulations 9, 13 and 15 of the Transfer of Undertakings (Protection of Employment) Regulations 2006], or
   (b)   a candidate in an election in which any person elected will, on being elected, be such an employee representative,
is entitled to be permitted by his employer to take reasonable time off during the employee's working hours in order to perform his functions as such an employee representative or candidate [or in order to undergo training to perform such functions].
(2)   For the purposes of this section the working hours of an employee shall be taken to be any time when, in accordance with his contract of employment, the employee is required to be at work.

**NOTES**

   Sub-s (1): words in square brackets in para (a) substituted by the Transfer of Undertakings (Protection of Employment) Regulations 2006, SI 2006/246, reg 20, Sch 2, para 10; words in second pair of square brackets added by the Collective Redundancies and Transfer of Undertakings (Protection of Employment) (Amendment) Regulations 1999, SI 1999/1925, reg 15.
   Conciliation: see the note following the Part heading *ante*.

**[1.835]**
## 62 Right to remuneration for time off under section 61

(1)   An employee who is permitted to take time off under section 61 is entitled to be paid remuneration by his employer for the time taken off at the appropriate hourly rate.

(2)   The appropriate hourly rate, in relation to an employee, is the amount of one week's pay divided by the number of normal working hours in a week for that employee when employed under the contract of employment in force on the day when the time off is taken.

(3)   But where the number of normal working hours differs from week to week or over a longer period, the amount of one week's pay shall be divided instead by—

   (a)   the average number of normal working hours calculated by dividing by twelve the total number of the employee's normal working hours during the period of twelve weeks ending with the last complete week before the day on which the time off is taken, or

   (b)   where the employee has not been employed for a sufficient period to enable the calculation to be made under paragraph (a), a number which fairly represents the number of normal working hours in a week having regard to such of the considerations specified in subsection (4) as are appropriate in the circumstances.

(4)   The considerations referred to in subsection (3)(b) are—

   (a)   the average number of normal working hours in a week which the employee could expect in accordance with the terms of his contract, and

   (b)   the average number of normal working hours of other employees engaged in relevant comparable employment with the same employer.

(5)   A right to any amount under subsection (1) does not affect any right of an employee in relation to remuneration under his contract of employment ("contractual remuneration").

(6)   Any contractual remuneration paid to an employee in respect of a period of time off under section 61 goes towards discharging any liability of the employer to pay remuneration under subsection (1) in respect of that period; and, conversely, any payment of remuneration under subsection (1) in respect of a period goes towards discharging any liability of the employer to pay contractual remuneration in respect of that period.

**NOTES**
   Conciliation: see the note following the Part heading *ante*.

**[1.836]**
## 63 Complaints to [employment tribunals]

(1)   An employee may present a complaint to an [employment tribunal] that his employer—

   (a)   has unreasonably refused to permit him to take time off as required by section 61, or

   (b)   has failed to pay the whole or any part of any amount to which the employee is entitled under section 62.

(2)   An [employment tribunal] shall not consider a complaint under this section unless it is presented—

   (a)   before the end of the period of three months beginning with the day on which the time off was taken or on which it is alleged the time off should have been permitted, or

   (b)   within such further period as the tribunal considers reasonable in a case where it is satisfied that it was not reasonably practicable for the complaint to be presented before the end of that period of three months.

[(2A)   Section 207A(3) (extension because of mediation in certain European cross-border disputes) *applies* for the purposes of subsection (2)(a).]

(3)   Where an [employment tribunal] finds a complaint under this section well-founded, the tribunal shall make a declaration to that effect.

(4)   If the complaint is that the employer has unreasonably refused to permit the employee to take time off, the tribunal shall also order the employer to pay to the employee an amount equal to the remuneration to which he would have been entitled under section 62 if the employer had not refused.

(5)   If the complaint is that the employer has failed to pay the employee the whole or part of any amount to which he is entitled under section 62, the tribunal shall also order the employer to pay to the employee the amount which it finds due to him.

**NOTES**
   Section heading, sub-ss (1)–(3): words in square brackets substituted by the Employment Rights (Dispute Resolution) Act 1998, s 1(2)(a), (b).
   Sub-s (2A): inserted by the Cross-Border Mediation (EU Directive) Regulations 2011, SI 2011/1133, regs 30, 40, as from 20 May 2011; for the word in italics there are substituted the words "and section 207B (extension of time limits to facilitate conciliation before institution of proceedings) apply", by the Enterprise and Regulatory Reform Act 2013, s 8, Sch 2, paras 15, 26, as from a day to be appointed.
   Conciliation: see the note following the Part heading *ante*.

**[1.837]**

**[63A   Right to time off for young person [in Wales or Scotland] for study or training**

(1)   An employee who—

(a)   is aged 16 or 17,

(b)   is not receiving full-time secondary or further education, and

(c)   has not attained such standard of achievement as is prescribed by regulations made by the Secretary of State,

is entitled to be permitted by his employer to take time off during the employee's working hours in order to undertake study or training leading to a relevant qualification.

(2)   In this section—

(a)   "secondary education"—

(i)   in relation to England and Wales, has the same meaning as in the Education Act 1996, and

(ii)   in relation to Scotland, has the same meaning as in section 135(2)(b) of the Education (Scotland) Act 1980;

(b)   "further education"—

(i)   in relation to England and Wales, [has the same meaning as in the Education Act 1996,] and

(ii)   in relation to Scotland, has the same meaning as in section 1(3) of the Further and Higher Education (Scotland) Act 1992; and

(c)   "relevant qualification" means an external qualification the attainment of which—

(i)   would contribute to the attainment of the standard prescribed for the purposes of subsection (1)(c), and

(ii)   would be likely to enhance the employee's employment prospects (whether with his employer or otherwise);

and for the purposes of paragraph (c) "external qualification" means an academic or vocational qualification awarded or authenticated by such person or body as may be specified in or under regulations made by the Secretary of State.

(3)   An employee who—

(a)   satisfies the requirements of paragraphs (a) to (c) of subsection (1), and

(b)   is for the time being supplied by his employer to another person ("the principal") to perform work in accordance with a contract made between the employer and the principal,

is entitled to be permitted by the principal to take time off during the employee's working hours in order to undertake study or training leading to a relevant qualification.

(4)   Where an employee—

(a)   is aged 18,

(b)   is undertaking study or training leading to a relevant qualification, and

(c)   began such study or training before attaining that age,

subsections (1) and (3) shall apply to the employee, in relation to that study or training, as if "or 18" were inserted at the end of subsection (1)(a).

(5)   The amount of time off which an employee is to be permitted to take under this section, and the occasions on which and any conditions subject to which time off may be so taken, are those that are reasonable in all the circumstances having regard, in particular, to—

(a)   the requirements of the employee's study or training, and

(b)   the circumstances of the business of the employer or the principal and the effect of the employee's time off on the running of that business.

[(5A)   References in this section to an employee do not include a person to whom Part 1 of the Education and Skills Act 2008 (duty to participate in education or training for 16 and 17 year olds in England) applies, or is treated by section 29 of that Act (extension for person reaching 18) as applying.]

(6)   Regulations made for the purposes of subsections (1)(c) and (2) may make different provision for different cases, and in particular may make different provision in relation to England, Wales and Scotland respectively.

(7)   References in this section to study or training are references to study or training on the premises of the employer or (as the case may be) principal or elsewhere.

(8)   For the purposes of this section the working hours of an employee shall be taken to be any time when, in accordance with his contract of employment, the employee is required to be at work.]

**NOTES**

Inserted by the Teaching and Higher Education Act 1998, s 32. Note that this section will effectively be replaced (as from a day to be appointed) by the provisions of the Education and Skills Act 2008, Pt 1 in relation to any person who is resident in England and who (a) has ceased to be of compulsory school age, (b) has not reached the age of 18, and (c) has not attained a level 3 qualification (see sub-s (5A) of this section above as inserted by the Education and Skills Act 2008 as noted below).

Section heading: words in square brackets inserted by the Education and Skills Act 2008, s 39(1), (2), as from a day to be appointed.

Sub-s (2): words in square brackets substituted by the Learning and Skills Act 2000, s 149, Sch 9, paras 1, 50.

Sub-s (5A): inserted by the Education and Skills Act 2008, s 39(1), (2), as from a day to be appointed.

Conciliation: see the note following the Part heading *ante*.

Transfer of functions: functions under sub-ss (1)(c) and (2) are transferred, in so far as they are exercisable in or as regards Scotland, to the Scottish Ministers subject to the requirement that they are exercisable only after consultation with the Secretary of State, by the Scotland Act 1998 (Transfer of Functions to the Scottish Ministers etc) Order 1999, SI 1999/1750, art 2, Sch 1.

Corresponding provision for Wales: see the note to s 47AA at **[1.807]**.

Regulations: the Right to Time Off for Study or Training (Scotland) Regulations 1999, SI 1999/1058; the Right to Time Off for Study or Training Regulations 2001, SI 2001/2801; the Right to Time Off for Study or Training (Scotland) Amendment Regulations 2001, SSI 2001/211; the Right to Time Off for Study or Training (Scotland) Amendment (No 2) Regulations 2001, SSI 2001/298.

## [1.838]
## [63B   Right to remuneration for time off under section 63A

(1)   An employee who is permitted to take time off under section 63A is entitled to be paid remuneration by his employer for the time taken off at the appropriate hourly rate.

(2)   The appropriate hourly rate, in relation to an employee, is the amount of one week's pay divided by the number of normal working hours in a week for that employee when employed under the contract of employment in force on the day when the time off is taken.

(3)   But where the number of normal working hours differs from week to week or over a longer period, the amount of one week's pay shall be divided instead by—

(a)   the average number of normal working hours calculated by dividing by twelve the total number of the employee's working hours during the period of twelve weeks ending with the last complete week before the day on which the time off is taken, or

(b)   where the employee has not been employed for a sufficient period to enable the calculation to be made under paragraph (a), a number which fairly represents the number of normal working hours in a week having regard to such of the considerations specified in subsection (4) as are appropriate in the circumstances.

(4)   The considerations referred to in subsection (3)(b) are—

(a)   the average number of normal working hours in a week which the employee could expect in accordance with the terms of his contract, and

(b)   the average number of normal working hours of other employees engaged in relevant comparable employment with the same employer.

(5)   A right to any amount under subsection (1) does not affect any right of an employee in relation to remuneration under his contract of employment ("contractual remuneration").

(6)   Any contractual remuneration paid to an employee in respect of a period of time off under section 63A goes towards discharging any liability of the employer to pay remuneration under subsection (1) in respect of that period; and, conversely, any payment of remuneration under subsection (1) in respect of a period goes towards discharging any liability of the employer to pay contractual remuneration in respect of that period.]

### NOTES
Inserted, together with s 63C, by the Teaching and Higher Education Act 1998, s 33.

Application to any person who is resident in England, etc: see the first note to s 63A at **[1.838]**.

Conciliation: see the note following the Part heading *ante*.

## [1.839]
## [63C   Complaints to employment tribunals

(1)   An employee may present a complaint to an employment tribunal that—

(a)   his employer, or the principal referred to in subsection (3) of section 63A, has unreasonably refused to permit him to take time off as required by that section, or

(b)   his employer has failed to pay the whole or any part of any amount to which the employee is entitled under section 63B.

(2)   An employment tribunal shall not consider a complaint under this section unless it is presented—

(a)   before the end of the period of three months beginning with the day on which the time off was taken or on which it is alleged the time off should have been permitted, or

(b)   within such further period as the tribunal considers reasonable in a case where it is satisfied that it was not reasonably practicable for the complaint to be presented before the end of that period of three months.

[(2A)   Section 207A(3) (extension because of mediation in certain European cross-border disputes) *applies* for the purposes of subsection (2)(a).]

(3)   Where an employment tribunal finds a complaint under this section well-founded, the tribunal shall make a declaration to that effect.

(4)   If the complaint is that the employer or the principal has unreasonably refused to permit the employee to take time off, the tribunal shall also order the employer or the principal, as the case may be, to pay to the employee an amount equal to the remuneration to which he would have been entitled under section 63B if the employer or the principal had not refused.

(5)   If the complaint is that the employer has failed to pay the employee the whole or part of any amount to which he is entitled under section 63B, the tribunal shall also order the employer to pay to the employee the amount which it finds due to him.]

Inserted as noted to s 63B at **[1.838]**.

Sub-s (2A): inserted by the Cross-Border Mediation (EU Directive) Regulations 2011, SI 2011/1133, regs 30, 41, as from 20 May 2011; for the word in italics there are substituted the words "and section 207B (extension of time limits to facilitate conciliation before institution of proceedings) apply", by the Enterprise and Regulatory Reform Act 2013, s 8, Sch 2, paras 15, 27, as from a day to be appointed.

Application to any person who is resident in England, etc: see the first note to s 63A at **[1.838]**.

Conciliation: see the note following the Part heading *ante*.

## [PART 6A
## STUDY AND TRAINING

**[1.840]**
### 63D Statutory right to make request in relation to study or training
(1)   A qualifying employee may make an application under this section to his or her employer.
(2)   An application under this section (a "section 63D application") is an application that meets—
  (a)   the conditions in subsections (3) to (5), and
  (b)   any further conditions specified by the Secretary of State in regulations.
(3)   The application must be made for the purpose of enabling the employee to undertake study or training (or both) within subsection (4).
(4)   Study or training is within this subsection if its purpose is to improve—
  (a)   the employee's effectiveness in the employer's business, and
  (b)   the performance of the employer's business.
(5)   The application must state that it is an application under this section.
(6)   An employee is a qualifying employee for the purposes of this section if the employee—
  (a)   satisfies any conditions about duration of employment specified by the Secretary of State in regulations, and
  (b)   is not a person within subsection (7).
(7)   The following persons are within this subsection—
  (a)   a person of compulsory school age (or, in Scotland, school age);
  (b)   a person to whom Part 1 of the Education and Skills Act 2008 (duty to participate in education or training for 16 and 17 year olds) applies;
  (c)   a person who, by virtue of section 29 of that Act, is treated as a person to whom that Part applies for the purposes specified in that section (extension for person reaching 18);
  (d)   a person to whom section 63A of this Act (right to time off for young person for study or training) applies;
  (e)   an agency worker;
  (f)   a person of a description specified by the Secretary of State in regulations.
(8)   Nothing in this Part prevents an employee and an employer from making any other arrangements in relation to study or training.
(9)   In this section—
  "agency worker" means a worker supplied by a person (the "agent") to do work for another person (the "principal") under a contract or other arrangement between the agent and principal;
  "compulsory school age" has the meaning given in section 8 of the Education Act 1996;
  "school age" has the meaning given in section 31 of the Education (Scotland) Act 1980.]

NOTES
Commencement: 6 April 2010 (except in relation to small employers and their employees); to be appointed (otherwise).

Part 6A (ss 63D–63K) was inserted by the Apprenticeships, Skills, Children and Learning Act 2009, s 40(1), (2), as from 6 April 2010 (except in relation to small employers and their employees), and as from a day to be appointed (otherwise) (see further the notes below).

Meaning of "small employers", etc: the Apprenticeships, Skills, Children and Learning Act 2009 (Commencement No 2 and Transitional and Saving Provisions) Order 2010, SI 2010/303, Sch 3 provides as follows—

  "(1)   "small employer" means an employer who employs fewer than 250 employees.
  (2)   For the purposes of (1) above—
    (a)   Subject to (3) below, the number of employees employed by an employer at any time shall be determined by ascertaining the average number of employees employed by the employer in the previous twelve months, calculated in accordance with (b).
    (b)   The average number of employees employed by an employer in a twelve month period is to be ascertained by determining the number of employees employed by the employer in each month in the twelve month period (whether they were employed throughout the month or not), adding together those monthly figures and dividing the number by 12.
    (3)   If the undertaking has been in existence for less than twelve months, the references to twelve months in (2)(a) and (b) and the divisor of 12 referred to in (2)(b), are to be replaced by the number of months the undertaking has been in existence.".

Note also that by virtue of the Apprenticeships, Skills, Children and Learning Act 2009 (Commencement No 2 and Transitional and Saving Provisions) Order 2010, SI 2010/303, art 7 and Sch 6, section 40 of the 2009 Act was due to come into force for all remaining purposes on 6 April 2011. However, art 7 of, and Sch 6 to, the 2010 Order were revoked by the Apprenticeships, Skills, Children and Learning Act 2009 (Commencement No 2 and Transitional and Saving Provisions) Order 2010 (Amendment) Order 2011, SI 2011/882, art 2, as from 21 March 2011. Therefore, section 40 did not come into force for all remaining purposes on 6 April 2011 and, as at 6 April 2013, has not been commenced for such other purposes.

Regulations: the Employee Study and Training (Qualifying Period of Employment) Regulations 2010, SI 2010/800 at **[2.1381]** (which provide that employees must have 26 weeks' continuous service in order to be a qualifying employee for the purposes of this section).

**[1.841]**
**[63E  Section 63D application: supplementary**
(1)  A section 63D application may—
   (a)  be made in relation to study or training of any description (subject to section 63D(3) and (4) and regulations under section 63D(2));
   (b)  relate to more than one description of study or training.
(2)  The study or training may (in particular) be study or training that (if undertaken)—
   (a)  would be undertaken on the employer's premises or elsewhere (including at the employee's home);
   (b)  would be undertaken by the employee while performing the duties of the employee's employment or separately;
   (c)  would be provided or supervised by the employer or by someone else;
   (d)  would be undertaken without supervision;
   (e)  would be undertaken within or outside the United Kingdom.
(3)  The study or training need not be intended to lead to the award of a qualification to the employee.
(4)  A section 63D application must—
   (a)  give the following details of the proposed study or training—
      (i)  its subject matter;
      (ii)  where and when it would take place;
      (iii)  who would provide or supervise it;
      (iv)  what qualification (if any) it would lead to;
   (b)  explain how the employee thinks the proposed study or training would improve—
      (i)  the employee's effectiveness in the employer's business, and
      (ii)  the performance of the employer's business;
   (c)  contain information of any other description specified by the Secretary of State in regulations.
(5)  The Secretary of State may make regulations about—
   (a)  the form of a section 63D application;
   (b)  when a section 63D application is to be taken to be received for the purposes of this Part.]

**NOTES**
Commencement: 6 April 2010 (except in relation to small employers and their employees); to be appointed (otherwise).
Inserted by the Apprenticeships, Skills, Children and Learning Act 2009, s 40 as noted to s 63D at **[1.840]** (see further the notes to that section regarding the meaning of "small employer" and the delayed commencement of s 40 of the 2009 Act).
Regulations: the Employee Study and Training (Eligibility, Complaints and Remedies) Regulations 2010, SI 2010/156 at **[2.1341]**.

**[1.842]**
**[63F  Employer's duties in relation to application**
(1)  Subsections (4) to (7) apply if—
   (a)  an employer receives a section 63D application (the "current application") from an employee, and
   (b)  during the relevant 12 month period the employer has not received another section 63D application (an "earlier application") from the employee.
(2)  The "relevant 12 month period" is the 12 month period ending with the day on which the employer receives the current application.
(3)  The Secretary of State may make regulations about circumstances in which, at an employee's request, an employer is to be required to ignore an earlier application for the purposes of subsection (1).
(4)  The employer must deal with the application in accordance with regulations made by the Secretary of State.
(5)  The employer may refuse a section 63D application only if the employer thinks that one or more of the permissible grounds for refusal applies in relation to the application.
(6)  The employer may refuse part of a section 63D application only if the employer thinks that one or more of the permissible grounds for refusal applies in relation to that part.
(7)  The permissible grounds for refusal are—
   (a)  that the proposed study or training to which the application, or the part in question, relates would not improve—
      (i)  the employee's effectiveness in the employer's business, or

(ii)   the performance of the employer's business;
(b)   the burden of additional costs;
(c)   detrimental effect on ability to meet customer demand;
(d)   inability to re-organise work among existing staff;
(e)   inability to recruit additional staff;
(f)   detrimental impact on quality;
(g)   detrimental impact on performance;
(h)   insufficiency of work during the periods the employee proposes to work;
(i)   planned structural changes;
(j)   any other grounds specified by the Secretary of State in regulations.]

**NOTES**
Commencement: 6 April 2010 (except in relation to small employers and their employees); to be appointed (otherwise).
Inserted by the Apprenticeships, Skills, Children and Learning Act 2009, s 40 as noted to s 63D at **[1.840]** (see further the notes to that section regarding the meaning of "small employer" and the delayed commencement of s 40 of the 2009 Act).
Conciliation: employment tribunal proceedings and claims which could be the subject of employment tribunal proceedings under sub-ss (4)–(6) are proceedings to which the Employment Tribunals Act 1996, s 18 applies; see s 18(1)(d) of that Act at **[1.706]**.
Regulations: the Employee Study and Training (Procedural Requirements) Regulations 2010, SI 2010/155 at **[2.1321]**.

**[1.843]**
**[63G   Regulations about dealing with applications**
(1)   Regulations under section 63F(4) may, in particular, include provision—
(a)   for the employee to have a right to be accompanied by a person of a specified description when attending meetings held in relation to a section 63D application in accordance with any such regulations;
(b)   for the postponement of such a meeting if the employee's companion under paragraph (a) is not available to attend it;
(c)   in relation to companions under paragraph (a), corresponding to section 10(6) and (7) of the Employment Relations Act 1999 (right to paid time off to act as companion, etc);
(d)   in relation to the rights under paragraphs (a) to (c), for rights to complain to an employment tribunal and not to be subjected to a detriment, and about unfair dismissal;
(e)   for section 63D applications to be treated as withdrawn in specified circumstances.
(2)   In this section "specified" means specified in the regulations.]

**NOTES**
Commencement: 6 April 2010 (except in relation to small employers and their employees); to be appointed (otherwise).
Inserted by the Apprenticeships, Skills, Children and Learning Act 2009, s 40 as noted to s 63D at **[1.840]** (see further the notes to that section regarding the meaning of "small employer" and the delayed commencement of s 40 of the 2009 Act).

**[1.844]**
**[63H   Employee's duties in relation to agreed study or training**
(1)   This section applies if an employer has agreed to a section 63D application, or part of a section 63D application, made by an employee in relation to particular study or training (the "agreed study or training").
(2)   The employee must inform the employer if the employee—
(a)   fails to start the agreed study or training;
(b)   fails to complete the agreed study or training;
(c)   undertakes, or proposes to undertake, study or training that differs from the agreed study or training in any respect (including those specified in section 63E(4)(a)).
(3)   The Secretary of State may make regulations about the way in which the employee is to comply with the duty under subsection (2).]

**NOTES**
Commencement: 6 April 2010 (except in relation to small employers and their employees); to be appointed (otherwise).
Inserted by the Apprenticeships, Skills, Children and Learning Act 2009, s 40 as noted to s 63D at **[1.840]** (see further the notes to that section regarding the meaning of "small employer" and the delayed commencement of s 40 of the 2009 Act).
Regulations: the Employee Study and Training (Procedural Requirements) Regulations 2010, SI 2010/155 at **[2.1321]**.

**[1.845]**
**[63I   Complaints to employment tribunals**
(1)   An employee who makes a section 63D application may present a complaint to an employment tribunal that—
(a)   the employer has failed to comply with section 63F(4), (5) or (6), or
(b)   the employer's decision to refuse the application, or part of it, is based on incorrect facts.
This is subject to the following provisions of this section.
(2)   No complaint under this section may be made in respect of a section 63D application which has been disposed of by agreement or withdrawn.

(3)   In the case of a section 63D application that has not been disposed of by agreement or withdrawn, a complaint under this section may only be made if the employer—
  (a)   notifies the employee of a decision to refuse the application (or part of it) on appeal, or
  (b)   commits a breach of regulations under section 63F(4), where the breach is of a description specified by the Secretary of State in regulations.
(4)   No complaint under this section may be made in respect of failure to comply with provision included in regulations under section 63F(4) because of—
  (a)   section 63G(1)(a) or (b), if provision is included in regulations under section 63F(4) by virtue of section 63G(1)(d), or
  (b)   section 63G(1)(c).
(5)   An employment tribunal may not consider a complaint under this section unless the complaint is presented—
  (a)   before the end of the period of three months beginning with the relevant date, or
  (b)   within any further period that the tribunal considers reasonable, if the tribunal is satisfied that it was not reasonably practicable for the complaint to be presented before the end of that period of three months.
(6)   The relevant date is—
  (a)   in the case of a complaint permitted by subsection (3)(a), the date on which the employee is notified of the decision on the appeal;
  (b)   in the case of a complaint permitted by subsection (3)(b), the date on which the breach was committed.
[(7)   Section 207A(3) (extension because of mediation in certain European cross-border disputes) *applies* to subsection (5)(a).]]

---

**NOTES**
  Commencement: 6 April 2010 (except in relation to small employers and their employees); to be appointed (otherwise).
  Inserted by the Apprenticeships, Skills, Children and Learning Act 2009, s 40 as noted to s 63D at **[1.840]** (see further the notes to that section regarding the meaning of "small employer" and the delayed commencement of s 40 of the 2009 Act).
  Sub-s (7): added by the Cross-Border Mediation (EU Directive) Regulations 2011, SI 2011/1133, regs 30, 42, as from 20 May 2011; for the word in italics there are substituted the words "and section 207B (extension of time limits to facilitate conciliation before institution of proceedings) apply", by the Enterprise and Regulatory Reform Act 2013, s 8, Sch 2, paras 15, 28, as from a day to be appointed.
  Conciliation: employment tribunal proceedings and claims which could be the subject of employment tribunal proceedings under this sub-s (1)(b) are proceedings to which the Employment Tribunals Act 1996, s 18 applies; see s 18(1)(d) of that Act at **[1.706]**.
  Regulations: the Employee Study and Training (Eligibility, Complaints and Remedies) Regulations 2010, SI 2010/156 at **[2.1341]**.

---

**[1.846]**
**[63J   Remedies**
(1)   If an employment tribunal finds a complaint under section 63I well-founded it must make a declaration to that effect and may—
  (a)   make an order for reconsideration of the section 63D application;
  (b)   make an award of compensation to be paid by the employer to the employee.
(2)   The amount of any compensation must be the amount the tribunal considers just and equitable in all the circumstances, but must not exceed the permitted maximum.
(3)   The permitted maximum is the number of weeks' pay specified by the Secretary of State in regulations.
(4)   If an employment tribunal makes an order under subsection (1)(a), section 63F and regulations under that section apply as if the application had been received on the date of the order (instead of on the date it was actually received).]

---

**NOTES**
  Commencement: 6 April 2010 (except in relation to small employers and their employees); to be appointed (otherwise).
  Inserted by the Apprenticeships, Skills, Children and Learning Act 2009, s 40 as noted to s 63D at **[1.840]** (see further the notes to that section regarding the meaning of "small employer" and the delayed commencement of s 40 of the 2009 Act).
  Regulations: the Employee Study and Training (Eligibility, Complaints and Remedies) Regulations 2010, SI 2010/156 at **[2.1341]**.

---

**[1.847]**
**[63K   Supplementary**
Regulations under this Part may make different provision for different cases.]

---

**NOTES**
  Commencement: 6 April 2010 (except in relation to small employers and their employees); to be appointed (otherwise).
  Inserted by the Apprenticeships, Skills, Children and Learning Act 2009, s 40 as noted to s 63D at **[1.840]** (see further the notes to that section regarding the meaning of "small employer" and the delayed commencement of s 40 of the 2009 Act).
  Regulations: the Employee Study and Training (Eligibility, Complaints and Remedies) Regulations 2010, SI 2010/156 at **[2.1341]**.

# PART VII
## SUSPENSION FROM WORK

**NOTES**

Conciliation: employment tribunal proceedings and claims which could be the subject of employment tribunal proceedings under this Part are proceedings to which the Employment Tribunals Act 1996, s 18 applies; see s 18(1)(d) of that Act at **[1.706]**.

Recoupment of social security benefits: as to the power to provide for recoupment of social security benefits in relation to payments by employers to employees under this Part, that are the subject of proceedings before employment tribunals, see the Employment Tribunals Act 1996, s 16 at **[1.704]**.

*Suspension on medical grounds*

**[1.848]**
### 64   Right to remuneration on suspension on medical grounds

(1)   An employee who is suspended from work by his employer on medical grounds is entitled to be paid by his employer remuneration while he is so suspended for a period not exceeding twenty-six weeks.

(2)   For the purposes of this Part an employee is suspended from work on medical grounds if he is suspended from work in consequence of—

    (a)   a requirement imposed by or under a provision of an enactment or of an instrument made under an enactment, or

    (b)   a recommendation in a provision of a code of practice issued or approved under section 16 of the Health and Safety at Work etc Act 1974,

and the provision is for the time being specified in subsection (3).

(3)   The provisions referred to in subsection (2) are—

    Regulation16 of the Control of Lead at Work Regulations 1980,

    [Regulation 24 of the Ionising Radiations Regulations 1999 (SI 1999/3232)], and

    Regulation 11 of the Control of Substances Hazardous to Health Regulations 1988.

(4)   The Secretary of State may by order add provisions to or remove provisions from the list of provisions specified in subsection (3).

(5)   For the purposes of this Part an employee shall be regarded as suspended from work on medical grounds only if and for so long as he—

    (a)   continues to be employed by his employer, but

    (b)   is not provided with work or does not perform the work he normally performed before the suspension.

**NOTES**

Sub-s (3): words in square brackets substituted by the Ionising Radiations Regulations 1999, SI 1999/3232, reg 41(1), Sch 9, para 2.

Conciliation: see the note following the Part heading *ante*.

Control of Lead at Work Regulations 1980, SI 1980/1248: revoked and replaced by the Control of Lead at Work Regulations 1998, SI 1998/543 (revoked). See now, the Control of Substances Hazardous to Health Regulations 2002, SI 2002/2677.

The reference to the Control of Substances Hazardous to Health Regulations 1988 is an apparent drafting error as these regulations had been revoked and replaced by the (largely consolidating) Control of Substances Hazardous to Health Regulations 1994, SI 1994/3246. See now, the Control of Substances Hazardous to Health Regulations 2002, SI 2002/2677.

**[1.849]**
### 65   Exclusions from right to remuneration

(1)   An employee is not entitled to remuneration under section 64 unless he has been continuously employed for a period of not less than one month ending with the day before that on which the suspension begins.

(2)   . . .

(3)   An employee is not entitled to remuneration under section 64 in respect of any period during which he is incapable of work by reason of disease or bodily or mental disablement.

(4)   An employee is not entitled to remuneration under section 64 in respect of any period if—

    (a)   his employer has offered to provide him with suitable alternative work during the period (whether or not it is work which the employee is under his contract, or was under the contract in force before the suspension, employed to perform) and the employee has unreasonably refused to perform that work, or

    (b)   he does not comply with reasonable requirements imposed by his employer with a view to ensuring that his services are available.

**NOTES**

Sub-s (2): repealed by the Fixed-term Employees (Prevention of Less Favourable Treatment) Regulations 2002, SI 2002/2034, reg 11, Sch 2, Pt 1, para 3(1), (3) (except in relation to Government training schemes, agency workers or apprentices; see regs 18–20 of the 2002 Regulations at **[2.614]** et seq).

Conciliation: see the note following the Part heading *ante*.

*Suspension on maternity grounds*

**[1.850]**
## 66 Meaning of suspension on maternity grounds

(1) For the purposes of this Part an employee is suspended from work on maternity grounds if, in consequence of any relevant requirement or relevant recommendation, she is suspended from work by her employer on the ground that she is pregnant, has recently given birth or is breastfeeding a child.

(2) In subsection (1)—

"relevant requirement" means a requirement imposed by or under a specified provision of an enactment or of an instrument made under an enactment, and

"relevant recommendation" means a recommendation in a specified provision of a code of practice issued or approved under section 16 of the Health and Safety at Work etc Act 1974;

and in this subsection "specified provision" means a provision for the time being specified in an order made by the Secretary of State under this subsection.

(3) For the purposes of this Part an employee shall be regarded as suspended from work on maternity grounds only if and for so long as she—

(a) continues to be employed by her employer, but

(b) is not provided with work or (disregarding alternative work for the purposes of section 67) does not perform the work she normally performed before the suspension.

**NOTES**

Modified, in relation to governing bodies with delegated budgets, by the Education (Modification of Enactments Relating to Employment) (England) Order 2003, SI 2003/1964, art 3, Schedule at **[2.746]**, **[2.750]** and the Education (Modification of Enactments Relating to Employment) (Wales) Order 2006, SI 2006/1073, art 3, Schedule at **[2.1043]**, **[2.1046]**.

Orders: the Suspension from Work on Maternity Grounds (Merchant Shipping and Fishing Vessels) Order 1998, SI 1998/587, specifying regs 8(3) and 9(2) of the Merchant Shipping and Fishing Vessels (Health and Safety at Work) Regulations 1997, SI 1997/2962, for the purposes of this section. Also, by virtue of s 241 of, and Sch 2, Pt I, paras 1–4 to, this Act, the Suspension from Work (on Maternity Grounds) Order 1994, SI 1994/2930 has effect as if made under this section. That Order now has the effect of specifying regs 16(3) and 17 of the Management of Health and Safety at Work Regulations 1999, SI 1999/3242 for the purposes of this section.

Conciliation: see the note following the Part heading *ante*.

**[1.851]**
## 67 Right to offer of alternative work

(1) Where an employer has available suitable alternative work for an employee, the employee has a right to be offered to be provided with the alternative work before being suspended from work on maternity grounds.

(2) For alternative work to be suitable for an employee for the purposes of this section—

(a) the work must be of a kind which is both suitable in relation to her and appropriate for her to do in the circumstances, and

(b) the terms and conditions applicable to her for performing the work, if they differ from the corresponding terms and conditions applicable to her for performing the work she normally performs under her contract of employment, must not be substantially less favourable to her than those corresponding terms and conditions.

**NOTES**

Modified as noted to s 66 at **[1.850]**.
Conciliation: see the note following the Part heading *ante*.

**[1.852]**
## 68 Right to remuneration

(1) An employee who is suspended from work on maternity grounds is entitled to be paid remuneration by her employer while she is so suspended.

(2) An employee is not entitled to remuneration under this section in respect of any period if—

(a) her employer has offered to provide her during the period with work which is suitable alternative work for her for the purposes of section 67, and

(b) the employee has unreasonably refused to perform that work.

**NOTES**

Modified as noted to s 66 at **[1.850]**.
Conciliation: see the note following the Part heading *ante*.

*[Ending the supply of an agency worker on maternity grounds*

**[1.853]**
**68A Meaning of ending the supply of an agency worker on maternity grounds**
(1) For the purposes of this Part the supply of an agency worker to a hirer is ended on maternity grounds if, in consequence of action taken pursuant to a provision listed in subsection (2), the supply of the agency worker to the hirer is ended on the ground that she is pregnant, has recently given birth or is breastfeeding a child.
(2) The provisions are—
 (a) regulations 8(3) or 9(2) of the Merchant Shipping and Fishing Vessels (Health and Safety at Work) Regulations 1997;
 (b) regulation 16A(2) or 17A of the Management of Health and Safety at Work Regulations 1999; or
 (c) regulation 20 of the Conduct of Employment Agencies and Employment Businesses Regulations 2003.]

**NOTES**
Commencement: 1 October 2011.
Inserted, together with the preceding heading and ss 68B–68D, by the Agency Workers Regulations 2010, SI 2010/93, reg 25, Sch 2, Pt 1, paras 9, 12, as from 1 October 2011.
Conciliation: see the note following the Part heading *ante*.

**[1.854]**
**[68B Right to offer of alternative work**
(1) Where the supply of an agency worker to a hirer is ended on maternity grounds and the temporary work agency has available suitable alternative work, the agency worker has a right to be offered to be proposed for such alternative work.
(2) For alternative work to be suitable for an agency worker for the purposes of this section—
 (a) the work must be of a kind which is both suitable in relation to her and appropriate for her to do in the circumstances, and
 (b) the terms and conditions applicable to her whilst performing the work, if they differ from the corresponding terms and conditions which would have applied to her but for the fact that the supply of the agency worker to the hirer was ended on maternity grounds, must not be substantially less favourable to her than those corresponding terms and conditions.
(3) Subsection (1) does not apply—
 (a) where the agency worker has confirmed in writing that she no longer requires the work-finding services of the temporary work agency, or
 (b) beyond the original intended duration, or likely duration, whichever is the longer, of the assignment which ended when the supply of the agency worker to the hirer was ended on maternity grounds.]

**NOTES**
Commencement: 1 October 2011.
Inserted as noted to s 68A at **[1.853]**.
Conciliation: see the note following the Part heading *ante*.

**[1.855]**
**[68C Right to remuneration**
(1) Where the supply of an agency worker to a hirer is ended on maternity grounds, that agency worker is entitled to be paid remuneration by the temporary work agency.
(2) An agency worker is not entitled to remuneration under this section in respect of any period if—
 (a) the temporary work agency has—
  (i) offered to propose the agency worker to a hirer that has alternative work available which is suitable alternative work for her for the purposes of section 68B, or
  (ii) proposed the agency worker to a hirer that has such suitable alternative work available, and that hirer has agreed to the supply of that agency worker, and
 (b) the agency worker has unreasonably refused that offer or to perform that work.
(3) Nothing in this section imposes a duty on the temporary work agency to pay remuneration beyond the original intended duration, or likely duration, whichever is the longer, of the assignment which ended when the supply of the agency worker to the hirer was ended on maternity grounds.]

**NOTES**
Commencement: 1 October 2011.
Inserted as noted to s 68A at **[1.853]**.
Conciliation: see the note following the Part heading *ante*.

**[1.856]**
**[68D   Agency workers: supplementary**
(1)   Without prejudice to any other duties of the hirer or temporary work agency under any enactment or rule of law sections 68A, 68B and 68C do not apply where the agency worker—
   (a)   has not completed the qualifying period, or
   (b)   is no longer entitled to the rights conferred by regulation 5 of the Agency Workers Regulations 2010 pursuant to regulation 8(a) or (b) of those Regulations.
(2)   Nothing in those sections imposes a duty on the hirer or temporary work agency beyond the original intended duration, or likely duration of the assignment, whichever is the longer.
(3)   Those sections do not apply where sections 66 to 68 apply.
(4)   In this section and sections 68A to 68C the following have the same meaning as in the Agency Workers Regulations 2010—
   "agency worker"
   "assignment";
   "hirer";
   "qualifying period";
   "temporary work agency".]

**NOTES**
Commencement: 1 October 2011.
Inserted as noted to s 68A at **[1.853]**.
Conciliation: see the note following the Part heading *ante*.

*General*

**[1.857]**
**69   Calculation of remuneration**
(1)   The amount of remuneration payable by an employer to an employee under section 64 or 68 is a week's pay in respect of each week of the period of suspension; and if in any week remuneration is payable in respect of only part of that week the amount of a week's pay shall be reduced proportionately.
(2)   A right to remuneration under section 64 or 68 does not affect any right of an employee in relation to remuneration under the employee's contract of employment ("contractual remuneration").
(3)   Any contractual remuneration paid by an employer to an employee in respect of any period goes towards discharging the employer's liability under section 64 or 68 in respect of that period; and, conversely, any payment of remuneration in discharge of an employer's liability under section 64 or 68 in respect of any period goes towards discharging any obligation of the employer to pay contractual remuneration in respect of that period.

**NOTES**
Conciliation: see the note following the Part heading *ante*.

**[1.858]**
**[69A   Calculation of remuneration (agency workers)**
(1)   The amount of remuneration payable by a temporary work agency to an agency worker under section 68C is a week's pay in respect of each week for which remuneration is payable in accordance with section 68C; and if in any week remuneration is payable in respect of only part of that week the amount of a week's pay shall be reduced proportionately.
(2)   A right to remuneration under section 68C does not affect any right of the agency worker in relation to remuneration under the contract with the temporary work agency ("contractual remuneration").
(3)   Any contractual remuneration paid by the temporary work agency to an agency worker in respect of any period goes towards discharging the temporary work agency's liability under section 68C in respect of that period; and, conversely, any payment of remuneration in discharge of a temporary work agency's liability under section 68C in respect of any period goes towards discharging any obligation of the temporary work agency to pay contractual remuneration in respect of that period.
(4)   For the purposes of subsection (1), a week's pay is the weekly amount that would have been payable to the agency worker for performing the work, according to the terms of the contract with the temporary work agency, but for the fact that the supply of the agency worker to the hirer was ended on maternity grounds.
(5)   Expressions used in this section and sections 68A to 68C have the same meaning as in those sections (see section 68D).]

**NOTES**
Commencement: 1 October 2011.
Inserted by the Agency Workers Regulations 2010, SI 2010/93, reg 25, Sch 2, Pt 1, paras 9, 13, as from 1 October 2011.
Conciliation: see the note following the Part heading *ante*.

**[1.859]**
**70   Complaints to [employment tribunals]**
(1)   An employee may present a complaint to an [employment tribunal] that his or her employer has failed to pay the whole or any part of remuneration to which the employee is entitled under section 64 or 68.
(2)   An [employment tribunal] shall not consider a complaint under subsection (1) relating to remuneration in respect of any day unless it is presented—
   (a)   before the end of the period of three months beginning with that day, or
   (b)   within such further period as the tribunal considers reasonable in a case where it is satisfied that it was not reasonably practicable for the complaint to be presented within that period of three months.
(3)   Where an [employment tribunal] finds a complaint under subsection (1) well-founded, the tribunal shall order the employer to pay the employee the amount of remuneration which it finds is due to him or her.
(4)   An employee may present a complaint to an [employment tribunal] that in contravention of section 67 her employer has failed to offer to provide her with work.
(5)   An [employment tribunal] shall not consider a complaint under subsection (4) unless it is presented—
   (a)   before the end of the period of three months beginning with the first day of the suspension, or
   (b)   within such further period as the tribunal considers reasonable in a case where it is satisfied that it was not reasonably practicable for the complaint to be presented within that period of three months.
(6)   Where an [employment tribunal] finds a complaint under subsection (4) well-founded, the tribunal may make an award of compensation to be paid by the employer to the employee.
(7)   The amount of the compensation shall be such as the tribunal considers just and equitable in all the circumstances having regard to—
   (a)   the infringement of the employee's right under section 67 by the failure on the part of the employer to which the complaint relates, and
   (b)   any loss sustained by the employee which is attributable to that failure.
[(8)   Section 207A(3) (extension because of mediation in certain European cross-border disputes) *applies* for the purposes of subsections (2)(a) and (5)(a).]

**NOTES**
   Section heading, sub-ss (1)–(6): words in square brackets substituted by the Employment Rights (Dispute Resolution) Act 1998, s 1(2)(a), (b).
   Sub-s (8): added by the Cross-Border Mediation (EU Directive) Regulations 2011, SI 2011/1133, regs 30, 42, as from 20 May 2011; for the word in italics there are substituted the words "and section 207B (extension of time limits to facilitate conciliation before institution of proceedings) apply", by the Enterprise and Regulatory Reform Act 2013, s 8, Sch 2, paras 15, 29, as from a day to be appointed.
   Modified as noted to s 66 at **[1.850]**.
   Conciliation: see the note following the Part heading *ante*.
   Recoupment of social security benefits: see the note at the beginning of this Part.

**[1.860]**
**[70A   Complaints to employment tribunals: agency workers**
(1)   An agency worker may present a complaint to an employment tribunal that the temporary work agency has failed to pay the whole or any part of remuneration to which the agency worker is entitled under section 68C.
(2)   An employment tribunal shall not consider a complaint under subsection (1) relating to remuneration in respect of any day unless it is presented—
   (a)   before the end of the period of three months beginning with the day on which the supply of the agency worker to a hirer was ended on maternity grounds, or
   (b)   within such further period as the tribunal considers reasonable in a case where it is satisfied that it was not reasonably practicable for the complaint to be presented within that period of three months.
(3)   Where an employment tribunal finds a complaint under subsection (1) well-founded, the tribunal shall order the temporary work agency to pay the agency worker the amount of remuneration which it finds is due to her.
(4)   An agency worker may present a complaint to an employment tribunal that in contravention of section 68B the temporary work agency has failed to offer to propose the agency worker to a hirer that has suitable alternative work available.
(5)   An employment tribunal shall not consider a complaint under subsection (4) unless it is presented—
   (a)   before the end of the period of three months beginning with the day on which the supply of the agency worker to a hirer was ended on maternity grounds, or

(b)    within such further period as the tribunal considers reasonable in a case where it is satisfied that it was not reasonably practicable for the complaint to be presented within that period of three months.

(6)    Where an employment tribunal finds a complaint under subsection (4) well-founded, the tribunal shall order the temporary work agency to pay the agency worker the amount of compensation which it finds is due to her.

(7)    The amount of the compensation shall be such as the tribunal considers just and equitable in all the circumstances having regard to—

(a)    the infringement of the agency worker's right under section 68B by the failure on the part of the temporary work agency to which the complaint relates, and

(b)    any loss sustained by the agency worker which is attributable to that failure.

[(7A)    Section 207A(3) (extension because of mediation in certain European cross-border disputes) and section 207B (extension of time limits to facilitate conciliation before institution of proceedings) apply for the purposes of subsections (2)(a) and (5)(a).]

(8)    Expressions used in this section and sections 68A to 68C have the same meaning as in those sections (see section 68D).]

**NOTES**

Commencement: 1 October 2011.

Inserted by the Agency Workers Regulations 2010, SI 2010/93, reg 25, Sch 2, Pt 1, paras 9, 14, as from 1 October 2011.

Sub-s (7A): inserted by the Enterprise and Regulatory Reform Act 2013, s 8, Sch 2, paras 15, 30, as from a day to be appointed.

Conciliation: see the note following the Part heading *ante*.

Recoupment of social security benefits: see the note at the beginning of this Part.

## [PART VIII

### CHAPTER I
### MATERNITY LEAVE]

**NOTES**

A new Pt VIII (ss 71–75, 76–80) was substituted for the original Pt VIII (ss 71–85) by the Employment Relations Act 1999, s 7, Sch 4, Pt I. Subsequently, various amendments have been made to this Part, including the insertion of ss 75A–75D and 80A–80E.

**[1.861]**
**[71    Ordinary maternity leave**

(1)    An employee may, provided that she satisfies any conditions which may be prescribed, be absent from work at any time during an ordinary maternity leave period.

(2)    An ordinary maternity leave period is a period calculated in accordance with regulations made by the Secretary of State.

[(3)    Regulations under subsection (2)—

(a)    shall secure that, where an employee has a right to leave under this section, she is entitled to an ordinary maternity leave period of at least 26 weeks;

(b)    may allow an employee to choose, subject to prescribed restrictions, the date on which an ordinary maternity leave period starts;

(c)    may specify circumstances in which an employee may work for her employer during an ordinary maternity leave period without bringing the period to an end.]

(4)    Subject to section 74, an employee who exercises her right under subsection (1)—

(a)    is entitled[, for such purposes and to such extent as may be prescribed,] to the benefit of the terms and conditions of employment which would have applied if she had not been absent,

(b)    is bound[, for such purposes and to such extent as may be prescribed,] by any obligations arising under those terms and conditions (except in so far as they are inconsistent with subsection (1)), and

[(c)    is entitled to return from leave to a job of a prescribed kind].

(5)    In subsection (4)(a) "terms and conditions of employment"—

(a)    includes matters connected with an employee's employment whether or not they arise under her contract of employment, but

(b)    does not include terms and conditions about remuneration.

(6)    The Secretary of State may make regulations specifying matters which are, or are not, to be treated as remuneration for the purposes of this section.

[(7)    The Secretary of State may make regulations making provision, in relation to the right to return under subsection (4)(c) above, about—

(a)    seniority, pension rights and similar rights;

(b)    terms and conditions of employment on return.]]

**NOTES**

Substituted as noted following the Part heading above.

Sub-s (3): substituted by the Work and Families Act 2006, s 11(1), Sch 1, para 31.

Sub-s (4): words in square brackets in paras (a), (b) inserted, and para (c) substituted, by the Employment Act 2002, s 17(1), (2).

Sub-s (7): substituted by the Employment Act 2002, s 17(1), (3).

Modified as noted to s 66 at **[1.850]**.

Regulations: the Maternity and Parental Leave etc Regulations 1999, SI 1999/3312 at **[2.484]**; the Maternity and Parental Leave (Amendment) Regulations 2002, SI 2002/2789; the Maternity and Parental Leave etc and the Paternity and Adoption Leave (Amendment) Regulations 2006, SI 2006/2014.

---

**[1.862]**
**[72 Compulsory maternity leave**

(1)   An employer shall not permit an employee who satisfies prescribed conditions to work during a compulsory maternity leave period.

(2)   A compulsory maternity leave period is a period calculated in accordance with regulations made by the Secretary of State.

(3)   Regulations under subsection (2) shall secure—

    (a)    that no compulsory leave period is less than two weeks, and

    (b)    that every compulsory maternity leave period falls within an ordinary maternity leave period.

(4)   Subject to subsection (5), any provision of or made under the Health and Safety at Work etc Act 1974 shall apply in relation to the prohibition under subsection (1) as if it were imposed by regulations under section 15 of that Act.

(5)   Section 33(1)(c) of the 1974 Act shall not apply in relation to the prohibition under subsection (1); and an employer who contravenes that subsection shall be—

    (a)    guilty of an offence, and

    (b)    liable on summary conviction to a fine not exceeding level 2 on the standard scale.]

**NOTES**

Substituted as noted following the Part heading above.

Regulations: the Maternity and Parental Leave etc Regulations 1999, SI 1999/3312 at **[2.484]**.

---

**[1.863]**
**[73 Additional maternity leave**

(1)   An employee who satisfies prescribed conditions may be absent from work at any time during an additional maternity leave period.

(2)   An additional maternity leave period is a period calculated in accordance with regulations made by the Secretary of State.

[(3)   Regulations under subsection (2)—

    (a)    may allow an employee to choose, subject to prescribed restrictions, the date on which an additional maternity leave period ends;

    (b)    may specify circumstances in which an employee may work for her employer during an additional maternity leave period without bringing the period to an end.]

(4)   Subject to section 74, an employee who exercises her right under subsection (1)—

    (a)    is entitled, for such purposes and to such extent as may be prescribed, to the benefit of the terms and conditions of employment which would have applied if she had not been absent,

    (b)    is bound, for such purposes and to such extent as may be prescribed, by obligations arising under those terms and conditions (except in so far as they are inconsistent with subsection (1)), and

    (c)    is entitled to return from leave to a job of a prescribed kind.

(5)   In subsection (4)(a) "terms and conditions of employment"—

    (a)    includes matters connected with an employee's employment whether or not they arise under her contract of employment, but

    (b)    does not include terms and conditions about remuneration.

[(5A)   In subsection (4)(c), the reference to return from leave includes, where appropriate, a reference to a continuous period of absence attributable partly to additional maternity leave and partly to ordinary maternity leave.]

(6)   The Secretary of State may make regulations specifying matters which are, or are not, to be treated as remuneration for the purposes of this section.

(7)   The Secretary of State may make regulations making provision, in relation to the right to return under subsection (4)(c), about—

    (a)    seniority, pension rights and similar rights;

    (b)    terms and conditions of employment on return.]

**NOTES**

Substituted as noted following the Part heading above.

Sub-s (3): substituted by the Work and Families Act 2006, s 11(1), Sch 1, para 32.

Sub-s (5A): inserted by the Employment Act 2002, s 17(1), (4).

Regulations: the Maternity and Parental Leave etc Regulations 1999, SI 1999/3312 at **[2.484]**; the Maternity and Parental Leave (Amendment) Regulations 2002, SI 2002/2689; the Maternity and Parental Leave etc and the Paternity and Adoption

Leave (Amendment) Regulations 2006, SI 2006/2014; the Maternity and Parental Leave etc and the Paternity and Adoption Leave (Amendment) Regulations 2008, SI 2008/1966.

**[1.864]**
**[74   Redundancy and dismissal**
(1)   Regulations under section 71 or 73 may make provision about redundancy during an ordinary or additional maternity leave period.
(2)   Regulations under section 71 or 73 may make provision about dismissal (other than by reason of redundancy) during an ordinary or additional maternity leave period.
(3)   Regulations made by virtue of subsection (1) or (2) may include—
  (a)   provision requiring an employer to offer alternative employment;
  (b)   provision for the consequences of failure to comply with the regulations (which may include provision for a dismissal to be treated as unfair for the purposes of Part X).
(4)   Regulations under section [71 or] 73 may make provision—
  (a)   for section [71(4)(c) or] 73(4)(c) not to apply in specified cases, and
  (b)   about dismissal at the conclusion of an [ordinary or] additional maternity leave period.]

**NOTES**
Substituted as noted following the Part heading above.
Sub-s (4): words in square brackets inserted by the Employment Act 2002, s 17(1), (5).

**[1.865]**
**[75   Sections 71 to 73: supplemental**
(1)   Regulations under section 71, 72 or 73 may—
  (a)   make provision about notices to be given, evidence to be produced and other procedures to be followed by employees and employers;
  (b)   make provision for the consequences of failure to give notices, to produce evidence or to comply with other procedural requirements;
  (c)   make provision for the consequences of failure to act in accordance with a notice given by virtue of paragraph (a);
  (d)   make special provision for cases where an employee has a right which corresponds to a right under this Chapter and which arises under her contract of employment or otherwise;
  (e)   make provision modifying the effect of Chapter II of Part XIV (calculation of a week's pay) in relation to an employee who is or has been absent from work on ordinary or additional maternity leave;
  (f)   make provision applying, modifying or excluding an enactment, in such circumstances as may be specified and subject to any conditions specified, in relation to a person entitled to ordinary, compulsory or additional maternity leave;
  (g)   make different provision for different cases or circumstances.
(2)   In sections 71 to 73 "prescribed" means prescribed by regulations made by the Secretary of State.]

**NOTES**
Substituted as noted following the Part heading above.

## [CHAPTER IA
## ADOPTION LEAVE

**[1.866]**
**75A   Ordinary adoption leave**
(1)   An employee who satisfies prescribed conditions may be absent from work at any time during an ordinary adoption leave period.
(2)   An ordinary adoption leave period is a period calculated in accordance with regulations made by the Secretary of State.
[(2A)   Regulations under subsection (2) may specify circumstances in which an employee may work for his employer during an ordinary adoption leave period without bringing the period to an end.]
(3)   Subject to section 75C, an employee who exercises his right under subsection (1)—
  (a)   is entitled, for such purposes and to such extent as may be prescribed, to the benefit of the terms and conditions of employment which would have applied if he had not been absent,
  (b)   is bound, for such purposes and to such extent as may be prescribed, by any obligations arising under those terms and conditions (except in so far as they are inconsistent with subsection (1)), and
  (c)   is entitled to return from leave to a job of a prescribed kind.
(4)   In subsection (3)(a) "terms and conditions of employment"—
  (a)   includes matters connected with an employee's employment whether or not they arise under his contract of employment, but
  (b)   does not include terms and conditions about remuneration.

(5) In subsection (3)(c), the reference to return from leave includes, where appropriate, a reference to a continuous period of absence attributable partly to ordinary adoption leave and partly to maternity leave.

(6) The Secretary of State may make regulations specifying matters which are, or are not, to be treated as remuneration for the purposes of this section.

(7) The Secretary of State may make regulations making provision, in relation to the right to return under subsection (3)(c), about—

(a) seniority, pension rights and similar rights;

(b) terms and conditions of employment on return.]

---

**NOTES**

Chapter IA (ss 75A–75D) inserted by the Employment Act 2002, s 3.

Sub-s (2A): inserted by the Work and Families Act 2006, s 11(1), Sch 1, para 33.

Regulations: the Paternity and Adoption Leave Regulations 2002, SI 2002/2788 at **[2.619]**; the Paternity and Adoption Leave (Adoptions from Overseas) Regulations 2003, SI 2003/921; the Paternity and Adoption Leave (Amendment) Regulations 2004, SI 2004/923; the Maternity and Parental Leave etc and the Paternity and Adoption Leave (Amendment) Regulations 2006, SI 2006/2014.

---

**[1.867]**

**[75B Additional adoption leave**

(1) An employee who satisfies prescribed conditions may be absent from work at any time during an additional adoption leave period.

(2) An additional adoption leave period is a period calculated in accordance with regulations made by the Secretary of State.

[(3) Regulations under subsection (2)—

(a) may allow an employee to choose, subject to prescribed restrictions, the date on which an additional adoption leave period ends;

(b) may specify circumstances in which an employee may work for his employer during an additional adoption leave period without bringing the period to an end.]

(4) Subject to section 75C, an employee who exercises his right under subsection (1)—

(a) is entitled, for such purposes and to such extent as may be prescribed, to the benefit of the terms and conditions of employment which would have applied if he had not been absent,

(b) is bound, for such purposes and to such extent as may be prescribed, by obligations arising under those terms and conditions (except in so far as they are inconsistent with subsection (1)), and

(c) is entitled to return from leave to a job of a prescribed kind.

(5) In subsection (4)(a) "terms and conditions of employment"—

(a) includes matters connected with an employee's employment whether or not they arise under his contract of employment, but

(b) does not include terms and conditions about remuneration.

(6) In subsection (4)(c), the reference to return from leave includes, where appropriate, a reference to a continuous period of absence attributable partly to additional adoption leave and partly to—

(a) maternity leave, or

(b) ordinary adoption leave,

or to both.

(7) The Secretary of State may make regulations specifying matters which are, or are not, to be treated as remuneration for the purposes of this section.

(8) The Secretary of State may make regulations making provision, in relation to the right to return under subsection (4)(c), about—

(a) seniority, pension rights and similar rights;

(b) terms and conditions of employment on return.]

---

**NOTES**

Inserted as noted to s 75A at **[1.866]**.

Sub-s (3): substituted by the Work and Families Act 2006, s 11(1), Sch 1, para 34.

Regulations: the Paternity and Adoption Leave Regulations 2002, SI 2002/2788 at **[2.619]**; the Paternity and Adoption Leave (Adoptions from Overseas) Regulations 2003, SI 2003/921; the Paternity and Adoption Leave (Amendment) Regulations 2004, SI 2004/923; the Maternity and Parental Leave etc and the Paternity and Adoption Leave (Amendment) Regulations 2006, SI 2006/2014; the Maternity and Parental Leave etc and the Paternity and Adoption Leave (Amendment) Regulations 2008, SI 2008/1966.

---

**[1.868]**

**[75C Redundancy and dismissal**

(1) Regulations under section 75A or 75B may make provision about—

(a) redundancy, or

(b) dismissal (other than by reason of redundancy),

during an ordinary or additional adoption leave period.

(2) Regulations made by virtue of subsection (1) may include—

(a)   provision requiring an employer to offer alternative employment;
(b)   provision for the consequences of failure to comply with the regulations (which may include provision for a dismissal to be treated as unfair for the purposes of Part 10).
(3)   Regulations under section 75A or 75B may make provision—
   (a)   for section 75A(3)(c) or 75B(4)(c) not to apply in specified cases, and
   (b)   about dismissal at the conclusion of an ordinary or additional adoption leave period.]

**NOTES**
Inserted as noted to s 75A at **[1.866]**.
Regulations under section 75A or 75B: see those sections *ante*.

**[1.869]**
**[75D   Chapter 1A: supplemental**
(1)   Regulations under section 75A or 75B may—
   (a)   make provision about notices to be given, evidence to be produced and other procedures to be followed by employees and employers;
   (b)   make provision requiring employers or employees to keep records;
   (c)   make provision for the consequences of failure to give notices, to produce evidence, to keep records or to comply with other procedural requirements;
   (d)   make provision for the consequences of failure to act in accordance with a notice given by virtue of paragraph (a);
   (e)   make special provision for cases where an employee has a right which corresponds to a right under this Chapter and which arises under his contract of employment or otherwise;
   (f)   make provision modifying the effect of Chapter 2 of Part 14 (calculation of a week's pay) in relation to an employee who is or has been absent from work on ordinary or additional adoption leave;
   (g)   make provision applying, modifying or excluding an enactment, in such circumstances as may be specified and subject to any conditions specified, in relation to a person entitled to ordinary or additional adoption leave;
   (h)   make different provision for different cases or circumstances.
(2)   In sections 75A and 75B "prescribed" means prescribed by regulations made by the Secretary of State.]

**NOTES**
Inserted as noted to s 75A at **[1.866]**.
Regulations under section 75A or 75B: see those sections *ante*.

[CHAPTER II
PARENTAL LEAVE

**[1.870]**
**76   Entitlement to parental leave**
(1)   The Secretary of State shall make regulations entitling an employee who satisfies specified conditions—
   (a)   as to duration of employment, and
   (b)   as to having, or expecting to have, responsibility for a child,
to be absent from work on parental leave for the purpose of caring for a child.
(2)   The regulations shall include provision for determining—
   (a)   the extent of an employee's entitlement to parental leave in respect of a child;
   (b)   when parental leave may be taken.
(3)   Provision under subsection (2)(a) shall secure that where an employee is entitled to parental leave in respect of a child he is entitled to a period or total period of leave of at least three months; but this subsection is without prejudice to any provision which may be made by the regulations for cases in which—
   (a)   a person ceases to satisfy conditions under subsection (1);
   (b)   an entitlement to parental leave is transferred.
(4)   Provision under subsection (2)(b) may, in particular, refer to—
   (a)   a child's age, or
   (b)   a specified period of time starting from a specified event.
(5)   Regulations under subsection (1) may—
   (a)   specify things which are, or are not, to be taken as done for the purpose of caring for a child;
   (b)   require parental leave to be taken as a single period of absence in all cases or in specified cases;
   (c)   require parental leave to be taken as a series of periods of absence in all cases or in specified cases;
   (d)   require all or specified parts of a period of parental leave to be taken at or by specified times;

(e)    make provision about the postponement by an employer of a period of parental leave which an employee wishes to take;

(f)    specify a minimum or maximum period of absence which may be taken as part of a period of parental leave.

(g)    specify a maximum aggregate of periods of parental leave which may be taken during a specified period of time.]

**NOTES**

Substituted as noted following the Part heading above.

Regulations: the Maternity and Parental Leave etc Regulations 1999, SI 1999/3312 at **[2.484]**; the Maternity and Parental Leave (Amendment) Regulations 2001, SI 2001/4010; the Maternity and Parental Leave (Amendment) Regulations 2002, SI 2002/2789; the Parental Leave (EU Directive) Regulations 2013, SI 2013/283 at **[2.1660]**.

**[1.871]**

**[77   Rights during and after parental leave**

(1)   Regulations under section 76 shall provide—

(a)    that an employee who is absent on parental leave is entitled, for such purposes and to such extent as may be prescribed, to the benefit of the terms and conditions of employment which would have applied if he had not been absent,

(b)    that an employee who is absent on parental leave is bound, for such purposes and to such extent as may be prescribed, by any obligations arising under those terms and conditions (except in so far as they are inconsistent with section 76(1)), and

(c)    that an employee who is absent on parental leave is entitled, subject to section 78(1), to return from leave to a job of such kind as the regulations may specify.

(2)   In subsection (1)(a) "terms and conditions of employment"—

(a)    includes matters connected with an employee's employment whether or not they arise under a contract of employment, but

(b)    does not include terms and conditions about remuneration.

(3)   Regulations under section 76 may specify matters which are, or are not, to be treated as remuneration for the purposes of subsection (2)(b) above.

(4)   The regulations may make provision, in relation to the right to return mentioned in subsection (1)(c), about—

(a)    seniority, pension rights and similar rights;

(b)    terms and conditions of employment on return.]

**NOTES**

Substituted as noted following the Part heading above.

Regulations under section 76: see that section *ante*.

**[1.872]**

**[78   Special cases**

(1)   Regulations under section 76 may make provision—

(a)    about redundancy during a period of parental leave;

(b)    about dismissal (other than by reason of redundancy) during a period of parental leave.

(2)   Provision by virtue of subsection (1) may include—

(a)    provision requiring an employer to offer alternative employment;

(b)    provision for the consequences of failure to comply with the regulations (which may include provision for a dismissal to be treated as unfair for the purposes of Part X).

(3)   Regulations under section 76 may provide for an employee to be entitled to choose to exercise all or part of his entitlement to parental leave—

(a)    by varying the terms of his contract of employment as to hours of work, or

(b)    by varying his normal working practice as to hours of work,

in a way specified in or permitted by the regulations for a period specified in the regulations.

(4)   Provision by virtue of subsection (3)—

(a)    may restrict an entitlement to specified circumstances;

(b)    may make an entitlement subject to specified conditions (which may include conditions relating to obtaining the employer's consent);

(c)    may include consequential and incidental provision.

(5)   Regulations under section 76 may make provision permitting all or part of an employee's entitlement to parental leave in respect of a child to be transferred to another employee in specified circumstances.

(6)   The reference in section 77(1)(c) to absence on parental leave includes, where appropriate, a reference to a continuous period of absence attributable partly [to parental leave and partly to—

(a)    maternity leave, or

(b)    adoption leave,

or to both].

(7)   Regulations under section 76 may provide for specified provisions of the regulations not to apply in relation to an employee if any provision of his contract of employment—

(a) confers an entitlement to absence from work for the purpose of caring for a child, and
(b) incorporates or operates by reference to all or part of a collective agreement, or workforce agreement, of a kind specified in the regulations.]

**NOTES**

Substituted as noted following the Part heading above.
Sub-s (6): words in square brackets substituted by the Employment Act 2002, s 53, Sch 7, paras 24, 28.
Regulations under section 76: see that section *ante*.

**[1.873]**
**[79  Supplemental**
(1) Regulations under section 76 may, in particular—
(a) make provision about notices to be given and evidence to be produced by employees to employers, by employers to employees, and by employers to other employers;
(b) make provision requiring employers or employees to keep records;
(c) make provision about other procedures to be followed by employees and employers;
(d) make provision (including provision creating criminal offences) specifying the consequences of failure to give notices, to produce evidence, to keep records or to comply with other procedural requirements;
(e) make provision specifying the consequences of failure to act in accordance with a notice given by virtue of paragraph (a);
(f) make special provision for cases where an employee has a right which corresponds to a right conferred by the regulations and which arises under his contract of employment or otherwise;
(g) make provision applying, modifying or excluding an enactment, in such circumstances as may be specified and subject to any conditions specified, in relation to a person entitled to parental leave;
(h) make different provision for different cases or circumstances.
(2) The regulations may make provision modifying the effect of Chapter II of Part XIV (calculation of a week's pay) in relation to an employee who is or has been absent from work on parental leave.
(3) Without prejudice to the generality of section 76, the regulations may make any provision which appears to the Secretary of State to be necessary or expedient—
(a) for the purpose of implementing Council Directive 96/34/EC on the framework agreement on parental leave, or
(b) for the purpose of dealing with any matter arising out of or related to the United Kingdom's obligations under that Directive.]

**NOTES**

Substituted as noted following the Part heading above.
Regulations under section 76: see that section *ante*.

**[1.874]**
**[80  Complaint to employment tribunal**
(1) An employee may present a complaint to an employment tribunal that his employer—
(a) has unreasonably postponed a period of parental leave requested by the employee, or
(b) has prevented or attempted to prevent the employee from taking parental leave.
(2) An employment tribunal shall not consider a complaint under this section unless it is presented—
(a) before the end of the period of three months beginning with the date (or last date) of the matters complained of, or
(b) within such further period as the tribunal considers reasonable in a case where it is satisfied that it was not reasonably practicable for the complaint to be presented before the end of that period of three months.
[(2A) Section 207A(3) (extension because of mediation in certain European cross-border disputes) *applies* for the purposes of subsection (2)(a).]
(3) Where an employment tribunal finds a complaint under this section well-founded it—
(a) shall make a declaration to that effect, and
(b) may make an award of compensation to be paid by the employer to the employee.
(4) The amount of compensation shall be such as the tribunal considers just and equitable in all the circumstances having regard to—
(a) the employer's behaviour, and
(b) any loss sustained by the employee which is attributable to the matters complained of.]

**NOTES**

Substituted as noted following the Part heading above.

Sub-s (2A): inserted by the Cross-Border Mediation (EU Directive) Regulations 2011, SI 2011/1133, regs 30, 44, as from 20 May 2011; for the word in italics there are substituted the words "and section 207B (extension of time limits to facilitate conciliation before institution of proceedings) apply", by the Enterprise and Regulatory Reform Act 2013, s 8, Sch 2, paras 15, 31, as from a day to be appointed.

Conciliation: employment tribunal proceedings and claims which could be the subject of employment tribunal proceedings under sub-s (1) are proceedings to which the Employment Tribunals Act 1996, s 18 applies; see s 18(1)(d) of that Act at **[1.706]**.

## [CHAPTER III
## PATERNITY LEAVE

**[1.875]**
**80A Entitlement to [ordinary] paternity leave: birth**
(1)  The Secretary of State shall make regulations entitling an employee who satisfies specified conditions—
 (a)  as to duration of employment,
 (b)  as to relationship with a newborn, or expected, child, and
 (c)  as to relationship with the child's mother,
to be absent from work on leave under this section for the purpose of caring for the child or supporting the mother.
(2)  The regulations shall include provision for determining—
 (a)  the extent of an employee's entitlement to leave under this section in respect of a child;
 (b)  when leave under this section may be taken.
(3)  Provision under subsection (2)(a) shall secure that where an employee is entitled to leave under this section in respect of a child he is entitled to at least two weeks' leave.
(4)  Provision under subsection (2)(b) shall secure that leave under this section must be taken before the end of a period of at least 56 days beginning with the date of the child's birth.
(5)  Regulations under subsection (1) may—
 (a)  specify things which are, or are not, to be taken as done for the purpose of caring for a child or supporting the child's mother;
 (b)  make provision excluding the right to be absent on leave under this section in respect of a child where more than one child is born as a result of the same pregnancy;
 (c)  make provision about how leave under this section may be taken.
(6)  Where more than one child is born as a result of the same pregnancy, the reference in subsection (4) to the date of the child's birth shall be read as a reference to the date of birth of the first child born as a result of the pregnancy.
(7)  In this section—
"newborn child" includes a child stillborn after twenty-four weeks of pregnancy;
"week" means any period of seven days.]

**NOTES**
Chapter III (ss 80A–80E) inserted by the Employment Act 2002, s 1.
Section heading: word in square brackets inserted by the Work and Families Act 2006, s 11(1), Sch 1, para 35, as from 6 April 2010.
Regulations: the Paternity and Adoption Leave Regulations 2002, SI 2002/2788 at **[2.619]**.

**[1.876]**
**[80AA Entitlement to additional paternity leave: birth**
(1)  The Secretary of State may make regulations entitling an employee who satisfies specified conditions—
 (a)  as to duration of employment,
 (b)  as to relationship with a child, and
 (c)  as to relationship with the child's mother,
to be absent from work on leave under this section for the purpose of caring for the child, at a time when the child's mother satisfies any conditions prescribed under subsection (2).
(2)  The conditions that may be prescribed under this subsection are conditions relating to any one or more of the following—
 (a)  any employment or self-employment of the child's mother;
 (b)  her entitlement (or lack of entitlement) to leave under this Part or to statutory maternity pay or maternity allowance;
 (c)  whether, and to what extent, she is exercising or has exercised any such entitlement.
(3)  Any regulations under this section shall include provision for determining—
 (a)  the extent of an employee's entitlement to leave under this section in respect of a child;
 (b)  when leave under this section may be taken.
(4)  Provision under subsection (3)(a) shall secure that an employee is not entitled to more than 26 weeks' leave in respect of a child.
(5)  Provision under subsection (3)(b) shall secure that leave under this section—

(a) may not be taken before the end of a specified period beginning with the date of the child's birth, but

(b) must be taken before the end of the period of twelve months beginning with that date.

(6) Subsections (4) and (5)(a) do not limit the provision that may be made under subsection (3) in relation to cases where the child's mother has died before the end of the period mentioned in subsection (5)(b).

(7) Regulations under subsection (1) may—

(a) specify things which are, or are not, to be taken as done for the purpose of caring for a child;

(b) make provision excluding the right to be absent on leave under this section in respect of a child where more than one child is born as a result of the same pregnancy;

(c) specify a minimum period which may be taken as leave under this section;

(d) make provision about how leave under this section may be taken;

(e) specify circumstances in which an employee may work for his employer during a period of leave under this section without bringing the period of leave to an end.

(8) Where more than one child is born as a result of the same pregnancy, the reference in subsection (5) to the date of the child's birth shall be read as a reference to the date of birth of the first child born as a result of the pregnancy.

(9) In this section "week" means any period of seven days.]

## NOTES
Commencement: 3 March 2010.

Inserted by the Work and Families Act 2006, s 3, as from 3 March 2010.

Regulations: the Additional Paternity Leave Regulations 2010, SI 2010/1055 at **[2.1415]**.

**[1.877]**
## [80B Entitlement to [ordinary] paternity leave: adoption

(1) The Secretary of State shall make regulations entitling an employee who satisfies specified conditions—

(a) as to duration of employment,

(b) as to relationship with a child placed, or expected to be placed, for adoption under the law of any part of the United Kingdom, and

(c) as to relationship with a person with whom the child is, or is expected to be, so placed for adoption,

to be absent from work on leave under this section for the purpose of caring for the child or supporting the person by reference to whom he satisfies the condition under paragraph (c).

(2) The regulations shall include provision for determining—

(a) the extent of an employee's entitlement to leave under this section in respect of a child;

(b) when leave under this section may be taken.

(3) Provision under subsection (2)(a) shall secure that where an employee is entitled to leave under this section in respect of a child he is entitled to at least two weeks' leave.

(4) Provision under subsection (2)(b) shall secure that leave under this section must be taken before the end of a period of at least 56 days beginning with the date of the child's placement for adoption.

(5) Regulations under subsection (1) may—

(a) specify things which are, or are not, to be taken as done for the purpose of caring for a child or supporting a person with whom a child is placed for adoption;

(b) make provision excluding the right to be absent on leave under this section in the case of an employee who exercises a right to be absent from work on adoption leave;

(c) make provision excluding the right to be absent on leave under this section in respect of a child where more than one child is placed for adoption as part of the same arrangement;

(d) make provision about how leave under this section may be taken.

(6) Where more than one child is placed for adoption as part of the same arrangement, the reference in subsection (4) to the date of the child's placement shall be read as a reference to the date of placement of the first child to be placed as part of the arrangement.

(7) In this section, "week" means any period of seven days.

(8) The Secretary of State may by regulations provide for this section to have effect in relation to cases which involve adoption, but not the placement of a child for adoption under the law of any part of the United Kingdom, with such modifications as the regulations may prescribe.]

## NOTES
Inserted as noted to s 80A at **[1.875]**.

Section heading: word in square brackets inserted by the Work and Families Act 2006, s 11(1), Sch 1, para 36, as from 6 April 2010.

Modified, in relation to adoptions from overseas, by the Employment Rights Act 1996 (Application of Section 80B to Adoptions from Overseas) Regulations 2003, SI 2003/920.

Regulations: the Paternity and Adoption Leave Regulations 2002, SI 2002/2788 at **[2.619]**; the Employment Rights Act 1996 (Application of Section 80B to Adoptions from Overseas) Regulations 2003, SI 2003/920; the Paternity and Adoption Leave (Adoptions from Overseas) Regulations 2003, SI 2003/921.

---

**[1.878]**
**[80BB  Entitlement to additional paternity leave: adoption**
(1)  The Secretary of State may make regulations entitling an employee who satisfies specified conditions—
    (a)    as to duration of employment,
    (b)    as to relationship with a child placed for adoption under the law of any part of the United Kingdom, and
    (c)    as to relationship with a person with whom the child is so placed for adoption ("the adopter"),
to be absent from work on leave under this section for the purpose of caring for the child, at a time when the adopter satisfies any conditions prescribed under subsection (2).
(2)  The conditions that may be prescribed under this subsection are conditions relating to any one or more of the following—
    (a)    any employment or self-employment of the adopter;
    (b)    the adopter's entitlement (or lack of entitlement) to leave under this Part or to statutory adoption pay;
    (c)    whether, and to what extent, the adopter is exercising or has exercised any such entitlement.
(3)  Any regulations under this section shall include provision for determining—
    (a)    the extent of an employee's entitlement to leave under this section in respect of a child;
    (b)    when leave under this section may be taken.
(4)  Provision under subsection (3)(a) shall secure that an employee is not entitled to more than 26 weeks' leave in respect of a child.
(5)  Provision under subsection (3)(b) shall secure that leave under this section—
    (a)    may not be taken before the end of a specified period beginning with the date of the child's placement for adoption, but
    (b)    must be taken before the end of the period of twelve months beginning with that date.
(6)  Subsections (4) and (5)(a) do not limit the provision that may be made under subsection (3) in relation to cases where the adopter has died before the end of the period mentioned in subsection (5)(b).
(7)  Regulations under subsection (1) may—
    (a)    specify things which are, or are not, to be taken as done for the purpose of caring for a child;
    (b)    make provision excluding the right to be absent on leave under this section in the case of an employee who exercises a right to be absent from work on adoption leave;
    (c)    make provision excluding the right to be absent on leave under this section in respect of a child where more than one child is placed for adoption as part of the same arrangement;
    (d)    specify a minimum period which may be taken as leave under this section;
    (e)    make provision about how leave under this section may be taken;
    (f)    specify circumstances in which an employee may work for his employer during a period of leave under this section without bringing the period of leave to an end.
(8)  Where more than one child is placed for adoption as part of the same arrangement, the reference in subsection (5) to the date of the child's placement shall be read as a reference to the date of placement of the first child to be placed as part of the arrangement.
(9)  In this section "week" means any period of seven days.
(10)  The Secretary of State may by regulations provide for this section to have effect in relation to cases which involve adoption, but not the placement of a child for adoption under the law of any part of the United Kingdom, with such modifications as the regulations may prescribe.]

---

**NOTES**
  Commencement: 3 March 2010.
  Inserted by the Work and Families Act 2006, s 4, as from 3 March 2010.
  Modified, in relation to adoptions from overseas, by the Employment Rights Act 1996 (Application of Section 80BB to Adoptions from Overseas) Regulations 2010, SI 2010/1058, reg 2, Schedule.
  Regulations: the Additional Paternity Leave Regulations 2010, SI 2010/1055 at **[2.1415]**; the Employment Rights Act 1996 (Application of Section 80BB to Adoptions from Overseas) Regulations 2010, SI 2010/1058; the Additional Paternity Leave (Adoptions from Overseas) Regulations 2010, SI 2010/1059.

---

**[1.879]**
**[80C  Rights during and after paternity leave**
(1)  Regulations under section 80A [or 80AA] shall provide—
    (a)    that an employee who is absent on leave under that section is entitled, for such purposes and to such extent as the regulations may prescribe, to the benefit of the terms and conditions of employment which would have applied if he had not been absent;

(b) that an employee who is absent on leave under that section is bound, for such purposes and to such extent as the regulations may prescribe, by obligations arising under those terms and conditions (except in so far as they are inconsistent with subsection (1) of that section), and

(c) that an employee who is absent on leave under that section is entitled to return from leave to a job of a kind prescribed by regulations, subject to section 80D(1).

(2) The reference in subsection (1)(c) to absence on leave under section 80A [or 80AA] includes, where appropriate, a reference to a continuous period of absence attributable partly to leave under that section and partly to any one or more of the following—

[(za) leave under the other section,]

(a) maternity leave,

(b) adoption leave, and

(c) parental leave.

(3) Subsection (1) shall apply to regulations under section 80B [or 80BB as it applies to regulations under section 80A or 80AA].

(4) In the application of subsection (1)(c) to regulations under section 80B [or 80BB], the reference to absence on leave under that section includes, where appropriate, a reference to a continuous period of absence attributable partly to leave under that section and partly to any one or more of the following—

[(za) leave under the other section,]

(a) maternity leave,

(b) adoption leave,

(c) parental leave, and

(d) leave under section 80A [or 80AA].

(5) In subsection (1)(a), "terms and conditions of employment"—

(a) includes matters connected with an employee's employment whether or not they arise under his contract of employment, but

(b) does not include terms and conditions about remuneration.

(6) Regulations under [any of sections 80A to 80BB] may specify matters which are, or are not, to be treated as remuneration for the purposes of this section.

(7) Regulations under [any of sections 80A to 80BB] may make provision, in relation to the right to return mentioned in subsection (1)(c), about—

(a) seniority, pension rights and similar rights;

(b) terms and conditions of employment on return.]

## NOTES

Inserted as noted to s 80A at **[1.875]**.

All words in square brackets were substituted or inserted by the Work and Families Act 2006, s 5, as from 3 March 2010.

Regulations under section 80A or 80AA: see those sections *ante*.

**[1.880]**
**[80D   Special cases**

[(1) Regulations under section [80A, 80AA, 80B or 80BB] may make provision about—

(a) redundancy, or

(b) dismissal (other than by reason of redundancy),

during a period of leave under that section.

(2) Provision by virtue of subsection (1) may include—

(a) provision requiring an employer to offer alternative employment;

(b) provision for the consequences of failure to comply with the regulations (which may include provision for a dismissal to be treated as unfair for the purposes of Part 10).]

## NOTES

Inserted as noted to s 80A at **[1.875]**.

Sub-s (1): words in square brackets substituted by the Work and Families Act 2006, s 11(1), Sch 1, para 37, as from 3 March 2010.

Regulations under section 80A, 80AA, 80B or 80BB: see those sections *ante*.

**[1.881]**
**[80E   Chapter 3: supplemental**

[(1)] Regulations under [any of sections 80A to 80BB] may—

(a) make provision about notices to be given, evidence to be produced and other procedures to be followed by employees and employers;

(b) make provision requiring employers or employees to keep records;

(c) make provision for the consequences of failure to give notices, to produce evidence, to keep records or to comply with other procedural requirements;

(d) make provision for the consequences of failure to act in accordance with a notice given by virtue of paragraph (a);

(e)    make special provision for cases where an employee has a right which corresponds to a right under [any of sections 80A to 80BB] and which arises under his contract of employment or otherwise;

(f)    make provision modifying the effect of Chapter 2 of Part 14 (calculation of a week's pay) in relation to an employee who is or has been absent from work on leave under [any of sections 80A to 80BB];

(g)    make provision applying, modifying or excluding an enactment, in such circumstances as may be specified and subject to any conditions which may be specified, in relation to a person entitled to take leave under [any of sections 80A to 80BB];

(h)    make different provision for different cases or circumstances.

[(2)   The persons on whom duties may be imposed by regulations under section 80AA or 80BB include not only employees exercising rights by virtue of that section and their employers but also—

(a)    in the case of section 80AA, the mother of the child in question and any employer or former employer of hers, and

(b)    in the case of section 80BB, the person by reference to whom the condition in subsection (1)(c) of that section is satisfied and any employer or former employer of that person.]]

**NOTES**

Inserted as noted to s 80A at **[1.875]**.

Sub-s (1) numbered as such, words in square brackets in that subsection substituted, and sub-s (2) added, by the Work and Families Act 2006, s 11(1), Sch 1, para 38, as from 3 March 2010.

Regulations under any of sections 80A to 80BB: see those sections *ante*.

## [PART VIIIA
## FLEXIBLE WORKING

**[1.882]**
**80F   Statutory right to request contract variation**

(1)   A qualifying employee may apply to his employer for a change in his terms and conditions of employment if—

(a)    the change relates to—
    (i)    the hours he is required to work,
    (ii)   the times when he is required to work,
    (iii)  where, as between his home and a place of business of his employer, he is required to work, or
    (iv)  such other aspect of his terms and conditions of employment as the Secretary of State may specify by regulations, and

[(b)    his purpose in applying for the change is to enable him to care for someone who, at the time of application, is—
    (i)    a child who has not reached the prescribed age or falls within a prescribed description and in respect of whom (in either case) the employee satisfies prescribed conditions as to relationship, or
    (ii)   a person aged 18 or over who falls within a prescribed description and in respect of whom the employee satisfies prescribed conditions as to relationship].

(2)   An application under this section must—

(a)    state that it is such an application,

(b)    specify the change applied for and the date on which it is proposed the change should become effective,

(c)    explain what effect, if any, the employee thinks making the change applied for would have on his employer and how, in his opinion, any such effect might be dealt with, and

(d)    explain how the employee meets, in respect of the [child or other person to be cared for, the conditions as to relationship mentioned in subsection (1)(b)(i) or (ii)].

(3)   . . .

(4)   If an employee has made an application under this section, he may not make a further application under this section to the same employer before the end of the period of twelve months beginning with the date on which the previous application was made.

(5)   The Secretary of State may by regulations make provision about—

(a)    the form of applications under this section, and

(b)    when such an application is to be taken as made.

(6), (7)   . . .

(8)   For the purposes of this section, an employee is—

(a)    a qualifying employee if he—
    (i)    satisfies such conditions as to duration of employment as the Secretary of State may specify by regulations, and
    (ii)   is not an agency worker [(other than an agency worker who is returning to work from a period of parental leave under regulations under section 76)];

(b) an agency worker if he is supplied by a person ("the agent") to do work for another ("the principal") under a contract or other arrangement made between the agent and the principal.]

[(9) Regulations under this section may make different provision for different cases.

(10) In this section—

"child" means a person aged under 18;

"prescribed" means prescribed by regulations made by the Secretary of State.]

**NOTES**

Part VIIIA (ss 80F–80I) inserted by the Employment Act 2002, s 47(1), (2).

Sub-s (1): para (b) substituted by the Work and Families Act 2006, s 12(1), (2).

Sub-s (2): words in square brackets in para (d) substituted by the Work and Families Act 2006, s 12(1), (3).

Sub-ss (3), (6), (7): repealed by the Work and Families Act 2006, ss 12(1), (4), 15, Sch 2.

Sub-s (8): words in square brackets inserted by the Parental Leave (EU Directive) Regulations 2013, SI 2013/283, reg 2, as from 8 March 2013.

Sub-ss (9), (10): added by the Work and Families Act 2006, s 12(1), (5).

Regulations: the Flexible Working (Eligibility, Complaints and Remedies) Regulations 2002, SI 2002/3236 at **[2.733]**; the Flexible Working (Eligibility, Complaints and Remedies) (Amendment) Regulations 2006, SI 2006/3314; the Flexible Working (Eligibility, Complaints and Remedies) (Amendment) Regulations 2007, SI 2007/1184; the Flexible Working (Eligibility, Complaints and Remedies) (Amendment) (No 2) Regulations 2007, SI 2007/2286; the Flexible Working (Eligibility, Complaints and Remedies) (Amendment) Regulations 2009, SI 2009/595; the Flexible Working (Eligibility, Complaints and Remedies) (Amendment) (Revocation) Regulations 2011, SI 2011/989.

**[1.883]**

**[80G Employer's duties in relation to application under section 80F**

(1) An employer to whom an application under section 80F is made—

(a) shall deal with the application in accordance with regulations made by the Secretary of State, and

(b) shall only refuse the application because he considers that one or more of the following grounds applies—

(i) the burden of additional costs,

(ii) detrimental effect on ability to meet customer demand,

(iii) inability to re-organise work among existing staff,

(iv) inability to recruit additional staff,

(v) detrimental impact on quality,

(vi) detrimental impact on performance,

(vii) insufficiency of work during the periods the employee proposes to work,

(viii) planned structural changes, and

(ix) such other grounds as the Secretary of State may specify by regulations.

(2) Regulations under subsection (1)(a) shall include—

(a) provision for the holding of a meeting between the employer and the employee to discuss an application under section 80F within twenty eight days after the date the application is made;

(b) provision for the giving by the employer to the employee of notice of his decision on the application within fourteen days after the date of the meeting under paragraph (a);

(c) provision for notice under paragraph (b) of a decision to refuse the application to state the grounds for the decision;

(d) provision for the employee to have a right, if he is dissatisfied with the employer's decision, to appeal against it within fourteen days after the date on which notice under paragraph (b) is given;

(e) provision about the procedure for exercising the right of appeal under paragraph (d), including provision requiring the employee to set out the grounds of appeal;

(f) provision for notice under paragraph (b) to include such information as the regulations may specify relating to the right of appeal under paragraph (d);

(g) provision for the holding, within fourteen days after the date on which notice of appeal is given by the employee, of a meeting between the employer and the employee to discuss the appeal;

(h) provision for the employer to give the employee notice of his decision on any appeal within fourteen days after the date of the meeting under paragraph (g);

(i) provision for notice under paragraph (h) of a decision to dismiss an appeal to state the grounds for the decision;

(j) provision for a statement under paragraph (c) or (i) to contain a sufficient explanation of the grounds for the decision;

(k) provision for the employee to have a right to be accompanied at meetings under paragraph (a) or (g) by a person of such description as the regulations may specify;

(l) provision for postponement in relation to any meeting under paragraph (a) or (g) which a companion under paragraph (k) is not available to attend;

(m) provision in relation to companions under paragraph (k) corresponding to section 10(6) and (7) of the Employment Relations Act 1999 (c 26) (right to paid time off to act as companion, etc);

(n) provision, in relation to the rights under paragraphs (k) and (l), for the application (with or without modification) of sections 11 to 13 of the Employment Relations Act 1999 (provisions ancillary to right to be accompanied under section 10 of that Act).

(3) Regulations under subsection (1)(a) may include—

(a) provision for any requirement of the regulations not to apply where an application is disposed of by agreement or withdrawn;

(b) provision for extension of a time limit where the employer and employee agree, or in such other circumstances as the regulations may specify;

(c) provision for applications to be treated as withdrawn in specified circumstances;

and may make different provision for different cases.

(4) The Secretary of State may by order amend subsection (2).]

**NOTES**

Inserted as noted to s 80F at **[1.882]**.

Conciliation: employment tribunal proceedings and claims which could be the subject of employment tribunal proceedings under sub-s (1) are proceedings to which the Employment Tribunals Act 1996, s 18 applies; see s 18(1)(d) of that Act at **[1.706]**.

Regulations: the Flexible Working (Procedural Requirements) Regulations 2002, SI 2002/3207 at **[2.716]**.

## [1.884]
## [80H   Complaints to employment tribunals

(1) An employee who makes an application under section 80F may present a complaint to an employment tribunal—

(a) that his employer has failed in relation to the application to comply with section 80G(1), or

(b) that a decision by his employer to reject the application was based on incorrect facts.

(2) No complaint under this section may be made in respect of an application which has been disposed of by agreement or withdrawn.

(3) In the case of an application which has not been disposed of by agreement or withdrawn, no complaint under this section may be made until the employer—

(a) notifies the employee of a decision to reject the application on appeal, or

(b) commits a breach of regulations under section 80G(1)(a) of such description as the Secretary of State may specify by regulations.

(4) No complaint under this section may be made in respect of failure to comply with provision included in regulations under subsection (1)(a) of section 80G because of subsection (2)(k), (l) or (m) of that section.

(5) An employment tribunal shall not consider a complaint under this section unless it is presented—

(a) before the end of the period of three months beginning with the relevant date, or

(b) within such further period as the tribunal considers reasonable in a case where it is satisfied that it was not reasonably practicable for the complaint to be presented before the end of that period of three months.

(6) In subsection (5)(a), the reference to the relevant date is—

(a) in the case of a complaint permitted by subsection (3)(a), the date on which the employee is notified of the decision on the appeal, and

(b) in the case of a complaint permitted by subsection (3)(b), the date on which the breach concerned was committed.

[(7) Section 207A(3) (extension because of mediation in certain European cross-border disputes) *applies* for the purposes of subsection (5)(a).]]

**NOTES**

Inserted as noted to s 80F at **[1.882]**.

Sub-s (7): added by the Cross-Border Mediation (EU Directive) Regulations 2011, SI 2011/1133, regs 30, 45, as from 20 May 2011; for the word in italics there are substituted the words "and section 207B (extension of time limits to facilitate conciliation before institution of proceedings) apply", by the Enterprise and Regulatory Reform Act 2013, s 8, Sch 2, paras 15, 32, as from a day to be appointed.

Conciliation: employment tribunal proceedings and claims which could be the subject of employment tribunal proceedings under sub-s (1)(b) are proceedings to which the Employment Tribunals Act 1996, s 18 applies; see s 18(1)(d) of that Act at **[1.706]**.

Regulations: the Flexible Working (Eligibility, Complaints and Remedies) Regulations 2002, SI 2002/3236 at **[2.733]**.

## [1.885]
## [80I   Remedies

(1) Where an employment tribunal finds a complaint under section 80H well-founded it shall make a declaration to that effect and may—

(a) make an order for reconsideration of the application, and

(b) make an award of compensation to be paid by the employer to the employee.

(2)   The amount of compensation shall be such amount, not exceeding the permitted maximum, as the tribunal considers just and equitable in all the circumstances.
(3)   For the purposes of subsection (2), the permitted maximum is such number of weeks' pay as the Secretary of State may specify by regulations.
(4)   Where an employment tribunal makes an order under subsection (1)(a), section 80G, and the regulations under that section, shall apply as if the application had been made on the date of the order.]

**NOTES**
Inserted as noted to s 80F at **[1.882]**.
Regulations: the Flexible Working (Eligibility, Complaints and Remedies) Regulations 2002, SI 2002/3236 at **[2.733]**.

## PART IX
## TERMINATION OF EMPLOYMENT
*Minimum period of notice*

**[1.886]**
**86   Rights of employer and employee to minimum notice**
(1)   The notice required to be given by an employer to terminate the contract of employment of a person who has been continuously employed for one month or more—
  (a)   is not less than one week's notice if his period of continuous employment is less than two years,
  (b)   is not less than one week's notice for each year of continuous employment if his period of continuous employment is two years or more but less than twelve years, and
  (c)   is not less than twelve weeks' notice if his period of continuous employment is twelve years or more.
(2)   The notice required to be given by an employee who has been continuously employed for one month or more to terminate his contract of employment is not less than one week.
(3)   Any provision for shorter notice in any contract of employment with a person who has been continuously employed for one month or more has effect subject to subsections (1) and (2); but this section does not prevent either party from waiving his right to notice on any occasion or from accepting a payment in lieu of notice.
(4)   Any contract of employment of a person who has been continuously employed for three months or more which is a contract for a term certain of one month or less shall have effect as if it were for an indefinite period; and, accordingly, subsections (1) and (2) apply to the contract.
(5)   . . .
(6)   This section does not affect any right of either party to a contract of employment to treat the contract as terminable without notice by reason of the conduct of the other party.

**NOTES**
Sub-s (5): repealed by the Fixed-term Employees (Prevention of Less Favourable Treatment) Regulations 2002, SI 2002/2034, reg 11, Sch 2, Pt 1, para 3(1), (4) (except in relation to Government training schemes, agency workers or apprentices; see regs 18–20 of the 2002 Regulations at **[2.614]** et seq).
General Note: the provisions of this Part of this Act relating to a minimum period of notice suggest that the intention of the Act is to incorporate into the contract of employment the statutory terms laid down and that an employee who wishes to enforce those terms should sue on his contract of employment as statutorily amended, and not on the statute; see *Secretary of State for Employment v Wilson* [1978] 3 All ER 137, [1978] 1 ICR 200, EAT (approved in *Westwood v Secretary of State for Employment* [1985] ICR 209, [1984] 1 All ER 874, HL), both cases being in relation to the statutory predecessors of this Part.

**[1.887]**
**87   Rights of employee in period of notice**
(1)   If an employer gives notice to terminate the contract of employment of a person who has been continuously employed for one month or more, the provisions of sections 88 to 91 have effect as respects the liability of the employer for the period of notice required by section 86(1).
(2)   If an employee who has been continuously employed for one month or more gives notice to terminate his contract of employment, the provisions of sections 88 to 91 have effect as respects the liability of the employer for the period of notice required by section 86(2).
(3)   In sections 88 to 91 "period of notice" means—
  (a)   where notice is given by an employer, the period of notice required by section 86(1), and
  (b)   where notice is given by an employee, the period of notice required by section 86(2).
(4)   This section does not apply in relation to a notice given by the employer or the employee if the notice to be given by the employer to terminate the contract must be at least one week more than the notice required by section 86(1).

**[1.888]**
**88   Employments with normal working hours**
(1)   If an employee has normal working hours under the contract of employment in force during the period of notice and during any part of those normal working hours—

(a)  the employee is ready and willing to work but no work is provided for him by his employer,

(b)  the employee is incapable of work because of sickness or injury,

(c)  the employee is absent from work wholly or partly because of pregnancy or childbirth [or on [adoption leave, parental leave or [ordinary or additional paternity leave]]], or

(d)  the employee is absent from work in accordance with the terms of his employment relating to holidays,

the employer is liable to pay the employee for the part of normal working hours covered by any of paragraphs (a), (b), (c) and (d) a sum not less than the amount of remuneration for that part of normal working hours calculated at the average hourly rate of remuneration produced by dividing a week's pay by the number of normal working hours.

(2)  Any payments made to the employee by his employer in respect of the relevant part of the period of notice (whether by way of sick pay, statutory sick pay, maternity pay, statutory maternity pay, [paternity pay, [ordinary statutory paternity pay, additional statutory paternity pay], adoption pay, statutory adoption pay,] holiday pay or otherwise) go towards meeting the employer's liability under this section.

(3)  Where notice was given by the employee, the employer's liability under this section does not arise unless and until the employee leaves the service of the employer in pursuance of the notice.

**NOTES**

Sub-s (1): words in first (outer) pair of square brackets in para (c) inserted by the Employment Relations Act 1999, s 9, Sch 4, Pt III, paras 1, 5, 10; words in second (inner) pair of square brackets in para (c) substituted by the Employment Act 2002, s 53, Sch 7, paras 24, 29(1), (2); words in third (inner) pair of square brackets in para (c) substituted by the Work and Families Act 2006, s 11(1), Sch 1, para 39(1), (2), as from 6 April 2010.

Sub-s (2): words in first (outer) pair of square brackets inserted by the Employment Act 2002, s 53, Sch 7, paras 24, 29(1), (3); words in second (inner) pair of square brackets substituted by the Work and Families Act 2006, s 11(1), Sch 1, para 39(1), (3), as from 6 April 2010.

**[1.889]**
## 89  Employments without normal working hours

(1)  If an employee does not have normal working hours under the contract of employment in force in the period of notice, the employer is liable to pay the employee for each week of the period of notice a sum not less than a week's pay.

(2)  The employer's liability under this section is conditional on the employee being ready and willing to do work of a reasonable nature and amount to earn a week's pay.

(3)  Subsection (2) does not apply—

(a)  in respect of any period during which the employee is incapable of work because of sickness or injury,

(b)  in respect of any period during which the employee is absent from work wholly or partly because of pregnancy or childbirth [or on [adoption leave, parental leave or [ordinary or additional paternity leave]]], or

(c)  in respect of any period during which the employee is absent from work in accordance with the terms of his employment relating to holidays.

(4)  Any payment made to an employee by his employer in respect of a period within subsection (3) (whether by way of sick pay, statutory sick pay, maternity pay, statutory maternity pay, [paternity pay, [ordinary statutory paternity pay, additional statutory paternity pay], adoption pay, statutory adoption pay,] holiday pay or otherwise) shall be taken into account for the purposes of this section as if it were remuneration paid by the employer in respect of that period.

(5)  Where notice was given by the employee, the employer's liability under this section does not arise unless and until the employee leaves the service of the employer in pursuance of the notice.

**NOTES**

Sub-s (3): words in first (outer) pair of square brackets in para (b) inserted by the Employment Relations Act 1999, s 9, Sch 4, Pt III, paras 1, 5, 11; words in second (inner) pair of square brackets in para (b) substituted by the Employment Act 2002, s 53, Sch 7, paras 24, 30(1), (2); words in third (inner) pair of square brackets in para (b) substituted by the Work and Families Act 2006, s 11(1), Sch 1, para 40(1), (2), as from 6 April 2010.

Sub-s (4): words in first (outer) pair of square brackets inserted by the Employment Act 2002, s 53, Sch 7, paras 24, 30(1), (3); words in second (inner) pair of square brackets substituted by the Work and Families Act 2006, s 11(1), Sch 1, para 40(1), (3), as from 6 April 2010.

**[1.890]**
## 90  Short-term incapacity benefit[, contributory employment and support allowance] and industrial injury benefit

(1)  This section has effect where the arrangements in force relating to the employment are such that—

(a)  payments by way of sick pay are made by the employer to employees to whom the arrangements apply, in cases where any such employees are incapable of work because of sickness or injury, and

   (b)   in calculating any payment so made to any such employee an amount representing, or treated as representing, short-term incapacity benefit[, contributory employment and support allowance] or industrial injury benefit is taken into account, whether by way of deduction or by way of calculating the payment as a supplement to that amount.

(2)  If—

   (a)   during any part of the period of notice the employee is incapable of work because of sickness or injury,

   (b)   one or more payments by way of sick pay are made to him by the employer in respect of that part of the period of notice, and

   (c)   in calculating any such payment such an amount as is referred to in paragraph (b) of subsection (1) is taken into account as mentioned in that paragraph,

for the purposes of section 88 or 89 the amount so taken into account shall be treated as having been paid by the employer to the employee by way of sick pay in respect of that part of that period, and shall go towards meeting the liability of the employer under that section accordingly.

**NOTES**

Section heading, sub-s (1): words in square brackets inserted by the Employment and Support Allowance (Consequential Provisions) (No 3) Regulations 2008, SI 2008/1879, reg 2, as from 27 October 2008.

**[1.891]**
**91 Supplementary**

(1)  An employer is not liable under section 88 or 89 to make any payment in respect of a period during which an employee is absent from work with the leave of the employer granted at the request of the employee, including any period of time off taken in accordance with—

   (a)   Part VI of this Act, or

   (b)   section 168 or 170 of the Trade Union and Labour Relations (Consolidation) Act 1992 (trade union duties and activities).

(2)  No payment is due under section 88 or 89 in consequence of a notice to terminate a contract given by an employee if, after the notice is given and on or before the termination of the contract, the employee takes part in a strike of employees of the employer.

(3)  If, during the period of notice, the employer breaks the contract of employment, payments received under section 88 or 89 in respect of the part of the period after the breach go towards mitigating the damages recoverable by the employee for loss of earnings in that part of the period of notice.

(4)  If, during the period of notice, the employee breaks the contract and the employer rightfully treats the breach as terminating the contract, no payment is due to the employee under section 88 or 89 in respect of the part of the period falling after the termination of the contract.

(5)  If an employer fails to give the notice required by section 86, the rights conferred by sections 87 to 90 and this section shall be taken into account in assessing his liability for breach of the contract.

(6)  Sections 86 to 90 and this section apply in relation to a contract all or any of the terms of which are terms which take effect by virtue of any provision contained in or having effect under an Act (whether public or local) as in relation to any other contract; and the reference in this subsection to an Act includes, subject to any express provision to the contrary, an Act passed after this Act.

*Written statement of reasons for dismissal*

**[1.892]**
**92 Right to written statement of reasons for dismissal**

(1)  An employee is entitled to be provided by his employer with a written statement giving particulars of the reasons for the employee's dismissal—

   (a)   if the employee is given by the employer notice of termination of his contract of employment,

   (b)   if the employee's contract of employment is terminated by the employer without notice, or

   [(c)   if the employee is employed under a limited-term contract and the contract terminates by virtue of the limiting event without being renewed under the same contract].

(2)  Subject to [subsections (4) and (4A)], an employee is entitled to a written statement under this section only if he makes a request for one; and a statement shall be provided within fourteen days of such a request.

(3)  Subject to [subsections (4) and (4A)], an employee is not entitled to a written statement under this section unless on the effective date of termination he has been, or will have been, continuously employed for a period of not less than [two years] ending with that date.

(4)  An employee is entitled to a written statement under this section without having to request it and irrespective of whether she has been continuously employed for any period if she is dismissed—

   (a)   at any time while she is pregnant, or

   (b)   after childbirth in circumstances in which her [ordinary or additional maternity leave period] ends by reason of the dismissal.

[(4A) An employee who is dismissed while absent from work during an ordinary or additional adoption leave period is entitled to a written statement under this section without having to request it and irrespective of whether he has been continuously employed for any period if he is dismissed in circumstances in which that period ends by reason of the dismissal.]

(5) A written statement under this section is admissible in evidence in any proceedings.

(6) Subject to subsection (7), in this section "the effective date of termination"—

(a) in relation to an employee whose contract of employment is terminated by notice, means the date on which the notice expires,

(b) in relation to an employee whose contract of employment is terminated without notice, means the date on which the termination takes effect, and

[(c) in relation to an employee who is employed under a limited-term contract which terminates by virtue of the limiting event without being renewed under the same contract, means the date on which the termination takes effect].

(7) Where—

(a) the contract of employment is terminated by the employer, and

(b) the notice required by section 86 to be given by an employer would, if duly given on the material date, expire on a date later than the effective date of termination (as defined by subsection (6)),

the later date is the effective date of termination.

(8) In subsection (7)(b) "the material date" means—

(a) the date when notice of termination was given by the employer, or

(b) where no notice was given, the date when the contract of employment was terminated by the employer.

**NOTES**

Sub-s (1): para (c) substituted by the Fixed-term Employees (Prevention of Less Favourable Treatment) Regulations 2002, SI 2002/2034, reg 11, Sch 2, Pt 1, para 3(1), (5) (except in relation to Government training schemes, agency workers or apprentices; see regs 18–20 of the 2002 Regulations at **[2.614]** et seq).

Sub-s (2): words in square brackets substituted by the Employment Act 2002, s 53, Sch 7, paras 24, 31.

Sub-s (3): words in first pair of square brackets substituted by the Employment Act 2002, s 53, Sch 7, paras 24, 31; words in second pair of square brackets substituted by the Unfair Dismissal and Statement of Reasons for Dismissal (Variation of Qualifying Period) Order 2012, SI 2012/989, art 2, as from 6 April 2012. Note that by virtue of art 4 of the 2012 Order, this amendment does not have effect in any case where the period of continuous employment began before that date (in such cases the previous period of one year continues to apply).

Sub-s (4): words in square brackets substituted by the Employment Relations Act 1999, s 9, Sch 4, Pt III, paras 1, 5, 12.

Sub-s (4A): inserted by the Employment Act 2002, s 53, Sch 7, paras 24, 31.

Sub-s (6): para (c) substituted by the Employment Relations Act 2004, s 57(1), Sch 1, para 28.

Modified as noted to s 66 at **[1.850]**.

Conciliation: employment tribunal proceedings and claims which could be the subject of employment tribunal proceedings under this section are proceedings to which the Employment Tribunals Act 1996, s 18 applies; see s 18(1)(d) of that Act at **[1.706]**.

**[1.893]**
**93 Complaints to [employment tribunal]**

(1) A complaint may be presented to an [employment tribunal] by an employee on the ground that—

(a) the employer unreasonably failed to provide a written statement under section 92, or

(b) the particulars of reasons given in purported compliance with that section are inadequate or untrue.

(2) Where an [employment tribunal] finds a complaint under this section well-founded, the tribunal—

(a) may make a declaration as to what it finds the employer's reasons were for dismissing the employee, and

(b) shall make an award that the employer pay to the employee a sum equal to the amount of two weeks' pay.

(3) An [employment tribunal] shall not consider a complaint under this section relating to the reasons for a dismissal unless it is presented to the tribunal at such a time that the tribunal would, in accordance with section 111, consider a complaint of unfair dismissal in respect of that dismissal presented at the same time.

**NOTES**

Words in square brackets substituted by the Employment Rights (Dispute Resolution) Act 1998, s 1(2)(a).

Modified as noted to s 66 at **[1.850]**.

# PART X
# UNFAIR DISMISSAL

**NOTES**

This Part (ss 94–134A) is applied, with modifications, in relation to governing bodies with delegated budgets, by the Education (Modification of Enactments Relating to Employment) (England) Order 2003, SI 2003/1964, art 3, Schedule at **[2.746]**, **[2.750]** and the Education (Modification of Enactments Relating to Employment) (Wales) Order 2006, SI 2006/1073, art 3, Schedule at **[2.1043]**, **[2.1046]**.

This Part is modified, in relation to an office holder who is dismissed in the circumstances described in reg 33(1) of the Ecclesiastical Offices (Terms of Service) Regulations 2009, SI 2009/2108 at **[2.1180]**; see as to the modifications, reg 33(2) of the 2009 Regulations.

Conciliation: employment tribunal proceedings and claims which could be the subject of employment tribunal proceedings under this Part are proceedings to which the Employment Tribunals Act 1996, s 18 applies; see s 18(1)(d) of that Act at **[1.706]**.

Recoupment of social security benefits: as to the power to provide for recoupment of social security benefits in relation to payments by employers to employees under this Part, that are the subject of proceedings before employment tribunals, see the Employment Tribunals Act 1996, s 16 at **[1.704]**.

# CHAPTER I
# RIGHT NOT TO BE UNFAIRLY DISMISSED

*The right*

**[1.894]**
**94   The right**
(1)   An employee has the right not to be unfairly dismissed by his employer.
(2)   Subsection (1) has effect subject to the following provisions of this Part (in particular sections 108 to 110) and to the provisions of the Trade Union and Labour Relations (Consolidation) Act 1992 (in particular sections 237 to 239).

**NOTES**

Conciliation; modification in relation to governing bodies with delegated budgets; application in relation to office holders within the meaning of the Ecclesiastical Offices (Terms of Service) Regulations 2009: see the notes following the Part heading *ante.*

*Dismissal*

**[1.895]**
**95   Circumstances in which an employee is dismissed**
(1)   For the purposes of this Part an employee is dismissed by his employer if (and, subject to subsection (2) . . . , only if)—
    (a)   the contract under which he is employed is terminated by the employer (whether with or without notice),
    [(b)   he is employed under a limited-term contract and that contract terminates by virtue of the limiting event without being renewed under the same contract, or]
    (c)   the employee terminates the contract under which he is employed (with or without notice) in circumstances in which he is entitled to terminate it without notice by reason of the employer's conduct.
(2)   An employee shall be taken to be dismissed by his employer for the purposes of this Part if—
    (a)   the employer gives notice to the employee to terminate his contract of employment, and
    (b)   at a time within the period of that notice the employee gives notice to the employer to terminate the contract of employment on a date earlier than the date on which the employer's notice is due to expire;
and the reason for the dismissal is to be taken to be the reason for which the employer's notice is given.

**NOTES**

Sub-s (1): words omitted repealed by the Employment Relations Act 2004, s 57, Sch 1, para 29, Sch 2; para (b) by the Fixed-term Employees (Prevention of Less Favourable Treatment) Regulations 2002, SI 2002/2034, reg para 3(1), (7) (except in relation to Government training schemes, agency workers or apprentices; see regs 18 Regulations at **[2.614]** et seq).

Conciliation; modification in relation to governing bodies with delegated budgets; application in relat' 5, 13, within the meaning of the Ecclesiastical Offices (Terms of Service) Regulations 2009: see the notes foll' 1, *ante.*

**96**   *(Repealed by the Employment Relations Act 1999, ss 9, 44, Sch 4 Sch 9(2).)*

the effective date of

**[1.896]**
**97   Effective date of termination**
(1)   Subject to the following provisions of this section, in / termination"—

    (a)    in relation to an employee whose contract of employment is terminated by notice, whether given by his employer or by the employee, means the date on which the notice expires,

    (b)    in relation to an employee whose contract of employment is terminated without notice, means the date on which the termination takes effect, and

    [(c)    in relation to an employee who is employed under a limited-term contract which terminates by virtue of the limiting event without being renewed under the same contract, means the date on which the termination takes effect].

(2)   Where—

    (a)    the contract of employment is terminated by the employer, and

    (b)    the notice required by section 86 to be given by an employer would, if duly given on the material date, expire on a date later than the effective date of termination (as defined by subsection (1)),

for the purposes of sections 108(1), 119(1) and 227(3) the later date is the effective date of termination.

(3)   In subsection (2)(b) "the material date" means—

    (a)    the date when notice of termination was given by the employer, or

    (b)    where no notice was given, the date when the contract of employment was terminated by the employer.

(4)   Where—

    (a)    the contract of employment is terminated by the employee,

    (b)    the material date does not fall during a period of notice given by the employer to terminate that contract, and

    (c)    had the contract been terminated not by the employee but by notice given on the material date by the employer, that notice would have been required by section 86 to expire on a date later than the effective date of termination (as defined by subsection (1)),

for the purposes of sections 108(1), 119(1) and 227(3) the later date is the effective date of termination.

(5)   In subsection (4) "the material date" means—

    (a)    the date when notice of termination was given by the employee, or

    (b)    where no notice was given, the date when the contract of employment was terminated by the employee.

(6)   . . .

**NOTES**

  Sub-s (1): para (c) substituted by the Fixed-term Employees (Prevention of Less Favourable Treatment) Regulations 2002, SI 2002/2034, reg 11, Sch 2, para 3(1), (8) (except in relation to Government training schemes, agency workers or apprentices; see regs 18–20 of the 2002 Regulations at [2.614] et seq).

  Sub-s (6): repealed by the Employment Relations Act 1999, ss 9, 44, Sch 4, Pt III, paras 1, 5, 14, Sch 9(2).

  Conciliation; modification in relation to governing bodies with delegated budgets; application in relation to office holders within the meaning of the Ecclesiastical Offices (Terms of Service) Regulations 2009: see the notes following the Part heading *ante.*

*Fairness*

**[1.897]**
**98   General**

(1)   In determining for the purposes of this Part whether the dismissal of an employee is fair or unfair, it is for the employer to show—

    (a)    the reason (or, if more than one, the principal reason) for the dismissal, and

    (b)    that it is either a reason falling within subsection (2) or some other substantial reason of a kind such as to justify the dismissal of an employee holding the position which the employee held.

(2)   A reason falls within this subsection if it—

    (a)    relates to the capability or qualifications of the employee for performing work of the kind which he was employed by the employer to do,

    (b)    relates to the conduct of the employee,

    (ba)  . . . ]

    is that the employee was redundant, or

    (s  that the employee could not continue to work in the position which he held without (d) contravention (either on his part or on that of his employer) of a duty or restriction imposed under an enactment.

    (b)  "qu..(2)(a)—

[(3A)  techni.. in relation to an employee, means his capability assessed by reference to skill, . . . ]  or any other physical or mental quality, and

     relation to an employee, means any degree, diploma or other academic, ..al qualification relevant to the position which he held.

(4)　[Where] the employer has fulfilled the requirements of subsection (1), the determination of the question whether the dismissal is fair or unfair (having regard to the reason shown by the employer)—

(a)　depends on whether in the circumstances (including the size and administrative resources of the employer's undertaking) the employer acted reasonably or unreasonably in treating it as a sufficient reason for dismissing the employee, and

(b)　shall be determined in accordance with equity and the substantial merits of the case.

(5)　. . .

(6)　[Subsection (4)] [is] subject to—

(a)　sections [98A] to 107 of this Act, and

(b)　sections 152, 153[, 238 and 238A] of the Trade Union and Labour Relations (Consolidation) Act 1992 (dismissal on ground of trade union membership or activities or in connection with industrial action).

---

**NOTES**

Sub-ss (2)(ba), (2A), (3A): inserted by the Employment Equality (Age) Regulations 2006, SI 2006/1031, reg 49(1), Sch 8, Pt 1, paras 21, 22(1)–(4), and repealed by the Employment Equality (Repeal of Retirement Age Provisions) Regulations 2011, SI 2011/1069, reg 3(1), (2)(a), as from 6 April 2011 (for savings in relation to the continued operation of these paragraphs, see regs 5, 6 of the 2011 Regulations at **[2.1603]**, **[2.1604]**).

Sub-s (4): words in square brackets substituted by SI 2011/1069, reg 3(1), (2)(b), as from 6 April 2011.

Sub-s (5): repealed by the Employment Relations Act 1999, ss 9, Sch 4, Pt III, paras 1, 5, 15(a), Sch 9(2).

Sub-s (6): words in first pair of square brackets substituted by the Employment Relations Act 1999, s 9, Sch 4, Pt III, paras 1, 5, 15(b); word in second pair of square brackets and figure in third pair of square brackets substituted by the Employment Act 2002, s 53, Sch 7, paras 24, 32; words in fourth pair of square brackets substituted by the Employment Relations Act 2004, s 57(1), Sch 1, para 30. Note that the reference to s 98A has not been amended despite the repeal of that section by the Employment Act 2008.

Conciliation; modification in relation to governing bodies with delegated budgets; application in relation to office holders within the meaning of the Ecclesiastical Offices (Terms of Service) Regulations 2009: see the notes following the Part heading *ante*.

**98ZA–98ZH**　*(Sections 98ZA–98ZH (Retirement) were inserted by the Employment Equality (Age) Regulations 2006, SI 2006/1031, reg 49(1), Sch 8, Pt 1, paras 21, 23, and repealed by the Employment Equality (Repeal of Retirement Age Provisions) Regulations 2011, SI 2011/1069, reg 3(1), (3), as from 6 April 2011 (for savings in relation to the continued operation of these sections, see regs 5, 6 of the 2011 Regulations at **[2.1603]**, **[2.1604]**.)*

*[Other dismissals]*

**98A**　*(Repealed by the Employment Act 2008, ss 2, 20, Schedule, Pt 1, as from as from 6 April 2009, subject to a variety of transitional provisions and savings in the Employment Act 2008 (Commencement No 1, Transitional Provisions and Savings) Order 2008, SI 2008/3232, Schedule, Pt 1.)*

**[1.898]**

**[98B　Jury Service**

(1)　An employee who is dismissed shall be regarded for the purposes of this Part as unfairly dismissed if the reason (or, if more than one, the principal reason) for the dismissal is that the employee—

(a)　has been summoned under the Juries Act 1974, *the Coroners Act 1988*, the Court of Session Act 1988 or the Criminal Procedure (Scotland) Act 1995 to attend for service as a juror, or

(b)　has been absent from work because he attended at any place in pursuance of being so summoned.

(2)　Subsection (1) does not apply in relation to an employee who is dismissed if the employer shows—

(a)　that the circumstances were such that the employee's absence in pursuance of being so summoned was likely to cause substantial injury to the employer's undertaking,

(b)　that the employer brought those circumstances to the attention of the employee,

(c)　that the employee refused or failed to apply to the appropriate officer for excusal from or a deferral of the obligation to attend in pursuance of being so summoned, and

(d)　that the refusal or failure was not reasonable.

(3)　In paragraph (c) of subsection (2) "the appropriate officer" means—

(a)　in the case of a person who has been summoned under the Juries Act 1974, the officer designated for the purposes of section 8, 9 or, as the case may be, 9A of that Act;

(b)　in the case of a person who has been summoned under the Coroners Act 1988, a person who is the appropriate officer for the purposes of any rules made under subsection (1) of section 32 of that Act by virtue of subsection (2) of that section;

(c)　in the case of a person who has been summoned under the Court of Session Act 1988, either—

(i)　the clerk of court issuing the citation to attend for jury service; or

(ii)　the clerk of the court before which the person is cited to attend for jury service;

(d) in the case of a person who has been summoned under the Criminal Procedure (Scotland) Act 1995, either—
   (i) the clerk of court issuing the citation to attend for jury service; or
   (ii) the clerk of the court before which the person has been cited to attend for jury service;

and references in that paragraph to a refusal or failure to apply include references to a refusal or failure to give a notice under section 1(2)(b) of the Law Reform (Miscellaneous Provisions) (Scotland) Act 1980.]

**NOTES**

Inserted by the Employment Relations Act 2004, s 40(3).

Sub-s (1): for the words in italics in para (a) there are substituted the words "Part 1 of the Coroners and Justice Act 2009" by the Coroners and Justice Act 2009, s 177(1), Sch 21, Pt 1, para 36(1), (3), as from a day to be appointed.

Conciliation; modification in relation to governing bodies with delegated budgets; application in relation to office holders within the meaning of the Ecclesiastical Offices (Terms of Service) Regulations 2009: see the notes following the Part heading *ante*.

---

**[1.899]**
**[99 Leave for family reasons**
(1) An employee who is dismissed shall be regarded for the purposes of this Part as unfairly dismissed if—
   (a) the reason or principal reason for the dismissal is of a prescribed kind, or
   (b) the dismissal takes place in prescribed circumstances.
(2) In this section "prescribed" means prescribed by regulations made by the Secretary of State.
(3) A reason or set of circumstances prescribed under this section must relate to—
   (a) pregnancy, childbirth or maternity,
   (b) ordinary, compulsory or additional maternity leave,
   [(ba) ordinary or additional adoption leave,]
   (c) parental leave,
   [(ca) ordinary or additional paternity leave, or]
   (d) time off under section 57A;
and it may also relate to redundancy or other factors.
(4) A reason or set of circumstances prescribed under subsection (1) satisfies subsection (3)(c) or (d) if it relates to action which an employee—
   (a) takes,
   (b) agrees to take, or
   (c) refuses to take,
under or in respect of a collective or workforce agreement which deals with parental leave.
(5) Regulations under this section may—
   (a) make different provision for different cases or circumstances
   (b) apply any enactment, in such circumstances as may be specified and subject to any conditions specified, in relation to persons regarded as unfairly dismissed by reason of this section.]

**NOTES**

Substituted by the Employment Relations Act 1999, s 9, Sch 4, Pt III, paras 1, 5, 16.

Sub-s (3): para (ba) inserted, and para (ca) substituted for the original word "or" at the end of para (c), by the Employment Act 2002, s 53, Sch 7, paras 24, 33; para (ca) further substituted by the Work and Families Act 2006, s 11(1), Sch 1, para 41, as from 3 March 2010.

Conciliation; modification in relation to governing bodies with delegated budgets; application in relation to office holders within the meaning of the Ecclesiastical Offices (Terms of Service) Regulations 2009: see the notes following the Part heading *ante*.

Regulations: the Maternity and Parental Leave etc Regulations 1999, SI 1999/3312 at **[2.484]**; the Paternity and Adoption Leave Regulations 2002, SI 2002/2788 at **[2.619]**; the Maternity and Parental Leave (Amendment) Regulations 2002, SI 2002/2789; the Paternity and Adoption Leave (Adoptions from Overseas) Regulations 2003, SI 2003/921; the Maternity and Parental Leave etc and the Paternity and Adoption Leave (Amendment) Regulations 2006, SI 2006/2014; the Maternity and Parental Leave etc and the Paternity and Adoption Leave (Amendment) Regulations 2008, SI 2008/1966; the Additional Paternity Leave Regulations 2010, SI 2010/1055 at **[2.1415]**; the Additional Paternity Leave (Adoptions from Overseas) Regulations 2010, SI 2010/1059.

---

**[1.900]**
**100 Health and safety cases**
(1) An employee who is dismissed shall be regarded for the purposes of this Part as unfairly dismissed if the reason (or, if more than one, the principal reason) for the dismissal is that—
   (a) having been designated by the employer to carry out activities in connection with preventing or reducing risks to health and safety at work, the employee carried out (or proposed to carry out) any such activities,
   (b) being a representative of workers on matters of health and safety at work or member of a safety committee—
      (i) in accordance with arrangements established under or by virtue of any enactment, or

    (ii)   by reason of being acknowledged as such by the employer,
the employee performed (or proposed to perform) any functions as such a representative or a member of such a committee,

[(ba)  the employee took part (or proposed to take part) in consultation with the employer pursuant to the Health and Safety (Consultation with Employees) Regulations 1996 or in the election of representatives of employee safety within the meaning of those Regulations (whether as a candidate or otherwise),]

  (c)   being an employee at a place where—
    (i)   there was no such representative or safety committee, or
    (ii)   there was such a representative or safety committee but it was not reasonably practicable for the employee to raise the matter by those means,
he brought to his employer's attention, by reasonable means, circumstances connected with his work which he reasonably believed were harmful or potentially harmful to health or safety,

  (d)   in circumstances of danger which the employee reasonably believed to be serious and imminent and which he could not reasonably have been expected to avert, he left (or proposed to leave) or (while the danger persisted) refused to return to his place of work or any dangerous part of his place of work, or

  (e)   in circumstances of danger which the employee reasonably believed to be serious and imminent, he took (or proposed to take) appropriate steps to protect himself or other persons from the danger.

(2)   For the purposes of subsection (1)(e) whether steps which an employee took (or proposed to take) were appropriate is to be judged by reference to all the circumstances including, in particular, his knowledge and the facilities and advice available to him at the time.

(3)   Where the reason (or, if more than one, the principal reason) for the dismissal of an employee is that specified in subsection (1)(e), he shall not be regarded as unfairly dismissed if the employer shows that it was (or would have been) so negligent for the employee to take the steps which he took (or proposed to take) that a reasonable employer might have dismissed him for taking (or proposing to take) them.

**NOTES**

Sub-s (1): para (ba) inserted by the Health and Safety (Consultation with Employees) Regulations 1996, SI 1996/1513, reg 8.

Conciliation; modification in relation to governing bodies with delegated budgets; application in relation to office holders within the meaning of the Ecclesiastical Offices (Terms of Service) Regulations 2009: see the notes following the Part heading *ante*.

**[1.901]**
**101  Shop workers and betting workers who refuse Sunday work**

(1)   Where an employee who is—
  (a)   a protected shop worker or an opted-out shop worker, or
  (b)   a protected betting worker or an opted-out betting worker,
is dismissed, he shall be regarded for the purposes of this Part as unfairly dismissed if the reason (or, if more than one, the principal reason) for the dismissal is that he refused (or proposed to refuse) to do shop work, or betting work, on Sunday or on a particular Sunday.

(2)   Subsection (1) does not apply in relation to an opted-out shop worker or an opted-out betting worker where the reason (or principal reason) for the dismissal is that he refused (or proposed to refuse) to do shop work, or betting work, on any Sunday or Sundays falling before the end of the notice period.

(3)   A shop worker or betting worker who is dismissed shall be regarded for the purposes of this Part as unfairly dismissed if the reason (or, if more than one, the principal reason) for the dismissal is that the shop worker or betting worker gave (or proposed to give) an opting-out notice to the employer.

(4)   For the purposes of section 36(2)(b) or 41(1)(b), the appropriate date in relation to this section is the effective date of termination.

**NOTES**

Conciliation; modification in relation to governing bodies with delegated budgets; application in relation to office holders within the meaning of the Ecclesiastical Offices (Terms of Service) Regulations 2009: see the notes following the Part heading *ante*.

**[1.902]**
**[101A  Working time cases**

[(1)]  An employee who is dismissed shall be regarded for the purposes of this Part as unfairly dismissed if the reason (or, if more than one, the principal reason) for the dismissal is that the employee—
  (a)   refused (or proposed to refuse) to comply with a requirement which the employer imposed (or proposed to impose) in contravention of the Working Time Regulations 1998,
  (b)   refused (or proposed to refuse) to forgo a right conferred on him by those Regulations,

(c)    failed to sign a workforce agreement for the purposes of those Regulations, or to enter into, or agree to vary or extend, any other agreement with his employer which is provided for in those Regulations, or

(d)   being—

    (i)    a representative of members of the workforce for the purposes of Schedule 1 to those Regulations, or

    (ii)   a candidate in an election in which any person elected will, on being elected, be such a representative,

    performed (or proposed to perform) any functions or activities as such a representative or candidate.]

[(2)   A reference in this section to the Working Time Regulations 1998 includes a reference to—

[(a)]  the Merchant Shipping (Working Time: Inland Waterways) Regulations 2003;]

[(b)  the Fishing Vessels (Working Time: Sea-fishermen) Regulations 2004];

[(c)  the Cross-border Railway Services (Working Time) Regulations 2008].]]

**NOTES**

Inserted by the Working Time Regulations 1998, SI 1998/1833, regs 2(1), 32(1).

Sub-s (1): numbered as such by the Merchant Shipping (Working Time: Inland Waterways) Regulations 2003, SI 2003/3049, reg 20, Sch 2, para 3(1), (3).

Sub-s (2): added by SI 2003/3049, reg 20, Sch 2, para 3(1), (3); letter "(a)" in square brackets and para (b) added by the Fishing Vessels (Working Time: Sea-fishermen) Regulations 2004, SI 2004/1713, reg 21, Sch 2, para 2(1), (3)(a); para (c) inserted by the Cross-border Railway Services (Working Time) Regulations 2008, SI 2008/1660, reg 19, Sch 3, para 2(1), (3), as from 27 July 2008.

Conciliation; modification in relation to governing bodies with delegated budgets; application in relation to office holders within the meaning of the Ecclesiastical Offices (Terms of Service) Regulations 2009: see the notes following the Part heading *ante*.

**[1.903]**
**[101B  Participation in education or training**
An employee who is dismissed shall be regarded for the purposes of this Part as unfairly dismissed if the reason (or, if more than one, the principal reason) for the dismissal is that, being a person entitled to be permitted to participate in education or training by section 27 or 28 of the Education and Skills Act 2008, the employee exercised, or proposed to exercise, that right.]

**NOTES**

Commencement: to be appointed.

Inserted by the Education and Skills Act 2008, s 38, as from a day to be appointed.

Corresponding provision for Wales: see the note to s 47AA at **[1.807]**.

Conciliation; modification in relation to governing bodies with delegated budgets; application in relation to office holders within the meaning of the Ecclesiastical Offices (Terms of Service) Regulations 2009: see the notes following the Part heading *ante*.

**[1.904]**
**102  Trustees of occupational pension schemes**
(1)   An employee who is dismissed shall be regarded for the purposes of this Part as unfairly dismissed if the reason (or, if more than one, the principal reason) for the dismissal is that, being a trustee of a relevant occupational pension scheme which relates to his employment, the employee performed (or proposed to perform) any functions as such a trustee.

[(1A)  This section applies to an employee who is a director of a company which is a trustee of a relevant occupational pension scheme as it applies to an employee who is a trustee of such a scheme (references to such a trustee being read for this purpose as references to such a director).]

(2)   In this section "relevant occupational pension scheme" means an occupational pension scheme (as defined in section 1 of the Pension Schemes Act 1993) established under a trust.

**NOTES**

Sub-s (1A): inserted by the Welfare Reform and Pensions Act 1999, s 18, Sch 2, para 19(1), (4).

Conciliation; modification in relation to governing bodies with delegated budgets; application in relation to office holders within the meaning of the Ecclesiastical Offices (Terms of Service) Regulations 2009: see the notes following the Part heading *ante*.

**[1.905]**
**103  Employee representatives**
[(1)]  An employee who is dismissed shall be regarded for the purposes of this Part as unfairly dismissed if the reason (or, if more than one, the principal reason) for the dismissal is that the employee, being—

(a)   an employee representative for the purposes of Chapter II of Part IV of the Trade Union and Labour Relations (Consolidation) Act 1992 (redundancies) or [regulations 9, 13 and 15 of the Transfer of Undertakings (Protection of Employment) Regulations 2006], or

(b) a candidate in an election in which any person elected will, on being elected, be such an employee representative,

performed (or proposed to perform) any functions or activities as such an employee representative or candidate.

[(2) An employee who is dismissed shall be regarded for the purposes of this Part as unfairly dismissed if the reason (or, if more than one, the principal reason) for the dismissal is that the employee took part in an election of employee representatives for the purposes of Chapter II of Part IV of the Trade Union and Labour Relations (Consolidation) Act 1992 (redundancies) or [regulations 9, 13 and 15 of the Transfer of Undertakings (Protection of Employment) Regulations 2006].]

**NOTES**

Sub-s (1): numbered as such by the Collective Redundancies and Transfer of Undertakings (Protection of Employment) (Amendment) Regulations 1999, SI 1999/1925, reg 13; words in square brackets in para (a) substituted by the Transfer of Undertakings (Protection of Employment) Regulations 2006, SI 2006/246, reg 20, Sch 2, para 10.

Sub-s (2): added by SI 1999/1925, reg 13; words in square brackets substituted by SI 2006/246, reg 20, Sch 2, para 10.

Conciliation; modification in relation to governing bodies with delegated budgets; application in relation to office holders within the meaning of the Ecclesiastical Offices (Terms of Service) Regulations 2009: see the notes following the Part heading *ante*.

**[1.906]**
**[103A Protected disclosure**
An employee who is dismissed shall be regarded for the purposes of this Part as unfairly dismissed if the reason (or, if more than one, the principal reason) for the dismissal is that the employee made a protected disclosure.]

**NOTES**

Inserted by the Public Interest Disclosure Act 1998, ss 5, 18(2).

Conciliation; modification in relation to governing bodies with delegated budgets; application in relation to office holders within the meaning of the Ecclesiastical Offices (Terms of Service) Regulations 2009: see the notes following the Part heading *ante*.

**[1.907]**
**104 Assertion of statutory right**
(1) An employee who is dismissed shall be regarded for the purposes of this Part as unfairly dismissed if the reason (or, if more than one, the principal reason) for the dismissal is that the employee—
  (a) brought proceedings against the employer to enforce a right of his which is a relevant statutory right, or
  (b) alleged that the employer had infringed a right of his which is a relevant statutory right.
(2) It is immaterial for the purposes of subsection (1)—
  (a) whether or not the employee has the right, or
  (b) whether or not the right has been infringed;
but, for that subsection to apply, the claim to the right and that it has been infringed must be made in good faith.
(3) It is sufficient for subsection (1) to apply that the employee, without specifying the right, made it reasonably clear to the employer what the right claimed to have been infringed was.
(4) The following are relevant statutory rights for the purposes of this section—
  (a) any right conferred by this Act for which the remedy for its infringement is by way of a complaint or reference to an [employment tribunal],
  (b) the right conferred by section 86 of this Act, . . .
  (c) the rights conferred by sections 68, 86, [145A, 145B,] 146, 168, [168A,] 169 and 170 of the Trade Union and Labour Relations (Consolidation) Act 1992 (deductions from pay, union activities and time off) [ . . .
  [(d) the rights conferred by the Working Time Regulations 1998, the Merchant Shipping (Working Time: Inland Waterway) Regulations 2003][, the Fishing Vessels (Working Time: Sea-fisherman) Regulations 2004 or the Cross-border Railway Services (Working Time) Regulations 2008]][, and
  (e) the rights conferred by the Transfer of Undertakings (Protection of Employment) Regulations 2006].
[(5) In this section any reference to an employer includes, where the right in question is conferred by section 63A, the principal (within the meaning of section 63A(3)).]

**NOTES**

Sub-s (4) is amended as follows:

Words in square brackets in para (a) substituted by the Employment Rights (Dispute Resolution) Act 1998, s 1(2)(a).

Word omitted from para (b) repealed, and para (d) and word immediately preceding it added, by the Working Time Regulations 1998, SI 1998/1833, regs 2(1), 32(2).

First figures in square brackets in para (c) inserted by the Employment Relations Act 2004, s 57(1), Sch 1, para 31.

Second figure in square brackets in para (c) inserted by the Employment Act 2002, s 53, Sch 7, paras 24, 34.

Word omitted from para (c) repealed, and para (e) and the word immediately preceding it added, by the Transfer of Undertakings (Protection of Employment) Regulations 2006, SI 2006/246, reg 19.

Para (d) substituted by the Fishing Vessels (Working Time: Sea-fishermen) Regulations 2004, SI 2004/1713, reg 21, Sch 2, para 2(1), (4).

Words in square brackets in para (d) substituted by the Cross-border Railway Services (Working Time) Regulations 2008, SI 2008/1660, reg 19, Sch 3, para 2(1), (4), as from 27 July 2008.

Sub-s (5): added by the Teaching and Higher Education Act 1998, s 44(1), Sch 3, para 13.

Conciliation; modification in relation to governing bodies with delegated budgets; application in relation to office holders within the meaning of the Ecclesiastical Offices (Terms of Service) Regulations 2009: see the notes following the Part heading *ante*.

## [1.908]
## [104A    The national minimum wage
(1)  An employee who is dismissed shall be regarded for the purposes of this Part as unfairly dismissed if the reason (or, if more than one, the principal reason) for the dismissal is that—

(a)    any action was taken, or was proposed to be taken, by or on behalf of the employee with a view to enforcing, or otherwise securing the benefit of, a right of the employee's to which this section applies; or

(b)    the employer was prosecuted for an offence under section 31 of the National Minimum Wage Act 1998 as a result of action taken by or on behalf of the employee for the purpose of enforcing, or otherwise securing the benefit of, a right of the employee's to which this section applies; or

(c)    the employee qualifies, or will or might qualify, for the national minimum wage or for a particular rate of national minimum wage.

(2)  It is immaterial for the purposes of paragraph (a) or (b) of subsection (1) above—

(a)    whether or not the employee has the right, or

(b)    whether or not the right has been infringed,

but, for that subsection to apply, the claim to the right and, if applicable, the claim that it has been infringed must be made in good faith.

(3)  The following are the rights to which this section applies—

(a)    any right conferred by, or by virtue of, any provision of the National Minimum Wage Act 1998 for which the remedy for its infringement is by way of a complaint to an employment tribunal; and

(b)    any right conferred by section 17 of the National Minimum Wage Act 1998 (worker receiving less than national minimum wage entitled to additional remuneration).]

**NOTES**

Inserted by the National Minimum Wage Act 1998, s 25(1).

Agricultural workers: as to the application of this section to agricultural workers, see the Agricultural Wages Act 1948, s 3A, and the Agricultural Wages (Scotland) Act 1949, s 3A.

Conciliation; modification in relation to governing bodies with delegated budgets; application in relation to office holders within the meaning of the Ecclesiastical Offices (Terms of Service) Regulations 2009: see the notes following the Part heading *ante*.

## [1.909]
## [104B    Tax credits
(1)  An employee who is dismissed shall be regarded for the purposes of this Part as unfairly dismissed if the reason (or, if more than one, the principal reason) for the dismissal is that—

(a)    any action was taken, or was proposed to be taken, by or on behalf of the employee with a view to enforcing, or otherwise securing the benefit of, a right conferred on the employee by regulations under section 25 of the Tax Credits Act 2002,

(b)    a penalty was imposed on the employer, or proceedings for a penalty were brought against him, under that Act, as a result of action taken by or on behalf of the employee for the purpose of enforcing, or otherwise securing the benefit of, such a right, or

(c)    the employee is entitled, or will or may be entitled, to working tax credit.

(2)  It is immaterial for the purposes of subsection (1)(a) or (b)—

(a)    whether or not the employee has the right, or

(b)    whether or not the right has been infringed,

but, for those provisions to apply, the claim to the right and (if applicable) the claim that it has been infringed must be made in good faith.]

**NOTES**

Inserted by the Tax Credits Act 1999, s 7, Sch 3, para 3(1); substituted by the Tax Credits Act 2002, s 27, Sch 1, para 3(1), (2).

Conciliation; modification in relation to governing bodies with delegated budgets; application in relation to office holders within the meaning of the Ecclesiastical Offices (Terms of Service) Regulations 2009: see the notes following the Part heading *ante*.

Part 1   Statutes

**[1.910]**
**[104C   Flexible working**
An employee who is dismissed shall be regarded for the purposes of this Part as unfairly dismissed if the reason (or, if more than one, the principal reason) for the dismissal is that the employee—
  (a)   made (or proposed to make) an application under section 80F,
  (b)   exercised (or proposed to exercise) a right conferred on him under section 80G,
  (c)   brought proceedings against the employer under section 80H, or
  (d)   alleged the existence of any circumstance which would constitute a ground for bringing such proceedings.]

NOTES
  Inserted by the Employment Act 2002, s 47(1), (4).
  Conciliation; modification in relation to governing bodies with delegated budgets; application in relation to office holders within the meaning of the Ecclesiastical Offices (Terms of Service) Regulations 2009: see the notes following the Part heading *ante*.

**[1.911]**
**[104D   Pension enrolment**
(1)   An employee who is dismissed shall be regarded for the purposes of this Part as unfairly dismissed if the reason (or, if more than one, the principal reason) for the dismissal is that—
  (a)   any action was taken, or was proposed to be taken, with a view to enforcing in favour of the employee a requirement to which this section applies;
  (b)   the employer was prosecuted for an offence under section 45 of the Pensions Act 2008 as a result of action taken for the purpose of enforcing in favour of the employee a requirement to which this section applies; or
  (c)   any provision of Chapter 1 of that Part of that Act applies to the employee, or will or might apply.
(2)   It is immaterial for the purposes of paragraph (a) or (b) of subsection (1) above—
  (a)   whether or not the requirement applies in favour of the employee, or
  (b)   whether or not the requirement has been contravened,
but, for that subsection to apply, the claim that the requirement applies and, if applicable, the claim that it has been contravened must be made in good faith.
(3)   This section applies to any requirement imposed on the employer by or under any provision of Chapter 1 of Part 1 of the Pensions Act 2008.
(4)   In this section references to enforcing a requirement include references to securing its benefit in any way.]

NOTES
  Commencement: 30 June 2012.
  Inserted by the Pensions Act 2008, s 57(1), (2), as from 30 June 2012.
  Conciliation; modification in relation to governing bodies with delegated budgets; application in relation to office holders within the meaning of the Ecclesiastical Offices (Terms of Service) Regulations 2009: see the notes following the Part heading *ante*.

**[1.912]**
**[104E   Study and training**
An employee who is dismissed is to be regarded for the purposes of this Part as unfairly dismissed if the reason (or, if more than one, the principal reason) for the dismissal is that the employee—
  (a)   made (or proposed to make) a section 63D application,
  (b)   exercised (or proposed to exercise) a right conferred on the employee under section 63F,
  (c)   brought proceedings against the employer under section 63I, or
  (d)   alleged the existence of any circumstance which would constitute a ground for bringing such proceedings.]

NOTES
  Commencement: 6 April 2010 (except in relation to small employers and their employees); to be appointed (otherwise).
  Inserted by the Apprenticeships, Skills, Children and Learning Act 2009, s 40(1), (4), as from 6 April 2010 (except in relation to small employers and their employees), and as from a day to be appointed (otherwise) (as to the meaning of "small employers" etc, see further the notes at **[1.840]**).
  Conciliation; modification in relation to governing bodies with delegated budgets; application in relation to office holders within the meaning of the Ecclesiastical Offices (Terms of Service) Regulations 2009: see the notes following the Part heading *ante*.

**[1.913]**
**[104F   Blacklists**
(1)   An employee who is dismissed shall be regarded for the purposes of this Part as unfairly dismissed if the reason (or, if more than one, the principal reason) for the dismissal relates to a prohibited list, and either—

(a) the employer contravenes regulation 3 of the 2010 Regulations in relation to that prohibited list, or
(b) the employer—
  (i) relies on information supplied by a person who contravenes that regulation in relation to that list, and
  (ii) knows or ought reasonably to know that the information relied on is supplied in contravention of that regulation.

(2) If there are facts from which the tribunal could conclude, in the absence of any other explanation, that the employer—
(a) contravened regulation 3 of the 2010 Regulations, or
(b) relied on information supplied in contravention of that regulation,
the tribunal must find that such a contravention or reliance on information occurred, unless the employer shows that it did not.

(3) In this section—
"the 2010 Regulations" means the Employment Relations Act 1999 (Blacklists) Regulations 2010, and
"prohibited list" has the meaning given in those Regulations (see regulation 3(2)).]

## NOTES
Commencement: 2 March 2010.

Inserted by the Employment Relations Act 1999 (Blacklists) Regulations 2010, SI 2010/493, reg 12(1), (2), as from 2 March 2010.

Conciliation; modification in relation to governing bodies with delegated budgets; application in relation to office holders within the meaning of the Ecclesiastical Offices (Terms of Service) Regulations 2009: see the notes following the Part heading *ante*.

## [1.914]
## [104G  Employee shareholder status
An employee who is dismissed is to be regarded for the purposes of this Part as unfairly dismissed if the reason (or, if more than one, the principal reason) for the dismissal is that the employee refused to accept an offer by the employer for the employee to become an employee shareholder (within the meaning of section 205A).]

## NOTES
Commencement: to be appointed.

Inserted by the Growth and Infrastructure Act 2013, s 31(4), as from a day to be appointed.

## [1.915]
## 105  Redundancy
(1) An employee who is dismissed shall be regarded for the purposes of this Part as unfairly dismissed if—
(a) the reason (or, if more than one, the principal reason) for the dismissal is that the employee was redundant,
(b) it is shown that the circumstances constituting the redundancy applied equally to one or more other employees in the same undertaking who held positions similar to that held by the employee and who have not been dismissed by the employer, and
[(c) it is shown that any of subsections [(2A) to [(7N)]] applies].
(2) . . .
[(2A) This subsection applies if the reason (or, if more than one, the principal reason) for which the employee was selected for dismissal was one of those specified in subsection (1) of section 98B (unless the case is one to which subsection (2) of that section applies).]
(3) This subsection applies if the reason (or, if more than one, the principal reason) for which the employee was selected for dismissal was one of those specified in subsection (1) of section 100 (read with subsections (2) and (3) of that section).
(4) This subsection applies if either—
(a) the employee was a protected shop worker or an opted-out shop worker, or a protected betting worker or an opted-out betting worker, and the reason (or, if more than one, the principal reason) for which the employee was selected for dismissal was that specified in subsection (1) of section 101 (read with subsection (2) of that section), or
(b) the employee was a shop worker or a betting worker and the reason (or, if more than one, the principal reason) for which the employee was selected for dismissal was that specified in subsection (3) of that section.
[(4A) This subsection applies if the reason (or, if more than one, the principal reason) for which the employee was selected for dismissal was one of those specified in section 101A.]
[(4B) This subsection applies if the reason (or, if more than one, the principal reason) for which the employee was selected for dismissal was that specified in section 101B.]
(5) This subsection applies if the reason (or, if more than one, the principal reason) for which the employee was selected for dismissal was that specified in section 102(1).

Part 1 Statutes

(6) This subsection applies if the reason (or, if more than one, the principal reason) for which the employee was selected for dismissal was that specified in section 103.

[(6A) This subsection applies if the reason (or, if more than one, the principal reason) for which the employee was selected for dismissal was that specified in section 103A.]

(7) This subsection applies if the reason (or, if more than one, the principal reason) for which the employee was selected for dismissal was one of those specified in subsection (1) of section 104 (read with subsections (2) and (3) of that section).

[(7A) This subsection applies if the reason (or, if more than one, the principal reason) for which the employee was selected for dismissal was one of those specified in subsection (1) of section 104A (read with subsection (2) of that section).]

[(7B) This subsection applies if the reason (or, if more than one, the principal reason) for which the employee was selected for dismissal was one of those specified in subsection (1) of section 104B (read with subsection (2) of that section).]

[(7BA) This subsection applies if the reason (or, if more than one, the principal reason) for which the employee was selected for dismissal was one of those specified in section 104C.]

[(7BB) This subsection applies if the reason (or, if more than one, the principal reason) for which the employee was selected for dismissal was one of those specified in section 104E.]

[(7C) This subsection applies if—
    (a) the reason (or, if more than one, the principal reason) for which the employee was selected for dismissal was the reason mentioned in section 238A(2) of the Trade Union and Labour Relations (Consolidation) Act 1992 (participation in official industrial action), and
    (b) subsection (3), (4) or (5) of that section applies to the dismissal.]

[(7D) This subsection applies if the reason (or, if more than one, the principal reason) for which the employee was selected for dismissal was one specified in paragraph (3) or (6) of regulation 28 of the Transnational Information and Consultation of Employees Regulations 1999 (read with paragraphs (4) and (7) of that regulation).]

[(7E) This subsection applies if the reason (or, if more than one, the principal reason) for which the employee was selected for dismissal was one specified in paragraph (3) of regulation 7 of the Part-time Workers (Prevention of Less Favourable Treatment) Regulations 2000 (unless the case is one to which paragraph (4) of that regulation applies).]

[(7F) This subsection applies if the reason (or, if more than one, the principal reason) for which the employee was selected for dismissal was one specified in paragraph (3) of regulation 6 of the Fixed-term Employees (Prevention of Less Favourable Treatment) Regulations 2002 (unless the case is one to which paragraph (4) of that regulation applies).]

[(7G) This subsection applies if the reason (or, if more than one, the principal reason) for which the employee was selected for dismissal was one specified in paragraph (3) or (6) of regulation 42 of the European Public Limited-Liability Company Regulations 2004 (read with paragraphs (4) and (7) of that regulation).]

[(7H) This subsection applies if the reason (or, if more than one, the principal reason) for which the employee was selected for dismissal was one specified in paragraph (3) or (6) of regulation 30 of the Information and Consultation of Employees Regulations 2004 (read with paragraphs (4) and (7) of that regulation).]

[(7I) This subsection applies if the reason (or, if more than one, the principal reason) for which the employee was selected for dismissal was one specified in paragraph 5(3) or (5) of the Schedule to the Occupational and Personal Pension Schemes (Consultation by Employers and Miscellaneous Amendment) Regulations 2006 (read with paragraph 5(6) of that Schedule).]

[(7IA) . . . ]

[(7J) This subsection applies if the reason (or, if more than one, the principal reason) for which the employee was selected for dismissal was one specified in paragraph (3) or (6) of regulation 31 of the European Cooperative Society (Involvement of Employees) Regulations 2006 (read with paragraphs (4) and (7) of that regulation).]

[(7JA) This subsection applies if the reason (or, if more than one, the principal reason) for which the employee was selected for dismissal was one of those specified in subsection (1) of section 104D (read with subsection (2) of that section).]

[(7K) This subsection applies if the reason (or, if more than one, the principal reason) for which the employee was selected for dismissal was one specified in—
    (a) paragraph (2) of regulation 46 of the Companies (Cross-Border Mergers) Regulations 2007 (read with paragraphs (3) and (4) of that regulation); or
    (b) paragraph (2) of regulation 47 of the Companies (Cross-Border Mergers) Regulations 2007 (read with paragraph (3) of that regulation).]

[(7L) This subsection applies if the reason (or, if more than one, the principal reason) for which the employee was selected for dismissal was one specified in paragraph (3) or (6) of regulation 29 of the European Public Limited-Liability Company (Employee Involvement) (Great Britain) Regulations 2009 (SI 2009/2401) (read with paragraphs (4) and (7) of that regulation).]

[(7M) This subsection applies if—
    (a) the reason (or, if more than one, the principal reason) for which the employee was selected for dismissal was the one specified in the opening words of section 104F(1), and

(b)   the condition in paragraph (a) or (b) of that subsection was met.]

[(7N)   This subsection applies if the reason (or, if more than one, the principal reason) for which the employee was selected for dismissal was one specified in paragraph (3) of regulation 17 of the Agency Workers Regulations 2010 (unless the case is one to which paragraph (4) of that regulation applies).]

(8)   For the purposes of section 36(2)(b) or 41(1)(b), the appropriate date in relation to this section is the effective date of termination.

(9)   In this Part "redundancy case" means a case where paragraphs (a) and (b) of subsection (1) of this section are satisfied.

## NOTES

Sub-s (1): para (c) substituted by the European Cooperative Society (Involvement of Employees) Regulations 2006, SI 2006/2059, reg 32(1)(a); words in first (outer) pair of square brackets in para (c) substituted by the Companies (Cross-Border Mergers) Regulations 2007, SI 2007/2974, reg 48(1)(a); reference to "(7N)" in second (inner) pair of square brackets substituted by the Agency Workers Regulations 2010, SI 2010/93, reg 25, Sch 2, Pt 1, paras 9, 15, as from 1 October 2011.

Sub-s (2): repealed by the Employment Relations Act 1999, ss 9, Sch 4, Pt III, paras 1, 5, 17, Sch 9(2).

Sub-s (2A): inserted by the Employment Relations Act 2004, s 40(5).

Sub-s (4A): inserted by the Working Time Regulations 1998, SI 1998/1833, regs 2(1), 32(3).

Sub-s (4B): inserted by the Education and Skills Act 2008, s 39(1), (3), as from a day to be appointed.

Sub-s (6A): inserted by the Public Interest Disclosure Act 1998, ss 6, 18(2).

Sub-s (7A): inserted by the National Minimum Wage Act 1998, s 25(2).

Sub-s (7B): inserted by the Tax Credits Act 1999, s 7, Sch 3, para 3(2).

Sub-s (7BA): inserted by the Employment Relations Act 2004, s 41(4).

Sub-s (7BB): inserted by the Apprenticeships, Skills, Children and Learning Act 2009, s 40(5), Sch 1, paras 1, 3, as from 6 April 2010 (except in relation to small employers and their employees), and as from a day to be appointed (otherwise) (as to the meaning of "small employers" etc, see further the notes at **[1.840]**).

Sub-s (7C): inserted by the Employment Relations Act 1999, s 16, Sch 5, para 5(1), (3).

Sub-s (7D): inserted by the Transnational Information and Consultation of Employees Regulations 1999, SI 1999/3323, reg 29(1).

Sub-s (7E): inserted by the Part-time Workers (Prevention of Less Favourable Treatment) Regulations 2000, SI 2000/1551, reg 10, Schedule, para 2(1).

Sub-s (7F): inserted by the Fixed-term Employees (Prevention of Less Favourable Treatment) Regulations 2002, SI 2002/2034, reg 11, Sch 2, Pt 1, para 3(1), (10) (except in relation to Government training schemes, agency workers or apprentices; see regs 18–20 of the 2002 Regulations at **[2.614]** et seq).

Sub-s (7G): inserted by the European Public Limited-Liability Company Regulations 2004, SI 2004/2326, reg 43(1)(b).

Sub-s (7H): inserted by the Information and Consultation of Employees Regulations 2004, SI 2004/3426, reg 31(1)(b).

Sub-s (7I): inserted by the Occupational and Personal Pension Schemes (Consultation by Employers and Miscellaneous Amendment) Regulations 2006, SI 2006/349, reg 17, Schedule, para 6(1)(b).

Sub-s (7IA): inserted by the Employment Equality (Age) (Consequential Amendments) Regulations 2007, SI 2007/825, reg 3, and repealed by the Employment Equality (Repeal of Retirement Age Provisions) Regulations 2011, SI 2011/1069, reg 3(1), (4), as from 6 April 2011 (for savings in relation to the continued operation of this subsection, see regs 5, 6 of the 2011 Regulations at **[2.1603]**, **[2.1604]**).

Sub-s (7J): inserted by SI 2006/2059, reg 32(1)(b).

Sub-s (7JA): inserted by the Pensions Act 2008, s 57(1), (4), as from 30 June 2012.

Sub-s (7K): inserted by SI 2007/2974, reg 48(1)(b).

Sub-s (7L): inserted by the European Public Limited-Liability Company (Employee Involvement) (Great Britain) Regulations 2009, SI 2009/2401, reg 30(1), (2), as from 1 October 2009.

Sub-s (7M): inserted by SI 2010/493, reg 12(1), (3)(b), as from 2 March 2010.

Sub-s (7N): inserted by SI 2010/93, reg 25, Sch 2, Pt 1, paras 9, 15, as from 1 October 2011.

Corresponding provision for Wales: see the note to s 47AA at **[1.807]**.

Conciliation; modification in relation to governing bodies with delegated budgets; application in relation to office holders within the meaning of the Ecclesiastical Offices (Terms of Service) Regulations 2009: see the notes following the Part heading *ante*.

**[1.916]**
## 106   Replacements

(1)   Where this section applies to an employee he shall be regarded for the purposes of section 98(1)(b) as having been dismissed for a substantial reason of a kind such as to justify the dismissal of an employee holding the position which the employee held.

(2)   This section applies to an employee where—

(a)   on engaging him the employer informs him in writing that his employment will be terminated on the resumption of work by another employee who is, or will be, absent wholly or partly because of pregnancy or childbirth, [or on adoption leave] [or leave under section 80AA or 80BB (additional paternity leave)] and

(b)   the employer dismisses him in order to make it possible to give work to the other employee.

(3)   This section also applies to an employee where—

(a)   on engaging him the employer informs him in writing that his employment will be terminated on the end of a suspension of another employee from work on medical grounds or maternity grounds (within the meaning of Part VII), and

(b)   the employer dismisses him in order to make it possible to allow the resumption of work by the other employee.

(4)   Subsection (1) does not affect the operation of section 98(4) in a case to which this section applies.

**Part 1   Statutes**

**NOTES**

Sub-s (2): words in first pair of square brackets in para (a) inserted by the Employment Act 2002, s 53, Sch 7, paras 24, 35; words in second pair of square brackets in that paragraph inserted by the Work and Families Act 2006, s 11(1), Sch 1, para 42, as from 6 April 2010.

Conciliation; modification in relation to governing bodies with delegated budgets; application in relation to office holders within the meaning of the Ecclesiastical Offices (Terms of Service) Regulations 2009: see the notes following the Part heading *ante*.

**[1.917]**
**107   Pressure on employer to dismiss unfairly**
(1)   This section applies where there falls to be determined for the purposes of this Part a question—
   (a)   as to the reason, or principal reason, for which an employee was dismissed,
   (b)   whether the reason or principal reason for which an employee was dismissed was a reason fulfilling the requirement of section 98(1)(b), or
   (c)   whether an employer acted reasonably in treating the reason or principal reason for which an employee was dismissed as a sufficient reason for dismissing him.
(2)   In determining the question no account shall be taken of any pressure which by calling, organising, procuring or financing a strike or other industrial action, or threatening to do so, was exercised on the employer to dismiss the employee; and the question shall be determined as if no such pressure had been exercised.

**NOTES**

Conciliation; modification in relation to governing bodies with delegated budgets; application in relation to office holders within the meaning of the Ecclesiastical Offices (Terms of Service) Regulations 2009: see the notes following the Part heading *ante*.

*Exclusion of right*

**[1.918]**
**108   Qualifying period of employment**
(1)   Section 94 does not apply to the dismissal of an employee unless he has been continuously employed for a period of not less than [two years] ending with the effective date of termination.
(2)   If an employee is dismissed by reason of any such requirement or recommendation as is referred to in section 64(2), subsection (1) has effect in relation to that dismissal as if for the words [two years] there were substituted the words "one month".
(3)   Subsection (1) does not apply if—
   (a)   . . .
   [(aa)  subsection (1) of section 98B (read with subsection (2) of that section) applies,]
   [(b)   subsection (1) of section 99 (read with any regulations made under that section) applies,]
   (c)   subsection (1) of section 100 (read with subsections (2) and (3) of that section) applies,
   (d)   subsection (1) of section 101 (read with subsection (2) of that section) or subsection (3) of that section applies,
   [(dd)  section 101A applies,]
   [(de)  section 101B applies,]
   (e)   section 102 applies,
   (f)   section 103 applies,
   [(ff)  section 103A applies,]
   (g)   subsection (1) of section 104 (read with subsections (2) and (3) of that section) applies, . . .
   [(gg)  subsection (1) of section 104A (read with subsection (2) of that section) applies, . . . ]
   [(gh)  subsection (1) of section 104B (read with subsection (2) of that section) applies, . . . ]
   [(gi)  section 104C applies,]
   [(gj)  subsection (1) of section 104D (read with subsection (2) of that section) applies,]
   [(gk)  subsection (1) of section 104F (read with subsection (2) of that section) applies,]
   [(gk)  section 104E applies,]
   [(gl)  subsection (1) of section 104F (read with subsection (2) of that section) applies,]
   [(gm) section 104G applies,]
   (h)   section 105 applies, [ . . .
   (hh)  paragraph (3) or (6) of regulation 28 of the Transnational Information and Consultation of Employees Regulations 1999 (read with paragraphs (4) and (7) of that regulation) applies], [ . . .
   (i)   paragraph (1) of regulation 7 of the Part-time Workers (Prevention of Less Favourable Treatment) Regulations 2000 applies], [ . . .
   (j)   paragraph (1) of regulation 6 of the Fixed-term Employees (Prevention of Less Favourable Treatment) Regulations 2002 applies], [ . . .

(k)    paragraph (3) or (6) of regulation 42 of the European Public Limited-Liability Company Regulations 2004 applies]; [ . . .

(l)    paragraph (3) or (6) of regulation 30 of the Information and Consultation of Employees Regulations 2004 (read with paragraphs (4) and (7) of that regulation) applies] [, . . .

(m)    paragraph 5(3) or (5) of the Schedule to the Occupational and Personal Pension Schemes (Consultation by Employers and Miscellaneous Amendment) Regulations 2006 (read with paragraph 5(6) of that Schedule) applies] [, . . .

(n)    . . . ][, . . .

(o)    paragraph (3) or (6) of regulation 31 of the European Cooperative Society (Involvement of Employees) Regulations 2006 (read with paragraphs (4) and (7) of that regulation) applies], [ . . .

(p)    regulation 46 or 47 of the Companies (Cross-Border Mergers) Regulations 2007 applies][, . . .

(q)    paragraph (1)(a) or (b) of regulation 29 of the European Public Limited-Liability Company (Employee Involvement) (Great Britain) Regulations 2009 (SI 2009/2401) applies,] [or

(r)    paragraph (1) of regulation 17 of the Agency Workers Regulations 2010 applies].

[(4)    Subsection (1) does not apply if the reason (or, if more than one, the principal reason) for the dismissal is, or relates to, the employee's political opinions or affiliation.]

---

**NOTES**

Sub-ss (1), (2): words in square brackets substituted by the Unfair Dismissal and Statement of Reasons for Dismissal (Variation of Qualifying Period) Order 2012, SI 2012/989, art 3, as from 6 April 2012. Note that by virtue of art 4 of the 2012 Order, this amendment does not have effect in any case where the period of continuous employment began before that date (in such cases the previous period of one year continues to apply).

Sub-s (3) is amended as follows:

Para (a) repealed by the Employment Relations Act 1999, ss 9, 44, Sch 4, Pt III, paras 1, 5, 18, Sch 9(2).

Para (aa) inserted by the Employment Relations Act 2004, s 40(6).

Para (b) substituted by the Employment Relations Act 2004, s 57(1), Sch 1, para 32.

Para (dd) inserted by the Working Time Regulations 1998, SI 1998/1833, regs 2(1), 32(4).

Para (de) inserted by the Education and Skills Act 2008, s 39(1), (4), as from a day to be appointed.

Para (ff) inserted by the Public Interest Disclosure Act 1998, ss 7(1), 18(2).

Word omitted from para (g) repealed, and para (gg) inserted, by the National Minimum Wage Act 1998, ss 25(3), 53, Sch 3.

Word omitted from para (gg) repealed, and para (gh) inserted, by the Tax Credits Act 1999, ss 7, 19(4), Sch 3, para 3(3), Sch 6.

Word omitted from para (gh) repealed, and para (hh) and the word immediately preceding it inserted, by the Transnational Information and Consultation of Employees Regulations 1999, SI 1999/3323, reg 29(2).

Para (gi) inserted by the Employment Relations Act 2004, s 41(5).

Para (gj) inserted by the Pensions Act 2008, s 57(1), (5), as from 30 June 2012.

First para (gk) inserted by the Employment Relations Act 1999 (Blacklists) Regulations 2010, SI 2010/493, reg 12(1), (4), as from 2 March 2010.

Second para (gk) inserted by the Apprenticeships, Skills, Children and Learning Act 2009, s 40(5), Sch 1, paras 1, 4, as from 6 April 2010 (except in relation to small employers and their employees), and as from a day to be appointed (otherwise) (as to the meaning of "small employers" etc, see further the notes at **[1.840]**).

Para (gl): inserted by the Employment Relations Act 1999 (Blacklists) Regulations 2010, SI 2010/493, reg 12(1), (4), as from 2 March 2010.

Para (gm): inserted by the Growth and Infrastructure Act 2013, s 31(5), as from a day to be appointed.

Word omitted from para (h) repealed, and para (i) and the word immediately preceding it added, by the Part-time Workers (Prevention of Less Favourable Treatment) Regulations 2000, SI 2000/1551, reg 10, Schedule, para 2(2).

Word omitted from para (hh) repealed, and para (j) and the word immediately preceding it added, by the Fixed-term Employees (Prevention of Less Favourable Treatment) Regulations 2002, SI 2002/2034, reg 11, Sch 2, Pt 1, para 3(1), (11) (except in relation to Government training schemes, agency workers or apprentices; see regs 18–20 of the 2002 Regulations at **[2.614]** et seq).

Word omitted from para (i) repealed, and para (k) and the word immediately preceding it added, by the European Public Limited-Liability Company Regulations 2004, SI 2004/2326, reg 43(2).

Word omitted from para (j) repealed, and para (l) and the word immediately preceding it added, by the Information and Consultation of Employees Regulations 2004, SI 2004/3426, reg 31(2).

Word omitted from para (k) repealed, and para (m) and the word immediately preceding it added, by the Occupational and Personal Pension Schemes (Consultation by Employers and Miscellaneous Amendment) Regulations 2006, SI 2006/349, reg 17, Schedule, para 6(2).

Word omitted following para (l) repealed, and para (n) and the word immediately preceding it added, by the Employment Equality (Age) Regulations 2006, SI 2006/1031, reg 49(1), Sch 8, Pt 1, paras 21, 24.

Para (n) repealed by the Employment Equality (Repeal of Retirement Age Provisions) Regulations 2011, SI 2011/1069, reg 3(1), (5), as from 6 April 2011 (for savings in relation to the continued operation of this paragraph, see regs 5, 6 of the 2011 Regulations at **[2.1603]**, **[2.1604]**).

Word omitted following para (m) repealed, and para (o) and the word immediately preceding it added, by the European Cooperative Society (Involvement of Employees) Regulations 2006, SI 2006/2059, reg 32(2).

Word omitted following para (n) repealed, and para (p) and the word immediately preceding it added, by the Companies (Cross-Border Mergers) Regulations 2007, SI 2007/2974, reg 48(2).

Word omitted following para (o) repealed, and para (q) and the word immediately preceding it added, by the European Public Limited-Liability Company (Employee Involvement) (Great Britain) Regulations 2009, SI 2009/2401, reg 30(3), as from 1 October 2009.

Word omitted following para (p) repealed and para (r) and the word immediately preceding it added, by the Agency Workers Regulations 2010, SI 2010/93, reg 25, Sch 2, Pt 1, paras 9, 16, as from 1 October 2011 (note that Sch 2, Pt 1, para 16 of the

2010 Regulations was amended by the Agency Workers (Amendment) Regulations 2011, SI 2011/1941, reg 2(1), (5), as from 1 September 2011 to correct a drafting error in the original Regulations which provided that the inserted paragraph should be paragraph (q) instead of paragraph (r)).

Sub-s (4): added by the Enterprise and Regulatory Reform Act 2013, s 13, as from 25 June 2013, subject to savings in s 24(3) of the 2013 Act at **[1.1855]**.

Conciliation; modification in relation to governing bodies with delegated budgets; application in relation to office holders within the meaning of the Ecclesiastical Offices (Terms of Service) Regulations 2009: see the notes following the Part heading *ante*.

Exclusion: this section is excluded in relation to dismissal on grounds related to union membership or activities; see the Trade Union and Labour Relations (Consolidation) Act 1992, s 154 at **[1.421]**.

Corresponding provision for Wales: see the note to s 47AA at **[1.807]**.

**109**　*(Repealed by the Employment Equality (Age) Regulations 2006, SI 2006/1031, reg 49(1), Sch 8, Pt 1, paras 21, 25.)*

**[1.919]**
**110　Dismissal procedures agreements**
(1)　Where a dismissal procedures agreement is designated by an order under subsection (3) which is for the time being in force—
(a)　the provisions of that agreement relating to dismissal shall have effect in substitution for any rights under section 94, and
(b)　accordingly, section 94 does not apply to the dismissal of an employee from any employment if it is employment to which, and he is an employee to whom, those provisions of the agreement apply.
[(2)　But if the agreement includes provision that it does not apply to dismissals of particular descriptions, subsection (1) does not apply in relation to a dismissal of any such description.]
(3)　An order designating a dismissal procedures agreement may be made by the Secretary of State, on an application being made to him jointly by all the parties to the agreement, if he is satisfied that—
(a)　every trade union which is a party to the agreement is an independent trade union,
(b)　the agreement provides for procedures to be followed in cases where an employee claims that he has been, or is in the course of being, unfairly dismissed,
(c)　those procedures are available without discrimination to all employees falling within any description to which the agreement applies,
(d)　the remedies provided by the agreement in respect of unfair dismissal are on the whole as beneficial as (but not necessarily identical with) those provided in respect of unfair dismissal by this Part,
[(e)　the agreement includes provision either for arbitration in every case or for—
(i)　arbitration where (by reason of equality of votes or for any other reason) a decision under the agreement cannot otherwise be reached, and
(ii)　a right to submit to arbitration any question of law arising out of such a decision, and]
(f)　the provisions of the agreement are such that it can be determined with reasonable certainty whether or not a particular employee is one to whom the agreement applies.
[(3A)　The Secretary of State may by order amend subsection (3) so as to add to the conditions specified in that subsection such conditions as he may specify in the order.]
(4)　If at any time when an order under subsection (3) is in force in relation to a dismissal procedures agreement the Secretary of State is satisfied, whether on an application made to him by any of the parties to the agreement or otherwise, either—
(a)　that it is the desire of all the parties to the agreement that the order should be revoked, or
(b)　that the agreement no longer satisfies all the conditions specified in subsection (3),
the Secretary of State shall revoke the order by an order under this subsection.
(5)　The transitional provisions which may be made in an order under subsection (4) include, in particular, provisions directing—
(a)　that an employee—
(i)　shall not be excluded from his right under section 94 where the effective date of termination falls within a transitional period which ends with the date on which the order takes effect and which is specified in the order, and
(ii)　shall have an extended time for presenting a complaint under section 111 in respect of a dismissal where the effective date of termination falls within that period, and
(b)　that, where the effective date of termination falls within such a transitional period, an [employment tribunal] shall, in determining any complaint of unfair dismissal presented by an employee to whom the dismissal procedures agreement applies, have regard to such considerations as are specified in the order (in addition to those specified in this Part and section 10(4) and (5) of [the Employment Tribunals Act 1996]).
[(6)　Where an award is made under a designated dismissal procedures agreement—

(a)    in England and Wales it may be enforced, by leave of *a county court*, in the same manner as a judgment of the court to the same effect and, where leave is given, judgment may be entered in terms of the award, and

(b)    in Scotland it may be recorded for execution in the Books of Council and Session and shall be enforceable accordingly.

**NOTES**

Sub-s (2): substituted by the Employment Rights (Dispute Resolution) Act 1998, s 12(1), (5).

Sub-s (3): words in square brackets substituted by the Employment Rights (Dispute Resolution) Act 1998, s 12(2), (5).

Sub-s (3A): inserted by the Employment Act 2002, s 44, as from a day to be appointed.

Sub-s (5): words in square brackets substituted by the Employment Rights (Dispute Resolution) Act 1998, s 1(2)(a), (b).

Sub-s (6): added by the Employment Rights (Dispute Resolution) Act 1998, s 12(3), (5); for the words in italics there are substituted the words "the county court" by the Crime and Courts Act 2013, s 17(5), Sch 9, Pt 3, para 52, as from a day to be appointed.

The only Order under the provisions re-enacted in this section (not made as a statutory instrument) is in relation to the electrical contracting industry. This order was revoked with effect from 1 June 2001 by the Dismissal Procedures Agreement Designation (Electrical Contracting Industry) Order 1991 Revocation Order 2001 (SI 2001/1752), subject to transitional provisions.

## CHAPTER II
## REMEDIES FOR UNFAIR DISMISSAL

*Introductory*

**[1.920]**

**111    Complaints to [employment tribunal]**

(1)    A complaint may be presented to an [employment tribunal] against an employer by any person that he was unfairly dismissed by the employer.

(2)    [Subject to the following provisions of this section], an [employment tribunal] shall not consider a complaint under this section unless it is presented to the tribunal—

(a)    before the end of the period of three months beginning with the effective date of termination, or

(b)    within such further period as the tribunal considers reasonable in a case where it is satisfied that it was not reasonably practicable for the complaint to be presented before the end of that period of three months.

[(2A)    Section 207A(3) (extension because of mediation in certain European cross-border disputes) *applies* for the purposes of subsection (2)(a).]

(3)    Where a dismissal is with notice, an [employment tribunal] shall consider a complaint under this section if it is presented after the notice is given but before the effective date of termination.

(4)    In relation to a complaint which is presented as mentioned in subsection (3), the provisions of this Act, so far as they relate to unfair dismissal, have effect as if—

(a)    references to a complaint by a person that he was unfairly dismissed by his employer included references to a complaint by a person that his employer has given him notice in such circumstances that he will be unfairly dismissed when the notice expires,

(b)    references to reinstatement included references to the withdrawal of the notice by the employer,

(c)    references to the effective date of termination included references to the date which would be the effective date of termination on the expiry of the notice, and

(d)    references to an employee ceasing to be employed included references to an employee having been given notice of dismissal.

[(5)    Where the dismissal is alleged to be unfair by virtue of section 104F (blacklists),

(a)    subsection (2)(b) does not apply, and

(b)    an employment tribunal may consider a complaint that is otherwise out of time if, in all the circumstances of the case, it considers that it is just and equitable to do so.]

**NOTES**

Words in first pair of square brackets in sub-s (2) substituted, and sub-s (5) added, by the Employment Relations Act 1999 (Blacklists) Regulations 2010, SI 2010/493, reg 12(1), (5), as from 2 March 2010.

Sub-s (2A): inserted by the Cross-Border Mediation (EU Directive) Regulations 2011, SI 2011/1133, regs 30, 46, as from 20 May 2011; for the word in italics there are substituted the words "and section 207B (extension of time limits to facilitate conciliation before institution of proceedings) apply", by the Enterprise and Regulatory Reform Act 2013, s 8, Sch 2, paras 15, 33, as from a day to be appointed.

All other words in square brackets this section (including in the section heading) were substituted by the Employment Rights (Dispute Resolution) Act 1998, s 1(2)(a).

Conciliation; modification in relation to governing bodies with delegated budgets; application in relation to office holders within the meaning of the Ecclesiastical Offices (Terms of Service) Regulations 2009: see the notes following the Part heading *ante*.

Tribunal jurisdiction: the Employment Act 2002, s 38 applies to proceedings before the employment tribunal relating to a claim under this section; see s 38(1) of, and Sch 5 to, the 2002 Act at **[1.1228]**, **[1.1236]**. See also the Trade Union and Labour Relations (Consolidation) Act 1992, s 207A at **[1.474]** (as inserted by the Employment Act 2008). That section provides that in proceedings before an employment tribunal relating to a claim by an employee under any of the jurisdictions listed in

Sch A2 to the 1992 Act at **[1.648]** (which includes this section) the tribunal may adjust any award given if the employer or the employee has unreasonably failed to comply with the relevant Code of Practice as defined by s 207A(4). See also the revised Acas Code of Practice 1 – Disciplinary and Grievance Procedures (2009) at **[4.1]**.

National security: for the effect of national security considerations on a complaint under this section, see the Employment Tribunals Act 1996, s 10(1) at **[1.694]**.

**[1.921]**
**[111A   Confidentiality of negotiations before termination of employment**
(1)   Evidence of pre-termination negotiations is inadmissible in any proceedings on a complaint under section 111.
This is subject to subsections (3) to (5).
(2)   In subsection (1) "pre-termination negotiations" means any offer made or discussions held, before the termination of the employment in question, with a view to it being terminated on terms agreed between the employer and the employee.
(3)   Subsection (1) does not apply where, according to the complainant's case, the circumstances are such that a provision (whenever made) contained in, or made under, this or any other Act requires the complainant to be regarded for the purposes of this Part as unfairly dismissed.
(4)   In relation to anything said or done which in the tribunal's opinion was improper, or was connected with improper behaviour, subsection (1) applies only to the extent that the tribunal considers just.
(5)   Subsection (1) does not affect the admissibility, on any question as to costs or expenses, of evidence relating to an offer made on the basis that the right to refer to it on any such question is reserved.]

**NOTES**
Commencement: to be appointed.
Inserted by the Enterprise and Regulatory Reform Act 2013, s 14, as from a day to be appointed, except in relation to any offer made or discussions held before this insertion comes into force (see s 24(4) of the 2013 Act at **[1.1855]**).

**[1.922]**
**112   The remedies: orders and compensation**
(1)   This section applies where, on a complaint under section 111, an [employment tribunal] finds that the grounds of the complaint are well-founded.
(2)   The tribunal shall—
   (a)   explain to the complainant what orders may be made under section 113 and in what circumstances they may be made, and
   (b)   ask him whether he wishes the tribunal to make such an order.
(3)   If the complainant expresses such a wish, the tribunal may make an order under section 113.
(4)   If no order is made under section 113, the tribunal shall make an award of compensation for unfair dismissal (calculated in accordance with sections 118 to [126] [ . . . ]) to be paid by the employer to the employee.
[(5), (6)   . . . ]

**NOTES**
Sub-s (1): words in square brackets substituted by the Employment Rights (Dispute Resolution) Act 1998, s 1(2)(a).
Sub-s (4): figure in square brackets substituted by the Employment Act 2002, s 53, Sch 7, paras 24, 36; words omitted (originally inserted by the Public Interest Disclosure Act 1998, s 8(1)) repealed by the Employment Relations Act 1999, s 44, Sch 9(11).
Sub-ss (5), (6): added by the Employment Act 2002, s 34(1), (3); repealed by the Employment Equality (Repeal of Retirement Age Provisions) Regulations 2011, SI 2011/1069, reg 3(1), (6), as from 6 April 2011 (for savings in relation to the continued operation of the provisions repealed, see regs 5–7 of the 2011 Regulations at **[2.1603]** et seq).

*Orders for Reinstatement or Re-engagement*

**[1.923]**
**113   The orders**
An order under this section may be—
   (a)   an order for reinstatement (in accordance with section 114), or
   (b)   an order for re-engagement (in accordance with section 115),
as the tribunal may decide.

**[1.924]**
**114   Order for reinstatement**
(1)   An order for reinstatement is an order that the employer shall treat the complainant in all respects as if he had not been dismissed.
(2)   On making an order for reinstatement the tribunal shall specify—
   (a)   any amount payable by the employer in respect of any benefit which the complainant might reasonably be expected to have had but for the dismissal (including arrears of pay) for the period between the date of termination of employment and the date of reinstatement,

(b)    any rights and privileges (including seniority and pension rights) which must be restored to the employee, and

(c)    the date by which the order must be complied with.

(3)   If the complainant would have benefited from an improvement in his terms and conditions of employment had he not been dismissed, an order for reinstatement shall require him to be treated as if he had benefited from that improvement from the date on which he would have done so but for being dismissed.

(4)   In calculating for the purposes of subsection (2)(a) any amount payable by the employer, the tribunal shall take into account, so as to reduce the employer's liability, any sums received by the complainant in respect of the period between the date of termination of employment and the date of reinstatement by way of—

(a)    wages in lieu of notice or ex gratia payments paid by the employer, or

(b)    remuneration paid in respect of employment with another employer,

and such other benefits as the tribunal thinks appropriate in the circumstances.

(5)    . . .

**NOTES**

Sub-s (5): repealed by the Employment Relations Act 1999, ss 9, 44, Sch 4, Pt III, paras 1, 5, 20, Sch 9(2).

**[1.925]**
**115   Order for re-engagement**

(1)   An order for re-engagement is an order, on such terms as the tribunal may decide, that the complainant be engaged by the employer, or by a successor of the employer or by an associated employer, in employment comparable to that from which he was dismissed or other suitable employment.

(2)   On making an order for re-engagement the tribunal shall specify the terms on which re-engagement is to take place, including—

(a)    the identity of the employer,

(b)    the nature of the employment,

(c)    the remuneration for the employment,

(d)    any amount payable by the employer in respect of any benefit which the complainant might reasonably be expected to have had but for the dismissal (including arrears of pay) for the period between the date of termination of employment and the date of re-engagement,

(e)    any rights and privileges (including seniority and pension rights) which must be restored to the employee, and

(f)    the date by which the order must be complied with.

(3)   In calculating for the purposes of subsection (2)(d) any amount payable by the employer, the tribunal shall take into account, so as to reduce the employer's liability, any sums received by the complainant in respect of the period between the date of termination of employment and the date of re-engagement by way of—

(a)    wages in lieu of notice or ex gratia payments paid by the employer, or

(b)    remuneration paid in respect of employment with another employer,

and such other benefits as the tribunal thinks appropriate in the circumstances.

(4)    . . .

**NOTES**

Sub-s (4): repealed by the Employment Relations Act 1999, ss 9, 44, Sch 4, Pt III, paras 1, 5, 21, Sch 9(2).

**[1.926]**
**116   Choice of order and its terms**

(1)   In exercising its discretion under section 113 the tribunal shall first consider whether to make an order for reinstatement and in so doing shall take into account—

(a)    whether the complainant wishes to be reinstated,

(b)    whether it is practicable for the employer to comply with an order for reinstatement, and

(c)    where the complainant caused or contributed to some extent to the dismissal, whether it would be just to order his reinstatement.

(2)   If the tribunal decides not to make an order for reinstatement it shall then consider whether to make an order for re-engagement and, if so, on what terms.

(3)   In so doing the tribunal shall take into account—

(a)    any wish expressed by the complainant as to the nature of the order to be made,

(b)    whether it is practicable for the employer (or a successor or an associated employer) to comply with an order for re-engagement, and

(c)    where the complainant caused or contributed to some extent to the dismissal, whether it would be just to order his re-engagement and (if so) on what terms.

(4)   Except in a case where the tribunal takes into account contributory fault under subsection (3)(c) it shall, if it orders re-engagement, do so on terms which are, so far as is reasonably practicable, as favourable as an order for reinstatement.

(5)　Where in any case an employer has engaged a permanent replacement for a dismissed employee, the tribunal shall not take that fact into account in determining, for the purposes of subsection (1)(b) or (3)(b), whether it is practicable to comply with an order for reinstatement or re-engagement.

(6)　Subsection (5) does not apply where the employer shows—

    (a)　that it was not practicable for him to arrange for the dismissed employee's work to be done without engaging a permanent replacement, or

    (b)　that—

        (i)　he engaged the replacement after the lapse of a reasonable period, without having heard from the dismissed employee that he wished to be reinstated or re-engaged, and

        (ii)　when the employer engaged the replacement it was no longer reasonable for him to arrange for the dismissed employee's work to be done except by a permanent replacement.

**[1.927]**

**117　Enforcement of order and compensation**

(1)　An [employment tribunal] shall make an award of compensation, to be paid by the employer to the employee, if—

    (a)　an order under section 113 is made and the complainant is reinstated or re-engaged, but

    (b)　the terms of the order are not fully complied with.

(2)　Subject to section 124 [ . . . ], the amount of the compensation shall be such as the tribunal thinks fit having regard to the loss sustained by the complainant in consequence of the failure to comply fully with the terms of the order.

[(2A)　There shall be deducted from any award under subsection (1) the amount of any award made under section 112(5) at the time of the order under section 113.]

(3)　Subject to subsections (1) and (2) [ . . . . ], if an order under section 113 is made but the complainant is not reinstated or re-engaged in accordance with the order, the tribunal shall make—

    (a)　an award of compensation for unfair dismissal (calculated in accordance with sections 118 to [126]), and

    (b)　except where this paragraph does not apply, an additional award of compensation of [an amount not less than twenty-six nor more than fifty-two weeks' pay],

to be paid by the employer to the employee.

(4)　Subsection (3)(b) does not apply where—

    (a)　the employer satisfies the tribunal that it was not practicable to comply with the order,

     . . .

    (b)　 . . .

(5), (6)　 . . .

(7)　Where in any case an employer has engaged a permanent replacement for a dismissed employee, the tribunal shall not take that fact into account in determining for the purposes of subsection (4)(a) whether it was practicable to comply with the order for reinstatement or re-engagement unless the employer shows that it was not practicable for him to arrange for the dismissed employee's work to be done without engaging a permanent replacement.

(8)　Where in any case an [employment tribunal] finds that the complainant has unreasonably prevented an order under section 113 from being complied with, in making an award of compensation for unfair dismissal . . . it shall take that conduct into account as a failure on the part of the complainant to mitigate his loss.

---

**NOTES**

Sub-s (1): words in square brackets substituted by the Employment Rights (Dispute Resolution) Act 1998, s 1(2)(a).

Sub-s (2): words omitted (originally inserted by the Public Interest Disclosure Act 1998, s 8(2)(a)) repealed by the Employment Relations Act 1999, s 44, Sch 9(11).

Sub-s (2A): inserted by the Employment Act 2002, s 34(1), (4).

Sub-s (3): words omitted (originally inserted by the Public Interest Disclosure Act 1998, s 8(2)(b)) repealed by the Employment Relations Act 1999, s 44, Sch 9(11); figure in square brackets in para (a) substituted by the Employment Act 2002, s 53, Sch 7, paras 24, 37; words in square brackets in para (b) substituted by the Employment Relations Act 1999, s 33(2).

Sub-s (4): para (b) and word immediately preceding it repealed by the Employment Relations Act 1999, ss 33(1)(a), 44, Sch 9(10).

Sub-ss (5), (6): repealed by the Employment Relations Act 1999, ss 33(2), 44, Sch 9(10).

Sub-s (8): words in square brackets substituted, and words omitted repealed, by the Employment Rights (Dispute Resolution) Act 1998, ss 1(2)(a), 15, Sch 2.

Modifications: for modifications in relation to arbitration schemes for unfair dismissal cases, see the ACAS Arbitration Scheme (Great Britain) Order 2004, SI 2004/753 at **[2.778]**.

---

*Compensation*

**[1.928]**

**118　General**

(1)　[ . . . ] where a tribunal makes an award of compensation for unfair dismissal under section 112(4) or 117(3)(a) the award shall consist of—

(a)   a basic award (calculated in accordance with sections 119 to 122 and 126), and
(b)   a compensatory award (calculated in accordance with sections 123, 124, [124A and 126]).
(2), (3), [(4)]   . . .

**NOTES**

Sub-s (1): words omitted (originally inserted by the Public Interest Disclosure Act 1998, s 8(3)) repealed by the Employment Relations Act 1999, s 44, Sch 9(11); words in square brackets in para (b) substituted by the Employment Act 2002, s 53, Sch 7, paras 24, 38.

Sub-ss (2), (3): repealed by the Employment Relations Act 1999, ss 33(1)(a), 44, Sch 9(10).

Sub-s (4): added by the Employment Rights (Dispute Resolution) Act 1998, s 15, Sch 1, para 21(1), (3); repealed by the Employment Act 2002, s 54, Sch 8(1).

**[1.929]**
**119   Basic award**
(1)   Subject to the provisions of this section, sections 120 to 122 and section 126, the amount of the basic award shall be calculated by—
   (a)   determining the period, ending with the effective date of termination, during which the employee has been continuously employed,
   (b)   reckoning backwards from the end of that period the number of years of employment falling within that period, and
   (c)   allowing the appropriate amount for each of those years of employment.
(2)   In subsection (1)(c) "the appropriate amount" means—
   (a)   one and a half weeks' pay for a year of employment in which the employee was not below the age of forty-one,
   (b)   one week's pay for a year of employment (not within paragraph (a)) in which he was not below the age of twenty-two, and
   (c)   half a week's pay for a year of employment not within paragraph (a) or (b).
(3)   Where twenty years of employment have been reckoned under subsection (1), no account shall be taken under that subsection of any year of employment earlier than those twenty years.
(4)–(6)   . . .

**NOTES**

Sub-ss (4), (5): repealed by the Employment Equality (Age) Regulations 2006, SI 2006/1031, reg 49(1), Sch 8, Pt 1, paras 21, 27.

Sub-s (6): repealed by the Employment Relations Act 1999, ss 9, 44, Sch 4, Pt III, paras 1, 5, 23, Sch 9(2).

**[1.930]**
**120   Basic award: minimum in certain cases**
(1)   The amount of the basic award (before any reduction under section 122) shall not be less than [£5,500] where the reason (or, if more than one, the principal reason)—
   (a)   in a redundancy case, for selecting the employee for dismissal, or
   (b)   otherwise, for the dismissal,
is one of those specified in section 100(1)(a) and (b), [101A(d),] 102(1) or 103.
[(1A), (1B)   . . .  ]
[(1C)   Where an employee is regarded as unfairly dismissed by virtue of section 104F (blacklists) (whether or not the dismissal is unfair or regarded as unfair for any other reason), the amount of the basic award of compensation (before any reduction is made under section 122) shall not be less than £5,000.]
(2)   . . .

**NOTES**

Sub-s (1): sum in first pair of square brackets substituted by the Employment Rights (Increase of Limits) Order 2012, SI 2012/3007, art 3, Schedule, as from 1 February 2013, in relation to any case where the appropriate date (as defined in the order) falls on or after that date (see SI 2012/3007, art 4 at **[2.1636]**). The previous sum was £5,300 (see SI 2011/3006). This sum may be varied by the Secretary of State (see the Employment Relations Act 1999, s 34(1)(a), (3)(b) at **[1.1202]**); figure in second pair of square brackets inserted by the Working Time Regulations 1998, SI 1998/1833, regs 2(1), 32(5).

Sub-ss (1A), (1B): inserted by the Employment Act 2002, s 34(1), (6); repealed by the Employment Equality (Repeal of Retirement Age Provisions) Regulations 2011, SI 2011/1069, reg 3(1), (7), as from 6 April 2011 (for savings in relation to its continued operation, see regs 5–7 of the 2011 Regulations at **[2.1603]** et seq).

Sub-s (1C): inserted by the Employment Relations Act 1999 (Blacklists) Regulations 2010, SI 2010/493, reg 12(1), (6), as from 2 March 2010.

Sub-s (2): repealed by the Employment Relations Act 1999, ss 36(1)(a), 44, Sch 9(10).

**[1.931]**
**121   Basic award of two weeks' pay in certain cases**
The amount of the basic award shall be two weeks' pay where the tribunal finds that the reason (or, where there is more than one, the principal reason) for the dismissal of the employee is that he was redundant and the employee—
   (a)   by virtue of section 138 is not regarded as dismissed for the purposes of Part XI, or

(b)  by virtue of section 141 is not, or (if he were otherwise entitled) would not be, entitled to a redundancy payment.

**[1.932]**
**122  Basic award: reductions**
(1)  Where the tribunal finds that the complainant has unreasonably refused an offer by the employer which (if accepted) would have the effect of reinstating the complainant in his employment in all respects as if he had not been dismissed, the tribunal shall reduce or further reduce the amount of the basic award to such extent as it considers just and equitable having regard to that finding.
(2)  Where the tribunal considers that any conduct of the complainant before the dismissal (or, where the dismissal was with notice, before the notice was given) was such that it would be just and equitable to reduce or further reduce the amount of the basic award to any extent, the tribunal shall reduce or further reduce that amount accordingly.
(3)  Subsection (2) does not apply in a redundancy case unless the reason for selecting the employee for dismissal was one of those specified in section 100(1)(a) and (b), [101A(d),] 102(1) or 103; and in such a case subsection (2) applies only to so much of the basic award as is payable because of section 120.
[(3A)  Where the complainant has been awarded any amount in respect of the dismissal under a designated dismissal procedures agreement, the tribunal shall reduce or further reduce the amount of the basic award to such extent as it considers just and equitable having regard to that award.]
(4)  The amount of the basic award shall be reduced or further reduced by the amount of—
    (a)  any redundancy payment awarded by the tribunal under Part XI in respect of the same dismissal, or
    (b)  any payment made by the employer to the employee on the ground that the dismissal was by reason of redundancy (whether in pursuance of Part XI or otherwise).
[(5)  Where a dismissal is regarded as unfair by virtue of section 104F (blacklists), the amount of the basic award shall be reduced or further reduced by the amount of any basic award in respect of the same dismissal under section 156 of the Trade Union and Labour Relations (Consolidation) Act 1992 (minimum basic award in case of dismissal on grounds related to trade union membership or activities).]

**NOTES**
   Sub-s (3): figure in square brackets inserted by the Working Time Regulations 1998, SI 1998/1833, regs 2(1), 32(5).
   Sub-s (3A): inserted by the Employment Rights (Dispute Resolution) Act 1998, s 15, Sch 1, para 22.
   Sub-s (5): added by the Employment Relations Act 1999 (Blacklists) Regulations 2010, SI 2010/493, reg 12(1), (7), as from 2 March 2010.

**[1.933]**
**123  Compensatory award**
(1)  Subject to the provisions of this section and sections 124[, 124A and 126], the amount of the compensatory award shall be such amount as the tribunal considers just and equitable in all the circumstances having regard to the loss sustained by the complainant in consequence of the dismissal in so far as that loss is attributable to action taken by the employer.
(2)  The loss referred to in subsection (1) shall be taken to include—
    (a)  any expenses reasonably incurred by the complainant in consequence of the dismissal, and
    (b)  subject to subsection (3), loss of any benefit which he might reasonably be expected to have had but for the dismissal.
(3)  The loss referred to in subsection (1) shall be taken to include in respect of any loss of—
    (a)  any entitlement or potential entitlement to a payment on account of dismissal by reason of redundancy (whether in pursuance of Part XI or otherwise), or
    (b)  any expectation of such a payment,
only the loss referable to the amount (if any) by which the amount of that payment would have exceeded the amount of a basic award (apart from any reduction under section 122) in respect of the same dismissal.
(4)  In ascertaining the loss referred to in subsection (1) the tribunal shall apply the same rule concerning the duty of a person to mitigate his loss as applies to damages recoverable under the common law of England and Wales or (as the case may be) Scotland.
(5)  In determining, for the purposes of subsection (1), how far any loss sustained by the complainant was attributable to action taken by the employer, no account shall be taken of any pressure which by—
    (a)  calling, organising, procuring or financing a strike or other industrial action, or
    (b)  threatening to do so,
was exercised on the employer to dismiss the employee; and that question shall be determined as if no such pressure had been exercised.
(6)  Where the tribunal finds that the dismissal was to any extent caused or contributed to by any action of the complainant, it shall reduce the amount of the compensatory award by such proportion as it considers just and equitable having regard to that finding.

[(6A) Where—

(a) the reason (or principal reason) for the dismissal is that the complainant made a protected disclosure, and

(b) it appears to the tribunal that the disclosure was not made in good faith,

the tribunal may, if it considers it just and equitable in all the circumstances to do so, reduce any award it makes to the complainant by no more than 25%.]

(7) If the amount of any payment made by the employer to the employee on the ground that the dismissal was by reason of redundancy (whether in pursuance of Part XI or otherwise) exceeds the amount of the basic award which would be payable but for section 122(4), that excess goes to reduce the amount of the compensatory award.

[(8) Where the amount of the compensatory award falls to be calculated for the purposes of an award under section 117(3)(a), there shall be deducted from the compensatory award any award made under section 112(5) at the time of the order under section 113.]

---

NOTES

Sub-s (1): words in square brackets substituted by the Employment Act 2002, s 53, Sch 7, paras 24, 39.

Sub-s (6A): inserted by the Enterprise and Regulatory Reform Act 2013, s 18(5), as from 25 June 2013, subject to savings in s 24(6) of the 2013 Act at [**1.1855**].

Sub-s (8): added by the Employment Act 2002, s 34(1), (5).

**[1.934]**
## 124 Limit of compensatory award etc

(1) The amount of—

(a) any compensation awarded to a person under section 117(1) and (2), or

(b) a compensatory award to a person calculated in accordance with section 123,

shall not exceed [£74,200].

[(1A) Subsection (1) shall not apply to compensation awarded, or a compensatory award made, to a person in a case where he is regarded as unfairly dismissed by virtue of section 100, 103A, 105(3) or 105(6A).]

(2) . . .

(3) In the case of compensation awarded to a person under section 117(1) and (2), the limit imposed by this section may be exceeded to the extent necessary to enable the award fully to reflect the amount specified as payable under section 114(2)(a) or section 115(2)(d).

(4) Where—

(a) a compensatory award is an award under paragraph (a) of subsection (3) of section 117, and

(b) an additional award falls to be made under paragraph (b) of that subsection,

the limit imposed by this section on the compensatory award may be exceeded to the extent necessary to enable the aggregate of the compensatory and additional awards fully to reflect the amount specified as payable under section 114(2)(a) or section 115(2)(d).

(5) The limit imposed by this section applies to the amount which the [employment tribunal] would, apart from this section, award in respect of the subject matter of the complaint after taking into account—

(a) any payment made by the respondent to the complainant in respect of that matter, and

(b) any reduction in the amount of the award required by any enactment or rule of law.

---

NOTES

Sub-s (1): sum in square brackets substituted by the Employment Rights (Increase of Limits) Order 2012, SI 2012/3007, art 3, Schedule, as from 1 February 2013, in relation to any case where the appropriate date (as defined in the order) falls on or after that date (see SI 2012/3007, art 4 at [**2.1636**]). Previous sums were as follows: £72,300 as from 1 February 2012 (see SI 2011/3006); £68,400 as from 1 February 2011 (see SI 2010/2926); £65,300 as from 1 February 2010 (see SI 2009/3274); £66,200, as from 1 February 2009 (see SI 2008/3055); £63,000 as from 1 February 2008 (SI 2007/3570); £60,600 as from 1 February 2007 (SI 2006/3045); £58,400 as from 1 February 2006 (SI 2005/3352); £56,800 as from 1 February 2005 (SI 2004/2989); and £55,000 as from 1 February 2004 (SI 2003/3038) in each case where the appropriate date fell after the commencement date). This sum may be varied by the Secretary of State, see the Employment Relations Act 1999, s 34(1)(a), (3)(c) at [**1.1202**].

Sub-s (1A): inserted by the Employment Relations Act 1999, s 37(1).

Sub-s (2): repealed by the Employment Relations Act 1999, ss 36(1)(a), 44, Sch 9(10).

Sub-s (5): words in square brackets substituted by the Employment Rights (Dispute Resolution) Act 1998, s 1(2)(a).

---

**[1.935]**
## [124A Adjustments under the Employment Act 2002

Where an award of compensation for unfair dismissal falls to be—

(a) reduced or increased under [section 207A of the Trade Union and Labour Relations (Consolidation) Act 1992 (effect of failure to comply with Code: adjustment of awards)], or

(b) increased under section 38 of that Act (failure to give statement of employment particulars), the adjustment shall be in the amount awarded under section 118(1)(b) and shall be applied immediately before any reduction under section 123(6) or (7).]

**NOTES**

Inserted by the Employment Act 2002, s 39.

Words in square brackets in para (a) substituted by the Employment Act 2008, s 3(4), as from 6 April 2009, subject to a variety of transitional provisions and savings in the Employment Act 2008 (Commencement No 1, Transitional Provisions and Savings) Order 2008, SI 2008/3232, Schedule, Pt 1.

Despite the amendment to para (a) of this section, there has been no corresponding amendment to the section heading nor the text in (b) (where the text "section 38 *of that Act*" should presumably now be read as "section 38 *of the Employment Act 2002*").

**125** *(Repealed by the Employment Relations Act 1999, ss 33(1)(a), 44, Sch 9(10).)*

**[1.936]**
**126 Acts which are both unfair dismissal and discrimination**
(1) This section applies where compensation falls to be awarded in respect of any act both under—
  (a) the provisions of this Act relating to unfair dismissal, and
  [(b) the Equality Act 2010].
(2) An [employment tribunal] shall not award compensation under [either of those Acts] in respect of any loss or other matter which is or has been taken into account under [the other] by the tribunal (or another [employment tribunal]) in awarding compensation on the same or another complaint in respect of that act.

**NOTES**

Sub-s (1): para (b) substituted by the Equality Act 2010, s 211(1), Sch 26, Pt 1, para 33(1), (2), as from 1 October 2010.

Sub-s (2): words "employment tribunal" in square brackets in both places they occur substituted by the Employment Rights (Dispute Resolution) Act 1998, s 1(2)(a); other words in square brackets substituted by the Equality Act 2010, s 211(1), Sch 26, Pt 1, para 33(1), (3), as from 1 October 2010.

**127, 127A, 127B** *(s 127 repealed by the Employment Relations Act 1999, ss 9, 44, Sch 4, Pt III, paras 1, 5, 24, Sch 9(2); s 127A originally inserted by the Employment Rights (Dispute Resolution) Act 1998, s 13, and repealed by the Employment Act 2002, ss 53, 54, Sch 7, paras 24, 40, Sch 8(1) s 127B originally inserted by the Public Interest Disclosure Act 1998, ss 8(4), 18(2), and repealed by the Employment Relations Act 1999, ss 37(2), 44, Sch 9(11).)*

*Interim relief*

**[1.937]**
**128 Interim relief pending determination of complaint**
[(1) An employee who presents a complaint to an employment tribunal that he has been unfairly dismissed and—
  (a) that the reason (or if more than one the principal reason) for the dismissal is one of those specified in—
    (i) section 100(1)(a) and (b), 101A(d), 102(1), 103 or 103A, or
    (ii) paragraph 161(2) of Schedule A1 to the Trade Union and Labour Relations (Consolidation) Act 1992, or
  (b) that the reason (or, if more than one, the principal reason) for which the employee was selected for dismissal was the one specified in the opening words of section 104F(1) and the condition in paragraph (a) or (b) of that subsection was met,
may apply to the tribunal for interim relief.]
(2) The tribunal shall not entertain an application for interim relief unless it is presented to the tribunal before the end of the period of seven days immediately following the effective date of termination (whether before, on or after that date).
(3) The tribunal shall determine the application for interim relief as soon as practicable after receiving the application.
(4) The tribunal shall give to the employer not later than seven days before the date of the hearing a copy of the application together with notice of the date, time and place of the hearing.
(5) The tribunal shall not exercise any power it has of postponing the hearing of an application for interim relief except where it is satisfied that special circumstances exist which justify it in doing so.

**NOTES**

Sub-s (1): substituted by the Employment Relations Act 1999 (Blacklists) Regulations 2010, SI 2010/493, reg 12(1), (8), as from 2 March 2010.

Conciliation; modification in relation to governing bodies with delegated budgets; application in relation to office holders within the meaning of the Ecclesiastical Offices (Terms of Service) Regulations 2009: see the notes following the Part heading *ante*.

**[1.938]**
**129 Procedure on hearing of application and making of order**
[(1)   This section applies where, on hearing an employee's application for interim relief, it appears to the tribunal that it is likely that on determining the complaint to which the application relates the tribunal will find—
(a)   that the reason (or if more than one the principal reason) for the dismissal is one of those specified in—
   (i)   section 100(1)(a) and (b), 101A(d), 102(1), 103 or 103A, or
   (ii)   paragraph 161(2) of Schedule A1 to the Trade Union and Labour Relations (Consolidation) Act 1992, or
(b)   that the reason (or, if more than one, the principal reason) for which the employee was selected for dismissal was the one specified in the opening words of section 104F(1) and the condition in paragraph (a) or (b) of that subsection was met.]
(2)   The tribunal shall announce its findings and explain to both parties (if present)—
(a)   what powers the tribunal may exercise on the application, and
(b)   in what circumstances it will exercise them.
(3)   The tribunal shall ask the employer (if present) whether he is willing, pending the determination or settlement of the complaint—
(a)   to reinstate the employee (that is, to treat him in all respects as if he had not been dismissed), or
(b)   if not, to re-engage him in another job on terms and conditions not less favourable than those which would have been applicable to him if he had not been dismissed.
(4)   For the purposes of subsection (3)(b) "terms and conditions not less favourable than those which would have been applicable to him if he had not been dismissed" means, as regards seniority, pension rights and other similar rights, that the period prior to the dismissal should be regarded as continuous with his employment following the dismissal.
(5)   If the employer states that he is willing to reinstate the employee, the tribunal shall make an order to that effect.
(6)   If the employer—
(a)   states that he is willing to re-engage the employee in another job, and
(b)   specifies the terms and conditions on which he is willing to do so,
the tribunal shall ask the employee whether he is willing to accept the job on those terms and conditions.
(7)   If the employee is willing to accept the job on those terms and conditions, the tribunal shall make an order to that effect.
(8)   If the employee is not willing to accept the job on those terms and conditions—
(a)   where the tribunal is of the opinion that the refusal is reasonable, the tribunal shall make an order for the continuation of his contract of employment, and
(b)   otherwise, the tribunal shall make no order.
(9)   If on the hearing of an application for interim relief the employer—
(a)   fails to attend before the tribunal, or
(b)   states that he is unwilling either to reinstate or re-engage the employee as mentioned in subsection (3),
the tribunal shall make an order for the continuation of the employee's contract of employment.

**NOTES**
Sub-s (1): substituted by the Employment Relations Act 1999 (Blacklists) Regulations 2010, SI 2010/493, reg 12(1), (9), as from 2 March 2010.

**[1.939]**
**130 Order for continuation of contract of employment**
(1)   An order under section 129 for the continuation of a contract of employment is an order that the contract of employment continue in force—
(a)   for the purposes of pay or any other benefit derived from the employment, seniority, pension rights and other similar matters, and
(b)   for the purposes of determining for any purpose the period for which the employee has been continuously employed,
from the date of its termination (whether before or after the making of the order) until the determination or settlement of the complaint.
(2)   Where the tribunal makes such an order it shall specify in the order the amount which is to be paid by the employer to the employee by way of pay in respect of each normal pay period, or part of any such period, falling between the date of dismissal and the determination or settlement of the complaint.
(3)   Subject to the following provisions, the amount so specified shall be that which the employee could reasonably have been expected to earn during that period, or part, and shall be paid—
(a)   in the case of a payment for any such period falling wholly or partly after the making of the order, on the normal pay day for that period, and

(b)　in the case of a payment for any past period, within such time as may be specified in the order.

(4)　If an amount is payable in respect only of part of a normal pay period, the amount shall be calculated by reference to the whole period and reduced proportionately.

(5)　Any payment made to an employee by an employer under his contract of employment, or by way of damages for breach of that contract, in respect of a normal pay period, or part of any such period, goes towards discharging the employer's liability in respect of that period under subsection (2); and, conversely, any payment under that subsection in respect of a period goes towards discharging any liability of the employer under, or in respect of breach of, the contract of employment in respect of that period.

(6)　If an employee, on or after being dismissed by his employer, receives a lump sum which, or part of which, is in lieu of wages but is not referable to any normal pay period, the tribunal shall take the payment into account in determining the amount of pay to be payable in pursuance of any such order.

(7)　For the purposes of this section, the amount which an employee could reasonably have been expected to earn, his normal pay period and the normal pay day for each such period shall be determined as if he had not been dismissed.

**[1.940]**
### 131　Application for variation or revocation of order
(1)　At any time between—
  (a)　the making of an order under section 129, and
  (b)　the determination or settlement of the complaint,
the employer or the employee may apply to an [employment tribunal] for the revocation or variation of the order on the ground of a relevant change of circumstances since the making of the order.

(2)　Sections 128 and 129 apply in relation to such an application as in relation to an original application for interim relief except that, in the case of an application by the employer, section 128(4) has effect with the substitution of a reference to the employee for the reference to the employer.

**NOTES**
Sub-s (1): words in square brackets substituted by the Employment Rights (Dispute Resolution) Act 1998, s 1(2)(a).

**[1.941]**
### 132　Consequence of failure to comply with order
(1)　If, on the application of an employee, an [employment tribunal] is satisfied that the employer has not complied with the terms of an order for the reinstatement or re-engagement of the employee under section 129(5) or (7), the tribunal shall—
  (a)　make an order for the continuation of the employee's contract of employment, and
  (b)　order the employer to pay compensation to the employee.

(2)　Compensation under subsection (1)(b) shall be of such amount as the tribunal considers just and equitable in all the circumstances having regard—
  (a)　to the infringement of the employee's right to be reinstated or re-engaged in pursuance of the order, and
  (b)　to any loss suffered by the employee in consequence of the non-compliance.

(3)　Section 130 applies to an order under subsection (1)(a) as in relation to an order under section 129.

(4)　If on the application of an employee an [employment tribunal] is satisfied that the employer has not complied with the terms of an order for the continuation of a contract of employment subsection (5) or (6) applies.

(5)　Where the non-compliance consists of a failure to pay an amount by way of pay specified in the order—
  (a)　the tribunal shall determine the amount owed by the employer on the date of the determination, and
  (b)　if on that date the tribunal also determines the employee's complaint that he has been unfairly dismissed, it shall specify that amount separately from any other sum awarded to the employee.

(6)　In any other case, the tribunal shall order the employer to pay the employee such compensation as the tribunal considers just and equitable in all the circumstances having regard to any loss suffered by the employee in consequence of the non-compliance.

**NOTES**
Sub-ss (1), (4): words in square brackets substituted by the Employment Rights (Dispute Resolution) Act 1998, s 1(2)(a).

## CHAPTER III
## SUPPLEMENTARY

**[1.942]**
### 133 Death of employer or employee

(1) Where—
  (a) an employer has given notice to an employee to terminate his contract of employment, and
  (b) before that termination the employee or the employer dies,
this Part applies as if the contract had been duly terminated by the employer by notice expiring on the date of the death.

(2) Where—
  (a) an employee's contract of employment has been terminated,
  (b) by virtue of subsection (2) or (4) of section 97 a date later than the effective date of termination as defined in subsection (1) of that section is to be treated for certain purposes as the effective date of termination, and
  (c) the employer or the employee dies before that date,
subsection (2) or (4) of section 97 applies as if the notice referred to in that subsection as required by section 86 expired on the date of the death.

(3) Where an employee has died, sections 113 to 116 do not apply; and, accordingly, if the [employment tribunal] finds that the grounds of the complaint are well-founded, the case shall be treated as falling within section 112(4) as a case in which no order is made under section 113.

(4) Subsection (3) does not prejudice an order for reinstatement or re-engagement made before the employee's death.

(5) Where an order for reinstatement or re-engagement has been made and the employee dies before the order is complied with—
  (a) if the employer has before the death refused to reinstate or re-engage the employee in accordance with the order, subsections (3) to (6) of section 117 apply, and an award shall be made under subsection (3)(b) of that section, unless the employer satisfies the tribunal that it was not practicable at the time of the refusal to comply with the order, and
  (b) if there has been no such refusal, subsections (1) and (2) of that section apply if the employer fails to comply with any ancillary terms of the order which remain capable of fulfilment after the employee's death as they would apply to such a failure to comply fully with the terms of an order where the employee had been reinstated or re-engaged.

**NOTES**

Sub-s (3): words in square brackets substituted by the Employment Rights (Dispute Resolution) Act 1998, s 1(2)(a).

**[1.943]**
### 134 Teachers in aided schools

(1) Where a teacher in [a foundation, voluntary aided or foundation special school is dismissed by the governing body of the school in pursuance of a requirement of the [local authority] under [paragraph 7 of Schedule 2 to the Education Act 2002]], this Part has effect in relation to the dismissal as if—
  (a) the [local authority] had at all material times been the teacher's employer,
  (b) the [local authority] had dismissed him, and
  (c) the reason or principal reason for which they did so had been the reason or principal reason for which they required his dismissal.

(2) For the purposes of a complaint under section 111 as it has effect by virtue of subsection (1)—
  (a) section 117(4)(a) applies as if for the words "not practicable to comply" there were substituted the words "not practicable for the [local authority] to permit compliance", and
  (b) section 123(5) applies as if the references in it to the employer were to the [local authority].
[(3) In this section "local authority" has the meaning given by section 579(1) of the Education Act 1996.]

**NOTES**

Sub-s (1): words in first (outer) pair of square brackets substituted by the School Standards and Framework Act 1998, s 140(1), Sch 30, para 55; words in third (inner) pair of square brackets substituted by the Education Act 2002, s 215(1), Sch 21, para 30; words "local authority" (in each place) substituted by the Local Education Authorities and Children's Services Authorities (Integration of Functions) Order 2010, SI 2010/1158, art 5, Sch 2, Pt 2, para 41(1), (3)(a), as from 5 May 2010.

Sub-s (2): words in square brackets substituted by SI 2010/1158, art 5(1), Sch 2, Pt 2, para 41(1), (3)(a), as from 5 May 2010.

Sub-s (3): added by SI 2010/1158, art 5, Sch 2, Pt 2, para 41(1), (3)(b), as from 5 May 2010.

Part 1 Statutes

**[1.944]**
**[134A Application to police**
(1) For the purposes of section 100, and of the other provisions of this Part so far as relating to the right not to be unfairly dismissed in a case where the dismissal is unfair by virtue of section 100, the holding, otherwise than under a contract of employment, of the office of constable or an appointment as police cadet shall be treated as employment by the relevant officer under a contract of employment.
[(2) In this section "the relevant officer", in relation to—
    (a)   a person holding the office of constable, or
    (b)   a person holding an appointment as a police cadet,
means the person who under section 51A of the Health and Safety at Work etc Act 1974 is to be treated as his employer for the purposes of Part 1 of that Act.]
[(3) Subsection (1) does not apply to the holding of the office of constable by a member of a police force on secondment to the *Serious Organised Crime Agency*.]]

**NOTES**
   Inserted by the Police (Health and Safety) Act 1997, s 4.
   Sub-s (2): substituted by the Serious Organised Crime and Police Act 2005, s 158(1), (2)(b), (3), (5).
   Sub-s (3): added by the Serious Organised Crime and Police Act 2005, s 59, Sch 4, paras 84, 87; for the words in italics there are substituted the words "National Crime Agency" by the Crime and Courts Act 2013, s 15(3), Sch 8, Pt 2, paras 49, 51, as from a day to be appointed.
   Note: this section was amended by the Police Reform Act 2002, s 95, as from a day to be appointed. Those amendments lapsed following the repeal of that section without being brought into force, by the Serious Organised Crime and Police Act 2005, ss 158(4)(a), 174(2), Sch 17, Pt 1.

## PART XI
## REDUNDANCY PAYMENTS ETC

### CHAPTER I
### RIGHT TO REDUNDANCY PAYMENT

**[1.945]**
**135 The right**
(1) An employer shall pay a redundancy payment to any employee of his if the employee—
    (a)   is dismissed by the employer by reason of redundancy, or
    (b)   is eligible for a redundancy payment by reason of being laid off or kept on short-time.
(2) Subsection (1) has effect subject to the following provisions of this Part (including, in particular, sections 140 to 144, 149 to 152, 155 to 161 and 164).

**NOTES**
   Conciliation: employment tribunal proceedings and claims which could be the subject of employment tribunal proceedings under this section are proceedings to which the Employment Tribunals Act 1996, s 18 applies; see s 18(1)(d) of that Act at **[1.706]**.
   Transfers of contracts of employment: the transfers of contracts of employment between certain bodies are not to be regarded as dismissals for the purposes of this Part; see the Enterprise Act 2002, s 13, Sch 3, Pt 2, para 15.

### CHAPTER II
### RIGHT ON DISMISSAL BY REASON OF REDUNDANCY
*Dismissal by reason of redundancy*

**[1.946]**
**136 Circumstances in which an employee is dismissed**
(1) Subject to the provisions of this section and sections 137 and 138, for the purposes of this Part an employee is dismissed by his employer if (and only if)—
    (a)   the contract under which he is employed by the employer is terminated by the employer (whether with or without notice),
    [(b)   he is employed under a limited term contract and that contract terminates by virtue of the limiting event without being renewed under the same contract, or]
    (c)   the employee terminates the contract under which he is employed (with or without notice) in circumstances in which he is entitled to terminate it without notice by reason of the employer's conduct.
(2) Subsection (1)(c) does not apply if the employee terminates the contract without notice in circumstances in which he is entitled to do so by reason of a lock-out by the employer.
(3) An employee shall be taken to be dismissed by his employer for the purposes of this Part if—
    (a)   the employer gives notice to the employee to terminate his contract of employment, and
    (b)   at a time within the obligatory period of notice the employee gives notice in writing to the employer to terminate the contract of employment on a date earlier than the date on which the employer's notice is due to expire.

(4)   In this Part the "obligatory period of notice", in relation to notice given by an employer to terminate an employee's contract of employment, means—
  (a)   the actual period of the notice in a case where the period beginning at the time when the notice is given and ending at the time when it expires is equal to the minimum period which (by virtue of any enactment or otherwise) is required to be given by the employer to terminate the contract of employment, and
  (b)   the period which—
      (i)    is equal to the minimum period referred to in paragraph (a), and
      (ii)   ends at the time when the notice expires,
    in any other case.
(5)   Where in accordance with any enactment or rule of law—
  (a)   an act on the part of an employer, or
  (b)   an event affecting an employer (including, in the case of an individual, his death),
operates to terminate a contract under which an employee is employed by him, the act or event shall be taken for the purposes of this Part to be a termination of the contract by the employer.

**NOTES**

Sub-s (1): para (b) substituted by the Fixed-term Employees (Prevention of Less Favourable Treatment) Regulations 2002, SI 2002/2034, reg 11, Sch 2, Pt 1, para 3(1), (13) (except in relation to Government training schemes, agency workers or apprentices; see regs 18–20 of the 2002 Regulations at **[2.614]** et seq).

**137**   *(Repealed by the Employment Relations Act 1999, ss 9, 44, Sch 4, Pt III, paras 1, 5, 25, Sch 9(2).)*

**[1.947]**
**138   No dismissal in cases of renewal of contract or re-engagement**
(1)   Where—
  (a)   an employee's contract of employment is renewed, or he is re-engaged under a new contract of employment in pursuance of an offer (whether in writing or not) made before the end of his employment under the previous contract, and
  (b)   the renewal or re-engagement takes effect either immediately on, or after an interval of not more than four weeks after, the end of that employment,
the employee shall not be regarded for the purposes of this Part as dismissed by his employer by reason of the ending of his employment under the previous contract.
(2)   Subsection (1) does not apply if—
  (a)   the provisions of the contract as renewed, or of the new contract, as to—
      (i)    the capacity and place in which the employee is employed, and
      (ii)   the other terms and conditions of his employment,
    differ (wholly or in part) from the corresponding provisions of the previous contract, and
  (b)   during the period specified in subsection (3)—
      (i)    the employee (for whatever reason) terminates the renewed or new contract, or gives notice to terminate it and it is in consequence terminated, or
      (ii)   the employer, for a reason connected with or arising out of any difference between the renewed or new contract and the previous contract, terminates the renewed or new contract, or gives notice to terminate it and it is in consequence terminated.
(3)   The period referred to in subsection (2)(b) is the period—
  (a)   beginning at the end of the employee's employment under the previous contract, and
  (b)   ending with—
      (i)    the period of four weeks beginning with the date on which the employee starts work under the renewed or new contract, or
      (ii)   such longer period as may be agreed in accordance with subsection (6) for the purpose of retraining the employee for employment under that contract;
and is in this Part referred to as the "trial period".
(4)   Where subsection (2) applies, for the purposes of this Part—
  (a)   the employee shall be regarded as dismissed on the date on which his employment under the previous contract (or, if there has been more than one trial period, the original contract) ended, and
  (b)   the reason for the dismissal shall be taken to be the reason for which the employee was then dismissed, or would have been dismissed had the offer (or original offer) of renewed or new employment not been made, or the reason which resulted in that offer being made.
(5)   Subsection (2) does not apply if the employee's contract of employment is again renewed, or he is again re-engaged under a new contract of employment, in circumstances such that subsection (1) again applies.
(6)   For the purposes of subsection (3)(b)(ii) a period of retraining is agreed in accordance with this subsection only if the agreement—
  (a)   is made between the employer and the employee or his representative before the employee starts work under the contract as renewed, or the new contract,
  (b)   is in writing,

(c)    specifies the date on which the period of retraining ends, and

(d)    specifies the terms and conditions of employment which will apply in the employee's case after the end of that period.

**[1.948]**
### 139  Redundancy

(1)  For the purposes of this Act an employee who is dismissed shall be taken to be dismissed by reason of redundancy if the dismissal is wholly or mainly attributable to—

(a)    the fact that his employer has ceased or intends to cease—

      (i)    to carry on the business for the purposes of which the employee was employed by him, or

      (ii)    to carry on that business in the place where the employee was so employed, or

(b)    the fact that the requirements of that business—

      (i)    for employees to carry out work of a particular kind, or

      (ii)    for employees to carry out work of a particular kind in the place where the employee was employed by the employer,

have ceased or diminished or are expected to cease or diminish.

(2)  For the purposes of subsection (1) the business of the employer together with the business or businesses of his associated employers shall be treated as one (unless either of the conditions specified in paragraphs (a) and (b) of that subsection would be satisfied without so treating them).

(3)  For the purposes of subsection (1) the activities carried on by a [local authority] with respect to the schools maintained by it, and the activities carried on by the [governing bodies] of those schools, shall be treated as one business (unless either of the conditions specified in paragraphs (a) and (b) of that subsection would be satisfied without so treating them).

(4)  Where—

(a)    the contract under which a person is employed is treated by section 136(5) as terminated by his employer by reason of an act or event, and

(b)    the employee's contract is not renewed and he is not re-engaged under a new contract of employment,

he shall be taken for the purposes of this Act to be dismissed by reason of redundancy if the circumstances in which his contract is not renewed, and he is not re-engaged, are wholly or mainly attributable to either of the facts stated in paragraphs (a) and (b) of subsection (1).

(5)  In its application to a case within subsection (4), paragraph (a)(i) of subsection (1) has effect as if the reference in that subsection to the employer included a reference to any person to whom, in consequence of the act or event, power to dispose of the business has passed.

(6)  In subsection (1) "cease" and "diminish" mean cease and diminish either permanently or temporarily and for whatever reason.

[(7)  In subsection (3) "local authority" has the meaning given by section 579(1) of the Education Act 1996.]

---

**NOTES**

Sub-s (3): words in first pair of square brackets substituted by the Local Education Authorities and Children's Services Authorities (Integration of Functions) Order 2010, SI 2010/1158, art 5, Sch 2, Pt 2, para 41(1), (4)(a), as from 5 May 2010; words in second pair of square brackets substituted by the Education Act 2002, s 215(1), Sch 21, para 31.

Sub-s (7): added by SI 2010/1158, art 5, Sch 2, Pt 2, para 41(1), (4)(b), as from 5 May 2010.

---

*Exclusions*

**[1.949]**
### 140  Summary dismissal

(1)  Subject to subsections (2) and (3), an employee is not entitled to a redundancy payment by reason of dismissal where his employer, being entitled to terminate his contract of employment without notice by reason of the employee's conduct, terminates it either—

(a)    without notice,

(b)    by giving shorter notice than that which, in the absence of conduct entitling the employer to terminate the contract without notice, the employer would be required to give to terminate the contract, or

(c)    by giving notice which includes, or is accompanied by, a statement in writing that the employer would, by reason of the employee's conduct, be entitled to terminate the contract without notice.

(2)  Where an employee who—

(a)    has been given notice by his employer to terminate his contract of employment, or

(b)    has given notice to his employer under section 148(1) indicating his intention to claim a redundancy payment in respect of lay-off or short-time,

takes part in a strike at any relevant time in circumstances which entitle the employer to treat the contract of employment as terminable without notice, subsection (1) does not apply if the employer terminates the contract by reason of his taking part in the strike.

(3)  Where the contract of employment of an employee who—

(a)    has been given notice by his employer to terminate his contract of employment, or

(b)  has given notice to his employer under section 148(1) indicating his intention to claim a redundancy payment in respect of lay-off or short-time,

is terminated as mentioned in subsection (1) at any relevant time otherwise than by reason of his taking part in a strike, an [employment tribunal] may determine that the employer is liable to make an appropriate payment to the employee if on a reference to the tribunal it appears to the tribunal, in the circumstances of the case, to be just and equitable that the employee should receive it.

(4)  In subsection (3) "appropriate payment" means—
  (a)  the whole of the redundancy payment to which the employee would have been entitled apart from subsection (1), or
  (b)  such part of that redundancy payment as the tribunal thinks fit.

(5)  In this section "relevant time"—
  (a)  in the case of an employee who has been given notice by his employer to terminate his contract of employment, means any time within the obligatory period of notice, and
  (b)  in the case of an employee who has given notice to his employer under section 148(1), means any time after the service of the notice.

---

**NOTES**

Sub-s (3): words in square brackets substituted by the Employment Rights (Dispute Resolution) Act 1998, s 1(2)(a).

---

**[1.950]**
**141  Renewal of contract or re-engagement**
(1)  This section applies where an offer (whether in writing or not) is made to an employee before the end of his employment—
  (a)  to renew his contract of employment, or
  (b)  to re-engage him under a new contract of employment,
with renewal or re-engagement to take effect either immediately on, or after an interval of not more than four weeks after, the end of his employment.

(2)  Where subsection (3) is satisfied, the employee is not entitled to a redundancy payment if he unreasonably refuses the offer.

(3)  This subsection is satisfied where—
  (a)  the provisions of the contract as renewed, or of the new contract, as to—
    (i)   the capacity and place in which the employee would be employed, and
    (ii)  the other terms and conditions of his employment,
    would not differ from the corresponding provisions of the previous contract, or
  (b)  those provisions of the contract as renewed, or of the new contract, would differ from the corresponding provisions of the previous contract but the offer constitutes an offer of suitable employment in relation to the employee.

(4)  The employee is not entitled to a redundancy payment if—
  (a)  his contract of employment is renewed, or he is re-engaged under a new contract of employment, in pursuance of the offer,
  (b)  the provisions of the contract as renewed or new contract as to the capacity or place in which he is employed or the other terms and conditions of his employment differ (wholly or in part) from the corresponding provisions of the previous contract,
  (c)  the employment is suitable in relation to him, and
  (d)  during the trial period he unreasonably terminates the contract, or unreasonably gives notice to terminate it and it is in consequence terminated.

**[1.951]**
**142  Employee anticipating expiry of employer's notice**
(1)  Subject to subsection (3), an employee is not entitled to a redundancy payment where—
  (a)  he is taken to be dismissed by virtue of section 136(3) by reason of giving to his employer notice terminating his contract of employment on a date earlier than the date on which notice by the employer terminating the contract is due to expire,
  (b)  before the employee's notice is due to expire, the employer gives him a notice such as is specified in subsection (2), and
  (c)  the employee does not comply with the requirements of that notice.

(2)  The employer's notice referred to in subsection (1)(b) is a notice in writing—
  (a)  requiring the employee to withdraw his notice terminating the contract of employment and to continue in employment until the date on which the employer's notice terminating the contract expires, and
  (b)  stating that, unless he does so, the employer will contest any liability to pay to him a redundancy payment in respect of the termination of his contract of employment.

(3)  An [employment tribunal] may determine that the employer is liable to make an appropriate payment to the employee if on a reference to the tribunal it appears to the tribunal, having regard to—
  (a)  the reasons for which the employee seeks to leave the employment, and
  (b)  the reasons for which the employer requires him to continue in it,
to be just and equitable that the employee should receive the payment.

(4) In subsection (3) "appropriate payment" means—

 (a) the whole of the redundancy payment to which the employee would have been entitled apart from subsection (1), or

 (b) such part of that redundancy payment as the tribunal thinks fit.

**NOTES**

 Sub-s (3): words in square brackets substituted by the Employment Rights (Dispute Resolution) Act 1998, s 1(2)(a).

**[1.952]**
### 143 Strike during currency of employer's notice

(1) This section applies where—

 (a) an employer has given notice to an employee to terminate his contract of employment ("notice of termination"),

 (b) after the notice is given the employee begins to take part in a strike of employees of the employer, and

 (c) the employer serves on the employee a notice of extension.

(2) A notice of extension is a notice in writing which—

 (a) requests the employee to agree to extend the contract of employment beyond the time of expiry by a period comprising as many available days as the number of working days lost by striking ("the proposed period of extension"),

 (b) indicates the reasons for which the employer makes that request, and

 (c) states that the employer will contest any liability to pay the employee a redundancy payment in respect of the dismissal effected by the notice of termination unless either—

  (i) the employee complies with the request, or

  (ii) the employer is satisfied that, in consequence of sickness or injury or otherwise, the employee is unable to comply with it or that (even though he is able to comply with it) it is reasonable in the circumstances for him not to do so.

(3) Subject to subsections (4) and (5), if the employee does not comply with the request contained in the notice of extension, he is not entitled to a redundancy payment by reason of the dismissal effected by the notice of termination.

(4) Subsection (3) does not apply if the employer agrees to pay a redundancy payment to the employee in respect of the dismissal effected by the notice of termination even though he has not complied with the request contained in the notice of extension.

(5) An [employment tribunal] may determine that the employer is liable to make an appropriate payment to the employee if on a reference to the tribunal it appears to the tribunal that—

 (a) the employee has not complied with the request contained in the notice of extension and the employer has not agreed to pay a redundancy payment in respect of the dismissal effected by the notice of termination, but

 (b) either the employee was unable to comply with the request or it was reasonable in the circumstances for him not to comply with it.

(6) In subsection (5) "appropriate payment" means—

 (a) the whole of the redundancy payment to which the employee would have been entitled apart from subsection (3), or

 (b) such part of that redundancy payment as the tribunal thinks fit.

(7) If the employee—

 (a) complies with the request contained in the notice of extension, or

 (b) does not comply with it but attends at his proper or usual place of work and is ready and willing to work on one or more (but not all) of the available days within the proposed period of extension,

the notice of termination has effect, and shall be deemed at all material times to have had effect, as if the period specified in it had been appropriately extended; and sections 87 to 91 accordingly apply as if the period of notice required by section 86 were extended to a corresponding extent.

(8) In subsection (7) "appropriately extended" means—

 (a) in a case within paragraph (a) of that subsection, extended beyond the time of expiry by an additional period equal to the proposed period of extension, and

 (b) in a case within paragraph (b) of that subsection, extended beyond the time of expiry up to the end of the day (or last of the days) on which he attends at his proper or usual place of work and is ready and willing to work.

**NOTES**

 Sub-s (5): words in square brackets substituted by the Employment Rights (Dispute Resolution) Act 1998, s 1(2)(a).

**[1.953]**
### 144 Provisions supplementary to section 143

(1) For the purposes of section 143 an employee complies with the request contained in a notice of extension if, but only if, on each available day within the proposed period of extension, he—

 (a) attends at his proper or usual place of work, and

 (b) is ready and willing to work,

whether or not he has signified his agreement to the request in any other way.

(2) The reference in section 143(2) to the number of working days lost by striking is a reference to the number of working days in the period—

(a) beginning with the date of service of the notice of termination, and

(b) ending with the time of expiry,

which are days on which the employee in question takes part in a strike of employees of his employer.

(3) In section 143 and this section—

"available day", in relation to an employee, means a working day beginning at or after the time of expiry which is a day on which he is not taking part in a strike of employees of the employer,

"available day within the proposed period of extension" means an available day which begins before the end of the proposed period of extension,

"time of expiry", in relation to a notice of termination, means the time at which the notice would expire apart from section 143, and

"working day", in relation to an employee, means a day on which, in accordance with his contract of employment, he is normally required to work.

(4) Neither the service of a notice of extension nor any extension by virtue of section 143(7) of the period specified in a notice of termination affects—

(a) any right either of the employer or of the employee to terminate the contract of employment (whether before, at or after the time of expiry) by a further notice or without notice, or

(b) the operation of this Part in relation to any such termination of the contract of employment.

*Supplementary*

**[1.954]**
**145 The relevant date**

(1) For the purposes of the provisions of this Act relating to redundancy payments "the relevant date" in relation to the dismissal of an employee has the meaning given by this section.

(2) Subject to the following provisions of this section, "the relevant date"—

(a) in relation to an employee whose contract of employment is terminated by notice, whether given by his employer or by the employee, means the date on which the notice expires,

(b) in relation to an employee whose contract of employment is terminated without notice, means the date on which the termination takes effect, and

[(c) in relation to an employee who is employed under a limited-term contract which terminates by virtue of the limiting event without being renewed under the same contract, means the date on which the termination takes effect].

(3) Where the employee is taken to be dismissed by virtue of section 136(3) the "relevant date" means the date on which the employee's notice to terminate his contract of employment expires.

(4) Where the employee is regarded by virtue of section 138(4) as having been dismissed on the date on which his employment under an earlier contract ended, "the relevant date" means—

(a) for the purposes of section 164(1), the date which is the relevant date as defined by subsection (2) in relation to the renewed or new contract or, where there has been more than one trial period, the last such contract, and

(b) for the purposes of any other provision, the date which is the relevant date as defined by subsection (2) in relation to the previous contract or, where there has been more than one such trial period, the original contract.

(5) Where—

(a) the contract of employment is terminated by the employer, and

(b) the notice required by section 86 to be given by an employer would, if duly given on the material date, expire on a date later than the relevant date (as defined by the previous provisions of this section),

for the purposes of sections 155, 162(1) and 227(3) the later date is the relevant date.

(6) In subsection (5)(b) "the material date" means—

(a) the date when notice of termination was given by the employer, or

(b) where no notice was given, the date when the contract of employment was terminated by the employer.

(7) . . .

**NOTES**

Sub-s (2): para (c) substituted by the Fixed-term Employees (Prevention of Less Favourable Treatment) Regulations 2002, SI 2002/2034, reg 11, Sch 2, Pt 1, para 3(1), (14) (except in relation to Government training schemes, agency workers or apprentices; see regs 18–20 of the 2002 Regulations at **[2.614]** et seq).

Sub-s (7): repealed by the Employment Relations Act 1999, ss 9, 44, Sch 4, Pt III, paras 1, 5, 26, Sch 9(2).

**[1.955]**
**146 Provisions supplementing sections 138 and 141**

(1) In sections 138 and 141—

(a)  references to re-engagement are to re-engagement by the employer or an associated employer, and

(b)  references to an offer are to an offer made by the employer or an associated employer.

(2)  For the purposes of the application of section 138(1) or 141(1) to a contract under which the employment ends on a Friday, Saturday or Sunday—

(a)  the renewal or re-engagement shall be treated as taking effect immediately on the ending of the employment under the previous contract if it takes effect on or before the next Monday after that Friday, Saturday or Sunday, and

(b)  the interval of four weeks to which those provisions refer shall be calculated as if the employment had ended on that next Monday.

(3)  . . .

**NOTES**

Sub-s (3): repealed by the Employment Relations Act 1999, ss 9, 44, Sch 4, Pt III, paras 1, 5, 27, Sch 9(2).

Modification: this section, and ss 155 and 162, are modified in relation to any person to whom the Redundancy Payments (Continuity of Employment in Local Government, etc) (Modification) Order 1999, SI 1999/2277 applies for the purposes of determining that person's entitlement to a redundancy payment under the this Act and the amount of such payment; see arts 2, 3 of, and Sch 2, Pt I to, the 1999 Order at **[2.447]**, **[2.448]**, **[2.452]**.

## CHAPTER III
## RIGHT BY REASON OF LAY-OFF OR SHORT-TIME

*Lay-off and short-time*

**[1.956]**
**147  Meaning of "lay-off" and "short-time"**

(1)  For the purposes of this Part an employee shall be taken to be laid off for a week if—

(a)  he is employed under a contract on terms and conditions such that his remuneration under the contract depends on his being provided by the employer with work of the kind which he is employed to do, but

(b)  he is not entitled to any remuneration under the contract in respect of the week because the employer does not provide such work for him.

(2)  For the purposes of this Part an employee shall be taken to be kept on short-time for a week if by reason of a diminution in the work provided for the employee by his employer (being work of a kind which under his contract the employee is employed to do) the employee's remuneration for the week is less than half a week's pay.

**[1.957]**
**148  Eligibility by reason of lay-off or short-time**

(1)  Subject to the following provisions of this Part, for the purposes of this Part an employee is eligible for a redundancy payment by reason of being laid off or kept on short-time if—

(a)  he gives notice in writing to his employer indicating (in whatever terms) his intention to claim a redundancy payment in respect of lay-off or short-time (referred to in this Part as "notice of intention to claim"), and

(b)  before the service of the notice he has been laid off or kept on short-time in circumstances in which subsection (2) applies.

(2)  This subsection applies if the employee has been laid off or kept on short-time—

(a)  for four or more consecutive weeks of which the last before the service of the notice ended on, or not more than four weeks before, the date of service of the notice, or

(b)  for a series of six or more weeks (of which not more than three were consecutive) within a period of thirteen weeks, where the last week of the series before the service of the notice ended on, or not more than four weeks before, the date of service of the notice.

*Exclusions*

**[1.958]**
**149  Counter-notices**

Where an employee gives to his employer notice of intention to claim but—

(a)  the employer gives to the employee, within seven days after the service of that notice, notice in writing (referred to in this Part as a "counter-notice") that he will contest any liability to pay to the employee a redundancy payment in pursuance of the employee's notice, and

(b)  the employer does not withdraw the counter-notice by a subsequent notice in writing,

the employee is not entitled to a redundancy payment in pursuance of his notice of intention to claim except in accordance with a decision of an [employment tribunal].

**NOTES**

Words in square brackets substituted by the Employment Rights (Dispute Resolution) Act 1998, s 1(2)(a).

**[1.959]**
**150 Resignation**
(1) An employee is not entitled to a redundancy payment by reason of being laid off or kept on short-time unless he terminates his contract of employment by giving such period of notice as is required for the purposes of this section before the end of the relevant period.
(2) The period of notice required for the purposes of this section—
  (a) where the employee is required by his contract of employment to give more than one week's notice to terminate the contract, is the minimum period which he is required to give, and
  (b) otherwise, is one week.
(3) In subsection (1) "the relevant period"—
  (a) if the employer does not give a counter-notice within seven days after the service of the notice of intention to claim, is three weeks after the end of those seven days,
  (b) if the employer gives a counter-notice within that period of seven days but withdraws it by a subsequent notice in writing, is three weeks after the service of the notice of withdrawal, and
  (c) if—
    (i) the employer gives a counter-notice within that period of seven days, and does not so withdraw it, and
    (ii) a question as to the right of the employee to a redundancy payment in pursuance of the notice of intention to claim is referred to an [employment tribunal],
  is three weeks after the tribunal has notified to the employee its decision on that reference.
(4) For the purposes of subsection (3)(c) no account shall be taken of—
  (a) any appeal against the decision of the tribunal, or
  (b) any proceedings or decision in consequence of any such appeal.

**NOTES**
Sub-s (3): words in square brackets substituted by the Employment Rights (Dispute Resolution) Act 1998, s 1(2)(a).

**[1.960]**
**151 Dismissal**
(1) An employee is not entitled to a redundancy payment by reason of being laid off or kept on short-time if he is dismissed by his employer.
(2) Subsection (1) does not prejudice any right of the employee to a redundancy payment in respect of the dismissal.

**[1.961]**
**152 Likelihood of full employment**
(1) An employee is not entitled to a redundancy payment in pursuance of a notice of intention to claim if—
  (a) on the date of service of the notice it was reasonably to be expected that the employee (if he continued to be employed by the same employer) would, not later than four weeks after that date, enter on a period of employment of not less than thirteen weeks during which he would not be laid off or kept on short-time for any week, and
  (b) the employer gives a counter-notice to the employee within seven days after the service of the notice of intention to claim.
(2) Subsection (1) does not apply where the employee—
  (a) continues or has continued, during the next four weeks after the date of service of the notice of intention to claim, to be employed by the same employer, and
  (b) is or has been laid off or kept on short-time for each of those weeks.

*Supplementary*

**[1.962]**
**153 The relevant date**
For the purposes of the provisions of this Act relating to redundancy payments "the relevant date" in relation to a notice of intention to claim or a right to a redundancy payment in pursuance of such a notice—
  (a) in a case falling within paragraph (a) of subsection (2) of section 148, means the date on which of the last of the four or more consecutive weeks before the service of the notice came to an end, and
  (b) in a case falling within paragraph (b) of that subsection, means the date on which the last of the series of six or more weeks before the service of the notice came to an end.

Part 1 Statutes

**[1.963]**
**154 Provisions supplementing sections 148 and 152**
For the purposes of sections 148(2) and 152(2)—
  (a)  it is immaterial whether a series of weeks consists wholly of weeks for which the employee is laid off or wholly of weeks for which he is kept on short-time or partly of the one and partly of the other, and
  (b)  no account shall be taken of any week for which an employee is laid off or kept on short-time where the lay-off or short-time is wholly or mainly attributable to a strike or a lock-out (whether or not in the trade or industry in which the employee is employed and whether in Great Britain or elsewhere).

CHAPTER IV
GENERAL EXCLUSIONS FROM RIGHT

**[1.964]**
**155 Qualifying period of employment**
An employee does not have any right to a redundancy payment unless he has been continuously employed for a period of not less than two years ending with the relevant date.

NOTES
  Modified as noted to s 146 at **[1.955]**.

**156**  *(Repealed by the Employment Equality (Age) Regulations 2006, SI 2006/1031, reg 49(1), Sch 8, Pt 1, paras 21, 30, 33.)*

**[1.965]**
**157 Exemption orders**
(1)  Where an order under this section is in force in respect of an agreement covered by this section, an employee who, immediately before the relevant date, is an employee to whom the agreement applies does not have any right to a redundancy payment.
(2)  An agreement is covered by this section if it is an agreement between—
  (a)  one or more employers or organisations of employers, and
  (b)  one or more trade unions representing employees,
under which employees to whom the agreement applies have a right in certain circumstances to payments on the termination of their contracts of employment.
(3)  Where, on the application of all the parties to an agreement covered by this section, the Secretary of State is satisfied, having regard to the provisions of the agreement, that the employees to whom the agreement applies should not have any right to a redundancy payment, he may make an order under this section in respect of the agreement.
(4)  The Secretary of State shall not make an order under this section in respect of an agreement unless the agreement indicates (in whatever terms) the willingness of the parties to it to submit to an [employment tribunal] any question arising under the agreement as to—
  (a)  the right of an employee to a payment on the termination of his employment, or
  (b)  the amount of such a payment.
(5)  An order revoking an earlier order under this section may be made in pursuance of an application by all or any of the parties to the agreement in question or in the absence of such an application.
(6)  . . .

NOTES
  Sub-s (4): words in square brackets substituted by the Employment Rights (Dispute Resolution) Act 1998, s 1(2)(a).
  Sub-s (6): repealed by the Employment Relations Act 1999, ss 9, 44, Sch 4, Pt III, paras 1, 5, 29, Sch 9(2).
  Orders: as of 6 April 2013 no Orders had been made under this section but, by virtue of s 241 of, and Sch 2, Pt I, paras 1–4 to, this Act, the Redundancy Payments (Exemption) (No 1) Order 1969, SI 1969/207, the Redundancy Payments (Exemption) (No 1) Order 1970, SI 1970/354, and the Redundancy Payments (Exemption) Order 1980, SI 1980/1052, have effect as if made under this section.

**158**  *(Repealed by the Employment Equality (Age) Regulations 2006, SI 2006/1031, reg 49(1), Sch 8, Pt 1, paras 21, 31, 33.)*

**[1.966]**
**159 Public offices etc**
A person does not have any right to a redundancy payment in respect of any employment which—
- (a) is employment in a public office within the meaning of section 39 of the Superannuation Act 1965, or
- (b) is for the purposes of pensions and other superannuation benefits treated (whether by virtue of that Act or otherwise) as service in the civil service of the State.

**[1.967]**
**160 Overseas government employment**
(1) A person does not have any right to a redundancy payment in respect of employment in any capacity under the Government of an overseas territory.
(2) The reference in subsection (1) to the Government of an overseas territory includes a reference to—
- (a) a Government constituted for two or more overseas territories, and
- (b) any authority established for the purpose of providing or administering services which are common to, or relate to matters of common interest to, two or more overseas territories.
(3) In this section references to an overseas territory are to any territory or country outside the United Kingdom.

**[1.968]**
**161 Domestic servants**
(1) A person does not have any right to a redundancy payment in respect of employment as a domestic servant in a private household where the employer is the parent (or step-parent), grandparent, child (or step-child), grandchild or brother or sister (or half-brother or half-sister) of the employee.
(2) Subject to that, the provisions of this Part apply to an employee who is employed as a domestic servant in a private household as if—
- (a) the household were a business, and
- (b) the maintenance of the household were the carrying on of that business by the employer.

**NOTES**
Step-parent; step-child: references to a step-parent or step-child include relationships arising through civil partnership; see the Civil Partnership Act 2004, ss 246, 247, Sch 21, para 42.

CHAPTER V
OTHER PROVISIONS ABOUT REDUNDANCY PAYMENTS

**[1.969]**
**162 Amount of a redundancy payment**
(1) The amount of a redundancy payment shall be calculated by—
- (a) determining the period, ending with the relevant date, during which the employee has been continuously employed,
- (b) reckoning backwards from the end of that period the number of years of employment falling within that period, and
- (c) allowing the appropriate amount for each of those years of employment.
(2) In subsection (1)(c) "the appropriate amount" means—
- (a) one and a half weeks' pay for a year of employment in which the employee was not below the age of forty-one,
- (b) one week's pay for a year of employment (not within paragraph (a)) in which he was not below the age of twenty-two, and
- (c) half a week's pay for each year of employment not within paragraph (a) or (b).
(3) Where twenty years of employment have been reckoned under subsection (1), no account shall be taken under that subsection of any year of employment earlier than those twenty years.
(4), (5) . . .
(6) [Subsections (1) to (3)] apply for the purposes of any provision of this Part by virtue of which an [employment tribunal] may determine that an employer is liable to pay to an employee—
- (a) the whole of the redundancy payment to which the employee would have had a right apart from some other provision, or
- (b) such part of the redundancy payment to which the employee would have had a right apart from some other provision as the tribunal thinks fit,
as if any reference to the amount of a redundancy payment were to the amount of the redundancy payment to which the employee would have been entitled apart from that other provision.
(7), (8) . . .

**NOTES**
Sub-ss (4), (5), (8): repealed by the Employment Equality (Age) Regulations 2006, SI 2006/1031, reg 49(1), Sch 8, Pt 1, paras 21, 32(1), (2), 33.

Sub-s (6): words in first pair of square brackets substituted by SI 2006/1031, reg 49(1), Sch 8, Pt 1, paras 21, 32(1), (3); words in second pair of square brackets substituted by the Employment Rights (Dispute Resolution) Act 1998, s 1(2)(a).

Sub-s (7): repealed by the Employment Relations Act 1999, ss 9, 44, Sch 4, Pt III, paras 1, 5, 30, Sch 9(2).

Modified as noted to s 146 at **[1.955]**.

**[1.970]**

**163 References to [employment tribunals]**

(1)  Any question arising under this Part as to—

(a)  the right of an employee to a redundancy payment, or

(b)  the amount of a redundancy payment,

shall be referred to and determined by an [employment tribunal].

(2)  For the purposes of any such reference, an employee who has been dismissed by his employer shall, unless the contrary is proved, be presumed to have been so dismissed by reason of redundancy.

(3)  Any question whether an employee will become entitled to a redundancy payment if he is not dismissed by his employer and he terminates his contract of employment as mentioned in section 150(1) shall for the purposes of this Part be taken to be a question as to the right of the employee to a redundancy payment.

(4)  Where an order under section 157 is in force in respect of an agreement, this section has effect in relation to any question arising under the agreement as to the right of an employee to a payment on the termination of his employment, or as to the amount of such a payment, as if the payment were a redundancy payment and the question arose under this Part.

[(5)  Where a tribunal determines under subsection (1) that an employee has a right to a redundancy payment it may order the employer to pay to the worker such amount as the tribunal considers appropriate in all the circumstances to compensate the worker for any financial loss sustained by him which is attributable to the non-payment of the redundancy payment.]

**NOTES**

Section heading, sub-s (1): words in square brackets substituted by the Employment Rights (Dispute Resolution) Act 1998, s 1(2)(a), (b).

Sub-s (5): added by the Employment Act 2008, s 7(2), as from 6 April 2009, except where the complaint has been presented to the employment tribunal before that date (see SI 2008/3232, Schedule, Pt 1, para 5).

Tribunal jurisdiction: the Employment Act 2002, s 38 applies to proceedings before the employment tribunal relating to a claim under this section; see s 38(1) of, and Sch 5 to, the 2002 Act at **[1.1228]**, **[1.1236]**. See also the Trade Union and Labour Relations (Consolidation) Act 1992, s 207A at **[1.474]** (as inserted by the Employment Act 2008). That section provides that in proceedings before an employment tribunal relating to a claim by an employee under any of the jurisdictions listed in Sch A2 to the 1992 Act at **[1.648]** (which includes this section) the tribunal may adjust any award given if the employer or the employee has unreasonably failed to comply with the relevant Code of Practice as defined by s 207A(4). See also the revised Acas Code of Practice 1 – Disciplinary and Grievance Procedures (2009) at **[4.1]**.

**[1.971]**

**164 Claims for redundancy payment**

(1)  An employee does not have any right to a redundancy payment unless, before the end of the period of six months beginning with the relevant date—

(a)  the payment has been agreed and paid,

(b)  the employee has made a claim for the payment by notice in writing given to the employer,

(c)  a question as to the employee's right to, or the amount of, the payment has been referred to an [employment tribunal], or

(d)  a complaint relating to his dismissal has been presented by the employee under section 111.

(2)  An employee is not deprived of his right to a redundancy payment by subsection (1) if, during the period of six months immediately following the period mentioned in that subsection, the employee—

(a)  makes a claim for the payment by notice in writing given to the employer,

(b)  refers to an [employment tribunal] a question as to his right to, or the amount of, the payment, or

(c)  presents a complaint relating to his dismissal under section 111,

and it appears to the tribunal to be just and equitable that the employee should receive a redundancy payment.

(3)  In determining under subsection (2) whether it is just and equitable that an employee should receive a redundancy payment an [employment tribunal] shall have regard to—

(a)  the reason shown by the employee for his failure to take any such step as is referred to in subsection (2) within the period mentioned in subsection (1), and

(b)  all the other relevant circumstances.

[(4)  Subsections (1)(c) and (2) are subject to section 207A (extension because of mediation in certain European cross-border disputes).]

[(5)  Section 207B (extension of time limits to facilitate conciliation before institution of proceedings) applies for the purposes of subsections (1)(c) and (2).]

**[1.972]**
**165   Written particulars of redundancy payment**
(1)   On making any redundancy payment, otherwise than in pursuance of a decision of a tribunal which specifies the amount of the payment to be made, the employer shall give to the employee a written statement indicating how the amount of the payment has been calculated.
(2)   An employer who without reasonable excuse fails to comply with subsection (1) is guilty of an offence and liable on summary conviction to a fine not exceeding level 1 on the standard scale.
(3)   If an employer fails to comply with the requirements of subsection (1), the employee may by notice in writing to the employer require him to give to the employee a written statement complying with those requirements within such period (not being less than one week beginning with the day on which the notice is given) as may be specified in the notice.
(4)   An employer who without reasonable excuse fails to comply with a notice under subsection (3) is guilty of an offence and liable on summary conviction to a fine not exceeding level 3 on the standard scale.

## CHAPTER VI
## PAYMENTS BY SECRETARY OF STATE

**[1.973]**
**166   Applications for payments**
(1)   Where an employee claims that his employer is liable to pay to him an employer's payment and either—
    (a)   that the employee has taken all reasonable steps, other than legal proceedings, to recover the payment from the employer and the employer has refused or failed to pay it, or has paid part of it and has refused or failed to pay the balance, or
    (b)   that the employer is insolvent and the whole or part of the payment remains unpaid,
the employee may apply to the Secretary of State for a payment under this section.
(2)   In this Part "employer's payment", in relation to an employee, means—
    (a)   a redundancy payment which his employer is liable to pay to him under this Part,  . . .
    [(aa) a payment which his employer is liable to make to him under an agreement to refrain from instituting or continuing proceedings for a contravention or alleged contravention of section 135 which has effect by virtue of section 203(2)(e) or (f), or]
    (b)   a payment which his employer is, under an agreement in respect of which an order is in force under section 157, liable to make to him on the termination of his contract of employment.
(3)   In relation to any case where (in accordance with any provision of this Part) an [employment tribunal] determines that an employer is liable to pay part (but not the whole) of a redundancy payment the reference in subsection (2)(a) to a redundancy payment is to the part of the redundancy payment.
(4)   In subsection (1)(a) "legal proceedings"—
    (a)   does not include any proceedings before an [employment tribunal], but
    (b)   includes any proceedings to enforce a decision or award of an [employment tribunal].
(5)   An employer is insolvent for the purposes of subsection (1)(b)—
    (a)   where the employer is an individual, if (but only if) subsection (6) is satisfied,  . . .
    (b)   where the employer is a company, if (but only if) subsection (7) is satisfied [, and
    (c)   where the employer is a limited liability partnership, if (but only if) subsection (8) is satisfied.]
(6)   This subsection is satisfied in the case of an employer who is an individual—
    (a)   in England and Wales if—
       (i)   he has been adjudged bankrupt or has made a composition or arrangement with his creditors, or
       (ii)  he has died and his estate falls to be administered in accordance with an order under section 421 of the Insolvency Act 1986, and
    (b)   in Scotland if—
       (i)   sequestration of his estate has been awarded or he has executed a trust deed for his creditors or has entered into a composition contract, or
       (ii)  he has died and a judicial factor appointed under section 11A of the Judicial Factors (Scotland) Act 1889 is required by that section to divide his insolvent estate among his creditors.
(7)   This subsection is satisfied in the case of an employer which is a company—

   (a)   if a winding up order  . . .  has been made, or a resolution for voluntary winding up has been passed, with respect to the company,

[(aa) if the company is in administration for the purposes of the Insolvency Act 1986,]

   (b)   if a receiver or (in England and Wales only) a manager of the company's undertaking has been duly appointed, or (in England and Wales only) possession has been taken, by or on behalf of the holders of any debentures secured by a floating charge, of any property of the company comprised in or subject to the charge, or

   (c)   if a voluntary arrangement proposed in the case of the company for the purposes of Part I of the Insolvency Act 1986 has been approved under that Part of that Act.

[(8)  This subsection is satisfied in the case of an employer which is a limited liability partnership—

   (a)   if a winding-up order, an administration order or a determination for a voluntary winding-up has been made with respect to the limited liability partnership,

   (b)   if a receiver or (in England and Wales only) a manager of the undertaking of the limited liability partnership has been duly appointed, or (in England and Wales only) possession has been taken, by or on behalf of the holders of any debentures secured by a floating charge, of any property of the limited liability partnership comprised in or subject to the charge, or

   (c)   if a voluntary arrangement proposed in the case of the limited liability partnership for the purpose of Part I of the Insolvency Act 1986 has been approved under that Part of that Act.]

[(9)  In this section—

   (a)   references to a company are to be read as including references to a charitable incorporated organisation, and

   (b)   any reference to the Insolvency Act 1986 in relation to a company is to be read as including a reference to that Act as it applies to charitable incorporated organisations.]

**NOTES**

   Sub-s (2): word omitted from para (a) repealed, and para (aa) inserted, by the Employment Rights (Dispute Resolution) Act 1998, ss 11(2), 15, Sch 2.

   Sub-ss (3), (4): words in square brackets substituted by the Employment Rights (Dispute Resolution) Act 1998, s 1(2)(a).

   Sub-s (5): word omitted from para (a) repealed, and para (c) and word immediately preceding it added, by the Limited Liability Partnerships Regulations 2001, SI 2001/1090, reg 9, Sch 5, para 18(1), (2).

   Sub-s (7): words omitted from para (a) repealed, and para (aa) inserted, by the Enterprise Act 2002, ss 248(3), 278(2), Sch 17, para 49(1), (2), Sch 26, except in relation to cases where a petition for an administration order was presented before 15 September 2003, and subject to savings in relation to special administration regimes (within the meaning of s 249 of the 2002 Act).

   Sub-s (8): added by SI 2001/1090, reg 9, Sch 5, para 18(1), (3).

   Sub-s (9): added by the Charitable Incorporated Organisations (Consequential Amendments) Order 2012, SI 2012/3014, art 3, as from 2 January 2013.

**[1.974]**
**167  Making of payments**

(1)  Where, on an application under section 166 by an employee in relation to an employer's payment, the Secretary of State is satisfied that the requirements specified in subsection (2) are met, he shall pay to the employee out of the National Insurance Fund a sum calculated in accordance with section 168 but reduced by so much (if any) of the employer's payment as has already been paid.

(2)  The requirements referred to in subsection (1) are—

   (a)   that the employee is entitled to the employer's payment, and

   (b)   that one of the conditions specified in paragraphs (a) and (b) of subsection (1) of section 166 is fulfilled,

and, in a case where the employer's payment is a payment such as is mentioned in subsection (2)(b) of that section, that the employee's right to the payment arises by virtue of a period of continuous employment (computed in accordance with the provisions of the agreement in question) which is not less than two years.

(3)  Where under this section the Secretary of State pays a sum to an employee in respect of an employer's payment—

   (a)   all rights and remedies of the employee with respect to the employer's payment, or (if the Secretary of State has paid only part of it) all the rights and remedies of the employee with respect to that part of the employer's payment, are transferred to and vest in the Secretary of State, and

   (b)   any decision of an [employment tribunal] requiring the employer's payment to be paid to the employee has effect as if it required that payment, or that part of it which the Secretary of State has paid, to be paid to the Secretary of State.

(4)  Any money recovered by the Secretary of State by virtue of subsection (3) shall be paid into the National Insurance Fund.

**NOTES**

   Sub-s (3): words in square brackets substituted by the Employment Rights (Dispute Resolution) Act 1998, s 1(2)(a).

**[1.975]**
**168 Amount of payments**
(1) The sum payable to an employee by the Secretary of State under section 167—
- (a) where the employer's payment to which the employee's application under section 166 relates is a redundancy payment or a part of a redundancy payment, is a sum equal to the amount of the redundancy payment or part, . . .
- [(aa) where the employer's payment to which the employee's application under section 166 relates is a payment which his employer is liable to make to him under an agreement having effect by virtue of section 203(2)(e) or (f), is a sum equal to the amount of the employer's payment or of any redundancy payment which the employer would have been liable to pay to the employee but for the agreement, whichever is less, and]
- (b) where the employer's payment to which the employee's application under section 166 relates is a payment which the employer is liable to make under an agreement in respect of which an order is in force under section 157, is a sum equal to the amount of the employer's payment or of the relevant redundancy payment, whichever is less.

(2) The reference in subsection (1)(b) to the amount of the relevant redundancy payment is to the amount of the redundancy payment which the employer would have been liable to pay to the employee on the assumptions specified in subsection (3).
(3) The assumptions referred to in subsection (2) are that—
- (a) the order in force in respect of the agreement had not been made,
- (b) the circumstances in which the employer's payment is payable had been such that the employer was liable to pay a redundancy payment to the employee in those circumstances,
- (c) the relevant date, in relation to any such redundancy payment, had been the date on which the termination of the employee's contract of employment is treated as having taken effect for the purposes of the agreement, and
- (d) in so far as the provisions of the agreement relating to the circumstances in which the continuity of an employee's period of employment is to be treated as broken, and the weeks which are to count in computing a period of employment, are inconsistent with the provisions of Chapter I of Part XIV, the provisions of the agreement were substituted for those provisions.

**NOTES**
Sub-s (1): word omitted from para (a) repealed, and para (aa) inserted, by the Employment Rights (Dispute Resolution) Act 1998, ss 11(3), 15, Sch 2.

**[1.976]**
**169 Information relating to applications for payments**
(1) Where an employee makes an application to the Secretary of State under section 166, the Secretary of State may, by notice in writing given to the employer, require the employer—
- (a) to provide the Secretary of State with such information, and
- (b) to produce for examination on behalf of the Secretary of State documents in his custody or under his control of such description,

as the Secretary of State may reasonably require for the purpose of determining whether the application is well-founded.
(2) Where a person on whom a notice is served under subsection (1) fails without reasonable excuse to comply with a requirement imposed by the notice, he is guilty of an offence and liable on summary conviction to a fine not exceeding level 3 on the standard scale.
(3) A person is guilty of an offence if—
- (a) in providing any information required by a notice under subsection (1), he makes a statement which he knows to be false in a material particular or recklessly makes a statement which is false in a material particular, or
- (b) he produces for examination in accordance with a notice under subsection (1) a document which to his knowledge has been wilfully falsified.

(4) A person guilty of an offence under subsection (3) is liable—
- (a) on summary conviction, to a fine not exceeding the statutory maximum or to imprisonment for a term not exceeding three months, or to both, or
- (b) on conviction on indictment, to a fine or to imprisonment for a term not exceeding two years, or to both.

**[1.977]**
**170 References to [employment tribunals]**
(1) Where on an application made to the Secretary of State for a payment under section 166 it is claimed that an employer is liable to pay an employer's payment, there shall be referred to an [employment tribunal]—
- (a) any question as to the liability of the employer to pay the employer's payment, and
- (b) any question as to the amount of the sum payable in accordance with section 168.

(2)   For the purposes of any reference under this section an employee who has been dismissed by his employer shall, unless the contrary is proved, be presumed to have been so dismissed by reason of redundancy.

**NOTES**

Section heading, sub-s (1): words in square brackets substituted by the Employment Rights (Dispute Resolution) Act 1998, s 1(2)(a), (b).

CHAPTER VII
SUPPLEMENTARY

*Application of Part to particular cases*

**[1.978]**
**171   Employment not under contract of employment**
(1)   The Secretary of State may by regulations provide that, subject to such exceptions and modifications as may be prescribed by the regulations, this Part and the provisions of this Act supplementary to this part have effect in relation to any employment of a description to which this section applies as may be so prescribed as if—
  (a)   it were employment under a contract of employment,
  (b)   any person engaged in employment of that description were an employee, and
  (c)   such person as may be determined by or under the regulations were his employer.
(2)   This section applies to employment of any description which—
  (a)   is employment in the case of which secondary Class 1 contributions are payable under Part I of the Social Security Contributions and Benefits Act 1992 in respect of persons engaged in it, but
  (b)   is not employment under a contract of service or of apprenticeship or employment of any description falling within subsection (3).
(3)   The following descriptions of employment fall within this subsection—
  (a)   any employment such as is mentioned in section 159 (whether as originally enacted or as modified by an order under section 209(1)),
  (b)   any employment remunerated out of the revenue of the Duchy of Lancaster or the Duchy of Cornwall,
  (c)   any employment remunerated out of [the Sovereign Grant], and
  (d)   any employment remunerated out of Her Majesty's Privy Purse.

**NOTES**

Sub-s (3): words in square brackets in para (c) substituted by the Sovereign Grant Act 2011, s 14, Sch 1, para 31, as from 1 April 2012.

Regulations: as of 6 April 2013 no Regulations had been made under this section but, by virtue of s 241 of, and Sch 2, Pt I, paras 1–4 to, this Act, the Redundancy Payments Office Holders Regulations 1965, SI 1965/2007 have effect as if made under this section.

**[1.979]**
**172   Termination of employment by statute**
(1)   The Secretary of State may by regulations provide that, subject to such exceptions and modifications as may be prescribed by the regulations, this Part has effect in relation to any person who by virtue of any statutory provisions—
  (a)   is transferred to, and becomes a member of, a body specified in those provisions, but
  (b)   at a time so specified ceases to be a member of that body unless before that time certain conditions so specified have been fulfilled,
as if the cessation of his membership of that body by virtue of those provisions were dismissal by his employer by reason of redundancy.
(2)   The power conferred by subsection (1) is exercisable whether or not membership of the body in question constitutes employment within the meaning of section 230(5); and, where that membership does not constitute such employment, that power may be exercised in addition to any power exercisable under section 171.

**NOTES**

Regulations: as of 6 April 2013 no Regulations had been made under this section but, by virtue of s 241 of, and Sch 2, Pt I, paras 1–4 to, this Act, the Redundancy Payments Termination of Employment Regulations 1965, SI 1965/2022 (concerning chief constables and chief or assistant chief fire officers), have effect as if made under this section.

**[1.980]**
**173   Employees paid by person other than employer**
(1)   For the purposes of the operation of the provisions of this Part (and Chapter I of Part XIV) in relation to any employee whose remuneration is, by virtue of any statutory provision, payable to him by a person other than his employer, each of the references to the employer specified in subsection (2) shall be construed as a reference to the person by whom the remuneration is payable.

(2)   The references referred to in subsection (1) are the first reference in section 135(1), the third reference in section 140(3), the first reference in section 142(3) and the first reference in section 143(2)(c) and the references in sections 142(2)(b), 143(4) and (5), 149(a) and (b), 150(3), 152(1)(b), 158(4), 162(6), 164 to 169, 170(1) and 214(5).

*Death of employer or employee*

**[1.981]**
**174   Death of employer: dismissal**
(1)   Where the contract of employment of an employee is taken for the purposes of this Part to be terminated by his employer by reason of the employer's death, this Part has effect in accordance with the following provisions of this section.
(2)   Section 138 applies as if—
   (a)   in subsection (1)(a), for the words "in pursuance" onwards there were substituted "by a personal representative of the deceased employer",
   (b)   in subsection (1)(b), for the words "either immediately" onwards there were substituted "not later than eight weeks after the death of the deceased employer", and
   (c)   in subsections (2)(b) and (6)(a), for the word "employer" there were substituted "personal representative of the deceased employer".
(3)   Section 141(1) applies as if—
   (a)   for the words "before the end of his employment" there were substituted "by a personal representative of the deceased employer", and
   (b)   for the words "either immediately" onwards there were substituted "not later than eight weeks after the death of the deceased employer."
(4)   For the purposes of section 141—
   (a)   provisions of the contract as renewed, or of the new contract, do not differ from the corresponding provisions of the contract in force immediately before the death of the deceased employer by reason only that the personal representative would be substituted for the deceased employer as the employer, and
   (b)   no account shall be taken of that substitution in determining whether refusal of the offer was unreasonable or whether the employee acted reasonably in terminating or giving notice to terminate the new or renewed employment.
(5)   Section 146 has effect as if—
   (a)   subsection (1) were omitted, and
   (b)   in subsection (2), paragraph (a) were omitted and, in paragraph (b), for the word "four" there were substituted "eight".
(6)   For the purposes of the application of this Part (in accordance with section 161(2)) in relation to an employee who was employed as a domestic servant in a private household, references in this section and sections 175 and 218(4) and (5) to a personal representative include a person to whom the management of the household has passed, otherwise than in pursuance of a sale or other disposition for valuable consideration, in consequence of the death of the employer.

**[1.982]**
**175   Death of employer: lay-off and short-time**
(1)   Where an employee is laid off or kept on short-time and his employer dies, this Part has effect in accordance with the following provisions of this section.
(2)   Where the employee—
   (a)   has been laid off or kept on short-time for one or more weeks before the death of the employer,
   (b)   has not given the deceased employer notice of intention to claim before the employer's death,
   (c)   after the employer's death has his contract of employment renewed, or is re-engaged under a new contract, by a personal representative of the deceased employer, and
   (d)   after renewal or re-engagement is laid off or kept on short-time for one or more weeks by the personal representative,
the week in which the employer died and the first week of the employee's employment by the personal representative shall be treated for the purposes of Chapter III as consecutive weeks (and references to four weeks or thirteen weeks shall be construed accordingly).
(3)   The following provisions of this section apply where—
   (a)   the employee has given the deceased employer notice of intention to claim before the employer's death,
   (b)   the employer's death occurred before the end of the period of four weeks after the service of the notice, and
   (c)   the employee has not terminated his contract of employment by notice expiring before the employer's death.
(4)   If the contract of employment is not renewed, and the employee is not re-engaged under a new contract, by a personal representative of the deceased employer before the end of the period of four weeks after the service of the notice of intention to claim—
   (a)   sections 149 and 152 do not apply, but

(b)    (subject to that) Chapter III applies as if the employer had not died and the employee had terminated the contract of employment by a week's notice, or by the minimum notice which he is required to give to terminate the contract (if longer than a week), expiring at the end of that period.

(5)    If—

    (a)    the contract of employment is renewed, or the employee is re-engaged under a new contract, by a personal representative of the deceased employer before the end of the period of four weeks after the service of the notice of intention to claim, and

    (b)    the employee was laid off or kept on short-time by the deceased employer for one or more of those weeks and is laid off or kept on short-time by the personal representative for the week, or for the next two or more weeks, following the renewal or re-engagement,

subsection (6) has effect.

(6)    Where this subsection has effect Chapter III applies as if—

    (a)    all the weeks mentioned in subsection (5) were consecutive weeks during which the employee was employed (but laid off or kept on short-time) by the same employer, and

    (b)    the periods specified by section 150(3)(a) and (b) as the relevant period were extended by any week or weeks any part of which was after the death of the employer and before the date on which the renewal or re-engagement took effect.

**[1.983]**
## 176   Death of employee

(1)    Where an employee whose employer has given him notice to terminate his contract of employment dies before the notice expires, this part applies as if the contract had been duly terminated by the employer by notice expiring on the date of the employee's death.

(2)    Where—

    (a)    an employee's contract of employment has been terminated by the employer,

    (b)    (by virtue of subsection (5) of section 145) a date later than the relevant date as defined by the previous provisions of that section is the relevant date for the purposes of certain provisions of this Act, and

    (c)    the employee dies before that date,

that subsection applies as if the notice to which it refers would have expired on the employee's death.

(3)    Where—

    (a)    an employer has given notice to an employee to terminate his contract of employment and has offered to renew his contract of employment or to re-engage him under a new contract, and

    (b)    the employee dies without having accepted or refused the offer and without the offer having been withdrawn,

section 141(2) applies as if for the words "he unreasonably refuses" there were substituted "it would have been unreasonable on his part to refuse".

(4)    Where an employee's contract of employment has been renewed or he has been re-engaged under a new contract—

    (a)    if he dies during the trial period without having terminated, or given notice to terminate, the contract, section 141(4) applies as if for paragraph (d) there were substituted—

        "(d)    it would have been unreasonable for the employee during the trial period to terminate or give notice to terminate the contract.", and

    (b)    if during that trial period he gives notice to terminate the contract but dies before the notice expires, sections 138(2) and 141(4) apply as if the notice had expired (and the contract had been terminated by its expiry) on the date of the employee's death.

(5)    Where in the circumstances specified in paragraphs (a) and (b) of subsection (3) of section 136 the employee dies before the notice given by him under paragraph (b) of that subsection expires—

    (a)    if he dies before his employer has given him a notice such as is specified in subsection (2) of section 142, subsections (3) and (4) of that section apply as if the employer had given him such a notice and he had not complied with it, and

    (b)    if he dies after his employer has given him such a notice, that section applies as if the employee had not died but did not comply with the notice.

(6)    Where an employee has given notice of intention to claim—

    (a)    if he dies before he has given notice to terminate his contract of employment and before the relevant period (as defined in subsection (3) of section 150) has expired, that section does not apply, and

    (b)    if he dies within the period of seven days after the service of the notice of intention to claim, and before the employer has given a counter-notice, Chapter III applies as if the employer had given a counter-notice within that period of seven days.

(7)    Where a claim for a redundancy payment is made by a personal representative of a deceased employee—

(a)    if the employee died before the end of the period of six months beginning with the relevant date, subsection (1) of section 164, and

(b)    if the employee died after the end of the period of six months beginning with the relevant date but before the end of the following period of six months, subsection (2) of that section,

applies as if for the words "six months" there were substituted "one year".

*Equivalent payments*

**[1.984]**
**177    References to [employment tribunals]**
(1)    Where the terms and conditions (whether or not they constitute a contract of employment) on which a person is employed in employment of any description mentioned in section 171(3) include provision—

(a)    for the making of a payment to which this section applies, and

(b)    for referring to an [employment tribunal] any question as to the right of any person to such a payment in respect of that employment or as to the amount of such a payment,

the question shall be referred to and determined by an [employment tribunal].

(2)    This section applies to any payment by way of compensation for loss of employment of any description mentioned in section 171(3) which is payable in accordance with arrangements falling within subsection (3).

(3)    The arrangements which fall within this subsection are arrangements made with the approval of the Treasury (or, in the case of persons whose service is for the purposes of pensions and other superannuation benefits treated as service in the civil service of the State, of the Minister for the Civil Service) for securing that a payment will be made—

(a)    in circumstances which in the opinion of the Treasury (or Minister) correspond (subject to the appropriate modifications) to those in which a right to a redundancy payment would have accrued if the provisions of this Part (apart from section 159 and this section) applied, and

(b)    on a scale which in the opinion of the Treasury (or Minister), taking into account any sums payable in accordance with—

(i)    a scheme made under section 1 of the Superannuation Act 1972, or

(ii)    the Superannuation Act 1965 as it continues to have effect by virtue of section 23(1) of the Superannuation Act 1972,

to or in respect of the person losing the employment in question, corresponds (subject to the appropriate modifications) to that on which a redundancy payment would have been payable if those provisions applied.

**NOTES**
Section heading, sub-s (1): words in square brackets substituted by the Employment Rights (Dispute Resolution) Act 1998, s 1(2)(a), (b).

*Other supplementary provisions*

**[1.985]**
**178    Old statutory compensation schemes**
(1)    The Secretary of State may make provision by regulations for securing that where—

(a)    (apart from this section) a person is entitled to compensation under a statutory provision to which this section applies, and

(b)    the circumstances are such that he is also entitled to a redundancy payment,

the amount of the redundancy payment shall be set off against the compensation to which he would be entitled apart from this section; and any statutory provision to which any such regulations apply shall have effect subject to the regulations.

(2)    This section applies to any statutory provision—

(a)    which was in force immediately before 6th December 1965, and

(b)    under which the holders of such situations, places or employments as are specified in that provision are, or may become, entitled to compensation for loss of employment, or for loss or diminution of emoluments or of pension rights, in consequence of the operation of any other statutory provision referred to in that provision.

**NOTES**
Regulations: as of 6 April 2013 no Regulations had been made under this section but, by virtue of s 241 of, and Sch 2, Pt I, paras 1–4 to, this Act, the Redundancy Payments Statutory Compensation Regulations 1965, SI 1965/1988, have effect as if made under this section.

**[1.986]**
**179    Notices**
(1)    Any notice which under this Part is required or authorised to be given by an employer to an employee may be given by being delivered to the employee, or left for him at his usual or last-known place of residence, or sent by post addressed to him at that place.

(2)   Any notice which under this Part is required or authorised to be given by an employee to an employer may be given either by the employee himself or by a person authorised by him to act on his behalf, and (whether given by or on behalf of the employee)—

(a)   may be given by being delivered to the employer, or sent by post addressed to him at the place where the employee is or was employed by him, or

(b)   if arrangements have been made by the employer, may be given by being delivered to a person designated by the employer in pursuance of the arrangements, left for such a person at a place so designated or sent by post to such a person at an address so designated.

(3)   In this section any reference to the delivery of a notice includes, in relation to a notice which is not required by this Part to be in writing, a reference to the oral communication of the notice.

(4)   Any notice which, in accordance with any provision of this section, is left for a person at a place referred to in that provision shall, unless the contrary is proved, be presumed to have been received by him on the day on which it was left there.

(5)   Nothing in subsection (1) or (2) affects the capacity of an employer to act by a servant or agent for the purposes of any provision of this Part (including either of those subsections).

(6)   In relation to an employee to whom section 173 applies, this section has effect as if—

(a)   any reference in subsection (1) or (2) to a notice required or authorised to be given by or to an employer included a reference to a notice which, by virtue of that section, is required or authorised to be given by or to the person by whom the remuneration is payable,

(b)   in relation to a notice required or authorised to be given to that person, any reference to the employer in paragraph (a) or (b) of subsection (2) were a reference to that person, and

(c)   the reference to an employer in subsection (5) included a reference to that person.

**[1.987]**
**180   Offences**

(1)   Where an offence under this Part committed by a body corporate is proved—

(a)   to have been committed with the consent or connivance of, or

(b)   to be attributable to any neglect on the part of,

any director, manager, secretary or other similar officer of the body corporate, or any person who was purporting to act in any such capacity, he (as well as the body corporate) is guilty of the offence and liable to be proceeded against and punished accordingly.

(2)   In this section "director", in relation to a body corporate established by or under any enactment for the purpose of carrying on under national ownership any industry or part of an industry or undertaking, being a body corporate whose affairs are managed by its members, means a member of that body corporate.

**[1.988]**
**181   Interpretation**

(1)   In this Part—

"counter-notice" shall be construed in accordance with section 149(a),

"dismissal" and "dismissed" shall be construed in accordance with sections 136 to 138,

"employer's payment" has the meaning given by section 166,

"notice of intention to claim" shall be construed in accordance with section 148(1),

"obligatory period of notice" has the meaning given by section 136(4), and

"trial period" shall be construed in accordance with section 138(3).

(2)   In this Part—

(a)   references to an employee being laid off or being eligible for a redundancy payment by reason of being laid off, and

(b)   references to an employee being kept on short-time or being eligible for a redundancy payment by reason of being kept on short-time,

shall be construed in accordance with sections 147 and 148.

## PART XII
## INSOLVENCY OF EMPLOYERS

**NOTES**

Bank insolvency or administration: in so far as any provision of this Act applies to liquidation or administration, it applies with specified modifications in the case of a bank insolvency or administration; see the Banking Act 2009 (Parts 2 and 3 Consequential Amendments) Order 2009, SI 2009/317.

**[1.989]**
**182   Employee's rights on insolvency of employer**

If, on an application made to him in writing by an employee, the Secretary of State is satisfied that—

(a)   the employee's employer has become insolvent,

(b)   the employee's employment has been terminated, and

(c)   on the appropriate date the employee was entitled to be paid the whole or part of any debt to which this Part applies, the Secretary of State shall, subject to section 186, pay the employee out of the National Insurance Fund the amount to which, in the opinion of the Secretary of State, the employee is entitled in respect of the debt.

**[1.990]**

**183 Insolvency**

(1) An employer has become insolvent for the purposes of this Part—
- (a) where the employer is an individual, if (but only if) subsection (2) is satisfied, . . .
- (b) where the employer is a company, if (but only if) subsection (3) is satisfied [, and
- (c) where the employer is a limited liability partnership, if (but only if) subsection (4) is satisfied].

(2) This subsection is satisfied in the case of an employer who is an individual—
- (a) in England and Wales if—
  - [(ai) a moratorium period under a debt relief order applies in relation to him,]
  - (i) he has been adjudged bankrupt or has made a composition or arrangement with his creditors, or
  - (ii) he has died and his estate falls to be administered in accordance with an order under section 421 of the Insolvency Act 1986, and
- (b) in Scotland if—
  - (i) sequestration of his estate has been awarded or he has executed a trust deed for his creditors or has entered into a composition contract, or
  - (ii) he has died and a judicial factor appointed under section 11A of the Judicial Factors (Scotland) Act 1889 is required by that section to divide his insolvent estate among his creditors.

(3) This subsection is satisfied in the case of an employer which is a company—
- (a) if a winding up order . . . has been made, or a resolution for voluntary winding up has been passed, with respect to the company,
- [(aa) if the company is in administration for the purposes of the Insolvency Act 1986,]
- (b) if a receiver or (in England and Wales only) a manager of the company's undertaking has been duly appointed, or (in England and Wales only) possession has been taken, by or on behalf of the holders of any debentures secured by a floating charge, of any property of the company comprised in or subject to the charge, or
- (c) if a voluntary arrangement proposed in the case of the company for the purposes of Part I of the Insolvency Act 1986 has been approved under that Part of that Act.

[(4) This subsection is satisfied in the case of an employer which is a limited liability partnership—
- (a) if a winding-up order, an administration order or a determination for a voluntary winding-up has been made with respect to the limited liability partnership,
- (b) if a receiver or (in England and Wales only) a manager of the undertaking of the limited liability partnership has been duly appointed, or (in England and Wales only) possession has been taken, by or on behalf of the holders of any debentures secured by a floating charge, of any property of the limited liability partnership comprised in or subject to the charge, or
- (c) if a voluntary arrangement proposed in the case of the limited liability partnership for the purposes of Part I of the Insolvency Act 1986 has been approved under that Part of that Act.]

[(5) In this section—
- (a) references to a company are to be read as including references to a charitable incorporated organisation, and
- (b) any reference to the Insolvency Act 1986 in relation to a company is to be read as including a reference to that Act as it applies to charitable incorporated organisations.]

**NOTES**

Sub-s (1): word omitted from para (a) repealed, and para (c) and word immediately preceding it added, by the Limited Liability Partnership Regulations, SI 2001/1090, reg 9, Sch 5, para 19(1), (2).

Sub-s (2): sub-para (a)(ai) inserted by the Tribunals, Courts and Enforcement Act 2007, s 108(3), Sch 20, Pt 2, para 17, as from 6 April 2009.

Sub-s (3): words omitted from para (a) repealed, and para (aa) inserted, by the Enterprise Act 2002, ss 248(3), 278(2), Sch 17, para 49(1), (3), Sch 26, except in relation to cases where a petition for an administration order was presented before 15 September 2003, and subject to savings in relation to special administration regimes (within the meaning of s 249 of the 2002 Act).

Sub-s (4): added by SI 2001/1090, reg 9, Sch 5, para 19(1), (3).

Sub-s (5): added by the Charitable Incorporated Organisations (Consequential Amendments) Order 2012, SI 2012/3014, art 4, as from 2 January 2013.

**[1.991]**

**184 Debts to which Part applies**

(1) This Part applies to the following debts—
- (a) any arrears of pay in respect of one or more (but not more than eight) weeks,

(b)  any amount which the employer is liable to pay the employee for the period of notice required by section 86(1) or (2) or for any failure of the employer to give the period of notice required by section 86(1),

(c)  any holiday pay—
    (i)  in respect of a period or periods of holiday not exceeding six weeks in all, and
    (ii)  to which the employee became entitled during the twelve months ending with the appropriate date,

(d)  any basic award of compensation for unfair dismissal [or so much of an award under a designated dismissal procedures agreement as does not exceed any basic award of compensation for unfair dismissal to which the employee would be entitled but for the agreement], and

(e)  any reasonable sum by way of reimbursement of the whole or part of any fee or premium paid by an apprentice or articled clerk.

(2)  For the purposes of subsection (1)(a) the following amounts shall be treated as arrears of pay—

(a)  a guarantee payment,

(b)  any payment for time off under Part VI of this Act or section 169 of the Trade Union and Labour Relations (Consolidation) Act 1992 (payment for time off for carrying out trade union duties etc),

(c)  remuneration on suspension on medical grounds under section 64 of this Act and remuneration on suspension on maternity grounds under section 68 of this Act, and

(d)  remuneration under a protective award under section 189 of the Trade Union and Labour Relations (Consolidation) Act 1992.

(3)  In subsection (1)(c) "holiday pay", in relation to an employee, means—

(a)  pay in respect of a holiday actually taken by the employee, or

(b)  any accrued holiday pay which, under the employee's contract of employment, would in the ordinary course have become payable to him in respect of the period of a holiday if his employment with the employer had continued until he became entitled to a holiday.

(4)  A sum shall be taken to be reasonable for the purposes of subsection (1)(e) in a case where a trustee in bankruptcy, or (in Scotland) a permanent or interim trustee (within the meaning of the Bankruptcy (Scotland) Act 1985), or liquidator has been or is required to be appointed—

(a)  as respects England and Wales, if it is admitted to be reasonable by the trustee in bankruptcy or liquidator under section 348 of the Insolvency Act 1986 (effect of bankruptcy on apprenticeships etc), whether as originally enacted or as applied to the winding up of a company by rules under section 411 of that Act, and

(b)  as respects Scotland, if it is accepted by the permanent or interim trustee or liquidator for the purposes of the sequestration or winding up.

**NOTES**

Sub-s (1): words in square brackets in para (d) inserted by the Employment Rights (Dispute Resolution) Act 1998, s 12(4).

**[1.992]**
**185   The appropriate date**
In this Part "the appropriate date"—

(a)  in relation to arrears of pay (not being remuneration under a protective award made under section 189 of the Trade Union and Labour Relations (Consolidation) Act 1992) and to holiday pay, means the date on which the employer became insolvent,

(b)  in relation to a basic award of compensation for unfair dismissal and to remuneration under a protective award so made, means whichever is the latest of—
    (i)  the date on which the employer became insolvent,
    (ii)  the date of the termination of the employee's employment, and
    (iii)  the date on which the award was made, and

(c)  in relation to any other debt to which this Part applies, means whichever is the later of—
    (i)  the date on which the employer became insolvent, and
    (ii)  the date of the termination of the employee's employment.

**[1.993]**
**186   Limit on amount payable under section 182**
(1)  The total amount payable to an employee in respect of any debt to which this Part applies, where the amount of the debt is referable to a period of time, shall not exceed—

(a)  [£450] in respect of any one week, or

(b)  in respect of a shorter period, an amount bearing the same proportion to [£450] as that shorter period bears to a week.

(2)  . . .

**NOTES**

Sub-s (1): sums in square brackets substituted by the Employment Rights (Increase of Limits) Order 2012, SI 2012/3007, art 3, Schedule, as from 1 February 2013, in relation to any case where the appropriate date (as defined in the order) falls on or after that date (see SI 2012/3007, art 4 at **[2.1636]**). Previous sums were as follows: £430 as from 1 February 2012 (see SI 2011/3006); £400 as from 1 February 2011 (see SI 2010/2926); £380 as from 1 October 2009 (see SI 2009/1903); £350 as from 1 February 2009 (see SI 2008/3055); £330 as from 1 February 2008 (SI 2007/3570); £310 as from 1 February 2007 (SI 2006/3045); £290 as from 1 February 2006 (SI 2005/3352); £280 as from 1 February 2005 (SI 2004/2989); £270 as from 1 February 2004 (SI 2003/3038), in each case where the appropriate date fell after the commencement date. This sum may be varied by the Secretary of State (see the Employment Relations Act 1999, s 34(1)(a), (3)(a) at **[1.1202]**). See also the Work and Families Act 2006, s 14 at **[1.1413]** (Increase of maximum amount of a week's pay for certain purposes).

Sub-s (2): repealed by the Employment Relations Act 1999, ss 36(1)(a), 44, Sch 9(10).

**[1.994]**
**187   Role of relevant officer**
(1)   Where a relevant officer has been, or is required to be, appointed in connection with an employer's insolvency, the Secretary of State shall not make a payment under section 182 in respect of a debt until he has received a statement from the relevant officer of the amount of that debt which appears to have been owed to the employee on the appropriate date and to remain unpaid.
(2)   If the Secretary of State is satisfied that he does not require a statement under subsection (1) in order to determine the amount of a debt which was owed to the employee on the appropriate date and remains unpaid, he may make a payment under section 182 in respect of the debt without having received such a statement.
(3)   A relevant officer shall, on request by the Secretary of State, provide him with a statement for the purposes of subsection (1) as soon as is reasonably practicable.
(4)   The following are relevant officers for the purposes of this section—
  (a)   a trustee in bankruptcy or a permanent or interim trustee (within the meaning of the Bankruptcy (Scotland) Act 1985),
  (b)   a liquidator,
  (c)   an administrator,
  (d)   a receiver or manager,
  (e)   a trustee under a composition or arrangement between the employer and his creditors, and
  (f)   a trustee under a trust deed for his creditors executed by the employer.
(5)   In subsection (4)(e) "trustee" includes the supervisor of a voluntary arrangement proposed for the purposes of, and approved under, Part I or VIII of the Insolvency Act 1986.

**[1.995]**
**188   Complaints to [employment tribunals]**
(1)   A person who has applied for a payment under section 182 may present a complaint to an [employment tribunal]—
  (a)   that the Secretary of State has failed to make any such payment, or
  (b)   that any such payment made by him is less than the amount which should have been paid.
(2)   An [employment tribunal] shall not consider a complaint under subsection (1) unless it is presented—
  (a)   before the end of the period of three months beginning with the date on which the decision of the Secretary of State on the application was communicated to the applicant, or
  (b)   within such further period as the tribunal considers reasonable in a case where it is not reasonably practicable for the complaint to be presented before the end of that period of three months.
(3)   Where an [employment tribunal] finds that the Secretary of State ought to make a payment under section 182, the tribunal shall—
  (a)   make a declaration to that effect, and
  (b)   declare the amount of any such payment which it finds the Secretary of State ought to make.

**NOTES**
Words in square brackets substituted by the Employment Rights (Dispute Resolution) Act 1998, s 1(2)(a), (b).

**[1.996]**
**189   Transfer to Secretary of State of rights and remedies**
(1)   Where, in pursuance of section 182, the Secretary of State makes a payment to an employee in respect of a debt to which this Part applies—
  (a)   on the making of the payment any rights and remedies of the employee in respect of the debt (or, if the Secretary of State has paid only part of it, in respect of that part) become rights and remedies of the Secretary of State, and
  (b)   any decision of an [employment tribunal] requiring an employer to pay that debt to the employee has the effect that the debt (or the part of it which the Secretary of State has paid) is to be paid to the Secretary of State.
(2)   Where a debt (or any part of a debt) in respect of which the Secretary of State has made a payment in pursuance of section 182 constitutes—

(a)    a preferential debt within the meaning of the Insolvency Act 1986 for the purposes of any provision of that Act (including any such provision as applied by any order made under that Act) or any provision of [the Companies Act 2006], or

(b)    a preferred debt within the meaning of the Bankruptcy (Scotland) Act 1985 for the purposes of any provision of that Act (including any such provision as applied by section 11A of the Judicial Factors (Scotland) Act 1889),

the rights which become rights of the Secretary of State in accordance with subsection (1) include any right arising under any such provision by reason of the status of the debt (or that part of it) as a preferential or preferred debt.

(3)   In computing for the purposes of any provision mentioned in subsection (2)(a) or (b) the aggregate amount payable in priority to other creditors of the employer in respect of—

(a)    any claim of the Secretary of State to be paid in priority to other creditors of the employer by virtue of subsection (2), and

(b)    any claim by the employee to be so paid made in his own right,

any claim of the Secretary of State to be so paid by virtue of subsection (2) shall be treated as if it were a claim of the employee.

(4)   . . .

(5)   Any sum recovered by the Secretary of State in exercising any right, or pursuing any remedy, which is his by virtue of this section shall be paid into the National Insurance Fund.

**NOTES**

Sub-s (1): words in square brackets substituted by the Employment Rights (Dispute Resolution) Act 1998, s 1(2)(a).

Sub-s (2): words in square brackets in para (a) substituted by the Companies Act 2006 (Consequential Amendments etc) Order 2008, SI 2008/948, arts 3(1)(b), 6, Sch 1, Pt 2, para 201.

Sub-s (4): repealed by the Enterprise Act 2002, ss 248(3), 278(2), Sch 17, para 49(1), (4), Sch 26, except in relation to cases where a petition for an administration order was presented before 15 September 2003, and subject to savings in relation to special administration regimes (within the meaning of s 249 of the 2002 Act).

**[1.997]**
### 190   Power to obtain information

(1)   Where an application is made to the Secretary of State under section 182 in respect of a debt owed by an employer, the Secretary of State may require—

(a)    the employer to provide him with such information as he may reasonably require for the purpose of determining whether the application is well-founded, and

(b)    any person having the custody or control of any relevant records or other documents to produce for examination on behalf of the Secretary of State any such document in that person's custody or under his control which is of such a description as the Secretary of State may require.

(2)   Any such requirement—

(a)    shall be made by notice in writing given to the person on whom the requirement is imposed, and

(b)    may be varied or revoked by a subsequent notice so given.

(3)   If a person refuses or wilfully neglects to furnish any information or produce any document which he has been required to furnish or produce by a notice under this section he is guilty of an offence and liable on summary conviction to a fine not exceeding level 3 on the standard scale.

(4)   If a person, in purporting to comply with a requirement of a notice under this section, knowingly or recklessly makes any false statement he is guilty of an offence and liable on summary conviction to a fine not exceeding level 5 on the standard scale.

(5)   Where an offence under this section committed by a body corporate is proved—

(a)    to have been committed with the consent or connivance of, or

(b)    to be attributable to any neglect on the part of,

any director, manager, secretary or other similar officer of the body corporate, or any person who was purporting to act in any such capacity, he (as well as the body corporate) is guilty of the offence and liable to be proceeded against and punished accordingly.

(6)   Where the affairs of a body corporate are managed by its members, subsection (5) applies in relation to the acts and defaults of a member in connection with his functions of management as if he were a director of the body corporate.

# PART XIII
# MISCELLANEOUS

## CHAPTER I
## PARTICULAR TYPES OF EMPLOYMENT

### *Crown employment etc*

**[1.998]**
**191 Crown employment**

(1) Subject to sections 192 and 193, the provisions of this Act to which this section applies have effect in relation to Crown employment and persons in Crown employment as they have effect in relation to other employment and other employees or workers.

(2) This section applies to—

    (a) Parts I to III,

    [(aa) Part IVA,]

    (b) Part V, apart from section 45,

    [(c) Parts 6 to 8A,]

    (d) in Part IX, sections 92 and 93,

    (e) Part X, apart from section 101, and

    (f) this Part and Parts XIV and XV.

(3) In this Act "Crown employment" means employment under or for the purposes of a government department or any officer or body exercising on behalf of the Crown functions conferred by a statutory provision.

(4) For the purposes of the application of provisions of this Act in relation to Crown employment in accordance with subsection (1)—

    (a) references to an employee or a worker shall be construed as references to a person in Crown employment,

    (b) references to a contract of employment, or a worker's contract, shall be construed as references to the terms of employment of a person in Crown employment,

    (c) references to dismissal, or to the termination of a worker's contract, shall be construed as references to the termination of Crown employment,

    (d) references to redundancy shall be construed as references to the existence of such circumstances as are treated, in accordance with any arrangements falling within section 177(3) for the time being in force, as equivalent to redundancy in relation to Crown employment, . . .

    [(da) the reference in section 98B(2)(a) to the employer's undertaking shall be construed as a reference to the national interest, and]

    (e) [any other reference] to an undertaking shall be construed—

        (i) in relation to a Minister of the Crown, as references to his functions or (as the context may require) to the department of which he is in charge, and

        (ii) in relation to a government department, officer or body, as references to the functions of the department, officer or body or (as the context may require) to the department, officer or body.

(5) Where the terms of employment of a person in Crown employment restrict his right to take part in—

    (a) certain political activities, or

    (b) activities which may conflict with his official functions,

nothing in section 50 requires him to be allowed time off work for public duties connected with any such activities.

(6) Sections 159 and 160 are without prejudice to any exemption or immunity of the Crown.

---

**NOTES**

Sub-s (2): para (aa) inserted by the Public Interest Disclosure Act 1998, ss 10, 18(2); para (c) substituted by the Employment Act 2002, s 53, Sch 7, paras 24, 41.

Sub-s (4): word omitted from para (d) repealed, para (da) inserted, and words in square brackets in para (e) substituted, by the Employment Relations Act 2004, s 57, Sch 1, para 34, Sch 2.

---

**[1.999]**
**192 Armed forces**

(1) Section 191—

    (a) applies to service as a member of the naval, military or air forces of the Crown but subject to the following provisions of this section, and

    (b) applies to employment by an association established for the purposes of Part XI of the Reserve Forces Act 1996.

(2) The provisions of this Act which have effect by virtue of section 191 in relation to service as a member of the naval, military or air forces of the Crown are—

    (a) Part I,

>     [(aa) in Part V, [sections [43M,] 45A, 47C and 47D] and sections 48 and 49 so far as relating to [those sections],
>     *[(ab) section 47C,]*
>     (b)   in Part VI, sections [55 to 57B],
>     (c)   Parts VII and VIII,
>     (d)   in Part IX, sections 92 and 93,
>     (e)   Part X, apart from sections [98B(2) and (3),] 100 to 103[, 104C] and 134, and
>     (f)   this Part and Parts XIV and XV.
> (3)   Her Majesty may by Order in Council—
>     (a)   amend subsection (2) by making additions to, or omissions from, the provisions for the time being specified in that subsection, and
>     (b)   make any provision for the time being so specified apply to service as a member of the naval, military or air forces of the Crown subject to such exceptions and modifications as may be specified in the Order in Council,
> but no provision contained in Part II may be added to the provisions for the time being specified in subsection (2).
> (4)   Modifications made by an Order in Council under subsection (3) may include provision precluding the making of a complaint or reference to any [employment tribunal] unless[—
>     (a)   the person aggrieved has made [a service complaint]; and
>     (b)   the Defence Council have made a determination with respect to the [service complaint]].
> [(5)   Where modifications made by an Order in Council under subsection (3) include provision such as is mentioned in subsection (4), the Order in Council shall also include provision—
>     (a)   enabling a complaint or reference to be made to an [employment tribunal] in such circumstances as may be specified in the Order, notwithstanding that provision such as is mentioned in subsection (4) would otherwise preclude the making of the complaint or reference; and
>     (b)   where a complaint or reference is made to an [employment tribunal] by virtue of provision such as is mentioned in paragraph (a), enabling [the service complaint procedures] to continue after the complaint or reference is made.]
> [(6A)   In subsections (4) and (5)—
>     "service complaint" means a complaint under section 334 of the Armed Forces Act 2006;
>     "the service complaint procedures" means the procedures prescribed by regulations under that section.]
> (7)   No provision shall be made by virtue of subsection (4) which has the effect of substituting a period longer than six months for any period specified as the normal period for a complaint or reference.
> (8)   In subsection (7) "the normal period for a complaint or reference", in relation to any matter within the jurisdiction of an [employment tribunal], means the period specified in the relevant enactment as the period within which the complaint or reference must be made (disregarding any provision permitting an extension of that period at the discretion of the tribunal).

---

**NOTES**

    Commencement: to be appointed (see the note below).

    By Sch 2, para 16 to this Act (at **[1.1050]**), until a day to be appointed by Order under sub-para (2)(b) of para 16, s 192 has effect as set out in para 16(1) of that Schedule, and the section set out above is not in force. This section, although not in force, has been amended as follows—

    Sub-s (2): para (aa) inserted by the Working Time Regulations 1998, SI 1998/1833, regs 2(1), 31(4); words in first (outer) and final pairs of square brackets in para (aa) substituted by the Tax Credits Act 2002, s 27, Sch 1, para 1(1), (5); figure in second (inner) pair of square paragraphs in para (aa) inserted by the Employment Relations Act 2004, s 57(1), Sch 1, para 35(a); para (ab) inserted, and words in square brackets in para (b) substituted, by the Employment Relations Act 1999, s 9, Sch 4, Pt III, paras 1, 5, 31; para (ab) repealed by the Tax Credits Act 2002, s 60, Sch 6, as from a day to be appointed; words in first pair of square brackets in para (e) inserted by the Employment Relations Act 2004, s 57(1), Sch 1, para 35(b); figure in second pair of square brackets in para (e) inserted by the Employment Act 2002, s 53, Sch 7, paras 24, 42.

    Sub-s (4): words in first pair of square brackets substituted by the Employment Rights (Dispute Resolution) Act 1998, s 1(2)(a); words in second (outer) pair of square brackets substituted by the Armed Forces Act 1996, s 26(1), (2); words in square brackets in paras (a), (b) substituted by the Armed Forces Act 2006, s 378(1), Sch 16, para 136(a).

    Sub-s (5): substituted by the Armed Forces Act 1996, s 26(1), (3); words "employment tribunal" in square brackets substituted by the Employment Rights (Dispute Resolution) Act 1998, s 1(2)(a); other words in square brackets substituted by the Armed Forces Act 2006, s 378(1), Sch 16, para 136(b).

    Sub-s (6A): substituted, for original sub-s (6), by the Armed Forces Act 2006, s 378(1), Sch 16, para 136(c).

    Sub-s (8): words in square brackets substituted by the Employment Rights (Dispute Resolution) Act 1998, s 1(2)(a).

    References to a service complaint, etc: see the Armed Forces Act 2006 (Transitional Provisions etc) Order 2009, SI 2009/1059, art 196, which provides: (i) references to a service complaint include a complaint made under the service redress procedures in sub-s (4) above, and (ii) references to the service complaint procedures include the service redress procedures in sub-s (5) above.

---

**[1.1000]**
**[193   National security**
Part IVA and section 47B of this Act do not apply in relation to employment for the purposes of—
    (a)   the Security Service,

(b)   the Secret Intelligence Service, or

(c)   the Government Communications Headquarters.]

**NOTES**

Substituted by the Employment Relations Act 1999, s 41, Sch 8, para 1.

*Parliamentary staff*

**[1.1001]**

**194   House of Lords staff**

(1)   The provisions of this Act to which this section applies have effect in relation to employment as a relevant member of the House of Lords staff as they have effect in relation to other employment.

(2)   This section applies to—

   (a)   Part I,

   (b)   Part III,

   (c)   in Part V, [sections [43M,] 44, 45A[, 47[, [47AA,] 47C[, 47D and 47E]]]], and sections 48 and 49 so far as relating to those sections,

   (d)   Part VI, apart from sections 58 to 60,

   [(e)   Parts [6A,] VII, VIII and VIIIA,]

   (f)   in Part IX, sections 92 and 93,

   (g)   Part X, apart from sections 101 and 102, and

   (h)   this Part and Parts XIV and XV.

[(2A)   For the purposes of the application of section 98B(2) in relation to a relevant member of the House of Lords staff, the reference to the employer's undertaking shall be construed as a reference to the national interest or, if the case so requires, the interests of the House of Lords.]

(3)   For the purposes of the application of [the other provisions] of this Act to which this section applies in relation to a relevant member of the House of Lords staff references to an undertaking shall be construed as references to the House of Lords.

(4)   Nothing in any rule of law or the law or practice of Parliament prevents a relevant member of the House of Lords staff from bringing before the High Court or *a county court*—

   (a)   a claim arising out of or relating to a contract of employment or any other contract connected with employment, or

   (b)   a claim in tort arising in connection with employment.

(5)   Where the terms of the contract of employment of a relevant member of the House of Lords staff restrict his right to take part in—

   (a)   certain political activities, or

   (b)   activities which may conflict with his official functions,

nothing in section 50 requires him to be allowed time off work for public duties connected with any such activities.

(6)   In this section "relevant member of the House of Lords staff" means any person who is employed under a contract of employment with the Corporate Officer of the House of Lords.

(7)   For the purposes of the application of—

   (a)   the provisions of this Act to which this section applies, or

   (b)   a claim within subsection (4),

in relation to a person continuously employed in or for the purposes of the House of Lords up to the time when he became so employed under a contract of employment with the Corporate Officer of the House of Lords, his employment shall not be treated as having been terminated by reason only of a change in his employer before or at that time.

**NOTES**

Sub-s (2) is amended as follows:

Words in first (outer) pair of square brackets in para (c) substituted by the Working Time Regulations 1998, SI 1998/1833, regs 2(1), 31(5).

Figure "43M," in para (c) inserted by the Employment Relations Act 2004, s 57(1), Sch 1, para 36(1), (2).

Figure ", 47" in para (c) substituted by the Employment Relations Act 1999, s 9, Sch 4, Pt II, paras 1, 5, 32.

Figure "47AA," in para (c) inserted by the Education and Skills Act 2008, s 39(1), (5), as from a day to be appointed.

Figure ", 47C" in para (c) substituted by both the Tax Credits Act 2002, s 27, Sch 1, para 1(1), (6)(a), and the Employment Act 2002, s 53, Sch 7, paras 24, 43(a).

Words ", 47D and 47E" in para (c) substituted by the Employment Relations Act 2004, s 41(7).

Para (e) substituted by the Employment Act 2002, s 53, Sch 7, paras 24, 43(b).

Figure "6A" in square brackets in para (e) inserted by the Apprenticeships, Skills, Children and Learning Act 2009, s 40(1), (5), Sch 1, paras 1, 5, as from 6 April 2010 (except in relation to small employers and their employees), and as from a day to be appointed (otherwise) (as to the meaning of "small employers" etc, see further the notes at **[1.840]**).

Sub-s (2A): inserted by the Employment Relations Act 2004, s 57(1), Sch 1, para 36(1), (3).

Sub-s (3): words in square brackets substituted by the Employment Relations Act 2004, s 57(1), Sch 1, para 36(1), (4).

Sub-s (4): for the words in italics there are substituted the words "the county court" by the Crime and Courts Act 2013, s 17(5), Sch 9, Pt 3, para 52, as from a day to be appointed.

**[1.1002]**
**195  House of Commons staff**
(1)   The provisions of this Act to which this section applies have in effect in relation to employment as a relevant member of the House of Commons staff as they have effect in relation to other employment.
(2)   This section applies to—
    (a)    Part I,
    (b)    Part III,
    (c)    in Part V, [sections [43M,] 44, 45A[, 47[, [47AA,] 47C[, 47D and 47E]]]], and sections 48 and 49 so far as relating to those sections,
    (d)    Part VI, apart from sections 58 to 60,
    [(e)    Parts [6A,] VII, VIII and VIIIA,]
    (f)    in Part IX, sections 92 and 93,
    (g)    Part X, apart from sections 101 and 102, and
    (h)    this Part and Parts XIV and XV.
[(2A)   For the purposes of the application of section 98B(2) in relation to a relevant member of the House of Commons staff, the reference to the employer's undertaking shall be construed as a reference to the national interest or, if the case so requires, the interests of the House of Commons.]
(3)   For the purposes of the application of the provisions of this Act to which this section applies in relation to a relevant member of the House of Commons staff—
    (a)    references to an employee shall be construed as references to a relevant member of the House of Commons staff,
    (b)    references to a contract of employment shall be construed as including references to the terms of employment of a relevant member of the House of Commons staff,
    (c)    references to dismissal shall be construed as including references to the termination of the employment of a relevant member of the House of Commons staff, and
    (d)    references to an undertaking [(other than in section 98B)] shall be construed as references to the House of Commons.
(4)   Nothing in any rule of law or the law or practice of Parliament prevents a relevant member of the House of Commons staff from bringing before the High Court or *a county court*—
    (a)    a claim arising out of or relating to a contract of employment or any other contract connected with employment, or
    (b)    a claim in tort arising in connection with employment.
(5)   In this section "relevant member of the House of Commons staff" means any person—
    (a)    who was appointed by the House of Commons Commission or is employed in the refreshment department, or
    (b)    who is a member of the Speaker's personal staff.
(6)   Subject to subsection (7), for the purposes of—
    (a)    the provisions of this Act to which this section applies,
    (b)    Part XI (where applicable to relevant members of the House of Commons staff), and
    (c)    a claim within subsection (4),
the House of Commons Commission is the employer of staff appointed by the Commission and the Speaker is the employer of his personal staff and of any person employed in the refreshment department and not appointed by the Commission.
(7)   Where the House of Commons Commission or the Speaker designates a person to be treated for all or any of the purposes mentioned in subsection (6) as the employer of any description of staff (other than the Speaker's personal staff), the person so designated shall be treated for those purposes as their employer.
(8)   Where any proceedings are brought by virtue of this section against—
    (a)    the House of Commons Commission,
    (b)    the Speaker, or
    (c)    any person designated under subsection (7),
the person against whom the proceedings are brought may apply to the court or [employment tribunal] concerned to have some other person against whom the proceedings could at the time of the application be properly brought substituted for him as a party to the proceedings.
(9)   For the purposes mentioned in subsection (6)—
    (a)    a person's employment in or for the purposes of the House of Commons shall not (provided he continues to be employed in such employment) be treated as terminated by reason only of a change in his employer, and
    (b)    (provided he so continues) his first appointment to such employment shall be deemed after the change to have been made by his employer for the time being.
(10)   In accordance with subsection (9)—
    (a)    an employee shall be treated for the purposes mentioned in subsection (6) as being continuously employed by his employer for the time being from the commencement of his employment until its termination, and

(b)    anything done by or in relation to his employer for the time being in respect of his employment before the change shall be so treated as having been done by or in relation to the person who is his employer for the time being after the change.

(11)    In subsections (9) and (10) "employer for the time being", in relation to a person who has ceased to be employed in or for the purposes of the House of Commons, means the person who was his employer immediately before he ceased to be so employed, except that where some other person would have been his employer for the time being if he had not ceased to be so employed it means that other person.

(12)    If the House of Commons resolves at any time that any provision of subsections (5) to (8) should be amended in its application to any member of the staff of that House, Her Majesty may by Order in Council amend that provision accordingly.

---

**NOTES**

Sub-s (2) is amended as follows:

Words in first (outer) pair of square brackets in para (c) substituted by the Working Time Regulations 1998, SI 1998/1833, regs 2(1), 31(5).

Figure "43M," in para (c) inserted by the Employment Relations Act 2004, s 57(1), Sch 1, para 36(1), (2).

Figure ", 47" in para (c) substituted by the Employment Relations Act 1999, s 9, Sch 4, Pt II, paras 1, 5, 33.

Figure "47AA," in para (c) inserted by the Education and Skills Act 2008, s 39(1), (6), as from a day to be appointed.

Figure ", 47C" in para (c) substituted by both the Tax Credits Act 2002, s 27, Sch 1, para 1(1), (6)(a), and the Employment Act 2002, s 53, Sch 7, paras 24, 43(a).

Words ", 47D and 47E" in para (c) substituted by the Employment Relations Act 2004, s 41(7).

Para (e) substituted by the Employment Act 2002, s 53, Sch 7, paras 24, 43(b).

Figure "6A" in square brackets in para (e) inserted by the Apprenticeships, Skills, Children and Learning Act 2009, s 40(1), (5), Sch 1, paras 1, 6, as from 6 April 2010 (except in relation to small employers and their employees), and as from a day to be appointed (otherwise) (as to the meaning of "small employers" etc, see further the notes at **[1.840]**).

Sub-s (2A): inserted by the Employment Relations Act 2004, s 57(1), Sch 1, para 37(1), (3).

Sub-s (3): words in square brackets in para (d) inserted by the Employment Relations Act 2004, s 57(1), Sch 1, para 37(1), (4).

Sub-s (4): for the words in italics there are substituted the words "the county court" by the Crime and Courts Act 2013, s 17(5), Sch 9, Pt 3, para 52, as from a day to be appointed.

Sub-s (8): words in square brackets substituted by the Employment Rights (Dispute Resolution) Act 1998, s 1(2)(a).

---

*Excluded classes of employment*

**196, 197**    *(S 196 repealed by the Employment Relations Act 1999, ss 32(3), 44, Sch 9(9); s 197 repealed by the Fixed-term Employees (Prevention of Less Favourable Treatment) Regulations 2002, SI 2002/2034, reg 11, Sch 2, Pt 1, para 3(1), (15) (except in relation to Government training schemes, agency workers or apprentices; see regs 18–20 of the 2002 Regulations at* **[2.614]** *et seq and subject to transitional provisions in Sch 2, Pt 2, para 5 thereto at* **[2.618]***) (sub-ss (1), (2) had been repealed previously by the Employment Relations Act 1999, ss 32(3), 44, Sch 9(9).)*

**[1.1003]**
**198    Short-term employment**
Sections 1 to 7 do not apply to an employee if his employment continues for less than one month.

**[1.1004]**
**199    Mariners**
(1)    Sections 1 to 7, Part II and sections 86 to 91 do not apply to a person employed as a seaman in a ship registered in the United Kingdom under a crew agreement the provisions and form of which are of a kind approved by the Secretary of State.

(2)    Sections 8 to 10, Part III, sections 44, 45, 47, [47C, [47E,] [47F,] 50 to 57B] and 61 to 63, [Parts [6A,] VII, VIII and VIIIA], sections 92 and 93 and  . . .  Parts X to XII do not apply to employment as master, or as a member of the crew, of a fishing vessel where the employee is remunerated only by a share in the profits or gross earnings of the vessel.

(3)    . . .

(4)    Sections 8 to 10 and 50 to 54 and Part XII do not apply to employment as a merchant seaman.

(5)    In subsection (4) "employment as a merchant seaman"—

(a)    does not include employment in the fishing industry or employment on board a ship otherwise than by the owner, manager or charterer of that ship except employment as a radio officer, but

(b)    subject to that, includes—

(i)    employment as a master or a member of the crew of any ship,

(ii)    employment as a trainee undergoing training for the sea service, and

(iii)    employment in or about a ship in port by the owner, manager or charterer of the ship to do work of the kind ordinarily done by a merchant seaman on a ship while it is in port.

(6)    . . .

[(7)    The provisions mentioned in subsection (8) apply to employment on board a ship registered in the register maintained under section 8 of the Merchant Shipping Act 1995 if and only if—

Part 1 Statutes

(a) the ship's entry in the register specifies a port in Great Britain as the port to which the vessel is to be treated as belonging,

(b) under his contract of employment the person employed does not work wholly outside Great Britain, and

(c) the person employed is ordinarily resident in Great Britain.

(8) The provisions are—

(a) sections 8 to 10,

(b) Parts II, III and V,

(c) Part VI, apart from sections 58 to 60,

[(d) Parts [6A,] VII, VIII and VIIIA,]

(e) sections 92 and 93, and

(f) Part X.]

**NOTES**

Sub-s (2) is amended as follows:

Words in first (outer) pair of square brackets substituted, and words omitted repealed, by the Employment Relations Act 1999, ss 9, 44, Sch 4, Pt III, paras 1, 5, 34(a), (b), Sch 9(2).

Figure "47E," in square brackets originally inserted by the Employment Act 2002, s 53, Sch 7, paras 24, 44(1), (2)(a), and substituted by the Employment Relations Act 2004, s 41(8).

Figures "47F," and "6A," in square brackets inserted by the Apprenticeships, Skills, Children and Learning Act 2009, s 40(5), Sch 1, paras 1, 7(a), (b), as from 6 April 2010 (except in relation to small employers and their employees), and as from a day to be appointed (otherwise) (as to the meaning of "small employers" etc, see further the notes at **[1.840]**).

Words in fourth pair of square brackets substituted by the Employment Act 2002, s 53, Sch 7, paras 24, 44(1), (2)(b).

Sub-s (3): repealed by the Employment Relations Act 1999, ss 9, 44, Sch 4, Pt III, paras 1, 5, 34(c), Sch 9(2).

Sub-s (6): repealed by the Fixed-term Employees (Prevention of Less Favourable Treatment) Regulations 2002, SI 2002/2034, reg 11, Sch 2, Pt 1, para 3(1), (16) (except in relation to Government training schemes, agency workers or apprentices; see regs 18–20 of the 2002 Regulations at **[2.614]** et seq, and subject to transitional provisions in Sch 2, Pt 2, para 5 thereto at **[2.618]**).

Sub-s (7): added by the Employment Relations Act 1999, s 32(4).

Sub-s (8): added by the Employment Relations Act 1999, s 32(4); para (d) substituted by the Employment Act 2002, s 53, Sch 7, paras 24, 44(1), (3); figure "6A," in square brackets inserted by the Apprenticeships, Skills, Children and Learning Act 2009, s 40(5), Sch 1, paras 1, 7(c), as from 6 April 2010 (except in relation to small employers and their employees), and as from a day to be appointed (otherwise) (as to the meaning of "small employers" etc, see further the notes at **[1.840]**).

**[1.1005]**
## 200 Police officers

(1) Sections 8 to 10, Part III[ . . . ], sections . . . , [43M,] 45, [45A,] 47[ . . . ], [47C,] 50 [to 57B] and 61 to 63, Parts VII and VIII, sections 92 and 93 [and], Part X [(except sections 100[, 103A] and 134A and the other provisions of that Part so far as relating to the right not to be unfairly dismissed in a case where the dismissal is unfair by virtue of section 100 [or 103A])] . . . do not apply to employment under a contract of employment in police service or to persons engaged in such employment.

(2) In subsection (1) "police service" means—

(a) service as a member of a constabulary maintained by virtue of an enactment, or

(b) subject to section 126 of the Criminal Justice and Public Order Act 1994 (prison staff not to be regarded as in police service), service in any other capacity by virtue of which a person has the powers or privileges of a constable.

**NOTES**

Sub-s (1) is amended as follows:

First and third words omitted originally inserted by the Public Interest Disclosure Act 1998, ss 13, 18(2), and repealed by the Police Reform Act 2002, ss 37(2)(a), 107, Sch 8.

Second word omitted repealed by the Police (Health and Safety) Act 1997, s 6(2)(a).

Figure "43M," in square brackets inserted by the Employment Relations Act 2004, s 57(1), Sch 1, para 38.

Figure "45A," in square brackets inserted by the Working Time Regulations 1998, SI 1998/1833, reg 31(6).

Figure "47C," in square brackets and the word "and" in square brackets inserted by the Employment Relations Act 1999, s 9, Sch 4, Pt III, paras 5, 35(a), (c).

Words "to 57B" in square brackets substituted by the Employment Relations Act 1999, s 9, Sch 4, Pt III, paras 5, 35(b).

Words in square brackets beginning with the words "(except sections 100" inserted by the Police (Health and Safety) Act 1997, s 6(2)(b).

Figure ", 103A" in square brackets and words "or 103A" in square brackets inserted by the Police Reform Act 2002, s 37(2)(b), (c).

Final words omitted repealed by the Employment Relations Act 1999, ss 9, 44, Sch 4, Pt III, paras 5, 35(d), Sch 9, Table 2.

Police service: a member of the staff of the Independent Police Complaints Commission, who is not a constable, is not treated as being in police service for the purposes of this section; see the Police Reform Act 2002, s 13, Sch 3, para 19(5). A member of staff of the Serious Organised Crime Agency who is designated under the Serious Organised Crime and Police Act 2005, s 43, as a person having the powers of a constable, is not treated as being in police service for the purpose of this section; see s 53(1), (2)(b) of the 2005 Act.

*Offshore employment*

**[1.1006]**
**201   Power to extend employment legislation to offshore employment**
(1)   In this section "offshore employment" means employment for the purposes of activities—
  (a)   in the territorial waters of the United Kingdom,
  (b)   connected with the exploration of the sea-bed or subsoil, or the exploitation of their natural resources, in the United Kingdom sector of the continental shelf, or
  (c)   connected with the exploration or exploitation, in a foreign sector of the continental shelf, of a cross-boundary petroleum field.
(2)   Her Majesty may by Order in Council provide that—
  (a)   the provisions of this Act, and
  (b)   any Northern Ireland legislation making provision for purposes corresponding to any of the purposes of this Act,
apply, to such extent and for such purposes as may be specified in the Order (with or without modification), to or in relation to a person in offshore employment.
(3)   An Order in Council under this section—
  (a)   may make different provision for different cases,
  (b)   may provide that all or any of the provisions referred to in subsection (2), as applied by such an Order in Council, apply—
    (i)   to individuals whether or not they are British subjects, and
    (ii)   to bodies corporate whether or not they are incorporated under the law of a part of the United Kingdom,
  and apply even where the application may affect their activities outside the United Kingdom,
  (c)   may make provision for conferring jurisdiction on any court or class of court specified in the Order in Council, or on [employment tribunals], in respect of offences, causes of action or other matters arising in connection with offshore employment,
  (d)   may (without prejudice to subsection (2) and paragraph (a)) provide that the provisions referred to in subsection (2), as applied by the Order in Council, apply in relation to any person in employment in a part of the areas referred to in subsection (1)(a) and (b),
  (e)   may exclude from the operation of section 3 of the Territorial Waters Jurisdiction Act 1878 (consents required for prosecutions) proceedings for offences under the provisions referred to in subsection (2) in connection with offshore employment,
  (f)   may provide that such proceedings shall not be brought without such consent as may be required by the Order in Council,
  (g)   may (without prejudice to subsection (2)) modify or exclude the operation of any or all of sections  . . .  199 and 215(2) to (6) or of any corresponding Northern Ireland legislation.
[(3A)   Where an Order in Council under this section confers jurisdiction on an employment tribunal, the jurisdiction conferred includes power to make an order under section 12A of the Employment Tribunals Act 1996 (financial penalties), and that section applies accordingly.]
(4)   Any jurisdiction conferred on a court or tribunal under this section is without prejudice to jurisdiction exercisable apart from this section by that or any other court or tribunal.
(5)   In this section—
  "cross-boundary petroleum field" means a petroleum field that extends across the boundary between the United Kingdom sector of the continental shelf and a foreign sector of the continental shelf,
  "foreign sector of the continental shelf" means an area outside the territorial waters of any state, within which rights with respect to the sea-bed and subsoil and their natural resources are exercisable by a state other than the United Kingdom,
  "petroleum field" means a geological structure identified as an oil or gas field by the Order in Council concerned, and
  "United Kingdom sector of the continental shelf" means the area designated under section 1(7) of the Continental Shelf Act 1964.

---

**NOTES**
Sub-s (1): substituted by the Petroleum Act 1998, s 50, Sch 4, para 40(1), (2), as from a day to be appointed, as follows—

  "(1)   In this section "offshore employment" means employment for the purposes of—
  (a)   any activities in the territorial sea adjacent to the United Kingdom, or
  (b)   any such activities as are mentioned in section 11(2) of the Petroleum Act 1998 in waters within subsection (8)(b) or (c) of that section.".

Sub-s (3): words in square brackets in para (c) substituted by the Employment Rights (Dispute Resolution) Act 1998, s 1(2)(b); figure omitted from para (g) repealed by the Employment Relations Act 1999, s 44, Sch 9(9).
Sub-s (3A): inserted by the Enterprise and Regulatory Reform Act 2013, s 16(2), Sch 3, para 5, as from 25 April 2013 (so far as is necessary for enabling the exercise of any power to make orders) and as from a day to be appointed (otherwise).
Sub-s (5): repealed by the Petroleum Act 1998, ss 50, 51(1), Sch 4, para 40(1), (3), Sch 5, Pt I, as from a day to be appointed.

Orders: the Employment Relations (Offshore Employment) Order 2000, SI 2000/1828. Also, by virtue of s 241 of, and Sch 2, Pt I, paras 1–4 to, this Act, the Employment Protection (Offshore Employment) Order 1976, SI 1976/766, has effect as if made under this section.

# CHAPTER II
# OTHER MISCELLANEOUS MATTERS

## *Restrictions on disclosure of information*

**[1.1007]**
### 202 National security

(1)   Where in the opinion of any Minister of the Crown the disclosure of any information would be contrary to the interests of national security—

(a)   nothing in any of the provisions to which this section applies requires any person to disclose the information, and

(b)   no person shall disclose the information in any proceedings in any court or tribunal relating to any of those provisions.

(2)   This section applies to—

(a)   Part I, so far as it relates to employment particulars,

(b)   in Part V, [sections [43M,] 44, 45A[, 47 and 47C]], and sections 48 and 49 so far as relating to those sections,

(c)   in Part VI, sections [55 to 57B] and 61 to 63,

(d)   in Part VII, sections 66 to 68, and sections 69 and 70 so far as relating to those sections,

(e)   Part VIII,

(f)   in Part IX, sections 92 and 93 where they apply by virtue of section 92(4),

(g)   Part X so far as relating to a dismissal which is treated as unfair—

[(i)   by section [98B,] 99, 100, 101A(d) or 103, or by section 104 in its application in relation to time off under section 57A.]

(ii)   by subsection (1) of section 105 by reason of the application of subsection [(2A)], (3) or (6) of that section [or by reason of the application of subsection (4A) in so far as it applies where the reason (or, if more than one, the principal reason) for which an employee was selected for dismissal was that specified in section 101A(d)], and

(h)   this Part and Parts XIV and XV (so far as relating to any of the provisions in paragraphs (a) to (g)).

### NOTES

Sub-s (2) is amended as follows:

Words in first (outer) pair of square brackets in para (b) substituted by the Working Time Regulations 1998, SI 1998/1833, reg 31(5).

Figure "43M," in square brackets in para (b) inserted by the Employment Relations Act 2004, s 57(1), Sch 1, para 39(1), (2).

Words ", 47 and 47C" in square brackets in para (b) substituted by the Employment Relations Act 1999, s 9, Sch 4, Pt III, paras 5, 36(a).

Words in square brackets in para (c) substituted by the Employment Relations Act 1999, s 9, Sch 4, Pt III, paras 5, 36(b).

Para (g)(i) substituted by the Employment Relations Act 1999, s 9, Sch 4, Pt III, paras 5, 36(c).

Figure "98B," in square brackets in para (g)(i) inserted by the Employment Relations Act 2004, s 57(1), Sch 1, para 39(1), (3)(a).

Figure "(2A)" in square brackets in para (g)(ii) substituted by the Employment Relations Act 2004, s 57(1), Sch 1, para 39(1), (3)(b).

Words in second pair of square brackets in para (g)(ii) inserted by SI 1998/1833, reg 32(6).

## *Contracting out etc and remedies*

**[1.1008]**
### 203 Restrictions on contracting out

(1)   Any provision in an agreement (whether a contract of employment or not) is void in so far as it purports—

(a)   to exclude or limit the operation of any provision of this Act, or

(b)   to preclude a person from bringing any proceedings under this Act before an [employment tribunal].

(2)   Subsection (1)—

(a)   does not apply to any provision in a collective agreement excluding rights under section 28 if an order under section 35 is for the time being in force in respect of it,

(b)   does not apply to any provision in a dismissal procedures agreement excluding the right under section 94 if that provision is not to have effect unless an order under section 110 is for the time being in force in respect of it,

(c)   does not apply to any provision in an agreement if an order under section 157 is for the time being in force in respect of it,

(d)   . . .

(e)   does not apply to any agreement to refrain from instituting or continuing proceedings where a conciliation officer has taken action under *section 18* of [the Employment Tribunals Act 1996], and

(f) does not apply to any agreement to refrain from instituting or continuing . . . any proceedings within [the following provisions of section 18(1) of the Employment Tribunals Act 1996 (cases where conciliation available)—

    (i) paragraph (d) (proceedings under this Act),

    (ii) paragraph (h) (proceedings arising out of the Part-time Workers (Prevention of Less Favourable Treatment) Regulations 2000,)]

    [(iii) paragraph (i) (proceedings arising out of the Fixed-term Employees (Prevention of Less Favourable Treatment) Regulations 2002),

    (iv) paragraph (j) (proceedings under those Regulations),]

if the conditions regulating *compromise* agreements under this Act are satisfied in relation to the agreement.

(3) For the purposes of subsection (2)(f) the conditions regulating *compromise* agreements under this Act are that—

(a) the agreement must be in writing,

(b) the agreement must relate to the particular [proceedings],

(c) the employee or worker must have received [advice from a relevant independent adviser] as to the terms and effect of the proposed agreement and, in particular, its effect on his ability to pursue his rights before an [employment tribunal],

(d) there must be in force, when the adviser gives the advice, a [contract of insurance, or an indemnity provided for members of a professional body,] covering the risk of a claim by the employee or worker in respect of loss arising in consequence of the advice,

(e) the agreement must identify the adviser, and

(f) the agreement must state that the conditions regulating *compromise* agreements under this Act are satisfied.

[(3A) A person is a relevant independent adviser for the purposes of subsection (3)(c)—

(a) if he is a qualified lawyer,

(b) if he is an officer, official, employee or member of an independent trade union who has been certified in writing by the trade union as competent to give advice and as authorised to do so on behalf of the trade union,

(c) if he works at an advice centre (whether as an employee or a volunteer) and has been certified in writing by the centre as competent to give advice and as authorised to do so on behalf of the centre, or

(d) if he is a person of a description specified in an order made by the Secretary of State.

(3B) But a person is not a relevant independent adviser for the purposes of subsection (3)(c) in relation to the employee or worker—

(a) if he is, is employed by or is acting in the matter for the employer or an associated employer,

(b) in the case of a person within subsection (3A)(b) or (c), if the trade union or advice centre is the employer or an associated employer,

(c) in the case of a person within subsection (3A)(c), if the employee or worker makes a payment for the advice received from him, or

(d) in the case of a person of a description specified in an order under subsection (3A)(d), if any condition specified in the order in relation to the giving of advice by persons of that description is not satisfied.

(4) In subsection (3A)(a) "qualified lawyer" means—

(a) as respects England and Wales, [a person who, for the purposes of the Legal Services Act 2007, is an authorised person in relation to an activity which constitutes the exercise of a right of audience or the conduct of litigation (within the meaning of that Act), and]

(b) as respects Scotland, an advocate (whether in practice as such or employed to give legal advice), or a solicitor who holds a practising certificate.]

[(5) An agreement under which the parties agree to submit a dispute to arbitration—

(a) shall be regarded for the purposes of subsection (2)(e) and (f) as being an agreement to refrain from instituting or continuing proceedings if—

    (i) the dispute is covered by a scheme having effect by virtue of an order under section 212A of the Trade Union and Labour Relations (Consolidation) Act 1992, and

    (ii) the agreement is to submit it to arbitration in accordance with the scheme, but

(b) shall be regarded as neither being nor including such an agreement in any other case.]

## NOTES

Sub-s (1): words in square brackets substituted by the Employment Rights (Dispute Resolution) Act 1998, s 1(2)(a).

Sub-s (2): para (d) repealed, and paras (f)(iii), (iv) inserted, by the Fixed-term Employees (Prevention of Less Favourable Treatment) Regulations 2002, SI 2002/2034, reg 11, Sch 2, Pt 1, para 3(1), (17) (except in relation to Government training schemes, agency workers or apprentices; see regs 18–20 of the 2002 Regulations at **[2.614]** et seq, and subject to transitional provisions in Sch 2, Pt 2, para 5 thereto at **[2.618]**); words in square brackets in para (e) substituted, and words omitted from para (f) repealed, by the Employment Rights (Dispute Resolution) Act 1998, ss 1(2)(c), 15, 44, Schs 2, 9(3); for the words in italics in para (e) there are substituted the words "any of sections 18A to 18C" by the Enterprise and Regulatory Reform Act 2013, s 7(2), Sch 1, para 10, as from a day to be appointed; words in first pair of square brackets in para (f) substituted by the

Part-time Workers (Prevention of Less Favourable Treatment) Regulations 2001, SI 2001/1107, reg 3; for the word "compromise" in italics in para (f) there is substituted the word "settlement" by the Enterprise and Regulatory Reform Act 2013, s 23(1)(b), as from a day to be appointed.

Sub-s (3): words in square brackets substituted by the Employment Rights (Dispute Resolution) Act 1998, ss 1(2)(a), 9(1), (2)(e), 10(1), (2)(e), 15, Sch 1, para 24(1), (2); for the word "compromise" in italics in both places it appears there is substituted the word "settlement" by the Enterprise and Regulatory Reform Act 2013, s 23(1)(b), as from a day to be appointed.

Sub-ss (3A), (3B): substituted (together with sub-s (4)), for the original sub-s (4), by the Employment Rights (Dispute Resolution) Act 1998, s 15, Sch 1, para 24(1), (3).

Sub-s (4): substituted as noted above: words in square brackets in para (a) substituted by the Legal Services Act 2007, s 208(1), Sch 21, para 120, as from 1 January 2010.

Sub-s (5): added by the Employment Rights (Dispute Resolution) Act 1998, s 8(5).

The Employment Relations Act 1999, ss 10–13, are to be treated as provisions of Pt V of this Act for the purposes of sub-ss (1), (2)(e), (f), (3), (4) above; see s 14 of that Act at **[1.1195]**.

Orders: the Compromise Agreements (Description of Person) Order 2004, SI 2004/754 at **[2.786]**; the Compromise Agreements (Description of Person) Order 2004 (Amendment) Order 2004, SI 2004/2515.

for the word "compromise" in italics there is substituted the word "settlement" by the Enterprise and Regulatory Reform Act 2013, s 23(1)(b), as from a day to be appointed.

## [1.1009]
## 204 Law governing employment

(1)  For the purposes of this Act it is immaterial whether the law which (apart from this Act) governs any person's employment is the law of the United Kingdom, or of a part of the United Kingdom, or not.

(2)  . . .

**NOTES**

Sub-s (2): repealed by the Employment Relations Act 1999, s 44, Sch 9(9).

## [1.1010]
## 205 Remedy for infringement of certain rights

(1)  The remedy of an employee for infringement of any of the rights conferred by section 8, Part III, Parts V to VIII, section 92, Part X and Part XII is, where provision is made for a complaint or the reference of a question to an [employment tribunal], by way of such a complaint or reference and not otherwise.

[(1ZA)  In relation to the right conferred by section 45A, the reference in subsection (1) to an employee has effect as a reference to a worker.]

[(1A)  In relation to the right conferred by section 47B, the reference in subsection (1) to an employee has effect as a reference to a worker.]

(2)  The remedy of a worker in respect of any contravention of section 13, 15, 18(1) or 21(1) is by way of a complaint under section 23 and not otherwise.

**NOTES**

Sub-s (1): words in square brackets substituted by the Employment Rights (Dispute Resolution) Act 1998, s 1(2)(a).

Sub-s (1ZA): inserted by the Working Time Regulations 1998, SI 1998/1833, regs 2(1), 31(7).

Sub-s (1A): inserted by the Public Interest Disclosure Act 1998, ss 14, 18(2).

*[Employee shareholder status*

## [1.1011]
## 205A Employee shareholders

(1)  An individual who is or becomes an employee of a company is an "employee shareholder" if—

   (a)   the company and the individual agree that the individual is to be an employee shareholder,

   (b)   in consideration of that agreement, the company issues or allots to the individual fully paid up shares in the company, or procures the issue or allotment to the individual of fully paid up shares in its parent undertaking, which have a value, on the day of issue or allotment, of no less than £2,000,

   (c)   the company gives the individual a written statement of the particulars of the status of employee shareholder and of the rights which attach to the shares referred to in paragraph (b) ("the employee shares") (see subsection (5)), and

   (d)   the individual gives no consideration other than by entering into the agreement.

(2)  An employee who is an employee shareholder does not have—

   (a)   the right to make an application under section 63D (request to undertake study or training),

   (b)   the right to make an application under section 80F (request for flexible working),

   (c)   the right under section 94 not to be unfairly dismissed, or

   (d)   the right under section 135 to a redundancy payment.

(3)  The following provisions are to be read in the case of an employee who is an employee shareholder as if for "8 weeks' notice", in each place it appears, there were substituted "16 weeks' notice"—

(a)  regulation 11 of the Maternity and Parental Leave etc Regulations 1999 (SI 1999/3312) (requirement for employee to notify employer of intention to return to work during maternity leave period), and

(b)  regulation 25 of the Paternity and Adoption Leave Regulations 2002 (SI 2002/2788) (corresponding provision for adoption leave).

(4)  Regulation 30 of the Additional Paternity Leave Regulations 2010 (SI 2010/1055) (requirement for employee to notify employer of intention to return to work during additional paternity leave period) is to be read in the case of an employee who is an employee shareholder as if for "six weeks' notice", in each place it appears, there were substituted "16 weeks' notice".

(5)  The statement referred to in subsection (1)(c) must—

(a)  state that, as an employee shareholder, the individual would not have the rights specified in subsection (2),

(b)  specify the notice periods that would apply in the individual's case as a result of subsections (3) and (4),

(c)  state whether any voting rights attach to the employee shares,

(d)  state whether the employee shares carry any rights to dividends,

(e)  state whether the employee shares would, if the company were wound up, confer any rights to participate in the distribution of any surplus assets,

(f)  if the company has more than one class of shares and any of the rights referred to in paragraphs (c) to (e) attach to the employee shares, explain how those rights differ from the equivalent rights that attach to the shares in the largest class (or next largest class if the class which includes the employee shares is the largest),

(g)  state whether the employee shares are redeemable and, if they are, at whose option,

(h)  state whether there are any restrictions on the transferability of the employee shares and, if there are, what those restrictions are,

(i)  state whether any of the requirements of sections 561 and 562 of the Companies Act 2006 are excluded in the case of the employee shares (existing shareholders' right of pre-emption), and

(j)  state whether the employee shares are subject to drag-along rights or tag-along rights and, if they are, explain the effect of the shares being so subject.

(6)  Agreement between a company and an individual that the individual is to become an employee shareholder is of no effect unless, before the agreement is made—

(a)  the individual, having been given the statement referred to in subsection (1)(c), receives advice from a relevant independent adviser as to the terms and effect of the proposed agreement, and

(b)  seven days have passed since the day on which the individual receives the advice.

(7)  Any reasonable costs incurred by the individual in obtaining the advice (whether or not the individual becomes an employee shareholder) which would, but for this subsection, have to be met by the individual are instead to be met by the company.

(8)  The reference in subsection (2)(b) to making an application under section 80F does not include a reference to making an application within the period of 14 days beginning with the day on which the employee shareholder returns to work from a period of parental leave under regulations under section 76.

(9)  The reference in subsection (2)(c) to unfair dismissal does not include a reference to a dismissal—

(a)  which is required to be regarded as unfair for the purposes of Part 10 by a provision (whenever made) contained in or made under this or any other Act, or

(b)  which amounts to a contravention of the Equality Act 2010.

(10)  The reference in subsection (2)(c) to the right not to be unfairly dismissed does not include a reference to that right in a case where section 108(2) (health and safety cases) applies.

(11)  The Secretary of State may by order amend subsection (1) so as to increase the sum for the time being specified there.

(12)  The Secretary of State may by regulations provide that any agreement for a company to buy back from an individual the shares referred to in subsection (1)(b) in the event that the individual ceases to be an employee shareholder or ceases to be an employee must be on terms which meet the specified requirements.

(13)  In this section—

"company" means—

(a)  a company or overseas company (within the meaning, in each case, of the Companies Act 2006) which has a share capital, or

(b)  a European Public Limited-Liability Company (or Societas Europaea) within the meaning of Council Regulation 2157/2001/EC of 8 October 2001 on the Statute for a European company;

"drag-along rights", in relation to shares in a company, means the right of the holders of a majority of the shares, where they are selling their shares, to require the holders of the minority to sell theirs;

"parent undertaking" has the same meaning as in the Companies Act 2006;

"relevant independent adviser" has the meaning that it has for the purposes of section 203(3)(c);

"tag-along rights", in relation to shares in a company, means the right of the holders of a minority of the shares to sell their shares, where the holders of the majority are selling theirs, on the same terms as those on which the holders of the majority are doing so.

(14)　The reference in this section to the value of shares in a company is a reference to their market value within the meaning of the Taxation of Chargeable Gains Act 1992 (see sections 272 and 273 of that Act).]

**NOTES**

Commencement: to be appointed.

Inserted, together with preceding cross-heading, by the Growth and Infrastructure Act 2013, s 31(1), as from a day to be appointed.

*General provisions about death of employer or employee*

**[1.1012]**
**206　Institution or continuance of tribunal proceedings**
(1)　Where an employer has died, any tribunal proceedings arising under any of the provisions of this Act to which this section applies may be defended by a personal representative of the deceased employer.
(2)　This section and section 207 apply to—
　　(a)　Part I, so far as it relates to itemised pay statements,
　　(b)　Part III,
　　(c)　Part V,
　　(d)　Part VI, apart from sections 58 to 60,
　　(e)　Parts VII and VIII,
　　(f)　in Part IX, sections 92 and 93, and
　　(g)　Parts X to XII.
(3)　Where an employee has died, any tribunal proceedings arising under any of the provisions of this Act to which this section applies may be instituted or continued by a personal representative of the deceased employee.
(4)　If there is no personal representative of a deceased employee, any tribunal proceedings arising under any of the provisions of this Act to which this section applies may be instituted or continued on behalf of the estate of the deceased employee by any appropriate person appointed by the [employment tribunal].
(5)　In subsection (4) "appropriate person" means a person who is—
　　(a)　authorised by the employee before his death to act in connection with the proceedings, or
　　(b)　the widow or widower, [surviving civil partner,] child, parent or brother or sister of the deceased employee;
and in Part XI and the following provisions of this section and section 207 references to a personal representative include a person appointed under subsection (4).
(6)　In a case where proceedings are instituted or continued by virtue of subsection (4), any award made by the [employment tribunal] shall be—
　　(a)　made in such terms, and
　　(b)　enforceable in such manner,
as the Secretary of State may by regulations provide.
(7)　Any reference in the provisions of this Act to which this section applies to the doing of anything by or in relation to an employer or employee includes a reference to the doing of the thing by or in relation to a personal representative of the deceased employer or employee.
(8)　Any reference in the provisions of this Act to which this section applies to a thing required or authorised to be done by or in relation to an employer or employee includes a reference to a thing required or authorised to be done by or in relation to a personal representative of the deceased employer or employee.
(9)　Subsections (7) and (8) do not prevent a reference to a successor of an employer including a personal representative of a deceased employer.

**NOTES**

Sub-ss (4), (6): words in square brackets substituted by the Employment Rights (Dispute Resolution) Act 1998, s 1(2)(a).

Sub-s (5): words in square brackets in para (b) inserted by the Civil Partnership Act 2004 (Overseas Relationships and Consequential, etc Amendments) Order 2005, SI 2005/3129, art 4(4), Sch 4, para 11.

Regulations: as of 6 April 2013 no Regulations had been made under this section but, by virtue of s 241 of, and Sch 2, Pt I, paras 1–4 to, this Act, the Employment Tribunal Awards (Enforcement in case of Death) Regulations 1976, SI 1976/663, have effect as if made under this section.

**[1.1013]**
**207　Rights and liabilities accruing after death**
(1)　Any right arising under any of the provisions of this Act to which this section applies which accrues after the death of an employee devolves as if it had accrued before his death.

(2)   Where an [employment tribunal] determines under any provision of Part XI that an employer is liable to pay to a personal representative of a deceased employee—
(a)   the whole of a redundancy payment to which he would have been entitled but for some provision of Part XI or section 206, or
(b)   such part of such a redundancy payment as the tribunal thinks fit,
the reference in subsection (1) to a right includes any right to receive it.
(3)   Where—
(a)   by virtue of any of the provisions to which this section applies a personal representative is liable to pay any amount, and
(b)   the liability has not accrued before the death of the employer,
it shall be treated as a liability of the deceased employer which had accrued immediately before his death.

NOTES
Sub-s (2): words in square brackets substituted by the Employment Rights (Dispute Resolution) Act 1998, s 1(2)(a).

*[Mediation in certain cross-border disputes*

**[1.1014]**
**207A   Extension of time limits because of mediation in certain cross-border disputes**
(1)   In this section—
(a)   "Mediation Directive" means Directive 2008/52/EC of the European Parliament and of the Council of 21 May 2008 on certain aspects of mediation in civil and commercial matters,
(b)   "mediation" has the meaning given by article 3(a) of the Mediation Directive,
(c)   "mediator" has the meaning given by article 3(b) of the Mediation Directive, and
(d)   "relevant dispute" means a dispute to which article 8(1) of the Mediation Directive applies (certain cross-border disputes).
(2)   Subsection (3) applies where—
(a)   this Act provides for that subsection to apply for the purposes of a provision of this Act,
(b)   a time limit is set by that provision in relation to the whole or part of a relevant dispute,
(c)   a mediation in relation to the relevant dispute starts before the time limit expires, and
(d)   if not extended by this section, the time limit would expire before the mediation ends or less than four weeks after it ends.
(3)   The time limit expires instead at the end of four weeks after the mediation ends (subject to subsection (4)).
(4)   If a time limit mentioned in subsection (2)(b) has been extended by this section, subsections (2) and (3) apply to the extended time limit as they apply to a time limit mentioned in subsection (2)(b).
(5)   Subsection (6) applies where—
(a)   a time limit is set by section 164(1)(c) or (2) in relation to the whole or part of a relevant dispute,
(b)   a mediation in relation to the relevant dispute starts before the time limit expires, and
(c)   if not extended by this section, the time limit would expire before the mediation ends or less than eight weeks after it ends.
(6)   The time limit expires instead at the end of eight weeks after the mediation ends (subject to subsection (7)).
(7)   If a time limit mentioned in subsection (5)(a) has been extended by this section, subsections (5) and (6) apply to the extended time limit as they apply to a time limit mentioned in subsection (5)(a).
(8)   Where more than one time limit applies in relation to a relevant dispute, the extension by subsection (3) or (6) of one of those time limits does not affect the others.
(9)   For the purposes of this section, a mediation starts on the date of the agreement to mediate that is entered into by the parties and the mediator.
(10)   For the purposes of this section, a mediation ends on the date of the first of these to occur—
(a)   the parties reach an agreement in resolution of the relevant dispute,
(b)   a party completes the notification of the other parties that it has withdrawn from the mediation,
(c)   a party to whom a qualifying request is made fails to give a response reaching the other parties within 14 days of the request,
(d)   the parties, after being notified that the mediator's appointment has ended (by death, resignation or otherwise), fail to agree within 14 days to seek to appoint a replacement mediator,
(e)   the mediation otherwise comes to an end pursuant to the terms of the agreement to mediate.
(11)   For the purpose of subsection (10), a qualifying request is a request by a party that another (A) confirm to all parties that A is continuing with the mediation.
(12)   In the case of any relevant dispute, references in this section to a mediation are references to the mediation so far as it relates to that dispute, and references to a party are to be read accordingly.

(13) Where an employment tribunal has power under this Act to extend a time limit to which subsection (3) applies, the power is exercisable in relation to the time limit as extended by this section.]

**NOTES**
Commencement: 20 May 2011.
Inserted by the Cross-Border Mediation (EU Directive) Regulations 2011, SI 2011/1133, regs 30, 48, as from 20 May 2011.

**[1.1015]**
**[207B   Extension of time limits to facilitate conciliation before institution of proceedings**
(1) This section applies where this Act provides for it to apply for the purposes of a provision of this Act (a "relevant provision").
But it does not apply to a dispute that is (or so much of a dispute as is) a relevant dispute for the purposes of section 207A.
(2) In this section—
    (a)   Day A is the day on which the complainant or applicant concerned complies with the requirement in subsection (1) of section 18A of the Employment Tribunals Act 1996 (requirement to contact ACAS before instituting proceedings) in relation to the matter in respect of which the proceedings are brought, and
    (b)   Day B is the day on which the complainant or applicant concerned receives or, if earlier, is treated as receiving (by virtue of regulations made under subsection (11) of that section) the certificate issued under subsection (4) of that section.
(3) In working out when a time limit set by a relevant provision expires the period beginning with the day after Day A and ending with Day B is not to be counted.
(4) If a time limit set by a relevant provision would (if not extended by this subsection) expire during the period beginning with Day A and ending one month after Day B, the time limit expires instead at the end of that period.
(5) Where an employment tribunal has power under this Act to extend a time limit set by a relevant provision, the power is exercisable in relation to the time limit as extended by this section.]

**NOTES**
Commencement: to be appointed.
Inserted by the Enterprise and Regulatory Reform Act 2013, s 8, Sch 2, paras 15, 35, as from a day to be appointed.

*Modifications of Act*

**208**   *(Repealed by the Employment Relations Act 1999, ss 36(2), 44, Sch 9(10).)*
**[1.1016]**
**209   Powers to amend Act**
(1) The Secretary of State may by order—
    (a)   provide that any provision of this Act, other than any to which this paragraph does not apply, which is specified in the order shall not apply to persons, or to employments, of such classes as may be prescribed in the order,
    (b)   provide that any provision of this Act, other than any to which this paragraph does not apply, shall apply to persons or employments of such classes as may be prescribed in the order subject to such exceptions and modifications as may be so prescribed, or
    (c)   vary, or exclude the operation of, any of the provisions to which this paragraph applies.
(2) Subsection (1)(a) does not apply to—
    (a)   Parts II and IV,
    (b)   in Part V, sections 45 and 46, and sections 48 and 49 so far as relating to those sections,
    (c)   in Part VI, sections 58 to 60,
    (d)   in Part IX, sections 87(3), 88 to 90, 91(1) to (4) and (6) and 92(6) to (8),
    (e)   in Part X, sections 95, 97(1) to (5), 98(1) to (4) and (6), 100, 101, [101A,] 102, 103, 105, 107, 110, 111, 120(2), 124(1), (2) and (5), 125(7) and 134,
    (f)   in Part XI, sections 143, 144, 160(2) and (3), 166 to 173 and 177 to 180,
    (g)   in Part XIII, sections . . . ,
    (h)   Chapter I of Part XIV, or
    (j)   in Part XV, section 236(3) so far as relating to sections 120(2), 124(2) and 125(7).
(3) Subsection (1)(b) does not apply to—
    (a)   any of the provisions to which subsection (1)(a) does not apply,
    (b)   sections 1 to 7, or
    (c)   the provisions of sections 86 to 91 not specified in subsection (2).
(4) The provision which may be made by virtue of paragraph (b) of subsection (1) in relation to section 94 does not include provision for application subject to exceptions or modifications; but this subsection does not prejudice paragraph (a) of that subsection.
(5) Subsection (1)(c) applies to sections 29(2), 65(2), 86(5), 92(3), 108(1), . . . 159, 160(1) . . . and 199(1), (2), (4) and (5).
(6), (7)   . . .

(8)   The provisions of this section are without prejudice to any other power of the Secretary of State to amend, vary or repeal any provision of this Act or to extend or restrict its operation in relation to any person or employment.

**NOTES**

Sub-s (2): figure in square brackets in para (e) inserted by the Working Time Regulations 1998, SI 1998/1833, regs 2(1), 32(7); words omitted from para (g) repealed by the Employment Relations Act 1999, s 44, Sch 9(3), (9) (it is unclear why the whole of para (g) was not repealed).

Sub-s (5): first words omitted repealed by the Employment Equality (Age) Regulations 2006, SI 2006/1031, reg 49(1), Sch 8, Pt 1, paras 21, 34; second words omitted repealed by the Employment Relations Act 1999, s 44, Sch 9(9).

Sub-s (6): repealed by the Employment Relations Act 1999, ss 9, 44, Sch 4, Pt III, paras 1, 5, 37, Sch 9(2).

Sub-s (7): repealed by the Employment Relations Act 1999, ss 23(6), 44, Sch 9(4).

Orders: the Redundancy Payments (Continuity of Employment in Local Government, etc) (Modification) Order 1999, SI 1999/2277 at **[2.446]**; the Redundancy Payments (Continuity of Employment in Local Government, etc) (Modification) (Amendment) Order 2001, SI 2001/866; the Redundancy Payments (Continuity of Employment in Local Government, etc) (Modification) (Amendment) Order 2002, SI 2002/532; the Redundancy Payments (Continuity of Employment in Local Government, etc) (Modification) (Amendment) Order 2004, SI 2004/1682; the Redundancy Payments (Continuity of Employment in Local Government, etc) (Modification) Order (Amendment) Order 2010, SI 2010/903; the Unfair Dismissal and Statement of Reasons for Dismissal (Variation of Qualifying Period) Order 2012, SI 2012/989 at **[2.1628]**; the Local Policing Bodies (Consequential Amendments and Transitional Provision) Order 2012, SI 2012/2733.

Also, by virtue of s 241 of, and Sch 2, Pt I, paras 1–4 to, this Act, the following Orders have effect as if made under this section: the Redundancy Payments (National Health Service) (Modification) Order 1993, SI 1993/3167 at **[2.204]**; the Employment Protection (Continuity of Employment of National Health Service Employees) (Modification) Order 1996, SI 1996/1023.

# PART XIV
# INTERPRETATION

## CHAPTER I
## CONTINUOUS EMPLOYMENT

**[1.1017]**
**210   Introductory**
(1)   References in any provision of this Act to a period of continuous employment are (unless provision is expressly made to the contrary) to a period computed in accordance with this Chapter.
(2)   In any provision of this Act which refers to a period of continuous employment expressed in months or years—
   (a)   a month means a calendar month, and
   (b)   a year means a year of twelve calendar months.
(3)   In computing an employee's period of continuous employment for the purposes of any provision of this Act, any question—
   (a)   whether the employee's employment is of a kind counting towards a period of continuous employment, or
   (b)   whether periods (consecutive or otherwise) are to be treated as forming a single period of continuous employment,
shall be determined week by week; but where it is necessary to compute the length of an employee's period of employment it shall be computed in months and years of twelve months in accordance with section 211.
(4)   Subject to sections 215 to 217, a week which does not count in computing the length of a period of continuous employment breaks continuity of employment.
(5)   A person's employment during any period shall, unless the contrary is shown, be presumed to have been continuous.

**[1.1018]**
**211   Period of continuous employment**
(1)   An employee's period of continuous employment for the purposes of any provision of this Act—
   (a)   (subject to [subsection] (3)) begins with the day on which the employee starts work, and
   (b)   ends with the day by reference to which the length of the employee's period of continuous employment is to be ascertained for the purposes of the provision.
(2)   . . .
(3)   If an employee's period of continuous employment includes one or more periods which (by virtue of section 215, 216 or 217) while not counting in computing the length of the period do not break continuity of employment, the beginning of the period shall be treated as postponed by the number of days falling within that intervening period, or the aggregate number of days falling within those periods, calculated in accordance with the section in question.

**NOTES**

Sub-s (1): word in square brackets in para (a) substituted by the Employment Equality (Age) Regulations 2006, SI 2006/1031, reg 49(1), Sch 8, Pt 1, paras 21, 35(1), (2).

Sub-s (2): repealed by SI 2006/1031, reg 49(1), Sch 8, Pt 1, paras 21, 35(1), (3).

**[1.1019]**
**212  Weeks counting in computing period**
(1)   Any week during the whole or part of which an employee's relations with his employer are governed by a contract of employment counts in computing the employee's period of employment.
(2)   . . .
(3)   Subject to subsection (4), any week (not within subsection (1)) during the whole or part of which an employee is—
  (a)   incapable of work in consequence of sickness or injury,
  (b)   absent from work on account of a temporary cessation of work, [or]
  (c)   absent from work in circumstances such that, by arrangement or custom, he is regarded as continuing in the employment of his employer for any purpose,  . . .
  (d)    . . .
counts in computing the employee's period of employment.
(4)   Not more than twenty-six weeks count under subsection (3)(a)  . . .  between any periods falling under subsection (1).

**NOTES**
  Sub-s (2): repealed by the Employment Relations Act 1999, ss 9, 44, Sch 4, Pt III, paras 1, 5, 38(1), (2), Sch 9(2).
  Sub-s (3): word in square brackets in para (b) inserted, and para (d) and word immediately preceding repealed, by the Employment Relations Act 1999, ss 9, 44, Sch 4, Pt III, paras 1, 5, 38(1), (3), Sch 9(2).
  Sub-s (4): words omitted repealed by the Employment Relations Act 1999, ss 9, Sch 4, Pt III, paras 1, 5, 38(1), (4), Sch 9(2).

**[1.1020]**
**213  Intervals in employment**
(1)   Where in the case of an employee a date later than the date which would be the effective date of termination by virtue of subsection (1) of section 97 is treated for certain purposes as the effective date of termination by virtue of subsection (2) or (4) of that section, the period of the interval between the two dates counts as a period of employment in ascertaining for the purposes of section 108(1) or 119(1) the period for which the employee has been continuously employed.
(2)   Where an employee is by virtue of section 138(1) regarded for the purposes of Part XI as not having been dismissed by reason of a renewal or re-engagement taking effect after an interval, the period of the interval counts as a period of employment in ascertaining for the purposes of section 155 or 162(1) the period for which the employee has been continuously employed (except so far as it is to be disregarded under section 214 or 215).
(3)   Where in the case of an employee a date later than the date which would be the relevant date by virtue of subsections (2) to (4) of section 145 is treated for certain purposes as the relevant date by virtue of subsection (5) of that section, the period of the interval between the two dates counts as a period of employment in ascertaining for the purposes of section 155 or 162(1) the period for which the employee has been continuously employed (except so far as it is to be disregarded under section 214 or 215).

**[1.1021]**
**214  Special provisions for redundancy payments**
(1)   This section applies where a period of continuous employment has to be determined in relation to an employee for the purposes of the application of section 155 or 162(1).
(2)   The continuity of a period of employment is broken where—
  (a)   a redundancy payment has previously been paid to the employee (whether in respect of dismissal or in respect of lay-off or short-time), and
  (b)   the contract of employment under which the employee was employed was renewed (whether by the same or another employer) or the employee was re-engaged under a new contract of employment (whether by the same or another employer).
(3)   The continuity of a period of employment is also broken where—
  (a)   a payment has been made to the employee (whether in respect of the termination of his employment or lay-off or short-time) in accordance with a scheme under section 1 of the Superannuation Act 1972 or arrangements falling within section 177(3), and
  (b)   he commenced new, or renewed, employment.
(4)   The date on which the person's continuity of employment is broken by virtue of this section—
  (a)   if the employment was under a contract of employment, is the date which was the relevant date in relation to the payment mentioned in subsection (2)(a) or (3)(a), and
  (b)   if the employment was otherwise than under a contract of employment, is the date which would have been the relevant date in relation to the payment mentioned in subsection (2)(a) or (3)(a) had the employment been under a contract of employment.
(5)   For the purposes of this section a redundancy payment shall be treated as having been paid if—
  (a)   the whole of the payment has been paid to the employee by the employer,
  (b)   a tribunal has determined liability and found that the employer must pay part (but not all) of the redundancy payment and the employer has paid that part, or

   (c)   the Secretary of State has paid a sum to the employee in respect of the redundancy payment under section 167.

**[1.1022]**
### 215  Employment abroad etc
(1)   This Chapter applies to a period of employment—
   (a)   (subject to the following provisions of this section) even where during the period the employee was engaged in work wholly or mainly outside Great Britain, and
   (b)   even where the employee was excluded by or under this Act from any right conferred by this Act.
(2)   For the purposes of sections 155 and 162(1) a week of employment does not count in computing a period of employment if the employee—
   (a)   was employed outside Great Britain during the whole or part of the week, and
   (b)   was not during that week an employed earner for the purposes of the Social Security Contributions and Benefits Act 1992 in respect of whom a secondary Class 1 contribution was payable under that Act (whether or not the contribution was in fact paid).
(3)   Where by virtue of subsection (2) a week of employment does not count in computing a period of employment, the continuity of the period is not broken by reason only that the week does not count in computing the period; and the number of days which, for the purposes of section 211(3), fall within the intervening period is seven for each week within this subsection.
(4)   Any question arising under subsection (2) whether—
   (a)   a person was an employed earner for the purposes of the Social Security Contributions and Benefits Act 1992, or
   (b)   if so, whether a secondary Class 1 contribution was payable in respect of him under that Act,
shall be determined by [an officer of the Commissioners of Inland Revenue].
[(5)   Part II of the Social Security Contributions (Transfer of Functions, etc) Act 1999 (decisions and appeals) shall apply in relation to the determination of any issue by the Inland Revenue under subsection (4) as if it were a decision falling within section 8(1) of that Act.]
(6)   Subsection (2) does not apply in relation to a person who is—
   (a)   employed as a master or seaman in a British ship, and
   (b)   ordinarily resident in Great Britain.

**NOTES**
Sub-s (4): words in square brackets substituted by the Social Security Contributions (Transfer of Functions, etc) Act 1999, s 18, Sch 7, para 21(1), (2).
Sub-s (5): substituted by the Social Security Contributions (Transfer of Functions, etc) Act 1999, s 18, Sch 7, para 21(1), (3).
Commissioners of Inland Revenue: a reference to the Commissioners of Inland Revenue is now to be taken as a reference to the Commissioners for Her Majesty's Revenue and Customs; see the Commissioners for Revenue and Customs Act 2005, s 50(1), (7).

**[1.1023]**
### 216  Industrial disputes
(1)   A week does not count under section 212 if during the week, or any part of the week, the employee takes part in a strike.
(2)   The continuity of an employee's period of employment is not broken by a week which does not count under this Chapter (whether or not by virtue only of subsection (1)) if during the week, or any part of the week, the employee takes part in a strike; and the number of days which, for the purposes of section 211(3), fall within the intervening period is the number of days between the last working day before the strike and the day on which work was resumed.
(3)   The continuity of an employee's period of employment is not broken by a week if during the week, or any part of the week, the employee is absent from work because of a lock-out by the employer; and the number of days which, for the purposes of section 211(3), fall within the intervening period is the number of days between the last working day before the lock-out and the day on which work was resumed.

**[1.1024]**
### 217  Reinstatement after military service
(1)   If a person who is entitled to apply to his former employer under the Reserve Forces (Safeguard of Employment) Act 1985 enters the employment of the employer not later than the end of the six month period mentioned in section 1(4)(b) of that Act, his period of service in the armed forces of the Crown in the circumstances specified in section 1(1) of that Act does not break his continuity of employment.
(2)   In the case of such a person the number of days which, for the purposes of section 211(3), fall within the intervening period is the number of days between the last day of his previous period of employment with the employer (or, if there was more than one such period, the last of them) and the first day of the period of employment beginning in the six month period.

**[1.1025]**
**218 Change of employer**
(1)  Subject to the provisions of this section, this Chapter relates only to employment by the one employer.
(2)  If a trade or business, or an undertaking (whether or not established by or under an Act), is transferred from one person to another—
(a)   the period of employment of an employee in the trade or business or undertaking at the time of the transfer counts as a period of employment with the transferee, and
(b)   the transfer does not break the continuity of the period of employment.
(3)  If by or under an Act (whether public or local and whether passed before or after this Act) a contract of employment between any body corporate and an employee is modified and some other body corporate is substituted as the employer—
(a)   the employee's period of employment at the time when the modification takes effect counts as a period of employment with the second body corporate, and
(b)   the change of employer does not break the continuity of the period of employment.
(4)  If on the death of an employer the employee is taken into the employment of the personal representatives or trustees of the deceased—
(a)   the employee's period of employment at the time of the death counts as a period of employment with the employer's personal representatives or trustees, and
(b)   the death does not break the continuity of the period of employment.
(5)  If there is a change in the partners, personal representatives or trustees who employ any person—
(a)   the employee's period of employment at the time of the change counts as a period of employment with the partners, personal representatives or trustees after the change, and
(b)   the change does not break the continuity of the period of employment.
(6)  If an employee of an employer is taken into the employment of another employer who, at the time when the employee enters the second employer's employment, is an associated employer of the first employer—
(a)   the employee's period of employment at that time counts as a period of employment with the second employer, and
(b)   the change of employer does not break the continuity of the period of employment.
(7)  If an employee of the [governing body] of a school maintained by a [local authority] is taken into the employment of the authority or an employee of a [local authority] is taken into the employment of the [governing body] of a school maintained by the authority—
(a)   his period of employment at the time of the change of employer counts as a period of employment with the second employer, and
(b)   the change does not break the continuity of the period of employment.
(8)  If a person employed in relevant employment by a health service employer is taken into relevant employment by another such employer, his period of employment at the time of the change of employer counts as a period of employment with the second employer and the change does not break the continuity of the period of employment.
(9)  For the purposes of subsection (8) employment is relevant employment if it is employment of a description—
(a)   in which persons are engaged while undergoing professional training which involves their being employed successively by a number of different health service employers, and
(b)   which is specified in an order made by the Secretary of State.
(10)   The following are health service employers for the purposes of subsections (8) and (9)—
[(za) the National Health Service Commissioning Board,
(zb)  a clinical commissioning group established under section 14D of the National Health Service Act 2006,]
(a)   . . .
(b)   Special Health Authorities established under [section 28 of [the National Health Service Act 2006] or section 22 of the National Health Service (Wales) Act 2006],
[(bb)  . . . ]
(c)   National Health Service trusts established under *[[the National Health Service Act 2006] or* the National Health Service (Wales) Act 2006],
[(ca) NHS foundation trusts,]
[(cb) Local Health Boards established under section 11 of the National Health Service (Wales) Act 2006,]
[(cc) the National Institute for Health and Care Excellence,]
[(cd) the Health and Social Care Information Centre,]
(d)   . . .
[(dd) . . . ]
(e)   . . .
[(11)   In subsection (7) "local authority" has the meaning given by section 579(1) of the Education Act 1996.]

**NOTES**

Sub-s (7): words "governing body" in square brackets substituted by the Education Act 2002, s 215(1), Sch 21, para 32; words "local authority" in square brackets substituted by the Local Education Authorities and Children's Services Authorities (Integration of Functions) Order 2010, SI 2010/1158, art 5, Sch 2, Pt 2, para 41(1), (5)(a), as from 5 May 2010.

Sub-s (10) is amended as follows:

Paras (za), (zb) inserted by the Health and Social Care Act 2012, s 55(2), Sch 5, para 75(a), as from 1 October 2012.

Para (a) repealed by the Health and Social Care Act 2012, s 55(2), Sch 5, para 75(b), as from 1 April 2013.

In para (b), words in first (outer) pair of square brackets substituted by the National Health Service (Consequential Provisions) Act 2006, s 2, Sch 1, paras 177, 180(b), and words in second (inner) pair of square brackets substituted by the Health and Social Care Act 2012, s 55(2), Sch 5, para 75(c), as from 1 April 2013.

Para (bb) inserted by the Health Act 1999 (Supplementary, Consequential etc Provisions) Order 2000, SI 2000/90, art 3(1), Sch 1, para 30(1), (3), and repealed by the Health and Social Care Act 2012, s 55(2), Sch 5, para 75(d), as from 1 April 2013.

In para (c), words in first (outer) pair of square brackets substituted by the National Health Service (Consequential Provisions) Act 2006, s 2, Sch 1, paras 177, 180(d), words in second (inner) pair of square brackets substituted by the Health and Social Care Act 2012, s 55(2), Sch 5, para 75(e), as from 1 April 2013, and words in italics repealed by the Health and Social Care Act 2012, s 179(6), Sch 14, Pt 2, paras 68, 70, as from a day to be appointed.

Para (ca) inserted by the Health and Social Care (Community Health and Standards) Act 2003, s 34, Sch 4, paras 99, 101.

Para (cb) inserted by SI 2007/961, art 3, Schedule, para 27(1), (4).

Para (cc) inserted by the Health and Social Care Act 2012, s 249, Sch 17, para 6(1), (3), as from 1 April 2013.

Para (cd) inserted by the Health and Social Care Act 2012, s 277, Sch 19, para 6(1), (3), as from 1 April 2013.

Paras (d), (e) (and the word immediately preceding para (e)) repealed by the Health and Social Care (Community Health and Standards) Act 2003, ss 190(2), 196, Sch 13, para 8, Sch 14, Pts 4, 7.

Para (dd) inserted by the Health Protection Agency Act 2004, s 11(1), Sch 3, para 13, and repealed by the Health and Social Care Act 2012, s 56(4), Sch 7, para 9, as from 1 April 2013.

Sub-s (11): inserted by SI 2010/1158, art 5(1), Sch 2, Pt 2, para 41(1), (5)(b), as from 5 May 2010.

Orders: as of 6 April 2013 no Orders had been made under this section but, by virtue of s 241 of, and Sch 2, Pt I, paras 1–4 to, this Act, the Employment Protection (National Health Service) Order 1996, SI 1996/638, has effect as if made under this section.

**[1.1026]**
### 219 Reinstatement or re-engagement of dismissed employee
(1) Regulations made by the Secretary of State may make provision—
    (a)   for preserving the continuity of a person's period of employment for the purposes of this Chapter or for the purposes of this Chapter as applied by or under any other enactment specified in the regulations, or
    (b)   for modifying or excluding the operation of section 214 subject to the recovery of any such payment as is mentioned in that section,
in cases where . . . a dismissed employee is reinstated [re-engaged or otherwise re-employed] by his employer or by a successor or associated employer of that employer [in any circumstances prescribed by the regulations].
(2)–(4)   . . .

**NOTES**

Sub-s (1): words omitted repealed, words in first pair of square brackets substituted, and words in second pair of square brackets inserted, by the Employment Rights (Dispute Resolution) Act 1998, s 15, Sch 1, para 25(1), (2), Sch 2.

Sub-ss (2)–(4): repealed by the Employment Rights (Dispute Resolution) Act 1998, s 15, Sch 1, para 25(1), (3), Sch 2.

Regulations: the Employment Protection (Continuity of Employment) Regulations 1996, SI 1996/3147 at **[2.265]**; the Employment Protection (Continuity of Employment) (Amendment) Regulations 2001, SI 2001/1188.

### CHAPTER II
### A WEEK'S PAY

*Introductory*

**[1.1027]**
### 220 Introductory
The amount of a week's pay of an employee shall be calculated for the purposes of this Act in accordance with this Chapter.

*Employments with normal working hours*

**[1.1028]**
### 221 General
(1) This section and sections 222 and 223 apply where there are normal working hours for the employee when employed under the contract of employment in force on the calculation date.
(2) Subject to section 222, if the employee's remuneration for employment in normal working hours (whether by the hour or week or other period) does not vary with the amount of work done in the period, the amount of a week's pay is the amount which is payable by the employer under the contract of employment in force on the calculation date if the employee works throughout his normal working hours in a week.

(3)   Subject to section 222, if the employee's remuneration for employment in normal working hours (whether by the hour or week or other period) does vary with the amount of work done in the period, the amount of a week's pay is the amount of remuneration for the number of normal working hours in a week calculated at the average hourly rate of remuneration payable by the employer to the employee in respect of the period of twelve weeks ending—

    (a)   where the calculation date is the last day of a week, with that week, and

    (b)   otherwise, with the last complete week before the calculation date.

(4)   In this section references to remuneration varying with the amount of work done includes remuneration which may include any commission or similar payment which varies in amount.

(5)   This section is subject to sections 227 and 228.

**[1.1029]**
## 222 Remuneration varying according to time of work

(1)   This section applies if the employee is required under the contract of employment in force on the calculation date to work during normal working hours on days of the week, or at times of the day, which differ from week to week or over a longer period so that the remuneration payable for, or apportionable to, any week varies according to the incidence of those days or times.

(2)   The amount of a week's pay is the amount of remuneration for the average number of weekly normal working hours at the average hourly rate of remuneration.

(3)   For the purposes of subsection (2)—

    (a)   the average number of weekly hours is calculated by dividing by twelve the total number of the employee's normal working hours during the relevant period of twelve weeks, and

    (b)   the average hourly rate of remuneration is the average hourly rate of remuneration payable by the employer to the employee in respect of the relevant period of twelve weeks.

(4)   In subsection (3) "the relevant period of twelve weeks" means the period of twelve weeks ending—

    (a)   where the calculation date is the last day of a week, with that week, and

    (b)   otherwise, with the last complete week before the calculation date.

(5)   This section is subject to sections 227 and 228.

**[1.1030]**
## 223 Supplementary

(1)   For the purposes of sections 221 and 222, in arriving at the average hourly rate of remuneration, only—

    (a)   the hours when the employee was working, and

    (b)   the remuneration payable for, or apportionable to, those hours,

shall be brought in.

(2)   If for any of the twelve weeks mentioned in sections 221 and 222 no remuneration within subsection (1)(b) was payable by the employer to the employee, account shall be taken of remuneration in earlier weeks so as to bring up to twelve the number of weeks of which account is taken.

(3)   Where—

    (a)   in arriving at the average hourly rate of remuneration, account has to be taken of remuneration payable for, or apportionable to, work done in hours other than normal working hours, and

    (b)   the amount of that remuneration was greater than it would have been if the work had been done in normal working hours (or, in a case within section 234(3), in normal working hours falling within the number of hours without overtime),

account shall be taken of that remuneration as if the work had been done in such hours and the amount of that remuneration had been reduced accordingly.

*Employments with no normal working hours*

**[1.1031]**
## 224 Employments with no normal working hours

(1)   This section applies where there are no normal working hours for the employee when employed under the contract of employment in force on the calculation date.

(2)   The amount of a week's pay is the amount of the employee's average weekly remuneration in the period of twelve weeks ending—

    (a)   where the calculation date is the last day of a week, with that week, and

    (b)   otherwise, with the last complete week before the calculation date.

(3)   In arriving at the average weekly remuneration no account shall be taken of a week in which no remuneration was payable by the employer to the employee and remuneration in earlier weeks shall be brought in so as to bring up to twelve the number of weeks of which account is taken.

(4)   This section is subject to sections 227 and 228.

*The calculation date*

**[1.1032]**
## 225 Rights during employment

(1) Where the calculation is for the purposes of section 30, the calculation date is—
 (a) where the employee's contract has been varied, or a new contract entered into, in connection with a period of short-time working, the last day on which the original contract was in force, and
 (b) otherwise, the day in respect of which the guarantee payment is payable.

(2) Where the calculation is for the purposes of section 53 or 54, the calculation date is the day on which the employer's notice was given.

(3) Where the calculation is for the purposes of section 56, the calculation date is the day of the appointment.

(4) Where the calculation is for the purposes of section 62, the calculation date is the day on which the time off was taken or on which it is alleged the time off should have been permitted.

[(4A) Where the calculation is for the purposes of section 63B, the calculation date is the day on which the time off was taken or on which it is alleged the time off should have been permitted.]

[(4B) Where the calculation is for the purposes of section 63J, the calculation date is the day on which the section 63D application was made.]

(5) Where the calculation is for the purposes of section 69—
 (a) in the case of an employee suspended on medical grounds, the calculation date is the day before that on which the suspension begins, and
 (b) in the case of an employee suspended on maternity grounds, the calculation date is—
  [(i) where the day before that on which the suspension begins falls during a period of ordinary or additional maternity leave, the day before the beginning of that period,]
  (ii) otherwise, the day before that on which the suspension begins.

[(6) Where the calculation is for the purposes of section 80I, the calculation date is the day on which the application under section 80F was made.]

**NOTES**

Sub-s (4A): inserted by the Teaching and Higher Education Act 1998, s 44(1), Sch 3, paras 10, 14.

Sub-s (4B): inserted by the Apprenticeships, Skills, Children and Learning Act 2009, s 40(5), Sch 1, paras 1, 8, as from 6 April 2010 (except in relation to small employers and their employees), and as from a day to be appointed (otherwise) (as to the meaning of "small employers" etc, see further the notes at **[1.840]**).

Sub-s (5): para (b)(i) substituted by the Employment Relations Act 1999, s 9, Sch 4, Pt III, paras 1, 5, 39.

Sub-s (6): added by the Employment Act 2002, s 53, Sch 7, paras 24, 45.

---

**[1.1033]**
## 226 Rights on termination

(1) Where the calculation is for the purposes of section 88 or 89, the calculation date is the day immediately preceding the first day of the period of notice required by section 86(1) or (2).

(2) Where the calculation is for the purposes of section 93, 117 or 125, the calculation date is—
 (a) if the dismissal was with notice, the date on which the employer's notice was given, and
 (b) otherwise, the effective date of termination.

(3) Where the calculation is for the purposes of section [112, 119, 120 or 121], the calculation date is—
 (a) . . .
 (b) if by virtue of subsection (2) or (4) of section 97 a date later than the effective date of termination as defined in subsection (1) of that section is to be treated for certain purposes as the effective date of termination, the effective date of termination as so defined, and
 (c) otherwise, the date specified in subsection (6).

(4) Where the calculation is for the purposes of section 147(2), the calculation date is the day immediately preceding the first of the four, or six, weeks referred to in section 148(2).

(5) Where the calculation is for the purposes of section 162, the calculation date is—
 (a) . . .
 (b) if by virtue of subsection (5) of section 145 a date is to be treated for certain purposes as the relevant date which is later than the relevant date as defined by the previous provisions of that section, the relevant date as so defined, and
 (c) otherwise, the date specified in subsection (6).

(6) The date referred to in subsections (3)(c) and (5)(c) is the date on which notice would have been given had—
 (a) the contract been terminable by notice and been terminated by the employer giving such notice as is required by section 86 to terminate the contract, and
 (b) the notice expired on the effective date of termination, or the relevant date,
(whether or not those conditions were in fact fulfilled).

**NOTES**

Sub-s (3): words in square brackets by the Employment Act 2002, s 53, Sch 7, paras 24, 46; para (a) repealed by the Employment Relations Act 1999, ss 9, 44, Sch 4, Pt III, paras 1, 5, 40, Sch 9(2).

Sub-s (5): para (a) repealed by the Employment Relations Act 1999, ss 9, 44, Sch 4, Pt III, paras 1, 5, 40, Sch 9(2).

*Maximum amount of week's pay*

**[1.1034]**
**227 Maximum amount**
(1)  For the purpose of calculating—
[(zza) an award of compensation under section 63J(1)(b),]
[(za) an award of compensation under section 80I(1)(b),]
(a)  a basic award of compensation for unfair dismissal,
(b)  an additional award of compensation for unfair dismissal,
[(ba) an award under section 112(5), or]
(c)  a redundancy payment,
the amount of a week's pay shall not exceed [£450].
(2)–(4)   . . .

**NOTES**
Sub-s (1) is amended as follows:
Para (zza) inserted by the Apprenticeships, Skills, Children and Learning Act 2009, s 40(5), Sch 1, paras 1, 9, as from 6 April 2010 (except in relation to small employers and their employees), and as from a day to be appointed (otherwise) (as to the meaning of "small employers" etc, see further the notes at **[1.840]**).
Para (za) inserted by the Employment Act 2002, s 53, Sch 7, paras 24, 47(1), (2).
Para (ba) substituted (for the original word "or" at the end of para (b)) by s 53 of, and Sch 7, paras 24, 47(1), (3) to, the 2002 Act.
Sum in square brackets substituted by the Employment Rights (Increase of Limits) Order 2012, SI 2012/3007, art 3, Schedule, as from 1 February 2013, in relation to any case where the appropriate date (as defined in the order) falls on or after that date (see SI 2012/3007, art 4 at **[2.1636]**). Previous sums were as follows: £430 as from 1 February 2012 (see SI 2011/3006); £400 as from 1 February 2011 (see SI 2010/2926); £380 as from 1 October 2009 (see SI 2009/1903); £350 as from 1 February 2009 (see SI 2008/3055); £330 as from 1 February 2008 (see SI 2007/3570); £310 as from 1 February 2007 (see SI 2006/3045); £290 as from 1 February 2006 (see SI 2005/3352); £280 as from 1 February 2005 (see SI 2004/2989); £270 as from 1 February 2004 (see SI 2003/3038) in each case where the appropriate date fell after the commencement date). This sum may be varied by the Secretary of State (see the Employment Relations Act 1999, s 34(1)(a), (3)(a) at **[1.1202]**).
Sub-ss (2)–(4): repealed by the Employment Relations Act 1999, ss 36(1)(a), 44, Sch 9(10).

*Miscellaneous*

**[1.1035]**
**228 New employments and other special cases**
(1)  In any case in which the employee has not been employed for a sufficient period to enable a calculation to be made under the preceding provisions of this Chapter, the amount of a week's pay is the amount which fairly represents a week's pay.
(2)  In determining that amount the [employment tribunal]—
(a)  shall apply as nearly as may be such of the preceding provisions of this Chapter as it considers appropriate, and
(b)  may have regard to such of the considerations specified in subsection (3) as it thinks fit.
(3)  The considerations referred to in subsection (2)(b) are—
(a)  any remuneration received by the employee in respect of the employment in question,
(b)  the amount offered to the employee as remuneration in respect of the employment in question,
(c)  the remuneration received by other persons engaged in relevant comparable employment with the same employer, and
(d)  the remuneration received by other persons engaged in relevant comparable employment with other employers.
(4)  The Secretary of State may by regulations provide that in cases prescribed by the regulations the amount of a week's pay shall be calculated in such manner as may be so prescribed.

**NOTES**
Sub-s (2): words in square brackets substituted by the Employment Rights (Dispute Resolution) Act 1998, s 1(2)(a).
Regulations: as of 6 April 2013 no Regulations had been made under this section.

**[1.1036]**
**229 Supplementary**
(1)  In arriving at—
(a)  an average hourly rate of remuneration, or
(b)  average weekly remuneration,
under this Chapter, account shall be taken of work for a former employer within the period for which the average is to be taken if, by virtue of Chapter I of this Part, a period of employment with the former employer counts as part of the employee's continuous period of employment.
(2)  Where under this Chapter account is to be taken of remuneration or other payments for a period which does not coincide with the periods for which the remuneration or other payments are calculated, the remuneration or other payments shall be apportioned in such manner as may be just.

## CHAPTER III
## OTHER INTERPRETATION PROVISIONS

**[1.1037]**
**230   Employees, workers etc**
(1)   In this Act "employee" means an individual who has entered into or works under (or, where the employment has ceased, worked under) a contract of employment.
(2)   In this Act "contract of employment" means a contract of service or apprenticeship, whether express or implied, and (if it is express) whether oral or in writing.
(3)   In this Act "worker" (except in the phrases "shop worker" and "betting worker") means an individual who has entered into or works under (or, where the employment has ceased, worked under)—
(a)   a contract of employment, or
(b)   any other contract, whether express or implied and (if it is express) whether oral or in writing, whereby the individual undertakes to do or perform personally any work or services for another party to the contract whose status is not by virtue of the contract that of a client or customer of any profession or business undertaking carried on by the individual;
and any reference to a worker's contract shall be construed accordingly.
(4)   In this Act "employer", in relation to an employee or a worker, means the person by whom the employee or worker is (or, where the employment has ceased, was) employed.
(5)   In this Act "employment"—
(a)   in relation to an employee, means (except for the purposes of section 171) employment under a contract of employment, and
(b)   in relation to a worker, means employment under his contract;
and "employed" shall be construed accordingly.
[(6)   This section has effect subject to sections 43K and 47B(3); and for the purposes of Part XIII so far as relating to Part IVA or section 47B, "worker", "worker's contract" and, in relation to a worker, "employer", "employment" and "employed" have the extended meaning given by section 43K.]

**NOTES**
Sub-s (6): added by the Public Interest Disclosure Act 1998, ss 15(1), 18(2).

**[1.1038]**
**231   Associated employers**
For the purposes of this Act any two employers shall be treated as associated if—
(a)   one is a company of which the other (directly or indirectly) has control, or
(b)   both are companies of which a third person (directly or indirectly) has control;
and "associated employer" shall be construed accordingly.

**[1.1039]**
**232   Shop workers**
(1)   In this Act "shop worker" means an employee who, under his contract of employment, is or may be required to do shop work.
(2)   In this Act "shop work" means work in or about a shop  .  .  .  on a day on which the shop is open for the serving of customers.
(3)   Subject to subsection (4), in this Act "shop" includes any premises where any retail trade or business is carried on.
(4)   Where premises are used mainly for purposes other than those of retail trade or business and would not (apart from subsection (3)) be regarded as a shop, only such part of the premises as—
(a)   is used wholly or mainly for the purposes of retail trade or business, or
(b)   is used both for the purposes of retail trade or business and for the purposes of wholesale trade and is used wholly or mainly for those two purposes considered together,
is to be regarded as a shop for the purposes of this Act.
(5)   In subsection (4)(b) "wholesale trade" means the sale of goods for use or resale in the course of a business or the hire of goods for use in the course of a business.
(6)   In this section "retail trade or business" includes—
(a)   the business of a barber or hairdresser,
(b)   the business of hiring goods otherwise than for use in the course of a trade or business, and
(c)   retail sales by auction,
but does not include catering business or the sale at theatres and places of amusement of programmes, catalogues and similar items.
(7)   In subsection (6) "catering business" means—
(a)   the sale of meals, refreshments or [alcohol] [  .  .  . ] for consumption on the premises on which they are sold, or
(b)   the sale of meals or refreshments prepared to order for immediate consumption off the premises;

and in paragraph (a) ["alcohol" has the same meaning as in the Licensing Act 2003] [except that in Scotland "alcohol" has the meaning given in section 2 of the Licensing (Scotland) Act 2005].
(8)  In this Act—
   "notice period", in relation to an opted-out shop worker, has the meaning given by section 41(3),
   "opted-out", in relation to a shop worker, shall be construed in accordance with section 41(1) and (2),
   "opting-in notice", in relation to a shop worker, has the meaning given by section 36(6),
   "opting-out notice", in relation to a shop worker, has the meaning given by section 40(2), and
   "protected", in relation to a shop worker, shall be construed in accordance with section 36(1) to (5).

**NOTES**

Sub-s (2): words omitted repealed by the Sunday Working (Scotland) Act 2003, s 1(1), (3)(a).

Sub-s (7) is amended as follows:

Word in first pair of square brackets in para (a) substituted by the Licensing Act 2003, s 198(1), Sch 6, para 114(a).

Words omitted from para (a) originally inserted by the Sunday Working (Scotland) Act 2003, s 1(1), (3)(b)(i), and repealed by the Licensing (Scotland) Act 2005 (Consequential Provisions) Order 2009, SSI 2009/248, art 2(1), Sch 1, Pt 1, para 7(a), as from 5am on 1 September 2009.

Penultimate words in square brackets substituted by the Licensing Act 2003, s 198(1), Sch 6, para 114(b).

Final words in square brackets substituted by SSI 2009/248, art 2(1), Sch 1, Pt 1, para 7(b), as from 5am on 1 September 2009.

**[1.1040]**
**[233  Betting workers**
(1)  In this Act "betting worker" means an employee who under his contract of employment is or may be required to do betting work.
(2)  In this Act "betting work" means—
   (a)  work which consists of or includes dealing with betting transactions at a track in England or Wales and which is carried out for a person who holds a general betting operating licence, a pool betting operating licence or a horse-race pool betting operating licence, and
   (b)  work on premises in respect of which a betting premises licence has effect at a time when the premises are used for betting transactions.
(3)  In subsection (2) "betting transactions" includes the collection or payment of winnings.
(4)  Expressions used in this section and in the Gambling Act 2005 have the same meaning in this section as in that Act.
(5)  In this Act—
   "notice period", in relation to an opted-out betting worker, has the meaning given by section 41(3),
   "opted-out", in relation to a betting worker, shall be construed in accordance with section 41(1) and (2),
   "opting-in notice", in relation to a betting worker, has the meaning given by section 36(6),
   "opting-out notice", in relation to a betting worker, has the meaning given by section 40(2), and
   "protected", in relation to a betting worker, shall be construed in accordance with section 36(1) to (5).]

**NOTES**

Substituted by the Gambling Act 2005, s 356(1), Sch 16, Pt 2, para 11.

**[1.1041]**
**234  Normal working hours**
(1)  Where an employee is entitled to overtime pay when employed for more than a fixed number of hours in a week or other period, there are for the purposes of this Act normal working hours in his case.
(2)  Subject to subsection (3), the normal working hours in such a case are the fixed number of hours.
(3)  Where in such a case—
   (a)  the contract of employment fixes the number, or minimum number, of hours of employment in a week or other period (whether or not it also provides for the reduction of that number or minimum in certain circumstances), and
   (b)  that number or minimum number of hours exceeds the number of hours without overtime,
   the normal working hours are that number or minimum number of hours (and not the number of hours without overtime).

**[1.1042]**
**235  Other definitions**
(1)  In this Act, except in so far as the context otherwise requires—
   "act" and "action" each includes omission and references to doing an act or taking action shall be construed accordingly,

"basic award of compensation for unfair dismissal" shall be construed in accordance with section 118,

"business" includes a trade or profession and includes any activity carried on by a body of persons (whether corporate or unincorporated),

"childbirth" means the birth of a living child or the birth of a child whether living or dead after twenty-four weeks of pregnancy,

"collective agreement" has the meaning given by section 178(1) and (2) of the Trade Union and Labour Relations (Consolidation) Act 1992,

"conciliation officer" means an officer designated by the Advisory, Conciliation and Arbitration Service under section 211 of that Act,

"dismissal procedures agreement" means an agreement in writing with respect to procedures relating to dismissal made by or on behalf of one or more independent trade unions and one or more employers or employers' associations,

"employers' association" has the same meaning as in the Trade Union and Labour Relations (Consolidation) Act 1992,

"expected week of childbirth" means the week, beginning with midnight between Saturday and Sunday, in which it is expected that childbirth will occur,

"guarantee payment" has the meaning given by section 28,

"independent trade union" means a trade union which—

(a)  is not under the domination or control of an employer or a group of employers or of one or more employers' associations, and

(b)  is not liable to interference by an employer or any such group or association (arising out of the provision of financial or material support or by any other means whatever) tending towards such control,

"job", in relation to an employee, means the nature of the work which he is employed to do in accordance with his contract and the capacity and place in which he is so employed,

["ordinary or additional paternity leave" means leave under any of sections 80A to 80BB,]

"position", in relation to an employee, means the following matters taken as a whole—

(a)  his status as an employee,

(b)  the nature of his work, and

(c)  his terms and conditions of employment,

["protected disclosure" has the meaning given by section 43A,]

"redundancy payment" has the meaning given by Part XI,

"relevant date" has the meaning given by sections 145 and 153,

"renewal" includes extension, and any reference to renewing a contract or a fixed term shall be construed accordingly,

["section 63D application" has the meaning given by section 63D(2);]

"statutory provision" means a provision, whether of a general or a special nature, contained in, or in any document made or issued under, any Act, whether of a general or special nature,

"successor", in relation to the employer of an employee, means (subject to subsection (2)) a person who in consequence of a change occurring (whether by virtue of a sale or other disposition or by operation of law) in the ownership of the undertaking, or of the part of the undertaking, for the purposes of which the employee was employed, has become the owner of the undertaking or part,

"trade union" has the meaning given by section 1 of the Trade Union and Labour Relations (Consolidation) Act 1992,

"week"—

(a)  in Chapter I of this Part means a week ending with Saturday, and

(b)  otherwise, except in [sections 80A, 80B and 86], means, in relation to an employee whose remuneration is calculated weekly by a week ending with a day other than Saturday, a week ending with that other day and, in relation to any other employee, a week ending with Saturday.

(2)  The definition of "successor" in subsection (1) has effect (subject to the necessary modifications) in relation to a case where—

(a)  the person by whom an undertaking or part of an undertaking is owned immediately before a change is one of the persons by whom (whether as partners, trustees or otherwise) it is owned immediately after the change, or

(b)  the persons by whom an undertaking or part of an undertaking is owned immediately before a change (whether as partners, trustees or otherwise) include the persons by whom, or include one or more of the persons by whom, it is owned immediately after the change,

as it has effect where the previous owner and the new owner are wholly different persons.

[(2A)  For the purposes of this Act a contract of employment is a "limited-term contract" if—

(a)  the employment under the contract is not intended to be permanent, and

(b)  provision is accordingly made in the contract for it to terminate by virtue of a limiting event.

(2B)  In this Act, "limiting event", in relation to a contract of employment means—

(a)    in the case of a contract for a fixed-term, the expiry of the term,

(b)    in the case of a contract made in contemplation of the performance of a specific task, the performance of the task, and

(c)    in the case of a contract which provides for its termination on the occurrence of an event (or the failure of an event to occur), the occurrence of the event (or the failure of the event to occur).]

(3)   References in this Act to redundancy, dismissal by reason of redundancy and similar expressions shall be construed in accordance with section 139.

(4)   In sections 136(2), 154 and 216(3) and paragraph 14 of Schedule 2 "lock-out" means—

(a)    the closing of a place of employment,

(b)    the suspension of work, or

(c)    the refusal by an employer to continue to employ any number of persons employed by him in consequence of a dispute,

done with a view to compelling persons employed by the employer, or to aid another employer in compelling persons employed by him, to accept terms or conditions of or affecting employment.

(5)   In sections 91(2), 140(2) and (3), 143(1), 144(2) and (3), 154 and 216(1) and (2) and paragraph 14 of Schedule 2 "strike" means—

(a)    the cessation of work by a body of employed persons acting in combination, or

(b)    a concerted refusal, or a refusal under a common understanding, of any number of employed persons to continue to work for an employer in consequence of a dispute,

done as a means of compelling their employer or any employed person or body of employed persons, or to aid other employees in compelling their employer or any employed person or body of employed persons, to accept or not to accept terms or conditions of or affecting employment.

**NOTES**

Sub-s (1) is amended as follows:

Definitions omitted repealed by the Employment Relations Act 1999, ss 9, 44, Sch 4, Pt III, paras 1, 5, 41, Sch 9(2).

Definition "ordinary or additional paternity leave" substituted (for the original definition "paternity leave" (as inserted by the Employment Act 2002, s 53, Sch 7, paras 24, 48)) by the Work and Families Act 2006, s 11(1), Sch 1, para 43, as from 3 March 2010.

Definition "protected disclosure" inserted by the Public Interest Disclosure Act 1998, ss 15(2), 18(2).

Definition "section 63D application" inserted by the Apprenticeships, Skills, Children and Learning Act 2009, s 40(5), Sch 1, paras 1, 10, as from 6 April 2010 (except in relation to small employers and their employees), and as from a day to be appointed (otherwise) (as to the meaning of "small employers" etc, see further the notes at **[1.840]**).

Sub-ss (2A), (2B): inserted by the Fixed-term Employees (Prevention of Less Favourable Treatment) Regulations 2002, SI 2002/2034, reg 11, Sch 2, Pt 1, para 3(1), (18) (except in relation to Government training schemes, agency workers or apprentices; see regs 18–20 of the 2002 Regulations at **[2.614]** et seq).

# PART XV
# GENERAL AND SUPPLEMENTARY

*General*

**[1.1043]**
## 236  Orders and regulations

(1)   Any power conferred by any provision of this Act to make any order (other than an Order in Council) or regulations is exercisable by statutory instrument.

(2)   A statutory instrument made under any power conferred by this Act to make an Order in Council or other order or regulations, except—

(a)    an Order in Council or other order [or regulations] to which subsection (3) applies,

(b)    an order under section 35 or Part II of Schedule 2, or

(c)    *an order made in accordance with section 208,*

is subject to annulment in pursuance of a resolution of either House of Parliament.

(3)   No recommendation shall be made to Her Majesty to make an Order in Council under section 192(3), and no order [or regulations] shall be made under section [43K(4)], [47C, [63D, 63F(7),], 71, 72, 73, [75A, 75B,] 76, [80A, 80AA, 80B, 80BB, 80G], 99,] *120(2), 124(2) or 125(7)* or (subject to subsection (4)) section 209, unless a draft of the Order in Council[, order or regulations] has been laid before Parliament and approved by a resolution of each House of Parliament.

(4)   Subsection (3) does not apply to an order under section 209(1)(b) which specifies only provisions contained in Part XI.

(5)   Any power conferred by this Act which is exercisable by statutory instrument includes power to make such incidental, supplementary or transitional provisions as appear to the authority exercising the power to be necessary or expedient.

**NOTES**

Sub-s (2): words in square brackets in para (a) inserted by the Employment Relations Act 1999, s 9, Sch 4, Pt III, paras 1, 5, 42(1), (2); para (c) repealed by the Employment Relations Act 1999, s 44, Sch 9(10), as from a day to be appointed.

Sub-s (3) is amended as follows:

Reference "43K(4)" inserted by the Enterprise and Regulatory Reform Act 2013, s 20(8), as from 25 June 2013, subject to savings in s 24(6) of the 2013 Act at [**1.1855**].

Words "or regulations" in square brackets inserted by the Employment Relations Act 1999, s 9, Sch 4, Pt III, paras 5, 42(1), (3)(a).

References from "47C," to "99," in square brackets substituted by the Employment Relations Act 1999, s 9, Sch 4, Pt III, paras 5, 42(1), (3)(b).

Reference "63D, 63F(7)," in square brackets inserted by the Apprenticeships, Skills, Children and Learning Act 2009, s 40(5), Sch 1, paras 1, 11, as from 6 April 2010 (except in relation to small employers and their employees), and as from a day to be appointed (otherwise) (as to the meaning of "small employers" etc, see further the notes at [**1.840**]).

References "75A, 75B" in square brackets inserted by the Employment Act 2002, s 53, Sch 7, paras 24, 49.

Reference "80A, 80AA, 80B, 80BB, 80G" in square brackets substituted (for the original reference "80A, 80B, 80G") by the Work and Families Act 2006, s 11(1), Sch 1, para 44, as from 3 March 2010. Note that the original reference "80A, 80B, 80G" was inserted by the Employment Act 2002, s 53, Sch 7, paras 24, 49.

Reference "120(2), 124(2)" in italics repealed by the Employment Relations Act 1999, s 44, Sch 9(10), as from a day to be appointed.

For the words "or 125(7)" in italics there are substituted the words ", 125(7) or 205A(11) or (12)" by the Growth and Infrastructure Act 2013, s 31(6), as from a day to be appointed.

Words ", order or regulations" in square brackets substituted by the Employment Relations Act 1999, s 9, Sch 4, Pt III, paras 5, 42(1), (3)(c).

An order made in accordance with section 208: note that s 208 was repealed by the Employment Relations Act 1999, ss 36(2), 44, Sch 9(10).

---

**[1.1044]**
## 237 Financial provisions
There shall be paid out of the National Insurance Fund into the Consolidated Fund sums equal to the amount of—
(a) any expenses incurred by the Secretary of State in consequence of Part XI, and
(b) any expenses incurred by the Secretary of State (or by persons acting on his behalf) in exercising his functions under Part XII.

**238, 239** *(S 238—provision for arrangements for co-ordinating provisions of Northern Ireland legislation corresponding to this Act (previously contained in s 157 of the 1978 Act), and s 239—provision for arrangements for co-ordinating provisions of Isle of Man legislation corresponding to this Act (previously contained in s 158 of the 1978 Act) outside the scope of this work.)*

### Final provisions

**240** *(Introduces Sch 1 (consequential amendments).)*

**[1.1045]**
## 241 Transitionals, savings and transitory provisions
Schedule 2 (transitional provisions, savings and transitory provisions) shall have effect.

**242** *(Introduces Sch 3 (repeals and revocations).)*

**[1.1046]**
## 243 Commencement
This Act shall come into force at the end of the period of three months beginning with the day on which it is passed.

**[1.1047]**
## 244 Extent
(1) Subject to the following provisions, this Act extends to England and Wales and Scotland but not to Northern Ireland.
(2) [Sections 36(2) and (4), 37(1) and (5), 38 and 39] extend to England and Wales only.
(3) Sections 201 and 238 (and sections 236 and 243, this section and section 245) extend to Northern Ireland (as well as to England and Wales and Scotland).
(4) Sections 240 and 242 and Schedules 1 and 3 have the same extent as the provisions amended or repealed by this Act.

---

**NOTES**
Sub-s (2): words in square brackets substituted by the Sunday Working (Scotland) Act 2003, s 1(1), (5).

**[1.1048]**
## 245 Short title
This Act may be cited as the Employment Rights Act 1996.

# SCHEDULES
## SCHEDULE 1

*(Schedule 1 (consequential amendments) in so far as these are within the scope of this work, they have been incorporated at the appropriate place.)*

## SCHEDULE 2
### TRANSITIONAL PROVISIONS, SAVINGS AND TRANSITORY PROVISIONS

Section 241

### PART I
### TRANSITIONAL PROVISIONS AND SAVINGS

*General transitionals and savings*

**[1.1049]**

**1.** The substitution of this Act for the provisions repealed or revoked by this Act does not affect the continuity of the law.

**2.** (1) Anything done, or having effect as done, (including the making of subordinate legislation) under or for the purposes of any provision repealed or revoked by this Act has effect as if done under or for the purposes of any corresponding provision of this Act.

(2) Sub-paragraph (1) does not apply to the making of any subordinate legislation to the extent that it is reproduced in this Act.

**3.** Any reference (express or implied) in this Act or any other enactment, or in any instrument or document, to a provision of this Act is (so far as the context permits) to be read as (according to the context) being or including in relation to times, circumstances and purposes before the commencement of this Act a reference to the corresponding provision repealed or revoked by this Act.

**4.** (1) Any reference (express or implied) in any enactment, or in any instrument or document, to a provision repealed or revoked by this Act is (so far as the context permits) to be read as (according to the context) being or including in relation to times, circumstances and purposes after the commencement of this Act a reference to the corresponding provision of this Act.

(2) In particular, where a power conferred by an Act is expressed to be exercisable in relation to enactments contained in Acts passed before or in the same Session as the Act conferring the power, the power is also exercisable in relation to provisions of this Act which reproduce such enactments.

**5.** Paragraphs 1 to 4 have effect in place of section 17(2) of the Interpretation Act 1978 (but are without prejudice to any other provision of that Act).

*Preservation of old transitionals and savings*

**6.** (1) The repeal by this Act of an enactment previously repealed subject to savings (whether or not in the repealing enactment) does not affect the continued operation of those savings.

(2) The repeal by this Act of a saving made on the previous repeal of an enactment does not affect the operation of the saving in so far as it remains capable of having effect.

(3) Where the purpose of an enactment repealed by this Act was to secure that the substitution of the provisions of the Act containing that enactment for provisions repealed by that Act did not affect the continuity of the law, the enactment repealed by this Act continues to have effect in so far as it is capable of doing so.

*Employment particulars*

**7.** (1) In this paragraph "pre-TURERA employee" means an employee whose employment with his employer began before 30th November 1993 (the day on which section 26 of the Trade Union Reform and Employment Rights Act 1993 came into force), whether or not the provisions of sections 1 to 6 of the Employment Protection (Consolidation) Act 1978, as they had effect before the substitution made by that section, applied to him before that date.

(2) Subject to the following provisions of this paragraph, sections 1 to 7 of this Act do not apply to a pre-TURERA employee (but the provisions of sections 1 to 6 of the Employment Protection (Consolidation) Act 1978, as they had effect before the substitution made by section 26 of the Trade Union Reform and Employment Rights Act 1993, continue in force in his case).

(3) Where a pre-TURERA employee, at any time—

    (a)   on or after the day on which this Act comes into force, and

    (b)   either before the end of his employment or within the period of three months beginning with the day on which his employment ends, requests from his employer a statement under section 1 of this Act, the employer shall (subject to section 5 and any other provision disapplying or having the effect of disapplying sections 1 to 4) be treated as being required by section 1 to give him a written statement under that section not later than two months after the request is made; and section 4 of this Act shall (subject to that) apply in relation to the employee after he makes the request.

(4)   An employer is not required to give an employee a statement under section 1 pursuant to sub-paragraph (3)—

(a)   on more than one occasion, or

(b)   if he has already given him a statement pursuant to paragraph 3(3) of Schedule 9 to the Trade Union Reform and Employment Rights Act 1993.

(5)   Where—

(a)   on or after the day on which this Act comes into force there is in the case of a pre-TURERA employee a change in any of the matters particulars of which would, had he been given a statement of particulars on 30th November 1993 under section 1 of the Employment Protection (Consolidation) Act 1978 (as substituted by section 26 of the Trade Union Reform and Employment Rights Act 1993), have been included or referred to in the statement, and

(b)   he has not previously requested a statement under sub-paragraph (3) or paragraph 3(3) of Schedule 9 to the Trade Union Reform and Employment Rights Act 1993,

subsections (1) and (6) of section 4 of this Act shall be treated (subject to section 5 and any other provision disapplying or having the effect of disapplying section 4) as requiring his employer to give him a written statement containing particulars of the change at the time specified in subsection (3) of section 4; and the other provisions of section 4 apply accordingly.

### Monetary limits in old cases

**8.** In relation to any case in which (but for this Act) a limit lower than that set by Article 3 of the Employment Protection (Increase of Limits) Order 1995 would have applied in accordance with Article 4 of that Order, this Act has effect as if it reproduced that lower limit.

### Shop workers and betting workers to whom old maternity provisions applied

**9.** (1)   This paragraph applies where an employee exercised a right to return to work under Part III of the Employment Protection (Consolidation) Act 1978 at a time when the amendments of that Part made by the Trade Union Reform and Employment Rights Act 1993 did not have effect in her case (so that her right was a right to return to work in the job in which she was employed under the original contract of employment).

(2)   Section 36(4) shall have effect as if for paragraph (b) there were substituted—

"(b)   under her original contract of employment, she was a shop worker, or a betting worker, but was not employed to work only on Sunday."

(3)   If the employee was employed as a shop worker under her original contract of employment, she shall not be regarded as failing to satisfy the condition in section 36(2)(a) or (c) or 41(1)(c) merely because during her pregnancy she was employed under a different contract of employment by virtue of section 60(2) of the Employment Protection (Consolidation) Act 1978 (as it had effect before the commencement of section 24 of the Trade Union Reform and Employment Rights Act 1993) or otherwise by reason of her pregnancy.

(4)   In this paragraph, and in section 36(4)(b) as substituted by sub-paragraph (2), "original contract of employment" has the meaning given by section 153(1) of the Employment Protection (Consolidation) Act 1978 as originally enacted.

### Validity of provisions deriving from certain regulations

**10.** Any question as to the validity of any of sections 47, 61, 62, 63 and 103, which derive from the Collective Redundancies and Transfer of Undertakings (Protection of Employment) (Amendment) Regulations 1995 made under subsection (2) of section 2 of the European Communities Act 1972, shall be determined as if those provisions were contained in regulations made under that subsection.

### Unfair dismissal

**11.** Part X does not apply to a dismissal from employment under a contract for a fixed term of two years or more (not being a contract of apprenticeship) if—

(a)   the contract was made before 28th February 1972, and

(b)   the dismissal consists only of the expiry of that term without its being renewed.

*Redundancy payments*

**12.** (1)   Section 135 does not apply to an employee who immediately before the relevant date is employed under a contract for a fixed term of two years or more (not being a contract of apprenticeship) if the contract was made before 6th December 1965.

(2)   Section 197(3) does not apply if the contract was made before 6th December 1965.

*Periods of employment*

**13.** (1)   The reference in section 215(2)(b) to a person being an employed earner for the purposes of the Social Security Contributions and Benefits Act 1992 in respect of whom a secondary Class 1 contribution was payable under that Act (whether or not it was in fact paid) shall be construed—

(a)   as respects a week of employment after 1st June 1976 and before 1st July 1992, as a reference to a person being an employed earner for the purposes of the Social Security Act 1975 in respect of whom a secondary Class 1 contribution was payable under that Act (whether or not it was in fact paid),

(b)   as respects a week of employment after 6th April 1975 and before 1st June 1976, as a reference to a person being an employed earner for the purposes of the Social Security Act 1975, and

(c)   as respects a week of employment before 6th April 1975, as a reference to a person being an employee in respect of whom an employer's contribution was payable in respect of the corresponding contribution week (whether or not it was in fact paid).

(2)   For the purposes of the application of sub-paragraph (1) to a week of employment where the corresponding contribution week began before 5th July 1948, an employer's contribution shall be treated as payable as mentioned in that sub-paragraph if such a contribution would have been so payable had the statutory provisions relating to national insurance in force on 5th July 1948 been in force in that contribution week.

(3)   The references in subsection (4) of section 215 to the Social Security Contributions and Benefits Act 1992 include the Social Security Act 1975; and that subsection applies to any question arising whether an employer's contribution was or would have been payable as mentioned in sub-paragraph (1) or (2).

(4)   In this paragraph—

"employer's contribution" has the same meaning as in the National Insurance Act 1965, and

"corresponding contribution week", in relation to a week of employment, means a contribution week (within the meaning of that Act) of which so much as falls within the period beginning with midnight between Sunday and Monday and ending with Saturday also falls within that week of employment.

**14.** (1)   Subject to paragraph 13 and sub-paragraphs (2) and (3) of this paragraph, Chapter I of Part XIV applies to periods before this Act comes into force as it applies to later periods.

(2)   If, during the whole or any part of a week beginning before 6th July 1964, an employee was absent from work—

(a)   because he was taking part in a strike, or

(b)   because of a lock-out by his employer,

the week counts as a period of employment.

(3)   Any week which counted as a period of employment in the computation of a period of employment for the purposes of the Employment Protection (Consolidation) Act 1978 counts as a period of employment for the purposes of this Act; and any week which did not break the continuity of a person's employment for the purposes of that Act shall not break the continuity of a period of employment for the purposes of this Act.

## PART II
## TRANSITORY PROVISIONS

**[1.1050]**
**15.**   . . .

*Armed forces*

**16.** (1)   If section 31 of the Trade Union Reform and Employment Rights Act 1993 has not come into force before the commencement of this Act, this Act shall have effect until the relevant commencement date as if for section 192 there were substituted—

**"192 Armed forces**

(1)   Section 191—

(a)   does not apply to service as a member of the naval, military or air forces of the Crown, but

(b)   does apply to employment by an association established for the purposes of Part XI of the Reserve Forces Act 1996."

(2)  The reference in sub-paragraph (1) to the relevant commencement date is a reference—

(a)  if an order has been made before the commencement of this Act appointing a day after that commencement as the day on which section 31 of the Trade Union Reform and Employment Rights Act 1993 is to come into force, to the day so appointed, and

(b)  otherwise, to such day as the Secretary of State may by order appoint.

**17.**  (1)  If Part XI of the Reserve Forces Act 1996 has not come into force before the commencement of this Act, section 192 of this Act shall have effect until the relevant commencement date as if for "Part XI of the Reserve Forces Act 1996" there were substituted "Part VI of the Reserve Forces Act 1980".

(2)  The reference in sub-paragraph (1) to the relevant commencement date is a reference—

(a)  if an order has been made before the commencement of this Act appointing a day after that commencement as the day on which Part XI of the Reserve Forces Act 1996 is to come into force, to the day so appointed, and

(b)  otherwise, to such day as the Secretary of State may by order appoint.

*Disability discrimination*

**18.**  . . .

**NOTES**

Para 15: repealed by the Statute Law (Repeals) Act 2004 (it was previously spent).

Para 16: s 31 of the 1993 Act was not brought into force prior to its repeal by Sch 3 to this Act, and as of 6 April 2013 no Orders had been made under para 16(2)(b); therefore, s 192 of the 1996 Act has effect as stated in para 16(1) until a date to be appointed by Order under para 16(2)(b).

Para 17: the Reserve Forces Act 1996, Pt XI was brought into force on 1 April 1997 by the Reserve Forces Act 1996 (Commencement No 1) Order 1997, SI 1997/305. That Order was made on 19 February 1997 (ie, after the commencement of this Act on 22 August 1996). As of 6 April 2013 no Orders had been made under para 17(2)(b).

Para 18: repealed by the Employment Rights (Dispute Resolution) Act 1998, s 15, Sch 2.

# SCHEDULE 3

*(Sch 3 (repeals and revocations) in so far as these are within the scope of this work, they have been incorporated at the appropriate place.)*

# EMPLOYMENT RIGHTS ACT 1996, DESTINATION TABLE

**[1.1051]**

---

## DESTINATION TABLE

This table shows in column (1) the enactments repealed by the Employment Rights Act 1996 and in column (2) the provisions of that Act corresponding thereto.

In certain cases the enactment in column (1), though having a corresponding provision in column (2) is not, or not wholly, repealed as it is still required, or partly required, for the purposes of other legislation.

| (1) | (2) | (1) | (2) |
|---|---|---|---|
| **Betting, Gaming and Lotteries Act 1963 (c 2)** | | **Betting, Gaming and Lotteries Act 1963 (c 2)** | |
| s 31A | Unnecessary | Sch 5A, para 10(6) | s 45(6)–(8) |
| Sch 5A, para 1(1) | ss 36(7), 45(4), 233(1)–(4), (6) | Sch 5A, para 11(1)–(3) | s 42(1)–(3) |
| | | Sch 5A, para 11(4) | s 42(5) |
| Sch 5A, para 1(2) | ss 210(1)–(3), 230(1), (2), (4), (5), 235(1) | Sch 5A, para 11(5) | s 42(6) |
| | | Sch 5A, para 11(6) | s 236(1), (2) |
| Sch 5A, para 1(3) | s 210(3) | Sch 5A, para 12(1)–(4) | s 37(1)–(4) |
| Sch 5A, para 1(4) | s 96(6) | Sch 5A, para 13(1)–(4) | s 43(1)–(4) |
| Sch 5A, para 2(1)–(3) | s 36(1)–(3) | Sch 5A, para 14 | s 38(1), (2) |
| Sch 5A, para 2(4)(a) | ss 101(4), 105(8) | Sch 5A, para 15(1) | s 39(1)–(3) |
| Sch 5A, para 2(4)(b) | s 45(9) | Sch 5A, para 15(2) | s 39(4) |
| Sch 5A, para 2(4)(c), (d) | s 37(5) | Sch 5A, para 16 | s 48(1) |
| | | Sch 5A, para 17(1) | s 203(1) |
| Sch 5A, para 2(4)(e) | s 38(3) | Sch 5A, para 17(2) | s 203(2) |
| Sch 5A, para 2(4)(f) | s 39(5) | Sch 5A, para 18 | Sch 2, para 9 |
| Sch 5A, para 2(5) | Spent | Sch 5A, para 19 | s 104(4) |
| Sch 5A, para 2(6) | s 45(10) | Sch 5A, para 20 | s 110(2) |
| Sch 5A, para 2(7) | s 36(4) | Sch 5A, para 22 | s 196(2), (3), 205(1), 206(2) |
| Sch 5A, para 3(1), (2) | s 36(5), (6) | | |
| Sch 5A, para 4(1) | s 40(3) | **Post Office Act 1969 (c 48)** | |
| Sch 5A, para 4(2) | s 40(1) | | |
| Sch 5A, para 4(3) | s 40(2) | Sch 9, para 33 | Spent |
| Sch 5A, para 5(1) | s 41(1) | **Atomic Energy Act 1971 (c 11)** | |
| Sch 5A, para 5(2)(a) | ss 101(4), 105(8) | | |
| Sch 5A, para 5(2)(b) | s 45(9) | s 10(1) | Spent |
| Sch 5A, para 5(2)(c), (d) | s 43(5) | **Race Relations Act 1976 (c 74)** | |
| Sch 5A, para 5(3) | Spent | Sch 2, paras 11(1)*, (2), (3), (5), 12, 13 | Spent |
| Sch 5A, para 5(4) | s 45(10) | **Employment Protection (Consolidation) Act 1978 (c 44)** | |
| Sch 5A, para 5(5) | s 41(2) | | |
| Sch 5A, para 6 | s 41(3) | | |
| Sch 5A, para 7(1)–(3) | s 101(1)–(3) | | |
| Sch 5A, para 7(4) | s 197(2) | s 1(1) | s 1(1), (2) |
| Sch 5A, para 8 | s 105(1), (4) | s 1(2)–(4) | s 1(3)–(5) |
| Sch 5A, para 9 | ss 108(3), 109(2) | s 2(1) | s 2(1) |
| Sch 5A, para 10(1)–(3) | s 45(1)–(3) | s 2(2)(a) | ss 2(2), 6 |
| Sch 5A, para 10(4) | s 45(4) | s 2(2)(b), (3) | ss 2(3), 6 |
| Sch 5A, para 10(5) | s 45(5) | s 2(4)–(6) | s 2(4)–(6) |

\* Repealed in part

| (1) | (2) | (1) | (2) |
|---|---|---|---|
| Employment Protection (Consolidation) Act 1978 (c 44) | | Employment Protection (Consolidation) Act 1978 (c 44) | |
| s 3(1)(a)–(c) | ss 3(1), 6 | s 18(4) | s 35(4), (5) |
| s 3(1)(d) | s 3(5) | s 18(5) | s 35(6) |
| s 3(2)–(4) | s 3(2)–(4) | s 19(1) | s 64(1)–(3) |
| s 4(1), (2) | s 4(1)–(3) | s 19(2) | s 64(5) |
| s 4(3)(a) | ss 4(4), 6 | s 19(3) | s 64(4) |
| s 4(3)(b), (4) | ss 4(5), 6 | s 20 | s 65 |
| s 4(5) | s 4(6), (7) | s 21(1) | s 69(1) |
| s 4(6) | s 4(8) | s 21(2) | s 69(2) |
| s 5(1)(a) | s 198 | s 21(3) | s 69(3) |
| s 5(1)(b) | Rep SI 1995/31 | s 22(1) | s 70(1) |
| s 5(2) | s 5(1) | s 22(2) | s 70(2) |
| s 5(3) | s 5(2) | s 22(3) | s 70(3) |
| s 6 | s 7 | s 22A | s 44 |
| s 8 | s 8 | s 22AA | s 47 |
| s 9(1) | s 9(1), (2) | s 22B(1) | s 48(1) |
| s 9(2)–(4) | s 9(3)–(5) | s 22B(2)–(4) | s 48(2)–(4) |
| s 10 | s 10 | s 22C | s 49 |
| s 11(1) | s 11(1) | s 29(1)(a) | s 50(1) |
| s 11(2) | s 11(2) | s 29(1)(b) | s 50(2)(a) |
| s 11(3) | Rep 1993 c 19, s 51, Sch 10 | s 29(1)(ba), (bb) | s 50(5) |
| | | s 29(1)(bc) | s 50(2)(c), (6) |
| s 11(4) | s 11(3) | s 29(1)(c) | s 50(2)(b) |
| s 11(5), (6) | s 12(1), (2) | s 29(1)(cc) | s 50(2)(d), (7) |
| s 11(7) | Rep 1993 c 19, s 51, Sch 10 | s 29(1)(d) | s 50(2)(e), (8) |
| | | s 29(1)(e), (ee), (ef) | s 50(2)(f), (9) |
| s 11(8) | s 12(3)–(5) | s 29(1)(f) | s 50(2)(g) |
| s 11(9) | s 11(4) | s 29(2)(a) | s 50(5) |
| s 12(1) | s 28(1)–(3) | s 29(2)(b) | s 50(2)(e), (8) |
| s 12(2) | s 28(4), (5) | s 29(2)(c) | s 50(9) (Unnecessary in part) |
| s 13(1), (2) | s 29(1), (2) | | |
| s 13(3) | s 29(3) | s 29(2)(d) | Rep SI 1996/973 |
| s 13(4) | s 29(4), (5) | s 29(3) | s 50(3) |
| s 14(1) | s 30(1) | s 29(4) | s 50(4) |
| s 14(2) | s 30(2)–(4) | s 29(5) | s 50(10) |
| s 14(3) | s 30(5) | s 29(6) | s 51(1) |
| s 15(1) | s 31(1) | s 30(1) | s 51(2) |
| s 15(2) | s 31(2) | s 30(2) | s 51(3), (4) |
| s 15(3) | s 31(3)–(5) | s 30(3) | Rep1992 c 52, s 300(1), (2), Sch 1, Sch 2, para 12 |
| s 15(4) | s 31(6) | | |
| s 15(5) | s 31(7) | s 31(1), (2) | s 52(1), (2) |
| s 16(1)–(3) | s 32(1)–(3) | s 31(3) | s 53(1) |
| s 16(4) | s 33 | s 31(4) | s 53(2), (3) |
| s 17(1)–(3) | s 34(1)–(3) | s 31(5) | s 53(4) |
| s 18(1)–(3) | s 35(1)–(3) | s 31(6)–(8) | s 54(1)–(3) |

\* Repealed in part

| (1) | (2) | (1) | (2) |
|---|---|---|---|
| Employment Protection (Consolidation) Act 1978 (c 44) | | Employment Protection (Consolidation) Act 1978 (c 44) | |
| s 31(9) | ss 53(5), 54(4) | s 47(3) | s 69(1) |
| s 31(10), (11) | s 53(6), (7) | s 47(4) | s 69(2) |
| s 31A(1)–(3) | s 55(1)–(3) | s 47(5) | s 69(3) |
| s 31A(4) | s 56(1) | s 47(6) | s 70(1) |
| s 31A(5) | s 56(2)–(4) | s 47(7) | s 70(2) |
| s 31A(6), (7) | s 57(1), (2) | s 47(8) | s 70(3) |
| s 31A(8) | s 57(3)–(5) | s 49(1)–(4) | s 86(1)–(4) |
| s 31A(9), (10) | s 56(5), (6) | s 49(4A) | s 86(5) |
| s 31A(11) | Spent | s 49(5) | s 86(6) |
| s 31AA(1) | s 61(1) | s 49(6) | s 235(1) |
| s 31AA(2), (3) | ss 62, 63 | s 50(1), (2) | s 87(1), (2) |
| s 32 | ss 50(11), 52(3), 55(4), 61(2) | s 50(3) | s 87(4) |
| | | s 51 | s 91(5) |
| s 33 | s 71 | s 52 | s 91(6) |
| s 34(1)–(3) | s 72 | s 53(1) | s 92(1), (2) |
| s 34(4) | s 236(3) | s 53(2) | s 92(3) |
| s 35(1) | s 73(1) | s 53(2A) | s 92(4) |
| s 35(2) | s 73(2), (4) | s 53(3) | s 92(5) |
| s 35(3) | s 73(3) | s 53(4) | s 93(1), (2) |
| s 35(4) | s 73(5) | s 53(5) | s 93(3) |
| s 35(5) | s 236(3) | s 54 | s 94 |
| s 36 | s 74 | s 55(1), (2) | s 95(1) |
| s 37 | s 75 | s 55(3) | s 95(2) |
| s 37A | s 76 | s 55(4) | s 97(1) |
| s 38(1) | s 77(1), (2) | s 55(5) | ss 92(7), 97(2) |
| s 38(2) | s 77(3) | s 55(6) | s 97(4) |
| s 38A | s 78 | s 55(7)(a) | s 97(3) |
| s 39(1)–(3) | s 79 | s 55(7)(b) | s 97(5) |
| s 39(4) | s 236(3) | s 56 | s 96(1) |
| s 40 | s 80 | s 56A | s 96(2)–(5) |
| s 41(1) | s 81(1), (2) | s 57(1), (2) | s 98(1), (2) |
| s 41(2) | s 81(3) | s 57(3) | s 98(4)–(6) |
| s 42(1), (2) | s 82(1), (2) | s 57(4) | s 98(3) |
| s 42(3) | s 82(3), (4) | s 57A | s 100 |
| s 42(4)–(6) | s 82(5)–(7) | s 57AA | s 103 |
| s 42(7) | s 82(8), (9) | s 59(1) | s 105(1), (4) |
| s 43(1), (2) | Unnecessary | s 59(2) | s 105(2), (3), (6), (7) |
| s 43(3), (4) | s 83 | s 59(3) | s 105(9) |
| s 44 | s 85 | s 60 | s 99(1)–(3) |
| s 45(1), (3) | s 66(1), (2) | s 60A(1)–(3) | s 104(1)–(3) |
| s 45(2) | s 66(3) | s 60A(4) | s 104(4) |
| s 46(1), (2) | s 67 | s 61 | s 106 |
| s 46(3)–(6) | s 70(4)–(7) | s 63 | s 107 |
| s 47(1), (2) | s 68 | s 64(1)(a) | s 108(1) |

\* Repealed in part

| (1) | (2) | (1) | (2) |
|---|---|---|---|
| Employment Protection (Consolidation) Act 1978 (c 44) | | Employment Protection (Consolidation) Act 1978 (c 44) | |
| s 64(1)(b) | s 109(1) | s 73(7) | Rep 1982 c 46, ss 4, 21(3), Sch 4 |
| s 64(2) | s 108(2) | | |
| s 64(3)–(5) | ss 108(3), 109(2) | s 73(7A) | s 122(1) |
| s 64A | Rep 1993 c 19, ss 49(1), 51, Sch 7, para 2, Sch 10 | s 73(7B) | s 122(2) |
| | | s 73(7C) | s 122(3) |
| | | s 73(8) | Rep 1980 c 42, ss 9(5), 20(3), Sch 2 |
| s 65(1), (2) | s 110(3) | | |
| s 65(3) | s 110(1) | s 73(9) | s 122(4) |
| s 65(4) | s 110(2) | s 74(1)–(7) | s 123 |
| s 66(1) | Rep 1980 c 42, s 20(2), (3), Sch 1, para 13, Sch 2 | s 74(8) | s 124(4) |
| | | s 75(1) | s 124(1) |
| | | s 75(2) | ss 124(2), 236(3) |
| s 66(2) | s 110(4) | s 75(3) | s 124(5) |
| s 66(3) | s 110(5) | s 75A(1)–(7) | s 125 |
| s 67(1), (2) | s 111(1), (2) | s 75A(8) | s 236(3) |
| s 67(3) | Rep 1992 c 52, s 300(1), Sch 1 | s 76(1) | s 126 |
| | | s 76(2) | Rep 1994 c 10, ss 1(2), 3(2), Schedule |
| s 67(4) | s 111(3), (4) | | |
| s 68 | s 112 | s 77 | s 128 |
| s 69(1) | ss 113, 115(1), (2) | s 77A(1) | s 129(1) |
| s 69(2) | s 114(1), (2) | s 77A(2) | s 129(2), (3) |
| s 69(3) | s 114(3) | s 77A(3) | s 129(4) |
| s 69(4) | s 115(1), (2) | s 77A(4) | s 129(5) |
| s 69(5) | s 116(1) | s 77A(5) | s 129(6)–(8) |
| s 69(6) | s 116(2)–(4) | s 77A(6) | s 129(9) |
| s 70(1) | s 116(5), (6) | s 78 | s 130 |
| s 70(2) | ss 114(4), 115(3) | s 78A | s 131 |
| s 71(1) | s 117(1), (2) | s 79(1) | s 132(1), (2) |
| s 71(1A) | s 124(3) | s 79(2) | s 132(3) |
| s 71(2), (2A), (2B) | s 117(3)–(5) | s 79(3) | s 132(4) |
| s 71(3) | s 117(6) | s 79(4), (5) | s 132(5) |
| s 71(4) | s 117(7) | s 79(6) | s 132(6) |
| s 71(5) | s 117(8) | s 80 | s 134 |
| s 72(1) | s 118(1) | s 81(1) | ss 135, 155, 162(1), (2) |
| s 72(2), (3) | s 118(2), (3) | s 81(2) | s 139(1), (2) |
| s 73(1), (3) | s 119(1), (2) | s 81(2A) | s 139(3) |
| s 73(2) | s 121 | s 81(3) | s 139(6) |
| s 73(4) | s 119(3) | s 81(4) | s 155 |
| s 73(4A), (4B) | Rep 1992 c 52, s 300(1), Sch 1 | s 82(1) | s 156(1) |
| | | s 82(2) | s 140(1) |
| s 73(5), (6) | s 119(4), (5) | s 82(3) | s 141(1) |
| s 73(6A), (6B) | s 120(1) | s 82(4) | s 146(2) |
| s 73(6C) | s 120(2) | s 82(5) | s 141(2), (3) |
| s 73(6D) | s 236(3) | s 82(6) | s 141(4) |

* Repealed in part

| (1) | (2) | (1) | (2) |
|---|---|---|---|
| Employment Protection (Consolidation) Act 1978 (c 44) | | Employment Protection (Consolidation) Act 1978 (c 44) | |
| s 82(7) | s 146(1) | s 98(3) | s 158(4) |
| s 83 | s 136(1), (2) | s 99(1) | ss 159, 191(6) |
| s 84(1) | s 138(1) | s 99(2) | s 160(1) |
| s 84(2) | s 146(2) | s 100 | s 161 |
| s 84(3), (6) | s 138(2), (4), (5) | s 101(1) | s 164(1) |
| s 84(4) | s 138(3) | s 101(2) | s 164(2), (3) |
| s 84(5) | s 138(6) | s 102(1), (2) | s 165(1), (2) |
| s 84(7) | s 146(1) | s 102(3) | s 165(3), (4) |
| s 85(1), (2) | s 136(3) | s 106(1) | s 166(1) |
| s 85(3) | s 142(1), (2) | s 106(1A), (1B) | s 166(2), (3) |
| s 85(4) | s 142(3), (4) | s 106(2) | s 167(1), (2) |
| s 85(5) | s 136(4) | s 106(3) | s 167(3), (4) |
| s 86 | s 137(1) | s 106(4) | Rep 1989 c 38, s 29(3), (4), Sch 6, para 21, Sch 7, Pt II |
| s 87 | s 147 | | |
| s 88(1) | s 148 | | |
| s 88(2) | ss 150(1), (2), 151 | s 106(5), (6) | s 166(5)–(7) |
| s 88(3) | s 152(1) | s 106(7) | s 166(4) |
| s 88(4) | ss 149, 152(1) | s 107(1)–(3) | s 169(1)–(3) |
| s 89(1) | s 152(2) | s 107(4), (5) | s 169(4) |
| s 89(2), (3) | s 154 | s 108 | s 170 |
| s 89(4) | s 149 | s 110(1), (2) | s 143(1), (2) |
| s 89(5) | s 150(3) | s 110(3) | s 144(1) |
| s 89(6) | s 150(4) | s 110(4) | s 143(7), (8) |
| s 90(1) | s 145(1)–(4) | s 110(5) | s 143(3), (4) |
| s 90(2) | s 153 | s 110(6) | s 143(5), (6) |
| s 90(3) | s 145(5), (6) | s 110(7) | s 144(4) |
| s 91(1)–(3) | s 163(1)–(3) | s 110(8) | s 144(2) |
| s 92(1) | s 140(2) | s 110(9) | s 144(3) |
| s 92(2) | s 140(5) | s 111(1) | s 171(3) |
| s 92(3) | s 140(3), (4) | s 111(2) | Spent |
| s 92(4) | s 136(1), (2) | s 111(3) | s 177(3) |
| s 92(5) | s 235(4), (5) | s 111(4)–(6) | Spent |
| s 93(1) | s 136(5) | s 112(1) | s 177(2) |
| s 93(2) | s 139(4) | s 112(2) | s 177(1) |
| s 93(3) | s 139(5) | s 114 | s 160(2), (3) |
| s 93(4) | Rep 1993 c 19, s 51, Sch 10 | s 115(1) | s 171(2) |
| | | s 115(2) | s 171(1) |
| s 96(1) | s 157(2), (3) | s 115(3) | Spent |
| s 96(2) | s 157(4) | s 116 | s 172 |
| s 96(3)(a) | s 157(1) | s 117(1), (2), (4) | s 173 |
| s 96(3)(b) | s 163(4) | s 117(2A), (2B) | Rep 1989 c 38, s 29(4), Sch 7, Pt II |
| s 96(4) | s 157(5) | | |
| s 98(1) | s 158(1), (2) | s 117(3) | s 179(6) |
| s 98(2) | s 158(3) | s 118(1) | s 178(2) |

\* Repealed in part

| (1) | (2) | (1) | (2) |
|---|---|---|---|
| Employment Protection (Consolidation) Act 1978 (c 44) | | Employment Protection (Consolidation) Act 1978 (c 44) | |
| s 118(2) | s 178(1) | s 139(4)–(6) | s 195(6)–(8) |
| s 119(1)–(5) | s 179(1)–(5) | s 139(7) | s 195(9), (10) |
| s 120 | s 180 | s 139(8), (9) | s 195(11), (12) |
| s 122(1) | s 182 | s 139A(1) | s 194(1), (2) |
| s 122(2) | s 185 | s 139A(2) | s 194(4) |
| s 122(3) | s 184(1) | s 139A(3)(b) | s 194(3) |
| s 122(4) | ss 27(1), 184(2) | s 139A(4) | s 194(5) |
| s 122(5) | s 186(1) | s 139A(5) | s 194(4), (6) |
| s 122(6) | s 186(2) | s 139A(6) | s 194(7) |
| s 122(7), (8) | s 184(4) | s 140(1) | s 203(1) |
| s 122(9), (10) | s 187(1), (3)–(5) | s 140(2) | s 203(2) |
| s 122(11) | s 187(2) | s 140(3), (4) | s 203(3), (4) |
| s 124(1) | s 188(1), (2) | s 141(1) | s 196(1) |
| s 124(2) | Rep 1993 c 48, s 188(1), Sch 5, Pt I | s 141(2) | s 196(2), (3) |
| | | s 141(2A) | s 196(7) |
| s 124(3) | s 188(3) | s 141(3), (4) | s 196(6) |
| s 125(1), (2) | s 189(1), (2) | s 141(5) | s 196(5) |
| s 125(2A) | s 189(3), (4) | s 142(1) | s 197(1) |
| s 125(3), (3A), (3B) | Rep 1993 c 48, s 188(1), Sch 5, Pt I | s 142(2)–(4) | s 197(3)–(5) |
| | | s 144(1) | s 199(1) |
| s 125(4) | s 189(5) | s 144(2) | s 199(2) |
| s 126(1)–(4) | s 190(1)–(4) | s 144(3) | s 199(6) |
| s 127(1), (2) | s 183 | s 144(4), (5) | s 199(4), (5) |
| s 127(3) | s 184(3) | s 146(1) | Rep 1982 c 46, s 21, Sch 3, Pt I, para 6, Sch 4 |
| s 129 | s 205(1) | | |
| s 137(1) | s 201(2) | | |
| s 137(2) | s 201(1), (5) | s 146(2) | s 200(1) |
| s 137(3) | s 201(3) | s 146(3) | s 200(2) |
| s 137(4) | s 201(4) | s 146(4)–(8) | Rep SI 1995/31 |
| s 137(5) | s 201(5) | s 146A | s 202 |
| s 138(1) | s 191(1), (2) | s 148(1)–(5) | s 208(1)–(5) |
| s 138(2) | s 191(3) | s 148(6) | s 208(6), (7) |
| s 138(3) | s 192(1) | s 149(1) | s 209(1), (4), (5) |
| s 138(4) | s 193 | s 149(2) | s 209(2), (3) |
| s 138(5) | Rep 1990 c 19, s 66(2), Sch 10 | s 149(2A) | s 209(7) |
| | | s 149(3) | s 209(8) |
| s 138(7)* | s 191(4) | s 149(4) | s 236(3) |
| s 138(8) | s 191(5) | s 149(5) | s 236(4) |
| s 138A(1)–(4) | s 192(2)–(5) | s 150 | Unnecessary |
| s 138A(5) | s 192(7) | s 151(1) | s 210(1), (2) |
| s 138A(6) | s 236(3) | s 151(2) | s 210(3) |
| s 138A(7) | s 192(6), (8) | s 151(3)–(5) | s 211 |
| s 139(1)* | s 195(1)–(3) | s 151(6)(a) | s 215(3) |
| s 139(2), (3) | s 195(4), (5) | s 151(6)(b) | s 216(2), (3) |

* Repealed in part

| (1) | (2) | (1) | (2) |
|---|---|---|---|
| **Employment Protection (Consolidation) Act 1978 (c 44)** | | **Employment Protection (Consolidation) Act 1978 (c 44)** | |
| s 151(6)(c) | s 217 | Sch 2, Pt II, para 4(1)(b), (c) | s 146(3) |
| s 152 | — | Sch 2, Pt II, para 4(2) | s 137(1) |
| s 153(1) | ss 230(1), (2), (4), (5), 235(1) (Unnecessary in part) | Sch 2, Pt II, para 4(3) | ss 156(2), 157(6), 162(7), 199(3), 226(5), 227(3), (4) |
| s 153(2) | s 235(3) | | |
| s 153(3) | Rep 1993 c 19, s 51, Sch 10 | Sch 2, Pt II, para 4(4) | s 226(5) |
| | | Sch 2, Pt II, para 5 | s 137(2) |
| s 153(4) | s 231 | Sch 2, Pt III, para 6(1) | |
| s 153(4A) | s 235(2) | (2) | s 84(1) |
| s 153(5) | s 204 | Sch 2, Pt III, para 6(3) | ss 108(3), 109(2), 110(2), 196(4), 199(3) |
| s 153(6), (7) | Unnecessary | | |
| s 154(1), (2) | s 236(1), (2) | Sch 2, Pt III, para 6(4)(a) | s 127 |
| s 154(3) | s 236(5) | | |
| s 154(4) | Unnecessary | Sch 2, Pt III, para 6(4)(b) | s 84(2) |
| s 155(1), (2) | s 190(5), (6) | | |
| s 156(1) | Rep 1986 c 50, s 86(2), Sch 11 | Sch 2, Pt III, para 7(1) | s 209(6) |
| | | Sch 2, Pt III, para 7(2) | s 236(3) |
| s 156(2) | s 237 (Spent in part) | Sch 3, para 1 | s 87(3) |
| s 156(3) | Spent | Sch 3, para 2(1) | s 88(1) |
| s 157(1) | s 238(1), (2) | Sch 3, para 2(2) | s 88(2) |
| s 157(2) | Rep 1990 c 38, s 16(2), Sch 3 | Sch 3, para 2(3) | s 88(3) |
| | | Sch 3, para 3(1), (2) | s 89(1), (2) |
| s 157(3) | s 238(3)–(5) | Sch 3, para 3(3) | s 89(3), (4) |
| s 157(4) | s 238(6) | Sch 3, para 3(4) | s 89(5) |
| s 158(1), (2) | s 239(1), (2) | Sch 3, para 4 | s 90 |
| s 158(3) | s 239(3), (4) | Sch 3, para 5 | s 91(1) |
| s 158(4) | s 239(5) | Sch 3, para 6 | s 91(2) |
| ss 159, 160 | Unnecessary | Sch 3, para 7 | s 91(3), (4) |
| Sch 1 | s 64(1)–(3) | Sch 4, paras 1, 2 | s 162(1), (2) |
| Sch 2, Pt I, para 1 | ss 97(6), 98(4)–(6), 99(4), 108(3), 109(2), 110(2), 114(5), 115(4), 119(6) | Sch 4, para 3 | s 162(3) |
| | | Sch 4, para 4 | s 162(4), (5) |
| | | Sch 4, para 5 | s 162(6) |
| | | Sch 4, para 6 | s 162(8) |
| Sch 2, Pt I, para 2(1) | s 98(4)–(6) | Sch 4, para 7 | Rep 1982 c 46, ss 20, 21(3), Sch 2, para 6(5), Sch 4 |
| Sch 2, Pt I, para 2(2) | s 99(4) | | |
| Sch 2, Pt I, para 2(3)(a) | s 97(6) | | |
| Sch 2, Pt I, para 2(3)(b) | ss 114(5), 115(4) | Sch 7 | s 168 |
| Sch 2, Pt I, para 2(4) | ss 97(6), 108(3), 109(2), 110(2), 119(6), 196(4), 199(3), 226(3), 227(3), (4) | Sch 8 | s 173 |
| | | Sch 12, Pt I, para 1 | s 206(2) |
| | | Sch 12, Pt I, para 2 | s 206(1), (3) |
| | | Sch 12, Pt I, para 3(1) | s 206(4), (5) |
| Sch 2, Pt I, para 2(5) | s 226(3) | Sch 12, Pt I, para 3(2) | s 206(6) |
| Sch 2, Pt II, para 3 | Unnecessary | Sch 12, Pt I, para 4(1) | s 206(7), (8) |
| Sch 2, Pt II, para 4(1)(a) | s 145(7) | Sch 12, Pt I, para 4(2) | s 206(9) |

\* Repealed in part

| (1) | (2) | (1) | (2) |
|---|---|---|---|
| Employment Protection (Consolidation) Act 1978 (c 44) | | Employment Protection (Consolidation) Act 1978 (c 44) | |
| Sch 12, Pt I, para 5 ....... | s 207(1) | Sch 13, para 14(3) ........ | s 215(3) |
| Sch 12, Pt I, para 6 ....... | s 207(3) | Sch 13, para 14(4) ........ | s 215(4), (5) |
| Sch 12, Pt II, paras 7, 8 .. | s 133(1) | Sch 13, para 14(5) ........ | cf Sch 2, Pt I, para 13 |
| Sch 12, Pt II, para 9 ...... | s 133(2) | Sch 13, para 14(6) ........ | s 215(6) |
| Sch 12, Pt II, para 10 .... | s 133(3), (4) | Sch 13, para 15(1) ........ | s 216(1) |
| Sch 12, Pt II, para 11 .... | s 133(5) | Sch 13, para 15(2), (3) .... | s 216(2) |
| Sch 12, Pt III, para 12... | ss 174(1), 175(1), (2) | Sch 13, para 15(4) ........ | s 216(3) |
| Sch 12, Pt III, para 13... | Rep 1993 c 19, s 51, Sch 10 | Sch 13, para 16(1) ........ | s 217 |
| Sch 12, Pt III, paras 14, 15.............................. | s 174(2), (3), (5) | Sch 13, para 16(2) ........ | Rep 1985 c 17, s 21, Sch 5 |
| Sch 12, Pt III, para 16... | s 174(4) | Sch 13, para 17(1) ........ | s 218(1) |
| Sch 12, Pt III, para 17... | s 175(1), (2) | Sch 13, para 17(2)–(5) .... | s 218(2)–(5) |
| Sch 12, Pt III, paras 18, 19.............................. | s 175(3), (4) | Sch 13, para 18............. | s 218(6) |
| Sch 12, Pt III, para 20(1), (2)............ | s 175(5), (6) | Sch 13, para 18A ......... | s 218(7) |
| | | Sch 13, para 18B ......... | s 218(8)–(10) |
| Sch 12, Pt III, para 21... | s 174(6) | Sch 13, para 19(1) ........ | s 191(1), (2) |
| Sch 12, Pt IV, para 22(1), (2)............ | s 176(1), (2) | Sch 13, para 19(2) ........ | s 191(3) |
| | | Sch 13, para 19(3) ........ | s 192(1) |
| Sch 12, Pt IV, para 23(1) | s 176(3) | Sch 13, para 19(4) ........ | Rep SI 1995/31 |
| Sch 12, Pt IV, paras 23(2), 24.......... | s 176(4) | Sch 13, para 19(5) ........ | s 191(4) |
| | | Sch 13, para 20............. | s 219 |
| Sch 12, Pt IV, paras 25–27 .............. | s 176(5)–(7) | Sch 13, paras 21, 22 .... | Cf Sch 2, para 14(1), (2) |
| | | Sch 13, para 23 ............. | Saved, Sch 2, para 6 |
| Sch 12, Pt IV, para 28 .. | s 207(2) | Sch 13, para 24(1) ........ | s 235(1), (4), (5) |
| Sch 13, para 1(1) .......... | s 210(4) | Sch 13, para 24(2) ........ | Rep SI 1995/31 |
| Sch 13, para 1(2) .......... | s 215(1) | Sch 14, Pt I, para 1 ....... | s 234(1), (2) |
| Sch 13, para 1(3) .......... | s 210(5) | Sch 14, Pt I, para 2 ....... | s 234(3) |
| Sch 13, para 3 ............... | Rep SI 1995/31 (there was no para 2) | Sch 14, Pt II, para 3 ...... | s 221(1)–(4) |
| Sch 13, para 4 ............... | s 212(1) | Sch 14, Pt II, para 4(1), (2).............................. | s 222(1), (2) |
| Sch 13, paras 5–8 ........ | Rep SI 1995/31 | Sch 14, Pt II, para 4(3), (4).............................. | s 222(3), (4) |
| Sch 13, para 9(1), (2).... | s 212(3), (4) | Sch 14, Pt II, para 5(1) ... | s 223(1), (2) |
| Sch 13, para 10............. | s 212(2) | Sch 14, Pt II, para 5(2), (3).............................. | s 223(3) |
| Sch 13, para 11(1) ....... | s 213(1) | | |
| Sch 13, para 11(2), (3).. | s 213(2), (3) | Sch 14, Pt II, para 6...... | s 224(1)–(3) |
| Sch 13, para 12(1), (2).. | s 214(1)–(4) | Sch 14, Pt II, para 7(1)(a)............... | s 225(1) |
| Sch 13, para 12(3) ....... | s 214(5) | | |
| Sch 13, para 13 ............. | Rep 1982 c 46, s 21, Sch 4 | Sch 14, Pt II, para 7(1)(b) .............. | s 225(5) |
| Sch 13, para 14(1)(a), (b)(ia)...................... | s 215(2) | Sch 14, Pt II, para 7(1)(c)............... | s 225(2) |
| Sch 13, para 14(1)(b)(i)–(iii), (2) .. | Cf Sch 2, Pt I, para 13 | Sch 14, Pt II, para 7(1)(cc)............. | s 225(3) |

\* Repealed in part

| (1) | (2) | (1) | (2) |
|---|---|---|---|
| **Employment Protection (Consolidation) Act 1978 (c 44)** | | **Employment Act 1980 (c 42)** | |
| Sch 14, Pt II, para 7(1)(ccc) | s 225(4) | s 8(2) | s 197(1) |
| Sch 14, Pt II, para 7(1)(d) | Rep 1986 c 50, s 86(2), Sch 11 | s 9(1) | Unnecessary |
| | | s 9(2) | s 119(1) |
| | | s 9(3) | s 119(2) |
| Sch 14, Pt II, para 7(1)(e) | s 226(1) | s 9(4) | s 122(1), (2) |
| Sch 14, Pt II, para 7(1)(ea) | s 225(5) | s 9(5) | Spent |
| | | s 12 | s 96(2)–(5) |
| Sch 14, Pt II, para 7(1)(f), (g) | s 226(2) | s 13 | ss 55(1)–(3), 56, 57 |
| | | s 14(1), (2) | s 31(2) |
| Sch 14, Pt II, para 7(1)(h) | s 226(3) | ss 20, 21 | Spent in part; unnecessary in part |
| Sch 14, Pt II, para 7(1)(i) | s 226(3), (6) | Sch 1, para 1 | Spent |
| Sch 14, Pt II, para 7(1)(ia), (ib) | s 226(2) | Sch 1, para 8 | s 31(7) |
| | | Sch 1, para 11 | s 96(1) |
| Sch 14, Pt II, para 7(1)(j) | s 226(4) | Sch 1, para 13(a) | Spent |
| | | Sch 1, para 13(b) | s 110(4) |
| Sch 14, Pt II, para 7(1)(k) | s 226(5) | Sch 1, para 20 | Spent |
| Sch 14, Pt II, para 7(1)(l) | s 226(5), (6) | Sch 1, para 22 | Spent in part; otherwise unnecessary |
| Sch 14, Pt II, para 7(2) | s 226(6) | Sch 1, para 23 | s 98(4)–(6) |
| Sch 14, Pt II, para 8(1), (2) | s 227(1), (2) | Sch 1, para 25 | Spent |
| | | Sch 1, para 31 | s 212(2) |
| Sch 14, Pt II, para 8(3), (4) | s 227(3), (4) | Sch 1, para 33 | s 225(3) |
| | | Sch 2 | Spent |
| Sch 14, Pt II, para 9 | s 228(1)–(3) | **Magistrates' Courts Act 1980 (c 43)** | |
| Sch 14, Pt II, para 10 | s 229(1) | | |
| Sch 14, Pt II, para 11 | s 229(2) | Sch 7, para 175 | s 169(4) |
| Sch 14, Pt II, para 12 | s 228(4) | **Finance Act 1980 (c 48)** | |
| Sch 15 | Superseded by Sch 2; repealed in part; spent in part | Sch 19, para 5(4) | Spent |
| | | **New Towns Act 1981 (c 64)** | |
| Sch 16 | Superseded by Sch 1; repealed in part; spent in part | s 54(6) | Spent |
| | | **Civil Aviation Act 1982 (c 16)** | |
| Sch 17 | Spent | Sch 3, paras 6, 8(1) | Spent |
| **Reserve Forces Act 1980 (c 9)** | | **Oil and Gas Enterprise Act 1982 (c 23)** | |
| Sch 9, para 17 | s 192(1) | Sch 3, para 40 | Unnecessary |
| **Education Act 1980 (c 20)** | | **Social Security and Housing Benefits Act 1982 (c 24)** | |
| Sch 1, para 30 | Unnecessary | | |
| **Employment Act 1980 (c 42)** | | Sch 2, para 13 | ss 88(2), 89(3), (4) |
| s 6 | s 98(4)–(6) | | |

\* Repealed in part

| (1) | (2) | (1) | (2) |
|-----|-----|-----|-----|
| **Employment Act 1982 (c 46)** | | **Mental Health (Scotland) Act 1984 (c 36)** | |
| ss 20, 21(2), (3) ............ | Spent in part; otherwise unnecessary | s 126(2)(c).................. | Spent |
| Sch 2, para 1 ................. | s 29(1), (2) | **Reserve Forces (Safeguard of Employment) Act 1985 (c 17)** | |
| Sch 2, para 2 ................. | s 65 | | |
| Sch 2, para 3(1) ........... | ss 86(1)–(3), 87(1), (2) | | |
| Sch 2, para 3(2) ........... | s 86(4) | Sch 4, para 6 ................ | s 217 |
| Sch 2, para 3(3) ........... | s 86(5) | **Local Government Act 1985 (c 51)** | |
| Sch 2, para 4 ................. | s 92(3) | | |
| Sch 2, para 5(1)(a)........ | Spent | ss 53*, 55*, 59*........... | Spent |
| Sch 2, para 5(1)(b)........ | s 108(2) | **Insolvency Act 1985 (c 65)** | |
| Sch 2, para 5(2) ........... | Spent | | |
| Sch 2, para 6(2) ........... | Spent | s 218(1) ...................... | Unnecessary |
| Sch 2, para 6(4) ........... | s 167(2) | s 218(2) ...................... | s 182 |
| Sch 2, para 6(5) ........... | Spent | s 218(3) ...................... | s 185 |
| Sch 2, para 7(1) ........... | ss 210(1)–(3), 211, 215(3), 216(2), (3), 217 | s 218(4) ...................... | ss 27(1), 184(2) |
| | | s 218(5) ...................... | s 184(4) |
| | | s 218(6)(a) .................. | s 187(4) |
| Sch 2, para 7(2) ........... | ss 210(4), (5), 215(1) | s 218(6)(b) .................. | s 187(5) |
| Sch 2, para 9(1) ........... | s 209(2), (5) | Sch 8, para 31(1) .......... | Unnecessary |
| Sch 2, para 9(2) ........... | s 238(1), (2) | Sch 8, para 31(2)(a)...... | s 166(6) |
| Sch 3, Pt I, para 1 ........ | ss 92(7), 97(2)–(5) | Sch 8, para 31(2)(b) ..... | s 166(7) |
| Sch 3, Pt I, para 2(1)..... | s 139(3) | Sch 8, para 31(5)(a)...... | s 183(2) |
| Sch 3, Pt I, para 2(2)..... | s 218(1) | Sch 8, para 31(5)(b) ..... | s 183(3) |
| Sch 3, Pt I, para 2(3)..... | s 218(7) | **Bankruptcy (Scotland) Act 1985 (c 66)** | |
| Sch 3, Pt I, para 4 ........ | s 184(1) | | |
| Sch 3, Pt I, para 6 ........ | Spent | Sch 7, Pt I, para 14(1), (2), (4) .................... | ss 16(6), 183(2), 184(4) |
| Sch 3, Pt II, para 15 ...... | s 29(3) | | |
| Sch 3, Pt II, para 21 ...... | s 112 | **Housing (Consequential Provisions) Act 1986 (c 71)** | |
| Sch 3, Pt II, para 22 ...... | s 117(3), (8) | | |
| Sch 3, Pt II, para 23 ...... | s 123(3) | | |
| Sch 3, Pt II, para 25 ...... | s 209(2) | Sch 4, para 7(2)(a)........ | Spent |
| Sch 3, Pt II, para 26 ...... | Unnecessary | **Insolvency Act 1986 (c 45)** | |
| Sch 3, Pt II, para 27(1).... | Spent | | |
| Sch 3, Pt II, para 28 ...... | s 133(1) | Sch 14*....................... | ss 166(6), (7), 183(2), (3), 184(4), 187(5) |
| Sch 3, Pt II, para 29 ...... | s 213(1) | | |
| Sch 3, Pt II, para 30(1).... | s 227(3) | **Legal Aid (Scotland) Act 1986 (c 47)** | |
| Sch 3, Pt II, para 30(2)(a), (b) ...... | s 226(3) | | |
| Sch 3, Pt II, para 30(3) . | s 227(3) | Sch 1, para 10(2)(a)*.... | Spent |
| Sch 4 ........................... | Spent | **Wages Act 1986 (c 48)** | |
| **Water Act 1983 (c 23)** | | | |
| Sch 2, Pt I, para 8(1)(b) .. | Spent | s 1(1) ......................... | s 13(1) |
| **Health and Social Services and Social Security Adjudications Act 1983 (c 41)** | | s 1(2) ......................... | s 15(1) |
| | | s 1(3) ......................... | ss 13(2), 15(2) |
| | | s 1(4) ......................... | ss 13(5), (6), 15(3), (4) |
| Sch 9, Pt I, para 25 ....... | Spent | s 1(5)(a) ...................... | ss 14(1), 16(1) |

\* Repealed in part

| (1) | (2) | (1) | (2) |
|---|---|---|---|
| **Wages Act 1986**<br>**(c 48)** | | **Wages Act 1986**<br>**(c 48)** | |
| s 1(5)(b) | ss 14(2), 16(2) | s 9(5) | s 191(4) |
| s 1(5)(c) | s 14(3) | s 10 | s 201 |
| s 1(5)(d) | s 14(4) | s 11 | Spent |
| s 1(5)(e) | ss 14(5), 16(3) | ss 28, 29 | Unnecessary; spent |
| s 1(5)(f) | ss 14(6), 16(4) | s 30(1) | s 196(2), (3) |
| s 1(6) | s 13(7) | s 30(2) | s 191(5) |
| s 2(1) | s 18(1) | s 30(3) | s 199(1) |
| s 2(2) | s 17(1)–(3), (6) | ss 32, 33 | Spent in part; otherwise unnecessary |
| s 2(3) | s 18(2), (3) | | |
| s 2(4) | s 19(1) | Sch 1 | Spent |
| s 2(5) | s 19(2)–(4) | Sch 4, para 4 | Superseded by Sch 1, para 3 |
| s 3(1)–(3) | s 20(1)–(3) | | |
| s 3(4), (5) | s 21(1), (2) | Sch 5 | Spent |
| s 3(6) | s 20(4) | Sch 6, para 10 | Unnecessary |
| s 4(1)–(3) | s 22(1)–(3) | **Social Security**<br>**Act 1986 (c 50)** | |
| s 4(4) | s 20(5) | | |
| s 4(5) | ss 21(3), 22(4) | Sch 10, Pt IV, para 76 .. | Spent |
| s 4(6) | s 17(4), (5) | Sch 10, Pt IV, para 81 .. | s 27(1) |
| s 5(1) | s 23(1) | **Sex Discrimination**<br>**Act 1986 (c 59)** | |
| s 5(2) | s 23(2), (4) | | |
| s 5(3) | s 23(3) | s 3(1) | s 109(1) |
| s 5(3A) | Rep 1992 c 52, s 300(1), Sch 1 | s 3(2) | s 119(4) |
| | | s 3(3) | Spent |
| s 5(4) | s 24 | **Housing (Scotland)**<br>**Act 1987 (c 26)** | |
| s 5(5) | s 25(1), (2) | | |
| s 5(6)–(8) | s 25(3)–(5) | Sch 22, Pt II,<br>para 10(2)(a) | Spent |
| s 6(1) | s 205(2) | | |
| s 6(2) | s 26 | **Income and Corporation**<br>**Taxes Act 1988 (c 1)** | |
| s 6(3) | s 203(1), (2) | | |
| s 6(4), (5) | s 203(3), (4) | ss 150(b), 579*, 580(2)... | Spent |
| s 6(6) | s 231 | **Norfolk and Suffolk**<br>**Broads Act 1988 (c 4)** | |
| s 7(1) | s 27(1) | | |
| s 7(2), (3) | s 27(2), (3) | Sch 6, para 19 | s 50(5) |
| s 7(4) | s 27(5) | **Dartford-Thurrock**<br>**Crossing Act 1988**<br>**(c 20)** | |
| s 8(1) | ss 27(4), 230(3)–(5), 235(1) (Unnecessary in part) | | |
| | | Sch 5, Pt I, para 2(2) | Spent |
| s 8(2) | s 230(3) | **Legal Aid Act 1988**<br>**(c 34)** | |
| s 8(3), (4) | s 13(3), (4) | | |
| s 8(5) | s 15(5) | Sch 7, para 7(3)* | Spent |
| s 9(1) | s 191(1), (2) | **Education Reform**<br>**Act 1988 (c 40)** | |
| s 9(2) | s 191(3) | | |
| s 9(3) | Rep 1993 c 19, s 51, Sch 10 | s 173* | Spent |
| | | s 178(1), (2) | Spent |
| s 9(4) | s 192(1) | | |

* Repealed in part

| (1) | (2) | (1) | (2) |
|---|---|---|---|
| Education Reform Act 1988 (c 40) | | National Health Service and Community Care Act 1990 (c 19) | |
| Sch 12, Pt I, para 23 ..... | s 50(2)(f), (9) | | |
| Sch 12, Pt III, para 80... | s 50(2)(f), (9) | Sch 9, para 20.............. | s 50(2)(e), (8) |
| Housing (Scotland) Act 1988 (c 26) | | Enterprise and New Towns (Scotland) Act 1990 (c 35) | |
| Sch 1, para 12(2) .......... | Spent | | |
| Housing Act 1988 (c 50) | | Sch 1, para 17(2) .......... | Spent |
| Sch 5, para 19(2)* ....... | Spent | Employment Act 1990 (c 38) | |
| Dock Work Act 1989 (c 13) | | ss 13(1), (2), (4), 16, 17*...................... | Spent in part; otherwise unnecessary |
| s 6(2)............................ | Spent | Sch 2, para 1(1) ........... | Spent |
| s 7(4)............................ | s 199(3) | Sch 2, para 1(3) ........... | s 167(1), (4) |
| Sch 2, paras 6, 7 .......... | Spent | Sch 2, para 1(4) ........... | ss 182, 189(5) |
| Water Act 1989 (c 15) | | Sch 2, para 1(5)(a)........ | s 237 |
| s 194(7)*...................... | Unnecessary | Sch 2, para 1(5)(b) ....... | Spent |
| Sch 25, para 56 ............. | s 50(2)(g) | Sch 2, para 1(6) ........... | s 239(2) |
| Electricity Act 1989 (c 29) | | Sch 3............................ | Spent |
| s 56(2)........................... | Spent | Environmental Protection Act 1990 (c 43) | |
| Employment Act 1989 (c 38) | | Sch 10, para 16*.......... | Spent |
| s 15(1)........................... | s 92(3) | Natural Heritage (Scotland) Act 1991 (c 28) | |
| s 15(2)........................... | s 209(5) | | |
| s 16(1)........................... | s 156(1) | | |
| s 16(2)........................... | s 162(5) | Sch 4, para 5*.............. | Spent |
| s 17 ............................. | Spent | Social Security (Consequential Provisions) Act 1992 (c 6) | |
| s 18(1)........................... | Unnecessary | | |
| s 18(2)........................... | s 187(2) | | |
| s 18(3)........................... | Spent | Sch 2, para 51(1) ......... | s 215(2), (4), (5) |
| s 19(1)........................... | s 189(2)–(4) | Sch 2, para 74.............. | s 27(1) |
| ss 27(1)*, 29(1)*, 30(3)(f) ..................... | Spent | Further and Higher Education Act 1992 (c 13) | |
| Sch 6, para 21(1) .......... | Spent | | |
| Sch 6, para 21(2) .......... | s 166(2), (3) | Sch 8, Pt II, para 89...... | s 50(2)(f), (9) |
| Sch 6, para 21(3) .......... | s 167(2) | Trade Union and Labour Relations (Consolidation) Act 1992 (c 52) | |
| Sch 6, para 21(4) .......... | Spent | | |
| Sch 6, para 22 ............... | s 170 | | |
| Sch 6, para 23 ............... | s 183(2) | | |
| Sch 6, para 24 ............... | Unnecessary | | |
| Sch 6, para 25 .............. | s 168 | Sch 2, para 11.............. | s 50(4) |
| Sch 9, paras 3–5 .......... | Spent | Sch 2, para 12(a) .......... | s 51(2) |
| Self-Governing Schools etc (Scotland) Act 1989 (c 39) | | Sch 2, para 12(b) .......... | s 51(3), (4) |
| | | Sch 2, para 12(c) ......... | Spent |
| Sch 10, para 7 ............... | s 50(9) | | |

\* Repealed in part

| (1) | (2) | (1) | (2) |
|---|---|---|---|
| **Trade Union and Labour Relations (Consolidation) Act 1992 (c 52)** | | **Trade Union Reform and Employment Rights Act 1993 (c 19)** | |
| Sch 2, para 13 | ss 50(11), 52(3), 55(4), 61(2) | Sch 4 | ss 1–7, 198 |
| | | Sch 5, para 1 | ss 44, 48(1), 49 |
| Sch 2, para 14 | s 98(4)–(6) | Sch 5, para 2 | s 98(4)–(6) |
| Sch 2, para 15† | s 117(4) | Sch 5, para 3 | s 100 |
| Sch 2, para 16 | s 118(1) | Sch 5, para 4 | s 105(3) |
| Sch 2, para 17 | s 122(3) | Sch 5, para 5 | ss 108(3), 109(2) |
| Sch 2, para 18 | ss 27(1), 184(2), 185 | Sch 5, para 6(a) | s 117(3) |
| Sch 2, para 21(1) | Spent | Sch 5, para 6(b) | s 117(4) |
| Sch 2, para 21(2) | s 235(1) | Sch 5, para 7 | s 118(2), (3) |
| Sch 2, para 21(3) | s 235(2) | Sch 5, para 8(a) | s 119(1) |
| Sch 2, para 22 | s 98(4)–(6) | Sch 5, para 8(b) | ss 120, 236(3) |
| Sch 2, para 23 | s 91(1) | Sch 5, para 8(c) | s 122(3) |
| Sch 2, paras 29(2), 30, 33 | Unnecessary | Sch 5, para 9 | ss 125, 236(3) |
| Sch 2, para 34(1), (2) | s 27(1) | Sch 5, para 10 | ss 128, 129, 130, 131, 132 |
| **Trade Union Reform and Employment Rights Act 1993 (c 19)** | | Sch 6, para 3(a) | s 203(2) |
| | | Sch 6, para 3(b) | ss 203(3), (4), 231 |
| s 23(1) | Unnecessary | Sch 7, para 2 | Spent |
| s 23(2) | ss 71, 72, 73, 74, 75, 76, 77, 78, 236(3) | Sch 7, para 3(a) | Spent |
| | | Sch 7, para 3(b) | s 193(1), (2) |
| s 24(1) | s 99(1)–(3) | Sch 7, para 4 | Spent |
| s 24(2) | s 105(1)–(3), (6), (7) | Sch 7, para 5 | s 202 |
| s 24(3) | ss 108(3), 109(2) | Sch 7, para 11 | s 194 |
| s 24(4) | s 92(4) | Sch 7, para 13 | s 209(7) |
| ss 25, 26, 28 | Unnecessary | Sch 7, para 14(a)–(c) | s 219(2) |
| s 29(1) | s 104 | Sch 7, para 14(d) | s 219(2)–(4) |
| s 29(2) | s 105(7) | Sch 7, para 16(a) | s 236(3) |
| s 29(3) | ss 108(3), 109(2) | Sch 7, para 16(b) | s 236(4) |
| s 30(1) | Unnecessary | Sch 8, para 10(a) | s 11(1) |
| s 30(2)(a) | s 117(1), (2) | Sch 8, para 10(b) | s 11(3) |
| s 30(2)(b) | s 124(3) | Sch 8, para 10(c) | s 11(4) |
| s 30(3)(a) | s 123(1) | Sch 8, para 11 | s 93(1), (2) |
| s 30(3)(b) | s 124(4) | Sch 8, para 12 | s 96(1) |
| s 30(4) | Unnecessary | Sch 8, para 13 | s 96(2)–(5) |
| s 31(1) | s 192(1) | Sch 8, para 14(a) | s 105(1), (4) |
| s 31(2) | ss 192(2)–(8), 236(3) | Sch 8, para 14(b) | Rep 1994 c 40, s 81(1), Sch 17 |
| s 39(1)(a) | s 203(2) | Sch 8, para 14(c) | s 105(9) |
| s 39(1)(b) | s 203(3), (4) | Sch 8, para 15 | s 106(2), (3) |
| s 39(2)* | Unnecessary | Sch 8, para 16 | s 110(2) |
| s 54* | Spent | Sch 8, para 17 | s 137(1) |
| Sch 2 | ss 79, 80, 81, 82, 83, 85, 236(3) | Sch 8, para 18 | ss 27(1), 184(2) |
| | | Sch 8, para 21 | s 203(2) |
| Sch 3 | ss 66, 67, 68, 69, 70 | Sch 8, para 22 | s 196(1) |

* Repealed in part

| (1) | (2) | (1) | (2) |
|---|---|---|---|
| **Trade Union Reform and Employment Rights Act 1993 (c 19)** | | **Sunday Trading Act 1994 (c 20)** | |
| | | Sch 4, para 1(5) ............. | s 210(3) |
| Sch 8, para 23 ............... | s 199(1) | Sch 4, para 1(6) ............ | s 96(6) |
| Sch 8, para 24 .............. | s 209(2) | Sch 4, para 2(1)–(3) ..... | s 36(1)–(3) |
| Sch 8, para 25(a)(i)–(iv) .. | s 235(1) | Sch 4, para 2(4)(a)........ | ss 101(4), 105(8) |
| Sch 8, para 25(a)(v) ...... | Unnecessary | Sch 4, para 2(4)(b) ....... | s 45(9) |
| Sch 8, para 25(b) .......... | s 204 | Sch 4, para 2(4)(c), (d).... | s 37(5) |
| Sch 8, para 26(a)(i)....... | s 98(4)–(6) | Sch 4, para 2(4)(e)........ | s 38(3) |
| Sch 8, para 26(a)(ii)...... | s 99(4) | Sch 4, para 2(4)(f)....... | s 39(5) |
| Sch 8, para 26(a)(iii)..... | s 226(3) | Sch 4, para 2(5) ............ | Unnecessary |
| Sch 8, para 26(b)(i)....... | s 146(3) | Sch 4, para 2(6) ............ | s 45(10) |
| Sch 8, para 26(b)(ii) ..... | s 226(5) | Sch 4, para 2(7) ............ | s 36(4) |
| Sch 8, para 26(c)........... | s 137(2) | Sch 4, para 3(1), (2) ..... | s 36(5), (6) |
| Sch 8, para 26(d) .......... | s 84(1) | Sch 4, para 4(1) ............ | s 40(3) |
| Sch 8, para 26(e)........... | s 209(6) | Sch 4, para 4(2) ............ | s 40(1) |
| Sch 8, para 27(a)(i), (ii) ... | s 88(1) | Sch 4, para 4(3) ............ | s 40(2) |
| Sch 8, para 27(a)(iii)..... | s 88(2) | Sch 4, para 5(1) ............ | s 41(1) |
| Sch 8, para 27(b) .......... | s 89(3), (4) | Sch 4, para 5(2)(a)........ | ss 101(4), 105(8) |
| Sch 8, para 31(a)........... | s 212(3) | Sch 4, para 5(2)(b) ....... | s 45(9) |
| Sch 8, para 31(b) .......... | s 212(2) | Sch 4, para 5(2)(c), (d).... | s 43(5) |
| Sch 8, para 32(a)........... | s 225(5) | Sch 4, para 5(3) ............ | Unnecessary |
| Sch 8, para 32(b) .......... | s 226(2) | Sch 4, para 5(4) ............ | s 45(10) |
| Sch 8, para 35 ............... | Unnecessary | Sch 4, para 5(5) ............ | s 41(2) |
| Sch 8, para 36 ............... | ss 196(2), (3), 199(1) | Sch 4, para 6 ................. | s 41(3) |
| Sch 8, paras 37, 67 ....... | Unnecessary | Sch 4, para 7(1)–(3) ..... | s 101(1)–(3) |
| Sch 9, para 3 ................. | Unnecessary | Sch 4, para 7(4) ............ | s 197(2) |
| **Pension Schemes Act 1993 (c 48)** | | Sch 4, para 8 ................. | s 105(1), (4) |
| | | Sch 4, para 9 ................. | ss 108(3), 109(2) |
| s 164(6)......................... | Spent | Sch 4, para 10(1)–(3) ... | s 45(1)–(3) |
| Sch 8, para 11(1) .......... | s 11(3) | Sch 4, para 10(4) .......... | s 45(4) |
| Sch 8, para 45(a)........... | Unnecessary | Sch 4, para 10(5) .......... | s 45(5) |
| **Race Relations (Remedies) Act 1994 (c 10)** | | Sch 4, para 10(6) .......... | s 45(6)–(8) |
| | | Sch 4, para 11(1)–(3) ... | s 42(1)–(3) |
| | | Sch 4, para 11(4) .......... | s 42(4) |
| s 1(2)............................. | Spent | Sch 4, para 11(5) .......... | s 42(6) |
| **Social Security (Incapacity for Work) Act 1994 (c 18)** | | Sch 4, para 11(6) .......... | s 236(1), (2) |
| | | Sch 4, para 12(1)–(4) ... | s 37(1)–(4) |
| | | Sch 4, para 13(1)–(4) ... | s 43(1)–(4) |
| Sch 1, Pt II, para 54 ...... | s 90(1) | Sch 4, para 14................ | s 38(1), (2) |
| **Sunday Trading Act 1994 (c 20)** | | Sch 4, para 15(1) .......... | s 39(1)–(3) |
| | | Sch 4, para 15(2) .......... | s 39(4) |
| Sch 4, para 1(1) ............ | ss 36(7), 45(4), 232(1)–(3), (6)–(8) | Sch 4, para 16................ | s 48(1) |
| | | Sch 4, para 17(1) .......... | s 203(1) |
| Sch 4, para 1(2), (3)...... | s 232(4), (5) | Sch 4, para 17(2) .......... | s 203(2) |
| Sch 4, para 1(4) ........... | ss 210(1)–(3), 230(1), (2), (4), (5), 235(1) | Sch 4, para 18............... | Sch 2, para 9 (spent in part) |

\* Repealed in part

| (1) | (2) | (1) | (2) |
|---|---|---|---|
| **Sunday Trading Act 1994 (c 20)** | | **Pensions Act 1995 (c 26)** | |
| Sch 4, para 19 | s 104(4) | s 46(6) | s 105(1), (5) |
| Sch 4, para 20 | s 110(2) | s 46(7) | ss 108(3), 109(2) |
| Sch 4, para 22 | ss 196(2), (3), 205(1), 206(2) | s 46(8) | s 203(1) |
| | | s 46(9) | s 203(2) |
| **Deregulation and Contracting Out Act 1994 (c 40)** | | s 46(10) | s 46(2) |
| | | s 46(11) | ss 230(1), (2), (4), (5), 235(1) |
| ss 20(3), (5), 36(1) | Unnecessary or spent | s 124(1)† | s 58(3) |
| Sch 8 | ss 36, 37, 38, 39, 40, 41, 42(1)–(3), (5), (6), 43, 45, 48(1), 96(6), 101, 104(4), 105(1), (4), (8), 108(3), 109(2), 110(2), 196(2), (3), 197(2), 203(1), (2), 205(1), 206(2), 210(1)–(3), 230(1), (2), (4), (5), 233(1)–(4), (6), 235(1), 236(1), (2) | Sch 3, para 1 | Unnecessary |
| | | Sch 3, para 2 | s 104(4) |
| | | Sch 3, para 3 | s 117(4) |
| | | Sch 3, para 4 | s 118(3) |
| | | Sch 3, para 5 | s 120(1) |
| | | Sch 3, para 6 | s 128(1) |
| | | Sch 3, para 7 | s 129(1) |
| | | Sch 3, para 10 | s 191(1), (2) |
| | | **Disability Discrimination Act 1995 (c 50)** | |
| **Health Authorities Act 1995 (c 17)** | | Sch 6, para 3(a) | s 219(3) |
| | | Sch 6, para 3(b) | s 219(2) |
| Sch 1, Pt III, para 103 | ss 50(8), 218(1), (8)–(10) | Sch 6, para 3(c) | s 219(4) |
| | | **Reserve Forces Act 1996 (c 14)** | |
| **Environment Act 1995 (c 25)** | | Sch 10, para 17 | s 192(1) |
| Sch 7, para 11(3)* | s 50(5) | **Employment Protection (Medical Suspension) Order 1980, SI 1980/1581** | s 64(1)–(3) |
| **Pensions Act 1995 (c 26)** | | | |
| s 42(1) | s 58(1) | | |
| s 42(2) | s 58(2) | **Insolvency of Employer (Excluded Classes) Regulations 1983, SI 1983/624** | |
| s 42(3) | s 60(1) | | |
| s 42(4) | s 58(4) | Reg 3 | ss 196(2), (3), (7), 200(1) |
| s 43(1)–(4) | s 59(1)–(4) | | |
| s 43(5) | s 59(5), (6) | | |
| s 43(6) | s 60(1) | **Employment Protection (Medical Suspension) Order 1985, SI 1985/1787** | s 64(1)–(3) |
| s 44 | s 60(2) | | |
| s 45(1)–(3) | s 60(3)–(5) | | |
| s 45(4) | s 205(1) | | |
| s 46(1), (2) | s 46(1), (2) | | |
| s 46(3) | s 48(1) | | |
| s 46(4)(a) | s 205(1) | **Employment Protection (Medical Suspension) Order 1988, SI 1988/1746** | s 64(1)–(3) |
| s 46(4)(b) | s 196(2), (3) | | |
| s 46(4)(c) | s 206(2) | | |
| s 46(5) | s 102(1) | | |

\* Repealed in part

| (1) | (2) | (1) | (2) |
|---|---|---|---|
| Time Off for Public Duties Order 1990, SI 1990/1870 | s 50(2)(d), (7) | Collective Redundancies and Transfer of Undertakings (Protection of Employment) (Amendment) Regulations 1995, SI 1995/2587 | |
| Sex Discrimination and Equal Pay (Remedies) Regulations 1993, SI 1993/2798* | | Reg 12(2) | s 48(1) |
| | | Reg 12(4) | s 209(7) |
| Sch 1, para 1*, 2 | Spent | Reg 13(1) | s 61(1) |
| Employment Protection (Part-time Employees) Regulations 1995, SI 1995/31 | | Reg 13(2) | s 61(2) |
| | | Reg 13(4) | s 193(1), (2) |
| | | Reg 13(5) | s 202(2) |
| | | Reg 13(6) | s 225(4) |
| Regs 1–3, 4(1) | Spent | Reg 14(1) | s 103 |
| Reg 4(2) | s 210(4) | Reg 14(2) | ss 105(6), 108(3), 109(2) |
| Regs 5, 6, Schedule | Spent | | |
| Insolvency of Employer (Excluded Classes) Regulations 1995, SI 1995/278 | | Reg 14(3) | ss 117(4), 118(3), 120(1), 128, 129(1) |
| | | Reg 14(4) | ss 193(1), (2), 202(2) |
| | | Reg 14(5) | s 192(2) |
| Regs 1, 2 | Unnecessary | Reg 14(6) | s 209(2) |
| Reg 3 | s 196(7) | Reg 14(7) | Unnecessary |
| Reg 4 | Spent | Environment Act 1995 (Consequential Amendments) Regulations 1996, SI 1996/593 | |
| Reg 5 | Unnecessary | | |
| Time Off for Public Duties Order 1995, SI 1995/694 | s 50(2)(c), (6) | | |
| | | Sch 1, para 19 | s 50(2)(g) |
| Collective Redundancies and Transfer of Undertakings (Protection of Employment) (Amendment) Regulations 1995, SI 1995/2587 | | Environment Act 1995 (Consequential and Transitional Provisions) (Scotland) Regulations 1996, SI 1996/973 | |
| | | Schedule, para 4(1) | Unnecessary |
| | | Schedule, para 4(2)(a) | s 50(2)(g) |
| Reg 12(1) | s 47 | Schedule, para 4(2)(b) | Unnecessary |

* Repealed in part

# ASYLUM AND IMMIGRATION ACT 1996 (NOTE)

## (1996 c 49)

**[1.1052]**

**NOTES**

Only ss 8 (Restrictions on employment), 8A (Code of practice) and 13 (Short title, etc) were reproduced in previous editions of this work. Sections 8 and 8A were repealed by the Immigration, Asylum and Nationality Act 2006, ss 26, 61, Sch 3, as from 29 February 2008, except in relation to employment which commenced before that date (see the transitional provisions note to s 15 of the 2006 Act at **[1.1399]**). Section 13 (short title, extent etc), although still in force, is now outside the scope of this work.

# PROTECTION FROM HARASSMENT ACT 1997

## (1997 c 40)

### ARRANGEMENT OF SECTIONS

#### England and Wales

*An Act to make provision for protecting persons from harassment and similar conduct*

[21 March 1997]

**NOTES**

Regulatory functions: the regulatory functions conferred by, or under, this Act are subject to the Legislative and Regulatory Reform Act 2006, ss 21, 22 at **[1.1495]**, **[1.1496]**; see the Legislative and Regulatory Reform (Regulatory Functions) Order 2007, SI 2007/3544 (made under s 24(2) of the 2006 Act) for details.

See *Harvey* L(3)(C)(1).

#### England and Wales

**[1.1053]**
**1 Prohibition of harassment**
(1) A person must not pursue a course of conduct—
  (a) which amounts to harassment of another, and
  (b) which he knows or ought to know amounts to harassment of the other.
[(1A) A person must not pursue a course of conduct—
  (a) which involves harassment of two or more persons, and
  (b) which he knows or ought to know involves harassment of those persons, and
  (c) by which he intends to persuade any person (whether or not one of those mentioned above)—
    (i) not to do something that he is entitled or required to do, or
    (ii) to do something that he is not under any obligation to do.]

(2)   For the purposes of this section [or section 2A(2)(c)], the person whose course of conduct is in question ought to know that it amounts to [or involves] harassment of another if a reasonable person in possession of the same information would think the course of conduct amounted to [or involved] harassment of the other.

(3)   Subsection (1) [or (1A)] does not apply to a course of conduct if the person who pursued it shows—

(a)   that it was pursued for the purpose of preventing or detecting crime,

(b)   that it was pursued under any enactment or rule of law or to comply with any condition or requirement imposed by any person under any enactment, or

(c)   that in the particular circumstances the pursuit of the course of conduct was reasonable.

**NOTES**

Sub-s (1A): inserted by the Serious Organised Crime and Police Act 2005, s 125(1), (2)(a).

Sub-s (2): words in first pair of square brackets inserted by the Protection of Freedoms Act 2012, s 115(1), Sch 9, Pt 11, para 143(1), (2), as from 25 November 2012; words in second and third pairs of square brackets inserted by the Serious Organised Crime and Police Act 2005, s 125(1), (2)(b).

Sub-s (3): words in square brackets inserted by the Serious Organised Crime and Police Act 2005, s 125(1), (2)(c).

**[1.1054]**
**2   Offence of harassment**

(1)   A person who pursues a course of conduct in breach of [section 1(1) or (1A)] is guilty of an offence.

(2)   A person guilty of an offence under this section is liable on summary conviction to imprisonment for a term not exceeding six months, or a fine not exceeding level 5 on the standard scale, or both.

(3)   . . .

**NOTES**

Sub-s (1): words in square brackets substituted by the Serious Organised Crime and Police Act 2005, s 125(1), (3).

Sub-s (3): repealed by the Police Reform Act 2002, s 107(2), Sch 8.

**[1.1055]**
**[2A   Offence of stalking**

(1)   A person is guilty of an offence if—

(a)   the person pursues a course of conduct in breach of section 1(1), and

(b)   the course of conduct amounts to stalking.

(2)   For the purposes of subsection (1)(b) (and section 4A(1)(a)) a person's course of conduct amounts to stalking of another person if—

(a)   it amounts to harassment of that person,

(b)   the acts or omissions involved are ones associated with stalking, and

(c)   the person whose course of conduct it is knows or ought to know that the course of conduct amounts to harassment of the other person.

(3)   The following are examples of acts or omissions which, in particular circumstances, are ones associated with stalking—

(a)   following a person,

(b)   contacting, or attempting to contact, a person by any means,

(c)   publishing any statement or other material—

(i)    relating or purporting to relate to a person, or

(ii)   purporting to originate from a person,

(d)   monitoring the use by a person of the internet, email or any other form of electronic communication,

(e)   loitering in any place (whether public or private),

(f)   interfering with any property in the possession of a person,

(g)   watching or spying on a person.

(4)   A person guilty of an offence under this section is liable on summary conviction to imprisonment for a term not exceeding 51 weeks, or a fine not exceeding level 5 on the standard scale, or both.

(5)   In relation to an offence committed before the commencement of section 281(5) of the Criminal Justice Act 2003, the reference in subsection (4) to 51 weeks is to be read as a reference to six months.

(6)   This section is without prejudice to the generality of section 2.]

**NOTES**

Commencement: 25 November 2012.

Inserted by the Protection of Freedoms Act 2012, s 111(1), as from 25 November 2012.

**[1.1056]**
## [2B Power of entry in relation to offence of stalking

(1) A justice of the peace may, on an application by a constable, issue a warrant authorising a constable to enter and search premises if the justice of the peace is satisfied that there are reasonable grounds for believing that—

   (a) an offence under section 2A has been, or is being, committed,

   (b) there is material on the premises which is likely to be of substantial value (whether by itself or together with other material) to the investigation of the offence,

   (c) the material—

      (i) is likely to be admissible in evidence at a trial for the offence, and

      (ii) does not consist of, or include, items subject to legal privilege, excluded material or special procedure material (within the meanings given by sections 10, 11 and 14 of the Police and Criminal Evidence Act 1984), and

   (d) either—

      (i) entry to the premises will not be granted unless a warrant is produced, or

      (ii) the purpose of a search may be frustrated or seriously prejudiced unless a constable arriving at the premises can secure immediate entry to them.

(2) A constable may seize and retain anything for which a search has been authorised under subsection (1).

(3) A constable may use reasonable force, if necessary, in the exercise of any power conferred by virtue of this section.

(4) In this section "premises" has the same meaning as in section 23 of the Police and Criminal Evidence Act 1984.]

---

### NOTES

Commencement: 25 November 2012.

Inserted by the Protection of Freedoms Act 2012, s 112, as from 25 November 2012.

Additional powers of seizure: the power of seizure conferred by sub-s (2) above is a power of seizure to which the Criminal Justice and Police Act 2001, s 50 (additional powers of seizure from premises) applies; see s 50 of, and Sch 1, Pt 1, para 63A to, the 2001 Act (as inserted by the Protection of Freedoms Act 2012).

**[1.1057]**
## 3 Civil remedy

(1) An actual or apprehended breach of [section 1(1)] may be the subject of a claim in civil proceedings by the person who is or may be the victim of the course of conduct in question.

(2) On such a claim, damages may be awarded for (among other things) any anxiety caused by the harassment and any financial loss resulting from the harassment.

(3) Where—

   (a) in such proceedings the High Court or *a county* court grants an injunction for the purpose of restraining the defendant from pursuing any conduct which amounts to harassment, and

   (b) the plaintiff considers that the defendant has done anything which he is prohibited from doing by the injunction,

the plaintiff may apply for the issue of a warrant for the arrest of the defendant.

(4) An application under subsection (3) may be made—

   (a) where the injunction was granted by the High Court, to a judge of that court, and

   (b) where the injunction was granted by *a county* court, to a judge *or district judge of that or any other county* court.

(5) The judge *or district judge* to whom an application under subsection (3) is made may only issue a warrant if—

   (a) the application is substantiated on oath, and

   (b) the judge *or district judge* has reasonable grounds for believing that the defendant has done anything which he is prohibited from doing by the injunction.

(6) Where—

   (a) the High Court or *a county* court grants an injunction for the purpose mentioned in subsection (3)(a), and

   (b) without reasonable excuse the defendant does anything which he is prohibited from doing by the injunction,

he is guilty of an offence.

(7) Where a person is convicted of an offence under subsection (6) in respect of any conduct, that conduct is not punishable as a contempt of court.

(8) A person cannot be convicted of an offence under subsection (6) in respect of any conduct which has been punished as a contempt of court.

(9) A person guilty of an offence under subsection (6) is liable—

   (a) on conviction on indictment, to imprisonment for a term not exceeding five years, or a fine, or both, or

   (b) on summary conviction, to imprisonment for a term not exceeding six months, or a fine not exceeding the statutory maximum, or both.

**NOTES**
Sub-s (1): words in square brackets substituted by the Serious Organised Crime and Police Act 2005, s 125(1), (4).
Sub-ss (3), (6): for the words "a county" in italics there are substituted the words "the county", by the Crime and Courts Act 2013, s 17(5), Sch 9, Pt 2, para 39(a), as from a day to be appointed.
Sub-s (4): for the first words in italics there are substituted the words "the county", and for the second words in italics there are substituted the words "of that", by the Crime and Courts Act 2013, s 17(5), Sch 9, Pt 2, para 39(a), (b), as from a day to be appointed.
Sub-s (5): words in italics repealed by the Crime and Courts Act 2013, s 17(5), Sch 9, Pt 2, para 39(c), as from a day to be appointed.

**[1.1058]**
**[3A  Injunctions to protect persons from harassment within section 1(1A)**
(1)  This section applies where there is an actual or apprehended breach of section 1(1A) by any person ("the relevant person").
(2)  In such a case—
  (a)  any person who is or may be a victim of the course of conduct in question, or
  (b)  any person who is or may be a person falling within section 1(1A)(c),
may apply to the High Court or *a county court* for an injunction restraining the relevant person from pursuing any conduct which amounts to harassment in relation to any person or persons mentioned or described in the injunction.
(3)  Section 3(3) to (9) apply in relation to an injunction granted under subsection (2) above as they apply in relation to an injunction granted as mentioned in section 3(3)(a).]

**NOTES**
Inserted by the Serious Organised Crime and Police Act 2005, s 125(1), (5).
Sub-s (2): for the words in italics there are substituted the words "the county court" by the Crime and Courts Act 2013, s 17(5), Sch 9, Pt 3, para 52, as from a day to be appointed.

**[1.1059]**
**4  Putting people in fear of violence**
(1)  A person whose course of conduct causes another to fear, on at least two occasions, that violence will be used against him is guilty of an offence if he knows or ought to know that his course of conduct will cause the other so to fear on each of those occasions.
(2)  For the purposes of this section, the person whose course of conduct is in question ought to know that it will cause another to fear that violence will be used against him on any occasion if a reasonable person in possession of the same information would think the course of conduct would cause the other so to fear on that occasion.
(3)  It is a defence for a person charged with an offence under this section to show that—
  (a)  his course of conduct was pursued for the purpose of preventing or detecting crime,
  (b)  his course of conduct was pursued under any enactment or rule of law or to comply with any condition or requirement imposed by any person under any enactment, or
  (c)  the pursuit of his course of conduct was reasonable for the protection of himself or another or for the protection of his or another's property.
(4)  A person guilty of an offence under this section is liable—
  (a)  on conviction on indictment, to imprisonment for a term not exceeding five years, or a fine, or both, or
  (b)  on summary conviction, to imprisonment for a term not exceeding six months, or a fine not exceeding the statutory maximum, or both.
(5)  If on the trial on indictment of a person charged with an offence under this section the jury find him not guilty of the offence charged, they may find him guilty of an offence under section 2 [or 2A].
(6)  The Crown Court has the same powers and duties in relation to a person who is by virtue of subsection (5) convicted before it of an offence under section 2 [or 2A] as a magistrates' court would have on convicting him of the offence.

**NOTES**
Sub-ss (5), (6): words in square brackets inserted by the Protection of Freedoms Act 2012, s 115(1), Sch 9, Pt 11, para 143(1), (3), as from 25 November 2012.

**[1.1060]**
**[4A  Stalking involving fear of violence or serious alarm or distress**
(1)  A person ("A") whose course of conduct—
  (a)  amounts to stalking, and
  (b)  either—
    (i)  causes another ("B") to fear, on at least two occasions, that violence will be used against B, or
    (ii)  causes B serious alarm or distress which has a substantial adverse effect on B's usual day-to-day activities,

is guilty of an offence if A knows or ought to know that A's course of conduct will cause B so to fear on each of those occasions or (as the case may be) will cause such alarm or distress.

(2)   For the purposes of this section A ought to know that A's course of conduct will cause B to fear that violence will be used against B on any occasion if a reasonable person in possession of the same information would think the course of conduct would cause B so to fear on that occasion.

(3)   For the purposes of this section A ought to know that A's course of conduct will cause B serious alarm or distress which has a substantial adverse effect on B's usual day-to-day activities if a reasonable person in possession of the same information would think the course of conduct would cause B such alarm or distress.

(4)   It is a defence for A to show that—

(a)   A's course of conduct was pursued for the purpose of preventing or detecting crime,

(b)   A's course of conduct was pursued under any enactment or rule of law or to comply with any condition or requirement imposed by any person under any enactment, or

(c)   the pursuit of A's course of conduct was reasonable for the protection of A or another or for the protection of A's or another's property.

(5)   A person guilty of an offence under this section is liable—

(a)   on conviction on indictment, to imprisonment for a term not exceeding five years, or a fine, or both, or

(b)   on summary conviction, to imprisonment for a term not exceeding twelve months, or a fine not exceeding the statutory maximum, or both.

(6)   In relation to an offence committed before the commencement of section 154(1) of the Criminal Justice Act 2003, the reference in subsection (5)(b) to twelve months is to be read as a reference to six months.

(7)   If on the trial on indictment of a person charged with an offence under this section the jury find the person not guilty of the offence charged, they may find the person guilty of an offence under section 2 or 2A.

(8)   The Crown Court has the same powers and duties in relation to a person who is by virtue of subsection (7) convicted before it of an offence under section 2 or 2A as a magistrates' court would have on convicting the person of the offence.

(9)   This section is without prejudice to the generality of section 4.]

**NOTES**

Commencement: 25 November 2012.

Inserted by the Protection of Freedoms Act 2012, s 111(2), as from 25 November 2012.

**[1.1061]**
## 5   Restraining orders [on conviction]

(1)   A court sentencing or otherwise dealing with a person ("the defendant") convicted of an offence  . . .  may (as well as sentencing him or dealing with him in any other way) make an order under this section.

(2)   The order may, for the purpose of protecting the victim [or victims] of the offence, or any other person mentioned in the order, from  . . .  conduct which—

(a)   amounts to harassment, or

(b)   will cause a fear of violence,

prohibit the defendant from doing anything described in the order.

(3)   The order may have effect for a specified period or until further order.

[(3A)   In proceedings under this section both the prosecution and the defence may lead, as further evidence, any evidence that would be admissible in proceedings for an injunction under section 3.]

(4)   The prosecutor, the defendant or any other person mentioned in the order may apply to the court which made the order for it to be varied or discharged by a further order.

[(4A)   Any person mentioned in the order is entitled to be heard on the hearing of an application under subsection (4).]

(5)   If without reasonable excuse the defendant does anything which he is prohibited from doing by an order under this section, he is guilty of an offence.

(6)   A person guilty of an offence under this section is liable—

(a)   on conviction on indictment, to imprisonment for a term not exceeding five years, or a fine, or both, or

(b)   on summary conviction, to imprisonment for a term not exceeding six months, or a fine not exceeding the statutory maximum, or both.

[(7)   A court dealing with a person for an offence under this section may vary or discharge the order in question by a further order.]

**NOTES**

Section heading: words in square brackets added by the Domestic Violence, Crime and Victims Act 2004, s 58(1), Sch 10, para 43(1), (2), as from 30 September 2009, except in relation to cases where the acquittal (or, where s 5A(5) applies, the allowing of the appeal) occurs before that date (see Sch 12, para 5(3)).

Sub-s (1): words omitted repealed by the Domestic Violence, Crime and Victims Act 2004, ss 12(1), 58(2), Sch 11, as from 30 September 2009, except in relation to cases where the conviction occurs before that date (see Sch 12, para 5(1)).

Sub-s (2): words in square brackets inserted by the Serious Organised Crime and Police Act 2005, s 125(1), (6); word omitted repealed by the Domestic Violence, Crime and Victims Act 2004, s 58(1), (2), Sch 10, para 43(1), (3), Sch 11, as from 30 September 2009, except in relation to cases where the conviction occurs before that date (see Sch 12, para 5(1)).

Sub-s (3A): inserted by the Domestic Violence, Crime and Victims Act 2004, s 12(2), 30 September 2009, in relation to applications made on or after that date (see Sch 12, para 5(2)).

Sub-s (4A): inserted by the Domestic Violence, Crime and Victims Act 2004, s 12(3), as from 30 September 2009.

Sub-s (7): added by the Domestic Violence, Crime and Victims Act 2004, s 12(4), as from 30 September 2009, except in relation to cases where the acquittal (or, where s 5A(5) applies, the allowing of the appeal) occurs before that date (see Sch 12, para 5(3)).

**[1.1062]**
**[5A   Restraining orders on acquittal**
(1)   A court before which a person ("the defendant") is acquitted of an offence may, if it considers it necessary to do so to protect a person from harassment by the defendant, make an order prohibiting the defendant from doing anything described in the order.
(2)   Subsections (3) to (7) of section 5 apply to an order under this section as they apply to an order under that one.
(3)   Where the Court of Appeal allow an appeal against conviction they may remit the case to the Crown Court to consider whether to proceed under this section.
(4)   Where—
   (a)   the Crown Court allows an appeal against conviction, or
   (b)   a case is remitted to the Crown Court under subsection (3),
the reference in subsection (1) to a court before which a person is acquitted of an offence is to be read as referring to that court.
(5)   A person made subject to an order under this section has the same right of appeal against the order as if—
   (a)   he had been convicted of the offence in question before the court which made the order, and
   (b)   the order had been made under section 5.]

**NOTES**
Commencement: 30 September 2009.
Inserted by the Domestic Violence, Crime and Victims Act 2004, s 12(5), as from 30 September 2009.

**6**   *(Amends the Limitation Act 1980, s 11 at* **[1.124]**.*)*

**[1.1063]**
**7   Interpretation of this group of sections**
(1)   This section applies for the interpretation of [sections 1 to 5A].
(2)   References to harassing a person include alarming the person or causing the person distress.
[(3)   A "course of conduct" must involve—
   (a)   in the case of conduct in relation to a single person (see section 1(1)), conduct on at least two occasions in relation to that person, or
   (b)   in the case of conduct in relation to two or more persons (see section 1(1A)), conduct on at least one occasion in relation to each of those persons.]
[(3A)   A person's conduct on any occasion shall be taken, if aided, abetted, counselled or procured by another—
   (a)   to be conduct on that occasion of the other (as well as conduct of the person whose conduct it is); and
   (b)   to be conduct in relation to which the other's knowledge and purpose, and what he ought to have known, are the same as they were in relation to what was contemplated or reasonably foreseeable at the time of the aiding, abetting, counselling or procuring.]
(4)   "Conduct" includes speech.
[(5)   References to a person, in the context of the harassment of a person, are references to a person who is an individual.]

**NOTES**
Sub-s (1): words in square brackets substituted by the Domestic Violence, Crime and Victims Act 2004, s 58(1), Sch 10, para 44, as from 30 September 2009, except in relation to cases where the acquittal (or, where s 5A(5) applies, the allowing of the appeal) occurs before that date (see Sch 12, para 5(3)).
Sub-s (3): substituted by the Serious Organised Crime and Police Act 2005, s 125(1), (7)(a).
Sub-s (3A): inserted by the Criminal Justice and Police Act 2001, s 44(1).
Sub-s (5): added by the Serious Organised Crime and Police Act 2005, s 125(1), (7)(b).

*Scotland*

**[1.1064]**
**8  Harassment**
(1)  Every individual has a right to be free from harassment and, accordingly, a person must not pursue a course of conduct which amounts to harassment of another and—
    (a)  is intended to amount to harassment of that person; or
    (b)  occurs in circumstances where it would appear to a reasonable person that it would amount to harassment of that person.
[(1A)  Subsection (1) is subject to section 8A.]
(2)  An actual or apprehended breach of subsection (1) may be the subject of a claim in civil proceedings by the person who is or may be the victim of the course of conduct in question; and any such claim shall be known as an action of harassment.
(3)  For the purposes of this section—
    "conduct" includes speech;
    "harassment" of a person includes causing the person alarm or distress; and
a course of conduct must involve conduct on at least two occasions.
(4)  It shall be a defence to any action of harassment to show that the course of conduct complained of—
    (a)  was authorised by, under or by virtue of any enactment or rule of law;
    (b)  was pursued for the purpose of preventing or detecting crime; or
    (c)  was, in the particular circumstances, reasonable.
(5)  In an action of harassment the court may, without prejudice to any other remedies which it may grant—
    (a)  award damages;
    (b)  grant—
        (i)  interdict or interim interdict;
        (ii)  if it is satisfied that it is appropriate for it to do so in order to protect the person from further harassment, an order, to be known as a "non-harassment order", requiring the defender to refrain from such conduct in relation to the pursuer as may be specified in the order for such period (which includes an indeterminate period) as may be so specified,
    but a person may not be subjected to the same prohibitions in an interdict or interim interdict and a non-harassment order at the same time.
(6)  The damages which may be awarded in an action of harassment include damages for any anxiety caused by the harassment and any financial loss resulting from it.
(7)  Without prejudice to any right to seek review of any interlocutor, a person against whom a non-harassment order has been made, or the person for whose protection the order was made, may apply to the court by which the order was made for revocation of or a variation of the order and, on any such application, the court may revoke the order or vary it in such manner as it considers appropriate.
(8)  . . .

**NOTES**
    Sub-s (1A): inserted by the Domestic Abuse (Scotland) Act 2011, s 1(1), as from 20 July 2011.
    Sub-s (8): repealed by the Damages (Scotland) Act 2011, s 16, Sch 2, as from 7 July 2011.

**[1.1065]**
**[8A  Harassment amounting to domestic abuse**
(1)  Every individual has a right to be free from harassment and, accordingly, a person must not engage in conduct which amounts to harassment of another and—
    (a)  is intended to amount to harassment of that person; or
    (b)  occurs in circumstances where it would appear to a reasonable person that it would amount to harassment of that person.
(2)  Subsection (1) only applies where the conduct referred to amounts to domestic abuse.
(3)  Subsections (2) to (7) of section 8 apply in relation to subsection (1) as they apply in relation to subsection (1) of that section but with the following modifications—
    (a)  in subsections (2) and (4), the words "course of" are omitted;
    (b)  for subsection (3) there is substituted—

    "(3)  For the purposes of this section—
        "conduct"—
            (a)  may involve behaviour on one or more than one occasion; and
            (b)  includes—
                (i)  speech; and
                (ii)  presence in any place or area; and
        "harassment" of a person includes causing the person alarm or distress."; and

    (c)  in subsection (4)(b), for "pursued" substitute "engaged in".]

NOTES
Commencement: 20 July 2011.
Inserted by the Domestic Abuse (Scotland) Act 2011, s 1(2), as from 20 July 2011.

**[1.1066]**
## 9 Breach of non-harassment order

(1)   Any person who is   . . .   in breach of a non-harassment order made under section 8 [or section 8A] is guilty of an offence and liable—

    (a)   on conviction on indictment, to imprisonment for a term not exceeding five years or to a fine, or to both such imprisonment and such fine; and

    (b)   on summary conviction, to imprisonment for a period not exceeding six months or to a fine not exceeding the statutory maximum, or to both such imprisonment and such fine.

(2)   A breach of a non-harassment order shall not be punishable other than in accordance with subsection (1).

[(3)   A constable may arrest without warrant any person he reasonably believes is committing or has committed an offence under subsection (1).

(4)   Subsection (3) is without prejudice to any power of arrest conferred by law apart from that subsection.]

NOTES
Sub-s (1): words omitted repealed by the Criminal Justice (Scotland) Act 2003, s 49(2)(a); words in square brackets inserted by the Domestic Abuse (Scotland) Act 2011, s 1(3), as from 20 July 2011.
Sub-ss (3), (4): added by the Criminal Justice (Scotland) Act 2003, s 49(2)(b).

**10–13**   *(Outside the scope of this work.)*

**[1.1067]**
## 14 Extent

(1)   Sections 1 to 7 extend to England and Wales only.

(2)   Sections 8 to 11 extend to Scotland only.

(3)   This Act (except section 13) does not extend to Northern Ireland.

**[1.1068]**
## 15 Commencement

(1)   Sections 1, 2, 4, 5 and 7 to 12 are to come into force on such day as the Secretary of State may by order made by statutory instrument appoint.

(2)   Sections 3 and 6 are to come into force on such day as the Lord Chancellor may by order made by statutory instrument appoint.

(3)   Different days may be appointed under this section for different purposes.

NOTES
Orders: the Protection from Harassment Act 1997 (Commencement) (No 1) Order 1997, SI 1997/1418; the Protection from Harassment Act 1997 (Commencement) (No 2) Order 1997, SI 1997/1498; the Protection from Harassment Act 1997 (Commencement) (No 3) Order 1998, SI 1998/1902.

**[1.1069]**
## 16 Short title

This Act may be cited as the Protection from Harassment Act 1997.

# EMPLOYMENT RIGHTS (DISPUTE RESOLUTION) ACT 1998

## (1998 c 8)

### ARRANGEMENT OF SECTIONS

#### PART I
#### EMPLOYMENT TRIBUNALS

*Renaming of tribunals*

*An Act to rename industrial tribunals and amend the law relating to those tribunals; to amend the law relating to dismissal procedures agreements and other alternative methods of resolving disputes about employment rights; to provide for the adjustment of awards of compensation for unfair dismissal in cases where no use is made of internal procedures for appealing against dismissal; to make provision about cases involving both unfair dismissal and disability discrimination; and for connected purposes*

[8 April 1998]

---

**NOTES**

Most of this Act comprises amendments to the Employment Tribunals Act 1996 and related legislation. The relevant amendments are incorporated in the text and noted below. Where these are enabling provisions any Orders are noted to the text of the provisions as inserted or amended.

See *Harvey* PI.

---

## PART I
## EMPLOYMENT TRIBUNALS

*Renaming of tribunals*

**[1.1070]**
**1    Industrial tribunals to be known as employment tribunals**
(1)    Industrial tribunals are renamed employment tribunals.
(2)    Accordingly, the Industrial Tribunals Act 1996 may be cited as the Employment Tribunals Act 1996; and (wherever they occur in any enactment)—
  (a)    for the words "industrial tribunal" substitute "employment tribunal",
  (b)    for the words "industrial tribunals" substitute "employment tribunals",
  (c)    for the words "the Industrial Tribunals Act 1996" substitute "the Employment Tribunals Act 1996",
  (d)    for the words "President of the Industrial Tribunals (England and Wales)" substitute "President of the Employment Tribunals (England and Wales)", and
  (e)    for the words "President of the Industrial Tribunals (Scotland)" substitute "President of the Employment Tribunals (Scotland)".

**2–6**    *(S 2 amends the Employment Tribunals Act 1996, s 7 at* **[1.689]***; ss 3–5 amend s 4 of the 1996 Act at* **[1.682]***; s 6 substitutes the Trade Union and Labour Relations (Consolidation) Act 1992, s 87 at* **[1.346]***.)*

## PART II
## OTHER METHODS OF DISPUTE RESOLUTION

**7–12**    *(S 7 inserts the Trade Union and Labour Relations (Consolidation) Act 1992, s 212A at* **[1.481]***; ss 8–10 amend s 288 of the 1992 Act at* **[1.568]***, the Employment Rights Act 1996, s 203 at* **[1.1008]***, and amended the Sex Discrimination Act 1975, s 77, the Race Relations Act 1976, s 72, and the Disability Discrimination Act 1995, s 9 (all repealed); s 11 amends the Employment Tribunals Act 1996, s 18(1) at* **[1.706]***, and the Employment Rights Act 1996, ss 166(2) and 168(1) at* **[1.973]***,* **[1.975]***; s 12 amends ss 110 and 184 of that Act at* **[1.919]** *and* **[1.991]***.)*

## PART III
## AWARDS OF COMPENSATION

**13, 14** *(S 13 inserted the Employment Rights Act 1996, s 127A (repealed), and was itself repealed by the Employment Act 2002, s 54, Sch 8; s 14(1) (repealed) originally amended s 117 of the 1996 Act; s 14(2) amends s 126 of the 1996 Act, at* **[1.936]**.*)*

## PART IV
## SUPPLEMENTARY AND GENERAL

**15, 16** *(S 15 introduces Sch 1 (minor and consequential amendments) and Sch 2 (repeals); s 16 relates to Northern Ireland.)*

**[1.1071]**
### 17 Commencement, transitional provisions and savings
(1) The provisions of this Act (apart from section 16, this section and section 18 and paragraph 17(2) of Schedule 1) shall not come into force until such day as the Secretary of State may by order made by statutory instrument appoint; and different days may be appointed for different purposes.
(2) An order under subsection (1) may contain such transitional provisions and savings as appear to the Secretary of State to be appropriate.
(3) The amendment made by paragraph 17(2) of Schedule 1 shall be deemed always to have had effect.
(4) . . .

**NOTES**
Sub-s (4): repealed by the Statute Law (Repeals) Act 2004.
Orders: the Employment Rights (Dispute Resolution) Act 1998 (Commencement No 1 and Transitional and Saving Provisions) Order 1998, SI 1998/1658.

**[1.1072]**
### 18 Short title
This Act may be cited as the Employment Rights (Dispute Resolution) Act 1998.

### SCHEDULES 1 AND 2

*(Schs 1 and 2 (minor and consequential amendments and repeals) are not reproduced. In so far as they amend or repeal any provision reproduced in this work, that amendment (etc) has been incorporated at the appropriate place.)*

# PUBLIC INTEREST DISCLOSURE ACT 1998

(1998 c 23)

*An Act to protect individuals who make certain disclosures of information in the public interest; to allow such individuals to bring action in respect of victimisation; and for connected purposes*

[2 July 1998]

**NOTES**
This Act consists almost entirely of provisions adding to or amending existing legislation, principally the Employment Rights Act 1996. The provisions so added or amended are incorporated at the relevant point in the text and are noted below. The provisions of the Act not brought into force at Royal Assent (see s 18(4) below) were brought into force on 2 July 1999 (SI 1999/1547). See also the Public Interest Disclosure (Prescribed Persons) Order 1999, SI 1999/1549, as amended (principally by SI 2003/1993) at **[2.443]** (made under the Employment Rights Act 1996, s 43F, as inserted by s 1 of this Act).
See *Harvey* CIII, DII(H).

**1–17** *(S 1 inserts the Employment Rights Act 1996, Pt IVA (ss 43A–43L) at* **[1.788]–[1.799]**, *s 2 inserts 47B of the 1996 Act at* **[1.808]**; *s 3 amends s 48 of the 1996 Act at* **[1.814]**; *s 4 amends s 49 of the 1996 Act at* **[1.815]**; *s 5 inserts s 103A of the 1996 Act at* **[1.906]**; *s 6 amends s 105 of the 1996 Act at* **[1.915]**; *s 7 amends ss 108 of the 1996 Act at* **[1.918]** *and amended s 109 of that Act (repealed); s 8 repealed by the Employment Relations Act 1999, s 44, Sch 9(11); s 9 amends s 128 and 129 of the 1996 Act at* **[1.937]** *and* **[1.938]**; *s 10 amends s 191 of the 1996 Act at* **[1.998]**; *s 11 repealed by the Employment Relations Act 1999, s 44, Sch 9(12); s 12 (which amended the repealed s 196 of the 1996 Act) is spent; s 13 repealed by the Police Reform Act 2002, ss 37(3), 107(2), Sch 8; s 14 amends s 205 of the 1996 Act at* **[1.1010]**; *s 15 amends ss 230, 235 of the 1996 Act at* **[1.1037]**, **[1.1042]**; *s 16 amends the Trade Union and Labour Relations (Consolidation) Act 1992, s 237 at* **[1.517]**; *s 17 (Northern Ireland) outside the scope of this work.)*

**[1.1073]**
**18 Short title, interpretation, commencement and extent**
(1) This Act may be cited as the Public Interest Disclosure Act 1998.
(2) In this Act "the 1996 Act" means the Employment Rights Act 1996.
(3) Subject to subsection (4), this Act shall come into force on such day or days as the Secretary of State may by order made by statutory instrument appoint, and different days may be appointed for different purposes.
(4) The following provisions shall come into force on the passing of this Act—
  (a) section 1 so far as relating to the power to make an order under section 43F of the 1996 Act,
  (b) . . .
  (c) section 17, and
  (d) this section.
(5) This Act, except section 17, does not extend to Northern Ireland.

**NOTES**
Sub-s (4): para (b) repealed by the Employment Relations Act 1999, s 44, Sch 9(11).
Orders: the Public Interest Disclosure Act 1998 (Commencement) Order 1999, SI 1999/1547.

# SCHOOL STANDARDS AND FRAMEWORK ACT 1998

(1998 c 31)

## ARRANGEMENT OF SECTIONS

### PART II
### NEW FRAMEWORK FOR MAINTAINED SCHOOLS

#### CHAPTER V
#### STAFFING AND CONDUCT OF SCHOOLS

*Appointment and dismissal of teachers of religious education*

*Religious opinions etc of staff*

#### PART VII
#### MISCELLANEOUS AND GENERAL

*Final provisions*

*An Act to make new provision with respect to school education and the provision of nursery education otherwise than at school; to enable arrangements to be made for the provision of further education for young persons partly at schools and partly at further education institutions; to make provision with respect to the Education Assets Board; and for connected purposes*

[24 July 1998]

**NOTES**
This is a major Act most parts of which are outside the scope of this work and are therefore omitted. Provisions omitted are not annotated. The provisions reproduced here only apply to England and Wales. They re-enact with amendments equivalent provisions of the Education Act 1996, which were repealed. Sections 54–57 of, and Schs 16, 17 to, this Act (staffing of schools) were repealed by the Education Act 2002; see now ss 35–37 of the 2002 Act at **[1.1237]**–**[1.1239]** and Regulations made thereunder.

## PART II
## NEW FRAMEWORK FOR MAINTAINED SCHOOLS

### CHAPTER V
### STAFFING AND CONDUCT OF SCHOOLS

*Appointment and dismissal of teachers of religious education*

**[1.1074]**
**58 Appointment and dismissal of certain teachers at schools with a religious character**
(1) In this section—

(a)   subsections (2) to (6) apply to a foundation or voluntary controlled school which has a religious character; and

(b)   subsection (7) applies (subject to subsection (8)) to a voluntary aided school which has a religious character;

and references in this Chapter to a school which has (or does not have) a religious character shall be construed in accordance with section 69(3).

(2)   Where the number of [teachers at] a school to which this subsection applies is more than two, [the teachers shall] include persons who—

(a)   are selected for their fitness and competence to give religious education as is required in accordance with arrangements under paragraph 3(3) of Schedule 19 (arrangements for religious education in accordance with the school's trust deed or with the tenets of the school's specified religion or religious denomination), and

(b)   are specifically appointed to do so.

(3)   The number of reserved teachers in such a school shall not exceed one-fifth of [the total number of teachers], including the head teacher (and for this purpose, where [the total number of teachers] is not a multiple of five, it shall be treated as if it were the next higher multiple of five).

(4)   . . .

(5)   Where the appropriate body propose to appoint a person to be a reserved teacher in such a school, that body—

(a)   shall consult the foundation governors, and

(b)   shall not so appoint that person unless the foundation governors are satisfied as to his fitness and competence to give such religious education as is mentioned in subsection (2)(a).

(6)   If the foundation governors of such a school consider that a reserved teacher has failed to give such religious education efficiently and suitably, they [may—

(a)   in the case of a teacher who is an employee, require the appropriate body to dismiss him from employment as a reserved teacher at the school, and

(b)   in the case of a teacher who is engaged otherwise than under a contract of employment, require the governing body to terminate his engagement].

(7)   If a teacher appointed to give religious education in a school to which this subsection applies fails to give such education efficiently and suitably, he may be dismissed on that ground by the governing body without the consent of the [local authority].

(8)   Subsection (7) does not apply—

(a)   where the school has a delegated budget, or

(b)   to religious education in accordance with an agreed syllabus.

(9)   In this section—

"the appropriate body" means—

(a)   in relation to a foundation school, the governing body, and

(b)   in relation to a voluntary controlled school, the [local authority];

"reserved teacher", in relation to a foundation or voluntary controlled school, means a person employed [or engaged] at the school in pursuance of subsection (2).

**NOTES**

Sub-ss (2), (3), (6): words in square brackets substituted by the Education Act 2002, s 40, Sch 3, paras 1, 6(1)–(3), (5).

Sub-s (4): repealed by the Education and Inspections Act 2006, ss 37(1), 184, Sch 18, Pt 6, as from 30 June 2008 (in relation to Wales), and as from 1 September 2008 (in relation to England).

Sub-s (7): words in square brackets substituted by the Local Education Authorities and Children's Services Authorities (Integration of Functions) Order 2010, SI 2010/1158, art 5(1), Sch 2, Pt 1, para 10(1), (2), as from 5 May 2010.

Sub-s (9): words in square brackets in definition "the appropriate body" substituted by SI 2010/1158, art 5(1), Sch 2, Pt 1, para 10(1), (2), as from 5 May 2010; words in square brackets in definition "reserved teacher" inserted by the Education Act 2002, s 40, Sch 3, para 6(1), (6).

*Religious opinions etc of staff*

**[1.1075]**
**59   Staff at community, secular foundation or voluntary, or special school**

(1)   This section applies to—

(a)   a community school or a community or foundation special school, or

(b)   a foundation or voluntary school which does not have a religious character.

(2)   No person shall be disqualified by reason of his religious opinions, or of his attending or omitting to attend religious worship—

(a)   from being a teacher at the school, or

(b)   from being employed [or engaged] for the purposes of the school otherwise than as a teacher.

(3)   No teacher at the school shall be required to give religious education.

(4)   No teacher at the school shall receive any less remuneration or be deprived of, or disqualified for, any promotion or other advantage—

(a)   by reason of the fact that he does or does not give religious education, or

(b) by reason of his religious opinions or of his attending or omitting to attend religious worship.

**NOTES**

Sub-s (2): words in square brackets inserted by the Education Act 2002, s 40, Sch 3, para 7.

**[1.1076]**
**60 Staff at foundation or voluntary school with religious character**
(1) This section applies to a foundation or voluntary school which has a religious character.
(2) If the school is a foundation or voluntary controlled school, then (subject to subsections (3) and (4) below) section 59(2) to (4) shall apply to the school as they apply to a foundation or voluntary controlled school which does not have a religious character.
(3) Section 59(2) to (4) shall not so apply in relation to a reserved teacher at the school; and instead subsection (5) below shall apply in relation to such a teacher as it applies in relation to a teacher at a voluntary aided school.
(4) In connection with the appointment of a person to be head teacher of the school (whether foundation or voluntary controlled) [in a case where the head teacher is not to be a reserved teacher] regard may be had to that person's ability and fitness to preserve and develop the religious character of the school.
(5) If the school is a voluntary aided school—
    (a) preference may be given, in connection with the appointment, remuneration or promotion of teachers at the school, to persons—
        (i) whose religious opinions are in accordance with the tenets of the religion or religious denomination specified in relation to the school under section 69(4), or
        (ii) who attend religious worship in accordance with those tenets, or
        (iii) who give, or are willing to give, religious education at the school in accordance with those tenets; and
    (b) regard may be had, in connection with the termination of the employment [or engagement] of any teacher at the school, to any conduct on his part which is incompatible with the precepts, or with the upholding of the tenets, of the religion or religious denomination so specified.
(6) If the school is a voluntary aided school [in Wales], no person shall be disqualified by reason of his religious opinions, or of his attending or omitting to attend religious worship, from being employed [or engaged] for the purposes of the school otherwise than as a teacher.
(7) Where immediately before the appointed day a teacher at a school which on that day becomes a school to which this section applies enjoyed, by virtue of section 304 or 305 of the Education Act 1996 (religious opinions of staff etc), any rights not conferred on him by this section as a teacher at a school to which it applies, he shall continue to enjoy those rights (in addition to those conferred by this section) until he ceases to be employed as a teacher at the school.
(8) In this section "reserved teacher", in relation to a foundation or voluntary controlled school, means a person employed at the school in pursuance of section 58(2).

**NOTES**

Sub-s (4): words in square brackets inserted by the Education and Inspections Act 2006, s 37(2)(a), as from 30 June 2008 (in relation to Wales), and as from 1 September 2008 (in relation to England).

Sub-s (5): words in square brackets in para (b) inserted by the Education Act 2002, s 40, Sch 3, para 8(1), (2).

Sub-s (6): words in first pair of square brackets inserted by the Education and Inspections Act 2006, s 37(2)(b), as from a day to be appointed (in relation to Wales), and as from 1 September 2008 (in relation to England); words in second pair of square brackets inserted by the Education Act 2002, s 40, Sch 3, para 8.

# PART VII
## MISCELLANEOUS AND GENERAL

*Final provisions*

**[1.1077]**
**145 Short title, commencement and extent**
(1) This Act may be cited as the School Standards and Framework Act 1998.
(2) *(Outside the scope of this work.)*
(3) Subject to subsections (4) and (5), this Act shall come into force on such day as the Secretary of State may by order appoint; and different days may be appointed for different provisions and for different purposes.
(4), (5) *(Outside the scope of this work.)*
(6) Subject to subsections (7) and (8), this Act extends to England and Wales only.
(7)–(9) *(Outside the scope of this work.)*

**NOTES**

Orders: the commencement order relevant to the provisions reproduced here is the School Standards and Framework Act 1998 (Commencement No 7 and Saving and Transitional Provisions) Order 1999, SI 1999/2323.

# DATA PROTECTION ACT 1998

## (1998 c 29)

### ARRANGEMENT OF SECTIONS

*An Act to make new provision for the regulation of the processing of information relating to individuals, including the obtaining, holding, use or disclosure of such information*

[16 July 1998]

**NOTES**
This Act is the domestic implementation of Council Directive 95/46/EC on data protection at **[3.203]**. The Directive required the domestic implementation of any necessary legislation by 24 October 1998 but this date was not achieved and the substantive provisions of the Act (other than those which came into force at Royal Assent by virtue of s 75(2) at **[1.1113]**) were brought into force on 1 March 2000 (SI 2000/183). Much of the Act relates to aspects of data protection in areas other than employment. Only those provisions of this Act relevant to employment law are reproduced. Provisions not reproduced are not annotated.

## PART I
## PRELIMINARY

**[1.1078]**
**1  Basic interpretative provisions**
(1)  In this Act, unless the context otherwise requires—
"data" means information which—
    (a)  is being processed by means of equipment operating automatically in response to instructions given for that purpose,
    (b)  is recorded with the intention that it should be processed by means of such equipment,
    (c)  is recorded as part of a relevant filing system or with the intention that it should form part of a relevant filing system, . . .
    (d)  does not fall within paragraph (a), (b) or (c) but forms part of an accessible record as defined by section 68, [or
    (e)  is recorded information held by a public authority and does not fall within any of paragraphs (a) to (d);]
"data controller" means, subject to subsection (4), a person who (either alone or jointly or in common with other persons) determines the purposes for which and the manner in which any personal data are, or are to be, processed;
"data processor", in relation to personal data, means any person (other than an employee of the data controller) who processes the data on behalf of the data controller;
"data subject" means an individual who is the subject of personal data;
"personal data" means data which relate to a living individual who can be identified—
    (a)  from those data, or
    (b)  from those data and other information which is in the possession of, or is likely to come into the possession of, the data controller,
and includes any expression of opinion about the individual and any indication of the intentions of the data controller or any other person in respect of the individual;
"processing", in relation to information or data, means obtaining, recording or holding the information or data or carrying out any operation or set of operations on the information or data, including—
    (a)  organisation, adaptation or alteration of the information or data,
    (b)  retrieval, consultation or use of the information or data,
    (c)  disclosure of the information or data by transmission, dissemination or otherwise making available, or
    (d)  alignment, combination, blocking, erasure or destruction of the information or data;
["public authority" means a public authority as defined by the Freedom of Information Act 2000 or a Scottish public authority as defined by the Freedom of Information (Scotland) Act 2002;]
"relevant filing system" means any set of information relating to individuals to the extent that, although the information is not processed by means of equipment operating automatically in response to instructions given for that purpose, the set is structured, either by reference to individuals or by reference to criteria relating to individuals, in such a way that specific information relating to a particular individual is readily accessible.

(2)　In this Act, unless the context otherwise requires—
- (a)　"obtaining" or "recording", in relation to personal data, includes obtaining or recording the information to be contained in the data, and
- (b)　"using" or "disclosing", in relation to personal data, includes using or disclosing the information contained in the data.

(3)　In determining for the purposes of this Act whether any information is recorded with the intention—
- (a)　that it should be processed by means of equipment operating automatically in response to instructions given for that purpose, or
- (b)　that it should form part of a relevant filing system,

it is immaterial that it is intended to be so processed or to form part of such a system only after being transferred to a country or territory outside the European Economic Area.

(4)　Where personal data are processed only for purposes for which they are required by or under any enactment to be processed, the person on whom the obligation to process the data is imposed by or under that enactment is for the purposes of this Act the data controller.

[(5)　In paragraph (e) of the definition of "data" in subsection (1), the reference to information "held" by a public authority shall be construed in accordance with section 3(2) of the Freedom of Information Act 2000.

(6)　Where—
- [(a)]　section 7 of the Freedom of Information Act 2000 prevents Parts I to V of that Act [or
- (b)　section 7(1) of the Freedom of Information (Scotland) Act 2002 prevents that Act,]

from applying to certain information held by a public authority, that information is not to be treated for the purposes of paragraph (e) of the definition of "data" in subsection (1) as held by a public authority.]

### NOTES

Sub-s (1): in definition "data" word omitted from para (c) repealed, and para (e) and the word immediately preceding it added, by the Freedom of Information Act 2000, ss 68(1), (2), 86, Sch 8, Pt III; definition "public authority" inserted by s 68(1), (2) of the 2000 Act, and substituted by the Freedom of Information (Scotland) Act 2002 (Consequential Modifications) Order 2004, SI 2004/3089, art 2(1), (2)(a).

Sub-ss (5), (6): added by the Freedom of Information Act 2000, s 68(1), (3); words in square brackets inserted by SI 2004/3089, art 2(1), (2)(b), (c).

### [1.1079]
### 2　Sensitive personal data
In this Act "sensitive personal data" means personal data consisting of information as to—
- (a)　the racial or ethnic origin of the data subject,
- (b)　his political opinions,
- (c)　his religious beliefs or other beliefs of a similar nature,
- (d)　whether he is a member of a trade union (within the meaning of the Trade Union and Labour Relations (Consolidation) Act 1992,
- (e)　his physical or mental health or condition,
- (f)　his sexual life,
- (g)　the commission or alleged commission by him of any offence, or
- (h)　any proceedings for any offence committed or alleged to have been committed by him, the disposal of such proceedings or the sentence of any court in such proceedings.

### [1.1080]
### 3　The special purposes
In this Act "the special purposes" means any one or more of the following—
- (a)　the purposes of journalism,
- (b)　artistic purposes, and
- (c)　literary purposes.

### [1.1081]
### 4　The data protection principles
(1)　References in this Act to the data protection principles are to the principles set out in Part I of Schedule 1.

(2)　Those principles are to be interpreted in accordance with Part II of Schedule 1.

(3)　Schedule 2 (which applies to all personal data) and Schedule 3 (which applies only to sensitive personal data) set out conditions applying for the purposes of the first principle; and Schedule 4 sets out cases in which the eighth principle does not apply.

(4)　Subject to section 27(1), it shall be the duty of a data controller to comply with the data protection principles in relation to all personal data with respect to which he is the data controller.

### [1.1082]
### 5　Application of Act
(1)　Except as otherwise provided by or under section 54, this Act applies to a data controller in respect of any data only if—

(a)  the data controller is established in the United Kingdom and the data are processed in the context of that establishment, or

(b)  the data controller is established neither in the United Kingdom nor in any other EEA State but uses equipment in the United Kingdom for processing the data otherwise than for the purposes of transit through the United Kingdom.

(2)  A data controller falling within subsection (1)(b) must nominate for the purposes of this Act a representative established in the United Kingdom.

(3)  For the purposes of subsections (1) and (2), each of the following is to be treated as established in the United Kingdom—

(a)  an individual who is ordinarily resident in the United Kingdom,

(b)  a body incorporated under the law of, or of any part of, the United Kingdom,

(c)  a partnership or other unincorporated association formed under the law of any part of the United Kingdom, and

(d)  any person who does not fall within paragraph (a), (b) or (c) but maintains in the United Kingdom—

(i)  an office, branch or agency through which he carries on any activity, or

(ii)  a regular practice;

and the reference to establishment in any other EEA State has a corresponding meaning.

**[1.1083]**
## 6  The Commissioner  . . .

[(1)  For the purposes of this Act and of the Freedom of Information Act 2000 there shall be an officer known as the Information Commissioner (in this Act referred to as "the Commissioner").]

(2)  The Commissioner shall be appointed by Her Majesty by Letters Patent.

(3)–(6)  . . .

(7)  Schedule 5 has effect in relation to the Commissioner  . . .

**NOTES**
The words omitted from the section heading and from sub-s (7) were repealed, and sub-s (3)–(6) were repealed, by the Transfer of Tribunal Functions Order 2010, SI 2010/22, art 5(1), Sch 2, paras 24, 25, as from 18 January 2010 (for transitional provisions and savings in relation to existing cases and appeals from the Information Tribunal, see Sch 5 to that Order).

Sub-s (1): substituted by the Freedom of Information Act 2000, s 18(4), Sch 2, Pt I, para 13.

# PART II
## RIGHTS OF DATA SUBJECTS AND OTHERS

**[1.1084]**
## 7  Right of access to personal data

(1)  Subject to the following provisions of this section and to [sections 8, 9 and 9A], an individual is entitled—

(a)  to be informed by any data controller whether personal data of which that individual is the data subject are being processed by or on behalf of that data controller,

(b)  if that is the case, to be given by the data controller a description of—

(i)  the personal data of which that individual is the data subject,

(ii)  the purposes for which they are being or are to be processed, and

(iii)  the recipients or classes of recipients to whom they are or may be disclosed,

(c)  to have communicated to him in an intelligible form—

(i)  the information constituting any personal data of which that individual is the data subject, and

(ii)  any information available to the data controller as to the source of those data, and

(d)  where the processing by automatic means of personal data of which that individual is the data subject for the purpose of evaluating matters relating to him such as, for example, his performance at work, his creditworthiness, his reliability or his conduct, has constituted or is likely to constitute the sole basis for any decision significantly affecting him, to be informed by the data controller of the logic involved in that decision-taking.

(2)  A data controller is not obliged to supply any information under subsection (1) unless he has received—

(a)  a request in writing, and

(b)  except in prescribed cases, such fee (not exceeding the prescribed maximum) as he may require.

[(3)  Where a data controller—

(a)  reasonably requires further information in order to satisfy himself as to the identity of the person making a request under this section and to locate the information which that person seeks, and

(b)  has informed him of that requirement,

the data controller is not obliged to comply with the request unless he is supplied with that further information.]

(4) Where a data controller cannot comply with the request without disclosing information relating to another individual who can be identified from that information, he is not obliged to comply with the request unless—

(a) the other individual has consented to the disclosure of the information to the person making the request, or

(b) it is reasonable in all the circumstances to comply with the request without the consent of the other individual.

(5) In subsection (4) the reference to information relating to another individual includes a reference to information identifying that individual as the source of the information sought by the request; and that subsection is not to be construed as excusing a data controller from communicating so much of the information sought by the request as can be communicated without disclosing the identity of the other individual concerned, whether by the omission of names or other identifying particulars or otherwise.

(6) In determining for the purposes of subsection (4)(b) whether it is reasonable in all the circumstances to comply with the request without the consent of the other individual concerned, regard shall be had, in particular, to—

(a) any duty of confidentiality owed to the other individual,

(b) any steps taken by the data controller with a view to seeking the consent of the other individual,

(c) whether the other individual is capable of giving consent, and

(d) any express refusal of consent by the other individual.

(7) An individual making a request under this section may, in such cases as may be prescribed, specify that his request is limited to personal data of any prescribed description.

(8) Subject to subsection (4), a data controller shall comply with a request under this section promptly and in any event before the end of the prescribed period beginning with the relevant day.

(9) If a court is satisfied on the application of any person who has made a request under the foregoing provisions of this section that the data controller in question has failed to comply with the request in contravention of those provisions, the court may order him to comply with the request.

(10) In this section—

"prescribed" means prescribed by the [Secretary of State] by regulations;

"the prescribed maximum" means such amount as may be prescribed;

"the prescribed period" means forty days or such other period as may be prescribed;

"the relevant day", in relation to a request under this section, means the day on which the data controller receives the request or, if later, the first day on which the data controller has both the required fee and the information referred to in subsection (3).

(11) Different amounts or periods may be prescribed under this section in relation to different cases.

**NOTES**

Sub-s (1): words in square brackets substituted by the Freedom of Information Act 2000, s 69(1).

Sub-s (3): substituted by the Freedom of Information Act 2000, s 73, Sch 6, para 1.

Sub-s (10): words in square brackets substituted by the Secretary of State for Constitutional Affairs Order 2003, SI 2003/1887, art 9, Sch 2, para 9(1)(a).

Exemptions: see, for certain exemptions from this section, the Data Protection (Subject Access Modification) (Health) Order 2000, SI 2000/413; the Data Protection (Subject Access Modification) (Education) Order 2000, SI 2000/414; the Data Protection (Subject Access Modification) (Social Work) Order 2000, SI 2000/415; the Data Protection (Miscellaneous Subject Access Exemptions) Order 2000, SI 2000/419, which modify s 7 in relation to data to which the respective orders apply. See also s 9 of this Act (application of s 7 where data controller is a credit reference agency), s 9A (limited exemptions in relation to data held by public authorities), and Sch 7 at **[1.1118]** (miscellaneous exemptions).

Regulations: the Data Protection (Subject Access) (Fees and Miscellaneous Provisions) Regulations 2000, SI 2000/191; the Data Protection (Subject Access) (Fees and Miscellaneous Provisions) (Amendment) Regulations 2001, SI 2001/3223.

**[1.1085]**

**8 Provisions supplementary to section 7**

(1) The [Secretary of State] may by regulations provide that, in such cases as may be prescribed, a request for information under any provision of subsection (1) of section 7 is to be treated as extending also to information under other provisions of that subsection.

(2) The obligation imposed by section 7(1)(c)(i) must be complied with by supplying the data subject with a copy of the information in permanent form unless—

(a) the supply of such a copy is not possible or would involve disproportionate effort, or

(b) the data subject agrees otherwise;

and where any of the information referred to in section 7(1)(c)(i) is expressed in terms which are not intelligible without explanation the copy must be accompanied by an explanation of those terms.

(3) Where a data controller has previously complied with a request made under section 7 by an individual, the data controller is not obliged to comply with a subsequent identical or similar request under that section by that individual unless a reasonable interval has elapsed between compliance with the previous request and the making of the current request.

(4)   In determining for the purposes of subsection (3) whether requests under section 7 are made at reasonable intervals, regard shall be had to the nature of the data, the purpose for which the data are processed and the frequency with which the data are altered.
(5)   Section 7(1)(d) is not to be regarded as requiring the provision of information as to the logic involved in any decision-taking if, and to the extent that, the information constitutes a trade secret.
(6)   The information to be supplied pursuant to a request under section 7 must be supplied by reference to the data in question at the time when the request is received, except that it may take account of any amendment or deletion made between that time and the time when the information is supplied, being an amendment or deletion that would have been made regardless of the receipt of the request.
(7)   For the purposes of section 7(4) and (5) another individual can be identified from the information being disclosed if he can be identified from that information, or from that and any other information which, in the reasonable belief of the data controller, is likely to be in, or to come into, the possession of the data subject making the request.

**NOTES**
   Sub-s (1): words in square brackets substituted by the Secretary of State for Constitutional Affairs Order 2003, SI 2003/1887, art 9, Sch 2, para 9(1)(a).
   Regulations: the Data Protection (Subject Access) (Fees and Miscellaneous Provisions) Regulations 2000, SI 2000/191.

**[1.1086]**
**10   Right to prevent processing likely to cause damage or distress**
(1)   Subject to subsection (2), an individual is entitled at any time by notice in writing to a data controller to require the data controller at the end of such period as is reasonable in the circumstances to cease, or not to begin, processing, or processing for a specified purpose or in a specified manner, any personal data in respect of which he is the data subject, on the ground that, for specified reasons—
   (a)   the processing of those data or their processing for that purpose or in that manner is causing or is likely to cause substantial damage or substantial distress to him or to another, and
   (b)   that damage or distress is or would be unwarranted.
(2)   subsection (1) does not apply—
   (a)   in a case where any of the conditions in paragraphs 1 to 4 of Schedule 2 is met, or
   (b)   in such other cases as may be prescribed by the [Secretary of State] by order.
(3)   The data controller must within twenty-one days of receiving a notice under subsection (1) ("the data subject notice") give the individual who gave it a written notice—
   (a)   stating that he has complied or intends to comply with the data subject notice, or
   (b)   stating his reasons for regarding the data subject notice as to any extent unjustified and the extent (if any) to which he has complied or intends to comply with it.
(4)   If a court is satisfied, on the application of any person who has given a notice under subsection (1) which appears to the court to be justified (or to be justified to any extent), that the data controller in question has failed to comply with the notice, the court may order him to take such steps for complying with the notice (or for complying with it to that extent) as the court thinks fit.
(5)   The failure by a data subject to exercise the right conferred by subsection (1) or section 11(1) does not affect any other right conferred on him by this Part.

**NOTES**
   Sub-s (2): words in square brackets substituted by the Secretary of State for Constitutional Affairs Order 2003, SI 2003/1887, art 9, Sch 2, para 9(1)(a).
   Orders: as of 6 April 2013 no Orders had been made under this section.

**[1.1087]**
**12   Rights in relation to automated decision-taking**
(1)   An individual is entitled at any time, by notice in writing to any data controller, to require the data controller to ensure that no decision taken by or on behalf of the data controller which significantly affects that individual is based solely on the processing by automatic means of personal data in respect of which that individual is the data subject for the purpose of evaluating matters relating to him such as, for example, his performance at work, his creditworthiness, his reliability or his conduct.
(2)   Where, in a case where no notice under subsection (1) has effect, a decision which significantly affects an individual is based solely on such processing as is mentioned in subsection (1)—
   (a)   the data controller must as soon as reasonably practicable notify the individual that the decision was taken on that basis, and
   (b)   the individual is entitled, within twenty-one days of receiving that notification from the data controller, by notice in writing to require the data controller to reconsider the decision or to take a new decision otherwise than on that basis.

(3)   The data controller must, within twenty-one days of receiving a notice under subsection (2)(b) ("the data subject notice") give the individual a written notice specifying the steps that he intends to take to comply with the data subject notice.

(4)   A notice under subsection (1) does not have effect in relation to an exempt decision; and nothing in subsection (2) applies to an exempt decision.

(5)   In subsection (4) "exempt decision" means any decision—

(a)   in respect of which the condition in subsection (6) and the condition in subsection (7) are met, or

(b)   which is made in such other circumstances as may be prescribed by the [Secretary of State] by order.

(6)   The condition in this subsection is that the decision—

(a)   is taken in the course of steps taken—

(i)    for the purpose of considering whether to enter into a contract with the data subject,

(ii)   with a view to entering into such a contract, or

(iii)  in the course of performing such a contract, or

(b)   is authorised or required by or under any enactment.

(7)   The condition in this subsection is that either—

(a)   the effect of the decision is to grant a request of the data subject, or

(b)   steps have been taken to safeguard the legitimate interests of the data subject (for example, by allowing him to make representations).

(8)   If a court is satisfied on the application of a data subject that a person taking a decision in respect of him ("the responsible person") has failed to comply with subsection (1) or (2)(b), the court may order the responsible person to reconsider the decision, or to take a new decision which is not based solely on such processing as is mentioned in subsection (1).

(9)   An order under subsection (8) shall not affect the rights of any person other than the data subject and the responsible person.

**NOTES**

Sub-s (5): words in square brackets substituted by the Secretary of State for Constitutional Affairs Order 2003, SI 2003/1887, art 9, Sch 2, para 9(1)(a).

Orders: as of 6 April 2013 no Orders had been made under this section.

## [1.1088]
### 13   Compensation for failure to comply with certain requirements

(1)   An individual who suffers damage by reason of any contravention by a data controller of any of the requirements of this Act is entitled to compensation from the data controller for that damage.

(2)   An individual who suffers distress by reason of any contravention by a data controller of any of the requirements of this Act is entitled to compensation from the data controller for that distress if—

(a)   the individual also suffers damage by reason of the contravention, or

(b)   the contravention relates to the processing of personal data for the special purposes.

(3)   In proceedings brought against a person by virtue of this section it is a defence to prove that he had taken such care as in all the circumstances was reasonably required to comply with the requirement concerned.

## [1.1089]
### 14   Rectification, blocking, erasure and destruction

(1)   If a court is satisfied on the application of a data subject that personal data of which the applicant is the subject are inaccurate, the court may order the data controller to rectify, block, erase or destroy those data and any other personal data in respect of which he is the data controller and which contain an expression of opinion which appears to the court to be based on the inaccurate data.

(2)   subsection (1) applies whether or not the data accurately record information received or obtained by the data controller from the data subject or a third party but where the data accurately record such information, then—

(a)   if the requirements mentioned in paragraph 7 of Part II of Schedule 1 have been complied with, the court may, instead of making an order under subsection (1), make an order requiring the data to be supplemented by such statement of the true facts relating to the matters dealt with by the data as the court may approve, and

(b)   if all or any of those requirements have not been complied with, the court may, instead of making an order under that subsection, make such order as it thinks fit for securing compliance with those requirements with or without a further order requiring the data to be supplemented by such a statement as is mentioned in paragraph (a).

(3)   Where the court—

(a)   makes an order under subsection (1), or

(b)   is satisfied on the application of a data subject that personal data of which he was the data subject and which have been rectified, blocked, erased or destroyed were inaccurate, it may, where it considers it reasonably practicable, order the data controller to notify third parties to whom the data have been disclosed of the rectification, blocking, erasure or destruction.

(4)  If a court is satisfied on the application of a data subject—
  (a)  that he has suffered damage by reason of any contravention by a data controller of any of the requirements of this Act in respect of any personal data, in circumstances entitling him to compensation under section 13, and
  (b)  that there is a substantial risk of further contravention in respect of those data in such circumstances,

the court may order the rectification, blocking, erasure or destruction of any of those data.

(5)  Where the court makes an order under subsection (4) it may, where it considers it reasonably practicable, order the data controller to notify third parties to whom the data have been disclosed of the rectification, blocking, erasure or destruction.

(6)  In determining whether it is reasonably practicable to require such notification as is mentioned in subsection (3) or (5) the court shall have regard, in particular, to the number of persons who would have to be notified.

**[1.1090]**
## 15  Jurisdiction and procedure
(1)  The jurisdiction conferred by sections 7 to 14 is exercisable [in England and Wales by the High Court or the county court or, in Northern Ireland,] by the High Court or a county court or, in Scotland, by the Court of Session or the sheriff.

(2)  For the purpose of determining any question whether an applicant under subsection (9) of section 7 is entitled to the information which he seeks (including any question whether any relevant data are exempt from that section by virtue of Part IV) a court may require the information constituting any data processed by or on behalf of the data controller and any information as to the logic involved in any decision-taking as mentioned in section 7(1)(d) to be made available for its own inspection but shall not, pending the determination of that question in the applicant's favour, require the information sought by the applicant to be disclosed to him or his representatives whether by discovery (or, in Scotland, recovery) or otherwise.

**NOTES**
  Sub-s (1): words in square brackets inserted by the Crime and Courts Act 2013, s 17(5), Sch 9, Pt 3, para 77, as from a day to be appointed.

## PART IV
## EXEMPTIONS

**[1.1091]**
## 27  Preliminary
(1)  References in any of the data protection principles or any provision of Parts II and III to personal data or to the processing of personal data do not include references to data or processing which by virtue of this Part are exempt from that principle or other provision.

(2)  In this Part "the subject information provisions" means—
  (a)  the first data protection principle to the extent to which it requires compliance with paragraph 2 of Part II of Schedule 1, and
  (b)  section 7.

(3)  In this Part "the non-disclosure provisions" means the provisions specified in subsection (4) to the extent to which they are inconsistent with the disclosure in question.

(4)  The provisions referred to in subsection (3) are—
  (a)  the first data protection principle, except to the extent to which it requires compliance with the conditions in Schedules 2 and 3,
  (b)  the second, third, fourth and fifth data protection principles, and
  (c)  sections 10 and 14(1) to (3).

(5)  Except as provided by this Part, the subject information provisions shall have effect notwithstanding any enactment or rule of law prohibiting or restricting the disclosure, or authorising the withholding, of information.

**[1.1092]**
## [33A  Manual data held by public authorities
(1)  Personal data falling within paragraph (e) of the definition of "data" in section 1(1) are exempt from—
  (a)  the first, second, third, fifth, seventh and eighth data protection principles,
  (b)  the sixth data protection principle except so far as it relates to the rights conferred on data subjects by sections 7 and 14,
  (c)  sections 10 to 12,
  (d)  section 13, except so far as it relates to damage caused by a contravention of section 7 or of the fourth data protection principle and to any distress which is also suffered by reason of that contravention,

(e)   Part III, and
(f)   section 55.
(2)   Personal data which fall within paragraph (e) of the definition of "data" in section 1(1) and relate to appointments or removals, pay, discipline, superannuation or other personnel matters, in relation to—
(a)   service in any of the armed forces of the Crown,
(b)   service in any office or employment under the Crown or under any public authority, or
(c)   service in any office or employment, or under any contract for services, in respect of which power to take action, or to determine or approve the action taken, in such matters is vested in Her Majesty, any Minister of the Crown, the National Assembly for Wales, any Northern Ireland Minister (within the meaning of the Freedom of Information Act 2000) or any public authority,
are also exempt from the remaining data protection principles and the remaining provisions of Part II.]

**NOTES**
Inserted by the Freedom of Information Act 2000, s 70(1).
As to the meaning of employment by or under the Crown, see also the National Assembly for Wales Commission (Crown Status) Order 2007, SI 2007/1118, art 5.

**[1.1093]**
**35   Disclosures required by law or made in connection with legal proceedings etc**
(1)   Personal data are exempt from the non-disclosure provisions where the disclosure is required by or under any enactment, by any rule of law or by the order of a court.
(2)   Personal data are exempt from the non-disclosure provisions where the disclosure is necessary—
(a)   for the purpose of, or in connection with, any legal proceedings (including prospective legal proceedings), or
(b)   for the purpose of obtaining legal advice,
or is otherwise necessary for the purposes of establishing, exercising or defending legal rights.

**[1.1094]**
**37   Miscellaneous exemptions**
Schedule 7 (which confers further miscellaneous exemptions) has effect.

**PART V**
**ENFORCEMENT**

**[1.1095]**
**40   Enforcement notices**
(1)   If the Commissioner is satisfied that a data controller has contravened or is contravening any of the data protection principles, the Commissioner may serve him with a notice (in this Act referred to as "an enforcement notice") requiring him, for complying with the principle or principles in question, to do either or both of the following—
(a)   to take within such time as may be specified in the notice, or to refrain from taking after such time as may be so specified, such steps as are so specified, or
(b)   to refrain from processing any personal data, or any personal data of a description specified in the notice, or to refrain from processing them for a purpose so specified or in a manner so specified, after such time as may be so specified.
(2)   In deciding whether to serve an enforcement notice, the Commissioner shall consider whether the contravention has caused or is likely to cause any person damage or distress.
(3)   An enforcement notice in respect of a contravention of the fourth data protection principle which requires the data controller to rectify, block, erase or destroy any inaccurate data may also require the data controller to rectify, block, erase or destroy any other data held by him and containing an expression of opinion which appears to the Commissioner to be based on the inaccurate data.
(4)   An enforcement notice in respect of a contravention of the fourth data protection principle, in the case of data which accurately record information received or obtained by the data controller from the data subject or a third party, may require the data controller either—
(a)   to rectify, block, erase or destroy any inaccurate data and any other data held by him and containing an expression of opinion as mentioned in subsection (3), or
(b)   to take such steps as are specified in the notice for securing compliance with the requirements specified in paragraph 7 of Part II of Schedule 1 and, if the Commissioner thinks fit, for supplementing the data with such statement of the true facts relating to the matters dealt with by the data as the Commissioner may approve.
(5)   Where—
(a)   an enforcement notice requires the data controller to rectify, block, erase or destroy any personal data, or

(b)   the Commissioner is satisfied that personal data which have been rectified, blocked, erased or destroyed had been processed in contravention of any of the data protection principles,

an enforcement notice may, if reasonably practicable, require the data controller to notify third parties to whom the data have been disclosed of the rectification, blocking, erasure or destruction; and in determining whether it is reasonably practicable to require such notification regard shall be had, in particular, to the number of persons who would have to be notified.

(6)   An enforcement notice must contain—

(a)   a statement of the data protection principle or principles which the Commissioner is satisfied have been or are being contravened and his reasons for reaching that conclusion, and

(b)   particulars of the rights of appeal conferred by section 48.

(7)   Subject to subsection (8), an enforcement notice must not require any of the provisions of the notice to be complied with before the end of the period within which an appeal can be brought against the notice and, if such an appeal is brought, the notice need not be complied with pending the determination or withdrawal of the appeal.

(8)   If by reason of special circumstances the Commissioner considers that an enforcement notice should be complied with as a matter of urgency he may include in the notice a statement to that effect and a statement of his reasons for reaching that conclusion; and in that event subsection (7) shall not apply but the notice must not require the provisions of the notice to be complied with before the end of the period of seven days beginning with the day on which the notice is served.

(9)   Notification regulations (as defined by section 16(2)) may make provision as to the effect of the service of an enforcement notice on any entry in the register maintained under section 19 which relates to the person on whom the notice is served.

(10)   This section has effect subject to section 46(1).

**NOTES**

Regulations: as of 6 April 2013 no Regulations had been made under this section.

**[1.1096]**
**41   Cancellation of enforcement notice**
(1)   If the Commissioner considers that all or any of the provisions of an enforcement notice need not be complied with in order to ensure compliance with the data protection principle or principles to which it relates, he may cancel or vary the notice by written notice to the person on whom it was served.

(2)   A person on whom an enforcement notice has been served may, at any time after the expiry of the period during which an appeal can be brought against that notice, apply in writing to the Commissioner for the cancellation or variation of that notice on the ground that, by reason of a change of circumstances, all or any of the provisions of that notice need not be complied with in order to ensure compliance with the data protection principle or principles to which that notice relates.

**[1.1097]**
**[41A   Assessment notices**
(1)   The Commissioner may serve a data controller within subsection (2) with a notice (in this Act referred to as an "assessment notice") for the purpose of enabling the Commissioner to determine whether the data controller has complied or is complying with the data protection principles.

(2)   A data controller is within this subsection if the data controller is—

(a)   a government department,

(b)   a public authority designated for the purposes of this section by an order made by the Secretary of State, or

(c)   a person of a description designated for the purposes of this section by such an order.

(3)   An assessment notice is a notice which requires the data controller to do all or any of the following—

(a)   permit the Commissioner to enter any specified premises;

(b)   direct the Commissioner to any documents on the premises that are of a specified description;

(c)   assist the Commissioner to view any information of a specified description that is capable of being viewed using equipment on the premises;

(d)   comply with any request from the Commissioner for—

(i)   a copy of any of the documents to which the Commissioner is directed;

(ii)   a copy (in such form as may be requested) of any of the information which the Commissioner is assisted to view;

(e)   direct the Commissioner to any equipment or other material on the premises which is of a specified description;

(f)   permit the Commissioner to inspect or examine any of the documents, information, equipment or material to which the Commissioner is directed or which the Commissioner is assisted to view;

(g) permit the Commissioner to observe the processing of any personal data that takes place on the premises;

(h) make available for interview by the Commissioner a specified number of persons of a specified description who process personal data on behalf of the data controller (or such number as are willing to be interviewed).

(4) In subsection (3) references to the Commissioner include references to the Commissioner's officers and staff.

(5) An assessment notice must, in relation to each requirement imposed by the notice, specify—

(a) the time at which the requirement is to be complied with, or

(b) the period during which the requirement is to be complied with.

(6) An assessment notice must also contain particulars of the rights of appeal conferred by section 48.

(7) The Commissioner may cancel an assessment notice by written notice to the data controller on whom it was served.

(8) Where a public authority has been designated by an order under subsection (2)(b) the Secretary of State must reconsider, at intervals of no greater than 5 years, whether it continues to be appropriate for the authority to be designated.

(9) The Secretary of State may not make an order under subsection (2)(c) which designates a description of persons unless—

(a) the Commissioner has made a recommendation that the description be designated, and

(b) the Secretary of State has consulted—

    (i) such persons as appear to the Secretary of State to represent the interests of those that meet the description;

    (ii) such other persons as the Secretary of State considers appropriate.

(10) The Secretary of State may not make an order under subsection (2)(c), and the Commissioner may not make a recommendation under subsection (9)(a), unless the Secretary of State or (as the case may be) the Commissioner is satisfied that it is necessary for the description of persons in question to be designated having regard to—

(a) the nature and quantity of data under the control of such persons, and

(b) any damage or distress which may be caused by a contravention by such persons of the data protection principles.

(11) Where a description of persons has been designated by an order under subsection (2)(c) the Secretary of State must reconsider, at intervals of no greater than 5 years, whether it continues to be necessary for the description to be designated having regard to the matters mentioned in subsection (10).

(12) In this section—

"public authority" includes any body, office-holder or other person in respect of which—

    (a) an order may be made under section 4 or 5 of the Freedom of Information Act 2000, or

    (b) an order may be made under section 4 or 5 of the Freedom of Information (Scotland) Act 2002;

"specified" means specified in an assessment notice.]

**NOTES**

Commencement: 6 April 2010.

Inserted by the Coroners and Justice Act 2009, s 173, as from 6 April 2010.

As of 6 April 2013 no Orders had been made under this section.

**[1.1098]**
**[41B  Assessment notices: limitations**

(1) A time specified in an assessment notice under section 41A(5) in relation to a requirement must not fall, and a period so specified must not begin, before the end of the period within which an appeal can be brought against the notice, and if such an appeal is brought the requirement need not be complied with pending the determination or withdrawal of the appeal.

(2) If by reason of special circumstances the Commissioner considers that it is necessary for the data controller to comply with a requirement in an assessment notice as a matter of urgency, the Commissioner may include in the notice a statement to that effect and a statement of the reasons for that conclusion; and in that event subsection (1) applies in relation to the requirement as if for the words from "within" to the end there were substituted "of 7 days beginning with the day on which the notice is served".

(3) A requirement imposed by an assessment notice does not have effect in so far as compliance with it would result in the disclosure of—

(a) any communication between a professional legal adviser and the adviser's client in connection with the giving of legal advice with respect to the client's obligations, liabilities or rights under this Act, or

(b)   any communication between a professional legal adviser and the adviser's client, or between such an adviser or the adviser's client and any other person, made in connection with or in contemplation of proceedings under or arising out of this Act (including proceedings before the Tribunal) and for the purposes of such proceedings.

(4)   In subsection (3) references to the client of a professional legal adviser include references to any person representing such a client.

(5)   Nothing in section 41A authorises the Commissioner to serve an assessment notice on—

    (a)   a judge,

    (b)   a body specified in section 23(3) of the Freedom of Information Act 2000 (bodies dealing with security matters), or

    (c)   the Office for Standards in Education, Children's Services and Skills in so far as it is a data controller in respect of information processed for the purposes of functions exercisable by Her Majesty's Chief Inspector of Education, Children's Services and Skills by virtue of section 5(1)(a) of the Care Standards Act 2000.

(6)   In this section "judge" includes—

    (a)   a justice of the peace (or, in Northern Ireland, a lay magistrate),

    (b)   a member of a tribunal, and

    (c)   a clerk or other officer entitled to exercise the jurisdiction of a court or tribunal;

and in this subsection "tribunal' means any tribunal in which legal proceedings may be brought.]

**NOTES**

Commencement: 6 April 2010.

Inserted by the Coroners and Justice Act 2009, s 173, as from 6 April 2010.

**[1.1099]**

**[41C   Code of practice about assessment notices**

(1)   The Commissioner must prepare and issue a code of practice as to the manner in which the Commissioner's functions under and in connection with section 41A are to be exercised.

(2)   The code must in particular—

    (a)   specify factors to be considered in determining whether to serve an assessment notice on a data controller;

    (b)   specify descriptions of documents and information that—

       (i)   are not to be examined or inspected in pursuance of an assessment notice, or

       (ii)   are to be so examined or inspected only by persons of a description specified in the code;

    (c)   deal with the nature of inspections and examinations carried out in pursuance of an assessment notice;

    (d)   deal with the nature of interviews carried out in pursuance of an assessment notice;

    (e)   deal with the preparation, issuing and publication by the Commissioner of assessment reports in respect of data controllers that have been served with assessment notices.

(3)   The provisions of the code made by virtue of subsection (2)(b) must, in particular, include provisions that relate to—

    (a)   documents and information concerning an individual's physical or mental health;

    (b)   documents and information concerning the provision of social care for an individual.

(4)   An assessment report is a report which contains—

    (a)   a determination as to whether a data controller has complied or is complying with the data protection principles,

    (b)   recommendations as to any steps which the data controller ought to take, or refrain from taking, to ensure compliance with any of those principles, and

    (c)   such other matters as are specified in the code.

(5)   The Commissioner may alter or replace the code.

(6)   If the code is altered or replaced, the Commissioner must issue the altered or replacement code.

(7)   *The Commissioner may not issue the code (or an altered or replacement code) without the approval of the Secretary of State.*

(8)   The Commissioner must arrange for the publication of the code (and any altered or replacement code) issued under this section in such form and manner as the Commissioner considers appropriate.

(9)   In this section "social care' has the same meaning as in Part 1 of the Health and Social Care Act 2008 (see section 9(3) of that Act).]

**NOTES**

Commencement:1 February 2010.

Inserted by the Coroners and Justice Act 2009, s 173, as from 1 February 2010.

Sub-s (7): substituted by the Protection of Freedoms Act 2012, s 106(1), as from a day to be appointed, as follows—

"(7)   The Commissioner must consult the Secretary of State before issuing the code (or an altered or replacement code).".

Code of Practice: The Assessment Notices Code of Practice (April 2010), not reproduced for reasons of space. See www.ico.gov.uk.

**[1.1100]**
## 42 Request for assessment
(1)   A request may be made to the Commissioner by or on behalf of any person who is, or believes himself to be, directly affected by any processing of personal data for an assessment as to whether it is likely or unlikely that the processing has been or is being carried out in compliance with the provisions of this Act.
(2)   On receiving a request under this section, the Commissioner shall make an assessment in such manner as appears to him to be appropriate, unless he has not been supplied with such information as he may reasonably require in order to—
  (a)   satisfy himself as to the identity of the person making the request, and
  (b)   enable him to identify the processing in question.
(3)   The matters to which the Commissioner may have regard in determining in what manner it is appropriate to make an assessment include—
  (a)   the extent to which the request appears to him to raise a matter of substance,
  (b)   any undue delay in making the request, and
  (c)   whether or not the person making the request is entitled to make an application under section 7 in respect of the personal data in question.
(4)   Where the Commissioner has received a request under this section he shall notify the person who made the request—
  (a)   whether he has made an assessment as a result of the request, and
  (b)   to the extent that he considers appropriate, having regard in particular to any exemption from section 7 applying in relation to the personal data concerned, of any view formed or action taken as a result of the request.

**[1.1101]**
## 47 Failure to comply with notice
(1)   A person who fails to comply with an enforcement notice, an information notice or a special information notice is guilty of an offence.
(2)   A person who, in purported compliance with an information notice or a special information notice—
  (a)   makes a statement which he knows to be false in a material respect, or
  (b)   recklessly makes a statement which is false in a material respect,
is guilty of an offence.
(3)   It is a defence for a person charged with an offence under subsection (1) to prove that he exercised all due diligence to comply with the notice in question.

**[1.1102]**
## 48 Rights of appeal
(1)   A person on whom an enforcement notice[, an assessment notice], an information notice or a special information notice has been served may appeal to the Tribunal against the notice.
(2)   A person on whom an enforcement notice has been served may appeal to the Tribunal against the refusal of an application under section 41(2) for cancellation or variation of the notice.
(3)   Where an enforcement notice[, an assessment notice], an information notice or a special information notice contains a statement by the Commissioner in accordance with section 40(8)[, 41B(2)], 43(5) or 44(6) then, whether or not the person appeals against the notice, he may appeal against—
  (a)   the Commissioner's decision to include the statement in the notice, or
  (b)   the effect of the inclusion of the statement as respects any part of the notice.
(4)   A data controller in respect of whom a determination has been made under section 45 may appeal to the Tribunal against the determination.
(5)   Schedule 6 has effect in relation to appeals under this section and the proceedings of the Tribunal in respect of any such appeal.

**NOTES**
Sub-ss (1), (3): words in square brackets inserted by the Coroners and Justice Act 2009, s 175, Sch 20, Pt 2, para 5, as from 6 April 2010.

**[1.1103]**
## 49 Determination of appeals
(1)   If on an appeal under section 48(1) the Tribunal considers—
  (a)   that the notice against which the appeal is brought is not in accordance with the law, or
  (b)   to the extent that the notice involved an exercise of discretion by the Commissioner, that he ought to have exercised his discretion differently,
the Tribunal shall allow the appeal or substitute such other notice or decision as could have been served or made by the Commissioner; and in any other case the Tribunal shall dismiss the appeal.

(2) On such an appeal, the Tribunal may review any determination of fact on which the notice in question was based.

(3) If on an appeal under section 48(2) the Tribunal considers that the enforcement notice ought to be cancelled or varied by reason of a change in circumstances, the Tribunal shall cancel or vary the notice.

(4) On an appeal under subsection (3) of section 48 the Tribunal may direct—

    (a) that the notice in question shall have effect as if it did not contain any such statement as is mentioned in that subsection, or

    (b) that the inclusion of the statement shall not have effect in relation to any part of the notice, and may make such modifications in the notice as may be required for giving effect to the direction.

(5) On an appeal under section 48(4), the Tribunal may cancel the determination of the Commissioner.

(6), (7) . . .

---

**NOTES**

Sub-ss (6), (7): repealed by the Transfer of Tribunal Functions Order 2010, SI 2010/22, art 5(1), Sch 2, paras 24, 27, as from 18 January 2010.

---

# PART VI
## MISCELLANEOUS AND GENERAL

*Functions of Commissioner*

**[1.1104]**
### 51 General duties of Commissioner

(1) It shall be the duty of the Commissioner to promote the following of good practice by data controllers and, in particular, so to perform his functions under this Act as to promote the observance of the requirements of this Act by data controllers.

(2) The Commissioner shall arrange for the dissemination in such form and manner as he considers appropriate of such information as it may appear to him expedient to give to the public about the operation of this Act, about good practice, and about other matters within the scope of his functions under this Act, and may give advice to any person as to any of those matters.

(3) Where—

    (a) the [Secretary of State] so directs by order, or

    (b) the Commissioner considers it appropriate to do so,

the Commissioner shall, after such consultation with trade associations, data subjects or persons representing data subjects as appears to him to be appropriate, prepare and disseminate to such persons as he considers appropriate codes of practice for guidance as to good practice.

(4) The Commissioner shall also—

    (a) where he considers it appropriate to do so, encourage trade associations to prepare, and to disseminate to their members, such codes of practice, and

    (b) where any trade association submits a code of practice to him for his consideration, consider the code and, after such consultation with data subjects or persons representing data subjects as appears to him to be appropriate, notify the trade association whether in his opinion the code promotes the following of good practice.

(5) An order under subsection (3) shall describe the personal data or processing to which the code of practice is to relate, and may also describe the persons or classes of persons to whom it is to relate.

[(5A) In determining the action required to discharge the duties imposed by subsections (1) to (4), the Commissioner may take account of any action taken to discharge the duty imposed by section 52A (data-sharing code).]

(6) The Commissioner shall arrange for the dissemination in such form and manner as he considers appropriate of—

    (a) any Community finding as defined by paragraph 15(2) of Part II of Schedule 1,

    (b) any decision of the European Commission, under the procedure provided for in Article 31(2) of the Data Protection Directive, which is made for the purposes of Article 26(3) or (4) of the Directive, and

    (c) such other information as it may appear to him to be expedient to give to data controllers in relation to any personal data about the protection of the rights and freedoms of data subjects in relation to the processing of personal data in countries and territories outside the European Economic Area.

(7) The Commissioner may, with the consent of the data controller, assess any processing of personal data for the following of good practice and shall inform the data controller of the results of the assessment.

(8) The Commissioner may charge such sums as he may *with the consent of the [Secretary of State]* determine for any [relevant] services provided by the Commissioner by virtue of this Part.

[(8A) In subsection (8) "relevant services" means—

(a) the provision to the same person of more than one copy of any published material where each of the copies of the material is either provided on paper, a portable disk which stores the material electronically or a similar medium,

(b) the provision of training, or

(c) the provision of conferences.

(8B) IThe Secretary of State may by order amend subsection (8A).]

(9) In this section—

"good practice" means such practice in the processing of personal data as appears to the Commissioner to be desirable having regard to the interests of data subjects and others, and includes (but is not limited to) compliance with the requirements of this Act;

"trade association" includes any body representing data controllers.

**NOTES**

Sub-s (3): words in square brackets substituted by the Secretary of State for Constitutional Affairs Order 2003, SI 2003/1887, art 9, Sch 2, para 9(1)(a).

Sub-s (5A): inserted by the Coroners and Justice Act 2009, s 174(2), as from 1 February 2010.

Sub-s (8): words "Secretary of State" in square brackets substituted by SI 2003/1887, art 9, Sch 2, para 9(1)(a); words in italics repealed, and word "relevant" in square brackets inserted, by the Protection of Freedoms Act 2012, ss 107(1)(a), 115(2), Sch 10, Pt 8, as from a day to be appointed.

Sub-ss (8A), (8B): inserted by the Protection of Freedoms Act 2012, s 107(1)(b), as from a day to be appointed.

Codes of Practice: see the Employment Practices Data Protection Code at **[4.171]** issued by the Information Commissioner under this section. Note that unlike other statutory provisions authorising the making of codes of practice, this section has no provision requiring an Order to bring the code into effect.

Orders: as of 6 April 2013 no Orders had been made under this section.

**[1.1105]**
**52 Reports and codes of practice to be laid before Parliament**

(1) The Commissioner shall lay annually before each House of Parliament a general report on the exercise of his functions under this Act.

(2) The Commissioner may from time to time lay before each House of Parliament such other reports with respect to those functions as he thinks fit.

(3) The Commissioner shall lay before each House of Parliament any code of practice prepared under section 51(3) for complying with a direction of the [Secretary of State], unless the code is included in any report laid under subsection (1) or (2).

**NOTES**

Sub-s (3): words in square brackets substituted by the Secretary of State for Constitutional Affairs Order 2003, SI 2003/1887, art 9, Sch 2, para 9(1)(a).

Codes of Practice: see the note to s 51 at **[1.1104]**.

*[Monetary penalties*

**[1.1106]**
**55A Power of Commissioner to impose monetary penalty**

(1) The Commissioner may serve a data controller with a monetary penalty notice if the Commissioner is satisfied that—

(a) there has been a serious contravention of section 4(4) by the data controller,

(b) the contravention was of a kind likely to cause substantial damage or substantial distress, and

(c) subsection (2) or (3) applies.

(2) This subsection applies if the contravention was deliberate.

(3) This subsection applies if the data controller—

(a) knew or ought to have known—

(i) that there was a risk that the contravention would occur, and

(ii) that such a contravention would be of a kind likely to cause substantial damage or substantial distress, but

(b) failed to take reasonable steps to prevent the contravention.

[(3A) The Commissioner may not be satisfied as mentioned in subsection (1) by virtue of any matter which comes to the Commissioner's attention as a result of anything done in pursuance of—

(a) an assessment notice;

(b) an assessment under section 51(7).]

(4) A monetary penalty notice is a notice requiring the data controller to pay to the Commissioner a monetary penalty of an amount determined by the Commissioner and specified in the notice.

(5) The amount determined by the Commissioner must not exceed the prescribed amount.

(6) The monetary penalty must be paid to the Commissioner within the period specified in the notice.

(7) The notice must contain such information as may be prescribed.

(8) Any sum received by the Commissioner by virtue of this section must be paid into the Consolidated Fund.

(9) In this section—

"data controller" does not include the Crown Estate Commissioners or a person who is a data controller by virtue of section 63(3);

"prescribed" means prescribed by regulations made by the Secretary of State.]

**NOTES**

Commencement: 1 October 2009 (sub-ss (4), (5), (7), (9)); 6 April 2010 (otherwise).

Inserted, together with the preceding heading and ss 55B–55E, by the Criminal Justice and Immigration Act 2008, s 144(1), as from 1 October 2009 (in so far as it relates to sub-ss (4), (5), (7), (9)), and as from 6 April 2010 (otherwise).

Sub-s (3A): inserted by the Coroners and Justice Act 2009, s 175, Sch 20, Pt 5, as from 6 April 2010.

Regulations: the Data Protection (Monetary Penalties) (Maximum Penalty and Notices) Regulations 2010, SI 2010/31 (which (i) prescribe £500,000 as the maximum amount the Information Commissioner may impose as a monetary penalty (reg 2); (ii) prescribe the information the Information Commissioner must include in a notice of intent, which he serves on a data controller when he intends to impose a monetary penalty (reg 3); and (iii) prescribe the information the Information Commissioner must include in a monetary penalty notice (reg 4)).

**[1.1107]**
**[55B Monetary penalty notices: procedural rights**
(1) Before serving a monetary penalty notice, the Commissioner must serve the data controller with a notice of intent.
(2) A notice of intent is a notice that the Commissioner proposes to serve a monetary penalty notice.
(3) A notice of intent must—
(a) inform the data controller that he may make written representations in relation to the Commissioner's proposal within a period specified in the notice, and
(b) contain such other information as may be prescribed.
(4) The Commissioner may not serve a monetary penalty notice until the time within which the data controller may make representations has expired.
(5) A person on whom a monetary penalty notice is served may appeal to the Tribunal against—
(a) the issue of the monetary penalty notice;
(b) the amount of the penalty specified in the notice.
(6) In this section, "prescribed" means prescribed by regulations made by the Secretary of State.]

**NOTES**

Commencement: 1 October 2009 (sub-ss (2), (3)(b), (6)); 6 April 2010 (otherwise).

Inserted as noted to s 55A at **[1.1106]**, as from 1 October 2009 (in so far as it relates to sub-ss (2), (3)(b), (6)), and as from 6 April 2010 (otherwise).

Regulations: the Data Protection (Monetary Penalties) (Maximum Penalty and Notices) Regulations 2010, SI 2010/31 (see the note to s 55A at **[1.1106]**).

**[1.1108]**
**[55C Guidance about monetary penalty notices**
(1) The Commissioner must prepare and issue guidance on how he proposes to exercise his functions under sections 55A and 55B.
(2) The guidance must, in particular, deal with—
(a) the circumstances in which he would consider it appropriate to issue a monetary penalty notice, and
(b) how he will determine the amount of the penalty.
(3) The Commissioner may alter or replace the guidance.
(4) If the guidance is altered or replaced, the Commissioner must issue the altered or replacement guidance.
(5) *The Commissioner may not issue guidance under this section without the approval of the Secretary of State.*
(6) The Commissioner must lay any guidance issued under this section before each House of Parliament.
(7) The Commissioner must arrange for the publication of any guidance issued under this section in such form and manner as he considers appropriate.
(8) In subsections (5) to (7), "guidance" includes altered or replacement guidance.]

**NOTES**

Commencement: 1 October 2009.

Inserted as noted to s 55A at **[1.1106]**, as from 1 October 2009.

Sub-s (5): substituted by the Protection of Freedoms Act 2012, s 106(3), as from a day to be appointed, as follows—

"(5) The Commissioner must consult the Secretary of State before issuing any guidance under this section.".

**[1.1109]**
**[55D Monetary penalty notices: enforcement**
(1) This section applies in relation to any penalty payable to the Commissioner by virtue of section 55A.
(2) In England and Wales, the penalty is recoverable—

(a) if *a county court* so orders, as if it were payable under an order of that court;

(b) if the High Court so orders, as if it were payable under an order of that court.

(3) In Scotland, the penalty may be enforced in the same manner as an extract registered decree arbitral bearing a warrant for execution issued by the sheriff court of any sheriffdom in Scotland.

(4) In Northern Ireland, the penalty is recoverable—

(a) if a county court so orders, as if it were payable under an order of that court;

(b) if the High Court so orders, as if it were payable under an order of that court.]

**NOTES**

Commencement: 6 April 2010.

Inserted as noted to s 55A at **[1.1106]**, as from 6 April 2010.

Sub-s (2): for the words in italics there are substituted the words "the county court" by the Crime and Courts Act 2013, s 17(5), Sch 9, Pt 3, para 52, as from a day to be appointed.

**[1.1110]**
**[55E    Notices under sections 55A and 55B: supplemental**
(1) The Secretary of State may by order make further provision in connection with monetary penalty notices and notices of intent.

(2) An order under this section may in particular—

(a) provide that a monetary penalty notice may not be served on a data controller with respect to the processing of personal data for the special purposes except in circumstances specified in the order;

(b) make provision for the cancellation or variation of monetary penalty notices;

(c) confer rights of appeal to the Tribunal against decisions of the Commissioner in relation to the cancellation or variation of such notices;

(d)    . . .

(e) make provision for the determination of [appeals made by virtue of paragraph (c)];

(f)    . . .

(3) An order under this section may apply any provision of this Act with such modifications as may be specified in the order.

(4) An order under this section may amend this Act.]

**NOTES**

Commencement: 1 October 2009.

Inserted as noted to s 55A at **[1.1106]**, as from 1 October 2009.

Sub-s (2): paras (d), (f) repealed, and words in square brackets in para (e) substituted, by the Transfer of Tribunal Functions Order 2010, SI 2010/22, art 5(1), Sch 2, paras 24, 28, as from 18 January 2010.

Orders: the Data Protection (Monetary Penalties) Order 2010, SI 2010/910.

*Records obtained under data subject's right of access*

**[1.1111]**
**56    Prohibition of requirement as to production of certain records**
(1) A person must not, in connection with—

(a) the recruitment of another person as an employee,

(b) the continued employment of another person, or

(c) any contract for the provision of services to him by another person,

require that other person or a third party to supply him with a relevant record or to produce a relevant record to him.

(2) A person concerned with the provision (for payment or not) of goods, facilities or services to the public or a section of the public must not, as a condition of providing or offering to provide any goods, facilities or services to another person, require that other person or a third party to supply him with a relevant record or to produce a relevant record to him.

(3) Subsections (1) and (2) do not apply to a person who shows—

(a) that the imposition of the requirement was required or authorised by or under any enactment, by any rule of law or by the order of a court, or

(b) that in the particular circumstances the imposition of the requirement was justified as being in the public interest.

(4) Having regard to the provisions of Part V of the Police Act 1997 (certificates of criminal records etc), the imposition of the requirement referred to in subsection (1) or (2) is not to be regarded as being justified as being in the public interest on the ground that it would assist in the prevention or detection of crime.

(5) A person who contravenes subsection (1) or (2) is guilty of an offence.

(6) In this section "a relevant record" means any record which—

(a) has been or is to be obtained by a data subject from any data controller specified in the first column of the Table below in the exercise of the right conferred by section 7, and

(b) contains information relating to any matter specified in relation to that data controller in the second column,

and includes a copy of such a record or a part of such a record.

*Table*

| Data controller | Subject-matter |
|---|---|
| 1. Any of the following persons— | (a) Convictions. |
| (a) a chief officer of police of a police force in England and Wales. | (b) Cautions. |
| (b) a chief constable of a police force in Scotland. | |
| (c) the [Chief Constable of the Police Service of Northern Ireland]. | |
| [(d) the *Director General of the Serious Organised Crime Agency*.] | |
| 2. The Secretary of State. | (a) Convictions. |
| | (b) Cautions. |
| | (c) His functions under [section 92 of the Powers of Criminal Courts (Sentencing) Act 2000], section 205(2) or 208 of the Criminal Procedure (Scotland) Act 1995 or section 73 of the Children and Young Persons Act (Northern Ireland) 1968 in relation to any person sentenced to detention. |
| | (d) His functions under the Prison Act 1952, the Prisons (Scotland) Act 1989 or the Prison Act (Northern Ireland) 1953 in relation to any person imprisoned or detained. |
| | (e) His functions under the Social Security Contributions and Benefits Act 1992, the Social Security Administration Act 1992[, the Jobseekers Act 1995 *or Part 1 of the Welfare Reform Act 2007* ]. |
| | (f) . . . |
| | [(g) . . . ] |
| 3. The Department of Health and Social Services for Northern Ireland. | Its functions under the Social Security Contributions and Benefits (Northern Ireland) Act 1992, the Social Security Administration (Northern Ireland) Act 1992 or the Jobseekers (Northern Ireland) Order 1995. |
| [4. [Disclosure and Barring Service]. | [(a) Its functions under the Safeguarding Vulnerable Groups Act 2006 [or the Safeguarding Vulnerable Groups (Northern Ireland) Order 2007].] |
| | [(b) Its functions under Part 5 of the Police Act 1997.] |
| [5 The Scottish Ministers. | Their functions under Parts 1 and 2 of the Protection of Vulnerable Groups (Scotland) Act 2007 (asp 14).] |

[(6A)   A record is not a relevant record to the extent that it relates, or is to relate, only to personal data falling within paragraph (e) of the definition of "data" in section 1(1).]

(7)   In the Table in subsection (6)—
    "caution" means a caution given to any person in England and Wales or Northern Ireland in respect of an offence which, at the time when the caution is given, is admitted;
    "conviction" has the same meaning as in the Rehabilitation of Offenders Act 1974 or the Rehabilitation of Offenders (Northern Ireland) Order 1978.

(8)   The [Secretary of State] may by order amend—
    (a)    the Table in subsection (6), and
    (b)    subsection (7).

(9)   For the purposes of this section a record which states that a data controller is not processing any personal data relating to a particular matter shall be taken to be a record containing information relating to that matter.

(10) In this section "employee" means an individual who—
  (a) works under a contract of employment, as defined by section 230(2) of the Employment Rights Act 1996, or
  (b) holds any office,
whether or not he is entitled to remuneration; and "employment" shall be construed accordingly.

___

**NOTES**

Commencement: 16 July 1998 (in so far as conferring power to make subordinate legislation); 7 July 2008 (in so far as relating to the entries in the table in sub-s (6) which relate to (a) the functions of the Secretary of State under the Safeguarding Vulnerable Groups Act 2006 or the Safeguarding Vulnerable Groups (Northern Ireland) Order 2007, and (b) the functions of the [Independent Safeguarding Authority] under the Safeguarding Vulnerable Groups Act 2006 or the Safeguarding Vulnerable Groups (Northern Ireland) Order 2007); 3 March 2011 (in so far as it relates to a record containing information relating to the Scottish Ministers' functions under Parts 1 and 2 of the Protection of Vulnerable Groups (Scotland) Act 2007); to be appointed (otherwise).

Sub-s (6), Table is amended as follows:

Words in square brackets in para 1(c) substituted by the Police (Northern Ireland) Act 2000, s 78(2)(a).

Para 1(d) substituted, for the original paras 1(d), (e), by the Serious Organised Crime and Police Act 2005, Sch 4, para 112.

For the words in italics in para 1(d) there are substituted the words "Director General of the National Crime Agency" by the Crime and Courts Act 2013, s 15(3), Sch 8, Pt 3, para 187, as from a day to be appointed.

Words in square brackets in para 2(c) substituted by the Powers of Criminal Courts (Sentencing) Act 2000, s 165(1), Sch 9, para 191.

In para 2(e), words in square brackets substituted by the Social Security (Miscellaneous Amendments) (No 3) Regulations 2011, SI 2011/2425, reg 4(a), as from 31 October 2011 and for the words in italics there are substituted the words ", Part 1 of the Welfare Reform Act 2007 or Part 1 of the Welfare Reform Act 2012" by the Universal Credit (Consequential, Supplementary, Incidental and Miscellaneous Provisions) Regulations 2013, SI 2013/630, reg 14(1), (2), as from 29 April 2013.

Para 2(f) repealed by the Protection of Freedoms Act 2012 (Disclosure and Barring Service Transfer of Functions) Order 2012, SI 2012/3006, arts 72, 73, as from 1 December 2012.

Para 2(g) inserted by the Safeguarding Vulnerable Groups Act 2006, s 63(1), Sch 9, Pt 2, para 15(1), (2)(a), as from 19 May 2008 and repealed by SI 2012/3006, arts 72, 73, as from 1 December 2012.

Para 4 inserted by the Safeguarding Vulnerable Groups Act 2006, s 63(1), Sch 9, Pt 2, para 15(1), (2)(b), as from 19 May 2008. Words in square brackets in column 1 substituted by SI 2012/3006, art 16, as from 1 December 2012. In column 2, para (a) numbered as such and para (b) added by SI 2012/3006, arts 72, 74, as from 1 December 2012 and words in square brackets in para (a) inserted by the Safeguarding Vulnerable Groups (Northern Ireland) Order 2007, SI 2007/1351, art 60, Sch 7, para 4(1), as from 29 May 2008.

Para 5 inserted by the Protection of Vulnerable Groups (Scotland) Act 2007 (Consequential Modifications) Order 2011, SI 2011/565, art 3(1), (2), as from 1 March 2011.

Sub-s (6A): inserted by the Freedom of Information Act 2000, s 68(4).

Sub-s (8): words in square brackets substituted by the Secretary of State for Constitutional Affairs Order 2003, SI 2003/1887, art 9, Sch 2, para 9(1)(a).

Orders: as of 6 April 2013 no Orders had been made under this section.

___

**[1.1112]**
**57 Avoidance of certain contractual terms relating to health records**
(1) Any term or condition of a contract is void in so far as it purports to require an individual—
  (a) to supply any other person with a record to which this section applies, or with a copy of such a record or a part of such a record, or
  (b) to produce to any other person such a record, copy or part.
(2) This section applies to any record which—
  (a) has been or is to be obtained by a data subject in the exercise of the right conferred by section 7, and
  (b) consists of the information contained in any health record as defined by section 68(2).

*General*

**[1.1113]**
**75 Short title, commencement and extent**
(1) This Act may be cited as the Data Protection Act 1998.
(2) The following provisions of this Act—
  (a) sections 1 to 3,
  (b) section 25(1) and (4),
  (c) section 26,
  (d) sections 67 to 71,
  (e) this section,
  (f) paragraph 17 of Schedule 5,
  (g) Schedule 11,
  (h) Schedule 12, and
  (i) so much of any other provision of this Act as confers any power to make subordinate legislation,
shall come into force on the day on which this Act is passed.
(3) The remaining provisions of this Act shall come into force on such day as the [Secretary of State] may by order appoint; and different days may be appointed for different purposes.

(4)   The day appointed under subsection (3) for the coming into force of section 56 must not be earlier than the first day on which [sections 112, 113A and 113B] of the Police Act 1997 (which provide for the issue   . . .   of criminal conviction certificates, criminal record certificates and enhanced criminal record certificates) are all in force.

[(4A)   Subsection (4) does not apply to section 56 so far as that section relates to a record containing information relating to—

(a)   the Secretary of State's functions under the Safeguarding Vulnerable Groups Act 2006 [or the Safeguarding Vulnerable Groups (Northern Ireland) Order 2007],   . . .

(b)   the [Independent Safeguarding Authority's] functions under that Act [or that Order][, or

(c)   the Scottish Ministers' functions under Parts 1 and 2 of the Protection of Vulnerable Groups (Scotland) Act 2007 (asp 14)].]

(5)   Subject to [subsections (5A) and (6)], this Act extends to Northern Ireland.

[(5A)   In section 56(6) (prohibition of requirement as to production of certain records), paragraph (2)(e) of the Table in that section, insofar as it relates to Part 1 of the Welfare Reform Act 2007 [and Part 1 of the Welfare Reform Act 2012], extends to England and Wales and Scotland only.]

(6)   Any amendment, repeal or revocation made by Schedule 15 or 16 has the same extent as that of the enactment or instrument to which it relates.

**NOTES**

Sub-s (3): words in square brackets substituted by the Secretary of State for Constitutional Affairs Order 2003, SI 2003/1887, art 9, Sch 2, para 9(1)(a).

Sub-s (4): words in square brackets substituted by the Protection of Freedoms Act 2012, s 86, as from 10 September 2012; words omitted repealed by the Protection of Freedoms Act 2012 (Disclosure and Barring Service Transfer of Functions) Order 2012, SI 2012/3006, arts 72, 75, as from 1 December 2012.

Sub-s (4A): inserted by the Safeguarding Vulnerable Groups Act 2006, s 63(1), Sch 9, Pt 2, para 15(1), (3), as from 19 May 2008; words in square brackets in para (a), and words in second pair of square brackets in para (b) inserted by the Safeguarding Vulnerable Groups (Northern Ireland) Order 2007, SI 2007/1351, art 60, Sch 7, para 4(2), as from 29 May 2008; word omitted from para (a) repealed, and para (c) (and the word immediately preceding it) added by the Protection of Vulnerable Groups (Scotland) Act 2007 (Consequential Modifications) Order 2011, SI 2011/565, art 3(1), (3)(b), as from 1 March 2011; words in first pair of square brackets in para (b) substituted by the Policing and Crime Act 2009, s 81(2), (3)(i), as from 12 November 2009.

Sub-s (5): words in square brackets substituted by the Social Security (Miscellaneous Amendments) (No 3) Regulations 2011, SI 2011/2425, reg 4(b)(i), as from 31 October 2011.

Sub-s (5A): inserted by SI 2011/2425, reg 4(b)(ii), as from 31 October 2011; words in square brackets inserted by the Universal Credit (Consequential, Supplementary, Incidental and Miscellaneous Provisions) Regulations 2013, SI 2013/630, reg 14(1), (3), as from 29 April 2013.

Orders: the Data Protection Act 1998 (Commencement) Order 2000, SI 2000/183; the Data Protection Act 1998 (Commencement No 2) Order 2008, SI 2008/1592; the Data Protection Act 1998 (Commencement No 3) Order 2011, SI 2011/601.

## SCHEDULES

## SCHEDULE 1
## THE DATA PROTECTION PRINCIPLES

### PART I
### THE PRINCIPLES

**[1.1114]**

**1.** Personal data shall be processed fairly and lawfully and, in particular, shall not be processed unless—

(a)   at least one of the conditions in Schedule 2 is met, and

(b)   in the case of sensitive personal data, at least one of the conditions in Schedule 3 is also met.

**2.** Personal data shall be obtained only for one or more specified and lawful purposes, and shall not be further processed in any manner incompatible with that purpose or those purposes.

**3.** Personal data shall be adequate, relevant and not excessive in relation to the purpose or purposes for which they are processed.

**4.** Personal data shall be accurate and, where necessary, kept up to date.

**5.** Personal data processed for any purpose or purposes shall not be kept for longer than is necessary for that purpose or those purposes.

**6.** Personal data shall be processed in accordance with the rights of data subjects under this Act.

**7.** Appropriate technical and organisational measures shall be taken against unauthorised or unlawful processing of personal data and against accidental loss or destruction of, or damage to, personal data.

**8.** Personal data shall not be transferred to a country or territory outside the European Economic Area unless that country or territory ensures an adequate level of protection for the rights and freedoms of data subjects in relation to the processing of personal data.

## PART II
## INTERPRETATION OF THE PRINCIPLES IN PART I

*The first principle*

**[1.1115]**

**1.** (1) In determining for the purposes of the first principle whether personal data are processed fairly, regard is to be had to the method by which they are obtained, including in particular whether any person from whom they are obtained is deceived or misled as to the purpose or purposes for which they are to be processed.

(2) Subject to paragraph 2, for the purposes of the first principle data are to be treated as obtained fairly if they consist of information obtained from a person who—

(a) is authorised by or under any enactment to supply it, or
(b) is required to supply it by or under any enactment or by any convention or other instrument imposing an international obligation on the United Kingdom.

**2.** (1) Subject to paragraph 3, for the purposes of the first principle personal data are not to be treated as processed fairly unless—

(a) in the case of data obtained from the data subject, the data controller ensures so far as practicable that the data subject has, is provided with, or has made readily available to him, the information specified in sub-paragraph (3), and
(b) in any other case, the data controller ensures so far as practicable that, before the relevant time or as soon as practicable after that time, the data subject has, is provided with, or has made readily available to him, the information specified in sub-paragraph (3).

(2) In sub-paragraph (1)(b) "the relevant time" means—

(a) the time when the data controller first processes the data, or
(b) in a case where at that time disclosure to a third party within a reasonable period is envisaged—
  (i) if the data are in fact disclosed to such a person within that period, the time when the data are first disclosed,
  (ii) if within that period the data controller becomes, or ought to become, aware that the data are unlikely to be disclosed to such a person within that period, the time when the data controller does become, or ought to become, so aware, or
  (iii) in any other case, the end of that period.

(3) The information referred to in sub-paragraph (1) is as follows, namely—

(a) the identity of the data controller,
(b) if he has nominated a representative for the purposes of this Act, the identity of that representative,
(c) the purpose or purposes for which the data are intended to be processed, and
(d) any further information which is necessary, having regard to the specific circumstances in which the data are or are to be processed, to enable processing in respect of the data subject to be fair.

**3.** (1) Paragraph 2(1)(b) does not apply where either of the primary conditions in sub-paragraph (2), together with such further conditions as may be prescribed by the [Secretary of State] by order, are met.

(2) The primary conditions referred to in sub-paragraph (1) are—

(a) that the provision of that information would involve a disproportionate effort, or
(b) that the recording of the information to be contained in the data by, or the disclosure of the data by, the data controller is necessary for compliance with any legal obligation to which the data controller is subject, other than an obligation imposed by contract.

**4.** (1) Personal data which contain a general identifier falling within a description prescribed by the [Secretary of State] by order are not to be treated as processed fairly and lawfully unless they are processed in compliance with any conditions so prescribed in relation to general identifiers of that description.

(2) In sub-paragraph (1) "a general identifier" means any identifier (such as, for example, a number or code used for identification purposes) which—

(a) relates to an individual, and
(b) forms part of a set of similar identifiers which is of general application.

*The second principle*

**5.** The purpose or purposes for which personal data are obtained may in particular be specified—

    (a)   in a notice given for the purposes of paragraph 2 by the data controller to the data subject, or

    (b)   in a notification given to the Commissioner under Part III of this Act.

**6.** In determining whether any disclosure of personal data is compatible with the purpose or purposes for which the data were obtained, regard is to be had to the purpose or purposes for which the personal data are intended to be processed by any person to whom they are disclosed.

### The fourth principle

**7.** The fourth principle is not to be regarded as being contravened by reason of any inaccuracy in personal data which accurately record information obtained by the data controller from the data subject or a third party in a case where—

    (a)   having regard to the purpose or purposes for which the data were obtained and further processed, the data controller has taken reasonable steps to ensure the accuracy of the data, and

    (b)   if the data subject has notified the data controller of the data subject's view that the data are inaccurate, the data indicate that fact.

### The sixth principle

**8.** A person is to be regarded as contravening the sixth principle if, but only if—

    (a)   he contravenes section 7 by failing to supply information in accordance with that section,

    (b)   he contravenes section 10 by failing to comply with a notice given under subsection (1) of that section to the extent that the notice is justified or by failing to give a notice under subsection (3) of that section,

    (c)   he contravenes section 11 by failing to comply with a notice given under subsection (1) of that section, or

    (d)   he contravenes section 12 by failing to comply with a notice given under subsection (1) or (2)(b) of that section or by failing to give a notification under subsection (2)(a) of that section or a notice under subsection (3) of that section.

### The seventh principle

**9.** Having regard to the state of technological development and the cost of implementing any measures, the measures must ensure a level of security appropriate to—

    (a)   the harm that might result from such unauthorised or unlawful processing or accidental loss, destruction or damage as are mentioned in the seventh principle, and

    (b)   the nature of the data to be protected.

**10.** The data controller must take reasonable steps to ensure the reliability of any employees of his who have access to the personal data.

**11.** Where processing of personal data is carried out by a data processor on behalf of a data controller, the data controller must in order to comply with the seventh principle—

    (a)   choose a data processor providing sufficient guarantees in respect of the technical and organisational security measures governing the processing to be carried out, and

    (b)   take reasonable steps to ensure compliance with those measures.

**12.** Where processing of personal data is carried out by a data processor on behalf of a data controller, the data controller is not to be regarded as complying with the seventh principle unless—

    (a)   the processing is carried out under a contract—

        (i)   which is made or evidenced in writing, and

        (ii)   under which the data processor is to act only on instructions from the data controller, and

    (b)   the contract requires the data processor to comply with obligations equivalent to those imposed on a data controller by the seventh principle.

### The eighth principle

**13.** An adequate level of protection is one which is adequate in all the circumstances of the case, having regard in particular to—

    (a)   the nature of the personal data,

    (b)   the country or territory of origin of the information contained in the data,

    (c)   the country or territory of final destination of that information,

    (d)   the purposes for which and period during which the data are intended to be processed,

    (e)   the law in force in the country or territory in question,

    (f)   the international obligations of that country or territory,

    (g)   any relevant codes of conduct or other rules which are enforceable in that country or territory (whether generally or by arrangement in particular cases), and

    (h)   any security measures taken in respect of the data in that country or territory.

**14.** The eighth principle does not apply to a transfer falling within any paragraph of Schedule 4, except in such circumstances and to such extent as the [Secretary of State] may by order provide.

**15.** (1)   Where—
(a)   in any proceedings under this Act any question arises as to whether the requirement of the eighth principle as to an adequate level of protection is met in relation to the transfer of any personal data to a country or territory outside the European Economic Area, and
(b)   a Community finding has been made in relation to transfers of the kind in question,
that question is to be determined in accordance with that finding.

(2)   In sub-paragraph (1) "Community finding" means a finding of the European Commission, under the procedure provided for in Article 31(2) of the Data Protection Directive, that a country or territory outside the European Economic Area does, or does not, ensure an adequate level of protection within the meaning of Article 25(2) of the Directive.

**NOTES**

Paras 3, 4, 14: words in square brackets substituted by the Secretary of State for Constitutional Affairs Order 2003, SI 2003/1887, art 9, Sch 2, para 9(1)(b).

Orders: the Data Protection (Conditions under Paragraph 3 of Part II of Schedule 1) Order 2000, SI 2000/185.

## SCHEDULE 2
### CONDITIONS RELEVANT FOR PURPOSES OF THE FIRST PRINCIPLE: PROCESSING OF ANY PERSONAL DATA

Section 4(3)

**[1.1116]**
**1.** The data subject has given his consent to the processing.

**2.** The processing is necessary—
(a)   for the performance of a contract to which the data subject is a party, or
(b)   for the taking of steps at the request of the data subject with a view to entering into a contract.

**3.** The processing is necessary for compliance with any legal obligation to which the data controller is subject, other than an obligation imposed by contract.

**4.** The processing is necessary in order to protect the vital interests of the data subject.

**5.** The processing is necessary—
(a)   for the administration of justice,
[(aa)  for the exercise of any functions of either House of Parliament,]
(b)   for the exercise of any functions conferred on any person by or under any enactment,
(c)   for the exercise of any functions of the Crown, a Minister of the Crown or a government department, or
(d)   for the exercise of any other functions of a public nature exercised in the public interest by any person.

**6.** (1)   The processing is necessary for the purposes of legitimate interests pursued by the data controller or by the third party or parties to whom the data are disclosed, except where the processing is unwarranted in any particular case by reason of prejudice to the rights and freedoms or legitimate interests of the data subject.

(2)   The [Secretary of State] may by order specify particular circumstances in which this condition is, or is not, to be taken to be satisfied.

**NOTES**

Para 5: sub-para (aa) inserted by the Freedom of Information Act 2000, s 73, Sch 6, para 4.

Para 6: words in square brackets substituted by the Secretary of State for Constitutional Affairs Order 2003, SI 2003/1887, art 9, Sch 2, para 9(1)(b).

As to the meaning of government department, see also the National Assembly for Wales Commission (Crown Status) Order 2007, SI 2007/1118, art 5.

Orders: as of 6 April 2013 no Orders had been made under para 6.

## SCHEDULE 3
### CONDITIONS RELEVANT FOR PURPOSES OF THE FIRST PRINCIPLE: PROCESSING OF SENSITIVE PERSONAL DATA

Section 4(3)

**[1.1117]**
**1.** The data subject has given his explicit consent to the processing of the personal data.

**2.** (1)  The processing is necessary for the purposes of exercising or performing any right or obligation which is conferred or imposed by law on the data controller in connection with employment.

(2)  The [Secretary of State] may by order—
- (a)  exclude the application of sub-paragraph (1) in such cases as may be specified, or
- (b)  provide that, in such cases as may be specified, the condition in subparagraph (1) is not to be regarded as satisfied unless such further conditions as may be specified in the order are also satisfied.

**3.**  The processing is necessary—
- (a)  in order to protect the vital interests of the data subject or another person, in a case where—
  - (i)  consent cannot be given by or on behalf of the data subject, or
  - (ii)  the data controller cannot reasonably be expected to obtain the consent of the data subject, or
- (b)  in order to protect the vital interests of another person, in a case where consent by or on behalf of the data subject has been unreasonably withheld.

**4.**  The processing—
- (a)  is carried out in the course of its legitimate activities by any body or association which—
  - (i)  is not established or conducted for profit, and
  - (ii)  exists for political, philosophical religious or trade-union purposes,
- (b)  is carried out with appropriate safeguards for the rights and freedoms of data subjects,
- (c)  relates only to individuals who either are members of the body or association or have regular contact with it in connection with its purposes, and
- (d)  does not involve disclosure of the personal data to a third party without the consent of the data subject.

**5.**  The information contained in the personal data has been made public as a result of steps deliberately taken by the data subject.

**6.**  The processing—
- (a)  is necessary for the purpose of, or in connection with, any legal proceedings (including prospective legal proceedings),
- (b)  is necessary for the purpose of obtaining legal advice, or
- (c)  is otherwise necessary for the purposes of establishing, exercising or defending legal rights.

**7.** (1)  The processing is necessary—
- (a)  for the administration of justice,
- [(aa)  for the exercise of any functions of either House of Parliament,]
- (b)  for the exercise of any functions conferred on any person by or under an enactment, or
- (c)  for the exercise of any functions of the Crown, a Minister of the Crown or a government department.

(2)  The [Secretary of State] may by order—
- (a)  exclude the application of sub-paragraph (1) in such cases as may be specified, or
- (b)  provide that, in such cases as may be specified, the condition in subparagraph (1) is not to be regarded as satisfied unless such further conditions as may be specified in the order are also satisfied.

**[7A.** (1)  The processing—
- (a)  is either—
  - (i)  the disclosure of sensitive personal data by a person as a member of an anti-fraud organisation or otherwise in accordance with any arrangements made by such an organisation; or
  - (ii)  any other processing by that person or another person of sensitive personal data so disclosed; and
- (b)  is necessary for the purposes of preventing fraud or a particular kind of fraud.

(2)  In this paragraph "an anti-fraud organisation" means any unincorporated association, body corporate or other person which enables or facilitates any sharing of information to prevent fraud or a particular kind of fraud or which has any of these functions as its purpose or one of its purposes.]

**8.** (1)  The processing is necessary for medical purposes and is undertaken by—
- (a)  a health professional, or
- (b)  a person who in the circumstances owes a duty of confidentiality which is equivalent to that which would arise if that person were a health professional.

(2)  In this paragraph "medical purposes" includes the purposes of preventative medicine, medical diagnosis, medical research, the provision of care and treatment and the management of healthcare services.

**9.** (1) The processing—
 (a) is of sensitive personal data consisting of information as to racial or ethnic origin,
 (b) is necessary for the purpose of identifying or keeping under review the existence or absence of equality of opportunity or treatment between persons of different racial or ethnic origins, with a view to enabling such equality to be promoted or maintained, and
 (c) is carried out with appropriate safeguards for the rights and freedoms of data subjects.

(2) The [Secretary of State] may by order specify circumstances in which processing falling within sub-paragraph (1)(a) and (b) is, or is not, to be taken for the purposes of sub-paragraph (1)(c) to be carried out with appropriate safeguards for the rights and freedoms of data subjects.

**10.** The personal data are processed in circumstances specified in an order made by the [Secretary of State] for the purposes of this paragraph

**NOTES**

Paras 2, 9, 10: words in square brackets substituted by the Secretary of State for Constitutional Affairs Order 2003, SI 2003/1887, art 9, Sch 2, para 9(1)(b).

Para 7: sub-para (1)(aa) inserted by the Freedom of Information Act 2000, s 73, Sch 6, para 5; words in square brackets in sub-para (2) substituted by SI 2003/1887, art 9, Sch 2, para 9(1)(b).

Para 7A: inserted by the Serious Crime Act 2007, s 72, as from 1 October 2008.

As to the meaning of government department, see also the National Assembly for Wales Commission (Crown Status) Order 2007, SI 2007/1118, art 5.

Orders: the Data Protection (Processing of Sensitive Personal Data) Order 2000, SI 2000/417 at **[2.563]**; the Data Protection (Processing of Sensitive Personal Data) (Elected Representatives) Order 2002, SI 2002/2905; the Data Protection (Processing of Sensitive Personal Data) Order 2006, SI 2006/2068; the Data Protection (Processing of Sensitive Personal Data) Order 2009, SI 2009/1811; the Data Protection (Processing of Sensitive Personal Data) Order 2012, SI 2012/1978.

## SCHEDULE 7
## MISCELLANEOUS EXEMPTIONS

Section 37

*Confidential references given by the data controller*

**[1.1118]**
**1.** Personal data are exempt from section 7 if they consist of a reference given or to be given in confidence by the data controller for the purposes of—
 (a) the education, training or employment, or prospective education, training or employment, of the data subject,
 (b) the appointment, or prospective appointment, of the data subject to any office, or
 (c) the provision, or prospective provision, by the data subject of any service.

**2.** (*Outside the scope of this work.*)

*Judicial appointments and honours*

**3.** Personal data processed for the purposes of—
 (a) assessing any person's suitability for judicial office or the office of Queen's Counsel, or
 (b) the conferring by the Crown of any honour [or dignity],
are exempt from the subject information provisions.

*Crown employment and Crown or Ministerial appointments*

**4.** [(1)] The [Secretary of State] may by order exempt from the subject information provisions personal data processed for the purposes of assessing any person's suitability for—
 (a) employment by or under the Crown, or
 (b) any office to which appointments are made by Her Majesty, by a Minister of the Crown or by a [Northern Ireland authority].

[(2) In this paragraph "Northern Ireland authority" means the First Minister, the deputy First Minister, a Northern Ireland Minister or a Northern Ireland department.]

*Management forecasts etc*

**5.** Personal data processed for the purposes of management forecasting or management planning to assist the data controller in the conduct of any business or other activity are exempt from the subject information provisions in any case to the extent to which the application of those provisions would be likely to prejudice the conduct of that business or other activity.

**6.** (*Outside the scope of this work.*)

## Negotiations

**7.** Personal data which consist of records of the intentions of the data controller in relation to any negotiations with the data subject are exempt from the subject information provisions in any case to the extent to which the application of those provisions would be likely to prejudice those negotiations.

**8, 9.** (*Outside the scope of this work.*)

## Legal professional privilege

**10.** Personal data are exempt from the subject information provisions if the data consist of information in respect of which a claim to legal professional privilege [or, in Scotland, to confidentiality of communications] could be maintained in legal proceedings.

## Self-incrimination

**11.** (1) A person need not comply with any request or order under section 7 to the extent that compliance would, by revealing evidence of the commission of any offence[, other than an offence under this Act or an offence within sub-paragraph (1A),] expose him to proceedings for that offence.

[(1A) The offences mentioned in sub-paragraph (1) are—
(a) an offence under section 5 of the Perjury Act 1911 (false statements made otherwise than on oath),
(b) an offence under section 44(2) of the Criminal Law (Consolidation) (Scotland) Act 1995 (false statements made otherwise than on oath), or
(c) an offence under Article 10 of the Perjury (Northern Ireland) Order 1979 (false statutory declarations and other false unsworn statements).]

(2) Information disclosed by any person in compliance with any request or order under section 7 shall not be admissible against him in proceedings for an offence under this Act.

**NOTES**

Para 3: words in square brackets in sub-para (b) inserted by the Freedom of Information Act 2000, s 73, Sch 6, para 6.

Para 4: sub-para (1) numbered as such, words in second pair of square brackets in that sub-paragraph substituted, and sub-para (2) added, by the Northern Ireland Act 1998, s 99, Sch 13, para 21; words in first pair of square brackets in sub-para (1) substituted by the Secretary of State for Constitutional Affairs Order 2003, SI 2003/1887, art 9, Sch 2, para 9(1)(e).

Para 10: words in square brackets substituted by the Freedom of Information Act 2000, s 73, Sch 6, para 7.

Para 11: words in square brackets in sub-para (1) substituted, and sub-para (1A) inserted, by the Coroners and Justice Act 2009, s 175, Sch 20, Pt 4, para 12(1), (2), as from 6 April 2010.

As to the meaning of employment by or under the Crown, see also the National Assembly for Wales Commission (Crown Status) Order 2007, SI 2007/1118, art 5.

Orders: the Data Protection (Corporate Finance Exemption) Order 2000, SI 2000/184; the Data Protection (Crown Appointments) Order 2000, SI 2000/416.

# NATIONAL MINIMUM WAGE ACT 1998

## (1998 c 39)

### ARRANGEMENT OF SECTIONS

*An Act to make provision for and in connection with a national minimum wage; to provide for the amendment of certain enactments relating to the remuneration of persons employed in agriculture; and for connected purposes*

[31 July 1998]

**NOTES**

This Act is reproduced in full apart from ss 5–8 (which relate to the Low Pay Commission), 25–27, 29 and 30 (amendments to other Acts, incorporated therein), 46 and 47 (which relate to agricultural wages), 50 (publicity for the National Minimum Wage) and 53 (repeals and revocations) and Schs 1–3 (the Low Pay Commission, agricultural wages and repeals and revocations). The principal Regulations under this Act are the National Minimum Wage Regulations 1999, SI 1999/584 at **[2.398]**.

Employment Appeal Tribunal: an appeal lies to the Employment Appeal Tribunal on any question of law arising from any decision of, or in any proceedings before, an employment tribunal under or by virtue of this Act; see the Employment Tribunals Act 1996, s 21(1)(ga) at **[1.713]**.

An employee who is dismissed is to be regarded as unfairly dismissed if the reason (or, if more than one, the principal reason) for the dismissal is that any action was taken, or was proposed to be taken, by or on behalf of the employee with a view to enforcing, or otherwise securing the benefit of, any right conferred by, or by virtue of, this Act for which the remedy for its infringement is by way of complaint to an employment tribunal; see the Employment Rights Act 1996, s 104A at **[1.908]**.

See *Harvey* BI(4).

*Entitlement to the national minimum wage*

**[1.1119]**
**1　Workers to be paid at least the minimum wage**
(1)　A person who qualifies for the national minimum wage shall be remunerated by his employer in respect of his work in any pay reference period at a rate which is not less than the national minimum wage.
(2)　A person qualifies for the national minimum wage if he is an individual who—
　(a)　is a worker;
　(b)　is working, or ordinarily works, in the United Kingdom under his contract; and
　(c)　has ceased to be of compulsory school age.
(3)　The national minimum wage shall be such single hourly rate as the Secretary of State may from time to time prescribe.
(4)　For the purposes of this Act a "pay reference period" is such period as the Secretary of State may prescribe for the purpose.
(5)　Subsections (1) to (4) above are subject to the following provisions of this Act.

**NOTES**

Regulations: the National Minimum Wage Regulations 1999, SI 1999/584 at **[2.398]**. Regulation 11 thereof at **[2.408]** (as last amended by the National Minimum Wage (Amendment) Regulations 2012, SI 2012/2397 (also made under this section)), prescribes £6.19 an hour as the single hourly rate of the national minimum wage, as from 1 October 2012. The Government has announced that the rate will increase from 1 October 2013 to £6.31, but the relevant Regulations had not, as at 6 April 2013, been made.

The previous rates were: £3.60 (from 1 April 1999); £3.70 (from 1 October 2000); £4.10 (from 1 October 2001); £4.20 (from 1 October 2002); £4.50 (from 1 October 2003); £4.85 (from 1 October 2004); £5.05 (from 1 October 2005); £5.35 (from 1 October 2006); £5.52 (from 1 October 2007); £5.73 (from 1 October 2008); £5.80 (from 1 October 2009); £5.93 (from 1 October 2010); £6.08 (from 1 October 2011). For provisions regarding those who do not qualify for the national minimum wage and those who qualify for it at a different rate, see regs 12, 13 of the 1999 Regulations at **[2.409]**, **[2.410]**.

*Regulations relating to the national minimum wage*

**[1.1120]**
**2　Determination of hourly rate of remuneration**
(1)　The Secretary of State may by regulations make provision for determining what is the hourly rate at which a person is to be regarded for the purposes of this Act as remunerated by his employer in respect of his work in any pay reference period.
(2)　The regulations may make provision for determining the hourly rate in cases where—
　(a)　the remuneration, to the extent that it is at a periodic rate, is at a single rate;
　(b)　the remuneration is, in whole or in part, at different rates applicable at different times or in different circumstances;
　(c)　the remuneration is, in whole or in part, otherwise than at a periodic rate or rates;
　(d)　the remuneration consists, in whole or in part, of benefits in kind.
(3)　The regulations may make provision with respect to—
　(a)　circumstances in which, times at which, or the time for which, a person is to be treated as, or as not, working, and the extent to which a person is to be so treated;
　(b)　the treatment of periods of paid or unpaid absence from, or lack of, work and of remuneration in respect of such periods.
(4)　The provision that may be made by virtue of paragraph (a) of subsection (3) above includes provision for or in connection with—

    (a)    treating a person as, or as not, working for a maximum or minimum time, or for a proportion of the time, in any period;

    (b)    determining any matter to which that paragraph relates by reference to the terms of an agreement.

(5)   The regulations may make provision with respect to—

    (a)    what is to be treated as, or as not, forming part of a person's remuneration, and the extent to which it is to be so treated;

    (b)    the valuation of benefits in kind;

    (c)    the treatment of deductions from earnings;

    (d)    the treatment of any charges or expenses which a person is required to bear.

(6)   The regulations may make provision with respect to—

    (a)    the attribution to a period, or the apportionment between two or more periods, of the whole or any part of any remuneration or work, whether or not the remuneration is received or the work is done within the period or periods in question;

    (b)    the aggregation of the whole or any part of the remuneration for different periods;

    (c)    the time at which remuneration is to be treated as received or accruing.

(7)   Subsections (2) to (6) above are without prejudice to the generality of subsection (1) above.

(8)   No provision shall be made under this section which treats the same circumstances differently in relation to—

    (a)    different areas;

    (b)    different sectors of employment;

    (c)    undertakings of different sizes;

    (d)    persons of different ages; or

    (e)    persons of different occupations.

**NOTES**

Regulations: the National Minimum Wage Regulations 1999, SI 1999/584 at **[2.398]**. Note that many Regulations have been made under this section that amend the principal 1999 Regulations, the most recent being the National Minimum Wage (Amendment) Regulations 2012, SI 2012/2397. The others are not listed here for reasons of space.

**[1.1121]**
## 3 Exclusion of, and modifications for, certain classes of person

(1)   This section applies to persons who have not attained the age of 26.

[(1A)   This section also applies to persons who have attained the age of 26 who are—

    (a)    within the first six months after the commencement of their employment with an employer by whom they have not previously been employed;

    (b)    participating in a scheme under which shelter is provided in return for work;

    (c)    participating in a scheme designed to provide training, work experience or temporary work;

    (d)    participating in a scheme to assist in the seeking or obtaining of work; . . .

    (e)    [undertaking] a course of higher education requiring attendance for a period of work experience; [or

    (f)    undertaking a course of further education requiring attendance for a period of work experience].]

(2)   The Secretary of State may by regulations make provision in relation to any of the persons to whom this section applies—

    (a)    preventing them being persons who qualify for the national minimum wage; or

    (b)    prescribing an hourly rate for the national minimum wage other than the single hourly rate for the time being prescribed under section 1(3) above.

(3)   No provision shall be made under subsection (2) above which treats persons differently in relation to—

    (a)    different areas;

    (b)    different sectors of employment;

    (c)    undertakings of different sizes; or

    (d)    different occupations.

(4)   If any description of persons who have attained the age of 26 is added by regulations under section 4 below to the descriptions of person to whom this section applies, no provision shall be made under subsection (2) above which treats persons of that description differently in relation to different ages over 26.

**NOTES**

Sub-s (1A): inserted by the National Minimum Wage Act 1998 (Amendment) Regulations 1999, SI 1999/583, reg 2; word omitted from para (d) repealed, word in square brackets in para (e) substituted, and para (f) (and the word immediately preceding it) inserted, by the National Minimum Wage Act 1998 (Amendment) Regulations 2007, SI 2007/2042, reg 2.

Regulations: the National Minimum Wage Regulations 1999, SI 1999/584 at **[2.398]**. Note that many Regulations have been made under this section that amend the principal 1999 Regulations, the most recent being the National Minimum Wage (Amendment) Regulations 2012, SI 2012/2397. The others are not listed here for reasons of space.

**[1.1122]**
### 4 Power to add to the persons to whom section 3 applies

(1) The Secretary of State may by regulations amend section 3 above by adding descriptions of persons who have attained the age of 26 to the descriptions of person to whom that section applies.
(2) No amendment shall be made under subsection (1) above which treats persons differently in relation to—
  (a) different areas;
  (b) different sectors of employment;
  (c) undertakings of different sizes;
  (d) different ages over 26; or
  (e) different occupations.

**NOTES**
  Regulations: National Minimum Wage Act 1998 (Amendment) Regulations 1999, SI 1999/583; the National Minimum Wage Act 1998 (Amendment) Regulations 2007, SI 2007/2042.

**5–8** ((*Establishment of, and references to, the Low Pay Commission) outside the scope of this work.*)

*Records*

**[1.1123]**
### 9 Duty of employers to keep records

For the purposes of this Act, the Secretary of State may by regulations make provision requiring employers—
  (a) to keep, in such form and manner as may be prescribed, such records as may be prescribed; and
  (b) to preserve those records for such period as may be prescribed.

**NOTES**
  Regulations: the National Minimum Wage Regulations 1999, SI 1999/584 at **[2.398]**.

**[1.1124]**
### 10 Worker's right of access to records

(1) A worker may, in accordance with the following provisions of this section,—
  (a) require his employer to produce any relevant records; and
  (b) inspect and examine those records and copy any part of them.
(2) The rights conferred by subsection (1) above are exercisable only if the worker believes on reasonable grounds that he is or may be being, or has or may have been, remunerated for any pay reference period by his employer at a rate which is less than the national minimum wage.
(3) The rights conferred by subsection (1) above are exercisable only for the purpose of establishing whether or not the worker is being, or has been, remunerated for any pay reference period by his employer at a rate which is less than the national minimum wage.
(4) The rights conferred by subsection (1) above are exercisable—
  (a) by the worker alone; or
  (b) by the worker accompanied by such other person as the worker may think fit.
(5) The rights conferred by subsection (1) above are exercisable only if the worker gives notice (a "production notice") to his employer requesting the production of any relevant records relating to such period as may be described in the notice.
(6) If the worker intends to exercise the right conferred by subsection (4)(b) above, the production notice must contain a statement of that intention.
(7) Where a production notice is given, the employer shall give the worker reasonable notice of the place and time at which the relevant records will be produced.
(8) The place at which the relevant records are produced must be—
  (a) the worker's place of work; or
  (b) any other place at which it is reasonable, in all the circumstances, for the worker to attend to inspect the relevant records; or
  (c) such other place as may be agreed between the worker and the employer.
(9) The relevant records must be produced—
  (a) before the end of the period of fourteen days following the date of receipt of the production notice; or
  (b) at such later time as may be agreed during that period between the worker and the employer.
(10) In this section—
  "records" means records which the worker's employer is required to keep and, at the time of receipt of the production notice, preserve in accordance with section 9 above;

"relevant records" means such parts of, or such extracts from, any records as are relevant to establishing whether or not the worker has, for any pay reference period to which the records relate, been remunerated by the employer at a rate which is at least equal to the national minimum wage.

**[1.1125]**
**11    Failure of employer to allow access to records**
(1)    A complaint may be presented to an employment tribunal by a worker on the ground that the employer—
    (a)    failed to produce some or all of the relevant records in accordance with subsections (8) and (9) of section 10 above; or
    (b)    failed to allow the worker to exercise some or all of the rights conferred by subsection (1)(b) or (4)(b) of that section.
(2)    Where an employment tribunal finds a complaint under this section well-founded, the tribunal shall—
    (a)    make a declaration to that effect; and
    (b)    make an award that the employer pay to the worker a sum equal to 80 times the hourly amount of the national minimum wage (as in force when the award is made).
(3)    An employment tribunal shall not consider a complaint under this section unless it is presented to the tribunal before the expiry of the period of three months following—
    (a)    the end of the period of fourteen days mentioned in paragraph (a) of subsection (9) of section 10 above; or
    (b)    in a case where a later day was agreed under paragraph (b) of that subsection, that later day.
(4)    Where the employment tribunal is satisfied that it was not reasonably practicable for a complaint under this section to be presented before the expiry of the period of three months mentioned in subsection (3) above, the tribunal may consider the complaint if it is presented within such further period as the tribunal considers reasonable.
[(4A)    Where the complaint is presented to an employment tribunal in England and Wales or Scotland, section 11A applies for the purposes of subsection (3).]
(5)    Expressions used in this section and in section 10 above have the same meaning in this section as they have in that section.

**NOTES**
Sub-s (4A): inserted by the Enterprise and Regulatory Reform Act 2013, s 8, Sch 2, paras 36, 37, as from a day to be appointed.
Conciliation: employment tribunal proceedings and claims which could be the subject of employment tribunal proceedings under or by virtue of this section are proceedings to which the Employment Tribunals Act 1996, s 18 applies; see s 18(1)(dd) of that Act at **[1.706]**.

**[1.1126]**
**[11A    Extension of time limit to facilitate conciliation before institution of proceedings**
(1)    In this section—
    (a)    Day A is the day on which the worker concerned complies with the requirement in subsection (1) of section 18A of the Employment Tribunals Act 1996 (requirement to contact ACAS before instituting proceedings) in relation to the matter in respect of which the proceedings are brought, and
    (b)    Day B is the day on which the worker concerned receives or, if earlier, is treated as receiving (by virtue of regulations made under subsection (11) of that section) the certificate issued under subsection (4) of that section.
(2)    In working out when the time limit set by section 11(3) expires the period beginning with the day after Day A and ending with Day B is not to be counted.
(3)    If the time limit set by section 11(3) would (if not extended by this subsection) expire during the period beginning with Day A and ending one month after Day B, the time limit expires instead at the end of that period.
(4)    The power conferred on the employment tribunal by subsection (4) of section 11 to extend the time limit set by subsection (3) of that section is exercisable in relation to that time limit as extended by this section.]

**NOTES**
Commencement: to be appointed.
Inserted by the Enterprise and Regulatory Reform Act 2013, s 8, Sch 2, paras 36, 38, as from a day to be appointed.

**[1.1127]**
**12    Employer to provide worker with national minimum wage statement**
(1)    Regulations may make provision for the purpose of conferring on a worker the right to be given by his employer, at or before the time at which any payment of remuneration is made to the worker, a written statement.

(2)   The regulations may make provision with respect to the contents of any such statement and may, in particular, require it to contain—
   (a)   prescribed information relating to this Act or any regulations under it; or
   (b)   prescribed information for the purpose of assisting the worker to determine whether he has been remunerated at a rate at least equal to the national minimum wage during the period to which the payment of remuneration relates.
(3)   Any statement required to be given under this section to a worker by his employer may, if the worker is an employee, be included in the written itemised pay statement required to be given to him by his employer under section 8 of the Employment Rights Act 1996 or Article 40 of the Employment Rights (Northern Ireland) Order 1996, as the case may be.
(4)   The regulations may make provision for the purpose of applying—
   (a)   sections 11 and 12 of the Employment Rights Act 1996 (references to employment tribunals and determination of references), or
   (b)   in relation to Northern Ireland, Articles 43 and 44 of the Employment Rights (Northern Ireland) Order 1996 (references to industrial tribunals and determination of references),
in relation to a worker and any such statement as is mentioned in subsection (1) above as they apply in relation to an employee and a statement required to be given to him by his employer under section 8 of that Act or Article 40 of that Order, as the case may be.

**NOTES**

Regulations: as of 6 April 2013 no Regulations had been made under this section.

*Officers*

**[1.1128]**
**13   Appointment of officers**
(1)   The Secretary of State—
   (a)   may appoint officers to act for the purposes of this Act; and
   (b)   may, instead of or in addition to appointing any officers under this section, arrange with any Minister of the Crown or government department, or any body performing functions on behalf of the Crown, that officers of that Minister, department or body shall act for those purposes.
(2)   When acting for the purposes of this Act, an officer shall, if so required, produce some duly authenticated document showing his authority so to act.
(3)   If it appears to an officer that any person with whom he is dealing while acting for the purposes of this Act does not know that he is an officer so acting, the officer shall identify himself as such to that person.

**[1.1129]**
**14   Powers of officers**
(1)   An officer acting for the purposes of this Act shall have power for the performance of his duties—
   (a)   to require the production by a relevant person of any records required to be kept and preserved in accordance with regulations under section 9 above and to inspect and examine those records and to copy   .  .  .   them;
   (b)   to require a relevant person to furnish to him (either alone or in the presence of any other person, as the officer thinks fit) an explanation of any such records;
   (c)   to require a relevant person to furnish to him (either alone or in the presence of any other person, as the officer thinks fit) any additional information known to the relevant person which might reasonably be needed in order to establish whether this Act, or any enforcement notice under section 19 below, is being or has been complied with;
   (d)   at all reasonable times to enter any relevant premises in order to exercise any power conferred on the officer by paragraphs (a) to (c) above.
(2)   No person shall be required under paragraph (b) or (c) of subsection (above to answer any question or furnish any information which might incriminate the person or, if [married or a civil partner, the person's spouse or civil partner].
(3)   The powers conferred by subsection (1) above include power, on reasonable written notice, to require a relevant person—
   (a)   to produce any such records as are mentioned in paragraph (a) of that subsection to an officer at such time and place as may be specified in the notice; or
   (b)   to attend before an officer at such time and place as may be specified in the notice to furnish any such explanation or additional information as is mentioned in paragraph (b) or (c) of that subsection.
[(3A)   The power of an officer to copy records under subsection (1)(a) includes a power to remove such records from the place where they are produced to him in order to copy them; but such records must be returned as soon as reasonably practicable to the relevant person by whom they are produced.]
(4)   In this section "relevant person" means any person whom an officer acting for the purposes of this Act has reasonable cause to believe to be—

(a) the employer of a worker;
(b) a person who for the purposes of section 34 below is the agent or the principal;
(c) a person who supplies work to an individual who qualifies for the national minimum wage;
(d) a worker, servant or agent of a person falling within paragraph (a), (b) or (c) above; or
(e) a person who qualifies for the national minimum wage.

(5) In this section "relevant premises" means any premises which an officer acting for the purposes of this Act has reasonable cause to believe to be—
(a) premises at which an employer carries on business;
(b) premises which an employer uses in connection with his business (including any place used, in connection with that business, for giving out work to home workers, within the meaning of section 35 below); or
(c) premises of a person who for the purposes of section 34 below is the agent or the principal.

**NOTES**

Sub-s (1): words omitted from para (a) repealed by the Employment Act 2008, s 10(1), (2), 20, Schedule, Pt 3, as from 13 January 2009 (subject to savings in s 10(4) of that Act in relation to the enforcement of the agricultural minimum wage in Scotland and Northern Ireland).

Sub-s (2): words in square brackets substituted by the Civil Partnership Act 2004, s 261(1), Sch 27, para 155.

Sub-s (3A): inserted by the Employment Act 2008, s 10(1), (3), as from 13 January 2009 (subject to savings in s 10(4) of that Act in relation to the enforcement of the agricultural minimum wage in Scotland and Northern Ireland).

*Information*

**[1.1130]**
**15 Information obtained by officers**
(1) This section applies to any information obtained by an officer acting for the purposes of this Act, whether by virtue of paragraph (a) or paragraph (b) of section 13(1) above.
(2) Information to which this section applies vests in the Secretary of State.
(3) Information to which this section applies may be used for any purpose relating to this Act by—
(a) the Secretary of State; or
(b) any relevant authority whose officer obtained the information.
(4) Information to which this section applies—
(a) may be supplied by, or with the authorisation of, the Secretary of State to any relevant authority for any purpose relating to this Act; and
(b) may be used by the recipient for any purpose relating to this Act.
(5) Information supplied under subsection (4) above—
(a) shall not be supplied by the recipient to any other person or body unless it is supplied for the purposes of any civil or criminal proceedings relating to this Act; and
(b) shall not be supplied in those circumstances without the authorisation of the Secretary of State.
[(5A) Information to which this section applies—
(a) may be supplied by, or with the authorisation of, the Secretary of State to an officer acting for the purposes of the Employment Agencies Act 1973 for any purpose relating to that Act; and
(b) may be used by an officer acting for the purposes of that Act for any purpose relating to that Act.]
[(6) This section—
(a) does not limit the circumstances in which information may be supplied or used apart from this section; and
(b) is subject to section 148 of the Finance Act 2000 (use of minimum wage information).]
[(6A) Nothing in this section prevents a disclosure in accordance with section 16A below.]
(7) Subsection (2) above does not affect the title or rights of—
(a) any person whose property the information was immediately before it was obtained as mentioned in subsection (1) above; or
(b) any person claiming title or rights through or under such a person otherwise than by virtue of any power conferred by or under this Act.
(8) In this section "relevant authority" means any Minister of the Crown who, or government department or other body which, is party to arrangements made with the Secretary of State which are in force under section 13(1)(b) above.

**NOTES**

Sub-s (5A): inserted by the Employment Act 2008, s 18(1), as from 6 April 2009, except in relation to any information obtained by an officer under this section before that date (see the Employment Act 2008 (Commencement No 2, Transitional Provisions and Savings) Order 2009, SI 2009/603, Schedule, para 3.

Sub-s (6): substituted by the Finance Act 2000, s 148(4).

Sub-s (6A): inserted by the Employment Relations Act 2004, s 57(1), Sch 1, para 40.

See further, as to the information to which this section applies, the Employment Relations Act 1999, s 39 at **[1.1205]**.

**[1.1131]**
**16   Information obtained by agricultural wages officers**
(1)   This section applies to information which has been obtained by an officer acting for the purposes of any of the agricultural wages legislation.
(2)   Information to which this section applies may, with the authorisation of the relevant authority, be supplied to the Secretary of State for use for any purpose relating to this Act.
(3)   Information supplied under subsection (2) above may be supplied by the recipient to any Minister of the Crown, government department or other body if—
  (a)   arrangements made between the recipient and that Minister, department or body under section 13(1)(b) above are in force; and
  (b)   the information is supplied for any purpose relating to this Act.
(4)   Except as provided by subsection (3) above, information supplied under subsection (2) or (3) above—
  (a)   shall not be supplied by the recipient to any other person or body unless it is supplied for the purposes of any civil or criminal proceedings relating to this Act; and
  (b)   shall not be supplied in those circumstances without the authorisation of the relevant authority.
(5)   This section does not limit the circumstances in which information may be supplied or used apart from this section.
[(5A)   Nothing in this section prevents a disclosure in accordance with section 16A below.]
(6)   In this section—
  "the agricultural wages legislation" means—
    *(a)   the Agricultural Wages Act 1948;*
    *(b)   the Agricultural Wages (Scotland) Act 1949; and*
    *(c)   the Agricultural Wages (Regulation) (Northern Ireland) Order 1977;*
  "relevant authority" means—
    *(a)   in relation to information obtained by an officer acting in England, the Minister of Agriculture, Fisheries and Food;*
    *(b)   in relation to information obtained by an officer acting in Wales, the Minister of the Crown with the function of appointing officers under section 12 of the Agricultural Wages Act 1948 in relation to Wales;*
    *(c)   in relation to information obtained by an officer acting in an area which is partly in England and partly in Wales, the Ministers mentioned in paragraphs (a) and (b) above acting jointly;*
    (d)   in relation to information obtained by an officer acting in Scotland, the Minister of the Crown with the function of appointing officers under section 12 of the Agricultural Wages (Scotland) Act 1949; and
    (e)   in relation to information obtained by an officer acting in Northern Ireland, the Department of Agriculture for Northern Ireland.

**NOTES**
Sub-s (5A): inserted by the Employment Relations Act 2004, s 57(1), Sch 1, para 41.
Sub-s (6): words in italics repealed by the Enterprise and Regulatory Reform Act 2013, s 72(4), Sch 20, as from a day to be appointed.
Transfer of functions in relation to Wales: as to the transfer of functions under this section from Ministers of the Crown to the National Assembly for Wales, see the National Assembly for Wales (Transfer of Functions) Order 1999, SI 1999/672.
Minister of Agriculture, Fisheries and Food: the Ministry of Agriculture, Fisheries and Food was dissolved and the functions of the Minister were transferred to the Secretary of State by the Ministry of Agriculture, Fisheries and Food (Dissolution) Order 2002, SI 2002/794.
See further the Employment Relations Act 1999, s 39 at **[1.1205]**.

**[1.1132]**
**[16A   Disclosure of information by officers**
(1)   Subsection (2) applies to information obtained for the purposes of the relevant legislation by an enforcement officer so far as that information relates to an identifiable worker or agency worker.
(2)   In order to enable or assist him to act for the purposes of the relevant legislation, the enforcement officer may disclose all or any of the information to the worker or, as the case may be, agency worker concerned.
(3)   Subsection (4) applies to information obtained for the purposes of the relevant legislation by an enforcement officer so far as that information relates to an identifiable employer or person who is the agent or the principal for the purposes of section 34 below.
(4)   In order to enable or assist him to act for the purposes of the relevant legislation, the officer may disclose all or any of the information to the employer, the agent or, as the case may be, the principal concerned.
(5)   In this section—
  "agency worker" shall be construed in accordance with section 34 below;
  "enforcement officer" means—

    (a)   an officer acting for the purposes of this Act, whether by virtue of paragraph (a) or (b) of section 13(1) above;

    *(b)   an officer acting for the purposes of the Agricultural Wages Act 1948; or*

    (c)   an officer acting for the purposes of the Agricultural Wages (Regulation) (Northern Ireland) Order 1977;

"the relevant legislation" means—

    (a)   in relation to an enforcement officer acting for the purposes of this Act, this Act;

    *(b)   in relation to an enforcement officer acting for the purposes of the Agricultural Wages Act 1948, that Act; and*

    (c)   in relation to an enforcement officer acting for the purposes of the Agricultural Wages (Regulation) (Northern Ireland) Order 1977, that Order.]

**NOTES**

Inserted by the Employment Relations Act 2004, s 44.

Sub-s (5): words in italics repealed by the Enterprise and Regulatory Reform Act 2013, s 72(4), Sch 20, as from a day to be appointed.

*Enforcement*

**[1.1133]**
**17   Non-compliance: worker entitled to additional remuneration**

(1)   If a worker who qualifies for the national minimum wage is remunerated for any pay reference period by his employer at a rate which is less than the national minimum wage, the worker shall [at any time ("the time of determination")] be taken to be entitled under his contract to be paid, as additional remuneration in respect of that period, [whichever is the higher of—

    (a)   the amount described in subsection (2) below, and

    (b)   the amount described in subsection (4) below].

(2)   [The amount referred to in subsection (1)(a) above] is the difference between—

    (a)   the relevant remuneration received by the worker for the pay reference period; and

    (b)   the relevant remuneration which the worker would have received for that period had he been remunerated by the employer at a rate equal to the national minimum wage.

(3)   In subsection (2) above, "relevant remuneration" means remuneration which falls to be brought into account for the purposes of regulations under section 2 above.

[(4)   The amount referred to in subsection (1)(b) above is the amount determined by the formula—

$$(A / R1) \times R2$$

where—

    A is the amount described in subsection (2) above,

    R1 is the rate of national minimum wage which was payable in respect of the worker during the pay reference period, and

    R2 is the rate of national minimum wage which would have been payable in respect of the worker during that period had the rate payable in respect of him during that period been determined by reference to regulations under section 1 and 3 above in force at the time of determination.

(5)   Subsection (1) above ceases to apply to a worker in relation to any pay reference period when he is at any time paid the additional remuneration for that period to which he is at that time entitled under that subsection.

(6)   Where any additional remuneration is paid to the worker under this section in relation to the pay reference period but subsection (1) above has not ceased to apply in relation to him, the amounts described in subsections (2) and (4) above shall be regarded as reduced by the amount of that remuneration.]

**NOTES**

Sub-s (1): words in first pair of square brackets inserted, and words in second pair of square brackets substituted, by the Employment Act 2008, s 8(1), (2), as from 6 April 2009 (subject to savings in s 8(7) of that Act in relation to the enforcement of the agricultural minimum wage in Scotland and Northern Ireland). Note also, that by s 8(8) of the 2008 Act, this amendment applies in relation to a pay reference period (within the meaning of this Act) ending before, as well as after, 6 April 2009.

Sub-s (2): words in square brackets substituted by the Employment Act 2008, s 8(1), (4), as from 6 April 2009 (subject to savings and transitional provisions in s 8(7), (8) of that Act as noted above).

Sub-ss (4)–(6): added by the Employment Act 2008, s 8(1), (5), as from 6 April 2009 (subject to savings and transitional provisions in s 8(7), (8) of that Act as noted above).

Transitional provisions and savings: see also the note to s 19 at **[1.1135]**.

**[1.1134]**
**18   Enforcement in the case of special classes of worker**

(1)   If the persons who are the worker and the employer for the purposes of section 17 above would not (apart from this section) fall to be regarded as the worker and the employer for the purposes of—

(a) Part II of the Employment Rights Act 1996 (protection of wages), or
(b) in relation to Northern Ireland, Part IV of the Employment Rights (Northern Ireland) Order 1996,

they shall be so regarded for the purposes of the application of that Part in relation to the entitlement conferred by that section.

(2) In the application by virtue of subsection (1) above of—
(a) Part II of the Employment Rights Act 1996, or
(b) Part IV of the Employment Rights (Northern Ireland) Order 1996,

in a case where there is or was, for the purposes of that Part, no worker's contract between the persons who are the worker and the employer for the purposes of section 17 above, it shall be assumed that there is or, as the case may be, was such a contract.

(3) For the purpose of enabling the amount described as additional remuneration in subsection (1) of section 17 above to be recovered in civil proceedings on a claim in contract in a case where in fact there is or was no worker's contract between the persons who are the worker and the employer for the purposes of that section, it shall be assumed for the purpose of any civil proceedings, so far as relating to that amount, that there is or, as the case may be, was such a contract.

**NOTES**

Conciliation: employment tribunal proceedings and claims which could be the subject of employment tribunal proceedings by virtue of this section are proceedings to which the Employment Tribunals Act 1996, s 18 applies; see s 18(1)(dd) of that Act at **[1.706]**.

**[1.1135]**
**[19 Notices of underpayment: arrears**
(1) Subsection (2) below applies where an officer acting for the purposes of this Act is of the opinion that, on any day ("the relevant day"), a sum was due under section 17 above for any one or more pay reference periods ending before the relevant day to a worker who at any time qualified for the national minimum wage.

(2) Where this subsection applies, the officer may, subject to this section, serve a notice requiring the employer to pay to the worker, within the 28-day period, the sum due to the worker under section 17 above for any one or more of the pay reference periods referred to in subsection (1) above.

(3) In this Act, "notice of underpayment" means a notice under this section.

(4) A notice of underpayment must specify, for each worker to whom it relates—
(a) the relevant day in relation to that worker;
(b) the pay reference period or periods in respect of which the employer is required to pay a sum to the worker as specified in subsection (2) above;
(c) the amount described in section 17(2) above in relation to the worker in respect of each such period;
(d) the amount described in section 17(4) above in relation to the worker in respect of each of such period;
(e) the sum due under section 17 above to the worker for each such period.

(5) Where a notice of underpayment relates to more than one worker, the notice may identify the workers by name or by description.

(6) The reference in subsection (1) above to a pay reference period includes (subject to subsection (7) below) a pay reference period ending before the coming into force of this section.

(7) A notice of underpayment may not relate to a pay reference period ending more than six years before the date of service of the notice.

(8) In this section and sections 19A to 19C below "the 28-day period" means the period of 28 days beginning with the date of service of the notice of underpayment.]

**NOTES**

Commencement: 6 April 2009.

Sections 19, 19A–19H were substituted for the original ss 19–22, and ss 22A–22F (as inserted by the Employment Relations Act 2004, s 46(1)), by the Employment Act 2008, s 9(1), as from 6 April 2009, subject to transitional provisions and savings as noted below.

Transitional provisions and savings:

(i) For savings in relation to the enforcement of the agricultural minimum wage in Scotland and Northern Ireland, see 9(7) of the 2008 Act.

(ii) The Employment Act 2008 (Commencement No 2, Transitional Provisions and Savings) Order 2009, SI 2009/603, Schedule, para 1 provides that the amendments to ss 17 and 19–22F of this Act made by ss 8 and 9 of the 2008 Act do not apply where an officer acting for the purposes of the Agricultural Wages Act 1948 required any person to produce records or provide information or explanations under s 14(1) of this Act before 6 April 2009 (except where an enforcement notice under s 19 of this Act is served after 6 April 2011).

(iii) SI 2009/603, Schedule, para 2 further provides that the substitution of ss 19–22F does not apply where an enforcement notice under s 19 of this Act is served before 6 April 2009.

**[1.1136]**
**[19A Notices of underpayment: financial penalty**
(1) A notice of underpayment must, subject to this section, require the employer to pay a financial penalty specified in the notice to the Secretary of State within the 28-day period.
(2) The Secretary of State may by directions specify circumstances in which a notice of underpayment is not to impose a requirement to pay a financial penalty.
(3) Directions under subsection (2) may be amended or revoked by further such directions.
(4) The amount of any financial penalty is, subject as follows, to be 50% of the total of the amounts referred to in subsection (5) below.
(5) Those amounts are the amounts specified under section 19(4)(c) above for all workers to whom the notice relates in respect of pay reference periods specified under section 19(4)(b) above which commence after the coming into force of this section.
(6) If a financial penalty as calculated under subsection (4) above would be less than £100, the financial penalty specified in the notice shall be that amount.
(7) If a financial penalty as calculated under subsection (4) above would be more than £5000, the financial penalty specified in the notice shall be that amount.
(8) The Secretary of State may by regulations—
   (a) amend subsection (4) above so as to substitute a different percentage for the percentage at any time specified there;
   (b) amend subsection (6) or (7) above so as to substitute a different amount for the amount at any time specified there.
(9) A notice of underpayment must, in addition to specifying the amount of any financial penalty, state how that amount was calculated.
(10) In a case where a notice of underpayment imposes a requirement to pay a financial penalty, if the employer on whom the notice is served, within the period of 14 days beginning with the day on which the notice was served—
   (a) pays the amount required under section 19(2) above, and
   (b) pays at least half the financial penalty,
he shall be regarded as having paid the financial penalty.
(11) A financial penalty paid to the Secretary of State pursuant to this section shall be paid by the Secretary of State into the Consolidated Fund.]

**NOTES**
Commencement: 6 April 2009.
Substituted subject to transitional provisions and savings as noted to s 19 at **[1.1135]**.
Regulations: as of 6 April 2013 no Regulations had been made under this section.

**[1.1137]**
**[19B Suspension of financial penalty**
(1) This section applies in any case where it appears to the officer serving a notice of underpayment which imposes a requirement to pay a financial penalty that—
   (a) relevant proceedings have been instituted; or
   (b) relevant proceedings may be instituted.
(2) In this section "relevant proceedings" means proceedings against the employer for an offence under section 31(1) below in relation to a failure to remunerate any worker to whom the notice relates for any pay reference period specified under section 19(4)(b) above in relation to that worker.
(3) The notice of underpayment may contain provision suspending the requirement to pay the financial penalty payable under the notice until a notice terminating the suspension is served on the employer.
(4) An officer acting for the purposes of this Act may serve on the employer a notice terminating the suspension ("a penalty activation notice") if it appears to the officer—
   (a) in a case referred to in subsection (1)(a) above, that relevant proceedings have concluded without the employer having been convicted of an offence under section 31(1) below, or
   (b) in a case referred to in subsection (1)(b) above—
      (i) that relevant proceedings will not be instituted; or
      (ii) that relevant proceedings have been concluded without the employer having been convicted of an offence under section 31(1) below.
(5) Where a penalty activation notice is served, the requirement to pay the financial penalty has effect as if the notice of underpayment had been served on the day on which the penalty activation notice was served.
(6) An officer acting for the purposes of this Act must serve on the employer a notice withdrawing the requirement to pay the financial penalty if it appears to the officer that, pursuant to relevant proceedings, the employer has been convicted of an offence under section 31(1) below.]

**NOTES**
Commencement: 6 April 2009.
Substituted subject to transitional provisions and savings as noted to s 19 at **[1.1135]**.

**[1.1138]**
**[19C  Notices of underpayment: appeals**
(1)  A person on whom a notice of underpayment is served may in accordance with this section appeal against any one or more of the following—
    (a)   the decision to serve the notice;
    (b)   any requirement imposed by the notice to pay a sum to a worker;
    (c)   any requirement imposed by the notice to pay a financial penalty.
(2)  An appeal under this section lies to an employment tribunal.
(3)  An appeal under this section must be made before the end of the 28-day period.
(4)  An appeal under subsection (1)(a) above must be made on the ground that no sum was due under section 17 above to any worker to whom the notice relates on the day specified under section 19(4)(a) above in relation to him in respect of any pay reference period specified under section 19(4)(b) above in relation to him.
(5)  An appeal under subsection (1)(b) above in relation to a worker must be made on either or both of the following grounds—
    (a)   that, on the day specified under section 19(4)(a) above in relation to the worker, no sum was due to the worker under section 17 above in respect of any pay reference period specified under section 19(4)(b) above in relation to him;
    (b)   that the amount specified in the notice as the sum due to the worker is incorrect.
(6)  An appeal under subsection (1)(c) above must be made on either or both of the following grounds—
    (a)   that the notice was served in circumstances specified in a direction under section 19A(2) above, or
    (b)   that the amount of the financial penalty specified in the notice of underpayment has been incorrectly calculated (whether because the notice is incorrect in some of the particulars which affect that calculation or for some other reason).
(7)  Where the employment tribunal allows an appeal under subsection (1)(a) above, it must rescind the notice.
(8)  Where, in a case where subsection (7) above does not apply, the employment tribunal allows an appeal under subsection (1)(b) or (c) above—
    (a)   the employment tribunal must rectify the notice, and
    (b)   the notice of underpayment shall have effect as rectified from the date of the employment tribunal's determination.]

**NOTES**
Commencement: 6 April 2009.
Substituted subject to transitional provisions and savings as noted to s 19 at **[1.1135]**.

**[1.1139]**
**[19D  Non-compliance with notice of underpayment: recovery of arrears**
(1)  If a requirement to pay a sum to a worker contained in a notice of underpayment is not complied with in whole or in part, an officer acting for the purposes of this Act may, on behalf of any worker to whom the requirement relates—
    (a)   present a complaint under section 23(1)(a) of the Employment Rights Act 1996 (deductions from worker's wages in contravention of section 13 of that Act) to an employment tribunal in respect of any sums due to the worker by virtue of section 17 above; or
    (b)   in relation to Northern Ireland, present a complaint under Article 55(1)(a) of the Employment Rights (Northern Ireland) Order 1996 (deductions from worker's wages in contravention of Article 45 of that Order) to an industrial tribunal in respect of any sums due to the worker by virtue of section 17 above; or
    (c)   commence other civil proceedings for the recovery, on a claim in contract, of any sums due to the worker by virtue of section 17 above.
(2)  The powers conferred by subsection (1) above for the recovery of sums due from an employer to a worker shall not be in derogation of any right which the worker may have to recover such sums by civil proceedings.]

**NOTES**
Commencement: 6 April 2009.
Substituted subject to transitional provisions and savings as noted to s 19 at **[1.1135]**.
Conciliation: employment tribunal proceedings and claims which could be the subject of employment tribunal proceedings by virtue of sub-s (1)(a) of this section are proceedings to which the Employment Tribunals Act 1996, s 18 applies; see s 18(1)(dd) of that Act at **[1.706]**. Note, however, that s 18(1)(dd) has not been amended to take account of the substitution of new ss 19, 19A–19H (for ss 19–22, 22A–22F) and that section still specifies s 20(1)(a) of this Act instead of the new s 19D(1)(a).

**[1.1140]**
**[19E  Non-compliance with notice of underpayment: recovery of penalty**
A financial penalty payable under a notice of underpayment—

(a)   in England and Wales, is recoverable, if *a county court* so orders, under section 85 of the County Courts Act 1984 or otherwise as if it were payable under an order of that court;

(b)   in Scotland, may be enforced in the same manner as an extract registered decree arbitral bearing a warrant for execution issued by the sheriff court of any sheriffdom in Scotland;

(c)   in Northern Ireland, is recoverable, if the county court so orders, as if it were payable under an order of that court.]

**NOTES**

Commencement: 6 April 2009.

Substituted subject to transitional provisions and savings as noted to s 19 at **[1.1135]**.

For the words in italics in para (a) there are substituted the words "the county court" by the Crime and Courts Act 2013, s 17(5), Sch 9, Pt 3, para 52, as from a day to be appointed.

Additional transitional provisions: before the coming into force of the Tribunals, Courts and Enforcement Act 2007, s 62, para (a) of this section has effect as if for the words "under section 85 of the County Courts Act 1984" there were substituted the words "by execution issued from the county court"; see the Employment Act 2008, s 9(2). As of 6 April 2013, s 62 had not come into force and no date for it to come into force had been appointed.

## [1.1141]
### [19F   Withdrawal of notice of underpayment

(1)   Where a notice of underpayment has been served (and not already withdrawn or rescinded) and it appears to an officer acting for the purposes of this Act that the notice incorrectly includes or omits any requirement or is incorrect in any particular, the officer may withdraw it by serving notice of the withdrawal on the employer.

(2)   Where a notice of underpayment is withdrawn and no replacement notice of underpayment is served in accordance with section 19G below—

(a)   any sum paid by or recovered from the employer by way of financial penalty payable under the notice must be repaid to him with interest at the appropriate rate running from the date when the sum was paid or recovered;

(b)   any appeal against the notice must be dismissed;

(c)   after the withdrawal no complaint may be presented or other civil proceedings commenced by virtue of section 19D above in reliance on any non-compliance with the notice before it was withdrawn;

(d)   any complaint or proceedings so commenced before the withdrawal may be proceeded with despite the withdrawal.

(3)   In a case where subsection (2) above applies, the notice of withdrawal must indicate the effect of that subsection (but a failure to do so does not make the withdrawal ineffective).

(4)   In subsection (2)(a) above, "the appropriate rate" means the rate that, on the date the sum was paid or recovered, was specified in section 17 of the Judgments Act 1838.]

**NOTES**

Commencement: 6 April 2009.

Substituted subject to transitional provisions and savings as noted to s 19 at **[1.1135]**.

## [1.1142]
### [19G   Replacement notice of underpayment

(1)   Where an officer acting for the purposes of this Act serves a notice of withdrawal under section 19F above and is of the opinion referred to in section 19(1) above in relation to any worker specified in the notice which is being withdrawn ("the original notice"), he may at the same time serve another notice under section 19 above ("the replacement notice").

(2)   The replacement notice may not relate to any worker to whom the original notice did not relate.

(3)   If the replacement notice contravenes subsection (2) above, that fact shall be an additional ground of appeal for the purposes of section 19C above.

(4)   The replacement notice may relate to a pay reference period ending after the date of service of the original notice.

(5)   Section 19(7) above applies in relation to the replacement notice as if the reference to six years before the date of service of the notice were a reference to six years before the date of service of the original notice.

(6)   The replacement notice must—

(a)   indicate the differences between it and the original notice that it is reasonable for the officer to consider are material; and

(b)   indicate the effect of section 19H below.

(7)   Failure to comply with subsection (6) above does not make the replacement notice ineffective.

(8)   Where a replacement notice is withdrawn under section 19F above, no further replacement notice may be served under subsection (1) above pursuant to the withdrawal.

(9)   Nothing in this section affects any power that arises apart from this section to serve a notice of underpayment in relation to any worker.]

**NOTES**
> Commencement: 6 April 2009.
> Substituted subject to transitional provisions and savings as noted to s 19 at **[1.1135]**.

**[1.1143]**
**[19H   Effect of replacement notice of underpayment**
(1) This section applies where a notice of underpayment is withdrawn under section 19F above and a replacement notice is served in accordance with section 19G above.
(2) If an appeal has been made under section 19C above against the original notice and the appeal has not been withdrawn or finally determined before the time when that notice is withdrawn—
   (a) that appeal ("the earlier appeal") shall have effect after that time as if it were against the replacement notice; and
   (b) the employer may exercise his right of appeal under section 19C above against the replacement notice only if he withdraws the earlier appeal.
(3) After the withdrawal no complaint may be presented or other civil proceedings commenced by virtue of section 19D above in reliance on any non-compliance with the notice before it was withdrawn; but any complaint or proceedings so commenced before the withdrawal may be proceeded with despite the withdrawal.
(4) If a sum was paid by or recovered from the employer by way of financial penalty under the original notice—
   (a) an amount equal to that sum (or, if more than one, the total of those sums) shall be treated as having been paid in respect of the replacement notice; and
   (b) any amount by which that sum (or total) exceeds the amount payable under the replacement notice must be repaid to the employer with interest at the appropriate rate running from the date when the sum (or, if more than one, the first of them) was paid or recovered.
(5) In subsection (4)(b) above "the appropriate rate" means the rate that, on the date mentioned in that provision, was specified in section 17 of the Judgments Act 1838.]

**NOTES**
> Commencement: 6 April 2009.
> Substituted subject to transitional provisions and savings as noted to s 19 at **[1.1135]**.

**20–22, 22A–22H** *(Substituted, subject to transitional provisions and savings, by new ss 19, 19A–19H, as noted to s 19 at* **[1.1135]**.*)*

*Rights not to suffer unfair dismissal or other detriment*

**[1.1144]**
**23   The right not to suffer detriment**
(1) A worker has the right not to be subjected to any detriment by any act, or any deliberate failure to act, by his employer, done on the ground that—
   (a) any action was taken, or was proposed to be taken, by or on behalf of the worker with a view to enforcing, or otherwise securing the benefit of, a right of the worker's to which this section applies; or
   (b) the employer was prosecuted for an offence under section 31 below as a result of action taken by or on behalf of the worker for the purpose of enforcing, or otherwise securing the benefit of, a right of the worker's to which this section applies; or
   (c) the worker qualifies, or will or might qualify, for the national minimum wage or for a particular rate of national minimum wage.
(2) It is immaterial for the purposes of paragraph (a) or (b) of subsection (1) above—
   (a) whether or not the worker has the right, or
   (b) whether or not the right has been infringed,
but, for that subsection to apply, the claim to the right and, if applicable, the claim that it has been infringed must be made in good faith.
(3) The following are the rights to which this section applies—
   (a) any right conferred by, or by virtue of, any provision of this Act for which the remedy for its infringement is by way of a complaint to an employment tribunal; and
   (b) any right conferred by section 17 above.
[(4) This section does not apply where the detriment in question amounts to dismissal within the meaning of—
   (a) Part X of the Employment Rights Act 1996 (unfair dismissal), or
   (b) Part XI of the Employment Rights (Northern Ireland) Order 1996 (corresponding provision for Northern Ireland),
  . . . ]

**[1.1145]**
**24   Enforcement of the right**
(1)   A worker may present a complaint to an employment tribunal that he has been subjected to a detriment in contravention of section 23 above.
(2)   Subject to the following provisions of this section, the provisions of—
  (a)   *sections 48(2) to (4)* and 49 of the Employment Rights Act 1996 (complaints to employment tribunals and remedies), or
  (b)   in relation to Northern Ireland, Articles 71(2) to (4) and 72 of the Employment Rights (Northern Ireland) Order 1996 (complaints to industrial tribunals and remedies),
shall apply in relation to a complaint under this section as they apply in relation to a complaint under section 48 of that Act or Article 71 of that Order (as the case may be), but taking references in those provisions to the employer as references to the employer within the meaning of section 23(1) above.
(3)   Where—
  (a)   the detriment to which the worker is subjected is the termination of his worker's contract, but
  (b)   that contract is not a contract of employment,
any compensation awarded under section 49 of the Employment Rights Act 1996 or Article 72 of the Employment Rights (Northern Ireland) Order 1996 by virtue of subsection (2) above must not exceed the limit specified in subsection (4) below.
(4)   The limit mentioned in subsection (3) above is the total of—
  (a)   the sum which would be the basic award for unfair dismissal, calculated in accordance with section 119 of the Employment Rights Act 1996 or Article 153 of the Employment Rights (Northern Ireland) Order 1996 (as the case may be), if the worker had been an employee and the contract terminated had been a contract of employment; and
  (b)   the sum for the time being specified in section 124(1) of that Act or Article 158(1) of that Order (as the case may be) which is the limit for a compensatory award to a person calculated in accordance with section 123 of that Act or Article 157 of that Order (as the case may be).
(5)   Where the worker has been working under arrangements which do not fall to be regarded as a worker's contract for the purposes of—
  (a)   the Employment Rights Act 1996, or
  (b)   in relation to Northern Ireland, the Employment Rights (Northern Ireland) Order 1996,
he shall be treated for the purposes of subsections (3) and (4) above as if any arrangements under which he has been working constituted a worker's contract falling within section 230(3)(b) of that Act or Article 3(3)(b) of that Order (as the case may be).

**25, 26**   (*S 25 inserts the Employment Rights Act 1996, s 104A at* **[1.908]**, *amends ss 105, 108 of that Act at* **[1.915]**, **[1.918]**, *and amended s 109 (repealed); s 26 applies to Northern Ireland (outside the scope of this work).*)

*Civil procedure, evidence and appeals*

**27**   (*Sub-s (1) amends the Employment Tribunals Act 1996, s 4(3) at* **[1.682]**; *sub-s (2) applies to Northern Ireland (outside the scope of this work).*)

**[1.1146]**
**28 Reversal of burden of proof**
(1)   Where in any civil proceedings any question arises as to whether an individual qualifies or qualified at any time for the national minimum wage, it shall be presumed that the individual qualifies or, as the case may be, qualified at that time for the national minimum wage unless the contrary is established.
(2)   Where—
   (a)   a complaint is made—
      (i)   to an employment tribunal under section 23(1)(a) of the Employment Rights Act 1996 (unauthorised deductions from wages), or
      (ii)   to an industrial tribunal under Article 55(1)(a) of the Employment Rights (Northern Ireland) Order 1996, and
   (b)   the complaint relates in whole or in part to the deduction of the amount described as additional remuneration in section 17(1) above,
it shall be presumed for the purposes of the complaint, so far as relating to the deduction of that amount, that the worker in question was remunerated at a rate less than the national minimum wage unless the contrary is established.
(3)   Where in any civil proceedings a person seeks to recover on a claim in contract the amount described as additional remuneration in section 17(1) above, it shall be presumed for the purposes of the proceedings, so far as relating to that amount, that the worker in question was remunerated at a rate less than the national minimum wage unless the contrary is established.

**29**   *(Amends the Employment Tribunals Act 1996, s 21(1) at* **[1.713]**.)

*Conciliation*

**30**   *(Sub-s (1) amends the Employment Tribunals Act 1996, s 18(1) at* **[1.706]**; *sub-s (2) applies to Northern Ireland (outside the scope of this work).)*

*Offences*

**[1.1147]**
**31 Offences**
(1)   If the employer of a worker who qualifies for the national minimum wage refuses or wilfully neglects to remunerate the worker for any pay reference period at a rate which is at least equal to the national minimum wage, that employer is guilty of an offence.
(2)   If a person who is required to keep or preserve any record in accordance with regulations under section 9 above fails to do so, that person is guilty of an offence.
(3)   If a person makes, or knowingly causes or allows to be made, in a record required to be kept in accordance with regulations under section 9 above any entry which he knows to be false in a material particular, that person is guilty of an offence.
(4)   If a person, for purposes connected with the provisions of this Act, produces or furnishes, or knowingly causes or allows to be produced or furnished, any record or information which he knows to be false in a material particular, that person is guilty of an offence.
(5)   If a person—
   (a)   intentionally delays or obstructs an officer acting for the purposes of this Act in the exercise of any power conferred by this Act, or
   (b)   refuses or neglects to answer any question, furnish any information or produce any document when required to do so under section 14(1) above,
that person is guilty of an offence.
(6)   Where the commission by any person of an offence under subsection (1) or (2) above is due to the act or default of some other person, that other person is also guilty of the offence.
(7)   A person may be charged with and convicted of an offence by virtue of subsection (6) above whether or not proceedings are taken against any other person.
(8)   In any proceedings for an offence under subsection (1) or (2) above it shall be a defence for the person charged to prove that he exercised all due diligence and took all reasonable precautions to secure that the provisions of this Act, and of any relevant regulations made under it, were complied with by himself and by any person under his control.
(9)   A person guilty of an offence under this section shall be liable—
   [(a)   on conviction on indictment, to a fine, or
   (b)   on summary conviction, to a fine not exceeding the statutory maximum].

**NOTES**
Sub-s (9): words in square brackets substituted by the Employment Act 2008, s 11(1), as from 6 April 2009 (subject to savings in s 11(3) of that Act in relation to the enforcement of the agricultural minimum wage in Scotland and Northern Ireland).

**[1.1148]**
**32 Offences by bodies corporate etc**
(1)   This section applies to any offence under this Act.
(2)   If an offence committed by a body corporate is proved—

(a)   to have been committed with the consent or connivance of an officer of the body, or

(b)   to be attributable to any neglect on the part of such an officer,

the officer as well as the body corporate is guilty of the offence and liable to be proceeded against and punished accordingly.

(3)   In subsection (2) above "officer", in relation to a body corporate, means a director, manager, secretary or other similar officer of the body, or a person purporting to act in any such capacity.

(4)   If the affairs of a body corporate are managed by its members, subsection (2) above applies in relation to the acts and defaults of a member in connection with his functions of management as if he were a director of the body corporate.

(5)   If an offence committed by a partnership in Scotland is proved—

(a)   to have been committed with the consent or connivance of a partner, or

(b)   to be attributable to any neglect on the part of a partner,

the partner as well as the partnership is guilty of the offence and liable to be proceeded against and punished accordingly.

(6)   In subsection (5) above, "partner" includes a person purporting to act as a partner.

**[1.1149]**
**33   Proceedings for offences**
(1)   The persons who may conduct proceedings for an offence under this Act—

(a)   . . .

(b)   in Northern Ireland, before a court of summary jurisdiction,

shall include any person authorised for the purpose by the Secretary of State even if that person is not a barrister or solicitor.

[(1A)   The persons who may conduct proceedings for an offence under this Act in England and Wales, before a magistrates' court, shall include any person authorised for the purpose by the Secretary of State.]

(2)–(5)   . . .

---

NOTES

Sub-s (1): para (a) repealed by the Legal Services Act 2007, ss 208(1), 210, Sch 21, paras 124, 125(a), Sch 23, as from 1 January 2010.

Sub-s (1A): inserted by the Legal Services Act 2007, s 208(1), Sch 21, paras 124, 125(b), as from 1 January 2010.

Sub-ss (2)–(5): repealed by the Employment Act 2008, ss 11(2), 20, Schedule, Pt 4, as from 6 April 2009 (subject to savings in s 11(3) of that Act in relation to the enforcement of the agricultural minimum wage in Scotland and Northern Ireland).

---

*Special classes of person*

**[1.1150]**
**34   Agency workers who are not otherwise "workers"**
(1)   This section applies in any case where an individual ("the agency worker")—

(a)   is supplied by a person ("the agent") to do work for another ("the principal") under a contract or other arrangements made between the agent and the principal; but

(b)   is not, as respects that work, a worker, because of the absence of a worker's contract between the individual and the agent or the principal; and

(c)   is not a party to a contract under which he undertakes to do the work for another party to the contract whose status is, by virtue of the contract, that of a client or customer of any profession or business undertaking carried on by the individual.

(2)   In a case where this section applies, the other provisions of this Act shall have effect as if there were a worker's contract for the doing of the work by the agency worker made between the agency worker and—

(a)   whichever of the agent and the principal is responsible for paying the agency worker in respect of the work; or

(b)   if neither the agent nor the principal is so responsible, whichever of them pays the agency worker in respect of the work.

**[1.1151]**
**35   Home workers who are not otherwise "workers"**
(1)   In determining for the purposes of this Act whether a home worker is or is not a worker, section 54(3)(b) below shall have effect as if for the word "personally" there were substituted "(whether personally or otherwise)".

(2)   In this section "home worker" means an individual who contracts with a person, for the purposes of that person's business, for the execution of work to be done in a place not under the control or management of that person.

**[1.1152]**
**36   Crown employment**
(1)   Subject to section 37 below, the provisions of this Act have effect in relation to Crown employment and persons in Crown employment as they have effect in relation to other employment and other workers.

(2)   In this Act, subject to section 37 below, "Crown employment" means employment under or for the purposes of a government department or any officer or body exercising on behalf of the Crown functions conferred by statutory provision.

(3)   For the purposes of the application of the other provisions of this Act in relation to Crown employment in accordance with subsection (1) above—

(a)   references to an employee or a worker shall be construed as references to a person in Crown employment;

(b)   references to a contract of employment or a worker's contract shall be construed as references to the terms of employment of a person in Crown employment; and

(c)   references to dismissal, or to the termination of a worker's contract, shall be construed as references to the termination of Crown employment.

## [1.1153]
## 37   Armed forces

(1)   A person serving as a member of the naval, military or air forces of the Crown does not qualify for the national minimum wage in respect of that service.

(2)   Section 36 above applies to employment by an association established for the purposes of Part XI of the Reserve Forces Act 1996, notwithstanding anything in subsection (1) above.

## [1.1154]
## [37A   Cadet Force Adult Volunteers

(1)   A person (not being a person to whom section 37(1) above applies) who—

(a)   is a member of any of the forces specified in subsection (2) below, and

(b)   assists the activities of those forces otherwise than in the course of Crown employment,

does not qualify for the national minimum wage in respect of anything done by him in so assisting those activities.

(2)   The forces referred to in subsection (1) above are—

(a)   the Combined Cadet Force;

(b)   the Sea Cadet Corps;

(c)   the Army Cadet Force;

(d)   the Air Training Corps.]

**NOTES**

Commencement: 13 January 2009.

Inserted by the Employment Act 2008, s 13, as from 13 January 2009.

## [1.1155]
## 38   House of Lords staff

(1)   Apart from section 21 above, the provisions of this Act have effect in relation to employment as a relevant member of the House of Lords staff as they have effect in relation to other employment.

(2)   Nothing in any rule of law or the law or practice of Parliament prevents a relevant member of the House of Lords staff from bringing before the High Court or *a county court* any claim under this Act.

(3)   In this section "relevant member of the House of Lords staff" means any person who is employed under a worker's contract with the Corporate Officer of the House of Lords.

**NOTES**

Sub-s (2): for the words in italics there are substituted the words "the county court" by the Crime and Courts Act 2013, s 17(5), Sch 9, Pt 3, para 52, as from a day to be appointed.

## [1.1156]
## 39   House of Commons staff

(1)   Apart from section 21 above, the provisions of this Act have effect in relation to employment as a relevant member of the House of Commons staff as they have effect in relation to other employment.

(2)   Nothing in any rule of law or the law or practice of Parliament prevents a relevant member of the House of Commons staff from bringing before the High Court or *a county court* any claim under this Act.

(3)   In this section "relevant member of the House of Commons staff" means any person—

(a)   who was appointed by the House of Commons Commission; or

(b)   who is a member of the Speaker's personal staff.

**NOTES**

Sub-s (2): for the words in italics there are substituted the words "the county court" by the Crime and Courts Act 2013, s 17(5), Sch 9, Pt 3, para 52, as from a day to be appointed.

**[1.1157]**
**40 Mariners**
For the purposes of this Act, an individual employed to work on board a ship registered in the United Kingdom under Part II of the Merchant Shipping Act 1995 shall be treated as an individual who under his contract ordinarily works in the United Kingdom unless—
(a) the employment is wholly outside the United Kingdom; or
(b) the person is not ordinarily resident in the United Kingdom;
and related expressions shall be construed accordingly.

*Extensions*

**[1.1158]**
**41 Power to apply Act to individuals who are not otherwise "workers"**
The Secretary of State may by regulations make provision for this Act to apply, with or without modifications, as if—
(a) any individual of a prescribed description who would not otherwise be a worker for the purposes of this Act were a worker for those purposes;
(b) there were in the case of any such individual a worker's contract of a prescribed description under which the individual works; and
(c) a person of a prescribed description were the employer under that contract.

**NOTES**
Regulations: as of 6 April 2013 no Regulations had been made under this section.

**[1.1159]**
**42 Power to apply Act to offshore employment**
(1) In this section "offshore employment" means employment for the purposes of activities—
(a) in the territorial waters of the United Kingdom, or
(b) connected with the exploration of the sea-bed or subsoil, or the exploitation of their natural resources, in the United Kingdom sector of the continental shelf, or
(c) connected with the exploration or exploitation, in a foreign sector of the continental shelf, of a cross-boundary petroleum field.
(2) Her Majesty may by Order in Council provide that the provisions of this Act apply, to such extent and for such purposes as may be specified in the Order (with or without modification), to or in relation to a person in offshore employment.
(3) An Order in Council under this section—
(a) may provide that all or any of the provisions of this Act, as applied by such an Order in Council, apply—
(i) to individuals whether or not they are British subjects, and
(ii) to bodies corporate whether or not they are incorporated under the law of a part of the United Kingdom,
and apply even where the application may affect their activities outside the United Kingdom,
(b) may make provision for conferring jurisdiction on any court or class of court specified in the Order in Council, or on employment tribunals, in respect of offences, causes of action or other matters arising in connection with offshore employment,
(c) may (without prejudice to subsection (2) above) provide that the provisions of this Act, as applied by the Order in Council, apply in relation to any person in employment in a part of the areas referred to in subsection (1)(a) and (b) above,
(d) may exclude from the operation of section 3 of the Territorial Waters Jurisdiction Act 1878 (consents required for prosecutions) proceedings for offences under this Act in connection with offshore employment,
(e) may provide that such proceedings shall not be brought without such consent as may be required by the Order in Council,
(f) may (without prejudice to subsection (2) above) modify or exclude the operation of sections 1(2)(b) and 40 above.
(4) Any jurisdiction conferred on a court or tribunal under this section is without prejudice to jurisdiction exercisable apart from this section by that or any other court or tribunal.
(5) In this section—
"cross-boundary petroleum field" means a petroleum field that extends across the boundary between the United Kingdom sector of the continental shelf and a foreign sector of the continental shelf,
"foreign sector of the continental shelf" means an area outside the territorial waters of any state, within which rights with respect to the sea-bed and subsoil and their natural resources are exercisable by a state other than the United Kingdom,
"petroleum field" means a geological structure identified as an oil or gas field by the Order in Council concerned, and

"United Kingdom sector of the continental shelf" means the area designated under section 1(7) of the Continental Shelf Act 1964.

**NOTES**

Orders: the National Minimum Wage (Offshore Employment) Order 1999, SI 1999/1128. This Order in Council has the effect of extending the provisions of this Act to workers who work, or ordinarily work, in the territorial waters of the UK. It also extends the operation of this Act to workers who work, or ordinarily work, in the UK sector of the continental shelf where the employment is: (a) connected with the exploration of the sea-bed or its subsoil, or the exploitation of their natural resources in the UK sector of the continental shelf; or (b) connected with the exploration or exploitation, in a foreign sector of the continental shelf, of a cross-boundary petroleum field. Note that the 1999 Order has no application in respect of ships in navigation, or engaged in fishing or dredging. As to the application of this Act to mariners, see s 40 *ante*.

*Exclusions*

**[1.1160]**
**43　Share fishermen**
A person—
  (a)　employed as master, or as a member of the crew, of a fishing vessel, and
  (b)　remunerated, in respect of that employment, only by a share in the profits or gross earnings of the vessel,
does not qualify for the national minimum wage in respect of that employment.

**[1.1161]**
**44　Voluntary workers**
(1)　A worker employed by a charity, a voluntary organisation, an associated fund-raising body or a statutory body does not qualify for the national minimum wage in respect of that employment if he receives, and under the terms of his employment (apart from this Act) is entitled to,—
  (a)　no monetary payments of any description, or no monetary payments except in respect of expenses—
　　(i)　actually incurred in the performance of his duties; or
　　(ii)　reasonably estimated as likely to be or to have been so incurred; and
  (b)　no benefits in kind of any description, or no benefits in kind other than the provision of some or all of his subsistence or of such accommodation as is reasonable in the circumstances of the employment.
[(1A)　For the purposes of subsection (1)(a) above, expenses which—
  (a)　are incurred in order to enable the worker to perform his duties,
  (b)　are reasonably so incurred, and
  (c)　are not accommodation expenses,
are to be regarded as actually incurred in the performance of his duties.]
(2)　A person who would satisfy the conditions in subsection (1) above but for receiving monetary payments made solely for the purpose of providing him with means of subsistence shall be taken to satisfy those conditions if—
  (a)　he is employed to do the work in question as a result of arrangements made between a charity acting in pursuance of its charitable purposes and the body for which the work is done; and
  (b)　the work is done for a charity, a voluntary organisation, an associated fund-raising body or a statutory body.
(3)　For the purposes of subsection (1)(b) above—
  (a)　any training (other than that which a person necessarily acquires in the course of doing his work) shall be taken to be a benefit in kind; but
  (b)　there shall be left out of account any training provided for the sole or main purpose of improving the worker's ability to perform the work which he has agreed to do.
(4)　In this section—
  "associated fund-raising body" means a body of persons the profits of which are applied wholly for the purposes of a charity or voluntary organisation;
  "charity" means a body of persons, or the trustees of a trust, established for charitable purposes only;
  "receive", in relation to a monetary payment or a benefit in kind, means receive in respect of, or otherwise in connection with, the employment in question (whether or not under the terms of the employment);
  "statutory body" means a body established by or under an enactment (including an enactment comprised in Northern Ireland legislation);
  "subsistence" means such subsistence as is reasonable in the circumstances of the employment in question, and does not include accommodation;
  "voluntary organisation" means a body of persons, or the trustees of a trust, which is established only for charitable purposes (whether or not those purposes are charitable within the meaning of any rule of law), benevolent purposes or philanthropic purposes, but which is not a charity.

**NOTES**

Sub-s (1A): inserted by the Employment Act 2008, s 14, as from 13 January 2009.

**[1.1162]**
**[44A Religious and other communities: resident workers**
(1)   A residential member of a community to which this section applies does not qualify for the national minimum wage in respect of employment by the community.
(2)   Subject to subsection (3), this section applies to a community if—
   (a)   it is a charity or is established by a charity,
   (b)   a purpose of the community is to practise or advance a belief of a religious or similar nature, and
   (c)   all or some of its members live together for that purpose.
(3)   This section does not apply to a community which—
   (a)   is an independent school [or an alternative provision Academy that is not an independent school], or
   (b)   provides a course of further or higher education.
(4)   The residential members of a community are those who live together as mentioned in subsection (2)(c).
(5)   In this section—
   (a)   "charity" has the same meaning as in section 44, and
   (b)   "independent school" has the same meaning as in section 463 of the Education Act 1996 (in England and Wales), section 135 of the Education (Scotland) Act 1980 (in Scotland) and Article 2 of the Education and Libraries (Northern Ireland) Order 1986 (in Northern Ireland).
(6)   In this section "course of further or higher education" means—
   (a)   in England and Wales, a course of a description referred to in Schedule 6 to the Education Reform Act 1988 or Schedule 2 to the Further and Higher Education Act 1992;
   (b)   in Scotland, a course or programme of a description mentioned in or falling within section 6(1) or 38 of the Further and Higher Education (Scotland) Act 1992;
   (c)   in Northern Ireland, a course of a description referred to in Schedule 1 to the Further Education (Northern Ireland) Order 1997 or a course providing further education within the meaning of Article 3 of that Order.]

**NOTES**

Inserted by the Employment Relations Act 1999, s 22.

Sub-s (3): words in square brackets inserted by the Alternative Provision Academies (Consequential Amendments to Acts) (England) Order 2012, SI 2012/976, art 2, Schedule, para 10, as from 1 April 2012.

Further and Higher Education Act 1992: Sch 2 to that Act was repealed by the Learning and Skills Act 2000, s 153, Sch 11.

**[1.1163]**
**45 Prisoners**
(1)   A prisoner does not qualify for the national minimum wage in respect of any work which he does in pursuance of prison rules.
(2)   In this section—
   "prisoner" means a person detained in, or on temporary release from, a prison;
   "prison" includes any other institution to which prison rules apply;
   "prison rules" means—
      (a)   in relation to England and Wales, rules made under section 47 [or 47A] of the Prison Act 1952;
      (b)   in relation to Scotland, rules made under section 39 of the Prisons (Scotland) Act 1989; and
      (c)   in relation to Northern Ireland, rules made under section 13 of the Prison Act (Northern Ireland) 1953.

**NOTES**

Sub-s (2): words in square brackets in the definition "prison rules" inserted by the Legal Aid, Sentencing and Punishment of Offenders Act 2012, s 129(9), as from a day to be appointed.

**[1.1164]**
**[45A Persons discharging fines by unpaid work**
A person does not qualify for the national minimum wage in respect of any work that he does in pursuance of a work order under Schedule 6 to the Courts Act 2003 (discharge of fines by unpaid work).]

**NOTES**

Inserted by the Courts Act 2003, s 109(1), Sch 8, para 382.

**[1.1165]**
**[45B   Immigration: detained persons**
Section 153A of the Immigration and Asylum Act 1999 (c 33) (persons detained in removal centres) disqualifies certain persons for the national minimum wage.]

**NOTES**
Inserted by the Immigration, Asylum and Nationality Act 2006, s 59(2).

**46, 47**   (*Agricultural workers: outside the scope of this work.*)

*Miscellaneous*

**[1.1166]**
**48   Application of Act to superior employers**
Where—
> (a)    the immediate employer of a worker is himself in the employment of some other person, and
> (b)    the worker is employed on the premises of that other person,

that other person shall be deemed for the purposes of this Act to be the employer of the worker jointly with the immediate employer.

**[1.1167]**
**49   Restrictions on contracting out**
(1)   Any provision in any agreement (whether a worker's contract or not) is void in so far as it purports—
> (a)    to exclude or limit the operation of any provision of this Act; or
> (b)    to preclude a person from bringing proceedings under this Act before an employment tribunal.

(2)   Subsection (1) above does not apply to any agreement to refrain from instituting or continuing proceedings where a conciliation officer has taken action under—
> (a)    *section 18* of the Employment Tribunals Act 1996 (conciliation), or
> (b)    in relation to Northern Ireland, Article 20 of the Industrial Tribunals (Northern Ireland) Order 1996.

(3)   Subsection (1) above does not apply to any agreement to refrain from instituting or continuing before an employment tribunal any proceedings within—
> (a)    section 18(1)(dd) of the Employment Tribunals Act 1996 (proceedings under or by virtue of this Act where conciliation is available), or
> (b)    in relation to Northern Ireland, Article 20(1)(cc) of the Industrial Tribunals (Northern Ireland) Order 1996,

if the conditions regulating *compromise* agreements under this Act are satisfied in relation to the agreement.

(4)   For the purposes of subsection (3) above the conditions regulating *compromise* agreements under this Act are that—
> (a)    the agreement must be in writing,
> (b)    the agreement must relate to the particular proceedings,
> (c)    the employee or worker must have received advice from a relevant independent adviser as to the terms and effect of the proposed agreement and, in particular, its effect on his ability to pursue his rights before an employment tribunal,
> (d)    there must be in force, when the adviser gives the advice, a contract of insurance, or an indemnity provided for members of a profession or a professional body, covering the risk of a claim by the employee or worker in respect of loss arising in consequence of the advice,
> (e)    the agreement must identify the adviser, and
> (f)    the agreement must state that the conditions regulating *compromise* agreements under this Act are satisfied.

(5)   A person is a relevant independent adviser for the purposes of subsection (4)(c) above—
> (a)    if he is a qualified lawyer,
> (b)    if he is an officer, official, employee or member of an independent trade union who has been certified in writing by the trade union as competent to give advice and as authorised to do so on behalf of the trade union,
> (c)    if he works at an advice centre (whether as an employee or a volunteer) and has been certified in writing by the centre as competent to give advice and as authorised to do so on behalf of the centre, or
> (d)    if he is a person of a description specified in an order made by the Secretary of State.

(6)   But a person is not a relevant independent adviser for the purposes of subsection (4)(c) above in relation to the employee or worker—
> (a)    if he is employed by, or is acting in the matter for, the employer or an associated employer,
> (b)    in the case of a person within subsection (5)(b) or (c) above, if the trade union or advice centre is the employer or an associated employer,

(c)   in the case of a person within subsection (5)(c) above, if the employee or worker makes a payment for the advice received from him, or

(d)   in the case of a person of a description specified in an order under subsection (5)(d) above, if any condition specified in the order in relation to the giving of advice by persons of that description is not satisfied.

(7)   In this section "qualified lawyer" means—

[(a)   as regards England and Wales, a person who, for the purposes of the Legal Services Act 2007, is an authorised person in relation to an activity which constitutes the exercise of a right of audience or the conduct of litigation (within the meaning of that Act);]

(b)   as respects Scotland—

(i)   an advocate (whether in practice as such or employed to give legal advice); or

(ii)   a solicitor who holds a practising certificate; and

(c)   as respects Northern Ireland—

(i)   a barrister (whether in practice as such or employed to give legal advice); or

(ii)   a solicitor who holds a practising certificate.

(8)   For the purposes of this section any two employers shall be treated as associated if—

(a)   one is a company of which the other (directly or indirectly) has control; or

(b)   both are companies of which a third person (directly or indirectly) has control;

and "associated employer" shall be construed accordingly.

(8A)–(11)   *(Apply to Northern Ireland: outside the scope of this work.)*

**NOTES**

Sub-s (2): for the words in italics in para (a) there are substituted the words "any of sections 18A to 18C" by the Enterprise and Regulatory Reform Act 2013, s 7(2), Sch 1, para 11, as from a day to be appointed.

Sub-ss (3), (4): for the word "compromise" in italics there is substituted the word "settlement" by the Enterprise and Regulatory Reform Act 2013, s 23(3)(a), as from a day to be appointed.

Sub-s (7): para (a) substituted by the Legal Services Act 2007, s 208(1), Sch 21, paras 124, 126, as from 1 January 2010.

Orders: the Compromise Agreements (Description of Person) Order 2004, SI 2004/754 at **[2.786]**; the Compromise Agreements (Description of Person) Order 2004 (Amendment) Order 2004, SI 2004/2515.

**50**   *((Publicity for the Act and Regulations) outside the scope of this work.)*

*Supplementary*

**[1.1168]**

**51   Regulations and orders**

(1)   Except to the extent that this Act makes provision to the contrary, any power conferred by this Act to make an Order in Council, regulations or an order includes power—

(a)   to make different provision for different cases or for different descriptions of person; and

(b)   to make incidental, consequential, supplemental or transitional provision and savings.

(2)   Paragraph (a) of subsection (1) above does not have effect in relation to regulations under section 1(3) above or an order under section 49 above.

(3)   No recommendation shall be made to Her Majesty to make an Order in Council under any provision of this Act unless a draft of the Order in Council has been laid before Parliament and approved by a resolution of each House of Parliament.

(4)   Any power of a Minister of the Crown to make regulations or an order under this Act shall be exercisable by statutory instrument.

(5)   A statutory instrument containing (whether alone or with other provisions) regulations under this Act shall not be made unless a draft of the instrument has been laid before, and approved by a resolution of, each House of Parliament.

(6)   Subsection (5) above shall not have effect in relation to a statutory instrument if the only regulations under this Act which the instrument contains are regulations under section . . . 47(2) or (4) above.

(7)   A statutory instrument—

(a)   which contains (whether alone or with other provisions) any regulations under section . . . 47(2) or (4) above or an order under section 49 above, and

(b)   which is not subject to any requirement that a draft of the instrument be laid before, and approved by a resolution of, each House of Parliament,

shall be subject to annulment in pursuance of a resolution of either House of Parliament.

(8)   The power—

(a)   of the Department of Economic Development to make an order under section 26(6) above, or

(b)   of the Department of Agriculture for Northern Ireland to make regulations under section 47 above,

shall be exercisable by statutory rule for the purposes of the Statutory Rules (Northern Ireland) Order 1979; and any such order or regulations shall be subject to negative resolution within the meaning of section 41(6) of the Interpretation Act (Northern Ireland) 1954.

**NOTES**

Sub-ss (6), (7): words omitted repealed by the Employment Act 2008, ss 9(3), 20, Schedule, Pt 2, as from 6 April 2009 (subject to savings in s 9(7) of that Act in relation to the enforcement of the agricultural minimum wage in Scotland and Northern Ireland).

**[1.1169]**
## 52 Expenses
There shall be paid out of money provided by Parliament—
   (a)   any expenditure incurred under this Act by a Minister of the Crown or government department or by a body performing functions on behalf of the Crown; and
   (b)   any increase attributable to the provisions of this Act in the sums payable out of such money under any other Act.

**53**   (*Introduces Sch 3 (repeals and revocations).*)

**[1.1170]**
## 54 Meaning of "worker", "employee" etc
(1)   In this Act "employee" means an individual who has entered into or works under (or, where the employment has ceased, worked under) a contract of employment.
(2)   In this Act "contract of employment" means a contract of service or apprenticeship, whether express or implied, and (if it is express) whether oral or in writing.
(3)   In this Act "worker" (except in the phrases "agency worker" and "home worker") means an individual who has entered into or works under (or, where the employment has ceased, worked under)—
   (a)   a contract of employment; or
   (b)   any other contract, whether express or implied and (if it is express) whether oral or in writing, whereby the individual undertakes to do or perform personally any work or services for another party to the contract whose status is not by virtue of the contract that of a client or customer of any profession or business undertaking carried on by the individual;
and any reference to a worker's contract shall be construed accordingly.
(4)   In this Act "employer", in relation to an employee or a worker, means the person by whom the employee or worker is (or, where the employment has ceased, was) employed.
(5)   In this Act "employment"—
   (a)   in relation to an employee, means employment under a contract of employment; and
   (b)   in relation to a worker, means employment under his contract;
and "employed" shall be construed accordingly.

**[1.1171]**
## 55 Interpretation
(1)   In this Act, unless the context otherwise requires,—
   "civil proceedings" means proceedings before an employment tribunal or civil proceedings before any other court;
   "enforcement notice" shall be construed in accordance with section 19 above;
   "government department" includes a Northern Ireland department, except in section 52(a) above;
   "industrial tribunal" means a tribunal established under Article 3 of the Industrial Tribunals (Northern Ireland) Order 1996;
   "notice" means notice in writing;
   "pay reference period" shall be construed in accordance with section 1(4) above;
   "penalty notice" shall be construed in accordance with section 21 above;
   "person who qualifies for the national minimum wage" shall be construed in accordance with section 1(2) above; and related expressions shall be construed accordingly;
   "prescribe" means prescribe by regulations;
   "regulations" means regulations made by the Secretary of State, except in the case of regulations under section 47(2) or (4) above made *by the Secretary of State and the Minister of Agriculture, Fisheries and Food acting jointly or* by the Department of Agriculture for Northern Ireland.
(2)   Any reference in this Act to a person being remunerated for a pay reference period is a reference to the person being remunerated by his employer in respect of his work in that pay reference period.
(3)   Any reference in this Act to doing work includes a reference to performing services; and "work" and other related expressions shall be construed accordingly.
(4)   For the purposes of this Act, a person ceases to be of compulsory school age in Scotland when he ceases to be of school age in accordance with sections 31 and 33 of the Education (Scotland) Act 1980.

(5)   Any reference in this Act to a person ceasing to be of compulsory school age shall, in relation to Northern Ireland, be construed in accordance with Article 46 of the Education and Libraries (Northern Ireland) Order 1986.

(6)   Any reference in this Act to an employment tribunal shall, in relation to Northern Ireland, be construed as a reference to an industrial tribunal.

**NOTES**

Sub-s (1): words in italics in the definition "regulations" repealed by the Enterprise and Regulatory Reform Act 2013, s 72(4), Sch 20, as from a day to be appointed.

Note: with regard to the definitions "enforcement notice" and "penalty notice", note that ss 19 and 21 of this Act have been substituted as noted *ante* and no longer make reference to these terms.

Minister of Agriculture, Fisheries and Food: the Ministry of Agriculture, Fisheries and Food was dissolved and the functions of the Minister were transferred to the Secretary of State by the Ministry of Agriculture, Fisheries and Food (Dissolution) Order 2002, SI 2002/794.

**[1.1172]**
**56   Short title, commencement and extent**
(1)   This Act may be cited as the National Minimum Wage Act 1998.
(2)   Apart from this section and any powers to make an Order in Council or regulations or an order (which accordingly come into force on the day on which this Act is passed) the provisions of this Act shall come into force on such day or days as the Secretary of State may by order appoint; and different days may be appointed for different purposes.
(3)   This Act extends to Northern Ireland.

**NOTES**

Orders: the National Minimum Wage Act 1998 (Commencement No 1 and Transitional Provisions) Order 1998, SI 1998/2574; the National Minimum Wage Act 1998 (Commencement No 2 and Transitional Provisions) Order 1999, SI 1999/685.

## SCHEDULES 1–3

*Sch 1 (provisions as to the Low Pay Commission), and Sch 2 (amendments to agricultural wages legislation) outside the scope of this work; Sch 3 contains repeals and revocations only and, in so far as relevant to this work, these have been incorporated at the appropriate place.)*

# HUMAN RIGHTS ACT 1998

## (1998 c 42)

### ARRANGEMENT OF SECTIONS

*Introduction*

## SCHEDULES

*An Act to give further effect to rights and freedoms guaranteed under the European Convention on Human Rights; to make provision with respect to holders of certain judicial offices who become judges of the European Court of Human Rights; and for connected purposes*

[9 November 1998]

**NOTES**

Only certain provisions of this Act are included: those omitted are outside the scope of this work for reasons given in notes thereto.

*Introduction*

**[1.1173]**
## 1 The Convention Rights
(1) In this Act "the Convention rights" means the rights and fundamental freedoms set out in—
    (a) Articles 2 to 12 and 14 of the Convention,
    (b) Articles 1 to 3 of the First Protocol, and
    (c) [Article 1 of the Thirteenth Protocol],
as read with Articles 16 to 18 of the Convention.
(2) Those Articles are to have effect for the purposes of this Act subject to any designated derogation or reservation (as to which see sections 14 and 15).
(3) The Articles are set out in Schedule 1.
(4) The [Secretary of State] may by order make such amendments to this Act as he considers appropriate to reflect the effect, in relation to the United Kingdom, of a protocol.
(5) In subsection (4) "protocol" means a protocol to the Convention—
    (a) which the United Kingdom has ratified; or
    (b) which the United Kingdom has signed with a view to ratification.
(6) No amendment may be made by an order under subsection (4) so as to come into force before the protocol concerned is in force in relation to the United Kingdom.

**NOTES**

Sub-s (1): words in square brackets in para (c) substituted by the Human Rights Act 1998 (Amendment) Order 2004, SI 2004/1574, art 2(1).

Sub-s (4): words in square brackets substituted by the Secretary of State for Constitutional Affairs Order 2003, SI 2003/1887, art 9, Sch 2, para 10(1).

Orders: the Human Rights Act 1998 (Amendment) Order 2004, SI 2004/1574.

**[1.1174]**
## 2 Interpretation of Convention rights
(1) A court or tribunal determining a question which has arisen in connection with a Convention right must take into account any—
    (a) judgment, decision, declaration or advisory opinion of the European Court of Human Rights,
    (b) opinion of the Commission given in a report adopted under Article 31 of the Convention,
    (c) decision of the Commission in connection with Article 26 or 27(2) of the Convention, or
    (d) decision of the Committee of Ministers taken under Article 46 of the Convention,
whenever made or given, so far as, in the opinion of the court or tribunal, it is relevant to the proceedings in which that question has arisen.
(2) Evidence of any judgment, decision, declaration or opinion of which account may have to be taken under this section is to be given in proceedings before any court or tribunal in such manner as may be provided by rules.
(3) In this section "rules" means rules of court or, in the case of proceedings before a tribunal, rules made for the purposes of this section—
    (a) by . . . [the Lord Chancellor or] the Secretary of State, in relation to any proceedings outside Scotland;
    (b) by the Secretary of State, in relation to proceedings in Scotland; or
    (c) by a Northern Ireland department, in relation to proceedings before a tribunal in Northern Ireland—
        (i) which deals with transferred matters; and
        (ii) for which no rules made under paragraph (a) are in force.

Part 1 Statutes

**NOTES**
Sub-s (3): words omitted from para (a) repealed by the Secretary of State for Constitutional Affairs Order 2003, SI 2003/1887, art 9, Sch 2, para 10(2); words in square brackets in para (a) inserted by the Transfer of Functions (Lord Chancellor and Secretary of State) Order 2005, SI 2005/3429, art 8, Schedule, para 3.
Rules: the Act of Adjournal (Criminal Procedure Rules Amendment No 2) (Human Rights Act 1998) 2000, SSI 2000/315; the Act of Sederunt (Rules of the Court of Session Amendment No 6) (Human Rights Act 1998) 2000, SSI 2000/316.

*Legislation*

**[1.1175]**
**3 Interpretation of legislation**
(1)  So far as it is possible to do so, primary legislation and subordinate legislation must be read and given effect in a way which is compatible with the Convention rights.
(2)  This section—
  (a)  applies to primary legislation and subordinate legislation whenever enacted;
  (b)  does not affect the validity, continuing operation or enforcement of any incompatible primary legislation; and
  (c)  does not affect the validity, continuing operation or enforcement of any incompatible subordinate legislation if (disregarding any possibility of revocation) primary legislation prevents removal of the incompatibility.

**[1.1176]**
**4 Declaration of incompatibility**
(1)  Subsection (2) applies in any proceedings in which a court determines whether a provision of primary legislation is compatible with a Convention right.
(2)  If the court is satisfied that the provision is incompatible with a Convention right, it may make a declaration of that incompatibility.
(3)  Subsection (4) applies in any proceedings in which a court determines whether a provision of subordinate legislation, made in the exercise of a power conferred by primary legislation, is compatible with a Convention right.
(4)  If the court is satisfied—
  (a)  that the provision is incompatible with a Convention right, and
  (b)  that (disregarding any possibility of revocation) the primary legislation concerned prevents removal of the incompatibility,
it may make a declaration of that incompatibility.
(5)  In this section "court" means—
  [(a)  the Supreme Court;]
  (b)  the Judicial Committee of the Privy Council;
  (c)  the [Court Martial Appeal Court];
  (d)  in Scotland, the High Court of Justiciary sitting otherwise than as a trial court or the Court of Session;
  (e)  in England and Wales or Northern Ireland, the High Court or the Court of Appeal;
  [(f)  the Court of Protection, in any matter being dealt with by the President of the Family Division, the *Vice-Chancellor* or a puisne judge of the High Court].
(6)  A declaration under this section ("a declaration of incompatibility")—
  (a)  does not affect the validity, continuing operation or enforcement of the provision in respect of which it is given; and
  (b)  is not binding on the parties to the proceedings in which it is made.

**NOTES**
Sub-s (5): para (a) substituted by the Constitutional Reform Act 2005, s 40, Sch 9, Pt 1, para 66(1), (2), as from 1 October 2009; words in square brackets in para (c) substituted by the Armed Forces Act 2006, s 378(1), Sch 16, para 156, as from 31 October 2009; para (f) added by the Mental Capacity Act 2005, s 67(1), Sch 6, para 43; for the words in italics in para (f) there are substituted the words "Chancellor of the High Court", by the Crime and Courts Act 2013, s 21(4), Sch 14, Pt 3, para 5(5), as from a day to be appointed.

**5**  (*Right of Crown to intervene in certain proceedings (outside the scope of this work).*)

*Public authorities*
**[1.1177]**
**6 Acts of public authorities**
(1)  It is unlawful for a public authority to act in a way which is incompatible with a Convention right.
(2)  Subsection (1) does not apply to an act if—
  (a)  as the result of one or more provisions of primary legislation, the authority could not have acted differently; or
  (b)  in the case of one or more provisions of, or made under, primary legislation which cannot be read or given effect in a way which is compatible with the Convention rights, the authority was acting so as to give effect to or enforce those provisions.

(3)   In this section "public authority" includes—
   (a)   a court or tribunal, and
   (b)   any person certain of whose functions are functions of a public nature,
but does not include either House of Parliament or a person exercising functions in connection with proceedings in Parliament.
(4)   . . .
(5)   In relation to a particular act, a person is not a public authority by virtue only of subsection (3)(b) if the nature of the act is private.
(6)   "An act" includes a failure to act but does not include a failure to—
   (a)   introduce in, or lay before, Parliament a proposal for legislation; or
   (b)   make any primary legislation or remedial order.

**NOTES**
  Sub-s (4): repealed by the Constitutional Reform Act 2005, ss 40, 146, Sch 9, Pt 1, para 66(1), (4), Sch 18, Pt 5, as from 1 October 2009.

**[1.1178]**
**7   Proceedings**
(1)   A person who claims that a public authority has acted (or proposes to act) in a way which is made unlawful by section 6(1) may—
   (a)   bring proceedings against the authority under this Act in the appropriate court or tribunal, or
   (b)   rely on the Convention right or rights concerned in any legal proceedings,
but only if he is (or would be) a victim of the unlawful act.
(2)   In subsection (1)(a) "appropriate court or tribunal" means such court or tribunal as may be determined in accordance with rules; and proceedings against an authority include a counterclaim or similar proceeding.
(3)   If the proceedings are brought on an application for judicial review, the applicant is to be taken to have a sufficient interest in relation to the unlawful act only if he is, or would be, a victim of that act.
(4)   If the proceedings are made by way of a petition for judicial review in Scotland, the applicant shall be taken to have title and interest to sue in relation to the unlawful act only if he is, or would be, a victim of that act.
(5)   Proceedings under subsection (1)(a) must be brought before the end of—
   (a)   the period of one year beginning with the date on which the act complained of took place; or
   (b)   such longer period as the court or tribunal considers equitable having regard to all the circumstances,
but that is subject to any rule imposing a stricter time limit in relation to the procedure in question.
(6)   In subsection (1)(b) "legal proceedings" includes—
   (a)   proceedings brought by or at the instigation of a public authority; and
   (b)   an appeal against the decision of a court or tribunal.
(7)   For the purposes of this section, a person is a victim of an unlawful act only if he would be a victim for the purposes of Article 34 of the Convention if proceedings were brought in the European Court of Human Rights in respect of that act.
(8)   Nothing in this Act creates a criminal offence.
(9)   In this section "rules" means—
   (a)   in relation to proceedings before a court or tribunal outside Scotland, rules made by  . . .  [the Lord Chancellor or] the Secretary of State for the purposes of this section or rules of court,
   (b)   in relation to proceedings before a court or tribunal in Scotland, rules made by the Secretary of State for those purposes,
   (c)   in relation to proceedings before a tribunal in Northern Ireland—
      (i)    which deals with transferred matters; and
      (ii)   for which no rules made under paragraph (a) are in force,
      rules made by a Northern Ireland department for those purposes,
and includes provision made by order under section 1 of the Courts and Legal Services Act 1990.
(10)   In making rules, regard must be had to section 9.
(11)   The Minister who has power to make rules in relation to a particular tribunal may, to the extent he considers it necessary to ensure that the tribunal can provide an appropriate remedy in relation to an act (or proposed act) of a public authority which is (or would be) unlawful as a result of section 6(1), by order add to—
   (a)   the relief or remedies which the tribunal may grant; or
   (b)   the grounds on which it may grant any of them.
(12)   An order made under subsection (11) may contain such incidental, supplemental, consequential or transitional provision as the Minister making it considers appropriate.
(13)   "The Minister" includes the Northern Ireland department concerned.

**NOTES**
Sub-s (9): words omitted from para (a) repealed by the Secretary of State for Constitutional Affairs Order 2003, SI 2003/1887, art 9, Sch 2, para 10(2); words in square brackets in para (a) inserted by the Transfer of Functions (Lord Chancellor and Secretary of State) Order 2005, SI 2005/3429, art 8, Schedule, para 3.
Rules: the Human Rights Act 1998 (Jurisdiction) (Scotland) Rules 2000, SSI 2000/301; the Proscribed Organisations Appeal Commission (Human Rights Act 1998 Proceedings) Rules 2006, SI 2006/2290.
Orders: as of 6 April 2013 no Orders had been made under sub-s (11).

**[1.1179]**
## 8 Judicial remedies

(1) In relation to any act (or proposed act) of a public authority which the court finds is (or would be) unlawful, it may grant such relief or remedy, or make such order, within its powers as it considers just and appropriate.

(2) But damages may be awarded only by a court which has power to award damages, or to order the payment of compensation, in civil proceedings.

(3) No award of damages is to be made unless, taking account of all the circumstances of the case, including—

    (a)    any other relief or remedy granted, or order made, in relation to the act in question (by that or any other court), and

    (b)    the consequences of any decision (of that or any other court) in respect of that act,

the court is satisfied that the award is necessary to afford just satisfaction to the person in whose favour it is made.

(4) In determining—

    (a)    whether to award damages, or

    (b)    the amount of an award,

the court must take into account the principles applied by the European Court of Human Rights in relation to the award of compensation under Article 41 of the Convention.

(5) A public authority against which damages are awarded is to be treated—

    (a)    in Scotland, for the purposes of section 3 of the Law Reform (Miscellaneous Provisions) (Scotland) Act 1940 as if the award were made in an action of damages in which the authority has been found liable in respect of loss or damage to the person to whom the award is made;

    (b)    for the purposes of the Civil Liability (Contribution) Act 1978 as liable in respect of damage suffered by the person to whom the award is made.

(6) In this section—

"court" includes a tribunal;

"damages" means damages for an unlawful act of a public authority; and

"unlawful" means unlawful under section 6(1).

**9** (*Proceedings and remedies in respect of judicial acts (outside the scope of this work).*)

*Remedial action*

**[1.1180]**
## 10 Power to take remedial action

(1) This section applies if—

    (a)    a provision of legislation has been declared under section 4 to be incompatible with a Convention right and, if an appeal lies—

        (i)    all persons who may appeal have stated in writing that they do not intend to do so;

        (ii)    the time for bringing an appeal has expired and no appeal has been brought within that time; or

        (iii)    an appeal brought within that time has been determined or abandoned; or

    (b)    it appears to a Minister of the Crown or Her Majesty in Council that, having regard to a finding of the European Court of Human Rights made after the coming into force of this section in proceedings against the United Kingdom, a provision of legislation is incompatible with an obligation of the United Kingdom arising from the Convention.

(2) If a Minister of the Crown considers that there are compelling reasons for proceeding under this section, he may by order make such amendments to the legislation as he considers necessary to remove the incompatibility.

(3) If, in the case of subordinate legislation, a Minister of the Crown considers—

    (a)    that it is necessary to amend the primary legislation under which the subordinate legislation in question was made, in order to enable the incompatibility to be removed, and

    (b)    that there are compelling reasons for proceeding under this section,

he may by order make such amendments to the primary legislation as he considers necessary.

(4) This section also applies where the provision in question is in subordinate legislation and has been quashed, or declared invalid, by reason of incompatibility with a Convention right and the Minister proposes to proceed under paragraph 2(b) of Schedule 2.

Part 1 Statutes

(5)   If the legislation is an Order in Council, the power conferred by subsection (2) or (3) is exercisable by Her Majesty in Council.
(6)   In this section "legislation" does not include a Measure of the Church Assembly or of the General Synod of the Church of England.
(7)   Schedule 2 makes further provision about remedial orders.

**NOTES**

Orders: the Marriage Act 1949 (Remedial) Order 2007, SI 2007/438; the Asylum and Immigration (Treatment of Claimants, etc) Act 2004 (Remedial) Order 2011, SI 2011/1158; the Sexual Offences Act 2003 (Remedial) Order 2012, SI 2012/1883.

*Other rights and proceedings*

**[1.1181]**
**11   Safeguard for existing human rights**
A person's reliance on a Convention right does not restrict—
(a)   any other right or freedom conferred on him by or under any law having effect in any part of the United Kingdom; or
(b)   his right to make any claim or bring any proceedings which he could make or bring apart from sections 7 to 9.

**12**   (*Restrictions on grant of relief affecting freedom of expression (outside the scope of this work).*)

**[1.1182]**
**13   Freedom of thought, conscience and religion**
(1)   If a court's determination of any question arising under this Act might affect the exercise by a religious organisation (itself or its members collectively) of the Convention right to freedom of thought, conscience and religion, it must have particular regard to the importance of that right.
(2)   In this section "court" includes a tribunal.

**14–18**   (*Ss 14–17 (derogations and reservations), s 18 (appointment of judges of the European Court of Human Rights) outside the scope of this work.*)

*Parliamentary procedure*

**[1.1183]**
**19   Statements of compatibility**
(1)   A Minister of the Crown in charge of a Bill in either House of Parliament must, before Second Reading of the Bill—
(a)   make a statement to the effect that in his view the provisions of the Bill are compatible with the Convention rights ("a statement of compatibility"); or
(b)   make a statement to the effect that although he is unable to make a statement of compatibility the government nevertheless wishes the House to proceed with the Bill.
(2)   The statement must be in writing and be published in such manner as the Minister making it considers appropriate.

*Supplemental*

**[1.1184]**
**20   Orders etc under this Act**
(1)   Any power of a Minister of the Crown to make an order under this Act is exercisable by statutory instrument.
(2)   The power of  . . .  [the Lord Chancellor or] the Secretary of State to make rules (other than rules of court) under section 2(3) or 7(9) is exercisable by statutory instrument.
(3)   Any statutory instrument made under section 14, 15 or 16(7) must be laid before Parliament.
(4)   No order may be made by  . . .  [the Lord Chancellor or] the Secretary of State under section 1(4), 7(11) or 16(2) unless a draft of the order has been laid before, and approved by, each House of Parliament.
(5)   Any statutory instrument made under section 18(7) or Schedule 4, or to which subsection (2) applies, shall be subject to annulment in pursuance of a resolution of either House of Parliament.
(6)   The power of a Northern Ireland department to make—
(a)   rules under section 2(3)(c) or 7(9)(c), or
(b)   an order under section 7(11),
is exercisable by statutory rule for the purposes of the Statutory Rules (Northern Ireland) Order 1979.
(7)   Any rules made under section 2(3)(c) or 7(9)(c) shall be subject to negative resolution; and section 41(6) of the Interpretation Act (Northern Ireland) 1954 (meaning of "subject to negative resolution") shall apply as if the power to make the rules were conferred by an Act of the Northern Ireland Assembly.
(8)   No order may be made by a Northern Ireland department under section 7(11) unless a draft of the order has been laid before, and approved by, the Northern Ireland Assembly.

**NOTES**

Sub-ss (2), (4): words omitted repealed by the Secretary of State for Constitutional Affairs Order 2003, SI 2003/1887, art 9, Sch 2, para 10(2); words in square brackets inserted by the Transfer of Functions (Lord Chancellor and Secretary of State) Order 2005, SI 2005/3429, art 8, Schedule, para 3.

**[1.1185]**
## 21 Interpretation, etc
(1) In this Act—

"amend" includes repeal and apply (with or without modifications);

"the appropriate Minister" means the Minister of the Crown having charge of the appropriate authorised government department (within the meaning of the Crown Proceedings Act 1947);

"the Commission" means the European Commission of Human Rights;

"the Convention" means the Convention for the Protection of Human Rights and Fundamental Freedoms, agreed by the Council of Europe at Rome on 4th November 1950 as it has effect for the time being in relation to the United Kingdom;

"declaration of incompatibility" means a declaration under section 4;

"Minister of the Crown" has the same meaning as in the Ministers of the Crown Act 1975;

"Northern Ireland Minister" includes the First Minister and the deputy First Minister in Northern Ireland;

"primary legislation" means any—
- (a) public general Act;
- (b) local and personal Act;
- (c) private Act;
- (d) Measure of the Church Assembly;
- (e) Measure of the General Synod of the Church of England;
- (f) Order in Council—
  - (i) made in exercise of Her Majesty's Royal Prerogative;
  - (ii) made under section 38(1)(a) of the Northern Ireland Constitution Act 1973 or the corresponding provision of the Northern Ireland Act 1998; or
  - (iii) amending an Act of a kind mentioned in paragraph (a), (b) or (c);

  and includes an order or other instrument made under primary legislation (otherwise than by the [Welsh Ministers, the First Minister for Wales, the Counsel General to the Welsh Assembly Government], a member of the Scottish Executive, a Northern Ireland Minister or a Northern Ireland department) to the extent to which it operates to bring one or more provisions of that legislation into force or amends any primary legislation;

"the First Protocol" means the protocol to the Convention agreed at Paris on 20th March 1952;

". . ."

"the Eleventh Protocol" means the protocol to the Convention (restructuring the control machinery established by the Convention) agreed at Strasbourg on 11th May 1994;

["the Thirteenth Protocol" means the protocol to the Convention (concerning the abolition of the death penalty in all circumstances) agreed at Vilnius on 3rd May 2002;]

"remedial order" means an order under section 10;

"subordinate legislation" means any—
- (a) Order in Council other than one—
  - (i) made in exercise of Her Majesty's Royal Prerogative;
  - (ii) made under section 38(1)(a) of the Northern Ireland Constitution Act 1973 or the corresponding provision of the Northern Ireland Act 1998; or
  - (iii) amending an Act of a kind mentioned in the definition of primary legislation;
- (b) Act of the Scottish Parliament;
- [(ba) Measure of the National Assembly for Wales;
- (bb) Act of the National Assembly for Wales;]
- (c) Act of the Parliament of Northern Ireland;
- (d) Measure of the Assembly established under section 1 of the Northern Ireland Assembly Act 1973;
- (e) Act of the Northern Ireland Assembly;
- (f) order, rules, regulations, scheme, warrant, byelaw or other instrument made under primary legislation (except to the extent to which it operates to bring one or more provisions of that legislation into force or amends any primary legislation);
- (g) order, rules, regulations, scheme, warrant, byelaw or other instrument made under legislation mentioned in paragraph (b), (c), (d) or (e) or made under an Order in Council applying only to Northern Ireland;
- (h) order, rules, regulations, scheme, warrant, byelaw or other instrument made by a member of the Scottish Executive[, Welsh Ministers, the First Minister for Wales,

the Counsel General to the Welsh Assembly Government], a Northern Ireland Minister or a Northern Ireland department in exercise of prerogative or other executive functions of Her Majesty which are exercisable by such a person on behalf of Her Majesty;

"transferred matters" has the same meaning as in the Northern Ireland Act 1998; and

"tribunal" means any tribunal in which legal proceedings may be brought.

(2)   The references in paragraphs (b) and (c) of section 2(1) to Articles are to Articles of the Convention as they had effect immediately before the coming into force of the Eleventh Protocol.

(3)   The reference in paragraph (d) of section 2(1) to Article 46 includes a reference to Articles 32 and 54 of the Convention as they had effect immediately before the coming into force of the Eleventh Protocol.

(4)   The references in section 2(1) to a report or decision of the Commission or a decision of the Committee of Ministers include references to a report or decision made as provided by paragraphs 3, 4 and 6 of Article 5 of the Eleventh Protocol (transitional provisions).

(5)    . . .

**NOTES**

Sub-s (1) is amended as follows:

Words in square brackets in the definition "primary legislation" substituted by the Government of Wales Act 2006, s 160(1), Sch 10, para 56(1), (2).

Definition "the Sixth Protocol" (omitted) repealed, and definition "the Thirteenth Protocol" inserted, by the Human Rights Act 1998 (Amendment) Order 2004, SI 2004/1574, art 2(2).

In definition "subordinate legislation" paras (ba), (bb) inserted, and words in square brackets in para (h) inserted, by the Government of Wales Act 2006, s 160(1), Sch 10, para 56(1), (3), (4).

Sub-s (5): repealed by the Armed Forces Act 2006, s 378(2), Sch 17, as from 31 October 2009.

**[1.1186]**
**22   Short title, commencement, application and extent**
(1)   This Act may be cited as the Human Rights Act 1998.
(2)   Sections 18, 20 and 21(5) and this section come into force on the passing of this Act.
(3)   The other provisions of this Act come into force on such day as the Secretary of State may by order appoint; and different days may be appointed for different purposes.
(4)   Paragraph (b) of subsection (1) of section 7 applies to proceedings brought by or at the instigation of a public authority whenever the act in question took place; but otherwise that subsection does not apply to an act taking place before the coming into force of that section.
(5)   This Act binds the Crown.
(6)   This Act extends to Northern Ireland.
(7)    . . .

**NOTES**

Sub-s (7): repealed by the Armed Forces Act 2006, s 378(2), Sch 17, as from 31 October 2009.

Orders: the Human Rights Act 1998 (Commencement) Order 1998, SI 1998/2882; the Human Rights Act 1998 (Commencement No 2) Order 2000, SI 2000/1851.

## SCHEDULES

## SCHEDULE 1
## THE ARTICLES

Section 1(3)

## PART I
## THE CONVENTION

### RIGHTS AND FREEDOMS

*Article 2*
*Right to life*

**[1.1187]**
1. Everyone's right to life shall be protected by law. No one shall be deprived of his life intentionally save in the execution of a sentence of a court following his conviction of a crime for which this penalty is provided by law.

2. Deprivation of life shall not be regarded as inflicted in contravention of this Article when it results from the use of force which is no more than absolutely necessary:
   (a)   in defence of any person from unlawful violence;
   (b)   in order to effect a lawful arrest or to prevent the escape of a person lawfully detained;
   (c)   in action lawfully taken for the purpose of quelling a riot or insurrection.

## Article 3
### *Prohibition of torture*

No one shall be subjected to torture or to inhuman or degrading treatment or punishment.

## Article 4
### *Prohibition of slavery and forced labour*

**1.** No one shall be held in slavery or servitude.

**2.** No one shall be required to perform forced or compulsory labour.

**3.** For the purpose of this Article the term "forced or compulsory labour" shall not include:
- (a) any work required to be done in the ordinary course of detention imposed according to the provisions of Article 5 of this Convention or during conditional release from such detention;
- (b) any service of a military character or, in case of conscientious objectors in countries where they are recognised, service exacted instead of compulsory military service;
- (c) any service exacted in case of an emergency or calamity threatening the life or well-being of the community;
- (d) any work or service which forms part of normal civic obligations.

## Article 5
### *Right to liberty and security*

**1.** Everyone has the right to liberty and security of person. No one shall be deprived of his liberty save in the following cases and in accordance with a procedure prescribed by law:
- (a) the lawful detention of a person after conviction by a competent court;
- (b) the lawful arrest or detention of a person for non-compliance with the lawful order of a court or in order to secure the fulfilment of any obligation prescribed by law;
- (c) the lawful arrest or detention of a person effected for the purpose of bringing him before the competent legal authority on reasonable suspicion of having committed an offence or when it is reasonably considered necessary to prevent his committing an offence or fleeing after having done so;
- (d) the detention of a minor by lawful order for the purpose of educational supervision or his lawful detention for the purpose of bringing him before the competent legal authority;
- (e) the lawful detention of persons for the prevention of the spreading of infectious diseases, of persons of unsound mind, alcoholics or drug addicts or vagrants;
- (f) the lawful arrest or detention of a person to prevent his effecting an unauthorised entry into the country or of a person against whom action is being taken with a view to deportation or extradition.

**2.** Everyone who is arrested shall be informed promptly, in a language which he understands, of the reasons for his arrest and of any charge against him.

**3.** Everyone arrested or detained in accordance with the provisions of paragraph 1(c) of this Article shall be brought promptly before a judge or other officer authorised by law to exercise judicial power and shall be entitled to trial within a reasonable time or to release pending trial. Release may be conditioned by guarantees to appear for trial.

**4.** Everyone who is deprived of his liberty by arrest or detention shall be entitled to take proceedings by which the lawfulness of his detention shall be decided speedily by a court and his release ordered if the detention is not lawful.

**5.** Everyone who has been the victim of arrest or detention in contravention of the provisions of this Article shall have an enforceable right to compensation.

## Article 6
### *Right to a fair trial*

**1.** In the determination of his civil rights and obligations or of any criminal charge against him, everyone is entitled to a fair and public hearing within a reasonable time by an independent and impartial tribunal established by law. Judgment shall be pronounced publicly but the press and public may be excluded from all or part of the trial in the interest of morals, public order or national security in a democratic society, where the interests of juveniles or the protection of the private life of the parties so require, or to the extent strictly necessary in the opinion of the court in special circumstances where publicity would prejudice the interests of justice.

**2.** Everyone charged with a criminal offence shall be presumed innocent until proved guilty according to law.

**3.** Everyone charged with a criminal offence has the following minimum rights:
- (a) to be informed promptly, in a language which he understands and in detail, of the nature and cause of the accusation against him;
- (b) to have adequate time and facilities for the preparation of his defence;
- (c) to defend himself in person or through legal assistance of his own choosing or, if he has not sufficient means to pay for legal assistance, to be given it free when the interests of justice so require;
- (d) to examine or have examined witnesses against him and to obtain the attendance and examination of witnesses on his behalf under the same conditions as witnesses against him;
- (e) to have the free assistance of an interpreter if he cannot understand or speak the language used in court.

### Article 7
#### No punishment without law

**1.** No one shall be held guilty of any criminal offence on account of any act or omission which did not constitute a criminal offence under national or international law at the time when it was committed. Nor shall a heavier penalty be imposed than the one that was applicable at the time the criminal offence was committed.

**2.** This Article shall not prejudice the trial and punishment of any person for any act or omission which, at the time when it was committed, was criminal according to the general principles of law recognised by civilised nations.

### Article 8
#### Right to respect for private and family life

**1.** Everyone has the right to respect for his private and family life, his home and his correspondence.

**2.** There shall be no interference by a public authority with the exercise of this right except such as is in accordance with the law and is necessary in a democratic society in the interests of national security, public safety or the economic well-being of the country, for the prevention of disorder or crime, for the protection of health or morals, or for the protection of the rights and freedoms of others.

### Article 9
#### Freedom of thought, conscience and religion

**1.** Everyone has the right to freedom of thought, conscience and religion; this right includes freedom to change his religion or belief and freedom, either alone or in community with others and in public or private, to manifest his religion or belief, in worship, teaching, practice and observance.

**2.** Freedom to manifest one's religion or beliefs shall be subject only to such limitations as are prescribed by law and are necessary in a democratic society in the interests of public safety, for the protection of public order, health or morals, or for the protection of the rights and freedoms of others.

### Article 10
#### Freedom of expression

**1.** Everyone has the right to freedom of expression. This right shall include freedom to hold opinions and to receive and impart information and ideas without interference by public authority and regardless of frontiers. This Article shall not prevent States from requiring the licensing of broadcasting, television or cinema enterprises.

**2.** The exercise of these freedoms, since it carries with it duties and responsibilities, may be subject to such formalities, conditions, restrictions or penalties as are prescribed by law and are necessary in a democratic society, in the interests of national security, territorial integrity or public safety, for the prevention of disorder or crime, for the protection of health or morals, for the protection of the reputation or rights of others, for preventing the disclosure of information received in confidence, or for maintaining the authority and impartiality of the judiciary.

## Article 11
### Freedom of assembly and association

**1.** Everyone has the right to freedom of peaceful assembly and to freedom of association with others, including the right to form and to join trade unions for the protection of his interests.

**2.** No restrictions shall be placed on the exercise of these rights other than such as are prescribed by law and are necessary in a democratic society in the interests of national security or public safety, for the prevention of disorder or crime, for the protection of health or morals or for the protection of the rights and freedoms of others. This Article shall not prevent the imposition of lawful restrictions on the exercise of these rights by members of the armed forces, of the police or of the administration of the State.

## Article 12
### Right to marry

Men and women of marriageable age have the right to marry and to found a family, according to the national laws governing the exercise of this right.

## Article 14
### Prohibition of discrimination

The enjoyment of the rights and freedoms set forth in this Convention shall be secured without discrimination on any ground such as sex, race, colour, language, religion, political or other opinion, national or social origin, association with a national minority, property, birth or other status.

## Article 16
### Restrictions on political activity of aliens

Nothing in Articles 10, 11 and 14 shall be regarded as preventing the High Contracting Parties from imposing restrictions on the political activity of aliens.

## Article 17
### Prohibition of abuse of rights

Nothing in this Convention may be interpreted as implying for any State, group or person any right to engage in any activity or perform any act aimed at the destruction of any of the rights and freedoms set forth herein or at their limitation to a greater extent than is provided for in the Convention.

## Article 18
### Limitation on use of restrictions on rights

The restrictions permitted under this Convention to the said rights and freedoms shall not be applied for any purpose other than those for which they have been prescribed.

# PART II
# THE FIRST PROTOCOL

## Article 1
### Protection of property

**[1.1188]**
Every natural or legal person is entitled to the peaceful enjoyment of his possessions. No one shall be deprived of his possessions except in the public interest and subject to the conditions provided for by law and by the general principles of international law.

The preceding provisions shall not, however, in any way impair the right of a State to enforce such laws as it deems necessary to control the use of property in accordance with the general interest or to secure the payment of taxes or other contributions or penalties.

### Article 2
### Right to education

No person shall be denied the right to education. In the exercise of any functions which it assumes in relation to education and to teaching, the State shall respect the right of parents to ensure such education and teaching in conformity with their own religious and philosophical convictions.

### Article 3
### Right to free elections

The High Contracting Parties undertake to hold free elections at reasonable intervals by secret ballot, under conditions which will ensure the free expression of the opinion of the people in the choice of the legislature.

### [PART III
### ARTICLE 1 OF THE THIRTEENTH PROTOCOL

#### Abolition of the Death Penalty

**[1.1189]**
The death penalty shall be abolished. No one shall be condemned to such penalty or executed.]

**NOTES**
Substituted by the Human Rights Act 1998 (Amendment) Order 2004, SI 2004/1574, art 2(3).

### SCHEDULES 2–4

*(Sch 2 (remedial orders), Sch 3 (derogations and reservations), Sch 4 (judicial pensions) outside the scope of this work.)*

# EMPLOYMENT RELATIONS ACT 1999

### (1999 c 26)

#### ARRANGEMENT OF SECTIONS

*An Act to amend the law relating to employment, to trade unions and to employment agencies and businesses*

[27 July 1999]

**NOTES**

Much of this Act amends other legislation; the amendments are incorporated therein so far as within the scope of this work, and noted below. The Act is otherwise printed in full except where (and for the reasons) noted.

Employment Appeal Tribunal: an appeal lies to the Employment Appeal Tribunal on any question of law arising from any decision of, or in any proceedings before, an employment tribunal under or by virtue of this Act; see the Employment Tribunals Act 1996, s 21(1)(gb) at **[1.713]**.

See *Harvey* AI(2), AII(7), NI(7).

*Trade unions*

**1, 2** *(S 1 adds the Trade Union and Labour Relations (Consolidation) Act 1992, Pt I, Ch VA (s 70A) and Sch A1, at **[1.325]**, **[1.582]**; s 2 introduces Sch 2 (Detriment related to trade union membership).)*

**[1.1190]**
**3 Blacklists**
(1) The Secretary of State may make regulations prohibiting the compilation of lists which—
   (a) contain details of members of trade unions or persons who have taken part in the activities of trade unions, and
   (b) are compiled with a view to being used by employers or employment agencies for the purposes of discrimination in relation to recruitment or in relation to the treatment of workers.
(2) The Secretary of State may make regulations prohibiting—
   (a) the use of lists to which subsection (1) applies;
   (b) the sale or supply of lists to which subsection (1) applies.
(3) Regulations under this section may, in particular—
   (a) confer jurisdiction (including exclusive jurisdiction) on employment tribunals and on the Employment Appeal Tribunal;
   (b) include provision for or about the grant and enforcement of specified remedies by courts and tribunals;
   (c) include provision for the making of awards of compensation calculated in accordance with the regulations;
   (d) include provision permitting proceedings to be brought by trade unions on behalf of members in specified circumstances;
   (e) include provision about cases where an employee is dismissed by his employer and the reason or principal reason for the dismissal, or why the employee was selected for dismissal, relates to a list to which subsection (1) applies;
   (f) create criminal offences;
   (g) in specified cases or circumstances, extend liability for a criminal offence created under paragraph (f) to a person who aids the commission of the offence or to a person who is an agent, principal, employee, employer or officer of a person who commits the offence;
   (h) provide for specified obligations or offences not to apply in specified circumstances;
   (i) include supplemental, incidental, consequential and transitional provision, including provision amending an enactment;
   (j) make different provision for different cases or circumstances.
(4) Regulations under this section creating an offence may not provide for it to be punishable—
   (a) by imprisonment,
   (b) by a fine in excess of level 5 on the standard scale in the case of an offence triable only summarily, or
   (c) by a fine in excess of the statutory maximum in the case of summary conviction for an offence triable either way.
(5) In this section—
   "list" includes any index or other set of items whether recorded electronically or by any other means, and
   "worker" has the meaning given by section 13.
(6) Subject to subsection (5), expressions used in this section and in the Trade Union and Labour Relations (Consolidation) Act 1992 have the same meaning in this section as in that Act.

**NOTES**

Regulations: the Employment Relations Act 1999 (Blacklists) Regulations 2010, SI 2010/493 at **[2.1347]**.

**4–9** *(S 4 introduces Sch 3 (Ballots and notices); s 5 inserts the Trade Union and Labour Relations (Consolidation) Act 1992, ss 70B, 70C at **[1.326]**, **[1.327]**; s 6 amends the Employment Rights Act*

*1996, ss 128, 129 at* **[1.937]**, **[1.938]**; *s 7 substitutes Pt VIII of the 1996 Act at* **[1.861]** *et seq; s 8 inserts ss 57A, 57B in the 1996 Act at* **[1.829]**, **[1.830]**; *s 9 introduces Sch 4, Pt III to this Act (amendments consequential on ss 7, 8).)*

*Disciplinary and grievance hearings*

**[1.1191]**
**10   Right to be accompanied**
(1)   This section applies where a worker—
   (a)   is required or invited by his employer to attend a disciplinary or grievance hearing, and
   (b)   reasonably requests to be accompanied at the hearing.
[(2A)   Where this section applies, the employer must permit the worker to be accompanied at the hearing by one companion who—
   (a)   is chosen by the worker; and
   (b)   is within subsection (3).
(2B)   The employer must permit the worker's companion to—
   (a)   address the hearing in order to do any or all of the following—
      (i)    put the worker's case;
      (ii)   sum up that case;
      (iii)  respond on the worker's behalf to any view expressed at the hearing;
   (b)   confer with the worker during the hearing.
(2C)   Subsection (2B) does not require the employer to permit the worker's companion to—
   (a)   answer questions on behalf of the worker;
   (b)   address the hearing if the worker indicates at it that he does not wish his companion to do so; or
   (c)   use the powers conferred by that subsection in a way that prevents the employer from explaining his case or prevents any other person at the hearing from making his contribution to it.]
(3)   A person is within this subsection if he is—
   (a)   employed by a trade union of which he is an official within the meaning of sections 1 and 119 of the Trade Union and Labour Relations (Consolidation) Act 1992,
   (b)   an official of a trade union (within that meaning) whom the union has reasonably certified in writing as having experience of, or as having received training in, acting as a worker's companion at disciplinary or grievance hearings, or
   (c)   another of the employer's workers.
(4)   If—
   (a)   a worker has a right under this section to be accompanied at a hearing,
   (b)   his chosen companion will not be available at the time proposed for the hearing by the employer, and
   (c)   the worker proposes an alternative time which satisfies subsection (5),
the employer must postpone the hearing to the time proposed by the worker.
(5)   An alternative time must—
   (a)   be reasonable, and
   (b)   fall before the end of the period of five working days beginning with the first working day after the day proposed by the employer.
(6)   An employer shall permit a worker to take time off during working hours for the purpose of accompanying another of the employer's workers in accordance with a request under subsection (1)(b).
(7)   Sections 168(3) and (4), 169 and 171 to 173 of the Trade Union and Labour Relations (Consolidation) Act 1992 (time off for carrying out trade union duties) shall apply in relation to subsection (6) above as they apply in relation to section 168(1) of that Act.

---

**NOTES**
  Sub-ss (2A)–(2C): substituted, for the original sub-s (2), by the Employment Relations Act 2004, s 37(1).
  See also the ACAS Code of Practice 1: Disciplinary and Grievance Procedures (2009) at **[4.1]**, and the accompanying Guide at **[4.6]**.

---

**[1.1192]**
**11   Complaint to employment tribunal**
(1)   A worker may present a complaint to an employment tribunal that his employer has failed, or threatened to fail, to comply with section [10(2A), (2B)] or (4).
(2)   A tribunal shall not consider a complaint under this section in relation to a failure or threat unless the complaint is presented—
   (a)   before the end of the period of three months beginning with the date of the failure or threat, or
   (b)   within such further period as the tribunal considers reasonable in a case where it is satisfied that it was not reasonably practicable for the complaint to be presented before the end of that period of three months.

[(2A)  Section 207A(3) (extension because of mediation in certain European cross-border disputes) and section 207B (extension of time limits to facilitate conciliation before institution of proceedings) of the Employment Rights Act 1996 apply for the purposes of subsection (2)(a).

(2B)  Subsections (2) and (2A) are to be treated as provisions of the Employment Rights Act 1996 for the purposes of sections 207A and 207B of that Act.]

(3)  Where a tribunal finds that a complaint under this section is well-founded it shall order the employer to pay compensation to the worker of an amount not exceeding two weeks' pay.

(4)  Chapter II of Part XIV of the Employment Rights Act 1996 (calculation of a week's pay) shall apply for the purposes of subsection (3); and in applying that Chapter the calculation date shall be taken to be—

   (a)   in the case of a claim which is made in the course of a claim for unfair dismissal, the date on which the employer's notice of dismissal was given or, if there was no notice, the effective date of termination, and

   (b)   in any other case, the date on which the relevant hearing took place (or was to have taken place).

(5)  The limit in section 227(1) of the Employment Rights Act 1996 (maximum amount of week's pay) shall apply for the purposes of subsection (3) above.

(6)  . . .

**NOTES**

Sub-s (1): figures in square brackets substituted by the Employment Relations Act 2004, s 37(2).

Sub-ss (2A), (2B): inserted by the Enterprise and Regulatory Reform Act 2013, s 8, Sch 2, para 40, as from a day to be appointed.

Sub-s (6): repealed by the Employment Act 2002, s 54, Sch 8.

Conciliation: by virtue of s 14 of this Act at [**1.1195**], this section (and ss 10, 12 and 13) is treated as a provision of Part V of the Employment Rights Act 1996 for the purposes of the Employment Tribunals Act 1996, s 18.

Application: as to the power of the Secretary of State to make Regulations under the Employment Rights Act 1996, s 80G(1) making provision for the application of this section (with or without modifications) and ss 12, 13 of this Act to requests made by qualifying employees under s 80F of that Act, see s 80G(1), (2)(n) of the 1996 Act at [**1.883**].

**[1.1193]**
## 12  Detriment and dismissal

(1)  A worker has the right not to be subjected to any detriment by any act, or any deliberate failure to act, by his employer done on the ground that he—

   (a)   exercised or sought to exercise the right under section [10(2A), (2B)] or (4), or

   (b)   accompanied or sought to accompany another worker (whether of the same employer or not) pursuant to a request under that section.

(2)  Section 48 of the Employment Rights Act 1996 shall apply in relation to contraventions of subsection (1) above as it applies in relation to contraventions of certain sections of that Act.

(3)  A worker who is dismissed shall be regarded for the purposes of Part X of the Employment Rights Act 1996 as unfairly dismissed if the reason (or, if more than one, the principal reason) for the dismissal is that he—

   (a)   exercised or sought to exercise the right under section [10(2A), (2B)] or (4), or

   (b)   accompanied or sought to accompany another worker (whether of the same employer or not) pursuant to a request under that section.

(4)  Sections 108 and 109 of that Act (qualifying period of employment and upper age limit) shall not apply in relation to subsection (3) above.

(5)  Sections 128 to 132 of that Act (interim relief) shall apply in relation to dismissal for the reason specified in subsection (3)(a) or (b) above as they apply in relation to dismissal for a reason specified in section 128(1)(b) of that Act.

(6)  In the application of Chapter II of Part X of that Act in relation to subsection (3) above, a reference to an employee shall be taken as a reference to a worker.

[(7)  References in this section to a worker having accompanied or sought to accompany another worker include references to his having exercised or sought to exercise any of the powers conferred by section 10(2A) or (2B).]

**NOTES**

Sub-ss (1), (3): figures in square brackets substituted by the Employment Relations Act 2004, s 37(3)(a).

Sub-s (7): added by the Employment Relations Act 2004, s 37(3)(b).

Application: see the note to s 11 at [**1.1192**].

**[1.1194]**
## 13  Interpretation

(1)  In sections 10 to 12 and this section "worker" means an individual who is—

   (a)   a worker within the meaning of section 230(3) of the Employment Rights Act 1996,

   (b)   an agency worker,

   (c)   a home worker,

   (d)   a person in Crown employment within the meaning of section 191 of that Act, other than a member of the naval, military, air or reserve forces of the Crown, or

(e)   employed as a relevant member of the House of Lords staff or the House of Commons staff within the meaning of section 194(6) or 195(5) of that Act.

(2)   In subsection (1) "agency worker" means an individual who—

(a)   is supplied by a person ("the agent") to do work for another ("the principal") by arrangement between the agent and the principal,

(b)   is not a party to a worker's contract, within the meaning of section 230(3) of that Act, relating to that work, and

(c)   is not a party to a contract relating to that work under which he undertakes to do the work for another party to the contract whose status is, by virtue of the contract, that of a client or customer of any professional or business undertaking carried on by the individual;

and, for the purposes of sections 10 to 12, both the agent and the principal are employers of an agency worker.

(3)   In subsection (1) "home worker" means an individual who—

(a)   contracts with a person, for the purposes of the person's business, for the execution of work to be done in a place not under the person's control or management, and

(b)   is not a party to a contract relating to that work under which the work is to be executed for another party to the contract whose status is, by virtue of the contract, that of a client or customer of any professional or business undertaking carried on by the individual;

and, for the purposes of sections 10 to 12, the person mentioned in paragraph (a) is the home worker's employer.

(4)   For the purposes of section 10 a disciplinary hearing is a hearing which could result in—

(a)   the administration of a formal warning to a worker by his employer,

(b)   the taking of some other action in respect of a worker by his employer, or

(c)   the confirmation of a warning issued or some other action taken.

(5)   For the purposes of section 10 a grievance hearing is a hearing which concerns the performance of a duty by an employer in relation to a worker.

(6)   For the purposes of section 10(5)(b) in its application to a part of Great Britain a working day is a day other than—

(a)   a Saturday or a Sunday,

(b)   Christmas Day or Good Friday, or

(c)   a day which is a bank holiday under the Banking and Financial Dealings Act 1971 in that part of Great Britain.

**NOTES**

Application: see the note to s 11 at **[1.1192]**.

**[1.1195]**
### 14   Contracting out and conciliation

Sections 10 to 13 of this Act shall be treated as provisions of Part V of the Employment Rights Act 1996 for the purposes of—

(a)   section 203(1), (2)(e) and (f), (3) and (4) of that Act (restrictions on contracting out), and

(b)   section 18(1)(d) of the Employment Tribunals Act 1996 (conciliation).

**[1.1196]**
### 15   National security employees

Sections 10 to 13 of this Act shall not apply in relation to a person employed for the purposes of—

(a)   the Security Service,

(b)   the Secret Intelligence Service, or

(c)   the Government Communications Headquarters.

*Other rights of individuals*

**16–18**   (*S 16 introduces Sch 5 (Unfair dismissal of striking workers); s 17 repealed by the Employment Relations Act 2004, ss 31(8), 57(2), Sch 2; s 18(1)–(4) amend the Employment Rights Act 1996, ss 44, 45A, 46, 47, 47A, 47B, at* **[1.801]**, **[1.803]**, **[1.804]**, **[1.805]**, **[1.806]**, **[1.808]**, *amended s 197 (repealed), and substitute the National Minimum Wage Act 1998, s 23(4) at* **[1.1144]**; *s 18(5) repealed by the Tax Credits Act 2002, s 60, Sch 6; s 18(6) repealed by Sch 9 to this Act.*)

**[1.1197]**
### 19   Part-time work: discrimination

(1)   The Secretary of State shall make regulations for the purpose of securing that persons in part-time employment are treated, for such purposes and to such extent as the regulations may specify, no less favourably than persons in full-time employment.

(2)   The regulations may—

(a)   specify classes of person who are to be taken to be, or not to be, in part-time employment;

(b)   specify classes of person who are to be taken to be, or not to be, in full-time employment;

(c)   specify circumstances in which persons in part-time employment are to be taken to be, or not to be, treated less favourably than persons in full-time employment;

    (d)    make provision which has effect in relation to persons in part-time employment generally or provision which has effect only in relation to specified classes of persons in part-time employment.

(3)   The regulations may—
    (a)    confer jurisdiction (including exclusive jurisdiction) on employment tribunals and on the Employment Appeal Tribunal;
    (b)    create criminal offences in relation to specified acts or omissions by an employer, by an organisation of employers, by an organisation of workers or by an organisation existing for the purposes of a profession or trade carried on by the organisation's members;
    (c)    in specified cases or circumstances, extend liability for a criminal offence created under paragraph (b) to a person who aids the commission of the offence or to a person who is an agent, principal, employee, employer or officer of a person who commits the offence;
    (d)    provide for specified obligations or offences not to apply in specified circumstances;
    (e)    make provision about notices or information to be given, evidence to be produced and other procedures to be followed;
    (f)    amend, apply with or without modifications, or make provision similar to any provision of the Employment Rights Act 1996 (including, in particular, Parts V, X and XIII) or the Trade Union and Labour Relations (Consolidation) Act 1992;
    (g)    provide for the provisions of specified agreements to have effect in place of provisions of the regulations to such extent and in such circumstances as may be specified;
    (h)    include supplemental, incidental, consequential and transitional provision, including provision amending an enactment;
    (i)    make different provision for different cases or circumstances.

(4)   Without prejudice to the generality of this section the regulations may make any provision which appears to the Secretary of State to be necessary or expedient—
    (a)    for the purpose of implementing Council Directive 97/81/EC on the framework agreement on part-time work in its application to terms and conditions of employment;
    (b)    for the purpose of dealing with any matter arising out of or related to the United Kingdom's obligations under that Directive;
    (c)    for the purpose of any matter dealt with by the framework agreement or for the purpose of applying the provisions of the framework agreement to any matter relating to part-time workers.

(5)   Regulations under this section which create an offence—
    (a)    shall provide for it to be triable summarily only, and
    (b)    may not provide for it to be punishable by imprisonment or by a fine in excess of level 5 on the standard scale.

**NOTES**

Regulations: the Part-time Workers (Prevention of Less Favourable Treatment) Regulations 2000, SI 2000/1551 at **[2.575]**; the Part-time Workers (Prevention of Less Favourable Treatment) Regulations 2001, SI 2001/1107.

**[1.1198]**
**20  Part-time work: code of practice**
(1)   The Secretary of State may issue codes of practice containing guidance for the purpose of—
    (a)    eliminating discrimination in the field of employment against part-time workers;
    (b)    facilitating the development of opportunities for part-time work;
    (c)    facilitating the flexible organisation of working time taking into account the needs of workers and employers;
    (d)    any matter dealt with in the framework agreement on part-time work annexed to Council Directive 97/81/EC.

(2)   The Secretary of State may revise a code and issue the whole or part of the revised code.

(3)   A person's failure to observe a provision of a code does not make him liable to any proceedings.

(4)   A code—
    (a)    is admissible in evidence in proceedings before an employment tribunal, and
    (b)    shall be taken into account by an employment tribunal in any case in which it appears to the tribunal to be relevant.

**NOTES**

Codes of Practice: as of 6 April 2013 no codes had been issued under this section.

**[1.1199]**
**21  Code of practice: supplemental**
(1)   Before issuing or revising a code of practice under section 20 the Secretary of State shall consult such persons as he considers appropriate.

(2)   Before issuing a code the Secretary of State shall—
    (a)    publish a draft code,
    (b)    consider any representations made to him about the draft,

(c)    if he thinks it appropriate, modify the draft in the light of any representations made to him.

(3)    If, having followed the procedure under subsection (2), the Secretary of State decides to issue a code, he shall lay a draft code before each House of Parliament.

(4)    If the draft code is approved by resolution of each House of Parliament, the Secretary of State shall issue the code in the form of the draft.

(5)    In this section and section 20(3) and (4)—

(a)    a reference to a code includes a reference to a revised code,

(b)    a reference to a draft code includes a reference to a draft revision, and

(c)    a reference to issuing a code includes a reference to issuing part of a revised code.

**22**    *(Inserts the National Minimum Wage Act 1998, s 44A at* **[1.1162]**.)

**[1.1200]**
## 23    Power to confer rights on individuals

(1)    This section applies to any right conferred on an individual against an employer (however defined) under or by virtue of any of the following—

(a)    the Trade Union and Labour Relations (Consolidation) Act 1992;

(b)    the Employment Rights Act 1996;

[(ba) the Employment Act 2002;]

(c)    this Act;

(d)    any instrument made under section 2(2) of the European Communities Act 1972.

(2)    The Secretary of State may by order make provision which has the effect of conferring any such right on individuals who are of a specified description.

(3)    The reference in subsection (2) to individuals includes a reference to individuals expressly excluded from exercising the right.

(4)    An order under this section may—

(a)    provide that individuals are to be treated as parties to workers' contracts or contracts of employment;

(b)    make provision as to who are to be regarded as the employers of individuals;

(c)    make provision which has the effect of modifying the operation of any right as conferred on individuals by the order;

(d)    include such consequential, incidental or supplementary provisions as the Secretary of State thinks fit.

(5)    An order under this section may make provision in such way as the Secretary of State thinks fit  . . .

[(5A)    The ways in which an order under this section may make provision include, in particular—

(a)    amending any enactment;

(b)    excluding or applying (whether with or without amendment) any enactment.

(5B)    In subsection (5A) "enactment" includes an enactment comprised in subordinate legislation made under an Act.]

(6)    Section 209(7) of the Employment Rights Act 1996 (which is superseded by this section) shall be omitted.

(7)    Any order made or having effect as if made under section 209(7), so far as effective immediately before the commencement of this section, shall have effect as if made under this section.

***

**NOTES**

Sub-s (1): para (ba) inserted by the Employment Act 2002, s 53, Sch 7, para 54.

Sub-s (5): words omitted repealed by a combination of the Employment Act 2002, s 41, and the Employment Relations Act 2004, ss 39(1), (2), 57(2), Sch 2.

Sub-ss (5A), (5B): inserted by the Employment Relations Act 2004, s 39(1), (3).

Orders: as of 6 April 2013 no Orders had been made under this section. As to Orders made or having effect as if made under the Employment Rights Act 1996, s 209(7) (and therefore having effect as if made under this section by virtue of sub-s (7) above) see the note to s 209 of the 1996 Act at **[1.1016]**.

***

### CAC, ACAS, Commissioners and Certification Officer

**24–29**    *(Ss 24–27 contain various amendments to the Trade Union and Labour Relations (Consolidation) Act 1992 at* **[1.241]** *et seq; s 28(1), (2) abolished the office of Commissioner for the Rights of Trade Union Members and the office of Commissioner for Protection Against Unlawful Industrial Action and repealed the Trade Union and Labour Relations (Consolidation) Act 1992, Pt I, Ch VIII, ss 235B, 235C and 266–271, and were themselves repealed by the Statute Law (Repeals) Act 2004; s 28(3) amends s 32A of the 1992 Act; s 29 introduces Sch 6 (the Certification Officer).)*

*Miscellaneous*

**[1.1201]**

## 30 Partnerships at work

(1) The Secretary of State may spend money or provide money to other persons for the purpose of encouraging and helping employers (or their representatives) and employees (or their representatives) to improve the way they work together.

(2) Money may be provided in such way as the Secretary of State thinks fit (whether as grants or otherwise) and on such terms as he thinks fit (whether as to repayment or otherwise).

**31–33** *(S 31 introduces Sch 7 (employment agencies); s 32 amends the Trade Union and Labour Relations (Consolidation) Act 1992, s 285 at* **[1.565]**, *inserts s 287(3A) of the 1992 Act at* **[1.567]**, *repeals the Employment Rights Act 1996, s 196 and amends s 199 of the 1996 Act at* **[1.1004]**; *s 33(1) repealed the Employment Rights Act 1996, ss 117(4)(b), 118(2), (3), 125 and the Trade Union and Labour Relations (Consolidation) Act 1992, ss 157, 158, and was repealed by the Statute Law (Repeals) Act 2004; s 33(2), (3) amend s 117 of the 1996 Act at* **[1.927]**, *and the Employment Rights (Dispute Resolution) Act 1998, s 14, and were repealed in part by the Statute Law (Repeals) Act 2004.)*

**[1.1202]**

## 34 Indexation of amounts, &c

(1) This section applies to the sums specified in the following of provisions—
  (a) section 31(1) of the Employment Rights Act 1996 (guarantee payments: limits);
  (b) section 120(1) of that Act (unfair dismissal: minimum amount of basic award);
  (c) section 124(1) of that Act (unfair dismissal: limit of compensatory award);
  (d) section 186(1)(a) and (b) of that Act (employee's rights on insolvency of employer: maximum amount payable);
  (e) section 227(1) of that Act (maximum amount of a week's pay for purposes of certain calculations);
  [(ea) section 145E(3) of the Trade Union and Labour Relations (Consolidation) Act 1992 (unlawful inducements: amount of award);
  (f) section 156(1) of that Act (unfair dismissal: minimum basic award);]
  (g) section [176(6A)] of that Act (right to membership of trade union: remedies).

(2) If the retail prices index for September of a year is higher or lower than the index for the previous September, the Secretary of State shall *as soon as practicable* make an order in relation to each sum mentioned in subsection (1)—
  (a) increasing each sum, if the new index is higher, or
  (b) decreasing each sum, if the new index is lower,
by the same percentage as the amount of the increase or decrease of the index[, with effect from the following 6th April].

(3) In making the calculation required by subsection (2) the Secretary of State shall—
  *(a) in the case of the sum mentioned in subsection (1)(a), round the result up to the nearest 10 pence,*
  *(b) in the case of the sums mentioned in subsection (1)(b), (c), [(ea),] (f) and (g), round the result up to the nearest £100, and*
  *(c) in the case of the sums mentioned in subsection (1)(d) and (e), round the result up to the nearest £10.*

(4) For the sum specified in section 124(1) of the Employment Rights Act 1996 (unfair dismissal: limit of compensatory award) there shall be substituted the sum of £50,000 (subject to subsection (2) above).

[(4A) A reference in this section to a sum specified in section 124(1) of the Employment Rights Act 1996 does not include anything specified by virtue of section 15(2)(b)(ii) of the Enterprise and Regulatory Reform Act 2013 (specified number multiplied by a week's pay of the individual concerned).

(4B) As regards a sum specified in section 124(1) of the Employment Rights Act 1996, the duty under subsection (2) to make an order with effect from 6 April in a particular year does not arise where an order varying such a sum with effect from a day within 12 months before that date has been made under section 15(1) of the Enterprise and Regulatory Reform Act 2013.]

(5) In this section "the retail prices index" means—
  (a) the general index of retail prices (for all items) published by the [Statistics Board], or
  (b) where that index is not published for a month, any substituted index or figures published by [the Board].

(6) An order under this section—
  (a) shall be made by statutory instrument,
  (b) may include transitional provision, and
  (c) shall be laid before Parliament after being made.

**NOTES**

Sub-s (1): paras (ea), (f) substituted, for the original para (f), by the Employment Relations Act 2004, s 57(1), Sch 1, para 42(1), (2); figure in square brackets in para (g) substituted by s 57(1) of, and Sch 1, para 42(1), (3) to, the 2004 Act.

Sub-s (2): words in italics repealed and words in square brackets added, by the Enterprise and Regulatory Reform Act 2013, s 22(1), (2), as from 25 June 2013.

Sub-s (3): words in square brackets in para (b) inserted by the Employment Relations Act 2004, s 57(1), Sch 1, para 42(1), (4); for the words in italics there are substituted the words "round the result to the nearest whole pound, taking 50p as nearest to the next whole pound above" by the Enterprise and Regulatory Reform Act 2013, s 22(1), (3), as from 25 June 2013.

Sub-ss (4A), (4B): inserted by the Enterprise and Regulatory Reform Act 2013, s 15(10), as from 25 June 2013.

Sub-s (5): words in square brackets substituted by the Statistics and Registration Service Act 2007, s 60(1), Sch 3, para 11.

Orders: the current Order is the Employment Rights (Increase of Limits) Order 2012, SI 2012/3007 at **[2.1634]**.

**35**  *(Amends the Employment Rights Act 1996, s 31 at* **[1.775]**.*)*

**[1.1203]**
**36  Sections 33 to 35: consequential**
(1), (2)   . . .
(3)   An increase effected, before section 34 comes into force, by virtue of a provision repealed by this section shall continue to have effect notwithstanding this section (but subject to section 34(2) and (4)).

**NOTES**

Sub-ss (1), (2): repeal the Employment Rights Act 1996, ss 120(2), 124(2), 186(2), 208, 227(2)–(4), and the Trade Union and Labour Relations (Consolidation) Act 1992, ss 159, 176(7), (8).

**37**  *(S 37(1) amends the Employment Rights Act 1996, s 124 at* **[1.934]**; *s 37(2) repealed s 127B of that Act, and was repealed by the Statute Law (Repeals) Act 2004.)*

**[1.1204]**
**38  Transfer of undertakings**
(1)   This section applies where regulations under section 2(2) of the European Communities Act 1972 (general implementation of Treaties) make provision for the purpose of implementing, or for a purpose concerning, [an] [EU] obligation of the United Kingdom which relates to the treatment of employees on the transfer of an undertaking or business or part of an undertaking or business.
(2)   The Secretary of State may by regulations make the same or similar provision in relation to the treatment of employees in circumstances other than those to which the [EU] obligation applies (including circumstances in which there is no transfer, or no transfer to which the [EU] obligation applies).
(3)   Regulations under this section shall be subject to annulment in pursuance of a resolution of either House of Parliament.

**NOTES**

Sub-ss (1), (2): words in square brackets substituted by the Treaty of Lisbon (Changes in Terminology) Order 2011, SI 2011/1043, art 6(1)(e), (3), as from 22 April 2011.

Regulations: the Transfer of Undertakings (Protection of Employment) (Rent Officer Service) Regulations 1999, SI 1999/2511; the Transfer of Undertakings (Protection of Employment) (Transfer to OFCOM) Regulations 2003, SI 2003/2715; the Transfer of Undertakings (Protection of Employment) Regulations 2006, SI 2006/246 at **[2.997]**; the Transfer of Undertakings (Protection of Employment) (Consequential Amendments) Regulations 2006, SI 2006/2405; the Transfer of Undertakings (Protection of Employment) (RCUK Shared Services Centre Limited) Regulations 2012, SI 2012/2413; the Transfer of Undertakings (Protection of Employment) (Transfers of Public Health Staff) Regulations 2013, SI 2013/278 at **[2.1654]**.

**[1.1205]**
**39  Minimum wage: information**
(1)   Information obtained by a revenue official in the course of carrying out a function of the Commissioners of Inland Revenue may be—
   (a)   supplied by the Commissioners of Inland Revenue to the Secretary of State for any purpose relating to the National Minimum Wage Act 1998;
   (b)   supplied by the Secretary of State with the authority of the Commissioners of Inland Revenue to any person acting under section 13(1)(b) of that Act;
   (c)   supplied by the Secretary of State with the authority of the Commissioners of Inland Revenue to an officer acting for the purposes of any of the agricultural wages legislation.
(2)   In this section—
"revenue official" means an officer of the Commissioners of Inland Revenue appointed under section 4 of the Inland Revenue Regulation Act 1890 (appointment of collectors, officers and other persons), and
"the agricultural wages legislation" has the same meaning as in section 16 of the National Minimum Wage Act 1998 (agricultural wages officers).

**40, 41**  *(S 40 repealed by the Education Act 2002, s 215(2), Sch 22, Pt 3; s 41 introduces Sch 8 (national security).)*

*General*

**[1.1206]**

### 42  Orders and regulations

(1)  Any power to make an order or regulations under this Act shall be exercised by statutory instrument.

(2)  No order or regulations shall be made under section 3, 17, 19 or 23 unless a draft has been laid before, and approved by resolution of, each House of Parliament.

**[1.1207]**

### 43  Finance

There shall be paid out of money provided by Parliament—

  (a)  any increase attributable to this Act in the sums so payable under any other enactment;

  (b)  any other expenditure of the Secretary of State under this Act.

**44**  *(Introduces Sch 9 (repeals).)*

**[1.1208]**

### 45  Commencement

(1)  The preceding provisions of this Act shall come into force in accordance with provision made by the Secretary of State by order made by statutory instrument.

(2)  An order under this section—

  (a)  may make different provision for different purposes;

  (b)  may include supplementary, incidental, saving or transitional provisions.

**[1.1209]**

### 46  Extent

(1)  Any amendment or repeal in this Act has the same extent as the provision amended or repealed.

(2)  An Order in Council under paragraph 1(1)(b) of Schedule 1 to the Northern Ireland Act 1974 (legislation for Northern Ireland in the interim period) which contains a statement that it is made only for purposes corresponding to any of the purposes of this Act—

  (a)  shall not be subject to paragraph 1(4) and (5) of that Schedule (affirmative resolution of both Houses of Parliament), but

  (b)  shall be subject to annulment in pursuance of a resolution of either House of Parliament.

(3)  Apart from sections 39 and 45 and subject to subsection (1), the preceding sections of this Act shall not extend to Northern Ireland.

**[1.1210]**

### 47  Citation

This Act may be cited as the Employment Relations Act 1999.

## SCHEDULES 1–9

*(In so far as still in force, Schedules 1–9 to this Act make a variety of amendments and repeals to (inter alia) the following: the Trade Union and Labour Relations (Consolidation) Act 1992, the*

*Employment Rights Act 1996, the Employment Tribunals Act 1996, and the Employment Agencies Act 1973; they also amended the Race Relations Act 1976 and the Disability Discrimination Act 1995 (both now repealed). All such amendments and repeals are noted at the appropriate place where they are within the scope of this work.)*

# CONTRACTS (RIGHTS OF THIRD PARTIES) ACT 1999

## (1999 c 31)

### ARRANGEMENT OF SECTIONS

*An Act to make provision for the enforcement of contractual terms by third parties*

[11 November 1999]

---

**NOTES**

As to the commencement and application of this Act, see s 10(2), (3) at **[1.1219]**.

---

**[1.1211]**
### 1   Right of third party to enforce contractual term
(1)   Subject to the provisions of this Act, a person who is not a party to a contract (a "third party") may in his own right enforce a term of the contract if—
  (a)   the contract expressly provides that he may, or
  (b)   subject to subsection (2), the term purports to confer a benefit on him.
(2)   subsection (1)(b) does not apply if on a proper construction of the contract it appears that the parties did not intend the term to be enforceable by the third party.
(3)   The third party must be expressly identified in the contract by name, as a member of a class or as answering a particular description but need not be in existence when the contract is entered into.
(4)   This section does not confer a right on a third party to enforce a term of a contract otherwise than subject to and in accordance with any other relevant terms of the contract.
(5)   For the purpose of exercising his right to enforce a term of the contract, there shall be available to the third party any remedy that would have been available to him in an action for breach of contract if he had been a party to the contract (and the rules relating to damages, injunctions, specific performance and other relief shall apply accordingly).
(6)   Where a term of a contract excludes or limits liability in relation to any matter references in this Act to the third party enforcing the term shall be construed as references to his availing himself of the exclusion or limitation.
(7)   In this Act, in relation to a term of a contract which is enforceable by a third party—
  "the promisor" means the party to the contract against whom the term is enforceable by the third party, and
  "the promisee" means the party to the contract by whom the term is enforceable against the promisor.

**[1.1212]**
### 2   Variation and rescission of contract
(1)   Subject to the provisions of this section, where a third party has a right under section 1 to enforce a term of the contract, the parties to the contract may not, by agreement, rescind the contract, or vary it in such a way as to extinguish or alter his entitlement under that right, without his consent if—
  (a)   the third party has communicated his assent to the term to the promisor,
  (b)   the promisor is aware that the third party has relied on the term, or
  (c)   the promisor can reasonably be expected to have foreseen that the third party would rely on the term and the third party has in fact relied on it.
(2)   The assent referred to in subsection (1)(a)—
  (a)   may be by words or conduct, and

(b)   if sent to the promisor by post or other means, shall not be regarded as communicated to the promisor until received by him.

(3)   subsection (1) is subject to any express term of the contract under which—

(a)   the parties to the contract may by agreement rescind or vary the contract without the consent of the third party, or

(b)   the consent of the third party is required in circumstances specified in the contract instead of those set out in subsection (1)(a) to (c).

(4)   Where the consent of a third party is required under subsection (1) or (3), the court or arbitral tribunal may, on the application of the parties to the contract, dispense with his consent if satisfied—

(a)   that his consent cannot be obtained because his whereabouts cannot reasonably be ascertained, or

(b)   that he is mentally incapable of giving his consent.

(5)   The court or arbitral tribunal may, on the application of the parties to a contract, dispense with any consent that may be required under subsection (1)(c) if satisfied that it cannot reasonably be ascertained whether or not the third party has in fact relied on the term.

(6)   If the court or arbitral tribunal dispenses with a third party's consent, it may impose such conditions as it thinks fit, including a condition requiring the payment of compensation to the third party.

(7)   The jurisdiction conferred on the court by subsections (4) to (6) is exercisable [in England and Wales by both the High Court and the county court and in Northern Ireland] by both the High Court and a county court.

## NOTES

Sub-s (7): words in square brackets inserted by the Crime and Courts Act 2013, s 17(5), Sch 9, Pt 3, para 71, as from a day to be appointed.

## [1.1213]
### 3   Defences etc available to promisor

(1)   Subsections (2) to (5) apply where, in reliance on section 1, proceedings for the enforcement of a term of a contract are brought by a third party.

(2)   The promisor shall have available to him by way of defence or set-off any matter that—

(a)   arises from or in connection with the contract and is relevant to the term, and

(b)   would have been available to him by way of defence or set-off if the proceedings had been brought by the promisee.

(3)   The promisor shall also have available to him by way of defence or set-off any matter if—

(a)   an express term of the contract provides for it to be available to him in proceedings brought by the third party, and

(b)   it would have been available to him by way of defence or set-off if the proceedings had been brought by the promisee.

(4)   The promisor shall also have available to him—

(a)   by way of defence or set-off any matter, and

(b)   by way of counterclaim any matter not arising from the contract,

that would have been available to him by way of defence or set-off or, as the case may be, by way of counterclaim against the third party if the third party had been a party to the contract.

(5)   Subsections (2) and (4) are subject to any express term of the contract as to the matters that are not to be available to the promisor by way of defence, set-off or counterclaim.

(6)   Where in any proceedings brought against him a third party seeks in reliance on section 1 to enforce a term of a contract (including, in particular, a term purporting to exclude or limit liability), he may not do so if he could not have done so (whether by reason of any particular circumstances relating to him or otherwise) had he been a party to the contract.

## [1.1214]
### 4   Enforcement of contract by promisee

Section 1 does not affect any right of the promisee to enforce any term of the contract.

## [1.1215]
### 5   Protection of party promisor from double liability

Where under section 1 a term of a contract is enforceable by a third party, and the promisee has recovered from the promisor a sum in respect of—

(a)   the third party's loss in respect of the term, or

(b)   the expense to the promisee of making good to the third party the default of the promisor,

then, in any proceedings brought in reliance on that section by the third party, the court or arbitral tribunal shall reduce any award to the third party to such extent as it thinks appropriate to take account of the sum recovered by the promisee.

**[1.1216]**
## 6   Exceptions
(1)   Section 1 confers no rights on a third party in the case of a contract on a bill of exchange, promissory note or other negotiable instrument.
(2)   Section 1 confers no rights on a third party in the case of any contract binding on a company and its members under [section 33 of the Companies Act 2006 (effect of company's constitution)].
[(2A)   Section 1 confers no rights on a third party in the case of any incorporation document of a limited liability partnership [or any agreement (express or implied) between the members of a limited liability partnership, or between a limited liability partnership and its members, that determines the mutual rights and duties of the members and their rights and duties in relation to the limited liability partnership].]
(3)   Section 1 confers no right on a third party to enforce—
   (a)   any term of a contract of employment against an employee,
   (b)   any term of a worker's contract against a worker (including a home worker), or
   (c)   any term of a relevant contract against an agency worker.
(4)   In subsection (3)—
   (a)   "contract of employment", "employee", "worker's contract", and "worker" have the meaning given by section 54 of the National Minimum Wage Act 1998,
   (b)   "home worker" has the meaning given by section 35(2) of that Act,
   (c)   "agency worker" has the same meaning as in section 34(1) of that Act, and
   (d)   "relevant contract" means a contract entered into, in a case where section 34 of that Act applies, by the agency worker as respects work falling within subsection (1)(a) of that section.
(5)–(8)   ((*Carriage of goods and cargo) outside the scope of this work.*)

**NOTES**
   Sub-s (2): words in square brackets substituted by the Companies Act 2006 (Consequential Amendments, Transitional Provisions and Savings) Order 2009, SI 2009/1941, art 2(1), Sch 1, para 179(1), (2)(a), as from 1 October 2009.
   Sub-s (2A): inserted by the Limited Liability Partnerships Regulations 2001, SI 2001/1090, reg 9(1), Sch 5, para 20; words in square brackets substituted by SI 2009/1941, art 2(1), Sch 1, para 179(1), (2)(b), as from 1 October 2009.

**[1.1217]**
## 7   Supplementary provisions relating to third party
(1)   Section 1 does not affect any right or remedy of a third party that exists or is available apart from this Act.
(2)   Section 2(2) of the Unfair Contract Terms Act 1977 (restriction on exclusion etc of liability for negligence) shall not apply where the negligence consists of the breach of an obligation arising from a term of a contract and the person seeking to enforce it is a third party acting in reliance on section 1.
(3)   In sections 5 and 8 of the Limitation Act 1980 the references to an action founded on a simple contract and an action upon a specialty shall respectively include references to an action brought in reliance on section 1 relating to a simple contract and an action brought in reliance on that section relating to specialty.
(4)   A third party shall not, by virtue of section 1(5) or 3(4) or (6), be treated as a party to the contract for the purposes of any other Act (or any instrument made under any other Act).

**[1.1218]**
## 8   Arbitration provisions
(1)   Where—
   (a)   a right under section 1 to enforce a term ("the substantive term") is subject to a term providing for the submission of disputes to arbitration ("the arbitration agreement"), and
   (b)   the arbitration agreement is an agreement in writing for the purposes of Part I of the Arbitration Act 1996,
the third party shall be treated for the purposes of that Act as a party to the arbitration agreement as regards disputes between himself and the promisor relating to the enforcement of the substantive term by the third party.
(2)   Where—
   (a)   a third party has a right under section 1 to enforce a term providing for one or more descriptions of dispute between the third party and the promisor to be submitted to arbitration ("the arbitration agreement"),
   (b)   the arbitration agreement is an agreement in writing for the purposes of Part I of the Arbitration Act 1996, and
   (c)   the third party does not fall to be treated under subsection (1) as a party to the arbitration agreement,
the third party shall, if he exercises the right, be treated for the purposes of that Act as a party to the arbitration agreement in relation to the matter with respect to which the right is exercised, and be treated as having been so immediately before the exercise of the right.

**9** *(Applies to Northern Ireland (outside the scope of this work).)*

**[1.1219]**
**10  Short title, commencement and extent**
(1)  This Act may be cited as the Contracts (Rights of Third Parties) Act 1999.
(2)  This Act comes into force on the day on which it is passed but, subject to subsection (3), does not apply in relation to a contract entered into before the end of the period of six months beginning with that day.
(3)  The restriction in subsection (2) does not apply in relation to a contract which—
  (a)  is entered into on or after the day on which this Act is passed, and
  (b)  expressly provides for the application of this Act.
(4)  This Act extends as follows—
  (a)  section 9 extends to Northern Ireland only;
  (b)  the remaining provisions extend to England and Wales and Northern Ireland only.

**NOTES**
"On or after the day on which this Act is passed" in sub-s (3): this was 11 November 1999.

# REGULATION OF INVESTIGATORY POWERS ACT 2000

(2000 c 23)

## ARRANGEMENT OF SECTIONS

### PART I
### COMMUNICATIONS

#### CHAPTER I
#### INTERCEPTION

*Unlawful and authorised interception*

*An Act to make provision for and about the interception of communications, the acquisition and disclosure of data relating to communications, the carrying out of surveillance, the use of covert human intelligence sources and the acquisition of the means by which electronic data protected by encryption or passwords may be decrypted or accessed; to provide for Commissioners and a tribunal with functions and jurisdiction in relation to those matters, to entries on and interferences with property or with wireless telegraphy and to the carrying out of their functions by the Security Service, the Secret Intelligence Service and the Government Communications Headquarters; and for connected purposes*

[28 July 2000]

**NOTES**
Only those provisions of this Act relevant to employment law are reproduced. Provisions not reproduced are not annotated.

### PART I
### COMMUNICATIONS

#### CHAPTER I
#### INTERCEPTION

*Unlawful and authorised interception*

**[1.1220]**
**1  Unlawful interception**
(1)  It shall be an offence for a person intentionally and without lawful authority to intercept, at any place in the United Kingdom, any communication in the course of its transmission by means of—
  (a)  a public postal service; or

(b)　　a public telecommunication system.

[(1A)　The Interception of Communications Commissioner may serve a monetary penalty notice on a person if the Commissioner—

   (a)　　considers that the person—

      (i)　　has without lawful authority intercepted, at any place in the United Kingdom, any communication in the course of its transmission by means of a public telecommunication system, and

      (ii)　　was not, at the time of the interception, making an attempt to act in accordance with an interception warrant which might, in the opinion of the Commissioner, explain the interception concerned, and

   (b)　　does not consider that the person has committed an offence under subsection (1).

(1B)　Schedule A1 (which makes further provision about monetary penalty notices) has effect.]

(2)　It shall be an offence for a person—

   (a)　　intentionally and without lawful authority, and

   (b)　　otherwise than in circumstances in which his conduct is excluded by subsection (6) from criminal liability under this subsection,

to intercept, at any place in the United Kingdom, any communication in the course of its transmission by means of a private telecommunication system.

(3)　Any interception of a communication which is carried out at any place in the United Kingdom by, or with the express or implied consent of, a person having the right to control the operation or the use of a private telecommunication system shall be actionable at the suit or instance of the sender or recipient, or intended recipient, of the communication if it is without lawful authority and is either—

   (a)　　an interception of that communication in the course of its transmission by means of that private system; or

   (b)　　an interception of that communication in the course of its transmission, by means of a public telecommunication system, to or from apparatus comprised in that private telecommunication system.

(4)　Where the United Kingdom is a party to an international agreement which—

   (a)　　relates to the provision of mutual assistance in connection with, or in the form of, the interception of communications,

   (b)　　requires the issue of a warrant, order or equivalent instrument in cases in which assistance is given, and

   (c)　　is designated for the purposes of this subsection by an order made by the Secretary of State,

it shall be the duty of the Secretary of State to secure that no request for assistance in accordance with the agreement is made on behalf of a person in the United Kingdom to the competent authorities of a country or territory outside the United Kingdom except with lawful authority.

(5)　Conduct has lawful authority for the purposes of this section if, and only if—

   (a)　　it is authorised by or under section 3 or 4;

   (b)　　it takes place in accordance with a warrant under section 5 ("an interception warrant"); or

   (c)　　it is in exercise, in relation to any stored communication, of any statutory power that is exercised (apart from this section) for the purpose of obtaining information or of taking possession of any document or other property;

and conduct (whether or not prohibited by this section) which has lawful authority for the purposes of this section by virtue of paragraph (a) or (b) shall also be taken to be lawful for all other purposes.

(6)　The circumstances in which a person makes an interception of a communication in the course of its transmission by means of a private telecommunication system are such that his conduct is excluded from criminal liability under subsection (2) if—

   (a)　　he is a person with a right to control the operation or the use of the system; or

   (b)　　he has the express or implied consent of such a person to make the interception.

(7)　A person who is guilty of an offence under subsection (1) or (2) shall be liable—

   (a)　　on conviction on indictment, to imprisonment for a term not exceeding two years or to a fine, or to both;

   (b)　　on summary conviction, to a fine not exceeding the statutory maximum.

(8)　No proceedings for any offence which is an offence by virtue of this section shall be instituted—

   (a)　　in England and Wales, except by or with the consent of the Director of Public Prosecutions;

   (b)　　in Northern Ireland, except by or with the consent of the Director of Public Prosecutions for Northern Ireland.

---

**NOTES**

Sub-ss (1A), (1B): inserted by the Regulation of Investigatory Powers (Monetary Penalty Notices and Consents for Interceptions) Regulations 2011, SI 2011/1340, reg 2(1), as from 16 June 2011.

Regulations: the Regulation of Investigatory Powers (Designation of an International Agreement) Order 2004, SI 2004/158.

**[1.1221]**
**2 Meaning and location of "interception" etc**
(1)   In this Act—
"postal service" means any service which—
(a)   consists in the following, or in any one or more of them, namely, the collection, sorting, conveyance, distribution and delivery (whether in the United Kingdom or elsewhere) of postal items; and
(b)   is offered or provided as a service the main purpose of which, or one of the main purposes of which, is to make available, or to facilitate, a means of transmission from place to place of postal items containing communications;
"private telecommunication system" means any telecommunication system which, without itself being a public telecommunication system, is a system in relation to which the following conditions are satisfied—
(a)   it is attached, directly or indirectly and whether or not for the purposes of the communication in question, to a public telecommunication system; and
(b)   there is apparatus comprised in the system which is both located in the United Kingdom and used (with or without other apparatus) for making the attachment to the public telecommunication system;
"public postal service" means any postal service which is offered or provided to, or to a substantial section of, the public in any one or more parts of the United Kingdom;
"public telecommunications service" means any telecommunications service which is offered or provided to, or to a substantial section of, the public in any one or more parts of the United Kingdom;
"public telecommunication system" means any such parts of a telecommunication system by means of which any public telecommunications service is provided as are located in the United Kingdom;
"telecommunications service" means any service that consists in the provision of access to, and of facilities for making use of, any telecommunication system (whether or not one provided by the person providing the service); and
"telecommunication system" means any system (including the apparatus comprised in it) which exists (whether wholly or partly in the United Kingdom or elsewhere) for the purpose of facilitating the transmission of communications by any means involving the use of electrical or electro-magnetic energy.
(2)   For the purposes of this Act, but subject to the following provisions of this section, a person intercepts a communication in the course of its transmission by means of a telecommunication system if, and only if, he—
(a)   so modifies or interferes with the system, or its operation,
(b)   so monitors transmissions made by means of the system, or
(c)   so monitors transmissions made by wireless telegraphy to or from apparatus comprised in the system,
as to make some or all of the contents of the communication available, while being transmitted, to a person other than the sender or intended recipient of the communication.
(3)   References in this Act to the interception of a communication do not include references to the interception of any communication broadcast for general reception.
(4)   For the purposes of this Act the interception of a communication takes place in the United Kingdom if, and only if, the modification, interference or monitoring or, in the case of a postal item, the interception is effected by conduct within the United Kingdom and the communication is either—
(a)   intercepted in the course of its transmission by means of a public postal service or public telecommunication system; or
(b)   intercepted in the course of its transmission by means of a private telecommunication system in a case in which the sender or intended recipient of the communication is in the United Kingdom.
(5)   References in this Act to the interception of a communication in the course of its transmission by means of a postal service or telecommunication system do not include references to—
(a)   any conduct that takes place in relation only to so much of the communication as consists in any traffic data comprised in or attached to a communication (whether by the sender or otherwise) for the purposes of any postal service or telecommunication system by means of which it is being or may be transmitted; or
(b)   any such conduct, in connection with conduct falling within paragraph (a), as gives a person who is neither the sender nor the intended recipient only so much access to a communication as is necessary for the purpose of identifying traffic data so comprised or attached.
(6)   For the purposes of this section references to the modification of a telecommunication system include references to the attachment of any apparatus to, or other modification of or interference with—
(a)   any part of the system; or

(b)    any wireless telegraphy apparatus used for making transmissions to or from apparatus comprised in the system.

(7)    For the purposes of this section the times while a communication is being transmitted by means of a telecommunication system shall be taken to include any time when the system by means of which the communication is being, or has been, transmitted is used for storing it in a manner that enables the intended recipient to collect it or otherwise to have access to it.

(8)    For the purposes of this section the cases in which any contents of a communication are to be taken to be made available to a person while being transmitted shall include any case in which any of the contents of the communication, while being transmitted, are diverted or recorded so as to be available to a person subsequently.

(9)    In this section "traffic data", in relation to any communication, means—
   (a)    any data identifying, or purporting to identify, any person, apparatus or location to or from which the communication is or may be transmitted,
   (b)    any data identifying or selecting, or purporting to identify or select, apparatus through which, or by means of which, the communication is or may be transmitted,
   (c)    any data comprising signals for the actuation of apparatus used for the purposes of a telecommunication system for effecting (in whole or in part) the transmission of any communication, and
   (d)    any data identifying the data or other data as data comprised in or attached to a particular communication,
but that expression includes data identifying a computer file or computer program access to which is obtained, or which is run, by means of the communication to the extent only that the file or program is identified by reference to the apparatus in which it is stored.

(10)    In this section—
   (a)    references, in relation to traffic data comprising signals for the actuation of apparatus, to a telecommunication system by means of which a communication is being or may be transmitted include references to any telecommunication system in which that apparatus is comprised; and
   (b)    references to traffic data being attached to a communication include references to the data and the communication being logically associated with each other;
and in this section "data", in relation to a postal item, means anything written on the outside of the item.

(11)    In this section "postal item" means any letter, postcard or other such thing in writing as may be used by the sender for imparting information to the recipient, or any packet or parcel.

**[1.1222]**
**3    Lawful interception without an interception warrant**
(1)    Conduct by any person consisting in the interception of a communication is authorised by this section if the communication is one which   . . .   is both—
   (a)    a communication sent by a person who has consented to the interception; and
   (b)    a communication the intended recipient of which has so consented.
(2)    Conduct by any person consisting in the interception of a communication is authorised by this section if—
   (a)    the communication is one sent by, or intended for, a person who has consented to the interception; and
   (b)    surveillance by means of that interception has been authorised under Part II.
(3)    Conduct consisting in the interception of a communication is authorised by this section if—
   (a)    it is conduct by or on behalf of a person who provides a postal service or a telecommunications service; and
   (b)    it takes place for purposes connected with the provision or operation of that service or with the enforcement, in relation to that service, of any enactment relating to the use of postal services or telecommunications services.
[(3A)    Conduct consisting in the interception of a communication in the course of its transmission by means of a public postal service is authorised by this section if it is conduct—
   (a)    under section 159 of the Customs and Excise Management Act 1979 as applied by virtue of—
      (i)    section 105 of the Postal Services Act 2000 (power to open postal items etc); or
      (ii)    that section 105 and another enactment; and
   (b)    by an officer of Revenue and Customs.]
(4)    Conduct by any person consisting in the interception of a communication in the course of its transmission by means of wireless telegraphy is authorised by this section if it takes place—
   (a)    with the authority of a designated person under [section 48 of the Wireless Telegraphy Act 2006 (interception and disclosure of wireless telegraphy messages)]; and
   (b)    for purposes connected with anything falling within subsection (5).
(5)    Each of the following falls within this subsection—
   [(a)    the grant of wireless telegraphy licences under the Wireless Telegraphy Act 2006;]

(b)    the prevention or detection of anything which constitutes interference with wireless telegraphy; and

(c)    the enforcement of[—
   (i)    any provision of Part 2 (other than Chapter 2 and sections 27 to 31) or Part 3 of that Act, or
   (ii)    any enactment not falling within sub-paragraph (i),]
   that relates to such interference.

**NOTES**

Sub-s (1): words omitted repealed by the Regulation of Investigatory Powers (Monetary Penalty Notices and Consents for Interceptions) Regulations 2011, SI 2011/1340, reg 3, as from 16 June 2011.

Sub-s (3A): inserted by the Policing and Crime Act 2009, s 100(1), as from 12 November 2009.

Sub-ss (4), (5): words in square brackets substituted by the Wireless Telegraphy Act 2006, s 123, Sch 7, paras 21, 22.

**[1.1223]**
**4    Power to provide for lawful interception**

(1)    Conduct by any person ("the interceptor") consisting in the interception of a communication in the course of its transmission by means of a telecommunication system is authorised by this section if—

(a)    the interception is carried out for the purpose of obtaining information about the communications of a person who, or who the interceptor has reasonable grounds for believing, is in a country or territory outside the United Kingdom;

(b)    the interception relates to the use of a telecommunications service provided to persons in that country or territory which is either—
   (i)    a public telecommunications service; or
   (ii)    a telecommunications service that would be a public telecommunications service if the persons to whom it is offered or provided were members of the public in a part of the United Kingdom;

(c)    the person who provides that service (whether the interceptor or another person) is required by the law of that country or territory to carry out, secure or facilitate the interception in question;

(d)    the situation is one in relation to which such further conditions as may be prescribed by regulations made by the Secretary of State are required to be satisfied before conduct may be treated as authorised by virtue of this subsection; and

(e)    the conditions so prescribed are satisfied in relation to that situation.

(2)    Subject to subsection (3), the Secretary of State may by regulations authorise any such conduct described in the regulations as appears to him to constitute a legitimate practice reasonably required for the purpose, in connection with the carrying on of any business, of monitoring or keeping a record of—

(a)    communications by means of which transactions are entered into in the course of that business; or

(b)    other communications relating to that business or taking place in the course of its being carried on.

(3)    Nothing in any regulations under subsection (2) shall authorise the interception of any communication except in the course of its transmission using apparatus or services provided by or to the person carrying on the business for use wholly or partly in connection with that business.

(4)    Conduct taking place in a prison is authorised by this section if it is conduct in exercise of any power conferred by or under any rules made under section 47 of the Prison Act 1952, section 39 of the Prisons (Scotland) Act 1989 or section 13 of the Prison Act (Northern Ireland) 1953 (prison rules).

(5)    Conduct taking place in any hospital premises where high security psychiatric services are provided is authorised by this section if it is conduct in pursuance of, and in accordance with, any direction given under [[section 4(3A)(a) of the National Health Service Act 2006], or section 19 or 23 of the National Health Service (Wales) Act 2006] (directions as to the carrying out of their functions by health bodies) to the body providing those services at those premises.

(6)    Conduct taking place in a state hospital is authorised by this section if it is conduct in pursuance of, and in accordance with, any direction given to the State Hospitals Board for Scotland under section 2(5) of the National Health Service (Scotland) Act 1978 (regulations and directions as to the exercise of their functions by health boards) as applied by Article 5(1) of and the Schedule to The State Hospitals Board for Scotland Order 1995 (which applies certain provisions of that Act of 1978 to the State Hospitals Board).

(7)    In this section references to a business include references to any activities of a government department, of any public authority or of any person or office holder on whom functions are conferred by or under any enactment.

(8)    In this section—

"government department" includes any part of the Scottish Administration, a Northern Ireland department and [the Welsh Assembly Government];

"high security psychiatric services" has the same meaning as in [section 4 of the National Health Service Act 2006];

"hospital premises" has the same meaning as in section 4(3) of that Act; and

"state hospital" has the same meaning as in the National Health Service (Scotland) Act 1978.

(9) In this section "prison" means—

(a) any prison, young offender institution, young offenders centre or remand centre which is under the general superintendence of, or is provided by, the Secretary of State under the Prison Act 1952 or the Prison Act (Northern Ireland) 1953, or

(b) any prison, young offenders institution or remand centre which is under the general superintendence of the Scottish Ministers under the Prisons (Scotland) Act 1989,

and includes any contracted out prison, within the meaning of Part IV of the Criminal Justice Act 1991 or section 106(4) of the Criminal Justice and Public Order Act 1994, and any legalised police cells within the meaning of section 14 of the Prisons (Scotland) Act 1989.

**NOTES**

Sub-s (5): words in first (outer) pair of square brackets substituted by the National Health Service (Consequential Provisions) Act 2006, s 2, Sch 1, paras 207, 208(a); words in second (inner) pair of square brackets substituted by the Health and Social Care Act 2012, s 55(2), Sch 5, para 98, as from 1 April 2013.

Sub-s (8): words in square brackets in definition "government department" substituted by the Government of Wales Act 2006 (Consequential Modifications and Transitional Provisions) Order 2007, SI 2007/1388, art 3, Sch 1, paras 76(1), (2); words in square brackets in definition "high security psychiatric services" substituted by the National Health Service (Consequential Provisions) Act 2006, s 2, Sch 1, paras 207, 208(b).

Construction of references to an office-holder in the Scottish Administration: unless the context otherwise requires, references to an office-holder in the Scottish Administration are to be taken to include a reference to the Scottish Court Service established by the Judiciary and Courts (Scotland) Act 2008, s 60(1): see the Judiciary and Courts (Scotland) Act 2008 (Consequential Provisions and Modifications) Order 2009, SI 2009/2231, art 3.

Regulations: the Telecommunications (Lawful Business Practice) (Interception of Communications) Regulations 2000, SI 2000/2699 at **[2.592]**; the Regulation of Investigatory Powers (Conditions for the Lawful Interception of Persons outside the United Kingdom) Regulations 2004, SI 2004/157.

## PART V
## MISCELLANEOUS AND SUPPLEMENTAL

**[1.1224]**
**83 Short title, commencement and extent**
(1) This Act may be cited as the Regulation of Investigatory Powers Act 2000.
(2) The provisions of this Act, other than this section, shall come into force on such day as the Secretary of State may by order appoint; and different days may be appointed under this subsection for different purposes.
(3) This Act extends to Northern Ireland.

**NOTES**

Orders: the commencement order relevant to the provisions reproduced here is the Regulation of Investigatory Powers Act 2000 (Commencement No 1 and Transitional Provisions) Order 2000, SI 2000/2543.

# EMPLOYMENT ACT 2002

## (2002 c 22)

### ARRANGEMENT OF SECTIONS

### PART 1
### STATUTORY LEAVE AND PAY

#### CHAPTER 1
#### PATERNITY AND ADOPTION

*Administration and enforcement: pay*

### PART 3
### DISPUTE RESOLUTION ETC

*Employment particulars*

*General*

## PART 4
## MISCELLANEOUS AND GENERAL

### *Miscellaneous*

## SCHEDULES

*An Act to make provision for statutory rights to paternity and adoption leave and pay; to amend the law relating to statutory maternity leave and pay; to amend the Employment Tribunals Act 1996; to make provision for the use of statutory procedures in relation to employment disputes; to amend the law relating to particulars of employment; to make provision about compromise agreements; to make provision for questionnaires in relation to equal pay; to make provision in connection with trade union learning representatives; to amend section 110 of the Employment Rights Act 1996; to make provision about fixed-term work; to make provision about flexible working; to amend the law relating to maternity allowance; to make provision for work-focused interviews for partners of benefit claimants; to make provision about the use of information for, or relating to, employment and training; and for connected purposes*

[8 July 2002]

### NOTES

Most of this major Act consists of amendments and additions to other legislation, principally the Employment Rights Act 1996 and the Social Security Contributions and Benefits Act 1992. These are cross referenced. The Act is otherwise printed in full save for those provisions that either have been repealed or are outside the scope of this work. In particular, ss 29–33 and Schs 2–4 were repealed by the Employment Act 2008, s 20, Schedule, Pt 1, as from 6 April 2009, subject to a variety of transitional provisions and savings in the Employment Act 2008 (Commencement No 1, Transitional Provisions and Savings) Order 2008, SI 2008/3232, Schedule, Pt 1.

## PART 1
## STATUTORY LEAVE AND PAY

### CHAPTER 1
### PATERNITY AND ADOPTION

**1–4**  *(S 1 inserts the Employment Rights Act 1996, ss 80A, 80B, 80C–80E at* **[1.875]** *et seq; s 2 inserts the Social Security Contributions and Benefits Act 1992, ss 171ZA–171ZE, 171ZF–171ZK at* **[1.209]** *et seq; s 3 inserts the Employment Rights Act 1996, ss 75A–75D at* **[1.866]** *et seq; s 4 inserts the Social Security Contributions and Benefits Act 1992, ss 171ZL–171ZT at* **[1.225]** *et seq.)*

*Administration and enforcement: pay*

**5, 6**  *(S 5 repealed by the Commissioners for Revenue and Customs Act 2005, ss 50(6), 52(2), Sch 4, para 93, Sch 5; s 6 (financial arrangements) outside the scope of this work.)*

### [1.1225]
### 7  Funding of employers' liabilities

(1)  The Secretary of State shall by regulations make provision for the payment by employers of [ordinary statutory paternity pay, additional statutory paternity pay] and statutory adoption pay to be funded by the Board to such extent as the regulations may specify.

(2)  Regulations under subsection (1) shall—

    (a)  make provision for a person who has made a payment of [ordinary statutory paternity pay, additional statutory paternity pay] or statutory adoption pay to be entitled, except in such circumstances as the regulations may provide, to recover an amount equal to the sum of—

        (i)  the aggregate of such of those payments as qualify for small employers' relief; and

        (ii)  an amount equal to 92 per cent of the aggregate of such of those payments as do not so qualify; and

    (b)  include provision for a person who has made a payment of [ordinary statutory paternity pay, additional statutory paternity pay] or statutory adoption pay qualifying for small employers' relief to be entitled, except in such circumstances as the regulations may

Part 1 Statutes

provide, to recover an additional amount equal to the amount to which the person would have been entitled under section 167(2)(b) of the Social Security Contributions and Benefits Act 1992 (corresponding provision for statutory maternity pay) had the payment been a payment of statutory maternity pay.

(3)   For the purposes of subsection (2), [a payment of ordinary statutory paternity pay, additional statutory paternity pay] or statutory adoption pay qualifies for small employers' relief if it would have so qualified were it a payment of statutory maternity pay, treating the period for which the payment is made, [in the case of ordinary statutory paternity pay or additional statutory paternity pay], or the payee's adoption pay period, in the case of statutory adoption pay, as the maternity pay period.

(4)   Regulations under subsection (1) may, in particular—

(a)   make provision for funding in advance as well as in arrear;

(b)   make provision for funding, or the recovery of amounts due under provision made by virtue of subsection (2)(b), by means of deductions from such amounts for which employers are accountable to the Board as the regulations may provide, or otherwise;

(c)   make provision for the recovery by the Board of any sums overpaid to employers under the regulations.

(5)   Where in accordance with any provision of regulations under subsection (1) an amount has been deducted from an employer's contributions payments, the amount so deducted shall (except in such cases as the Secretary of State may by regulations provide) be treated for the purposes of any provision made by or under any enactment in relation to primary or secondary Class 1 contributions—

(a)   as having been paid (on such date as may be determined in accordance with the regulations), and

(b)   as having been received by the Board,

towards discharging the employer's liability in respect of such contributions.

(6)   Regulations under this section must be made with the concurrence of the Board.

(7)   In this section, "contributions payments", in relation to an employer, means any payments which the employer is required, by or under any enactment, to make in discharge of any liability in respect of primary or secondary Class 1 contributions.

**NOTES**

Sub-ss (1)–(3): words in square brackets substituted by the Work and Families Act 2006, s 11(1), Sch 1, para 50, as from 3 March 2010.

Regulations: the Statutory Paternity Pay and Statutory Adoption Pay (Administration) Regulations 2002, SI 2002/2820 at **[2.654]**; the Statutory Paternity Pay (Adoption) and Statutory Adoption Pay (Adoptions from Overseas) (Administration) Regulations 2003, SI 2003/1192; the Additional Statutory Paternity Pay (Birth, Adoption and Adoptions from Overseas) (Administration) Regulations 2010, SI 2010/154 at **[2.1307]**.

**[1.1226]**
## 8   Regulations about payment

(1)   The Secretary of State may make regulations with respect to the payment by employers of [ordinary statutory paternity pay, additional statutory paternity pay] and statutory adoption pay.

(2)   Regulations under subsection (1) may, in particular, include provision—

(a)   about the records to be kept by employers in relation to payments of [ordinary statutory paternity pay, additional statutory paternity pay] and statutory adoption pay, including the length of time for which they are to be retained;

(b)   for the production of wages sheets and other documents and records to officers of the Board for the purpose of enabling them to satisfy themselves that [ordinary statutory paternity pay, additional statutory paternity pay] and statutory adoption pay have been paid and are being paid, in accordance with the regulations, to employees who are entitled to them;

(c)   for requiring employers to provide information to employees (in their itemised pay statements or otherwise);

(d)   for requiring employers to make returns to the Board containing such particulars with respect to payments of [ordinary statutory paternity pay, additional statutory paternity pay] and statutory adoption pay as the regulations may provide.

(3)   Regulations under subsection (1) must be made with the concurrence of the Board.

**NOTES**

Sub-ss (1), (2): words in square brackets substituted by the Work and Families Act 2006, s 11(1), Sch 1, para 51, as from 3 March 2010.

Regulations: the Statutory Paternity Pay and Statutory Adoption Pay (Administration) Regulations 2002, SI 2002/2820 at **[2.654]**; the Statutory Paternity Pay (Adoption) and Statutory Adoption Pay (Adoptions from Overseas) (Administration) Regulations 2003, SI 2003/1192; the Additional Statutory Paternity Pay (Birth, Adoption and Adoptions from Overseas) (Administration) Regulations 2010, SI 2010/154 at **[2.1307]**.

**9–15** *(S 9 amends the Social Security Contributions (Transfer of Functions, etc) Act 1999; ss 10–15 (powers to require information, penalties and supply and use of information) outside the scope of this work.)*

**[1.1227]**
## 16 Interpretation
In sections 5 to 15—
"the Board" means the Commissioners of Inland Revenue;
"the Department" means the Department for Social Development or the Department for Employment and Learning;
"employer" and "employee" have the same meanings as in Parts 12ZA and 12ZB of the Social Security Contributions and Benefits Act 1992.

**NOTES**
Commissioners of Inland Revenue: a reference to the Commissioners of Inland Revenue is now to be taken as a reference to the Commissioners for Her Majesty's Revenue and Customs; see the Commissioners for Revenue and Customs Act 2005, s 50(1), (7).

**17–28** *(In so far as these sections are still in force and not outside the scope of this work, they contain various amendments to the Employment Rights Act 1996 and the Social Security Contributions and Benefits Act 1992 which have been incorporated where appropriate.)*

## PART 3
## DISPUTE RESOLUTION ETC

*Statutory procedures*

**29–34** *(Ss 29–33 repealed by the Employment Act 2008, s 20, Schedule, Pt 1, as from 6 April 2009, subject to a variety of transitional provisions and savings in the Employment Act 2008 (Commencement No 1, Transitional Provisions and Savings) Order 2008, SI 2008/3232, Schedule, Pt 1 (with regard to s 30 (Contracts of employment) note that prior to its repeal, only sub-s (3) (Secretary of State's power to make provision by Regulations about the application of the statutory procedures) had been brought into force (see SI 2003/1190, art 2)); s 34(1) introduces the amendments that follow; s 34(2) inserted the Employment Rights Act 1996, s 98A, and was repealed by the Employment Act 2008, as from 6 April 2009 (subject to a variety of transitional provisions and savings in SI 2008/3232, Schedule, Pt 1); s 34(3)–(6) amend ss 112, 117, 120, 123 of the 1996 Act at* **[1.922]**, **[1.927]**, **[1.930]**, **[1.933]**.*)*

*Employment particulars*

**35–37** *(Ss 35, 36 amend the Employment Rights Act 1996, s 3 at* **[1.745]**; *s 37 inserts ss 7A, 7B of the 1996 Act at* **[1.750]**, **[1.751]**.*)*

**[1.1228]**
## 38 Failure to give statement of employment particulars etc
(1) This section applies to proceedings before an employment tribunal relating to a claim by an employee under any of the jurisdictions listed in Schedule 5.
(2) If in the case of proceedings to which this section applies—
    (a) the employment tribunal finds in favour of the employee, but makes no award to him in respect of the claim to which the proceedings relate, and
    (b) when the proceedings were begun the employer was in breach of his duty to the employee under section 1(1) or 4(1) of the Employment Rights Act 1996 (c 18) (duty to give a written statement of initial employment particulars or of particulars of change),
the tribunal must, subject to subsection (5), make an award of the minimum amount to be paid by the employer to the employee and may, if it considers it just and equitable in all the circumstances, award the higher amount instead.
(3) If in the case of proceedings to which this section applies—
    (a) the employment tribunal makes an award to the employee in respect of the claim to which the proceedings relate, and
    (b) when the proceedings were begun the employer was in breach of his duty to the employee under section 1(1) or 4(1) of the Employment Rights Act 1996,
the tribunal must, subject to subsection (5), increase the award by the minimum amount and may, if it considers it just and equitable in all the circumstances, increase the award by the higher amount instead.
(4) In subsections (2) and (3)—
    (a) references to the minimum amount are to an amount equal to two weeks' pay, and
    (b) references to the higher amount are to an amount equal to four weeks' pay.
(5) The duty under subsection (2) or (3) does not apply if there are exceptional circumstances which would make an award or increase under that subsection unjust or inequitable.
(6) The amount of a week's pay of an employee shall—

(a)  be calculated for the purposes of this section in accordance with Chapter 2 of Part 14 of the Employment Rights Act 1996 (c 18), and

(b)  not exceed the amount for the time being specified in section 227 of that Act (maximum amount of week's pay).

(7)  For the purposes of Chapter 2 of Part 14 of the Employment Rights Act 1996 as applied by subsection (6), the calculation date shall be taken to be—

(a)  if the employee was employed by the employer on the date the proceedings were begun, that date, and

(b)  if he was not, the effective date of termination as defined by section 97 of that Act.

(8)  The Secretary of State may by order—

(a)  amend Schedule 5 for the purpose of—

(i)  adding a jurisdiction to the list in that Schedule, or

(ii)  removing a jurisdiction from that list;

(b)  make provision, in relation to a jurisdiction listed in Schedule 5, for this section not to apply to proceedings relating to claims of a description specified in the order;

(c)  make provision for this section to apply, with or without modifications, as if—

(i)  any individual of a description specified in the order who would not otherwise be an employee for the purposes of this section were an employee for those purposes, and

(ii)  a person of a description specified in the order were, in the case of any such individual, the individual's employer for those purposes.

**NOTES**

The tribunal must . . . make an award, etc (sub-s (2)): where an award of compensation for unfair dismissal falls to be increased under this section, the adjustment is to be in the amount awarded under the Employment Rights Act 1996, s 118(1)(b), and is to be applied immediately before any reduction under s 123(6), (7) of that Act; see s 124A of the 1996 Act at **[1.935]**.

Orders: the Employment Act 2002 (Amendment of Schedules 3, 4 and 5) Order 2007, SI 2007/30 (note that Schs 3 and 4 have been repealed as noted *post*).

*General*

**39**  *(Inserts the Employment Rights Act 1996, s 124A at **[1.935]**.)*

**[1.1229]**

**40  Interpretation of Part 3**

In this Part—

"employer" and "employee" have the same meanings as in the Employment Rights Act 1996 (c 18);

. . .

**NOTES**

Definition "statutory procedure" (omitted) repealed by the Employment Act 2008, s 20, Schedule, Pt 1, as from 6 April 2009, subject to a variety of transitional provisions and savings in the Employment Act 2008 (Commencement No 1, Transitional Provisions and Savings) Order 2008, SI 2008/3232, Schedule, Pt 1.

## PART 4
## MISCELLANEOUS AND GENERAL

*Miscellaneous*

**41–44**  *(S 41 repealed by the Employment Relations Act 2004, s 57(2); s 42 repealed by the Equality Act 2010, s 211(2), Sch 27, Pt 1, as from 1 October 2010; s 43 inserts the Trade Union and Labour Relations (Consolidation) Act 1992, s 168A at **[1.433]**, and amends ss 169, 170, 173, 199, 200, 203 of that Act; s 44 amends the Employment Rights Act 1996, s 110 at **[1.919]**.)*

**[1.1230]**

**45  Fixed-term work**

(1)  The Secretary of State shall make regulations—

(a)  for the purpose of securing that employees in fixed-term employment are treated, for such purposes and to such extent as the regulations may specify, no less favourably than employees in permanent employment, and

(b)  for the purpose of preventing abuse arising from the use of successive periods of fixed-term employment.

(2)  The regulations may—

(a)  specify classes of employee who are to be taken to be, or not to be, in fixed-term employment;

(b)  specify classes of employee who are to be taken to be, or not to be, in permanent employment;

(c)  specify circumstances in which employees in fixed-term employment are to be taken to be, or not to be, treated less favourably than employees in permanent employment;

(d)  specify circumstances in which periods of fixed-term employment are to be taken to be, or not to be, successive;

  (e)    specify circumstances in which fixed-term employment is to have effect as permanent employment;

  (f)    make provision which has effect in relation to employees in fixed-term employment generally or provision which has effect only in relation to specified classes of employee in fixed-term employment.

(3)  The regulations may—

  (a)    confer jurisdiction (including exclusive jurisdiction) on employment tribunals;

  (b)    provide for specified obligations not to apply in specified circumstances;

  (c)    make provision about notices or information to be given, evidence to be produced and other procedures to be followed;

  (d)    amend, apply with or without modifications, or make provision similar to any provision of—

      (i)    the Employment Rights Act 1996 (c 18) (including, in particular, Parts 5, 10 and 13),

      (ii)   the Trade Union and Labour Relations (Consolidation) Act 1992 (c 52), or

      (iii)  the Social Security Contributions and Benefits Act 1992 (c 4);

  (e)    provide for the provisions of specified agreements to have effect in place of provisions of the regulations to such extent and in such circumstances as may be specified.

(4)  Without prejudice to the generality of this section, the regulations may make any provision in relation to employees which appears to the Secretary of State to be necessary or expedient—

  (a)    for the purpose of implementing Council Directive 99/70/EC on the framework agreement on fixed-term work in its application to terms and conditions of employment;

  (b)    for the purpose of dealing with any matter arising out of or related to the United Kingdom's obligations under that Directive;

  (c)    for the purpose of any matter dealt with by the framework agreement or for the purpose of applying the provisions of the framework agreement to any matter relating to fixed term workers.

(5)  In its application to this section, section 51(1)(b) includes power to amend an enactment.

(6)  In this section—

  (a)    "employee" means an individual who has entered into or works under (or, where the employment has ceased, worked under) a contract of employment, and

  (b)    "contract of employment" means a contract of service or apprenticeship, whether express or implied, and (if it is express) whether oral or in writing.

**NOTES**

Regulations: the Fixed-term Employees (Prevention of Less Favourable Treatment) Regulations 2002, SI 2002/2034 at **[2.597]**; the Fixed-term Employees (Prevention of Less Favourable Treatment) (Amendment) Regulations 2008, SI 2008/2776.

**46–50**  *(S 46 applies to Northern Ireland only; s 47 inserts the Employment Rights Act 1996, ss 47E, 80F–80I, 104C at* **[1.811]**, **[1.882]–[1.885]**, **[1.910]**; *s 48 (Rate of maternity allowance), s 49 (Work-focused interviews for partners), s 50 (introduces Sch 6 (Use of information for, or relating to, employment and training)) outside the scope of this work. Note also that s 49 is repealed by the Welfare Reform Act 2012, s 147, Sch 14, Pt 1, as from a day to be appointed.)*

*General*

**[1.1231]**
**51  Orders and regulations**
(1)  Any power of the Secretary of State to make orders or regulations under this Act includes power—

  (a)    to make different provision for different cases or circumstances;

  (b)    to make such incidental, supplementary, consequential or transitional provision as the Secretary of State thinks fit.

(2)  Any power of the Secretary of State to make orders or regulations under this Act is exercisable by statutory instrument.

(3)  No order may be made under this Act unless a draft of the order has been laid before and approved by resolution of each House of Parliament.

(4)  No regulations may be made under section . . . 45 unless a draft of the regulations has been laid before and approved by resolution of each House of Parliament.

(5)  A statutory instrument containing regulations under any other provision of this Act shall be subject to annulment in pursuance of a resolution of either House of Parliament.

(6)  This section does not apply to orders under section 55(2).

**NOTES**

Sub-s (4): words omitted repealed by the Employment Act 2008, s 20, Schedule, Pt 1, as from 6 April 2009.

**[1.1232]**
**52  Financial provisions**
(1)  There shall be paid out of money provided by Parliament—

(a)    any expenses incurred by a Minister of the Crown or government department in consequence of this Act, and

(b)    any increase attributable to this Act in the sums so provided under any other Act.

(2)    There shall be paid into the Consolidated Fund any increase attributable to this Act in the sums payable into that Fund under any other Act.

**[1.1233]**
### 53 Minor and consequential amendments
Schedule 7 (which makes minor and consequential amendments) has effect.

**[1.1234]**
### 54 Repeals and revocations
The enactments and instruments specified in Schedule 8 are hereby repealed or revoked to the extent specified there.

**[1.1235]**
### 55 Short title etc
(1)    This Act may be cited as the Employment Act 2002.

(2)    This Act, except sections 45, 46, 51 and 52 and this section, shall come into force on such day as the Secretary of State may by order made by statutory instrument appoint, and different days may be so appointed for different purposes.

(3)    An order under subsection (2) may contain such transitional provisions and savings as the Secretary of State considers necessary or expedient in connection with the coming into force of any of the provisions of this Act.

(4)    The Secretary of State may by regulations make such transitional provisions and savings as he considers necessary or expedient for the purposes of or in connection with—

(a)    the coming into force of section 19 or 48, or Schedule 7 so far as relating to any amendment made in consequence of either of those sections; or

(b)    the operation of any enactment amended by any of those provisions during any period when the amendment is not wholly in force.

(5)    Subject to subsections (6) and (7), this Act extends to England and Wales and Scotland only.

(6)–(8)    *(Apply to Northern Ireland only.)*

---

**NOTES**

Orders: the Employment Act 2002 (Commencement No 1) Order 2002, SI 2002/1989; the Employment Act 2002 (Commencement No 2) Order 2002, SI 2002/2256; the Employment Act 2002 (Commencement No 3 and Transitional and Saving Provisions) Order 2002, SI 2002/2866; the Employment Act 2002 (Commencement No 4 and Transitional Provisions) Order 2003, SI 2003/1190; the Employment Act 2002 (Commencement No 5) Order 2003, SI 2003/1666; the Employment Act 2002 (Commencement No 6 and Transitional Provision) Order 2004, SI 2004/1717; the Employment Act 2002 (Commencement No 7) Order 2004, SI 2004/2185; the Employment Act 2002 (Commencement No 8) Order 2004, SI 2004/2822.

---

## SCHEDULES

## SCHEDULES 1–4

*(Sch 1 (Penalties: procedure and appeals) outside the scope of this work; Schs 2–4 repealed by the Employment Act 2008, s 20, Schedule, Pt 1, as from 6 April 2009, subject to a variety of transitional provisions and savings in the Employment Act 2008 (Commencement No 1, Transitional Provisions and Savings) Order 2008, SI 2008/3232, Schedule, Pt 1.)*

## SCHEDULE 5
## TRIBUNAL JURISDICTIONS TO WHICH SECTION 38 APPLIES

Section 38

**[1.1236]**

. . .

. . .

[Section 145A of the Trade Union and Labour Relations (Consolidation) Act 1992 (inducements relating to union membership or activities)

Section 145B of that Act (inducements relating to collective bargaining)

Section 146 of that Act (detriment in relation to union membership and activities)]

Paragraph 156 of Schedule A1 to that Act (detriment in relation to union recognition rights)

. . .

Section 23 of the Employment Rights Act 1996 (c 18) (unauthorised deductions and payments)

Section 48 of that Act (detriment in employment)

Section 111 of that Act (unfair dismissal)

Section 163 of that Act (redundancy payments)

Section 24 of the National Minimum Wage Act 1998 (c 39) (detriment in relation to national minimum wage)

. . .

[Sections 120 and 127 of the Equality Act 2010 (discrimination etc in work cases)]

The Employment Tribunal Extension of Jurisdiction (England and Wales) Order 1994 (SI 1994/1623) (breach of employment contract and termination)

The Employment Tribunal Extension of Jurisdiction (Scotland) Order 1994 (SI 1994/1624) (corresponding provision for Scotland)

Regulation 30 of the Working Time Regulations 1998 (SI 1998/1833) (breach of regulations)

Regulation 32 of the Transnational Information and Consultation of Employees Regulations 1999 (SI 1999/3323) (detriment relating to European Works Councils)

[ . . . ]

[ . . . ]

[Regulation 45 of the European Public Limited-Liability Company Regulations 2004 (SI 2004/2326) (detriment in employment)

Regulation 33 of the Information and Consultation of Employees Regulations 2004 (SI 2004/3426) (detriment in employment)

Paragraph 8 of the Schedule to the Occupational and Personal Pension Schemes (Consultation by Employers and Miscellaneous Amendment) Regulations 2006 (SI 2006/349) (detriment in employment)]

[ . . . ]

[Regulation 34 of the European Cooperative Society (Involvement of Employees) Regulations 2006 (detriment in relation to involvement in a European Cooperative Society)]

[Regulation 51 of the Companies (Cross-Border Mergers) Regulations 2007 (detriment in relation to special negotiating body or employee participation)]

[Regulation 17 of the Cross-border Railways Services (Working Time) Regulations 2008 (breach of regulations)].

**NOTES**

Entries relating to the Equal Pay Act 1970, the Sex Discrimination Act 1975, the Race Relations Act 1976, and the Disability Discrimination Act 1995 (all omitted) repealed by the Equality Act 2010, s 211, Sch 26, Pt 1, para 49(1), (2)(a)–(d), Sch 27, Pt 1, as from 1 October 2010 (see further the final note below).

Entries relating to the Trade Union and Labour Relations (Consolidation) Act 1992 substituted by the Employment Relations Act 2004, s 57(1), Sch 1, para 43.

Entry relating to the Tax Credits Act 1999 (omitted) repealed by the Tax Credits Act 2002, s 60, Sch 6.

Entry relating to the Equality Act 2010 inserted by the Equality Act 2010, s 211(1), Sch 26, Pt 1, para 49(1), (3), as from 1 October 2010 (see further the final note below).

Entry relating to the Employment Equality (Sexual Orientation) Regulations 2003 (omitted) originally inserted by the Employment Equality (Sexual Orientation) Regulations 2003, SI 2003/1661, reg 39, Sch 5, para 4(c), and repealed by the Equality Act 2010, s 211, Sch 26, Pt 1, para 49(1), (2)(e), Sch 27, Pt 1, as from 1 October 2010 (see further the final note below).

Entry relating to the Employment Equality (Religion or Belief) Regulations 2003 (omitted) originally inserted by the Employment Equality (Religion or Belief) Regulations 2003, SI 2003/1660, reg 39(2), Sch 5, para 4(c), and repealed by the Equality Act 2010, s 211, Sch 26, Pt 1, para 49(1), (2)(f), Sch 27, Pt 1, as from 1 October 2010 (see further the final note below).

Entries relating to the European Public Limited-Liability Company Regulations 2004, the Information and Consultation of Employees Regulations 2004, and the Occupational and Personal Pension Schemes (Consultation by Employers and Miscellaneous Amendment) Regulations 2006 inserted by the Employment Act 2002 (Amendment of Schedules 3, 4 and 5) Order 2007, SI 2007/30, art 2.

Entry relating to the Employment Equality (Age) Regulations 2006 (omitted) originally inserted by the Employment Equality (Age) Regulations 2006, SI 2006/1031, reg 49(1), Sch 8, Pt 1, para 36(1), (2), and repealed by the Equality Act 2010, s 211, Sch 26, Pt 1, para 49(1), (2)(g), Sch 27, Pt 1, as from 1 October 2010 (see further the final note below).

Entry relating to the European Cooperative Society (Involvement of Employees) Regulations 2006 inserted by the European Cooperative Society (Involvement of Employees) Regulations 2006, SI 2006/2059, reg 34(4).

Entry relating to the Companies (Cross-Border Mergers) Regulations 2007 inserted by the Companies (Cross-Border Mergers) Regulations 2007, SI 2007/2974, reg 63(c).

Entry relating to the Cross-border Railways Services (Working Time) Regulations 2008 inserted by the Cross-border Railways Services (Working Time) Regulations 2008, SI 2008/1660, reg 19, Sch 3, para 3(c), as from 27 July 2008.

Savings: for savings in relation to the operation of the Equal Pay Act 1970, the Sex Discrimination Act 1975, the Race Relations Act 1976, the Disability Discrimination Act 1995, the Employment Equality (Sexual Orientation) Regulations 2003, the Employment Equality (Religion or Belief) Regulations 2003, and the Employment Equality (Age) Regulations 2006 (all of which were repealed or revoked by the Equality Act 2010, as from 1 October 2010), see the Equality Act 2010 (Commencement No 4, Savings, Consequential, Transitional, Transitory and Incidental Provisions and Revocation) Order 2010, SI 2010/2317, art 15 at **[2.1568]** which provides that the 2010 Act does not apply where the act complained of occurs wholly before 1 October 2010 so that (a) nothing in the 2010 Act affects (i) the operation of a previous enactment or anything duly done or suffered under a previous enactment; (ii) any right, obligation or liability acquired or incurred under a previous enactment; (iii) any penalty incurred in relation to any unlawful act under a previous enactment; (iv) any investigation, legal proceeding or remedy in respect of any such right, obligation, liability or penalty; and (b) any such investigation, legal proceeding or remedy may be instituted, continued or enforced, and any such penalty may be imposed, as if the 2010 Act had not been commenced.

## SCHEDULE 6

*(Sch 6 (Miscellaneous amendments concerning the use of information for, or relating to, employment and training) outside the scope of this work; Schs 7 and 8 contain minor and consequential amendments and repeals respectively and, where relevant to this work, have been incorporated at the appropriate place.)*

# EDUCATION ACT 2002

## (2002 c 32)

### ARRANGEMENT OF SECTIONS

*An Act to make provision about education, training and childcare*

[24 July 2002]

### NOTES

Most of this Act covers matters outside the scope of this work, and only those provisions most directly relevant to employment law are printed. For reasons of space, the subject matter of sections not printed is not annotated. The provisions printed here apply only to England and Wales.

## PART 3
## MAINTAINED SCHOOLS

### CHAPTER 1
### GOVERNMENT OF MAINTAINED SCHOOLS

**[1.1237]**
**35 Staffing of community, voluntary controlled, community special and maintained nursery schools**
(1)   This section applies to—
   (a)   community schools,
   (b)   voluntary controlled schools,
   (c)   community special schools, and
   (d)   maintained nursery schools.

(2) Any teacher or other member of staff who is appointed to work under a contract of employment at a school to which this section applies is to be employed by the [local authority].

(3) The teaching staff of any school to which this section applies shall include—

    (a) a person appointed as head teacher, or

    (b) a person appointed to carry out the functions of the head teacher of the school—

       (i) pending the appointment of a head teacher, or

       (ii) in the absence of the head teacher.

(4) Regulations may make further provision with respect to the staffing of schools to which this section applies.

(5) Regulations under subsection (4) may, in particular—

    (a) make provision with respect to the appointment, discipline, suspension and dismissal of teachers and other staff,

    (b) make provision with respect to the appointment of teachers and other staff to work at a school otherwise than under a contract of employment,

    (c) make provision with respect to staff employed, or engaged otherwise than under a contract of employment, wholly or partly for the purposes of—

       (i) the provision of facilities and services under section 27, or

       (ii) any other activities which are not school activities but are carried on the school premises under the management or control of the governing body, and

    (d) confer functions on [local authorities], governing bodies and head teachers.

(6) In relation to teachers at a voluntary controlled school who are reserved teachers within the meaning of section 58 of the School Standards and Framework Act 1998 (c 31) (appointment and dismissal of certain teachers at schools with a religious character), regulations under subsection (4) shall have effect subject to the provisions of that section.

(7) If at any time a school to which this section applies does not have a delegated budget by virtue of any suspension under section 17 of, or Schedule 15 to, the School Standards and Framework Act 1998[, or section 66 of the Education and Inspections Act 2006]—

    (a) regulations under subsection (4) shall not apply, and

    (b) the provisions of Part 1 of Schedule 2 shall apply instead.

(8) In discharging any function conferred by regulations under subsection (4), a [local authority] or the governing body or head teacher of a maintained school shall have regard to any guidance given from time to time—

    (a) in relation to England, by the Secretary of State, or

    (b) in relation to Wales, by the National Assembly for Wales.

**NOTES**

Sub-ss (2), (5), (8): words in square brackets substituted by the Local Education Authorities and Children's Services Authorities (Integration of Functions) Order 2010, SI 2010/1158, art 5(1), Sch 2, Pt 1, para 11(1)–(3), as from 5 May 2010.

Sub-s (7): words in square brackets inserted by the Education Act 2011, s 19(1), as from 1 February 2012.

Regulations: the Staffing of Maintained Schools (Wales) Regulations 2006, SI 2006/873; the Staffing of Maintained Schools (Miscellaneous Amendments) (Wales) Regulations 2007, SI 2007/944; the Education (Miscellaneous Amendments relating to Safeguarding Children) (England) Regulations 2009, SI 2009/1924; the Education (Miscellaneous Amendments relating to Safeguarding Children) (Wales) Regulations 2009, SI 2009/2544; the School Staffing (England) Regulations 2009, SI 2009/2680 at **[2.1221]**; the Staffing of Maintained Schools (Wales) (Amendment) Regulations 2009, SI 2009/2708; the Staffing of Maintained Schools (Wales) (Amendment No 2) Regulations 2009, SI 2009/3161; the Federation of Maintained Schools and Miscellaneous Amendments (Wales) Regulations 2010, SI 2010/638; the School Governance (Federations) (England) Regulations 2012, SI 2012/1035; the School Staffing (England) (Amendment) Regulations 2012, SI 2012/1740.

**[1.1238]**
**36 Staffing of foundation, voluntary aided and foundation special schools**

(1) This section applies to—

    (a) foundation schools,

    (b) voluntary aided schools, and

    (c) foundation special schools.

(2) Except as provided by regulations under subsection (4), any teacher or other member of staff who is appointed to work under a contract of employment at a school to which this section applies is to be employed by the governing body of the school.

(3) The teaching staff of any school to which this section applies shall include—

    (a) a person appointed as head teacher, or

    (b) a person appointed to carry out the functions of the head teacher of the school—

       (i) pending the appointment of a head teacher, or

       (ii) in the absence of the head teacher.

(4) Regulations may make further provision with respect to the staffing of schools to which this section applies.

(5) Regulations under subsection (4) may, in particular—

    (a) make provision with respect to the appointment, discipline, suspension and dismissal of teachers and other staff,

(b) make provision with respect to the appointment of teachers and other staff to work at a school otherwise than under a contract of employment,

(c) make provision with respect to staff employed, or engaged otherwise than under a contract of employment, wholly or partly for the purposes of—

    (i) the provision of facilities and services under section 27, or

    (ii) any other activities which are not school activities but are carried on the school premises under the management or control of the governing body,

(d) enable teachers and other staff to be employed by the [local authority] in prescribed cases, and

(e) confer functions on [local authorities], governing bodies and head teachers.

(6) Regulations under subsection (4) shall have effect subject to section 58 of the School Standards and Framework Act 1998 (c 31) (appointment and dismissal of certain teachers at schools with a religious character).

(7) If at any time a school to which this section applies does not have a delegated budget by virtue of any suspension under section 17 of, or Schedule 15 to, the School Standards and Framework Act 1998[, or section 66 of the Education and Inspections Act 2006], regulations under subsection (4) shall have effect subject to the provisions of Part 2 of Schedule 2.

(8) In discharging any function conferred by regulations under subsection (4), a [local authority] or the governing body or head teacher of a maintained school shall have regard to any guidance given from time to time

(a) in relation to England, by the Secretary of State, or

(b) in relation to Wales, by the National Assembly for Wales.

**NOTES**

Sub-ss (5), (8): words in square brackets substituted by the Local Education Authorities and Children's Services Authorities (Integration of Functions) Order 2010, SI 2010/1158, art 5(1), Sch 2, Pt 1, para 11(1)–(3), as from 5 May 2010.

Sub-s (7): words in square brackets inserted by the Education Act 2011, s 19(2), as from 1 February 2012.

Regulations: see the note to s 35 *ante*.

**[1.1239]**
## 37 Payments in respect of dismissal, etc

(1) It shall be for the governing body of a maintained school to determine—

(a) whether any payment should be made by the [local authority] in respect of the dismissal, or for the purpose of securing the resignation, of any member of the staff of the school, and

(b) the amount of any such payment.

(2) Subsection (1) does not, however, apply in relation to a payment which the [local authority] are required to make—

(a) by virtue of any contract other than one made in contemplation of the impending dismissal or resignation of the member of staff concerned, or

(b) under any statutory provision.

(3) The [local authority]—

(a) shall take such steps as may be required for giving effect to any determination of the governing body under subsection (1), and

(b) shall not make, or agree to make, a payment in relation to which that subsection applies except in accordance with such a determination.

(4) Subject to subsection (7), costs incurred by the [local authority] in respect of any premature retirement of a member of the staff of a maintained school shall be met from the school's budget share for one or more [funding periods] except in so far as the authority agree with the governing body in writing (whether before or after the retirement occurs) that they shall not be so met.

(5) Subject to subsection (7), costs incurred by the [local authority] in respect of the dismissal, or for the purpose of securing the resignation, of any member of the staff of a maintained school shall not be met from the school's budget share for any [funding period] except in so far as the authority have good reason for deducting those costs, or any part of those costs, from that share.

(6) The fact that the authority have a policy precluding dismissal of their employees by reason of redundancy is not to be regarded as a good reason for the purposes of subsection (5); and in this subsection the reference to dismissal by reason of redundancy shall be read in accordance with section 139 of the Employment Rights Act 1996 (c 18).

(7) Where a [local authority] incur costs

(a) in respect of any premature retirement of any member of the staff of a maintained school who is employed for community purposes, or

(b) in respect of the dismissal, or for the purpose of securing the resignation, of any member of the staff of a maintained school who is employed for those purposes,

they shall recover those costs from the governing body except in so far as the authority agree with the governing body in writing (whether before or after the retirement, dismissal or resignation occurs) that they shall not be so recoverable.

[(7A) Any amount payable by virtue of subsection (7) by the governing body of a maintained school in England to the local authority may be met by the governing body out of the school's budget share for any funding period if and to the extent that the condition in subsection (7B) is met.

(7B) The condition is that the governing body are satisfied that meeting the amount out of the school's budget share will not to a significant extent interfere with the performance of any duty imposed on them by section 21(2) or by any other provision of the Education Acts.]

(8) Any amount payable by virtue of subsection (7) by the governing body of a maintained school [in Wales] to the [local authority] shall not be met by the governing body out of the school's budget share for any [funding period].

(9) Where a person is employed partly for community purposes and partly for other purposes, any payment or costs in respect of that person is to be apportioned between the two purposes; and the preceding provisions of this section shall apply separately to each part of the payment or costs.

(10) Regulations may make provision with respect to the recovery from governing bodies of amounts payable by virtue of subsection (7).

(11) Subsections (1) to (6) do not apply to a maintained school at any time when the school does not have a delegated budget by virtue of any suspension under section 17 of, or Schedule 15 to, the School Standards and Framework Act 1998 (c 31).

[(12) In this section—

"community purposes" means the purposes of the provision of facilities or services under section 27;

"funding period" has the meaning given by section 45(1B) of the School Standards and Framework Act 1998.]

**NOTES**

The words "funding periods" in sub-s (4), "funding period" in sub-ss (5), (8), and the whole of sub-s (12) were substituted by the Education Act 2005, s 117, Sch 18, para 14(1), (3), (4), as from 1 November 2005 (in relation to England), and as from 1 April 2010 (in relation to Wales).

Sub-ss (7A), (7B) were inserted, and the words "in Wales" in square bracket in sub-s (8) were inserted, by the Education Act 2011, s 47(1), as from 15 January 2012.

All other words in square brackets were substituted by the Local Education Authorities and Children's Services Authorities (Integration of Functions) Order 2010, SI 2010/1158, art 5(1), Sch 2, Pt 1, para 11(1), (2), as from 5 May 2010.

## PART 11
## MISCELLANEOUS AND GENERAL

*General*

**[1.1240]**
### 216 Commencement

(1) The following provisions shall come into force on the day on which this Act is passed—
(*outside the scope of this work*),
this section and section 217.

(2), (3) (*Outside the scope of this work.*)

(4) Subject to subsections (1) to (3), this Act shall come into force—
  (a) except in relation to Wales, in accordance with provision made by the Secretary of State by order, and
  (b) in relation to Wales, in accordance with provision made by the National Assembly for Wales by order.

(5) An order under this section may—
  (a) make provision generally or for specified purposes only,
  (b) make different provision for different purposes, and
  (c) contain such transitional provisions and savings as the person making the order thinks fit.

**NOTES**

Orders: commencement orders made under this section are outside the scope of this work.

**[1.1241]**
### 217 Short title and extent

(1) This Act may be cited as the Education Act 2002.

(2) This Act shall be included in the list of Education Acts set out in section 578 of the Education Act 1996 (c 56).

(3) Any amendment or repeal in this Act has the same extent as the provision amended or repealed.

(4) Except as provided by subsection (3), this Act extends to England and Wales only.

# INCOME TAX (EARNINGS AND PENSIONS) ACT 2003

## (2003 c 1)

### ARRANGEMENT OF SECTIONS

PART 6
EMPLOYMENT INCOME: INCOME WHICH IS NOT EARNINGS OR SHARE-RELATED

CHAPTER 3
PAYMENTS AND BENEFITS ON TERMINATION OF EMPLOYMENT ETC

*An Act to restate, with minor changes, certain enactments relating to income tax on employment income, pension income and social security income; and for connected purposes*

[6 March 2003]

**NOTES**

This substantial Act is essentially a re-enactment of the provisions of the Income and Corporation Taxes Act 1988 (referred to in this Act as ICTA) and later legislation, so far as relating to the taxation of earnings and pensions. Most of this Act covers matters outside the scope of this work, and only those provisions most directly relevant to employment law are printed. For reasons of space, the subject matter of sections not printed is not annotated.

The provisions printed here, unless noted otherwise, came into force on 6 April 2003 and have effect for the purposes of income tax for the year 2003–04 and subsequent years of assessment, and for the purposes of corporation tax for accounting periods ending after 5 April 2003. This Act is reproduced as amended, in particular, by the Income Tax Act 2007, as from 6 April 2007, with effect for the purposes of income tax for the year 2007–08 and subsequent tax years, and for the purposes of corporation tax for accounting periods ending after 5 April 2007 (see s 1034(1)). For transitional provisions and savings see s 1034(2) of, and Sch 2 to, the 2007 Act.

PART 1
OVERVIEW

**[1.1242]**
**1   Overview of contents of this Act**
(1)   This Act imposes charges to income tax on—
   (a)   employment income (see Parts 2 to [7A]),
   (b)   pension income (see Part 9), and
   (c)   social security income (see [Chapters 1 to 7 of] Part 10).
(2)   .
(3)   This Act also—
   (a)   confers certain reliefs in respect of liabilities of former employees (see Part 8),

[(aa) makes provision for the high income child benefit charge (see Chapter 8 of Part 10),]
(b) provides for the assessment, collection and recovery of income tax in respect of employment, pension or social security income that is PAYE income (see Part 11), . . .
[(ba) allows deductions to be made from such income in respect of certain debts payable to the Commissioners for Her Majesty's Revenue and Customs (see Part 11), and]
(c) allows deductions to be made from such income in respect of payroll giving (see Part 12).

**NOTES**

Sub-s (1): figure "7A" in square brackets in para (a) substituted by the Finance Act 2011, s 26, Sch 2, paras 2, 3 (note that Part 7A of this Act (as inserted by Sch 2, para 1 to the 2011 Act) has effect in relation to relevant steps taken on or after 6 April 2011 and that all other amendments made by that Schedule have effect accordingly (for transitional provisions etc in relation to the new Part 7A see Sch 2, para 52 et seq); words in square brackets in para (c) inserted by the Finance Act 2012, s 8, Sch 1, paras 5(1), (2)(a), 7(1), with effect for the tax year 2012–13 and subsequent tax years.

Sub-s (2): repealed by the Income Tax Act 2007, ss 1027, 1031, Sch 1, Pt 2, paras 425, 426, Sch 3, Pt 1 (for effect and transitional provisions see the introductory note to this Act).

Sub-s (3): para (aa) inserted by the Finance Act 2012, s 8, Sch 1, paras 5(1), (2)(b), 7(1), with effect for the tax year 2012–13 and subsequent tax years; word omitted from para (b) repealed, and para (ba) inserted, by the Finance Act 2009 (Consequential Amendments) Order 2011, SI 2011/1583, art 2(1), (2), as from 20 July 2011.

## PART 2
## EMPLOYMENT INCOME: CHARGE TO TAX

### CHAPTER 1
### INTRODUCTION

**[1.1243]**
**3 Structure of employment income Parts**
(1) The structure of the employment income Parts is as follows—
this Part imposes the charge to tax on employment income, and sets out—
    (a) how the amount charged to tax for a tax year is to be calculated, and
    (b) who is liable for the tax charged;
Part 3 sets out what are earnings and provides for amounts to be treated as earnings;
Part 4 deals with exemptions from the charge to tax under this Part (and, in some cases, from other charges to tax);
Part 5 deals with deductions from taxable earnings;
Part 6 deals with employment income other than earnings or share-related income; and
Part 7 deals with [income and exemptions relating to securities and securities options acquired in connection with an employment].
(2) In this Act "the employment income Parts" means this Part and Parts 3 to 7.

**NOTES**

Sub-s (1): words in square brackets in the entry relating to Part 7 substituted by the Finance Act 2003, s 140, Sch 22, paras 1, 16(1); entry relating to Part 7A inserted by the Finance Act 2011, s 26, Sch 2, paras 2, 4(1), (3), as from 6 April 2011 (for effect, etc, see the note to s 1 at **[1.1242]**).

Sub-s (2): figure "7A" in square brackets substituted by the Finance Act 2011, s 26, Sch 2, paras 2, 4(1), (3), as from 6 April 2011 (for effect, etc, see the note to s 1 at **[1.1242]**).

**[1.1244]**
**4 "Employment" for the purposes of the employment income Parts**
(1) In the employment income Parts "employment" includes in particular—
    (a) any employment under a contract of service,
    (b) any employment under a contract of apprenticeship, and
    (c) any employment in the service of the Crown.
(2) In those Parts "employed", "employee" and "employer" have corresponding meanings.

**[1.1245]**
**5 Application to offices and office-holders**
(1) The provisions of the employment income Parts that are expressed to apply to employments apply equally to offices, unless otherwise indicated.
(2) In those provisions as they apply to an office—
    (a) references to being employed are to being the holder of the office;
    (b) "employee" means the office-holder;
    (c) "employer" means the person under whom the office-holder holds office.
(3) In the employment income Parts "office" includes in particular any position which has an existence independent of the person who holds it and may be filled by successive holders.

## CHAPTER 8
## APPLICATION OF PROVISIONS TO WORKERS UNDER ARRANGEMENTS MADE BY INTERMEDIARIES

### *Application of this Chapter*

**[1.1246]**
### 49   Engagements to which this Chapter applies
(1)   This Chapter applies where—
  (a)   an individual ("the worker") personally performs, or is under an obligation personally to perform, services [for another person] ("the client"),
  (b)   the services are provided not under a contract directly between the client and the worker but under arrangements involving a third party ("the intermediary"), and
  (c)   the circumstances are such that, if the services were provided under a contract directly between the client and the worker, the worker would be regarded for income tax purposes as an employee of the client.
(2)   . . .
(3)   The reference in subsection (1)(b) to a "third party" includes a partnership or unincorporated body of which the worker is a member.
(4)   The circumstances referred to in subsection (1)(c) include the terms on which the services are provided, having regard to the terms of the contracts forming part of the arrangements under which the services are provided.
(5)   In this Chapter "engagement to which this Chapter applies" means any such provision of services as is mentioned in subsection (1).

**NOTES**
  Sub-s (1): words in square brackets in para (a) substituted by the Finance Act 2003, s 136(1), (2).
  Sub-s (2): repealed by the Finance Act 2003, ss 216, 136(1), (3)(a), Sch 43, Pt 3(1).

**[1.1247]**
### 50   Worker treated as receiving earnings from employment
(1)   If, in the case of an engagement to which this Chapter applies, in any tax year—
  (a)   the conditions specified in section 51, 52 or 53 are met in relation to the intermediary, and
  (b)   the worker, or an associate of the worker—
    (i)    receives from the intermediary, directly or indirectly, a payment or benefit that is not employment income, or
    (ii)   has rights which entitle, or which in any circumstances would entitle, the worker or associate to receive from the intermediary, directly or indirectly, any such payment or benefit,
the intermediary is treated as making to the worker, and the worker is treated as receiving, in that year a payment which is to be treated as earnings from an employment ("the deemed employment payment").
(2)   A single payment is treated as made in respect of all engagements in relation to which the intermediary is treated as making a payment to the worker in the tax year.
(3)   The deemed employment payment is treated as made at the end of the tax year, unless section 57 applies (earlier date of deemed payment in certain cases).
(4)   In this Chapter "the relevant engagements", in relation to a deemed employment payment, means the engagements mentioned in subsection (2).

**[1.1248]**
### 51   Conditions of liability where intermediary is a company
(1)   Where the intermediary is a company the conditions are that the intermediary is not an associated company of the client that falls within subsection (2) and either—
  (a)   the worker has a material interest in the intermediary, or
  (b)   the payment or benefit mentioned in section 50(1)(b)—
    (i)    is received or receivable by the worker directly from the intermediary, and
    (ii)   can reasonably be taken to represent remuneration for services provided by the worker to the client.
(2)   An associated company of the client falls within this subsection if it is such a company by reason of the intermediary and the client being under the control—
  (a)   of the worker, or
  (b)   of the worker and other persons.
(3)   A worker is treated as having a material interest in a company if—
  (a)   the worker, alone or with one or more associates of the worker, or
  (b)   an associate of the worker, with or without other such associates,
has a material interest in the company.
(4)   For this purpose a material interest means—

(a) beneficial ownership of, or the ability to control, directly or through the medium of other companies or by any other indirect means, more than 5% of the ordinary share capital of the company; or

(b) possession of, or entitlement to acquire, rights entitling the holder to receive more than 5% of any distributions that may be made by the company; or

(c) where the company is a close company, possession of, or entitlement to acquire, rights that would in the event of the winding up of the company, or in any other circumstances, entitle the holder to receive more than 5% of the assets that would then be available for distribution among the participators.

(5) In subsection (4)(c) "participator" has the meaning given by [section 454 of CTA 2010].

**NOTES**

Sub-s (5): words in square brackets substituted by the Corporation Tax Act 2010, s 1177, Sch 1, Pt 2, paras 378, 380 (note that the 2010 Act came into force on 1 April 2010 and applies (a) for corporation tax purposes, for accounting periods ending on or after that day, and (b) for income tax and capital gains tax purposes, for the tax year 2010–11 and subsequent tax years; for general transitional provisions and savings see s 1180(1), Sch 2, Pts 1, 2).

**[1.1249]**
## 52 Conditions of liability where intermediary is a partnership
(1) Where the intermediary is a partnership the conditions are as follows.
(2) In relation to any payment or benefit received or receivable by the worker as a member of the partnership the conditions are—
(a) that the worker, alone or with one or more relatives, is entitled to 60% or more of the profits of the partnership; or
(b) that most of the profits of the partnership concerned derive from the provision of services under engagements to which this Chapter applies—
(i) to a single client, or
(ii) to a single client together with associates of that client; or
(c) that under the profit sharing arrangements the income of any of the partners is based on the amount of income generated by that partner by the provision of services under engagements to which this Chapter applies.

In paragraph (a) "relative" means [spouse or civil partner], parent or child or remoter relation in the direct line, or brother or sister.
(3) In relation to any payment or benefit received or receivable by the worker otherwise than as a member of the partnership, the conditions are that the payment or benefit—
(a) is received or receivable by the worker directly from the intermediary, and
(b) can reasonably be taken to represent remuneration for services provided by the worker to the client.

**NOTES**

Sub-s (2): words in square brackets substituted by the Tax and Civil Partnership Regulations 2005, SI 2005/3229, regs 137, 138.

**[1.1250]**
## 53 Conditions of liability where intermediary is an individual
Where the intermediary is an individual the conditions are that the payment or benefit—
(a) is received or receivable by the worker directly from the intermediary, and
(b) can reasonably be taken to represent remuneration for services provided by the worker to the client.

*The deemed employment payment*

**[1.1251]**
## 54 Calculation of deemed employment payment
(1) The amount of the deemed employment payment for a tax year ("the year") is the amount resulting from the following steps—
*Step 1*
Find (applying section 55) the total amount of all payments and benefits received by the intermediary in the year in respect of the relevant engagements, and reduce that amount by 5%.
*Step 2*
Add (applying that section) the amount of any payments and benefits received by the worker in the year in respect of the relevant engagements, otherwise than from the intermediary, that—
(a) are not chargeable to income tax as employment income, and
(b) would be so chargeable if the worker were employed by the client.
*Step 3*
Deduct (applying Chapters 1 to 5 of Part 5) the amount of any expenses met in the year by the intermediary that would have been deductible from the taxable earnings from the employment if—
(a) the worker had been employed by the client, and
(b) the expenses had been met by the worker out of those earnings.

If the result at this or any later point is nil or a negative amount, there is no deemed employment payment.

*Step 4*

Deduct the amount of any capital allowances in respect of expenditure incurred by the intermediary that could have been deducted from employment income under section 262 of CAA 2001 (employments and offices) if the worker had been employed by the client and had incurred the expenditure.

*Step 5*

Deduct any contributions made in the year for the benefit of the worker by the intermediary to a [registered pension scheme] that if made by an employer for the benefit of an employee would not be chargeable to income tax as income of the employee.

This does not apply to excess contributions made and later repaid.

*Step 6*

Deduct the amount of any employer's national insurance contributions paid by the intermediary for the year in respect of the worker.

*Step 7*

Deduct the amount of any payments and benefits received in the year by the worker from the intermediary—

    (a)   in respect of which the worker is chargeable to income tax as employment income, and

    (b)   which do not represent items in respect of which a deduction was made under step 3.

*Step 8*

Assume that the result of step 7 represents an amount together with employer's national insurance contributions on it, and deduct what (on that assumption) would be the amount of those contributions.

The result is the deemed employment payment.

(2)   If [section 61 of the Finance Act 2004] applies (sub-contractors in the construction industry: payments to be made under deduction), the intermediary is treated for the purposes of step 1 of subsection (1) as receiving the amount that would have been received had no deduction been made under that section.

(3)   In step 3 of subsection (1), the reference to expenses met by the intermediary includes—

    (a)   expenses met by the worker and reimbursed by the intermediary, and

    (b)   where the intermediary is a partnership and the worker is a member of the partnership, expenses met by the worker for and on behalf of the partnership.

(4)   In step 3 of subsection (1), the expenses deductible include the amount of any mileage allowance relief for the year which the worker would have been entitled to in respect of the use of a vehicle falling within subsection (5) if—

    (a)   the worker had been employed by the client, and

    (b)   the vehicle had not been a company vehicle (within the meaning of Chapter 2 of Part 4).

(5)   A vehicle falls within this subsection if—

    (a)   it is provided by the intermediary for the worker, or

    (b)   where the intermediary is a partnership and the worker is a member of the partnership, it is provided by the worker for the purposes of the business of the partnership.

(6)   Where, on the assumptions mentioned in paragraphs (a) and (b) of step 3 of subsection (1), the deductibility of the expenses is determined under sections 337 to 342 (travel expenses), the duties performed under the relevant engagements are treated as duties of a continuous employment with the intermediary.

(7)   In step 7 of subsection (1), the amounts deductible include any payments received in the year from the intermediary that—

    (a)   are exempt from income tax by virtue of section 229 or 233 (mileage allowance payments and passenger payments), and

    (b)   do not represent items in respect of which a deduction was made under step 3.

(8)   For the purposes of subsection (1) any necessary apportionment is to be made on a just and reasonable basis of amounts received by the intermediary that are referable—

    (a)   to the services of more than one worker, or

    (b)   partly to the services of the worker and partly to other matters.

---

**NOTES**

Sub-s (1): words in square brackets in step 5 substituted by the Finance Act 2004, s 281(1), Sch 35, paras 54, 56.

Sub-s (2): words in square brackets substituted by the Finance Act 2004, s 76, Sch 12, para 17.

See further, the Pension Protection Fund (Tax) Regulations 2006, SI 2006/575, reg 39, which provides as follows—

"39.   Step 5 of section 54(1) of ITEPA 2003 (calculation of deemed employment payment under arrangements made by intermediaries) applies in relation to a payment, by the intermediary, of any sum in respect of any of the Pensions Act levies in the same way as it applies in relation to any contributions that may be deducted under that step.".

**[1.1252]**
**55 Application of rules relating to earnings from employment**
(1) The following provisions apply in relation to the calculation of the deemed employment payment.
(2) A "payment or benefit" means anything that, if received by an employee for performing the duties of an employment, would be earnings from the employment.
(3) The amount of a payment or benefit is taken to be—
  (a) in the case of a payment or cash benefit, the amount received, and
  (b) in the case of a non-cash benefit, the cash equivalent of the benefit.
(4) The cash equivalent of a non-cash benefit is taken to be—
  (a) the amount that would be earnings if the benefit were earnings from an employment, or
  (b) in the case of living accommodation, whichever is the greater of that amount and the cash equivalent determined in accordance with section 398(2).
(5) A payment or benefit is treated as received—
  (a) in the case of a payment or cash benefit, when payment is made of or on account of the payment or benefit;
  (b) in the case of a non-cash benefit that is calculated by reference to a period within the tax year, at the end of that period;
  (c) in the case of a non-cash benefit that is not so calculated, when it would have been treated as received for the purposes of Chapter 4 or 5 of this Part (see section 19 or 32) if—
    (i) the worker had been an employee, and
    (ii) the benefit had been provided by reason of the employment.

**[1.1253]**
**56 Application of Income Tax Acts in relation to deemed employment**
(1) The Income Tax Acts (in particular, the PAYE provisions) apply in relation to the deemed employment payment as follows.
(2) They apply as if—
  (a) the worker were employed by the intermediary, and
  (b) the relevant engagements were undertaken by the worker in the course of performing the duties of that employment.
(3) The deemed employment payment is treated in particular—
  (a) as taxable earnings from the employment for the purpose of securing that any deductions under Chapters 2 to 5 of Part 5 do not exceed the deemed employment payment; and
  (b) as taxable earnings from the employment for the purposes of section 232.
(4) The worker is not chargeable to tax in respect of the deemed employment payment if, or to the extent that, by reason of any combination of the factors mentioned in subsection (5), the worker would not be chargeable to tax if—
  (a) the client employed the worker,
  (b) the worker performed the services in the course of that employment, and
  (c) the deemed employment payment were a payment by the client of earnings from that employment.
(5) The factors are—
  (a) the worker being resident, ordinarily resident or domiciled outside the United Kingdom,
  (b) the client being resident or ordinarily resident outside the United Kingdom, and
  (c) the services in question being provided outside the United Kingdom.
(6) Where the intermediary is a partnership or unincorporated association, the deemed employment payment is treated as received by the worker in the worker's personal capacity and not as income of the partnership or association.
(7) Where—
  (a) the worker is resident in the United Kingdom, [and]
  (b) the services in question are provided in the United Kingdom, . . .
  (c) . . .
the intermediary is treated as having a place of business in the United Kingdom, whether or not it in fact does so.
(8) . . .

**NOTES**
Sub-s (7): word in square brackets in para (a) inserted, and para (c) and the word immediately preceding it repealed, by the Finance Act 2003, ss 136(1), (3)(b)(ii), 216, Sch 43, Pt 3(1).
Sub-s (8): repealed by the Finance Act 2004, s 326, Sch 42, Pt 3.

*Supplementary provisions*

**[1.1254]**
**57 Earlier date of deemed employment payment in certain cases**
(1) If in any tax year—
  (a) a deemed employment payment is treated as made, and

(b)    before the date on which the payment would be treated as made under section 50(2) any
relevant event (as defined below) occurs in relation to the intermediary,
the deemed employment payment for that year is treated as having been made immediately before
that event or, if there is more than one, immediately before the first of them.
(2)    Where the intermediary is a company the following are relevant events—
    (a)    the company ceasing to trade;
    (b)    where the worker is a member of the company, the worker ceasing to be such a member;
    (c)    where the worker holds an office with the company, the worker ceasing to hold such an
office;
    (d)    where the worker is employed by the company, the worker ceasing to be so employed.
(3)    Where the intermediary is a partnership the following are relevant events—
    (a)    the dissolution of the partnership or the partnership ceasing to trade or a partner ceasing to
act as such;
    (b)    where the worker is employed by the partnership, the worker ceasing to be so employed.
(4)    Where the intermediary is an individual and the worker is employed by the intermediary, it is
a relevant event if the worker ceases to be so employed.
(5)    The fact that the deemed employment payment is treated as made before the end of the tax
year does not affect what receipts and other matters are taken into account in calculating its amount.

**[1.1255]**
**58    Relief in case of distributions by intermediary**
(1)    A claim for relief may be made under this section where the intermediary—
    (a)    is a company,
    (b)    is treated as making a deemed employment payment in any tax year, and
    (c)    either in that tax year (whether before or after that payment is treated as made), or in a
subsequent tax year, makes a distribution (a "relevant distribution").
(2)    A claim for relief under this section must be made—
    (a)    by the intermediary by notice to [an officer of Revenue and Customs], and
    (b)    within 5 years after the 31st January following the tax year in which the distribution is
made.
(3)    If on a claim being made [an officer of Revenue and Customs] [is] satisfied that relief should
be given in order to avoid a double charge to tax, [the officer] must direct the giving of such relief
by way of amending any assessment, by discharge or repayment of tax, or otherwise, as appears to
[the officer] appropriate.
(4)    Relief under this section is given by setting the amount of the deemed employment payment
against the relevant distribution so as to reduce the distribution.
(5)    In the case of more than one relevant distribution, [an officer of Revenue and Customs] must
exercise the power conferred by this section so as to secure that so far as practicable relief is given
by setting the amount of a deemed employment payment—
    (a)    against relevant distributions of the same tax year before those of other years,
    (b)    against relevant distributions received by the worker before those received by another
person, and
    (c)    against relevant distributions of earlier years before those of later years.
(6)    Where the amount of a relevant distribution is reduced under this section, the amount of any
associated tax credit is reduced accordingly.

**NOTES**
    Sub-ss (2), (3), (5): words in square brackets substituted by the Commissioners for Revenue and Customs Act 2005, s 50(6),
Sch 4, paras 101, 102(1), 103(1)(a), 105.

**[1.1256]**
**59    Provisions applicable to multiple intermediaries**
(1)    The provisions of this section apply where in the case of an engagement to which this Chapter
applies the arrangements involve more than one relevant intermediary.
(2)    All relevant intermediaries in relation to the engagement are jointly and severally liable,
subject to subsection (3), to account for any amount required under the PAYE provisions to be
deducted from a deemed employment payment treated as made by any of them—
    (a)    in respect of that engagement, or
    (b)    in respect of that engagement together with other engagements.
(3)    An intermediary is not so liable if it has not received any payment or benefit in respect of that
engagement or any such other engagement as is mentioned in subsection (2)(b).
(4)    Subsection (5) applies where a payment or benefit has been made or provided, directly or
indirectly, from one relevant intermediary to another in respect of the engagement.
(5)    In that case, the amount taken into account in relation to any intermediary in step 1 or step 2
of section 54(1) is reduced to such extent as is necessary to avoid double-counting having regard to
the amount so taken into account in relation to any other intermediary.
(6)    Except as provided by subsections (2) to (5), the provisions of this Chapter apply separately in
relation to each relevant intermediary.

(7) In this section "relevant intermediary" means an intermediary in relation to which the conditions specified in section 51, 52 or 53 are met.

**[1.1257]**
**60 Meaning of "associate"**
(1) In this Chapter "associate"—
  (a) in relation to an individual, has the meaning given by [section 448 of CTA 2010], subject to the following provisions of this section;
  (b) in relation to a company, means a person connected with the company; and
  (c) in relation to a partnership, means any associate of a member of the partnership.
(2) Where an individual has an interest in shares or obligations of the company as a beneficiary of an employee benefit trust, the trustees are not regarded as associates of the individual by reason only of that interest except in the following circumstances.
(3) The exception is where—
  (a) the individual, either alone or with any one or more associates of the individual, or
  (b) any associate of the individual, with or without other such associates,
has at any time on or after 14th March 1989 been the beneficial owner of, or able (directly or through the medium of other companies or by any other indirect means) to control more than 5% of the ordinary share capital of the company.
(4) In subsection (3) "associate" does not include the trustees of an employee benefit trust as a result only of the individual's having an interest in shares or obligations of the trust.
(5) Sections 549 to 554 (attribution of interests in companies to beneficiaries of employee benefit trusts) apply for the purposes of subsection (3) as they apply for the purposes of the provisions listed in section 549(2).
(6) In this section "employee benefit trust" has the meaning given by sections 550 and 551.

**NOTES**
Sub-s (1): words in square brackets substituted by the Corporation Tax Act 2010, s 1177, Sch 1, Pt 2, paras 378, 381 (note that the 2010 Act came into force on 1 April 2010 and applies (a) for corporation tax purposes, for accounting periods ending on or after that day, and (b) for income tax and capital gains tax purposes, for the tax year 2010–11 and subsequent tax years; for general transitional provisions and savings see s 1180(1), Sch 2, Pts 1, 2).

**[1.1258]**
**61 Interpretation**
(1) In this Chapter—
  "associate" has the meaning given by section 60;
  "associated company" has the meaning given by [section 449 of CTA 2010];
  "business" means any trade, profession or vocation and includes a [UK property business [within the meaning of Chapter 2 of Part 3 of ITTOIA 2005 or Chapter 2 of Part 4 of CTA 2009]];
  "company" means a body corporate or unincorporated association, and does not include a partnership;
  "employer's national insurance contributions" means secondary Class 1 or Class 1A national insurance contributions;
  "engagement to which this Chapter applies" has the meaning given by section 49(5);
  "national insurance contributions" means contributions under Part 1 of SSCBA 1992 or Part 1 of SSCB(NI)A 1992;
  "PAYE provisions" means the provisions of Part 11 or PAYE regulations;
  "the relevant engagements" has the meaning given by section 50(4).
(2) References in this Chapter to payments or benefits received or receivable from a partnership or unincorporated association include payments or benefits to which a person is or may be entitled in the person's capacity as a member of the partnership or association.
(3) For the purposes of this Chapter—
  (a) anything done by or in relation to an associate of an intermediary is treated as done by or in relation to the intermediary, and
  (b) a payment or other benefit provided to a member of an individual's family or household is treated as provided to the individual.
(4) For the purposes of this Chapter a man and a woman living together as husband and wife are treated as if they were married to each other.
[(5) For the purposes of this Chapter two people of the same sex living together as if they were civil partners of each other are treated as if they were civil partners of each other.
  For the purposes of this Chapter, two people of the same sex are to be regarded as living together as if they were civil partners if, but only if, they would be regarded as living together as husband and wife were they instead two people of the opposite sex.]

**NOTES**
Sub-s (1): in definition "associated company" words in square brackets substituted by the Corporation Tax Act 2010, s 1177, Sch 1, Pt 2, paras 378, 382 (note that the 2010 Act came into force on 1 April 2010 and applies (a) for corporation tax purposes, for accounting periods ending on or after that day, and (b) for income tax and capital gains tax purposes, for the tax year

2010–11 and subsequent tax years; in definition "business" words in first (outer) pair of square brackets inserted by the Income Tax (Trading and Other Income) Act 2005, s 882, Sch 1, Pt 2, paras 584, 586; words in second (inner) pair of square brackets substituted by the Corporation Tax Act 2009, s 1322, Sch 1, Pt 2, paras 548, 549, for the purposes of income tax and capital gains tax for the tax year 2009–10 and subsequent tax years, and for corporation tax purposes for accounting periods ending on or after 1 April 2009.

Sub-s (5): added by the Tax and Civil Partnership Regulations 2005, SI 2005/3229, regs 137, 139.

ICTA: Income and Corporation Taxes Act 1988.

ITTOIA 2005: the Income Tax (Trading and Other Income) Act 2005.

CTA 2009: the Corporation Tax Act 2009.

'SSCBA 1992' and 'SSCB(NI)A 1992': the Social Security Contributions and Benefits Act 1992 and the Social Security Contributions and Benefits (Northern Ireland) Act 1992, respectively.

# PART 3
# EMPLOYMENT INCOME: EARNINGS AND BENEFITS ETC TREATED AS EARNINGS

## CHAPTER 1
## EARNINGS

**[1.1259]**
**62  Earnings**
(1)  This section explains what is meant by "earnings" in the employment income Parts.
(2)  In those Parts "earnings", in relation to an employment, means—
  (a)  any salary, wages or fee,
  (b)  any gratuity or other profit or incidental benefit of any kind obtained by the employee if it is money or money's worth, or
  (c)  anything else that constitutes an emolument of the employment.
(3)  For the purposes of subsection (2) "money's worth" means something that is—
  (a)  of direct monetary value to the employee, or
  (b)  capable of being converted into money or something of direct monetary value to the employee.
(4)  Subsection (1) does not affect the operation of statutory provisions that provide for amounts to be treated as earnings (and see section 721(7)).

## CHAPTER 2
## TAXABLE BENEFITS: THE BENEFITS CODE

### *The benefits code*

**[1.1260]**
**63  The benefits code**
(1)  In the employment income Parts "the benefits code" means—
  this Chapter,
  Chapter 3 (expenses payments),
  Chapter 4 (vouchers and credit-tokens),
  Chapter 5 (living accommodation),
  Chapter 6 (cars, vans and related benefits),
  Chapter 7 (loans),
  . . .
  . . .
  Chapter 10 (residual liability to charge), and
  Chapter 11 (exclusion of lower-paid employments from parts of benefits code).
(2)  If an employment is an excluded employment, the general effect of section 216(1) (provisions not applicable to lower-paid employments) is that only the following Chapters apply to the employment—
  this Chapter,
  Chapter 4 (vouchers and credit-tokens),
  Chapter 5 (living accommodation), and
  Chapter 11 (exclusion of lower-paid employments from parts of benefits code).
(3)  section 216(5) and (6) explain and restrict the effect of section 216(1).
(4)  In the benefits code "excluded employment" means an employment to which the exclusion in section 216(1) applies.
[(5)  The benefits code has effect subject to section 554Z2(2).]

---

**NOTES**

Sub-s (1): entries relating to Chapters 8 and 9 (omitted) repealed by the Finance Act 2003, ss 140, 216, Sch 22, paras 1, 20(1), Sch 43, Pt 3(4).

Sub-s (5): added by the Finance Act 2011, s 26, Sch 2, paras 2, 8, as from 6 April 2011 (for effect, etc, see the note to s 1 at **[1.1242]**).

## CHAPTER 3
## TAXABLE BENEFITS: EXPENSES PAYMENTS

**[1.1261]**
**70 Sums in respect of expenses**
(1)  This Chapter applies to a sum paid to an employee in a tax year if the sum—
  (a)  is paid to the employee in respect of expenses, and
  (b)  is so paid by reason of the employment.
(2)  This Chapter applies to a sum paid away by an employee in a tax year if the sum—
  (a)  was put at the employee's disposal in respect of expenses,
  (b)  was so put by reason of the employment, and
  (c)  is paid away by the employee in respect of expenses.
(3)  For the purposes of this Chapter it does not matter whether the employment is held at the time when the sum is paid or paid away so long as it is held at some point in the tax year in which the sum is paid or paid away.
(4)  References in this Chapter to an employee accordingly include a prospective or former employee.
(5)  This Chapter does not apply to the extent that the sum constitutes earnings from the employment by virtue of any other provision.

**[1.1262]**
**71 Meaning of paid or put at disposal by reason of the employment**
(1)  If an employer pays a sum in respect of expenses to an employee it is to be treated as paid by reason of the employment unless—
  (a)  the employer is an individual, and
  (b)  the payment is made in the normal course of the employer's domestic, family or personal relationships.
(2)  If an employer puts a sum at an employee's disposal in respect of expenses it is to be treated as put at the employee's disposal by reason of the employment unless—
  (a)  the employer is an individual, and
  (b)  the sum is put at the employee's disposal in the normal course of the employer's domestic, family or personal relationships.

**[1.1263]**
**72 Sums in respect of expenses treated as earnings**
(1)  If this Chapter applies to a sum, the sum is to be treated as earnings from the employment for the tax year in which it is paid or paid away.
(2)  Subsection (1) does not prevent the making of a deduction allowed under any of the provisions listed in subsection (3).
(3)  The provisions are—
  section 336 (deductions for expenses: the general rule);
  section 337 (travel in performance of duties);
  section 338 (travel for necessary attendance);
  section 340 (travel between group employments);
  section 341 (travel at start or finish of overseas employment);
  section 342 (travel between employments where duties performed abroad);
  section 343 (deduction for professional membership fees);
  section 344 (deduction for annual subscriptions);
  section 346 (deduction for employee liabilities);
  section 351 (expenses of ministers of religion);
  section 353 (deductions from earnings charged on remittance).

## CHAPTER 5
## TAXABLE BENEFITS: LIVING ACCOMMODATION

*Living accommodation*

**[1.1264]**
**97 Living accommodation to which this Chapter applies**
(1)  This Chapter applies to living accommodation provided for—
  (a)  an employee, or
  (b)  a member of an employee's family or household,
by reason of the employment.
(2)  Living accommodation provided for any of those persons by the employer is to be regarded as provided by reason of the employment unless—
  (a)  the employer is an individual, and
  (b)  the provision is made in the normal course of the employer's domestic, family or personal relationships.

*Exceptions*

**[1.1265]**
**98   Accommodation provided by local authority**
This Chapter does not apply to living accommodation provided for an employee if—
  (a)   the employer is a local authority,
  (b)   it is provided for the employee by the authority, and
  (c)   the terms on which it is provided are no more favourable than those on which similar accommodation is provided by the authority for persons who are not their employees but whose circumstances are otherwise similar to those of the employee.

**[1.1266]**
**99   Accommodation provided for performance of duties**
(1)   This Chapter does not apply to living accommodation provided for an employee if it is necessary for the proper performance of the employee's duties that the employee should reside in it.
(2)   This Chapter does not apply to living accommodation provided for an employee if—
  (a)   it is provided for the better performance of the duties of the employment, and
  (b)   the employment is one of the kinds of employment in the case of which it is customary for employers to provide living accommodation for employees.
(3)   But if the accommodation is provided by a company and the employee ("E") is a director of the company or of an associated company, the exception in subsection (1) or (2) only applies if, in the case of each company of which E is a director—
  (a)   E has no material interest in the company, and
  (b)   either—
      (i)   E's employment is as a full-time working director, or
      (ii)   the company is non-profit-making or is [a charitable company].
(4)   "Non-profit-making" means that the company does not carry on a trade and its functions do not consist wholly or mainly in the holding of investments or other property.
(5)   A company is "associated" with another if—
  (a)   one has control of the other, or
  (b)   both are under the control of the same person.

---

**NOTES**
Sub-s (3): words in square brackets in para (b) substituted by the Finance Act 2010, s 30, Sch 6, Pt 2, para 17(1), (2), with effect for the tax year 2012–13 and subsequent tax years (see SI 2012/736).

---

CHAPTER 6
TAXABLE BENEFITS: CARS, VANS AND RELATED BENEFITS
*General*

**[1.1267]**
**114   Cars, vans and related benefits**
(1)   This Chapter applies to a car or a van in relation to a particular tax year if in that year the car or van—
  (a)   is made available (without any transfer of the property in it) to an employee or a member of the employee's family or household,
  (b)   is so made available by reason of the employment (see section 117), and
  (c)   is available for the employee's or member's private use (see section 118).
(2)   Where this Chapter applies to a car or van—
  (a)   sections 120 to 148 provide for the cash equivalent of the benefit of the car to be treated as earnings,
  (b)   sections 149 to 153 provide for the cash equivalent of the benefit of any fuel provided for the car to be treated as earnings,  . . .
  (c)   sections 154 to [159] provide for the cash equivalent of the benefit of the van to be treated as earnings[; and
  (d)   sections 160 to 164 provide for the cash equivalent of the benefit of any fuel provided for the van to be treated as earnings in certain circumstances].
(3)   This Chapter does not apply if an amount constitutes earnings from the employment in respect of the benefit of the car or van by virtue of any other provision (see section 119).
[(3A)   This Chapter does not apply to a van in relation to a tax year if the private use of the van during the tax year by the employee or member of the employee's family or household is insignificant.]
(4)   The following provisions of this Chapter provide for further exceptions—
    section 167 (pooled cars);
    section 168 (pooled vans);
    section 169 (car available to more than one member of family or household employed by same employer);

[section 169A (van available to more than one member of family or household employed by same employer)].

**NOTES**
Sub-s (2): word omitted from para (b) repealed, figure in square brackets in para (c) substituted, and para (d) and the word immediately preceding it added, by the Finance Act 2004, ss 80(1), 326, Sch 14, paras 1, 2(1)–(3), Sch 42, Pt 2(9).
Sub-s (3A): inserted by the Finance Act 2004, s 80(1), Sch 14, paras 1, 2(1), (4).
Sub-s (4): words in square brackets added by the Finance Act 2004, s 80(1), Sch 14, paras 1, 2(1), (4).

**[1.1268]**
**115 Meaning of "car" and "van"**
(1) In this Chapter—
"car" means a mechanically propelled road vehicle which is not—
 (a) a goods vehicle,
 (b) a motor cycle,
 (c) an invalid carriage, or
 (d) a vehicle of a type not commonly used as a private vehicle and unsuitable to be so used;
"van" means a mechanically propelled road vehicle which—
 (a) is a goods vehicle, and
 (b) has a design weight not exceeding 3,500 kilograms,
and which is not a motor cycle.
(2) For the purposes of subsection (1)—
"design weight" means the weight which a vehicle is designed or adapted not to exceed when in normal use and travelling on a road laden;
"goods vehicle" means a vehicle of a construction primarily suited for the conveyance of goods or burden of any description;
"invalid carriage" has the meaning given by section 185(1) of the Road Traffic Act 1988 (c 52);
"motor cycle" has the meaning given by section 185(1) of the Road Traffic Act 1988.

**[1.1269]**
**116 Meaning of when car or van is available to employee**
(1) For the purposes of this Chapter a car or van is available to an employee at a particular time if it is then made available, by reason of the employment and without any transfer of the property in it, to the employee or a member of the employee's family or household.
(2) References in this Chapter to—
 (a) the time when a car [or van] is first made available to an employee are to the earliest time when the car [or van] is made available as mentioned in subsection (1), and
 (b) the last day in a year on which a car [or van] is available to an employee are to the last day in the year on which the car [or van] is made available as mentioned in subsection (1).
(3) This section does not apply to section [124A or] 138 (automatic car for a disabled employee).

**NOTES**
Sub-s (2): words in square brackets inserted by the Finance Act 2004, s 80(1), Sch 14, paras 1, 3.
Sub-s (3): words in square brackets inserted by the Finance Act 2009, s 54(1), (2), with effect for the year 2009–10 and subsequent tax years.

**[1.1270]**
**117 Meaning of car or van made available by reason of employment**
For the purposes of this Chapter a car or van made available by an employer to an employee or a member of the employee's family or household is to be regarded as made available by reason of the employment unless—
 (a) the employer is an individual, and
 (b) it is so made available in the normal course of the employer's domestic, family or personal relationships.

**[1.1271]**
**118 Availability for private use**
(1) For the purposes of this Chapter a car or van made available in a tax year to an employee or a member of the employee's family or household is to be treated as available for the employee's or member's private use unless in that year—
 (a) the terms on which it is made available prohibit such use, and
 (b) it is not so used.
(2) In this Chapter "private use", in relation to a car or van made available to an employee or a member of the employee's family or household, means any use other than for the employee's business travel (see section 171(1)).

## CHAPTER 10
## TAXABLE BENEFITS: RESIDUAL LIABILITY TO CHARGE

### *Introduction*

**[1.1272]**
### 201   Employment-related benefits
(1)   This Chapter applies to employment-related benefits.

(2)   In this Chapter—

"benefit" means a benefit or facility of any kind;

"employment-related benefit" means a benefit, other than an excluded benefit, which is provided
    in a tax year—
      (a)   for an employee, or
      (b)   for a member of an employee's family or household,
    by reason of the employment.

For the definition of "excluded benefit" see section 202.

(3)   A benefit provided by an employer is to be regarded as provided by reason of the employment
unless—
      (a)   the employer is an individual, and
      (b)   the provision is made in the normal course of the employer's domestic, family or personal
         relationships.

(4)   For the purposes of this Chapter it does not matter whether the employment is held at the time
when the benefit is provided so long as it is held at some point in the tax year in which the benefit
is provided.

(5)   References in this Chapter to an employee accordingly include a prospective or former
employee.

**[1.1273]**
### 202   Excluded benefits
(1)   A benefit is an "excluded benefit" for the purposes of this Chapter if—
      (a)   any of Chapters 3 to 9 of the benefits code applies to the benefit,
      (b)   any of those Chapters would apply to the benefit but for an exception, or
      (c)   the benefit consists in the right to receive, or the prospect of receiving, sums treated as
         earnings under section 221 (payments where employee absent because of sickness or
         disability).

(2)   In this section "exception", in relation to the application of a Chapter of the benefits code to
a benefit, means any enactment in the Chapter which provides that the Chapter does not apply to the
benefit.

But for this purpose section 86 (transport vouchers under pre-26th March 1982 arrangements) is
not an exception.

### *Cash equivalent of benefit treated as earnings*

**[1.1274]**
### 203   Cash equivalent of benefit treated as earnings
(1)   The cash equivalent of an employment-related benefit is to be treated as earnings from the
employment for the tax year in which it is provided.

(2)   The cash equivalent of an employment-related benefit is the cost of the benefit less any part of
that cost made good by the employee to the persons providing the benefit.

(3)   The cost of an employment-related benefit is determined in accordance with section 204
unless—
      (a)   section 205 provides that the cost is to be determined in accordance with that section, or
      (b)   section 206 provides that the cost is to be determined in accordance with that section.

### *Determination of the cost of the benefit*

**[1.1275]**
### 204   Cost of the benefit: basic rule
The cost of an employment-related benefit is the expense incurred in or in connection with
provision of the benefit (including a proper proportion of any expense relating partly to provision of
the benefit and partly to other matters).

### *Supplementary provisions*

**[1.1276]**
### 210   Power to exempt minor benefits
(1)   The Treasury may make provision by regulations for exempting from the application of this
Chapter such minor benefits as may be specified in the regulations.

(2)   An exemption conferred by such regulations is conditional on the benefit being made available
to the employer's employees generally on similar terms.

NOTES

Regulations: the Income Tax (Exemption of Minor Benefits) (Amendment) Regulations 2003, SI 2003/1434; the Income Tax (Exemption of Minor Benefits) (Amendment) Regulations 2004, SI 2004/3087; the Income Tax (Exemption of Minor Benefits) (Revocation) Regulations 2009, SI 2009/695; the Income Tax (Exemption of Minor Benefits) (Amendment) Regulations 2012, SI 2012/1808. Note also that the Income Tax (Benefits in Kind) (Exemption for Welfare Counselling) Regulations 2000, SI 2000/2080, the Income Tax (Exemption of Minor Benefits) Regulations 2002, SI 2002/205, and the Income Tax (Benefits in Kind) (Exemption for Employment Costs resulting from Disability) Regulations 2002, SI 2002/1596, all have effect as if made under this section by virtue of s 723(2) of, and Sch 7, para 3 to, this Act.

## CHAPTER 11
## TAXABLE BENEFITS: EXCLUSION OF LOWER-PAID EMPLOYMENTS FROM PARTS OF BENEFITS CODE

### *Introduction*

**[1.1277]**
### 216  Provisions not applicable to lower-paid employments
(1)   The Chapters of the benefits code listed in subsection (4) do not apply to an employment in relation to a tax year if—
 (a)   it is lower-paid employment in relation to that year (see section 217), and
 (b)   condition A or B is met.
(2)   Condition A is that the employee is not employed as a director of a company.
(3)   Condition B is that the employee is employed as a director of a company but has no material interest in the company and either—
 (a)   the employment is as a full-time working director, or
 (b)   the company is non-profit-making or is [a charitable company].
  "Non-profit-making" means that the company does not carry on a trade and its functions do not consist wholly or mainly in the holding of investments or other property.
(4)   The Chapters referred to in subsection (1) are—
  Chapter 3 (taxable benefits: expenses payments);
  Chapter 6 (taxable benefits: cars, vans and related benefits);
  Chapter 7 (taxable benefits: loans);
  . . .
  . . .
  Chapter 10 (taxable benefits: residual liability to charge).
(5)   Subsection (1)—
 (a)   means that in any of those Chapters a reference to an employee does not include an employee whose employment is within the exclusion in that subsection, if the context is such that the reference is to an employee in relation to whom the Chapter applies, but
 (b)   does not restrict the meaning of references to employees in other contexts.
(6)   Subsection (1) has effect subject to—
  section 188(2) (discharge of loan: where employment becomes lower-paid),
  . . .
  . . . and
  section 220 (employment in two or more related employments).

NOTES

Sub-s (3): words in square brackets substituted by the Finance Act 2010, s 30, Sch 6, Pt 2, para 17(1), (3), with effect for the tax year 2012–13 and subsequent tax years (see SI 2012/736).

Sub-s (4): entries relating to Chapters 8 and 9 (omitted) repealed by the Finance Act 2003, ss 140, 216, Sch 22, paras 1, 24(1), (2), Sch 43, Pt 3(4).

Sub-s (6): entries relating to sections 195(3) and 199(4) (omitted) repealed by the Finance Act 2003, ss 140, 216, Sch 22, paras 1, 24(1), (3), Sch 43, Pt 3(4).

## PART 4
## EMPLOYMENT INCOME: EXEMPTIONS

## CHAPTER 10
## EXEMPTIONS: TERMINATION OF EMPLOYMENT

### *Redundancy payments*

**[1.1278]**
### 309  Limited exemptions for statutory redundancy payments
(1)   No liability to income tax in respect of earnings arises by virtue of a redundancy payment or an approved contractual payment, except where subsection (2) applies.
(2)   Where an approved contractual payment exceeds the amount which would have been due if a redundancy payment had been payable, the excess is liable to income tax.

(3)  No liability to income tax in respect of employment income other than earnings arises by virtue of a redundancy payment or an approved contractual payment, except where it does so by virtue of Chapter 3 of Part 6 (payments and benefits on termination of employment etc).

(4)  For the purposes of this section—

    (a)    a statutory payment in respect of a redundancy payment is to be treated as paid on account of the redundancy payment, and

    (b)    a statutory payment in respect of an approved contractual payment is to be treated as paid on account of the approved contractual payment.

(5)  In this section—

    "approved contractual payment" means a payment to a person on the termination of the person's employment under an agreement in respect of which an order is in force under section 157 of ERA 1996 or Article 192 of ER(NI)O 1996,

    "redundancy payment" means a redundancy payment under Part 11 of ERA 1996 or Part 12 of ER(NI)O 1996, and

    "statutory payment" means a payment under section 167(1) of ERA 1996 or Article 202(1) of ER(NI)O 1996.

(6)  In subsection (5) "employment", in relation to a person, has the meaning given in section 230(5) of ERA 1996 or Article 3(5) of ER(NI)O 1996.

**NOTES**

'ERA 1996' and 'ER(NI)O 1996': the Employment Rights Act 1996 and the Employment Rights (Northern Ireland) Order 1996, respectively.

*Outplacement benefits*

**[1.1279]**
**310  Counselling and other outplacement services**

(1)  No liability to income tax arises in respect of—

    (a)    the provision of services to a person in connection with the cessation of the person's employment, or

    (b)    the payment or reimbursement of—

        (i)    fees for such provision, or

        (ii)    travelling expenses incurred in connection with such provision,

if conditions A to D and, in the case of travel expenses, condition E are met.

(2)  Condition A is that the only or main purpose of the provision of the services is to enable the person to do either or both of the following—

    (a)    to adjust to the cessation of the employment, or

    (b)    to find other gainful employment (including self-employment).

(3)  Condition B is that the services consist wholly of any or all of the following—

    (a)    giving advice and guidance,

    (b)    imparting or improving skills,

    (c)    providing or making available the use of office equipment or similar facilities.

(4)  Condition C is that the person has been employed  . . .  in the employment which is ceasing throughout the period of 2 years ending—

    (a)    at the time when the services begin to be provided, or

    (b)    if earlier, at the time when the employment ceases.

(5)  Condition D is that the opportunity to receive the services, on similar terms as to payment or reimbursement of any expenses incurred in connection with their provision, is available—

    (a)    generally to employees or former employees of the person's employer in that employment, or

    (b)    to a particular class or classes of them.

(6)  Condition E is that the travel expenses are expenses—

    (a)    in respect of which, on the assumptions in subsection (7), mileage allowance relief under Chapter 2 of this Part would be available if no mileage allowance payments had been made, or

    (b)    which, on those assumptions, would be deductible under Part 5.

(7)  The assumptions are—

    (a)    that receiving the services is one of the duties of the employee's employment,

    (b)    that the employee incurs and pays the expenses, and

    (c)    if the employment has in fact ceased, that it continues.

(8)  In this section "mileage allowance payments" has the meaning given by section 229(2).

**NOTES**

Sub-s (4): words omitted repealed by the Finance Act 2005, ss 18(1), (2), 104, Sch 11, Pt 2(1).

# PART 5
# EMPLOYMENT INCOME: DEDUCTIONS ALLOWED FROM EARNINGS

## CHAPTER 1
## DEDUCTIONS ALLOWED FROM EARNINGS: GENERAL RULES

*Introduction*

**[1.1280]**
**327 Deductions from earnings: general**

(1) This Part provides for deductions that are allowed from the taxable earnings from an employment in a tax year in calculating the net taxable earnings from the employment in the tax year for the purposes of Part 2 (see section 11(1)).

(2) In this Part, unless otherwise indicated by the context—
   (a) references to the earnings from which deductions are allowed are references to the taxable earnings mentioned in subsection (1), and
   (b) references to the tax year are references to the tax year mentioned there.

(3) The deductions for which this Part provides are those allowed under—
   Chapter 2 (deductions for employee's expenses),
   Chapter 3 (deductions from benefits code earnings),
   Chapter 4 (fixed allowances for employee's expenses),
   Chapter 5 (deductions for earnings representing benefits or reimbursed expenses), and
   Chapter 6 (deductions from seafarers' earnings).

(4) Further provision about deductions from earnings is made in—
   section 232 (giving effect to mileage allowance relief),
   . . .
   section 262 of CAA 2001 (capital allowances to be given effect by treating them as deductions from earnings).

(5) Further provision about deductions from income including earnings is made in—
   Part 12 (payroll giving),
   [and sections 188 to 194 of FA 2004 (contributions to registered pension schemes)]

---

**NOTES**

Sub-s (4): words omitted repealed by the Finance Act 2004, ss 281, 326, Sch 35, paras 54, 60(1), (2), Sch 42, Pt 3.
Sub-s (5): words in square brackets substituted by the Finance Act 2004, s 281(1), Sch 35, paras 54, 60(1), (3).

## CHAPTER 2
## DEDUCTIONS FOR EMPLOYEE'S EXPENSES

*Introduction*

**[1.1281]**
**333 Scope of this Chapter: expenses paid by the employee**

(1) A deduction from a person's earnings for an amount is allowed under the following provisions of this Chapter only if the amount—
   (a) is paid by the person, or
   (b) is paid on the person's behalf by someone else and is included in the earnings.

(2) In the following provisions of this Chapter, in relation to a deduction from a person's earnings, references to the person paying an amount include references to the amount being paid on the person's behalf by someone else if or to the extent that the amount is included in the earnings.

(3) Subsection (1)(b) does not apply to the deductions under—
   (a) section 351(2) and (3) (expenses of ministers of religion), and
   (b) section 355 (deductions for corresponding payments by non-domiciled employees with foreign employers),
and subsection (2) does not apply in the case of those deductions.

(4) Chapter 3 of this Part provides for deductions where—
   (a) a person's earnings include an amount treated as earnings under Chapter 4, 5 or 10 of Part 3 (taxable benefits: vouchers etc, living accommodation and residual liability to charge), and
   (b) an amount in respect of the benefit in question would be deductible under this Chapter if the person had incurred and paid it.

**[1.1282]**
**334 Effect of reimbursement etc**

(1) For the purposes of this Chapter, a person may be regarded as paying an amount despite—
   (a) its reimbursement, or
   (b) any other payment from another person in respect of the amount.

(2) But where a reimbursement or such other payment is made in respect of an amount, a deduction for the amount is allowed under the following provisions of this Chapter only if or to the extent that—

(a)   the reimbursement, or
(b)   so much of the other payment as relates to the amount,
is included in the person's earnings.
(3)   This section does not apply to a deduction allowed under section 351 (expenses of ministers of religion).
(4)   This section is to be disregarded for the purposes of the deductibility provisions.

*General rule for deduction of employee's expenses*

**[1.1283]**
**336   Deductions for expenses: the general rule**
(1)   The general rule is that a deduction from earnings is allowed for an amount if—
(a)   the employee is obliged to incur and pay it as holder of the employment, and
(b)   the amount is incurred wholly, exclusively and necessarily in the performance of the duties of the employment.
(2)   The following provisions of this Chapter contain additional rules allowing deductions for particular kinds of expenses and rules preventing particular kinds of deductions.
(3)   No deduction is allowed under this section for an amount that is deductible under sections 337 to 342 (travel expenses).

*Travel expenses*

**[1.1284]**
**337   Travel in performance of duties**
(1)   A deduction from earnings is allowed for travel expenses if—
(a)   the employee is obliged to incur and pay them as holder of the employment, and
(b)   the expenses are necessarily incurred on travelling in the performance of the duties of the employment.
(2)   This section needs to be read with section 359 (disallowance of travel expenses: mileage allowances and reliefs).

**[1.1285]**
**338   Travel for necessary attendance**
(1)   A deduction from earnings is allowed for travel expenses if—
(a)   the employee is obliged to incur and pay them as holder of the employment, and
(b)   the expenses are attributable to the employee's necessary attendance at any place in the performance of the duties of the employment.
(2)   Subsection (1) does not apply to the expenses of ordinary commuting or travel between any two places that is for practical purposes substantially ordinary commuting.
(3)   In this section "ordinary commuting" means travel between—
(a)   the employee's home and a permanent workplace, or
(b)   a place that is not a workplace and a permanent workplace.
(4)   Subsection (1) does not apply to the expenses of private travel or travel between any two places that is for practical purposes substantially private travel.
(5)   In subsection (4) "private travel" means travel between—
(a)   the employee's home and a place that is not a workplace, or
(b)   two places neither of which is a workplace.
(6)   This section needs to be read with section 359 (disallowance of travel expenses: mileage allowances and reliefs).

**[1.1286]**
**339   Meaning of "workplace" and "permanent workplace"**
(1)   In this Part "workplace", in relation to an employment, means a place at which the employee's attendance is necessary in the performance of the duties of the employment.
(2)   In this Part "permanent workplace", in relation to an employment, means a place which—
(a)   the employee regularly attends in the performance of the duties of the employment, and
(b)   is not a temporary workplace.
This is subject to subsections (4) and (8).
(3)   In subsection (2) "temporary workplace", in relation to an employment, means a place which the employee attends in the performance of the duties of the employment—
(a)   for the purpose of performing a task of limited duration, or
(b)   for some other temporary purpose.
This is subject to subsections (4) and (5).
(4)   A place which the employee regularly attends in the performance of the duties of the employment is treated as a permanent workplace and not a temporary workplace if—
(a)   it forms the base from which those duties are performed, or
(b)   the tasks to be carried out in the performance of those duties are allocated there.
(5)   A place is not regarded as a temporary workplace if the employee's attendance is—
(a)   in the course of a period of continuous work at that place—
(i)   lasting more than 24 months, or

    (ii)   comprising all or almost all of the period for which the employee is likely to hold the employment, or

(b)   at a time when it is reasonable to assume that it will be in the course of such a period.

(6)  For the purposes of subsection (5), a period is a period of continuous work at a place if over the period the duties of the employment are performed to a significant extent at the place.

(7)  An actual or contemplated modification of the place at which duties are performed is to be disregarded for the purposes of subsections (5) and (6) if it does not, or would not, have any substantial effect on the employee's journey, or expenses of travelling, to and from the place where they are performed.

(8)  An employee is treated as having a permanent workplace consisting of an area if—

    (a)   the duties of the employment are defined by reference to an area (whether or not they also require attendance at places outside it),

    (b)   in the performance of those duties the employee attends different places within the area,

    (c)   none of the places the employee attends in the performance of those duties is a permanent workplace, and

    (d)   the area would be a permanent workplace if subsections (2), (3), (5), (6) and (7) referred to the area where they refer to a place.

## PART 6
## EMPLOYMENT INCOME: INCOME WHICH IS NOT EARNINGS OR SHARE-RELATED

### CHAPTER 3
### PAYMENTS AND BENEFITS ON TERMINATION OF EMPLOYMENT ETC

*Preliminary*

**[1.1287]**
**401 Application of this Chapter**

(1)  This Chapter applies to payments and other benefits which are received directly or indirectly in consideration or in consequence of, or otherwise in connection with—

    (a)   the termination of a person's employment,

    (b)   a change in the duties of a person's employment, or

    (c)   a change in the earnings from a person's employment,

by the person, or the person's spouse [or civil partner], blood relative, dependant or personal representatives.

(2)  Subsection (1) is subject to subsection (3) and sections 405 to [413A] (exceptions for certain payments and benefits).

(3)  This Chapter does not apply to any payment or other benefit chargeable to income tax apart from this Chapter.

(4)  For the purposes of this Chapter—

    (a)   a payment or other benefit which is provided on behalf of, or to the order of, the employee or former employee is treated as received by the employee or former employee, and

    (b)   in relation to a payment or other benefit—

        (i)   any reference to the employee or former employee is to the person mentioned in subsection (1), and

        (ii)   any reference to the employer or former employer is to be read accordingly.

**NOTES**

Sub-s (1): words in square brackets inserted by the Tax and Civil Partnership Regulations 2005, SI 2005/3229, regs 137, 152.

Sub-s (2): figure in square brackets substituted by the Enactment of Extra-Statutory Concessions Order 2011, SI 2011/1037, art 10(1), (2), (4), as from 1 April 2011, in relation to payments made on or after 6 April 2011.

**[1.1288]**
**402 Meaning of "benefit"**

(1)  In this Chapter "benefit" includes anything in respect of which, were it received for performance of the duties of the employment, an amount—

    (a)   would be taxable earnings from the employment, or

    (b)   would be such earnings apart from an earnings-only exemption.

This is subject to subsections (2) to (4).

(2)  In this Chapter "benefit" does not include a benefit received in connection with the termination of a person's employment that is a benefit which, were it received for performance of the duties of the employment, would fall within—

    (a)   section 239(4) (exemption of benefits connected with taxable cars and vans and exempt heavy goods vehicles), so far as that section applies to a benefit connected with a car or van,

    (b)   section 269 (exemption where benefits or money obtained in connection with taxable car or van or exempt heavy goods vehicle),

    (c)   section 319 (mobile telephones), or

(d)   section 320 (limited exemption for computer equipment).

(3)   In this Chapter "benefit" does not include a benefit received in connection with any change in the duties of, or earnings from, a person's employment to the extent that it is a benefit which, were it received for performance of the duties of the employment, would fall within section 271(1) (limited exemption of removal benefits and expenses).

(4)   The right to receive a payment or benefit is not itself a benefit for the purposes of this Chapter.

*Payments and benefits treated as employment income*

**[1.1289]**
**403   Charge on payment or other benefit**

(1)   The amount of a payment or benefit to which this Chapter applies counts as employment income of the employee or former employee for the relevant tax year if and to the extent that it exceeds the £30,000 threshold.

(2)   In this section "the relevant tax year" means the tax year in which the payment or other benefit is received.

(3)   For the purposes of this Chapter—
  (a)   a cash benefit is treated as received—
     (i)   when it is paid or a payment is made on account of it, or
     (ii)   when the recipient becomes entitled to require payment of or on account of it, and
  (b)   a non-cash benefit is treated as received when it is used or enjoyed.

(4)   For the purposes of this Chapter the amount of a payment or benefit in respect of an employee or former employee exceeds the £30,000 threshold if and to the extent that, when it is aggregated with other such payments or benefits to which this Chapter applies, it exceeds £30,000 according to the rules in section 404 (how the £30,000 threshold applies).

(5)   If it is received after the death of the employee or former employee—
  (a)   the amount of a payment or benefit to which this Chapter applies counts as the employment income of the personal representatives for the relevant year if or to the extent that it exceeds £30,000 according to the rules in section 404, and
  (b)   the tax is accordingly to be assessed and charged on them and is a debt due from and payable out of the estate.

(6)   In this Chapter references to the taxable person are to the person in relation to whom subsection (1) or (5) provides for an amount to count as employment income.

**[1.1290]**
**404   How the £30,000 threshold applies**

(1)   For the purpose of the £30,000 threshold in section 403(4) and (5), the payments and other benefits provided in respect of an employee or former employee which are to be aggregated are those provided—
  (a)   in respect of the same employment,
  (b)   in respect of different employments with the same employer, and
  (c)   in respect of employments with employers who are associated.

(2)   For this purpose employers are "associated" if on a termination or change date—
  (a)   one of them is under the control of the other, or
  (b)   one of them is under the control of a third person who on that termination or change date or another such date controls or is under the control of the other.

(3)   In subsection (2)—
  (a)   references to an employer, or to a person controlling or controlled by an employer, include the successors of the employer or person, and
  (b)   "termination or change date" means a date on which a termination or change occurs in connection with which a payment or other benefit to which this Chapter applies is received in respect of the employee or former employee.

(4)   If payments and other benefits are received in different tax years, the £30,000 is set against the amount of payments and other benefits received in earlier years before those received in later years.

(5)   If more than one payment or other benefit is received in a tax year in which the threshold is exceeded—
  (a)   the £30,000 (or the balance of it) is set against the amounts of cash benefits as they are received, and
  (b)   any balance at the end of the year is set against the aggregate amount of non-cash benefits received in the year.

**[1.1291]**
**[404A   Amounts charged to be treated as highest part of total income**

(1)   A payment or other benefit which counts as a person's employment income as a result of section 403 is treated as the highest part of the person's total income.

(2)   Subsection (1) has effect for all income tax purposes except the purposes of sections 535 to 537 of ITTOIA 2005 (gains from contracts for life insurance etc: top slicing relief).

(3)   See section 1012 of ITA 2007 (relationship between highest part rules) for the relationship between—

(a)  the rule in subsection (1), and
(b)  other rules requiring particular income to be treated as the highest part of a person's total income]

**NOTES**

Inserted by the Income Tax Act 2007, s 1027, Sch 1, Pt 2, paras 425, 437 (for effect and transitional provisions see the introductory note to this Act).

ITTOIA 2005: the Income Tax (Trading and Other Income) Act 2005.

ITA 2007: the Income Tax Act 2007.

*Exceptions and reductions*

**[1.1292]**
**405  Exception for certain payments exempted when received as earnings**
(1)  This Chapter does not apply to any payment received in connection with the termination of a person's employment which, were it received for the performance of the duties of the employment, would fall within section 308 (exemption of contributions to approved personal pension arrangements).
(2)  This Chapter does not apply to any payment received in connection with any change in the duties of, or earnings from, a person's employment to the extent that, were it received for the performance of the duties of the employment, it would fall within section 271(1) (limited exemption of removal benefits and expenses).

**[1.1293]**
**406  Exception for death or disability payments and benefits**
This Chapter does not apply to a payment or other benefit provided—
(a)  in connection with the termination of employment by the death of an employee, or
(b)  on account of injury to, or disability of, an employee.

**[1.1294]**
**407  Exception for payments and benefits under tax-exempt pension schemes**
(1)  This Chapter does not apply to a payment or other benefit provided under a tax-exempt pension scheme if—
(a)  the payment or other benefit is by way of compensation—
  (i)  for loss of employment, or
  (ii)  for loss or diminution of earnings, and
  the loss or diminution is due to ill-health, or
(b)  the payment or other benefit is properly regarded as earned by past service.
(2)  For this purpose "tax-exempt pension scheme" means—
[(a)  a registered pension scheme,
(aa)  a scheme set up by a government outside the United Kingdom for the benefit of employees or primarily for their benefit, or]
(b)  any such scheme or fund as was described in section 221(1) and (2) of ICTA 1970 (schemes to which payments could be made without charge to tax under section 220 of ICTA 1970).
(3)  . . .

**NOTES**

Sub-s (2): paras (a), (aa) substituted, for the original para (a), by the Finance Act 2004, s 281(1), Sch 35, paras 54, 62(1), (2).

Sub-s (3): repealed by the Finance Act 2004, ss 281(1), 326, Sch 35, paras 54, 62(1), (3), Sch 42, Pt 3.

ICTA 1970: the Income and Corporation Taxes Act 1970 (repealed).

**[1.1295]**
**408  Exception for contributions to [registered pension schemes]**
(1)  This Chapter does not apply to a contribution to a [registered pension scheme] [or an employer-financed retirement benefit scheme] if the contribution is made—
(a)  as part of an arrangement relating to the termination of a person's employment, and
(b)  in order to provide benefits for the person in accordance with the terms of the scheme or approved personal pension arrangements.
(2)  . . .

**NOTES**

The words in square brackets in the section heading and the words in the first pair of square brackets in sub-s (1) were substituted, and sub-s (2) was repealed, by the Finance Act 2004, ss 281(1), 326, Sch 35, paras 54, 63, Sch 42, Pt 3.

The words in the second pair of square brackets in sub-s (1) were inserted by the Taxation of Pension Schemes (Consequential Amendments) (No 2) Order 2006, SI 2006/1963, art 2.

**[1.1296]**
**409 Exception for payments and benefits in respect of employee liabilities and indemnity insurance**
(1) This Chapter does not apply to a payment or other benefit received by an individual if or to the extent that—
  (a) in the case of a cash benefit, it is provided for meeting the cost of a deductible amount, or
  (b) in the case of a non-cash benefit, it is or represents a benefit equivalent to the cost of paying a deductible amount.
(2) For the purposes of this section "deductible amount" means an amount which meets conditions A to C.
(3) Condition A is that the amount is paid by the individual.
(4) Condition B is that a deduction for the amount would have been allowed under section 346 from earnings from the relevant employment, if the individual still held the employment when the amount was paid.
(5) Condition C is that the amount is paid at a time which falls within the run-off period.
(6) In this section and section 410—
  "relevant employment" means the employment mentioned in section 401(1);
  "run-off period" means the period which—
  (a) starts with the day on which the relevant employment terminated, and
  (b) ends with the last day of the sixth tax year following the tax year in which the period started.

**[1.1297]**
**410 Exception for payments and benefits in respect of employee liabilities and indemnity insurance: individual deceased**
(1) This Chapter does not apply to a payment or other benefit received by an individual's personal representatives if or to the extent that—
  (a) in the case of a cash benefit, it is provided for meeting the cost of a deductible amount, or
  (b) in the case of a non-cash benefit, it is or represents a benefit equivalent to the cost of paying a deductible amount.
(2) For the purposes of this section "deductible amount" means an amount which meets conditions A to C.
(3) Condition A is that the amount is paid by the individual's personal representatives.
(4) Condition B is that a deduction for the amount would have been allowed under section 346 from earnings from the relevant employment, if—
  (a) the individual had not died,
  (b) the amount had been paid by the individual, and
  (c) the individual still held the employment when the amount was paid.
(5) Condition C is that the amount is paid at a time which falls within the run-off period.

**[1.1298]**
**411 Exception for payments and benefits for forces**
[(1)] This Chapter does not apply to a payment or other benefit provided—
  (a) under a Royal Warrant, Queen's Order or Order in Council relating to members of Her Majesty's forces, or
  (b) by way of payment in commutation of annual or other periodical payments authorised by any such Warrant or Order.
[(2) This Chapter does not apply to a payment or other benefit provided under a scheme established by an order under section 1(1) of the Armed Forces (Pensions and Compensation) Act 2004.]

**NOTES**
Sub-s (1) numbered as such, and sub-s (2) added, by the Finance Act 2007, s 63.

**[1.1299]**
**412 Exception for payments and benefits provided by foreign governments etc**
(1) This Chapter does not apply to—
  (a) a benefit provided under a pension scheme administered by the government of an overseas territory within the Commonwealth, or
  (b) a payment of compensation for loss of career, interruption of service or disturbance made—
  (i) in connection with any change in the constitution of any such overseas territory, and
  (ii) to a person who was employed in the public service of the territory before the change.
(2) References in subsection (1) to—
  (a) an overseas territory,
  (b) the government of such a territory, and
  (c) employment in the public service of such a territory,

have the meanings given in section 615 of ICTA.

**[1.1300]**
### 413 Exception in certain cases of foreign service
(1) This Chapter does not apply if the service of the employee or former employee in the employment in respect of which the payment or other benefit is received included foreign service comprising—
  (a) three-quarters or more of the whole period of service ending with the date of the termination or change in question, or
  (b) if the period of service ending with that date exceeded 10 years, the whole of the last 10 years, or
  (c) if the period of service ending with that date exceeded 20 years, one-half or more of that period, including any 10 of the last 20 years.
(2) In subsection (1) "foreign service" means service to which subsection (3), (4) or (6) applies.
(3) This subsection applies to service in or after the tax year 2003–04 such that—
  [(a) any earnings from the employment would not be relevant earnings, or]
  (b) a deduction equal to the whole amount of the earnings from the employment was or would have been allowable under Chapter 6 of Part 5 (deductions from seafarers' earnings).
[(3A) In subsection (3)(a) "relevant earnings" means—
  (a) for service in or after the tax year 2008–09, earnings—
    (i) which are for a tax year in which the employee is ordinarily UK resident,
    (ii) to which section 15 applies, and
    (iii) to which that section would apply, even if the employee made a claim under section 809B of ITA 2007 (claim for remittance basis) for that year, and
  (b) for service before the tax year 2008–09, general earnings to which section 15 or 21 as originally enacted applies.]
(4) This subsection applies to service before the tax year 2003–04 and after the tax year 1973–74 such that—
  (a) the emoluments from the employment were not chargeable under Case I of Schedule E, or would not have been so chargeable had there been any, or
  (b) a deduction equal to the whole amount of the emoluments from the employment was or would have been allowable under a foreign earnings deduction provision.
(5) In subsection (4) "foreign earnings deduction provision" means—
  (a) paragraph 1 of Schedule 2 to FA 1974,
  (b) paragraph 1 of Schedule 7 to FA 1977, or
  (c) section 192A or 193(1) of ICTA.
(6) This subsection applies to service before the tax year 1974–75 such that tax was not chargeable in respect of the emoluments of the employment—
  (a) in the tax year 1956–57 or later, under Case I of Schedule E, or
  (b) in earlier tax years, under Schedule E,
or it would not have been so chargeable had there been any such emoluments.

**NOTES**
Sub-s (3)(a) substituted, and sub-s (3A) inserted, by the Finance Act 2008, s 25, Sch 7, Pt 1, paras 2, 30, with effect for the tax year 2008–09 and subsequent tax years.

**[1.1301]**
### [413A Exception for payment of certain legal costs
(1) This Chapter does not apply to a payment which meets conditions A and B.
(2) Condition A is that the payment meets the whole or part of legal costs incurred by the employee exclusively in connection with the termination of the employee's employment.
(3) Condition B is that either—
  (a) the payment is made pursuant to an order of a court or tribunal, or
  (b) the termination of the employee's employment results in a [settlement] agreement between the employer and the employee and—
    (i) the [settlement] agreement provides for the payment to be made by the employer, and
    (ii) the payment is made directly to the employee's lawyer.
(4) In this section—

  "lawyer" has the same meaning as "qualified lawyer" in section 203(4) of the Employment Rights Act 1996 or article 245(4) of the Employment Rights (Northern Ireland) Order 1996;
  "legal costs" means fees payable for the services and disbursements of a lawyer.]

**NOTES**

Commencement: 1 April 2011 (see below).

Inserted by the Enactment of Extra-Statutory Concessions Order 2011, SI 2011/1037, art 10(1), (3), (4), as from 1 April 2011, in relation to payments made on or after 6 April 2011.

Sub-s (3): words in square brackets substituted by the Enactment of Extra-Statutory Concessions Order 2013, SI 2013/234, art 3(1)(a), (2), as from 1 March 2013, in relation to payments made on or after that date.

Sub-s (4): definition "compromise agreement" (omitted) repealed by SI 2013/234, art 3(1)(b), (2), as from 1 March 2013, in relation to payments made on or after that date.

**[1.1302]**
### 414  Reduction in other cases of foreign service
(1)   This section applies if—
  (a)   the service of the employee or former employee in the employment in respect of which the payment or other benefit is received includes foreign service, and
  (b)   section 413 (exception in certain cases of foreign service) does not apply.
(2)   The taxable person may claim relief in the form of a proportionate reduction of the amount that would otherwise count as employment income under this Chapter.
(3)   The proportion is that which the length of the foreign service bears to the whole length of service in the employment before the date of the termination or change in question.
(4)   A person's entitlement to relief under this section is limited as mentioned in subsection (5) if the person is entitled—
  (a)   to deduct, retain or satisfy income tax out of a payment which the person is liable to make, or
  (b)   to charge any income tax against another person.
(5)   The relief must not reduce the amount of income tax for which the person is liable below the amount the person is entitled so to deduct, retain, satisfy or charge.
(6)   In this section "foreign service" has the same meaning as in section 413(2).

*General and supplementary provisions*

**[1.1303]**
### 415  Valuation of benefits
(1)   In the case of a cash benefit, for the purposes of this Chapter the amount of a payment or other benefit is taken to be the amount received.
(2)   In the case of a non-cash benefit, for the purposes of this Chapter the amount of a payment or other benefit is taken to be the greater of—
  (a)   the amount of earnings (as defined in Chapter 1 of Part 3) that the benefit would give rise to if it were received by an employee within section 15 for performance of the duties of an employment (money's worth), and
  (b)   the cash equivalent of the benefit under the benefits code if it were so received and the code applied to it.
(3)   For the purposes of subsection (2), the benefits code has effect with the modifications in subsections (4), (6) and (7).
(4)   References in the benefits code to the employee are to be taken as references to the taxable person and any other person by whom the benefit is received.
(5)   For the purposes of subsection (4), section 401(4)(a) is to be disregarded.
(6)   References in the benefits code to the employer are to be taken as including references to the former employer.
(7)   Where—
  (a)   section 106 (cash equivalent: cost of accommodation over £75,000) applies, and
  (b)   the sum referred to in section 105(2)(b) (the sum made good) exceeds the amount referred to in section 105(2)(a) (the rental value),
the amount to be subtracted under paragraph (b) of step 4 of the calculation in section 106(2) is that excess (and not only the excess rent referred to there).

**[1.1304]**
### 416  Notional interest treated as paid if amount charged for beneficial loan
(1)   This section applies if an amount ("the taxable amount") consisting of, or including, an amount representing the benefit of a loan counts as a person's employment income in a tax year under section 403.
(2)   That person is to be treated for the purposes of the Tax Acts (other than this Chapter) as having paid interest on the loan in the tax year equal to the lesser of—
  (a)   the amount representing the cash equivalent of the loan, and
  (b)   the taxable amount.
(3)   The interest is to be treated—
  (a)   as accruing during the period in the tax year during which the loan is outstanding, and
  (b)   as paid at the end of the period.
(4)   The interest is not to be treated—

(a)  as income of the person making the loan, or

(b)  as relevant loan interest to which section 369 of ICTA applies (mortgage interest payable under deduction of tax).

## PART 13
## SUPPLEMENTARY PROVISIONS

*Amendments, repeals, citation etc*

**[1.1305]**
### 723  Commencement and transitional provisions and savings

(1)  This Act comes into force on 6th April 2003 and has effect—

(a)  for the purposes of income tax, for the tax year 2003–04 and subsequent tax years, and

(b)  for the purposes of corporation tax, for accounting periods ending after 5th April 2003.

(2)  Subsection (1) is subject to Schedule 7, which contains transitional provisions and savings.

**[1.1306]**
### 725  Citation

This Act may be cited as the Income Tax (Earnings and Pensions) Act 2003.

# LOCAL GOVERNMENT ACT 2003

(2003 c 26)

*An Act to make provision about finance, and other provision, in connection with local and certain other authorities; to provide for changing the dates of local elections in 2004; to amend the Audit Commission Act 1998; and for connected purposes*

[18 September 2003]

**NOTES**

Most of this Act covers matters outside the scope of this work, and only those provisions most directly relevant to employment law are printed. For reasons of space, the subject matter of sections not printed is not annotated. All provisions of the Act printed here apply to England, Wales and Scotland, except where the contrary appears.

The Code of Practice on Workforce Matters in Local Authority Service Contracts, which was given legislative status by ss 101, 102 of his Act, was revoked on 23 March 2011 with immediate effect. However, the Best Value Authorities Staff Transfers (Pensions) Direction 2007, made under ss 101 and 102, remains in place.

## PART 8
## MISCELLANEOUS AND GENERAL

### CHAPTER 1
### MISCELLANEOUS

*Contracting-out*

**[1.1307]**
### 101  Staff transfer matters: general

(1)  In exercising a power to contract with a person for the provision of services, [a relevant authority] must—

(a)  deal with matters affecting—

(i)  who will be the employer of existing staff if a contract is entered into and carried out, or

(ii)  what will be the terms and conditions of employment of existing staff, or the arrangements for their pensions, if their employer changes as a result of a contract being entered into and carried out,

in accordance with directions given to it by the appropriate person;

(b)  have regard to guidance issued to it by the appropriate person on matters relating to the employment or pensions of existing staff.

(2)  In subsection (1), references to existing staff, in relation to a contract for the provision of services, are to staff who before the contract is carried out are engaged in the provision of any of the services.

(3)  Where the provision of any services under a contract with [a relevant authority] for their provision is to cease in circumstances where they are to be provided instead by members of the authority's staff, the authority shall comply with directions given to it by the appropriate person for the purpose of requiring it to offer employment to staff who, before the services cease to be provided under the contract, are engaged in the provision of any of the services.

(4)  The duties under Part 1 of the Local Government Act 1999 (c 27) (best value) of a best value authority have effect subject to subsections (1) and (3).

(5)  The duties under sections 1 and 2 of the Local Government in Scotland Act 2003 (asp 1) (best value) of a relevant authority have effect subject to subsections (1) and (3).

[(5A)  The duties under Part 1 of the Local Government (Wales) Measure 2009 (local government improvement) have effect subject to subsections (1) and (3).]

(6)  Directions given, or guidance issued, for the purposes of subsection (1) or (3)—

    (a)   may be addressed to—

       (i)   [all relevant authorities], or

       (ii)  authorities of a particular description;

    (b)   may be different for different cases or authorities.

[(7)   . . . ]

[(7A)  In this section, in relation to England and Wales, "relevant authority" means—

    (a)   a best value authority;

    [(aa) a Welsh improvement authority;]

    (b)   a parish council;

    (c)   a parish meeting of a parish which does not have a separate parish council; or

    (d)   a community council.]

(8)  In this section[, in relation to Scotland]—

    "appropriate person"  . . .  means the Scottish Ministers; and

    "relevant authority" means—

        (a)   a council constituted under section 2 of the Local Government etc (Scotland) Act 1994 (c 39),

        (b)   the Strathclyde Passenger Transport Authority, or

        (c)   any other body to which Part 1 of the Local Government in Scotland Act 2003 (asp 1) (best value and accountability) applies.

**NOTES**

Commencement: 18 November 2003 (so far as relating to England and to a best value authority in Wales mentioned in sub-s (7)); 27 November 2003 (so far as relating to a best value authority in Wales, other than one mentioned in sub-s (7)); to be appointed (so far as relating to Scotland).

Sub-ss (1), (3), (6): words in square brackets substituted by the Local Government and Public Involvement in Health Act 2007, s 136(3), Sch 7, para 3(1), (9)(a), (b).

Sub-s (5A): inserted by the Local Government (Wales) Measure 2009, s 51(1), Sch 1, paras 23, 30(a), as from 1 April 2010.

Sub-s (7): substituted by the Local Government and Public Involvement in Health Act 2007, s 144(2), Sch 8, Pt 2, para 25(1), (4); repealed by the Police Reform and Social Responsibility Act 2011, s 99, Sch 16, Pt 3, paras 316, 321, as from 22 November 2012 (for general transitional provisions relating to police reform and the abolition of existing police authorities, see Sch 15 to the 2011 Act).

Sub-s (7A): inserted by the Local Government and Public Involvement in Health Act 2007, s 136(3), Sch 7, para 3(1), (9)(c); para (aa) inserted by the Local Government (Wales) Measure 2009, s 51(1), Sch 1, paras 23, 30(b), as from 1 April 2010.

Sub-s (8): words in square brackets inserted, and words omitted repealed, by the Local Government and Public Involvement in Health Act 2007, s 136(3), Sch 7, para 3(1), (9)(d).

See further, the final note at the beginning of this Act.

**[1.1308]**
**102  Staff transfer matters: pensions**

(1)  The appropriate person shall exercise his power to give directions under section 101(1) so as to secure that where a local authority is contracting with a person ("the contractor") for the provision of services that are to be provided under a contract instead of by employees of the authority, it does so on terms—

    (a)   that require the contractor, in the event of there being any transferring employees, to secure pension protection for each of them, and

    (b)   that, so far as relating to the securing of pension protection for a transferring employee, are enforceable by the employee.

(2)  For the purposes of subsection (1)—

    (a)   "transferring employee" means an employee of the authority whose contract of employment becomes, by virtue of the application of the TUPE regulations in relation to what is done for the purposes of carrying out the contract between the authority and the contractor, a contract of employment with someone other than the authority, and

    (b)   "pension protection" is secured for a transferring employee if after that change in his employer he has, as an employee of his new employer, rights to acquire pension benefits and those rights—

       (i)   are the same as, or

       (ii)  under the directions count as being broadly comparable to or better than,

       those that he had as an employee of the authority.

(3)  The appropriate person shall exercise his power to give directions under section 101(1) so as to secure that where—

    (a)   a local authority has contracted with a person ("the first contractor") for the provision of services,

(b) the application of the TUPE regulations in relation to what was done for the purposes of carrying out the contract between the authority and the first contractor resulted in employees of the authority ("the original employees") becoming employees of someone other than the authority, and

(c) the authority is contracting with a person ("the subsequent contractor") for the provision of any of the services,

the authority contracts with the subsequent contractor on terms satisfying the requirements of subsection (4).

(4) Those requirements are that the terms—

(a) require the subsequent contractor, in the event of there being any transferring original employees, to secure pension protection for each of them, and

(b) so far as relating to the securing of pension protection for an original employee, are enforceable by the employee.

(5) For the purposes of subsection (4)—

(a) "transferring original employee" means an original employee—

(i) whose contract of employment becomes, by virtue of the application of the TUPE regulations in relation to what is done for the purposes of carrying out the contract between the authority and the subsequent contractor, a contract of employment with someone other than his existing employer, and

(ii) whose contract of employment on each occasion when an intervening contract was carried out became, by virtue of the application of the TUPE regulations in relation to what was done for the purposes of carrying out the intervening contract, a contract of employment with someone other than his existing employer;

(b) "pension protection" is secured for a transferring original employee if after the change in his employer mentioned in paragraph (a)(i) he has, as an employee of his new employer, rights to acquire pension benefits and those rights—

(i) are the same as, or

(ii) under the directions count as being broadly comparable to or better than,

those that he had before that change.

(6) In subsection (5)(a)(ii), "intervening contract" means a contract with the authority for the provision, at times after they are provided under the contract with the first contractor and before they are to be provided under a contract with the subsequent contractor, of the services to be provided under the contract with the subsequent contractor.

(7) Any expression used in this section, and in the TUPE regulations, has in this section the meaning that it has in the TUPE regulations.

[(7A) In this section, in relation to England, "local authority" means—

(a) a county council in England, a district council, a London borough council, a parish council or a parish meeting of a parish which does not have a separate parish council;

(b) the Council of the Isles of Scilly;

(c) the Common Council of the City of London in its capacity as a local authority; and

(d) the Greater London Authority so far as it exercises its functions through the Mayor.

(7B) In this section, in relation to Wales, "local authority" means a county council, county borough council or community council in Wales.]

(8) In this section[, in relation to Scotland]—

"appropriate person" . . . means the Scottish Ministers;

"local authority"—

(a) . . .

(b) . . . means a council constituted under section 2 of the Local Government etc (Scotland) Act 1994 (c 39);

[(9) In this section,]

"the TUPE regulations" means the [Transfer of Undertakings (Protection of Employment) Regulations 2006], or any regulations replacing those regulations, as from time to time amended.

**NOTES**

Commencement: 27 November 2003 (in relation to Wales); 1 April 2004 (in relation to England); to be appointed (in relation to Scotland).

Sub-ss (7A), (7B): inserted by the Local Government and Public Involvement in Health Act 2007, s 136(3), Sch 7, para 3(1), (10).

Sub-s (8): words in square brackets inserted, and words omitted repealed, by the Local Government and Public Involvement in Health Act 2007, s 136(3), Sch 7, para 3(1), (11)(a)–(c).

Sub-s (9): numbered as such, and words "In this section," in square brackets inserted, by the Local Government and Public Involvement in Health Act 2007, s 136(3), Sch 7, para 3(1), (11)(d); words in square brackets in definition "the TUPE regulations" substituted by the Transfer of Undertakings (Protection of Employment) Regulations 2006, SI 2006/246, Sch 2, para 1(i).

See further, the final note at the beginning of this Act.

CHAPTER 2
GENERAL

**[1.1309]**
## 124   General interpretation
In this Act—

"appropriate person" means—

(a)    in relation to England, the Secretary of State, and

(b)    in relation to Wales, the National Assembly for Wales;

"best value authority" means an authority or body which is a best value authority for the purposes of Part 1 of the Local Government Act 1999 (c 27);

"financial year" means a period of 12 months beginning with 1st April;

. . .

["Welsh improvement authority" means an authority which is a Welsh improvement authority within the meaning of section 1 of the Local Government (Wales) Measure 2009].

**NOTES**
Definition "valuation tribunal" (omitted) repealed by the Local Government and Public Involvement in Health Act 2007, ss 220(1), 241, Sch 16, paras 10, 12, Sch 18, Pt 17, as from 1 October 2009.

Definition "Welsh improvement authority" inserted by the Local Government (Wales) Measure 2009, s 51(1), Sch 1, paras 23, 31, as from 1 April 2010.

**[1.1310]**
## 128   Commencement
(1)   The following provisions shall come into force on the day on which this Act is passed—

(a)    this section and sections 30, 34, 35, 72, 73, 103, 104, 110, 114, 121, 123, 124 and 129;

(b), (c) *(outside the scope of this work.)*

(2)   *(Outside the scope of this work.)*

(3)   The following provisions shall come into force on such day as the Secretary of State may by order appoint—

(a)    *(outside the scope of this work)*;

(b)    section 101, so far as relating to England and so far as relating to a best value authority in Wales mentioned in subsection (7) of that section;

(c)–(f) *(outside the scope of this work.)*

(4)   The following provisions shall come into force on such day as the National Assembly for Wales may by order appoint—

(a), (b) *(outside the scope of this work)*;

(c)    section 101, so far as relating to a best value authority in Wales, other than one mentioned in subsection (7) of that section;

(d)–(g) *(outside the scope of this work.)*

(5)   So far as relating to Scotland, sections 101 and 102 shall come into force on such day as the Scottish Ministers may by order appoint.

(6)   The remaining provisions of this Act—

(a)    so far as relating to England, shall come into force on such day as the Secretary of State may by order appoint, and

(b)    so far as relating to Wales, shall come into force on such day as the National Assembly for Wales may by order appoint.

(7)   Power to make orders under this section is exercisable by statutory instrument.

(8)   Orders under this section may make different provision for different purposes.

(9)   A person who has power under this section to appoint a day for the coming into force of a provision may by order make in connection with the coming into force of that provision such transitional provision or saving as the person considers necessary or expedient.

**NOTES**
Orders: the commencement orders relevant to the sections reproduced here are the Local Government Act 2003 (Commencement No 1 and Transitional Provisions and Savings) Order 2003, SI 2003/2938, and the Local Government Act 2003 (Commencement) (Wales) Order 2003, SI 2003/3034.

**[1.1311]**
## 129   Short title and extent
(1)   This Act may be cited as the Local Government Act 2003.

(2)   Subject to the following provisions, this Act extends to England and Wales only.

(3)   Sections 83(2), 101 and 102 extend also to Scotland.

(4)   The following provisions extend also to Scotland, Northern Ireland and Gibraltar—

(a)    sections 103, 104 and 128,

(b)    this section, and

(c)    *(outside the scope of this work.)*

(5)–(8)   *(Outside the scope of this work.)*

# GENDER RECOGNITION ACT 2004

(2004 c 7)

## ARRANGEMENT OF SECTIONS

*An Act to make provision for and in connection with change of gender*

[1 July 2004]

**NOTES**

Most of this Act covers matters outside the scope of this work, and only those provisions most directly relevant to employment law are printed. For reasons of space, the subject matter of sections not printed is not annotated. The provisions reproduced here apply to the whole of the United Kingdom (s 28). All provisions which did not come into force on Royal assent came into force on 4 April 2005 (see SI 2005/54).

*Consequences of issue of gender recognition certificate etc*

**[1.1312]**
**9  General**
(1)  Where a full gender recognition certificate is issued to a person, the person's gender becomes for all purposes the acquired gender (so that, if the acquired gender is the male gender, the person's sex becomes that of a man and, if it is the female gender, the person's sex becomes that of a woman).
(2)  Subsection (1) does not affect things done, or events occurring, before the certificate is issued; but it does operate for the interpretation of enactments passed, and instruments and other documents made, before the certificate is issued (as well as those passed or made afterwards).
(3)  Subsection (1) is subject to provision made by this Act or any other enactment or any subordinate legislation.

**[1.1313]**
**13  Social security benefits and pensions**
Schedule 5 (entitlement to benefits and pensions) has effect.

**[1.1314]**
**15  Succession etc**
The fact that a person's gender has become the acquired gender under this Act does not affect the disposal or devolution of property under a will or other instrument made before the appointed day.

**19**  *(Repealed by the Equality Act 2010, s 211(2), Sch 27, Pt 1, as from 1 October 2010.)*

*Supplementary*

**[1.1315]**
**29  Short title**
This Act may be cited as the Gender Recognition Act 2004.

# SCHEDULES

## SCHEDULE 5
## BENEFITS AND PENSIONS

Section 13

## PART 1
## INTRODUCTORY

**[1.1316]**

**1.** This Schedule applies where a full gender recognition certificate is issued to a person.

## PART 3
## OCCUPATIONAL PENSION SCHEMES

**[1.1317]**

**14   Guaranteed minimum pensions etc: Great Britain**

(1) In this paragraph "the 1993 Act" means the Pension Schemes Act 1993 (c 48); and expressions used in this paragraph and in that Act have the same meaning in this paragraph as in that Act.

(2) The fact that the person's gender has become the acquired gender does not affect the operation of section 14 of the 1993 Act (guaranteed minimum) in relation to the person, except to the extent that its operation depends on section 16 of the 1993 Act (revaluation); and sub-paragraphs (3) and (5) have effect subject to that.

(3) If (immediately before the certificate is issued) the person is a woman who is entitled to a guaranteed minimum pension but has not attained the age of 65—

    (a) the person is for the purposes of section 13 of the 1993 Act and the guaranteed minimum pension provisions to be treated after it is issued as not having attained pensionable age (so that the entitlement ceases) but as attaining pensionable age on subsequently attaining the age of 65, and

    (b) in a case where the person's guaranteed minimum pension has commenced before the certificate is issued, it is to be treated for the purposes of Chapter 3 of Part 4 of the 1993 Act (anti-franking) as if it had not.

(4) But sub-paragraph (3)(a) does not—

    (a) affect any pension previously paid to the person, or

    (b) prevent section 15 of the 1993 Act (increase of guaranteed minimum where commencement of guaranteed minimum pension postponed) operating to increase the person's guaranteed minimum by reason of a postponement of the commencement of the person's guaranteed minimum pension for a period ending before the certificate is issued.

(5) If (immediately before the certificate is issued) the person is a man who—

    (a) has attained the age of 60, but

    (b) has not attained the age of 65,

the person is to be treated for the purposes of section 13 of the 1993 Act and the guaranteed minimum pension provisions as attaining pensionable age when it is issued.

(6) If at that time the person has attained the age of 65, the fact that the person's gender has become the acquired gender does not affect the person's pensionable age for those purposes.

(7) The fact that the person's gender has become the acquired gender does not affect any guaranteed minimum pension to which the person is entitled as a widow or widower immediately before the certificate is issued (except in consequence of the operation of the previous provisions of this Schedule).

(8) If a transaction to which section 19 of the 1993 Act applies which is carried out before the certificate is issued discharges a liability to provide a guaranteed minimum pension for or in respect of the person, it continues to do so afterwards.

(9) "The guaranteed minimum pension provision" means so much of the 1993 Act (apart from section 13) and of any other enactment as relates to guaranteed minimum pensions.

**15.** *(Applies to Northern Ireland only.)*

**16   Equivalent pension benefits: Great Britain**

(1) The provision that may be made by regulations under paragraph 15 of Schedule 3 to the Social Security (Consequential Provisions) Act 1992 (c 6) (power to retain provisions repealed by Social Security Act 1973 (c 38), with or without modification, for transitional purposes) includes provision modifying the preserved equivalent pension benefits provisions in consequence of this Act.

(2) "The preserved equivalent pension benefits provisions" are the provisions of the National Insurance Act 1965 (c 51) relating to equivalent pension benefits continued in force, with or without modification, by regulations having effect as if made under that paragraph.

**17.** *(Applies to Northern Ireland only.)*

# HIGHER EDUCATION ACT 2004

## (2004 c 8)

*An Act to make provision about research in the arts and humanities and about complaints by students against institutions providing higher education; to make provision about fees payable by students in higher education; to provide for the appointment of a Director of Fair Access to Higher Education; to make provision about grants and loans to students in higher or further education; to limit the jurisdiction of visitors of institutions providing higher education; and for connected purposes*

[1 July 2004]

**NOTES**

Most of this Act covers matters outside the scope of this work, and only s 46 is reproduced here. For reasons of space, the subject matter of sections not printed is not annotated. Section 46 came into force on 1 January 2005 in relation to both England and Wales (see SI 2004/2781 and SI 2004/3144) and applies to England and Wales only (s 53).

## PART 5
## MISCELLANEOUS AND GENERAL

*Staff disputes: jurisdiction of visitor*

**[1.1318]**
### 46 Exclusion of visitor's jurisdiction in relation to staff disputes
(1) The visitor of a qualifying institution has no jurisdiction in respect of—
  (a) any dispute relating to a member of staff which concerns his appointment or employment or the termination of his appointment or employment,
  (b) any other dispute between a member of staff and the qualifying institution in respect of which proceedings could be brought before any court or tribunal, or
  (c) any dispute as to the application of the statutes or other internal laws of the institution in relation to a matter falling within paragraph (a) or (b).
(2) In subsection (1) "qualifying institution" has the meaning given by section 11.
(3) In determining whether a dispute falls within subsection (1)(b) it is to be assumed that the visitor does not have jurisdiction to determine the dispute.
(4) Section 206 of the Education Reform Act 1988 (c 40) (which is superseded by subsection (1)) shall cease to have effect.

**NOTES**

Note for the purposes of this section that s 11 of this Act in Pt 2 provides as follows—

**"11 Qualifying institutions**
In this Part "qualifying institution" means any of the following institutions in England or Wales—
  (a) a university (whether or not receiving financial support under section 65 of the 1992 Act) whose entitlement to grant awards is conferred or confirmed by—
    (i) an Act of Parliament,
    (ii) a Royal Charter, or
    (iii) an order under section 76 of the 1992 Act;
  (b) a constituent college, school or hall or other institution of a university falling within paragraph (a);
  (c) an institution conducted by a higher education corporation;
  (d) a designated institution, as defined by section 72(3) of the 1992 Act.".

# GANGMASTERS (LICENSING) ACT 2004

## (2004 c 11)

### ARRANGEMENT OF SECTIONS

*Scope of Act*

*An Act to make provision for the licensing of activities involving the supply or use of workers in connection with agricultural work, the gathering of wild creatures and wild plants, the harvesting of fish from fish farms, and certain processing and packaging; and for connected purposes*

[8 July 2004]

**1, 2**    *((The Gangmasters Licensing Authority) outside the scope of this work.)*

*Scope of Act*

**[1.1319]**
## 3 Work to which this Act applies
(1) The work to which this Act applies is—
- (a) agricultural work,
- (b) gathering shellfish, and
- (c) processing or packaging—
  - (i) any produce derived from agricultural work, or
  - (ii) shellfish, fish or products derived from shellfish or fish.

This is subject to any provision made by regulations under subsection (5) below and to section 5 (territorial scope of application).

(2) In subsection (1)(a) "agricultural work" means work in agriculture.

(3) In this Act "agriculture" includes—
- (a) dairy-farming,
- (b) the production for the purposes of any trade, business or other undertaking (whether carried on for profit or not) of consumable produce,
- (c) the use of land as grazing, meadow or pasture land,
- (d) the use of land as an orchard or as osier land or woodland, and
- (e) the use of land for market gardens or nursery grounds.

In paragraph (b) "consumable produce" means produce grown for sale, consumption or other use after severance from the land on which it is grown.

(4) In this Act "shellfish" means crustaceans and molluscs of any kind, and includes any part of a shellfish and any (or any part of any) brood, ware, halfware or spat of shellfish, and any spawn of shellfish, and the shell, or any part of the shell, of a shellfish.

(5) The Secretary of State may by regulations make provision—
- (a) excluding work of a prescribed description from being work to which this Act applies;
- (b) including work of the following nature as being work to which this Act applies—
  - (i) the gathering (by any manner) of wild creatures, or wild plants, of a prescribed description and the processing and packaging of anything so gathered, and
  - (ii) the harvesting of fish from a fish farm (within the meaning of [the Salmon and Freshwater Fisheries Act 1975]).

---

**NOTES**

Sub-s (5): words in square brackets in sub-para (b)(ii) substituted in relation to England and Wales by the Aquatic Animal Health (England and Wales) Regulations 2009, SI 2009/463, reg 45, Sch 2, para 10, and in relation to Scotland by the Aquatic Animal Health (Scotland) Regulations 2009, SSI 2009/85, reg 48, Sch 2, para 11, as from (in both cases) 27 March 2009.

Regulations: as of 6 April 2013 no Regulations had been made under this section.

---

**[1.1320]**
## 4 Acting as a gangmaster
(1) This section defines what is meant in this Act by a person acting as a gangmaster.
(2) A person ("A") acts as a gangmaster if he supplies a worker to do work to which this Act applies for another person ("B").

(3)   For the purposes of subsection (2) it does not matter—

(a)   whether the worker works under a contract with A or is supplied to him by another person,

(b)   whether the worker is supplied directly under arrangements between A and B or indirectly under arrangements involving one or more intermediaries,

(c)   whether A supplies the worker himself or procures that the worker is supplied,

(d)   whether the work is done under the control of A, B or an intermediary,

(e)   whether the work done for B is for the purposes of a business carried on by him or in connection with services provided by him to another person.

(4)   A person ("A") acts as a gangmaster if he uses a worker to do work to which this Act applies in connection with services provided by him to another person.

(5)   A person ("A") acts as a gangmaster if he uses a worker to do any of the following work to which this Act applies for the purposes of a business carried on by him—

(a)   harvesting or otherwise gathering agricultural produce following—

(i)   a sale, assignment or lease of produce to A, or

(ii)   the making of any other agreement with A,

where the sale, assignment, lease or other agreement was entered into for the purpose of enabling the harvesting or gathering to take place;

(b)   gathering shellfish;

(c)   processing or packaging agricultural produce harvested or gathered as mentioned in paragraph (a).

In this subsection "agricultural produce" means any produce derived from agriculture.

(6)   For the purposes of subsection (4) or (5) A shall be treated as using a worker to do work to which this Act applies if he makes arrangements under which the worker does the work—

(a)   whether the worker works for A (or for another) or on his own account, and

(b)   whether or not he works under a contract (with A or another).

(7)   Regulations under section 3(5)(b) may provide for the application of subsections (5) and (6) above in relation to work that is work to which this Act applies by virtue of the regulations.

**[1.1321]**
## 5   Territorial scope of application
(1)   The work to which this Act applies is work—

(a)   in the United Kingdom,

(b)   on any portion of the shore or bed of the sea, or of an estuary or tidal river, adjacent to the United Kingdom, whether above or below (or partly above and partly below) the low water mark, or

(c)   in UK coastal waters.

(2)   In subsection (1)(c) "UK coastal waters" means waters adjacent to the United Kingdom to a distance of six miles measured from the baselines from which the breadth of the territorial sea is measured.

In this subsection "miles" means international nautical miles of 1,852 metres.

(3)   The provisions of this Act apply where a person acts as a gangmaster, whether in the United Kingdom or elsewhere, in relation to work to which this Act applies.

*Licensing*

**[1.1322]**
## 6   Prohibition of unlicensed activities
(1)   A person shall not act as a gangmaster except under the authority of a licence.

(2)   Regulations made by the Secretary of State may specify circumstances in which a licence is not required.

**NOTES**

Regulations: the Gangmasters Licensing (Exclusions) Regulations 2010, SI 2010/649.

**[1.1323]**
## 7   Grant of licence
(1)   The Authority may grant a licence if it thinks fit.

(2)   A licence shall describe the activities authorised by it and shall be granted for such period as the Authority thinks fit.

(3)   A licence authorises activities—

(a)   by the holder of the licence, and

(b)   by persons employed or engaged by the holder of the licence who are named or otherwise specified in the licence.

(4)   In the case of a licence held otherwise than by an individual, the reference in subsection (3)(a) to activities by the holder of the licence shall be read as a reference only to such activities as are mentioned in whichever of the following provisions applies—

section 20(2) (body corporate);

section 21(2) (unincorporated association);

Part 1 Statutes

section 22(4) (partnership that is regarded as a legal person under the law of the country or territory under which it is formed).

(5) A licence shall be granted subject to such conditions as the Authority considers appropriate.

**[1.1324]**
**8 General power of Authority to make rules**
(1) The Authority may make such rules as it thinks fit in connection with the licensing of persons acting as gangmasters.
(2) The rules may, in particular—
 (a) prescribe the form and contents of applications for licences and other documents to be filed in connection with applications;
 (b) regulate the procedure to be followed in connection with applications and authorise the rectification of procedural irregularities;
 (c) prescribe time limits for doing anything required to be done in connection with an application and provide for the extension of any period so prescribed;
 (d) prescribe the requirements which must be met before a licence is granted;
 (e) provide for the manner in which the meeting of those requirements is to be verified;
 (f) allow for the grant of licences on a provisional basis before it is determined whether the requirements for the grant of a licence are met and for the withdrawal of such licences (if appropriate) if it appears that those requirements are not met;
 (g) prescribe the form of licences and the information to be contained in them;
 (h) require the payment of such fees as may be prescribed or determined in accordance with the rules;
 (i) provide that licences are to be granted subject to conditions requiring the licence holder—
  (i) to produce, in prescribed circumstances, evidence in a prescribed form of his being licensed, and
  (ii) to comply with any prescribed requirements relating to the recruitment, use and supply of workers.
(3) The Authority must consult the Secretary of State before making any rules about fees.
(4) In subsection (2) "prescribed" means prescribed by the rules.

**NOTES**
Rules: the Gangmasters (Licensing Conditions) Rules 2009, SI 2009/307 at **[2.1143]**.

**[1.1325]**
**9 Modification, revocation or transfer of licence**
(1) The Authority may by notice in writing to the licensee modify or revoke any licence granted to him (including any of the conditions of that licence)—
 (a) with the consent of the licensee, or
 (b) where it appears to him that a condition of the licence or any requirement of this Act has not been complied with.
(2) The modifications that may be made include one suspending the effect of the licence for such period as the Authority may determine.
(3) A licence may be transferred with the written consent of the Authority and in such other cases as may be determined by the Authority.

**[1.1326]**
**10 Appeals**
(1) The Secretary of State shall by regulations make provision for an appeal against any decision of the Authority—
 (a) to refuse an application for a licence,
 (b) as to the conditions to which the grant of the licence is subject,
 (c) to refuse consent to the transfer of a licence, or
 (d) to modify or revoke a licence.
(2) The regulations shall make provision—
 (a) for and in connection with the appointment of a person to hear and determine such appeals (including provision for the payment of remuneration and allowances to such a person), and
 (b) as to the procedure to be followed in connection with an appeal.

**NOTES**
Regulations: the Gangmasters (Appeals) Regulations 2006, SI 2006/662.

**[1.1327]**
**11 Register of licences**
(1) The Authority shall establish and maintain a register of persons licensed under this Act.

(2)   The register shall contain such particulars as the Authority may determine of every person who for the time being holds a licence or whose activities are authorised by a licence (whether or not they are named in the licence).

(3)   The Authority shall ensure that appropriate arrangements are in force for allowing members of the public to inspect the contents of the register.

*Offences*

**[1.1328]**

**12   Offences: acting as a gangmaster, being in possession of false documents etc**

(1)   A person commits an offence if he acts as a gangmaster in contravention of section 6 (prohibition of unlicensed activities).

For this purpose a person acting as a gangmaster does not contravene section 6 by reason only of the fact that he breaches a condition of the licence which authorises him to so act.

(2)   A person commits an offence if he has in his possession or under his control—

    (a)   a relevant document that is false and that he knows or believes to be false,

    (b)   a relevant document that was improperly obtained and that he knows or believes to have been improperly obtained, or

    (c)   a relevant document that relates to someone else,

with the intention of inducing another person to believe that he or another person acting as a gangmaster in contravention of section 6 is acting under the authority of a licence.

(3)   A person guilty of an offence under subsection (1) or (2) is liable on summary conviction—

    (a)   in England and Wales, to imprisonment for a term not exceeding twelve months, or to a fine not exceeding the statutory maximum, or to both;

    (b)   in Scotland or Northern Ireland, to imprisonment for a term not exceeding six months, or to a fine not exceeding the statutory maximum, or to both.

In relation to an offence committed before the commencement of section 154(1) of the Criminal Justice Act 2003 (c 44), for "twelve months" in paragraph (a) substitute "six months".

(4)   A person guilty of an offence under subsection (1) or (2) is liable on conviction on indictment to imprisonment for a term not exceeding ten years, or to a fine, or to both.

(5)   For the purposes of this section—

    (a)   except in Scotland, a document is false only if it is false within the meaning of Part 1 of the Forgery and Counterfeiting Act 1981 (c 45) (see section 9(1) of that Act), and

    (b)   a document was improperly obtained if false information was provided, in or in connection with the application for its issue or an application for its modification, to the person who issued it or (as the case may be) to a person entitled to modify it,

and references to the making of a false document include references to the modification of a document so that it becomes false.

(6)   In this section "relevant document" means—

    (a)   a licence, or

    (b)   any document issued by the Authority in connection with a licence.

**[1.1329]**

**13   Offences: entering into arrangements with gangmasters**

(1)   A person commits an offence if—

    (a)   he enters into arrangements under which a person ("the gangmaster") supplies him with workers or services, and

    (b)   the gangmaster in supplying the workers or services contravenes section 6 (prohibition of unlicensed activities).

(2)   In proceedings against a person for an offence under subsection (1) it is a defence for him to prove that he—

    (a)   took all reasonable steps to satisfy himself that the gangmaster was acting under the authority of a valid licence, and

    (b)   did not know, and had no reasonable grounds for suspecting that the gangmaster was not the holder of a valid licence.

(3)   The Secretary of State may by regulations make provision as to what constitutes "reasonable steps" for the purposes of subsection (2)(a).

(4)   A person guilty of an offence under subsection (1) is liable—

    (a)   on summary conviction in England and Wales, to imprisonment for a term not exceeding 51 weeks, or to a fine not exceeding the statutory maximum, or to both,

    (b)   on summary conviction in Scotland or Northern Ireland, to imprisonment for a term not exceeding six months, or to a fine not exceeding the statutory maximum, or to both.

In relation to an offence committed before the commencement of section 281(5) of the Criminal Justice Act 2003 (c 44), for "51 weeks" in paragraph (a) substitute "six months".

**NOTES**

Regulations: as of 6 April 2013 no Regulations had been made under sub-s (3).

**[1.1330]**
**14   Offences: supplementary provisions**
(1)   An enforcement officer (see section 15) has the powers of arrest mentioned in subsection (2) (in addition to powers under [section 24A] of the Police and Criminal Evidence Act 1984 (c 60)) in relation to any of the following offences—
 (a)   an offence under section 12(1) or (2),
 (b)   conspiring to commit any such offence,
 (c)   attempting to commit any such offence,
 (d)   inciting, aiding, abetting, counselling or procuring the commission of any such offence.
(2)   Those powers are as follows—
 (a)   if he has reasonable grounds for suspecting that such an offence has been committed, he may arrest without warrant anyone whom he has reasonable grounds for suspecting to be guilty of the offence;
 (b)   he may arrest without warrant—
  (i)   anyone who is about to commit such an offence;
  (ii)  anyone whom he has reasonable grounds for suspecting to be about to commit such an offence.
(3)   Subsections (1) and (2) do not apply in Scotland.
(4)   . . .

**NOTES**
 Sub-s (1): words in square brackets substituted by the Serious Organised Crime and Police Act 2005, s 111, Sch 7, Pt 4, para 62(a).
 Sub-s (4): amends the Proceeds of Crime Act 2002, Schs 2, 4, 5.
 Attempt, conspiracy or incitement to commit an offence: see the Serious Crime Act 2007, s 63(1), (2), Sch 6, Pt 1, para 50 which provides that any reference however expressed to (or to conduct amounting to) the offence abolished by s 59 of the 2007 Act (abolition of common law offence of inciting the commission of another offence) has effect as a reference to (or to conduct amounting to) the offences of encouraging or assisting the commission of an offence.

**15–22**   (*Ss 15–19 (Enforcement), ss 20–22 (supplementary) outside the scope of this work.*)

*Miscellaneous and general*

**23–25**   (*S 23 (Annual report), s 24 (financial provision), s 25 (general provisions about the making of Regulations, etc) outside the scope of this work.*)

**[1.1331]**
**26   Meaning of "worker"**
(1)   In this Act "worker" means an individual who does work to which this Act applies.
(2)   A person is not prevented from being a worker for the purposes of this Act by reason of the fact that he has no right to be, or to work, in the United Kingdom.

**[1.1332]**
**27   Exclusion of provisions relating to employment agencies and businesses**
(1)   The Employment Agencies Act 1973 (c 35) does not apply to an employment agency or an employment business in so far as it consists of activities for which a licence is required under this Act.
(2)   In subsection (1) "employment agency" and "employment business" have the same meaning as in that Act.

**28**   (*(Application to Northern Ireland) Outside the scope of this work.*)

**[1.1333]**
**29   Commencement and transitional provision**
(1)   The provisions of this Act come into force on such day as the Secretary of State may by order appoint.
(2)   Different days may be appointed for different purposes and for different areas.
(3)   The Secretary of State may by order make such transitional provision as he considers appropriate in connection with the coming into force of any provision of this Act.

**NOTES**
 Commencement: to be appointed.
 Orders: the Gangmasters (Licensing) Act 2004 (Commencement No 1) Order 2004, SI 2004/2857; the Gangmasters (Licensing) Act 2004 (Commencement No 2) Order 2005, SI 2005/447; the Gangmasters (Licensing) Act 2004 (Commencement No 3) Order 2006, SI 2006/2406; the Gangmasters (Licensing) Act 2004 (Commencement No 4) Order 2006, SI 2006/2906; the Gangmasters (Licensing) Act 2004 (Commencement No 5) Order 2007, SI 2007/695.
 Note that this section has never technically been brought into force; for the statutory basis of orders made under a section not yet in force, see the Interpretation Act 1978, s 13 (anticipatory exercise of powers).

**[1.1334]**

**30 Short title and extent**

(1) This Act may be cited as the Gangmasters (Licensing) Act 2004.

(2) This Act extends to England and Wales, Scotland and Northern Ireland.

## SCHEDULES 1 AND 2

*(Sch 1 (Consequential amendments), Sch 2 (Application to Northern Ireland) outside the scope of this work.)*

# EMPLOYMENT RELATIONS ACT 2004

### (2004 c 24)

*An Act to amend the law relating to the recognition of trade unions and the taking of industrial action; to make provision about means of voting in ballots under the Trade Union and Labour Relations (Consolidation) Act 1992; to amend provisions of that Act relating to rights of members and non-members of trade unions and to make other provision about rights of trade union members, employees and workers; to make further provision concerning the enforcement of legislation relating to minimum wages; to make further provision about proceedings before and appeals from the Certification Officer; to make further provision about the amalgamation of trade unions; to make provision facilitating the administration of trade unions and the carrying out by them of their functions; and for connected purposes*

[16 September 2004]

**NOTES**

Most of this Act consists of amendments to other Acts and, where relevant, they have been incorporated at the appropriate place. The rest of the Act is printed in full save for provisions that have been repealed and ss 43, 47, and 58 which are outside the scope of this work.

**1–28** *(Pt 1 (ss 1–21: Union Recognition) inserts the Trade Union and Labour Relations (Consolidation) Act 1992, s 210A at* **[1.478]**, *and amends Sch A1 to the 1992 Act at* **[1.582]** *et seq; Pt 2 (ss 22–28: Law Relating to Industrial Action) contains various amendments to the 1992 Act (these amendments have been incorporated at the appropriate place.))*

### PART 3
### RIGHTS OF TRADE UNION MEMBERS, WORKERS AND EMPLOYEES

**29–34** *(S 29 inserts the Trade Union and Labour Relations (Consolidation) Act 1992, s 145A–145F at* **[1.407]** *et seq; ss 30–34 contain various amendments to the 1992 Act (these amendments have been incorporated at the appropriate place) and repeal the Employment Relations Act 1999, s 17.)*

*Other rights of workers and employees*

**35–41** *(Substitute the Trade Union and Labour Relations (Consolidation) Act 1992, s 154 at* **[1.421]**, *and amend ss 237, 238 of that Act at* **[1.517]**, **[1.518]**, *amend the Employment Tribunals Act 1996, ss 10, 21 at* **[1.694]**, **[1.713]**, *amend the Employment Relations Act 1999, ss 10–12, 23 at* **[1.1191]–[1.1193]**, **[1.1200]**, *insert the Employment Rights Act 1996, ss 43M, 98B at* **[1.800]**, **[1.898]**, *amend ss 48, 105, 108, 194, 195, 199 of that Act at* **[1.814]**, **[1.915]**, **[1.918]**, **[1.1001]**, **[1.1002]**, **[1.1004]**, *and amended s 109 (repealed). Note that s 41(1), (2) (amendments to ss 237(1A), 238(2A) of the 1992 Act) are repealed by the Pensions Act 2008, s 148, Sch 11, Pt 1, as from a day to be appointed.)*

**[1.1335]**

**42 Information and consultation: Great Britain**

(1) The Secretary of State may make regulations for the purpose of conferring on employees of an employer to whom the regulations apply, or on representatives of those employees, rights—

   (a) to be informed by the employer about prescribed matters;

   (b) to be consulted by the employer about prescribed matters.

(2) Regulations made under subsection (1) must make provision as to the employers to whom the regulations apply which may include provision—

   (a) applying the regulations by reference to factors including the number of employees in the United Kingdom in the employer's undertaking;

   (b) as to the method by which the number of employees in an employer's undertaking is to be calculated; and

   (c) applying the regulations to different descriptions of employer with effect from different dates.

Part 1 Statutes

(3) Regulations made under subsection (1) may make provision—
   (a) as to the circumstances in which the rights mentioned in subsection (1) arise and the extent of those rights;
   (b) for and about the initiation and conduct of negotiations between employers to whom the regulations apply and their employees for the purposes of reaching an agreement satisfying prescribed conditions about the provision of information to the employees, and consultation of them (whether that provision or consultation is to be direct or through representatives);
   (c) about the representatives the employees may have for the purposes of the regulations and the method by which those representatives are to be selected;
   (d) as to the resolution of disputes and the enforcement of obligations imposed by the regulations or by an agreement of the kind mentioned in paragraph (b).
(4) Regulations made under subsection (1) may—
   (a) confer jurisdiction (including exclusive jurisdiction) on employment tribunals and on the Employment Appeal Tribunal;
   (b) confer functions on the Central Arbitration Committee;
   (c) require or authorise the holding of ballots;
   (d) amend, apply with or without modifications, or make provision similar to any provision of the Employment Rights Act 1996 (c 18) (including, in particular, Parts 5, 10 and 13), the Employment Tribunals Act 1996 (c 17) or the 1992 Act;
   (e) include supplemental, incidental, consequential and transitional provision, including provision amending any enactment;
   (f) make different provision for different cases or circumstances.
(5) Regulations made under subsection (1) may make any provision which appears to the Secretary of State to be necessary or expedient—
   (a) for the purpose of implementing Directive 2002/14/EC of the European Parliament and of the Council of 11 March 2002 establishing a general framework for informing and consulting employees in the European Community;
   (b) for the purpose of dealing with any matter arising out of or related to the United Kingdom's obligations under that Directive.
(6) Nothing in subsections (2) to (5) prejudices the generality of this section.
(7) Regulations under this section shall be made by statutory instrument.
(8) No such regulations may be made unless a draft of the regulations has been laid before Parliament and approved by a resolution of each House of Parliament.
(9) In this section "prescribed" means prescribed by regulations under this section.

**NOTES**
  Regulations: the Information and Consultation of Employees Regulations 2004, SI 2004/3426 at **[2.896]**; the Information and Consultation of Employees (Amendment) Regulations 2006, SI 2006/514.

**43–51** _(S 43 (Information and consultation: Northern Ireland) outside the scope of this work; ss 44–47 (Pt 4 Enforcement of Minimum Wage Legislation) are as follows: s 44 inserts the National Minimum Wage Act 1998,s 16A at_ **[1.1132]**_; ss 45, 46 repealed by the Employment Act 2008, s 20, Schedule, Pt 2, as from 6 April 2009; s 47 contains miscellaneous amendments to agricultural wages legislation that are outside the scope of this work; ss 48–51 (Pt 5 The Certification Officer) insert the Trade Union and Labour Relations (Consolidation) Act 1992, ss 101A, 101B, 256ZA at_ **[1.365]**, **[1.366]**, **[1.541]**_, contain various other amendments to the 1992 Act (incorporated as appropriate), and amend the Employment Tribunals Act 1996, ss 33, 42 at_ **[1.727]**, **[1.736]**_.)_

## PART 6
## MISCELLANEOUS

**52, 53** _(Amend the Trade Union and Labour Relations (Consolidation) Act 1992, ss 34, 36, 37, 46 at_ **[1.276]**, **[1.278]**, **[1.279]**, **[1.297]**_.)_

**[1.1336]**
### 54 Means of voting in ballots and elections
(1) The Secretary of State may by order provide, in relation to any description of ballot or election authorised or required by the 1992 Act, that any ballot or election of that description is to be conducted by such one or more permissible means as the responsible person determines.
(2) A "permissible means" is a means of voting that the order provides is permissible for that description of ballot or election.
(3) "The responsible person" is a person specified, or of a description specified, by the order.
(4) An order under this section may—
   (a) include provision about the determinations that may be made by the responsible person, including provision requiring specified factors to be taken into account, or specified criteria to be applied, in making a determination;
   (b) allow the determination of different means of voting for voters in different circumstances;

   (c)   allow a determination to be such that voters have a choice of means of voting.

(5)   The means that an order specifies as permissible means must, in the case of any description of ballot or election, include (or consist of) postal voting.

(6)   An order under this section may—
   (a)   include supplemental, incidental and consequential provisions;
   (b)   make different provision for different cases or circumstances.

(7)   An order under this section may—
   (a)   modify the provisions of the 1992 Act;
   (b)   exclude or apply (with or without modifications) any provision of that Act;
   (c)   make provision as respects any ballot or election conducted by specified means which is similar to any provision of that Act relating to ballots or elections.

(8)   The power to make an order under this section is exercisable by statutory instrument.

(9)   No order may be made under this section unless a draft of the order has been laid before Parliament and approved by a resolution of each House.

(10)   The Secretary of State shall not make an order under this section which provides that a means of voting is permissible for a description of ballot or election unless he considers—
   (a)   that a ballot or election of that description conducted by that means could, if particular conditions were satisfied, meet the required standard; and
   (b)   that, in relation to any ballot or election of that description held after the order comes into force, the responsible person will not be permitted to determine that that means must or may be used by any voters unless he has taken specified factors into account or applied specified criteria.

(11)   In specifying in an order under this section factors to be taken into account or criteria to be applied by the responsible person, the Secretary of State must have regard to the need for ballots and elections to meet the required standard.

(12)   For the purposes of subsections (10) and (11) a ballot or election meets "the required standard" if it is such that—
   (a)   those entitled to vote have an opportunity to do so;
   (b)   votes cast are secret;
   (c)   the risk of any unfairness or malpractice is minimised.

(13)   In this section "specified" means specified in an order under this section.

**NOTES**

   Orders: as of 6 April 2013, no Orders had been made under this section.

**55**   (*Inserts the Trade Union and Labour Relations (Consolidation) Act 1992, ss 116A, 118(8) at* **[1.377]**, **[1.379]**.)

# PART 7
# SUPPLEMENTARY PROVISIONS

**[1.1337]**
**56  Meaning of "the 1992 Act"**
In this Act "the 1992 Act" means the Trade Union and Labour Relations (Consolidation) Act 1992 (c 52).

**57, 58**   (*S 57 introduces Schs 1, 2 (Minor and consequential amendments and repeals); s 58 (Corresponding provision for Northern Ireland) outside the scope of this work.*)

**[1.1338]**
**59  Citation, commencement and extent**
(1)   This Act may be cited as the Employment Relations Act 2004.

(2)   This section and sections 42, 43, 56 and 58 shall come into force on the day on which this Act is passed.

(3)   The other provisions of this Act shall not come into force until such day as the Secretary of State may by order made by statutory instrument appoint, and different days may be appointed for different purposes.

(4)   An order under subsection (3) may contain such transitional provisions and savings as the Secretary of State considers necessary or expedient in connection with the coming into force of any of the provisions of this Act.

(5)   Subject to subsections (6) and (7), this Act extends to England and Wales and to Scotland.

(6)   Any amendment by this Act of an enactment (including an enactment contained in Northern Ireland legislation) has the same extent as the enactment amended.

(7)   Sections 43 and 58 extend to Northern Ireland only.

**NOTES**

   Orders: the Employment Relations Act 2004 (Commencement No 1 and Transitional Provisions) Order 2004, SI 2004/2566; the Employment Relations Act 2004 (Commencement No 2 and Transitional Provisions) Order 2004, SI 2004/3342; the

Employment Relations Act 2004 (Commencement No 3 and Transitional Provisions) Order 2005, SI 2005/872; the Employment Relations Act 2004 (Commencement No 4 and Transitional Provisions) Order 2005, SI 2005/2419.

## SCHEDULES 1 AND 2

(*Schs 1, 2 contain minor and consequential amendments and repeals; in so far as these are relevant to this work, they have been taken in at the appropriate place.*)

# PENSIONS ACT 2004

## (2004 c 35)

### ARRANGEMENT OF SECTIONS

#### PART 4
#### FINANCIAL PLANNING AND RETIREMENT

*Employee information and advice*

#### PART 5
#### OCCUPATIONAL AND PERSONAL PENSION SCHEMES: MISCELLANEOUS PROVISIONS

*Requirements for member-nominated trustees and directors*

*Pension protection on transfer of employment*

*Consultation by employers*

#### PART 9
#### MISCELLANEOUS AND SUPPLEMENTARY

*Miscellaneous and Supplementary*

*An Act to make provision relating to pensions and financial planning for retirement and provision relating to entitlement to bereavement payments, and for connected purposes*

[18 November 2004]

**NOTES**

Most of this Act covers matters outside the scope of this work, and only those provisions most directly relevant to employment law are printed. For reasons of space, the subject matter of sections not printed is not annotated. The substantive provisions reproduced here apply to Great Britain only (s 323), and come into force in accordance with provision made by the Secretary of State by order (s 322(1)).

See *Harvey* BI(9), F2(F).

## PART 4
## FINANCIAL PLANNING AND RETIREMENT

*Employee information and advice*

**[1.1339]**
**238  Information and advice to employees**
(1)  Regulations may require employers to take action for the purpose of enabling employees to obtain information and advice about pensions and saving for retirement.
(2)  Regulations under subsection (1) may in particular—
   (a)  provide that they are to apply in relation to employers of a prescribed description and employees of a prescribed description;
   (b)  make different provision for different descriptions of employers and employees;
   (c)  make provision as to the action to be taken by employers (including the frequency at which, and the time and place at which, action is to be taken);

(d)    make provision as to the description of information and advice in relation to which requirements apply;

(e)    make provision about the description of person authorised to provide any such information and advice.

(3)   Employers to whom regulations under subsection (1) apply must provide information to the Regulator about the action taken by them for the purpose of complying with the regulations.

(4)   Regulations may make provision as to—

(a)    the information to be provided under subsection (3);

(b)    the form and manner in which the information is to be provided;

(c)    the period within which the information is to be provided.

(5)   Section 10 of the Pensions Act 1995 (c 26) (civil penalties) applies to any person who, without reasonable excuse, fails to comply with subsection (3).

(6)   In this section "employer" means any employer, whether or not resident or incorporated in any part of the United Kingdom.

---

**NOTES**

Commencement: to be appointed.

---

# PART 5
## OCCUPATIONAL AND PERSONAL PENSION SCHEMES: MISCELLANEOUS PROVISIONS

*Requirements for member-nominated trustees and directors*

**[1.1340]**
**241   Requirement for member-nominated trustees**

(1)   The trustees of an occupational trust scheme must secure—

(a)    that, within a reasonable period of the commencement date, arrangements are in place which provide for at least one-third of the total number of trustees to be member-nominated trustees, and

(b)    that those arrangements are implemented.

(2)   "Member-nominated trustees" are trustees of an occupational trust scheme who—

(a)    are nominated as the result of a process in which at least the following are eligible to participate—

    (i)    all the active members of the scheme or an organisation which adequately represents the active members, and

    (ii)   all the pensioner members of the scheme or an organisation which adequately represents the pensioner members, and

(b)    are selected as a result of a process which involves some or all of the members of the scheme.

(3)   The "commencement date", in relation to a scheme, is—

(a)    the date upon which this section first applies in relation to the scheme, or

(b)    in the case of a scheme to which this section has ceased to apply and then reapplies, the date on which the section reapplies to it.

(4)   The arrangements may provide for a greater number of member-nominated trustees than that required to satisfy the one-third minimum mentioned in subsection (1)(a) only if the employer has approved the greater number.

(5)   The arrangements—

(a)    must provide for the nomination and selection process to take place within a reasonable period of any requirement arising under the arrangements to appoint a member-nominated trustee,

(b)    must provide, where a vacancy is not filled because insufficient nominations are received, for the nomination and selection process to be repeated at reasonable intervals until the vacancy is filled,

(c)    must provide that where the employer so requires, a person who is not a member of the scheme must have the employer's approval to qualify for selection as a member-nominated trustee, and

(d)    subject to paragraph (c), may provide that, where the number of nominations received is equal to or less than the number of appointments required, the nominees are deemed to be selected.

(6)   The arrangements must provide that the removal of a member-nominated trustee requires the agreement of all the other trustees.

(7)   Nothing in the arrangements or in the provisions of the scheme may exclude member-nominated trustees from the exercise of functions exercisable by other trustees by reason only of the fact that they are member-nominated trustees.

(8)   This section does not apply in relation to an occupational trust scheme if—

(a)    every member of the scheme is a trustee of the scheme and no other person is such a trustee,

(b) every trustee of the scheme is a company, or
(c) the scheme is of a prescribed description.
(9) If, in the case of an occupational trust scheme, the arrangements required by subsection (1)—
    (a) are not in place as required by subsection (1)(a), or
    (b) are not being implemented,
section 10 of the Pensions Act 1995 (c 26) (civil penalties) applies to any trustee who has failed to take all reasonable steps to secure compliance.

**NOTES**

Regulations: the Occupational Pension Schemes (Member-nominated Trustees and Directors) Regulations 2006, SI 2006/714 (reg 5 of which modifies this section and s 242 in respect of schemes whose existing scheme rules require a higher proportion of trustees or directors to be member-nominated; it also provides for transitional provisions for schemes that were exempted under the Occupational Pension Schemes (Member-nominated Trustees and Directors) Regulations 1996 (SI 1996/1216)); the Occupational and Personal Pension Schemes (Miscellaneous Amendments) Regulations 2007, SI 2007/814; the Occupational Pension Schemes (Scottish Parliamentary Pensions Act 2009) Regulations 2009, SI 2009/1906.

**[1.1341]**
**242 Requirement for member-nominated directors of corporate trustees**
(1) Where a company is a trustee of an occupational trust scheme and every trustee of the scheme is a company, the company must secure—
    (a) that, within a reasonable period of the commencement date, arrangements are in place which provide for at least one-third of the total number of directors of the company to be member-nominated directors, and
    (b) that those arrangements are implemented.
(2) "Member-nominated directors" are directors of the company in question who—
    (a) are nominated as the result of a process in which at least the following are eligible to participate—
        (i) all the active members of the occupational trust scheme or an organisation which adequately represents the active members, and
        (ii) all the pensioner members of the occupational trust scheme or an organisation which adequately represents the pensioner members, and
    (b) are selected as a result of a process which involves some or all of the members of that scheme.
(3) The "commencement date", in relation to a company, is—
    (a) the date upon which this section first applies in relation to the company, or
    (b) in the case of a company to which this section has ceased to apply and then reapplies, the date on which the section reapplies to it.
(4) The arrangements may provide for a greater number of member-nominated directors than that required to satisfy the one-third minimum mentioned in subsection (1)(a) only if the employer has approved the greater number.
(5) The arrangements—
    (a) must provide for the nomination and selection process to take place within a reasonable period of any requirement arising under the arrangements to appoint a member-nominated director,
    (b) must provide, where a vacancy is not filled because insufficient nominations are received, for the nomination and selection process to be repeated at reasonable intervals until the vacancy is filled,
    (c) must provide that where the employer so requires, a person who is not a member of the scheme must have the employer's approval to qualify for selection as a member-nominated director, and
    (d) subject to paragraph (c), may provide that, where the number of nominations received is equal to or less than the number of appointments required, the nominees are deemed to be selected.
(6) The arrangements must provide that the removal of a member-nominated director requires the agreement of all the other directors.
(7) Nothing in the arrangements may exclude member-nominated directors from the exercise of functions exercisable by other directors by reason only of the fact that they are member-nominated directors.
(8) Where the same company is a trustee of two or more occupational trust schemes by reference to each of which this section applies to the company, then, subject to subsection (9), the preceding provisions of this section have effect as if—
    (a) the schemes were a single scheme,
    (b) the members of each of the schemes were members of that single scheme, and
    (c) the references to "the employer" were references to all the employers in relation to the schemes.
(9) Where, apart from this subsection, subsection (8) would apply in relation to a company, the company may elect that subsection (8)—
    (a) is not to apply as mentioned in that subsection, or

(b)   is to apply but only in relation to some of the schemes to which it would otherwise apply.

(10)   This section does not apply in relation to an occupational trust scheme if the scheme is of a prescribed description.

(11)   If, in the case of a company which is a trustee of an occupational trust scheme, the arrangements required by subsection (1)—

(a)   are not in place as required by subsection (1)(a), or

(b)   are not being implemented,

section 10 of the Pensions Act 1995 (c 26) (civil penalties) applies to the company.

**NOTES**

Regulations: the Occupational Pension Schemes (Member-nominated Trustees and Directors) Regulations 2006, SI 2006/714 (see the note to s 241 *ante*); the Occupational and Personal Pension Schemes (Miscellaneous Amendments) Regulations 2007, SI 2007/814; the Occupational, Personal and Stakeholder Pensions (Miscellaneous Amendments) Regulations 2009, SI 2009/615.

**[1.1342]**
**243   Member-nominated trustees and directors: supplementary**

(1)   The Secretary of State may, by order, amend sections 241(1)(a) and (4) and 242(1)(a) and (4) by substituting, in each of those provisions, "one-half" for "one-third".

(2)   Regulations may modify sections 241 and 242 (including any of the provisions mentioned in subsection (1)) in their application to prescribed cases.

(3)   In sections 241 and 242—

"company" means a company [as defined in section 1(1) of the Companies Act 2006] or a
        company which may be wound up under Part 5 of the Insolvency Act 1986 (c 45)
        (unregistered companies);

"occupational trust scheme" means an occupational pension scheme established under a trust.

**NOTES**

Sub-s (3): words in square brackets in the definition "company" substituted by the Companies Act 2006 (Consequential Amendments, Transitional Provisions and Savings) Order 2009, SI 2009/1941, art 2(1), Sch 1, para 243(1), (9), as from 1 October 2009.

Regulations: the Occupational Pension Schemes (Member-nominated Trustees and Directors) Regulations 2006, SI 2006/714 (see the note to s 241 *ante*); the Occupational, Personal and Stakeholder Pensions (Miscellaneous Amendments) Regulations 2009, SI 2009/615.

*Pension protection on transfer of employment*

**[1.1343]**
**257   Conditions for pension protection**

(1)   This section applies in relation to a person ("the employee") where—

[(a)   there is a relevant transfer within the meaning of the TUPE regulations,]

(b)   by virtue of the transfer the employee ceases to be employed by the transferor and becomes
        employed by the transferee, and

(c)   at the time immediately before the employee becomes employed by the transferee—

(i)    there is an occupational pension scheme ("the scheme") in relation to which the
        transferor is the employer, and

(ii)   one of subsections (2), (3) and (4) applies.

(2)   This subsection applies where—

(a)   the employee is an active member of the scheme, and

(b)   if any of the benefits that may be provided under the scheme are money purchase
        benefits—

(i)    the transferor is required to make contributions to the scheme in respect of the
        employee, or

(ii)   the transferor is not so required but has made one or more such contributions.

(3)   This subsection applies where—

(a)   the employee is not an active member of the scheme but is eligible to be such a member,
        and

(b)   if any of the benefits that may be provided under the scheme are money purchase benefits,
        the transferor would have been required to make contributions to the scheme in respect of
        the employee if the employee had been an active member of it.

(4)   This subsection applies where—

(a)   the employee is not an active member of the scheme, nor eligible to be such a member, but
        would have been an active member of the scheme or eligible to be such a member if, after
        the date on which he became employed by the transferor, he had been employed by the
        transferor for a longer period, and

(b)   if any of the benefits that may be provided under the scheme are money purchase benefits,
        the transferor would have been required to make contributions to the scheme in respect of
        the employee if the employee had been an active member of it.

(5) For the purposes of this section, the condition in subsection (1)(c) is to be regarded as satisfied in any case where it would have been satisfied but for any action taken by the transferor by reason of the transfer.

(6) . . .

(7) . . .

(8) In this section—

the "TUPE Regulations" means the [Transfer of Undertakings (Protection of Employment) Regulations 2006];

references to the transferor include any associate of the transferor, and section 435 of the Insolvency Act 1986 (c 45) applies for the purposes of this section as it applies for the purposes of that Act.

**NOTES**

Sub-s (1): para (a) substituted by the Transfer of Undertakings (Protection of Employment) Regulations 2006, SI 2006/246, reg 20(3), Sch 2, paras 13(1), (2).

Sub-s (6): repealed by SI 2006/246, reg 20(3), Sch 2, paras 13(1), (3) (for transitional provisions see the note above).

Sub-s (7): repealed by the Pensions Act 2007, ss 15(3)(a), 27(2), Sch 4, Pt 1, para 41, Sch 7, Pt 6, as from 6 April 2012.

Sub-s (8): words in square brackets in the definition "TUPE Regulations" substituted by SI 2006/246, reg 20(3), Sch 2, paras 13(1), (4) (for transitional provisions see the note above).

Note: as to the application of this section to certain specified banks, see the Banking (Special Provisions) Act 2008, the Banking Act 2009, and Orders made under those Acts.

**[1.1344]**
**258 Form of protection**
(1) In a case where section 257 applies, it is a condition of the employee's contract of employment with the transferee that the requirements in subsection (2) or the requirement in subsection (3) are complied with.

(2) The requirements in this subsection are that—

(a) the transferee secures that, as from the relevant time, the employee is, or is eligible to be, an active member of an occupational pension scheme in relation to which the transferee is the employer, and

(b) in a case where the scheme is a money purchase scheme, as from the relevant time—

(i) the transferee makes relevant contributions to the scheme in respect of the employee, or

(ii) if the employee is not an active member of the scheme but is eligible to be such a member, the transferee would be required to make such contributions if the employee were an active member, and

(c) in a case where the scheme is not a money purchase scheme, as from the relevant time the scheme—

(i) satisfies the statutory standard referred to in section 12A of the Pension Schemes Act 1993 (c 48), or

(ii) if regulations so provide, complies with such other requirements as may be prescribed.

(3) The requirement in this subsection is that, as from the relevant time, the transferee makes relevant contributions to a stakeholder pension scheme of which the employee is a member.

(4) The requirement in subsection (3) is for the purposes of this section to be regarded as complied with by the transferee during any period in relation to which the condition in subsection (5) is satisfied.

(5) The condition in this subsection is that the transferee has offered to make relevant contributions to a stakeholder pension scheme of which the employee is eligible to be a member (and the transferee has not withdrawn the offer).

(6) Subsection (1) does not apply in relation to a contract if or to the extent that the employee and the transferee so agree at any time after the time when the employee becomes employed by the transferee.

(7) In this section—

"the relevant time" means—

(a) in a case where section 257 applies by virtue of the application of subsection (2) or (3) of that section, the time when the employee becomes employed by the transferee;

(b) in a case where that section applies by virtue of the application of subsection (4) of that section, the time at which the employee would have been a member of the scheme referred to in subsection (1)(c)(i) of that section or (if earlier) would have been eligible to be such a member;

"relevant contributions" means such contributions in respect of such period or periods as may be prescribed;

"stakeholder pension scheme" means a pension scheme which is registered under section 2 of the Welfare Reform and Pensions Act 1999 (c 30).

*Consultation by employers*

**[1.1345]**

**259 Consultation by employers: occupational pension schemes**

(1)   Regulations may require any prescribed person who is the employer in relation to an occupational pension scheme and who—

  (a)   proposes to make a prescribed decision in relation to the scheme, or

  (b)   has been notified by the trustees or managers of the scheme that they propose to make a prescribed decision in relation to the scheme,

to consult prescribed persons in the prescribed manner before the decision is made.

(2)   Regulations may require the trustees or managers of an occupational pension scheme not to make a prescribed decision in relation to the scheme unless—

  (a)   they have notified the employer of the proposed decision, and

  (b)   they are satisfied that the employer has undertaken any consultation required by virtue of subsection (1).

(3)   The validity of any decision made in relation to an occupational pension scheme is not affected by any failure to comply with regulations under this section.

(4)   Section 261 contains further provisions about regulations under this section.

**[1.1346]**

**260 Consultation by employers: personal pension schemes**

(1)   Regulations may require any prescribed person who—

  (a)   is the employer in relation to a personal pension scheme where direct payment arrangements exist in respect of one or more members of the scheme who are his employees, and

  (b)   proposes to make a prescribed decision affecting the application of the direct payment arrangements in relation to those employees,

to consult prescribed persons in the prescribed manner before he makes the decision.

(2)   The validity of any decision prescribed for the purposes of subsection (1)(b) is not affected by any failure to comply with regulations under this section.

(3)   Section 261 contains further provisions about regulations under this section.

**[1.1347]**

**261 Further provisions about regulations relating to consultation**

(1)   In this section "consultation regulations" means regulations under section 259 or 260.

(2)   Consultation regulations may—

  (a)   make provision about the time to be allowed for consultation;

  (b)   prescribe the information which must be provided to the persons who are required to be consulted;

  (c)   confer a discretion on the employer in prescribed cases as to the persons who are to be consulted;

  (d)   make provision about the representatives the employees may have for the purposes of the regulations and the methods by which those representatives are to be selected;

(e)    require or authorise the holding of ballots;

(f)    amend, apply with or without modifications, or make provision similar to, any provision of the Employment Rights Act 1996 (c 18) (including, in particular, Parts 5, 10 and 13), the Employment Tribunals Act 1996 (c 17) or the Trade Union and Labour Relations (Consolidation) Act 1992 (c 52);

(g)    enable any requirement for consultation imposed by the regulations to be waived or relaxed by order of the Regulator;

(h)    require the employer to communicate to the trustees and managers of the scheme any representations received by the employer in response to any consultation required by the regulations.

(3)   Persons on whom obligations are imposed by consultation regulations, either as employers or as the trustees or managers of occupational pension schemes, must, if so required by the Regulator, provide information to the Regulator about the action taken by them for the purpose of complying with the regulations.

(4)   Consultation regulations may make provision as to—

(a)    the information to be provided under subsection (3);

(b)    the form and manner in which the information is to be provided;

(c)    the period within which the information is to be provided.

(5)   Nothing in consultation regulations is to be regarded as affecting any duty to consult arising otherwise than under the regulations.

**NOTES**

Multi-employer Schemes: see the note to s 259 at **[1.1345]**.

Regulations: the Occupational and Personal Pension Schemes (Consultation by Employers and Miscellaneous Amendment) Regulations 2006, SI 2006/349 at **[2.1017]**.

## PART 9
## MISCELLANEOUS AND SUPPLEMENTARY

*Miscellaneous and Supplementary*

**[1.1348]**
**325   Short title**

This Act may be cited as the Pensions Act 2004.

# DISABILITY DISCRIMINATION ACT 2005 (NOTE)

(2005 c 13)

**[1.1349]**

**NOTES**

The whole of this Act was repealed by the Equality Act 2010, s 211(2), Sch 27, Pt 1, as from 1 October 2010, subject to the following exceptions: (i) s 3 (Duties of public authorities) which inserted the Disability Discrimination Act 1995, Part 5A; (ii) s 9 (Recognition of disabled persons' badges issued outside Great Britain) which inserts the Chronically Sick and Disabled Persons Act 1970, ss 21A–21C; (iii) Sch 1, Pt 1, paras 31, 33, 34(1), (6) (Minor and consequential amendments: Amendments of the Disability Discrimination Act 1995) which amend ss 64, 67 and 68 of the 1995 Act (all repealed by the Equality Act 2010 subject to savings); (iv) Sch 1, Pt 2 (Minor and consequential amendments: Amendments relating to disabled persons' badges) which amends the 1970 Act.

Section 3 of this Act was repealed, as from 4 April 2011, by the Equality Act 2010, s 211(2), Sch 27, Pt 1A (as inserted by the Equality Act 2010 (Public Authorities and Consequential and Supplementary Amendments) Order 2011, SI 2011/1060, art 3(1), (3)(a), Sch 3, as from 4 April 2011).

In so far as the above-mentioned provisions are still in force, they are outside the scope of this work.

# EQUALITY ACT 2006

## (2006 c 3)

### ARRANGEMENT OF SECTIONS

#### PART 1
#### THE COMMISSION FOR EQUALITY AND HUMAN RIGHTS

*An Act to make provision for the establishment of the Commission for Equality and Human Rights; to dissolve the Equal Opportunities Commission, the Commission for Racial Equality and the Disability Rights Commission; to make provision about discrimination on grounds of religion or belief; to enable provision to be made about discrimination on grounds of sexual orientation; to impose duties relating to sex discrimination on persons performing public functions; to amend the Disability Discrimination Act 1995; and for connected purposes*

[16 February 2006]

### NOTES

Part 1 of this Act, which establishes the Commission for Equality and Human Rights (which has subsequently adopted the name 'Equality and Human Rights Commission'), is reproduced in full. Only those other provisions of most relevance to employment law are reproduced.

Regulatory functions: the regulatory functions conferred by, or under, this Act are subject to the Legislative and Regulatory Reform Act 2006, ss 21, 22 at **[1.1495]**, **[1.1496]**; see the Legislative and Regulatory Reform (Regulatory Functions) Order 2007, SI 2007/3544 (made under s 24(2) of the 2006 Act) for details.

Transfer of functions: (i) as to the transfer of the functions of the Secretary of State for Trade and Industry under Part 1 of this Act to the Secretary of State for Communities and Local Government, see the Secretary of State for Communities and Local Government Order 2006, SI 2006/1926, arts 7(1), (2), (3)(c), 8; (ii) see also the Transfer of Functions (Equality) Order 2007, SI 2007/2914, art 3(1), (2)(f), regarding the transfer of the functions of the Secretary of State under this Act (except s 66(2) and Sch 2, para 14(4)) to the Lord Privy Seal; (iii) see also the Transfer of Functions (Equality) Order 2010, SI 2010/1839 which makes provision in connection with the transfer (as from 18 August 2010) of certain statutory functions relating to equality from the Lord Privy Seal to the Secretary of State (the Government Equalities Office, previously the department of the Lord Privy Seal, is now headed by the Secretary of State entrusted with responsibility for equality, ie, the Home Secretary).

See *Harvey* L

## PART 1
## THE COMMISSION FOR EQUALITY AND HUMAN RIGHTS

### *The Commission*

**[1.1350]**
### 1   Establishment
There shall be a body corporate known as the Commission for Equality and Human Rights.

**[1.1351]**
### 2   Constitution, &c
Schedule 1 (constitution of the Commission, proceedings, money, &c) shall have effect.

**[1.1352]**
### 3   General duty
The Commission shall exercise its functions under this Part with a view to encouraging and supporting the development of a society in which—
  (a)   people's ability to achieve their potential is not limited by prejudice or discrimination,
  (b)   there is respect for and protection of each individual's human rights,
  (c)   there is respect for the dignity and worth of each individual,
  (d)   each individual has an equal opportunity to participate in society, and
  (e)   there is mutual respect between groups based on understanding and valuing of diversity and on shared respect for equality and human rights.

**[1.1353]**
### 4   Strategic plan
(1)   The Commission shall prepare a plan showing—
  (a)   activities or classes of activity to be undertaken by the Commission in pursuance of its functions under this Act,
  (b)   an expected timetable for each activity or class, and
  (c)   priorities for different activities or classes, or principles to be applied in determining priorities.
(2)   The Commission shall review the plan—

(a)    at least once during the period of three years beginning with its completion,

(b)    at least once during each period of three years beginning with the completion of a review, and

(c)    at such other times as the Commission thinks appropriate.

(3)   If the Commission thinks it appropriate as a result of a review, the Commission shall revise the plan.

(4)   The Commission shall send the plan and each revision to the [Secretary of State], who shall lay a copy before Parliament.

(5)   The Commission shall publish the plan and each revision.

**NOTES**

Sub-s (4): words in square brackets substituted by the Transfer of Functions (Equality) Order 2010, SI 2010/1839, arts 3(1)(f), 7, Schedule, para 14(1), (2)(a), as from 18 August 2010.

**[1.1354]**
## 5   Strategic plan: consultation

Before preparing or reviewing a plan in accordance with section 4 the Commission shall—

(a)    consult   such   persons   having   knowledge   or   experience   relevant   to the Commission's functions as the Commission thinks appropriate,

(b)    consult such other persons as the Commission thinks appropriate,

(c)    issue a general invitation to make representations, in a manner likely in the Commission's opinion to bring the invitation to the attention of as large a class of persons who may wish to make representations as is reasonably practicable, and

(d)    take account of any representations made.

**[1.1355]**
## 6   Disclosure

(1)   A person who is or was a Commissioner, an Investigating Commissioner, an employee of the Commission or a member of a committee established by the Commission commits an offence if he discloses information to which this section applies unless subsection (3) authorises the disclosure.

(2)   This section applies to information acquired by the Commission—

(a)    by way of representations made in relation to, or otherwise in the course of, an inquiry under section 16,

(b)    by way of representations made in relation to, or otherwise in the course of, an investigation under section 20,

(c)    by way of representations made in relation to, or otherwise in the course of, an assessment under section 31,

(d)    by way of representations made in relation to, or otherwise in connection with, a notice under section 32, or

(e)    from a person with whom the Commission enters into, or considers entering into, an agreement under section 23.

(3)   This subsection authorises a disclosure made—

(a)    for the purpose of the exercise of a function of the Commission under any of sections 16, 20, 21, 24, 25, 31 and 32,

(b)    in a report of an inquiry, investigation or assessment published by the Commission,

(c)    in pursuance of an order of a court or tribunal,

(d)    with the consent of each person to whom the disclosed information relates,

(e)    in a manner that ensures that no person to whom the disclosed information relates can be identified,

(f)    for the purpose of civil or criminal proceedings to which the Commission is party, or

(g)    if the information was acquired by the Commission more than 70 years before the date of the disclosure.

(4)   But subsection (3) does not authorise, nor may the Commission make, a disclosure of information provided by or relating to an intelligence service unless the service has authorised the disclosure.

(5)   In subsection (4) "intelligence service" means—

(a)    the Security Service,

(b)    the Secret Intelligence Service, and

(c)    the Government Communications Headquarters.

(6)   A person guilty of an offence under subsection (1) shall be liable on summary conviction to a fine not exceeding level 5 on the standard scale.

**NOTES**

Discloses information: in so far as it authorises the disclosure of information, this section is subject to the Anti-terrorism, Crime and Security Act 2001, s 17 (extension of existing disclosure powers); see Sch 4, Pt 1, para 53B to that Act.

**[1.1356]**
**7  Scotland: human rights**
(1)   The Commission shall not take human rights action in relation to a matter if the Scottish Parliament has legislative competence to enable a person to take action of that kind in relation to that matter.
(2)   In subsection (1) "human rights action" means action taken—
   (a)   in accordance with section 9(1), and
   (b)   under, by virtue of or in pursuance of—
      (i)   section 11(1) in so far as it relates to the Human Rights Act 1998 (c 42),
      (ii)   section 11(2)(c) or (d),
      (iii)   section 12,
      (iv)   section 13,
      (v)   section 16,
      (vi)   section 17, or
      (vii)   section 30.
(3)   Despite section 9(4), the Commission shall not, in the course of fulfilling a duty under section 8 *or 10*, consider the question whether a person's human rights have been contravened if the Scottish Parliament has legislative competence to enable a person to consider that question.
(4)   Subsections (1) and (3) shall not prevent the Commission from taking action with the consent (whether general or specific) of a person if—
   (a)   the person is established by Act of the Scottish Parliament, and
   (b)   the person's principal duties relate to human rights and are similar to any of the Commission's duties under section 9.
(5)   Subsections (1) and (3) shall not prevent the Commission from relying on section 13(1)(f) so as to act jointly or cooperate (but not assist) for a purpose relating to human rights and connected with Scotland.

**NOTES**

Sub-s (3): words in italics repealed by the Enterprise and Regulatory Reform Act 2013, s 64(3), (4), as from 25 June 2013.

*Duties*

**[1.1357]**
**8  Equality and diversity**
(1)   The Commission shall, by exercising the powers conferred by this Part—
   (a)   promote understanding of the importance of equality and diversity,
   (b)   encourage good practice in relation to equality and diversity,
   (c)   promote equality of opportunity,
   (d)   promote awareness and understanding of rights under the [Equality Act 2010],
   (e)   enforce [that Act],
   (f)   work towards the elimination of unlawful discrimination, and
   (g)   work towards the elimination of unlawful harassment.
(2)   In subsection (1)—
"diversity" means the fact that individuals are different,
"equality" means equality between individuals, and
"unlawful" is to be construed in accordance with section 34.
(3)   In promoting equality of opportunity between disabled persons and others, the Commission may, in particular, promote the favourable treatment of disabled persons.
(4)   In this Part "disabled person" means a person who—
   (a)   is a disabled person within the meaning of the [Equality Act 2010], or
   (b)   has been a disabled person within that meaning (whether or not at a time when that Act had effect).

**NOTES**

Sub-ss (1), (4): words in square brackets substituted by the Equality Act 2010, s 211(1), Sch 26, paras 61, 62, as from 1 October 2010.

**[1.1358]**
**9  Human rights**
(1)   The Commission shall, by exercising the powers conferred by this Part—
   (a)   promote understanding of the importance of human rights,
   (b)   encourage good practice in relation to human rights,
   (c)   promote awareness, understanding and protection of human rights, and
   (d)   encourage public authorities to comply with section 6 of the Human Rights Act 1998 (c 42) (compliance with Convention rights).
(2)   In this Part "human rights" means—
   (a)   the Convention rights within the meaning given by section 1 of the Human Rights Act 1998, and
   (b)   other human rights.

(3)   In determining what action to take in pursuance of this section the Commission shall have particular regard to the importance of exercising the powers conferred by this Part in relation to the Convention rights.

(4)   In fulfilling a duty under section 8 *or 10* the Commission shall take account of any relevant human rights.

(5)   A reference in this Part (including this section) to human rights does not exclude any matter by reason only of its being a matter to which section 8 *or 10* relates.

**NOTES**

Sub-ss (4), (5): words in italics repealed by the Enterprise and Regulatory Reform Act 2013, s 64(3), (5), as from 25 June 2013.

**[1.1359]**
**10   Groups**
*(1)   The Commission shall, by exercising the powers conferred by this Part—*
   *(a)   promote understanding of the importance of good relations—*
      *(i)      between members of different groups, and*
      *(ii)     between members of groups and others,*
   *(b)   encourage good practice in relation to relations—*
      *(i)      between members of different groups, and*
      *(ii)     between members of groups and others,*
   *(c)   work towards the elimination of prejudice against, hatred of and hostility towards members of groups, and*
   *(d)   work towards enabling members of groups to participate in society.*
(2)   In this Part "group" means a group or class of persons who share a common attribute in respect of any of the following matters—
   (a)   age,
   (b)   disability,
   (c)   gender,
   [(d)   gender reassignment (within the meaning of section 7 of the Equality Act 2010),]
   (e)   race,
   (f)   religion or belief, and
   (g)   sexual orientation.
(3)   For the purposes of this Part a reference to a group (as defined in subsection (2)) includes a reference to a smaller group or smaller class, within a group, of persons who share a common attribute (in addition to the attribute by reference to which the group is defined) in respect of any of the matters specified in subsection (2)(a) to (g).
*(4)   In determining what action to take in pursuance of this section the Commission shall have particular regard to the importance of exercising the powers conferred by this Part in relation to groups defined by reference to race, religion or belief.*
*(5)   The Commission may, in taking action in pursuance of subsection (1) in respect of groups defined by reference to disability and others, promote or encourage the favourable treatment of disabled persons.*
*(6)   The [Secretary of State] may by order amend the list in subsection (2) so as to—*
   *(a)   add an entry, or*
   *(b)   vary an entry.*
*(7)   This section is without prejudice to the generality of section 8.*

**NOTES**

Sub-s (1): repealed by the Enterprise and Regulatory Reform Act 2013, s 64(1)(a), as from 25 June 2013.

Sub-s (2): para (d) substituted by the Equality Act 2010, s 211(1), Sch 26, paras 61, 63, as from 1 October 2010.

Sub-ss (4), (5), (7): repealed by the Enterprise and Regulatory Reform Act 2013, s 64(1)(a), as from 25 June 2013.

Sub-s (6): words in square brackets substituted by the Transfer of Functions (Equality) Order 2010, SI 2010/1839, arts 3(1)(f), 7, Schedule, para 14(1), (2)(b), as from 18 August 2010; repealed by the Enterprise and Regulatory Reform Act 2013, s 64(1)(a), as from 25 June 2013.

Orders: as of 6 April 2013 no Orders had been made under this section.

Note: the Enterprise and Regulatory Reform Act 2013, s 64(1)(a), states that sub-s (8) of this section is repealed, but sub-s (8) does not exist.

**[1.1360]**
**11   Monitoring the law**
(1)   The Commission shall monitor the effectiveness of the equality and human rights enactments.
(2)   The Commission may—
   (a)   advise central government about the effectiveness of any of the equality and human rights enactments;
   (b)   recommend to central government the amendment, repeal, consolidation (with or without amendments) or replication (with or without amendments) of any of the equality and human rights enactments;

(c) advise central or devolved government about the effect of an enactment (including an enactment in or under an Act of the Scottish Parliament);
(d) advise central or devolved government about the likely effect of a proposed change of law.
(3) In this section—
  (a) "central government" means Her Majesty's Government,
  (b) "devolved government" means—
    (i) the Scottish Ministers, and
    (ii) the [Welsh Ministers, the First Minister for Wales and the Counsel General to the Welsh Assembly Government], and
  [(c) a reference to the equality and human rights enactments is a reference to the Human Rights Act 1998, this Act and the Equality Act 2010].

**NOTES**
Sub-s (3): words in square brackets in para (b)(ii) substituted by the Government of Wales Act 2006 (Consequential Modifications and Transitional Provisions) Order 2007, SI 2007/1388, art 3, Sch 1, paras 112, 113; para (c) substituted by the Equality Act 2010, s 211(1), Sch 26, paras 61, 64, as from 1 October 2010.

**[1.1361]**
**12 Monitoring progress**
(1) The Commission shall from time to time identify—
  (a) changes in society that have occurred or are expected to occur and are relevant to *the aim specified in section 3*,
  (b) results at which to aim for the purpose of encouraging and supporting *the development of the society described in section 3* ("outcomes"), and
  (c) factors by reference to which progress towards those results may be measured ("indicators").
(2) In identifying outcomes and indicators the Commission shall—
  (a) consult such persons having knowledge or experience relevant to the Commission's functions as the Commission thinks appropriate,
  (b) consult such other persons as the Commission thinks appropriate,
  (c) issue a general invitation to make representations, in a manner likely in the Commission's opinion to bring the invitation to the attention of as large a class of persons who may wish to make representations as is reasonably practicable, and
  (d) take account of any representations made.
(3) The Commission shall from time to time monitor progress towards each identified outcome by reference to any relevant identified indicator.
(4) The Commission shall publish a report on progress towards the identified outcomes by reference to the identified indicators—
  (a) within the period of three years beginning with the date on which this section comes into force, and
  (b) within each period of *three* years beginning with the date on which a report is published under this subsection.
(5) The Commission shall send each report to the [Secretary of State], who shall lay a copy before Parliament.

**NOTES**
Sub-s (1): for the words in italics in paras (a), (b) there are substituted the words "the duties specified in sections 8 and 9" and "changes in society that are consistent with those duties" respectively, by the Enterprise and Regulatory Reform Act 2013, s 64(3), (6), as from 25 June 2013.
Sub-s (4): for the words in italics in para (b) there is substituted the word "five" by the Enterprise and Regulatory Reform Act 2013, s 64(2), as from 25 June 2013.
Sub-s (5): words in square brackets substituted by the Transfer of Functions (Equality) Order 2010, SI 2010/1839, arts 3(1)(f), 7, Schedule, para 14(1), (2)(c), as from 18 August 2010.

*General powers*

**[1.1362]**
**13 Information, advice, &c**
(1) In pursuance of its duties under sections 8 *to 10* the Commission may—
  (a) publish or otherwise disseminate ideas or information;
  (b) undertake research;
  (c) provide education or training;
  (d) give advice or guidance (whether about the effect or operation of an enactment or otherwise);
  (e) arrange for a person to do anything within paragraphs (a) to (d);
  (f) act jointly with, co-operate with or assist a person doing anything within paragraphs (a) to (d).
(2) The reference to giving advice in subsection (1)(d) does not include a reference to preparing, or assisting in the preparation of, a document to be used for the purpose of legal proceedings.

NOTES

Sub-s (1): for the words in italics there are substituted the words "and 9" by the Enterprise and Regulatory Reform Act 2013, s 64(3), (7), as from 25 June 2013.

**[1.1363]**
**14   Codes of practice**
[(1)   The Commission may issue a code of practice in connection with any matter addressed by the Equality Act 2010.]
(2)   A code of practice under subsection (1) shall contain provision designed—
   (a)   to ensure or facilitate compliance with [the Equality Act 2010 or an enactment made under that Act], or
   (b)   to promote equality of opportunity.
(3)   The Commission may issue a code of practice giving practical guidance to landlords and tenants in England or Wales about—
   (a)   circumstances in which a tenant requires the consent of his landlord to make a relevant improvement, within the meaning of [section 190(7) of the Equality Act 2010] (improvements), to a dwelling house,
   (b)   reasonableness in relation to that consent, and
   (c)   the application in relation to relevant improvements (within that meaning) to dwelling houses of—
      (i)   section 19(2) of the Landlord and Tenant Act 1927 (c 36) (consent to improvements),
      (ii)   sections 81 to 85 of the Housing Act 1980 (c 51) (tenant's improvements),
      (iii)   sections 97 to 99 of the Housing Act 1985 (c 68) (tenant's improvements), and
      [(iv)   section 190 of the Equality Act 2010].
(4)   The Commission may issue a code of practice giving practical guidance to landlords and tenants of houses (within the meaning of the Housing (Scotland) Act 2006 (asp 01)) in Scotland about—
   (a)   circumstances in which the tenant requires the consent of the landlord to carry out work in relation to the house for the purpose of making the house suitable for the accommodation, welfare or employment of any disabled person who occupies, or intends to occupy, the house as a sole or main residence,
   (b)   circumstances in which it is unreasonable to withhold that consent,
   (c)   circumstances in which any condition imposed on the granting of that consent is unreasonable, and
   (d)   the application in relation to such work of—
      (i)   sections 28 to 31 and 34(6) of the Housing (Scotland) Act 2001 (asp 10), and
      (ii)   sections 52, 53 and 64(6) of the Housing (Scotland) Act 2006 (asp 01).
(5)   The Commission shall comply with a direction of the [Secretary of State] to issue a code under this section in connection with a specified matter if—
   (a)   the matter is not [a matter addressed by the Equality Act 2010], but
   (b)   the [Secretary of State] expects to add it by order under section 15(6).
(6)   Before issuing a code under this section the Commission shall—
   (a)   publish proposals, and
   (b)   consult such persons as it thinks appropriate.
(7)   Before issuing a code under this section the Commission shall submit a draft to the [Secretary of State], who shall—
   (a)   if he approves the draft—
      (i)   notify the Commission, and
      (ii)   lay a copy before Parliament, or
   (b)   otherwise, give the Commission written reasons why he does not approve the draft.
(8)   Where a draft is laid before Parliament under subsection (7)(a)(ii), if neither House passes a resolution disapproving the draft within 40 days—
   (a)   the Commission may issue the code in the form of the draft, and
   (b)   it shall come into force in accordance with provision made by the [Secretary of State] by order.
(9)   If, or in so far as, a code relates to a duty imposed by or under [section 149, 153 or 154 of the Equality Act 2010 (public sector equality duty)] the [Secretary of State] shall consult the Scottish Ministers and the [Welsh Ministers] before—
   (a)   approving a draft under subsection (7)(a) above, or
   (b)   making an order under subsection (8)(b) above.
(10)   In relation to a code of practice under subsection (4), the [Secretary of State] shall consult the Scottish Ministers before—
   (a)   approving a draft under subsection (7)(a) above, or
   (b)   making an order under subsection (8)(b) above.

**NOTES**

Words "Secretary of State" in square brackets in every place they occur substituted by the Transfer of Functions (Equality) Order 2010, SI 2010/1839, arts 3(1)(f), 7, Schedule, para 14(1), (2)(d), as from 18 August 2010.

Other amendments to this section are as follows:

Sub-s (1): substituted by the Equality Act 2010, s 211(1), Sch 26, paras 61, 65(1), (2), as from 6 July 2010.

Sub-ss (2), (3): words in square brackets substituted by the Equality Act 2010, s 211(1), Sch 26, paras 61, 65(1), (3), (4), as from 6 July 2010 (in the case of the sub-s (2) amendment), and as from 1 October 2010 (in the case of the sub-s (3) amendments).

Sub-s (5): words "a matter addressed by the Equality Act 2010" in square brackets substituted by the Equality Act 2010, s 211(1), Sch 26, paras 61, 65(1), (5) , as from 6 July 2010.

Sub-s (9): words "Welsh Ministers" in square brackets substituted by the Government of Wales Act 2006 (Consequential Modifications and Transitional Provisions) Order 2007, SI 2007/1388, art 3, Sch 1, paras 112, 114; words "section 149, 153 or 154 of the Equality Act 2010 (public sector equality duty)" substituted by the Equality Act 2010, s 211(1), Sch 26, paras 61, 65(1), (6), as from 5 April 2011.

Orders: (i) the Disability Discrimination Code of Practice (Trade Organisations, Qualifications Bodies and General Qualifications Bodies) (Commencement) Order 2008, SI 2008/1335. This Order brings the revised Disability Discrimination Act 1995 Code of Practice for Trade Organisations, Qualifications Bodies and General Qualifications Bodies into force on 23 June 2008 (see **[4.123]**). (ii) the Equality Act 2010 Codes of Practice (Services, Public Functions and Associations, Employment, and Equal Pay) Order 2011, SI 2011/857. This Order brings into force (on 6 April 2011) the Equality Act 2010 Code of Practice on Services, Public Functions and Associations, the Equality Act 2010 Code of Practice on Employment at **[4.138]** and the Equality Act 2010 Code of Practice on Equal Pay at **[4.134]**.

**[1.1364]**
## 15   Codes of practice: supplemental

(1) The Commission may revise a code issued under section 14; and a reference in this section or in that section to the issue of a code shall be treated as including a reference to the revision of a code.

(2) The 40 day period specified in section 14(8)—

    (a)   shall begin with the date on which the draft is laid before both Houses (or, if laid before each House on a different date, with the later date), and

    (b)   shall be taken not to include a period during which—

        (i)   Parliament is prorogued or dissolved, or

        (ii)   both Houses are adjourned for more than four days.

(3) A code issued under section 14 may be revoked by the [Secretary of State], at the request of the Commission, by order.

(4) A failure to comply with a provision of a code shall not of itself make a person liable to criminal or civil proceedings; but a code—

    (a)   shall be admissible in evidence in criminal or civil proceedings, and

    (b)   shall be taken into account by a court or tribunal in any case in which it appears to the court or tribunal to be relevant.

(5) Subsection (4)(b) does not apply in relation to a code issued under section 14(4).

(6) The [Secretary of State] may by order amend section 14 so as to vary the range of matters that codes of practice under that section may address.

**NOTES**

Sub-ss (3), (6): words in square brackets substituted by the Transfer of Functions (Equality) Order 2010, SI 2010/1839, arts 3(1)(f), 7, Schedule, para 14(1), (2)(e), as from 18 August 2010.

Orders: as of 6 April 2013 no Orders had been made under this section.

**[1.1365]**
## 16   Inquiries

(1) The Commission may conduct an inquiry into a matter relating to any of the Commission's duties under sections 8, *9 and 10*.

(2) If in the course of an inquiry the Commission begins to suspect that a person may have committed an unlawful act—

    (a)   in continuing the inquiry the Commission shall, so far as possible, avoid further consideration of whether or not the person has committed an unlawful act,

    (b)   the Commission may commence an investigation into that question under section 20,

    (c)   the Commission may use information or evidence acquired in the course of the inquiry for the purpose of the investigation, and

    (d)   the Commission shall so far as possible ensure (whether by aborting or suspending the inquiry or otherwise) that any aspects of the inquiry which concern the person investigated, or may require his involvement, are not pursued while the investigation is in progress.

(3) The report of an inquiry—

    (a)   may not state (whether expressly or by necessary implication) that a specified or identifiable person has committed an unlawful act, and

    (b)   shall not otherwise refer to the activities of a specified or identifiable person unless the Commission thinks that the reference—

(i)    will not harm the person, or
(ii)   is necessary in order for the report adequately to reflect the results of the inquiry.
(4)   Subsections (2) and (3) shall not prevent an inquiry from considering or reporting a matter relating to human rights (whether or not a necessary implication arises in relation to the [Equality Act 2010]).
(5)   Before settling a report of an inquiry which records findings which in the Commission's opinion are of an adverse nature and relate (whether expressly or by necessary implication) to a specified or identifiable person the Commission shall—
(a)   send a draft of the report to the person,
(b)   specify a period of at least 28 days during which he may make written representations about the draft, and
(c)   consider any representations made.
(6)   Schedule 2 makes supplemental provision about inquiries.

**NOTES**
Sub-s (1): for the words in italics there are substituted the words "and 9" by the Enterprise and Regulatory Reform Act 2013, s 64(3), (8), as from 25 June 2013.
Sub-s (4): words in square brackets substituted by the Equality Act 2010, s 211(1), Sch 26, paras 61, 66, as from 1 October 2010.

**[1.1366]**
**17   Grants**
(1)   In pursuance of any of its duties under sections 8 *to 10* the Commission may make grants to another person.
(2)   A grant under subsection (1) may be made subject to conditions (which may, in particular, include conditions as to repayment).
(3)   A power under this Part to co-operate with or assist a person may not be exercised by the provision of financial assistance otherwise than in accordance with this section.

**NOTES**
Sub-s (1): for the words in italics there are substituted the words "and 9" by the Enterprise and Regulatory Reform Act 2013, s 64(3), (9), as from 25 June 2013.

**[1.1367]**
**18   Human rights**
In pursuance of its duties under section 9 the Commission may (without prejudice to the generality of section 13) co-operate with persons interested in human rights within the United Kingdom or elsewhere.

**[1.1368]**
*19   Groups*
*(1)   In pursuance of its duties under section 10 the Commission may do anything specified in this section (without prejudice to the generality of section 13).*
*(2)   The Commission may make, co-operate with or assist in arrangements—*
*(a)   for the monitoring of kinds of crime affecting certain groups;*
*(b)   designed to prevent or reduce crime within or affecting certain groups;*
*(c)   for activities (whether social, recreational, sporting, civic, educational or otherwise) designed to involve members of groups.*

**NOTES**
Repealed by the Enterprise and Regulatory Reform Act 2013, s 64(1)(a), as from 25 June 2013.

*Enforcement powers*
**[1.1369]**
**20   Investigations**
(1)   The Commission may investigate whether or not a person—
(a)   has committed an unlawful act,
(b)   has complied with a requirement imposed by an unlawful act notice under section 21, or
(c)   has complied with an undertaking given under section 23.
(2)   The Commission may conduct an investigation under subsection (1)(a) only if it suspects that the person concerned may have committed an unlawful act.
(3)   A suspicion for the purposes of subsection (2) may (but need not) be based on the results of, or a matter arising during the course of, an inquiry under section 16.
(4)   Before settling a report of an investigation recording a finding that a person has committed an unlawful act or has failed to comply with a requirement or undertaking the Commission shall—
(a)   send a draft of the report to the person,
(b)   specify a period of at least 28 days during which he may make written representations about the draft, and

(c)  consider any representations made.

(5)  Schedule 2 makes supplemental provision about investigations.

**[1.1370]**
**21  Unlawful act notice**
(1)  The Commission may give a person a notice under this section (an "unlawful act notice") if—
  (a)  he is or has been the subject of an investigation under section 20(1)(a), and
  (b)  the Commission is satisfied that he has committed an unlawful act.
(2)  A notice must specify—
  (a)  the unlawful act, and
  (b)  the provision of the [Equality Act 2010] by virtue of which the act is unlawful.
(3)  A notice must inform the recipient of the effect of—
  (a)  subsections (5) to (7),
  (b)  section 20(1)(b), and
  (c)  section 24(1).
(4)  A notice may—
  (a)  require the person to whom the notice is given to prepare an action plan for the purpose of avoiding repetition or continuation of the unlawful act;
  (b)  recommend action to be taken by the person for that purpose.
(5)  A person who is given a notice may, within the period of six weeks beginning with the day on which the notice is given, appeal to the appropriate court or tribunal on the grounds—
  (a)  that he has not committed the unlawful act specified in the notice, or
  (b)  that a requirement for the preparation of an action plan imposed under subsection (4)(a) is unreasonable.
(6)  On an appeal under subsection (5) the court or tribunal may—
  (a)  affirm a notice;
  (b)  annul a notice;
  (c)  vary a notice;
  (d)  affirm a requirement;
  (e)  annul a requirement;
  (f)  vary a requirement;
  (g)  make an order for costs or expenses.
(7)  In subsection (5) "the appropriate court or tribunal" means—
  (a)  an employment tribunal, if a claim in respect of the alleged unlawful act could be made to it, or
  (b)  *a county court* (in England and Wales) or the sheriff (in Scotland), if a claim in respect of the alleged unlawful act could be made to it or to him.

**NOTES**
Sub-s (2): words in square brackets substituted by the Equality Act 2010, s 211(1), Sch 26, paras 61, 67, as from 1 October 2010; for transitory provisions relating to ships and hovercraft, see the Equality Act 2010 (Commencement No 4, Savings, Consequential, Transitional, Transitory and Incidental Provisions and Revocation) Order 2010, SI 2010/2317, arts 10(4), 11(2) at **[2.1563]**, **[2.1564]**.
Sub-s (7): for the words in italics there are substituted the words "the county court" by the Crime and Courts Act 2013, s 17(5), Sch 9, Pt 3, para 52, as from a day to be appointed.

**[1.1371]**
**22  Action plans**
(1)  This section applies where a person has been given a notice under section 21 which requires him (under section 21(4)(a)) to prepare an action plan.
(2)  The notice must specify a time by which the person must give the Commission a first draft plan.
(3)  After receiving a first draft plan from a person the Commission shall—
  (a)  approve it, or
  (b)  give the person a notice which—
    (i)  states that the draft is not adequate,
    (ii)  requires the person to give the Commission a revised draft by a specified time, and
    (iii)  may make recommendations about the content of the revised draft.
(4)  Subsection (3) shall apply in relation to a revised draft plan as it applies in relation to a first draft plan.
(5)  An action plan comes into force—
  (a)  if the period of six weeks beginning with the date on which a first draft or revised draft is given to the Commission expires without the Commission—
    (i)  giving a notice under subsection (3)(b), or
    (ii)  applying for an order under subsection (6)(b), or
  (b)  upon a court's declining to make an order under subsection (6)(b) in relation to a revised draft of the plan.

(6)   The Commission may apply to *a county court* (in England and Wales) or to the sheriff (in Scotland)—
- (a)   for an order requiring a person to give the Commission a first draft plan by a time specified in the order,
- (b)   for an order requiring a person who has given the Commission a revised draft plan to prepare and give to the Commission a further revised draft plan—
  - (i)   by a time specified in the order, and
  - (ii)   in accordance with any directions about the plan's content specified in the order, or
- (c)   during the period of five years beginning with the date on which an action plan prepared by a person comes into force, for an order requiring the person—
  - (i)   to act in accordance with the action plan, or
  - (ii)   to take specified action for a similar purpose.

(7)   An action plan may be varied by agreement between the Commission and the person who prepared it.

(8)   Paragraphs 10 to 14 of Schedule 2 apply (but omitting references to oral evidence) in relation to consideration by the Commission of the adequacy of a draft action plan as they apply in relation to the conduct of an inquiry.

(9)   A person commits an offence if without reasonable excuse he fails to comply with an order under subsection (6); and a person guilty of an offence under this subsection shall be liable on summary conviction to a fine not exceeding level 5 on the standard scale.

**NOTES**

Sub-s (6): for the words in italics there are substituted the words "the county court" by the Crime and Courts Act 2013, s 17(5), Sch 9, Pt 3, para 52, as from a day to be appointed.

**[1.1372]**
### 23   Agreements

(1)   The Commission may enter into an agreement with a person under which—
- (a)   the person undertakes—
  - (i)   not to commit an unlawful act of a specified kind, and
  - (ii)   to take, or refrain from taking, other specified action (which may include the preparation of a plan for the purpose of avoiding an unlawful act), and
- (b)   the Commission undertakes not to proceed against the person under section 20 or 21 in respect of any unlawful act of the kind specified under paragraph (a)(i).

(2)   The Commission may enter into an agreement with a person under this section only if it thinks that the person has committed an unlawful act.

(3)   But a person shall not be taken to admit to the commission of an unlawful act by reason only of entering into an agreement under this section.

(4)   An agreement under this section—
- (a)   may be entered into whether or not the person is or has been the subject of an investigation under section 20,
- (b)   may include incidental or supplemental provision (which may include provision for termination in specified circumstances), and
- (c)   may be varied or terminated by agreement of the parties.

(5)   This section shall apply in relation to the breach of a duty specified in section 34(2) as it applies in relation to the commission of an unlawful act; and for that purpose the reference in subsection (1)(b) above to section 20 or 21 shall be taken as a reference to section 32.

**[1.1373]**
### 24   Applications to court

(1)   If the Commission thinks that a person is likely to commit an unlawful act, it may apply—
- (a)   in England and Wales, to *a county court* for an injunction restraining the person from committing the act, or
- (b)   in Scotland, to the sheriff for an interdict prohibiting the person from committing the act.

(2)   Subsection (3) applies if the Commission thinks that a party to an agreement under section 23 has failed to comply, or is likely not to comply, with an undertaking under the agreement.

(3)   The Commission may apply to *a county court* (in England and Wales) or to the sheriff (in Scotland) for an order requiring the person—
- (a)   to comply with his undertaking, and
- (b)   to take such other action as the court or the sheriff may specify.

**NOTES**

Sub-ss (1), (3): for the words in italics there are substituted the words "the county court" by the Crime and Courts Act 2013, s 17(5), Sch 9, Pt 3, para 52, as from a day to be appointed.

**[1.1374]**
### [24A   Enforcement powers: supplemental

(1)   This section has effect in relation to—

(a)   an act which is unlawful because, by virtue of any of sections 13 to 18 of the Equality Act 2010, it amounts to a contravention of any of Parts 3, 4, 5, 6 or 7 of that Act,

(b)   an act which is unlawful because it amounts to a contravention of section 60(1) of that Act (or to a contravention of section 111 or 112 of that Act that relates to a contravention of section 60(1) of that Act) (enquiries about disability and health),

(c)   an act which is unlawful because it amounts to a contravention of section 106 of that Act (information about diversity in range of election candidates etc),

(d)   an act which is unlawful because, by virtue of section 108(1) of that Act, it amounts to a contravention of any of Parts 3, 4, 5, 6 or 7 of that Act, or

(e)   the application of a provision, criterion or practice which, by virtue of section 19 of that Act, amounts to a contravention of that Act.

(2)   For the purposes of sections 20 to 24 of this Act, it is immaterial whether the Commission knows or suspects that a person has been or may be affected by the unlawful act or application.

(3)   For those purposes, an unlawful act includes making arrangements to act in a particular way which would, if applied to an individual, amount to a contravention mentioned in subsection (1)(a).

(4)   Nothing in this Act affects the entitlement of a person to bring proceedings under the Equality Act 2010 in respect of a contravention mentioned in subsection (1).]

**NOTES**

Commencement: 1 October 2010.

Inserted by the Equality Act 2010, s 211(1), Sch 26, paras 61, 68, as from 1 October 2010.

**25, 26**   *(Repealed by the Equality Act 2010, s 211, Sch 26, paras 61, 69, 70, Sch 27, Pt 1, as from 1 October 2010; for transitory provisions relating to ships and hovercraft, see the Equality Act 2010 (Commencement No 4, Savings, Consequential, Transitional, Transitory and Incidental Provisions and Revocation) Order 2010, SI 2010/2317, arts 10(4), 11(2) at* **[2.1563]**, **[2.1564]**.)

**[1.1375]**
**27   Conciliation**
[(1)   The Commission may make arrangements for the provision of conciliation services for disputes in respect of which proceedings have been or could be determined by virtue of section 114 [or 116] of the Equality Act 2010.]

[(1A)   The Commission may make arrangements for the provision of conciliation services for disputes in respect of which proceedings have been or could be brought in England and Wales or Scotland under regulation 9 of the Civil Aviation (Access to Air Travel for Disabled Persons and Persons with Reduced Mobility) Regulations 2007 (civil proceedings).]

[(1B)   The Commission may make arrangements for the provision of conciliation services for disputes in respect of which proceedings have been or could be brought in England and Wales or Scotland under regulation 11 of the Rail Passengers' Rights and Obligations Regulations 2010 (compensation claims by disabled persons and persons with reduced mobility).]

(2)   The Commission may make arrangements for the provision of conciliation services for disputes about a landlord's reasonableness in relation to consent to the making of an improvement to a dwelling in England or Wales where the improvement would be likely to facilitate the enjoyment of the premises by the tenant or another lawful occupier having regard to a disability.

(3)   The Commission may make arrangements for the provision of conciliation services for disputes about whether—

(a)   it is unreasonable for a landlord of a house (within the meaning of the Housing (Scotland) Act 2006 (asp 01)) in Scotland to withhold consent to the carrying out of work in relation to the house for the purpose of making the house suitable for the accommodation, welfare or employment of any disabled person who occupies, or intends to occupy, the house as a sole or main residence, or

(b)   any condition imposed by such a landlord on consenting to the carrying out of such work is unreasonable.

(4)   The Commission shall aim to exercise the powers in subsections (1) to (3) so as to ensure that, so far as is reasonably practicable, conciliation services are available to parties who want them.

(5)   Information communicated to a person providing conciliation services in accordance with arrangements under this section may not be adduced in legal proceedings without the consent of the person who communicated the information.

(6)   None of the following shall participate in the provision of conciliation services for which arrangements are made under this section—

(a)   a Commissioner,

(b)   a member of the Commission's staff,

(c)   a member of a committee established by the Commission, and

(d)   an Investigating Commissioner.

(7)   The Commission shall make administrative arrangements designed to secure that information in connection with conciliation services provided in accordance with arrangements made under this section is not disclosed to—

(a)   a Commissioner, or

(b)   a member of the Commission's staff.

(8)   But subsection (7) shall not apply to a disclosure—

(a)   made with the consent of the parties to the dispute to which it relates,

(b)   which does not identify individuals or enable them to be identified, or

(c)   of information without which arrangements under this section cannot be made.

(9)   In this section "conciliation services" means a service which is provided—

(a)   by a person who is not party to a dispute,

(b)   to the parties to the dispute, and

(c)   with the aim of enabling the dispute to be settled by agreement and without legal proceedings.

(10)   The [Secretary of State] may by order amend this section so as to vary the range of disputes in respect of which the Commission may make arrangements for the provision of conciliation services.

**NOTES**

Repealed by the Enterprise and Regulatory Reform Act 2013, s 64(1)(b), as from 25 June 2013.

Sub-s (1): substituted by the Equality Act 2010, s 211(1), Sch 26, paras 61, 71, as from 1 October 2010; words in square brackets inserted by the Equality Act 2010 (Public Authorities and Consequential and Supplementary Amendments) Order 2011, SI 2010/1060, art 7, as from 4 April 2011.

Sub-s (1A): inserted by the Civil Aviation (Access to Air Travel for Disabled Persons and Persons with Reduced Mobility) Regulations 2007, SI 2007/1895, reg 10.

Sub-s (1B): inserted by the Rail Passengers' Rights and Obligations Regulations 2010, SI 2010/1504, reg 12, as from 25 June 2010.

Sub-s (10): words in square brackets substituted by the Transfer of Functions (Equality) Order 2010, SI 2010/1839, arts 3(1)(f), 7, Schedule, para 14(1), (2)(f), as from 18 August 2010.

Orders: as of 6 April 2013 no Orders had been made under this section.

**[1.1376]**
**28   Legal assistance**

(1)   The Commission may assist an individual who is or may become party to legal proceedings if—

(a)   the proceedings relate or may relate (wholly or partly) to a provision of the [Equality Act 2010], and

(b)   the individual alleges that he has been the victim of behaviour contrary to a provision of [that Act].

(2)   The Commission may assist an individual who is or may become party to legal proceedings in England and Wales if and in so far as the proceedings concern or may concern the question of a landlord's reasonableness in relation to consent to the making of an improvement to a dwelling where the improvement would be likely to facilitate the enjoyment of the premises by the tenant or another lawful occupier having regard to a disability.

(3)   The Commission may assist an individual who is or may become a party to legal proceedings in Scotland if and in so far as the proceedings concern or may concern the question whether—

(a)   it is unreasonable for a landlord to withhold consent to the carrying out of work in relation to a house (within the meaning of the Housing (Scotland) Act 2006 (asp 01)) for the purpose of making the house suitable for the accommodation, welfare or employment of any disabled person who occupies, or intends to occupy, the house as a sole or main residence, or

(b)   any condition imposed by a landlord on consenting to the carrying out of such work is unreasonable.

(4)   In giving assistance under this section the Commission may provide or arrange for the provision of—

(a)   legal advice;

(b)   legal representation;

(c)   facilities for the settlement of a dispute;

(d)   any other form of assistance.

(5)   Assistance may not be given under subsection (1) in relation to alleged behaviour contrary to a provision of [Part 12 of the Equality Act 2010 (disabled persons:] transport).

(6)   Where proceedings relate or may relate partly to a provision of [the Equality Act 2010] and partly to other matters—

(a)   assistance may be given under subsection (1) in respect of any aspect of the proceedings while they relate to a provision of [that Act], but

(b)   if the proceedings cease to relate to a provision of [that Act], assistance may not be continued under subsection (1) in respect of the proceedings (except in so far as it is permitted by virtue of subsection (7) or (8)).

(7)   The Lord Chancellor may by order disapply subsection (6)(b), and enable the Commission to give assistance under subsection (1), in respect of legal proceedings which—

(a)   when instituted, related (wholly or partly) to a provision of the [Equality Act 2010],

(b)   have ceased to relate to the provision of [that Act], and

(c)    relate (wholly or partly) to any of the Convention rights within the meaning given by section 1 of the Human Rights Act 1998 (c 42).

(8)    The [Secretary of State] may by order enable the Commission to give assistance under this section in respect of legal proceedings in the course of which an individual who is or has been a disabled person relies or proposes to rely on a matter relating to his disability; but an order under this subsection may not permit assistance in relation to alleged behaviour contrary to a provision of [Part 12 of the Equality Act 2010].

(9)    An order under subsection (7) or (8) may make provision generally or only in relation to proceedings of a specified kind or description (which in the case of an order under subsection (7) may, in particular, refer to specified provisions of the [Equality Act 2010]) or in relation to specified circumstances.

(10)    This section is without prejudice to the effect of any restriction imposed, in respect of representation—

(a)    by virtue of an enactment (including an enactment in or under an Act of the Scottish Parliament), or

(b)    in accordance with the practice of a court.

(11)    A legislative provision which requires insurance or an indemnity in respect of advice given in connection with a *compromise contract or agreement* shall not apply to advice provided by the Commission under this section.

(12)    [This section applies] to a provision of [EU] law which—

(a)    relates to discrimination on grounds of sex (including reassignment of gender), racial origin, ethnic origin, religion, belief, disability, age or sexual orientation, and

(b)    confers rights on individuals
          [as it applies to the Equality Act 2010].

(13)    In its application by virtue of subsection (12), subsection (1)(b) shall have effect as if it referred to an allegation by an individual that he is disadvantaged by—

(a)    an enactment (including an enactment in or under an Act of the Scottish Parliament) which is contrary to a provision of [EU] law, or

(b)    a failure by the United Kingdom to implement a right as required by [EU] law.

**NOTES**

Sub-ss (1), (5)–(7), (9): words in square brackets substituted by the Equality Act 2010, s 211(1), Sch 26, paras 61, 72(1)–(5), (7), as from 1 October 2010.

Sub-s (8): words in first pair of square brackets substituted by the Transfer of Functions (Equality) Order 2010, SI 2010/1839, arts 3(1)(f), 7, Schedule, para 14(1), (2)(g), as from 18 August 2010; words in second pair of square brackets substituted by the Equality Act 2010, s 211(1), Sch 26, paras 61, 72(1), (6), as from 1 October 2010.

Sub-s (11): for the words in italics there are substituted the words "settlement agreement" by the Enterprise and Regulatory Reform Act 2013, s 23(4), as from a day to be appointed.

Sub-s (12): words in first pair of square brackets substituted and words in third pair of square brackets added by the Equality Act 2010, s 211(1), Sch 26, paras 61, 72(1), (8), as from 1 October 2010; reference in second pair of square brackets substituted by the Treaty of Lisbon (Changes in Terminology) Order 2011, SI 2011/1043, art 6(2)(a), as from 22 April 2011.

Sub-s (13): references in square brackets substituted by SI 2011/1043, art 6(2)(a), as from 22 April 2011.

**[1.1377]**
**29   Legal assistance: costs**

(1)    This section applies where—

(a)    the Commission has assisted an individual under section 28 in relation to proceedings, and

(b)    the individual becomes entitled to some or all of his costs in the proceedings (whether by virtue of an award or by virtue of an agreement).

(2)    The Commission's expenses in providing the assistance—

(a)    shall be charged on sums paid to the individual by way of costs, and

(b)    may be enforced as a debt due to the Commission.

(3)    A requirement to pay money to the Commission under subsection (2) ranks, in England and Wales, after a requirement imposed by virtue of [section 25 of the Legal Aid, Sentencing and Punishment of Offenders Act 2012 (statutory charge in connection with civil legal aid)].

(4)    Subsection (2), in its application to Scotland, shall not affect the operation of section 17(2A) of the Legal Aid (Scotland) Act 1986 (c 47) (requirement in certain cases to pay to the Scottish Legal Aid Board sums recovered under awards of, or agreements as to, expenses).

(5)    For the purposes of subsection (2) the Commission's expenses shall be calculated in accordance with such provision (if any) as the [Secretary of State] makes for the purpose by regulations; and regulations may, in particular, provide for the apportionment of expenditure incurred by the Commission—

(a)    partly for one purpose and partly for another, or

(b)    for general purposes.

(6)    In the application of this section to Scotland a reference to costs shall be taken as a reference to expenses.

**NOTES**

Sub-s (3): words in square brackets substituted by the Legal Aid, Sentencing and Punishment of Offenders Act 2012, s 39, Sch 5, Pt 1, para 67, as from 1 April 2013.

Sub-s (5): words in square brackets substituted by the Transfer of Functions (Equality) Order 2010, SI 2010/1839, arts 3(1)(f), 7, Schedule, para 14(1), (2)(h), as from 18 August 2010.

Regulations: as of 6 April 2013 no Regulations had been made under this section.

**[1.1378]**
**30  Judicial review and other legal proceedings**
(1)   The Commission shall have capacity to institute or intervene in legal proceedings, whether for judicial review or otherwise, if it appears to the Commission that the proceedings are relevant to a matter in connection with which the Commission has a function.
(2)   The Commission shall be taken to have title and interest in relation to the subject matter of any legal proceedings in Scotland which it has capacity to institute, or in which it has capacity to intervene, by virtue of subsection (1).
(3)   The Commission may, in the course of legal proceedings for judicial review which it institutes (or in which it intervenes), rely on section 7(1)(b) of the Human Rights Act 1998 (c 42) (breach of Convention rights); and for that purpose—
   (a)   the Commission need not be a victim or potential victim of the unlawful act to which the proceedings relate,
   (b)   the Commission may act only if there is or would be one or more victims of the unlawful act,
   (c)   section 7(3) and (4) of that Act shall not apply, and
   (d)   no award of damages may be made to the Commission (whether or not the exception in section 8(3) of that Act applies);
and an expression used in this subsection and in section 7 of the Human Rights Act 1998 has the same meaning in this subsection as in that section.
(4)   Subsections (1) and (2)—
   (a)   do not create a cause of action, and
   (b)   are, except as provided by subsection (3), subject to any limitation or restriction imposed by virtue of an enactment (including an enactment in or under an Act of the Scottish Parliament) or in accordance with the practice of a court.

**[1.1379]**
**31  Public sector duties: assessment**
[(1)   The Commission may assess the extent to which or the manner in which a person has complied with a duty under or by virtue of section 149, 153 or 154 of the Equality Act 2010 (public sector equality duty).]
(2)   Schedule 2 makes supplemental provision about assessments.
(3)   This section is without prejudice to the generality of sections 16 and 20.

**NOTES**

Sub-s (1): substituted by the Equality Act 2010, s 211(1), Sch 26, paras 61, 73, as from 5 April 2011.

**[1.1380]**
**32  Public sector duties: compliance notice**
[(1)   This section applies where the Commission thinks that a person has failed to comply with a duty under or by virtue of section 149, 153 or 154 of the Equality Act 2010 (public sector equality duty).]
(2)   The Commission may give the person a notice requiring him—
   (a)   to comply with the duty, and
   (b)   to give the Commission, within the period of 28 days beginning with the date on which he receives the notice, written information of steps taken or proposed for the purpose of complying with the duty.
(3)   A notice under this section may require a person to give the Commission information required by the Commission for the purposes of assessing compliance with the duty; in which case the notice shall specify—
   (a)   the period within which the information is to be given (which shall begin with the date on which the notice is received and shall not exceed three months), and
   (b)   the manner and form in which the information is to be given.
(4)   The Commission may not give a notice under this section in respect of a duty under [section 149 of the Equality Act 2010] unless—
   (a)   the Commission has carried out an assessment under section 31 above, and
   (b)   the notice relates to the results of the assessment.
(5)   A person who receives a notice under this section shall comply with it.
(6)   But a notice under this section shall not oblige a person to give information—
   (a)   that he is prohibited from disclosing by virtue of an enactment, or

(b)    that he could not be compelled to give in proceedings before the High Court or the Court of Session.

(7)    Paragraphs 11 and 14 of Schedule 2 shall have effect (with any necessary modifications) in relation to a requirement imposed by a notice under this section as they have effect in relation to a requirement imposed by a notice under paragraph 9 of that Schedule.

(8)    If the Commission thinks that a person, to whom a notice under this section has been given, has failed to comply with a requirement of the notice, the Commission may apply to the court for an order requiring the person to comply.

(9)    In subsection (8) "the court" means—

(a)    where the notice related to a duty under [section 149 of the Equality Act 2010], the High Court (in England and Wales) or (in Scotland) the Court of Session, and

(b)    [where the notice related to a duty by virtue of section 153 or 154 of that Act], *a county court* (in England and Wales) or the sheriff (in Scotland).

(10)    A notice under this section shall specify a time before which the Commission may not make an application under subsection (8) in respect of the notice.

(11)    Legal proceedings in relation to a duty by virtue of [section 153 or 154 of the Equality Act 2010]—

(a)    may be brought by the Commission in accordance with subsection (8) above, and

(b)    may not be brought in any other way.

**NOTES**

Sub-s (1): substituted by the Equality Act 2010, s 211(1), Sch 26, paras 61,74(1), (2), as from 5 April 2011.

Sub-ss (4), (9), (11): words in square brackets substituted by the Equality Act 2010, s 211(1), Sch 26, paras 61,74(1), (3)–(6), as from 5 April 2011; for the words in italics in sub-s (9) there are substituted the words "the county court" by the Crime and Courts Act 2013, s 17(5), Sch 9, Pt 3, para 52, as from a day to be appointed.

*Interpretation*

**33**    *(Repealed by the Equality Act 2010, s 211, Sch 26, paras 61, 75, Sch 27, Pt 1, as from 1 October 2010; for transitory provisions relating to the public sector equality duty, see the Equality Act 2010 (Commencement No 4, Savings, Consequential, Transitional, Transitory and Incidental Provisions and Revocation) Order 2010, SI 2010/2317, art 9 at* **[2.1562]**.)

**[1.1381]**
**34    Unlawful**
(1)    In this Part (except section 30(3)) "unlawful" means contrary to a provision of the [Equality Act 2010].

(2)    But action is not unlawful for the purposes of this Part by reason only of the fact that it contravenes a duty under or by virtue of [any of the following provisions of the Equality Act 2010]—

[(a)    section 1 (public sector duty regarding socio-economic inequalities),

(b)    section 149, 153 or 154 (public sector equality duty),

(c)    Part 12 (disabled persons: transport), or

(d)    section 190 (disability: improvements to let dwelling houses).]

**NOTES**

Sub-s (1): words in square brackets substituted by the Equality Act 2010, s 211(1), Sch 26, paras 61, 76(1), (2), as from 1 October 2010.

Sub-s (2): words in first pair of square brackets inserted, and words in second pair of square brackets substituted, by the Equality Act 2010, s 211(1), Sch 26, paras 61, 76(1), (3). Note that these amendments came into force on 1 October 2010, except in so far as relating to the substituted paras (a), (b). Note also that in so far as it relates to para (b), this amendment was further commenced on 5 April 2011. It is still to be appointed in so far as relating to para (a). See the Equality Act 2010 (Commencement No 4, Savings, Consequential, Transitional, Transitory and Incidental Provisions and Revocation) Order 2010, SI 2010/2317, art 2(15)(e)(vii) at **[2.1559]** and the Equality Act 2010 (Commencement No 6) Order, SI 2011/1066, art 2. For for transitory provisions relating to the public sector equality duty, see art 9 of the 2010 Order at **[2.1562]**.

**[1.1382]**
**35    General**
In this Part—
"act" includes deliberate omission,
"groups" has the meaning given by section 10,
"the Commission" means the Commission for Equality and Human Rights,
"disabled person" has the meaning given by section 8,
"human rights" has the meaning given by section 9,
[ . . . ]
"race" includes colour, nationality, ethnic origin and national origin,
"religion or belief" has the same meaning as in [section 10 of the Equality Act 2010], and
["sexual orientation" has the same meaning as in section 12 of the Equality Act 2010].

**NOTES**
Definition "the Minister" (omitted) originally inserted by the Transfer of Functions (Equality) Order 2007, SI 2007/2914, art 8, Schedule, para 15(1), and repealed by the Transfer of Functions (Equality) Order 2010, SI 2010/1839, arts 3(1)(f), 7, Schedule, para 14(1), (3), as from 18 August 2010.

Words in square brackets in definition "religion or belief" substituted, and definition "sexual orientation" substituted, by the Equality Act 2010, s 211(1), Sch 26, paras 61, 77, as from 1 October 2010.

*Dissolution of Existing Commissions*

**[1.1383]**

**36 Dissolution**

(1) The Secretary of State may by order provide for—

(a) any of the former Commissions to cease to exist, or

(b) the removal from any of the former Commissions of a specified function.

(2) In this Part "the former Commissions" means—

(a) the Equal Opportunities Commission,

(b) the Commission for Racial Equality, and

(c) the Disability Rights Commission.

(3) The Secretary of State shall by exercising the power under subsection (1) ensure that each of the former Commissions ceases to exist not later than the end of 31st March 2009.

**NOTES**

"The Secretary of State": see the note on transfer of functions immediately before Part 1 of this Act.

Orders: the Equality Act 2006 (Dissolution of Commissions and Consequential and Transitional Provisions) Order 2007, SI 2007/2602; the Equality Act 2006 (Dissolution of Commissions and Consequential and Transitional Provisions) (Amendment) Order 2007, SI 2007/3555.

**[1.1384]**

**37 Transfer of property, &c**

(1) An order under section 36(1) in respect of any of the former Commissions may provide for the transfer to the Commission for Equality and Human Rights of specified property, rights and liabilities of the former Commission.

(2) The Secretary of State may give a former Commission any direction that the Secretary of State thinks appropriate in connection with the dissolution of the former Commission or the establishment of the Commission for Equality and Human Rights; and a direction may, in particular, require the former Commission—

(a) to provide information in connection with property, rights or liabilities;

(b) to provide information in connection with the exercise of functions;

(c) to transfer specified property, rights and liabilities to a specified person;

(d) to make property, staff or facilities available, on such terms or conditions as may be specified in the direction, to the Commission for Equality and Human Rights;

(e) not to take action of a specified kind or in specified circumstances.

(3) The Secretary of State may direct a former Commission to prepare a scheme for the transfer of specified property, rights and liabilities to—

(a) the Commission for Equality and Human Rights, or

(b) another person specified in the direction.

(4) If the Secretary of State gives a direction under subsection (3)—

(a) the former Commission shall prepare a scheme in accordance with the direction, having consulted either the Commission for Equality and Human Rights or the person specified under subsection (3)(b), and

(b) the scheme shall have effect—

(i) when approved by the Secretary of State, and

(ii) subject to any modifications made by him, having consulted the former Commission and either the Commission for Equality and Human Rights or the person specified under subsection (3)(b).

(5) Where a former Commission ceases to exist by virtue of section 36(1)(a), its property, rights and liabilities shall by virtue of this subsection vest in the Commission for Equality and Human Rights (and this subsection operates in addition to any transfer provided for by virtue of subsection (1) above).

(6) An order, direction or scheme under or by virtue of this section may, in particular—

(a) specify property, rights or liabilities;

(b) specify a class or description of property, rights or liabilities;

(c) specify property, rights or liabilities to a specified extent.

**NOTES**

"The Secretary of State": see the note on transfer of functions immediately before Part 1 of this Act.

**[1.1385]**
## 38 Transfer of property: supplemental
(1)  A direction under section 37—
- (a)  shall be in writing,
- (b)  may be given only following consultation with the former Commission to which the direction relates and, where the Secretary of State thinks it appropriate, the Commission for Equality and Human Rights, and
- (c)  may be varied or revoked by a further direction.

(2)  In so far as is appropriate as a consequence of a transfer effected by or by virtue of section 37—
- (a)  anything done by or in relation to any of the former Commissions which has effect immediately before the transfer shall continue to have effect as if done by or in relation to the Commission for Equality and Human Rights, and
- (b)  anything (including any legal proceedings) which immediately before the transfer is in the process of being done by or in relation to any of the former Commissions may be continued by or in relation to the Commission for Equality and Human Rights.

(3)  In so far as is appropriate in consequence of a transfer effected by or by virtue of section 37 a reference to any of the former Commissions in an agreement, instrument or other document shall be treated as a reference to the Commission for Equality and Human Rights.

(4)  Section 37, and a direction, scheme or order under or by virtue of that section, shall operate in relation to property, rights or liabilities—
- (a)  whether or not they would otherwise be capable of being transferred,
- (b)  without any instrument or other formality being required, and
- (c)  irrespective of any requirement for consent that would otherwise apply.

(5)  A scheme or order under or by virtue of section 37 which relates to rights or liabilities under a contract of employment—
- (a)  must provide for the application of the [Transfer of Undertakings (Protection of Employment) Regulations 2006], and
- (b)  must provide that for any purpose relating to an employee of a former commission who becomes an employee of the Commission for Equality and Human Rights by virtue of the scheme or order—
  - (i)  a period of employment with the former commission shall be treated as a period of employment with the Commission for Equality and Human Rights, and
  - (ii)  the transfer to that Commission shall not be treated as a break in service.

**NOTES**

Sub-s (5): the Transfer of Undertakings (Protection of Employment) Regulations 2006, SI 2006/246, reg 20, Sch 2, para 1(l) provides that the words "Transfer of Undertakings (Protection of Employment) Regulations 2006" should be substituted for the words "Transfer of Undertakings (Protection of Employment) Regulations 1981 (SI 1981/1794)" in s 39(5) of this Act. It appears that this is a drafting error as the words in question occur in sub-s (5) of this section and not in s 39(5). The amendment has been taken in above.

"The Secretary of State": see the note on transfer of functions immediately before Part 1 of this Act.

*Miscellaneous*

**[1.1386]**
## 39 Orders and regulations
(1)  An order of a Minister of the Crown under this Part and regulations under this Part shall be made by statutory instrument.

(2)  An order of a Minister of the Crown under this Part and regulations under this Part—
- (a)  may make provision generally or only for specified purposes,
- (b)  may make different provision for different purposes, and
- (c)  may include transitional, incidental or consequential provision.

(3)  An order or regulations under any of the following provisions shall be subject to annulment in pursuance of a resolution of either House of Parliament—
- (a)  section 15(3),
- (b)  section 28,
- (c)  section 29,
- (d)  section 36, and
- (e)  Part 5 of Schedule 1.

(4)  An order under section *10(6), 15(6) [or 27(10)]*—
- (a)  may, in particular, make consequential amendment of an enactment (including this Act and including an enactment in or under an Act of the Scottish Parliament), and
- (b)  may not be made unless a draft has been laid before and approved by resolution of each House of Parliament.

(5)  An incidental provision included in an order or regulations by virtue of subsection (2)(c) may, in particular, impose a requirement for consent to action under or by virtue of the order or regulations.

**NOTES**

Sub-s (4): words in square brackets substituted by the Equality Act 2010, s 211(1), Sch 26, paras 61, 78, as from 1 October 2010; for the words in italics there is substituted "15(6)" by the Enterprise and Regulatory Reform Act 2013, s 64(3), (10), as from 25 June 2013.

**40**   *(Introduces Sch 3 (consequential amendments).)*

**[1.1387]**
## 41   Transitional: the Commission

(1)   If an order under section 93 provides for any of sections 1 to 3 and Schedule 1 to come into force (to any extent) at a time before any of sections 8 to 32 come into force (to any extent)—

   (a)   the period between that time and the commencement of any of sections 8 to 32 (to any extent) is the "transitional period" for the purposes of this section, and

   (b)   the following provisions of this section shall have effect.

(2)   During the transitional period the minimum number of Commissioners shall be five (and not as provided by paragraph 1 of Schedule 1).

(3)   The Secretary of State shall, as soon as is reasonably practicable after making the first appointments under that paragraph, appoint as additional members of the Commission (to be known as Transition Commissioners)—

   (a)   a commissioner of the Equal Opportunities Commission nominated by its chairman,

   (b)   a commissioner of the Commission for Racial Equality nominated by its chairman, and

   (c)   a commissioner of the Disability Rights Commission nominated by its chairman.

(4)   A person may nominate himself as a Transition Commissioner.

(5)   If a Transition Commissioner ceases to be a commissioner of the Commission whose chairman nominated him—

   (a)   he shall cease to be a Transition Commissioner,

   (b)   the chairman of that Commission shall nominate a replacement, and

   (c)   the Secretary of State shall appoint the nominated replacement.

(6)   A person shall hold appointment as a Transition Commissioner until a time specified by order of the Secretary of State (subject to subsection (5)); and the Secretary of State shall specify a time which in his opinion is not more than two years after the time when, by virtue of section 36, the Commission whose chairman nominated the Transition Commissioner—

   (a)   ceases to exist, or

   (b)   loses its principal functions.

(7)   In all other respects the provisions of this Part apply in relation to a Transition Commissioner as in relation to another Commissioner.

**NOTES**

"The Secretary of State": see the note on transfer of functions immediately before Part 1 of this Act.
Orders: the Equality Act 2006 (Termination of Appointments) Order 2007, SI 2007/2604.

**[1.1388]**
## 42   Transitional: functions of the dissolved Commissions

(1)   An order under section 36(1)(a) or (b) may—

   (a)   provide for a former Commission to continue to exercise a function in respect of a transitional case of a kind specified;

   (b)   provide for the Commission for Equality and Human Rights to exercise a function of a former Commission in respect of a transitional case of a kind specified.

(2)   An order under section 93 commencing a provision of Schedule 3 or 4 may include a saving or a consequential or incidental provision for the purpose of the operation of provision made by virtue of subsection (1) above; and the saving, consequential or incidental provision may, in particular, include provision applying, disapplying or modifying the application of a provision of this Act or of another enactment (including an enactment in or under an Act of the Scottish Parliament).

(3)   A code of practice issued by a Commission dissolved by virtue of section 36, or which relates to a function of a Commission removed by virtue of section 36(1)(b)—

   (a)   shall continue to have effect until revoked by the Secretary of State, at the request of the Commission for Equality and Human Rights, by order made by statutory instrument, and

   (b)   may be revised by the Commission for Equality and Human Rights as if it had been issued under section 14.

(4)   Consultation undertaken by a former Commission in relation to the issue or revision of a code of practice may be relied upon by the Commission for Equality and Human Rights for a purpose of section 14.

(5)   An order under subsection (3)(a) shall be subject to annulment in pursuance of a resolution of either House of Parliament.

**NOTES**

"The Secretary of State": see the note on transfer of functions immediately before Part 1 of this Act.

Orders: the Equality Act 2006 (Dissolution of Commissions and Consequential and Transitional Provisions) Order 2007, SI 2007/2602; the Disability Discrimination Code of Practice (Trade Organisations and Qualifications Bodies) (Revocation) Order 2008, SI 2008/1336 (which revokes, with effect from 23 June 2008 but subject to transitional provisions, the Disability Discrimination Act 1995 Code of Practice for Trade Organisations and Qualifications Bodies); the Former Equality Commissions' Codes of Practice (Employment, Equal Pay, and Rights of Access for Disabled Persons) (Revocation) Order 2011, SI 2011/776.

**43–80**    (*S 43 repealed by the Equality Act 2010, s 211, Sch 26, paras 61, 79, Sch 27, Pt 1, as from 1 October 2010; ss 44–80 (Pt 2: Discrimination on grounds of religion or belief in relation to goods, facilities and services) repealed by the Equality Act 2010, s 211, Sch 26, paras 61, 80, Sch 27, Pt 1, as from 1 October 2010.*)

**PART 3**
**DISCRIMINATION ON GROUNDS OF SEXUAL ORIENTATION**

**81**    (*Repealed by the Equality Act 2010, s 211, Sch 26, paras 61, 81, Sch 27, Pt 1, as from 1 October 2010; for transitory provisions relating to ships and hovercraft, see the Equality Act 2010 (Commencement No 4, Savings, Consequential, Transitional, Transitory and Incidental Provisions and Revocation) Order 2010, SI 2010/2317, art 10(2), Sch 1 at* **[2.1563]**, **[2.1575]**.)

**82–90**    (*S 82 (Regulations for Northern Ireland) outside the scope of this work; ss 83–90 (Pt 4) contain various amendments to the Sex Discrimination Act 1975, the Race Relations Act 1976, and the Disability Discrimination Act 1995 (all repealed).*)

**PART 5**
**GENERAL**

**91**    (*Introduces Schedule 4 (Repeals).*)

**[1.1389]**
**92   Crown application**
This Act applies (except as is otherwise expressly provided) to—
     (a)    Ministers of the Crown,
     (b)    government departments,
     (c)    office-holders in the Scottish Administration (within the meaning of section 126(7) of the Scotland Act 1998 (c 46)),
     [(ca)   the Welsh Ministers, the First Minister for Wales and the Counsel General to the Welsh Assembly Government,] and
     (d)    other agents of the Crown.

**NOTES**

Para (ca) inserted by the Government of Wales Act 2006 (Consequential Modifications and Transitional Provisions) Order 2007, SI 2007/1388, art 3, Sch 1, paras 112, 119.

Construction of references to an office-holder in the Scottish Administration: unless the context otherwise requires, references to an office-holder in the Scottish Administration are to be taken to include a reference to the Scottish Court Service established by the Judiciary and Courts (Scotland) Act 2008, s 60(1): see the Judiciary and Courts (Scotland) Act 2008 (Consequential Provisions and Modifications) Order 2009, SI 2009/2231, art 3.

**[1.1390]**
**93   Commencement**
(1)    The preceding provisions of this Act, except for sections 41, 42 and 86, shall come into force in accordance with provision made by the Secretary of State by order.
(2)    An order under subsection (1)—
     (a)    shall be made by statutory instrument,
     (b)    may make provision generally or only for a specified purpose,
     (c)    may make different provision for different purposes, and
     (d)    may include transitional provisions and savings.

**NOTES**

"The Secretary of State": see the note on transfer of functions immediately before Part 1 of this Act.

Orders: the Equality Act 2006 (Commencement No 1) Order 2006, SI 2006/1082; the Equality Act 2006 (Commencement No 2) Order 2007, SI 2007/1092; the Equality Act 2006 (Commencement No 3 and Savings) Order 2007, SI 2007/2603.

**[1.1391]**
**94   Extent**
(1)    This Act extends only to—
     (a)    England and Wales, and

(b)   Scotland.
(2)   But—
    (a)   section 82 extends only to Northern Ireland, and
    (b)   except as provided by subsection (3), an amendment of an enactment by this Act shall have the same extent as the enactment amended (or as the relevant part of the enactment amended).
(3)   Paragraphs 36 to 38 . . . of Schedule 3 (which amend the Estate Agents Act 1979 (c 38) . . . ), together with corresponding entries in Schedule 4, shall not extend to Northern Ireland.

**NOTES**

Sub-s (3): words omitted repealed by the Equality Act 2010, s 211, Sch 26, paras 61, 83, Sch 27, Pt 1, as from 1 October 2010.

**[1.1392]**
**95   Short title**
This Act may be cited as the Equality Act 2006.

**SCHEDULES**

**SCHEDULE 1**
**THE COMMISSION: CONSTITUTION, &C**

Section 2

**PART 1**
**CONSTITUTION**

*Membership*

**[1.1393]**
**1.** (1)   The [Secretary of State] shall appoint not less than 10 or more than 15 individuals as members of the Commission (to be known as Commissioners).
(2)   The chief executive of the Commission (appointed under paragraph 7 below) shall be a Commissioner *ex officio*.

**2.** (1)   In appointing Commissioners the [Secretary of State] shall—
    (a)   appoint an individual only if the [Secretary of State] thinks that the individual—
        (i)   has experience or knowledge relating to a relevant matter, or
        (ii)   is suitable for appointment for some other special reason, and
    (b)   have regard to the desirability of the Commissioners together having experience and knowledge relating to the relevant matters.
(2)   For the purposes of sub-paragraph (1) the relevant matters are those matters in respect of which the Commission has functions including, in particular—
    (a)   discrimination (whether on grounds of age, disability, gender, gender reassignment, race, religion or belief, sexual orientation or otherwise), and
    (b)   human rights.
(3)   The [Secretary of State] shall ensure that the Commission includes—
    (a)   a Commissioner appointed under paragraph 1(1) who is (or has been) a disabled person,
    (b)   a Commissioner appointed under paragraph 1(1), with the consent of the Scottish Ministers, who knows about conditions in Scotland, and
    (c)   a Commissioner appointed under paragraph 1(1), with the consent of the [Welsh Ministers], who knows about conditions in Wales.
(4)   A person may not be appointed for the purpose of satisfying more than one paragraph of sub-paragraph (3).

*Tenure*

**3.** (1)   A Commissioner shall hold and vacate office in accordance with the terms of his appointment (subject to this Schedule).
(2)   The appointment of a Commissioner must be expressed to be for a specified period of not less than two years or more than five years.
(3)   A Commissioner whose period of membership has expired may be re-appointed.
(4)   A Commissioner may resign by notice in writing to the [Secretary of State].
(5)   The [Secretary of State] may dismiss a Commissioner who is, in the opinion of the [Secretary of State], unable, unfit or unwilling to perform his functions.
(6)   This paragraph does not apply to the chief executive.

*Chairman*

**4.** (1)   The [Secretary of State] shall appoint—

(a)    a Commissioner as Chairman, and

(b)    one or more Commissioners as deputy Chairman.

(2)    The Chairman shall—

(a)    preside over meetings of the Commission,

(b)    perform such functions as may be specified in the terms of his appointment, and

(c)    perform such other functions as may be assigned to him by the Commission.

(3)    A deputy Chairman—

(a)    may act for the Chairman when he is unavailable, and

(b)    shall perform—

(i)    such functions as may be specified in the terms of his appointment, and

(ii)   such other functions as the Chairman may delegate or assign to him.

(4)    The Chairman or a deputy Chairman—

(a)    shall vacate office if he ceases to be a Commissioner,

(b)    may resign by notice in writing to the [Secretary of State], and

(c)    otherwise, shall hold and vacate office in accordance with the terms of his appointment (and may be reappointed).

(5)    If the Chairman resigns he shall cease to be a Commissioner (but he may be reappointed as a Commissioner).

(6)    The chief executive may not be appointed Chairman or deputy Chairman.

**NOTES**

The words "Secretary of State" in square brackets in every place they occur were substituted by the Transfer of Functions (Equality) Order 2010, SI 2010/1839, arts 3(1)(f), 7, Schedule, para 14(1), (2)(o), as from 18 August 2010.

The words in the second pair of square brackets in para 2(3) were substituted by the Government of Wales Act 2006 (Consequential Modifications and Transitional Provisions) Order 2007, SI 2007/1388, art 3, Sch 1, paras 112, 120.

## PART 2
## PROCEEDINGS

*Procedure*

**[1.1394]**

5.  The Commission may regulate its own proceedings (subject to this Schedule).

6.  (1)    The Commission shall determine a quorum for its meetings.

(2)    At least five Commissioners must participate in the process by which a determination under sub-paragraph (1) is made.

*Staff*

7.  (1)    The Commission—

(a)    shall appoint a chief executive, and

(b)    may appoint other staff.

(2)    A person may be appointed under sub-paragraph (1)(a) only with the consent of the [Secretary of State].

(3)    An appointment may be made under sub-paragraph (1)(b) only if consistent with arrangements determined by the Commission and approved by the [Secretary of State] as to—

(a)    numbers, and

(b)    terms and conditions of appointment.

8.   . . .

*Investigating Commissioners*

9.  (1)    The Commission may appoint one or more Investigating Commissioners.

(2)    An Investigating Commissioner may be appointed only—

(a)    for the purpose of having delegated to him by the Commission the function of taking action of a kind listed in sub-paragraph (3), and

(b)    with the consent of the [Secretary of State].

(3)    The kinds of action referred to in sub-paragraph (2)(a) are—

(a)    carrying out an inquiry under section 16,

(b)    carrying out an investigation under section 20,

(c)    giving an unlawful act notice under section 21, and

(d)    entering into an agreement under section 23.

(4)    An Investigating Commissioner is not a Commissioner; but paragraphs 3(1), (4) and (5) and 33 apply to him as if he were (and with the substitution of references to the Commission for references to the [Secretary of State]).

*Delegation*

**10.** (1)  The Commission may delegate a function—
  (a)   to a Commissioner,
  (b)   to staff, or
  (c)   in accordance with paragraph 9, to an Investigating Commissioner.
(2)  Paragraphs 15, 21, 22, 29, 30 and 52 make provision about delegation to committees.

*Committees*

**11.** (1)  The Commission may establish one or more committees (to be known as advisory committees) to advise—
  (a)   the Commission, or
  (b)   an Investigating Commissioner.
(2)  An advisory committee may include any of the following—
  (a)   Commissioners;
  (b)   staff;
  (c)   other non-Commissioners.

**12.** (1)  The Commission may establish one or more committees to whom the Commission may delegate functions (to be known as decision-making committees).
(2)  A decision-making committee may include any of the following—
  (a)   Commissioners;
  (b)   staff;
  (c)   other non-Commissioners.
(3)  The Commission shall ensure that the Chairman of each decision-making committee is a Commissioner.
(4)  In allocating its resources the Commission shall ensure that each decision-making committee receives a share sufficient to enable it to exercise its functions.

**13.**  A member of a committee shall hold and vacate office in accordance with the terms of his appointment by the Commission (which may include provision for dismissal).

**14.**  The Commission—
  (a)   may, to any extent, regulate the proceedings of a committee (and may, in particular, determine a quorum for meetings),
  (b)   may, to any extent, permit a committee to regulate its own proceedings (and may, in particular, enable a committee to determine a quorum for meetings), and
  (c)   may dissolve a committee.

**15.** (1)  The Commission may delegate a function to a decision-making committee.
(2)  This paragraph is subject to paragraphs 21, 22, 29, 30 and 52.

*Scotland Committee*

**16.** (1)  The Commission shall establish a decision-making committee to be known as the Scotland Committee.
(2)  The Commission shall ensure that the Scotland Committee is established before any of sections 8 to 12 comes into force (to any extent).

**17.**  The Commission shall appoint as the Chairman of the Scotland Committee a Commissioner appointed for the purpose of satisfying paragraph 2(3)(b).

**18.**  The Commission shall appoint each member of the Scotland Committee for a period of not less than two years or more than 5 years, subject to the possibilities of—
  (a)   reappointment, and
  (b)   dismissal in accordance with the terms of appointment.

**19.**  The Scotland Committee shall advise the Commission about the exercise of the Commission's functions in so far as they affect Scotland.

**20.**  Before exercising a function in a manner which in the opinion of the Commission is likely to affect persons in Scotland, the Commission shall consult the Scotland Committee.

**21.** (1)  The power under section 13—
  (a)   shall be treated by virtue of this paragraph as having been delegated by the Commission to the Scotland Committee in so far as its exercise, in the opinion of the Commission, affects Scotland, and
  (b)   to that extent shall not be exercisable by the Commission.

(2) Sub-paragraph (1) shall not apply to the power under section 13 in so far as it is treated as delegated to the Disability Committee in accordance with paragraph 52.

(3) Sub-paragraph (1) shall not prevent the Commission from making arrangements under section 13(1)(d) or (e) for the provision of advice or guidance to persons anywhere in Great Britain.

**22.** (1) The power under section 11(2)(c)—
  (a)  shall be treated by virtue of this paragraph as having been delegated by the Commission to the Scotland Committee in so far as it concerns the giving of advice to devolved government about enactments which, in the opinion of the Commission, affect only Scotland, and
  (b)  to that extent shall not be exercisable by the Commission.

(2) The power under section 11(2)(d)—
  (a)  shall be treated by virtue of this paragraph as having been delegated by the Commission to the Scotland Committee in so far as it concerns the giving of advice to devolved government about proposed changes in the law which, in the opinion of the Commission, would affect only Scotland, and
  (b)  to that extent shall not be exercisable by the Commission.

(3) Sub-paragraphs (1) and (2) shall not apply to the powers under section 11(2)(c) and (d) in so far as they are treated as delegated to the Disability Committee in accordance with paragraph 52.

**23.** In allocating its resources the Commission shall ensure that the Scotland Committee receives a share sufficient to enable it to exercise its functions.

### Wales Committee

**24.** (1) The Commission shall establish a decision-making committee to be known as the Wales Committee.

(2) The Commission shall ensure that the Wales Committee is established before any of sections 8 to 12 comes into force (to any extent).

**25.** The Commission shall appoint as the Chairman of the Wales Committee a Commissioner appointed for the purpose of satisfying paragraph 2(3)(c).

**26.** The Commission shall appoint each member of the Wales Committee for a period of not less than two years or more than 5 years, subject to the possibilities of—
  (a)  reappointment, and
  (b)  dismissal in accordance with the terms of appointment.

**27.** The Wales Committee shall advise the Commission about the exercise of its functions in so far as they affect Wales.

**28.** Before exercising a function in a manner which in the opinion of the Commission is likely to affect persons in Wales, the Commission shall consult the Wales Committee.

**29.** (1) The power under section 13—
  (a)  shall be treated by virtue of this paragraph as having been delegated by the Commission to the Wales Committee in so far as its exercise, in the opinion of the Commission, affects Wales, and
  (b)  to that extent shall not be exercisable by the Commission.

(2) Sub-paragraph (1) does not apply to the power under section 13 in so far as it is treated as delegated to the Disability Committee in accordance with paragraph 52.

(3) Sub-paragraph (1) shall not prevent the Commission from making arrangements under section 13(1)(d) or (e) for the provision of advice or guidance to persons anywhere in Great Britain.

**30.** (1) The power under section 11(2)(c)—
  (a)  shall be treated by virtue of this paragraph as having been delegated by the Commission to the Wales Committee in so far as it concerns the giving of advice to devolved government about enactments which, in the opinion of the Commission, affect only Wales, and
  (b)  to that extent shall not be exercisable by the Commission.

(2) The power under section 11(2)(d)—
  (a)  shall be treated by virtue of this paragraph as having been delegated by the Commission to the Wales Committee in so far as it concerns the giving of advice to devolved government about proposed changes in the law which, in the opinion of the Commission, would affect only Wales, and
  (b)  to that extent shall not be exercisable by the Commission.

(3) Sub-paragraphs (1) and (2) shall not apply to the powers under section 11(2)(c) and (d) in so far as they are treated as delegated to the Disability Committee in accordance with paragraph 52.

**31.** In allocating its resources the Commission shall ensure that the Wales Committee receives a share sufficient to enable it to exercise its functions.

*Annual report*

**32.** (1) The Commission shall for each financial year prepare a report on the performance of its functions in that year (to be known as its annual report).

(2) An annual report shall, in particular, indicate in what manner and to what extent the Commission's performance of its functions has accorded to the plan under section 4.

(3) The matters addressed by an annual report shall, in particular, include the Commission's activities in relation to—

    (a) Scotland, and

    (b) Wales.

(4) The Commission shall send each annual report to the [Secretary of State] within such period, beginning with the end of the financial year to which the report relates, as he may specify.

(5) The [Secretary of State] shall lay before Parliament a copy of each annual report received under sub-paragraph (4).

(6) The Commission shall send a copy of each annual report to—

    (a) the Scottish Parliament, and

    (b) the National Assembly for Wales.

*Savings*

**33.** The validity of proceedings of the Commission shall not be affected by—

    (a) a vacancy (whether for Commissioner, Chairman, deputy Chairman or chief executive), or

    (b) a defect in relation to an appointment.

**34.** The validity of proceedings of a committee of the Commission shall not be affected by—

    (a) a vacancy (including a vacancy in the office of Chairman), or

    (b) a defect in relation to an appointment (including a defect in relation to the office of Chairman).

---

**NOTES**

The words "Secretary of State" in square brackets in every place they occur were substituted by the Transfer of Functions (Equality) Order 2010, SI 2010/1839, arts 3(1)(f), 7, Schedule, para 14(1), (2)(o), as from 18 August 2010.

Para 8: amends the Employers' Liability (Compulsory Insurance) Act 1969, s 3.

---

# PART 3
# MONEY

*Remuneration, &c*

**[1.1395]**

**35.** (1) The Commission may pay to the Chairman, a deputy Chairman or another Commissioner—

    (a) such remuneration as the [Secretary of State] may determine, and

    (b) such travelling and other allowances as the [Secretary of State] may determine.

(2) The Commission may pay to or in respect of the Chairman, a deputy Chairman or another Commissioner such sums as the [Secretary of State] may determine by way of, or in respect of, pensions, allowances or gratuities.

(3) If the [Secretary of State] thinks that there are special circumstances that make it right for a person ceasing to hold office as Chairman, deputy Chairman or Commissioner to receive compensation, the Commission may pay to him such compensation as the [Secretary of State] may determine.

(4) This paragraph does not apply to the Chief Executive.

**36.** (1) The Commission may pay sums to or in respect of a member or former member of staff by way of or in respect of—

    (a) remuneration,

    (b) allowances,

    (c) pensions,

    (d) gratuities, or

    (e) compensation for loss of employment.

(2) . . .

(3) The Commission shall pay to the Minister for the Civil Service such sums as he may determine in respect of any increase attributable to sub-paragraph (2) in the sums payable out of money provided by Parliament under the Superannuation Act 1972 (c 11).

**37.** (1)   The Commission may, with the approval of the [Secretary of State], pay sums to or in respect of a member or former member of an advisory or decision-making committee by way of or in respect of —
  (a)   remuneration,
  (b)   allowances, or
  (c)   gratuities.
(2)   This paragraph does not apply in relation to a person who is a member of staff of the Commission.
(3)   Approval for the purposes of sub-paragraph (1) may be general or specific.

*Funding by [Secretary of State]*

**38.**   The [Secretary of State] shall pay to the Commission such sums as appear to the [Secretary of State] reasonably sufficient for the purpose of enabling the Commission to perform its functions.

*Charging*

**39.**   The Commission may make a charge for a service provided under section 13 *or 27*.

*Accounts*

**40.** (1)   The Commission shall—
  (a)   keep proper accounting records, and
  (b)   prepare a statement of accounts in respect of each financial year in such form as the [Secretary of State] may direct.
(2)   The Commission shall send a copy of a statement under sub-paragraph (1)(b) to—
  (a)   the [Secretary of State], and
  (b)   the Comptroller and Auditor General.
(3)   A copy of a statement must be sent under sub-paragraph (2) within such period, beginning with the end of the financial year to which the statement relates, as the [Secretary of State] may direct.
(4)   The Comptroller and Auditor General shall—
  (a)   examine, certify and report on a statement received under this paragraph, and
  (b)   lay a copy of the statement and his report before Parliament.
(5)   The [Secretary of State] may make a direction under sub-paragraph (1)(b) only with the consent of the Treasury.

*Financial year*

**41.** (1)   The financial year of the Commission shall be the period of 12 months ending with 31st March.
(2)   But the first financial year of the Commission shall be the period—
  (a)   beginning with the coming into force of section 1, and
  (b)   ending with—
    (i)    the following 31st March, if that section comes into force on 1st April, and
    (ii)   the second following 31st March, in any other case.

---

**NOTES**
   The words "Secretary of State" in square brackets in every place they occur were substituted by the Transfer of Functions (Equality) Order 2010, SI 2010/1839, arts 3(1)(f), 7, Schedule, para 14(1), (2)(o), as from 18 August 2010.
   Para 36: sub-para (2) amends the Superannuation Act 1972, Sch 1.
   Para 39: words in italics repealed by the Enterprise and Regulatory Reform Act 2013, s 64(3), (11)(a), as from 25 June 2013.

---

**PART 4**
**STATUS, &C**

*Status*

**[1.1396]**
**42.** (1)   The Commission shall not—
  (a)   be regarded as the servant or agent of the Crown, or
  (b)   enjoy any status, immunity or privilege of the Crown.
(2)   Service as Commissioner, Investigating Commissioner or employee of the Commission is not employment in the civil service of the State.
(3)   The [Secretary of State] shall have regard to the desirability of ensuring that the Commission is under as few constraints as reasonably possible in determining—
  (a)   its activities,
  (b)   its timetables, and
  (c)   its priorities.

*Supervision*

**43.**   . . .

*Disqualifications*

**44, 45.**   . . .

**46.** A Commissioner or Investigating Commissioner, and a member of a decision-making committee of the Commission, shall be disqualified from being a member of the National Assembly for Wales.

*Records*

**47, 48.**   . . .

**NOTES**

Para 42: words in square brackets substituted by the Transfer of Functions (Equality) Order 2010, SI 2010/1839, arts 3(1)(f), 7, Schedule, para 14(1), (2)(o), as from 18 August 2010.

Paras 43–45, 47, 48: amend the Parliamentary Commissioner Act 1967, Sch 2, the House of Commons Disqualification Act 1975, Sch 1, Pts II, III, the Northern Ireland Assembly Disqualification Act 1975, Sch 1, Pts II, III, the Public Records Act 1958, Sch 1, and the Freedom of Information Act 2000, Sch 1, Pt VI.

# PART 5
# DISABILITY COMMITTEE

*Establishment*

**[1.1397]**
**49.** (1)   The Commission shall establish a decision-making committee to be known as the Disability Committee.

(2)   The Commission shall ensure that the Disability Committee is established before either section 8 or section 10, in so far as they relate to disability, comes into force (to any extent).

*Membership*

**50.** (1)   The Commission shall ensure that—
   (a)   there are not less than 7 or more than 9 members of the Disability Committee,
   (b)   at least one half of the members are (or have been) disabled persons, and
   (c)   the Chairman is (or has been) a disabled person.

(2)   The Transition Commissioner nominated by the chairman of the Disability Rights Commission may not be a member of the Disability Committee.

**51.**   The appointment of each member of the Disability Committee shall be for a period of not less than two years or more than 5 years, subject to the possibilities of—
   (a)   reappointment,
   (b)   dismissal in accordance with the terms of appointment, and
   (c)   the lapsing of the appointment upon the dissolution of the Committee.

*Functions*

**52.** (1)   The Commission shall by virtue of this paragraph be treated as having delegated to the Disability Committee—
   (a)   the Commission's duty under section 8 in so far as it relates to disability matters and may be fulfilled by the exercise of the powers conferred by or referred to in—
         (i)     section 11,
         (ii)    section 13(1)(a), (c) or (d) (or paragraph (e) or (f) in so far as it relates to paragraph (a), (c) or (d)),
         (iii)   section 14,
         (iv)    section 15,
         *(v)    section 19, in so far as it relates to disability,*
         *(vi)   section 27,*
         (vii)   section 28, or
         (viii)  section 30,
   *(b)   the Commission's duty under section 10 in so far as it relates to disability and may be fulfilled by the exercise of those powers, and*
   (c)   those powers in so far as they are or may be exercised for the purpose of disability matters.

(2)   Delegation under this paragraph shall not prevent the exercise by the Commission of a power, or the fulfilment by the Commission of a duty, by action which relates partly to disability matters and partly to other matters.

(3)   In this paragraph "disability matters" means—

  (a)    matters provided for in [Parts 2, 3, 4, 6, 7, 12 and 13 of the Equality Act 2010, in so far as they relate to disability],

  *(b)    sections 8 and 10 above, in so far as they relate to disability, and*

  (c)    matters addressed in sections 14(3) and (4), *27(2) and (3)* and 28(2) and (3).

(4)    Before exercising a power to which paragraph 21(2) or 22(3) applies the Disability Committee shall consult the Scotland Committee.

(5)    Before exercising a power to which paragraph 29(2) or 30(3) applies the Disability Committee shall consult the Wales Committee.

**53.**  Before exercising a power or fulfilling a duty wholly or partly in relation to a matter affecting disabled persons (including, in particular, any matter provided for in [Part 5 of the Equality Act 2010]) the Commission shall consult the Disability Committee.

**54.**  The Disability Committee shall advise the Commission about the exercise of the Commission's functions in so far as they affect disabled persons (including, in particular, in so far as they relate to any matter provided for in [Part 5 of the Equality Act 2010]).

### Resources

**55.**  In allocating its resources the Commission shall ensure that the Disability Committee receives a share sufficient to enable it to exercise its functions.

### Report

**56.**  (1)  The Disability Committee shall for each financial year of the Commission submit to the Commission a report on the Committee's activities in that year.

(2)    The Commission shall incorporate each report of the Disability Committee under sub-paragraph (1) into the relevant annual report of the Commission.

### 5-year review

**57.**  The Commission shall arrange for a review of the activities of the Disability Committee to be conducted as soon as is reasonably practicable after the end of the period of five years beginning with the date of the commencement for all purposes of sections 8 and 10 in so far as they relate to disability.

**58.**  The following may not participate in the review (although those conducting the review may seek views from any of the following)—

  (a)    a Commissioner or former Commissioner,

  (b)    staff or former staff of the Commission,

  (c)    a person who is or has been an Investigating Commissioner, and

  (d)    a person who is or has been a member of a committee established by the Commission.

**59.**  The Commission shall ensure—

  (a)    that those conducting the review consult disabled persons and other persons whom they think likely to have an interest,

  (b)    that those conducting the review submit a report to the Commission which, in particular, recommends for how long the Disability Committee should continue in existence, and

  (c)    that the report is published.

**60.**  As soon as is reasonably practicable after receiving a report under paragraph 59 the Commission shall recommend to the [Secretary of State] for how long the Disability Committee should continue in existence.

**61.**  As soon as is reasonably practicable after receiving a recommendation under paragraph 60 the [Secretary of State] shall by order—

  (a)    dissolve the Disability Committee with effect from such time as shall be specified in the order, and

  (b)    repeal this Part of this Schedule with effect from that time.

**62.**  An order under paragraph 61 may include provision about—

  (a)    the conduct of the business of the Disability Committee before its dissolution;

  (b)    the conduct of the Commission after the dissolution of the Disability Committee in relation to functions formerly delegated to that committee.

**63.**  The dissolution of the Disability Committee is without prejudice to any power of the Commission under this Schedule—

  (a)    to establish a committee, or

  (b)    to delegate to a committee.

**64.**  The Disability Committee may not be dissolved under paragraph 14(c).

NOTES

Para 52: words in square brackets in sub-para (3)(a) substituted by the Equality Act 2010, s 211(1), Sch 26, paras 61, 84(1), (2), as from 1 October 2010; sub-paras (1)(a)(v), (vi), (b) are repealed, sub-para (3)(b) is substituted as follows, and words in italics in sub-para (3)(c) are repealed by the Enterprise and Regulatory Reform Act 2013, s 64(3), (11)(b)–(d), as from 25 June 2013:

"(b)    section 8, in so far as it relates to disability, and".

Paras 53, 54: words in square brackets substituted by the Equality Act 2010, s 211(1), Sch 26, paras 61, 84(1), (3), (4), as from 1 October 2010.

Paras 60, 61: words in square brackets substituted by the Transfer of Functions (Equality) Order 2010, SI 2010/1839, arts 3(1)(f), 7, Schedule, para 14(1), (2)(o), as from 18 August 2010.

Orders: as of 6 April 2013 no Orders had been made under this Part of this Schedule.

## SCHEDULE 2
## INQUIRIES, INVESTIGATIONS AND ASSESSMENTS

Sections 16, 20 and 31

*Introduction*

**[1.1398]**

**1.** This Schedule applies to—
(a)    inquiries under section 16,
(b)    investigations under section 20, and
(c)    assessments under section 31.

*Terms of reference*

**2.** Before conducting an inquiry the Commission shall—
(a)    publish the terms of reference of the inquiry in a manner that the Commission thinks is likely to bring the inquiry to the attention of persons whom it concerns or who are likely to be interested in it, and
(b)    in particular, give notice of the terms of reference to any persons specified in them.

**3.** Before conducting an investigation the Commission shall—
(a)    prepare terms of reference specifying the person to be investigated and the nature of the unlawful act which the Commission suspects,
(b)    give the person to be investigated notice of the proposed terms of reference,
(c)    give the person to be investigated an opportunity to make representations about the proposed terms of reference,
(d)    consider any representations made, and
(e)    publish the terms of reference once settled.

**4.** Before conducting an assessment of a person's compliance with a duty the Commission shall—
(a)    prepare terms of reference,
(b)    give the person notice of the proposed terms of reference,
(c)    give the person an opportunity to make representations about the proposed terms of reference,
(d)    consider any representations made, and
(e)    publish the terms of reference once settled.

**5.** Paragraphs 2 to 4 shall apply in relation to revised terms of reference as they apply in relation to original terms of reference.

*Representations*

**6.** (1)    The Commission shall make arrangements for giving persons an opportunity to make representations in relation to inquiries, investigations and assessments.

(2)    In particular, in the course of an investigation, inquiry or assessment the Commission must give any person specified in the terms of reference an opportunity to make representations.

**7.** Arrangements under paragraph 6 may (but need not) include arrangements for oral representations.

**8.** (1)    The Commission shall consider representations made in relation to an inquiry, investigation or assessment.

(2)    But the Commission may, where they think it appropriate, refuse to consider representations—
(a)    made neither by nor on behalf of a person specified in the terms of reference, or
(b)    made on behalf of a person specified in the terms of reference by a person who is not [a relevant lawyer].

[(2A)    "Relevant lawyer" means—
(a)    an advocate or solicitor in Scotland, or

(b) a person who, for the purposes of the Legal Services Act 2007, is an authorised person in relation to an activity which constitutes the exercise of a right of audience or the conduct of litigation (within the meaning of that Act).]

(3) If the Commission refuse to consider representations in reliance on sub-paragraph (2) they shall give the person who makes them written notice of the Commission's decision and the reasons for it.

*Evidence*

**9.** In the course of an inquiry, investigation or assessment the Commission may give a notice under this paragraph to any person.

**10.** (1) A notice given to a person under paragraph 9 may require him—
(a) to provide information in his possession,
(b) to produce documents in his possession, or
(c) to give oral evidence.

(2) A notice under paragraph 9 may include provision about—
(a) the form of information, documents or evidence;
(b) timing.

(3) A notice under paragraph 9—
(a) may not require a person to provide information that he is prohibited from disclosing by virtue of an enactment,
(b) may not require a person to do anything that he could not be compelled to do in proceedings before the High Court or the Court of Session, and
(c) may not require a person to attend at a place unless the Commission undertakes to pay the expenses of his journey.

**11.** The recipient of a notice under paragraph 9 may apply to *a county court* (in England and Wales) or to the sheriff (in Scotland) to have the notice cancelled on the grounds that the requirement imposed by the notice is—
(a) unnecessary having regard to the purpose of the inquiry, investigation or assessment to which the notice relates, or
(b) otherwise unreasonable.

**12.** (1) Sub-paragraph (2) applies where the Commission thinks that a person—
(a) has failed without reasonable excuse to comply with a notice under paragraph 9, or
(b) is likely to fail without reasonable excuse to comply with a notice under paragraph 9.

(2) The Commission may apply to *a county court* (in England and Wales) or to the sheriff (in Scotland) for an order requiring a person to take such steps as may be specified in the order to comply with the notice.

**13.** (1) A person commits an offence if without reasonable excuse he—
(a) fails to comply with a notice under paragraph 9 or an order under paragraph 12(2),
(b) falsifies anything provided or produced in accordance with a notice under paragraph 9 or an order under paragraph 12(2), or
(c) makes a false statement in giving oral evidence in accordance with a notice under paragraph 9.

(2) A person who is guilty of an offence under this paragraph shall be liable on summary conviction to a fine not exceeding level 5 on the standard scale.

**14.** (1) Where a person is given a notice under paragraph 9 he shall disregard it, and notify the Commission that he is disregarding it, in so far as he thinks it would require him—
(a) to disclose sensitive information within the meaning of *paragraph 4 of Schedule 3 to the Intelligence Services Act 1994 (c 13)* (Intelligence and Security Committee [of Parliament]),
(b) to disclose information which might lead to the identification of an employee or agent of an intelligence service (other than one whose identity is already known to the Commission),
(c) to disclose information which might provide details of processes used in recruiting, selecting or training employees or agents of an intelligence service,
(d) to disclose information which might provide details of, or cannot practicably be separated from, information falling within any of paragraphs (a) to (c), or
(e) to make a disclosure of information relating to an intelligence service which would prejudice the interests of national security.

(2) In sub-paragraph (1) "intelligence service" means—
(a) the Security Service,
(b) the Secret Intelligence Service, and
(c) the Government Communications Headquarters.

(3)   Where in response to a notice under paragraph 9 a person gives a notice to the Commission under sub-paragraph (1) above—

(a)   paragraphs 12 and 13 shall not apply in relation to that part of the notice under paragraph 9 to which the notice under sub-paragraph (1) above relates,

(b)   the Commission may apply to the tribunal established by section 65 of the Regulation of Investigatory Powers Act 2000 (c 23) for an order requiring the person to take such steps as may be specified in the order to comply with the notice,

(c)   the following provisions of that Act shall apply in relation to proceedings under this paragraph as they apply in relation to proceedings under that Act (with any necessary modifications)—

(i)   section 67(7), (8) and (10) to (12) (determination),

(ii)   section 68 (procedure), and

(iii)   section 69 (rules), and

(d)   the tribunal shall determine proceedings under this paragraph by considering the opinion of the person who gave the notice under sub-paragraph (1) above in accordance with the principles that would be applied by a court on an application for judicial review of the giving of the notice.

(4)   Where the Commission receives information or documents from or relating to an intelligence service in response to a notice under paragraph 9, the Commission shall store and use the information or documents in accordance with any arrangements specified by the Secretary of State.

(5)   The recipient of a notice under paragraph 9 may apply to the High Court (in England and Wales) or the Court of Session (in Scotland) to have the notice cancelled on the grounds that the requirement imposed by the notice is undesirable for reasons of national security, other than for the reason that it would require a disclosure of a kind to which sub-paragraph (1) above applies.

### Reports

**15.** The Commission shall publish a report of its findings on an inquiry, investigation or assessment.

### Recommendations

**16.**   (1)   The Commission may make recommendations—

(a)   as part of a report of an inquiry, investigation or assessment under paragraph 15, or

(b)   in respect of a matter arising in the course of an inquiry, investigation or assessment.

(2)   A recommendation may be addressed to any class of person.

### Effect of report

**17.**   (1)   A court or tribunal—

(a)   may have regard to a finding of the report of an inquiry, investigation or assessment, but

(b)   shall not treat it as conclusive.

**18.**   A person to whom a recommendation in the report of an inquiry, investigation or assessment is addressed shall have regard to it.

### Courts and tribunals

**19.**   An inquiry, investigation or assessment may not question (whether expressly or by necessary implication) the findings of a court or tribunal.

### Intelligence services

**20.**   (1)   An inquiry may not consider—

(a)   whether an intelligence service has acted (or is acting) in a way which is incompatible with a person's human rights, or

(b)   other matters concerning human rights in relation to an intelligence service.

(2)   In this paragraph "intelligence service" has the same meaning as in paragraph 14.

**NOTES**

Para 8: words in square brackets in sub-para (2)(b) substituted, and sub-para (2A) added, by the Legal Services Act 2007, s 208(1), Sch 21, para 152, as from 1 January 2010.

Paras 11, 12: for the words in italics there are substituted the words "the county court" by the Crime and Courts Act 2013, s 17(5), Sch 9, Pt 3, para 52, as from a day to be appointed.

Para 14: for the words in italics there are substituted the words "paragraph 5 of Schedule 1 to the Justice and Security Act 2013" and words in square brackets inserted, by the Justice and Security Act 2013, s 19(1), Sch 2, Pt 1, para 6, as from a day to be appointed.

## SCHEDULES 3 AND 4

*(Sch 3 (Amendments Consequential on Part 1) and Sch 4 (Repeals) contains various amendments and repeals; in so far as these are still in force and relevant to this Handbook, they have been incorporated at the appropriate place.)*

# IMMIGRATION, ASYLUM AND NATIONALITY ACT 2006

(2006 c 13)

### ARRANGEMENT OF SECTIONS

*Employment*

*An Act to make provision about immigration, asylum and nationality; and for connected purposes*

[30 March 2006]

### NOTES

Only those provisions of this Act relevant to employment law are reproduced. Provisions not reproduced are not annotated. The provisions reproduced here extend to the whole of the United Kingdom (s 63).

See *Harvey* AI(5).

*Employment*

**[1.1399]**

**15  Penalty**

(1)   It is contrary to this section to employ an adult subject to immigration control if—
   (a)   he has not been granted leave to enter or remain in the United Kingdom, or
   (b)   his leave to enter or remain in the United Kingdom—
      (i)   is invalid,
      (ii)   has ceased to have effect (whether by reason of curtailment, revocation, cancellation, passage of time or otherwise), or
      (iii)   is subject to a condition preventing him from accepting the employment.
(2)   The Secretary of State may give an employer who acts contrary to this section a notice requiring him to pay a penalty of a specified amount not exceeding the prescribed maximum.
(3)   An employer is excused from paying a penalty if he shows that he complied with any prescribed requirements in relation to the employment.
(4)   But the excuse in subsection (3) shall not apply to an employer who knew, at any time during the period of the employment, that it was contrary to this section.
(5)   The Secretary of State may give a penalty notice without having established whether subsection (3) applies.
(6)   A penalty notice must—
   (a)   state why the Secretary of State thinks the employer is liable to the penalty,
   (b)   state the amount of the penalty,
   (c)   specify a date, at least 28 days after the date specified in the notice as the date on which it is given, before which the penalty must be paid,
   (d)   specify how the penalty must be paid,
   (e)   explain how the employer may object to the penalty, and
   (f)   explain how the Secretary of State may enforce the penalty.
(7)   An order prescribing requirements for the purposes of subsection (3) may, in particular—
   (a)   require the production to an employer of a document of a specified description;

    (b)    require the production to an employer of one document of each of a number of specified descriptions;

    (c)    require an employer to take specified steps to verify, retain, copy or record the content of a document produced to him in accordance with the order;

    (d)    require action to be taken before employment begins;

    (e)    require action to be taken at specified intervals or on specified occasions during the course of employment.

**NOTES**

Orders: the Immigration (Restrictions on Employment) Order 2007, SI 2007/3290 at **[2.1122]**; the Immigration (Employment of Adults Subject to Immigration Control) (Maximum Penalty) Order 2008, SI 2008/132 at **[2.1135]**; the Immigration (Restrictions on Employment) (Amendment) Order 2009, SI 2009/2908.

**[1.1400]**
## 16 Objection
(1)    This section applies where an employer to whom a penalty notice is given objects on the ground that—

    (a)    he is not liable to the imposition of a penalty,

    (b)    he is excused payment by virtue of section 15(3), or

    (c)    the amount of the penalty is too high.

(2)    The employer may give a notice of objection to the Secretary of State.

(3)    A notice of objection must—

    (a)    be in writing,

    (b)    give the objector's reasons,

    (c)    be given in the prescribed manner, and

    (d)    be given before the end of the prescribed period.

(4)    Where the Secretary of State receives a notice of objection to a penalty he shall consider it and—

    (a)    cancel the penalty,

    (b)    reduce the penalty,

    (c)    increase the penalty, or

    (d)    determine to take no action.

(5)    Where the Secretary of State considers a notice of objection he shall—

    (a)    have regard to the code of practice under section 19 (in so far as the objection relates to the amount of the penalty),

    (b)    inform the objector of his decision before the end of the prescribed period or such longer period as he may agree with the objector,

    (c)    if he increases the penalty, issue a new penalty notice under section 15, and

    (d)    if he reduces the penalty, notify the objector of the reduced amount.

**NOTES**

Orders: the Immigration (Restrictions on Employment) Order 2007, SI 2007/3290 at **[2.1122]**.

**[1.1401]**
## 17 Appeal
(1)    An employer to whom a penalty notice is given may appeal to the court on the ground that—

    (a)    he is not liable to the imposition of a penalty,

    (b)    he is excused payment by virtue of section 15(3), or

    (c)    the amount of the penalty is too high.

(2)    The court may—

    (a)    allow the appeal and cancel the penalty,

    (b)    allow the appeal and reduce the penalty, or

    (c)    dismiss the appeal.

(3)    An appeal shall be a re-hearing of the Secretary of State's decision to impose a penalty and shall be determined having regard to—

    (a)    the code of practice under section 19 that has effect at the time of the appeal (in so far as the appeal relates to the amount of the penalty), and

    (b)    any other matters which the court thinks relevant (which may include matters of which the Secretary of State was unaware);

and this subsection has effect despite any provision of rules of court.

(4)    An appeal must be brought within the period of 28 days beginning with—

    (a)    the date specified in the penalty notice as the date upon which it is given, or

    (b)    if the employer gives a notice of objection and the Secretary of State reduces the penalty, the date specified in the notice of reduction as the date upon which it is given, or

    (c)    if the employer gives a notice of objection and the Secretary of State determines to take no action, the date specified in the notice of that determination as the date upon which it is given.

(5)    An appeal may be brought by an employer whether or not—

(a)   he has given a notice of objection under section 16;
(b)   the penalty has been increased or reduced under that section.
(6)   In this section "the court" means—
   (a)   where the employer has his principal place of business in England and Wales, *a county court*,
   (b)   where the employer has his principal place of business in Scotland, the sheriff, and
   (c)   where the employer has his principal place of business in Northern Ireland, a county court.

**NOTES**
   Sub-s (6): for the words in italics in para (a) there are substituted the words "the county court" by the Crime and Courts Act 2013, s 17(5), Sch 9, Pt 3, para 52, as from a day to be appointed.

**[1.1402]**
**18   Enforcement**
(1)   A sum payable to the Secretary of State as a penalty under section 15 may be recovered by the Secretary of State as a debt due to him.
(2)   In proceedings for the enforcement of a penalty no question may be raised as to—
   (a)   liability to the imposition of the penalty,
   (b)   the application of the excuse in section 15(3), or
   (c)   the amount of the penalty.
(3)   Money paid to the Secretary of State by way of penalty shall be paid into the Consolidated Fund.

**[1.1403]**
**19   Code of practice**
(1)   The Secretary of State shall issue a code of practice specifying factors to be considered by him in determining the amount of a penalty imposed under section 15.
(2)   The code—
   (a)   shall not be issued unless a draft has been laid before Parliament, and
   (b)   shall come into force in accordance with provision made by order of the Secretary of State.
(3)   The Secretary of State shall from time to time review the code and may revise and re-issue it following a review; and a reference in this section to the code includes a reference to the code as revised.

**NOTES**
   Orders: the Immigration (Restrictions on Employment) Order 2007, SI 2007/3290 at **[2.1122]**.
   Code of practice: see the Border & Immigration Agency Code of Practice: Civil Penalties for Employers (2008) at **[4.107]**.

**[1.1404]**
**20   Orders**
(1)   An order of the Secretary of State under section 15, 16 or 19—
   (a)   may make provision which applies generally or only in specified circumstances,
   (b)   may make different provision for different circumstances,
   (c)   may include transitional or incidental provision, and
   (d)   shall be made by statutory instrument.
(2)   An order under section 15(2) may not be made unless a draft has been laid before and approved by resolution of each House of Parliament.
(3)   Any other order shall be subject to annulment in pursuance of a resolution of either House of Parliament.

**[1.1405]**
**21   Offence**
(1)   A person commits an offence if he employs another ("the employee") knowing that the employee is an adult subject to immigration control and that—
   (a)   he has not been granted leave to enter or remain in the United Kingdom, or
   (b)   his leave to enter or remain in the United Kingdom—
      (i)    is invalid,
      (ii)   has ceased to have effect (whether by reason of curtailment, revocation, cancellation, passage of time or otherwise), or
      (iii)  is subject to a condition preventing him from accepting the employment.
(2)   A person guilty of an offence under this section shall be liable—
   (a)   on conviction on indictment—
      (i)    to imprisonment for a term not exceeding two years,
      (ii)   to a fine, or
      (iii)  to both, or
   (b)   on summary conviction—
      (i)    to imprisonment for a term not exceeding 12 months in England and Wales or 6 months in Scotland or Northern Ireland,

      (ii)   to a fine not exceeding the statutory maximum, or

      (iii)  to both.

(3)   An offence under this section shall be treated as—

   (a)   a relevant offence for the purpose of sections 28B and 28D of the Immigration Act 1971 (c 77) (search, entry and arrest), and

   (b)   an offence under Part III of that Act (criminal proceedings) for the purposes of sections 28E, 28G and 28H (search after arrest).

(4)   In relation to a conviction occurring before the commencement of section 154(1) of the Criminal Justice Act 2003 (c 44) (general limit on magistrates' powers to imprison) the reference to 12 months in subsection (2)(b)(i) shall be taken as a reference to 6 months.

**[1.1406]**

## 22  Offence: bodies corporate, &c

(1)   For the purposes of section 21(1) a body (whether corporate or not) shall be treated as knowing a fact about an employee if a person who has responsibility within the body for an aspect of the employment knows the fact.

(2)   If an offence under section 21(1) is committed by a body corporate with the consent or connivance of an officer of the body, the officer, as well as the body, shall be treated as having committed the offence.

(3)   In subsection (2) a reference to an officer of a body includes a reference to—

   (a)   a director, manager or secretary,

   (b)   a person purporting to act as a director, manager or secretary, and

   (c)   if the affairs of the body are managed by its members, a member.

(4)   Where an offence under section 21(1) is committed by a partnership (whether or not a limited partnership) subsection (2) above shall have effect, but as if a reference to an officer of the body were a reference to—

   (a)   a partner, and

   (b)   a person purporting to act as a partner.

**[1.1407]**

## 23  Discrimination: code of practice

(1)   The Secretary of State shall issue a code of practice specifying what an employer should or should not do in order to ensure that, while avoiding liability to a penalty under section 15 and while avoiding the commission of an offence under section 21, he also avoids contravening—

   (a)   [the Equality Act 2010, so far as relating to race], or

   (b)   the Race Relations (Northern Ireland) Order 1997 (SI 869 (NI 6)).

(2)   Before issuing the code the Secretary of State shall—

   (a)   consult—

      (i)   the Commission for Equality and Human Rights,

      (ii)  the Equality Commission for Northern Ireland,

      (iii)  such bodies representing employers as he thinks appropriate, and

      (iv)  such bodies representing workers as he thinks appropriate,

   (b)   publish a draft code (after that consultation),

   (c)   consider any representations made about the published draft, and

   (d)   lay a draft code before Parliament (after considering representations under paragraph (c) and with or without modifications to reflect the representations).

(3)   The code shall come into force in accordance with provision made by order of the Secretary of State; and an order—

   (a)   may include transitional provision,

   (b)   shall be made by statutory instrument, and

   (c)   shall be subject to annulment in pursuance of a resolution of either House of Parliament.

(4)   A breach of the code—

   (a)   shall not make a person liable to civil or criminal proceedings, but

   (b)   may be taken into account by a court or tribunal.

(5)   The Secretary of State shall from time to time review the code and may revise and re-issue it following a review; and a reference in this section to the code includes a reference to the code as revised.

(6)   Until the dissolution of the Commission for Racial Equality, the reference in subsection (2)(a)(i) to the Commission for Equality and Human Rights shall be treated as a reference to the Commission for Racial Equality.

---

**NOTES**

  Sub-s (1): words in square brackets in para (a) substituted by the Equality Act 2010, s 211(1), Sch 26, Pt 1, para 86, as from 1 October 2010.

  Code of practice: see the Border & Immigration Agency Code of Practice: Guidance for Employers on the Avoidance of Unlawful Discrimination in Employment Practice while Seeking to Prevent Illegal Working (2008) at **[4.114]**.

**[1.1408]**
**24 Temporary admission, &c**
Where a person is at large in the United Kingdom by virtue of paragraph 21(1) of Schedule 2 to the Immigration Act 1971 (c 77) (temporary admission or release from detention)—
(a) he shall be treated for the purposes of sections 15(1) and 21(1) as if he had been granted leave to enter the United Kingdom, and
(b) any restriction as to employment imposed under paragraph 21(2) shall be treated for those purposes as a condition of leave.

**[1.1409]**
**25 Interpretation**
In sections 15 to 24—
(a) "adult" means a person who has attained the age of 16,
(b) a reference to employment is to employment under a contract of service or apprenticeship, whether express or implied and whether oral or written,
(c) a person is subject to immigration control if under the Immigration Act 1971 he requires leave to enter or remain in the United Kingdom, and
(d) "prescribed" means prescribed by order of the Secretary of State.

**[1.1410]**
**26 Repeal**
Sections 8 and 8A of the Asylum and Immigration Act 1996 (c 49) (restrictions on employment) shall cease to have effect.

# WORK AND FAMILIES ACT 2006

## (2006 c 18)

### ARRANGEMENT OF SECTIONS

*Leave and pay related to birth or adoption: further amendments*

*An Act to make provision about statutory rights to leave and pay in connection with the birth or adoption of children; to amend section 80F of the Employment Rights Act 1996; to make provision about workers' entitlement to annual leave; to provide for the increase in the sums specified in section 186(1) and 227(1) of that Act; and for connected purposes*

[21 June 2006]

**NOTES**
See *Harvey* CI(1), H(2).

**1–10** *(S 1 amends the Social Security Contributions and Benefits Act 1992, s 165 at* **[1.202]***; s 2 amends s 171ZN of the 1992 Act at* **[1.227]***; ss 3, 4 add the Employment Rights Act 1996, ss 80AA, 80BB, at* **[1.876]**, **[1.878]***; s 5 amends s 80C of the 1996 Act at* **[1.879]***; ss 6–10 add ss 171ZEA–171ZEE of the 1992 Act at* **[1.214]–[1.218]**.*)*

*Leave and pay related to birth or adoption: further amendments*

**[1.1411]**
**11 Leave and pay related to birth or adoption: further amendments**
(1) Schedule 1 (which contains further amendments relating to statutory leave and pay) has effect.
(2) Any reference to statutory paternity pay in any instrument or document made before the commencement of paragraphs 12 and 13 of Schedule 1 is to be read, in relation to any time after that commencement, as a reference to ordinary statutory paternity pay.

(3)   Any reference to ordinary statutory paternity pay in any enactment (including this Act and any enactment amended by this Act) or any instrument or document is to be read, in relation to any time before the commencement of paragraphs 12 and 13 of Schedule 1, as a reference to statutory paternity pay.

**NOTES**

Commencement: 27 June 2006 (specified paragraphs of Sch 1 (see SI 2006/1682)); 1 October 2006 (specified paragraphs of Sch 1 (see SI 2006/1682 and SI 2006/2232)); 3 March 2010 (specified paragraphs of Sch 1 (see SI 2010/495)); 6 April 2010 (otherwise).

*Miscellaneous provisions about employment rights*

**12**   *(Amends the Employment Rights Act 1996, s 80F at* **[1.882]**.*)*

**[1.1412]**
**13   Annual leave**
(1)   The Secretary of State may by regulations make provision conferring on workers the right, except in prescribed cases, to a prescribed amount of annual leave in each leave year, as defined for the purposes of the regulations.
(2)   The regulations may in particular—
  (a)   make provision for determining the amount of annual leave to which workers are to be entitled;
  (b)   make provision for determining the amount of pay in respect of any period of leave which is required by the regulations to be paid leave;
  (c)   make provision enabling a worker to elect when to take leave to which he is entitled by virtue of the regulations, subject to any provision of the regulations enabling his employer to require him to take, or not to take, that leave at a particular time;
  (d)   make provision for the payment of compensation in prescribed cases to a worker who has not taken leave to which he is entitled;
  (e)   make provision as to the relationship between the rights conferred by the regulations and a worker's rights to leave, pay or compensation under any contract or under any Act or subordinate legislation;
  (f)   enable a worker to present a complaint to an employment tribunal that his employer has refused to permit him to exercise any right he has under the regulations, or has failed to pay him any amount due to him under the regulations;
  (g)   make, in connection with any right conferred by the regulations (including any right to payment), any other provision which is the same as or similar to any provision made, in connection with any right relating to annual leave conferred in pursuance of any [EU] obligation, by any regulations under section 2(2) of the 1972 Act made at any time before the day on which the first regulations under this section are made.
(3)   Regulations under this section may make provision as to—
  (a)   who is to be treated as a worker for the purposes of the regulations, and
  (b)   who is to be treated as the worker's employer.
(4)   Regulations under this section may in particular—
  (a)   make provision applying to—
     (i)   Crown employment and persons in Crown employment;
     (ii)   service as a member of the armed forces;
  (b)   make provision conferring rights to and in connection with annual leave on persons falling within any other categories of persons on whom any [EU] obligation of the United Kingdom requires a right to annual leave to be conferred.
(5)   Regulations under this section may not make provision in relation to the subject-matter of the Agricultural Wages (Scotland) Act 1949 (c 30) (as that Act had effect on 1st July 1999).
(6)   Regulations under this section—
  (a)   are to be made by statutory instrument;
  (b)   may make different provision for different cases;
  (c)   may contain incidental, supplemental, consequential, transitional or saving provision, including provision amending any Act or subordinate legislation.
(7)   No statutory instrument containing regulations under this section may be made unless a draft of the instrument has been laid before, and approved by a resolution of, each House of Parliament.
(8)   In this section—
  "the 1972 Act" means the European Communities Act 1972 (c 68);
  "the armed forces" means any of the naval, military or air forces of the Crown;
  "Crown employment" has the meaning given by section 191(3) of ERA 1996;
  "subordinate legislation" has the same meaning as in the Interpretation Act 1978 (c 30).

**NOTES**

Sub-s (2): reference in square brackets in para (g) substituted by the Treaty of Lisbon (Changes in Terminology) Order 2011, SI 2011/1043, art 6(1)(e), as from 22 April 2011.

Sub-s (4): reference in square brackets in para (b) substituted by SI 2011/1043, art 6(1)(e), as from 22 April 2011.

Regulations: the Working Time (Amendment) Regulations 2007, SI 2007/2079 amending the Working Time Regulations 1998, SI 1998/1833 at **[2.269]**.

**[1.1413]**

**14 Increase of maximum amount of a week's pay for certain purposes**

(1)   This section applies to the sums specified in the following provisions—

(a)   section 186(1)(a) and (b) of ERA 1996 (employee's rights on insolvency of employer: maximum amount payable);

(b)   section 227(1) of ERA 1996 (maximum amount of a week's pay for the purposes of certain provisions of the Act relating to awards of compensation and redundancy payments).

(2)   The Secretary of State may, on one occasion only, by order substitute for each of the sums mentioned in subsection (1) such higher sum as may be specified in the order.

(3)   An order under this section—

(a)   is to be made by statutory instrument;

(b)   may include transitional provision;

(c)   may exclude, on a single occasion specified in the order under this section, any duty to make an order under section 34 of the 1999 Act (indexation of certain amounts, &c), so far as relating to the sums mentioned in subsection (1).

(4)   Subject to any provision made under subsection (3)(c), this section does not affect the operation of section 34 of the 1999 Act in relation to the sums substituted by the order under this section in the provisions mentioned in subsection (1).

(5)   No statutory instrument containing an order under this section may be made unless a draft of the instrument has been laid before, and approved by a resolution of, each House of Parliament.

(6)   In this section "the 1999 Act" means the Employment Relations Act 1999 (c 26).

**NOTES**

Orders: the Work and Families (Increase of Maximum Amount) Order 2009, SI 2009/1903 was made under this section and increased the sums specified in the Employments Rights Act 1996, ss 186(1)(a), (b) and 227(1). It has effectively been superseded by the Employment Rights (Increase of Limits) Order 2010, SI 2010/2926 (revoked), the Employment Rights (Increase of Limits) Order 2011, SI 2011/3006 (revoked) and the Employment Rights (Increase of Limits) Order 2012, SI 2012/3007.

*Supplementary*

**15**   *(Introduces Sch 2 (repeals).)*

**[1.1414]**

**16   Interpretation**

In this Act—

"ERA 1996" means the Employment Rights Act 1996 (c 18);

"SSCBA 1992" means the Social Security Contributions and Benefits Act 1992 (c 4).

**17**   *((Corresponding provision for Northern Ireland) outside the scope of this work.)*

**[1.1415]**

**18   Financial provisions**

(1)   There shall be paid out of money provided by Parliament—

(a)   any expenses incurred by a Minister of the Crown or government department under this Act, and

(b)   any increase attributable to this Act in the sums which under any other Act are payable out of money so provided.

(2)   There shall be paid into the Consolidated Fund any increase attributable to this Act in the sums payable into that Fund under any other Act.

**[1.1416]**

**19   Commencement**

(1)   Sections 16 to 18, this section and section 20 come into force on the day on which this Act is passed.

(2)   The other provisions of this Act come into force in accordance with provision made by the Secretary of State by order made by statutory instrument.

(3)   An order under this section—

(a)   may make different provision for different purposes;

(b)   may include supplementary, incidental, saving or transitional provisions.

**NOTES**

Orders: the Work and Families Act 2006 (Commencement No 1) Order 2006, SI 2006/1682; the Work and Families Act 2006 (Commencement No 2) Order 2006, SI 2006/2232; the Work and Families Act 2006 (Commencement No 4) Order 2010, SI 2010/495.

**[1.1417]**
**20 Short title and extent**
(1) This Act may be cited as the Work and Families Act 2006.
(2) Subject to subsection (3), this Act extends to England and Wales and Scotland only.
(3) The following provisions extend also to Northern Ireland—
  (a) this section and sections 17 to 19;
  (b) paragraphs 2, 45, 49, and 55 to 61 of Schedule 1, and section 11 so far as relating to those paragraphs;
  (c) the entry in Schedule 2 relating to the Income Tax (Earnings and Pensions) Act 2003 (c 1), and section 15 so far as relating to that entry.

## SCHEDULE 1 AND 2

*(Sch 1 (Leave and pay related to birth or adoptions: further amendments) contains various consequential amendments to the Social Security Act 1989, the Finance Act 1989, the Social Security Contributions and Benefits Act 1992, the Social Security Administration Act 1992, the Employment Rights Act 1996, the Finance Act 1997, the Social Security Contributions (Transfer of Functions, etc) Act 1999, the Finance Act 1999, the Employment Act 2002, the Proceeds of Crime Act 2002, the Income Tax (Earnings and Pensions) Act 2003, and the Commissioners for Revenue and Customs Act 2005; in so far as relevant to this work, these have been incorporated at the appropriate place. Sch 2 repeals certain provisions in the Social Security Contributions and Benefits Act 1992, the Employment Rights Act 1996, the Employment Act 2002, and the Income Tax (Earnings and Pensions) Act 2003 (incorporated as appropriate).)*

# COMPENSATION ACT 2006

## (2006 c 29)

### ARRANGEMENT OF SECTIONS

#### PART 1
#### STANDARD OF CARE

#### PART 2
#### CLAIMS MANAGEMENT SERVICES

#### PART 3
#### GENERAL

*An Act to specify certain factors that may be taken into account by a court determining a claim in negligence or breach of statutory duty; to make provision about damages for mesothelioma; and to make provision for the regulation of claims management services*

[25 July 2006]

**NOTES**
  This Act (apart from s 3 (not reproduced) and s 16(3), (6) does not extend to Scotland).

# PART 1
## STANDARD OF CARE

**[1.1419]**
**1    Deterrent effect of potential liability**
A court considering a claim in negligence or breach of statutory duty may, in determining whether the defendant should have taken particular steps to meet a standard of care (whether by taking precautions against a risk or otherwise), have regard to whether a requirement to take those steps might—
   (a)    prevent a desirable activity from being undertaken at all, to a particular extent or in a particular way, or
   (b)    discourage persons from undertaking functions in connection with a desirable activity.

**[1.1420]**
**2    Apologies, offers of treatment or other redress**
An apology, an offer of treatment or other redress, shall not of itself amount to an admission of negligence or breach of statutory duty.

**3**    ((*Mesothelioma: damages) outside the scope of this work.*)

# PART 2
## CLAIMS MANAGEMENT SERVICES

**[1.1421]**
**4    Provision of regulated claims management services**
(1)    A person may not provide regulated claims management services unless—
   (a)    he is an authorised person,
   (b)    he is an exempt person,
   (c)    the requirement for authorisation has been waived in relation to him in accordance with regulations under section 9, or
   (d)    he is an individual acting otherwise than in the course of a business.
(2)    In this Part—
   (a)    "authorised person" means a person authorised by the Regulator under section 5(1)(a),
   (b)    "claims management services" means advice or other services in relation to the making of a claim,
   (c)    "claim" means a claim for compensation, restitution, repayment or any other remedy or relief in respect of loss or damage or in respect of an obligation, whether the claim is made or could be made—
      (i)    by way of legal proceedings,
      (ii)    in accordance with a scheme of regulation (whether voluntary or compulsory), or
      (iii)    in pursuance of a voluntary undertaking,
   (d)    "exempt person" has the meaning given by section 6(5), and
   (e)    services are regulated if they are—
      (i)    of a kind prescribed by order of the Secretary of State, or
      (ii)    provided in cases or circumstances of a kind prescribed by order of the Secretary of State.
[(2A)    The Secretary of State may not make an order under subsection (2)(e) unless—
   (a)    it is made in accordance with a recommendation made by the Legal Services Board, or
   (b)    the Secretary of State has consulted the Legal Services Board about the making of the order.]
(3)    For the purposes of this section—
   (a)    a reference to the provision of services includes, in particular, a reference to—
      (i)    the provision of financial services or assistance,
      (ii)    the provision of services by way of or in relation to legal representation,
      (iii)    referring or introducing one person to another, and
      (iv)    making inquiries, and
   (b)    a person does not provide claims management services by reason only of giving, or preparing to give, evidence (whether or not expert evidence).
(4)    For the purposes of subsection (1)(d) an individual acts in the course of a business if, in particular—
   (a)    he acts in the course of an employment, or
   (b)    he otherwise receives or hopes to receive money or money's worth as a result of his action.
(5)    The Secretary of State may by order provide that a claim for a specified benefit shall be treated as a claim for the purposes of this Part.
(6)    The Secretary of State may specify a benefit under subsection (5) only if it appears to him to be a United Kingdom social security benefit designed to provide compensation for industrial injury.

**NOTES**
Sub-s (2A): inserted by the Legal Services Act 2007, s 187, Sch 19, paras 1, 2, as from a day to be appointed.

Orders: the Compensation (Regulated Claims Management Services) Order 2006, SI 2006/3319 at **[2.1061]**; the Compensation (Specification of Benefits) Order 2006, SI 2006/3321.

## [1.1422]
## 5   The Regulator

(1)   The Secretary of State may by order designate a person ("the Regulator")—
  (a)   to authorise persons to provide regulated claims management services,
  (b)   to regulate the conduct of authorised persons, and
  (c)   to exercise such other functions as are conferred on the Regulator by or under this Part.

[(1A)   The Secretary of State may designate a person only on the recommendation of the Legal Services Board.]

(2)   *The Secretary of State may designate a person* only if satisfied that the person—
  (a)   is competent to perform the functions of the Regulator,
  (b)   will make arrangements to avoid any conflict of interest between the person's functions as Regulator and any other functions, and
  (c)   will promote the interests of persons using regulated claims management services (including, in particular, by—
    (i)    setting and monitoring standards of competence and professional conduct for persons providing regulated claims management services,
    (ii)   promoting good practice by persons providing regulated claims management services, in particular in relation to the provision of information about charges and other matters to persons using or considering using the services,
    (iii)  promoting practices likely to facilitate competition between different providers of regulated claims management services, and
    (iv)   ensuring that arrangements are made for the protection of persons using regulated claims management services (including arrangements for the handling of complaints about the conduct of authorised persons)).

(3)   . . .
(4)   The Regulator shall—
  (a)   comply with any directions given to him by the *Secretary of State*;
  (b)   have regard to any guidance given to him by the *Secretary of State*;
  (c)   . . .
  (d)   try to meet any targets set for him by the *Secretary of State*;
  (e)   provide the *Secretary of State* with any report or information requested (but this paragraph does not require or permit disclosure of information in contravention of any other enactment).

(5)   . . .
(6)   The Secretary of State may pay grants to the Regulator (which may be on terms or conditions, including terms and conditions as to repayment with or without interest).
(7)   A reference in this Part to the Regulator includes a reference to a person acting on behalf of the Regulator or with his authority.
(8)   The Secretary of State may[, on the recommendation of the Legal Services Board,] by order revoke a person's designation under subsection (1).
(9)   While no person is designated under subsection (1) the *Secretary of State* shall exercise functions of the Regulator.
(10)   The Secretary of State may[, on the recommendation of the Legal Services Board,] by order transfer (whether for a period of time specified in the order or otherwise) a function of the Regulator to the *Secretary of State*.
[(11)   In discharging any function by virtue of subsection (9) or (10), the Legal Services Board must take such steps as are necessary to ensure an appropriate financial and organisational separation between the activities of the Board that relate to the carrying out of those functions and the other activities of the Board.]

### NOTES

Sub-s (1A): inserted by the Legal Services Act 2007, s 187, Sch 19, paras 1, 3(1), (2), as from a day to be appointed.

Sub-s (2): for the words in italics there are substituted the words "The Legal Services Board may recommend a person for designation" by the Legal Services Act 2007, s 187, Sch 19, paras 1, 3(1), (3), as from a day to be appointed.

Sub-s (3): repealed by the Legal Services Act 2007, ss 187, 210, Sch 19, paras 1, 3(1), (4), Sch 23, as from 1 January 2010 (see further the final note below).

Sub-s (4): for the words "Secretary of State" in italics in paras (a), (b), (d), (e) there are substituted the words "Legal Services Board", and para (c) is repealed, by the Legal Services Act 2007, ss 187, 210, Sch 19, paras 1, 3(1), (5), Sch 23, as from a day to be appointed (in the case of the amendments to paras (a), (b), (d), (e)), and as from 1 January 2010 (in the case of the repeal of para (c); see further the final note below).

Sub-s (5): repealed by the Legal Services Act 2007, s 210, Sch 23, as from 1 January 2010.

Sub-s (8): words in square brackets inserted by the Legal Services Act 2007, s 187, Sch 19, paras 1, 3(1), (6), as from a day to be appointed.

Sub-s (9): for the words in italics there are substituted the words "Legal Services Board" by the Legal Services Act 2007, s 187, Sch 19, paras 1, 3(1), (7), as from a day to be appointed.

Sub-s (10): words in square brackets inserted, and for the words in italics there are substituted the words "Legal Services Board", by the Legal Services Act 2007, s 187, Sch 19, paras 1, 3(1), (8), as from a day to be appointed.

Sub-s (11): added by the Legal Services Act 2007, s 187, Sch 19, paras 1, 3(1), (9), as from a day to be appointed.

Note that Sch 19, para 3 to the 2007 Act is not (as at 6 April 2013) in force. However, the repeals of sub-ss (3), (4)(c) (but not sub-s (5)) contained in that paragraph were also made by Sch 23 to the 2007 Act and those repeals were brought into force on 1 January 2010 as noted above).

## [1.1423]
## 6   Exemptions

(1)   The Secretary of State may by order provide that section 4(1) shall not prevent the provision of regulated claims management services by a person who is a member of a specified body.

(2)   The Secretary of State may by order provide that section 4(1) shall not prevent the provision of regulated claims management services—

   (a)   by a specified person or class of person,

   (b)   in specified circumstances, or

   (c)   by a specified person or class of person in specified circumstances.

(3)   Provision by virtue of subsection (1) or (2) may be expressed to have effect subject to compliance with specified conditions.

[(3A)   The Secretary of State may not make an order under subsection (1) or (2) unless—

   (a)   it is made in accordance with a recommendation made by the Legal Services Board, or

   (b)   the Secretary of State has consulted the Legal Services Board about the making of the order.]

(4)   Section 4(1) shall not prevent the provision of regulated claims management services by a person who is established or appointed by virtue of an enactment.

(5)   For the purposes of this Part a person is "exempt" if, or in so far as, section 4(1) does not, by virtue of this section, prevent him from providing regulated claims management services.

**NOTES**

Sub-s (3A): inserted by the Legal Services Act 2007, s 187, Sch 19, paras 1, 4, as from a day to be appointed.

Orders: the Compensation (Exemptions) Order 2007, SI 2007/209 at **[2.1065]**; the Compensation (Exemptions) (Amendment) (No 1) Order 2007, SI 2007/1090.

## [1.1424]
## 7   Enforcement: offence

(1)   A person commits an offence if he contravenes section 4(1).

(2)   A person who is guilty of an offence under subsection (1) shall be liable—

   (a)   on conviction on indictment—

      (i)   to imprisonment for a term not exceeding two years,

      (ii)   to a fine, or

      (iii)   to both, or

   (b)   on summary conviction—

      (i)   to imprisonment for a term not exceeding [12 months],

      (ii)   to a fine not exceeding [the statutory maximum], or

      (iii)   to both.

[(3)   In relation to an offence committed before the commencement of section 154(1) of the Criminal Justice Act 2003 the reference in subsection (2)(b)(i) to 12 months is to be read as a reference to 6 months.]

**NOTES**

Sub-s (2): words in square brackets substituted by the Legal Services Act 2007, s 187, Sch 19, paras 1, 5(1), (2).

Sub-s (3): substituted by the Legal Services Act 2007, s 187, Sch 19, paras 1, 5(1), (3).

## [1.1425]
## 8   Enforcement: the Regulator

(1)   The Regulator may apply to the court for an injunction restraining a person from providing regulated claims management services if he is not—

   (a)   an authorised person,

   (b)   an exempt person, or

   (c)   the subject of a waiver in accordance with regulations under section 9.

(2)   In subsection (1) "the court" means the High Court or *a county court*.

(3)   The Regulator may—

   (a)   investigate whether an offence has been committed under this Part;

   (b)   institute criminal proceedings in respect of an offence under this Part.

(4)   For the purpose of investigating whether an offence has been committed under this Part the Regulator may require the provision of information or documents.

(5)   On an application by the Regulator a judge of the High Court, Circuit judge or justice of the peace may issue a warrant authorising the Regulator[—

(a)] to enter and search premises on which a person conducts or is alleged to conduct regulated claims management business, for the purposes of investigating whether an offence has been committed under this Part[, and

(b) to take possession of any written or electronic records found on the search for the purposes of subsection (6)].

(6) The Regulator may take copies of written or electronic records found on a search by virtue of subsection (5) for a purpose specified in subsection (3)(a) or (b).

(7) In subsections (4) to (6) a reference to the Regulator includes a reference to a person authorised by him in writing.

(8) The Secretary of State shall make regulations—

(a) specifying matters of which a judge or justice of the peace must be satisfied, or to which he must have regard, before issuing a warrant under subsection (5), and

(b) regulating the exercise of a power under or by virtue of subsection (4) or (5) (whether by restricting the circumstances in which a power may be exercised, by specifying conditions to be complied with in the exercise of a power, or otherwise).

[(9) The Secretary of State may not make regulations under subsection (8) unless—

(a) they are made in accordance with a recommendation made by the Legal Services Board, or

(b) the Secretary of State has consulted the Legal Services Board about the making of the regulations.]

**NOTES**

Sub-s (2): for the words in italics there are substituted the words "the county court" by the Crime and Courts Act 2013, s 17(5), Sch 9, Pt 3, para 52, as from a day to be appointed.

Sub-s (5): words in square brackets inserted by the Legal Services Act 2007, s 187, Sch 19, paras 1, 6(1), (2), as from 30 June 2008.

Sub-s (9): inserted by the Legal Services Act 2007, s 187, Sch 19, paras 1, 6(1), (3), as from a day to be appointed.

Regulations: the Compensation (Claims Management Services) Regulations 2006, SI 2006/3322; the Compensation (Claims Management Services) (Amendment) Regulations 2008, SI 2008/1441.

## [1.1426]
## 9 Regulations

(1) The Secretary of State shall make regulations about—

(a) authorisations under section 5(1);

(b) the functions of the Regulator.

(2) The Schedule specifies particular provision that may be made by the regulations.

[(2A) The Secretary of State may not make regulations under this section unless—

(a) they are made in accordance with a recommendation made by the Legal Services Board, or

(b) the Secretary of State has consulted the Legal Services Board about the making of the regulations.]

(3) Transitional provision of regulations under this section may, in particular, make provision about the extent to which functions under this Part or under the regulations may be exercised in respect of matters arising before the commencement of a provision made by or by virtue of this Part.

**NOTES**

Sub-s (2A): inserted by the Legal Services Act 2007, s 187, Sch 19, paras 1, 7, as from a day to be appointed.

Regulations: the Compensation (Claims Management Services) Regulations 2006, SI 2006/3322; the Compensation (Claims Management Services) (Amendment) Regulations 2008, SI 2008/1441.

## [1.1427]
## 10 Obstructing the Regulator

(1) A person commits an offence if without reasonable excuse he obstructs the Regulator in the exercise of a power—

(a) under section 8(4) to (6), or

(b) by virtue of paragraph 14 of the Schedule.

(2) A person who is guilty of an offence under subsection (1) shall be liable on summary conviction to a fine not exceeding level 5 on the standard scale.

## [1.1428]
## 11 Pretending to be authorised, &c

(1) A person commits an offence if he falsely holds himself out as being—

(a) an authorised person,

(b) an exempt person, or

(c) the subject of a waiver in accordance with regulations under section 9.

(2) A person commits an offence if—

(a) he offers to provide regulated claims management services, and

(b) provision by him of those services would constitute an offence under this Part.

(3) For the purposes of subsection (2) a person offers to provide services if he—

(a) makes an offer to a particular person or class of person,

(b)    makes arrangements for an advertisement in which he offers to provide services, or

(c)    makes arrangements for an advertisement in which he is described or presented as competent to provide services.

(4)    A person who is guilty of an offence under subsection (1) or (2) shall be liable—

    (a)    on conviction on indictment—

        (i)     to imprisonment for a term not exceeding two years,

        (ii)    to a fine, or

        (iii)   to both, or

    (b)    on summary conviction—

        (i)     to imprisonment for a term not exceeding [12 months],

        (ii)    to a fine not exceeding [the statutory maximum], or

        (iii)   to both.

(5)    Where a person commits an offence under this section by causing material to be displayed or made accessible, he shall be treated as committing the offence on each day during any part of which the material is displayed or made accessible.

[(6)    In relation to an offence committed before the commencement of section 154(1) of the Criminal Justice Act 2003 the reference in subsection (4)(b)(i) to 12 months is to be read as a reference to 6 months.]

**NOTES**

Sub-s (4): words in square brackets substituted by the Legal Services Act 2007, s 187, Sch 19, paras 1, 8(1), (2).

Sub-s (6): substituted by the Legal Services Act 2007, s 187, Sch 19, paras 1, 8(1), (3).

**12**    *(Repealed by the Transfer of Tribunal Functions Order 2010, SI 2010/22, art 5(1), Sch 2, paras 106, 107, as from 6 April 2010 (for transitional provisions and savings in relation to existing cases and appeals from the Claims Management Services Tribunal, see Sch 5 to that Order).)*

**[1.1429]**
### 13    Appeals and references to Tribunal

(1)    A person may appeal to the [First-tier Tribunal ("the Tribunal")] if the Regulator—

    (a)    refuses the person's application for authorisation,

    (b)    grants the person authorisation on terms or subject to conditions,

    (c)    imposes conditions on the person's authorisation,

    (d)    suspends the person's authorisation, or

    (e)    cancels the person's authorisation.

(2)    The Regulator may refer to the Tribunal (with or without findings of fact or recommendations)—

    (a)    a complaint about the professional conduct of an authorised person, or

    (b)    the question whether an authorised person has complied with a rule of professional conduct.

(3)    On a reference or appeal under this section the Tribunal—

    (a)    may take any decision on an application for authorisation that the Regulator could have taken;

    (b)    may impose or remove conditions on a person's authorisation;

    (c)    may suspend a person's authorisation;

    (d)    may cancel a person's authorisation;

    (e)    may remit a matter to the Regulator;

    (f)    may not award costs.

[(3A)    In the case of appeals under subsection (1), Tribunal Procedure Rules—

    (a)    shall include provision for the suspension of decisions of the Regulator while an appeal could be brought or is pending;

    (b)    shall include provision about the making of interim orders;

    (c)    shall enable the Tribunal to suspend or further suspend (wholly or partly) the effect of a decision of the Regulator;

    (d)    shall permit the Regulator to apply for the termination of the suspension of a decision made by the Regulator.]

(4)    . . .

**NOTES**

Commencement: 23 January 2007 (sub-ss (1), (3), (4)); to be appointed (sub-s (2)).

Words in square brackets in sub-s (1) substituted, sub-s (3A) inserted, and sub-s (4) repealed, by the Transfer of Tribunal Functions Order 2010, SI 2010/22, art 5(1), Sch 2, paras 106, 108, as from 6 April 2010 (for transitional provisions and savings in relation to existing cases and appeals from the Claims Management Services Tribunal, see Sch 5 to that Order).

**[1.1430]**
### 14    Interpretation

In this Part—

    "action" includes omission,

"authorised person" has the meaning given by section 4,
"claim" has the meaning given by section 4,
"claims management services" has the meaning given by section 4,
"exempt person" has the meaning given by section 6(5),
"regulated claims management services" shall be construed in accordance with section 4(2)(e),
"specified", in relation to an order or regulations, means specified in the order or regulations, and
"the Regulator" means (subject to section 5(7)) the person designated under section 5(1) or, where no person is designated or in so far as is necessary having regard to any order under section 5(10), the *Secretary of State*.

**NOTES**

For the words in italics in the definition "the Regulator" there are substituted the words "Legal Services Board" by the Legal Services Act 2007, s 187, Sch 19, paras 1, 10, as from a day to be appointed.

**[1.1431]**
**15  Orders and regulations**
(1)   An order or regulations under this Part—
   (a)   may make provision that applies generally or only in specified cases or circumstances,
   (b)   may make different provision for different cases or circumstances, and
   (c)   may include transitional, incidental or consequential provision.
(2)   An order or regulations under this Part shall be made by statutory instrument.
(3)   An order under section 4(2)(e)—
   (a)   may not be made unless the Secretary of State has consulted—
      (i)    the Office of Fair Trading, and
      (ii)   such other persons as he thinks appropriate, and
   (b)   may not be made unless a draft has been laid before and approved by resolution of each House of Parliament.
(4)   An order under section 4(5) may not be made unless a draft has been laid before, and approved by resolution of, each House of Parliament.
(5)   An order under section 5 may not be made unless a draft has been laid before, and approved by resolution of, each House of Parliament.
(6)   . . .
(7)   The first order made under section 6 may not be made unless a draft has been laid before, and approved by resolution of, each House of Parliament.
(8)   An order under section 6 which has the effect of removing or restricting an exemption from section 4(1) may not be made unless a draft has been laid before, and approved by resolution of, each House of Parliament.
(9)   Any other order under section 6 shall be subject to annulment in pursuance of a resolution of either House of Parliament.
(10)   Regulations under section 8 or 9 may not be made unless a draft has been laid before, and approved by resolution of, each House of Parliament.

**NOTES**

Sub-s (6): repealed by the Legal Services Act 2007, s 210, Sch 23, as from 1 January 2010.

**PART 3**
**GENERAL**

**[1.1432]**
**16  Commencement**
(1)   The preceding provisions of this Act, other than sections 1, 2 and 3, shall come into force in accordance with provision made by order of the Secretary of State.
(2)   An order under subsection (1)—
   (a)   may make provision generally or only for specified purposes,
   (b)   may make different provision for different purposes,
   (c)   may make transitional, consequential or incidental provision, and
   (d)   shall be made by statutory instrument.
(3)   Section 3 shall be treated as having always had effect.
(4)   But the section shall have no effect in relation to—
   (a)   a claim which is settled before 3rd May 2006 (whether or not legal proceedings in relation to the claim have been instituted), or
   (b)   legal proceedings which are determined before that date.
(5)   Where a claim is settled on or after that date and before the date on which this Act is passed, a party to the settlement may apply to a relevant court to have the settlement varied; and—
   (a)   a court is a relevant court for that purpose if it had, or would have had, jurisdiction to determine the claim by way of legal proceedings,
   (b)   an application shall be brought as an application in, or by way of, proceedings on the claim, and